BLA

COMPLETE WRITINGS

Oxford University Press, Walton Street, Oxford, OX2 6DP

OXFORD LONDON GLASGOW NEW YORK
TORONTO MELBOURNE WELLINGTON CAPE TOWN
IBADAN NAIROBI DAR ES SALAAM LUSAKA ADDIS ABABA
KUALA LUMPUR SINGAPORE JAKARTA HONG KONG TOKYO
DELHI BOMBAY CALCUTTA MADRAS KARACHI

BLAKE
COMPLETE WRITINGS

WITH VARIANT READINGS

EDITED BY

GEOFFREY KEYNES

LONDON
OXFORD UNIVERSITY PRESS

WILLIAM BLAKE

Born in London 28 November 1757
Died at Fountain Court in the Strand,
London 12 August 1827

This Oxford Standard Authors edition of The Complete Writings of William Blake, *edited by Geoffrey Keynes, is reprinted photographically from the Nonesuch Press edition first published in 1957. A number of additions and corrections have been made, a new Preface added, and a supplement containing newly discovered material printed at the end. This Oxford edition was first published in 1966 and reprinted the same year and in 1967, 1969 (with corrections) 1972, and 1976*

This edition was also issued in Oxford Paperbacks in 1969 and was reprinted in that series, with corrections, in 1971, 1972, 1974, and 1976

ISBN 0 19 254157 9

Printed in Great Britain
at the University Press, Oxford
by Vivian Ridler
Printer to the University
O.S.A.

The Contents

The Editor's Preface

WILLIAM BLAKE *was born two hundred years ago on November* 28 1757, *and died at the age of seventy on August* 12 1827. *Many people at the present time share the opinion that he was one of the greatest of Englishmen, his contribution to the art and literature of his country being of the very highest order. Certainly no artist has ever brought to his creative work a deeper assurance of the importance of imaginative art in human affairs, and none has dedicated his life and spirit more completely to his allotted task—the expression of his message with pen, graver, and paint-brush.*

Blake suffered neglect and even ridicule during his life, and was almost forgotten for nearly forty years after his death; but in 1863 *the publication of Alexander Gilchrist's* Life *brought his work again to notice and initiated the growth of an interest which has spread far beyond the confines of his country and seems to be for ever growing. Nevertheless it was many years before this heightened sense of Blake's powers as a writer produced a scholar determined to present his poems as he wrote them. His earlier editors tended to abuse their office by insufficient attention to accuracy of transcription or by actually falsifying the text. Not until* 1905, *when the late Dr John Sampson published his Oxford edition of the* Poetical Works, *was a proper standard of Blake scholarship established. Even then this was restricted to the shorter poems; the symbolic epics, which Blake himself would have regarded as his major works, being excluded. In* 1925 *the Nonesuch Press decided to render to Blake the justice that he deserved by publishing the entire body of his writings as they were then known, with every variation and deletion recorded as completely as possible. As editor, I attempted to emulate Sampson's scholarship by working wherever possible from original sources and by careful attention to accurate transcription. The three illustrated volumes embodying the results of this very extensive piece of research have remained as a tribute to Blake's genius which has not been superseded, though their rather monumental character has to some extent defeated their purpose. The high cost and limitation of the size of the edition has prevented their reaching much of the public for whom they were intended. A compromise was effected two years later by the publication in* 1927 *of the complete* Poetry and Prose *in a single unillustrated volume, but this compression was effected by sacrificing all variant readings and all notes, some poems being given in an "editor's version" which made for easier reading but eliminated much of the furnace-force of Blake's creative workshop. The single volume edition has been reprinted many times, and on several occasions partially revised, up to* 1939, *when the whole text was reset. Since that date no further revision has been possible. Now, after eighteen years, a fresh effort has been made by the Nonesuch Press to satisfy all legitimate demands by providing in a single volume under the same editorship as before a complete text with variant readings and notes. This new venture is a brave one, since it seeks to provide in a popular form fare which has been thought in the past to have little appeal to the popular palate. But Blake's following is now large enough, it is believed, to provide adequate support for this experiment, so much more ambitious than the "compendious edition" of* 1927. *It has moreover provided the editor with an opportunity of making a complete revision of the text; for no conscientious editor can long remain fully satisfied with the results of his labours—certainly not for so long as eighteen years.*

THE TEXT

Almost everything that was printed in the edition of 1925 *has been included in the present text. The only omissions are a debtor-and-creditor account,* 1805-6, *between Blake and his patron, Thomas Butts, and an index to the* Songs of Innocence and of Experience, c. 1818. *These do not now seem to belong among Blake's* Writings *and are available with similar documents in my recent edition of the* Letters, *London,* 1956. *On the other hand there are a few interesting, if minor, additions, such as a recently discovered advertisement of* A Descriptive Catalogue, 1809 *; some letters which have been collected only in the recent edition mentioned above, with one short one newly discovered ; and Blake's list of subjects for* A History of England. *More important additions than these are the two series of annotations written as marginalia in his copies of* Bacon's Essays, 1798, *and of Boyd's translation of* Dante's Inferno, 1785 (*annotations* *about* 1800). *Only a small part of the annotations to Bacon were previously known, and those to Boyd's* Dante *were completely unknown until their publication in* The Times Literary Supplement, 3 *May* 1957. *During the revision of the text as a whole some errors have been corrected, and a fresh collation of the* MS Note-book *has resulted in the deciphering of additional lines, as recorded in the notes. The text of* An Island in the Moon *has also acquired a few additional passages which had previously been found illegible.*

In 1925 *some sort of justification of editorial pedantry apparent in the reproduction of many variant readings was deemed necessary. At the present time no kind of apology is offered. Some of the poems, in which the lines are loaded with deletions and rearrangements, may seem rather difficult to read and appreciate, but for many of them Blake provided his own solution by making fair copies or printed texts, which are all given here in their appropriate places. In two instances where no such elucidation was made by the author, a "reader's text" has been supplied by the editor in the notes. Some readers may also be grateful for the very difficulties put in their way. Reading a poem by Blake with the lines broken up by his hesitations and alterations will often be found to give fresh beauty and new light to its meaning by engaging the reader's closer attention and illustrating the poet's method of composition. The outstanding example of the second advantage is, of course, in "The Tyger" where the* MS Note-book *provides two early versions and the printed* Songs of Experience *gives the final form.*

THE ARRANGEMENT

In 1925 *it was decided after much thought to print Blake's writings, whether poetry or prose, as far as possible in chronological sequence instead of grouping the poems, prose pieces, annotations, and so forth under these headings. It was pointed out that Blake's writings, whatever form they take, are so interdependent that "any other attempt at classification must result in the violent and arbitrary separation of pieces which should properly come together". It was claimed in addition that "the development of Blake's symbolic system and of his doctrines is also elucidated by this plan". In the smaller compendious edition of* 1927 *the more usual arrangement in groups was used, but in the present edition the considerations previously urged have seemed convincing and a return has been made to the chronological sequence—with one important change. In* 1925 *even Blake's letters to his friends were interspersed according to their dates among his other writings. It is true that many of his letters are of great importance in elucidating his ideas, but on the whole their distribution in this manner was seen to give them a certain incongruity, and they have now all been grouped together at the end. For the rest of the writings the warning must again be given that a chronological arrangement can only be approximate, for it is inevitable that the shorter poems should be presented in large groups and that a work such as* Jerusalem, *the composition of which occupied many years, cannot be placed with any precision. Further, the dates assigned to some of the pieces are necessarily conjectural.*

EMENDATIONS

As in 1925, *this text contains very few editorial emendations. Those that have been made will be found in texts such as the* Poetical Sketches, *which had suffered at the hands of a compositor and had plainly not been corrected by the author. All changes of this kind have been recorded either in foot-notes or in the notes at the end of the book. All Blake's manuscripts have been reproduced as far as possible with fidelity to the originals and any editorial alterations are indicated by square brackets. Blake's corrections are also included in square brackets with added indications such as* del., *though the great difficulty, or impossibility, of always shewing exactly what Blake was doing is confessed in the note on the manuscript of* Vala, or the Four Zoas. *This manuscript, however, presents special problems which do not occur on a comparable scale elsewhere.*

SPELLING, CAPITALS, ABBREVIATIONS

Fidelity to the original manuscripts or etched texts has necessitated the reproduction of Blake's peculiarities of spelling, frequent use of capitals, and abbreviations. Throughout his life he was consistent in his archaic or irregular spellings, and words that may seem at first to have been misprinted here will usually be found to be as he wrote them. Thus the reader will have to become accustomed to seeing "recieve" for "receive", "perswade" for "persuade", "lilly" for "lily", "desart" for "desert", "tyger" for "tiger", and so on. Blake was not altogether consistent in his prose writings in his use of ed and 'd in past participles. In his poetry or blank verse, however, his consistency in this respect is almost always to be relied upon, and it may usually be assumed that where ed is printed it should be sounded.

In the profusion of his capitals Blake rivalled some of the authors of earlier days. Although he may have been influenced by his reading of Swedenborg's writings, where capitals were very freely used, he certainly had in his mind some idea of indicating emphasis, and for that reason it is justifiable to preserve this peculiarity, though it cannot be claimed that he followed any very systematic plan. Moreover, Blake's calligraphy sometimes leaves room for doubt whether a capital or small letter is intended, especially in his writing of c, d, k, and s. Some mistakes, therefore, have probably been made ; it is not a matter of great importance, though inattention to this point has led some editors to credit Blake with having used a capital when referring to the Deity. This he seldom did, though he usually employed one when writing Me or My.

A few abbreviations, such as "tho" for "though" and "thro" for "through", are usually found in the original texts, but without the apostrophe which has here been supplied ; Blake also very frequently used an ampersand. Most previous editors have ignored these peculiarities. It may therefore be assumed that, wherever in the present text they do not appear, or are only partially reproduced, as in some of the letters to Hayley, the original manuscript was not available, so recourse has been had to that of an earlier editor.

PUNCTUATION

A major difficulty had to be faced in editing the Writings *of* 1925 *owing to Blake's peculiar method of punctuating his works. If his irregular use of the colon and other uncertain marks had been reproduced, his meaning would have been greatly obscured. With the help of the late Max Plowman a bold attempt was therefore made to supply punctuation, with the admitted risk of sometimes conveying a meaning not intended by Blake. The result did not attract any serious criticism, and the punctuation in this edition has been left substantially as it was in 1925. In reprinting works such as* Poetical Sketches *and* The French Revolution *the punctuation supplied by the contemporary compositor has been allowed to stand except where obvious alterations were demanded by the sense.*

FACSIMILES

Blake's insistence on printing most of his works from etched copper plates with designs coloured by a method of his own invention, or with water-colour washes added, shews that he did not intend that text and designs should ever be divorced. For technical reasons it has proved impossible to maintain this association except in the expensive forms published by William Muir in the last century and by the William Blake Trust in recent years. Students are urged to study these facsimiles or, better still, Blake's original volumes where they are available, since for present purposes the ideal cannot be attained ; a partial exception has been made, as in the previous Nonesuch editions, where Blake has woven words or sentences into his designs, or has etched a sentence, or even a stanza, in reversed writing. He certainly intended to indicate by reverse script that these passages were to be read from another spiritual, or inside, aspect of existence. All such passages have been reproduced in line blocks inserted in the text, and the same has been done for the emblem book known as The Gates of Paradise, *where the designs are essential to the understanding of the text.*

LINE NUMBERS

In other editions great inconvenience has been caused by the absence of line numbering. An important feature of the present text is the numbering of the lines of all metrical writings or blank verse. The numbering of the lines of the Illuminated Books has in general been done plate by plate in accordance with the numbering as set out in the Census of the Illuminated Books *by Keynes and Wolf,* 1953. Vala, or the Four Zoas, *has been numbered by "Nights" without reference to the pages of the manuscript. Erased lines indicated in the text are included in the numbering.*

THE NOTES

As in 1925, *the notes supplied here are mainly textual and bibliographical, though a partial exception has been made in those on the symbolic works. Here a clue to the theme of each book has been given in a few lines. For the rest Blake has been left to speak for himself. He has had many interpreters, beginning with A. C. Swinburne in* 1868. *After him came E. J. Ellis and W. B. Yeats in* 1895, *followed after an interval of nearly thirty years by S. Foster Damon,* 1924, *and D. J. Sloss and J. P. R. Wallis,* 1926. *More recently Northrop Frye, Mark Schorer, and David V. Erdman have made notable contributions in this field, all of them having profited by the labours of Joseph Wicksteed,* 1910 *and* 1928, *and readers of this edition of Blake's writings are advised to refer to these authorities if they wish for further interpretive studies. Blake has often been classed as a "mystic", but neither this nor any other single term can define the astonishing and varied qualities of his mind.*

1957 *GEOFFREY KEYNES*

Preface to this Edition

THE PUBLISHERS *of the Nonesuch edition of Blake's* Complete Writings, 1957, *not wishing to reprint the book, the publishing rights have been transferred to the Oxford University Press. Recently a group of American scholars, led by Dr David Erdman, has been compiling a Concordance of Blake's writings based on the Nonesuch edition. They have verified in great detail every part of the text and have laboured to decipher all passages obliterated by Blake in his manuscripts or erased from his etched plates. Numerous corrections and some additions have been made, notably among the lines erased from the plates of* Jerusalem, *and the results have been generously put at my disposal by Dr Erdman. A great many of the corrections and variants are admittedly trivial and for technical reasons it has not been feasible to use them all in this edition. The opportunity has been taken, however, to correct the misprints which had escaped me in the former edition, and substantive corrections or additions have been incorporated. Apart from technical limitations, it seemed reasonable to be selective, because the readings of so many of the deleted or altered words are, to say the least, dubious and some "corrections" remain a matter of opinion. Nevertheless changes have been made in* 124 *pages of the text, affecting the numbering of the lines in only two instances (pp.* 110 *and* 420*). The text as a whole has, therefore, greatly benefited and I am most grateful to all those scholars who have made their contribution.*

The present reprinting of this edition has made it possible to rearrange the additions made since the first printing of 1966. A lightly pencilled passage detected by Dr Erdman in the Note-Book *has been placed in its approximately correct position on p.* 559. *Other additions include Blake's brief annotations to his copy of Swedenborg's* Heaven and Hell, *Dr Erdman's decipherings, partly conjectural, of obliterated passages in the annotations to Reynolds's* Discourses, *some curious notes written in Varley's, rather than Blake's, hand in the recently rediscovered Varley-Blake sketchbook, and the chapter headings to Blake's manuscript of* Genesis *previously omitted. Finally, the few additional letters are now arranged in their proper order. Some of the Notes at the end of the volume have been revised in accordance with the latest knowledge.*

1969 *GEOFFREY KEYNES*

Another reprinting has allowed the incorporation of a number of further corrections, mostly of a minor kind, but all helping to bring the text nearer to Blake's apparent intention. As before the stimulus has come from Dr D. V. Erdman, though technical difficulties have limited the use of his conjectural readings of obliterated passages.

An emendation in Jerusalem (*p.* 654, *line 28*) *has been adopted at the suggestion of Miss Joanne Witke of the University of California.*

1970 *GEOFFREY KEYNES*

This 1972 reprinting contains further minor corrections and revision of a passage in the indistinctly written annotations to Dr. Thornton's New Translation of the Lord's Prayer (*p.* 788).

1972 *GEOFFREY KEYNES*

A very few further corrections, all minor, have been made in the text for this reprinting. A few notes have been brought up to date.

1974 *GEOFFREY KEYNES*

POETICAL SKETCHES

By W. B.

[1769-1778]

LONDON: Printed in the Year MDCCLXXXIII

MISCELLANEOUS POEMS

TO SPRING

O thou with dewy locks, who lookest down
Thro' the clear windows of the morning, turn
Thine angel eyes upon our western isle,
Which in full choir hails thy approach, O Spring!

The hills tell each other, and the list'ning
Vallies hear; all our longing eyes are turned
Up to thy bright pavillions: issue forth,
And let thy holy feet visit our clime.

Come o'er the eastern hills, and let our winds
Kiss thy perfumed garments; let us taste
Thy morn and evening breath; scatter thy pearls
Upon our love-sick land that mourns for thee.

O deck her forth with thy fair fingers; pour
Thy soft kisses on her bosom; and put
Thy golden crown upon her languish'd head,
Whose modest tresses were bound up for thee!

TO SUMMER

O thou, who passest thro' our vallies in
Thy strength, curb thy fierce steeds, allay the heat
That flames from their large nostrils! thou, O Summer,
Oft pitched'st here thy golden tent, and oft
Beneath our oaks hast slept, while we beheld
With joy thy ruddy limbs and flourishing hair.

Beneath our thickest shades we oft have heard
Thy voice, when noon upon his fervid car
Rode o'er the deep of heaven; beside our springs
Sit down, and in our mossy vallies, on
Some bank beside a river clear, throw thy
Silk draperies off, and rush into the stream:
Our vallies love the Summer in his pride.

Our bards are fam'd who strike the silver wire:
Our youths are bolder than the southern swains:
Our maidens fairer in the sprightly dance:
We lack not songs, nor instruments of joy,
Nor echoes sweet, nor waters clear as heaven,
Nor laurel wreaths against the sultry heat.

TO AUTUMN

O autumn, laden with fruit, and stained
With the blood of the grape, pass not, but sit
Beneath my shady roof; there thou may'st rest,
And tune thy jolly voice to my fresh pipe;
And all the daughters of the year shall dance!
Sing now the lusty song of fruits and flowers.

"The narrow bud opens her beauties to
"The sun, and love runs in her thrilling veins;
"Blossoms hang round the brows of morning, and
"Flourish down the bright cheek of modest eve,
"Till clust'ring Summer breaks forth into singing,
"And feather'd clouds strew flowers round her head.

"The spirits of the air live on the smells
"Of fruit; and joy, with pinions light, roves round
"The gardens, or sits singing in the trees."
Thus sang the jolly Autumn as he sat;
Then rose, girded himself, and o'er the bleak
Hills fled from our sight; but left his golden load.

TO WINTER

O Winter! bar thine adamantine doors:
The north is thine; there hast thou built thy dark
Deep-founded habitation. Shake not thy roofs,
Nor bend thy pillars with thine iron car.

He hears me not, but o'er the yawning deep
Rides heavy; his storms are unchain'd, sheathed
In ribbed steel; I dare not lift mine eyes,
For he hath rear'd his sceptre o'er the world.

Lo! now the direful monster, whose skin clings
To his strong bones, strides o'er the groaning rocks:
He withers all in silence, and in[1] his hand
Unclothes the earth, and freezes up frail life.

He takes his seat upon the cliffs; the mariner
Cries in vain. Poor little wretch! that deal'st
With storms, till heaven smiles, and the monster
Is driv'n yelling to his caves beneath mount Hecla.

TO THE EVENING STAR

Thou fair-hair'd angel of the evening,
Now, whilst[2] the sun rests on the mountains, light
Thy bright torch of love; thy radiant crown
Put on, and smile upon our evening bed!
Smile on our loves, and, while thou drawest the
Blue curtains of the sky, scatter thy silver dew
On every flower that shuts its sweet eyes
In timely sleep. Let thy west wind sleep on
The lake; speak silence with thy glimmering eyes,
And wash the dusk with silver. Soon, full soon,
Dost thou withdraw; then the wolf rages wide,
And the lion glares thro' the dun forest:
The fleeces of our flocks are cover'd with
Thy sacred dew: protect them with thine influence.

TO MORNING

O holy virgin! clad in purest white,
Unlock heav'n's golden gates, and issue forth;
Awake the dawn that sleeps in heaven; let light
Rise from the chambers of the east, and bring
The honied dew that cometh on waking day.
O radiant morning, salute the sun,
Rouz'd like a huntsman to the chace, and, with
Thy buskin'd feet, appear upon our hills.

[1] This word is deleted by pen in some copies.

[2] *Altered by pen to* while *in one copy.*

FAIR ELENOR

The bell struck one, and shook the silent tower;
The graves give up their dead: fair Elenor
Walk'd by the castle gate, and looked in.
A hollow groan ran thro' the dreary vaults.

She shriek'd aloud, and sunk upon the steps
On the cold stone her pale cheek[1]. Sickly smells
Of death issue as from a sepulchre,
And all is silent but the sighing vaults.

Chill death withdraws his hand, and she revives;
Amaz'd, she finds herself upon her feet,
And, like a ghost, thro' narrow passages
Walking, feeling the cold walls with her hands.

Fancy returns, and now she thinks of bones,
And grinning skulls, and corruptible death,
Wrap'd in his shroud; and now fancies she hears
Deep sighs, and sees pale sickly ghosts gliding.

At length, no fancy, but reality
Distracts her. A rushing sound, and the feet
Of one that fled, approaches—Ellen stood,
Like a dumb statue, froze to stone with fear.

The wretch approaches, crying, "The deed is done;
"Take this, and send it by whom thou wilt send;
"It is my life—send it to Elenor:—
"He's dead, and howling after me for blood!

"Take this", he cry'd; and thrust into her arms
A wet napkin, wrap'd about; then rush'd
Past, howling: she receiv'd into her arms
Pale death, and follow'd on the wings of fear.

They pass'd swift thro' the outer gate; the wretch,
Howling, leap'd o'er the wall into the moat,
Stifling in mud. Fair Ellen pass'd the bridge,
And heard a gloomy voice cry, "Is it done?"

[1] *Altered by pen in some copies from* cheeks.

As the deer wounded, Ellen flew over
The pathless plain; as the arrows that fly
By night, destruction flies, and strikes in darkness.
She fled from fear, till at her house arriv'd.

Her maids await her; on her bed she falls,
That bed of joy, where erst her lord hath press'd:
"Ah, woman's-fear!" she cry'd; "Ah, cursed duke!
"Ah, my dear lord! ah, wretched Elenor!

"My lord was like a flower upon the brows
"Of lusty May! Ah, life as frail as flower!
"O ghastly death! withdraw thy cruel hand,
"Seek'st thou that flow'r to deck thy horrid temples?

"My lord was like a star, in highest heav'n
"Drawn down to earth by spells and wickedness;
"My lord was like the opening eyes of day,
"When western winds creep softly o'er the flowers:

"But he is darken'd; like the summer's noon,
"Clouded; fall'n like the stately tree, cut down;
"The breath of heaven dwelt among his leaves.
"O Elenor, weak woman, fill'd with woe!"

Thus having spoke, she raised up her head,
And saw the bloody napkin by her side,
Which in her arms she brought; and now, tenfold
More terrified, saw it unfold itself.

Her eyes were fix'd; the bloody cloth unfolds,
Disclosing to her sight the murder'd head
Of her dear lord, all ghastly pale, clotted
With gory blood; it groan'd, and thus it spake:

"O Elenor, I am thy husband's head[1],
"Who, sleeping on the stones of yonder tower,
"Was 'reft of life by the accursed duke!
"A hired villain turn'd my sleep to death!

[1] *Altered by pen in some copies to:*
O Elenor, behold thy husband's head.

"O Elenor, beware the cursed duke;
"O give not him thy hand now I am dead;
"He seeks thy love, who, coward, in the night,
"Hired a villain to bereave my life."

She sat with dead cold limbs, stiffen'd to stone;
She took the gory head up in her arms;
She kiss'd the pale lips; she had no tears to shed;
She hugg'd it to her breast, and groan'd her last.

SONG

How sweet I roam'd from field to field,
And tasted all the summer's pride,
'Till I the prince of love beheld,
Who in the sunny beams did glide!

He shew'd me lilies for my hair,
And blushing roses for my brow;
He led me through his gardens fair,
Where all his golden pleasures grow.

With sweet May dews my wings were wet,
And Phœbus fir'd my vocal rage;
He caught me in his silken net,
And shut me in his golden cage.

He loves to sit and hear me sing,
Then, laughing, sports and plays with me;
Then stretches out my golden wing,
And mocks my loss of liberty.

SONG

My silks and fine array,
My smiles and languish'd air,
By love are driv'n away;
And mournful lean Despair
Brings me yew to deck my grave:
Such end true lovers have.

His face is fair as heav'n,
When springing buds unfold;
O why to him was't giv'n,
Whose heart is wintry cold?
His breast is love's all worship'd tomb,
Where all love's pilgrims come.

Bring me an axe and spade,
  Bring me a winding sheet;
When I my grave have made,
  Let winds and tempests beat:
Then down I'll lie, as cold as clay.
True love doth pass away!

SONG

Love and harmony combine,
And around our souls intwine,
While thy branches mix with mine,
And our roots together join.

Joys upon our branches sit,
Chirping loud, and singing sweet;
Like gentle streams beneath our feet
Innocence and virtue meet.

Thou the golden fruit dost bear,
I am clad in flowers fair;
Thy sweet boughs perfume the air,
And the turtle buildeth there.

There she sits and feeds her young,
Sweet I hear her mournful song;
And thy lovely leaves among,
There is love: I hear his[1] tongue.

There his charming nest doth lay,
There he sleeps the night away;
There he sports along the day,
And doth among our branches play.

SONG

I love the jocund dance,
  The softly-breathing song,
Where innocent eyes do glance,
  And where lisps the maiden's tongue.

I love the laughing vale,
  I love the echoing hill,
Where mirth does never fail,
  And the jolly swain laughs his fill.

[1] *Altered by pen from* her *in one copy.*

I love the pleasant cot,
   I love the innocent bow'r,
Where white and brown is our lot,
   Or fruit in the mid-day hour.

I love the oaken seat,
   Beneath the oaken tree,
Where all the old villagers meet,
   And laugh our sports to see.

I love our neighbours all,
   But, Kitty, I better love thee;
And love them I ever shall;
   But thou art all to me.

SONG

Memory, hither come,
   And tune your merry notes;
And, while upon the wind
   Your music floats,

I'll pore upon the stream,
Where sighing lovers dream,
And fish for fancies as they pass
Within the watery glass.

I'll drink of the clear stream,
   And hear the linnet's song;
And there I'll lie and dream
   The day along:

And, when night comes, I'll go
   To places fit for woe,
Walking along the darken'd valley
   With silent Melancholy.

MAD SONG

The wild winds weep,
   And the night is a-cold;
Come hither, Sleep,
   And my griefs infold[1]:

[1] *Printed* unfold, *altered by pen in some copies.*

But lo! the morning peeps
Over the eastern steeps,
And the rustling birds[1] of dawn
The earth do scorn.

Lo! to the vault
Of paved heaven
With sorrow fraught
My notes are driven:
They strike the ear of night,
Make weep the eyes of day;
They make mad the roaring winds,
And with tempests play.

Like a fiend in a cloud,
With howling woe,
After night I do croud,
And with night will go;
I turn my back to the east,
From whence comforts have increas'd;
For light doth seize my brain
With frantic pain.

SONG

Fresh from the dewy hill, the merry year
Smiles on my head, and mounts his flaming car;
Round my young brows the laurel wreathes a shade,
And rising glories beam around my head.

My feet are wing'd, while o'er the dewy lawn
I meet my maiden, risen like the morn:
Oh bless those holy feet, like angels' feet;
Oh bless those limbs, beaming with heav'nly light!

Like as an angel glitt'ring in the sky
In times of innocence and holy joy;
The joyful shepherd stops his grateful song
To hear thc music of an angel's tongue.

So when she speaks, the voice of Heaven I hear:
So when we walk, nothing impure comes near;
Each field seems Eden, and each calm retreat;
Each village seems the haunt of holy feet.

[1] *Printed* beds, *altered by pen in some copies.*

But that sweet village, where my black-ey'd maid
Closes her eyes in sleep beneath night's shade,
Whene'er I enter, more than mortal fire
Burns in my soul, and does my song inspire.

SONG

When early morn walks forth in sober grey,
Then to my black ey'd maid I haste away;
When evening sits beneath her dusky bow'r,
And gently sighs away the silent hour,
The village bell alarms, away I go,
And the vale darkens at my pensive woe.

To that sweet village, where my black ey'd maid
Doth drop a tear beneath the silent shade,
I turn my eyes; and, pensive as I go,
Curse my black stars, and bless my pleasing woe.

Oft when the summer sleeps among the trees,
Whisp'ring faint murmurs to the scanty breeze,
I walk the village round; if at her side
A youth doth walk in stolen joy and pride,
I curse my stars in bitter grief and woe,
That made my love so high, and me so low.

O should she e'er prove false, his limbs I'd tear,
And throw all pity on the burning air;
I'd curse bright fortune for my mixed lot,
And then I'd die in peace, and be forgot.

TO THE MUSES

Whether on Ida's shady brow,
   Or in the chambers of the East,
The chambers of the sun, that now
   From antient melody have ceas'd;

Whether in Heav'n ye wander fair,
   Or the green corners of the earth,
Or the blue regions of the air,
   Where the melodious winds have birth;

Whether on chrystal rocks ye rove,
  Beneath the bosom of the sea
Wand'ring in many a coral grove,
  Fair Nine, forsaking Poetry!

How have you left the antient love
  That bards of old enjoy'd in you!
The languid strings do scarcely move!
  The sound is forc'd, the notes are few!

GWIN, KING OF NORWAY

Come, Kings, and listen to my song:
  When Gwin, the son of Nore,
Over the nations of the North
  His cruel sceptre bore,

The Nobles of the land did feed
  Upon the hungry Poor;
They tear the poor man's lamb, and drive
  The needy from their door!

"The land is desolate; our wives
  "And children cry for bread;
"Arise, and pull the tyrant down!
  "Let Gwin be humbled!"

Gordred the giant rous'd himself
  From sleeping in his cave;
He shook the hills, and in the clouds
  The troubl'd banners wave.

Beneath them roll'd, like tempests black,
  The num'rous sons of blood;
Like lions' whelps, roaring abroad,
  Seeking their nightly food.

Down Bleron's hills they dreadful rush,
  Their cry ascends the clouds;
The trampling horse, and clanging arms
  Like rushing mighty floods!

Their wives and children, weeping loud,
  Follow in wild array,
Howling like ghosts, furious as wolves
  In the bleak wintry day.

"Pull down the tyrant to the dust,
"Let Gwin be humbled,"
They cry, "and let ten thousand lives
"Pay for the tyrant's head."

From tow'r to tow'r the watchmen cry:
"O Gwin, the son of Nore,
"Arouse thyself! the nations, black
"Like clouds, come rolling o'er!"

Gwin rear'd his shield, his palace shakes,
His chiefs come rushing round;
Each, like an awful thunder cloud,
With voice of solemn sound:

Like reared stones around a grave
They stand around the King;
Then suddenly each seiz'd his spear,
And clashing steel does ring.

The husbandman does leave his plow,
To wade thro' fields of gore;
The merchant binds his brows in steel,
And leaves the trading shore;

The shepherd leaves his mellow pipe,
And sounds the trumpet shrill;
The workman throws his hammer down
To heave the bloody bill.

Like the tall ghost of Barraton,
Who sports in stormy sky,
Gwin leads his host, as black as night,
When pestilence does fly,

With horses and with chariots—
And all his spearmen bold
March to the sound of mournful song,
Like clouds around him roll'd.

Gwin lifts his hand—the nations halt;
"Prepare for war," he cries——
"Gordred appears!—his frowning brow
"Troubles our northern skies."

The armies stand, like balances
  Held in th' Almighty's hand:
"Gwin, thou hast fill'd thy measure up,
  "Thou'rt swept from out the land."

And now the raging armies rush'd,
  Like warring mighty seas;
The Heav'ns are shook with roaring war,
  And dust ascends the skies!

Earth smokes with blood, and groans, and shakes
  To drink her children's gore,
A sea of blood; nor can the eye
  See to the trembling shore!

And on the verge of this wild sea
  Famine and death doth cry;
The cries of women and of babes
  Over the field doth fly.

The King is seen raging afar,
  With all his men of might,
Like blazing comets, scattering death
  Thro' the red fev'rous night.

Beneath his arm like sheep they die,
  And groan upon the plain;
The battle faints, and bloody men
  Fight upon hills of slain.

Now death is sick, and riven men
  Labour and toil for life;
Steed rolls on steed, and shield on shield,
  Sunk in this sea of strife!

The god of war is drunk with blood;
The earth doth faint and fail;
The stench of blood makes sick the heav'ns;
  Ghosts glut the throat of hell!

O what have Kings to answer for,
  Before that awful throne!
When thousand deaths for vengeance cry,
  And ghosts accusing groan!

Like blazing comets in the sky,
  That shake the stars of light,
Which drop like fruit unto the earth
  Thro' the fierce burning night;

Like these did Gwin and Gordred meet,
  And the first blow decides;
Down from the brow unto the breast
  Gordred his head divides!

Gwin fell; the Sons of Norway fled,
  All that remain'd alive;
The rest did fill the vale of death,
  For them the eagles strive.

The river Dorman roll'd their blood
  Into the northern sea,
Who mourn'd his sons, and overwhelm'd
  The pleasant south country.

AN IMITATION OF SPENSER

Golden Apollo, that thro' heaven wide
  Scatter'st the rays of light and truth's beams!
In lucent words my darkling verses dight,
  And wash my earthy mind in thy clear streams,
  That wisdom may descend in fairy dreams:
All while the jocund hours in thy train
  Scatter their fancies at thy poet's feet;
And when thou yields to night thy wide domain,
Let rays of truth enlight his sleeping brain.

For brutish Pan in vain might thee assay
  With tinkling sounds to dash thy nervous verse,
Sound without sense; yet in his rude affray,
  (For ignorance is Folly's leasing nurse,
  And love of Folly needs none other[1] curse;)

Midas the praise hath gain'd of lengthen'd ears[2],
  For which himself might deem him ne'er the worse
To sit in council with his modern peers,
  And judge of tinkling rhimes, and elegances terse.

[1] *Altered by pen from* other's *in some copies.*

[2] *Altered by pen in one copy from* cares.

And thou, Mercurius, that with winged brow
  Dost mount aloft into the yielding sky,
And thro' Heav'n's halls thy airy flight dost throw,
  Entering with holy feet to where on high
  Jove weighs the counsel of futurity;
Then, laden with eternal fate, dost go
  Down, like a falling star, from autumn sky,
  And o'er the surface of the silent deep dost fly:

If thou arrivest at the sandy shore,
  Where nought but envious hissing adders dwell,
Thy golden rod, thrown on the dusty floor,
  Can charm to harmony with potent spell;
  Such is sweet Eloquence, that does dispel
Envy and Hate, that thirst for human gore;
  And cause in sweet society to dwell
  Vile savage minds that lurk in lonely cell.

O Mercury, assist my lab'ring sense,
  That round the circle of the world wou'd fly!
As the wing'd eagle scorns the tow'ry fence
  Of Alpine hills round his high aery,
  And searches thro' the corners of the sky,
Sports in the clouds to hear the thunder's sound,
  And see the winged lightnings as they fly;
Then, bosom'd in an amber cloud, around
  Plumes his wide wings, and seeks Sol's palace high.

And thou, O warrior maid invincible,
  Arm'd with the terrors of Almighty Jove!
Pallas, Minerva, maiden terrible,
  Lov'st thou to walk the peaceful solemn grove,
  In solemn gloom of branches interwove?
Or bear'st thy Egis o'er the burning field,
  Where, like the sea, the waves of battle move?
Or have thy soft piteous eyes beheld
  The weary wanderer thro' the desert rove?
  Or does th' afflicted man thy heav'nly bosom move?

BLIND-MAN'S BUFF

When silver Snow decks Susan's cloaths,
And jewel hangs at th' shepherd's nose,
The blushing bank is all my care,
With hearth so red, and walls so fair;

"Heap the sea-coal; come, heap it higher,
"The oaken log lay on the fire:"
The well-wash'd stools, a circling row,
With lad and lass, how fair the show!
The merry can of nut-brown ale,
The laughing jest, the love-sick tale,
'Till, tir'd of chat, the game begins.
The lasses prick the lads with pins;
Roger from Dolly twitch'd the stool,
She, falling, kiss'd the ground, poor fool!
She blush'd so red, with side-long glance
At hob-nail Dick, who griev'd the chance.
But now for Blind-man's Buff they call;
Of each incumbrance clear the hall—
Jenny her silken 'kerchief folds,
And blear-ey'd Will the black lot holds;
Now laughing, stops, with "Silence! hush!"
And Peggy Pout gives Sam a push.——
The Blind-man's arms, extended wide,
Sam slips between:—"O woe betide
"Thee, clumsy Will!"—but titt'ring Kate
Is pen'd up in the corner strait!
And now Will's eyes beheld the play;
He thought his face was t'other way.——
"Now, Kitty, now; what chance hast thou,
"Roger so near thee? Trips, I vow!"
She catches him—then Roger ties
His own head up—but not his eyes;
For thro' the slender cloth he sees,
And runs at Sam, who slips with ease
His clumsy hold, and, dodging round,
Sukey is tumbled on the ground!——
"See what it is to play unfair!
"Where cheating is, there's mischief there."
But Roger still pursues the chace,——
"He sees! he sees!" cries softly, Grace;
"O Roger, thou, unskill'd in art,
"Must, surer bound, go thro' thy part!"
Now Kitty, pert, repeats the rhymes,
And Roger turns him round three times;
Then pauses ere he starts——but Dick
Was mischief bent upon a trick:
Down on his hands and knees he lay,
Directly in the Blind-man's way——
Then cries out, "Hem!" Hodge heard, and ran

With hood-wink'd chance—sure of his man;
But down he came.—Alas, how frail
Our best of hopes, how soon they fail!
With crimson drops he stains the ground;
Confusion startles all around!
Poor piteous Dick supports his head,
And fain would cure the hurt he made;
But Kitty hasted with a key,
And down his back they strait convey
The cold relief—the blood is stay'd,
And Hodge again holds up his head.
Such are the fortunes of the game,
And those who play should stop the same
By wholesome laws, such as—all those
Who on the blinded man impose
Stand in his stead; as, long a-gone,
When men were first a nation grown,
Lawless they liv'd—till wantonness
And liberty began t'increase,
And one man lay in another's way;
Then laws were made to keep fair play.

KING EDWARD THE THIRD

PERSONS

KING EDWARD.	SIR WALTER MANNY.
THE BLACK PRINCE.	LORD AUDLEY.
QUEEN PHILIPPA.	LORD PERCY.
DUKE OF CLARENCE.	BISHOP.
SIR JOHN CHANDOS.	WILLIAM, *Dagworth's Man.*
SIR THOMAS DAGWORTH.	PETER BLUNT, *a common Soldier.*

[1]

SCENE: *The Coast of France*, KING EDWARD *and Nobles before it. The Army.*

King.

O thou, to whose fury the nations are
But as dust, maintain thy servant's right!
Without thine aid, the twisted mail, and spear,
And forged helm, and shield of seven times beaten brass,
Are idle trophies of the vanquisher.

When confusion rages, when the field is in a flame,
When the cries of blood tear horror from heav'n,
And yelling death runs up and down the ranks,
Let Liberty, the charter'd right of Englishmen,
Won by our fathers in many a glorious field,
Enerve my soldiers; let Liberty
Blaze in each countenance, and fire the battle.
The enemy fight in chains, invisible chains, but heavy;
Their minds are fetter'd; then how can they be free?
While, like the mounting flame,
We spring to battle o'er the floods of death,
And these fair youths, the flow'r of England,
Vent'ring their lives in my most righteous cause.
O sheathe their hearts with triple steel, that they
May emulate their fathers' virtues!
And thou, my son, be strong; thou fightest for a crown
That death can never ravish from thy brow,
A crown of glory; but from thy very dust
Shall beam a radiance, to fire the breasts
Of youth unborn! Our names are written equal
In fame's wide trophied hall; 'tis ours to gild
The letters, and to make them shine with gold
That never tarnishes: whether Third Edward,
Or the Prince of Wales, or Montacute, or Mortimer,
Or ev'n the least by birth, shall gain the brightest fame,
Is in his hand to whom all men are equal.
The world of men are like the num'rous stars,
That beam and twinkle in the depth of night,
Each clad in glory according to his sphere;—
But we, that wander from our native seats,
And beam forth lustre on a darkling world,
Grow larger as we advance! and some perhaps
The most obscure at home, that scarce were seen
To twinkle in their sphere, may so advance,
That the astonish'd world, with up-turn'd eyes,
Regardless of the moon, and those that once were bright,
Stand only for to gaze upon their splendor!

[*He here knights the* PRINCE, *and other young Nobles.*

Now let us take a just revenge for those
Brave Lords, who fell beneath the bloody axe
At Paris. Thanks, noble Harcourt, for 'twas
By your advice we landed here in Brittany—
A country not yet sown with destruction,
And where the fiery whirlwind of swift war
Has not yet swept its desolating wing.——

Into three parties we divide by day,
And separate march, but join again at night:
Each knows his rank, and Heav'n marshal all. [*Exeunt.*

[2]

SCENE: *English Court.* LIONEL, DUKE OF CLARENCE; QUEEN PHILIPPA, LORDS, BISHOP, *etc.*

Clarence. My lords, I have, by the advice of her
Whom I am doubly bound to obey, my Parent
And my Sovereign, call'd you together.
My task is great, my burden heavier than
My unfledg'd years;
Yet, with your kind assistance, Lords, I hope
England shall dwell in peace; that while my father
Toils in his wars, and turns his eyes on this
His native shore, and sees commerce fly round
With his white wings, and sees his golden London,
And her silver Thames, throng'd with shining spires
And corded ships, her merchants buzzing round
Like summer bees, and all the golden cities
In his land overflowing with honey,
Glory may not be dimm'd with clouds of care.
Say, Lords, should not our thoughts be first to commerce?
My Lord Bishop, you would recommend us agriculture?
Bishop. Sweet Prince! the arts of peace are great,
And no less glorious than those of war,
Perhaps more glorious in the ph[i]losophic mind.
When I sit at my home, a private man,
My thoughts are on my gardens, and my fields,
How to employ the hand that lacketh bread.
If Industry is in my diocese,
Religion will flourish; each man's heart
Is cultivated, and will bring forth fruit:
This is my private duty and my pleasure.
But as I sit in council with my prince,
My thoughts take in the gen'ral good of the whole,
And England is the land favour'd by Commerce;
For Commerce, tho' the child of Agriculture,
Fosters his parent, who else must sweat and toil,
And gain but scanty fare. Then, my dear Lord,
Be England's trade our care; and we, as tradesmen,
Looking to the gain of this our native land.

Clarence. O my good Lord, true wisdom drops like honey
From your tongue, as from a worship'd oak!
Forgive, my Lords, my talkative youth, that speaks
Not merely what my narrow observation has
Pick'd up, but what I have concluded from your lessons:
Now, by the Queen's advice, I ask your leave
To dine to-morrow with the Mayor of London:
If I obtain your leave, I have another boon
To ask, which is, the favour of your company;
I fear Lord Percy will not give me leave.
Percy. Dear Sir, a prince should always keep his state,
And grant his favours with a sparing hand,
Or they are never rightly valued.
These are my thoughts, yet it were best to go;
But keep a proper dignity, for now
You represent the sacred person of
Your father; 'tis with princes as 'tis with the sun,
If not sometimes o'er-clouded, we grow weary
Of his officious glory.
Clarence. Then you will give me leave to shine sometimes,
My Lord?
Lord. Thou hast a gallant spirit, which I fear
Will be imposed on by the closer sort! [*Aside.*
Clarence. Well, I'll endeavour to take
Lord Percy's advice; I have been used so much
To dignity, that I'm sick on't.
Queen Philippa. Fie, Fie, Lord Clarence; you proceed not to business,
But speak of your own pleasures.
I hope their Lordships will excuse your giddiness.
Clarence. My Lords, the French have fitted out many
Small ships of war, that, like to ravening wolves,
Infest our English seas, devouring all
Our burden'd vessels, spoiling our naval flocks.
The merchants do complain, and beg our aid.
Percy. The merchants are rich enough;
Can they not help themselves?
Bishop. They can, and may; but how to gain their will,
Requires our countenance and help.
Percy. When that they find they must, my Lord, they will:
Let them but suffer awhile, and you shall see
They will bestir themselves.
Bishop. Lord Percy cannot mean that we should suffer
This disgrace; if so, we are not sovereigns
Of the sea; our right, that Heaven gave

To England, when at the birth of nature
She was seated in the deep, the Ocean ceas'd
His mighty roar; and, fawning, play'd around
Her snowy feet, and own'd his awful Queen.
Lord Percy, if the heart is sick, the head
Must be aggriev'd; if but one member suffer,
The heart doth fail. You say, my Lord, the merchants
Can, if they will, defend themselves against
These rovers: this is a noble scheme,
Worthy the brave Lord Percy, and as worthy
His generous aid to put it into practice.

Percy. Lord Bishop, what was rash in me, is wise
In you; I dare not own the plan. 'Tis not
Mine. Yet will I, if you please,
Quickly to the Lord Mayor, and work him onward
To this most glorious voyage, on which cast
I'll set my whole estate.
But we will bring these Gallic rovers under.

Queen Philippa. Thanks, brave Lord Percy; you have the thanks
Of England's Queen, and will, ere long, of England. [*Exeunt.*

[3]

SCENE: *At Cressy.* SIR THOMAS DAGWORTH *and* LORD AUDLEY, *meeting.*

Audley. Good morrow, brave Sir Thomas; the bright morn
Smiles on our army, and the gallant sun
Springs from the hills like a young hero
Into the battle, shaking his golden locks
Exultingly; this is a promising day.

Dagworth. Why, my Lord Audley, I don't know.
Give me your hand, and now I'll tell you what
I think you do not know—Edward's afraid of Philip.

Audley. Ha, Ha, Sir Thomas! you but joke;
Did you e'er see him fear? At Blanchetaque,
When almost singly he drove six thousand
French from the ford, did he fear then?

Dagworth. Yes, fear; that made him fight so.

Audley. By the same reason I might say, 'tis fear
That makes you fight.

Dagworth. Mayhap you may; look upon Edward's face—
No one can say he fears. But when he turns
His back, then I will say it to his face,
He is afraid; he makes us all afraid.

I cannot bear the enemy at my back.
Now here we are at Cressy; where, to-morrow,
To-morrow we shall know. I say, Lord Audley,
That Edward runs away from Philip.
Audley. Perhaps you think the Prince too is afraid?
Dagworth. No; God forbid! I'm sure he is not—
He is a young lion. O I have seen him fight,
And give command, and lightning has flashed
From his eyes across the field; I have seen him
Shake hands with death, and strike a bargain for
The enemy; he has danc'd in the field
Of battle, like the youth at morrice play.
I'm sure he's not afraid, nor Warwick, nor none,
None of us but me; and I am very much afraid.
Audley. Are you afraid too, Sir Thomas?
I believe that as much as I believe
The King's afraid; but what are you afraid of?
Dagworth. Of having my back laid open; we turn
Our backs to the fire till we shall burn our skirts.
Audley. And this, Sir Thomas, you call fear? Your fear
Is of a different kind then from the King's;
He fears to turn his face, and you to turn your back.—
I do not think, Sir Thomas, you know what fear is.

Enter SIR JOHN CHANDOS.

Chandos. Good morrow, Generals; I give you joy:
Welcome to the fields of Cressy. Here we stop,
And wait for Philip.
Dagworth. I hope so.
Audley. There, Sir Thomas; do you call that fear?
Dagworth. I don't know; perhaps he takes it by fits.
Why, noble Chandos, look you here—
One rotten sheep spoils the whole flock;
And if the bell-weather is tainted, I wish
The Prince may not catch the distemper too.
Chandos. Distemper, Sir Thomas! what distemper?
I have not heard.
Dagworth. Why, Chandos, you are a wise man,
I know you understand me; a distemper
The King caught here in France of running away.
Audley. Sir Thomas, you say you have caught it too.
Dagworth. And so will the whole army; 'tis very catching,
For when the coward runs, the brave man totters.
Perhaps the air of the country is the cause.—
I feel it coming upon me, so I strive against it;

You yet are whole, but after a few more
Retreats, we all shall know how to retreat
Better than fight.—To be plain, I think retreating
Too often, takes away a soldier's courage.
Chandos. Here comes the King himself; tell him your thoughts
Plainly, Sir Thomas.
Dagworth. I've told him before, but his disorder
Makes him deaf.

Enter KING EDWARD *and* BLACK PRINCE.

King. Good morrow, Generals; when English courage fails,
Down goes our right to France;
But we are conquerors every where; nothing
Can stand our soldiers; each man is worthy
Of a triumph. Such an army of heroes
Ne'er shouted to the Heav'ns, nor shook the field.
Edward, my son, thou art
Most happy, having such command; the man
Were base who were not fir'd to deeds
Above heroic, having such examples.
Prince. Sire! with respect and deference I look
Upon such noble souls, and wish myself
Worthy the high command that Heaven and you
Have given me. When I have seen the field glow,
And in each countenance the soul of war
Curb'd by the manliest reason, I have been wing'd
With certain victory; and 'tis my boast,
And shall be still my glory, I was inspir'd
By these brave troops.
Dagworth. Your Grace had better make
Them all Generals.
King. Sir Thomas Dagworth, you must have your joke,
And shall, while you can fight as you did at
The Ford.
Dagworth. I have a small petition to your Majesty.
King. What can Sir Thomas Dagworth ask, that Edward
Can refuse?
Dagworth. I hope your Majesty cannot refuse so great
A trifle; I've gilt your cause with my best blood,
And would again, were I not forbid
By him whom I am bound to obey; my hands
Are tied up, my courage shrunk and wither'd,
My sinews slacken'd, and my voice scarce heard;
Therefore I beg I may return to England.
King. I know not what you could have ask'd, Sir Thomas,

That I would not have sooner parted with
Than such a soldier as you have been, and such a friend;
Nay, I will know the most remote particulars
Of this your strange petition; that, if I can,
I still may keep you here.

Dagworth. Here on the fields of Cressy we are settled,
'Till Philip springs the tim'rous covey again.
The Wolf is hunted down by causeless fear;
The Lion flees, and fear usurps his heart,
Startled, astonish'd at the clam'rous Cock;
The Eagle, that doth gaze upon the sun,
Fears the small fire that plays about the fen;
If, at this moment of their idle fear,
The Dog doth seize the Wolf, the Forester the Lion,
The Negro in the crevice of the rock
Doth seize the soaring Eagle; undone by flight,
They tame submit: such the effect flight has
On noble souls. Now hear its opposite:
The tim'rous Stag starts from the thicket wild,
The fearful Crane springs from the splashy fen,
The shining Snake glides o'er the bending grass,
The Stag turns head! and bays the crying Hounds;
The Crane o'ertaken, fighteth with the Hawk;
The Snake doth turn, and bite the padding foot;
And, if your Majesty's afraid of Philip,
You are more like a Lion than a Crane:
Therefore I beg I may return to England.

King. Sir Thomas, now I understand your mirth,
Which often plays with Wisdom for its pastime,
And brings good counsel from the breast of laughter.
I hope you'll stay, and see us fight this battle,
And reap rich harvest in the fields of Cressy;
Then go to England, tell them how we fight,
And set all hearts on fire to be with us.
Philip is plum'd, and thinks we flee from him,
Else he would never dare to attack us. Now,
Now the quarry's set! and Death doth sport
In the bright sunshine of this fatal day.

Dagworth. Now my heart dances, and I am as light
As the young bridegroom going to be married.
Now must I to my soldiers, get them ready,
Furbish our armours bright, new plume our helms,
And we will sing, like the young housewives busied
In the dairy; my feet are wing'd, but not
For flight, an please your grace.

King. If all my soldiers are as pleas'd as you,
'Twill be a gallant thing to fight or die;
Then I can never be afraid of Philip.

Dagworth. A raw-bon'd fellow t'other day pass'd by me;
I told him to put off his hungry looks—
He answer'd me, "I hunger for another battle."
I saw a little Welchman with a fiery face;
I told him he look'd like a candle half
Burn'd out; he answer'd, he was "pig enough
"To light another pattle." Last night, beneath
The moon I walk'd abroad, when all had pitch'd
Their tents, and all were still;
I heard a blooming youth singing a song
He had compos'd, and at each pause he wip'd
His dropping eyes. The ditty was, "if he
"Return'd victorious, he should wed a maiden
"Fairer than snow, and rich as midsummer."
Another wept, and wish'd health to his father.
I chid them both, but gave them noble hopes.
These are the minds that glory in the battle,
And leap and dance to hear the trumpet sound.

King. Sir Thomas Dagworth, be thou near our person;
Thy heart is richer than the vales of France:
I will not part with such a man as thee.
If Philip came arm'd in the ribs of death,
And shook his mortal dart against my head,
Thoud'st laugh his fury into nerveless shame!
Go now, for thou art suited to the work,
Throughout the camp; enflame the timorous,
Blow up the sluggish into ardour, and
Confirm the strong with strength, the weak inspire,
And wing their brows with hope and expectation:
Then to our tent return, and meet to council. [*Exit* DAGWORTH.

Chandos. That man's a hero in his closet, and more
A hero to the servants of his house
Than to the gaping world; he carries windows
In that enlarged breast of his, that all
May see what's done within.

Prince. He is a genuine Englishman, my Chandos,
And hath the spirit of Liberty within him.
Forgive my prejudice, Sir John; I think
My Englishmen the bravest people on
The face of the earth.

Chandos. Courage, my Lord, proceeds from self-dependence:
Teach man to think he's a free agent,

Give but a slave his liberty, he'll shake
Off sloth, and build himself a hut, and hedge
A spot of ground; this he'll defend; 'tis his
By right of nature: thus set in action,
He will still move onward to plan conveniences,
'Till glory fires his breast to enlarge his castle,
While the poor slave drudges all day, in hope
To rest at night.

King. O Liberty, how glorious art thou!
I see thee hov'ring o'er my army, with
Thy wide-stretch'd plumes; I see thee
Lead them on to battle;
I see thee blow thy golden trumpet, while
Thy sons shout the strong shout of victory!
O noble Chandos! think thyself a gardener,
My son a vine, which I commit unto
Thy care; prune all extravagant shoots, and guide
Th' ambitious tendrils in the paths of wisdom;
Water him with thy advice, and Heav'n
Rain fresh'ning dew upon his branches. And,
O Edward, my dear son! learn to think lowly of
Thyself, as we may all each prefer other—
'Tis the best policy, and 'tis our duty. [*Exit*[1] KING EDWARD.

Prince. And may our duty, Chandos, be our pleasure.
Now we are alone, Sir John, I will unburden,
And breathe my hopes into the burning air,
Where thousand deaths are posting up and down,
Commission'd to this fatal field of Cressy;
Methinks I see them arm my gallant soldiers,
And gird the sword upon each thigh, and fit
Each shining helm, and string each stubborn bow,
And dance to the neighing of our steeds.
Methinks the shout begins, the battle burns;
Methinks I see them perch on English crests,
And roar the wild flame of fierce war upon
The thronged enemy! In truth, I am too full;
It is my sin to love the noise of war.
Chandos, thou seest my weakness; strong nature
Will bend or break us; my blood, like a springtide,
Does rise so high, to overflow all bounds
Of moderation; while Reason, in her[2]
Frail bark, can see no shore or bound for vast

[1] Corrected from *Exeunt*.

[2] *Altered by pen to* his *in some copies.*

Ambition. Come, take the helm, my Chandos,
That my full-blown sails overset me not
In the wild tempest; condemn my 'vent'rous youth,
That plays with danger, as the innocent child
Unthinking plays upon the viper's den;
I am a coward in my reason, Chandos.
Chandos. You are a man, my prince, and a brave man,
If I can judge of actions; but your heat
Is the effect of youth, and want of use;
Use makes the armed field and noisy war
Pass over as a summer cloud, unregarded,
Or but expected as a thing of course.
Age is contemplative; each rolling year
Brings forth fruit to the mind's treasure-house;
While vacant youth doth crave and seek about
Within itself, and findeth discontent:
Then, tir'd of thought, impatient takes the wing,
Seizes the fruits of time, attacks experience,
Roams round vast Nature's forest, where no bounds
Are set, the swiftest may have room, the strongest
Find prey; till tir'd at length, sated and tired
With the changing sameness, old variety,
We sit us down, and view our former joys
With distaste and dislike.
Prince. Then if we must tug for experience,
Let us not fear to beat round Nature's wilds,
And rouze the strongest prey; then if we fall,
We fall with glory; I know the wolf
Is dangerous to fight, not good for food,
Nor is the hide a comely vestment; so
We have our battle for our pains. I know
That youth has need of age to point fit prey,
And oft the stander-by shall steal the fruit
Of th' other's labour. This is philosophy;
These are the tricks of the world; but the pure soul
Shall mount on native wings, disdaining
Little sport, and cut a path into the heaven of glory,
Leaving a track of light for men to wonder at.
I'm glad my father does not hear me talk;
You can find friendly excuses for me, Chandos;
But do you not think, Sir John, that if it please
Th' Almighty to stretch out my span of life,
I shall with pleasure view a glorious action,
Which my youth master'd.
Chandos. Considerate age, my Lord, views motives,

And not acts; when neither warbling voice
Nor trilling pipe is heard, nor pleasure sits
With trembling age; the voice of Conscience then,
Sweeter than music in a summer's eve,
Shall warble round the snowy head, and keep
Sweet symphony to feather'd angels, sitting
As guardians round your chair; then shall the pulse
Beat slow, and taste, and touch, and sight, and sound, and smell,
That sing and dance round Reason's fine-wrought throne,
Shall flee away, and leave him[1] all forlorn;
Yet not forlorn if Conscience is his friend. [*Exeunt.*

[4]

SCENE *in* SIR THOMAS DAGWORTH'S *Tent.* DAGWORTH *and* WILLIAM *his Man.*

Dagworth. Bring hither my armour, William;
Ambition is the growth of ev'ry clime.
William. Does it grow in England, Sir?
Dagworth. Aye, it grows most in lands most cultivated.
William. Then it grows most in France; the vines here
Are finer than any we have in England.
Dagworth. Aye, but the oaks are not.
William. What is the tree you mentioned? I don't think
I ever saw it.
Dagworth. Ambition.
William. Is it a little creeping root that grows in ditches?
Dagworth. Thou dost not understand me, William.
It is a root that grows in every breast;
Ambition is the desire or passion that one man
Has to get before another in any pursuit after glory;
But I don't think you have any of it.
William. Yes, I have; I have a great ambition to know every thing, Sir.

Dagworth. But when our first ideas are wrong, what follows must all be wrong of course; 'tis best to know a little, and to know that little aright.

William. Then, Sir, I should be glad to know if it was not ambition that brought over our King to France to fight for his right?

Dagworth. Tho' the knowledge of that will not profit thee much, yet I will tell you that it was ambition.

William. Then if ambition is a sin, we are all guilty in coming with him, and in fighting for him.

[1] *Altered by pen from* them *in some copies.*

Dagworth. Now, William, thou dost thrust the question home; but I must tell you, that guilt being an act of the mind, none are guilty but those whose minds are prompted by that same ambition.

William. Now I always thought that a man might be guilty of doing wrong, without knowing it was wrong.

Dagworth. Thou art a natural philosopher, and knowest truth by instinct, while reason runs aground, as we have run our argument. Only remember, William, all have it in their power to know the motives of their own actions, and 'tis a sin to act without some reason.

William. And whoever acts without reason, may do a great deal of harm without knowing it.

Dagworth. Thou art an endless moralist.

William. Now there's a story come into my head, that I will tell your honour, if you'll give me leave.

Dagworth. No, William, save it till another time; this is no time for story-telling; but here comes one who is as entertaining as a good story.

Enter PETER BLUNT.

Peter. Yonder's a musician going to play before the King; it's a new song about the French and English, and the Prince has made the minstrel a 'squire, and given him I don't know what, and I can't tell whether he don't mention us all one by one; and he is to write another about all us that are to die, that we may be remembered in Old England, for all our blood and bones are in France; and a great deal more that we shall all hear by and by; and I came to tell your honour, because you love to hear war-songs.

Dagworth. And who is this minstrel, Peter, do'st know?

Peter. O aye, I forgot to tell that; he has got the same name as Sir John Chandos, that the prince is always with—the wise man, that knows us all as well as your honour, only e'nt so good natur'd.

Dagworth. I thank you, Peter, for your information, but not for your compliment, which is not true; there's as much difference between him and me, as between glittering sand and fruitful mould; or shining glass and a wrought diamond, set in rich gold, and fitted to the finger of an emperor: such is that worthy Chandos.

Peter. I know your honour does not think any thing of yourself, but every body else does.

Dagworth. Go, Peter, get you gone; flattery is delicious, even from the lips of a babbler. [*Exit* PETER.

William. I never flatter your honour.

Dagworth. I don't know that.

William. Why you know, Sir, when we were in England at the tournament at Windsor, and the Earl of Warwick was tumbled over, you ask'd me if he did not look well when he fell? and I said, No, he look'd very foolish; and you was very angry with me for not flattering you.

Dagworth. You mean that I was angry with you for not flattering the Earl of Warwick. [*Exeunt.*

[5]

SCENE: SIR THOMAS DAGWORTH'S *Tent.*

SIR THOMAS DAGWORTH—*to him.*

Enter SIR WALTER MANNY.

Sir Walter. Sir Thomas Dagworth, I have been weeping
Over the men that are to die to-day.
Dagworth. Why, brave Sir Walter, you or I may fall.
Sir Walter. I know this breathing flesh must lie and rot,
Cover'd with silence and forgetfulness.—
Death wons in cities' smoke, and in still night,
When men sleep in their beds, walketh about!
How many in walled cities lie and groan,
Turning themselves upon their beds,
Talking with death, answering his hard demands!
How many walk in darkness, terrors are round
The curtains of their beds, destruction is
Ready at the door! How many sleep
In earth, cover'd with stones and deathy dust,
Resting in quietness, whose spirits walk
Upon the clouds of heaven, to die no more!
Yet death is terrible, tho' borne on angels' wings!
How terrible then is the field of death,
Where he doth rend the vault of heaven,
And shake the gates of hell!
O Dagworth, France is sick! the very sky,
Tho' sunshine light it, seems to me as pale
As the pale fainting man on his death-bed,
Whose face is shewn by light of sickly taper!
It makes me sad and sick at very heart,
Thousands must fall to-day!
Dagworth. Thousands of souls must leave this prison-house
To be exalted to those heavenly fields,
Where songs of triumph, palms of victory,
Where peace, and joy, and love, and calm content,
Sit singing in the azure clouds, and strew
Flowers of heaven's growth over the banquet-table;
Bind ardent Hope upon your feet like shoes,

Put on the robe of preparation,
The table is prepar'd in shining heaven,
The flowers of immortality are blown;
Let those that fight, fight in good stedfastness,
And those that fall shall rise in victory.
Sir Walter. I've often seen the burning field of war,
And often heard the dismal clang of arms;
But never, till this fatal day of Cressy,
Has my soul fainted with these views of death!
I seem to be in one great charnel-house,
And seem to scent the rotten carcases!
I seem to hear the dismal yells of death,
While the black gore drops from his horrid jaws:
Yet I not fear the monster in his pride.——
But O the souls that are to die to-day!
Dagworth. Stop, brave Sir Walter; let me drop a tear,
Then let the clarion of war begin;
I'll fight and weep, 'tis in my country's cause;
I'll weep and shout for glorious liberty.
Grim war shall laugh and shout, decked in tears,
And blood shall flow like streams across the meadows,
That murmur down their pebbly channels, and
Spend their sweet lives to do their country service:
Then shall England's verdure shoot, her fields shall smile,
Her ships shall sing across the foaming sea,
Her mariners shall use the flute and viol,
And rattling guns, and black and dreary war,
Shall be no more.
Sir Walter. Well, let the trumpet sound, and the drum beat;
Let war stain the blue heavens with bloody banners,
I'll draw my sword, nor ever sheath it up
'Till England blow the trump of victory,
Or I lay stretch'd upon the field of death! [*Exeunt*.

[6]

SCENE, *in the Camp. Several of the Warriors met at the King's Tent with a* MINSTREL, *who sings the following song:*

O Sons of Trojan Brutus, cloath'd in war,
Whose voices are the thunder of the field,
Rolling dark clouds o'er France, muffling the sun
In sickly darkness like a dim eclipse,
Threatening as the red brow of storms, as fire
Burning up nations in your wrath and fury!

Your ancestors came from the fires of Troy,
(Like lions rouz'd by light'ning from their dens,
Whose eyes do glare against the stormy fires)
Heated with war, fill'd with the blood of Greeks,
With helmets hewn, and shields covered with gore,
In navies black, broken with wind and tide!

They landed in firm array upon the rocks
Of Albion; they kiss'd the rocky shore;
"Be thou our mother, and our nurse," they said;
"Our children's mother, and thou shalt be our grave;
"The sepulchre of ancient Troy, from whence
"Shall rise cities, and thrones, and arms, and awful pow'rs."

Our fathers swarm from the ships. Giant voices
Are heard from the hills, the enormous sons
Of Ocean run from rocks and caves: wild men,
Naked and roaring like lions, hurling rocks,
And wielding knotty clubs, like oaks entangled
Thick as a forest, ready for the axe.

Our fathers move in firm array to battle;
The savage monsters rush like roaring fire;
Like as a forest roars, with crackling flames,
When the red lightning, borne by furious storms,
Lights on some woody shore; the parched heavens
Rain fire into the molten raging sea!

The smoaking trees are strewn upon the shore,
Spoil'd of their verdure! O how oft have they
Defy'd the storm that howled o'er their heads!
Our fathers, sweating, lean on their spears, and view
The mighty dead: giant bodies streaming blood,
Dread visages frowning in silent death!

Then Brutus spoke, inspir'd; our fathers sit
Attentive on the melancholy shore:——
Hear ye the voice of Brutus—"The flowing waves
"Of time come rolling o'er my breast," he said;
"And my heart labours with futurity:
"Our sons shall rule the empire of the sea.

"Their mighty wings shall stretch from east to west,
"Their nest is in the sea; but they shall roam
"Like eagles for the prey; nor shall the young
"Crave or be heard; for plenty shall bring forth,
"Cities shall sing, and vales in rich array
"Shall laugh, whose fruitful laps bend down with fulness.

"Our sons shall rise from thrones in joy,
"Each one buckling on his armour; Morning
"Shall be prevented by their swords gleaming,
"And Evening hear their song of victory!
"Their towers shall be built upon the rocks,
"Their daughters shall sing, surrounded with shining spears!

"Liberty shall stand upon the cliffs of Albion,
"Casting her blue eyes over the green ocean;
"Or, tow'ring, stand upon the roaring waves,
"Stretching her mighty spear o'er distant lands;
"While, with her eagle wings, she covereth
"Fair Albion's shore, and all her families."

PROLOGUE

INTENDED FOR A DRAMATIC PIECE OF

KING EDWARD THE FOURTH

O for a voice like thunder, and a tongue
To drown the throat of war!—When the senses
Are shaken, and the soul is driven to madness,
Who can stand? When the souls of the oppressed
Fight in the troubled air that rages, who can stand?
When the whirlwind of fury comes from the
Throne of God, when the frowns of his countenance
Drive the nations together, who can stand?
When Sin claps his broad wings over the battle,
And sails rejoicing in the flood of Death;
When souls are torn to everlasting fire,
And fiends of Hell rejoice upon the slain,
O who can stand? O who hath caused this?
O who can answer at the throne of God?
The Kings and Nobles of the Land have done it!
Hear it not, Heaven, thy Ministers have done it!

PROLOGUE TO KING JOHN

Justice hath heaved a sword to plunge in Albion's breast; for Albion's sins are crimson dy'd, and the red scourge follows her desolate sons! Then Patriot rose; full oft did Patriot rise, when Tyranny hath stain'd fair Albion's breast with her own children's gore. Round his majestic feet deep thunders roll; each heart does tremble, and each knee grows slack. The stars of heaven tremble: the roaring voice of war, the trumpet, calls to battle! Brother in brother's blood must bathe, rivers of death! O land, most hapless! O beauteous island, how forsaken! Weep from thy silver fountains; weep from thy gentle rivers! The angel of the island weeps! Thy widowed virgins weep beneath thy shades! Thy aged fathers gird themselves for war! The sucking infant lives to die in battle; the weeping mother feeds him for the slaughter! The husbandman doth leave his bending harvest! Blood cries afar! The land doth sow itself! The glittering youth of courts must gleam in arms! The aged senators their ancient swords assume! The trembling sinews of old age must work the work of death against their progeny; for Tyranny hath stretch'd his purple arm, and "blood," he cries; "the chariots and the horses, the noise of shout, and dreadful thunder of the battle heard afar!"—Beware, O Proud! thou shalt be humbled; thy cruel brow, thine iron heart is smitten, though lingering Fate is slow. O yet may Albion smile again, and stretch her peaceful arms, and raise her golden head, exultingly! Her citizens shall throng about her gates, her mariners shall sing upon the sea, and myriads shall to her temples crowd! Her sons shall joy as in the morning! Her daughters sing as to the rising year!

A WAR SONG TO ENGLISHMEN

Prepare, prepare the iron helm of war,
Bring forth the lots, cast in the spacious orb;
Th' Angel of Fate turns them with mighty hands,
And casts them out upon the darken'd earth!
Prepare, prepare.

Prepare your hearts for Death's cold hand! prepare
Your souls for flight, your bodies for the earth!
Prepare your arms for glorious victory!
Prepare your eyes to meet a holy God!
Prepare, prepare.

Whose fatal scroll is that? Methinks 'tis mine!
Why sinks my heart, why faultereth my tongue?

Had I three lives, I'd die in such a cause,
And rise, with ghosts, over the well-fought field.
Prepare, prepare.

The arrows of Almighty God are drawn!
Angels of Death stand in the low'ring heavens!
Thousands of souls must seek the realms of light,
And walk together on the clouds of heaven!
Prepare, prepare.

Soldiers, prepare! Our cause is Heaven's cause;
Soldiers, prepare! Be worthy of our cause:
Prepare to meet our fathers in the sky:
Prepare, O troops, that are to fall to-day!
Prepare, prepare.

Alfred shall smile, and make his harp rejoice;
The Norman William, and the learned Clerk,
And Lion Heart, and black-brow'd Edward with
His loyal queen shall rise, and welcome us!
Prepare, prepare.

THE COUCH OF DEATH

The veiled Evening walked solitary down the western hills, and Silence reposed in the valley; the birds of day were heard in their nests, rustling in brakes and thickets; and the owl and bat flew round the darkening trees: all is silent when Nature takes her repose.—In former times, on such an evening, when the cold clay breathed with life, and our ancestors, who now sleep in their graves, walked on the stedfast globe, the remains of a family of the tribes of Earth, a mother and a sister were gathered to the sick bed of a youth: Sorrow linked them together, leaning on one another's necks alternately—like lilies, dropping tears in each other's bosom, they stood by the bed like reeds bending over a lake, when the evening drops trickle down. His voice was low as the whisperings of the woods when the wind is asleep, and the visions of Heaven unfold their visitation. "Parting is hard, and "death is terrible; I seem to walk through a deep valley, far from the "light of day, alone and comfortless! The damps of death fall thick "upon me! Horrors stare me in the face! I look behind, there is no "returning; Death follows after me; I walk in regions of Death, where "no tree is; without a lantern to direct my steps, without a staff to "support me."—Thus he laments through the still evening, till the curtains of darkness were drawn! Like the sound of a broken pipe, the aged woman raised her voice. "O my son, my son, I know but "little of the path thou goest! But lo, there is a God, who made the "world; stretch out thy hand to Him." The youth replied, like a voice heard from a sepulchre, "My hand is feeble, how should I stretch it "out? My ways are sinful, how should I raise mine eyes? My voice "hath used deceit, how should I call on Him who is Truth? My "breath is loathsome, how should he not be offended? If I lay my "face in the dust, the grave opens its mouth for me; if I lift up my "head, sin covers me as a cloak! O my dear friends, pray ye for me! "Stretch forth your hands, that my helper may come! Through the "void space I walk between the sinful world and eternity! Beneath "me burns eternal fire! O for a hand to pluck me forth!" As the voice of an omen heard in the silent valley, when the few inhabitants cling trembling together: as the voice of the Angel of Death, when the thin beams of the moon give a faint light, such was this young man's voice to his friends! Like the bubbling waters of the brook in the dead of night, the aged woman raised her cry, and said, "O Voice, that "dwellest in my breast, can I not cry, and lift my eyes to Heaven? "Thinking of this, my spirit is turned within me into confusion! "O my child, my child! is thy breath infected? So is mine. As the "deer, wounded by the brooks of water, so the arrows of sin stick in "my flesh; the poison hath entered into my marrow."—Like rolling waves, upon a desert shore, sighs succeeded sighs; they covered their faces, and wept! The youth lay silent—his mother's arm was under his head; he was like a cloud tossed by the winds, till the sun shine, and the drops of rain glisten, the yellow harvest breathes, and the thankful eyes of the villagers are turned up in smiles. The traveller that hath taken shelter under an oak, eyes the distant country with joy! Such smiles were seen upon the face of the youth; a visionary hand wiped away his tears, and a ray of light beamed around his head! All was still. The moon hung not out her lamp, and the stars faintly glimmered in the summer sky; the breath of night slept among the leaves of the forest; the bosom of the lofty hill drank in the silent dew, while on his majestic brow the voice of Angels is heard, and stringed sounds ride upon the wings of night. The sorrowful pair lift up their heads, hovering Angels are around them, voices of comfort are heard over the Couch of Death, and the youth breathes out his soul with joy into eternity.

CONTEMPLATION

Who is this, that with unerring step dares tempt the wilds, where only Nature's foot hath trod? 'Tis Contemplation, daughter of the grey Morning! Majestical she steppeth, and with her pure quill on every flower writeth Wisdom's name. Now lowly bending, whispers in mine ear, "O man, how great, how little thou! O man, slave of each "moment, lord of eternity! seest thou where Mirth sits on the painted "cheek? doth it not seem ashamed of such a place, and grow im- "moderate to brave it out? O what an humble garb true Joy puts on! "Those who want Happiness must stoop to find it; it is a flower that "grows in every vale. Vain foolish man, that roams on lofty rocks, "where, 'cause his garments are swoln with wind, he fancies he is "grown into a giant! Lo then, Humility, take it, and wear it in thine "heart; lord of thyself, thou then art lord of all. Clamour brawls "along the streets, and destruction hovers in the city's smoak; but "on these plains, and in these silent woods, true joys descend: here "build thy nest; here fix thy staff; delights blossom around; number- "less beauties blow; the green grass springs in joy, and the nimble air "kisses the leaves; the brook stretches its arms along the velvet "meadow, its silver inhabitants sport and play; the youthful sun "joys like a hunter rouzed to the chace: he rushes up the sky, and "lays hold on the immortal coursers of day; the sky glitters with the "jingling trappings! Like a triumph, season follows season, while "the airy music fills the world with joyful sounds." I answered "Heavenly goddess! I am wrapped in mortality, my flesh is a prison, "my bones the bars of death; Misery builds over our cottage roofs, "and Discontent runs like a brook. Even in childhood Sorrow slept "with me in my cradle; he followed me up and down in the house "when I grew up; he was my school-fellow: thus he was in my steps "and in my play, till he became to me as my brother. I walked through "dreary places with him, and in church-yards; and I oft found my- "self sitting by Sorrow on a tomb-stone!"

SAMSON

Samson, the strongest of the children of men, I sing; how he was foiled by woman's arts, by a false wife brought to the gates of death! O Truth, that shinest with propitious beams, turning our earthly night to heavenly day, from presence of the Almighty Father! thou visitest our darkling world with blessed feet, bringing good news of Sin and Death destroyed! O white-robed Angel, guide my timorous hand to write as on a lofty rock with iron pens the words of truth, that all who pass may read.—Now Night, noon-tide of damned spirits, over the silent earth spreads her pavilion, while in dark council sat Philista's lords; and where strength failed, black thoughts in ambush lay. Their helmed youth and aged warriors in dust together lie[1], and Desolation spread his wings over the land of Palestine; from side to side the land groans, her prowess lost, and seeks to hide

---

[1] *Corrected from* ly.

her bruised head under the mists of night, breeding dark plots. For Dalila's fair arts have long been tried in vain; in vain she wept in many a treacherous tear. "Go on, fair traitress; do thy guileful work; "ere once again the changing moon her circuit hath performed, thou "shalt overcome, and conquer him by force unconquerable, and "wrest his secret from him. Call thine alluring arts and honest-"seeming brow, the holy kiss of love, and the transparent tear; put "on fair linen, that with the lily vies, purple and silver; neglect thy "hair, to seem more lovely in thy loose attire; put on thy country's "pride, deceit; and eyes of love decked in mild sorrow, and sell thy "Lord for gold."—For now, upon her sumptuous couch reclined, in gorgeous pride, she still intreats, and still she grasps his vigorous knees with her fair arms.—"Thou lov'st me not! thou'rt war, thou "art not love! O foolish Dalila! O weak woman! it is death cloathed "in flesh thou lovest, and thou hast been incircled in his arms!— "Alas, my Lord, what am I calling thee? Thou art my God! To thee "I pour my tears for sacrifice morning and evening: My days are "covered with sorrow! Shut up, darkened. By night I am deceived! "Who says that thou wast born of mortal kind? Destruction was thy "father, a lioness suckled thee, thy young hands tore human limbs, "and gorged human flesh! Come hither, Death; art thou not Samson's "servant? 'Tis Dalila that calls, thy master's wife; no, stay, and let "thy master do the deed: one blow of that strong arm would ease "my pain; then should I lay at quiet, and have rest. Pity forsook thee "at thy birth! O Dagon furious, and all ye gods of Palestine, with-"draw your hand! I am but a weak woman. Alas, I am wedded to "your enemy! I will go mad, and tear my crisped hair; I'll run about, "and pierce the ears o' th' gods! O Samson, hold me not; thou lovest "me not! Look not upon me with those deathful eyes! Thou wouldst "my death, and death approaches fast."—Thus, in false tears, she bath'd his feet, and thus she day by day oppressed his soul: he seemed a mountain, his brow among the clouds; she seemed a silver stream, his feet embracing. Dark thoughts rolled to and fro in his mind, like thunder clouds, troubling the sky; his visage was troubled; his soul was distressed.—"Though I should tell her all my heart, what can "I fear? Though I should tell this secret of my birth, the utmost may "be warded off as well when told as now." She saw him moved, and thus resumes her wiles.—"Samson, I'm thine; do with me what "thou wilt; my friends are enemies; my life is death; I am a traitor "to my nation, and despised; my joy is given into the hands of him "who hates me, using deceit to the wife of his bosom. Thrice hast "thou mocked me, and grieved my soul. Didst thou not tell me with "green withes[1] to bind thy nervous arms, and after that, when I had

[1] *Corrected from* withs.

"found thy falsehood, with new ropes to bind thee fast? I knew thou "didst but mock me. Alas, when in thy sleep I bound thee with them "to try thy truth, I cried, 'The Philistines be upon thee, Samson!' "Then did suspicion wake thee; how didst thou rend the feeble ties! "Thou fearest nought, what shouldst thou fear? Thy power is more "than mortal, none can hurt thee; thy bones are brass, thy sinews are "iron! Ten thousand spears are like the summer grass; an army of "mighty men are as flocks in the vallies; what canst thou fear? I drink "my tears like water; I live upon sorrow! O worse than wolves and "tygers, what canst thou give when such a trifle is denied me? But "O at last thou mockest me, to shame my over-fond inquiry! Thou "toldest me to weave thee to the beam by thy strong hair; I did even "that to try thy truth: but when I cried, 'The Philistines be upon " thee!' then didst thou leave me to bewail that Samson loved me "not."—He sat, and inward griev'd; he saw and lov'd the beauteous suppliant, nor could conceal aught that might appease her; then, leaning on her bosom, thus he spoke: "Hear, O Dalila! doubt no "more of Samson's love; for that fair breast was made the ivory palace "of my inmost heart, where it shall lie at rest; for sorrow is the lot "of all of woman born: for care was I brought forth, and labour is "my lot: nor matchless might, nor wisdom, nor every gift enjoyed, "can from the heart of man hide sorrow.—Twice was my birth fore-"told from heaven, and twice a sacred vow enjoined me that I should "drink no wine, nor eat of any unclean thing, for holy unto Israel's "God I am, a Nazarite even from my mother's womb. Twice was it "told, that it might not be broken. 'Grant me a son, kind Heaven', "Manoa cried; but Heaven refused! Childless he mourned, but "thought his God knew best. In solitude, though not obscure, in "Israel he lived, till venerable age came on: his flocks increased, and "plenty crowned his board: beloved, revered of man! But God hath "other joys in store. Is burdened Israel his grief? The son of his old "age shall set it free! The venerable sweetner of his life receives the "promise first from Heaven. She saw the maidens play, and blessed "their innocent mirth; she blessed each new-joined pair; but from "her the long-wished deliverer shall spring. Pensive, alone she sat "within the house, when busy day was fading, and calm evening, "time for contemplation, rose from the forsaken east, and drew the "curtains of heaven; pensive she sat, and thought on Israel's grief, "and silent prayed to Israel's God; when lo, an angel from the fields "of light entered the house! His form was manhood in the prime, and "from his spacious brow shot terrors through the evening shade! "But mild he hailed her——'Hail, highly favoured!' said he, 'for lo, " 'thou shalt conceive, and bear a son, and Israel's strength shall be " 'upon his shoulders, and he shall be called Israel's Deliverer! Now " 'therefore drink no wine, and eat not any unclean thing, for he shall

" 'be a Nazarite to God.'—Then as a neighbour, when his evening "tale is told, departs, his blessing leaving, so seemed he to depart: "she wondered with exceeding joy, nor knew he was an angel. Manoa "left his fields to sit in the house, and take his evening's rest from "labour—the sweetest time that God has allotted mortal man. He "sat, and heard with joy, and praised God who Israel still doth keep. "The time rolled on, and Israel groaned oppressed. The sword was "bright, while the plow-share rusted, till hope grew feeble, and was "ready to give place to doubting: then prayed Manoa—'O Lord, thy " 'flock is scattered on the hills! The wolf teareth them, Oppression " 'stretches his rod over our land, our country is plowed with swords, " 'and reaped in blood! The echoes of slaughter reach from hill to " 'hill! Instead of peaceful pipe, the shepherd bears a sword; the ox " 'goad is turned into a spear! O when shall our Deliverer come? The " 'Philistine riots on our flocks, our vintage is gathered by bands of " 'enemies! Stretch forth thy hand, and save.'——Thus prayed "Manoa. The aged woman walked into the field, and lo, again the "angel came! Clad as a traveller fresh risen on his journey; she ran "and called her husband, who came and talked with him.——'O man " 'of God,' said he, 'thou comest from far! Let us detain thee while " 'I make ready a kid, that thou mayest sit and eat, and tell us of thy " 'name and warfare[1]; that when thy sayings come to pass, we may " 'honour thee.' The Angel answered, 'My name is wonderful; " 'enquire not after it, seeing it is a secret: but, if thou wilt, offer an " 'offering unto the Lord.' "

[END OF POETICAL SKETCHES]

[THEN SHE BORE PALE DESIRE]

Written before 1777

then she bore Pale desire, father of Curiosity, a Virgin ever young. And after, Leaden Sloth, from whom came Ignorance, who brought forth Wonder. These are the Gods which came from fear, for Gods like these nor male nor female are, but single Pregnate, or, if they list, together mingling bring forth mighty pow'rs. She knew them not; yet they all war with Shame, and strengthen her weak arm. [Now day arose, the Golden Sun his mighty Race began, Refreshing the Cold earth with beaming Joy *del.*]. But Pride awoke, nor knew that Joy was born, and taking Pois'nous Seed from her own Bowels in the

[1] *Probably a misprint for* wayfare.

Monster Shame infus'd; forth came Ambition, crawling like a toad. Pride Bears it in her Bosom, and the Gods all bow to it. So Great its Power that Pride, inspir'd by it, Prophetic saw the Kingdoms of the World & all their Glory, Giants of Mighty arm, before the flood, Cain's city built with Murder. Then Babel mighty Rear'd him to the Skies, Babel with thousand tongues. Confusion it was call'd and Given to Shame; this Pride observing inly Griev'd, but knew not that the rest was Giv'n to Shame as well as this. [*words del.*]

Then Nineva & Babylon and costly tyre and ev'n Jerusalem was shewn, the holy City. Then Athens' learning, & the Pride of Greece; and, further from the Rising Sun, was Rome, seated on seven hills, the mistress of the world, Emblem of Pride. She saw the Arts their treasures Bring, and luxury his bounteous table spread: but now a cloud o'er casts and back to th'East, to Constantine's Great City, Empire fled, Ere long to bleed & die, A sacrifice done by a Priestly hand. So, once, the Sun his Chariot drew back to prolong a Good King's life. The cloud o'er past & Rome now shone again, Miter'd and Crown'd with triple crown. Then Pride was better Pleas'd. She saw the World fall down in Adoration [Nor could Refrain but Cry'd, "O this is the blest time when Pride shall hold the sway" *del.*]. But now, full to the Setting Sun, a Sun arose out of the Sea; it rose, & shed Sweet Influence o'er the Earth. Pride feared for her City, but not long, for looking stedfastly, she saw that Pride Reign'd here. Now Direful Pains accost her, and still pregnant, so Envy came, & Hate, twin progeny. Envy hath a serpent's head of fearful bulk, hissing with hundred tongues; her pois'nous breath breeds Satire, foul contagion, from which none are free: o'er whelm'd by ever During Thirst she swalloweth her own Poison, which consumes her nether Parts, from Whence a River Springs. Most Black & loathsom through the land it Runs, Rolling with furious Noise; but at the last it settles in a lake called Oblivion: 'tis at this River's fount where ev'ry mortal's Cup is Mix't. My cup is fill'd with Envy's Rankest Draught [and Death is in the Pot *del.*]; a miracle, No less, can set me Right. Desire still pines but for one Cooling Drop, and 'tis Deny'd; while others in Contentment's downy Nest do sleep, it is the cursed thorn wounding my breast that makes me sing: however sweet, 'tis Envy that Inspires my Song: prickt by the fame of others how I mourn, and my complaints are Sweeter than their Joys; but O, could I at Envy Shake my hands, my notes should Rise to meet the New born Day. Hate, Meager hag, sets Envy on, Unable to Do ought herself, but Worn away, a Bloodless Daemon. The Gods all Serve her at her will; so great her Power is, like fabled hecate, she doth bind them to her law. Far in a Direful Cave she lives unseen, Clos'd from the Eye of Day, to the hard Rock transfixt by fate, and here she works her witcheries, that when she Groans she shakes the Solid Ground. Now Envy she controlls with numming trance, & Melancholy, sprung from her dark womb. There is a Melancholy, O how lovely 'tis, whose heaven is in the heavenly Mind, for she from heaven came, and where she goes heaven still doth follow her. She brings true Joy once fled, & Contemplation is her Daughter. Sweet Contemplation! [She teacheth knowledge how to know *del.*] She brings humility to man. "Take her," she says, "& wear her in thine heart, lord of thyself, thou then "art lord of all." [humility, her Daughter *del.*] 'Tis Contemplation teacheth knowledge truly how to know, and Reinstates him on his throne, once lost; how lost, I'll tell. But stop the motley Song. I'll shew how Conscience Came from heaven. But O, who listens to his Voice. 'Twas Conscience who brought Melancholy down, Conscience was sent, a Guard to Reason, Reason once fairer than the light, till foul'd in Knowledge's dark Prison house. For knowledge drove sweet Innocence away, and Reason would have follow'd, but fate suffer'd not; then down came Conscience with his lovely band. The Eager Song Goes on, telling how Pride against her father Warr'd & Overcame. Down his white Beard the silver torrents Roll and swelling sighs burst forth, his Children all in arms appear to tear him from his throne. Black was the deed, most Black. Shame in a Mist sat Round his troubled head, & fill'd him with confusion. Fear as a torrent wild Roar'd Round his throne; the mighty pillars shake. Now all the Gods in black'ning Ranks appear, like a tempestuous thunder Cloud. Pride leads them on. Now they surround the God and bind him fast. Pride bound him, then usurp'd o'er all the Gods. She Rode upon the swelling wind, and scatter'd all who durst t'oppose; but Shame opposing fierce and hovering over her in the darkning storm, She brought forth Rage. And Shame bore honour, & made league with Pride[1]. Meanwhile Strife, Mighty Prince, was born. Envy in direful Pains him bore; then Envy brought forth Care. Care sitteth in the wrinkled brow. Strife, shapeless, sitteth under thrones of kings, like smould'ring fire, or in the Buzz of cities flies abroad. Care brought forth Covet, Eyeless & prone to th'Earth, and Strife brought forth Revenge. Hate, brooding in her Dismal den, grew Pregnant, & [brought forth *del.*] bore Scorn & Slander. Scorn waits on Pride, but Slander flies around the World to do the Work of hate, her drudge & Elf: but Policy doth drudge for hate, as well as Slander, & oft makes use of her, Policy, Son of Shame. Indeed hate controlls all the Gods at will. Policy brought forth Guile & fraud; these Gods last nam'd live in the Smoke of Cities, on Dusky wing breathing forth Clamour & Destruction; alas, in Cities where's the man whose face is not a mask unto his heart? Pride made a Goddess fair, or Image rather, till knowledge animated it; 'twas call'd Self love. The Gods admiring

[1] *This sentence is marked for insertion in two places. See below.*

loaded her with Gifts, as once Pandora. She 'mongst men was sent, and worser ills attended her by far. She was a Goddess Powerful & bore Conceit & Emulation. Conceit and Shame bore honour & made league with Pride, & Policy doth dwell with her, by whom she had Mistrust and Suspition; [by Shame she had a Son call'd Honour who bore Revenge *del.*] then [Self love *del.*] bore a Daughter called Emulation, who married honour; these follow her around the World. Go see the city, friends Join'd Hand in Hand. Go see the Natural tie of flesh & blood. Go see more strong the ties of marriage love—thou Scarce Shall find, but Self love Stands Between.

[WOE, CRIED THE MUSE]

Written before 1777

Woe, cried the muse, tears Started at the Sound. Grief percht upon my brow and thought Embrac'd Her. "What does this mean," I cried, "when all around Summer hath spred her Plumes and tunes her "[*word del.*] Notes, When Buxom Joy doth fan his wings & Golden "Pleasures Beam around my head? Why, Grief, dost thou accost "me?" The Muse then struck her Deepest [note *del.*] string & Sympathy Came forth. She spre'd her [shadowy *del.*] awful Wings & gave me up; my Nerves with trembling Curdle all my blood, & ev'ry piece of flesh doth Cry out Woe. [hark *del.*] how soon the Winds Sing round the Dark'ning Storm, ere while so fair; and now they fall & beg the skies will weep; a Day like this laid Elfrid in the Dust, Sweet Elfrid, fairer than the Beaming Sun, O Soon cut off i'th' morning of her days; 'twas the Rude thunder stroke that Clos'd her Eyes, and laid her lilied Beauties on the Green. The dance was broke, the Circle just Begun; the flower was Pluck'd & yet it was not blown. "But what art thou?" I could no more till mute attention struck my [trembling *del.*] list'ning Ear. It spoke: "I come my friend to take my "last farewell, Sunk by the hand of Death in Wat'ry tomb. O'er "yonder [ruffling *del.*] lake [*several words del.*] the winds their sad "complainings bear for Conrade lost, untimely lost, thy Conrade "once. When living thee I lov'd ev'n unto Death; now Dead, I'll "guard thee from approaching ill; farewell my time is gone." It said no more, but vanished ever from my Sight.

. . . swift as the Nightly Blast that Blights the Infant Bud [*not marked for insertion, but probably intended to precede* the winds *five lines above*].

[AN ISLAND IN THE MOON]

Written about 1784-5

In the Moon is a certain Island near by a mighty continent, which small island seems to have some affinity to England, &, what is more extraordinary, the people are so much alike, & their language so much the same, that you would think you was among your friends. In this Island dwells three Philosophers—Suction the Epicurean, Quid the Cynic, & Sipsop the Pythagorean. I call them by the names of those sects, tho' the sects are not ever mention'd there, as being quite out of date; however, the things still remain, and the vanities are the same. The three Philosophers sat together thinking of nothing. In comes Etruscan Column the Antiquarian, & after an abundance of Enquiries to no purpose, sat himself down & described something that nobody listen'd to. So they were employ'd when Mrs Gimblet came in [tipsy *del.*]. The corners of her mouth seem'd—I don't know how, but very odd, as if she hoped you had not an ill opinion of her,—to be sure, we are all poor creatures! Well, she seated [herself] & [listen'd *del.*] seem'd to listen with great attention while the Antiquarian seem'd to be talking of virtuous cats. But it was not so; she was thinking of the shape of her eyes & mouth, & he was thinking of his eternal fame. The three Philosophers at this time were each endeavouring to conceal [the *blotted*] his laughter (not at them but) at his own imagination. This was the situation of this improving company when, in a great hurry, Inflammable Gass the Wind-finder enter'd. They seem'd to rise & salute each other. Etruscan Column & Inflammable Gass fix'd their eyes on each other; their tongues went in question & answer, but their thoughts were otherwise employ'd. "I don't like his eyes," said Etruscan Column. "He's a foolish puppy," said Inflammable Gass, smiling on him. The 3 Philosophers—the Cynic smiling, the Epicurean seeming [not *del.*] studying the flame of the candle, & the Pythagorean playing with the cat—listen'd with open mouths to the edifying discourses.

"Sir," said the Antiquarian, "I have seen these works, & I do "affirm that they are no such thing. They seem to me to be the most "wretched, paltry, flimsy stuff that ever——"

"What d'ye say? What d'ye say?" said Inflammable Gass. "Why "—why, I wish I could see you write so."

"Sir," said the Antiquarian, "according to my opinion the author "is an errant blockhead."

"Your reason—Your reason?" said Inflammable Gass. "Why—"why, I think it very abominable to call a man a blockhead that you "know nothing of."

"Reason, Sir?" said the Antiquarian. "I'll give you an example "for your reason. As I was walking along the street I saw a vast "number of swallows on the [top of an house *del.*] rails of an old "Gothic square. They seem'd to be going on their passage, as Pliny "says. As I was looking up, a little *outré* fellow, pulling me by the "sleeve, cries, 'Pray, Sir, who do all they belong to?' I turn'd myself "about with great contempt. Said I, 'Go along, you fool!' 'Fool!' said "he, 'who do you call fool? I only ask'd you a civil question.' [*words* "*del.*] I had a great mind to have thrash'd the fellow, only he was "bigger than I."

Here Etruscan Column left off—Inflammable Gass, recollecting himself [said], "Indeed I do not think the man was a fool, for he "seems to me to have been desirous of enquiring into the works of "nature!"

"Ha! Ha! Ha!" said the Pythagorean.

It was re-echo'd by [the *del.*] Inflammable Gass to overthrow the argument.

Etruscan Column then, star[t]ing up & clenching both his fists, was prepared to give a formal answer to the company. But Ob[t]use Angle, entering the room, having made a gentle bow, proceeded to empty his pockets of a vast number of papers, turned about & sat down, wiped his [head *del.*] face with his pocket handkerchief, & shutting his eyes, began to scratch his head.

"Well, gentlemen," said he, "what is the cause of strife?"

The Cynic answer'd, "They are only quarreling about Voltaire."

"Yes," said the Epicurean, "& having a bit of fun with him."

"And," said the Pythagorean, "endeavoring to incorporate their "souls with their bodies."

Obtuse Angle, giving a grin, said, "Voltaire understood nothing "of the Mathematics, and a man must be a fool i'faith not to under-"stand the Mathematics."

Inflammable Gass, turning round hastily in his chair, said, "Mathematics! He found out a number of Queries in Philosophy."

Obtuse Angle, shutting his eyes & saying that he always understood better when he shut his eyes, [replied], ["It is not of use to make *del.*] "In the first place, it is of no use for a man to make Queries, but to "solve them; for a man may be a fool & make Queries, but a man "must have good sound sense to solve them. A query & an answer are "as different as a strait line & a crooked one. Secondly——"

"I—I—I—aye! Secondly, Voltaire's a fool," says the Epicurean.

"Pooh!" says the Mathematician, scratching his head with double violence, "It is not worth Quarreling about."

The Antiquarian here got up, & hemming twice to shew the strength of his Lungs, said, "But, my Good Sir, Voltaire was im-"mersed in matter, & seems to have understood very little but what "he saw before his eyes, like the Animal upon the Pythagorean's "lap, always playing with its own tail."

"Ha! Ha! Ha!" said Inflammable Gass. "He was the Glory of "France. I have got a bottle of air that would spread a Plague."

Here the Antiquarian shrugg'd up his shoulders, & was silent [talk'd for half an hour *del.*] while Inflammable Gass talk'd for half an hour.

When Steelyard, the lawgiver, coming in stalking—with an act of parliament in his hand, said that it was a shameful thing that acts of parliament should be in a free state, it had so engrossed his mind that he did not salute the company.

M[rs]. Gimblet drew her mouth downwards.

Chap 2[d]

Tilly Lally, the Siptippidist, Aradobo, the Dean of Morocco, Miss Gittipin, [& *del.*] M[rs] Nannicantipot, M[rs] Sistagatist, [& the three Philosophers . . . Quid the Cynic, Sipsop the Pythagorean, Suction the Epicurean enter'd the room *del.*] Gibble Gabble, the wife of Inflammable Gass, [enter'd the room *del.*] & Little Scopprell enter'd the room.

(If I have not presented you with every character in the piece, call me [Ass* Arse *del.*] Ass.)

Chap 3[d]

In the Moon, as Phebus stood over his oriental Gardening, "O ay, come, I'll sing you a song," said the Cynic.

" 'The trumpeter shit in his hat,' " said the Epicurean.

"——& clapt it on his head," said the Pythagorean.

"I'll begin again," said the Cynic.

"Little Phebus came strutting in
"With his fat belly & his round chin,
"What is it you would please to have?
"Ho! Ho!
"I won't let it go at only so & so."

M[rs] Gimblet look'd as if they meant her. Tilly Lally laught like a cherry clapper. Aradobo ask'd, "Who was Phebus, Sir?"

Obtuse Angle answer'd quickly, "He was the God of Physic, "Painting, Perspective, Geometry, Geography, Astronomy, Cookery, "Chymistry [*word del.*], Mechanics, Tactics, Pathology, Phraseology, "Theology, Mythology, Astrology, Osteology, Somatology—in "short, every art & science adorn'd him as beads round his neck."

Here Aradobo look'd Astonish'd & ask'd if he understood Engraving.

Obtuse Angle Answer'd, indeed he did.

"Well," said the other, "he was as great as Chatterton."

Tilly Lally turn'd round to Obtuse Angle & ask'd who it was that was as great as Chatterton. [Obtuse Angle answer'd *del.*]

"Hay! How should I know?" Answer'd Obtuse Angle. "Who was "It, Aradobo?"

"Why sir," said he, "the Gentleman that the song was about."

"Ah," said Tilly Lally, "I did not hear it. What was it, Obtuse "Angle?"

"Pooh," said he. "Nonsense!"

"Mhm," said Tilly Lally.

"It was Phebus," said the Epicurean.

"Ah, that was the Gentleman," said Aradobo.

"Pray, Sir," said Tilly Lally, "who was Phebus?"

Obtuse Angle answer'd, "The heathens in the old ages us'd to "have Gods that they worship'd, & they us'd to sacrifice to them. "You have read about that in the bible."

"Ah," said Aradobo, "I thought I had read of Phebus in the "Bible."

"Aradobo, you should always think [of what you *del.*] before you "speak," said Obtuse Angle.

"Ha! Ha! Ha! He means Pharaoh," said Tilly Lally.

"I am asham'd of you,—making use of the names in the Bible," said M^rs^. Sistagatist.

"I'll tell you what, Mrs. Sinagain. I don't think there's any harm "in it," said Tilly Lally.

"No," said Inflammable Gass. "I have got a camera obscura at "home. What was it you was talking about?"

"Law!" said Tilly Lally. "What has that to do with Pharaoh?"

"Pho! nonsense! hang Pharoh & all his host," said the Pythagorean. "Sing away, Quid."

Then the Cynic sung—

> "Honour & Genius is all I ask,
> "And I ask the Gods no more.
> "No more, No more, } the three Philosophers
> "No more, No more." } bear Chorus.

Here Aradobo suck'd his under lip.

Chap 4

"Hang names!" said the Pythagorean. "What's Pharoh better than "Phebus, or Phebus than Pharoh?"

"Hang them both," said the Cynic.

"Don't be prophane," said Mrs Sistagatist.

"Why?" said Mrs Nannicantipot, "I don't think it's prophane to "say 'Hang Pharoh.' "

"Oh," said Mrs Sinagain. "I'm sure you ought to hold your "tongue, for you never say any thing about the scriptures, & you "hinder your husband from going to church."

"Ha, ha!" said Inflammable Gass. "What! don't you like to go to church?"

"No," said Mrs Nannicantipot. "I think a person may be as good "at home."

"If I had not a place of profit that forces me to go to church," said Inflammable Gass, "I'd see the parsons all hang'd,—a parcel of "lying——"

"O!" said Mrs Sistagatist. "If it was not for churches & chapels "I should not have liv'd so long. There was I, up in a Morning at "four o'clock, when I was a Girl. I would run like the dickins till I "was all in a heat. I would stand till I was ready to sink into the earth. "Ah, Mr Huffcap would kick the bottom of the Pulpit out with "Passion—would tear off the sleeve of his Gown & set his wig on fire "& throw it at the people. He'd cry & stamp & kick & sweat, and all "for the good of their souls."

"I'm sure he must be a wicked villain," said Mrs Nannicantipot, "a passionate wretch. If I was a man I'd wait at the bottom of the "pulpit stairs & knock him down & run away!"

"You would, you Ignorant jade? I wish I could see you hit any of "the ministers! You deserve to have your ears boxed, you do."

"I'm sure this is not religion," answers the other.

Then Mr Inflammable Gass ran & shov'd his head into the fire & set his [head *del.*] hair all in a flame, & ran about the room No—— no, he did not; I was only making a fool of you.

Chap 5

Obtuse Angle, Scopprell, Aradobo, & Tilly Lally are all met in Obtuse Angle's study.

"Pray," said Aradobo, "is Chatterton a Mathematician?"

"No," said Obtuse Angle. "How can you be so foolish as to think "he was?"

"Oh, I did not think he was—I only ask'd," said Aradobo.

"How could you think he was not, & ask if he was?" said Obtuse Angle.

"Oh no, Sir. I did think he was, before you told me, but afterwards "I thought he was not."

Obtuse Angle said, "In the first place you thought he was [not *del.*], "& then afterwards when I said he was not, you thought he was not. "[*Several words del.*] Why, I know that——"

"Oh no, sir, I thought that he was not, but I ask'd to know whether "he was."

"How can that be?" said Obtuse Angle. "How could you ask & "think that he was not?"

"Why," said he, "it came into my head that he was not."

"Why then," said Obtuse Angle, "you said that he was."

"Did I say so? Law! I did not think I said that."

"Did not he?" said Obtuse Angle.

"Yes," said Scopprell.

"But I meant——" said Aradobo, "I—I—I can't think. Law! "Sir, I wish you'd tell me how it is."

Then Obtuse Angle put his chin in his hand & said, "Whenever "you think, you must always think for yourself."

"How, sir!" said Aradobo. "Whenever I think, I must think my-"self? I think I do. In the first place——" said he with a grin.

"Poo! Poo!" said Obtuse Angle. "Don't be a fool."

Then Tilly Lally took up a Quadrant & ask'd, "[what is this gim-"crank for *del.*] Is not this a sun-dial?"

"Yes," said Scopprell, "but it's broke."

At this moment the three Philosophers enter'd, and low'ring darkness hover'd o'er th' assembly.

"Come," said the Epicurean, "let's have some rum & water, & "hang the mathematics! Come, Aradobo! Say some thing."

Then Aradobo began, "In the first place I think, I think in the "first place that Chatterton was clever at Fissic, Follogy, Pistinology, "Aridology, Arography, Transmography, Phizography, Hogamy, "Hatomy, & hall that, but, in the first place, he eat wery little, wickly "—that is, he slept very little, which he brought into a consumsion; "& what was that that he took? [*word del.*] Fissic or somethink,—& "so died!"

So all the people in the book enter'd into the room, & they could not talk any more to the present purpose.

Chap 6

They all went home & left the Philosophers. Then Suction Ask'd if Pindar was not a better Poet than Ghiotto was a Painter.

"Plutarch has not the life of Ghiotto," said Sipsop.

"No," said Quid, "to be sure, he was an Italian."

"Well," said Suction, "that is not any proof."

"Plutarch was a nasty ignorant puppy," said Quid. "I hate your "sneaking rascals. There's Aradobo in [*word del.*] ten or twelve years "will be a far superior genius."

"Ah!" said the Pythagorean, "Aradobo will make a very clever "fellow."

"Why," said Quid, "I think that [a *del.*] any natural fool would "make a clever fellow, if he was properly brought up."

"Ah, hang your reasoning!" said the Epicurean. "I hate reasoning. "I do everything by my feelings."

"Ah!" said Sipsop, "I only wish Jack [Hunter *del.*] Tearguts had "had the cutting of Plutarch. He understands anatomy better than "any of the Ancients. He'll plunge his knife up to the hilt in a single "drive, and thrust his fist in, and all in the space of a Quarter of an "hour. He does not mind their crying, tho' they cry ever so. He'll "swear at them & keep them down with his fist, & tell them that he'll "scrape their bones if they don't lay still & be quiet. What the devil "should the people in the hospital that have it done for nothing make "such a piece of work for?"

"Hang that," said Suction; "let us have a song."

Then [Sipsop sang *del.*] the Cynic sang—

1.

"When old corruption first begun,
"Adorn'd in yellow vest,
"He committed on flesh a whoredom—
"O, what a wicked beast!

2.

"From them a callow babe did spring,
"And old corruption smil'd
"To think his race should never end.
"For now he had a child.

3.

"He call'd him surgery, & fed
"The babe with his own milk,
"For flesh & he could ne'er agree,
"She would not let him suck.

4.

"And this he always kept in mind,
"And form'd a crooked knife,
"And ran about with bloody hands
"To seek his mother's life.

5.

"And as he ran to seek his mother
"He met with a dead woman,
"He fell in love & married her,
"A deed which is not common.

6.

"She soon grew pregnant & brought forth
"Scurvy & spott'd fever.
"The father grin'd & skipt about,
"And said, 'I'm made for ever!

7.

" 'For now I have procur'd these imps
" 'I'll try experiments.'
"With that he tied poor scurvy down
"& stopt up all its vents.

8.

"And when the child began to swell,
"He shouted out aloud,
" 'I've found the dropsy out, & soon
" 'Shall do the world more good.'

9.

"He took up fever by the neck
"And cut out all its spots,
"And thro' the holes which he had made
"He first discover'd guts."

"Ah," said Sipsop, "you think we are rascals—& we think you are "rascals. I do as I chuse. What is it to any body what I do? I am always "unhappy too. When I think of Surgery—I don't know. I do it be-"cause I like it. My father does what he likes & so do I. I think, "somehow, I'll leave it off. There was a woman having her cancer "cut, & she shriek'd so that I was quite sick."

CHAP 7

"Good-night," said Sipsop. "Good-night," said the other two.

Then [they *del.*] Quid & Suction were left alone. Then said Quid, "I think that Homer is bombast, & Shakespeare is too wild, & "Milton has no feelings: they might be easily outdone. Chatterton "never writ those poems! A parcel of fools, going to Bristol! If I was "to go, I'd find it out in a minute, but I've found it out already."

"If I don't knock them all up next year in the Exhibition, I'll be "hang'd," said Suction. "Hang Philosophy! I would not give a "farthing for it! Do all by your feelings, and never think at all about "it. I'm hang'd if I don't get up to-morrow morning by four o'clock "& work Sir Joshua."

"Before ten years are at an end," said Quid, "how I will work those "poor milksop devils,—an ignorant pack of wretches!"

So they went to bed.

Chap 8

Steelyard the Lawgiver, sitting at his table, taking extracts from Hervey's Meditations among the tombs & Young's Night thoughts [*several words del.*].

"He is not able to hurt me," said he, "more than making me "Constable or taking away the parish business. Hah!

"[O, what a scene is here! What a disguise! *del.*]
" 'My crop of corn is but a field of tares',

"says Jerome. Happiness is not for us, poor crawling reptiles of the "earth [*word del.*]. Talk of happiness & happiness! It's no such thing. "Every person has as something.

"Hear then the pride & knowledge of a Sailor,
"His sprit sail, fore sail, main sail, & his mizen.
"A poor frail man! God wot, I know none frailer.
"I know no greater sinner than John Taylor.

"If I had only myself to care for I'd soon make Double Elephant look "foolish, & Filligree work. I hope [I] shall live to see—

" 'The wreck of matter & the crush of worlds',

"as Young says."

Obtuse Angle enter'd the Room.

"What news, Mr Steelyard?"

"I am Reading Theron & Aspasio," said he.

Obtuse Angle took up the books one by one.

"I don't find it here," said he.

"O no," said the other, "it was the meditations!"

Obtuse Angle took up the book & read till the other was quite tir'd out.

Then Scopprell & Miss Gittipin coming in, Scopprell took up a book & read the following passage:—

"An Easy of Huming Understanding, by John Lookye [Gentleman "*altered to*] Gent."

"John Locke," said Obtuse Angle.

"O, ay—Lock," said Scopprell [It's a book about *del.*].

"Now here," said Miss Gittipin,—"I never saw such company in "my life. You are always talking of your books. I like to be where we "talk. You had better take a walk, that we may have some pleasure. I "am sure I never see any pleasure. There's Double Elephant's Girls, "they have their own way; & there's Miss Filligreework, she goes out "in her coaches, & her footman & her maids, & Stormonts & Balloon "hats, & a pair of Gloves every day, & the Sorrows of Werter, & "Robinsons, & the Queen of France's Puss colour, & my Cousin "Gibble Gabble says that I am like nobody else. I might as well be "in a nunnery. There they go [to *altered to*] in Postchaises & Stages to "Vauxhall & Ranelagh. And I hardly know what a coach is, except "when I go to Mr Jacko's. He knows what riding is, [& he does not "*del.*] & his wife is the most agreeable woman. You hardly know she "has a tongue in her head, and he is the funniest fellow, & I do believe "he'll go in partnership with his master, & they have black servants "lodge at their house. I never saw such a place in my life. He says he "has six & twenty rooms in his house, and I believe it, & he is not such "a liar as Quid thinks he is." [but he is always Envying *del.*]

"Poo! Poo! Hold your tongue. Hold your tongue," said the Lawgiver.

This quite provok'd Miss Gittipin, to interrupt her in her favourite topic, & she proceeded to use every Provoking speech that ever she could, & he bore it more like a Saint than a Lawgiver, and with great solemnity he address'd the company in these words:—

"They call women the weakest vessel, but I think they are the "strongest. A girl has always more tongue than a boy. I have seen a "little brat no higher than a nettle, & she had as much tongue as a "city clark; but a boy would be such a fool, not have any thing to say, "and, if any body ask'd him a question he would put his head into a "hole & hide it. I am sure I take but little pleasure. You have as much "pleasure as I have. There I stand & bear every fool's insult. If I had "only myself to care for, I'd wring off their noses."

To this Scopprell answer'd, "I think the Ladies' discourses, Mr "Steelyard, are some of them more improving than any book. That "is the way I have got some of my knowledge."

"Then," said Miss Gittipin, "Mr Scopprell, do you know the "song of Phebe and Jellicoe?"

"No, Miss," said Scopprell.

Then she repeated these verses, while Steelyard walk'd about the room:

"Phebe, drest like beautie's Queen,
"Jellicoe in faint pea green,
"Sitting all beneath a grot
"Where the little lambkins trot;

"Maidens dancing, loves asporting,
"All the country folks acourting,
"Susan, Johnny, Bet, & Joe
"Lightly tripping on a row.

"Happy people, who can be
"In happiness compar'd with ye?
"The Pilgrim with his crook & hat
"Sees your happiness compleat."

"A charming song, indeed, miss," said Scopprell. [That was all for *del.*] here they receiv'd a summons for a merry making at the Philosopher's house.

Chap 9

"I say, this evening we'll all get drunk—I say—dash! an Anthem, "an Anthem!" said Suction.

"Lo the Bat with Leathern wing,
"Winking & blinking,
"Winking & blinking,
"Winking & blinking,
"Like Doctor Johnson."

Quid. " 'Oho', said Doctor Johnson
"To Scipio Africanus,
" 'If you don't own me a Philosopher,
" 'I'll kick your Roman Anus'."

Suction. " 'Aha', To Doctor Johnson
"Said Scipio Africanus,
" 'Lift up my Roman Petticoat
" 'And kiss my Roman Anus'."

"And the Cellar goes down with a step." (Grand Chorus.)

"Ho, Ho, Ho, Ho, Ho, Ho, Ho, Hooooo, my poooooor siiides! "I I should die if I was to live here!" said Scopprell. "Ho, Ho, Ho, "Ho, Ho!"

1st Vo. "Want Matches?"
2nd Vo. "Yes, yes, yes."
1st Vo. "Want Matches?"
2nd Vo. "No."

1st Vo. "Want Matches?"
2nd Vo. "Yes, yes, yes."
1st Vo. "Want Matches?"
2nd Vo. "No."

Here was great confusion & disorder. Aradobo said that the boys in the street sing something very pretty & funny [about London—O no *del.*] about Matches. Then Mrs Nannicantipot sung:

"I cry my matches as far as Guild hall;
"God bless the duke & his aldermen all!"

Then sung Scopprell:

"I ask the Gods no more,—
"no more, no more."

"Then," said Suction, "come, Mr Lawgiver, your song"; and the Lawgiver sung:

"As I walk'd forth one may morning
"To see the fields so pleasant & so gay,
"O there did I spy a young maiden sweet,
"Among the Violets that smell so sweet,
"Smell so sweet,
"Smell so sweet,
"Among the Violets that smell so sweet."

"Hang your Violets! Here's your Rum & water [sweeter *del.*]. "O "ay," said Tilly Lally, "Joe Bradley & I was going along one day in "the sugar-house. Joe Bradley saw—for he had but one eye—[*word* "*del.*] saw a treacle Jar. So he goes of his blind side & dips his hand "up to the shoulder in treacle. 'Here, lick, lick, lick!' said he. Ha! Ha! "Ha! Ha! Ha! For he had but one eye. Ha! Ha! Ha! Ho!"

Then sung Scopprell:

"And I ask the Gods no more,—
"no more, no more,
"no more, no more.

"Miss Gittipin," said he, "you sing like a harpsichord. Let your "bounty descend to our fair ears and favour us with a fine song."

Then she sung:

"This frog he would a-wooing ride,
"Kitty alone,—Kitty alone,—
"This frog he would a-wooing ride,—
"Kitty alone & I!
"Sing cock I cary, Kitty alone,
"Kitty alone,—Kitty alone,—
"Cock I cary, Kitty alone,—
"Kitty alone & I!"

"Charming! Truly elegant!" said Scopprell.

"And I ask the gods no more!"

"Hang your serious songs!" said Sipsop, & he sung as follows:—

"Fa ra so bo ro
"Fa ra bo ra
"Sa ba ra ra ba rare roro
"Sa ra ra ra bo ro ro ro
"Radara
"Sarapodo no flo ro."

"Hang Italian songs! Let's have English!" said Quid. "[Sing a "Mathematical Song Obtuse Angle then he sung *del.*] English genius "for ever! Here I go:

"Hail Matrimony, made of Love,
"To thy wide gates how great a drove
"On purpose to be yok'd do come!
"Widows & maids & youths also,
"That lightly trip on beauty's toe,
"Or sit on beauty's bum.

"Hail, fingerfooted lovely Creatures!
"The females of our human Natures,
"Formed to suckle all Mankind.
"'Tis you that come in time of need;
"Without you we shoud never Breed,
"Or any Comfort find.

"For if a Damsel's blind or lame,
"Or Nature's hand has crooked her frame,
"Or if she's deaf, or is wall eyed,
"Yet if her heart is well inclined,
"Some tender lover she shall find
"That panteth for a Bride.

"The universal Poultice this,
"To cure whatever is amiss
"In damsel or in widow gay.
"It makes them smile, it makes them skip,
"Like Birds just cured of the pip,
"They chirp, & hop away.

"Then come ye maidens, come ye swains,
"Come & be eased of all your pains
"In Matrimony's Golden cage."

"[None of *del.*] Go & be hanged!" said Scopprell. "How can you have the face to make game of matrimony?"

["What you skipping flea, how dare ye? I'll dash you through your "chair," says the Cynic. "This Quid" (cries out Miss Gittipin), "always spoils good company in this manner & it's a shame." *del.*]

Then Quid call'd upon Obtuse Angle for a Song, & he, wiping his face & looking on the corner of the ceiling, sang:

"To be, or not to be
"Of great capacity,
"Like Sir Isaac Newton,
"Or Locke, or Doctor South,
"Or Sherlock upon death?
"I'd rather be Sutton.

"For he did build a house
"For aged men & youth,
"With walls of brick & stone.
"He furnish'd it within
"With whatever he could win,
"And all his own.

"He drew out of the Stocks
"His money in a box,
"And sent his servant
"To Green the Bricklayer
"And to the Carpenter:
"He was so fervent.

"The chimneys were three score,
"The windows many more,
"And for convenience
"He sinks & gutters made,
"And all the way he pav'd
"To hinder pestilence.

"Was not this a good man,
"Whose life was but a span,
"Whose name was Sutton,—
"As Locke, or Doctor South,
"Or Sherlock upon Death,
"Or Sir Isaac Newton?"

The Lawgiver was very attentive & beg'd to have it sung over again & again, till the company were tired & insisted on the Lawgiver singing a song himself, which he readily complied with.

"This city & this country has brought forth many mayors,
"To sit in state & give forth laws out of their old oak chairs,
"With face as brown as any nut with drinking of strong ale;
"Good English hospitality, O then it did not fail!

"With scarlet gowns & broad gold lace would make a yeoman sweat,
"With stockings roll'd above their knees & shoes as black as jet,
"With eating beef & drinking beer, O they were stout & hale!
"Good English hospitality, O then it did not fail!

"Thus sitting at the table wide, the Mayor & Aldermen
"Were fit to give law to the city; each eat as much as ten.
"The hungry poor enter'd the hall, to eat good beef & ale.
"Good English hospitality, O then it did not fail!"

Here they gave a shout, & the company broke up.

Chap 10

Thus these happy Islanders spent their time. But felicity does not last long, for being met at the house of Inflammable Gass the wind-finder, the following affairs happen'd.

"Come, Flammable," said Gibble Gabble, "& let's enjoy ourselves. "Bring the Puppets."

"Hay,—Hay," said he, "you—sho—why—ya, ya. How can you "be so foolish? Ha! Ha! Ha! She calls the experiments puppets!"

Then he went up stairs & loaded the maid with glasses, & brass tubes, & magic pictures.

"Here, ladies & gentlemen," said he, "I'll shew you a louse, or a "flea, or a butterfly, or a cockchafer, the blade bone of a tittleback. "No, No. Here's a bottle of wind that I took up in the boghouse, "O dear, O dear, the water's got into the sliders! Look here, Gibble "Gabble! Lend me your handkerchief, Tilly Lally."

Tilly Lally took out his handkerchief, which smear'd the glass worse than ever. Then he screw'd it on. Then he took the sliders, & then he set up the glasses for the Ladies to view the pictures. Thus he was employ'd, & quite out of breath. While Tilly Lally & Scopprell were pumping at the airpump, Smack went the glass.

"Hang!" said Tilly Lally.

Inflammable Gass turn'd short round & threw down the table & Glasses, & Pictures, & broke the bottles of wind, & let out the Pestilence. He saw the Pestilence fly out of the bottle, & cried out, while he ran out of the room:

"Come out! Come out! We are putrified! We are corrupted! Our "lungs are destroy'd with the Flogiston. This will spread a plague all "thro' the Island!"

He was downstairs the very first. On the back of him came all the others in a heap.

So they need not bidding go.

CHAP II

Another merry meeting at the house of Steelyard the Lawgiver. After supper, Steelyard & Obtuse Angle had pump'd Inflammable Gass quite dry. They play'd at forfeits, & try'd every method to get good humour.

Said Miss Gittipin, "Pray, M[r] Obtuse Angle, sing us a song."

Then he sung:

"Upon a holy thursday, their innocent faces clean,
"The children walking two & two in grey & blue & green,
"Grey headed beadles walk'd before with wands as white as snow,
"Till into the high dome of Paul's they like thames' waters flow.

"O what a multitude they seem'd, these flowers of London town!
"Seated in companies, they sit with radiance all their own.
"The hum of multitudes were there, but multitudes of lambs,
"[And all in order sit waiting the chief chanter's commands *del.*]
"Thousands of little girls & boys raising their innocent hands.

"[Then like a mighty wind they raise to heav'n the voice of song,
"Or like harmonious thunderings the seats of heav'n among,
"When the whole multitude of innocents their voices raise
"Like angels on the throne of heav'n, raising the voice of praise *del.*]

"[Let Cherubim & Seraphim now raise their voices high *del.*]
"Then like a mighty wind they raise to heav'n the voice of song,
"Or like harmonious thunderings the seats of heav'n among.
"Beneath them sit the rev'rend men, the guardians of the poor;
"Then cherish pity lest you drive an angel from your door."[1]

After this they all sat silent for a quarter of an hour, [& M[rs] Sistagatist *del.*] & M[rs] Nannicantipot said, "It puts me in Mind of my "[Grand *del.*] mother's song,

[1] First draft of "Holy Thursday" in *Songs of Innocence*; see p. 121.

[The voice *del.*]
"When the tongues of children are heard on the green,
"And laughing [upon *del.*] is heard on the hill,
"My heart is at rest within my breast,
"And every thing else is still.

" 'Then come home, my children, the sun is gone down,
" 'And the dews of night arise;
" 'Come, Come, leave off play, & let us away
" ' Till the morning appears in the skies.'

" 'No, No, let us play, for it is yet day,
" 'And we cannot [go to *del.*] go to sleep [till it's dark *del.*]
" '[The flocks are at play & we can't go away *del.*]
" 'Besides in the sky the little birds fly,
" 'And the meadows are cover'd with sheep.'

" 'Well, Well, go & play till the light fades away,
" 'And then go home to bed.'
"The little ones leaped, & shouted, & laugh'd,
"And all the hills ecchoed."[1]

Then [Miss Gittipin Tilly Lally sung; Quid *del.*] sung Quid:

"O father, father, where are you going?
"Oh do not walk so fast;
"Oh, speak, father, speak to your little boy,
"Or else I shall be lost.

"The night it was dark & no father was there,
"And the child was wet with dew.
"The mire was deep, & the child did weep,
"And away the vapour flew."[2]

Here nobody could sing any longer, till Tilly Lally pluck'd up a spirit & he sung:

"O I say, you Joe,
"Throw us the ball.
"I've a good mind to go,
"And leave you all.

[1] First draft of "Nurse's Song" in *Songs of Innocence;* see p. 121.
[2] First draft of "The Little Boy lost" in *Songs of Innocence;* see p. 120.

"I never saw such a bowler,
"To bowl the ball in a [turd *del.*] tansey,
"And to clean it with my handkercher
"Without saying a word.

"That Bill's a foolish fellow,
"[To hit me with the bat *del.*]
"He has given me a black eye.
"He does not know how to handle a bat
"Any more than a [*word del.*] dog or a cat.

"He has knock'd down the wicket
"And broke the stumps,
"And runs without shoes to save his pumps."

Here a laugh began, and Miss Gittipin sung:

"Leave, O leave [me] to my sorrows,
"Here I'll sit & fade away;
"Till I'm nothing but a spirit,
"And I lose this form of clay.

"Then if chance along this forest
"Any walk in pathless ways,
"Thro' the gloom he'll see my shadow,
"Hear my voice upon the Breeze."

The Lawgiver all the while sat delighted to see them in such a serious humour. "Mr Scopprell," said he, "you must be acquainted "with a great many songs."

"O, dear sir! Ho, Ho, Ho, I am no singer. I must beg of one of "these tender-hearted ladies to sing for me."

They all declined, & he was forced to sing himself:

"There's Doctor Clash
"And Signior Falalasole:
"O they sweep in the cash
"Into their purse hole.
"Fa me la sol, La me fa sol.

[how many Blackamoors
cou'd sing with their thick lips *del.*]

"Great A, little A,
"Bouncing B.
"Play away, Play away,
"You're out of the key.
"Fa me la sol, La me fa sol.

"Musicians should have
"A pair of very good ears,
"And Long fingers & thumbs,
"And not like clumsy bears.
"Fa me la sol, La me fa sol.

"Gentlemen, Gentlemen!
"Rap, rap, rap,
"Fiddle, Fiddle, Fiddle,
"Clap, Clap, Clap.
"Fa me la sol, La me fa sol."

"Hm," said the Lawgiver, "Funny enough! Let's have handel's "water piece." Then Sipsop sung:

"A crowned king,
"On a white horse sitting,
"With his trumpets sounding,
"And Banners flying,
"Thro' the clouds of smoke he makes his way,
"And the shout of his thousands fills his heart with rejoicing & victory:
"And the shout of his thousands fills his heart with rejoicing & victory.
"Victory! Victory! 'twas William, the prince of Orange,—"

[*Here a leaf, or more, is missing.*]

"—them Illuminating the Manuscript."

"Ay," said she, "that would be excellent."

"Then," said he, "I would have all the writing Engraved instead "of Printed, & at every other [*word del.*] leaf a high finish'd print—all "in three Volumes folio—& sell them a hundred pounds apiece. They "would print off two thousand."

"Then," said she, "whoever will not have them will be ignorant "fools & will not deserve to live."

"Don't you think I have something of the Goat's face?" says he.

"Very like a Goat's face," she answer'd.

"I think your face," said he, "is like that noble beast the Tyger. "Oh, I was at Mrs Sicknaker's, & I was speaking of my abilities, "but their nasty hearts, poor devils, are eat up with envy. They "envy me my abilities, & all the women envy your abilities."

"My dear, they hate people who are of higher abilities than their "nasty, filthy [souls *del.*] selves. But do you outface them, & then strangers will see you have an opinion."

"Now I think we should do as much good as we can when we are "at Mr Femality's. Do you snap, & take me up, and I will fall into "such a passion. I'll hollow and stamp, & frighten all the People "there, & show them what truth is."

At this Instant Obtuse Angle came in.

"Oh, I am glad you are come," said Quid.

POEMS WRITTEN IN A COPY OF "POETICAL SKETCHES"

Composed about 1787

SONG 1ST BY A SHEPHERD

Welcome, stranger, to this place,
Where joy doth sit on every bough,
Paleness flies from every face;
We reap not what we do not sow.

Innocence doth like a rose
Bloom on every maiden's cheek;
Honour twines around her brows,
The jewel health adorns her neck.

SONG 2ND BY A YOUNG SHEPHERD

When the trees do laugh with our merry wit,
And the green hill laughs with the noise of it,
When the meadows laugh with lively green
And the grasshopper laughs in the merry scene,

When the greenwood laughs with the voice of joy,
And the dimpling stream runs laughing by,
When Edessa, and Lyca, and Emilie,
With their sweet round mouths sing ha, ha, he,

When the painted Birds laugh in the shade,
Where our table with cherries and nuts is spread;
Come live and be merry and join with me
To sing the sweet chorus of ha, ha, he.

SONG 3D BY AN OLD SHEPHERD

When silver snow decks Sylvio's clothes
And jewel hangs at shepherd's nose,
We can abide life's pelting storm
That makes our limbs quake, if our hearts be warm.

Whilst Virtue is our walking-staff
And Truth a lantern to our path,
We can abide life's pelting storm
That makes our limbs quake, if our hearts be warm.

Blow, boisterous wind, stern winter frown,
Innocence is a winter's gown;
So clad, we'll abide life's pelting storm
That makes our limbs quake, if our hearts be warm.

ANNOTATIONS TO LAVATER'S APHORISMS ON MAN
London MDCCLXXXVIII

Written about 1788

[*Blake's remarks are here printed in larger type after the aphorisms to which they refer. Passages underlined by Blake are printed in italic.*]

For the reason of these remarks see the last aphorism.

[643

If you mean to know yourself, interline such of these aphorisms as affect you agreeably in reading, and set a mark to such as left a sense of uneasiness with you; and then shew your copy to whom you please.]

1.

Know, in the first place, that mankind agree in essence, as they do in their limbs and senses.

2.

Mankind differ as much in essence as they do in form, limbs, and senses—and only so, and not more.

This is true Christian philosophy far above all abstraction.

3.

As in looking upward each beholder thinks himself the centre of the sky; so Nature formed her individuals, that each must see himself the centre of being.

Let me refer here to a remark on aphorism 533 & another on 630.

8.

Who pursues means of enjoyment contradictory, irreconcilable, and self-destructive, is a fool, or what is called a sinner—*Sin and destruction of order are the same.*

A golden sentence.

11.

The less you can enjoy, the poorer, the scantier yourself—the more you can enjoy, the richer, the more vigorous.
You enjoy with wisdom or with folly, as the gratification of your appetites capacitates or unnerves your powers.

False, for weak is the joy that is never wearied.

13.

Joy and grief decide character. What exalts prosperity? what imbitters grief? what leaves us indifferent? what interests us? As the interest of *man, so his God—as his God, so he.*

All gold!

14.

What is a man's interest? what constitutes his God, the ultimate of his wishes, his end of existence? Either that which on every occasion he communicates with the most unrestrained cordiality, or hides from every profane eye and ear with mysterious awe; to which he makes every other thing a mere appendix;—the vortex, the centre, the comparative point from which he sets out, on which he fixes, to which he irresistably returns;—that, at the loss of which you may safely think him inconsolable;—that which he rescues from the gripe of danger with equal anxiety and boldness.

Pure gold!

. . . of thousands it may be decided what loss, what gain, would affect them most. And suppose we cannot pronounce on others, cannot we determine on ourselves? This the sage of Nazareth meant when he said, "Where thy treasure is, there will thy heart be also"—The object of your love is your God.

This should be written in gold letters on our temples.

16.

The greatest of characters, no doubt, was he, who, free of all trifling accidental helps, could see objects through one grand immutable medium, always at hand, and proof against illusion and time, reflected by every object, and invariably traced through all the fluctuation of things.

This was Christ.

20.

Distinguish with exactness, in thyself and others, between WISHES and WILL, in the strictest sense.

Who has many wishes has generally but little will. Who has energy of will has few diverging wishes. Whose will is bent with energy on ONE, MUST renounce the wishes for MANY things. Who cannot do this is not stamped with the majesty of human nature.

Admirable. [*probably written by another hand*]

The energy of choice, the unison of various powers for one is only WILL, born under the agonies of self-denial and renounced desires.

Regeneration.

21.

Calmness of will is a sign of grandeur. The vulgar, far from hiding their WILL, blab their wishes—a single spark of occasion discharges the child of passions into a thousand crackers of desire.

Uneasy. See 384 [the serenely serious alone are formed for friendship]

23.

Who in the same given time can produce more than many others, has VIGOUR; who can produce more and *better*, has TALENTS; *who can produce what none else can, has GENIUS.*

28.

The glad gladdens—who gladdens not is not glad. Who is fatal to others is so to himself —to him, heaven, earth, wisdom, folly, virtue, *vice, are equally* so—to such an one tell neither good nor bad of yourself.

32.

Let the degree of egotism be the measure of confidence.

Uneasy.

36.

Who begins with severity, in judging of another, ends commonly with falsehood.

False! Severity of judgment is a great virtue.

37.

The smiles that encourage severity of judgment, hide malice and insincerity.

False! Aphorisms should be universally true.

39.

Who, without pressing temptation, tells a lie, will, without pressing temptation, act ignobly and meanly.

Uneasy.

False! A man may lie for his own pleasure, but if any one is hurt by his lying, will confess his lie: see no. 124.

40.

Who, under pressing temptations to lie, adheres to truth, nor to the profane betrays aught of a sacred trust, is near the summit of wisdom and virtue.

Excellent.

43.

As the present character of a man, so his past, so his future. Who knows intuitively the history of the past, knows his destiny to come.

44.

You can depend on no man, on no friend, but him who can depend on himself. *He only* who acts consequentially *toward himself* will act so toward others, and VICE VERSA.

Man is for ever the same; the same under every form, in all situations and relations that admit of free and unrestrained exertion. The same regard which you have for *yourself, you have for others, for nature, for the invisible NUMEN, which you call God—Who has witnessed one free* and unconstrained act of yours, has witnessed all.

54.

Frequent laughing has been long called a sign of a little mind—whilst the scarcer smile of harmless quiet has been complimented as the mark of a noble heart—But to abstain from laughing, and exciting laughter, merely not to offend, or to risk giving offence, or not to debase the inward dignity of character—is a power unknown to many a vigorous mind.

I hate scarce smiles: I love laughing.

59.

A sneer is often the sign of heartless malignity.

Damn sneerers!

60.

Who courts the intimacy of a *professed sneerer, is a professed knave.*

61.

I know not which of these two I should wish to avoid most; the scoffer at virtue and religion, who, with heartless villainy, butchers innocence and truth; *or the pietist, who crawls, groans, blubbers, and secretly says to gold, thou art* my hope! and to his belly, thou art my god!

I hate crawlers.

62.

All moral dependence on him, who has been guilty of ONE act of positive cool villainy, against an acknowledged, virtuous and noble character, is credulity, imbecility, or insanity.

Is being like him, rather.

63.

The most stormy ebullitions of passion, *from blasphemy to murder, are less terrific than one single act of cool villany : a still RABIES is more dangerous than the paroxisms of a fever—Fear the boisterous savage of passion less than the sedate grin of villany.*

Bravo!

66.

Can he love truth who can take a knave to his bosom?

No!

67.

There are offences against individuals, to all appearance trifling, which are capital offences against the human race—fly him who can commit them.

68.

There ought to be a perpetual whisper in the ear of plain honesty—take heed not even to pronounce the name of a knave—he will make the very sound of his name a handle of mischief. And do you think a knave begins mischief to leave off? Know this—whether he overcome or be foiled, he will wrangle on.

Therefore pronounce him a knave: why should honesty fear a knave?

69.

Humility and love, whatever obscurities may involve religious tenets, constitute the essence of true religion. *The humble is formed to adore; the loving to associate with eternal love.*

Sweet!

70.

Have you ever seen a vulgar mind warm or humble? or a proud one that could love?—where pride begins, love ceases—as love, so humility—as both, so the still real power of man.

Pride may love.

71.

Every thing may be mimicked by hypocrisy, but humility and love united. The humblest star twinkles most in the darkest night—the more rare humility and love united, the more radiant where they meet.

All this may be mimicked very well; this Aphorism certainly was an oversight, for what are all crawlers but mimickers of humility & love?

73.

Modesty is silent when it would not be improper to speak: the humble, without being called upon, never recollects to say any thing of himself.

Uneasy.

78.

The wrath that on conviction subsides into mildness, is the wrath of a generous mind.

80.

Thousands are hated, *whilst none are ever loved, without a real cause. The amiable alone can be loved.*

81.

He who is loved and commands love, when he corrects or is the cause of uneasiness, must be loveliness itself; and

82.

He who can love him, in the moment of correction, is the most amiable of mortals.

83.

He, to whom you may tell any thing, may see every thing, and will betray nothing.

86.

The freer you feel yourself in the presence of another, the more free is he: who is free makes free.

Rather uneasy.

92.

Who instantly does the best that can be done, what no other could have done, and what all must acknowledge to be the best, is a genius and a hero at once.

Uneasy.

93.

The discovery of truth, by slow progressive meditation, is wisdom—*Intuition of truth, not preceded by perceptible meditation, is genius.*

94.

The degree of genius is determined by its velocity, clearness, depth, simplicity, copiousness, extent of glance (COUP D'OEIL), and instantaneous intuition of the whole at once.

Copiousness of glance.

96.

Dread more the blunderer's friendship than the calumniator's enmity.

I doubt this.

97.

He only, who can give durability to his exertions, has genuine power and energy of mind.

Uneasy. Sterling!

98.

Before thou callest a man hero or genius, investigate whether his exertion has features of indelibility; for all that is celestial, all genius, *is the offspring of immortality.*

Uneasy. Sterling!

99.

Who despises all that is despicable, is made to be impressed with all that is grand.

107.

Who takes from you, ought to give in his turn, or he is a thief; I distinguish taking and accepting, robbing and receiving: many give already by the mere wish to give; their still unequivocal wish of improvement and gratitude, whilst it draws *from us, opens treasures within us, that might have remained locked up, even to ourselves.*

Noble & Generous.

114.

Who writes as he speaks, speaks as he writes, looks as he speaks and writes—is honest.

115.

A habit of sneering marks the egotist, or the fool, or the knave—or all three.

—all three!

121.

Who knows not how to wait with YES, will often be with shame reduced to say NO —Letting "I DARE NOT wait upon I WOULD."

Uneasy.

124.

Who has a daring eye, tells downright truths and downright lies.

Contrary to N. 39, but most True.

141.

Many trifling inattentions, neglects, indiscretions—are so many unequivocal proofs of dull frigidity, hardness, or extreme egotism.

Rather uneasy.

150.

As your enemies and your friends, so are you.

Very uneasy.

151.

You may depend upon it that he is a good man whose intimate friends are all good, and whose enemies are characters decidedly bad.

Uneasy: I fear I have not many enemies.

157.

Say not you know another entirely, till you have divided an inheritance with him.

! !

163.

Who, at the pressing solicitation of bold and noble confidence, hesitates one moment before he consents, proves himself at once inexorable.

Uneasy: I do not believe it.

164.

Who, at the solicitations of cunning, self-interest, silliness, or impudence, hesitates one moment before he refuses, proves himself at once a silly giver.

Uneasy.

168.

Whenever a man undergoes a considerable change, in consequence of being observed by others, whenever he assumes another gait, another language, than what he had before he thought himself observed, be advised to guard yourself against him.

Rather uneasy.

170.

I am prejudiced in favour of him who can solicit boldly, without impudence—he has faith in humanity—he has faith in himself. No one, who is not accustomed to give grandly, can ask nobly and with boldness.

176.

As a man's salutation, so the total of his character : in nothing do we lay ourselves so open as in our manner of meeting and salutation.

177.

Be afraid of him who meets you with friendly aspect, and, in the midst of a flattering salutation, *avoids your direct open look.*

185.

All finery is a sign of littleness.

Not always.

200.

The more honesty a man has, the less he affects the air of a saint—the affectation of sanctity is a blotch on the face of piety.

Bravo!

201.

There are more heroes than saints; (heroes I call rulers over the minds and destinies of men); more saints than humane characters. Him, who humanises all that is within and around himself, adore: I know but of one such by tradition.

Sweet!

203.

Who seeks those that are greater than himself, their greatness enjoys, and forgets his greatest qualities in their greater ones, is already truly great.

I hope I do not flatter my self that this is pleasant to me.

219.

None love without being loved; *and none* beloved *is without loveliness.*

225.

The friend of *order has made half his way to virtue.*

226.

There is no mortal truly wise and restless at once—wisdom is the repose of minds.

Rather uneasy.

242.

The connoisseur in painting discovers an original by some great line, though covered with dust, and disguised by daubing; so he who studies man discovers a valuable character by some original trait, though unnoticed, disguised, or debased

—ravished at the discovery, he feels it his duty to restore it to its own genuine splendour. *Him who, in spite of contemptuous pretenders, has the boldness to do this, choose for your friend.*

244.

Who writes what he should tell, and dares not tell what he writes, is either like a wolf in sheep's clothing, or like a sheep in a wolf's skin.

Some cannot tell what they can write, tho' they dare.

248.

Know that the great art to love your enemy consists in never losing sight of MAN in him: humanity has power over all that is human; the most inhuman man still remains man, and never CAN throw off all taste for what becomes a man—but you must learn to wait.

None can see the man in the enemy; if he is ignorantly so, he is not truly an enemy; if maliciously, not a man. I cannot love my enemy, for my enemy is not man, but beast & devil, if I have any. I can love him as a beast & wish to beat him.

253.

Who welcomes the look of the good is good himself.

254.

I know deists, whose religiousness I venerate, and atheists, whose honesty and nobleness of mind I wish for; but I have not yet seen the man who could have tempted *me to think him honest whom I knew publicly acted the Christian whilst privately he was a positive deist.*

Bravo!

256.

He who laughed at you till he got to your door, flattered you as you opened it—felt the force of your argument whilst he was with you—applauded when he rose, and, after he went away, blasts you—has the most indisputable title to an arch-dukedom in hell.

Such a one I can never forgive while he continues such a one.

261.

Ask not only, am I hated? but, by whom?—am I loved? but why?—*as the GOOD love thee, the BAD will hate thee.*

Uneasy.

272.

Who can *act or perform* as if each work *or action were the first*, *the last, and only one in his life, is great* in his sphere. [*the last three words deleted.*]

276.

We can do all by speech and silence. He, who understands the double art of speaking opportunely to the moment, and of saying not a syllable more or less than it demanded—and he who can wrap himself up in silence when every word would be in vain—will understand to connect energy with patience.

Uneasy.

278.

Let the unhappiness you feel at another's *errors,* and the happiness you *enjoy in their perfections, be the measure of your progress in wisdom and virtue.*

Excellent!

279.

Who becomes every day more sagacious, in observing his own faults, and the perfections of another, without either envying him or despairing of himself, is ready to mount the ladder on which angels ascend and descend.

Noble!

282.

The more there is of mind in your solitary employments, the more dignity there is in your character.

285.

He, who can at all times sacrifice pleasure to duty, approaches sublimity. [*scored in the margin.*]

287.

The most eloquent speaker, the most ingenious writer, and the most accomplished statesman, cannot effect so much as the mere presence of the man who tempers his wisdom and his vigour with humanity. [*the last nine words deleted.*]

Unsophisticated!

289.

Between the best and the worst, there are, you say, innumerable degrees—and you are right; but admit that I am right too, in saying that the best and the worst differ only in one thing—*in the object of their love.*

Would to God that every one would consider this.

290.

What is it you love in him you love? what is it you hate in him you hate? Answer this closely to yourself, pronounce it loudly, and you will know yourself and him.

All Gold.

292.

If you see one cold and vehement at the same time, set him down for a fanatic.

i.e, hypocrite.

295.

Who can hide magnanimity, stands on the supreme degree of human nature, and is admired by the world of spirits.

301.

He has not a little of the devil in him who prays and bites.

There is no other devil; he who bites without praying is only a beast.

302.

He who, when called upon to speak a *disagreeable truth, tells it boldly and has done, is both bolder and milder than he who nibbles in a low voice,* and never ceases *nibbling.*

Damn such!

305.

Be not the fourth friend of him who had three before and lost them.

An excellent rule.

308.

Want of friends argues either want of humility or courage, or both.

Uneasy.

309.

He who, at a table of forty covers, thirty-nine of which are exquisite, and one indifferent, lays hold of that, and with a "damn your dinner" dashes it in the landlord's face, should be sent to Bethlem or to Bridewell—and whither he, who blasphemes a book, a work of art, or perhaps a man of nine-and-thirty good and but one bad quality, and calls those fools or flatterers who, engrossed by the superior number of good qualities, would fain forget the bad one.

To hell till he behaves better! mark that I do not believe there is such a thing litterally, but hell is the being shut up in the possession of corporeal desires which shortly weary the man, *for* ALL LIFE IS HOLY.

328.

Keep him at least three paces distant who hates bread, music, and the laugh of a child.

The best in the book!

333.

Between passion and lie there is not a finger's breadth.

Lie is the contrary to Passion.

334.

Avoid, *like a serpent, him who writes impertinently, yet speaks politely.*

A dog! get a stick to him!

338.

Search carefully if one patiently finishes what he boldly began.

Uneasy.

339.

Who comes from the kitchen smells of its smoke; *who adheres to a sect has something of its cant:* The college-air pursues the student, and dry inhumanity him who herds with literary pedants.

341.

Call him truly religious who believes in something higher, more powerful, more living, than visible *nature; and who, clear as* his own *existence, feels his conformity to that superior being.*

342.

Superstition always inspires littleness, religion grandeur of mind: the superstitious raises beings inferiour to himself to deities. [Superstition *altered to* Hipocrisy; superstitious *to* hypocrite.]

No man was ever truly superstitious who was not truly religious as far as he knew.
True superstition is ignorant honesty & this is beloved of god and man.
I do not allow that there is such a thing as superstition taken in the strict sense of the word.
A man must first decieve himself before he is thus Superstitious and so he is a hypocrite.
Hipocrisy is as distant from superstition as the wolf from the lamb.

343.

Who are the saints of humanity? those whom perpetual habits of goodness and of grandeur have made nearly unconscious that what they do is good or grand—heroes with infantine simplicity.

This is heavenly.

345.

The jealous is possessed by a "fine mad devil"* and a dull spirit at once.

Pity the jealous!

352.

He alone has *energy that cannot be deprived of it.*

353.

Sneers are the blasts that precede quarrels.

Hate the sneerer!

354.

Who loves will not be adored.

False!

359.

No great character cavils.

365.

He can love who can forget all and nothing.

366.

The purest religion is the most refined Epicurism. He, who in the smallest given time can enjoy *most of what he never shall repent, and what furnishes* enjoyments, still more unexhausted, still less changeable—is the most religious and the most voluptuous of men.

True Christian philosophy.

370.

The generous, who is always just—and the just, who is always generous—*may, unannounced, approach the throne of God.*

---

*Shakspeare.

375.

Let me once more, in other words, repeat it—he is the king of kings who longs for nothing, *and wills but one at once.*

376.

Spare the lover without flattering his passion; to make the pangs of love the butt of ridicule, is unwise and harsh—soothing meekness and wisdom subdue in else unconquerable things.

And consider that LOVE IS LIFE.

377.

There is none so bad to do the twentieth part of the evil he might, nor any so good as to do the tenth part of the good it is in his power to do. Judge of yourself by the good you might do and neglect—and of others by the evil they might do and omit—and your judgment will be poised between too much indulgence for yourself and too much severity on others.

Most Excellent!

380.

To him who is simple, and inexhaustible, *like nature*, *simple and inexhausted nature resigns her sway.*

383.

How can he be pious who loves not the beautiful, whilst piety is nothing but the love of beauty? Beauty we call the MOST VARIED ONE, the MOST UNITED VARIETY. Could there be a man who should harmoniously unite each variety of knowledge and of powers—were he not the most beautiful? were he not your *god*?

This is our Lord.

385.

The unloved cannot love.

Doubtful.

386.

Let the object of love be careful to lose none of its loveliness. [*Marked with a cross.*]

389.

We cannot be great, if we calculate how great we and how little others are, and calculate not how great others, how minute, how impotent ourselves.

Uneasy.

391.

He loves unalterably who keeps within the bounds of love; who always shews somewhat less than what he *is possessed of*—nor ever utters a *syllable*, or gives a hint, of *more than* what in fact remains *behind*—is just and friendly in the same degree.

396.

Who kindles love loves warmly.

400.

There is a manner of forgiving so divine, that you are ready to embrace the offender for having called it forth.

This I cannot concieve.

401.

Expect the secret resentment of him whom your forgiveness has impressed with a sense of his inferiority; expect the resentment of the woman whose proffered love you have repulsed; yet surer still expect the unceasing rancour of envy against the progress of genius and merit—renounce the hopes of reconciling him: but know, that whilst you steer on, mindless of his grin, allruling destiny will either change his rage to awe, or blast his powers to their deepest root.

If you expect his resentment you do not forgive him *now*, tho' you did once; forgiveness of enemies can only come upon their repentance.

407.

Whatever is visible is the vessel or veil of the invisible past, present, future—as man penetrates to this more, or perceives it less, he raises or depresses his dignity of being.

A vision of the Eternal Now.

408.

Let none turn over books, or roam the stars *in quest of God, who sees him not in man.*

409.

He alone is good, who, though possessed of energy, prefers virtue, *with the appearance of weakness, to the invitation of acting brilliantly ill.*

Noble! But Mark! Active Evil is better than Passive Good.

410.

Clearness, rapidity, comprehension of look, glance (what the French call COUP D'OEIL), is the greatest, simplest, most inexhausted gift a mortal can receive from heaven: who has that has all; and who has it not has little of what constitutes the good and great.

Uneasy: doubtful.

413.

As the presentiment of the possible, deemed impossible, so genius, so heroism—*every genius, every hero, is a prophet.*

414.

He who goes one step beyond his real faith, or presentiment, is in danger of deceiving himself and others.

Uneasy.

416.

He, who to obtain much will suffer little or nothing, can never be called great; and none ever little, who, to obtain one great object, will suffer much.

The man who does this is a Sectary: therefore not great.

419.

You beg as you question; you give as you answer.

Excellent!

424.

Love sees what no eye sees; *love hears what no ear hears; and what never rose in the heart of man love prepares for its object.*

Most Excellent!

426.

Him, who arrays malignity in good nature and treachery in familiarity, a miracle of Omnipotence alone can make an honest man.

No Omnipotence can act against order.

427.

He, who sets fire to one part of a town to rob more safely in another, is, no doubt, a villain: what will you call him, who, to avert suspicion from himself, accuses the innocent of a crime he knows himself guilty of, and means to commit again?

Damn him!

432.

The richer you are, the more calmly you bear the reproach of poverty: *the more genius you have, the more easily you bear the imputation of mediocrity.*

435.

There is no instance of a miser becoming a prodigal without losing his intellect; but there are thousands of prodigals becoming misers; *if, therefore, your turn be profuse, nothing is so much to be avoided as avarice :* and, if you be a miser, procure a physician who can cure an irremediable disorder.

Excellent!

437.

Avarice has sometimes been the flaw of great men, but never of great minds; great men produce effects that cannot be produced by a thousand of the vulgar; but great minds are stamped *with expanded benevolence*, unattainable by most.

440.

He is much greater and more authentic, who produces one thing entire and perfect, than he who does many by halves.

Uneasy.

444.

Say what you please of your humanity, no wise man will ever believe a syllable while I and MINE are the two only gates at which you sally forth and enter, and through which alone all must pass who seek admittance.

Uneasy.

447.

Who hides love, to bless with unmixed happiness, is great, like the king of heaven.

I do not understand this or else I do not agree to it. I know not what hiding love means.

449.

Trust not him with your secrets, who, when left alone in your room, turns over your papers.

Uneasy, yet I hope I should not do it.

450.

A woman whose ruling passion *is not vanity, is superior to any man of equal faculties.*

Such a woman I adore.

451.

He who has but one way of seeing every thing, is as important for him who studies man as fatal to friendship.

This I do not understand.

452.

Who has written will write again, says the Frenchman; he who has written against you will write against you again: he who has begun certain things is under the curse of leaving off no more. [*The second clause is deleted; the word* curse *is altered to* blessing.]

460.

Nothing is more impartial than the stream-like public; always the same and never the same; of whom, sooner or later, each misrepresented character obtains justice, and each calumniated, honour: he who cannot wait for that, is either ignorant of human nature, or feels that he was not made for honour.

Uneasy.

462.

The obstinacy of the indolent and weak is less conquerable than that of the fiery and bold.

463.

Who, with calm wisdom alone, imperceptibly directs the obstinacy of others, will be the most eligible friend or the most dreadful enemy.

This must be a grand fellow.

465.

He is condemned to depend on no man's modesty and honour who dares not depend on his own.

Uneasy.

477.

The frigid smiler, crawling, indiscreet, obtrusive, brazen-faced, is a scorpion whip of destiny—avoid him!

& never forgive him till he mends.

486.

Distrust your heart and the durability of your fame, if from the stream of occasion you snatch a handful of foam; deny the stream, and give its name to the frothy bursting bubble.

Uneasy: this I lament that I have done.

478.

If you ask me which is the real hereditary sin of human nature, do you imagine I shall answer pride? or luxury? or ambition? or egotism? no; I shall say indolence—who conquers indolence will conquer all the rest.

Pride, fullness of bread, & *abundance of Idleness* was the sin of Sodom. See Ezekiel, Ch. xvi, 49 ver.

489.

An entirely honest man, in the severe sense of the word, exists no more than an entirely dishonest knave: the best and the worst are only approximations of those qualities. Who are those that never contradict themselves? yet honesty never contradicts itself: who are those that always contradict themselves? yet knavery is mere self-contradiction. Thus the knowledge of man determines not the things themselves, but their proportions, the quantum of congruities and incongruities.

Man is a twofold being, one part capable of evil & the other capable of good; that which is capable of good is not also capable of evil, but that which is capable of evil is also capable of good. This aphorism seems to consider man as simple & yet capable of evil: now both evil & good cannot exist in a simple being, for thus 2 contraries would spring from one essence, which is impossible; but if man is consider'd as only evil & god only good, how then is regeneration effected which turns the evil to good? by casting out the evil by the good? See Matthew xii Ch., 26, 27, 28, 29 v.

496.

Sense seeks and finds the thought; the thought seeks and finds genius.

& vice versa, genius finds thought without seek[g] & thought thus produc'd finds sense.

506.

The poet, who composes not before the moment of inspiration, and as that leaves him ceases—composes, and he alone, for all men, all classes, all ages.

Most Excellent!

507.

He, who has frequent moments of complete existence, is a hero, though not laurelled; is crowned, and without crowns, a king: he only who has enjoyed immortal moments can reproduce them.

O that men would seek immortal moments! O that men would converse with God!

508.

The greater that which you can hide, the greater yourself.

Pleasant!

514.

He, who cannot forgive a trespass of malice to his enemy, has never yet tasted the most sublime enjoyment of love.

Uneasy: this I know not.

518.

You may have hot enemies without having a warm friend; but not a fervid friend without a bitter enemy. The qualities of your friends will be those of your enemies: cold friends, cold enemies—half friends, half enemies—fervid enemies, warm friends.

Very Uneasy indeed, but *truth*.

521.

He, who reforms himself, has done more toward reforming the public than a crowd of noisy, impotent patriots.

Excellent!

523.

He will do great things who can avert his words and thoughts from past irremediable evils.

Not if evils are past sins, for these a man should never avert his thoughts from.

526.

He, who is ever intent on great ends, has an eagle-eye for great means, and scorns not the smallest.

Great ends never look at means, but produce them spontaneously.

532.

Take from LUTHER his roughness and fiery courage; from CALVIN his hectic obstinacy; from ERASMUS his timid prudence; hypocrisy and fanaticism from CROMWELL; from HENRY IV his sanguine character; mysticism from FENELON; from HUME his all-unhinging wit; love of paradox and brooding suspicion from ROUSSEAU; naivetè and elegance of knavery from VOLTAIRE; from MILTON the extravagance of his all-personifying fancy; from RAFAELLE his dryness and nearly hard precision; and from RUBENS his supernatural luxury of colours:—deduct this oppressive EXUBERANCE from each; rectify them according to your own taste —what will be the result? your own correct, pretty, flat, useful—for me, to be sure, quite convenient vulgarity. And why this amongst maxims of humanity? that you may learn to know this EXUBERANCE, this LEVEN, of each great character, and its effects on contemporaries and posterity—that you may know where d, e, f, is, there must be a, b, c: he alone has knowledge of man, who knows the ferment that raises each character, and makes it that which it shall be, and some thing more or less than it shall be.

Deduct from a rose its redness, from a lilly its whiteness, from a diamond its hardness, from a spunge its softness, from an oak its heighth, from a daisy its lowness, & rectify every thing in Nature as the Philosophers do, & then we shall return to Chaos, & God will be compell'd to be Excentric if he Creates, O happy Philosopher.

Variety does not necessarily suppose deformity, for a rose & a lilly are various & both beautiful. Beauty is exuberant, but not of ugliness, but of beauty, and if ugliness is adjoin'd to beauty it is not the exuberance of beauty; so, if Rafael is hard & dry, it is not his genius but an accident acquired, for how can Substance and Accident be predicated of the same Essence? I cannot concieve. But substance gives tincture to the accident, and makes it physiognomic. Aphorism 47* speaks of the heterogeneous, which all extravagance is, but exuberance not.

---

*Man has an inward sense of consequence—of all that is pertinent. This sense is the essence of humanity: this, developed and determined, characterises him— this, displayed, is his education. The more strict you are in observing what is pertinent and impertinent, (or heterogeneous) in character, actions, works of art and literature—the wiser, nobler, greater, the more humane yourself.

533.

I have often, too often, been tempted, at the daily relation of new knaveries, to despise human nature in every individual, till, on minute anatomy of each trick, I found that the knave was only an ENTHUSIAST or MOMENTARY FOOL. This discovery of momentary folly, symptoms of which assail the wisest and the best, has thrown a great consolatory light on my inquiries into man's moral nature: by this the theorist is enabled to assign to each class and each individual its own peculiar fit of vice or folly; and, by the same, he has it in his power to contrast the ludicrous or dismal catalogue with the more pleasing one of sentiment and virtue, more properly their own.

Man is the ark of God; the mercy seat is above, upon the ark; cherubims guard it on either side, & in the midst is the holy law; man is either the ark of God or a phantom of the earth & of the water; if thou seekest by human policy to guide this ark, remember Uzzah, II Sam[l] vi ch: knaveries are not human nature; knaveries are knaveries. See N. 554; this aphorism seems to me to want discrimination.

534.

He, who is master of the fittest moment to crush his enemy, and magnanimously neglects it, is born to be a conqueror.

This was old George the second.

539.

A great woman not imperious, a fair woman not vain, a woman of common talents not jealous, an accomplished woman, who scorns to shine—are four wonders, just great enough to be divided among the four quarters of the globe.

Let the men do their duty & the women will be such wonders; the female life lives from the light of the male: see a man's female dependants, you know the man.

543.

Depend not much upon your rectitude, if you are uneasy in the presence of the good;

Easy.

nor trust to your humility if you are mortified when you are not noticed.

Uneasy.

549.

He, who hates [*altered to* loves] the wisest and best of men, hates [*altered to* loves] the Father of men; for, where is *the Father of men to be seen but in the most perfect of his children?*

This is true worship.

552.

He, who adores an impersonal God, has none; and, without guide or rudder, launches on an immense abyss that first absorbs his powers, and next himself.

Most superlatively beautiful & most affectionately Holy & pure; would to God that all men would consider it.

554.

The enemy of art is the enemy of nature; art is nothing but the highest sagacity and exertion of human nature; *and what nature will he honour who honours not the human?*

Human nature is the image of God.

556.

Where there is much pretension, much has been borrowed—*nature never pretends.*

557.

Do you think *him common man who can make what is common exquisite?*

559.

Whose promise may you depend upon? his who dares refuse what he knows he cannot perform; who promises calmly, strictly, conditionally, and never excites a hope which he may disappoint.

560.

You promise as you speak.

562.

Avoid him *who speaks softly, and writes sharply.*

Ah rogue! I could be thy hangman!

566.

Neither patience nor inspiration can give wings to a snail—you waste your own force, you destroy what remained of energy in the indolent, by urging him to move beyond his rate of power.

573.

Your humility is equal to your desire of being unnoticed, unobserved in your acts of virtue.

True humility.

574.

There are certain light characteristic momentary features of man, which, in spite of masks and all exterior mummery, represent him as he is and shall be. If once in an individual you have discovered one ennobling feature, let him debase it, *let it at times shrink from him, no matter; he will, in the end, prove superior to thousands of his critics,*

The wise man falleth 7 times in a day, and riseth again, &c.

576.

The man who has and uses but one scale for every thing, for himself and his enemy, the past and the future, the grand and the trifle, for truth and error, virtue and vice, religion, superstition, infidelity; for nature, art, and works of genius and art—is truly wise, just, great.

This is most true, but how does this agree with 451?

577.

The infinitely little constitutes the infinite difference in works of art, and in the degrees of morals and religion; the greater the rapidity, precision, acuteness, with which this is observed and determined, the more authentic, the greater the observer.

Uneasy.

580.

Range him high amongst your saints, who, with all-acknowledged powers, and his own stedfast scale for every thing, can, on the call of judgment or advice, submit to transpose *himself into another's situation, and to adopt* his point of sight.

582.

No communications and no gifts can exhaust genius, or impoverish charity.

Most Excellent.

585.

Distrust yourself if you fear the eye of the sincere; *but be afraid of neither God or man, if you have no reason to distrust yourself.*

586.

Who comes as he goes, and is present as he came and went, is sincere.

588.

He loves grandly (I speak of friendship) who is not jealous when he has partners of love.

Uneasy, but I hope to mend.

590.

He knows himself greatly who never opposes his genius.

Most Excellent!

596.

"Love as if you could hate and might be hated";—maxim of detested prudence in real friendship, the bane of all tenderness, the death of all familiarity. Consider the *fool who follows it as nothing inferior to him who at every bit of bread trembles at the thought of its being poisoned.*

Excellent!

597.

"Hate as if you could love or should be loved";—him who follows this maxim, if all the world were to declare an idiot and enthusiast, I shall esteem, of all men, the most eminently formed for friendship.

Better than Excellent!

600.

Distinguish with exactness, if you mean to know yourself and others, what is so often mistaken—the SINGULAR, *the ORIGINAL, the EXTRAORDINARY, the GREAT, and the SUBLIME man: the SUBLIME alone unites the singular, original, extraordinary, and great, with his own uniformity and simplicity : the GREAT, with many powers, and uniformity of ends, is destitute of that superior calmness* and inward harmony which soars above the atmosphere of praise: the EXTRAORDINARY is distinguished by copiousness, and a wide range of energy: the ORIGINAL need not be *very rich, only* that which he produces is unique, and has the exclusive stamp of individuality: the SINGULAR, as such, is placed between originality and whim, and often makes a trifle the medium of fame.

601.

Forwardness nips affection in the bud.

The more is the pity.

602.

If you mean to be loved, give more than what is asked, but not more than what is wanted; and ask less than what is expected. [*the last clause deleted.*]

This whole aphorism is an oversight; this is human policy, as it is call'd.

603.

Whom smiles and tears make equally lovely, all hearts may court.

[*Altered to read:*] Whom smiles and frowns make equally lovely, only good hearts can or dare court.

604.

Take here the grand secret—if not of pleasing all, yet of displeasing none—court mediocrity, avoid originality, and sacrifice to fashion.

& go to hell.

605.

He who pursues the glimmering steps of hope, with stedfast, not presumptuous, eye, may pass the gloomy rock, on either side of which superstition [*altered to* hypocrisy] and incredulity their dark abysses spread.

Superstition has been long a bugbear by reason of its being united with hypocrisy; but let them be fairly seperated & then superstition will be honest feeling, & God, who loves all honest men, will lead the poor enthusiast in the paths of holiness.

606.

The public seldom forgive twice.

Let us take their example.

607.

Him who is hurried on by the furies of immature, impetuous wishes, stern repentance shall drag bound and reluctant, back to the place from which he sallied: where you hear the crackling of wishes expect intolerable vapours or repining grief.

Uneasy.

608.

He submits to be seen through a microscope, who suffers himself to be caught in a fit of passion.

& such a one I dare love.

609.

Venerate four characters; the sanguine, who has checked volatility *and the rage for pleasure; the choleric, who has subdued passion and pride; the phlegmatic, emerged from indolence; and the melancholy, who has dismissed avarice, suspicion, and asperity.*

4 most holy men.

610.

All *great minds sympathize.*

612.

Men carry their character not seldom in their pockets: you might decide on more than half of your acquaintance, had you will or right to turn their pockets inside out.

I seldom carry money in my pockets; they are generally full of paper. [*several words erased*]

615.

Not he who forces himself on opportunity, but he who watches its approach, and welcomes its arrival by immediate use, is wise.

616.

Love and hate are the genius of invention, the parents of virtue and of vice—*forbear to decide on yourself till you have had opportunities of warm attachment or deep dislike.*

True Experience.

619.

Each heart is a world of nations, classes, and individuals; full of friendships, enmities, indifferences; . . . the world that surrounds you is the magic glass of the world, and of its forms within you; the brighter you are yourself, so much brighter are your friends—so much more polluted your enemies. Be assured then, that to know yourself perfectly you have only to set down a true statement of those that ever loved or hated you.

Uneasy because I cannot do this.

623.

Avoid connecting yourself with characters whose good and bad sides are unmixed, and have not fermented together; they resemble phials of vinegar and oil, or pallets set with colours: they are either excellent at home and intolerable abroad, or insufferable within doors and excellent in public: . . .

Most Excellent!

624.

The fool separates his object from all surrounding ones; all abstraction is temporary folly.

Uneasy, because I once thought otherwise but now know it is truth.

626.

Let me repeat it—He only is great who has the habits of greatness; who, after performing *what none in ten thousand could accomplish, passes, on like Samson, and "tells neither father nor mother of it."*

This is Excellent.

630.

A GOD, an ANIMAL, a PLANT, are not companions of man; nor is the FAULTLESS —then judge with lenity of all; the coolest, wisest, best, all without exception, have their points, their moments of enthusiasm, fanaticism, absence of mind, faint-heartedness, stupidity—if you allow not for these, your criticisms on man will be a mass of accusations or caricatures.

It is the God in *all* that is our companion & friend, for our God himself says: "you are my brother, my sister & my mother," & St. John: "Whoso dwelleth in love dwelleth in God & God in him," & such an one cannot judge of any but in love, & his feelings will be attractions or repulses. See Aphorisms 549, 554. God is in the lowest effects as well as in the highest causes; for he is become a worm that he may nourish the weak. For let it be remember'd that creation is God descending according to the weakness of man, for our Lord is the word of God & every thing on earth is the word of God & in its essence is God.

633.

You think to meet with some additions here to your stock of moral knowledge—and not in vain, I hope: but know, a great many rules cannot be given by him who means not to offend, and many of mine have perhaps offended already; believe me, for him who has an open ear and eye, every minute teems with observations of precious import, yet scarcely communicable to the most faithful friend; so incredibly weak, so vulnerable in certain points, is man; forbear to meddle with these at your first setting out, and make amusement the minister of reflection: sacrifice all egotism—sacrifice ten points to one, if that one have the value of twenty; and if you are happy enough to impress your disciple with respect for himself, with probability of success in his exertions of growing better; and, above all, with the idea of your disinterestedness—you may perhaps succeed in making one proselyte to virtue.

—lovely!

Those who are offended with any thing in this book would be offended with the innocence of a child & for the same reason, because it reproaches him with the errors of acquired folly.

635.

Keep your heart from him who begins his acquaintance with you by indirect flattery of your favourite paradox or foible.

Unless you find it to be his also, previous to your acquaintance.

636.

Receive no satisfaction for premeditated impertinence—forget it, forgive it— but keep him inexorably at a distance who offered it.

This is a paradox.

638.

Let the cold, who offers the nauseous mimickry of warm affection, meet with what he deserves—a repulse; but from that moment depend on his irreconcilable enmity.

Uneasy because I do not know how to do this, but I will try to do it the first opportunity.

640.

The moral enthusiast, who in the maze of his refinements loses or despises the plain paths of honesty and duty, is on the brink of crimes.

Most True!

I hope no one will call what I have written cavilling because he may think my remarks of small consequence. For I write from the warmth of my heart, & cannot resist the impulse I feel to rectify what I think false in a book I love so much & approve so generally.

Man is bad or good as he unites himself with bad or good spirits: tell me with whom you go & I'll tell you what you do.

As we cannot experience pleasure but by means of others [so we are *del.*], who experience either pleasure or pain thro' us, And as all of us on earth are united in thought, for it is impossible to think without images of somewhat on earth—So it is impossible to know God or heavenly things without conjunction with those who know God & heavenly things; therefore all who converse in the spirit, converse with spirits. [& they converse with the spirit of God. *del.*]

For these reasons I say that this Book is written by consultation with Good Spirits, because it is Good, & that the name Lavater is the amulet of those who purify the heart of man.

There is a strong objection to Lavater's principles (as I understand them) & that is He makes every thing originate in its accident; he makes the vicious propensity not only a leading feature of the man, but the stamina on which all his virtues grow. But as I understand Vice it is a Negative. It does not signify what the laws of Kings & Priests have call'd Vice; we who are philosophers ought not to call the Staminal Virtues of Humanity by the same name that we call the omissions of intellect springing from poverty.

Every man's leading propensity ought to be call'd his leading Virtue & his good Angel. But the Philosophy of Causes & Consequences misled Lavater as it has all his Cotemporaries. Each thing is its own cause & its own effect. Accident is the omission of act in self & the hindering of act in another; This is Vice, but all Act [from Individual propensity *inserted and del.*] is Virtue. To hinder another is not an act; it is the contrary; it is a restraint on action both in ourselves & in the person hinder'd, for he who hinders another omits his own duty at the same time.

Murder is Hindering Another.

Theft is Hindering Another.

Backbiting, Undermining, Circumventing, & whatever is Negative is Vice. But the origin of this mistake in Lavater & his cotemporaries is, They suppose that Woman's Love is Sin; in consequence all the Loves & Graces with them are Sin.

ANNOTATIONS TO SWEDENBORG'S WISDOM OF ANGELS CONCERNING DIVINE LOVE AND DIVINE WISDOM

London MDCCLXXXVIII

Written about 1789

There can be no Good Will. Will is always Evil; it is pernicious to others or selfish. If God is anything he is Understanding. He is the Influx from that into the Will. Good to others or benevolent Understanding can & does [?] Work harm [?] ignorantly but never can the [?] Truth be evil because Man is only Evil . . . H. & Hell Chapter 425

Understanding or Thought is not natural to Man; it is acquir'd by means of Suffering & Distress i.e. Experience. Will, Desire, Love, Rage, Envy, & all other affections are Natural, but Understanding is Acquired But Observe: without these is to be less than Man. Man could . . . affections; one would be . . . in different periods of time. Wisdom of Angels 10

[*The subsequent annotations are marginal, and are here printed after the corresponding passages from Swedenborg's text, these being given in smaller type. Words underlined by Blake are printed in italic.*]

Page 2.
Doth it not happen that in Proportion as the Affection which is of Love groweth cold, the Thought, Speech and Action grow cold also? And that in Proportion as it is heated, they also are heated? But this a wise Man perceiveth, not from a Knowledge that Love is the Life of Man, but from Experience of this Fact.

They also percieve this from Knowledge, but not with the natural part.

Page 3.
No one knowth what is the Life of Man, unless he knoweth that it is Love.

This was known to me & thousands.

Page 7.
That the Divine or God is not in Space . . . cannot be comprehended by any merely natural Idea, but it may by a spiritual Idea: The Reason why it cannot be comprehended by a natural Idea is because in that Idea there is Space.

What a natural Idea is.

Nevertheless, Man may comprehend this by natural Thought, if he will only admit into such Thought somewhat of spiritual Light.

Mark this.

A spiritual Idea doth not derive any Thing from Space, but it derives every Thing appertaining to it from State.

Poetic idea.

Pages 8–9.
Hence it may appear, that Man from a *merely natural* Idea cannot comprehend that the Divine is every where, and yet not in Space; and yet that Angels and Spirits clearly comprehend this; consequently *that Man also may,* if so be he will admit something of spiritual Light into his Thought; the Reason why Man may comprehend it is because his Body doth not think, but his Spirit, therefore not his natural but his spiritual Part.

Observe the distinction here between Natural & Spiritual as seen by Man. Man may comprehend, but not the natural or external man.

Page 10.
It hath been said, that in the spiritual World Spaces appear equally as in the natural World. . . . Hence it is that the Lord, although he is in the Heavens with the Angels everywhere, nevertheless appears high above them as a Sun: And whereas the reception of Love and Wisdom constitutes Affinity with him, therefore those Heavens appear nearer to him where the Angels are in a nearer Affinity from Reception, than where they are in a more remote Affinity.

He who Loves feels love descend into him & if he has wisdom may percieve it is from the Poetic Genius, which is the Lord.

Page 11.
In all the Heavens there is no other Idea of God than that of a Man.

Man can have no idea of any thing greater than Man, as a cup cannot contain more than its capaciousness. But God is a man, not because he is so perciev'd by man, but because he is the creator of man.

Page 12.
"The Gentiles, particularly the Africans . . . entertain an Idea of God as of a Man, and say that no one can have any other Idea of God: When they hear that many form an Idea of God as existing in the Midst of a Cloud, they ask where such are. . . ."

Think of a white cloud as being holy, you cannot love it; but think of a holy man within the cloud, love springs up in your thoughts, for to think of holiness distinct from man is impossible to the affections. Thought alone can make monsters, but the affections cannot.

Page 13.
They who are wiser than the common People pronounce God to be invisible.

Worldly wisdom, or demonstration by the senses is the cause of this.

Page 14.
The Negation of God constitutes Hell, and in the Christian World the Negation of the Lord's Divinity.

The Negation of the Poetic Genius.

Page 15.
When Love is in Wisdom, then it existeth. These two are such a ONE, that they may be distinguished indeed in Thought, but not in Act.

Thought without affection makes a distinction between Love & Wisdom, as it does between body & Spirit.

Page 24.
What Person of Sound Reason doth not perceive, that the Divine is not divisible . . . If another, who hath no Reason, should say that it is possible there may be several Infinities, Uncreates, Omnipotents and Gods, provided they have the same Essence, and that thereby there is one Infinite, Uncreate, Omnipotent and God—is not one and the same Essence one and the same Identity?

Answer: Essence is not Identity, but from Essence proceeds Identity & from one Essence may proceed many Identities, as from one Affection may proceed many thoughts. Surely this is an oversight.

That there is but one Omnipotent, Uncreate & God I agree, but that there is but one Infinite I do not; for if all but God is not Infinite, they shall come to an End, which God forbid.

If the Essence was the same as the Identity, there could be but one Identity, which is false. Heaven would upon this plan be but a Clock; but one & the same Essence is therefore Essence & not Identity.

Page 33.
Appearances are the first Things from which the human Mind forms its Understanding, and it cannot shake them off but by an Investigation of the Cause, and if the Cause is very deep, it cannot investigate it, *without keeping the Understanding some Time in spiritual Light*. . . .

This Man can do while in the body.

It cannot be demonstrated except by such Things as a Man can perceive by his bodily Senses.

Demonstration is only by bodily Senses.

Page 40.
With respect to God, it is not possible that he can love and be reciprocally beloved by others, in whom . . . there is any Thing Divine; for if there was any Thing Divine in them, then it would not be beloved by others, but it would love itself.

False. Take it so or the contrary, it comes to the same, for if a thing loves it is infinite. Perhaps we only differ in the meaning of the words Infinity & Eternal.

Page 56.
Man is only a Recipient of Life. From this Cause it is, that Man, from his own hereditary Evil, reacts against God; but so far as he believes that all his Life is from God, and every Good of Life from the Action of God, and every Evil of Life from the Reaction of Man, Reaction thus becomes correspondent with Action, and Man acts with God as from himself.

Good & Evil are here both Good & the two contraries Married.

Page 57.
But he who knows how to elevate his Mind above the Ideas of Thought which are derived from Space and Time, such a Man passes from Darkness to Light, and becomes wise in Things spiritual and Divine . . . and then by Virtue of that Light he shakes off the Darkness of natural Light, and removes *its Fallacies* from the Center to the Circumference.

When the fallacies of darkness are in the circumference they cast a bound about the infinite.

Page 58.
Now inasmuch as the Thoughts of the Angels derive nothing from Space and Time, but from States of Life, it is evident that they do not comprehend what is meant when it is said, that the Divine fills Space, for they do not know what Space is, but that they comprehend clearly, when it is said, without any Idea of Space that the Divine fills all Things.

Excellent.

Page 131.
That without two Suns, the one living and the other dead, there can be no Creation.

False philosophy according to the letter, but true according to the spirit.

Page 133.
It follows that the one Sun is living and that the other Sun is dead, also that the dead Sun itself was created by the living Sun from the Lord.

How could Life create death?

The reason why a dead Sun was created is to the End that in the Ultimate all Things may be fixed. . . . On this and no other Ground Creation is founded. The terraqueous Globe . . . is as it were the Basis and Firmament.

They exist literally about the sun & not about the earth.

That all Things were created from the Lord by the living Sun, *and nothing by the dead Sun*, may appear from this Consideration. . . .

The dead Sun is only a phantasy of evil Man.

Page 146.
It is the same upon Earth with Men, but with this Difference, that the Angels feel that Heat and see that Light, whereas Men do not. . . .

He speaks of Men as meer earthly Men, not as receptacles of spirit, or else he contradicts N. 257 [p. 220].

Now forasmuch as Man, whilst he is in natural Heat and Light, knoweth nothing of spiritual Heat and Light in himself, and this cannot be known but by Experience from the spiritual World. . . .

This is certainly not to be understood according to the letter, for it is false by all experience. Who does not or may not know of love & wisdom in himself?

Page 181.
From these Consideration a Conclusion was drawn, that the Whole of Charity and Faith is in Works. . . .

The Whole of the New Church is in the Active Life & not in Ceremonies at all.

Pages 195-6.
These three Degrees of Altitude are named Natural, Spiritual and Celestial. . . . Man, at his Birth, first comes into the natural Degree, and this increases in him by

Continuity according to the Sciences, and according to the Understanding acquired by them, to the Summit of Understanding which is called Rational.

Study Sciences till you are blind, Study intellectuals till you are cold, Yet science cannot teach intellect. Much less can intellect teach Affection. How foolish then is it to assert that Man is born in only one degree, when that one degree is reception of the 3 degrees, two of which he must destroy or close up or they will descend; if he closes up the two superior, then he is not truly in the 3[d], but descends out of it into meer Nature or Hell. See N. 239. [p. 198]. Is it not also evident that one degree will not open the other, & that science will not open intellect, but that they are discrete & not continuous so as to explain each other except by correspondence, which has nothing to do with demonstration; for you cannot demonstrate one degree by the other; for how can science be brought to demonstrate intellect without making them continuous & not discrete?

Page 196.

Man, so long as he lives in the World, does not know any Thing of the opening of these Degrees in himself.

See N. 239 [p. 198].

Page 198.

In every Man there is a natural, spiritual and celestial Will and Understanding, in Power from his Birth, and in Act whilst they are opening.

Mark this; it explains no. 238 [p. 196].

In a Word the Mind of Man . . . is of three Degrees, so that . . . a Man may be elevated thereby to Angelic Wisdom and possess it, while he lives in the World, but nevertheless he does not come into it till after Death, if he becomes an Angel *and then he speaks Things ineffable and incomprehensible to the natural Man.*

Not to a Man, but to the natural Man.

Page 200.

Every one who consults his Reason, *whilst it is in the Light*, may see that Man's Love is the End of all Things appertaining to him.

Page 204.

And hence it also follows that the Understanding does not lead the Will, or that Wisdom does not produce Love, but that it only teaches and shows the Way, it teaches how a Man ought to live, and shows the Way in which he ought to walk.

Mark this.

Page 219.

From this it is evident, that Man, *so long as he lives in the World, and is thereby in the natural Degree,* cannot be elevated into Wisdom itself, . . .

See Sect. 4 of the next Number.

Page 220.

But still Man, in whom the spiritual Degree is open, comes into that Wisdom when he dies, and may also come into it by laying asleep the Sensations of the Body, and by Influx from above at the Same time into the Spirituals of his Mind.

This is while in the Body.

This is to be understood as unusual in our time, but common in ancient.

The natural Mind of Man consists of spiritual Substances, and at the same Time of natural Substances; from its *spiritual Substances* Thought is produced, but not from its *natural Substances;* . . .

Many perversely understand him as if man, while in the body, was only conversant with natural Substances, because themselves are mercenary & worldly & have no idea of any but worldly gain.

Page 233.

. . . for the natural Man can elevate his Understanding to superior Light as far as he desires it, but he who is principled in Evils and thence in Things false, does not elevate it higher than to the superior Region of his natural Mind; . . .

Who shall dare to say after this that all elevation is of self & is Enthusiasm & Madness, & is it not plain that self-derived intelligence is worldly demonstration?

Page 268.

Forasmuch as the Things, which constitute the Sun of the spiritual World, are from the Lord, and not the Lord, therefore they are not Life in itself, . . .

This assertion that the spiritual Sun is not Life explains how the natural Sun is dead.

This is an Arcanum which the Angels by their spiritual Ideas can see in Thought, and also express in Speech, but not Men by their *natural Ideas;* . . .

How absurd then would it be to say that no man on earth has a spiritual idea after reading N. 257 [p. 220].

Page 269.

That there is such a Difference between the Thoughts of Angels and Men, was made known to me by this Experience. They were told to think of something spiritually, and afterwards to tell me what they thought of; when this was done and would have told me, they could not, . . .

They could not tell him in natural ideas; how absurd must men be to understand him as if he said the angels could not express themselves at all to him.

Page 276.

Forasmuch as there is such a Progression of the Fibres and Vessels in a Man from first Principles to Ultimates, therefore there is a similar Progression of their States; their States are the Sensations, Thoughts and Affections; these also from their first Principles *where they are in the Light,* pervade to their Ultimates, where they are in Obscurity; or from their first Principles, where they are in Heat, to their Ultimates where they are not *in Heat.*

We see here that the cause of an ultimate is the absence from heat & light.

Page 285.

It is to be observed, that the Heat, Light and Atmospheres of the natural World conduce nothing to this Image of Creation, . . .

Therefore the Natural Earth & Atmosphere is a Phantasy.

The Heat, Light and Atmospheres of the natural World only open Seeds; . . . but this not by Powers derived from their own Sun . . .

Mark this.

Page 286.
. . . but by Powers from the spiritual Sun, . . . *for the Image of Creation is Spiritual,* nevertheless that it may appear, and furnish Use *in the natural World,* . . . it must be clothed in Matter . . .
. . . it is evident, that as there is a Resemblance of Creation in the Forms of Vegetables, so there is also in the Forms of Animals, viz. that there is a Progression from first Principles to Ultimates, and from Ultimates to first Principles.

A going forth & returning.

Page 295.
. . . there doth not exist any Thing in the created Universe, which hath not Correspondence with Something of Man, not only with his Affections and his Thoughts thence derived, but also with the Organs and Viscera of his Body, not with them as Substances, but with them as Uses.

Uses & substances are so different as not to correspond.

Pages 410–411.
Thought indeed exists first, because it is of the natural Mind, but Thought from the Perception of Truth, which is from the Affection *of Truth, exists last; this Thought is the Thought of Wisdom, but the other is Thought from the Memory by the Sight of the natural Mind.*

Note this.

Page 421.
From these Things it may be seen, that Love or the Will joins itself to Wisdom or the Understanding, and not that Wisdom or the Understanding joins itself to Love or the Will.

Mark this.

Page 422.
Thoughts, Perceptions, and Knowledge, thence derived, flow indeed from the spiritual World, *but still they are not received by the Understanding, but by the Love according to its Affections in the Understanding.*

Mark this.

It appears also as if the Understanding joined itself to Love or the Will, *but this also is a Fallacy;* Love or the Will joins itself to the Understanding and causeth the Understanding to be reciprocally joined to it.

Mark this.

Page 423.
For the Life of Man is his Love, . . . that is, according as he has exalted his Affections by Truths, . . .

Mark this.

Page 424.
From these Considerations it is also evident, *that Love joins itself to the Understanding, and not vice versa.* . . .

Mark this.

Page 425.
He who knows all the Fabric of the Lungs from Anatomy, if he compares them with the Understanding, may clearly see that the *Understanding does nothing from itself,* that it does not *perceive nor think from itself, but all from Affections which are of the Love,* which in the Understanding are called the Affection of knowing, . . .

Mark.

Page 426.
From the Structure of the Lungs . . . *I was fully convinced that the Love by its Affections joins itself to the Understanding, and that the Understanding does not join itself to any Affection of the Love.* . . .

Mark this.

Pages 426–427.
That Wisdom or the Understanding by Means of the Power given it by Love, can be elevated, and receive the Things which are of the Light from Heaven, and perceive them.

Mark this.

Page 429.
. . . when Man shuns Evils as Sins, therefore by these Means Love or the Will also can be elevated, and without these Means it cannot.

Is it not false then, that love recieves influx thro' the understanding, as was asserted in the society?

Page 435.
. . . and moreover this Love became impure by Reason of the Separation of celestial Love from it in the Parents.

Therefore it was not created impure & is not naturally so.

Page 436.
. . . so far the Love is purged of its Uncleannesses, and purified, that is, so far it is elevated into the Heat of Heaven, . . . in which the Understanding is.

Therefore it does not recieve influx thro' the understanding.

Page 440.
That Love or the Will is defiled in the Understanding, and by it, if they are not elevated together.

Mark this: they are elevated together.

Page 441.
The Understanding is not made spiritual and celestial, but the Love is; . . .

Page 458.
Moreover it was shown in the Light of Heaven, . . . that the interior Compages of this little Brain was . . . in the Order and Form of Heaven; and that its exterior Compages was in Opposition to that Order and Form.

Heaven & Hell are born together.

THERE IS NO NATURAL RELIGION

[FIRST SERIES]

Etched about 1788

The Argument. Man has no notion of moral fitness but from Education. Naturally he is only a natural organ subject to Sense.

I. Man cannot naturally Percieve but through his natural or bodily organs.

II. Man by his reasoning power can only compare & judge of what he has already perciev'd.

III. From a perception of only 3 senses or 3 elements none could deduce a fourth or fifth.

IV. None could have other than natural or organic thoughts if he had none but organic perceptions.

V. Man's desires are limited by his perceptions, none can desire what he has not perciev'd.

VI. The desires & perceptions of man, untaught by any thing but organs of sense, must be limited to objects of sense.

Conclusion. If it were not for the Poetic or Prophetic character the Philosophic & Experimental would soon be at the ratio of all things, & stand still, unable to do other than repeat the same dull round over again.

THERE IS NO NATURAL RELIGION

[SECOND SERIES]

Etched about 1788

I. Man's perceptions are not bounded by organs of perception; he percieves more than sense (tho' ever so acute) can discover.

II. Reason, or the ratio of all we have already known, is not the same that it shall be when we know more.

III. [*This proposition has been lost.*]

IV. The bounded is loathed by its possessor. The same dull round, even of a universe, would soon become a mill with complicated wheels.

V. If the many become the same as the few when possess'd, More! More! is the cry of a mistaken soul; less than All cannot satisfy Man.

VI. If any could desire what he is incapable of possessing, despair must be his eternal lot.

VII. The desire of Man being Infinite, the possession is Infinite & himself Infinite.

Application. He who sees the Infinite in all things, sees God. He who sees the Ratio only, sees himself only.

Therefore God becomes as we are, that we may be as he is.

ALL RELIGIONS are ONE

Etched about 1788

The Voice of one crying in the Wilderness

The Argument. As the true method of knowledge is experiment, the true faculty of knowing must be the faculty which experiences. This faculty I treat of.

PRINCIPLE 1st. That the Poetic Genius is the true Man, and that the body or outward form of Man is derived from the Poetic Genius. Likewise that the forms of all things are derived from their Genius, which by the Ancients was call'd an Angel & Spirit & Demon.

PRINCIPLE 2[d]. As all men are alike in outward form, So (and with the same infinite variety) all are alike in the Poetic Genius.

PRINCIPLE 3[d]. No man can think, write, or speak from his heart, but he must intend truth. Thus all sects of Philosophy are from the Poetic Genius adapted to the weaknesses of every individual.

PRINCIPLE 4th. As none by travelling over known lands can find out the unknown, So from already acquired knowledge Man could not acquire more: therefore an universal Poetic Genius exists.

PRINCIPLE 5th. The Religions of all Nations are derived from each Nation's different reception of the Poetic Genius, which is every where call'd the Spirit of Prophecy.

PRINCIPLE 6th. The Jewish & Christian Testaments are An original derivation from the Poetic Genius; this is necessary from the confined nature of bodily sensation.

PRINCIPLE 7th. As all men are alike (tho' infinitely various), So all Religions &, as all similars, have one source.

The true Man is the source, he being the Poetic Genius.

TIRIEL

Written about 1789

I

And Aged Tiriel stood before the Gates of his beautiful palace
[But dark were his once piercing eyes *del.*]
With Myratana, once the Queen of all the western plains;
But now his eyes were dark'ned & his wife fading in death.
They stood before their once delightful palace, & thus the Voice
Of aged Tiriel arose, that his sons might hear in their gates:

"Accursed race of Tiriel! behold your [aged *del.*] father;
"Come forth & look on her that bore you! come, you accursed sons!
"In my weak [aged *del.*] arms I here have borne your dying mother.
"Come forth, sons of the Curse, come forth! see the death of Myratana!"

His sons ran from their gates & saw their aged parents stand,
And thus the eldest son of Tiriel rais'd his mighty voice:

"Old man! unworthy to be call'd the father of Tiriel's race!
"For every one of those thy wrinkles, each of those grey hairs
"Are cruel as death & as obdurate as the devouring pit!
"Why should thy sons care for thy curses, thou accursed man?
"Were we not slaves till we rebel'd? Who cares for Tiriel's curse?
"His blessing was a cruel curse. His curse may be a blessing."

He ceast: the aged man rais'd up his right hand to the heavens,
His left supported Myratana, [heaving *del.*] shrinking in pangs of death:
The orbs of his large eyes he open'd, & thus his voice went forth:

"Serpents, not sons, wreathing around the bones of Tiriel!
"Ye worms of death, feasting upon your aged parent's flesh!
"Listen! & hear your mother's groans! No more accursed Sons
"She bears; she groans not at the birth of Heuxos or Yuva.
"These are the groans of death, ye serpents! These are the groans of death!
"Nourish'd with milk, ye serpents, nourish'd with mother's tears & cares!
"Look at my eyes, blind as the orbless scull among the stones!
"Look at my bald head! Hark! listen, ye serpents, listen!
"What, Myratana! What, my wife! O Soul! O Spirit! O fire!

"What, Myratana! art thou dead? Look here, ye serpents, look!
"The serpents sprung from her own bowels have drain'd her dry as this.
"Curse on your ruthless heads, for I will bury her even here!"

So saying, he began to dig a grave with his aged hands;
But Heuxos call'd a Son of Zazel to dig their mother a grave.

"Old Cruelty, desist! & let us dig a grave for thee.
"Thou hast refus'd our charity, thou hast refus'd our food,
"Thou hast refus'd our clothes, our beds, our houses for thy dwelling,
"Chusing to wander like a Son of Zazel in the rocks.
"Why dost thou curse? is not the curse now come upon your head?
"Was it not you enslav'd the sons of Zazel? & they have curs'd,
"And now you feel it. Dig a grave, & let us bury our mother,"

"There, take the body, cursed sons! & may the heavens rain wrath
"As thick as northern fogs around your gates, to choke you up!
"That you may lie as now your mother lies, like dogs cast out,
"The stink of your dead carcases annoying man & beast,
"Till your white bones are bleach'd with age for a memorial.
"No! your remembrance shall perish; for, when your carcases
"Lie stinking on the earth, the buriers shall arise from the east,
"And not a bone of all the sons of Tiriel remain.
"Bury your mother! but you cannot bury the curse of Tiriel."

He ceast & darkling o'er the mountains sought his pathless way.

2

He wander'd day & night: to him both day & night were dark.
The sun he felt, but the bright moon was now a useless globe:
O'er mountains & thro' vales of woe the blind & aged man
Wander'd, till he that leadeth all led him to the vales of Har.

And Har & Heva, like two children, sat beneath the Oak:
Mnetha, now aged, waited on them & brought them food & clothing;
But they were as the shadow of Har & as the years forgotten.
Playing with flowers & running after birds they spent the day,
And in the night like infants slept, delighted with infant dreams.

Soon as the blind wanderer enter'd the pleasant gardens of Har,
[The aged father & mother saw him as they sat at play *del.*]
They ran weeping, like frighted infants, for refuge in Mnetha's arms.

The blind man felt his way & cried: "peace to these open doors!
"Let no one fear, for poor blind Tiriel hurts none but himself.
"Tell me, O friends, where am I now & in what pleasant place?"

"This is the valley of Har," said Mnetha, "& this the tent of Har.
"Who art thou, poor blind man, that takest the name of Tiriel on thee?
"Tiriel is king of all the west: who art thou? I am Mnetha,
"And this is Har & Heva, trembling like infants by my side."

"I know Tiriel is king of the west, & there he lives in joy.
"No matter who I am; O Mnetha, if thou hast any food,
"Give it me, for I cannot stay; my journey is far from hence."

Then Har said: "O my mother Mnetha, venture not so near him;
"For he is the king of rotten wood & of the bones of death;
"He wanders without eyes & passes thro' thick walls & doors.
"Thou shalt not smite my mother Mnetha, O thou eyeless man!"

"[O venerable, O most piteous, O most woeful day! *del.*]
"A wanderer, I beg for food: you see I cannot weep:
"[But I can kneel down at your door, I am a harmless man. *del.*]
"I cast away my staff, the kind companion of my travel,
"And I kneel down that you may see I am a harmless man."

He kneeled down, & Mnetha said: "Come, Har & Heva, rise!
"He is an innocent old man & hungry with his travel."

Then Har arose & laid his hand upon old Tiriel's head.

"God bless thy poor bald pate! God bless thy hollow winking eyes!
"God bless thy shrivel'd beard! God bless thy many-wrinkled fore-head!
"Thou hast no teeth, old man, & thus I kiss thy sleek bald head.
"Heva, come kiss his bald head, for he will not hurt us, Heva."

Then Heva came & took old Tiriel in her mother's arms.

"Bless thy poor eyes, old man, & bless the old father of Tiriel!
"Thou art my Tiriel's old father; I know thee thro' thy wrinkles,
"Because thou smellest like the fig-tree, thou smellest like ripe figs.
"How didst thou lose thy eyes, old Tiriel? bless thy wrinkled face!"

[The aged Tiriel could not speak, his heart was full of grief;
He strove against his rising passions, but still he could not speak. *del.*]

Mnetha said: "Come in, aged wanderer! tell us of thy name.
"Why shouldest thou conceal thyself from those of thine own flesh?"

"I am not of this region," said Tiriel dissemblingly,
[Fearing to tell them who he was, because of the weakness of Har. *del.*]
"I am an aged wanderer, once father of a race
"Far in the north; but they were wicked & were all destroy'd,
"And I their father sent an outcast. I have told you all.
"Ask me no more, I pray, for grief hath seal'd my precious sight."

"O Lord!" said Mnetha, "how I tremble! are there then more people,
"More human creatures on this earth, beside the sons of Har?"

"No more," said Tiriel, "but I, remain on all this globe;
"And I remain an outcast; hast thou any thing to drink?"

Then Mnetha gave him milk & fruits, & they sat down together.

3

They sat & eat, & Har & Heva smil'd on Tiriel.

"Thou art a very old old man, but I am older than thou.
"How came thine hair to leave thy forehead? how came thy face so brown?
"My hair is very long, my beard doth cover all my breast.
"God bless thy piteous face! to count the wrinkles in thy face
"Would puzzle [Har *del.*] Mnetha: bless thy face! for thou art Tiriel."

[Tiriel could scarce dissemble more, & his tongue could scarce refrain,
But still he fear'd that Har & Heva would die of joy & grief. *del.*]

"Tiriel I never saw but once: I sat with him & eat;
"He was as chearful as a prince & gave me entertainment;
"But long I staid not at his palace, for I am forc'd to wander."

"What! wilt thou leave us too?" said Heva: "thou shalt not leave us too,
"For we have many sports to shew thee & many songs to sing,
"And after dinner we will walk into the cage of Har,
"And thou shalt help us to catch birds & gather them ripe cherries.
"Then let thy name be Tiriel & never leave us more."

"If thou dost go," said Har, "I wish thine eyes may see thy folly.
"My sons have left me; did thine leave thee? O, 'twas very cruel!"

"No! venerable man," said Tiriel, "ask me not such things,
"For thou dost make my heart to bleed: my sons were not like thine,
"But worse. O never ask me more, or I must flee away!"

"Thou shalt not go," said Heva, "till thou hast seen our singing birds,
"And heard Har sing in the great cage & slept upon our fleeces.
"Go not! for thou art so like Tiriel that I love thine head,
"Tho' it is wrinkled like the earth parch'd with the summer heat."

Then Tiriel rose up from the seat & said: "God bless these tents!
"[God bless my benefactors, for I cannot tarry longer. *del.*]
"My Journey is o'er rocks & mountains, not in pleasant vales:
"I must not sleep nor rest, because of madness & dismay."

[Then Mnetha led him to the door & gave to him his staff,
And Har & Heva stood & watch'd him till he enter'd the wood,
And then they went & wept to Mnetha; but they soon forgot their tears. *del.*]

And Mnetha said: "Thou must not go to wander dark, alone;
"But dwell with us & let us be to thee instead of eyes,
"And I will bring thee food, old man, till death shall call thee hence."

Then Tiriel frown'd & answer'd: "Did I not command you, saying,
" 'Madness & deep dismay possess the heart of the blind man,
" 'The wanderer who [*word del.*] seeks the woods, leaning upon his staff?' "

Then Mnetha, trembling at his frowns, led him to the tent door
And gave to him his staff & blest him: he went on his way.

But Har & Heva stood & watch'd him till he enter'd the wood,
And then they went & wept to Mnetha: but they soon forgot their tears.

4

Over the weary hills the blind man took his lonely way;
To him the day & night alike was dark & desolate;
But far he had not gone when Ijim from his woods come down,
Met him at entrance of the forest in a dark & lonely way.

"Who art thou, Eyeless wretch, that thus obstruct'st the lion's path?
"Ijim shall rend thy feeble joints, thou tempter of dark Ijim!
"Thou hast the form of Tiriel, but I know thee well enough.
"Stand from my path, foul fiend! is this the last of thy deceits,
"To be a hypocrite & stand in shape of a blind beggar?"

The blind man heard his brother's voice & kneel'd down on his knee.

"O brother Ijim, if it is thy voice that speaks to me,
"Smite not thy brother Tiriel, tho' weary of his life.
"My sons have smitten me already; and, if thou smitest me,
"The curse that rolls over their heads will rest itself on thine.
"'Tis now seven years since in my palace I beheld thy face.
"[Seven years of sorrow; then the curse of Zazel *del.*]"

"Come, thou dark fiend, I dare thy cunning! know that Ijim scorns
"To smite thee in the form of helpless age & eyeless policy.
"Rise up! for I discern thee & I dare thy eloquent tongue.
"Come! I will lead thee on thy way & use thee as a scoff."

"O Brother Ijim, thou beholdest wretched Tiriel:
"Kiss me, my brother, & then leave me to wander desolate!"

"No! artful fiend, but I will lead thee; dost thou want to go?
"Reply not, lest I bind thee with the green flags of the brook.
"Ay! now thou art discover'd, I will use thee like a slave."

When Tiriel heard the words of Ijim, he sought not to reply:
He knew 'twas vain, for Ijim's words were as the voice of Fate.

And they went on together, over hills, thro' woody dales,
Blind to the pleasures of the sight & deaf to warbling birds:
All day they walk'd & all the night beneath the pleasant Moon,
Westwardly journeying, till Tiriel grew weary with his travel.

"O Ijim, I am faint & weary, for my knees forbid
"To bear me further: urge me not, lest I should die with travel.
"A little rest I crave, a little water from a brook,
"Or I shall soon discover that I am a mortal man,
"And you will lose your once lov'd Tiriel: alas! how faint I am!"

"Impudent fiend!" said Ijim, "hold thy glib & eloquent tongue!
"Tiriel is a king, & thou the tempter of dark Ijim.
"Drink of this running brook & I will bear thee on my shoulders."

He drank, & Ijim rais'd him up & bore him on his shoulders:
All day he bore him, & when evening drew her solemn curtain,
Enter'd the gates of Tiriel's palace & stood & call'd aloud:

"Heuxos, come forth! I here have brought the fiend that troubles Ijim.
"Look! know'st thou aught of this grey beard, or of these blinded eyes?"

Heuxos & Lotho ran forth at the sound of Ijim's voice,
And saw their aged father borne upon his mighty shoulders.
Their eloquent tongues were dumb, & sweat stood on their trembling limbs:
They knew 'twas vain to strive with Ijim; they bow'd & silent stood.

"What, Heuxos! call thy father, for I [must *del.*] mean to sport to-night.
"This is the hypocrite that sometimes roars a dreadful lion;
"Then I have rent his limbs & left him rotting in the forest
"For birds to eat; but I have scarce departed from the place,
"But like a tyger he would come: & so I rent him too.
"Then like a river he would seek to drown me in his waves;
"But soon I buffetted the torrent: anon like to a cloud
"Fraught with the swords of lightning; but I brav'd the vengeance too.
"Then he would creep like a bright serpent, till around my neck,
"While I was sleeping, he would twine: I squeez'd his pois'nous soul.
"Then like a toad, or like a newt, would whisper in my ears;
"Or like a rock stood in my way, or like a pois'nous shrub.
"At last I caught him in the form of Tiriel, blind & old,
"And so I'll keep him! fetch your father, fetch forth Myratana!"

They stood confounded, and Thus Tiriel rais'd his silver voice:

"Serpents, not sons, [you see . . . your father *del.*] why do you stand? fetch hither Tiriel!
"Fetch hither Myratana! & delight yourselves with scoffs;
"For poor blind Tiriel is return'd, & this much injur'd head
"Is ready for your bitter taunts: come forth, sons of the curse!"

Mean time the other sons of Tiriel ran around their father,
Confounded at the terrible strength of Ijim: they knew 'twas vain,
Both spear & shield were useless & the coat of iron mail,
When Ijim stretch'd his mighty arm; the arrow from his limbs
Rebounded & the piercing sword broke on his naked [limbs *del.*] flesh.
[Then Ijim said: "Lotho, Clthyma, Makuth, fetch your father!
"Why do you stand confounded thus? Heuxos, why art thou silent?"

"O noble Ijim, thou hast brought our father to (the gates *del.*) our eyes,
"That we may tremble & repent before thy mighty knees.
"O! we are but the slaves of Fortune, & that most cruel man
"Desires our deaths, O Ijim! ('tis one whose aged tongue
"Decieve the noble & *del.*) if the eloquent voice of Tiriel
"Hath work'd our ruin, we submit nor strive against stern fate."

He spoke & kneel'd upon his knee. Then Ijim on the pavement
Set aged Tiriel in deep thought whether these things were so. *del.*]

"Then is it true, Heuxos, that thou hast turn'd thy aged parent
"To be the sport of wintry winds?" (said Ijim), "is this true?
"It is a lie & I am [*word del.*] like the tree torn by the wind,
"Thou eyeless fiend, & you dissemblers! Is this Tiriel's house?
"It is as false & [as] Matha & as dark as vacant Orcus.
"Escape, ye fiends! for Ijim will not lift his hand against ye."

So saying, Ijim gloomy turn'd his back, & silent sought
The [gloom *del.*] secret forests & all night wander'd in desolate ways.

5

And aged Tiriel stood & said: "Where does the thunder sleep?
"Where doth he hide his terrible head? & his swift & fiery daughters,
"Where do they shroud their fiery wings & the terrors of their hair?
"Earth, thus I stamp thy bosom! rouse the earthquake from his den,
"[Display thy *del.*] To raise his dark & burning visage thro' the cleaving [earth *del.*] ground,
"To thrust these towers with his shoulders! let his fiery dogs
"Rise from the center, belching flames & roarings, dark smoke!
"Where art thou, Pestilence, that bathest in fogs & standing lakes?
"Rise up thy sluggish limbs & let the loathsomest of poisons
"Drop from thy garments as thou walkest, wrapt in yellow clouds!
"Here take thy seat in this wide court; let it be strown with dead;
"And sit & smile upon these cursed sons of Tiriel!
"Thunder & fire & pestilence, hear[1] you not Tiriel's curse?"

He ceast: the heavy clouds confus'd roll'd round the lofty towers,
Discharging their enormous voices at the father's curse.
The earth trembled; fires belched from the yawning clefts;
And when the shaking ceast, a fog possest the accursed clime.

The cry was great in Tiriel's palace: his five daughters ran
And caught him by the garments, weeping with cries of bitter woe.

"Aye, now you feel the curse, you cry! but may all ears be deaf
"As Tiriel's, & all eyes as blind as Tiriel's to your woes!
"May never stars shine on your roofs! may never sun nor moon
"Visit you, but eternal fogs hover around your walls!
"Hela, my youngest daughter, you shall lead me from this place,
"And let the curse fall on the rest & wrap them up together!"

[1] *Written* here.

He ceast, & Hela led her father from the noisom place.
In haste they fled, while all the sons & daughters of Tiriel,
Chain'd in thick darkness, utter'd cries of mourning all the night;
And in the morning, Lo! an hundred men in ghastly death!
The four daughters [& all the children in their silent beds
. . . *del.*] stretch'd on the marble pavement, silent all,
[And *del.*] fall'n by the pestilence!—the rest moped round in [ghastly *del.*] guilty fears;
And all the children in their beds were cut off in one night.
Thirty of Tiriel's sons remain'd, to wither in the palace,
Desolate, Loathed, Dumb, Astonish'd, waiting for black death.

6

And Hela led her father thro' the silent of the night,
Astonish'd, silent, till the morning beams began to spring.

"Now, Hela, I can go with pleasure & dwell with Har & Heva,
"Now that the curse shall clean devour all those guilty sons.
"This is the right & ready way; I know it by the sound
"That our feet make. Remember, Hela, I have sav'd thee from death;
"Then be obedient to thy father, for the curse is taken off thee.
"I dwelt with Myratana five years in the desolate rock,
"And all that time we waited for the fire to fall from heaven,
"Or for the torrents of the sea to overwhelm you all.
"But now my wife is dead & all the time of grace is past:
"You see the parent's curse. Now lead me where I have commanded."

"O leagued with evil spirits, thou accursed man of sin!
"True, I was born thy [child *del.*] slave! who ask'd thee to save me from death?
"'Twas for thy self, thou cruel man, because thou wantest eyes."

"True, Hela, this is the desert of all those cruel ones.
"Is Tiriel cruel? look! his daughter & his youngest daughter
"Laughs at affection, glories in rebellion, scoffs at Love.
"I have not eat these two days; lead me to Har & Heva's tent,
"Or I will wrap the[e] up in such a terrible father's curse
"That thou shalt feel worms in thy marrow creeping thro' thy bones.
"Yet thou shalt lead me! Lead me, I command, to Har & Heva!"

"O cruel! O destroyer! O consumer! O avenger!
"To Har & Heva I will lead thee: then would that they would curse!
"Then would they curse as thou hast cursed! but they are not like thee!

"O! they are holy & forgiving, fill'd with loving mercy,
"Forgetting the offences of their most rebellious children,
"Or else thou wouldest not have liv'd to curse thy helpless children."

"Look on my eyes, Hela, & see, for thou hast eyes to see,
"The tears swell from my stony fountains: wherefore do I weep?
"Wherefore from my blind orbs art thou not siez'd with pois'nous stings?
"Laugh, serpent, youngest venomous reptile of the flesh of Tiriel!
"Laugh! for thy father Tiriel shall give the[e] cause to laugh,
"Unless thou lead me to the tent of Har, child of the curse!"

"Silence thy evil tongue, thou murderer of thy helpless children!
"I lead thee to the tent of Har; not that I mind thy curse,
"But that I feel they will curse thee & hang upon thy bones
"Fell shaking agonies, & in each wrinkle of that face
"Plant worms of death to feast upon the tongue of terrible curses."

"Hela, my daughter, listen! thou art the daughter of Tiriel.
"Thy father calls. Thy father lifts his hand unto the [air *del.*] heavens,
"For thou hast laughed at my tears & curst thy aged father.
"Let snakes rise from thy bedded locks & laugh among thy curls!"

He ceast; her dark hair upright stood, while snakes infolded round
Her madding brows: her shrieks apall'd the soul of Tiriel.

"What have I done, Hela, my daughter? fear'st thou now the curse,
"Or wherefore dost thou cry? Ah, wretch, to curse thy aged father!
"Lead me to Har & Heva, & the curse of Tiriel
"Shall fail. If thou refuse, howl in the desolate mountains!"

7

She, howling, led him over mountains & thro' frighted vales,
Till to the caves of Zazel they approach'd at even tide.
Forth from their caves [the sons of Zazel *del.*] Old Zazel & his sons ran; [& *del.*] when they saw
Their tyrant prince blind, & his daughter howling & leading him,
They laugh'd & mocked; some threw dirt & stones as they pass'd by;
But when Tiriel turn'd around & rais'd his awful voice,
[They *del.*] Some fled away [& hid themselves *del.*]; but [some *del.*] Zazel stood still, & thus [scoffing *del.*] begun:

"Bald tyrant, wrinkled, cunning [wretch *del.*], listen to Zazel's chains!
"'Twas thou that chain'd thy brother Zazel! where are now thine eyes?

"Shout, beautiful daughter of Tiriel! thou singest a sweet song!
"Where are you going? come & eat some roots & drink some water.
"Thy crown is bald, old man; the sun will dry thy brains away,
"And thou wilt be as foolish as thy foolish brother Zazel."

The blind man heard, & smote his breast, & trembling passed on.
They threw dirt after them, till to the covert of a wood
[They *del.*] The howling maiden led her father, where wild beasts resort,
Hoping to end her [life *del.*] woes; but from her cries the tygers fled.
All night they wander'd thro' the wood, & when the sun arose,
They enter'd on the mountains of Har: at Noon the happy tents
Were frighted by the dismal cries of Hela on the mountains.

But Har & Heva slept fearless as babes on loving breasts.
Mnetha awoke: she ran & stood at the tent door, & saw
The aged wanderer led towards the tents; she took her bow,
And chose her arrows, then advanc'd to meet the terrible pair.

8

And Mnetha hasted & met them at the gate of the lower garden.

"Stand still, or from my bow recieve a sharp & winged death!"

Then Tiriel stood, saying: "What soft voice threatens such bitter things?
"Lead me to Har & Heva; I am Tiriel, king of the west."

And Mnetha led them to the tent of Har, and Har & Heva
Ran to the door; when Tiriel felt the ankles of aged Har,
He said: "O weak mistaken father of a lawless race,
"Thy laws, O Har, & Tiriel's wisdom, end together in a curse.
"[Thy God of Love, thy Heaven of Joy *del.*]

"Why is one law given to the lion & the patient Ox?
"[Dost thou not see that men cannot be formed all alike,
"Some nostril'd wide, breathing out blood. Some close shut up
"In silent deceit, poisons inhaling from the morning rose,
"With daggers hid beneath their lips & poison in their tongue;
"Or eyed with little sparks of Hell, or with infernal brands
"Flinging flames of discontent & plagues of dark despair;
"Or those whose mouths are graves, whose teeth the gates of eternal death.

"Can wisdom be put in a silver rod, or love in a golden bowl?
"Is the son of a king warmed without wool? or does he cry with a voice
"Of thunder? does he look upon the sun & laugh or stretch
"His little hands into the depths of the sea, to bring forth
"The deadly cunning of the [scaly tribe *del.*] flatterer & spread it to the morning? *del.*]
"And why men bound beneath the heavens in a reptile form,
"A worm of sixty winters creeping on the dusky ground?
"The child springs from the womb; the father ready stands to form
"The infant head, while the mother idle plays with her dog on her couch:
"The young bosom is cold for lack of mother's nourishment, & milk
"Is cut off from the weeping mouth: with difficulty & pain
"The little lids are lifted & the little nostrils open'd:
"The father forms a whip to rouze the sluggish senses to act
"And scourges off all youthful fancies from the new-born man.
"Then walks the weak infant in sorrow, compell'd to number footsteps
"Upon the sand &c.
"And when the [foolish, crawling *del.*] drone has reach'd his crawling length,
"Black berries appear that poison all around him. Such [is *del.*] was Tiriel,
"[Hypocrisy, the idiot's wisdom & the wise man's folly. *del.*]
"Compell'd to pray repugnant & to humble the immortal spirit
"Till I am subtil as a serpent in a paradise,
"Consuming all, both flowers & fruits, insects & warbling birds.
"And now my paradise is fall'n & a drear sandy plain
"Returns my thirsty hissings in a curse on thee, O Har,
"Mistaken father of a lawless race, my voice is past."

He ceast, outstretch'd at Har & Heva's feet in awful death.

SONGS of Innocence
The Author & Printer W. Blake
Etched 1789

Introduction

Piping down the valleys wild,
Piping songs of pleasant glee,
On a cloud I saw a child,
And he laughing said to me:

"Pipe a song about a Lamb!"
So I piped with merry chear.
"Piper, pipe that song again;"
So I piped: he wept to hear.

"Drop thy pipe, thy happy pipe;
"Sing thy songs of happy chear:"
So I sung the same again,
While he wept with joy to hear.

"Piper, sit thee down and write
"In a book that all may read."
So he vanish'd from my sight,
And I pluck'd a hollow reed,

And I made a rural pen,
And I stain'd the water clear,
And I wrote my happy songs
Every child may joy to hear.

A Dream

Once a dream did weave a shade
O'er my Angel-guarded bed,
That an Emmet lost its way
Where on grass methought I lay.

Troubled, 'wilder'd, and fo[r]lorn,
Dark, benighted, travel-worn,
Over many a tangled spray,
All heart-broke I heard her say:

"O, my children! do they cry?
"Do they hear their father sigh?
"Now they look abroad to see:
"Now return and weep for me."

Pitying, I drop'd a tear;
But I saw a glow-worm near,
Who replied: "What wailing wight
"Calls the watchman of the night?

"I am set to light the ground,
"While the beetle goes his round:
"Follow now the beetle's hum;
"Little wanderer, hie thee home."

The Little Girl Lost

In futurity
I prophetic see
That the earth from sleep
(Grave the sentence deep)

Shall arise and seek
For her maker meek;
And the desart wild
Become a garden mild.

In the southern clime,
Where the summer's prime
Never fades away,
Lovely Lyca lay.

Seven summers old
Lovely Lyca told;
She had wander'd long
Hearing wild birds' song.

"Sweet sleep, come to me
"Underneath this tree.
"Do father, mother weep,
"Where can Lyca sleep?

"Lost in desart wild
"Is your little child.
"How can Lyca sleep
"If her mother weep?

"If her heart does ake
"Then let Lyca wake;
"If my mother sleep,
"Lyca shall not weep.

"Frowning, frowning night,
"O'er this desart bright
"Let thy moon arise
"While I close my eyes."

Sleeping Lyca lay
While the beasts of prey,
Come from caverns deep,
View'd the maid asleep.

The kingly lion stood
And the virgin view'd,
Then he gambol'd round
O'er the hallow'd ground.

Leopards, tygers, play
Round her as she lay,
While the lion old
Bow'd his mane of gold

And her bosom lick,
And upon her neck
From his eyes of flame
Ruby tears there came;

While the lioness
Loos'd her slender dress,
And naked they convey'd
To caves the sleeping maid.

The Little Girl Found

All the night in woe
Lyca's parents go
Over vallies deep,
While the desarts weep.

Tired and woe-begone,
Hoarse with making moan,
Arm in arm seven days
They trac'd the desart ways.

Seven nights they sleep
Among shadows deep,
And dream they see their child
Starv'd in desart wild.

Pale, thro' pathless ways
The fancied image strays
Famish'd, weeping, weak,
With hollow piteous shriek.

Rising from unrest,
The trembling woman prest
With feet of weary woe:
She could no further go.

In his arms he bore
Her, arm'd with sorrow sore;
Till before their way
A couching lion lay.

Turning back was vain:
Soon his heavy mane
Bore them to the ground.
Then he stalk'd around,

Smelling to his prey;
But their fears allay
When he licks their hands,
And silent by them stands.

They look upon his eyes
Fill'd with deep surprise,
And wondering behold
A Spirit arm'd in gold.

On his head a crown,
On his shoulders down
Flow'd his golden hair.
Gone was all their care.

"Follow me," he said;
"Weep not for the maid;
"In my palace deep
"Lyca lies asleep."

Then they followed
Where the vision led,
And saw their sleeping child
Among tygers wild.

To this day they dwell
In a lonely dell;
Nor fear the wolvish howl
Nor the lions' growl.

The Lamb

Little Lamb, who made thee?
Dost thou know who made thee?
Gave thee life, & bid thee feed
By the stream & o'er the mead;
Gave thee clothing of delight,
Softest clothing, wooly, bright;
Gave thee such a tender voice,
Making all the vales rejoice?
Little Lamb, who made thee?
Dost thou know who made thee?

Little Lamb, I'll tell thee,
Little Lamb, I'll tell thee:
He is called by thy name,
For he calls himself a Lamb.
He is meek, & he is mild;
He became a little child.
I a child, & thou a lamb,
We are called by his name.
Little Lamb, God bless thee!
Little Lamb, God bless thee!

The Blossom

Merry, Merry Sparrow!
Under leaves so green
A happy Blossom
Sees you swift as arrow
Seek your cradle narrow
Near my Bosom.

Pretty, Pretty Robin!
Under leaves so green
A happy Blossom
Hears you sobbing, sobbing
Pretty, Pretty Robin,
Near my Bosom.

The Ecchoing Green

The Sun does arise,
And make happy the skies;
The merry bells ring
To welcome the Spring;
The skylark and thrush,
The birds of the bush,
Sing louder around
To the bells' chearful sound,
While our sports shall be seen
On the Ecchoing Green.

Old John, with white hair,
Does laugh away care,
Sitting under the oak,
Among the old folk.
They laugh at our play,
And soon they all say:
"Such, such were the joys
"When we all, girls & boys,
"In our youth time were seen
"On the Ecchoing Green."

Till the little ones, weary,
No more can be merry;
The sun does descend,
And our sports have an end.
Round the laps of their mothers
Many sisters and brothers,
Like birds in their nest,
Are ready for rest,
And sport no more seen
On the darkening Green.

The Divine Image

To Mercy, Pity, Peace, and Love
All pray in their distress;
And to these virtues of delight
Return their thankfulness.

For Mercy, Pity, Peace, and Love
Is God, our father dear,
And Mercy, Pity, Peace, and Love
Is Man, his child and care.

For Mercy has a human heart,
Pity a human face,
And Love, the human form divine,
And Peace, the human dress.

Then every man, of every clime,
That prays in his distress,
Prays to the human form divine,
Love, Mercy, Pity, Peace.

And all must love the human form,
In heathen, turk, or jew;
Where Mercy, Love, & Pity dwell
There God is dwelling too.

The Chimney Sweeper

When my mother died I was very young,
And my Father sold me while yet my tongue
Could scarcely cry "'weep! 'weep! 'weep! 'weep!"
So your chimneys I sweep, & in soot I sleep.

There's little Tom Dacre, who cried when his head,
That curl'd like a lamb's back, was shav'd: so I said
"Hush, Tom! never mind it, for when your head's bare
"You know that the soot cannot spoil your white hair."

And so he was quiet, & that very night
As Tom was a-sleeping, he had such a sight!
That thousands of sweepers, Dick, Joe, Ned, & Jack,
Were all of them lock'd up in coffins of black.

And by came an Angel who had a bright key,
And he open'd the coffins & set them all free;
Then down a green plain leaping, laughing, they run,
And wash in a river, and shine in the Sun.

Then naked & white, all their bags left behind,
They rise upon clouds and sport in the wind;
And the Angel told Tom, if he'd be a good boy,
He'd have God for his father, & never want joy.

And so Tom awoke; and we rose in the dark,
And got with our bags & our brushes to work.
Tho' the morning was cold, Tom was happy & warm;
So if all do their duty they need not fear harm.

Infant Joy

"I have no name:
"I am but two days old."
What shall I call thee?
"I happy am,
"Joy is my name."
Sweet joy befall thee!

Pretty joy!
Sweet joy but two days old,
Sweet joy I call thee:
Thou dost smile,
I sing the while,
Sweet joy befall thee!

The Shepherd

How sweet is the Shepherd's sweet lot!
From the morn to the evening he strays;
He shall follow his sheep all the day,
And his tongue shall be filled with praise.

For he hears the lamb's innocent call,
And he hears the ewe's tender reply;
He is watchful while they are in peace,
For they know when their Shepherd is nigh.

Night

The sun descending in the west,
The evening star does shine;
The birds are silent in their nest,
And I must seek for mine.
The moon like a flower
In heaven's high bower,
With silent delight
Sits and smiles on the night.

Farewell, green fields and happy groves,
Where flocks have took delight.
Where lambs have nibbled, silent moves
The feet of angels bright;
Unseen they pour blessing
And joy without ceasing,
On each bud and blossom,
And each sleeping bosom.

They look in every thoughtless nest,
Where birds are cover'd warm;
They visit caves of every beast.
To keep them all from harm.
If they see any weeping
That should have been sleeping,
They pour sleep on their head,
And sit down by their bed.

When wolves and tygers howl for prey,
They pitying stand and weep;
Seeking to drive their thirst away,
And keep them from the sheep;
But if they rush dreadful,
The angels, most heedful,
Recieve each mild spirit,
New worlds to inherit.

And there the lion's ruddy eyes
Shall flow with tears of gold,
And pitying the tender cries,
And walking round the fold,
Saying "Wrath, by his meekness,
"And by his health, sickness
"Is driven away
"From our immortal day.

"And now beside thee, bleating lamb,
"I can lie down and sleep;
"Or think on him who bore thy name,
"Graze after thee and weep.
"For, wash'd in life's river,
"My bright mane for ever
"Shall shine like the gold
"As I guard o'er the fold."

A CRADLE SONG

Sweet dreams, form a shade
O'er my lovely infant's head;
Sweet dreams of pleasant streams
By happy, silent, moony beams.

Sweet sleep, with soft down
Weave thy brows an infant crown.
Sweet sleep, Angel mild,
Hover o'er my happy child.

Sweet smiles, in the night
Hover over my delight;
Sweet smiles, Mother's smiles,
All the livelong night beguiles.

Sweet moans, dovelike sighs,
Chase not slumber from thy eyes.
Sweet moans, sweeter smiles,
All the dovelike moans beguiles.

Sleep, sleep, happy child,
All creation slept and smil'd;
Sleep, sleep, happy sleep,
While o'er thee thy mother weep.

Sweet babe, in thy face
Holy image I can trace.
Sweet babe, once like thee,
Thy maker lay and wept for me,

Wept for me, for thee, for all,
When he was an infant small.
Thou his image ever see,
Heavenly face that smiles on thee,

Smiles on thee, on me, on all;
Who became an infant small.
Infant smiles are his own smiles;
Heaven & earth to peace beguiles.

The Little Boy lost

"Father! father! where are you going?
"O do not walk so fast.
"Speak, father, speak to your little boy,
"Or else I shall be lost."

The night was dark, no father was there;
The child was wet with dew;
The mire was deep, & the child did weep,
And away the vapour flew.

The Little Boy found

The little boy lost in the lonely fen,
Led by the wand'ring light,
Began to cry; but God, ever nigh,
Appear'd like his father in white.

He kissed the child & by the hand led
And to his mother brought,
Who in sorrow pale, thro' the lonely dale,
Her little boy weeping sought.

Nurse's Song

When the voices of children are heard on the green
And laughing is heard on the hill,
My heart is at rest within my breast
  And everything else is still.

"Then come home, my children, the sun is gone down
"And the dews of night arise;
"Come, come, leave off play, and let us away
"Till the morning appears in the skies."

"No, no, let us play, for it is yet day
"And we cannot go to sleep;
"Besides, in the sky the little birds fly
"And the hills are all cover'd with sheep."

"Well, well, go & play till the light fades away
"And then go home to bed."
The little ones leaped & shouted & laugh'd
  And all the hills ecchoed.

HOLY THURSDAY

'Twas on a Holy Thursday, their innocent faces clean,
The children walking two & two, in red & blue & green,
Grey-headed beadles walk'd before, with wands as white as snow,
Till into the high dome of Paul's they like Thames' waters flow.

O what a multitude they seem'd, these flowers of London town!
Seated in companies they sit with radiance all their own.
The hum of multitudes was there, but multitudes of lambs,
Thousands of little boys & girls raising their innocent hands.

Now like a mighty wind they raise to heaven the voice of song,
Or like harmonious thunderings the seats of heaven among.
Beneath them sit the aged men, wise guardians of the poor;
Then cherish pity, lest you drive an angel from your door.

On Another's Sorrow

Can I see another's woe,
And not be in sorrow too?
Can I see another's grief,
And not seek for kind relief?

Can I see a falling tear,
And not feel my sorrow's share?
Can a father see his child
Weep, nor be with sorrow fill'd?

Can a mother sit and hear
An infant groan, an infant fear?
No, no! never can it be!
Never, never can it be!

And can he who smiles on all
Hear the wren with sorrows small,
Hear the small bird's grief & care,
Hear the woes that infants bear,

And not sit beside the nest,
Pouring pity in their breast;
And not sit the cradle near,
Weeping tear on infant's tear;

And not sit both night & day,
Wiping all our tears away?
O! no never can it be!
Never, never can it be!

He doth give his joy to all;
He becomes an infant small;
He becomes a man of woe;
He doth feel the sorrow too.

Think not thou canst sigh a sigh
And thy maker is not by;
Think not thou canst weep a tear
And thy maker is not near.

O! he gives to us his joy
That our grief he may destroy;
Till our grief is fled & gone
He doth sit by us and moan.

Spring

Sound the Flute!
Now it's mute.
Birds delight
Day and Night;
Nightingale
In the dale,
Lark in Sky,
Merrily,
Merrily, Merrily, to welcome in the Year.

Little Boy,
Full of joy;
Little Girl,
Sweet and small;
Cock does crow,
So do you;
Merry voice,
Infant noise,
Merrily, Merrily, to welcome in the Year.

Little Lamb,
Here I am;
Come and lick
My white neck;
Let me pull
Your soft Wool;
Let me kiss
Your soft face:
Merrily, Merrily, we welcome in the Year.

The School Boy

I love to rise in a summer morn
When the birds sing on every tree;
The distant huntsman winds his horn,
And the sky-lark sings with me.
O! what sweet company.

But to go to school in a summer morn,
O! it drives all joy away;
Under a cruel eye outworn,
The little ones spend the day
In sighing and dismay.

Ah! then at times I drooping sit,
And spend many an anxious hour,
Nor in my book can I take delight,
Nor sit in learning's bower,
Worn thro' with the dreary shower.

How can the bird that is born for joy
Sit in a cage and sing?
How can a child, when fears annoy,
But droop his tender wing,
And forget his youthful spring?

O! father & mother, if buds are nip'd
And blossoms blown away,
And if the tender plants are strip'd
Of their joy in the springing day,
By sorrow and care's dismay,

How shall the summer arise in joy,
Or the summer fruits appear?
Or how shall we gather what griefs destroy,
Or bless the mellowing year,
When the blasts of winter appear?

Laughing Song

When the green woods laugh with the voice of joy,
And the dimpling stream runs laughing by;
When the air does laugh with our merry wit,
And the green hill laughs with the noise of it;

When the meadows laugh with lively green,
And the grasshopper laughs in the merry scene,
When Mary and Susan and Emily
With their sweet round mouths sing "Ha, Ha, He!"

When the painted birds laugh in the shade,
Where our table with cherries and nuts is spread,
Come live & be merry, and join with me,
To sing the sweet chorus of "Ha, Ha, He!"

The Little Black Boy

My mother bore me in the southern wild,
And I am black, but O! my soul is white;
White as an angel is the English child,
But I am black, as if bereav'd of light.

My mother taught me underneath a tree,
And sitting down before the heat of day,
She took me on her lap and kissed me,
And pointing to the east, began to say:

"Look on the rising sun: there God does live,
"And gives his light, and gives his heat away;
"And flowers and trees and beasts and men recieve
"Comfort in morning, joy in the noonday.

"And we are put on earth a little space,
"That we may learn to bear the beams of love;
"And these black bodies and this sunburnt face
"Is but a cloud, and like a shady grove.

"For when our souls have learn'd the heat to bear,
"The cloud will vanish; we shall hear his voice,
"Saying: 'Come out from the grove, my love & care,
" 'And round my golden tent like lambs rejoice.' "

Thus did my mother say, and kissed me;
And thus I say to little English boy.
When I from black and he from white cloud free,
And round the tent of God like lambs we joy,

I'll shade him from the heat, till he can bear
To lean in joy upon our father's knee;
And then I'll stand and stroke his silver hair,
And be like him, and he will then love me.

The Voice of the Ancient Bard

Youth of delight, come hither,
And see the opening morn,
Image of truth new born.
Doubt is fled, & clouds of reason,
Dark disputes & artful teazing.
Folly is an endless maze,
Tangled roots perplex her ways.
How many have fallen there!
They stumble all night over bones of the dead,
And feel they know not what but care,
And wish to lead others, when they should be led.

THE BOOK of THEL

The Author & Printer Willm Blake, 1789

Plate i

THEL'S MOTTO.

Does the Eagle know what is in the pit?
Or wilt thou go ask the Mole?
Can Wisdom be put in a silver rod?
Or Love in a golden bowl?

Plate 1

I

The daughters of Mne Seraphim led round their sunny flocks,
All but the youngest: she in paleness sought the secret air,
To fade away like morning beauty from her mortal day:
Down by the river of Adona her soft voice is heard,
And thus her gentle lamentation falls like morning dew:

"O life of this our spring! why fades the lotus of the water,
"Why fade these children of the spring, born but to smile & fall?
"Ah! Thel is like a wat'ry bow, and like a parting cloud;
"Like a reflection in a glass; like shadows in the water;
"Like dreams of infants, like a smile upon an infant's face;
"Like the dove's voice; like transient day; like music in the air.
"Ah! gentle may I lay me down, and gentle rest my head,
"And gentle sleep the sleep of death, and gentle hear the voice
"Of him that walketh in the garden in the evening time."

The Lilly of the valley, breathing in the humble grass,
Answer'd the lovely maid and said: "I am a wat'ry weed,
"And I am very small and love to dwell in lowly vales;
"So weak, the gilded butterfly scarce perches on my head.
"Yet I am visited from heaven, and he that smiles on all
"Walks in the valley and each morn over me spreads his hand,
"Saying, 'Rejoice, thou humble grass, thou new-born lilly flower,
" 'Thou gentle maid of silent valleys and of modest brooks;
" 'For thou shalt be clothed in light, and fed with morning manna,
" 'Till summer's heat melts thee beside the fountains and the springs
" 'To flourish in eternal vales.' Then why should Thel complain?

Plate 2

"Why should the mistress of the vales of Har utter a sigh?"

She ceas'd & smil'd in tears, then sat down in her silver shrine.

Thel answer'd: "O thou little virgin of the peaceful valley,
"Giving to those that cannot crave, the voiceless, the o'ertired;
"Thy breath doth nourish the innocent lamb, he smells thy milky garments,
"He crops thy flowers while thou sittest smiling in his face,
"Wiping his mild and meekin mouth from all contagious taints.
"Thy wine doth purify the golden honey; thy perfume,
"Which thou dost scatter on every little blade of grass that springs,
"Revives the milked cow, & tames the fire-breathing steed.
"But Thel is like a faint cloud kindled at the rising sun:
"I vanish from my pearly throne, and who shall find my place?"

"Queen of the vales," the Lilly answer'd, "ask the tender cloud,
"And it shall tell thee why it glitters in the morning sky,
"And why it scatters its bright beauty thro' the humid air,
"Descend, O little Cloud, & hover before the eyes of Thel."

The Cloud descended, and the Lilly bow'd her modest head
And went to mind her numerous charge among the verdant grass.

Plate 3

II

"O little Cloud," the virgin said, "I charge thee tell to me
"Why thou complainest not when in one hour thou fade away:
"Then we shall seek thee, but not find. Ah! Thel is like to thee:
"I pass away: yet I complain, and no one hears my voice."

The Cloud then shew'd his golden head & his bright form emerg'd,
Hovering and glittering on the air before the face of Thel.

"O virgin, know'st thou not our steeds drink of the golden springs
"Where Luvah doth renew his horses? Look'st thou on my youth,
"And fearest thou, because I vanish and am seen no more,
"Nothing remains? O maid, I tell thee, when I pass away
"It is to tenfold life, to love, to peace and raptures holy:
"Unseen descending, weigh my light wings upon balmy flowers,
"And court the fair-eyed dew to take me to her shining tent:
"The weeping virgin, trembling kneels before the risen sun,
"Till we arise link'd in a golden band and never part,
"But walk united, bearing food to all our tender flowers."

"Dost thou, O little Cloud? I fear that I am not like thee,
"For I walk through the vales of Har, and smell the sweetest flowers,
"But I feed not the little flowers; I hear the warbling birds,
"But I feed not the warbling birds; they fly and seek their food:
"But Thel delights in these no more, because I fade away;
"And all shall say, 'Without a use this shining woman liv'd,
" 'Or did she only live to be at death the food of worms?' "

The Cloud reclin'd upon his airy throne and answer'd thus:

"Then if thou art the food of worms, O virgin of the skies,
"How great thy use, how great thy blessing! Every thing that lives
"Lives not alone nor for itself. Fear not, and I will call
"The weak worm from its lowly bed, and thou shalt hear its voice.
"Come forth, worm of the silent valley, to thy pensive queen."

The helpless worm arose, and sat upon the Lilly's leaf,
And the bright Cloud sail'd on, to find his partner in the vale.

Plate 4

III

Then Thel astonish'd view'd the Worm upon its dewy bed.

"Art thou a Worm? Image of weakness, art thou but a Worm?
"I see thee like an infant wrapped in the Lilly's leaf.
"Ah! weep not, little voice, thou canst not speak, but thou canst weep.
"Is this a Worm? I see thee lay helpless & naked, weeping,
"And none to answer, none to cherish thee with mother's smiles."

The Clod of Clay heard the Worm's voice & rais'd her pitying head:
She bow'd over the weeping infant, and her life exhal'd
In milky fondness: then on Thel she fix'd her humble eyes.

"O beauty of the vales of Har! we live not for ourselves.
"Thou seest me the meanest thing, and so I am indeed.
"My bosom of itself is cold, and of itself is dark;

Plate 5

"But he, that loves the lowly, pours his oil upon my head,
"And kisses me, and binds his nuptial bands around my breast,
"And says: 'Thou mother of my children, I have loved thee
" 'And I have given thee a crown that none can take away.'
"But how this is, sweet maid, I know not, and I cannot know;
"I ponder, and I cannot ponder; yet I live and love."

The daughter of beauty wip'd her pitying tears with her white veil,
And said: "Alas! I knew not this, and therefore did I weep.
"That God would love a Worm I knew, and punish the evil foot
"That wilful bruis'd its helpless form; but that he cherish'd it
"With milk and oil I never knew, and therefore did I weep;
"And I complain'd in the mild air, because I fade away,
"And lay me down in thy cold bed, and leave my shining lot."

"Queen of the vales," the matron Clay answer'd, "I heard thy sighs,
"And all thy moans flew o'er my roof, but I have call'd them down.
"Wilt thou, O Queen, enter my house? 'Tis given thee to enter
"And to return: fear nothing, enter with thy virgin feet."

Plate 6

IV

The eternal gates' terrific porter lifted the northern bar:
Thel enter'd in & saw the secrets of the land unknown.
She saw the couches of the dead, & where the fibrous roots
Of every heart on earth infixes deep its restless twists:
A land of sorrows & of tears where never smile was seen.

She wander'd in the land of clouds thro' valleys dark, list'ning
Dolours & lamentations; waiting oft beside a dewy grave
She stood in silence, list'ning to the voices of the ground,
Till to her own grave plot she came, & there she sat down,
And heard this voice of sorrow breathed from the hollow pit.

"Why cannot the Ear be closed to its own destruction?
"Or the glist'ning Eye to the poison of a smile?
"Why are Eyelids stor'd with arrows ready drawn,
"Where a thousand fighting men in ambush lie?
"Or an Eye of gifts & graces show'ring fruits & coined gold?
"Why a Tongue impress'd with honey from every wind?
"Why an Ear, a whirlpool fierce to draw creations in?
"Why a Nostril wide inhaling terror, trembling, & affright?
"Why a tender curb upon the youthful burning boy?
"Why a little curtain of flesh on the bed of our desire?"

The Virgin started from her seat, & with a shriek
Fled back unhinder'd till she came into the vales of Har.

THE END

ANNOTATIONS TO SWEDENBORG'S THE WISDOM OF ANGELS CONCERNING DIVINE PROVIDENCE

London MDCCXC

Written about 1790

[*Blake's annotations here follow the passages from Swedenborg to which they refer, these being printed in smaller type. Words scored by Blake are printed in italic.*]

Page v. Translator's Preface

Perhaps there never was a Period in any Age of the World, which required a Vindication and Elucidation of the Divine Providence of the Lord, more than the present. Not that the Divine Providence is at this Day generally denied IN WORD, for none except absolute Atheists do this; but because it is allowed in so partial and confined a Manner and Measure of Operation, as borders upon a Denial, and indeed when rightly considered IS a Denial.

For if we allow a GENERAL Providence, and yet deny a PARTICULAR one, or if we allow a PARTICULAR one, and yet deny a SINGULAR one, that is, one extending to Things and Circumstances most SINGULAR and minute, what is this but denying a GENERAL Providence?

Is not this Predestination?

Pages xviii–xix.

. . . if he [the reader] be one of a sincere and humble Mind . . . his Humility and Sincerity will teach him, that Nothing doth IN GENERAL so contradict Man's natural and favourite Opinions as TRUTH, and that all the grandest and purest Truths of Heaven must needs seem obscure and perplexing to the natural Man at first View—

Lies & Priestcraft. Truth is Nature.

—until his intellectual Eye becomes accustomed to the Light, and can thereby behold it with Satisfaction—

—that is: till he agrees to the Priests' interest.

Page 82. § 69.

But the Man who doth not suffer himself to be led to, and enrolled in Heaven, is prepared for his Place in Hell; for Man from himself continually tends to the lowest Hell, but is continually with-held by the Lord; and he, who cannot be with-held, is prepared for a certain Place there, in which he is also enrolled immediately after his Departure out of the World; and this Place there is opposite to a certain Place in Heaven, for Hell is in Opposition to Heaven; wherefore as a Man Angel, according to the Affection of Good and Truth, hath his Place assigned him in Heaven, so a Man Devil, according to the Affection of Evil and the False, hath his Place assigned him in Hell; for two Opposites, disposed in a similar Situation against each other, are contained in Connection. This is the INTIMUM of the Divine Providence concerning Hell.

What is Enrolling but Predestination? Query does he also occupy that place in Heaven. See N. 185 & 329 at the End. See 277 & 307 & 203, where he says that a Place for Every Man is Foreseen & at the same time provided.

§ 185.

Page 254.

That this is the Case, cannot better be known than from the Case of Men after Death in the spiritual World, where the greatest Part of those, who in the natural World became great and rich, and in Honours respected themselves alone, and also in Riches, at first speak of God, and of the Divine Providence, as if they acknowledged them in their Hearts; But whereas they then manifestly see the Divine Providence, and from it their final Portion, which is that they are to be in Hell, they connect themselves with Devils there, and then not only deny God, but also blaspheme;

What could Calvin Say more than is Said in this Number? Final Portion is Predestination. See N. 69 & 329 at the End, & 277 & 203, Where he says, A Place for Each Man is Foreseen & at the same time Provided.

§ 203.

Pages 280-281.

Since every Man therefore lives after Death to Eternity, and according to his Life here hath his Place assigned to him either in Heaven or in Hell, and both these, as well Heaven as Hell, must be in such a Form as to act as one, as was said before; and no one can occupy any other Place in that Form, but his own, it follows, that the human Race throughout the whole World is under the Auspices of the Lord, and that everyone, from his Infancy even to the End of his Life, is led of Him in the most minute Particulars, and his *Place foreseen,* and at the same *Time provided.*

Devils & Angels are Predestinated.

§ 220.

Page 317.

. . . Dignities with their Honours are natural and temporary, when a Man personally respects himself in them, and not the State and Uses, for then a Man cannot but think interiorly with himself, that the State was made for him, and not he for the State; he is like a King *who* thinks his Kingdom and all the Men in it are for him, *and not he for the* Kingdom and all the Men of which it consists . . .

He says at N. 201: No King hath such a Government as this; for all Kings are Universal in their Government, otherwise they are No Kings.

[§ 201.

If it should be alledged, that the Divine Providence is an universal Government, and that not any Thing is governed, but only kept in it's Connection, and the Things which relate to Government are disposed by others, can this be called an universal Government? No King hath such a Government as this; for if a King were to allow his Subjects to govern every Thing in his Kingdom, he would no longer be a King, but would only be called a King, therefore would have only a nominal Dignity and no real Dignity: Such a King cannot be said to hold the Government, much less universal Government.]

§ 274.

Page 426.

That a Doubt may be inferred against *Divine Providence, because it was not known heretofore, that Man liveth after Death; and this* was not discovered till now. . . . *But yet all who have any Religion, have in them an inherent Knowledge,* that *Men live after Death;* the Idea that they live as Souls, and not as Men, takes Place only with those who are infatuated by their own Self-derived Intelligence, and with no others.

It was not Known & yet All Know.

§ 277.

Page 434.

That Man is to be withdrawn from Evil, in Order that he may be reformed, is evident without Explanation; for he who is in Evil in the World, the same is in Evil after he goes out of *the World; wherefore if Evil be not removed* in the *World, it cannot be removed afterwards;* where the Tree falls, there it lieth; so also it is with the Life of Man; as it was at his Death, such it remaineth; everyone also is judged according to his Actions, not that they are enumerated, but because he returns to them, and does the like again; for Death is a Continuation of Life; with this Difference, that then Man cannot be reformed.

Predestination after this Life is more Abominable than Calvin's, & Swedenborg is Such a Spiritual Predestinarian—witness this Number & many others, In 69 & 185 & 329 & 307.
Cursed Folly!

§ 307.

Pages 496-497.

... That the Wicked, who are in the World, are governed in Hell by the Lord; the Reason is, because Man with Respect to his Spirit is in the spiritual World, and there in some Society, in an infernal Society if he is wicked, and in a celestial Society if good; for the Mind of Man, which in itself is Spiritual, cannot be any where but among Spirits, into whose Society it comes also after Death; that this is the Case, hath also been said and shewn above. But Man is not there like one of the Spirits who is inscribed into the Society, for Man is continually in a State of Reformation, wherefore according to his Life and the Changes thereof, he is translated by the Lord from one Society of Hell to another, if he is wicked; but if he suffers himself to be reformed, he is led out of Hell and introduced into Heaven, and there also he is translated from one Society to another, and this until the Time of his Death, after which he is no longer carried from one Society to another, because he is then no longer in any State of Reformation, but remains in that in which he is according to his Life; wherefore when a Man dies, he is inscribed in his own Place...

Predestination!

§ 329.

Page 566.

... there is not wanting to any Man a Knowledge of the Means whereby he may be saved, nor the Power of being saved if he will; from which it follows, that all are predestined or intended for Heaven, and none for Hell. But forasmuch as there prevails among some a Belief in Predestination to no Salvation, which is Predestination to Damnation, and such a Belief is hurtful, and cannot be dispelled, unless Reason also sees the Madness and Cruelty of it, therefore it shall be treated of in the following Series. 1. That any other Predestination, than Predestination to Heaven, is contrary to the Divine Love and it's Infinity. 2. That any other Predestination, than Predestination to Heaven, is contrary to the Divine Wisdom and it's Infinity. 3. That it is an insane Heresy, to suppose that they only are saved who are born within the Church. 4. That it is a cruel Heresy, to suppose that any of the human Race are predestined to be damned.

Read N. 185 & There See how Swedenborg contradicts himself & N. 69. See also 277 & 203 where he Says that a Place for Each Man is foreseen & at the same time provided.

THE FRENCH REVOLUTION

A POEM IN SEVEN BOOKS

BOOK THE FIRST

LONDON: PRINTED FOR J. JOHNSON. MDCCXCI.

ADVERTISEMENT.

The remaining Books of this Poem are finished, and will be published in their Order[1].

BOOK THE FIRST

The dead brood over Europe, the cloud and vision descends over chearful France;
O cloud well appointed! Sick, sick, the Prince on his couch, wreath'd in dim
And appalling mist, his strong hand outstretch'd, from his shoulder down the bone
Runs aching cold into the scepter, too heavy for mortal grasp, No more
To be swayed by visible hand, nor in cruelty bruise the mild flourishing mountains.

Sick the mountains, and all their vineyards weep, in the eyes of the kingly mourner;
Pale is the morning cloud in his visage. Rise, Necker! the ancient dawn calls us
To awake from slumbers of five thousand years. I awake, but my soul is in dreams;
From my window I see the old mountains of France, like aged men, fading away.

Troubled, leaning on Necker, descends the King to his chamber of council; shady mountains
In fear utter voices of thunder; the woods of France embosom the sound;
Clouds of wisdom prophetic reply, and roll over the palace roof heavy.
Forty men, each conversing with woes in the infinite shadows of his soul,
Like our ancient fathers in regions of twilight, walk, gathering round the King;
Again the loud voice of France cries to the morning; the morning prophecies to its clouds.

For the Commons convene in the Hall of the Nation. France shakes! And the heavens of France

---

[1] No more were printed.

Perplex'd vibrate round each careful countenance! Darkness of old times around them
Utters loud despair, shadowing Paris; her grey towers groan, and the Bastile trembles.
In its terrible towers the Governor stood, in dark fogs list'ning the horror;
A thousand his soldiers, old veterans of France, breathing red clouds of power and dominion.
Sudden seiz'd with howlings, despair, and black night, he stalk'd like a lion from tower
To tower; his howlings were heard in the Louvre; from court to court restless he dragg'd
His strong limbs; from court to court curs'd the fierce torment unquell'd,
Howling and giving the dark command; in his soul stood the purple plague,
Tugging his iron manacles, and piercing through the seven towers dark and sickly,
Panting over the prisoners like a wolf gorg'd; and the den nam'd Horror held a man
Chain'd hand and foot, round his neck an iron band, bound to the impregnable wall.
In his soul was the serpent coil'd round in his heart, hid from the light, as in a cleft rock:
And the man was confin'd for a writing prophetic: in the tower nam'd Darkness was a man
Pinion'd down to the stone floor, his strong bones scarce cover'd with sinews; the iron rings
Were forg'd smaller as the flesh decay'd, a mask of iron on his face hid the lineaments
Of ancient Kings, and the frown of the eternal lion was hid from the oppressed earth.
In the tower named Bloody, a skeleton yellow remained in its chains on its couch
Of stone, once a man who refus'd to sign papers of abhorrence; the eternal worm
Crept in the skeleton. In the den nam'd Religion, a loathsome sick woman bound down
To a bed of straw; the seven diseases of earth, like birds of prey, stood on the couch
And fed on the body. She refus'd to be whore to the Minister, and with a knife smote him.
In the tower nam'd Order, an old man, whose white beard cover'd the stone floor like weeds

On margin of the sea, shrivel'd up by heat of day and cold of night; his den was short
And narrow as a grave dug for a child, with spiders' webs wove, and with slime
Of ancient horrors cover'd, for snakes and scorpions are his companions; harmless they breathe
His sorrowful breath: he, by conscience urg'd, in the city of Paris rais'd a pulpit,
And taught wonders to darken'd souls. In the den nam'd Destiny a strong man sat,
His feet and hands cut off, and his eyes blinded; round his middle a chain and a band
Fasten'd into the wall; fancy gave him to see an image of despair in his den,
Eternally rushing round, like a man on his hands and knees, day and night without rest:
He was friend to the favourite. In the seventh tower, nam'd the tower of God, was a man
Mad, with chains loose, which he dragg'd up and down; fed with hopes year by year, he pined
For liberty; vain hopes! his reason decay'd, and the world of attraction in his bosom
Center'd, and the rushing of chaos overwhelm'd his dark soul. He was confin'd
For a letter of advice to a King, and his ravings in winds are heard over Versailles.

But the dens shook and trembled: the prisoners look up and assay to shout; they listen,
Then laugh in the dismal den, then are silent, and a light walks round the dark towers:
For the Commons convene in the Hall of the Nation, like spirits of fire in the beautiful
Porches of the Sun, to plant beauty in the desart craving abyss, they gleam
On the anxious city; all children new-born first behold them; tears are fled,
And they nestle in earth-breathing bosoms. So the city of Paris, their wives and children,
Look up to the morning Senate, and visions of sorrow leave pensive streets.

But heavy brow'd jealousies lower o'er the Louvre, and terrors of ancient Kings
Descend from the gloom and wander thro' the palace, and weep round the King and his Nobles.

While loud thunders roll, troubling the dead, Kings are sick throughout all the earth.
The voice ceas'd: the Nation sat: And the triple forg'd fetters of times were unloos'd.
The voice ceas'd: the Nation sat: but ancient darkness and trembling wander thro' the palace.

As in day of havock and routed battle, among thick shades of discontent,
On the soul-skirting mountains of sorrow, cold waving the Nobles fold round the King;
Each stern visage lock'd up as with strong bands of iron, each strong limb bound down as with marble,
In flames of red wrath burning, bound in astonishment a quarter of an hour.

Then the King glow'd: his Nobles fold round, like the sun of old time quench'd in clouds;
In their darkness the King stood; his heart flam'd, and utter'd a with'ring heat, and these words burst forth:

"The nerves of five thousand years' ancestry tremble, shaking the heavens of France;
"Throbs of anguish beat on brazen war foreheads, they descend and look into their graves.
"I see thro' darkness, thro' clouds rolling round me, the spirits of ancient Kings
"Shivering over their bleached bones; round them their counsellors look up from the dust,
"Crying: 'Hide from the living! Our bonds and our prisoners shout in the open field,
" 'Hide in the nether earth! Hide in the bones! Sit obscured in the hollow scull!
" 'Our flesh is corrupted, and we wear away. We are not numbered among the living. Let us hide
" 'In stones, among roots of trees. The prisoners have burst their dens.
" 'Let us hide; let us hide in the dust; and plague and wrath and tempest shall cease.' "

He ceas'd, silent pond'ring; his brows folded heavy, his forehead was in affliction,
Like the central fire: from the window he saw his vast armies spread over the hills,
Breathing red fires from man to man, and from horse to horse: then his bosom

Expanded like starry heaven; he sat down: his Nobles took their ancient seats.

Then the ancientest Peer, Duke of Burgundy, rose from the Monarch's right hand, red as wines
From his mountains; an odor of war, like a ripe vineyard, rose from his garments,
And the chamber became as a clouded sky; o'er the council he stretch'd his red limbs,
Cloth'd in flames of crimson; as a ripe vineyard stretches over sheaves of corn,
The fierce Duke hung over the council; around him croud, weeping in his burning robe,
A bright cloud of infant souls; his words fall like purple autumn on the sheaves:

"Shall this marble built heaven become a clay cottage, this earth an oak stool, and these mowers
"From the Atlantic mountains mow down all this great starry harvest of six thousand years?
"And shall Necker, the hind of Geneva, stretch out his crook'd sickle o'er fertile France
"Till our purple and crimson is faded to russet, and the kingdoms of earth bound in sheaves,
"And the ancient forests of chivalry hewn, and the joys of the combat burnt for fuel;
"Till the power and dominion is rent from the pole, sword and scepter from sun and moon,
"The law and gospel from fire and air, and eternal reason and science
"From the deep and the solid, and man lay his faded head down on the rock
"Of eternity, where the eternal lion and eagle remain to devour?
"This to prevent—urg'd by cries in day, and prophetic dreams hovering in night,
"To enrich the lean earth that craves, furrow'd with plows, whose seed is departing from her—
"Thy Nobles have gather'd thy starry hosts round this rebellious city,
"To rouze up the ancient forests of Europe, with clarions of cloud breathing war,
"To hear the horse neigh to the drum and trumpet, and the trumpet and war shout reply.
"Stretch the hand that beckons the eagles of heaven; they cry over Paris, and wait
"Till Fayette point his finger to Versailles; the eagles of heaven must have their prey!"

He ceas'd, and burn'd silent; red clouds roll round Necker; a weeping is heard o'er the palace.
Like a dark cloud Necker paus'd, and like thunder on the just man's burial day he paus'd;
Silent sit the winds, silent the meadows, while the husbandman and woman of weakness
And bright children look after him into the grave, and water his clay with love,
Then turn towards pensive fields; so Necker paus'd, and his visage was cover'd with clouds.

The King lean'd on his mountains, then lifted his head and look'd on his armies, that shone
Through heaven, tinging morning with beams of blood; then turning to Burgundy, troubled:
"Burgundy, thou wast born a lion! My soul is o'ergrown with distress
"For the Nobles of France, and dark mists roll round me and blot the writing of God
"Written in my bosom. Necker rise! leave the kingdom, thy life is surrounded with snares.
"We have call'd an Assembly, but not to destroy; we have given gifts, not to the weak;
"I hear rushing of muskets, and bright'ning of swords, and visages redd'ning with war,
"Frowning and looking up from brooding villages and every dark'ning city.
"Ancient wonders frown over the kingdom, and cries of women and babes are heard,
"And tempests of doubt roll around me, and fierce sorrows, because of the Nobles of France.
"Depart! answer not! for the tempest must fall, as in years that are passed away."

Dropping a tear the old man his place left, and when he was gone out
He set his face toward Geneva to flee; and the women and children of the city
Kneel'd round him and kissed his garments and wept: he stood a short space in the street,
Then fled, and the whole city knew he was fled to Geneva, and the Senate heard it.

But the Nobles burn'd wrathful at Necker's departure, and wreath'd their clouds and waters
In dismal volumes, as, risen from beneath, the Archbishop of Paris arose

In the rushing of scales and hissing of flames and rolling of sulphurous smoke:

"Hearken, Monarch of France, to the terrors of heaven, and let thy soul drink of my counsel!
"Sleeping at midnight in my golden tower, the repose of the labours of men
"Wav'd its solemn cloud over my head. I awoke; a cold hand passed over my limbs, and behold
"An aged form, white as snow, hov'ring in mist, weeping in the uncertain light.
"Dim the form almost faded, tears fell down the shady cheeks; at his feet, many cloth'd
"In white robes; strewn in air, censers and harps; silent they lay prostrated;
"Beneath, in the awful void, myriads descending and weeping thro' dismal winds;
"Endless the shady train shiv'ring descended from the gloom where the aged form wept.
"At length, trembling, the vision, sighing in a low voice like the voice of the grasshopper, whisper'd:
" 'My groaning is heard in the abbeys, and God, so long worshipp'd, departs as a lamp
" 'Without oil; for a curse is heard hoarse thro' the land from a godless race
" 'Descending to beasts; they look downward and labour and forget my holy law;
" 'The sound of prayer fails from lips of flesh, and the holy hymn from thicken'd tongues;
" 'For the bars of Chaos are burst; her millions prepare their fiery way
" 'Thro' the orbed abode of the holy dead, to root up and pull down and remove,
" 'And Nobles and Clergy shall fail from before me, and my cloud and vision be no more;
" 'The mitre become black, the crown vanish, and the scepter and ivory staff
" 'Of the ruler wither among bones of death; they shall consume from the thistly field,
" 'And the sound of the bell, and voice of the sabbath, and singing of the holy choir
" 'Is turn'd into songs of the harlot in day, and cries of the virgin in night.
" 'They shall drop at the plow and faint at the harrow, unredeem'd, unconfess'd, unpardon'd;

" 'The priest rot in his surplice by the lawless lover, the holy beside the accursed,
" 'The King, frowning in purple, beside the grey plowman, and their worms embrace together.'
"The voice ceas'd: a groan shook my chamber; I slept, for the cloud of repose returned,
"But morning dawn'd heavy upon me. I rose to bring my Prince heaven utter'd counsel.
"Hear my counsel, O King, and send forth thy Generals; the command of Heaven is upon thee!
"Then do thou command, O King, to shut up this Assembly in their final home;
"Let thy soldiers possess this city of rebels, that threaten to bathe their feet
"In the blood of Nobility, trampling the heart and the head; let the Bastile devour
"These rebellious seditious; seal them up, O Anointed, in everlasting chains."
He sat down: a damp cold pervaded the Nobles, and monsters of worlds unknown
Swam round them, watching to be delivered; When Aumont, whose chaos-born soul
Eternally wand'ring a Comet and swift-falling fire, pale enter'd the chamber.
Before the red Council he stood, like a man that returns from hollow graves:

"Awe-surrounded, alone thro' the army, a fear and a with'ring blight blown by the north,
"The Abbé de Sieyès from the Nation's Assembly, O Princes and Generals of France,
"Unquestioned, unhindered! awe-struck are the soldiers; a dark shadowy man in the form
"Of King Henry the Fourth walks before him in fires; the captains like men bound in chains
"Stood still as he pass'd: he is come to the Louvre, O King, with a message to thee!
"The strong soldiers tremble, the horses their manes bow, and the guards of thy palace are fled!"

Up rose awful in his majestic beams Bourbon's strong Duke; his proud sword from his thigh
Drawn, he threw on the Earth! the Duke of Bretagne and the Earl of Borgogne
Rose inflam'd, to and fro in the chamber, like thunder-clouds ready to burst.

"What! damp all our fires, O spectre of Henry?" said Bourbon, "and rend the flames
"From the head of our King? Rise, Monarch of France! command me, and I will lead
"This army of superstition at large, that the ardor of noble souls, quenchless,
"May yet burn in France, nor our shoulders be plow'd with the furrows of poverty."

Then Orleans, generous as mountains, arose and unfolded his robe, and put forth
His benevolent hand, looking on the Archbishop who, changed as pale as lead,
Would have risen but could not: his voice issued harsh grating; instead of words harsh hissings
Shook the chamber; he ceas'd abash'd. Then Orleans spoke; all was silent.
He breath'd on them, and said: "O princes of fire, whose flames are for growth, not consuming,
"Fear not dreams, fear not visions, nor be you dismay'd with sorrows which flee at the morning!
"Can the fires of Nobility ever be quench'd, or the stars by a stormy night?
"Is the body diseas'd when the members are healthful? can the man be bound in sorrow
"Whose ev'ry function is fill'd with its fiery desire? can the soul whose brain and heart
"Cast their rivers in equal tides thro' the great Paradise, languish because the feet,
"Hands, head, bosom, and parts of love follow their high breathing joy?
"And can Nobles be bound when the people are free, or God weep when his children are happy?
"Have you never seen Fayette's forehead, or Mirabeau's eyes, or the shoulders of Target,
"Or Bailly the strong foot of France, or Clermont the terrible voice? and your robes
"Still retain their own crimson: mine never yet faded, for fire delights in its form.
"But go, merciless man! enter into the infinite labyrinth of another's brain
"Ere thou measure the circle that he shall run. Go, thou cold recluse, into the fires
"Of another's high flaming rich bosom, and return unconsum'd, and write laws.

"If thou canst not do this, doubt thy theories; learn to consider all men as thy equals,
"Thy brethren, and not as thy foot or thy hand, unless thou first fearest to hurt them."

The Monarch stood up; the strong Duke his sword to its golden scabbard return'd;
The Nobles sat round like clouds on the mountains, when the storm is passing away:
"Let the Nation's Ambassador come among Nobles, like incense of the valley!"

Aumont went out and stood in the hollow porch, his ivory wand in his hand;
A cold orb of disdain revolv'd round him, and covered his soul with snows eternal.
Great Henry's soul shuddered, a whirlwind and fire tore furious from his angry bosom;
He indignant departed on horses of heav'n. Then the Abbé de Sieyès rais'd his feet
On the steps of the Louvre; like a voice of God following a storm, the Abbé follow'd
The pale fires of Aumont into the chamber; as a father that bows to his son,
Whose rich fields inheriting spread their old glory, so the voice of the people bowed
Before the ancient seat of the kingdom and mountains to be renewed.

"Hear, O Heavens of France, the voice of the people arising from valley and hill,
"O'erclouded with power. Hear the voice of vallies, the voice of meek cities,
"Mourning oppressed on village and field, till the village and field is a waste.
"For the husbandman weeps at blights of the fife, and blasting of trumpets consume
"The souls of mild France; the pale mother nourishes her child to the deadly slaughter.
"When the heavens were seal'd with a stone, and the terrible sun clos'd in an orb, and the moon
"Rent from the nations, and each star appointed for watchers of night,
"The millions of spirits immortal were bound in the ruins of sulphur heaven
"To wander enslav'd; black, deprest in dark ignorance, kept in awe with the whip

"To worship terrors, bred from the blood of revenge and breath of desire
"In bestial forms, or more terrible men; till the dawn of our peaceful morning,
"Till dawn, till morning, till the breaking of clouds, and swelling of winds, and the universal voice;
"Till man raise his darken'd limbs out of the caves of night: his eyes and his heart
"Expand: where is Space? where, O Sun, is thy dwelling? where thy tent, O faint slumb'rous Moon?
"Then the valleys of France shall cry to the soldier: 'Throw down thy sword and musket,
" 'And run and embrace the meek peasant.' Her Nobles shall hear and shall weep, and put off
"The red robe of terror, the crown of oppression, the shoes of contempt, and unbuckle
"The girdle of war from the desolate earth; then the Priest in his thund'rous cloud
"Shall weep, bending to earth, embracing the valleys, and putting his hand to the plow,
"Shall say: 'No more I curse thee; but now I will bless thee: No more in deadly black
" 'Devour thy labour; nor lift up a cloud in thy heavens, O laborious plow,
" 'That the wild raging millions, that wander in forests, and howl in law blasted wastes,
" 'Strength madden'd with slavery, honesty bound in the dens of superstition,
" 'May sing in the village, and shout in the harvest, and woo in pleasant gardens
" 'Their once savage loves, now beaming with knowledge, with gentle awe adorned;
" 'And the saw, and the hammer, the chisel, the pencil, the pen, and the instruments
" 'Of heavenly song sound in the wilds once forbidden, to teach the laborious plowman
" 'And shepherd, deliver'd from clouds of war, from pestilence, from night-fear, from murder,
" 'From falling, from stifling, from hunger, from cold, from slander, discontent and sloth,
" 'That walk in beasts and birds of night, driven back by the sandy desart,
" 'Like pestilent fogs round cities of men; and the happy earth sing in its course,

" 'The mild peaceable nations be opened to heav'n, and men walk with their fathers in bliss.'
"Then hear the first voice of the morning: 'Depart, O clouds of night, and no more
" 'Return; be withdrawn cloudy war, troops of warriors depart, nor around our peaceable city
" 'Breathe fires, but ten miles from Paris let all be peace, nor a soldier be seen!' "

He ended: the wind of contention arose, and the clouds cast their shadows; the Princes,
Like the mountains of France, whose aged trees utter an awful voice, and their branches
Are shatter'd, till gradual a murmur is heard descending into the valley,
Like a voice in the vineyards of Burgundy when grapes are shaken on grass,
Like the low voice of the labouring man, instead of the shout of joy;
And the palace appear'd like a cloud driven abroad; blood ran down the ancient pillars.
Thro' the cloud a deep thunder, the Duke of Burgundy, delivers the King's command:

"Seest thou yonder dark castle, that moated around, keeps this city of Paris in awe?
"Go command yonder tower, saying: 'Bastile, depart! and take thy shadowy course;
" 'Overstep the dark river, thou terrible tower, and get thee up into the country ten miles.
" 'And thou black southern prison, move along the dusky road to Versailles; there
" 'Frown on the gardens'; and if it obey and depart, then the King will disband
"This war-breathing army; but if it refuse, let the Nation's Assembly thence learn
"That this army of terrors, that prison of horrors, are the bands of the murmuring kingdom."

Like the morning star arising above the black waves, when a ship-wreck'd soul sighs for morning,
Thro' the ranks, silent, walk'd the Ambassador back to the Nation's Assembly, and told
The unwelcome message; silent they heard; then a thunder roll'd round loud and louder;
Like pillars of ancient halls and ruins of times remote, they sat.

Like a voice from the dim pillars Mirabeau rose; the thunders subsided away;
A rushing of wings around him was heard as he brighten'd, and cried out aloud:
"Where is the General of the Nation?" The walls re-echo'd: "Where is the General of the Nation?"

Sudden as the bullet wrapp'd in his fire, when brazen cannons rage in the field,
Fayette sprung from his seat saying "Ready!" Then bowing like clouds, man toward man, the Assembly
Like a council of ardors seated in clouds, bending over the cities of men,
And over the armies of strife, where their children are marshall'd together to battle,
They murmuring divide; while the wind sleeps beneath, and the numbers are counted in silence,
While they vote the removal of War, and the pestilence weighs his red wings in the sky.

So Fayette stood silent among the Assembly, and the votes were given, and the numbers numb'red;
And the vote was that Fayette should order the army to remove ten miles from Paris.

The aged sun rises appall'd from dark mountains, and gleams a dusky beam
On Fayette; but on the whole army a shadow, for a cloud on the eastern hills
Hover'd, and stretch'd across the city, and across the army, and across the Louvre.
Like a flame of fire he stood before dark ranks, and before expecting captains:
On pestilent vapours around him flow frequent spectres of religious men, weeping
In winds; driven out of the abbeys, their naked souls shiver in keen open air;
Driven out by the fiery cloud of Voltaire, and thund'rous rocks of Rousseau,
They dash like foam against the ridges of the army, uttering a faint feeble cry.

Gleams of fire streak the heavens, and of sulphur the earth, from Fayette as he lifted his hand;
But silent he stood, till all the officers rush round him like waves

Round the shore of France, in day of the British flag, when heavy cannons
Affright the coasts, and the peasant looks over the sea and wipes a tear;
Over his head the soul of Voltaire shone fiery; and over the army Rousseau his white cloud
Unfolded, on souls of war, living terrors, silent list'ning toward Fayette.
His voice loud inspir'd by liberty, and by spirits of the dead, thus thunder'd:

"The Nation's Assembly command that the Army remove ten miles from Paris;
"Nor a soldier be seen in road or in field, till the Nation command return."

Rushing along iron ranks glittering, the officers each to his station
Depart, and the stern captain strokes his proud steed, and in front of his solid ranks
Waits the sound of trumpet; captains of foot stand each by his cloudy drum:
Then the drum beats, and the steely ranks move, and trumpets rejoice in the sky.
Dark cavalry, like clouds fraught with thunder, ascend on the hills, and bright infantry, rank
Behind rank, to the soul shaking drum and shrill fife, along the roads glitter like fire.

The noise of trampling, the wind of trumpets, smote the palace walls with a blast.
Pale and cold sat the King in midst of his peers, and his noble heart sunk, and his pulses
Suspended their motion; a darkness crept over his eye-lids, and chill cold sweat
Sat round his brows faded in faint death; his peers pale, like mountains of the dead
Cover'd with dews of night, groaning, shaking forests and floods. The cold newt,
And snake, and damp toad on the kingly foot crawl, or croak on the awful knee,
Shedding their slime; in folds of the robe the crown'd adder builds and hisses
From stony brows; shaken the forests of France, sick the kings of the nations,

And the bottoms of the world were open'd, and the graves of arch-angels unseal'd:
The enormous dead lift up their pale fires and look over the rocky cliffs.

A faint heat from their fires reviv'd the cold Louvre; the frozen blood reflow'd.
Awful up rose the king; him the peers follow'd; they saw the courts of the Palace
Forsaken, and Paris without a soldier, silent; for the noise was gone up
And follow'd the army, and the Senate in peace sat beneath morning's beam.

END OF THE FIRST BOOK

THE MARRIAGE of HEAVEN and HELL

Etched about 1790–1793

Plate 2

The Argument

Rintrah roars & shakes his fires in the burden'd air;
Hungry clouds swag on the deep.

Once meek, and in a perilous path,
The just man kept his course along
The vale of death.
Roses are planted where thorns grow,
And on the barren heath
Sing the honey bees.

Then the perilous path was planted,
And a river and a spring
On every cliff and tomb,
And on the bleached bones
Red clay brought forth;

Till the villain left the paths of ease,
To walk in perilous paths, and drive
The just man into barren climes.

Now the sneaking serpent walks
In mild humility,
And the just man rages in the wilds
Where lions roam.

Rintrah roars & shakes his fires in the burden'd air;
Hungry clouds swag on the deep.

Plate 3

As a new heaven is begun, and it is now thirty-three years since its advent, the Eternal Hell revives. And lo! Swedenborg is the Angel sitting at the tomb: his writings are the linen clothes folded up. Now is the dominion of Edom, & the return of Adam into Paradise; see Isaiah xxxiv & xxxv Chap.

Without Contraries is no progression. Attraction and Repulsion, Reason and Energy, Love and Hate, are necessary to Human existence.

From these contraries spring what the religious call Good & Evil. Good is the passive that obeys Reason. Evil is the active springing from Energy.

Good is Heaven. Evil is Hell.

Plate 4

The voice of the Devil

All Bibles or sacred codes have been the causes of the following Errors:

1. That Man has two real existing principles: Viz: a Body & a Soul.

2. That Energy, call'd Evil, is alone from the Body; & that Reason, call'd Good, is alone from the Soul.

3. That God will torment Man in Eternity for following his Energies.

But the following Contraries to these are True:

1. Man has no Body distinct from his Soul; for that call'd Body is a portion of Soul discern'd by the five Senses, the chief inlets of Soul in this age.

2. Energy is the only life, and is from the Body; and Reason is the bound or outward circumference of Energy.

3. Energy is Eternal Delight.

Plates 5-6

Those who restrain desire, do so because theirs is weak enough to be restrained; and the restrainer or reason usurps its place & governs the unwilling.

And being restrain'd, it by degrees becomes passive, till it is only [illegible] shadow of desire.

The history of this is written in Paradise Lost, & the Governor or Reason is call'd Messiah.

And the original Archangel, or possessor of the command of the heavenly host, is call'd the Devil or Satan, and his children are call'd Sin & Death.

But in the Book of Job, Milton's Messiah is call'd Satan.

For this history has been adopted by both parties.

It indeed appear'd to Reason as if Desire was cast out; but the Devil's account is, that the Messiah fell, & formed a heaven of what he stole from the Abyss.

This is shewn in the Gospel, where he prays to the Father to send the comforter, or Desire, that Reason may have Ideas to build on; the Jehovah of the Bible being no other than [the Devil *del.*] he who dwells in flaming fire.

Know that after Christ's death, he became Jehovah.

But in Milton, the Father is Destiny, the Son a Ratio of the five senses, & the Holy-ghost Vacuum!

Note: The reason Milton wrote in fetters when he wrote of Angels & God, and at liberty when of Devils & Hell, is because he was a true Poet and of the Devil's party without knowing it.

Plates 6–7

A MEMORABLE FANCY

As I was walking among the fires of hell, delighted with the enjoyments of Genius, which to Angels look like torment and insanity, I collected some of their Proverbs; thinking that as the sayings used in a nation mark its character, so the Proverbs of Hell show the nature of Infernal wisdom better than any description of buildings or garments.

When I came home: on the abyss of the five senses, where a flat sided steep frowns over the present world, I saw a mighty Devil folded in black clouds, hovering on the sides of the rock: with corroding fires he wrote the following sentence now percieved by the minds of men, & read by them on earth:

> How do you know but ev'ry Bird that cuts the airy way,
> Is an immense world of delight, clos'd by your senses five?

Plate 7

PROVERBS OF HELL

In seed time learn, in harvest teach, in winter enjoy.
Drive your cart and your plow over the bones of the dead.
The road of excess leads to the palace of wisdom.

Prudence is a rich, ugly old maid courted by Incapacity.
He who desires but acts not, breeds pestilence.
The cut worm forgives the plow.
Dip him in the river who loves water.
A fool sees not the same tree that a wise man sees.
He whose face gives no light, shall never become a star.
Eternity is in love with the productions of time.
The busy bee has no time for sorrow.
The hours of folly are measur'd by the clock; but of wisdom, no clock can measure.
All wholesom food is caught without a net or a trap.
Bring out number, weight & measure in a year of dearth.
No bird soars too high, if he soars with his own wings.
A dead body revenges not injuries.
The most sublime act is to set another before you.
If the fool would persist in his folly he would become wise.
Folly is the cloke of knavery.
Shame is Pride's cloke.

Plate 8

Prisons are built with stones of Law, Brothels with bricks of Religion.
The pride of the peacock is the glory of God.
The lust of the goat is the bounty of God.
The wrath of the lion is the wisdom of God.
The nakedness of woman is the work of God.
Excess of sorrow laughs. Excess of joy weeps.
The roaring of lions, the howling of wolves, the raging of the stormy sea, and the destructive sword, are portions of eternity, too great for the eye of man.
The fox condemns the trap, not himself.
Joys impregnate. Sorrows bring forth.
Let man wear the fell of the lion, woman the fleece of the sheep.
The bird a nest, the spider a web, man friendship.
The selfish, smiling fool, & the sullen, frowning fool shall be both thought wise, that they may be a rod.
What is now proved was once only imagin'd.
The rat, the mouse, the fox, the rabbet watch the roots; the lion, the tyger, the horse, the elephant watch the fruits.
The cistern contains: the fountain overflows.
One thought fills immensity.
Always be ready to speak your mind, and a base man will avoid you.
Every thing possible to be believ'd is an image of truth.
The eagle never lost so much time as when he submitted to learn of the crow.

Plate 9

The fox provides for himself, but God provides for the lion.

Think in the morning. Act in the noon. Eat in the evening. Sleep in the night.

He who has suffer'd you to impose on him, knows you.

As the plow follows words, so God rewards prayers.

The tygers of wrath are wiser than the horses of instruction.

Expect poison from the standing water.

You never know what is enough unless you know what is more than enough.

Listen to the fool's reproach! it is a kingly title!

The eyes of fire, the nostrils of air, the mouth of water, the beard of earth.

The weak in courage is strong in cunning.

The apple tree never asks the beech how he shall grow; nor the lion, the horse, how he shall take his prey.

The thankful reciever bears a plentiful harvest.

If others had not been foolish, we should be so.

The soul of sweet delight can never be defil'd.

When thou seest an Eagle, thou seest a portion of Genius; lift up thy head!

As the catterpiller chooses the fairest leaves to lay her eggs on, so the priest lays his curse on the fairest joys.

To create a little flower is the labour of ages.

Damn braces: Bless relaxes.

The best wine is the oldest, the best water the newest.

Prayers plow not! Praises reap not!

Joys laugh not! Sorrows weep not!

Plate 10

The head Sublime, the heart Pathos, the genitals Beauty, the hands & feet Proportion.

As the air to a bird or the sea to a fish, so is contempt to the contemptible.

The crow wish'd every thing was black, the owl that every thing was white.

Exuberance is Beauty.

If the lion was advised by the fox, he would be cunning.

Improve[me]nt makes strait roads; but the crooked roads without Improvement are roads of Genius.

Sooner murder an infant in its cradle than nurse unacted desires.

Where man is not, nature is barren.

Truth can never be told so as to be understood, and not be believ'd.

Enough! or Too much.

Plate 11

The ancient Poets animated all sensible objects with Gods or Geniuses, calling them by the names and adorning them with the properties of woods, rivers, mountains, lakes, cities, nations, and whatever their enlarged & numerous senses could percieve.

And particularly they studied the genius of each city & country, placing it under its mental deity;

Till a system was formed, which some took advantage of, & enslav'd the vulgar by attempting to realize or abstract the mental deities from their objects: thus began Priesthood;

Choosing forms of worship from poetic tales.

And at length they pronounc'd that the Gods had order'd such things.

Thus men forgot that All deities reside in the human breast.

Plates 12–13

A memorable Fancy

The Prophets Isaiah and Ezekiel dined with me, and I asked them how they dared so roundly to assert that God spake to them; and whether they did not think at the time that they would be misunderstood, & so be the cause of imposition.

Isaiah answer'd: "I saw no God, nor heard any, in a finite organical "perception; but my senses discover'd the infinite in every thing, and "as I was then perswaded, & remain confirm'd, that the voice of "honest indignation is the voice of God, I cared not for consequences, "but wrote."

Then I asked: "does a firm perswasion that a thing is so, make it so?"

He replied: "All poets believe that it does, & in ages of imagination "this firm perswasion removed mountains; but many are not capable "of a firm perswasion of any thing."

Then Ezekiel said: "The philosophy of the east taught the first "principles of human perception: some nations held one principle "for the origin, & some another: we of Israel taught that the Poetic "Genius (as you now call it) was the first principle and all the others "merely derivative, which was the cause of our despising the Priests "& Philosophers of other countries, and prophecying that all Gods "would at last be proved to originate in ours & to be the tributaries "of the Poetic Genius; it was this that our great poet, King David, "desired so fervently & invokes so pathetic'ly, saying by this he "conquers enemies & governs kingdoms; and we so loved our God, "that we cursed in his name all the deities of surrounding nations, "and asserted that they had rebelled: from these opinions the vulgar "came to think that all nations would at last be subject to the jews."

"This," said he, "like all firm perswasions, is come to pass; for "all nations believe the jews' code and worship the jews' god, and "what greater subjection can be?"

I heard this with some wonder, & must confess my own conviction. After dinner I ask'd Isaiah to favour the world with his lost works; he said none of equal value was lost. Ezekiel said the same of his.

I also asked Isaiah what made him go naked and barefoot three years? he answer'd: "the same that made our friend Diogenes, "the Grecian."

I then asked Ezekiel why he eat dung, & lay so long on his right & left side? he answer'd, "the desire of raising other men into a "perception of the infinite: this the North American tribes practise, "& is he honest who resists his genius or conscience only for the sake "of present ease or gratification?"

Plate 14

The ancient tradition that the world will be consumed in fire at the end of six thousand years is true, as I have heard from Hell.

For the cherub with his flaming sword is hereby commanded to leave his guard at tree of life; and when he does, the whole creation will be consumed and appear infinite and holy, whereas it now appears finite & corrupt.

This will come to pass by an improvement of sensual enjoyment.

But first the notion that man has a body distinct from his soul is to be expunged; this I shall do by printing in the infernal method, by corrosives, which in Hell are salutary and medicinal, melting apparent surfaces away, and displaying the infinite which was hid.

If the doors of perception were cleansed every thing would appear to man as it is, infinite.

For man has closed himself up, till he sees all things thro' narrow chinks of his cavern.

Plates 15-17

A MEMORABLE FANCY

I was in a Printing house in Hell, & saw the method in which knowledge is transmitted from generation to generation.

In the first chamber was a Dragon-Man, clearing away the rubbish from a cave's mouth; within, a number of Dragons were hollowing the cave.

In the second chamber was a Viper folding round the rock & the cave, and others adorning it with gold, silver and precious stones.

In the third chamber was an Eagle with wings and feathers of air: he caused the inside of the cave to be infinite; around were numbers of Eagle-like men who built palaces in the immense cliffs.

In the fourth chamber were Lions of flaming fire, raging around & melting the metals into living fluids.

In the fifth chamber were Unnam'd forms, which cast the metals into the expanse.

There they were reciev'd by Men who occupied the sixth chamber, and took the forms of books & were arranged in libraries.

The Giants who formed this world into its sensual existence, and now seem to live in it in chains, are in truth the causes of its life & the sources of all activity; but the chains are the cunning of weak and tame minds which have power to resist energy; according to the proverb, the weak in courage is strong in cunning.

Thus one portion of being is the Prolific, the other the Devouring: to the devourer it seems as if the producer was in his chains; but it is not so, he only takes portions of existence and fancies that the whole.

But the Prolific would cease to be Prolific unless the Devourer, as a sea, recieved the excess of his delights.

Some will say: "Is not God alone the Prolific?" I answer: "God "only Acts & Is, in existing beings or Men."

These two classes of men are always upon earth, & they should be enemies: whoever tries to reconcile them seeks to destroy existence.

Religion is an endeavour to reconcile the two.

Note: Jesus Christ did not wish to unite, but to seperate them, as in the Parable of sheep and goats! & he says: "I came not to send Peace, but a Sword."

Messiah or Satan or Tempter was formerly thought to be one of the Antediluvians who are our Energies.

Plates 17-20

A Memorable Fancy

An Angel came to me and said: "O pitiable foolish young man! O "horrible! O dreadful state! consider the hot burning dungeon thou "art preparing for thyself to all eternity, to which thou art going in "such career."

I said: "perhaps you will be willing to shew me my eternal lot, & "we will contemplate together upon it, and see whether your lot or "mine is most desirable."

So he took me thro' a stable & thro' a church & down into the church vault, at the end of which was a mill: thro' the mill we went, and came to a cave: down the winding cavern we groped our tedious way, till a void boundless as a nether sky appear'd beneath us, & we held by the roots of trees and hung over this immensity; but I said: "if you please, we will commit ourselves to this void, and see "whether providence is here also: if you will not, I will:" but he answer'd: "do not presume, O young man, but as we here remain, "behold thy lot which will soon appear when the darkness passes "away."

So I remain'd with him, sitting in the twisted root of an oak; he was suspended in a fungus, which hung with the head downward into the deep.

By degrees we beheld the infinite Abyss, fiery as the smoke of a burning city; beneath us, at an immense distance, was the sun, black but shining; round it were fiery tracks on which revolv'd vast spiders, crawling after their prey, which flew, or rather swum, in the infinite deep, in the most terrific shapes of animals sprung from corruption; & the air was full of them, & seem'd composed of them: these are Devils, and are called Powers of the air. I now asked my companion which was my eternal lot? he said: "between the black & white spiders."

But now, from between the black & white spiders, a cloud and fire burst and rolled thro' the deep, black'ning all beneath, so that the nether deep grew black as a sea, & rolled with a terrible noise; beneath us was nothing now to be seen but a black tempest, till looking east between the clouds & the waves, we saw a cataract of blood mixed with fire, and not many stones' throw from us appear'd and sunk again the scaly fold of a monstrous serpent; at last, to the east, distant about three degrees, appear'd a fiery crest above the waves; slowly it reared like a ridge of golden rocks, till we discover'd two globes of crimson fire, from which the sea fled away in clouds of smoke; and now we saw it was the head of Leviathan; his forehead was divided into streaks of green & purple like those on a tyger's forehead: soon we saw his mouth & red gills hang just above the raging foam, tinging the black deep with beams of blood, advancing toward us with all the fury of a spiritual existence.

My friend the Angel climb'd up from his station into the mill: I remain'd alone; & then this appearance was no more, but I found myself sitting on a pleasant bank beside a river by moonlight, hearing a harper, who sung to the harp; & his theme was: "The man who "never alters his opinion is like standing water, & breeds reptiles of "the mind."

But I arose and sought for the mill, & there I found my Angel, who, surprised, asked me how I escaped?

I answer'd: "All that we saw was owing to your metaphysics; for "when you ran away, I found myself on a bank by moonlight hearing "a harper. But now we have seen my eternal lot, shall I shew you "yours?" he laugh'd at my proposal; but I by force suddenly caught him in my arms, & flew westerly thro' the night, till we were elevated above the earth's shadow; then I flung myself with him directly into the body of the sun; here I clothed myself in white, & taking in my hand Swedenborg's volumes, sunk from the glorious clime, and passed all the planets till we came to saturn: here I stay'd to rest, & then leap'd into the void between saturn & the fixed stars.

"Here," said I, "is your lot, in this space—if space it may be "call'd." Soon we saw the stable and the church, & I took him to the altar and open'd the Bible, and lo! it was a deep pit, into which I descended, driving the Angel before me; soon we saw seven houses of brick; one we enter'd; in it were a number of monkeys, baboons, & all of that species, chain'd by the middle, grinning and snatching at one another, but witheld by the shortness of their chains: however, I saw that they sometimes grew numerous, and then the weak were caught by the strong, and with a grinning aspect, first coupled with, & then devour'd, by plucking off first one limb and then another, till the body was left a helpless trunk; this, after grinning & kissing it with seeming fondness, they devour'd too; and here & there I saw one savourily picking the flesh off of his own tail; as the stench terribly annoy'd us both, we went into the mill, & I in my hand brought the skeleton of a body, which in the mill was Aristotle's Analytics.

So the Angel said: "thy phantasy has imposed upon me, & thou "oughtest to be ashamed."

I answer'd: "we impose on one another, & it is but lost time to "converse with you whose works are only Analytics."

Opposition is true Friendship[1].

Plates 21-22

I have always found that Angels have the vanity to speak of themselves as the only wise; this they do with a confident insolence sprouting from systematic reasoning.

Thus Swedenborg boasts that what he writes is new; tho' it is only the Contents or Index of already publish'd books.

A man carried a monkey about for a shew, & because he was a little wiser than the monkey, grew vain, and conciev'd himself as much wiser than seven men. It is so with Swedenborg: he shews the folly of churches, & exposes hypocrites, till he imagines that all are religious, & himself the single one on earth that ever broke a net.

Now hear a plain fact: Swedenborg has not written one new truth. Now hear another: he has written all the old falshoods.

And now hear the reason. He conversed with Angels who are all religious, & conversed not with Devils who all hate religion, for he was incapable thro' his conceited notions.

---

[1] This line is obliterated in some copies.

Thus Swedenborg's writings are a recapitulation of all superficial opinions, and an analysis of the more sublime—but no further.

Have now another plain fact. Any man of mechanical talents may, from the writings of Paracelsus or Jacob Behmen, produce ten thousand volumes of equal value with Swedenborg's, and from those of Dante or Shakespear an infinite number.

But when he has done this, let him not say that he knows better than his master, for he only holds a candle in sunshine.

A Memorable Fancy

Plates 22-24

Once I saw a Devil in a flame of fire, who arose before an Angel that sat on a cloud, and the Devil utter'd these words: "The worship of God is: Honouring his gifts in other men, each according to his "genius, and loving the greatest men best: those who envy or "calumniate great men hate God; for there is no other God."

The Angel hearing this became almost blue; but mastering himself he grew yellow, & at last white, pink, & smiling, and then replied:

"Thou Idolater! is not God One? & is not he visible in Jesus "Christ? and has not Jesus Christ given his sanction to the law of "ten commandments? and are not all other men fools, sinners, & "nothings?"

The Devil answer'd: "bray a fool in a morter with wheat, yet shall "not his folly be beaten out of him; if Jesus Christ is the greatest "man, you ought to love him in the greatest degree; now hear how "he has given his sanction to the law of ten commandments: did he "not mock at the sabbath, and so mock the sabbath's God? murder "those who were murder'd because of him? turn away the law from "the woman taken in adultery? steal the labor of others to support "him? bear false witness when he omitted making a defence before "Pilate? covet when he pray'd for his disciples, and when he bid "them shake off the dust of their feet against such as refused to lodge "them? I tell you, no virtue can exist without breaking these ten "commandments. Jesus was all virtue, and acted from impulse, not "from rules."

When he had so spoken, I beheld the Angel, who stretched out his arms, embracing the flame of fire, & he was consumed and arose as Elijah.

Note: This Angel, who is now become a Devil, is my particular friend; we often read the Bible together in its infernal or diabolical sense, which the world shall have if they behave well.

I have also The Bible of Hell, which the world shall have whether they will or no.

One Law for the Lion & Ox is Oppression.

Plates 25-27

A Song of Liberty

I

1. The Eternal Female groan'd! it was heard over all the Earth.

2. Albion's coast is sick silent; the American meadows faint!

3. Shadows of Prophecy shiver along by the lakes and the rivers and mutter across the ocean: France, rend down thy dungeon!

4. Golden Spain, burst the barriers of old Rome!

5. Cast thy keys, O Rome, into the deep down falling, even to eternity down falling.

6. And weep and bow thy reverend locks[1].

7. In her trembling hands she took the new born terror, howling:

8. On those infinite mountains of light, now barr'd out by the atlantic sea, the new born fire stood before the starry king!

9. Flag'd with grey brow'd snows and thunderous visages, the jealous wings wav'd over the deep.

10. The speary hand burned aloft, unbuckled was the shield; forth went the hand of jealousy among the flaming hair, and hurl'd the new born wonder thro' the starry night.

11. The fire, the fire is falling!

12. Look up! look up! O citizen of London, enlarge thy countenance! O Jew, leave counting gold! return to thy oil and wine. O African! black African! (go, winged thought, widen his forehead.)

13. The fiery limbs, the flaming hair, shot like the sinking sun into the western sea.

14. Wak'd from his eternal sleep, the hoary element roaring fled away:

15. Down rush'd, beating his wings in vain, the jealous king; his grey brow'd councellors, thunderous warriors, curl'd veterans, among helms, and shields, and chariots, horses, elephants, banners, castles, slings, and rocks,

16. Falling, rushing, ruining! buried in the ruins, on Urthona's dens;

17. All night beneath the ruins; then, their sullen flames faded, emerge round the gloomy King.

18. With thunder and fire, leading his starry hosts thro' the waste wilderness, he promulgates his ten commands, glancing his beamy eyelids over the deep in dark dismay,

---

[1] The last five words afterwards erased from the plate.

19. Where the son of fire in his eastern cloud, while the morning plumes her golden breast,

20 Spurning the clouds written with curses, stamps the stony law to dust, loosing the eternal horses from the dens of night, crying:

EMPIRE IS NO MORE! AND NOW THE LION & WOLF SHALL CEASE.

Chorus

Let the Priests of the Raven of dawn, no longer in deadly black, with hoarse note curse the sons of joy. Nor his accepted brethren—whom, tyrant, he calls free—lay the bound or build the roof. Nor pale religious letchery call that virginity that wishes but acts not!

For every thing that lives is Holy.

THE DANCE OF ALBION

Inscription to the design known as "The Dance of Albion" or "Glad Day"

Engraved about 1793

Albion rose from where he labour'd at the Mill with Slaves:
Giving himself for the Nations he danc'd the dance of Eternal Death.

POEMS AND FRAGMENTS FROM THE NOTE-BOOK

Written about 1793

P. 115, reversed.

I

First draft of "My Pretty Rose-tree" in Songs of Experience; *see p.* 215

A flower was offer'd to me
Such a flower as may never bore;
But I said, "I've a pretty rose tree,"
And I passed the sweet flower o'er.

Then I went to my pretty rose tree
[In the silent of the night *del.*]
To tend it by day & by night
But my rose [was turned from me *del.*]
[was fill'd *del.*] turn'd away with Jealousy
And her thorns were my only delight.

P. 115, reversed.

2

[Never (seek *del.*) pain to tell thy love
Love that never told can be;
For the gentle wind does move
Silently, invisibly. *del.*]

I told my love, I told my love,
I told her all my heart,
Trembling, cold, in ghastly fears—
Ah, she doth depart.

Soon as she was gone from me
A traveller came by
Silently, invisibly—
[He took her with a sigh *del.*]
O, was no deny.

P. 115, reversed.

3

First draft of "The Clod and the Pebble" in Songs of Experience; *see p.* 211

"Love seeketh not itself to please,
"Nor for itself hath any care
"But for another gives its ease
"And builds a heaven in hell's despair."

So sung a little clod of clay,
Trodden with the cattle's feet,
But a pebble of the brook
Warbled out these metres meet:

"Love seeketh only self to please
"To bind another to its delight,
"Joys in another's loss of ease
"And builds a hell in heaven's despite."

P. 115, reversed.

4

I laid me down upon a bank
Where love lay sleeping.
I heard among the rushes dank
Weeping, Weeping.

Then I went to the heath & the wild
To the thistles & thorns of the waste
And they told how they were beguil'd,
Driven out, & compel'd to be chaste.

P. 115, reversed.

5

First draft of "The Garden of Love" in Songs of Experience; *see p.* 215

I went to the garden of love,
And I saw what I never had seen:
A chapel was built in the midst,
Where I used to play on the green.

And the gates of the chapel were shut,
And "thou shalt not" writ over the door,
[And *del.*] So I turn'd to the garden of love
That so many sweet flowers bore;

And I saw it was filled with graves,
And tomb stones where flowers should be,
And priests in black gounds were walking their rounds
And binding with briars my joys & desires.

P. 115, reversed.

6

I saw a chapel all of gold
That none did dare to enter in,
And many weeping stood without,
Weeping, mourning, worshipping.

I saw a serpent rise between
The white pillars of the door,
And he forc'd & forc'd & forc'd,
[Till he broke the pearly door *del.*]
Down the golden hinges tore.

And along the pavement sweet,
Set with pearls & rubies bright,
All his slimy length he drew,
Till upon the altar white

Vomiting his poison out
On the bread & on the wine.
So I turn'd into a sty
And laid me down among the swine.

P. 114, reversed.

7

I asked a thief [if he'd *del.*] to steal me a peach
[And *del.*] He turned up his eyes.
I ask'd a lithe lady to lie her down
[And *del.*] Holy & meek she cries.

As soon as I went an angel came:
[And *del.*] He wink'd at the thief
And [he *del.*] smil'd at the dame,
And without one word [spoke *del.*] said
Had a peach from the tree,
[And 'twixt earnest & joke *del.*]
And still as a maid
[He *del.*] Enjoy'd the Lady[1].

[1] Blake retained most of the second readings in a fair copy dated 1796; *see p.* 261

P. 114, reversed.

8

I heard an Angel singing
When the day was springing,
"Mercy, Pity, [& *del.*] Peace
"Is the world's release."

Thus he sung all day
Over the new mown hay,
Till the sun went down
And haycocks looked brown.

I heard a Devil curse
Over the heath & the furze,
"Mercy could be no more,
"If there was nobody poor,

"And pity no more could be,
"If all were as happy as we."
[Thus he sang & *del.*]
At his curse the sun went down,
And the heavens gave a frown.

[(And *del.*) Down pour'd the heavy rain
Over the new reap'd grain,
And Mercy & Pity & Peace descended
The Farmers were ruin'd & harvest was ended. *del.*]

[And Mercy, Pity, (& *del.*) Peace
Joy'd at their increase
With Poverty's Increase
Are . . .
And by distress increase
Mercy, Pity, Peace,
By Misery to increase
Mercy, Pity, Peace. *del.*]
And Miseries' increase
Is Mercy, Pity, Peace.

P. 114, reversed.

9

A cradle song

1 3 Sleep, Sleep: in thy sleep
4 Little sorrows sit & weep.
[Thou wilt every secret keep *del.*]
[Cans't thou any secret keep *del.*]

1 Sleep, Sleep, beauty bright
[Thou shalt taste the joys of night *del.*]
2 Dreaming o'er the joys of night

[Yet a little while the moon
Silent . . . *del.*]
3 As thy softest limbs I [touch *del.*] [stroke *del.*] feel
Smiles as of the morning [broke *del.*] steal
O'er thy cheek & o'er thy breast
Where thy little heart does rest.

4 O, the cunning wiles that creep
In thy little heart asleep.
When thy little heart does wake,
Then the dreadful lightnings break.

2 Sweet Babe, in thy face
Soft desires I can trace
Secret joys & secret smiles
[Such as burning youth beguiles *del.*]
Little pretty infant wiles.

5 From thy cheek & from thy eye
O'er the youthful harvests nigh
[Female *del.*] Infant wiles & [female *del.*] infant smiles
Heaven & Earth of peace beguiles.

P. 114, reversed.

10

Christian Forbearance

First draft of "A Poison Tree" in Songs of Experience; *see p.* 218

I was angry with my friend:
I told my wrath, my wrath did end.
I was angry with my foe:
I told it not, my wrath did grow.

And I water'd it in fears
Night & morning with my tears;
And I sunned it with smiles
And with soft deceitful wiles.

And it grew by day & night
Till it bore an apple bright;
[And I gave it to my foe *del.*]
And my foe beheld it shine,
And he knew that it was mine,

And into my garden stole,
When the night had veil'd the pole.
In the morning Glad I see
My foe outstretch'd beneath the tree.

P. 113, reversed.

11

I fear'd the [roughness *del.*] fury of my wind
Would blight all blossoms fair & true;
And my sun it shin'd & shin'd
[But *del.*] and my wind it never blew.

But a blossom fair or true
Was not found on any tree;
For all blossoms grew & grew
Fruitless, false, tho' fair to see.

P. 113, reversed.

12

Why should I care for the men of thames,
Or the cheating waves of charter'd streams,
Or shrink at the little blasts of fear
That the hireling blows into my ear?

Tho' born on the cheating banks of Thames,
Tho' his waters bathed my infant limbs,
[I spurn'd his waters away from me *del.*]
The Ohio shall wash his stains from me:
I was born a slave, but I [long *del.*] go to be free.

P. 113, reversed.

13

Infant Sorrow

My mother groan'd, my father wept;
Into the dangerous world I leapt,
Helpless, naked, piping loud,
Like a fiend hid in a cloud.

Struggling in my father's hands
Striving against my swaddling bands,
Bound & weary, I thought best
To sulk upon my mother's breast.

When I saw that rage was vain,
And to sulk would nothing gain,
[I began to so *del.*] [Seeking many an artful wile *del.*]
Turning many a trick & wile,
I began to soothe & smile.

And I [grew *del.*] [smil'd *del.*] sooth'd day after day
Till upon the ground I stray;
And I [grew *del.*] smil'd night after night,
Seeking only for delight.

[But upon the nettly ground
No delight was to be found *del.*]
And I saw before me shine
Clusters of the wand'ring vine
[And beyond a mirtle tree *del.*]
And many a lovely flower & tree
Stretch'd [its *del.*] their blossoms out to me.

[But a *del.*] [But many a Priest *del.*]
My father then with holy look,
In [their *del.*] his hands a holy book,
Pronounc'd curses on [his *del.*] my head
[Who the fruit or blossoms shed *del.*]
And bound me in a mirtle shade.

[I beheld the Priests by night;
They embrac'd (my mirtle *del.*) the blossoms bright:
I beheld the Priests by day;
(Where beneath my *del.*)
Underneath the vines (he *del.*) they lay *del.*]

[3 Like (a *del.*) to serpents in the night,
4 They (*altered to* He) embrac'd my (mirtle *del.*)
blossoms bright *del.*]
1 Like [a *del.*] to [serpents in the *del.*] holy men by day,
2 Underneath [my *del.*] the vines [he *del.*] they lay.

So I smote them & [his *del.*] their gore
Stain'd the roots my mirtle bore;
But the time of youth is fled,
And grey hairs are on my head.

The first two stanzas were used with the same title in Songs of Experience; *see p.* 217

P. 113, reversed.

14

Silent, Silent Night
Quench the holy light
Of thy torches bright.

For possess'd of Day
Thousand spirits stray
That sweet joys betray.

Why should joys be sweet
Used with deceit
Nor with sorrows meet?

But an honest joy
Does itself destroy
For a harlot coy.

P. 113, reversed.

15

O Lapwing, thou fliest around the heath,
Nor seest the net that is spread beneath.
Why dost thou not fly among the corn fields?
They cannot spread nets where a harvest yields.

P. 111, reversed.

16

Thou hast a lap full of seed,
And this is a fine country.
Why dost thou not cast thy seed
And live in it merrily?
[Oft I've *del.*] Shall I cast it on the sand
And [turn'd *del.*] turn it into fruitful land?
[But *del.*] For on no other ground [can *del.*]
Can I sow my seed,
Without [pulling *del.*] tearing up
Some stinking weed.

P. 111, reversed.

17

[The *del.*] Earth's Answer

First draft of the poem with the same title in Songs of Experience; *see p.* 210

Earth rais'd up her head
From the darkness dread & drear.
Her [eyes fled *del.*] [orbs dead *del.*] light fled,
Stony dread!
And her locks cover'd with grey despair.

Prison'd on wat'ry shore
Starry jealousy does keep my den
Cold & hoar
Weeping o'er
I hear the [father of the *del.*] ancient men.

[(Cruel *del.*) Selfish father of men
Cruel jealous (wintry *del.*) selfish fear
Cān delight,
(Clos'd *del.*) Chain'd in night,
The virgins of youth & morning bear? *del.*]

Does spring hide its [delight *del.*] joy
When buds & blossom grow?
Does the sower [sow *del.*]
[His seed *del.*] Sow by night
Or the plowman in darkness plow?

Break this heavy chain
That does [close *del.*] freeze my bones around.
Selfish, vain!
[Thou my *del.*] Eternal bane,
[Hast my *del.*] That free love with bondage bound.

P. 111, reversed.

18

in a mirtle shade

[To a lovely mirtle bound
Blossoms show'ring all around *del.*]
2 O, how sick & weary I
Underneath my mirtle lie,
Like to dung upon the ground
Underneath my mirtle bound.

1 Why should I be bound to thee,
O my lovely mirtle tree?
Love, free love, cannot be bound
To any tree that grows on ground.

3 Oft my mirtle sigh'd in vain
To behold my heavy chain
Oft [the priest beheld *del.*] my father saw us sigh,
And laugh'd at our simplicity.

So I smote him & his gore
Stain'd the roots my mirtle bore.
But the time of youth is fled,
And grey hairs are on my head.

P. 109, reversed.

19

London

First draft of the poem with the same title in Songs of Experience; *see p.* 216

I wander thro' each dirty street,
Near where the dirty Thames does flow,
And [see *del.*] mark in every face I meet
Marks of weakness, marks of woe.

In every cry of every man
In [every voice of every child *del.*]
every infant's cry of fear
In every voice, in every ban
The [german *del.*] mind forg'd [links I hear *del.*]
manacles I hear.

[But most *del.*] How the chimney sweeper's cry
[Blackens o'er the churches' walls, *del.*]
Every black'ning church appalls,
And the hapless soldier's sigh
Runs in blood down palace walls.

[But most the midnight harlot's curse
From every dismal street I hear,
Weaves around the marriage hearse
And blasts the new born infant's tear. *del.*]

But most [from every *del.*] thro' wintry streets I hear
How the midnight harlot's curse
Blasts the new born infant's tear,
And [hangs *del.*] smites with plagues the marriage hearse.

But most the shrieks of youth I hear
But most thro' midnight & . . . .
How the youthful . . .

P. 109, reversed.

20

Stanzas 2 and 3 of no. 30

I [was found *del.*] slept in the dark
In the silent night
I murmur'd my fears
And I felt delight.

In the morning I went
As rosy as morn
To seek for new Joy,
But I met with scorn.

P. 109, reversed.

21

To Nobodaddy

Why art thou silent & invisible,
[Man *del.*] Father of Jealousy?
Why dost thou hide thyself in clouds
From every searching Eye?

Why darkness & obscurity
In all thy words & laws,
That none dare eat the fruit but from
The wily serpents jaws?
Or is it because Secresy gains [feminine *del.*]
  females' loud applause?

P. 109, reversed.

22

First draft of "The Lilly" in Songs of Experience; *see p.* 215

The [rose puts envious *del.*]
  [lustful *del.*] modest rose puts forth a thorn,
The [coward *del.*] humble sheep a threatn'ing horn,
While the lilly white shall in love delight,
[And the lion increase freedom & peace. *del.*]
[The priest loves war & the soldier peace. *del.*]
Nor a thorn, nor a threat, stain her beauty bright.

P. 109, reversed.

23

First draft of "Nurse's Song" in Songs of Experience; *see p.* 212

When the voices of children are heard on the green
And whisp'rings are in the dale,
The [desires *del.*] days of youth rise fresh in my mind,
My face turns green & pale.

Then come home, my children, the sun is gone down
And the dews of night arise;
Your spring & your day are wasted in play,
And your winter & night in disguise.

P. 109, reversed.

24

Are not the joys of morning sweeter
Than the joys of night?
And are the vig'rous joys of youth
Ashamed of the light?

Let age & sickness silent rob
The vineyards in the night;
But those who burn with vig'rous youth
Pluck fruits before the light.

P. 109–108, reversed.

25

The Tyger

First draft of "The Tyger" in Songs of Experience; *see p.* 214

1 Tyger, Tyger, burning bright
In the forests of the night,
What immortal hand or eye
[Could *del.*] [Dare *del.*] frame thy fearful symmetry?

2 [In what *del.*] [Burnt in *del.*] distant deeps or skies
[Burnt the *del.*] [The cruel *del.*] fire of thine eyes?
On what wings dare he aspire?
What the hand dare sieze the fire?

3 And what shoulder & what art
Could twist the sinews of thy heart?
And when thy heart began to beat
What dread hand & what dread feet

[Could fetch it from the furnace deep
And in [the *altered to*] thy horrid ribs dare steep
In the well of sanguine woe?
In what clay & in what mould
Were thy eyes of fury roll'd? *del.*]

4 [What *del.*] Where the hammer? [What *del.*] Where the chain?
In what furnace was thy brain?
What the anvil? What [the arm *del.*] [arm *del.*] [grasp *del.*] [clasp *del.*] dread grasp?
[Could *del.*] Dare its deadly terrors [clasp *del.*] [grasp *del.*] clasp?

6 Tyger, Tyger, burning bright
In the forests of the night,
What Immortal hand [or *del.*] & eye
Dare [form *del.*] frame thy fearful symmetry?

5 3 And [did he laugh *del.*] dare he [smile *del.*] [laugh *del.*] his work
to see?
[What the (shoulder *del.*) ankle? What the knee? *del.*]
4 [Did *del.*] Dare he who made the lamb make thee?
1 When the stars threw down their spears
2 And water'd heaven with their tears

P. 108, reversed.

26

Second draft of the same

Tyger, Tyger, burning bright
In the forests of the night,
What Immortal hand [or *del.*] & eye
Dare frame thy fearful symmetry?

Burnt in distant deeps or skies
The cruel fire of thine eyes?
Could heart descend or wings aspire?
What the hand dare sieze the fire?

And what shoulder & what art
Could twist the sinews of thy heart?
And when thy heart began to beat
What dread hand? & what dread feet?

When the stars threw down their spears,
And water'd heaven with their tears,
Did he smile his work to see?
Did he who made the lamb make thee?

Tyger, Tyger, burning bright
In the forests of the night,
What immortal hand & eye
Dare frame thy fearful symmetry?

P. 107, reversed.

27

[How came pride in Man
From Mary it began
How Contempt & Scorn

What a world is Man
His Earth . . . *del.*]

P. 107, reversed.

28

The human Image

First draft of "The Human Abstract" in Songs of Experience; *see p.* 217

Pity [*written over* Mercy] could be no more,
[If there was nobody poor *del.*]
If we did not make somebody poor;
And Mercy no more could be,
If all were as happy as we.

And mutual fear brings Peace,
Till the selfish Loves increase;
Then Cruelty knits a snare,
And spreads his [nets *del.*] baits with care.

He sits down with holy fears
And waters the ground with tears;
Then humility takes its root
Underneath his foot.

Soon spreads the dismal shade
Of Mystery over his head;
And the catterpiller & fly
Feed on the Mystery.

And it bears the fruit of deceit,
Ruddy & sweet to eat;
And the raven his nest has made
In its thickest shade.

The Gods of the Earth & Sea
Sought thro' nature to find this tree;
But their search was all in vain:
[Till they sought in the human brain. *del.*]
There grows one in the human brain.

They said this mystery never shall cease;
The priest [loves *del.*] promotes war & the soldier peace.

There souls of men are bought & sold,
And [cradled *del.*] milk fed infancy [is sold *del.*] for gold;
And youths to slaughter houses led,
And [maidens *del.*] beauty for a bit of bread.

P. 107–106, reversed.

29

[How to know Love from Deceit *del.*]

Love to faults is always blind,
Always is to joy inclin'd,
[Always *del.*] Lawless, wing'd, & unconfin'd,
And breaks all chains from every mind.

Deceit to secresy [inclin'd *del.*] confin'd,
[Modest, prudish, & confin'd *del.*]
Lawful, cautious, [*word del.*] & refin'd;
[Never is to *del.*] To every thing but interest blind
[And chains in fetters every mind *del.*]
And forges fetters for the mind.

P. 107, reversed.

30

The wild flower's song

As I wander'd the forest,
The green leaves among,
I heard a wild [thistle *del.*] flower
Singing a song:

"I slept in the [dark *del.*] earth, &c."

See no. 20, *page* 170.

P. 107, reversed.

31

The sick rose

First draft of the poem with the same title in Songs of Experience; *see p.* 213

O Rose, thou art sick;
The invisible worm,
That flies in the night,
In the howling storm,

Hath found out thy bed
Of crimson joy;
[O, dark secret love
Doth life destroy. *del.*]
And [his *del.*] her dark secret love
Does thy life destroy.

P. 107, reversed.

32

Soft Snow

I walked abroad in a snowy day:
I ask'd the soft snow with me to play:
She play'd & she melted in all her prime,
[Ah, that sweet love should be thought a crime! *del.*]
And the winter call'd it a dreadful crime.

P. 107, reversed.

33

An ancient Proverb

Remove away that black'ning church:
Remove away that marriage hearse:
Remove away that [place *del.*] man of blood:
['Twill *del.*] You'll quite remove the ancient curse.

P. 106, reversed.

34

To my Mirtle

5 Why should I be bound to thee,
6 O, my lovely mirtle tree?
[Love, free love, cannot be bound
To any tree that grows on ground. *del.*]
1 To a lovely mirtle bound,
2 Blossoms show'ring all around,
[Like to dung upon the ground,
Underneath my mirtle bound. *del.*]
3 O, how sick & weary I
4 Underneath my mirtle lie.

Copied from no. 18, p. 169

P. 106, reversed.

35

First draft of "A Little Boy Lost" in Songs of Experience; *see p.* 218

"Nought loves another as itself,
"Nor venerates another so,
"Nor is it possible to Thought
"A greater than itself to know:

"[Then *del.*] And father [I cannot *del.*] how
can I love you
"[Nor *del.*] Or any of my brothers more?
"I love [myself, so does the bird *del.*]
you like the little bird
"That picks up crumbs around the door."

The Priest sat by and heard the child.
In trembling zeal he siez'd his hair:
[The mother follow'd, weeping loud:
"O, that I such a fiend should bear." *del.*]
[Then *del.*] He led him by his little coat
[To show his zealous, priestly care. *del.*]
And all admir'd his priestly care.

And standing on the altar high:
"Lo, what a fiend is here," said he,
"One who sets reason up for judge
"Of our most holy mystery."

The weeping child could not be heard;
The weeping parents wept in vain.
[They bound his little ivory limbs
In a cruel Iron chain. *del.*]
[And *del.*] They strip'd him to his little shirt
& bound him in an iron chain.

[They *del.*] And burn'd him in a holy [fire *del.*] place,
Where many had been burn'd before.
The weeping parents wept in vain.
Are Such things [are *del.*] done on Albion's shore?

P. 106, reversed.

36

Merlin's prophecy

The harvest shall flourish in wintry weather
When two virginities meet together:

The King & the Priest must be tied in a tether
Before two virgins can meet together.

P. 105, reversed.

37

Day

The [day *del.*] Sun arises in the East,
Cloth'd in robes of blood & gold;
Swords & spears & wrath increast
All around his [ancles *del.*] bosom roll'd,
Crown'd with warlike fires & raging desires.

P. 105, reversed.

38

[The Marriage Ring *del.*] The Fairy

"Come hither my sparrows,
"My little arrows.
"If a tear or a smile
"Will a man beguile,
"If an amorous delay
"Clouds a sunshiny day,
"If the [tread *del.*] step of a foot
"Smites the heart to its root,
" 'Tis the marriage ring
"Makes each fairy a king."

So a fairy sung.
From the leaves I sprung.
He leap'd from the spray
To flee away.
But in my hat caught
He soon shall be taught.
Let him laugh, let him cry,
He's my butterfly;
For I've pull'd out the sting
[And *del.*] Of the marriage ring
[(Is a foolish thing *del.*) Is a childs play thing *del.*]

P. 105, reversed.

39

The sword sung on the barren heath,
The sickle in the fruitful field:
The sword he sung a song of death,
But could not make the sickle yield.

P. 105, reversed.

40

Abstinence sows sand all over
The ruddy limbs & flaming hair,
But Desire Gratified
Plants fruits of life & beauty there.

P. 105, reversed.

41

In a wife I would desire
What in whores is always found—
The lineaments of Gratified desire.

P. 105, reversed.

42

If you [catch *del.*] trap the moment before it's ripe,
The tears of repentance you'll certainly wipe;
But if once you let the ripe moment go
You ['ll *del.*] can never wipe off the tears of woe.

P. 105, reversed.

43

Eternity

He who binds to himself [to *del.*] a joy
Does the winged life destroy;
But he who [just *del.*] kisses the joy as it flies
Lives in [an eternal *del.*] eternity's sun rise.

P. 105, reversed.

44

The Kid

Thou, little Kid, didst play
&c.

Not found elsewhere.

P. 105, reversed.

45

The little [A pretty *del.*] Vagabond

First draft of the poem with the same title in Songs of Experience; *see p.* 216

Dear Mother, Dear Mother, the church is cold
But the alehouse is healthy & pleasant & warm;
Besides I can tell where I am us'd well.
[Such usage in heaven makes all go to hell. *del.*]
The poor parsons with wind like a blown bladder swell.

But if at the Church they would give us some Ale,
And a pleasant fire our souls to regale,
We'd sing and we'd pray all the livelong day,
Nor ever once wish from the Church to stray.

Then the parson might preach, & drink, & sing,
And we'd be as happy as birds in the spring;
And Modest dame Lurch, who is always at Church,
Would not have bandy children, nor fasting, nor birch.

Then God, like a father, [that joys for *del.*] rejoicing to see
His children as pleasant & happy as he,
Would have no more quarrel with the devil or the Barrel,
[But shake hands & kiss him & there'd be no more hell. *del.*]
But kiss him & give him both [food *del.*] drink & apparel.

P. 103, reversed.

46

The Question Answer'd

What is it men [of *del.*] in women do require?
The lineaments of Gratified Desire.
What is it women do [of *del.*] in men require?
The lineaments of Gratified Desire.

P. 106 & 103, reversed.

47

The Chimney Sweeper

First draft of the poem with the same title in Songs of Experience; *see p.* 212

A little black thing among the snow
Crying "'weep! 'weep!" in notes of woe.
"Where are thy father & mother, say?"
"They are both gone up to Church to pray.

"Because I was happy upon the heath,
"And smil'd among the winter's [wind *del.*] snow,
"They clothed me in the clothes of death
"And taught me to sing the notes of woe.

"And because I am happy & dance & sing,
"They think they have done me no injury,
"And are gone to praise God & his Priest & King,
"[Who wrap themselves up in our misery. *del.*]
"Who make up a heaven of our misery."

P. 103, reversed.

48

Lacedemonian Instruction

"Come hither, my boy, tell me what thou seest there."
"A fool tangled in a religious snare."

P. 103, reversed.

49

Riches

The [*word del.*] countless gold of a merry heart,
The rubies & pearls of a loving eye,
The [idle man *del.*] indolent never can bring to the mart,
Nor the [cunning *del.*] secret hoard up in his treasury.

P. 103, reversed.

50

An answer to the parson

"Why of the sheep do you not learn peace?"
"Because I don't want you to shear my fleece."

P. 103, reversed.

51

Holy Thursday

First draft of the poem with the same title in Songs of Experience; *see p.* 211

Is this a holy thing to see
In a rich & fruitful land,
Babes reduced to misery,
Fed with cold & usurous hand?

Is that trembling cry a song?
Can it be a song of joy?
And so great a number poor?
'Tis a land of poverty.

And their sun does never shine,
And their fields are bleak & bare,
And their ways are fill'd with thorns.
'Tis eternal winter there.

But where'er the sun does shine,
And where'er the rain does fall,
Babe can never hunger there,
Nor poverty the mind appall.

P. 103, reversed.

52

The Angel

First draft of "The Angel" in Songs of Experience; *see p.* 213

I dreamt a dream! what can it mean?
And that I was a maiden queen
Guarded by an angel mild.
Witless woe was ne'er beguil'd!

And I wept both night & day,
And he wiped my tears away,
And I wept both day & night,
And hid from him my heart's delight.

So he took his wings & fled;
Then the morn blush'd rosy red;
I dried my tears & arm'd my fears
With ten thousand shields & spears.

Soon my angel came again.
I was arm'd, he came in vain,
[But *del.*] For the time of youth was fled,
And grey hairs were on my head.

P. 103, reversed.

53

The look of love alarms,
Because 'tis fill'd with fire;
But the look of soft deceit
Shall win the lover's hire.

P. 103, reversed.

54

[Which are beauties sweetest dress? *del.*]
Soft deceit & idleness,
These are beauties sweetest dress.

P. 101, reversed.

55

First draft of "The Fly" in Songs of Experience; *see p.* 213

[Woe, alas! my guilty hand
Brush'd across thy summer joy;
All thy gilded, painted pride
Shatter'd, fled . . . *del.*]

1 Little fly,
Thy summer play
My [guilty hand *del.*] thoughtless hand
Hath brush'd away.

[The cut worm
Forgives the plow,
And dies in peace,
And so do thou. *del.*]

2 Am not I
A fly like thee?
Or art not thou
A man like me?

3 For I dance,
And drink, & sing,
Till some blind hand
Shall brush my wing.

5 Then am I
A happy fly,
If I live,
Or if I die.

[4 Thought is life
And strength & breath;
But the want (of *del.*)
Of Thought is death. *del.*]

4 If thought is life
And strength & breath
And the want [of *del.*]
Of Thought is death;

P. 101, reversed.

56

Motto to the Songs of Innocence & of Experience

The Good are attracted by Men's perceptions,
And Think not for themselves;
Till Experience teaches them to catch
And to cage the Fairies & Elves.

And then the Knave begins to snarl
And the Hypocrite to howl;
And all his good Friends shew their private ends,
And the Eagle is known from the Owl.

P. 100, reversed.

57

Her whole Life is an Epigram, smack, smooth, & neatly pen'd,
Platted quite neat to catch applause with a sliding noose at the end.

P. 100, reversed.

58

2 O, I cannot, cannot find
The undaunted courage of a Virgin Mind,
For Early I in love was crost,
Before my flower of love was lost.

1 An old maid early—e'er I knew
Ought but the love that on me grew;
And now I'm cover'd o'er & o'er
And wish that I had been a Whore.

P. 99, reversed.

59

Several Questions Answered

Copies of nos. 46, 53, 54, 43 and 33

4 What is it men in women do require?
The lineaments of Gratified Desire.
What is it women do in men require?
The lineaments of Gratified Desire.

2 The look of love alarms
Because 'tis fill'd with fire;
But the look of soft deceit
Shall Win the lover's hire.

3 Soft deceit & Idleness,
These are Beauty's sweetest dress.

1 He who binds to himself a joy
Doth the winged life destroy;
But he who kisses the joy as it flies
Lives in Eternity's sun rise.

5 An ancient Proverb:
Remove away that black'ning church,
Remove away that marriage hearse,
Remove away that — of blood,
You'll quite remove the ancient curse.

P. 99–98, reversed

60

1 1 "Let the Brothels of Paris be opened
2 "With many an alluring dance,
3 "To awake the [Pestilence *del.*] Physicians thro' the city,"
4 Said the beautiful Queen of France.

4 9 The King awoke on his couch of gold,
10 As soon as he heard these tidings told:
11 "Arise & come, both fife & drum,
12 "And the [Famine *del.*] shall eat both crust & crumb."

[2 Then old Nobodaddy aloft
Farted & belch'd & cough'd,
7 And said, "I love hanging & drawing & quartering
8 "Every bit as well as war & slaughtering.
"(Damn praying & singing,
"Unless they will bring in
"The blood of ten thousand by fighting or swinging." *del.*)

3 5 Then he swore a great & solemn Oath:
6 "To kill the people I am loth,
"But If they rebel, they must go to hell:
"They shall have a Priest & a passing bell." *del.*]

The Queen of France just touched this Globe,
And the Pestilence darted from her robe;
[But the bloodthirsty people across the water
Will not submit to the gibbet & halter. *del.*]
But our good Queen quite grows to the ground,
[There is just such a tree at Java found. *del.*]
And a great many suckers grow all around.

[Fayette beside King Lewis stood:
He saw him sign his hand;
And soon he saw the famine rage
About the fruitful land. *del.*]
[Fayette beheld the Queen to smile
And wink her lovely eye;
And soon he saw the pestilence
From street to street to fly. *del.*]

Fayette beheld the King & Queen
In tears & iron bound;
But mute Fayette wept tear for tear,
And guarded them around.

[Fayette, Fayette, thou'rt bought & sold,
For well I see thy tears
Of Pity are exchanged for those
Of selfish slavish fears. *del.*]

[Fayette beside his banner stood,
His captains false around
Thou'rt bought & sold . . . *del.*]

3 Who will exchange his own fire side
For the steps of another's door?
Who will exchange his wheaten loaf
For the links of a dungeon floor?

[Who will exchange his own heart's blood
For the drops of a harlot's eye? *del.*]

[2 Will the mother exchange her new born babe
For the dog at the wintry door?
Yet thou dost exchange thy pitying tears
For the links of a dungeon floor. *del.*]

[1 Fayette, Fayette, thou'rt bought & sold,
And sold is thy happy morrow;
Thou gavest the tears of Pity away
In exchange for the tears of sorrow. *del.*]

2 Fayette beheld the King & Queen
In [tears *del.*] curses & iron bound;
But mute Fayette wept tear for tear,
And guarded them around.

1 Who will exchange his own fire side
For the [steps *del.*] stone of another's door?
Who will exchange his wheaten loaf
For the links of a dungeon floor?

3 O, who would smile on the wintry seas,
[Or *del.*] & Pity the stormy roar?
Or who will exchange his new born child
For the dog at the wintry door?

P. 5.

61

When Klopstock England defied,
Uprose terrible Blake in his pride;
For old Nobodaddy aloft
Farted & Belch'd & cough'd;

Then swore a great oath that made heaven quake,
And call'd aloud to English Blake.
Blake was giving his body ease
At Lambeth beneath the poplar trees.
From his seat then started he,
And turned himself round three times three.
The Moon at that sight blush'd scarlet red,
The stars threw down their cups & fled,
And all the devils that were in hell
Answered with a ninefold yell.
Klopstock felt the [ninefold *del.*] intripled turn,
And all his bowels began to [burn *del.*] churn,
[And they *del.*] And his bowels turned round three times three,
And lock'd in his soul with a ninefold key,
That from his body it ne'er could be parted
Till to the last trumpet it was farted.
Then again old Nobodaddy swore
He ne'er had seen such a thing before,
Since Noah was shut in the ark,
Since Eve first chose her hellfire spark,
Since 'twas the fashion to go naked,
Since the old anything was created,
And so feeling, he beg'd him to turn again
And ease poor Klopstock's ninefold pain.

[*four lines illegible*]

If Blake could do this when he [sat down to *del.*] rose up from shite,
What might he not do if he sat down to write?

P. 10.

62

I say I shan't live five years, And if I live one it will be a Wonder.

June 1793

P. 39.

63

The Hebrew Nation did not write it.
Avarice & Chastity did shite it.

[END OF NOTE-BOOK 1793]

[FRAGMENT]

Written about 1793

A fairy [leapt *del.*] skipt upon my knee
Singing & dancing merrily;
I said, "Thou thing of patches, rings,
"Pins, Necklaces, & such like things,
"Disguiser of the Female Form,
"Thou paltry, gilded, poisnous worm!"
Weeping, he fell upon my thigh,
And thus in tears did soft reply:
"Knowest thou not, O Fairies' Lord!
"How much by us Contemn'd, Abhorr'd,
"Whatever hides the Female form
"That cannot bear the Mental storm?
"Therefore in Pity still we give
"Our lives to make the Female live;
"And what would turn into disease
"We turn to what will joy & please."

VISIONS of the Daughters of Albion

The Eye sees more than the Heart knows

Printed by Willm Blake: 1793

Plate iii

The Argument

I loved Theotormon,
And I was not ashamed;
I trembled in my virgin fears,
And I hid in Leutha's vale!

I plucked Leutha's flower,
And I rose up from the vale;
But the terrible thunders tore
My virgin mantle in twain.

Plate 1

Visions

Enslav'd, the Daughters of Albion weep; a trembling lamentation
Upon their mountains; in their valleys, sighs toward America.

For the soft soul of America, Oothoon, wander'd in woe,
Along the vales of Leutha seeking flowers to comfort her;
And thus she spoke to the bright Marygold of Leutha's vale:

"Art thou a flower? art thou a nymph? I see thee now a flower,
"Now a nymph! I dare not pluck thee from thy dewy bed!"

The Golden nymph replied: "Pluck thou my flower, Oothoon the mild!
"Another flower shall spring, because the soul of sweet delight
"Can never pass away." She ceas'd, & clos'd her golden shrine.
Then Oothoon pluck'd the flower, saying: "I pluck thee from thy bed,
"Sweet flower, and put thee here to glow between my breasts,
"And thus I turn my face to where my whole soul seeks."

Over the waves she went in wing'd exulting swift delight,
And over Theotormon's reign took her impetuous course.

Bromion rent her with his thunders; on his stormy bed
Lay the faint maid, and soon her woes appall'd his thunders hoarse.

Bromion spoke: "Behold this harlot here on Bromion's bed,
"And let the jealous dolphins sport around the lovely maid!
"Thy soft American plains are mine, and mine thy north & south:
"Stampt with my signet are the swarthy children of the sun;
"They are obedient, they resist not, they obey the scourge;
"Their daughters worship terrors and obey the violent.

Plate 2

"Now thou maist marry Bromion's harlot, and protect the child
"Of Bromion's rage, that Oothoon shall put forth in nine moons' time."

Then storms rent Theotormon's limbs: he roll'd his waves around
And folded his black jealous waters round the adulterate pair.
Bound back to back in Bromion's caves, terror & meekness dwell:

At entrance Theotormon sits, wearing the threshold hard
With secret tears; beneath him sound like waves on a desart shore
The voice of slaves beneath the sun, and children bought with money,
That shiver in religious caves beneath the burning fires
Of lust, that belch incessant from the summits of the earth.

Oothoon weeps not; she cannot weep! her tears are locked up;
But she can howl incessant writhing her soft snowy limbs,
And calling Theotormon's Eagles to prey upon her flesh.

"I call with holy voice! Kings of the sounding air,
"Rend away this defiled bosom that I may reflect
"The image of Theotormon on my pure transparent breast."

The Eagles at her call descend & rend their bleeding prey:
Theotormon severely smiles; her soul reflects the smile,
As the clear spring, mudded with feet of beasts, grows pure & smiles.

The Daughters of Albion hear her woes, & eccho back her sighs.

"Why does my Theotormon sit weeping upon the threshold,
"And Oothoon hovers by his side, perswading him in vain?
"I cry: arise, O Theotormon! for the village dog
"Barks at the breaking day; the nightingale has done lamenting;
"The lark does rustle in the ripe corn, and the Eagle returns
"From nightly prey and lifts his golden beak to the pure east,
"Shaking the dust from his immortal pinions to awake

"The sun that sleeps too long. Arise, my Theotormon, I am pure,
"Because the night is gone that clos'd me in its deadly black.
"They told me that the night & day were all that I could see;
"They told me that I had five senses to inclose me up,
"And they inclos'd my infinite brain into a narrow circle,
"And sunk my heart into the Abyss, a red, round globe, hot burning,
"Till all from life I was obliterated and erased.
"Instead of morn arises a bright shadow, like an eye
"In the eastern cloud; instead of night a sickly charnel house:
"That Theotormon hears me not! to him the night and morn
"Are both alike; a night of sighs, a morning of fresh tears,

Plate 3

"And none but Bromion can hear my lamentations.

"With what sense is it that the chicken shuns the ravenous hawk?
"With what sense does the tame pigeon measure out the expanse?
"With what sense does the bee form cells? have not the mouse & frog
"Eyes and ears and sense of touch? yet are their habitations
"And their pursuits as different as their forms and as their joys.
"Ask the wild ass why he refuses burdens, and the meek camel
"Why he loves man: is it because of eye, ear, mouth, or skin,
"Or breathing nostrils? No, for these the wolf and tyger have.
"Ask the blind worm the secrets of the grave, and why her spires
"Love to curl round the bones of death; and ask the rav'nous snake
"Where she gets poison, & the wing'd eagle why he loves the sun;
"And then tell me the thoughts of man, that have been hid of old.

"Silent I hover all the night, and all day could be silent
"If Theotormon once would turn his loved eyes upon me.
"How can I be defil'd when I reflect thy image pure?
"Sweetest the fruit that the worm feeds on, & the soul prey'd on by woe,
"The new wash'd lamb ting'd with the village smoke, & the bright swan
"By the red earth of our immortal river. I bathe my wings,
"And I am white and pure to hover round Theotormon's breast."

Then Theotormon broke his silence, and he answered:—

"Tell me what is the night or day to one o'erflow'd with woe?
"Tell me what is a thought, & of what substance is it made?
"Tell me what is a joy, & in what gardens do joys grow?
"And in what rivers swim the sorrows? and upon what mountains

Plate 4

"Wave shadows of discontent? and in what houses dwell the wretched,
"Drunken with woe forgotten, and shut up from cold despair?

"Tell me where dwell the thoughts forgotten till thou call them forth?
"Tell me where dwell the joys of old? & where the ancient loves,
"And when will they renew again, & the night of oblivion past,
"That I might traverse times & spaces far remote, and bring
"Comforts into a present sorrow and a night of pain?
"Where goest thou, O thought? to what remote land is thy flight?
"If thou returnest to the present moment of affliction
"Wilt thou bring comforts on thy wings, and dews and honey and balm,
"Or poison from the desart wilds, from the eyes of the envier?"

Then Bromion said, and shook the cavern with his lamentation:

"Thou knowest that the ancient trees seen by thine eyes have fruit,
"But knowest thou that trees and fruits flourish upon the earth
"To gratify senses unknown? trees, beasts and birds unknown;
"Unknown, not unperciev'd, spread in the infinite microscope,
"In places yet unvisited by the voyager, and in worlds
"Over another kind of seas, and in atmospheres unknown:
"Ah! are there other wars beside the wars of sword and fire?
"And are there other sorrows beside the sorrows of poverty?
"And are there other joys beside the joys of riches and ease?
"And is there not one law for both the lion and the ox?
"And is there not eternal fire and eternal chains
"To bind the phantoms of existence from eternal life?"

Then Oothoon waited silent all the day and all the night;

Plate 5

But when the morn arose, her lamentation renew'd.
The Daughters of Albion hear her woes, & eccho back her sighs.

"O Urizen! Creator of men! mistaken Demon of heaven!
"Thy joys are tears, thy labour vain to form men to thine image.
"How can one joy absorb another? are not different joys
"Holy, eternal, infinite? and each joy is a Love.

"Does not the great mouth laugh at a gift, & the narrow eyelids mock
"At the labour that is above payment? and wilt thou take the ape
"For thy councellor, or the dog for a schoolmaster to thy children?
"Does he who contemns poverty and he who turns with abhorrence

"From usury feel the same passion, or are they moved alike?
"How can the giver of gifts experience the delights of the merchant?
"How the industrious citizen the pains of the husbandman?
"How different far the fat fed hireling with hollow drum,
"Who buys whole corn fields into wastes, and sings upon the heath!
"How different their eye and ear! how different the world to them!
"With what sense does the parson claim the labour of the farmer?
"What are his nets & gins & traps; & how does he surround him
"With cold floods of abstraction, and with forests of solitude,
"To build him castles and high spires, where kings & priests may dwell;
"Till she who burns with youth, and knows no fixed lot, is bound
"In spells of law to one she loathes? and must she drag the chain
"Of life in weary lust? must chilling, murderous thoughts obscure
"The clear heaven of her eternal spring; to bear the wintry rage
"Of a harsh terror, driv'n to madness, bound to hold a rod
"Over her shrinking shoulders all the day, & all the night
"To turn the wheel of false desire, and longings that wake her womb
"To the abhorred birth of cherubs in the human form,
"That live a pestilence & die a meteor, & are no more;
"Till the child dwell with one he hates, and do the deed he loaths,
"And the impure scourge force his seed into its unripe birth
"Ere yet his eyelids can behold the arrows of the day?

"Does the whale worship at thy footsteps as the hungry dog;
"Or does he scent the mountain prey because his nostrils wide
"Draw in the ocean? does his eye discern the flying cloud
"As the raven's eye? or does he measure the expanse like the vulture?
"Does the still spider view the cliffs where eagles hide their young;
"Or does the fly rejoice because the harvest is brought in?
"Does not the eagle scorn the earth & despise the treasures beneath?
"But the mole knoweth what is there, & the worm shall tell it thee.
"Does not the worm erect a pillar in the mouldering church yard

Plate 6

"And a palace of eternity in the jaws of the hungry grave?
"Over his porch these words are written: 'Take thy bliss, O Man!
" 'And sweet shall be thy taste, & sweet thy infant joys renew!'

"Infancy! fearless, lustful, happy, nestling for delight
"In laps of pleasure: Innocence! honest, open, seeking
"The vigorous joys of morning light; open to virgin bliss.
"Who taught thee modesty, subtil modesty, child of night & sleep?
"When thou awakest wilt thou dissemble all thy secret joys,
"Or wert thou not awake when all this mystery was disclos'd?

"Then com'st thou forth a modest virgin, knowing to dissemble,
"With nets found under thy night pillow, to catch virgin joy
"And brand it with the name of whore, & sell it in the night,
"In silence, ev'n without a whisper, and in seeming sleep.
"Religious dreams and holy vespers light thy smoky fires:
"Once were thy fires lighted by the eyes of honest morn.
"And does my Theotormon seek this hypocrite modesty,
"This knowing, artful, secret, fearful, cautious, trembling hypocrite?
"Then is Oothoon a whore indeed! and all the virgin joys
"Of life are harlots, and Theotormon is a sick man's dream;
"And Oothoon is the crafty slave of selfish holiness.

"But Oothoon is not so: a virgin fill'd with virgin fancies,
"Open to joy and to delight where ever beauty appears;
"If in the morning sun I find it, there my eyes are fix'd

Plate 7

"In happy copulation; if in evening mild, wearied with work,
"Sit on a bank and draw the pleasures of this free born joy.

"The moment of desire! the moment of desire! The virgin
"That pines for man shall awaken her womb to enormous joys
"In the secret shadows of her chamber: the youth shut up from
"The lustful joy shall forget to generate & create an amorous image
"In the shadows of his curtains and in the folds of his silent pillow.
"Are not these the places of religion, the rewards of continence,
"The self enjoyings of self denial? why dost thou seek religion?
"Is it because acts are not lovely that thou seekest solitude
"Where the horrible darkness is impressed with reflections of desire?

"Father of Jealousy, be thou accursed from the earth!
"Why hast thou taught my Theotormon this accursed thing?
"Till beauty fades from off my shoulders, darken'd and cast out,
"A solitary shadow wailing on the margin of non-entity.

"I cry: Love! Love! Love! happy happy Love! free as the mountain wind!
"Can that be Love that drinks another as a sponge drinks water,
"That clouds with jealousy his nights, with weepings all the day,
"To spin a web of age around him, grey and hoary, dark,
"Till his eyes sicken at the fruit that hangs before his sight?
"Such is self-love that envies all, a creeping skeleton
"With lamplike eyes watching around the frozen marriage bed.

"But silken nets and traps of adamant will Oothoon spread,
"And catch for thee girls of mild silver, or of furious gold.

"I'll lie beside thee on a bank & view their wanton play
"In lovely copulation, bliss on bliss, with Theotormon:
"Red as the rosy morning, lustful as the first born beam,
"Oothoon shall view his dear delight, nor e'er with jealous cloud
"Come in the heaven of generous love, nor selfish blightings bring.

"Does the sun walk in glorious raiment on the secret floor

Plate 8

"Where the cold miser spreads his gold; or does the bright cloud drop
"On his stone threshold? does his eye behold the beam that brings
"Expansion to the eye of pity? or will he bind himself
"Beside the ox to thy hard furrow? does not that mild beam blot
"The bat, the owl, the glowing tyger, and the king of night?
"The sea fowl takes the wintry blast for a cov'ring to her limbs,
"And the wild snake the pestilence to adorn him with gems & gold;
"And trees & birds & beasts & men behold their eternal joy.
"Arise, you little glancing wings, and sing your infant joy!
"Arise, and drink your bliss, for every thing that lives is holy!"

Thus every morning wails Oothoon; but Theotormon sits
Upon the margin'd ocean conversing with shadows dire.

The Daughters of Albion hear her woes, & eccho back her sighs.

The End

AMERICA

a PROPHECY

LAMBETH Printed by William Blake in the year 1793

Plate 1

Preludium

The shadowy Daughter of Urthona stood before red Orc,
When fourteen suns had faintly journey'd o'er his dark abode:
His food she brought in iron baskets, his drink in cups of iron:
Crown'd with a helmet & dark hair the nameless female stood;

A quiver with its burning stores, a bow like that of night,
When pestilence is shot from heaven: no other arms she need!
Invulnerable tho' naked, save where clouds roll round her loins
Their awful folds in the dark air: silent she stood as night;
For never from her iron tongue could voice or sound arise,
But dumb till that dread day when Orc assay'd his fierce embrace.

"Dark Virgin," said the hairy youth, "thy father stern, abhorr'd,
"Rivets my tenfold chains while still on high my spirit soars;
"Sometimes an eagle screaming in the sky, sometimes a lion
"Stalking upon the mountains, & sometimes a whale, I lash
"The raging fathomless abyss; anon a serpent folding
"Around the pillars of Urthona, and round thy dark limbs
"On the Canadian wilds I fold; feeble my spirit folds,
"For chain'd beneath I rend these caverns: when thou bringest food
"I howl my joy, and my red eyes seek to behold thy face—
"In vain! these clouds roll to & fro, & hide thee from my sight."

Plate 2

Silent as despairing love, and strong as jealousy,
The hairy shoulders rend the links; free are the wrists of fire;
Round the terrific loins he siez'd the panting, struggling womb;
It joy'd: she put aside her clouds & smiled her first-born smile,
As when a black cloud shews its lightnings to the silent deep.

Soon as she saw the terrible boy, then burst the virgin cry:

"I know thee, I have found thee, & I will not let thee go:
"Thou art the image of God who dwells in darkness of Africa,
"And thou art fall'n to give me life in regions of dark death.
"On my American plains I feel the struggling afflictions
"Endur'd by roots that writhe their arms into the nether deep.
"I see a Serpent in Canada who courts me to his love,
"In Mexico an Eagle, and a Lion in Peru;
"I see a Whale in the South-sea, drinking my soul away.
"O what limb rending pains I feel! thy fire & my frost
"Mingle in howling pains, in furrows by thy lightnings rent.
"This is eternal death, and this the torment long foretold."

The stern Bard ceas'd, asham'd of his own song; enrag'd he swung
His harp alóft sounding, then dash'd its shining frame against
A ruin'd pillar in glitt'ring fragments; silent he turn'd away,
And wander'd down the vales of Kent in sick & drear lamentings.[1]

[1] These four lines are omitted from most copies of the book.

Plate 3

A PROPHECY

The Guardian Prince of Albion burns in his nightly tent:
Sullen fires across the Atlantic glow to America's shore,
Piercing the souls of warlike men who rise in silent night.
Washington, Franklin, Paine & Warren, Gates, Hancock & Green
Meet on the coast glowing with blood from Albion's fiery Prince.

Washington spoke: "Friends of America! look over the Atlantic sea;
"A bended bow is lifted in heaven, & a heavy iron chain
"Descends, link by link, from Albion's cliffs across the sea, to bind
"Brothers & sons of America till our faces pale and yellow,
"Heads deprest, voices weak, eyes downcast, hands work-bruis'd,
"Feet bleeding on the sultry sands, and the furrows of the whip
"Descend to generations that in future times forget."

The strong voice ceas'd, for a terrible blast swept over the heaving sea:
The eastern cloud rent: on his cliffs stood Albion's wrathful Prince,
A dragon form, clashing his scales: at midnight he arose,
And flam'd red meteors round the land of Albion beneath;
His voice, his locks, his awful shoulders, and his glowing eyes

Plate 4

Appear to the Americans upon the cloudy night.

Solemn heave the Atlantic waves between the gloomy nations,
Swelling, belching from its deeps red clouds & raging fires.
Albion is sick! America faints! enrag'd the Zenith grew.
As human blood shooting its veins all round the orbed heaven,
Red rose the clouds from the Atlantic in vast wheels of blood,
And in the red clouds rose a Wonder o'er the Atlantic sea,
Intense! naked! a Human fire, fierce glowing, as the wedge
Of iron heated in the furnace: his terrible limbs were fire
With myriads of cloudy terrors, banners dark & towers
Surrounded: heat but not light went thro' the murky atmosphere.

The King of England looking westward trembles at the vision.

Plate 5

Albion's Angel stood beside the Stone of night, and saw
The terror like a comet, or more like the planet red
That once enclos'd the terrible wandering comets in its sphere.
Then, Mars, thou wast our center, & the planets three flew round

Thy crimson disk: so e'er the Sun was rent from thy red sphere.
The Spectre glow'd, his horrid length staining the temple long
With beams of blood; & thus a voice came forth, and shook the
temple:

Plate 6

"The morning comes, the night decays, the watchmen leave their
stations;
"The grave is burst, the spices shed, the linen wrapped up;
"The bones of death, the cov'ring clay, the sinews shrunk & dry'd
"Reviving shake, inspiring move, breathing, awakening,
"Spring like redeemed captives when their bonds & bars are burst.
"Let the slave grinding at the mill run out into the field,
"Let him look up into the heavens & laugh in the bright air;
"Let the inchained soul, shut up in darkness and in sighing,
"Whose face has never seen a smile in thirty weary years,
"Rise and look out; his chains are loose, his dungeon doors are open;
"And let his wife and children return from the oppressor's scourge.

"They look behind at every step & believe it is a dream,
"Singing: 'The Sun has left his blackness & has found a fresher
morning,
" 'And the fair Moon rejoices in the clear & cloudless night;
" 'For Empire is no more, and now the Lion & Wolf shall cease.' "

Plate 7

In thunders ends the voice. Then Albion's Angel wrathful burnt
Beside the Stone of Night, and like the Eternal Lion's howl
In famine & war, reply'd: "Art thou not Orc, who serpent-form'd
"Stands at the gate of Enitharmon to devour her children?
"Blasphemous Demon, Antichrist, hater of Dignities,
"Lover of wild rebellion, and transgressor of God's Law,
"Why dost thou come to Angel's eyes in this terrific form?"

Plate 8

The Terror answer'd: "I am Orc, wreath'd round the accursed tree:
"The times are ended; shadows pass, the morning 'gins to break;
"The fiery joy, that Urizen perverted to ten commands,
"What night he led the starry hosts thro' the wide wilderness,
"That stony law I stamp to dust; and scatter religion abroad
"To the four winds as a torn book, & none shall gather the leaves;

"But they shall rot on desart sands, & consume in bottomless deeps,
"To make the desarts blossom, & the deeps shrink to their fountains,
"And to renew the fiery joy, and burst the stony roof;
"That pale religious le[t]chery, seeking Virginity,
"May find it in a harlot, and in coarse-clad honesty
"The undefil'd, tho' ravish'd in her cradle night and morn;
"For every thing that lives is holy, life delights in life;
"Because the soul of sweet delight can never be defil'd.
"Fires inwrap the earthly globe, yet man is not consum'd;
"Amidst the lustful fires he walks; his feet become like brass,
"His knees and thighs like silver, & his breast and head like gold."

Plate 9

"Sound! sound! my loud war-trumpets, & alarm my Thirteen Angels!
"Loud howls the eternal Wolf! the eternal Lion lashes his tail!
"America is darken'd; and my punishing Demons, terrified,
"Crouch howling before their caverns deep, like skins dry'd in the wind.
"They cannot smite the wheat, nor quench the fatness of the earth;
"They cannot smite with sorrows, nor subdue the plow and spade;
"They cannot wall the city, nor moat round the castle of princes;
"They cannot bring the stubbed oak to overgrow the hills;
"For terrible men stand on the shores, & in their robes I see
"Children take shelter from the lightnings: there stands Washington
"And Paine and Warren with their foreheads rear'd toward the east.
"But clouds obscure my aged sight. A vision from afar!
"Sound! Sound! my loud war-trumpets, & alarm my thirteen Angels!
"Ah vision from afar! Ah rebel form that rent the ancient
"Heavens! Eternal Viper, self-renew'd, rolling in clouds,
"I see thee in thick clouds and darkness on America's shore,
"Writhing in pangs of abhorred birth; red flames the crest rebellious
"And eyes of death; the harlot womb, oft opened in vain,
"Heaves in enormous circles: now the times are return'd upon thee,
"Devourer of thy parent, now thy unutterable torment renews.
"Sound! sound! my loud war trumpets, & alarm my thirteen Angels!
"Ah terrible birth! a young one bursting! where is the weeping mouth,
"And where the mother's milk? instead, those ever-hissing jaws
"And parched lips drop with fresh gore: now roll thou in the clouds;
"Thy mother lays her length outstretch'd upon the shore beneath.
"Sound! sound! my loud war-trumpets, & alarm my thirteen Angels!
"Loud howls the eternal Wolf! the eternal Lion lashes his tail!"

Plate 10

Thus wept the Angel voice, & as he wept, the terrible blasts
Of trumpets blew a loud alarm across the Atlantic deep.
No trumpets answer; no reply of clarions or of fifes:
Silent the Colonies remain and refuse the loud alarm.

On those vast shady hills between America & Albion's shore,
Now barr'd out by the Atlantic sea, call'd Atlantean hills,
Because from their bright summits you may pass to the Golden world,
An ancient palace, archetype of mighty Emperies,
Rears its immortal pinnacles, built in the forest of God
By Ariston, the king of beauty, for his stolen bride.

Here on their magic seats the thirteen Angels sat perturb'd,
For clouds from the Atlantic hover o'er the solemn roof.

Plate 11

Fiery the Angels rose, & as they rose deep thunder roll'd
Around their shores, indignant burning with the fires of Orc;
And Boston's Angel cried aloud as they flew thro' the dark night.

He cried: "Why trembles honesty, and like a murderer
"Why seeks he refuge from the frowns of his immortal station?
"Must the generous tremble & leave his joy to the idle, to the pestilence,
"That mock him? who commanded this? what God? what Angel?
"To keep the gen'rous from experience till the ungenerous
"Are unrestrain'd performers of the energies of nature;
"Till pity is become a trade, and generosity a science
"That men get rich by; & the sandy desart is giv'n to the strong?
"What God is he writes laws of peace & clothes him in a tempest?
"What pitying Angel lusts for tears and fans himself with sighs?
"What crawling villain preaches abstinence & wraps himself
"In fat of lambs? no more I follow, no more obedience pay!"

Plate 12

So cried he, rending off his robe & throwing down his scepter
In sight of Albion's Guardian; and all the thirteen Angels
Rent off their robes to the hungry wind, & threw their golden scepters
Down on the land of America; indignant they descended
Headlong from out their heav'nly heights, descending swift as fires
Over the land; naked & flaming are their lineaments seen
In the deep gloom; by Washington & Paine & Warren they stood;
And the flame folded, roaring fierce within the pitchy night

Before the Demon red, who burnt towards America,
In black smoke, thunders, and loud winds, rejoicing in its terror,
Breaking in smoky wreaths from the wild deep, & gath'ring thick
In flames as of a furnace on the land from North to South,

Plate 13

What time the thirteen Governors that England sent, convene
In Bernard's house; the flames cover'd the land, they rouze, they cry;
Shaking their mental chains, they rush in fury to the sea
To quench their anguish; at the feet of Washington down fall'n
They grovel on the sand and writhing lie, while all
The British soldiers thro' the thirteen states sent up a howl
Of anguish, threw their swords & muskets to the earth, & ran
From their encampments and dark castles, seeking where to hide
From the grim flames, and from the visions of Orc, in sight
Of Albion's Angel; who, enrag'd, his secret clouds open'd
From north to south and burnt outstretch'd on wings of wrath, cov'ring
The eastern sky, spreading his awful wings across the heavens.
Beneath him roll'd his num'rous hosts, all Albion's Angels camp'd
Darken'd the Atlantic mountains; & their trumpets shook the valleys,
Arm'd with diseases of the earth to cast upon the Abyss,
Their numbers forty millions, must'ring in the eastern sky.

Plate 14

In the flames stood & view'd the armies drawn out in the sky,
Washington, Franklin, Paine, & Warren, Allen, Gates, & Lee,
And heard the voice of Albion's Angel give the thunderous command;
His plagues, obedient to his voice, flew forth out of their clouds,
Falling upon America, as a storm to cut them off,
As a blight cuts the tender corn when it begins to appear.
Dark is the heaven above, & cold & hard the earth beneath:
And as a plague wind fill'd with insects cuts off man & beast,
And as a sea o'erwhelms a land in the day of an earthquake,
Fury! rage! madness! in a wind swept through America;
And the red flames of Orc, that folded roaring, fierce, around
The angry shores; and the fierce rushing of th' inhabitants together!
The citizens of New York close their books & lock their chests;
The mariners of Boston drop their anchors and unlade;
The scribe of Pensylvania casts his pen upon the earth;
The builder of Virginia throws his hammer down in fear.

Then had America been lost, o'erwhelm'd by the Atlantic,
And Earth had lost another portion of the infinite,
But all rush together in the night in wrath and raging fire.
The red fires rag'd! the plagues recoil'd! then roll'd they back with fury

Plate 15

On Albion's Angels: then the Pestilence began in streaks of red
Across the limbs of Albion's Guardian; the spotted plague smote Bristol's
And the Leprosy London's Spirit, sickening all their bands:
The millions sent up a howl of anguish and threw off their hammer'd mail,
And cast their swords & spears to earth, & stood, a naked multitude:
Albion's Guardian writhed in torment on the eastern sky,
Pale, quiv'ring toward the brain his glimmering eyes, teeth chattering,
Howling & shuddering, his legs quivering, convuls'd each muscle & sinew:
Sick'ning lay London's Guardian, and the ancient miterd York,
Their heads on snowy hills, their ensigns sick'ning in the sky.
The plagues creep on the burning winds driven by flames of Orc,
And by the fierce Americans rushing together in the night,
Driven o'er the Guardians of Ireland, and Scotland and Wales.
They, spotted with plagues, forsook the frontiers; & their banners, sear'd
With fires of hell, deform their ancient heavens with shame & woe.
Hid in his caves the Bard of Albion felt the enormous plagues,
And a cowl of flesh grew o'er his head, & scales on his back & ribs;
And, rough with black scales, all his Angels fright their ancient heavens.
The doors of marriage are open, and the Priests in rustling scales
Rush into reptile coverts, hiding from the fires of Orc,
That play around the golden roofs in wreaths of fierce desire,
Leaving the females naked and glowing with the lusts of youth.

For the female spirits of the dead, pining in bonds of religion,
Run from their fetters reddening, & in long drawn arches sitting,
They feel the nerves of youth renew, and desires of ancient times
Over their pale limbs, as a vine when the tender grape appears.

Plate 16

Over the hills, the vales, the cities, rage the red flames fierce:
The Heavens melted from north to south: and Urizen, who sat

Above all heavens, in thunders wrap'd, emerg'd his leprous head
From out his holy shrine, his tears in deluge piteous
Falling into the deep sublime; flag'd with grey-brow'd snows
And thunderous visages, his jealous wings wav'd over the deep;
Weeping in dismal howling woe, he dark descended, howling
Around the smitten bands, clothed in tears & trembling, shudd'ring cold.
His stored snows he poured forth, and his icy magazines
He open'd on the deep, and on the Atlantic sea white shiv'ring
Leprous his limbs, all over white, and hoary was his visage,
Weeping in dismal howlings before the stern Americans,
Hiding the Demon red with clouds & cold mists from the earth;
Till Angels & weak men twelve years should govern o'er the strong;
And then their end should come, when France reciev'd the Demon's light.

Stiff shudderings shook the heav'nly thrones! France, Spain, & Italy
In terror view'd the bands of Albion, and the ancient Guardians,
Fainting upon the elements, smitten with their own plagues.
They slow advance to shut the five gates of their law-built heaven,
Filled with blasting fancies and with mildews of despair,
With fierce disease and lust, unable to stem the fires of Orc.
But the five gates were consum'd, & their bolts and hinges melted;
And the fierce flames burnt round the heavens, & round the abodes of men.

FINIS

AMERICA

Cancelled plates etched about 1793

Plate a

A Prophecy

The Guardian Prince of Albion burns in his nightly tent:
Sullen fires across the Atlantic glow to America's shore,
Piercing the souls of warlike men who rise in silent night.
Washington, Hancock, Paine & Warren, Gates, Franklin & Green
Meet on the coast glowing with blood from Albion's fiery Prince.

Washington spoke: "Friends of America! look, over the Atlantic sea;
"A bended bow in heaven is lifted, & a heavy iron chain
"Descends, link by link, from Albion's cliffs across the sea, to bind
"Brothers & sons of America till our faces pale and yellow,
"Heads deprest, voices weak, eyes downcast, hands work-bruised,
"Feet bleeding on the sultry sands, & the furrows of the whip
"Descend to generations that in future times forget."

The strong voice ceas'd, for a terrible blast swept over the heaving sea:
The eastern cloud rent: on his cliffs stood Albions fiery Prince,
A dragon form, clashing his scales: at midnight he arose,
And flam'd fierce meteors round the land of Albion beneath;
His voice, his locks, his awful shoulders, & his glowing eyes

Plate b

Reveal the dragon thro' the human; coursing swift as fire
To the close hall of counsel, where his Angel form renews.
In a sweet vale shelter'd with cedars, that eternal stretch
Their unmov'd branches, stood the hall, built when the moon shot forth,
In that dread night when Urizen call'd the stars round his feet;
Then burst the center from its orb, and found a place beneath;
And Earth conglob'd, in narrow room, roll'd round its sulphur Sun.
To this deep valley situated by the flowing Thames,
Where George the third holds council & his Lords & Commons meet,
Shut out from mortal sight the Angel came; the vale was dark
With clouds of smoke from the Atlantic, that in volumes roll'd
Between the mountains; dismal visions mope around the house
On chairs of iron, canopied with mystic ornaments
Of life by magic power condens'd; infernal forms art-bound
The council sat; all rose before the aged apparition,
His snowy beard that streams like lambent flames down his wide breast
Wetting with tears, & his white garments cast a wintry light.
Then, as arm'd clouds arise terrific round the northern drum,
The world is silent at the flapping of the folding banners.
So still terrors rent the house, as when the solemn globe
Launch'd to the unknown shore, while Sotha held the northern helm,
Till to that void it came & fell; so the dark house was rent.
The valley mov'd beneath; its shining pillars split in twain,
And its roofs crack across down falling on th' Angelic seats.

Plate c[1]

[Then Albion's Angel *del.*] rose resolv'd to the cove of armoury:
His shield that bound twelve demons & their cities in its orb
He took down from its trembling pillar; from its cavern deep,
His helm was brought by London's Guardian, & his thirsty spear
By the wise spirit of London's river; silent stood the King breathing [with flames *del.*] [hoar frosts *del.*] damp mists,
And on his [shining *del.*] aged limbs they clasp'd the armour of terrible gold.
Infinite London's awful spires cast a dreadful [gleam *del.*] cold
Even [to *del.*] on rational things beneath and from the palace walls
Around Saint James's [glow the fires *del.*], chill & heavy, even to the city gate.
On the vast stone whose name is Truth he stood, his cloudy shield
Smote with his scepter, the scale bound orb loud howl'd; th' [eternal *del.*] pillar
Trembling sunk, an earthquake roll'd along the mossy pile.
In glitt'ring armour, swift as winds, intelligent as [flames *del.*] clouds
Four winged heralds mount the furious blasts & blow their trumps;
Gold, silver, brass & iron [ardors *del.*] clangors clamoring rend the shores.
Like white clouds rising from the deeps his fifty-two armies
From the four cliffs of Albion rise, [glowing *del.*] mustering around their Prince;
Angels of cities and of parishes and villages and families,
In armour as the nerves of wisdom, each his station [fires *del.*] holds.
In opposition dire, a warlike cloud, the myriads stood
In the red air before the Demon [seen even by mortal men,
Who call it Fancy, (& *del.*) or shut the gates of sense, (& *del.*) or in their chambers
Sleep like the dead. *del.*] But like a constellation ris'n and blazing
Over the rugged ocean, so the Angels of Albion hung
[Over the *del.*] A frowning shadow like [a *altered to*] an aged King in arms of gold,
Who wept over a den, in which his only son outstretch'd
By rebels' hands was slain; his white beard wav'd in the wild wind.

On mountains & cliffs of snow the awful apparition hover'd,
And like the voices of religious dead heard in the mountains
When holy zeal scents the sweet valleys of ripe virgin bliss,
Such was the hollow voice that o'er [the red Demon *del.*] America lamented.

---

[1] With alterations made in pencil.

[FRAGMENT]

probably intended for America

Etched about 1793

As when a dream of Thiralatha flies the midnight hour:
In vain the dreamer grasps the joyful images, they fly
Seen in obscured traces in the Vale of Leutha, So
The British Colonies beneath the woful Princes fade.

And so the Princes fade from earth, scarce seen by souls of men,
But tho' obscur'd, this is the form of the Angelic land.

PROSPECTUS

Etched 1793

TO THE PUBLIC *October* 10, 1793.

The Labours of the Artist, the Poet, the Musician, have been proverbially attended by poverty and obscurity; this was never the fault of the Public, but was owing to a neglect of means to propagate such works as have wholly absorbed the Man of Genius. Even Milton and Shakespeare could not publish their own works.

This difficulty has been obviated by the Author of the following productions now presented to the Public; who has invented a method of Printing both Letter-press and Engraving in a style more ornamental, uniform, and grand, than any before discovered, while it produces works at less than one fourth of the expense.

If a method of Printing which combines the Painter and the Poet is a phenomenon worthy of public attention, provided that it exceeds in elegance all former methods, the Author is sure of his reward.

Mr. Blake's powers of invention very early engaged the attention of many persons of eminence and fortune; by whose means he has been regularly enabled to bring before the Public works (he is not afraid to say) of equal magnitude and consequence with the productions of any age or country: among which are two large highly finished engravings (and two more are nearly ready) which will commence a Series of subjects from the Bible, and another from the History of England.

The following are the Subjects of the several Works now published and on Sale at Mr. Blake's, No. 13, Hercules Buildings, Lambeth.

1. Job, a Historical Engraving. Size 1 ft. 7½ in. by 1 ft. 2 in.: price 12*s*.
2. Edward and Elinor, a Historical Engraving. Size 1 ft. 6½ in. by 1 ft.: price 10*s*. 6*d*.
3. America, a Prophecy, in Illuminated Printing. Folio, with 18 designs: price 10*s*. 6*d*.
4. Visions of the Daughters of Albion, in Illuminated Printing. Folio, with 8 designs, price 7*s*. 6*d*.
5. The Book of Thel, a Poem in Illuminated Printing. Quarto, with 6 designs, price 3*s*.
6. The Marriage of Heaven and Hell, in Illuminated Printing. Quarto, with 14 designs, price 7*s*. 6*d*.

7. Songs of Innocence, in Illuminated Printing. Octavo, with 25 designs, price 5*s*.
8. Songs of Experience, in Illuminated Printing. Octavo, with 25 designs, price 5*s*.
9. The History of England, a small book of Engravings. Price 3*s*.
10. The Gates of Paradise, a small book of Engravings. Price 3*s*.

The Illuminated Books are Printed in Colours, and on the most beautiful wove paper that could be procured.

No Subscriptions for the numerous great works now in hand are asked, for none are wanted; but the Author will produce his works, and offer them to sale at a fair price.

[Subjects for "The History of England, a small book of Engravings"]

From the Note-Book, p. 116, *written* 1793

1. Giants ancient inhabitants of England.
2. The Landing of Brutus.
3. Corineus throws Gogmagog the Giant into the Sea.
4. King Lear.
5. The Ancient Britons according to Caesar [The frontispiece *del.*]
6. The Druids.
7. The Landing of Julius Caesar.
8. Boadicea inspiring the Britons against the Romans.
   The Britons' distress & depopulation.
   Women fleeing from War.
   Women in a Siege.
9. Alfred in the countryman's house.
10. Edwin & Morcar stirring up the Londoners to resist W. the Conq[r].
11. W. the Conq. Crown'd.
12. King John & Mag. Charta.
    A Famine occasion'd by the Popish interdict.

13. Edward at Calais.
14. Edward the Black Prince brings his Captives to his father.
15. The Penance of Jane Shore.
[16, 17 *del.*] 19. The Plague. [17. The Reformation by H. VIII. *del.*]
[17, 18 *del.*] 20. The fire of London. [18. Ch. I beheaded. *del.*]
[18 *del.*] 16. The Cruelties used by Kings & Priests [whose arts *del.*]
[19 *del.*] 21. A prospect of Liberty.
[20 *del.*] 22. A Cloud.

FOR CHILDREN
THE GATES OF PARADISE

Engraved 1793

Frontispiece. What is Man!
1. I found him beneath a Tree.
2. Water.
3. Earth.
4. Air.
5. Fire.
6. At length for hatching ripe he breaks the shell.
7. Alas!
8. My Son! my Son!
9. I want! I want!
10. Help! Help!
11. Aged Ignorance.
12. Does thy God O Priest take such vengeance as this?
13. Fear & Hope are—Vision.
14. The Traveller hasteth in the Evening.
15. Death's Door.
16. I have said to the Worm: Thou art my mother & my sister.

[*The Emblems accompanying these legends will be found at* *p.* 760 *with the later work,* For the Sexes: The Gates of Paradise, 1818.]

SONGS Of INNOCENCE and Of EXPERIENCE

Shewing the Two Contrary States of the Human Soul

Etched 1789-1794

SONGS OF INNOCENCE: *see pages* 111-126

SONGS of EXPERIENCE

The Author & Printer W. Blake

Introduction

Hear the voice of the Bard!
Who Present, Past, & Future, sees;
Whose ears have heard
The Holy Word
That walk'd among the ancient trees,

Calling the lapsed Soul,
And weeping in the evening dew;
That might controll
The starry pole,
And fallen, fallen light renew!

"O Earth, O Earth, return!
"Arise from out the dewy grass;
"Night is worn,
"And the morn
"Rises from the slumberous mass.

"Turn away no more;
"Why wilt thou turn away?
"The starry floor,
"The wat'ry shore,
"Is giv'n thee till the break of day."

EARTH'S Answer

Earth rais'd up her head
From the darkness dread & drear.
Her light fled,
Stony dread!
And her locks cover'd with grey despair.

"Prison'd on wat'ry shore,
"Starry Jealousy does keep my den:
"Cold and hoar,
"Weeping o'er,
"I hear the Father of the ancient men.

"Selfish father of men!
"Cruel, jealous, selfish fear!
"Can delight,
"Chain'd in night,
"The virgins of youth and morning bear?

"Does spring hide its joy
"When buds and blossoms grow?
"Does the sower
"Sow by night,
"Or the plowman in darkness plow?

"Break this heavy chain
"That does freeze my bones around.
"Selfish! vain!
"Eternal bane!
"That free Love with bondage bound."

The CLOD & the PEBBLE

"Love seeketh not Itself to please,
"Nor for itself hath any care,
"But for another gives its ease,
"And builds a Heaven in Hell's despair."

So sang a little Clod of Clay
Trodden with the cattle's feet,
But a Pebble of the brook
Warbled out these metres meet:

"Love seeketh only Self to please,
"To bind another to Its delight,
"Joys in another's loss of ease,
"And builds a Hell in Heaven's despite."

HOLY THURSDAY

Is this a holy thing to see
In a rich and fruitful land,
Babes reduc'd to misery,
Fed with cold and usurous hand?

Is that trembling cry a song?
Can it be a song of joy?
And so many children poor?
It is a land of poverty!

And their sun does never shine,
And their fields are bleak & bare,
And their ways are fill'd with thorns:
It is eternal winter there.

For where-e'er the sun does shine,
And where-e'er the rain does fall,
Babe can never hunger there,
Nor poverty the mind appall.

The Chimney Sweeper

A little black thing among the snow,
Crying ''weep! 'weep!' in notes of woe!
"Where are thy father & mother? say?"
"They are both gone up to the church to pray.

"Because I was happy upon the heath,
"And smil'd among the winter's snow,
"They clothed me in the clothes of death,
"And taught me to sing the notes of woe.

"And because I am happy & dance & sing,
"They think they have done me no injury,
"And are gone to praise God & his Priest & King,
"Who make up a heaven of our misery."

NURSE'S Song

When the voices of children are heard on the green
And whisp'rings are in the dale,
The days of my youth rise fresh in my mind,
My face turns green and pale.

Then come home, my children, the sun is gone down,
And the dews of night arise;
Your spring & your day are wasted in play,
And your winter and night in disguise.

The SICK ROSE

O Rose, thou art sick!
The invisible worm
That flies in the night,
In the howling storm,

Has found out thy bed
Of crimson joy:
And his dark secret love
Does thy life destroy.

THE FLY

Little Fly,
Thy summer's play
My thoughtless hand
Has brush'd away.

Am not I
A fly like thee?
Or art not thou
A man like me?

For I dance,
And drink, & sing,
Till some blind hand
Shall brush my wing.

If thought is life
And strength & breath,
And the want
Of thought is death;

Then am I
A happy fly,
If I live
Or if I die.

The Angel

I Dreamt a Dream! what can it mean?
And that I was a maiden Queen,
Guarded by an Angel mild;
Witless woe was ne'er beguil'd!

And I wept both night and day,
And he wip'd my tears away,
And I wept both day and night,
And hid from him my heart's delight.

So he took his wings and fled;
Then the morn blush'd rosy red;
I dried my tears, & arm'd my fears
With ten thousand shields and spears.

Soon my Angel came again:
I was arm'd, he came in vain;
For the time of youth was fled,
And grey hairs were on my head.

The Tyger

Tyger! Tyger! burning bright
In the forests of the night,
What immortal hand or eye
Could frame thy fearful symmetry?

In what distant deeps or skies
Burnt the fire of thine eyes?
On what wings dare he aspire?
What the hand dare sieze the fire?

And what shoulder, & what art,
Could twist the sinews of thy heart?
And when thy heart began to beat,
What dread hand? & what dread feet?[1]

What the hammer? what the chain?
In what furnace was thy brain?
What the anvil? what dread grasp
Dare its deadly terrors clasp?

When the stars threw down their spears,
And water'd heaven with their tears,
Did he smile his work to see?
Did he who made the Lamb make thee?

Tyger! Tyger! burning bright
In the forests of the night,
What immortal hand or eye
Dare frame thy fearful symmetry?

[1] *Altered in one copy to:* What dread hand Form'd thy dread feet?

My pretty ROSE TREE

A flower was offer'd to me,
Such a flower as May never bore;
But I said "I've a Pretty Rose-tree,"
And I passed the sweet flower o'er.

Then I went to my Pretty Rose-tree,
To tend her by day and by night;
But my Rose turn'd away with jealousy,
And her thorns were my only delight.

AH! SUN-FLOWER

Ah, Sun-flower, weary of time,
Who countest the steps of the Sun,
Seeking after that sweet golden clime
Where the traveller's journey is done:

Where the Youth pined away with desire,
And the pale Virgin shrouded in snow
Arise from their graves, and aspire
Where my Sun-flower wishes to go.

THE LILLY

The modest Rose puts forth a thorn,
The humble Sheep a threat'ning horn;
While the Lilly white shall in Love delight,
Nor a thorn, nor a threat, stain her beauty bright.

The GARDEN of LOVE

I went to the Garden of Love,
And saw what I never had seen:
A Chapel was built in the midst,
Where I used to play on the green.

And the gates of this Chapel were shut,
And "Thou shalt not" writ over the door;
So I turn'd to the Garden of Love
That so many sweet flowers bore;

And I saw it was filled with graves,
And tomb-stones where flowers should be;
And Priests in black gowns were walking their rounds,
And binding with briars my joys & desires.

The Little Vagabond

Dear Mother, dear Mother, the Church is cold,
But the Ale-house is healthy & pleasant & warm;
Besides I can tell where I am used well,
Such usage in heaven will never do well.

But if at the Church they would give us some Ale,
And a pleasant fire our souls to regale,
We'd sing and we'd pray all the live-long day,
Nor ever once wish from the Church to stray.

Then the Parson might preach, & drink, & sing,
And we'd be as happy as birds in the spring;
And modest dame Lurch, who is always at Church,
Would not have bandy children, nor fasting, nor birch.

And God, like a father rejoicing to see
His children as pleasant and happy as he,
Would have no more quarrel with the Devil or the Barrel,
But kiss him, & give him both drink and apparel.

LONDON

I wander thro' each charter'd street,
Near where the charter'd Thames does flow,
And mark in every face I meet
Marks of weakness, marks of woe.

In every cry of every Man,
In every Infant's cry of fear,
In every voice, in every ban,
The mind-forg'd manacles I hear.

How the Chimney-sweeper's cry
Every black'ning Church appalls;
And the hapless Soldier's sigh
Runs in blood down Palace walls.

But most thro' midnight streets I hear
How the youthful Harlot's curse
Blasts the new born Infant's tear,
And blights with plagues the Marriage hearse.

The Human Abstract

Pity would be no more
If we did not make somebody Poor;
And Mercy no more could be
If all were as happy as we.

And mutual fear brings peace,
Till the selfish loves increase:
Then Cruelty knits a snare,
And spreads his baits with care.

He sits down with holy fears,
And waters the ground with tears;
Then Humility takes its root
Underneath his foot.

Soon spreads the dismal shade
Of Mystery over his head;
And the Catterpiller and Fly
Feed on the Mystery.

And it bears the fruit of Deceit,
Ruddy and sweet to eat;
And the Raven his nest has made
In its thickest shade.

The Gods of the earth and sea
Sought thro' Nature to find this Tree;
But their search was all in vain:
There grows one in the Human Brain.

INFANT SORROW

My mother groan'd! my father wept.
Into the dangerous world I leapt:
Helpless, naked, piping loud:
Like a fiend hid in a cloud.

Struggling in my father's hands,
Striving against my swadling bands,
Bound and weary I thought best
To sulk upon my mother's breast.

A POISON TREE

I was angry with my friend:
I told my wrath, my wrath did end.
I was angry with my foe:
I told it not, my wrath did grow.

And I water'd it in fears,
Night & morning with my tears;
And I sunned it with smiles,
And with soft deceitful wiles.

And it grew both day and night,
Till it bore an apple bright;
And my foe beheld it shine,
And he knew that it was mine,

And into my garden stole
When the night had veil'd the pole:
In the morning glad I see
My foe outstretch'd beneath the tree.

A Little BOY Lost

"Nought loves another as itself,
"Nor venerates another so,
"Nor is it possible to Thought
"A greater than itself to know:

"And Father, how can I love you
"Or any of my brothers more?
"I love you like the little bird
"That picks up crumbs around the door."

The Priest sat by and heard the child,
In trembling zeal he siez'd his hair:
He led him by his little coat,
And all admir'd the Priestly care.

And standing on the altar high,
"Lo! what a fiend is here!" said he,
"One who sets reason up for judge
"Of our most holy Mystery."

The weeping child could not be heard,
The weeping parents wept in vain;
They strip'd him to his little shirt,
And bound him in an iron chain;

And burn'd him in a holy place,
Where many had been burn'd before:
The weeping parents wept in vain.
Are such things done on Albion's shore?

A Little GIRL Lost

Children of the future Age
Reading this indignant page,
Know that in a former time
Love! sweet Love! was thought a crime.

In the Age of Gold,
Free from winter's cold,
Youth and maiden bright
To the holy light,
Naked in the sunny beams delight.

Once a youthful pair,
Fill'd with softest care,
Met in garden bright
Where the holy light
Had just remov'd the curtains of the night.

There, in rising day
On the grass they play;
Parents were afar,
Strangers came not near,
And the maiden soon forgot her fear.

Tired with kisses sweet,
They agree to meet,
When the silent sleep
Waves o'er heaven's deep,
And the weary tired wanderers weep.

To her father white
Came the maiden bright;
But his loving look,
Like the holy book,
All her tender limbs with terror shook.

"Ona! pale and weak!
"To thy father speak:
"O, the trembling fear!
"O, the dismal care!
"That shakes the blossoms of my hoary hair."

To Tirzah

Probably added about 1801

Whate'er is Born of Mortal Birth
Must be consumed with the Earth
To rise from Generation free:
Then what have I to do with thee?

The Sexes sprung from Shame & Pride,
Blow'd in the morn; in evening died;
But Mercy chang'd Death into Sleep;
The Sexes rose to work & weep.

Thou, Mother of my Mortal part,
With cruelty didst mould my Heart,
And with false self-decieving tears
Didst bind my Nostrils, Eyes, & Ears:

Didst close my Tongue in senseless clay,
And me to Mortal Life betray.
The Death of Jesus set me free:
Then what have I to do with thee?

ADDITIONAL POEM

Etched about 1791, *but not included by Blake.*

A DIVINE IMAGE

Cruelty has a Human Heart,
And Jealousy a Human Face;
Terror the Human Form Divine,
And Secrecy the Human Dress.

The Human Dress is forged Iron,
The Human Form a fiery Forge,
The Human Face a Furnace seal'd,
The Human Heart its hungry Gorge.

THE FIRST[1] BOOK of URIZEN

LAMBETH. Printed by Will Blake 1794

Plate 2

PRELUDIUM TO THE FIRST[1] BOOK OF URIZEN

Of the primeval Priest's assum'd power,
When Eternals spurn'd back his religion
And gave him a place in the north,
Obscure, shadowy, void, solitary.

Eternals! I hear your call gladly.
Dictate swift winged words & fear not
To unfold your dark visions of torment.

Plate 3

Chap: I

1. Lo, a shadow of horror is risen
In Eternity! Unknown, unprolific,
Self-clos'd, all-repelling: what Demon
Hath form'd this abominable void,
This soul-shudd'ring vacuum? Some said
"It is Urizen." But unknown, abstracted,
Brooding, secret, the dark power hid.

2. Times on times he divided & measur'd
Space by space in his ninefold darkness,
Unseen, unknown; changes appear'd
Like[2] desolate mountains, rifted furious
By the black winds of perturbation.

3. For he strove in battles dire,
In unseen conflictions with shapes
Bred from his forsaken wilderness
Of beast, bird, fish, serpent & element,
Combustion, blast, vapour and cloud.

---

[1] This word afterwards deleted.

[2] *Later altered to* In his.

4. Dark, revolving in silent activity:
Unseen in tormenting passions:
An activity unknown and horrible,
A self-contemplating shadow,
In enormous labours occupied.

5. But Eternals beheld his vast forests;
Age on ages he lay, clos'd, unknown,
Brooding shut in the deep; all avoid
The petrific, abominable chaos.

6. His cold horrors silent, dark Urizen
Prepar'd; his ten thousands of thunders,
Rang'd in gloom'd array, stretch out across
The dread world; & the rolling of wheels,
As of swelling seas, sound in his clouds,
In his hills of stor'd snows, in his mountains
Of hail & ice; voices of terror
Are heard, like thunders of autumn
When the cloud blazes over the harvests.

Chap: II

1. Earth was not: nor globes of attraction;
The will of the Immortal expanded
Or contracted his all flexible senses;
Death was not, but eternal life sprung.

2. The sound of a trumpet the heavens
Awoke, & vast clouds of blood roll'd
Round the dim rocks of Urizen, so nam'd
That solitary one in Immensity.

3. Shrill the trumpet: & myriads of Eternity

Plate 4[1]

Muster around the bleak desarts,
Now fill'd with clouds, darkness, & waters,
That roll'd perplex'd, lab'ring; & utter'd
Words articulate bursting in thunders
That roll'd on the tops of his mountains:

[1] This plate was omitted from four of the seven copies of the book.

4. "From the depths of dark solitude, From
"The eternal abode in my holiness,
"Hidden, set apart, in my stern counsels,
"Reserv'd for the days of futurity,
"I have sought for a joy without pain,
"For a solid without fluctuation.
"Why will you die, O Eternals?
"Why live in unquenchable burnings?

5. "First I fought with the fire, consum'd
"Inwards into a deep world within:
"A void immense, wild, dark & deep,
"Where nothing was: Nature's wide womb;
"And self balanc'd, stretch'd o'er the void,
"I alone, even I! the winds merciless
"Bound; but condensing in torrents
"They fall & fall; strong I repell'd
"The vast waves, & arose on the waters
"A wide world of solid obstruction.

6. "Here alone I, in books form'd of metals,
"Have written the secrets of wisdom,
"The secrets of dark contemplation,
"By fightings and conflicts dire
"With terrible monsters Sin-bred
"Which the bosoms of all inhabit,
"Seven deadly Sins of the soul.[1]

7. "Lo! I unfold my darkness, and on
"This rock place with strong hand the Book
"Of eternal brass, written in my solitude:

8. "Laws of peace, of love, of unity,
"Of pity, compassion, forgiveness;
"Let each chuse one habitation,
"His ancient infinite mansion,
"One command, one joy, one desire,
"One curse, one weight, one measure,
"One King, one God, one Law."

Chap: III

1. The voice ended: they saw his pale visage
Emerge from the darkness, his hand
On the rock of eternity unclasping
The Book of brass. Rage siez'd the strong,

[1] This line erased in one copy.

2. Rage, fury, intense indignation,
In cataracts of fire, blood, & gall,
In whirlwinds of sulphurous smoke,
And enormous forms of energy,
All the seven deadly sins of the soul[1]

Plate 5

In living creations appear'd,
In the flames of eternal fury.

3. Sund'ring, dark'ning, thund'ring,
Rent away with a terrible crash,
Eternity roll'd wide apart,
Wide asunder rolling;
Mountainous all around
Departing, departing, departing,
Leaving ruinous fragments of life
Hanging, frowning cliffs, &, all between,
An ocean of voidness unfathomable.

4. The roaring fires ran o'er the heav'ns
In whirlwinds & cataracts of blood,
And o'er the dark desarts of Urizen
Fires pour thro' the void on all sides
On Urizen's self-begotten armies.[1]

5. But no light from the fires: all was darkness
In the flames of Eternal fury.

6. In fierce anguish & quenchless flames
To the desarts and rocks he ran raging
To hide; but he could not: combining,
He dug mountains & hills in vast strength,
He piled them in incessant labour,
In howlings & pangs & fierce madness,
Long periods in burning fires labouring
Till hoary, and age-broke, and aged,
In despair and the shadows of death.

7. And a roof vast, petrific around
On all sides he fram'd, like a womb,
Where thousands of rivers in veins
Of blood pour down the mountains to cool

---

[1] This line erased in one copy.

The eternal fires, beating without
From Eternals; & like a black globe,
View'd by sons of Eternity standing
On the shore of the infinite ocean,
Like a human heart, strugling & beating,
The vast world of Urizen appear'd.

8. And Los, round the dark globe of Urizen,
Kept watch for Eternals to confine
The obscure separation alone;
For Eternity stood wide apart,

Plate 6

As the stars are apart from the earth.

9. Los wept, howling around the dark Demon,
And cursing his lot; for in anguish
Urizen was rent from his side,
And a fathomless void for his feet,
And intense fires for his dwelling.

10. But Urizen laid in a stony sleep,
Unorganiz'd, rent from Eternity.
[*Two lines erased from the plate*]

11. The Eternals said: "What is this? Death.
"Urizen is a clod of clay."

Plate 7

12. Los howl'd in a dismal stupor,
Groaning, gnashing, groaning,
Till the wrenching apart was healed.

13. But the wrenching of Urizen heal'd not.
Cold, featureless, flesh or clay,
Rifted with direful changes
He lay in a dreamless night,

14. Till Los rouz'd his fires, affrighted
At the formless, unmeasurable death.

Plate 8

Chap: IV [a]

1. Los, smitten with astonishment,
Frighten'd at the hurtling bones

2. And at the surging, sulphureous,
Perturbed Immortal, mad raging

3. In whirlwinds & pitch & nitre
Round the furious limbs of Los.

4. And Los formed nets & gins
And threw the nets round about.

5. He watch'd in shudd'ring fear
The dark changes, & bound every change
With rivets of iron & brass.

6. And these were the changes of Urizen:

Plate 10

Chap: IV [b]

1. Ages on ages roll'd over him;
In stony sleep ages roll'd over him,
Like a dark waste stretching, chang'able,
By earthquakes riv'n, belching sullen fires:
On ages roll'd ages in ghastly
Sick torment; around him in whirlwinds
Of darkness the eternal Prophet howl'd,
Beating still on his rivets of iron,
Pouring sodor of iron; dividing
The horrible night into watches.

2. And Urizen (so his eternal name)
His prolific delight obscur'd more & more
In dark secresy, hiding in surgeing
Sulphureous fluid his phantasies.
The Eternal Prophet heav'd the dark bellows,
And turn'd restless the tongs, and the hammer
Incessant beat, forging chains new & new,
Numb'ring with links hours, days & years.

3. The Eternal mind, bounded, began to roll
Eddies of wrath ceaseless round & round,
And the sulphureous foam, surgeing thick,
Settled, a lake, bright & shining clear,
White as the snow on the mountains cold.

4. Forgetfulness, dumbness, necessity,
In chains of the mind locked up,
Like fetters of ice shrinking together,
Disorganiz'd, rent from Eternity,
Los beat on his fetters of iron,
And heated his furnaces, & pour'd
Iron sodor and sodor of brass.

5. Restless turn'd the Immortal inchain'd,
Heaving dolorous, anguish'd unbearable;
Till a roof, shaggy wild, inclos'd
In an orb his fountain of thought.

6. In a horrible, dreamful slumber,
Like the linked infernal chain,
A vast Spine writh'd in torment
Upon the winds, shooting pain'd
Ribs, like a bending cavern;
And bones of solidness Froze
Over all his nerves of joy.
And a first Age passed over,
And a state of dismal woe.

Plate 11

7. From the caverns of his jointed Spine
Down sunk with fright a red
Round Globe, hot burning, deep,
Deep down into the Abyss;
Panting, Conglobing, Trembling,

Shooting out ten thousand branches
Around his solid bones.
And a second Age passed over,
And a state of dismal woe.

8. In harrowing fear rolling round,
His nervous brain shot branches
Round the branches of his heart
On high into two little orbs,
And fixed in two little caves,
Hiding carefully from the wind,
His Eyes beheld the deep.
And a third Age passed over,
And a state of dismal woe.

9. The pangs of hope began.
In heavy pain, striving, struggling,
Two Ears in close volutions
From beneath his orbs of vision
Shot spiring out and petrified
As they grew. And a fourth Age passed,
And a state of dismal woe.

10. In ghastly torment sick,
Hanging upon the wind,

Plate 13

Two Nostrils bent down to the deep.
And a fifth Age passed over,
And a state of dismal woe.

11. In ghastly torment sick,
Within his ribs bloated round,
A craving Hungry Cavern;
Thence arose his channel'd Throat,
And, like a red flame, a Tongue
Of thirst & of hunger appear'd.
And a sixth Age passed over,
And a state of dismal woe.

12. Enraged & stifled with torment,
He threw his right Arm to the north,
His left Arm to the south
Shooting out in anguish deep,
And his feet stamp'd the nether Abyss
In trembling & howling & dismay.
And a seventh Age passed over,
And a state of dismal woe.

Chap: V

1. In terrors Los shrunk from his task:
His great hammer fell from his hand.
His fires beheld, and sickening
Hid their strong limbs in smoke;
For with noises, ruinous, loud,
With hurtlings & clashings & groans,
The Immortal endur'd his chains,
Tho' bound in a deadly sleep.

2. All the myriads of Eternity,
All the wisdom & joy of life
Roll like a sea around him,
Except what his little orbs
Of sight by degrees unfold.

3. And now his eternal life
Like a dream was obliterated.

4. Shudd'ring, the Eternal Prophet smote
With a stroke from his north to south region.
The bellows & hammer are silent now;
A nerveless silence his prophetic voice
Siez'd; a cold solitude & dark void
The Eternal Prophet & Urizen clos'd.

5. Ages on ages roll'd over them,
Cut off from life & light, frozen
Into horrible forms of deformity.
Los suffer'd his fires to decay;
Then he look'd back with anxious desire,
But the space, undivided by existence,
Struck horror into his soul.

6. Los wept obscur'd with mourning,
His bosom earthquak'd with sighs;
He saw Urizen deadly black
In his chains bound, & Pity began,

7. In anguish dividing & dividing,
For pity divides the soul
In pangs, eternity on eternity,
Life in cataracts pour'd down his cliffs.
The void shrunk the lymph into Nerves
Wand'ring wide on the bosom of night
And left a round globe of blood
Trembling upon the Void.

Plate 15

Thus the Eternal Prophet was divided
Before the death image of Urizen;
For in changeable clouds and darkness,
In a winterly night beneath,
The Abyss of Los stretch'd immense;
And now seen, now obscur'd, to the eyes

Of Eternals the visions remote
Of the dark seperation appear'd:
As glasses discover Worlds
In the endless Abyss of space,
So the expanding eyes of Immortals
Beheld the dark visions of Los
And the globe of life blood trembling.

Plate 18

8. The globe of life blood trembled
Branching out into roots,
Fibrous, writhing upon the winds,
Fibres of blood, milk and tears,
In pangs, eternity on eternity.
At length in tears & cries imbodied,
A female form, trembling and pale,
Waves before his deathy face.

9. All Eternity shudder'd at sight
Of the first female now separate,
Pale as a cloud of snow
Waving before the face of Los.

10. Wonder, awe, fear, astonishment
Petrify the eternal myriads
At the first female form now separate.

Plate 19

They call'd her Pity, and fled.

11. "Spread a Tent with strong curtains around them.
"Let cords & stakes bind in the Void,
"That Eternals may no more behold them."

12. They began to weave curtains of darkness,
They erected large pillars round the Void,
With golden hooks fasten'd in the pillars;
With infinite labour the Eternals
A woof wove, and called it Science.

Chap: VI

1. But Los saw the Female & pitied;
He embrac'd her; she wept, she refus'd;
In perverse and cruel delight
She fled from his arms, yet he follow'd.

2. Eternity shudder'd when they saw
Man begetting his likeness
On his own divided image.

3. A time passed over: the Eternals
Began to erect the tent,
When Enitharmon, sick,
Felt a Worm within her womb.

4. Yet helpless it lay like a Worm
In the trembling womb
To be moulded into existence.

5. All day the worm lay on her bosom;
All night within her womb
The worm lay till it grew to a serpent,
With dolorous hissings & poisons
Round Enitharmon's loins folding.

6. Coil'd within Enitharmon's womb
The serpent grew, casting its scales;
With sharp pangs the hissings began
To change to a grating cry:
Many sorrows and dismal throes,
Many forms of fish, bird & beast
Brought forth an Infant form
Where was a worm before.

7. The Eternals their tent finished
Alarm'd with these gloomy visions,
When Enitharmon groaning
Produc'd a man Child to the light.

8. A shriek ran thro' Eternity,
And a paralytic stroke,
At the birth of the Human shadow.

9. Delving earth in his resistless way,
Howling, the Child with fierce flames
Issu'd from Enitharmon.

10. The Eternals closed the tent;
They beat down the stakes, the cords

Plate 20

Stretch'd for a work of eternity.
No more Los beheld Eternity.

11. In his hands he siez'd the infant,
He bathed him in springs of sorrow,
He gave him to Enitharmon.

Chap: VII

1. They named the child Orc; he grew,
Fed with milk of Enitharmon.

2. Los awoke her. O sorrow & pain!
A tight'ning girdle grew
Around his bosom. In sobbings
He burst the girdle in twain;
But still another girdle
Oppress'd his bosom. In sobbings
Again he burst it. Again
Another girdle succeeds.
The girdle was form'd by day,
By night was burst in twain.

3. These falling down on the rock
Into an iron Chain
In each other link by link lock'd.

4. They took Orc to the top of a mountain.
O how Enitharmon wept!
They chain'd his young limbs to the rock
With the Chain of Jealousy
Beneath Urizen's deathful shadow.

5. The dead heard the voice of the child
And began to awake from sleep;
All things heard the voice of the child
And began to awake to life.

6. And Urizen, craving with hunger,
Stung with the odours of Nature,
Explor'd his dens around.

7. He form'd a line & a plummet
To divide the Abyss beneath;
He form'd a dividing rule;

8. He formed scales to weigh,
He formed massy weights;
He formed a brazen quadrant;
He formed golden compasses,
And began to explore the Abyss;
And he planted a garden of fruits.

9. But Los encircled Enitharmon
With fires of Prophecy
From the sight of Urizen & Orc.

10. And she bore an enormous race.

Chap: VIII

1. Urizen explor'd his dens,
Mountain, moor & wilderness,
With a globe of fire lighting his journey,
A fearful journey, annoy'd
By cruel enormities, forms

Plate 23

Of life on his forsaken mountains.

2. And his world teem'd vast enormities,
Fright'ning, faithless, fawning
Portions of life, similitudes
Of a foot, or a hand, or a head,
Or a heart, or an eye; they swam mischevous,
Dread terrors, delighting in blood.

3. Most Urizen sicken'd to see
His eternal creations appear,
Sons & daughters of sorrow on mountains
Weeping, wailing. First Thiriel appear'd,
Astonish'd at his own existence,
Like a man from a cloud born; & Utha,
From the waters emerging, laments:
Grodna rent the deep earth, howling
Amaz'd; his heavens immense cracks
Like the ground parch'd with heat, then Fuzon
Flam'd out, first begotten, last born;
All his eternal sons in like manner;
His daughters from green herbs & cattle,
From monsters & worms of the pit.

4. He in darkness clos'd view'd all his race,
And his soul sicken'd! he curs'd
Both sons & daughters; for he saw
That no flesh nor spirit could keep
His iron laws one moment.

5. For he saw that life liv'd upon death:

Plate 25

The Ox in the slaughter house moans,
The Dog at the wintry door;
And he wept & he called it Pity,
And his tears flowed down on the winds.

6. Cold he wander'd on high, over their cities
In weeping & pain & woe;
And where ever he wander'd, in sorrows
Upon the aged heavens,
A cold shadow follow'd behind him
Like a spider's web, moist, cold & dim,
Drawing out from his sorrowing soul,
The dungeon-like heaven dividing,
Where ever the footsteps of Urizen
Walked over the cities in sorrow;

7. Till a Web, dark & cold, throughout all
The tormented element stretch'd
From the sorrows of Urizen's soul.
And the Web is a Female in embrio.[1]
None could break the Web, no wings of fire,

8. So twisted the cords, & so knotted
The meshes, twisted like to the human brain.

9. And all call'd it The Net of Religion.

Chap: IX

1. Then the Inhabitants of those Cities
Felt their Nerves change into Marrow,
And hardening Bones began
In swift diseases and torments,

[1] This line was erased in most copies of the book.

In throbbings & shootings & grindings
Thro' all the coasts; till weaken'd
The Senses inward rush'd, shrinking
Beneath the dark net of infection;

2. Till the shrunken eyes, clouded over,
Discern'd not the woven hipocrisy;
But the streaky slime in their heavens,
Brought together by narrowing perceptions,
Appear'd transparent air; for their eyes
Grew small like the eyes of a man,
And in reptile forms shrinking together,
Of seven feet stature they remain'd.

3. Six days they shrunk up from existence,
And on the seventh day they rested,
And they bless'd the seventh day, in sick hope,
And forgot their eternal life.

4. And their thirty cities divided
In form of a human heart.
No more could they rise at will
In the infinite void, but bound down
To earth by their narrowing perceptions

Plate 28

They lived a period of years;
Then left a noisom body
To the jaws of devouring darkness.

5. And their children wept, & built
Tombs in the desolate places,
And form'd laws of prudence, and call'd them
The eternal laws of God.

6. And the thirty cities remain'd,
Surrounded by salt floods, now call'd
Africa: its name was then Egypt.

7. The remaining sons of Urizen
Beheld their brethren shrink together
Beneath the Net of Urizen.
Perswasion was in vain;
For the ears of the inhabitants
Were wither'd & deafen'd & cold,
And their eyes could not discern
Their brethren of other cities.

8. So Fuzon call'd all together
The remaining children of Urizen,
And they left the pendulous earth.
They called it Egypt, & left it.

9. And the salt Ocean rolled englob'd.

The End of the first[1] book of Urizen

EUROPE

a PROPHECY

LAMBETH Printed by Will: Blake, 1794

Plate iii[2]

"Five windows light the cavern'd Man: thro' one he breathes the air;
"Thro' one hears music of the spheres; thro' one the eternal vine
"Flourishes, that he may recieve the grapes; thro' one can look
"And see small portions of the eternal world that ever groweth;
"Thro' one himself pass out what time he please; but he will not,
"For stolen joys are sweet & bread eaten in secret pleasant."

So sang a Fairy, mocking, as he sat on a streak'd Tulip,
Thinking none saw him: when he ceas'd I started from the trees
And caught him in my hat, as boys knock down a butterfly.
"How know you this," said I, "small Sir? where did you learn this song?"
Seeing himself in my possession, thus he answer'd me:
"My master, I am yours! command me, for I must obey."

"Then tell me, what is the material world, and is it dead?"
He, laughing, answer'd: "I will write a book on leaves of flowers,
"If you will feed me on love-thoughts & give me now and then
"A cup of sparkling poetic fancies; so, when I am tipsie,
"I'll sing to you to this soft lute, and shew you all alive
"The world, when every particle of dust breathes forth its joy."

[1] This word afterwards deleted.
[2] This plate was omitted from most copies of the book.

I took him home in my warm bosom: as we went along
Wild flowers I gather'd, & he shew'd me each eternal flower:
He laugh'd aloud to see them whimper because they were pluck'd.
They hover'd round me like a cloud of incense: when I came
Into my parlour and sat down and took my pen to write,
My Fairy sat upon the table and dictated EUROPE.

Plate 1

PRELUDIUM

The nameless shadowy female rose from out the breast of Orc,
Her snaky hair brandishing in the winds of Enitharmon;
And thus her voice arose:

"O mother Enitharmon, wilt thou bring forth other sons?
"To cause my name to vanish, that my place may not be found,
"For I am faint with travel,[1]
"Like the dark cloud disburden'd in the day of dismal thunder.

"My roots are brandish'd in the heavens, my fruits in earth beneath
"Surge, foam and labour into life, first born & first consum'd!
"Consumed and consuming!
"Then why shouldst thou, accursed mother, bring me into life?

"I wrap my turban of thick clouds around my lab'ring head,
"And fold the sheety waters as a mantle round my limbs;
"Yet the red sun and moon
"And all the overflowing stars rain down prolific pains.

Plate 2

"Unwilling I look up to heaven, unwilling count the stars:
"Sitting in fathomless abyss of my immortal shrine
"I sieze their burning power
"And bring forth howling terrors, all devouring fiery kings,

"Devouring & devoured, roaming on dark and desolate mountains,
"In forests of eternal death, shrieking in hollow trees.
"Ah mother Enitharmon!
"Stamp not with solid form this vig'rous progeny of fires.

"I bring forth from my teeming bosom myriads of flames,
"And thou dost stamp them with a signet; then they roam abroad
"And leave me void as death.
"Ah! I am drown'd in shady woe and visionary joy.

---

[1] *Probably an error for* travail.

"And who shall bind the infinite with an eternal band?
"To compass it with swaddling bands? and who shall cherish it
"With milk and honey?
"I see it smile, & I roll inward, & my voice is past."

She ceast, & roll'd her shady clouds
Into the secret place.

Plate 3

A PROPHECY

The deep of winter came,
What time the secret child
Descended thro' the orient gates of the eternal day:
War ceas'd, & all the troops like shadows fled to their abodes.

Then Enitharmon saw her sons & daughters rise around;
Like pearly clouds they meet together in the crystal house;
And Los, possessor of the moon, joy'd in the peaceful night,
Thus speaking, while his num'rous sons shook their bright fiery
wings:

"Again the night is come
"That strong Urthona takes his rest;
"And Urizen, unloos'd from chains,
"Glows like a meteor in the distant north.
"Stretch forth your hands and strike the elemental strings!
"Awake the thunders of the deep!"

Plate 4

The shrill winds wake,
Till all the sons of Urizen look out and envy Los:
"Sieze all the spirits of life, and bind
"Their warbling joys to our loud strings!
"Bind all the nourishing sweets of earth
"To give us bliss, that we may drink the sparkling wine of Los!
"And let us laugh at war,
"Despising toil and care,
"Because the days and nights of joy in lucky hours renew."

"Arise, O Orc, from thy deep den!
"First born of Enitharmon, rise!
"And we will crown thy head with garlands of the ruddy vine;
"For now thou art bound,
"And I may see thee in the hour of bliss, my eldest born."

The horrent Demon rose surrounded with red stars of fire
Whirling about in furious circles round the immortal fiend.

Then Enitharmon down descended into his red light,
And thus her voice rose to her children: the distant heavens reply:

Plate 5

"Now comes the night of Enitharmon's joy!
"Who shall I call? Who shall I send,
"That Woman, lovely Woman, may have dominion?
"Arise, O Rintrah, thee I call! & Palamabron, thee!
"Go! tell the Human race that Woman's love is Sin;
"That an Eternal life awaits the worms of sixty winters
"In an allegorical abode where existence hath never come.
"Forbid all Joy, & from her childhood shall the little female
"Spread nets in every secret path.

"My weary eyelids draw towards the evening; my bliss is yet but new.

Plate 8

"Arise! O Rintrah, eldest born, second to none but Orc!
"O lion Rintrah, raise thy fury from thy forests black!
"Bring Palamabron, horned priest, skipping upon the mountains,
"And silent Elynittria, the silver bowed queen.
"Rintrah, where hast thou hid thy bride?
"Weeps she in desart shades?
"Alas! my Rintrah, bring the lovely jealous Ocalythron.

"Arise, my son! bring all thy brethren, O thou king of fire!
"Prince of the sun! I see thee with thy innumerable race,
"Thick as the summer stars;
"But each, ramping, his golden mane shakes,
"And thine eyes rejoice because of strength, O Rintrah, furious king!"

Plate 9

Enitharmon slept
Eighteen hundred years. Man was a Dream!
The night of Nature and their harps unstrung!
She slept in middle of her nightly song
Eighteen hundred years, a female dream.

Shadows of men in fleeting bands upon the winds
Divide the heavens of Europe
Till Albion's Angel, smitten with his own plagues, fled with his bands.
The cloud bears hard on Albion's shore,
Fill'd with immortal demons of futurity:
In council gather the smitten Angels of Albion;
The cloud bears hard upon the council house, down rushing
On the heads of Albion's Angels.

One hour they lay buried beneath the ruins of that hall;
But as the stars rise from the salt lake, they arise in pain,
In troubled mists, o'erclouded by the terrors of strugling times.

Plate 10

In thoughts perturb'd they rose from the bright ruins, silent following
The fiery King, who sought his ancient temple, serpent-form'd,
That stretches out its shady length along the Island white.
Round him roll'd his clouds of war; silent the Angel went
Along the infinite shores of Thames to golden Verulam.
There stand the venerable porches that high-towering rear
Their oak-surrounded pillars, form'd of massy stones, uncut
With tool, stones precious, such eternal in the heavens,
Of colours twelve, few known on earth, give light in the opake,
Plac'd in the order of the stars, when the five senses whelm'd
In deluge o'er the earth-born man; then turn'd the fluxile eyes
Into two stationary orbs, concentrating all things:
The ever-varying spiral ascents to the heavens of heavens
Were bended downward, and the nostrils' golden gates shut,
Turn'd outward, barr'd and petrify'd against the infinite.

Thought chang'd the infinite to a serpent, that which pitieth
To a devouring flame; and man fled from its face and hid
In forests of night: then all the eternal forests were divided
Into earths rolling in circles of space, that like an ocean rush'd
And overwhelmed all except this finite wall of flesh.
Then was the serpent temple form'd, image of infinite
Shut up in finite revolutions, and man became an Angel,
Heaven a mighty circle turning, God a tyrant crown'd.

Now arriv'd the ancient Guardian at the southern porch
That planted thick with trees of blackest leaf & in a vale
Obscure enclos'd the Stone of Night; oblique it stood, o'erhung
With purple flowers and berries red, image of that sweet south

Once open to the heavens, and elevated on the human neck,
Now overgrown with hair and cover'd with a stony roof.
Downward 'tis sunk beneath th' attractive north, that round the feet,
A raging whirlpool, draws the dizzy enquirer to his grave.

Plate 11

Albion's Angel rose upon the Stone of Night.
He saw Urizen on the Atlantic;
And his brazen Book
That Kings & Priests had copied on Earth,
Expanded from North to South.

Plate 12

And the clouds & fires pale roll'd round in the night of Enitharmon,
Round Albion's cliffs & London's walls: still Enitharmon slept.
Rolling volumes of grey mist involve Churches, Palaces, Towers;
For Urizen unclasp'd his Book, feeding his soul with pity.
The youth of England, hid in gloom, curse the pain'd heavens, compell'd
Into the deadly night to see the form of Albion's Angel.
Their parents brought them forth, & aged ignorance preaches, canting,
On a vast rock, perciev'd by those senses that are clos'd from thought:
Bleak, dark, abrupt it stands & overshadows London city.
They saw his boney feet on the rock, the flesh consum'd in flames;
They saw the Serpent temple lifted above, shadowing the Island white;
They heard the voice of Albion's Angel howling in flames of Orc,
Seeking the trump of the last doom.

Above the rest the howl was heard from Westminster louder & louder:
The Guardian of the secret codes forsook his ancient mansion,
Driven out by the flames of Orc; his furr'd robes & false locks
Adhered and grew one with his flesh, and nerves & veins shot thro' them.
With dismal torment sick, hanging upon the wind, he fled
Groveling along Great George Street thro' the Park gate: all the soldiers
Fled from his sight: he drag'd his torments to the wilderness.

Thus was the howl thro' Europe!
For Orc rejoic'd to hear the howling shadows;
But Palamabron shot his lightnings, trenching down his wide back;
And Rintrah hung with all his legions in the nether deep.

Enitharmon laugh'd in her sleep to see (O woman's triumph!)
Every house a den, every man bound: the shadows are fill'd
With spectres, and the windows wove over with curses of iron:
Over the doors "Thou shalt not," & over the chimneys "Fear" is written:
With bands of iron round their necks fasten'd into the walls
The citizens, in leaden gyves the inhabitants of suburbs
Walk heavy; soft and bent are the bones of villagers.

Between the clouds of Urizen the flames of Orc roll heavy
Around the limbs of Albion's Guardian, his flesh consuming:
Howlings & hissings, shrieks & groans, & voices of despair
Arise around him in the cloudy heavens of Albion. Furious,

Plate 13

The red limb'd Angel siez'd in horror and torment
The Trump of the last doom; but he could not blow the iron tube!
Thrice he assay'd presumptuous to awake the dead to Judgment.

A mighty Spirit leap'd from the land of Albion,
Nam'd Newton: he siez'd the trump & blow'd the enormous blast!
Yellow as leaves of Autumn, the myriads of Angelic hosts
Fell thro' the wintry skies seeking their graves,
Rattling their hollow bones in howling and lamentation.

Then Enitharmon woke, nor knew that she had slept;
And eighteen hundred years were fled
As if they had not been.
She call'd her sons & daughters
To the sports of night
Within her crystal house,
And thus her song proceeds:

"Arise, Ethinthus! tho' the earth-worm call,
"Let him call in vain,
"Till the night of holy shadows
"And human solitude is past!

Plate 14

"Ethinthus, queen of waters, how thou shinest in the sky!
"My daughter, how do I rejoice! for thy children flock around
"Like the gay fishes on the wave, when the cold moon drinks the dew.
"Ethinthus! thou art sweet as comforts to my fainting soul,
"For now thy waters warble round the feet of Enitharmon.

"Manathu-Vorcyon! I behold thee flaming in my halls,
"Light of thy mother's soul! I see thy lovely eagles round;
"Thy golden wings are my delight, & thy flames of soft delusion.

"Where is my lureing bird of Eden? Leutha, silent love!
"Leutha, the many colour'd bow delights upon thy wings:
"Soft soul of flowers, Leutha!
"Sweet smiling pestilence! I see thy blushing light;
"Thy daughters, many changing,
"Revolve like sweet perfumes ascending, O Leutha, silken queen!

"Where is the youthful Antamon, prince of the pearly dew?
"O Antamon! why wilt thou leave thy mother Enitharmon?
"Alone I see thee, crystal form,
"Flo[a]ting upon the bosom'd air
"With lineaments of gratified desire.
"My Antamon, the seven churches of Leutha seek thy love.

"I hear the soft Oothoon in Enitharmon's tents;
"Why wilt thou give up woman's secrecy, my melancholy child?
"Between two moments bliss is ripe.
"O Theotormon! robb'd of joy, I see thy salt tears flow
"Down the steps of my crystal house.

"Sotha & Thiralatha! secret dwellers of dreamful caves,
"Arise and please the horrent fiend with your melodious songs;
"Still all your thunders, golden-hoof'd, & bind your horses black.
"Orc! smile upon my children!
"Smile, son of my afflictions.
"Arise, O Orc, and give our mountains joy of thy red light!"

She ceas'd; for All were forth at sport beneath the solemn moon[1]
Waking the stars of Urizen with their immortal songs,
That nature felt thro' all her pores the enormous revelry
Till morning oped the eastern gate;[2]
Then every one fled to his station, & Enitharmon wept.

But terrible Orc, when he beheld the morning in the east, .

---

[1] *The first form of this line on a proof of the plate was:*
She ceas'd and all went forth to sport . . .
Blake then altered this in ink to:
She ceas'd All were forth in sport . . .

[2] *On another proof of the plate Blake has erased the last six lines from the paper, but it can be seen that six words of the last line but two have been erased from the plate; on another proof these are:*
Till morning ope'd the eastern gate, and the angel trumpet blew.

Plate 15

Shot from the heights of Enitharmon, [before the Trumpet blew *erased*]
And in the vineyards of red France appear'd the light of his fury.

The sun glow'd fiery red!
The furious terrors flew around
On golden chariots raging with red wheels dropping with blood!
The Lions lash their wrathful tails!
The Tigers couch upon the prey & suck the ruddy tide,
And Enitharmon groans & cries in anguish and dismay.

Then Los arose: his head he rear'd in snaky thunders clad;
And with a cry that shook all nature to the utmost pole,
Call'd all his sons to the strife of blood.

FINIS

THE SONG of LOS

LAMBETH Printed by W Blake 1795

Plate 3

AFRICA

I will sing you a song of Los, the Eternal Prophet:
He sung it to four harps at the tables of Eternity.
In heart-formed Africa.
Urizen faded! Ariston shudder'd!
And thus the Song began:

Adam stood in the garden of Eden
And Noah on the mountains of Ararat;
They saw Urizen give his Laws to the Nations
By the hands of the children of Los.

Adam shudder'd! Noah faded! black grew the sunny African
When Rintrah gave Abstract Philosophy to Brama in the East.
(Night spoke to the Cloud:
"Lo these Human form'd spirits, in smiling hipocrisy, War
"Against one another; so let them War on, slaves to the eternal Elements.")
Noah shrunk beneath the waters;
Abram fled in fires from Chaldea;
Moses beheld upon Mount Sinai forms of dark delusion.

To Trismegistus, Palamabron gave an abstract Law:
To Pythagoras, Socrates & Plato.

Times rolled on o'er all the sons of Har: time after time
Orc on Mount Atlas howl'd, chain'd down with the Chain of Jealousy;
Then Oothoon hover'd over Judah & Jerusalem,
And Jesus heard her voice (a man of sorrows) he reciev'd
A Gospel from wretched Theotormon.

The human race began to wither, for the healthy built
Secluded places, fearing the joys of Love,
And the diseased only propagated.
So Antamon call'd up Leutha from her valleys of delight
And to Mahomet a loose Bible gave.
But in the North, to Odin, Sotha gave a Code of War,
Because of Diralada, thinking to reclaim his joy.

Plate 4

These were the Churches, Hospitals, Castles, Palaces,
Like nets & gins & traps to catch the joys of Eternity,
And all the rest a desart;
Till, like a dream, Eternity was obliterated & erased.

Since that dread day when Har and Heva fled
Because their brethren & sisters liv'd in War & Lust;
And as they fled they shrunk
Into two narrow doleful forms
Creeping in reptile flesh upon
The bosom of the ground;
And all the vast of Nature shrunk
Before their shrunken eyes.

Thus the terrible race of Los & Enitharmon gave
Laws & Religions to the sons of Har, binding them more
And more to Earth, closing and restraining,
Till a Philosophy of Five Senses was complete.
Urizen wept & gave it into the hands of Newton & Locke.

Clouds roll heavy upon the Alps round Rousseau & Voltaire,
And on the mountains of Lebanon round the deceased Gods
Of Asia, & on the desarts of Africa round the Fallen Angels
The Guardian Prince of Albion burns in his nightly tent.

Plate 6

ASIA

The Kings of Asia heard
The howl rise up from Europe,
And each ran out from his Web,
From his ancient woven Den;
For the darkness of Asia was startled
At the thick-flaming, thought-creating fires of Orc.

And the Kings of Asia stood
And cried in bitterness of soul:

"Shall not the King call for Famine from the heath,
"Nor the Priest for Pestilence from the fen,
"To restrain, to dismay, to thin
"The inhabitants of mountain and plain,
"In the day of full-feeding prosperity
"And the night of delicious songs?

"Shall not the Councellor throw his curb
"Of Poverty on the laborious,
"To fix the price of labour,
"To invent allegoric riches?

"And the privy admonishers of men
"Call for fires in the City,
"For heaps of smoking ruins
"In the night of prosperity & wantonness?

"To turn man from his path,
"To restrain the child from the womb,

Plate 7

"To cut off the bread from the city,
"That the remnant may learn to obey,

"That the pride of the heart may fail,
"That the lust of the eyes may be quench'd,
"That the delicate ear in its infancy
"May be dull'd, and the nostrils clos'd up,
"To teach mortal worms the path
"That leads from the gates of the Grave?"

Urizen heard them cry,
And his shudd'ring, waving wings
Went enormous above the red flames,
Drawing clouds of despair thro' the heavens
Of Europe as he went.
And his Books of brass, iron & gold
Melted over the land as he flew,
Heavy-waving, howling, weeping.

And he stood over Judea,
And stay'd in his ancient place,
And stretch'd his clouds over Jerusalem;

For Adam, a mouldering skeleton,
Lay bleach'd on the garden of Eden;
And Noah, as white as snow,
On the mountains of Ararat.

Then the thunders of Urizen bellow'd aloud
From his woven darkness above.

Orc, raging in European darkness,
Arose like a pillar of fire above the Alps,
Like a serpent of fiery flame!
The sullen Earth
Shrunk!

Forth from the dead dust, rattling bones to bones
Join; shaking convuls'd, the shiv'ring clay breathes,
And all flesh naked stands: Fathers and Friends,
Mothers & Infants, Kings & Warriors.

The Grave shrieks with delight & shakes
Her hollow womb & clasps the solid stem:
Her bosom swells with wild desire,
And milk & blood & glandous wine
In rivers rush & shout & dance,
On mountain, dale and plain.

The SONG of LOS is Ended.

Urizen Wept.

THE BOOK of AHANIA

LAMBETH Printed by W. Blake 1795

Plate 2

Chap: I[st]

1. Fuzon on a chariot iron-wing'd
On spiked flames rose; his hot visage
Flam'd furious; sparkles his hair & beard
Shot down his wide bosom and shoulders.
On clouds of smoke rages his chariot
And his right hand burns red in its cloud
Moulding into a vast Globe his wrath,
As the thunder-stone is moulded.
Son of Urizen's silent burnings:

2. "Shall we worship this Demon of smoke,"
Said Fuzon, "this abstract non-entity,
"This cloudy God seated on waters,
"Now seen, now obscur'd, King of sorrow?"

3. So he spoke in a fiery flame,
On Urizen frowning indignant,
The Globe of wrath shaking on high;
Roaring with fury he threw
The howling Globe; burning it flew
Length'ning into a hungry beam. Swiftly

4. Oppos'd to the exulting flam'd beam,
The broad Disk of Urizen upheav'd
Across the Void many a mile.

5. It was forg'd in mills where the winter
Beats incessant: ten winters the disk
Unremitting endur'd the cold hammer.

6. But the strong arm that sent it remember'd
The sounding beam: laughing, it tore through
That beaten mass, keeping its direction,
The cold loins of Urizen dividing.

7. Dire shriek'd his invisible Lust;
Deep groan'd Urizen! stretching his awful hand,
Ahania (so name his parted soul)
He siez'd on his mountains of Jealousy.

He groan'd anguish'd, & called her Sin,
Kissing her and weeping over her;
Then hid her in darkness, in silence,
Jealous, tho' she was invisible.

8. She fell down a faint shadow wand'ring
In chaos and circling dark Urizen,
As the moon anguish'd circles the earth,
Hopeless! abhorr'd! a death-shadow,
Unseen, unbodied, unknown,
The mother of Pestilence.

9. But the fiery beam of Fuzon
Was a pillar of fire to Egypt
Five hundred years wand'ring on earth,
Till Los siez'd it and beat in a mass
With the body of the sun.

Plate 3

Chap: II[d]

1. But the forehead of Urizen gathering,
And his eyes pale with anguish, his lips
Blue & changing, in tears and bitter
Contrition he prepar'd his Bow,

2. Form'd of Ribs, that in his dark solitude,
When obscur'd in his forests, fell monsters
Arose. For his dire Contemplations
Rush'd down like floods from his mountains,
In torrents of mud settling thick,
With Eggs of unnatural production:
Forthwith hatching, some howl'd on his hills,
Some in vales, some aloft flew in air.

3. Of these, an enormous dread Serpent,
Scaled and poisonous horned,
Approach'd Urizen, even to his knees,
As he sat on his dark rooted Oak.

4. With his horns he push'd furious:
Great the conflict & great the jealousy
In cold poisons, but Urizen smote him.

5. First he poison'd the rocks with his blood,
Then polish'd his ribs, and his sinews
Dried, laid them apart till winter;
Then a Bow black prepar'd: on this Bow
A poisoned rock plac'd in silence.
He utter'd these words to the Bow:

6. "O Bow of the clouds of secresy!
"O nerve of that lust-form'd monster!
"Send this rock swift, invisible thro'
"The black clouds on the bosom of Fuzon."

7. So saying, In torment of his wounds
He bent the enormous ribs slowly,
A circle of darkness! then fixed
The sinew in its rest; then the Rock,
Poisonous source, plac'd with art, lifting difficult
Its weighty bulk; silent the rock lay,

8. While Fuzon, his tygers unloosing,
Thought Urizen slain by his wrath.
"I am God!" said he, "eldest of things."

9. Sudden sings the rock; swift & invisible
On Fuzon flew, enter'd his bosom;
His beautiful visage, his tresses
That gave light to the mornings of heaven,
Were smitten with darkness, deform'd
And outstretch'd on the edge of the forest.

10. But the rock fell upon the Earth,
Mount Sinai in Arabia.

Chap: III

1. The Globe shook, and Urizen seated
On black clouds his sore wound anointed;
The ointment flow'd down on the void
Mix'd with blood—here the snake gets her poison.

2. With difficulty & great pain Urizen
Lifted on high the dead corse:
On his shoulders he bore it to where
A Tree hung over the Immensity.

3. For when Urizen shrunk away
From Eternals, he sat on a rock
Barren: a rock which himself
From redounding fancies had petrified.
Many tears fell on the rock,
Many sparks of vegetation.
Soon shot the pained root
Of Mystery under his heel:

It grew a thick tree: he wrote
In silence his book of iron,
Till the horrid plant bending its boughs
Grew to roots when it felt the earth,
And again sprung to many a tree.

4. Amaz'd started Urizen when
He beheld himself compassed round
And high roofed over with trees.
He arose, but the stems stood so thick
He with difficulty and great pain
Brought his Books, all but the Book

Plate 4

Of iron, from the dismal shade.

5. The Tree still grows over the Void
Enrooting itself all around,
An endless labyrinth of woe!

6. The corse of his first begotten
On the accursed Tree of Mystery,
On the topmost stem of this Tree,
Urizen nail'd Fuzon's corse.

Chap: IV

1. Forth flew the arrows of pestilence
Round the pale living Corse on the tree.

2. For in Urizen's slumbers of abstraction
In the infinite ages of Eternity,
When his Nerves of Joy melted & flow'd,
A white Lake on the dark blue air
In perturb'd pain and dismal torment
Now stretching out, now swift conglobing,

3. Effluvia vapor'd above
In noxious clouds; these hover'd thick
Over the disorganiz'd Immortal,
Till petrific pain scurf'd o'er the Lakes
As the bones of man, solid & dark.

4. The clouds of disease hover'd wide
Around the Immortal in torment,
Perching around the hurtling bones,
Disease on disease, shape on shape
Winged screaming in blood & torment.

5. The Eternal Prophet beat on his anvils;
Enrag'd in the desolate darkness
He forg'd nets of iron around
And Los threw them around the bones.

6. The shapes screaming flutter'd vain:
Some combin'd into muscles & glands,
Some organs for craving and lust;
Most remain'd on the tormented void,
Urizen's army of horrors.

7. Round the pale living Corse on the Tree
Forty years flew the arrows of pestilence.

8. Wailing and terror and woe
Ran thro' all his dismal world;
Forty years all his sons & daughters
Felt their skulls harden; then Asia
Arose in the pendulous deep.

9. They reptilize upon the Earth.

10. Fuzon groan'd on the Tree.

Chap: V

1. The lamenting voice of Ahania
Weeping upon the void!
And round the Tree of Fuzon,
Distant in solitary night,
Her voice was heard, but no form
Had she; but her tears from clouds
Eternal fell round the Tree.

2. And the voice cried: "Ah, Urizen! Love!
"Flower of morning! I weep on the verge
"Of Non-entity; how wide the Abyss
"Between Ahania and thee!

3. "I lie on the verge of the deep;
"I see thy dark clouds ascend;
"I see thy black forests and floods,
"A horrible waste to my eyes!

4. "Weeping I walk over rocks,
"Over dens & thro' valleys of death
"Why didst thou despise Ahania
"To cast me from thy bright presence
"Into the World of Loneness?

5. "I cannot touch his hand,
"Nor weep on his knees, nor hear
"His voice & bow, nor see his eyes
"And joy, nor hear his footsteps and
"My heart leap at the lovely sound!
"I cannot kiss the place
"Whereon his bright feet have trod,

Plate 5

"But I wander on the rocks
"With hard necessity.

6. "Where is my golden palace?
"Where my ivory bed?
"Where the joy of my morning hour?
"Where the sons of eternity singing

7. "To awake bright Urizen, my king,
"To arise to the mountain sport,
"To the bliss of eternal valleys;

8. "To awake my king in the morn,
"To embrace Ahania's joy
"On the bredth of his open bosom?
"From my soft cloud of dew to fall
"In showers of life on his harvests,

9. "When he gave my happy soul
"To the sons of eternal joy,
"When he took the daughters of life
"Into my chambers of love,

10. "When I found babes of bliss on my beds
"And bosoms of milk in my chambers
"Fill'd with eternal seed.
"O eternal births sung round Ahania
"In interchange sweet of their joys!

11. "Swell'd with ripeness & fat with fatness,
"Bursting on winds, my odors,
"My ripe figs and rich pomegranates
"In infant joy at thy feet,
"O Urizen, sported and sang.

12. "Then thou with thy lap full of seed,
"With thy hand full of generous fire
"Walked forth from the clouds of morning,
"On the virgins of springing joy,
"On the human soul to cast
"The seed of eternal science.

13. "The sweat poured down thy temples;
"To Ahania return'd in evening,
"The moisture awoke to birth
"My mothers-joys, sleeping in bliss.

14. "But now alone over rocks, mountains,
"Cast out from thy lovely bosom,
"Cruel jealousy! selfish fear!
"Self-destroying, how can delight
"Renew in these chains of darkness,
"Where bones of beasts are strown
"On the bleak and snowy mountains,
"Where bones from the birth are buried
"Before they see the light?"

FINIS

THE BOOK OF LOS

LAMBETH Printed by W. Blake 1795

Plate 3

Chap: I

1. Eno, aged Mother,
Who the chariot of Leutha guides
Since the day of thunders in old time,

2. Sitting beneath the eternal Oak
Trembled and shook the steadfast Earth,
And thus her speech broke forth:

3. "O Times remote!
"When Love & Joy were adoration,
"And none impure were deem'd:
"Not Eyeless Covet,
"Nor Thin-lip'd Envy,
"Nor Bristled Wrath,
"Nor Curled Wantonness;

4. "But Covet was poured full,
"Envy fed with fat of lambs,
"Wrath with lion's gore,
"Wantonness lull'd to sleep
"With the virgin's lute
"Or sated with her love;

5. "Till Covet broke his locks & bars
"And slept with open doors;
"Envy sung at the rich man's feast;
"Wrath was follow'd up and down
"By a little ewe lamb,
"And Wantonness on his own true love
"Begot a giant race."

6. Raging furious, the flames of desire
Ran thro' heaven & earth, living flames
Intelligent, organiz'd, arm'd
With destruction & plagues. In the midst
The Eternal Prophet, bound in a chain,
Compell'd to watch Urizen's shadow,

7. Rag'd with curses & sparkles of fury:
Round the flames roll, as Los hurls his chains,
Mounting up from his fury, condens'd,
Rolling round & round, mounting on high
Into vacuum, into non-entity
Where nothing was; dash'd wide apart,
His feet stamp the eternal fierce-raging
Rivers of wide flame; they roll round
And round on all sides, making their way
Into darkness and shadowy obscurity.

8. Wide apart stood the fires: Los remain'd
In the void between fire and fire:
In trembling and horror they beheld him;
They stood wide apart, driv'n by his hands
And his feet, which the nether abyss
Stamp'd in fury and hot indignation.

9. But no light from the fires! all was

Plate 4

Darkness round Los: heat was not; for bound up
Into fiery spheres from his fury,
The gigantic flames trembled and hid.

10. Coldness, darkness, obstruction, a Solid
Without fluctuation, hard as adamant,
Black as marble of Egypt, impenetrable,
Bound in the fierce raging Immortal;
And the seperated fires froze in:
A vast solid without fluctuation
Bound in his expanding clear senses.

Chap: II

1. The Immortal stood frozen amidst
The vast rock of eternity times
And times, a night of vast durance,
Impatient, stifled, stiffen'd, hard'ned;

2. Till impatience no longer could bear
The hard bondage: rent, rent, the vast solid,
With a crash from immense to immense,

3. Crack'd across into numberless fragments.
The Prophetic wrath, strugling for vent,
Hurls apart, stamping furious to dust
And crumbling with bursting sobs, heaves
The black marble on high into fragments.

4. Hurl'd apart on all sides as a falling
Rock, the innumerable fragments away
Fell asunder; and horrible vacuum
Beneath him, & on all sides round,

5. Falling, falling, Los fell & fell,
Sunk precipitant, heavy, down, down,
Times on times, night on night, day on day—
Truth has bounds, Error none—falling, falling,
Years on years, and ages on ages
Still he fell thro' the void, still a void
Found for falling, day & night without end;
For tho' day or night was not, their spaces
Were measur'd by his incessant whirls
In the horrid vacuity bottomless.

6. The Immortal revolving, indignant,
First in wrath threw his limbs like the babe
New born into our world: wrath subsided,
And contemplative thoughts first arose;
Then aloft his head rear'd in the Abyss
And his downward-borne fall chang'd oblique

7. Many ages of groans, till there grew
Branchy forms organizing the Human
Into finite inflexible organs;

8. Till in process from falling he bore
Sidelong on the purple air, wafting
The weak breeze in efforts o'erwearied.

9. Incessant the falling Mind labour'd,
Organizing itself, till the Vacuum
Became element, pliant to rise
Or to fall or to swim or to fly,
With ease searching the dire vacuity.

Chap: III

1. The Lungs heave incessant, dull, and heavy;
For as yet were all other parts formless,
Shiv'ring, clinging around like a cloud,
Dim & glutinous as the white Polypus
Driv'n by waves & englob'd on the tide.

2. And the unformed part crav'd repose;
Sleep began; the Lungs heave on the wave:
Weary, overweigh'd, sinking beneath
In a stifling black fluid, he woke.

3. He arose on the waters; but soon
Heavy falling, his organs like roots
Shooting out from the seed, shot beneath,
And a vast world of waters around him
In furious torrents began.

4. Then he sunk, & around his spent Lungs
Began intricate pipes that drew in
The spawn of the waters, Outbranching

Plate 5

An immense Fibrous Form, stretching out
Thro' the bottoms of immensity raging.

5. He rose on the floods; then he smote
The wild deep with his terrible wrath,
Seperating the heavy and thin.

6. Down the heavy sunk, cleaving around
To the fragments of solid: up rose
The thin, flowing round the fierce fires
That glow'd furious in the expanse.

Chap: IV

1. Then Light first began: from the fires,
Beams, conducted by fluid so pure,
Flow'd around the Immense. Los beheld
Forthwith, writhing upon the dark void,
The Back bone of Urizen appear
Hurtling upon the wind
Like a serpent! like an iron chain
Whirling about in the Deep.

2. Upfolding his Fibres together
To a Form of impregnable strength,
Los, astonish'd and terrified, built
Furnaces; he formed an Anvil,
A Hammer of adamant: then began
The binding of Urizen day and night.

3. Circling round the dark Demon with howlings,
Dismay & sharp blightings, the Prophet
Of Eternity beat on his iron links.

4. And first from those infinite fires,
The light that flow'd down on the winds
He siez'd, beating incessant, condensing
The subtil particles in an Orb.

5. Roaring indignant, the bright sparks
Endur'd the vast Hammer; but unwearied
Los beat on the Anvil, till glorious
An immense Orb of fire he fram'd.

6. Oft he quench'd it beneath in the Deeps,
Then survey'd the all bright mass, Again
Siezing fires from the terrific Orbs,
He heated the round Globe, then beat,
While, roaring, his Furnaces endur'd
The chain'd Orb in their infinite wombs.

7. Nine ages completed their circles
When Los heated the glowing mass, casting
It down into the Deeps: the Deeps fled
Away in redounding smoke: the Sun
Stood self-balanc'd. And Los smil'd with joy.
He the vast Spine of Urizen siez'd,
And bound down to the glowing illusion.

8. But no light! for the Deep fled away
On all sides, and left an unform'd
Dark vacuity: here Urizen lay
In fierce torments on his glowing bed;

9. Till his Brain in a rock & his Heart
In a fleshy slough formed four rivers
Obscuring the immense Orb of fire
Flowing down into night: till a Form
Was completed, a Human Illusion
In darkness and deep clouds involv'd.

The end of the Book of LOS

"I ASKED A THIEF"

Fair copy, written 1796[1]

I askéd a thief to steal me a peach:
He turned up his eyes.
I ask'd a lithe lady to lie her down:
Holy & meek she cries—

As soon as I went
An angel came.
He wink'd at the thief
And smil'd at the dame.

And without one word said
Had a peach from the tree
And still as a maid
Enjoy'd the lady.

W Blake
Lambeth
1796

LEGENDS IN A SMALL BOOK OF DESIGNS

Written 1796

Urizen, title-page design:

Which is the Way
The Right or the Left.

The Marriage of Heaven and Hell, pl. 11:

Death & Hell
Team with Life.

The same, pl. 14:

a Flaming Sword
Revolving every way.

---

[1] For first draft see p. 163.

Urizen, pl. 2:

Teach these Souls to Fly.

The same, pl. 10:

Does the Soul labour thus
In Caverns of The Grave.

Visions of the Daughters of Albion, pl. 7:

Wait Sisters
Tho' all is Lost.

Urizen, pl. 5:

The Book of my Remembrance.

The same, pl. 9:

Eternally I labour on.

The same, pl. 12:

I labour upwards into futurity.

LEGEND IN A LARGE BOOK OF DESIGNS

Written about 1796

Urizen, pl. 22:

Frozen doors to mock
The World: while they within torments uplock.

THE FOUR ZOAS

Written and Revised 1795-1804

Dated 1797

[*Title, first form*]

VALA

OR

The Death and Judgement

of the [Eternal *del.*] Ancient Man

a DREAM of Nine Nights

by William Blake 1797

[*Title, second form*]

The Four Zoas

The torments of Love & Jealousy in

The Death and Judgement

of *Albion* the Ancient Man

Rest before Labour

"Οτι οὐκ ἐστιν ἡμῖν ἡ πάλη πρὸς αἷμα καὶ σάρκα, ἀλλὰ πρὸς τὰς ἀρχάς, πρὸς τὰς ἐξουσίας, πρὸς τοὺς κοσμοκράτορας τοῦ σκότους τοῦ αἰῶνος τούτου, πρὸς τὰ πνευματικὰ τῆς πονηρίας ἐν τοῖς ἐπουρανιοις.

'Εφεσ. 5 [6] κεφ. 12 [*V.*][1]

[1] For our contention is not with the blood and the flesh,
but with dominion, with authority, with the blind world—
rulers of this life, with the spirit of evil in things heavenly.
Ephes., 6 chap., 12.

VALA

Night the First

[This is the Song of Eno . . . . Vala *del.*]
The Song of the Aged Mother which shook the heavens with wrath,
[And thus beginneth the Book of Vala, which whosoever reads
If with his intellect he comprehend the terrible sentence *del.*]
Hearing the march of long resounding, strong heroic Verse
Marshall'd in order for the day of Intellectual Battle.
The heavens [shall *del.*] quake, the earth [shall *del.*] was moved & shudder'd, & the mountains
With all their woods, the streams & valleys wail'd in dismal fear.

Four Mighty Ones are in every Man; a Perfect Unity
Cannot Exist but from the Universal Brotherhood of Eden,
The Universal Man, to Whom be Glory Evermore. Amen.

John xvii c., 21, 22, 23 v
John i c., 14 v
Καὶ ἐσκήνωσεν ἐν ἡμῖν.[1]

What are the Natures of those Living Creatures the Heav'nly Father only
Knoweth. No Individual [*Man* del.] *knoweth* (*not*), *nor can know in all Eternity.*[2]

Los was the fourth immortal starry one, & in the Earth
Of a bright Universe, Empery attended day & night,
Days & nights of revolving joy. Urthona was his name
In Eden; in the Auricular Nerves of Human Life,
Which is the Earth of Eden, he his Emanations propagated,
[Like Sons & Daughters *del.*] *Fairies of Albion, afterwards Gods of the Heathen.*
Daughter of Beulah, Sing
His fall into Division & his Resurrection to Unity:
His fall into the Generation of decay & death, & his
Regeneration by the Resurrection from the dead.

Begin with Tharmas, Parent pow'er, dark'ning in the West.

"Lost! Lost! Lost! are my Emanations! Enion, [come forth, *del.*] O Enion,
"We are become a Victim to the Living. We hide in secret.
"I have hidden [thee, Enion, in jealous despair *del.*] Jerusalem in silent Contrition, O Pity Me.

---

[1] And he dwelt among us.

[2] Blake's late additions and corrections in the MS, made in pencil, are printed throughout in italic.

"I will build thee a Labyrinth [where we may remain for ever alone *del.*] also: O pity me. O Enion,
"Why hast thou taken sweet Jerusalem from my inmost Soul?
"Let her Lay secret in the soft recess of darkness & silence.
"It is not Love I bear to Enitharmon. It is Pity.
"She hath taken refuge in my bosom & I cannot cast her out.

"The Men have reciev'd their death wounds & their Emanations are fled
"To me for refuge & I cannot turn them out for Pity's sake."

Enion said: "Thy fear has made me tremble, thy terrors have surrounded me.
"All Love is lost: Terror succeeds, & Hatred instead of Love,
"And stern demands of Right & Duty instead of Liberty.
"Once thou wast to Me the loveliest son of heaven—But now
"Why art thou Terrible? and yet I love thee in thy terror till
"I am almost Extinct & soon shall be a shadow in Oblivion,
"Unless some way can be found that I may look upon thee & live.
"Hide me some shadowy semblance, secret whisp'ring in my Ear,
"In secret of soft wings, in mazes of delusive beauty.
"I have look'd into the secret soul of him I lov'd,
"And in the Dark recesses found Sin & cannot return."

Trembling & pale sat Tharmas, weeping in his clouds.

"Why wilt thou Examine every little fibre of my soul,
"Spreading them out before the sun like stalks of flax to dry?
"The infant joy is beautiful, but its anatomy
"Horrible, Ghast & Deadly; nought shalt thou find in it
"But Death, Despair & Everlasting brooding Melancholy.
"Thou wilt go mad with horror if thou dost Examine thus
"Every moment of my secret hours. Yea, I know
"That I have sinn'd, & that my Emanations are become harlots.
"I am already distracted at their deeds, & if I look
"Upon them more, Despair will bring self-murder on my soul.
"O Enion, thou art thyself a root growing in hell,
"Tho' thus heavenly beautiful to draw me to destruction.
"*Sometimes I think thou art a flower expanding,*
"*Sometimes I think thou art fruit, breaking from its bud*
"*In dreadful dolor & pain; & I am like an atom,*
"*A Nothing, left in darkness; yet I am an identity:*
"*I wish & feel & weep & groan. Ah, terrible! terrible!*"

In [Beulah *del.*] Eden, Females sleep the winter in soft silken veils
Woven by their own hands to hide them in the darksom grave;
But Males immortal live renew'd by female deaths; in soft
Delight they die, & they revive in spring with music & songs.
Enion said: "Farewell, I die. I hide from thy searching eyes."

So saying, From her bosom weaving soft in sinewy threads
A tabernacle [of delight *del.*] *for Jerusalem*, she sat among the Rocks
Singing her lamentation. Tharmas groan'd among his Clouds
Weeping; [and *del.*] then bending from his Clouds, he stoop'd his
[holy *del.*] innocent head,
And stretching out his holy hand in the vast deep sublime,
Turn'd round the circle of Destiny with tears & bitter sighs
And said: "Return, O wanderer, when the day of Clouds is o'er."

So saying, he sunk down into the sea, a pale white corse.
[So saying *del.*] In torment he sunk down & flow'd among her
filmy Woof,
His spectre issuing from his feet in flames of fire.
In [dismal *del.*] gnawing pain drawn out by her lov'd fingers, every
nerve
She counted, every vein & lacteal, threading them among
Her woof of terror. Terrified & drinking tears of woe
Shudd'ring she wove nine days & nights, sleepless; her food was
tears.

Wond'ring she saw her woof begin to animate, & not
As Garments woven subservient to her hands, but having a will
Of its own, perverse & wayward. Enion lov'd & wept.
Nine days she labour'd at her work, & nine dark sleepless nights;
But on the tenth [bright *del.*] trembling morn, the Circle of Destiny
complete,
Round roll'd the sea, Englobing in a wat'ry Globe, self balanc'd.
A Frowning Continent appear'd where Enion in the desart,
Terrified in her own Creation, viewing her woven shadow,
Sat in a [sweet *del.*] dread intoxication of [false woven bliss *del.*]
[self woven sorrow *del.*] Repentance & Contrition.
[He spurn'd Enion with his foot; he sprang aloft in Clouds
Alighting in his drunken joy in a far distant Grove. *del.*]

There is from Great Eternity a mild & pleasant rest
Nam'd Beulah, a soft Moony Universe, feminine, lovely,
Pure, mild & Gentle, given in Mercy to those who sleep,
Eternally created by the Lamb of God around,
On all sides, within & without the Universal Man.

The daughters of Beulah follow sleepers in all their Dreams,
Creating spaces, lest they fall into Eternal Death.
The Circle of Destiny complete, they gave to it a space,
And nam'd the space Ulro, & brooded over it in care & love.
They said: "The Spectre is in every man insane & most
"Deform'd. Thro' the three heavens descending in fury & fire
"We meet it with our songs & loving blandishments, & give
"To it a form of vegetation. But this Spectre of Tharmas
"Is Eternal Death. What shall we do? O God, [help *del.*] pity & help!"
So spoke they, & clos'd the Gate of the Tongue in trembling fear.

["What have I done," said Enion, "accursed wretch! What deed?
"Is this a deed of Love? I know what I have done. I know
"Too late now to repent. Love is chang'd to deadly Hate,
"A life is blotted out, & I alone remain, possess'd with Fears.
"I see the [remembrance *del.*] shadow of the dead within my [eyes *del.*] soul, wandering
"In darkness & solitude, forming Seas of Doubt & rocks of Repentance.
"Already are my Eyes reverted; all that I behold
"Within my soul has lost its splendor, & a brooding Fear
"Shadows me o'er & drives me outward to a world of woe."
So wail'd she, trembling before her own Created Phantasm *del.*]
[But standing on the Rocks her woven shadow glowing bright *del.*]
Who animating times on times by the force of her sweet song . . .
Rear'd . . .

She drew the Spectre forth from Tharmas in [her silken *del.*] her shining loom
Of Vegetation, weeping in wayward infancy & sullen youth.
List'ning to her soft lamentations, soon his tongue began
To lisp out words & soon, in masculine strength augmenting, he
Rear'd up a form of gold & stood upon the glittering rock
A shadowy human form winged, & in his depths
The dazzlings as of gems shone clear; rapturous in [joy *del.*] fury,
Glorying in his own eyes, Exalted in terrific Pride,
[Searching for glory, wishing that the heavens had eyes to see,
And courting that the Earth would ope her Eyelids & behold
Such wondrous beauty, repining in the midst of all his glory
That nought but Enion could be found to praise, adore, & love.

Three days in self admiring raptures on the rocks he flam'd,
And three dark nights repin'd the solitude, but the third morn
Astonish'd he found Enion hidden in the darksom Cave.

She spoke: "What am I? wherefore was I put forth on these rocks
"Among the Clouds to tremble in the wind in solitude?
"Where is the voice that lately woke the desart? where the Face
"That wept among the clouds, & where the voice that shall reply?
"No other living thing is here. The Sea, the Earth, the Heaven,
"And Enion, desolate; where art thou, Tharmas? O return."

Three days she wail'd & three dark nights, sitting among the Rocks
While the bright spectre hid himself among the trailing clouds.
Then sleep fell on her eyelids in a Chasm of the Valley.
The sixteenth morn the Spectre stood before her manifest. *del.*]

The Spectre thus spoke: "[Art thou not my slave & shalt thou dare
To smite me with thy tongue? beware lest I sting also thee *del.*]
Who art thou, Diminutive husk & shell
"Broke from my bonds? I scorn my prison, I scorn & yet I love.
"If thou hast sinn'd & art polluted, know that I am pure
"And unpolluted, & will bring to rigid strict account
"All thy past deeds; hear what I tell thee! mark it well! remember!
"This world is Thine in which thou dwellest; that within thy soul,
"That dark & dismal infinite where Thought roams up & down,
"Is Mine, & there thou goest when with one Sting of my tongue
"Envenom'd thou roll'st inwards to the place [of death & hell *del.*] *whence I emerg'd.*"

She trembling answer'd: "Wherefore was I born, and what am I?
"A sorrow & a fear, a living torment, & naked Victim.
["I thought to weave a Covering (from *del.*) for my Sins from wrath of Tharmas. *del.*]

"[Examining the sins of Tharmas I (have *del.*) soon found my own.
"O slay me not! thou art his wrath embodied in Deceit *del.*]
"I thought Tharmas a sinner & I murder'd his Emanations,
"His secret loves & Graces. Ah me wretched! What have I done?
"For now I find that all those Emanations were my Children's souls,
"And I have murder'd these with Cruelty above atonement.
"Those that remain have fled from my cruelty into the desarts,
"[Among wild beasts to roam *del.*]
"And thou, the delusive tempter to these deeds, sitt'st before me.
"[But where is *del.*] [Thou art not *del.*] And art thou Tharmas? all thy soft delusive beauty cannot
"Tempt me to murder [honest love *del.*] my own soul & wipe my tears & smile
"In this thy world, [for ah! how *del.*] not mine: tho' dark I feel my world within."[*del., but marked : This line to come in.*]

The Spectre said: "Thou sinful Woman, was it thy desire
"That I should hide thee with my power & delight thee with my beauty?
"And now thou dark'nest in my presence; never from my sight
"Shalt thou depart to weep in secret. In my jealous wings
"I evermore will hold thee, when thou goest out or comest in.
"'Tis thou hast darken'd all My World, O Woman, lovely bane."

[Thus they contended all the day among the Caves of Tharmas,
Twisting in fearful forms & howling, howling, harsh shrieking,
Howling, harsh shrieking; mingling, their bodies join in burning anguish. *del.*]
Mingling his [horrible *del.*] brightness with her tender limbs, then high she soar'd
[Shrieking *del.*] Above the ocean; a bright wonder, [that Beulah *del.*] Nature, [shudder'd at , *del.*]
Half Woman & half Spectre; all his lovely changing colours mix
With her fair crystal clearness; in her lips & cheeks his poisons rose
In blushes like the morning, and his scaly armour softening,
A monster lovely in the heavens or wandering on the earth,
[With spectre voice incessant wailing, in incessant thirst,
Beauty all blushing with desire, mocking her fell despair.

Wandering desolate, a wonder abhorr'd by Gods & Men, *del.*]
Till, with fierce pain, she brought forth on the rocks her sorrow & woe:
Behold two little Infants wept upon the desolate wind.

The first state weeping they began, & helpless as a wave
Beaten along its sightless way, growing enormous in its motion to
Its utmost goal, till strength from Enion, like richest summer shining,
Rais'd the [bright, *del.*] *fierce* boy & girl with glories from their heads out-beaming,
Drawing forth drooping mother's pity, drooping mother's sorrow.

[But those in Great Eternity Met in the Council of God
As One Man, hovering over Gilead & Hermon.
He is the Good Shepherd, He is the Lord & Master
To Create Man Morning by Morning, to give gifts at Noon day.

Enion brooded o'er the rocks; the rough rocks groaning vegetate.
Such power was given to the Solitary wanderer:
The barked Oak, the long limb'd Beech, the Chestnut tree, the Pine,
The Pear tree mild, the frowning Walnut, the sharp Crab, & Apple sweet,

The rough bark opens; twittering peep forth little beaks & wings,
The Nightingale, the Goldfinch, Robin, Lark, Linnet & Thrush.
The Goat leap'd from the craggy cliff, the Sheep awoke from the mould,
Upon its green stalk rose the Corn, waving innumerable,
Infolding the bright Infants from the desolating winds. *del.*]

They sulk upon her breast, her hair became like snow on mountains:
Weaker & weaker, weeping woful, wearier and wearier,
Faded, & her bright Eyes decay'd, melted with pity & love.
And then they wander'd far away, she sought for them in vain:
In weeping blindness, stumbling, she follow'd them o'er rocks & mountains,
Rehumanizing from the Spectre in pangs of maternal love.
Ingrate they wander'd, scorning her, drawing her [life; ingrate *del.*] *spectrous Life,*
Repelling her away & away by a dread repulsive power
Into Non Entity, revolving round in dark despair
And drawing in the spectrous life in pride and haughty joy.
Thus Enion gave them all her spectrous life [*in deep despair.* del.]

Then Eno, a daughter of Beulah, took a Moment of Time
And drew it out to [*twenty years* del.] *seven thousand years with much care & affliction*
And many tears, & in (*the*) [*twenty* del.] *every year*(*s*) [*gave visions toward heaven* del.] *made windows into Eden.*
She also took an atom of space & opened its centre
Into Infinitude & ornamented it with wondrous art.
Astonish'd sat her sisters of Beulah to see her soft affections
To Enion & her children, & they ponder'd these things wond'ring,
And they Alternate kept watch over the Youthful terrors.
They saw not yet the Hand Divine, for it was not yet reveal'd,
But they went on in silent Hope & Feminine repose.

But Los & Enitharmon delighted in the Moony spaces of [Ona *del.*] *Eno,*
Nine Times they liv'd among the forests, feeding on sweet fruits,
And nine bright Spaces wander'd, weaving mazes of delight,
Snaring the wild Goats for their milk, they eat the flesh of Lambs:
A male & female, naked & ruddy as the pride of summer.

Alternate Love & Hate his breast: hers Scorn & Jealousy
In embryon passions; they kiss'd not nor embrac'd for shame & fear.
His head beam'd light & in his vigorous voice was prophecy.
He could controll the times & seasons & the days & years;

She could controll the spaces, regions, desart, flood & forest,
But had no power to weave a Veil of covering for her sins.
She drave the Females all away from Los,
And Los drave all the Males from her away.
They wander'd long, till they sat down upon the margin'd sea,
Conversing with the visions of Beulah in dark slumbrous bliss.
[Nine years they view the living spheres, reading the Visions of Beulah. *del.*]

[*marked:* Night the Second]

But the two youthful wonders wander'd in the world of Tharmas.
"Thy name is Enitharmon," said the [bright *del.*] fierce prophetic boy.
"While thy mild voice fills all these caverns with sweet harmony,
"O how [thy *del.*] our Parents sit & [weep *del.*] mourn in their silent secret bowers!"
But Enitharmon answer'd with a dropping tear & frowning
Dark as a dewy morning when the crimson light appears,
"To make us happy [how they *del.*] *let them* weary their immortal powers . .
"While we draw in their sweet delights, while we return them scorn
"On scorn to feed our discontent; for if we grateful prove
"They will withhold sweet love, whose food is thorns & bitter roots.
"We hear the warlike clarions, we view the turning spheres,
"Yet Thou in indolence reposest, holding me in bonds.
"Hear! I will sing a Song of Death! it is a Song of Vala!
"The Fallen Man takes his repose, Urizen sleeps in the porch,
"Luvah and Vala wake & [flew *del.*] *fly* up from the Human Heart
"Into the Brain from thence; upon the pillow Vala slumber'd,
"And Luvah siez'd the Horses of Light & rose into the Chariot of Day.
"Sweet laughter siez'd me in my sleep; silent & close I laugh'd,
"For in the visions of Vala I walk'd with the mighty Fallen One,
"I heard his voice among the branches & among sweet flowers:
" 'Why is the light of Enitharmon darken'd in [her *del.*] dewy morn?
" 'Why is the silence of Enitharmon a [cloud *del.*] terror, & her smile a whirlwind,
" 'Uttering this darkness in my halls, in the pillars of my Holy-ones?
" 'Why dost thou weep as Vala & wet thy veil with dewy tears,
" 'In slumbers of my night-repose infusing a false morning,
" 'Driving the Female Emanations all away from Los?
" 'I have refus'd to look upon the Universal Vision.
" 'And wilt thou slay with death him who devotes himself to thee

" '[If thou drivest all the (Males *del.*) Females away from (Los *del.*) Luvah, I will drive all
" 'The Males away from thee. *del.*]
" 'Once born for the sport & amusement of Man, now born to drink up all his Powers?'
"I heard the sounding sea, I heard the voice weaker and weaker,
"The voice came & went like a dream: I awoke in my sweet bliss."

Then Los smote her upon the Earth; 'twas long e'er she reviv'd.
[Los *del.*] *He* answer'd, dark'ning *more*, with [foul *del.*] indignation hid in smiles:
"I die not, Enitharmon, tho' thou sing'st thy song of Death,
"Nor shalt thou me torment; For I behold the Fallen Man
"Seeking to comfort Vala: she will not be comforted.
"She rises from his throne and seeks the shadows of her garden
"Weeping for Luvah lost in bloody beams of your false morning;
"Sick'ning lies the Fallen Man, his head sick, his heart faint:
"Mighty atchievement of your power! Beware the punishment!

"Refusing to behold the Divine Image which all behold
"And live thereby, he is sunk down into a deadly sleep.
"But we, immortal in our own strength, survive by stern debate
"Till we have drawn the Lamb of God into a mortal form.
"And that he must be born is certain, for One must be All
"And comprehend within himself all things both small & great,
"We therefore, for whose sake all things aspire to be & live,
"Will so recieve the Divine Image that amongst the Reprobate
"He may be devoted to destruction from his mother's womb.

"I see, invisible descend into the Gardens of Vala,
"Luvah walking on the winds! I see the invisible knife,
"I see the shower of blood, I see the swords & spears of futurity.

"Tho' in the Brain of Man we live & in his circling Nerves,
"Tho' this bright world of all our joy is in the Human Brain
"Where Urizen & all his Hosts hang their immortal lamps,
"Thou ne'er shalt leave this cold expanse where wat'ry Tharmas mourns."

So spoke Los. Scorn & Indignation rose upon Enitharmon.

Then Enitharmon, redd'ning fierce, stretch'd her immortal hands:
"Descend, O Urizen, descend with horse & chariots!
"Threaten not me, O visionary; thine the punishment.
"The Human Nature shall no more remain, nor Human acts
"Form the [free *del.*] rebellious Spirits of Heaven, but War & Princedom, & Victory & Blood."

Night darken'd as she spoke; a shudd'ring ran from East to West;
A Groan was heard on high. The warlike clarions ceast, the Spirits
Of Luvah & Vala shudder'd in their Orb, an orb of blood.

Eternity groan'd & was troubled at the Image of Eternal Death.
The Wandering Man bow'd his faint head and Urizen descended—
And *the one must have murder'd the other if he had not descended—*
Indignant, muttering low thunders, Urizen descended,
Gloomy sounding: "Now I am God from Eternity to Eternity."

Sullen sat Los plotting Revenge. Silent he [Urizen *del.*] eyed the Prince
Of Light. Silent the Prince of Light view'd Los; at length a brooded
Smile broke from Urizen, for Enitharmon brighten'd more & more.
Sullen he lower'd on Enitharmon, but he smil'd on Los,
Saying: "Thou art the Lord of Luvah: into thine hands I give
"The prince of Love, the murderer; his soul is in thine hands.
"Pity not Vala, for she pitied not the Eternal Man,
"Nor pity thou the cries of Luvah. Lo, these starry hosts,
"They are thy servants if thou wilt obey my awful Law."

So spoke the Prince of Light & sat beside the seat of Los.
Upon the sandy shore rested his chariot of fire.

Los answer'd furious: "Art thou one of those who when most complacent
"Mean mischief most? If you are such, Lo! I am also such.
"One must be master. Try thy Arts. I also will try mine,
"For I percieve thou hast Abundance which I claim as mine."

Urizen startled stood, but not Long; Soon he cried:
"Obey my voice, young Demon; I am God from Eternity to Eternity.
"*Art thou a visionary of Jesus, the soft delusion of Eternity?*
"*Lo I am God, the terrible destroyer, & not the Saviour.*
"*Why should the Divine Vision compell the sons of Eden*
"*To forego each his own delight, to war against his spectre?*
"*The Spectre is the Man. The rest is only delusion & fancy.*"
Thus Urizen spoke, collected in himself in awful pride.
Ten thousand thousand were his hosts of spirits on the wind,
Ten thousand thousand glittering Chariots shining in the sky.
They pour upon the golden shore beside the silent ocean,
Rejoicing in the Victory, & the heavens were fill'd with blood.

The Earth spread forth her table wide; the Night, a silver cup
Fill'd with the wine of anguish, waited at the golden feast.
But the bright Sun was not as yet; he, filling all the expanse,
Slept as a bird in the blue shell that soon shall burst away.

Los saw the wound of his blow: he saw, he pitied, he wept.
Los now repented that he had smitten Enitharmon; he felt love
Arise in all his Veins; he threw his arms around her loins
To heal the wound of his smiting.

They eat the fleshly bread, they drank the nervous wine;
They listen'd to the Elemental Harps & Sphery Song:
They view'd the dancing Hours quick sporting thro' the sky,
With winged radiance scattering joys thro' the ever changing light.

But Luvah and Vala standing in the bloody sky
On high remain'd alone, forsaken, in fierce jealousy.
They stood above the heavens, forsaken, desolate, suspended in blood.
Descend they could not, nor from Each other avert their eyes.
Eternity appear'd above them as One Man infolded
In Luvah's robes of blood & bearing all his afflictions;
As the sun shines down on the misty earth, such was the Vision.

But purple night and crimson morning & golden day descending
Thro' the clear changing atmosphere display'd green fields among
The varying clouds, like paradises stretch'd in the expanse,
With towns & villages and temples, tents, sheepfolds and pastures
Where dwell the children of the elemental worlds in harmony.

Not long in harmony they dwell, their life is drawn away
And wintry woes succeed, successive driven into the Void
Where Enion craves, successive drawn into the golden feast.

And Los & Enitharmon sat in discontent & scorn.
The Nuptial Song arose from all the thousand thousand spirits
Over the joyful Earth & Sea & ascended into the Heavens;
For Elemental Gods their thunderous Organs blew, creating
Delicious Viands. Demons of Waves their wat'ry Echoes woke.
Bright Souls of vegetative life budding and blossoming
Stretch their immortal hands to smite the gold & silver Wires,
And with immortal Voice soft warbling, fill all Earth & Heaven.
With doubling voices, & loud Horns wound round, sounding,
Cavernous dwellers fill'd the enormous Revelry, Responsing,
And Spirits of Flaming fire on high govern'd the mighty Song.

And This the Song sung at The Feast of Los & Enitharmon:

"[The Mountain *del.*] *Ephraim* call'd out [to the Mountain *del.*] *to Zion:* 'Awake, O Brother Mountain!
" 'Let us refuse the Plow & Spade, the heavy Roller & spiked
" 'Harrow; burn all these Corn fields, throw down all these fences!
" 'Fatten'd on Human blood & drunk with wine of life is better far

" 'Than all these labours of the harvest & the vintage. See the river,
" 'Red with the blood of Men, swells lustful round my rocky knees;
" 'My clouds are not the clouds of verdant fields & groves of fruit,
" 'But Clouds of Human Souls: my nostrils drink the lives of Men.'

"The Villages Lament: they faint, outstretch'd upon the plain.
"Wailing runs round the Valleys from the Mill & from the Barn.
"But most the polish'd Palaces, dark, silent, bow with dread,
"Hiding their books & pictures underneath the dens of Earth.

"The Cities send to one another saying: 'My sons are Mad
" 'With wine of cruelty. Let us plat a scourge, O Sister City.'
"Children are nourish'd for the Slaughter; once the Child was fed
"With Milk, but wherefore now are Children fed with blood?

"The Horse is of more value than the Man. The Tyger fierce
"Laughs at the Human form; the Lion mocks & thirsts for blood.
"They cry, 'O Spider, spread thy web! Enlarge thy bones &, fill'd
" 'With marrow, sinews & flesh, Exalt thyself, attain a voice.

" 'Call to thy dark arm'd hosts; for all the sons of Men muster together
" 'To desolate their cities! Man shall be no more!' 'Awake, O Hosts!'
"The bow string sang upon the hills, 'Luvah & Vala ride
" 'Triumphant in the bloody sky, & the Human form is no more.'

"The list'ning Stars heard, & the first beam of the morning started back:
"He cried out to his Father 'depart! depart!' but sudden Siez'd,
"And clad in steel, & his Horse proudly neigh'd; he smelt the battle
"Afar off. Rushing back, redd'ning with rage, the Mighty Father

"Siez'd his bright sheephook studded with gems & gold; he swung it round
"His head, shrill sounding in the sky; down rush'd the Sun with noise
"Of war; the Mountains fled away; they sought a place beneath.
"Vala remain'd in desarts of dark solitude, nor Sun nor Moon

"By night nor day to comfort her; she labour'd in thick smoke.
"Tharmas endur'd not; he fled howling; then, a barren waste, sunk down
"Conglobing in the dark confusion. Mean time Los was born
"And thou, O Enitharmon! Hark, I hear the hammers of Los.

"They melt the bones of Vala & the bones of Luvah into wedges;
"The innumerable sons & daughters of Luvah, clos'd in furnaces,
"Melt into furrows; winter blows his bellows: Ice & snow
"Tend the dire anvils: Mountains mourn, & Rivers faint & fail.

"There is no City, nor Cornfield, nor Orchard; all is Rock & Sand.
"There is no Sun, nor Moon, nor Star, but rugged wintry rocks
"Justling together in the void, suspended by inward fires.
"Impatience now no longer can endure. Distracted Luvah,

"Bursting forth from the loins of Enitharmon, Thou fierce Terror,
"Go howl in vain! Smite, smite his fetters! smite, O wintry hammers!
"Smite, Spectre of Urthona! mock the fiend who drew us down
"From heavens of joy into this deep. Now rage, but rage in vain!"

Thus sang the demons of the deep; the Clarions of war blew loud.
The Feast redounds, & Crown'd with roses & the circling vine
The Enormous Bride & Bridegroom sat; beside them Urizen,
With faded radiance sigh'd, forgetful of the flowing wine
And of Ahania, his Pure Bride; but she was distant far.

But Los & Enitharmon sat in discontent & scorn,
Craving the more, the more enjoying, drawing out sweet bliss
From all the turning wheels of heaven & the chariots of the Slain.

At distance, Far in Night repell'd, in direful hunger craving,
Summers & winters round revolving in the frightful deep,
Enion, blind & age-bent, wept upon the desolate wind:

"Why does the Raven cry aloud and no eye pities her?
"Why fall the Sparrow & the Robin in the foodless winter?
"Faint, shivering, they sit on leafless bush or frozen stone

"Wearied with seeking food across the snowy waste, the little
"Heart cold, and the little tongue consum'd that once in thoughtless joy
"Gave songs of gratitude to waving cornfields round their nest.

"Why howl the Lion & the Wolf? why do they roam abroad?
"Deluded by [the *del.*] summer's heat, they sport in enormous love
"And cast their young out to the hungry wilds & sandy desarts.

"Why is the Sheep given to the knife? the Lamb plays in the Sun:
"He starts! he hears the foot of Man! he says: Take thou my wool,
"But spare my life: *but* he knows not that [the *del.*] winter cometh fast.

"The Spider sits in his labour'd Web, eager watching for the Fly.
"Presently comes a famish'd Bird & takes away the Spider.
"His Web is left all desolate that his little anxious heart
"So careful wove & spread it out with sighs and weariness."

This was the Lamentation of Enion round the golden Feast.
Eternity groan'd and was troubled at the image of Eternal Death
Without the body of Man, an Exudation from his sick'ning limbs.

Now Man was come to the Palm tree & to the Oak of Weeping
Which stand upon the edge of Beulah, & he sunk down
From the supporting arms of the Eternal Saviour who dispos'd
The pale limbs of his Eternal Individuality
Upon The Rock of Ages, Watching over him with Love & Care.

End of The First Night [*first draft*]

Then those in Great Eternity met in the Council of God
As one Man, for contracting their Exalted Senses
They behold Multitude, or Expanding they behold as one,
As One Man all the Universal family; & that One Man
They call Jesus the Christ, & they in him & he in them
Live in Perfect harmony, in Eden the land of life,
Consulting as One Man above [Mount Gilead *del.*] the Mountain of Snowdon Sublime.

For messengers from Beulah come in tears & dark'ning clouds
Saying, "Shiloh is in ruins, our brother is sick: Albion, He
"Whom thou lovest, is sick; he wanders from his house of Eternity.
"The Daughters of Beulah, terrified, have clos'd the Gate of the Tongue.
"Luvah & Urizen contend in war around the holy tent."

So spoke the Ambassadors from Beulah, & with solemn mourning
They were introduc'd to the divine presence, & they kneeled down
In [Beth Peor *del.*] Conway's Vale, thus recounting the Wars of Death Eternal:

"The Eternal Man wept in the holy tent: Our Brother in Eternity,
"Even Albion whom thou lovest, wept in pain; his family
"Slept round on hills & valleys in the regions of his love.
"But Urizen awoke, & Luvah woke, & thus conferr'd:

" 'Thou Luvah,' said the Prince of Light, 'behold our sons & daughters
" 'Repos'd on beds; let them sleep on; do thou alone depart
" 'Into thy wished Kingdom, where in Majesty & Power

" 'We may erect a throne; deep in the North I place my lot,
" 'Thou in the South; listen attentive. In silent of this night
" 'I will infold the Eternal tent in clouds opake, while thou,
" 'Siezing the chariots of the morning, Go, outfleeting ride
" 'Afar into the Zenith high, bending thy furious course
" 'Southward, with half the tents of men inclos'd in clouds
" 'Of Tharmas & Urthona. I, remaining in porches of the brain,
" 'Will lay my scepter on Jerusalem, the Emanation,
" 'On all her sons, & on thy sons, O Luvah, & on mine
" 'Till dawn was wont to wake them; then my trumpet sounding loud,
" 'Ravish'd away in night; my strong command shall be obey'd
" 'For I have plac'd my centinels in stations; each tenth man
" 'Is bought & sold, & in dim night my word shall be their law.'

" Luvah replied: 'Dictate to thy Equals; am not I
" 'The Prince of all the hosts of Men, nor equal know in Heaven?
" 'If I arise into the Zenith, leaving thee to watch
" 'The Emanation & her Sons, the Satan & the Anak,
" 'Sihon and Og, wilt thou not, rebel to my laws, remain
" 'In darkness building thy strong throne, & in my ancient night
" 'Daring my power wilt arm my sons against me in the [deep *del.*] Atlantic,
" 'My deep, My night, which thou assuming hast assum'd my Crown?
" 'I will remain as well as thou, & here with hands of blood
" 'Smite this dark sleeper in his tent, then try my strength with thee.'

"While thus he spoke his fires redden'd [round *del.*] o'er the holy tent.
"Urizen cast deep darkness round him, silent brooding death,
"Eternal death to Luvah; raging, Luvah pour'd
"The Lances of Urizen from chariots round the holy tent.
"Discord began, & yells & cries shook the wide firmament.

"Beside his anvil stood Urthona dark; a mass of iron
"Glow'd furious on the anvil prepar'd for spades & coulters. All
"His sons fled from his side to join the conflict; pale he heard
"The Eternal voice; he stood, the sweat chill'd on his mighty limbs.
"He drop'd his hammer: dividing from his aking bosom fled
"A portion of his life; shrieking upon the wind she fled,
"And Tharmas took her in, pitying. Then Enion in jealous fear
"Murder'd her & hid her in her bosom, embalming her for fear
"She should arise again to life. Embalm'd in Enion's bosom
"Enitharmon remains a corse; such thing was never known
"*In Eden, that one died a death never to be reviv'd.*
"Urthona stood in terror, but not long; his spectre fled

"To Enion, & his body fell. Tharmas beheld him fall
"Endlong, a raging serpent rolling round the holy tent.
"The sons of war, astonish'd at the Glitt'ring monster, drove
"Him far into the world of Tharmas, into a cavern'd rock.

"But Urizen, with darkness overspreading all the armies,
"Sent round his heralds secretly commanding to depart
"Into the north. Sudden with thunder's sound his multitudes
"Retreat from the fierce conflict, all the sons of Urizen at once
"Must'ring together in thick clouds, leaving the rage of Luvah
"To pour its fury on himself & on the Eternal Man.

"Sudden down fell they all together into an unknown Space,
"Deep, horrible, without End, separated from Beulah, far beneath.
"The Man's exteriors are become indefinite, open'd to pain
"In a fierce hungring void, & none can visit his regions.

"Jerusalem, his Emanation, [will soon *del.*] *is* become a ruin,
"Her little ones [will be *del.*] *are* slain on the top of every street,
"And she herself let (led) captive & scatter'd into [all nations *del.*] the indefinite.
"Gird on thy sword, O thou most mighty in glory & majesty!
"Destroy these oppressors of Jerusalem & those who ruin Shiloh."

So spoke the Messengers of Beulah. Silently removing,
The Family Divine drew up the Universal tent
Above [Mount Gilead *del.*] High Snowdon, & clos'd the Messengers in clouds around
Till the time of the End. Then they Elected Seven, called the Seven
Eyes of God & the Seven Lamps of the Almighty.
The Seven are one within the other; the Seventh is named Jesus,
The Lamb of God, blessed for ever, & he follow'd the Man
Who wander'd in mount Ephraim seeking a Sepulcher,
His inward eyes closing from the Divine vision, & all
His children wandering outside, from his bosom fleeing away.

End of The First Night [*second draft*]

The Daughters of Beulah beheld the Emanation; they pitied,
They wept before the Inner gates of Enitharmon's bosom,
And of her fine wrought brain, & of her bowels within her loins.
Three gates within, Glorious & bright, open into [*Eternity* del.] *Beulah*
From Enitharmon's inward parts; but the bright female terror
Refus'd to open the bright gates; she clos'd and barr'd them fast
Lest Los should enter into Beulah thro' her beautiful gates.

The Emanation stood before the Gates of Enitharmon,
Weeping; the Daughters of Beulah silent in the Porches
Spread her a couch unknown to Enitharmon; here repos'd
Jerusalem in slumbers soft, lull'd into silent rest.

Terrific rag'd the Eternal wheels of intellect, terrific rag'd
The living creatures of the wheels, in the Wars of Eternal life.
But perverse roll'd the wheels of Urizen & Luvah, back revers'd
Downwards & outwards, [*bending* del.] *consuming in the wars of Eternal Death.*

[*Additional lines*]

VALA

Night the [Second] [First *del.*]

Rising upon his Couch of death Albion beheld his Sons.
Turning his Eyes outward to Self, losing the Divine Vision,
[Man *del.*] Albion call'd Urizen & said: "Behold these sick'ning Spheres,
"Whence is this voice of Enion that soundeth in my [ears *del.*] *Porches*?
"Take thou possession! take this Scepter! go forth in my might,
"For I am weary & must sleep in the dark sleep of Death.
"Thy brother Luvah hath smitten me, but pity thou his youth
"Tho' thou hast not piti'd my Age, O Urizen, Prince of Light."

Urizen rose from the bright Feast like a star thro' the evening sky,
Exulting at the voice that call'd him from the Feast of envy.
First he beheld the body of Man, pale, cold; the horrors of death
Beneath his feet shot thro' him as he stood in the Human Brain,
And all its golden porches grew pale with his sickening light,
No more Exulting, for he saw Eternal Death beneath.
Pale, he beheld futurity: pale, he beheld the Abyss
Where Enion, blind & age bent, wept in direful hunger craving,
All rav'ning like the hungry worm & like the silent grave.
Mighty was the draught of Voidness to draw Existence in.

Terrific Urizen strode above in fear & pale dismay.
He saw the indefinite space beneath & his soul shrunk with horror,
His feet upon the verge of Non Existence; his voice went forth:

Luvah & Vala trembling & shrinking beheld the great Work master
And heard his Word: "Divide, ye bands, influence by influence.
"Build we a Bower for heaven's darling in the grizly deep:
"*Build we the Mundane Shell around the Rock of Albion.*"

The Bands of Heaven flew thro' the air singing & shouting to Urizen.
Some fix'd the anvil, some the loom erected, some the plow
And harrow form'd & fram'd the harness of silver & ivory,
The golden compasses, the quadrant, & the rule & balance.
They erected the furnaces, they form'd the anvils of gold beaten in mills
Where winter beats incessant, fixing them firm on their base.
The bellows began to blow, & the Lions of Urizen stood round the anvil
And the leopards cover'd with skins of beasts tended the roaring fires,
Sublime, distinct, their lineaments divine of human beauty.
The tygers of wrath called the horses of instruction from their mangers,
They unloos'd them & put on the harness of gold & silver & ivory,
In human forms distinct they stood round Urizen, prince of Light,
Petrifying all the Human Imagination into rock & sand.
Groans ran along Tyburn's brook and along the River of Oxford
Among the Druid Temples. Albion groan'd on Tyburn's brook:
Albion gave his loud death groan. The Atlantic Mountains trembled.
Aloft the Moon fled with a cry: the Sun with streams of blood.
From Albion's Loins fled all Peoples and Nations of this Earth,
Fled with the noise of Slaughter, & the stars of heaven fled.
Jerusalem came down in a dire ruin over all the Earth,
She fell cold from Lambeth's Vales in groans & dewy death—
The dew of anxious souls, the death-sweat of the dying—
In every pillar'd hall & arched roof of Albion's skies.
The brother & the brother bathe in blood upon the Severn,
The Maiden weeping by. The father & the mother with
The Maiden's father & her mother fainting over the body,
And the Young Man, the Murderer, fleeing over the mountains.

Reuben slept on Penmaenmawr & Levi slept on Snowdon.
Their eyes, their ears, nostrils & tongues roll outward, they behold
What is within now seen without; they are raw to the hungry wind.
They become Nations far remote, in a little & dark Land.
The daughters of Albion girded around their garments of Needle-work,
Stripping Jerusalem's curtains from mild demons of the hills;
Across Europe & Asia to China & Japan like lightnings
They go forth & return to Albion on his rocky couch:
Gwendolen, Ragan, Sabrina, Gonorill, Mehetabel, Cordella,
Boadicea, Conwenna, Estrild, Gwinefrid, Ignoge, Cambel,
Binding Jerusalem's Children in the dungeons of Babylon;
They play before the Armies, before the hounds of Nimrod,
While the Prince of Light on Salisbury plain among the Druid Stones.

Rattling, the adamantine chains & hooks heave up the ore,
In mountainous masses plung'd in furnaces, & they shut & seal'd
The furnaces a time & times; all the while blew the North
His cloudy bellows, & the South & East & dismal West,
And all the while the plow of iron cut the dreadful furrows
In Ulro, beneath Beulah, where the dead wail Night & Day.

Luvah was cast into the Furnaces of affliction & sealed,
And Vala fed in cruel delight the furnaces with fire.
Stern Urizen beheld, urg'd by necessity to keep
The evil day afar, & if perchance with iron power
He might avert his own despair; in woe & fear he saw
Vala incircle round the furnaces where Luvah was clos'd.
In joy she heard his howlings & forgot he was her Luvah,
With whom she walk'd in bliss in times of innocence & youth.

Hear ye the voice of Luvah from the furnaces of Urizen:

"If I indeed am Vala's King, & ye, O sons of Men,
"The workmanship of Luvah's hands in times of Everlasting,
"When I call'd forth the Earth-worm from the cold & dark obscure
"I nurtur'd her, I fed her with my rains & dews; she grew
"A scaled Serpent, yet I fed her tho' she hated me;
"Day after day she fed upon the mountains in Luvah's sight,
"I brought her thro' the Wilderness, a dry & thirsty land,
"And I commanded springs to rise for her in the black desart,
"Till she became a Dragon, winged, bright & poisonous.
"I open'd all the floodgates of the heavens to quench her thirst,
"And I commanded the Great deep to hide her in his hand
"Till she became a little weeping Infant a span long.
"I carried her in my bosom as a man carries a lamb,
"I loved her, I gave her all my soul & my delight,
"I hid her in soft gardens & in secret bowers of summer,
"Weaving mazes of delight along the sunny paradise,
"Inextricable labyrinths. She bore me sons & daughters,
"And they have taken her away & hid her from my sight.
"They have surrounded me with walls of iron & brass. O Lamb
"Of God clothed in Luvah's garments! little knowest thou
"Of death Eternal, that we all go to Eternal Death,
"To our Primeval Chaos in fortuitous concourse of incoherent
"Discordant principles of Love & Hate. I suffer affliction
"Because I love, for I [am *del.*] was love, but hatred awakes in me,
"And Urizen, who was Faith & certainty, is chang'd to Doubt;
"The hand of Urizen is upon me because I blotted out
"That Human [terror *del.*] delusion to deliver all the sons of God

"From bondage of the Human form. O first born Son of Light,
"O Urizen my enemy, I weep for thy stern ambition,
"But weep in vain. O when will you return, Vala the Wanderer?"

These were the words of Luvah, patient in afflictions,
Reasoning from the loins in the unreal forms of Ulro's night.

And when Luvah, age after age, was quite melted with woe,
The fires of Vala faded like a shadow cold & pale,
An evanescent shadow; last she fell, a heap of Ashes
Beneath the furnaces, a woful heap in living death.

Then were the furnaces unseal'd with spades, & pickaxes
Roaring let out the fluid: the molten metal ran in channels
Cut by the plow of ages held in Urizen's strong hand
In many a valley, for the Bulls of Luvah drag'd the Plow.

With trembling horror pale, aghast the Children of Man
Stood on the infinite Earth & saw these visions in the air,
In waters & in earth beneath; they cried to one another,
"What! are we terrors to one another? Come, O brethren, wherefore
"Was this wide Earth spread all abroad? not for wild beasts to roam."
But many stood silent, & busied in their families.
And many said, "We see no Visions in the darksom air.
"Measure the course of that sulphur orb that lights the [dismal *del.*] darksom day;
"Set stations on this breeding Earth & let us buy & sell."
Others arose & schools erected, forming Instruments
To measure out the course of heaven. Stern Urizen beheld
In woe his brethren & his sons, in dark'ning woe lamenting
Upon the winds in clouds involv'd, Uttering his voice in thunders,
Commanding all the work with care & power & severity.

Then siez'd the Lions of Urizen their work, & heated in the forge
Roar the bright masses; thund'ring beat the hammers, many a [Globe *del.*] pyramid
Is form'd & thrown down thund'ring into the deeps of Non Entity.
Heated red hot they, hizzing, rend their way down many a league
Till resting, each his [center *del.* basement *del.*] finds; suspended there they stand
Casting their sparkles dire abroad into the dismal deep.
For, measur'd out in order'd spaces, the Sons of Urizen
With compasses divide the deep; they the strong scales erect
That Luvah rent from the faint Heart of the Fallen Man,
And weigh the massy [Globes *del.*] Cubes, then fix them in their awful stations.

And all the time, in Caverns shut, the golden Looms erected
First spun, then wove the Atmospheres; there the Spider & Worm
Plied the wing'd shuttle, piping shrill thro' all the list'ning threads;
Beneath the Caverns roll the weights of lead & spindles of iron,
The enormous warp & woof rage direful in the affrighted deep.

While far into the vast unknown the strong wing'd Eagles bend
Their venturous flight in Human forms distinct; thro' darkness deep
They bear the woven draperies; on golden hooks they hang abroad
The universal curtains & spread out from Sun to Sun
The vehicles of light; they separate the furious particles
Into mild currents as the water mingles with the wine.

While thus the Spirits of strongest wing enlighten the dark deep,
The threads are spun & the cords twisted & drawn out; then the weak
Begin their work, & many a net is netted, many a net
Spread, & many a Spirit caught; innumerable the nets,
Innumerable the gins & traps, & many a soothing flute
Is form'd, & many a corded lyre outspread over the immense.
In cruel delight they trap the listeners, & in cruel delight
Bind them, condensing the strong energies into little compass.
Some became seed of every plant that shall be planted; some
The bulbous roots, thrown up together into barns & garners.

Then rose the Builders. First the Architect divine his plan
Unfolds. The wondrous scaffold rear'd all round the infinite,
Quadrangular the building rose, the heavens squared by a line,
Trigons & cubes divide the elements in finite bonds.
Multitudes without number work incessant: the hewn stone
Is plac'd in beds of mortar mingled with the ashes of Vala.
Severe the labour; female slaves the mortar trod oppressed.

Twelve halls after the names of his twelve sons compos'd
The [golden *del.*] wondrous building, & three Central Domes after the Names
Of his three daughters were encompass'd by the twelve bright halls.
Every hall surrounded by bright Paradises of Delight
In which were towns & Cities, Nations, Seas, Mountains & Rivers.
Each Dome open'd toward four halls, & the Three Domes Encompass'd
The Golden Hall of Urizen, whose western side glow'd bright
With ever streaming fires beaming from his awful limbs.
His Shadowy Feminine Semblance here repos'd on a White Couch,
Or hover'd over his starry head; & when he smil'd she brighten'd
Like a bright Cloud in harvest; but when Urizen frown'd she wept

In mists over his carved throne; & when he turn'd his back
Upon his Golden hall & sought the Labyrinthine porches
Of his wide heaven, Trembling, cold, in paling fears she sat
A shadow of Despair; therefore toward the West, Urizen form'd
A recess in the wall for fires to glow upon the pale
Female's limbs in his absence, & her Daughters oft upon
A Golden Altar burnt perfumes: with Art Celestial form'd
Foursquare, sculptur'd & sweetly Engrav'd to please their shadowy mother.
Ascending into her [cloudy *del.*] misty garments the blue smoke roll'd to revive
Her cold limbs in the absence of her Lord. Also her sons,
With lives of Victims sacrificed upon an altar of brass
On the East side, Reviv'd her soul with lives of beasts & birds
Slain on the Altar, up ascending into her cloudy bosom.
Of terrible workmanship the Altar, labour of ten thousand Slaves,
One thousand Men of wondrous power spent their lives in its formation.
It stood on twelve steps nam'd after the names of her twelve sons,
And was Erected at the chief entrance of Urizen's hall.

When Urizen [descended *del.*] return'd from his immense labours & travels,
Descending she repos'd beside him, folding him around
In her bright skirts. Astonish'd & Confounded he beheld
Her shadowy form now separate; he shudder'd & was silent
Till her caresses & her tears reviv'd him to life & joy.
Two wills they had, two intellects, & not as in times of old.
This Urizen perciev'd, & silent brooded in dark'ning Clouds.
To him his Labour was but Sorrow & his Kingdom was Repentance.
He drave the Male Spirits all away from Ahania,
And she drave all the Females from him away.

Los joy'd, & Enitharmon laugh'd, saying, "Let us go down
"And see this labour & sorrow." They went down to see the woes
Of Vala & the woes of Luvah, to draw in their delights.

And Vala like a shadow oft appear'd to Urizen.
The King of Light beheld her mourning among the Brick kilns, compell'd
To labour night & day among the fires; her lamenting voice
Is heard when silent night returns & the labourers take their rest.

"O Lord, wilt thou not look upon our sore afflictions
"Among these flames incessant labouring? our hard masters laugh
"At all our sorrow. We are made to turn the wheel for water,

"To carry the heavy basket on our scorched shoulders, to sift
"The sand & ashes, & to mix the clay with tears & repentance.
"The times are now return'd upon us; we have given ourselves
"To scorn, and now are scorned by the slaves of our enemies.
"Our beauty is cover'd over with clay & ashes, & our backs
"Furrow'd with whips, & our flesh bruised with the heavy basket.
"Forgive us, O thou piteous one whom we have offended! forgive
"The weak remaining shadow of Vala that returns in sorrow to thee.

"*I see not Luvah as of old, I only see his feet*
"*Like pillars of fire travelling thro' darkness & non entity.*"

Thus she lamented day & night, compell'd to labour & sorrow.
Luvah in vain her lamentations heard: in vain his love
Brought him in various forms before her, still she knew him not,
Still she despis'd him, calling on his name & knowing him not,
Still hating, still professing love, still labouring in the smoke.

[And Los & Enitharmon joy'd; they drank in tenfold joy
From all the sorrow of Luvah & the labour of Urizen. *del. and afterwards marked :* To Come in.]
And Enitharmon joy'd, Plotting to rend the secret cloud,
To plant divisions in the soul of Urizen & Ahania.

[For *del.*] But infinitely beautiful the wondrous work arose
In sorrow and care, a Golden World whose porches round the heavens
And pillar'd halls & rooms reciev'd the eternal wandering stars.
A wondrous golden Building, many a window, many a door.
And many a division let in & out into the vast unknown.
[*words erased and illegible*] immoveable, within its [arches all *del.*] walls & cielings
The heavens were clos'd, [& *del.*] and spirits mourn'd their bondage night & day,
And the Divine Vision appear'd in Luvah's robes of blood.

Thus was the Mundane shell builded by Urizen's strong Power.

[Then *del.*] Sorrowing went the Planters forth to plant, the Sowers [forth *del.*] to sow;
They dug the channels for the rivers, & they pour'd abroad
The seas & lakes; they rear'd the mountains & the rocks & hills
On broad pavilions, on pillar'd roofs & porches & high towers,
In beauteous order; thence arose soft clouds & exhalations
Wandering even to the sunny [orbs *del.*] Cubes of light & heat,
For many a window ornamented with sweet ornaments
Look'd out into the World of Tharmas, where in ceaseless torrents
His billows roll, where monsters wander in the foamy paths.

On clouds the Sons of Urizen beheld Heaven walled round;
They weigh'd & order'd all, & Urizen comforted saw
The wondrous work flow forth like visible out of the invisible;
For the Divine Lamb, Even Jesus who is the Divine Vision,
Permitted all, lest Man should fall into Eternal Death;
For when Luvah sunk down, himself put on the robes of blood
Lest the state call'd Luvah should cease; & the Divine Vision
Walked in robes of blood till he who slept should awake.

Thus were the stars of heaven created like a golden chain
To bind the Body of Man to heaven from falling into the Abyss.
Each took his station & his course began with sorrow & care.

In sevens & tens & fifties, hundreds, thousands, number'd all
According to their various powers, subordinate to Urizen
And to his sons in their degrees & to his beauteous daughters,
Travelling in silent majesty along their order'd ways
In right lined paths outmeasur'd by proportions of [weight & measure *del.*] number, weight
And measure, mathematic motion wondrous along the deep,
In fiery pyramid, or Cube, or unornamented pillar square
Of fire, far shining, travelling along even to its destin'd end;
Then falling down a terrible space, recovering in winter dire
Its wasted strength, it back returns upon a nether course,
Till fir'd with ardour fresh recruited in its humble [spring *del.*] season,
It rises up on high all summer, till its wearied course
Turns into autumn. Such the period of many worlds.
Others triangular, [their *del.*] right angled course maintain. Others obtuse,
Acute [& Oblong *del.*], Scalene, in simple paths; but others move
In intricate ways, biquadrate, Trapeziums, Rhombs, Rhomboids,
Paralellograms triple & quadruple, polygonic
In their amazing [fructifying *del.*] hard subdu'd course in the vast deep.

And Los & Enitharmon were drawn down by their desires,
Descending sweet upon the wind among soft harps & voices
To plant divisions in the Soul of Urizen & Ahania,
To conduct the Voice of Enion to Ahania's midnight pillow.

Urizen saw & envied, & his imagination was filled.
Repining he contemplated the past in his bright sphere,
Terrified with his heart & spirit at the visions of futurity
That his dread fancy form'd before him in the unform'd void.

[Now *del.*] For Los & Enitharmon walk'd forth on the dewy Earth
Contracting or expanding their all flexible senses
At will to murmur in the flowers small as the honey bee,
At will to stretch across the heavens & step from star to star,
Or standing on the Earth erect, or on the stormy waves
Driving the storms before them, or delighting in sunny beams,
While round their heads the Elemental Gods kept harmony.
And Los said: "Lo, the Lilly pale & the rose redd'ning fierce
"Reproach thee, & the beamy gardens sicken at thy beauty;
"I grasp thy vest in my strong hand in vain, like water springs
"In the bright sands of Los evading my embrace; then I alone
"Wander among the virgins of the summer. Look, they cry,
"The poor forsaken Los, mock'd by the worm, the shelly snail,
"The Emmet & the beetle, hark! they laugh, & mock at Los."

Enitharmon answer'd: "Secure now from the smitings of thy Power, demon of fury,
"If the God enraptur'd me infolds
"In clouds of sweet obscurity my beauteous form dissolving,
"Howl thou over the body of death; 'tis thine. But if among the virgins
"Of summer I have seen thee sleep & turn thy cheek delighted
"Upon the rose or lilly pale, or on a bank where sleep
"The beamy daughters of the light, starting, they rise, they flee
"From thy fierce love, for tho' I am dissolv'd in the bright God,
"My spirit still pursues thy false love over rocks & valleys."

Los answer'd: "Therefore fade I thus dissolv'd in raptur'd trance.
"Thou canst repose on clouds of secrecy, while o'er my limbs
"Cold dews & hoary frost creep tho' I lie on banks of summer
"Among the beauties of the World. Cold & repining Los
"Still dies for Enitharmon, nor a spirit springs from my dead corse;
"Then I am dead till thou revivest me with thy sweet song.
"Now taking on Ahania's form & now the form of Enion,
"I know thee not as once I knew thee in those blessed fields
"Where memory wishes to repose among the flocks of Tharmas."

Enitharmon answer'd, "Wherefore didst thou throw thine arms around
"Ahania's Image? I deciev'd thee & will still decieve.
"Urizen saw thy sin & hid his beams in dark'ning clouds.
"I still keep watch altho' I tremble & wither across the heavens
"In strong vibrations of fierce jealousy; for thou art mine,
"Created for my will, my slave, tho' strong, tho' I am weak.
"Farewell, the God calls me away. I depart in my sweet bliss."

She fled, vanishing on the wind, And left a dead cold corse
In Los's arms; howlings began over the body of death.
Los spoke. "Thy God in vain shall call thee if by my strong power
"I can infuse my dear revenge into his glowing breast.
"Then jealousy shall shadow all his mountains & Ahania
"Curse thee, thou plague of woful Los, & seek revenge on thee."

So saying in deep sobs he languish'd till dead he also fell.
Night passed, & Enitharmon, e'er the dawn, return'd in bliss.
She sang O'er Los reviving him to Life: his groans were terrible;
But thus she sang:
"I sieze the sphery harp. I strike the strings.

"At the first sound the Golden sun arises from the deep
"And shakes his awful hair,
"The Eccho wakes the moon to unbind her silver locks,
"The golden sun bears on my song
"And nine bright spheres of harmony rise round the fiery king.

"The joy of woman is the death of her most best beloved
"Who dies for Love of her
"In torments of fierce jealousy & pangs of adoration.
"The Lovers' night bears on my song
"And the nine spheres rejoice beneath my powerful controll.

"They sing unceasing to the notes of my immortal hand.
"The solemn, silent moon
"Reverberates the living harmony upon my limbs,
"The birds & beasts rejoice & play,
"And every one seeks for his mate to prove his inmost joy.

"Furious & terrible they sport & rend the nether deeps;
"The deep lifts up his rugged head,
"And lost in infinite hum[m]ing wings vanishes with a cry.
"The fading cry is ever dying,
"The living voice is ever living in its inmost joy.

"Arise, you little glancing wings & sing your infant joy!
"Arise & drink your bliss!
"For every thing that lives is holy; for the source of life
"Descends to be a weeping babe;
"For the Earthworm renews the moisture of the sandy plain.

"Now my left hand I stretch to earth beneath,
"And strike the terrible string.
"I wake sweet joy in dens of sorrow & I plant a smile
"In forests of affliction,
"And wake the bubbling springs of life in regions of dark death.

"O, I am weary! lay thine hand upon me or I faint,
"I faint beneath these beams of thine,
"For thou hast touch'd my five senses & they answer'd thee.
"Now I am nothing, & I sink
"And on the bed of silence sleep till thou awakest me."

Thus sang the Lovely one in Rapturous delusive trance.
Los heard, reviving; he siez'd her in his arms; delusive hopes
Kindling, she led him into shadows & thence fled outstretch'd
Upon the immense like a bright rainbow, weeping & smiling & fading.

Thus liv'd Los, driving Enion far into the *deathful* infinite
That he may also draw Ahania's spirit into her Vortex.
Ah, happy blindness! Enion sees not the terrors of the uncertain,
And [oft *del.*] thus she wails from the dark deep; the golden heavens tremble:

"I am made to sow the thistle for wheat, the nettle for a nourishing dainty.
"I have planted a false oath in the earth; it has brought forth a poison tree.
"I have chosen the serpent for a councellor, & the dog
"For a schoolmaster to my children.
"I have blotted out from light & living the dove & nightingale,
"And I have caused the earth worm to beg from door to door.

"I have taught the thief a secret path into the house of the just.
"I have taught pale artifice to spread his nets upon the morning.
"My heavens are brass, my earth is iron, my moon a clod of clay,
"My sun a pestilence burning at noon & a vapour of death in night.

"What is the price of Experience? do men buy it for a song?
"Or wisdom for a dance in the street? No, it is bought with the price
"Of all that a man hath, his house, his wife, his children.
"Wisdom is sold in the desolate market where none come to buy,
"And in the wither'd field where the farmer plows for bread in vain.

"It is an easy thing to triumph in the summer's sun
"And in the vintage & to sing on the waggon loaded with corn.
"It is an easy thing to talk of patience to the afflicted,
"To speak the laws of prudence to the houseless wanderer,
"To listen to the hungry raven's cry in wintry season
"When the red blood is fill'd with wine & with the marrow of lambs.

"It is an easy thing to laugh at wrathful elements,
"To hear the dog howl at the wintry door, the ox in the slaughter house moan;

"To see a god on every wind & a blessing on every blast;
"To hear sounds of love in the thunder storm that destroys our enemies' house;
"To rejoice in the blight that covers his field, & the sickness that cuts off his children,
"While our olive & vine sing & laugh round our door, & our children bring fruits & flowers.

"Then the groan & the dolor are quite forgotten, & the slave grinding at the mill,
"And the captive in chains, & the poor in the prison, & the soldier in the field
"When the shatter'd bone hath laid him groaning among the happier dead.

"It is an easy thing to rejoice in the tents of prosperity:
"Thus could I sing & thus rejoice: but it is not so with me."

Ahania heard the Lamentation, & a swift Vibration
Spread thro' her Golden frame. She rose up e'er the dawn of day
When Urizen slept on his couch: drawn thro' unbounded space
On to the margin of Non Entity the bright Female came.
There she beheld the [terrible *del.*] *Spectrous* form of Enion in the Void,
And never from that moment could she rest upon her pillow.

End of the Second Night

VALA

Night the Third

Now sat the King of Light on high upon his starry throne,
And bright Ahania bow'd herself before his splendid feet.

"O Urizen, look on [thy wife that *del.*] *Me;* like a mournful stream
"*I* Embrace[s *del.*] round thy knees & wet[s her *del.*] *My* bright hair with [her *del.*] *My* tears.
"Why sighs my Lord? are not the morning stars thy obedient Sons?
"Do they not bow their bright heads at thy voice? at thy command
"Do they not fly into their stations & return their light to thee?
"The immortal Atmospheres are thine; there thou art seen in glory
"Surrounded by the ever changing Daughters of the Light.
"[Thou sit'st in harmony, for God hath set thee over all. *del.*]
"Why wilt thou look upon futurity, dark'ning present joy?"

She ceas'd; the Prince his light obscur'd & the splendors of his crown
Infolded in thick clouds from whence his mighty voice burst forth:

"O bright Ahania [shadow *del.*], a Boy is born of the dark Ocean
"Whom Urizen doth serve, with Light replenishing his darkness.
"I am set here a King of trouble, commanded here to serve
"And do my ministry to those who eat of my wide table.
"All this is mine, yet I must serve, & that Prophetic boy
"Must grow up to command his Prince; [& all my Kingly power *del.*]
but hear my determin'd decree:
"[But *del.*] Vala shall become a Worm in Enitharmon's Womb,
"Laying her seed upon the fibres, soon to issue forth,
"And Luvah in the loins of Los a dark & furious death.
"Alas for me! what will become of me at that dread time?"

Ahania bow'd her head & wept seven days before the King;
And on the eighth day, when his clouds unfolded from his throne,
She rais'd her bright head sweet perfum'd & thus with heavenly voice:

"O Prince, the Eternal One hath set thee leader of his hosts,
"[Raise then thy radiant eyes to him, raise thy obedient hands,
"And comforts shall descend from heaven into thy dark'ning clouds. *del.*]
"Leave all futurity to him. Resume thy fields of Light.
"Why didst thou listen to the voice of Luvah that dread morn
"To give the immortal steeds of light to his deceitful hands?
"No longer now obedient to thy will, thou art compell'd
"To forge the curbs of iron & brass, to build the iron mangers,
"To feed them with intoxication from the wine presses of Luvah
"Till the Divine Vision & Fruition is quite obliterated.
"They call thy lions to the field of blood; they rouze thy tygers
"Out of the halls of justice, till these dens thy wisdom fram'd
"Golden & beautiful, but O how unlike those sweet fields of bliss
"Where liberty was justice, & eternal science was mercy.
"Then, O my dear lord, listen to Ahania, listen to the vision,
"The vision of Ahania in the slumbers of Urizen
"When Urizen slept in the porch & the Ancient Man was smitten.

"The Dark'ning Man walk'd on the steps of fire before his halls,
"And Vala walk'd with him in dreams of soft deluding slumber.
"He looked up & saw thee, Prince of Light, [with *del.*] thy splendor faded,
"[But saw not Los nor Enitharmon for Luvah hid them in shadow
"[Of *del.*] *In* a soft cloud outstretch'd across, & Luvah dwelt in the cloud. *del.*]

"Then Man ascended mourning into the splendors of his palace,
"Above him rose a Shadow from his wearied intellect
"Of living gold, pure, perfect, holy; in white linen pure he hover'd,
"A sweet entrancing self delusion, a wat'ry vision of Man
"Soft exulting in existence, all the Man absorbing.

"Man fell upon his face prostrate before the wat'ry shadow,
"Saying 'O Lord, whence is this change? thou knowest I am nothing.'
"And Vala trembled & cover'd her face, & her locks were spread on the pavement.
"[I *del.*] *We* heard astonish'd at the Vision, & [my *del.*] *our* hearts trembled within [me *del.*] *us.*
"[I *del.*] *We* heard the voice of the Slumberous Man, & thus he spoke
"Idolatrous to his own Shadow, words of Eternity uttering:
" 'O I am nothing when I enter into judgment with thee.
" 'If thou withdraw thy breath I die & vanish into Hades;
" 'If thou dost lay thine hand upon me, behold I am silent;
" 'If thou withhold thine hand I perish like a fallen leaf.
" 'O I am nothing, & to nothing must return again.
" 'If thou withdraw thy breath, behold I am oblivion.'

"He ceas'd: the shadowy voice was silent, but the cloud hover'd over their heads
"In golden wreathes, the sorrow of Man, & the balmy drops fell down,
"And Lo, that Son of Man, that shadowy Spirit of the Fallen One [*alt. readg. Albion*]
"Luvah, descended from the cloud. In terror [Man arose. *del.*] *Albion rose :*
"Indignant rose the Awful Man & turn'd his back on Vala.

"[I *del.*] We heard the Voice of the [fall'n One *del.*] Albion starting from his sleep:
" 'Why roll thy clouds in sick'ning mists? I can no longer hide
" 'The dismal vision of mine eyes. O love & life & light!
" 'Prophetic dreads urge me to speak: futurity is before me
" 'Like a dark lamp. Eternal death haunts all my expectation.
" 'Rent from Eternal Brotherhood we die & are no more.

" 'Whence is this voice crying, Enion! that soundeth in my ears?
" 'O cruel pity! O dark deceit! can Love seek for dominion?'

"And Luvah strove to gain dominion over the Ancient Man [*alt. readg. mighty Albion*].

"They strove together above the Body where Vala was inclos'd
"And the dark Body of [Man *del.*] *Albion* left prostrate upon the crystal pavement,
"Cover'd with boils from head to foot, the terrible smitings of Luvah.

"Then frown'd the Fallen Man, [*alt. readg. Albion*] & put forth Luvah from his presence
"(I heard him: frown not, Urizen, but listen to my Vision)
"Saying, 'Go & die the Death of Man for Vala the sweet wanderer.
" 'I will turn the volutions of your Ears outward, & bend your Nostrils
" 'Downward, & your fluxile Eyes englob'd roll round in fear;
" 'Your with'ring Lips & Tongue shrink up into a narrow circle
" 'Till into narrow forms you creep. Go take your fiery way
" 'And learn what 'tis to absorb the Man, you Spirits of Pity & Love.'
"O Urizen, why art thou pale at the visions of Ahania?
"Listen to her who loves thee, lest we also are driven away.

"They heard the Voice & fled, swift as the winter's setting sun.
"And now the Human Blood foam'd high. I saw that Luvah & Vala
"Went down the Human Heart, where Paradise & its joys abounded,
"In jealous fears, in fury & rage, & flames roll'd round their fervid feet,
"And the vast form of Nature like a Serpent play'd before them;
"And as they went, in folding fires & thunders of the deep,
"Vala shrunk in like the dark sea that leaves its slimy banks,
"And from her bosom Luvah fell far as the east & west
"And the vast form of Nature, like a Serpent, roll'd between.
"*Whether this is Jerusalem or Babylon we know not.*
"*All is Confusion. All is tumult, & we alone are escaped.*"
She ended, for his wrathful throne burst forth the black hail storm.

(Albion clos'd the Western Gate, & shut America out by the Atlantic, for a curse, and hidden horror, and an altar of victims to Sin and Repentance.)

"Am I not God?" said Urizen, "Who is Equal to me?
"Do I not stretch the heavens abroad, or fold them up like a garment?"
He spoke, mustering his heavy clouds around him, black, opake.
Then thunders roll'd around & lightnings darted to & fro;
His visage chang'd to darkness, & his strong right hand came forth
To cast Ahania to the Earth: he siez'd her by the hair
And threw her from the steps of ice that froze around his throne,

Saying, "Art thou also become like Vala? thus I cast thee out!
"Shall the feminine indolent bliss, the indulgent self of weariness,
"The passive idle sleep, the enormous night & darkness of Death
"Set herself up to give her laws to the active masculine virtue?
"Thou little diminutive portion that dar'st be a counterpart,
"Thy passivity, thy laws of obedience & insincerity
"Are my abhorrence. Wherefore hast thou taken that fair form?
"Whence is this power given to thee? Once thou wast in my breast
"A sluggish current of dim waters on whose verdant margin
"A cavern shagg'd with horrid shades, dark, cool & deadly, where
"I laid my head in the hot noon after the broken clods
"Had wearied me; there I laid my plow, & there my horses fed:
"And thou hast risen with thy moist locks into a wat'ry image
"Reflecting all my indolence, my weakness & my death,
"To weigh me down beneath the grave into non Entity
"Where Luvah strives, scorned by Vala, age after age wandering,
"Shrinking & shrinking from her Lord & calling him the Tempter.
"And art thou also become like Vala? thus I cast thee out!"

So loud in thunders spoke the King, folded in dark despair,
And threw Ahania from his bosom obdurate. She fell like lightning.
Then fled the sons of Urizen from his thunderous throne petrific;
They fled to East & West & left the North & South of Heaven.
A crash ran thro' the immense. The bounds of Destiny were broken.
The bounds of Destiny crash'd direful, & the swelling sea
Burst from its bonds in whirlpools fierce, roaring with Human voice,
Triumphing even to the stars at bright Ahania's fall.

Down from the dismal North the Prince in thunders & thick clouds—
As when the thunderbolt down falleth on the appointed place—
Fell down, down rushing, ruining, thundering, [*word del.*] shuddering,
Into the Caverns of the Grave & places of Human Seed
Where the impressions of Despair & Hope enroot for ever:
A world of Darkness. Ahania fell far into Non Entity.

She Continued falling. Loud the Crash continu'd, loud & Hoarse.
From the Crash roared a flame of blue sulphureous fire, from the flame
A dolorous groan that struck with dumbness all confusion,
Swallowing up the horrible din in agony on agony.
Thro' the Confusion, like a crack across from immense to immense,
Loud, strong, a universal groan of death, louder
Than all the wracking elements, deafen'd & rended worse

Than Urizen & all his hosts in curst despair down rushing.
But from the Dolorous Groan one like a shadow of smoke appear'd
And human bones rattling together in the smoke & stamping
The nether Abyss, & gnashing in fierce despair, panting in sobs,
Thick, short, incessant, bursting, sobbing, deep despairing,
stamping, struggling,
Struggling to utter the voice of Man, struggling to take the features
of Man, struggling
To take the limbs of Man, at length emerging from the smoke
Of Urizen dashed in pieces from his precipitant fall,
Tharmas rear'd up his hands & stood on the affrighted Ocean:
The dead rear'd up his Voice & stood on the resounding shore,

Crying: "Fury in my limbs! destruction in my bones & marrow!
"My skull riven into filaments, my eyes into sea jellies
"Floating upon the tide wander bubbling & bubbling,
"Uttering my lamentations & begetting little monsters
"Who sit mocking upon the little pebbles of the tide
"In all my rivers & on dried shells that the fish
"Have quite forsaken. O fool! fool! to lose my sweetest bliss.
"Where art thou, Enion? ah, too near to cunning, too far off
"And yet too near. Dash'd down I send thee into distant darkness
"Far as my strength can hurl thee; wander there & laugh & play
"Among the frozen arrows; they will tear thy tender flesh.
"Fall off afar from Tharmas, come not too near my strong fury.
"Scream & fall off & laugh at Tharmas, lovely summer beauty,
"Till winter rends thee into Shivers as thou hast rended me."

So Tharmas bellow'd o'er the ocean, thund'ring, sobbing, bursting.
The bounds of Destiny were broken, & hatred now began
Instead of love to Enion. Enion, blind & age bent,
Plung'd into the cold billows, living a life in midst of waters;
In terrors she wither'd away to Entuthon Benithon,
A world of deep darkness where all things in horrors are rooted.

These are the words of Enion, heard from the cold waves of despair:
"O Tharmas, I had lost thee, & when I hoped I had found thee,
"O Tharmas, do not thou destroy me quite, but let
"A little shadow, but a little showery form of Enion
"Be near thee, loved Terror; let me still remain, & then do thou
"Thy righteous doom upon me; only let me hear thy voice.
"Driven by thy rage I wander like a cloud into the deep
"Where never yet Existence came; there losing all my life
"I back return weaker & weaker; consume me not away

"In thy great wrath; tho' I have sinned, tho' I have rebell'd
"Make me not like the things forgotten as they had not been.
"Make not the thing that loveth thee a tear wiped away."

Tharmas replied, riding on storms, [the *del.*] his voice of [Tharmas *del.*] Thunder roll'd:
"Image of grief, thy fading lineaments make my eyelids fail.
"What have I done? both rage & mercy are alike to me;
"Looking upon thee, Image of faint waters, I recoil
"From my fierce rage into thy semblance. Enion, return.
"Why does thy piteous face Evanish like a rainy cloud
"Melting, a shower of falling tears, nothing but tears! Enion,
"Substanceless, voiceless, weeping, vanish'd, nothing but tears! Enion,
"Art thou for ever vanish'd from the wat'ry eyes of Tharmas?
"Rage, Rage shall never from my bosom: winds & waters of woe
"Consuming all, to the end consuming. Love and [Joy *del.*] Hope are ended."

For now no more remain'd of Enion in the dismal air,
Only a voice eternal wailing in the Elements.

Where Enion, blind & age bent, wander'd, Ahania wanders now:
She wanders in Eternal fear of falling into the indefinite,
For her bright eyes behold the Abyss. Sometimes a little sleep
Weighs down her eyelids; then she falls; then starting, wakes in fears
Sleepless to wander round, repell'd on the margin of Non Entity.

The End of the Third Night

Vala

Night The Fourth

But Tharmas rode on the dark Abyss; the voice of Tharmas roll'd
Over the heaving deluge; he saw Los & Enitharmon Emerge
In strength & brightness from the Abyss; his bowels yearn'd over them.
They rose in strength above the heaving deluge in mighty scorn,
Red as the Sun in the hot morning of the bloody day
Tharmas beheld them; his bowels yearn'd over them.

And he said: "Wherefore do I feel such love & pity?
"Ah, Enion! Ah, Enion! Ah, lovely, lovely Enion!
"How is this? All my hope is gone! [Enion *del.*] for ever fled!
"Like a famish'd Eagle, Eyeless, raging in the vast expanse,

"Incessant tears are now my food, incessant rage & tears.
"Deathless for ever now I wander seeking oblivion
"In torrents of despair: in vain; for if I plunge beneath,
"Stifling I live: If dash'd in pieces from a rocky height,
"I reunite in endless torment; would I had never risen
"From death's cold sleep [upon *del.*] beneath the bottom of the raging Ocean.
"And cannot those who once have lov'd ever forget their Love?
"Are love & rage the same passion? they are the same in me.
"Are those who love like those who died, risen again from death,
"Immortal in immortal torment, never to be deliver'd?
"Is it not possible that one risen again from death
"Can die? When dark despair comes over, can I not
"Flow down into the sea & slumber in oblivion? Ah Enion,
"Deform'd I see these lineaments of ungratified desire.
"The all powerful curse of an honest man be upon Urizen & Luvah.
"But thou, My Son, Glorious in brightness, comforter of Tharmas,
"Go forth, Rebuild this Universe beneath my indignant power,
"A Universe of Death & Decay. Let Enitharmon's hands
"Weave soft delusive forms of Man above my wat'ry world;
"Renew these ruin'd souls of Men thro' Earth, Sea, Air & Fire,
"To waste in endless corruption, renew thou, I will destroy.
"Perhaps Enion may resume some little semblance
"To ease my pangs of heart & to restore some peace to Tharmas."

Los answer'd in his furious pride, sparks issuing from his hair:
"Hitherto shalt thou come, no further; here thy proud waves cease.
"We have drunk up the Eternal Man by our unbounded power,
"Beware lest we also drink up thee, rough Demon of the waters.
"Our God is Urizen the King, King of the Heavenly hosts;
"We have no other God but he, thou father of worms & clay,
"And he is fall'n into the Deep, rough Demon of the waters,
"And Los remains God over all, weak father of worms & clay.
"I know I was Urthona, keeper of the gates of heaven,
"But now I am all powerful Los, & Urthona is but my shadow."

Doubting stood Tharmas in the solemn darkness; his dim Eyes
Swam in red tears; he rear'd his waves above the head of Los
In wrath, but pitying back withdrew with many a sigh.
Now he resolv'd to destroy Los, & now his tears flow'd down.

In scorn stood Los, red sparks of blighting from his furious head
Flew over the waves of Tharmas; pitying, Tharmas stayed his Waves,
For Enitharmon shriek'd amain, crying: "O my sweet world
"Built by the Architect divine, whose love to Los & Enitharmon

"Thou rash abhorred Demon in thy fury hast o'erthrown!"
"What Sovereign Architect," said Tharmas, "dare my will controll?
"For if I will, I urge these waters. If I will, they sleep
"In peace beneath my awful frown; my will shall be my Law."

So saying, in a Wave he rap'd bright Enitharmon far
Apart from Los, but cover'd her with softest brooding care
On a broad wave in the warm west, balming her bleeding wound.

O how Los howl'd at the rending asunder! All the fibres rent,
Where Enitharmon join'd to his left side, in griding pain.
He, falling on the rocks, bellow'd his dolor till the blood
Stanch'd: then in ululation wail'd his woes upon the wind.

And Tharmas call'd to the Dark Spectre who upon the shores
With dislocated Limbs had fall'n. The Spectre rose in pain,
A shadow blue, obscure & dismal; like a statue of lead,
Bent by its fall from a high tower, the dolorous shadow rose.

"Go forth," said Tharmas, "works of joy are thine: obey & live,
"So shall the spungy marrow issuing from thy splinter'd bones
"Bonify, & thou shalt have rest when this thy labour is done.
"Go forth, bear Enitharmon back to the Eternal Prophet,
"Build her a bower in the midst of all my dashing waves;
"Make first a resting place for Los & Enitharmon, then
"Thou shalt have rest. If thou refusest, dash'd abroad on all
"My waves, thy limbs shall separate in stench & rotting, & thou
"Become a prey to all my demons of despair & hope."

The Spectre of Urthona [answers *del.*] seeing Enitharmon, writh'd
His cloudy form in jealous fear, & muttering thunders hoarse
And casting round thick glooms, thus utter'd his fierce pangs of heart:

"Tharmas, I know thee: how are we alter'd, our beauty decay'd!
"But still I know thee, tho' in this horrible ruin whelm'd.
"Thou, once the mildest son of heaven, art now become a Rage,
"A terror to all living things; think not that I am ignorant
"That thou art risen from the dead, or that, my power forgot,
"I slumber here in weak repose. I well remember the Day,
"The day of terror & abhorrence [eternal *del.*] . . .
"When fleeing from the battle, thou fleeting like the raven
"Of dawn, outstretching an expanse where ne'er expanse had been,
"Drew'st all the Sons of Beulah into thy [great *del.*] dread vortex, following

"Thy Eddying spirit down the hills of Beulah. All my sons
"Stood round me at the anvil, where, new heated, the wedge
"Of iron glow'd furious, prepar'd for spades & mattocks.
"Hearing the symphonies of war loud sounding, All my sons
"Fled from my side; then pangs smote me unknown before. I saw
"My loins begin to break forth into veiny pipes & writhe
"Before me in the wind englobing, trembling with strong vibrations,
"The bloody mass began to animate. I, bending over,
"Wept bitter tears incessant. Still beholding how the piteous form
"Dividing & dividing from my loins, a weak & piteous
"Soft cloud of snow, a female pale & weak, I soft embrac'd
"My counter part & call'd it Love. I nam'd her Enitharmon,
"But found myself & her together issuing down the tide
"Which now our rivers were become, delving thro' caverns huge
"Of goary blood, strugg[l]ing to be deliver'd from our bonds.
"She strove in vain; not so Urthona strove, for breaking forth,
"A shadow blue, obscure & dismal, from the breathing Nostrils
"Of Enion I issued into the air, divided from Enitharmon.
"I howl'd in sorrow. I beheld thee rotting upon the Rocks.
"I, pitying, hover'd over thee; I protected thy ghastly corse
"From Vultures of the deep; then wherefore shouldst thou rage
"Against me who thee guarded in the night of death from harm?"

Tharmas replied: "Art thou Urthona, My friend, my old companion
"With whom I liv'd in happiness before that deadly night
"When Urizen gave the horses of Light into the hands of Luvah?
"Thou knowest not what Tharmas knows. O I could tell thee tales
"That would enrage thee as it has Enraged me, even
"From death in wrath & fury. But now, come, bear back
"Thy loved Enitharmon. For thou hast her here before thine eyes;
"But my sweet Enion is vanish'd, & I never more
"Shall see her, unless thou, O Shadow, wilt protect this Son
"Of Enion & him assist to bind the fallen King,
"Lest he should rise again from death in all his [dismal *del.*] dreary pow'r.
"Bind him; take Enitharmon for thy sweet reward, while I
"In vain am driven on false hope, hope sister of despair."

Groaning the terror rose & drave his solid rocks before
Upon the tide, till underneath the feet of Los a World
Dark dreadful rose, & Enitharmon lay at Los's feet.
The dolorous shadow joy'd; weak hope appear'd around his head.

Tharmas before Los stood, & thus the Voice of Tharmas roll'd:

"Now all comes into the power of Tharmas. Urizen is fall'n
"And Luvah hidden in the Elemental forms of Life & Death.
"Urthona is My Son. O Los, thou art Urthona, & Tharmas
"Is God. The Eternal Man is seal'd, never to be deliver'd.
"I roll my floods over his body, my billows & waves pass over him,
"The sea encompasses him & monsters of the deep are his companions.
"Dreamer of furious oceans, cold sleeper of weeds & shells,
"Thy Eternal form shall never renew, my uncertain prevails against thee.
"Yet tho' I rage, God over all, A portion of my Life
"That in Eternal fields in comfort wander'd with my flocks
"At noon & laid her head upon my wearied bosom at night,
"She is divided. She is vanish'd, even like Luvah & Vala.
"O why did foul ambition sieze thee, Urizen, Prince of Light?
"And thee, O Luvah, prince of Love, till Tharmas was divided?
"And I, what can I now behold but an Eternal Death
"Before my Eyes, & an Eternal weary work to strive
"Against the monstrous forms that breed among my silent waves?
"Is this to be A God? far rather would I be a Man,
"To know sweet Science, & to do with simple companions
"Sitting beneath a tent & viewing sheepfolds & soft pastures.
"Take thou the hammer of Urthona: rebuild these furnaces.
"Dost thou refuse? mind I the sparks that issue from thy hair?
"I will compell thee to rebuild by these my furious waves.
"Death choose or life; thou strugglest in my waters; now choose life,
"And all the Elements shall serve thee to their soothing flutes:
"Their sweet inspiriting lyres thy labours shall administer,
"And they to thee; only remit not, faint not thou, my son.
"Now thou dost know what 'tis to strive against the God of waters."

So saying, Tharmas on his furious chariots of the Deep
Departed far into the Unknown & left a wondrous void
Round Los; afar his waters bore on all sides round with noise
Of wheels & horses' hoofs, & Trumpets, Horns & Clarions.

Terrified, Los beheld the ruins of Urizen beneath,
A horrible Chaos to his eyes, a formless unmeasurable Death
Whirling up broken rocks on high into the dismal air
And fluctuating all beneath in Eddies of molten fluid.

Then Los with terrible hands siez'd on the Ruin'd Furnaces
Of Urizen: Enormous work, he builded them anew,
Labour of Ages in the Darkness & the war of Tharmas;
And Los form'd Anvils of Iron petrific, for his blows
Petrify with incessant beating many a rock, many a planet.

But Urizen slept in a stoned stupor in the nether Abyss,
A dreamful, horrible state in tossings on his icy bed
Freezing to solid all beneath; his grey oblivious form,
Stretch'd over the immense, heaves in strong shudders, silent his voice,
In brooding contemplation stretching out from North to South
In mighty power. Round him Los roll'd furious
His thunderous wheels from furnace to furnace, tending diligent
The contemplative terror frighten'd in his scornful sphere,
Frighten'd with cold infectious madness; in his hand the thundering
Hammer of Urthona forming under his heavy hand the hours,
The days & years, in chains of iron round the limbs of Urizen
Link'd hour to hour & day to night & night to day & year to year,
In periods of pulsative furor; mills he form'd & works
Of many wheels resistless in the power of dark Urthona.

But Enitharmon wrap'd in clouds, wail'd loud, for as Los beat
The anvils of Urthona, link by link the chains of sorrow,
Warping upon the winds & whirling round in the dark deep,
Lash'd on the limbs of Enitharmon, & the sulphur fires,
Belch'd from the furnaces, wreath'd round her, chain'd in ceaseless fire.

The lovely female howl'd, & Urizen beneath, deep groan'd
Deadly between the hammer's beating, grateful to the Ears
Of Los absorb'd in dire revenge; he drank with joy the cries
Of Enitharmon & the groans of Urizen, fuel for his wrath
And for his pity, secret feeding on thoughts of cruelty.

The Spectre wept at his dire labours when from [*word del.*] Ladles huge
He pour'd the molten iron round the limbs of Enitharmon.
But when he pour'd it round the bones of Urizen, he laugh'd
Hollow upon the hollow wind, his shadowy form obeying
The voice of Los; compell'd he labour'd round the Furnaces.

And thus began the binding of Urizen; day & night in fear
Circling round the dark Demon, with howlings, dismay & sharp blightings,
The Prophet of Eternity beat on his iron links & links of brass;
And as he beat round the hurtling Demon, terrified at the Shapes
Enslav'd humanity put on, he became what he beheld.
Raging against Tharmas his God, & uttering
Ambiguous words, blasphemous, fill'd with envy, firm resolv'd
On hate Eternal, in his vast disdain he labour'd beating
The Links of fate, link after link, an endless chain of sorrows.

The Eternal Mind, bounded, began to roll eddies of wrath ceaseless
Round & round, & the sulphureous foam surgeing thick,
Settled, a Lake bright & shining clear, White as the snow.

Forgetfulness, dumbness, necessity, in chains of the mind lock'd up,
In fetters of ice shrinking, disorganiz'd, rent from Eternity,
Los beat on his fetters & [pour'd *del.*] heated his furnaces,
And pour'd iron sodor & sodor of brass.

Restless the immortal inchain'd, heaving dolorous,
Anguish'd unbearable till a roof, shaggy wild, inclos'd
In an orb his fountain of thought.

In a horrible dreamful slumber, like the linked chain,
A vast spine writh'd in torment upon the wind,
Shooting pain'd ribbs, like a bending Cavern,
And bones of solidness froze over all his nerves of joy.
A first age passed, a state of dismal woe.

From the Caverns of his jointed spine, down sunk with fright
A red round globe, hot burning, deep deep down into the Abyss,
Panting, conglobing, trembling, shooting out ten thousand branches
Around his solid bones, & a second age passed over.

In harrowing fear rolling, his nervous brain shot branches
[Round the branches of his heart *del.*]
On high into two little orbs hiding in two little caves,
Hiding carefully from the wind; his eyes beheld the deep,
And a third age passed, a state of dismal woe.

The pangs of hope began; in heavy pain striving, struggling,
Two Ears in close volutions from beneath his orbs of vision
Shot spiring out & petrified as they grew. And a Fourth
Age passed over & a state of dismal woe.

In ghastly torment sick, hanging upon the wind,
Two nostrils bent down to the deeps,
And a fifth age passed & a state of dismal woe.

In ghastly torment sick, within his ribs bloated round,
A craving hungry cavern. Thence arose his channel'd
Throat; then like a red flame a tongue of hunger
And thirst appear'd, and a sixth age pass'd of dismal woe.

Enraged & stifled with torment, he threw his right arm to the north,
His left arm to the south, shooting out in anguish deep,
And his feet stamp'd the nether abyss in trembling, howling & dismay,
And a seventh age passed over & a state of dismal woe.

The Council of God on high watching over the Body
Of Man cloth'd in Luvah's robes of blood, saw & wept.
Descending over Beulah's mild moon cover'd regions,
The daughters of Beulah saw the Divine Vision; they were comforted,
And as a double female form, loveliness & perfection of beauty,
They bow'd the head & worshipp'd, & with mild voice spoke these words:

"Lord Saviour, if thou hadst been here our brother had not died,
"And now we know that whatsoever thou wilt ask of God
"He will give it thee; for we are weak women & dare not lift
"Our eyes to the Divine pavilions; therefore in mercy thou
"Appearest cloth'd in Luvah's garments that we may behold thee
"And live. Behold Eternal Death is in Beulah. Behold
"We perish & shall not be found unless thou grant a place
"In which we may be hidden under the shadow of wings.
"For if we, who are but for a time & who pass away in winter,
"Behold these wonders of Eternity, we shall consume."

Such were the words of Beulah, of the Feminine Emanation.
The Empyrean groan'd throughout. All Eden was darken'd.
The Corse of [Man *del.*] Albion lay on the Rock; the sea of Time & Space
Beat round the Rock in mighty waves, & as a Polypus
That vegetates beneath the Sea, the limbs of Man vegetated
In monstrous forms of Death, a Human polypus of Death.

The Saviour mild & gentle bent over the corse of Death,
Saying, "If ye will Believe, your Brother shall rise again."
And first he found the Limit of Opacity, & nam'd it Satan,
In Albion's bosom, for in every human bosom these limits stand.
And next he found the Limit of Contraction, & nam'd it Adam,
While yet those beings were not born nor knew of good or Evil.

Then wondrously the [Deep beneath *del.*] *Starry Wheels* felt the divine hand. Limit
Was put to Eternal Death. Los felt the Limit & saw
The Finger of God touch the Seventh furnace in terror.
And Los beheld the hand of God over his furnaces
Beneath the Deeps in dismal Darkness beneath immensity.

In terrors Los shrank from his task; his great hammer
Fell from his hand, his fires hid their strong limbs in smoke;
For [in *del.*] with noises ruinous, hurtlings & clashings & groans,
The immortal endur'd, tho' bound in a deadly sleep.

Pale terror siezed the Eyes of Los as he beat round
The hurtling demon; terrified at the shapes
Enslav'd humanity put on, he became what he beheld:
He became what he was doing: he was himself transform'd.

(*Bring in here the Globe of Blood as in the B. of Urizen.*)

Spasms siez'd his muscular fibres writhing to & fro: his pallid lips
Unwilling mov'd as Urizen howl'd: his loins wav'd like the sea
At Enitharmon's shrieks: his knees each other smote, & then he look'd
With stony Eyes on Urizen, & then swift writh'd his neck
Involuntary to the Couch where Enitharmon lay.
The bones of Urizen hurtle on the wind; the bones of Los
Twinge & his iron sinews bend like lead & fold
Into unusual forms, dancing & howling, stamping the abyss.

End of the Fourth Night

Vala

Night The Fifth

Infected, Mad, he danc'd on his mountains high & dark as heaven,
Now fix'd into one stedfast bulk his features stonify,
From his mouth curses, & from his eyes sparks of blighting,
Beside the anvil cold he danc'd with the hammer of Urthona,
Terrific pale. Enitharmon stretched on the [dismal *del.*] *dreary* earth.
Felt her immortal limbs freeze, stiffening, pale, inflexible.
His feet shrunk with'ring from the deep, shrinking & withering,
And Enitharmon shrunk up, all their fibres with'ring beneath,
As plants wither'd by winter, leaves & stems & roots decaying
Melt into thin air, while the seed, driv'n by the furious wind,
Rests on the distant Mountain's top. So Los & Enitharmon,
Shrunk into fixed space, stood trembling on a Rocky cliff,
Yet mighty bulk & majesty & beauty remain'd, but unexpansive.
As far as highest Zenith from the lowest Nadir, so far shrunk
Los from the furnaces, a space immense, & left the cold
Prince of Light bound in chains of intellect among the furnaces;
But all the furnaces were out & the bellows had ceast to blow.

He stood trembling & Enitharmon clung around his knees,
Their senses unexpansive in one stedfast bulk remain.
The night blew cold, & Enitharmon shriek'd on the dismal wind.
Her pale hands cling around her husband, & over her weak head
Shadows of Eternal Death sit in the leaden air.

But the soft pipe, the flute, the viol, organ, harp, & cymbal,
And the sweet sound of silver voices calm the weary couch
Of Enitharmon; but her groans drown the immortal harps.
Loud & more loud the living music floats upon the air,
Faint & more faint the daylight wanes; the wheels of turning darkness
Began in solemn revolutions. Earth, convuls'd with rending pangs,
Rock'd to & fro & cried sore at the groans of Enitharmon.
Still the faint harps & silver voices calm the weary couch,
But from the caves of deepest night, ascending in clouds of mist,
The winter spread his wide black wings across from pole to pole:
Grim frost beneath & terrible snow, link'd in a marriage chain,
Began a dismal dance. The winds around on pointed rocks
Settled like bats innumerable, ready to fly abroad.
The groans of Enitharmon shake the skies, the lab'ring Earth,
Till from her heart rending his way, a terrible child sprang forth
In thunder, smoke & sullen flames, & howlings & fury & blood.

Soon as his burning Eyes were open'd on the Abyss,
The horrid trumpets of the deep bellow'd with bitter blasts.
The Enormous Demons woke & howl'd around the [youthful *del.*] new born King,
Crying, "Luvah, King of Love, thou art the King of rage & death."
Urizen cast deep darkness round him; raging, Luvah pour'd
The spears of Urizen from Chariots round the Eternal tent.
Discord began, [& *del.*] then yells & cries shook the wide firmament:

"Where is sweet Vala, gloomy prophet? where the lovely form
"That drew the body of Man from heaven into this dark Abyss?
"Soft tears & sighs, where are you? come forth! shout on bloody fields.
"Shew thy soul, Vala! shew thy bow & quiver of secret fires.

"Draw thy bow, Vala! from the depths of hell thy black bow draw,
"And twang the bowstring to our howlings; let thine arrows black
"Sing in the Sky as once they sang upon the hills of Light
"When dark Urthona wept in torment of the secret pain:

"He wept & he divided & he laid his gloomy head
"Down on the Rock of Eternity on darkness of the deep,
"Torn by black storms & ceaseless torrents of consuming fire,
"Within his breast his fiery sons chain'd down & fill'd with cursings.

"And breathing terrible blood & vengeance, gnashing his teeth with pain,
"Let loose the Enormous Spirit in the darkness of the deep,
"And his dark wife, that once fair crystal form divinely clear,
"Within his ribs producing serpents whose souls are flames of fire.

"But now the times return upon thee. Enitharmon's womb
"Now holds thee, soon to issue forth. Sound, Clarions of war!
"Call Vala from her close recess in all her dark deceit,
"Then rage on rage shall fierce redound out of her crystal quiver."

So sung the Demons round red Orc & round faint Enitharmon.
Sweat & blood stood on the limbs of Los in globes; his fiery Eyelids
Faded; he rouz'd, he siez'd the wonder in his hands & went
Shudd'ring & weeping thro' the Gloom & down into the deeps.

Enitharmon nurs'd her fiery child in the dark deeps
Sitting in darkness: over her Los mourn'd in anguish fierce
Cover'd with gloom; the fiery boy grew, fed by the milk
Of Enitharmon. Los around her builded pillars of iron
And brass & silver & gold fourfold, in dark prophetic fear,
For now he fear'd Eternal Death & uttermost Extinction:
He builded Golgonooza on the Lake of Udan Adan.
Upon the Limit of Translucence then he builded Luban.
Tharmas laid the Foundation & Los finish'd it in howling woe.

But when fourteen summers & winters had revolved over
Their solemn habitation, Los beheld the ruddy boy
Embracing his bright mother, & beheld malignant fires
In his young eyes, discerning plain that Orc plotted his death.
Grief rose upon his ruddy brows; a tightening girdle grew
Around his bosom like a bloody cord; in secret sobs
He burst it, but next morn another girdle succeeds
Around his bosom. Every day he view'd the fiery youth
With silent fear, & his immortal cheeks grew deadly pale,
Till many a morn & many a night pass'd over in dire woe
Forming a girdle in the day & bursting it at night.
The girdle was form'd by day, by night was burst in twain,
Falling down on the rock, an iron chain link by link lock'd.

Enitharmon beheld the bloody chain of nights & days
Depending from the bosom of Los, & how with [dismal *del.*] *griding* pain
He went each morning to his labours with the spectre dark,
Call'd it the chain of Jealousy. Now Los began to speak
His woes aloud to Enitharmon, since he could not hide
His uncouth plague. He siez'd the boy in his immortal hands,
While Enitharmon follow'd him, weeping in dismal woe,
Up to the iron mountain's top, & there the jealous chain
Fell from his bosom on the mountain. The spectre dark
Held the fierce boy. Los nail'd him down, binding around his limbs

The [dismal *del.*] *accursed* chain. O how bright Enitharmon howl'd & cried
Over her son! Obdurate, Los bound down her loved Joy.

The hammer of Urthona smote the rivets in terror, of brass
Tenfold; the Demon's rage flam'd tenfold forth, rending,
Roaring, redounding, Loud, Loud, Louder & Louder, & fir'd
The darkness, warring with the waves of Tharmas & Snows of Urizen.
Crackling the flames went up with fury from the immortal demon.
Surrounded with flames the Demon grew, loud howling in his fires;
Los folded Enitharmon in a cold white cloud in fear,
Then led her down into the deeps & into his labyrinth,
Giving the Spectre sternest charge over the howling fiend,
Concenter'd into Love of Parent, Storgous Appetite, Craving.

His limbs bound down mock at his chains, for over them a flame
Of circling fire unceasing plays; to feed them with life & bring
The virtues of the Eternal worlds, ten thousand thousand spirits
Of life [*word del.*] lament around the Demon, going forth & returning.
At his enormous call they flee into the heavens of heavens
And back return with wine & food, or dive into the deeps
To bring the thrilling joys of sense to quell his ceaseless rage.
His eyes, the lights of his large soul, contract or else expand:
Contracted they behold the secrets of the infinite mountains,
The veins of gold & silver & the hidden things of Vala,
Whatever grows from its pure bud or breathes a fragrant soul:
Expanded they behold the terrors of the Sun & Moon,
The Elemental Planets & the orbs of eccentric fire.
His nostrils breathe [with *del.*] a fiery flame, his locks are like the forests
Of wild beasts; there the lion glares, the tyger & wolf howl there,
And there the Eagle hides her young in cliffs & precipices.
His bosom is like starry heaven expanded; all the stars
Sing round; there waves the harvest & the vintage rejoices; the springs
Flow into rivers of delight; there the spontaneous flowers
Drink, laugh & sing, the grasshopper, the Emmet & the Fly;
The golden Moth builds there a house & spreads her silken bed.
His loins inwove with silken fires are like a furnace fierce:
As the strong Bull in summer time when bees sing round the heath
Where the herds low after the shadow & after the water spring,
The num'rous flocks cover the mountain & shine along the valley.
His knees are rocks of adamant & rubie & emerald:
Spirits of strength [rejoice *del.*] in Palaces rejoice in golden armour
Armed with spear & shield they drink & rejoice over the slain.
Such is the Demon, such his terror in the nether deep.

But, when return'd to Golgonooza, Los & Enitharmon
Felt all the sorrow Parents feel, they wept toward one another
And Los repented that he had chain'd Orc upon the mountain.
And Enitharmon's tears prevail'd; parental love return'd,
Tho' terrible his dread of that infernal chain. They rose
At midnight hasting to their much beloved care.
Nine days they travel'd thro' the Gloom of Entuthon Benithon.
Los, taking Enitharmon by the hand, led her along
The dismal vales & up to the iron mountain's top where Orc
Howl'd in the furious wind; he thought to give to Enitharmon
Her son in tenfold joy, & to compensate for her tears
Even if his own death resulted, so much pity him pain'd.

But when they came to the dark rock & to the spectrous cave,
Lo, the young limbs had strucken root into the rock, & strong
Fibres had from the Chain of Jealousy inwove themselves
In a swift vegetation round the rock & round the Cave
And over the immortal limbs of the terrible fiery boy.
In vain they strove now to unchain, In vain with bitter tears
To melt the chain of Jealousy; not Enitharmon's death,
Nor the Consummation of Los could ever melt the chain
Nor unroot the infernal fibres from their rocky bed,
Nor all Urthona's strength, nor all the power of Luvah's Bulls,
Tho' they each morning drag the unwilling Sun out of the deep,
Could uproot the infernal chain, for it had taken root
Into the iron rock & grew a chain beneath the Earth
Even to the Center, wrapping round the Center; & the limbs
Of Orc entering with fibres became one with him, a living Chain
Sustained by the Demon's life. Despair & Terror & Woe & Rage
Inwrap the Parents in cold clouds as they bend howling over
The terrible boy, till fainting by his side, the Parents fell.

Not long they lay; Urthona's spectre found herbs of the pit.
Rubbing their temples, he reviv'd them; all their lamentations
I write not here, but all their after life was lamentation.

When satiated with grief they return'd back to Golgonooza,
Enitharmon on the road of Dranthon felt the inmost gate
Of her bright heart burst open & again close with a deadly pain.
Within her heart Vala began to reanimate in bursting sobs;
And when the Gate was open she beheld that dreary deep
Where bright Ahania wept. She also saw the infernal roots
Of the chain of Jealousy, & felt the rendings of fierce howling Orc
Rending the Caverns like a mighty wind pent in the Earth.
Tho' wide apart as furthest north is from the furthest south,

Urizen trembled where he lay to hear the howling terror.
The rocks shook, the Eternal bars tugg'd to & fro were rifted.
Outstretch'd upon the stones of ice, the ruins of his throne,
Urizen shudd'ring heard, his trembling limbs shook the strong caves.

The Woes of Urizen shut up in the deep dens of Urthona:

"Ah! how shall Urizen the King submit to this dark mansion?
"Ah! how is this? Once on the heights I stretch'd my throne sublime;
"The mountains of Urizen, once of silver, where the sons of wisdom dwelt,
"And on whose tops the Virgins sang, are rocks of desolation.

"My fountains, once the haunt of swans, now breed the scaly tortoise,
"The houses of my harpers are become a haunt of crows,
"The gardens of wisdom are become a field of horrid graves,
"And on the bones I drop my tears & water them in vain.

"Once how I walked from my palace in gardens of delight,
"The sons of wisdom stood around, the harpers follow'd with harps,
"Nine virgins cloth'd in light compos'd the song to their immortal voices,
"And at my banquets of new wine my head was crown'd with joy.

"Then in my ivory pavilions I slumber'd [with *del.*] in the noon
"And walked in the silent night among sweet smelling flowers,
"Till on my silver bed I slept & sweet dreams round me hover'd,
"But now my land is darken'd & my wise men are departed.

"My songs are turned into cries of Lamentation
"Heard on my Mountains, & deep sighs under my palace roofs,
"Because the Steeds of Urizen, once swifter than the light,
"Were kept back from my Lord & from his chariot of mercies.

"O did I keep the horses of the day in silver pastures!
"O I refus'd the lord of day the horses of his prince!
"O did I close my treasuries with roofs of solid stone
"And darken all my Palace walls with envyings & hate!

"O Fool! to think that I could hide from his all piercing eyes
"The gold & silver & costly stones, his holy workmanship!
"O Fool! could I forget the light that filled my bright spheres
"Was a reflection of his face who call'd me from the deep!

"I well remember, for I heard the mild & holy voice
"Saying, 'O light, spring up & shine,' & I sprang up from the deep.
"He gave to me a silver scepter, & crown'd me with a golden crown,
"[Saying *del.*] *& said,* 'Go forth & guide my Son who wanders on the ocean.'

"I went not forth: I hid myself in black clouds of my wrath;
"I call'd the stars around my feet in the night of councils dark;
"The stars threw down their spears & fled naked away.
"We fell. I siez'd thee, dark Urthona. In my left hand falling

"I siez'd thee, beauteous Luvah; thou art faded like a flower
"And like a lilly is thy wife Vala wither'd by winds.
"When thou didst bear the golden cup at the immortal tables
"Thy children smote their fiery wings, crown'd with the gold of heaven.

"Thy pure feet step'd on the steps divine, too pure for other feet,
"And thy fair locks shadow'd thine eyes from the divine effulgence,
"Then thou didst keep with Strong Urthona the living gates of heaven,
"But now thou art bound down with him, even to the gates of hell.

"Because thou gavest Urizen the wine of the Almighty
"For Steeds of Light, that they might run in thy golden chariot of pride,
"I gave to thee the Steeds, I pour'd the stolen wine
"And drunken with the immortal draught fell from my throne sublime.

"I will arise, Explore these dens, & find that deep pulsation
"That shakes my caverns with strong shudders; perhaps this is the night
"Of Prophecy, & Luvah hath burst his way from Enitharmon.
"When Thought is clos'd in Caves Then love shall shew its root in deepest Hell."

End of the Fifth [Book *del.*] Night

Vala

Night the Sixth

So Urizen arose, & leaning on his spear explor'd his dens.
He threw his flight thro' the dark air to where a river flow'd,
And taking off his silver helmet filled it & drank;
But when, unsatiated his thirst, he assay'd to gather more,
Lo, three terrific women at the verge of the bright flood,
Who would not suffer him to approach, but drove him back with storms.

Urizen knew them not, & thus addressed the spirits of darkness:

"Who art thou, Eldest Woman, sitting in thy clouds?
"What is that name written on thy forehead? what art thou?
"And wherefore dost thou pour this water forth in sighs & care?"

She answer'd not, but fill'd her urn & pour'd it forth abroad.

"Answerest thou not?" said Urizen. "Then thou maist answer me,
"Thou terrible woman, clad in blue, whose strong attractive power
"Draws all into a fountain at the rock of thy attraction;
"With frowning brow thou sittest, mistress of these mighty waters."

She answer'd not, but stretched her arms & threw her limbs abroad.

"Or wilt thou answer, youngest Woman, clad in shining green?
"With labour & care thou dost divide the [river *del.*] current into four.
"Queen of these dreadful rivers, speak, & let me hear thy voice."

[Then *del.*] *And* Urizen rais'd his spear, [but *del.*] they rear'd up a wall of rocks.
They gave a scream, they knew their father: Urizen knew his daughters.
They shrunk into their channels, dry the rocky strand beneath his feet,
Hiding themselves in rocky forms from the Eyes of Urizen.

Then Urizen wept & thus his lamentation poured forth:

"O horrible, O dreadful state! those whom I loved best,
"On whom I pour'd the beauties of my light, adorning them
"With jewels & precious ornament labour'd with art divine,
"Vests of the radiant colours of heaven & crowns of golden fire.
"I gave sweet lillies to their breasts & roses to their hair,
"I taught them songs of sweet delight, I gave their tender voices
"Into the blue expanse, & I invented with laborious art
"Sweet instruments of sound; in pride encompassing my knees
"They pour'd their radiance above all; the daughters of Luvah envied
"At their exceeding brightness, & the sons of eternity sent them gifts.
"Now will I pour my fury on them, & I will reverse
"The precious benediction; for their colours of loveliness
"I will give blackness; for jewels, hoary frost; for ornament, deformity;
"For crowns, wreath'd serpents; for sweet odors, stinking corruptibility;
"For voices of delight, hoarse croakings inarticulate thro' frost;
"For labour'd fatherly care & sweet instruction, I will give
"Chains of dark ignorance & cords of twisted self-conceit

"And whips of stern repentance & food of stubborn obstinacy,
"That they may curse Tharmas their God, & Los his adopted son;
"That they may curse & worship the obscure demon of destruction;
"That they may worship terrors & obey the violent.
"Go forth, sons of my curse. Go forth, daughters of my abhorrence."

Tharmas heard the deadly scream across his wat'ry world
And Urizen's loud sounding voice lamenting on the wind,
And he came riding in his fury; froze to solid were his waves,
Silent in ridges he beheld them stand round Urizen,
A dreary waste of solid waters; for the King of Light
Darken'd his brows with his cold helmet, & his gloomy spear
Darken'd before him. Silent on the ridgy waves he took
His gloomy way; before him Tharmas fled, & flying fought,
Crying: "What & who art thou, Cold Demon? art thou Urizen?
"Art thou, like me, risen again from death? or art thou deathless?
"If thou art he, my desperate purpose hear, & give me death,
"For death to me is better far than life, death my desire
"That I in vain in various paths have sought, but still I live.
"The Body of Man is given to me. I seek in vain to destroy,
"For still it surges forth in fish & monsters of the deeps,
"And in these monstrous forms I Live in an Eternal woe,
"And thou, O Urizen, art fall'n, never to be deliver'd.
"Withhold thy light from me for ever, & I will withhold
"From thee thy food; so shall we cease to be, & all our sorrows
"[Cease *del.*] End, & the Eternal Man no more renew beneath our power.
"If thou refusest, in eternal flight thy beams in vain
"Shall pursue Tharmas, & in vain shalt crave for food. I will
"Pour down my flight thro' dark immensity Eternal falling.
"Thou shalt pursue me but in vain, till starv'd upon the void
"Thou hang'st, a dried skin, shrunk up, weak wailing in the wind."

So Tharmas spoke, but Urizen replied not. On his way
He took, high bounding over hills & desarts, floods & horrible chasms.
Infinite was his labour, without end his travel; he strove
In vain, for hideous monsters of the deeps annoy'd him sore,
Scaled & finn'd with iron & brass, they devour'd the path before him.
Incessant was the conflict. On he bent his weary steps
Making a path toward the dark world of Urthona; he rose
With pain upon the dreary mountains & with pain descended
And saw their grizly fears, & his eyes sicken'd at the sight:
The howlings, gnashings, groanings, shriekings, shudderings, sobbings, burstings
Mingle together to create a world for Los. In cruel delight

Los brooded on the darkness, nor saw Urizen with a Globe of fire
Lighting his dismal journey thro' the pathless world of death,
Writing in bitter tears & groans in books of iron & brass
The enormous wonders of the Abysses, once his brightest joy.

For Urizen beheld the terrors of the Abyss wandering among
The ruin'd spirits, once his children & the children of Luvah.
Scar'd at the sound of their own sigh that seems to shake the immense
They wander Moping, in their heart a sun, a dreary moon,
A Universe of fiery constellations in their brain,
An earth of wintry woe beneath their feet, & round their loins
Waters or winds or clouds or brooding lightnings & pestilential plagues.
Beyond the bounds of their own self their senses cannot penetrate:
As the tree knows not what is outside of its leaves & bark
And yet it drinks the summer joy & fears the winter sorrow,
So, in the regions of the grave, none knows his dark compeer
Tho' he partakes of his dire woes & mutual returns the pang,
The throb, the dolor, the convulsion, in soul-sickening woes.

[Not so clos'd up the Prince of Light now darken'd, wandering among
The Ruin'd Spirits, once his Children & the Children of Luvah:
For Urizen beheld the terrors of the Abyss, wandering among *del.*]
The horrid shapes & sights of torment in burning dungeons & in
Fetters of red hot iron; some with crowns of serpents & some
With monsters girding round their bosoms; some lying on beds of sulphur,
On racks & wheels; he beheld women marching o'er burning wastes
Of Sand in bands of hundreds & of fifties & of thousands, strucken with
Lightnings which blazed after them upon their shoulders in their march
In successive volleys with loud thunders: swift flew the King of Light
Over the burning desarts; Then, the desarts pass'd, involv'd in clouds
Of smoke with myriads moping in the stifling vapours, Swift
Flew the King, tho' flag'd his powers, labouring till over rocks
And Mountains faint weary he wander'd where multitudes were shut
Up in the solid mountains & in rocks which heav'd with their torments.
Then came he among fiery cities & castles built of burning steel.
Then he beheld the forms of tygers & of Lions, dishumaniz'd men.
Many in serpents & in worms, stretched out enormous length
Over the sullen mould & slimy tracks, obstruct his way
Drawn out from deep to deep, woven by ribb'd
And scaled monsters or arm'd in iron shell, or shell of brass

Or gold; a glittering torment shining & hissing in eternal pain;
Some, columns of fire or of water, sometimes stretch'd out in [length *del.*] heighth,
Sometimes in [breadth *del.*] length, sometimes englobing, wandering in vain seeking for ease.
His voice to them was but an inarticulate thunder, for their Ears
Were heavy & dull, & their eyes & nostrils closed up.
Oft he stood by a howling victim Questioning in words
Soothing or Furious; no one answer'd; every one wrap'd up
In his own sorrow howl'd regardless of his words, nor voice
Of sweet response could he obtain, tho' oft assay'd with tears.
He knew they were his Children ruin'd in his ruin'd world.

Oft would he stand & question a fierce scorpion glowing with gold;
In vain; the terror heard not. Then a lion he would sieze
By the fierce mane, staying his howling course; in vain the voice
Of Urizen, in vain the Eloquent tongue. A Rock, a Cloud, a Mountain,
Were now not Vocal as in Climes of happy Eternity
Where the lamb replies to the infant voice, & the lion to the man of years
Giving them sweet instructions; where the Cloud, the River & the Field
Talk with the husbandman & shepherd. But these attack'd him sore,
Siezing upon his feet, & rending the sinews, that in Caves
He hid to recure his obstructed powers with rest & oblivion.

Here he had time enough to repent of his rashly threaten'd curse.
He saw them curs'd beyond his Curse: his soul melted with fear.
He could not take their fetters off, for they grew from the soul,
Nor could he quench the fires, for they flam'd out from the heart,
Nor could he calm the Elements, because himself was subject;
So he threw his flight in terror & pain, & in repentant tears.

When he had pass'd these southern terrors he approach'd the East,
Void, pathless, beaten with [eternal *del.*] iron sleet, & eternal hail & [snow *del.*] rain.
No form was there, no living thing, & yet his way lay thro'
This dismal world; he stood a while & look'd back over his former
Terrific voyage, Hills & Vales of torment & despair!
Sighing, & wiping a fresh tear, then turning round, he threw
Himself into the dismal void; falling he fell & fell,
Whirling in unresistible revolutions down & down
In the horrid bottomless vacuity, falling, falling, falling,
Into the Eastern vacuity, the empty world of Luvah.

The ever pitying one who seeth all things, saw his fall,
And in the dark vacuity created a bosom of [slime *del.*] clay;
When wearied, dead he fell, his limbs repos'd in the bosom of slime;
As the seed falls from the sower's hand, so Urizen fell, & death
Shut up his powers in oblivion; then as the seed shoots forth
In pain & sorrow, so the slimy bed his limbs renew'd.
At first an infant weakness; periods pass'd; he gather'd strength,
But still in solitude he sat; then rising, threw his flight
Onward, tho' falling, thro' the waste of night & ending in death
And in another resurrection to sorrow & weary travel.
But still his books he bore in his strong hands, & his iron pen,
For when he died they lay beside his grave, & when he rose
He siez'd them with a [dismal *del.*] *gloomy* smile; for wrap'd in his death clothes
He hid them when he slept in death, when he reviv'd, the clothes
Were rotted by the winds; the books remain'd still unconsum'd,
Still to be written & interleav'd with brass & iron & gold,
Time after time, for such a journey none but iron pens
Can write And adamantine leaves recieve, nor can the man who goes
The journey obstinate refuse to write time after time.

Endless had been his travel, but the Divine hand him led,
For infinite the distance & obscur'd by Combustions dire,
By rocky masses frowning in the abysses, revolving erratic
Round Lakes of fire in the dark deep, the ruins of Urizen's world.

Oft would he sit in a dark rift & regulate his books,
Or sleep such sleep as spirits eternal, wearied in his dark
Tearful & sorrowful state; then rise, look out & ponder
His dismal voyage, eyeing the next sphere tho' far remote;
Then darting into the Abyss of night his venturous limbs
Thro' lightnings, thunders, earthquakes & concussions, fires & floods
Stemming his downward fall, labouring up against futurity,
Creating many a Vortex, fixing many a Science in the deep,
And thence throwing his venturous limbs into the vast unknown,
Swift, swift from Chaos to chaos, from void to void, a road immense.
For when he came to where a Vortex ceas'd to operate,
Nor down nor up remain'd, then if he turn'd & look'd back
From whence he came, 'twas upward all; & if he turn'd and view'd
The unpass'd void, upward was still his mighty wand'ring,
The midst between, an Equilibrium grey of air serene
Where he might live in peace & where his life might meet repose.

But Urizen said: "Can I not leave this world of Cumbrous wheels,
"Circle o'er Circle, nor on high attain a void

"Where self sustaining I may view all things beneath my feet?
"Or sinking thro' these Elemental wonders, swift to fall,
"I thought perhaps to find an End, a world beneath of voidness
"Whence I might travel round the outside of this dark confusion.
"When I bend downward, bending my head downward into the deep,
"'Tis upward all which way soever I my course begin;
"But when A Vortex, form'd on high by labour & sorrow & care
"And weariness, begins on all my limbs, then sleep revives
"My wearied spirits; waking then 'tis downward all which way
"Soever I my spirits turn, no end I find of all
"O what a world is here, unlike those climes of bliss
"Where my sons gather'd round my knees! O, thou poor ruin'd world!
"Thou horrible ruin! once like me thou wast all glorious,
"And now like me partaking desolate thy master's lot.
"Art thou, O ruin, the once glorious heaven? are these thy rocks
"Where joy sang in the trees & pleasure sported on the rivers,
"And laughter sat beneath the Oaks, & innocence sported round
"Upon the green plains, & sweet friendship met in palaces,
"And books & instruments of song & pictures of delight?
"Where are they, whelmed beneath these ruins in horrible [confusion *del.*] destruction?
"And if, Eternal falling, I repose on the dark bosom
"Of winds & waters, or thence fall into a Void where air
"Is not, down falling thro' immensity ever & ever,
"I lose my powers, weaken'd every revolution, till a death
"Shuts up my powers; then a seed in the vast womb of darkness
"I dwell in dim oblivion; brooding over me, the Enormous worlds
"Reorganize me, shooting forth in bones & flesh & blood,
"I am regenerated, to fall or rise at will, or to remain
"A labourer of ages, a dire discontent, a living woe
"Wandering in vain. Here will I fix my foot & here rebuild.
"Here Mountains of Brass promise much riches in their dreadful bosoms."

So [saying *del.*] he began to form of gold, silver & [brass *del.*] iron
And brass, vast instruments to measure out the immense & fix
The whole into another world better suited to obey
His will, where none should dare oppose his will, himself being King
Of All, & all futurity be bound in his vast chain.
And the Sciences were fix'd & the Vortexes began to operate
On all the sons of men, & every human soul terrified
At the turning wheels of heaven shrunk away inward, with'ring away.
Gaining a New dominion over all his Sons & Daughters, & over the Sons & Daughters of Luvah in the horrible Abyss.
For Urizen lamented over them in a selfish lamentation

Till a white woof cover'd his cold limbs from head to feet,
Hair white as snow cover'd him in flaky locks terrific
Overspreading his limbs; in pride he wander'd weeping,
Clothed in aged venerableness, obstinately resolv'd,
Travelling thro' darkness; & wherever he travel'd a dire Web
Follow'd behind him, as the Web of a Spider, dusky & cold,
Shivering across from Vortex to Vortex, drawn out from his mantle of years:
A living Mantle adjoined to his life & growing from his soul.
And the Web of Urizen stre[t]ch'd direful, shivering in clouds,
And uttering such woes, such [burstings *del.*] bursts, such thunderings.

The eyelids expansive as morning & the Ears
As a golden ascent winding round to the heavens of heavens
Within the dark horrors of the Abysses, lion or tyger, or scorpion;
For every one open'd within into Eternity at will,
But they refus'd, because their outward forms were in the Abyss;
And the wing-like tent of the Universe, beautiful, surrounding all,
Or drawn up or let down at the will of the immortal man,
Vibrated in such anguish the eyelids quiver'd,
Weak & Weaker their expansive orbs began shrinking;
Pangs smote thro' the brain & a universal shriek
Ran thro' the Abysses rending the web, torment on torment.

Thus Urizen in sorrows wander'd many a dreary way
Warring with monsters of the deeps in his most hideous pilgrimage,
Till, his bright hair scatter'd in snows, his skin bark'd o'er with wrinkles,
Four Caverns rooting downwards their foundations, thrusting forth
The metal, rock & stone in ever painful throes of vegetation.
The Cave of Orc stood to the South, a furnace of dire flames,
Quenchless, unceasing. In the west the Cave of Urizen;
For Urizen fell, as the Midday sun falls down, into the West.
North stood Urthona's stedfast throne, a World of Solid darkness
Shut up in stifling obstruction, rooted in dumb despair.
The East was Void. But Tharmas roll'd his billows in ceaseless eddies,
Void, pathless, beat with Snows eternal & iron hail & rain
All thro' the caverns of fire & air & Earth, Seeking
For Enion's limbs, nought finding but the black sea weed & sick'ning slime:
Flying away from Urizen that he might not give him food,
Above, beneath, on all sides round in the vast deep of immensity,
That he might starve the sons & daughters of Urizen on the winds,
Making between, horrible chasms into the vast unknown.
All these around the world of Los cast forth their monstrous births.

But in Eternal times the Seat of Urizen is in the South,
Urthona in the North, Luvah in East, Tharmas in West.

And now he came into the Abhorred world of Dark Urthona,
By Providence Divine conducted, not bent from his own will
Lest Death Eternal should be the result, for the Will cannot be violated:
Into the doleful vales where no tree grew nor river flow'd,
Nor man nor beast nor creeping thing, nor sun nor cloud nor star;
Still he, with his globe of fire immense in his venturous hand,
Bore on thro' the Affrighted vales, ascending & descending,
O'erwearied or in cumbrous flight he ventur'd o'er dark rifts,
Or down dark precipices, or climb'd with pain and labour huge
Till he beheld the world of Los from the Peaked rock of Urthona
And heard the howlings of red Orc distincter & distincter.

Redoubling his immortal efforts, thro' the narrow vales
With difficulty down descending, guided by his Ear
And [with *del.*] by his globe of fire, he went down the Vale of Urthona
Between the enormous iron walls built by the Spectre dark.
Dark grew his globe redd'ning with mists, & full before his path,
Striding across the narrow vale, the Shadow of Urthona
A spectre Vast appear'd, whose feet & legs with iron scaled,
Stamp'd the hard rocks expectant of the unknown wanderer
Whom he had seen wandering his nether world when distant far,
And watch'd his swift approach; collected, dark, the Spectre stood.
Beside him Tharmas stay'd his flight & stood in stern defiance,
Communing with the Spectre who rejoic'd along the vale.
Round his loins a girdle glow'd with many colour'd fires,
In his hand a knotted Club whose knots like mountains frown'd
Desart among the stars, them withering with its ridges cold.
Black scales of iron arm the dread visage; iron spikes instead
Of hair shoot from his orbed scull; his glowing eyes
Burn like two furnaces; he call'd with Voice of Thunder.
Four winged heralds mount the furious blasts & blow their trumps;
Gold, Silver, Brass & iron clangors, clamoring rend the [deeps *del.*] *shores*.
Like white clouds rising from the Vales, his fifty two armies
From the four Cliffs of Urthona rise glowing around the Spectre.
Four sons of Urizen the Squadrons of Urthona led, in arms
Of gold & silver, brass & iron: he knew his mighty sons.

Then Urizen arose upon the wind, back many a mile
Retiring into his dire Web, scattering fleecy snows:
As he ascended, howling loud, the Web vibrated strong,

From heaven to heaven, from globe to globe. In vast excentric paths
Compulsive roll'd the Comets at his dread command, the dreary way
Falling with wheel impetuous down among Urthona's vales
And round red Orc; returning back to Urizen, gorg'd with blood.
Slow roll the massy Globes at his command, & slow o'erwheel
The dismal squadrons of Urthona weaving the dire Web
In their progressions, & preparing Urizen's path before him.

End of The Sixth Night

Vala

Night the Seventh[1]

Then Urizen arose. The Spectre fled, & Tharmas fled;
The dark'ning Spectre of Urthona hid beneath a rock.
Tharmas threw his impetuous flight thro' the deeps of immensity
Revolving round in whirlpools fierce, all round the cavern'd worlds.

But Urizen silent descended to the Caves of Orc & saw
A Cavern'd Universe of flaming fire; the horses of Urizen
Here bound to fiery mangers, furious dash their golden hoofs,
Striking fierce sparkles from their brazen fetters; fierce his lions
Howl in the burning dens; his tygers roam in the redounding smoke
In forests of affliction; the adamantine scales of justice
Consuming in the raging lamps of mercy, pour'd in rivers.
The holy oil rages thro' all the cavern'd rocks; fierce flames
Dance on the rivers & the rocks; howling & drunk with fury
The plow of ages & the golden harrow wade thro' fields
Of goary blood; the immortal seed is nourish'd for the slaughter.
The bulls of Luvah, breathing fire, bellow on burning pastures
Round howling Orc, whose awful limbs cast forth red smoke & fire,
That Urizen approach'd not near but took his seat on a rock
And rang'd his books around him, brooding Envious over Orc.

Howling & rending his dark caves the awful Demon lay:
Pulse after pulse beat on his fetters, pulse after pulse his spirit
Darted & darted higher & higher to the shrine of Enitharmon;
As when the thunder folds himself in thickest clouds,
The wat'ry nations couch & hide in the profoundest deeps,
Then bursting from his troubled head, with terrible visages & flaming hair,
His swift wing'd daughters sweep across the vast black ocean.

[1] Blake wrote two versions of Night the Seventh, but did not finally reject either. The one that was probably written later is here distinguished as Seventh [*b*].

Los felt the Envy in his limbs like to a blighted tree,
For Urizen fix'd in envy sat brooding & cover'd with snow;
His book of iron on his knees, he trac'd the dreadful letters
While his snows fell & his storms beat to cool the flames of Orc
Age after Age, till underneath his heel a deadly root
Struck thro' the rock, the root of Mystery accursed shooting up
Branches into the heaven of Los: they, pipe form'd, bending down
Take root again where ever they touch, again branching forth
In intricate labyrinths o'erspreading many a grizly deep.

Amaz'd started Urizen when he found himself compass'd round
And high roofed over with trees; he arose, but the stems
Stood so thick he with difficulty & great pain brought
His books out of the dismal shade, all but the book of iron.
Again he took his seat & rang'd his [*word del.*] Books around
On a rock of iron frowning over the foaming fires of Orc.
And Urizen hung over Orc & view'd his terrible wrath;
Sitting upon [his *del.*] an iron Crag, at length his words broke forth:

"Image of dread, whence art thou? whence is this most woful place?
"Whence these fierce fires, but from thyself? No other living thing
"In all this Chasm I behold. No other living thing
"Dare thy most terrible wrath abide. Bound here to waste in pain
"Thy vital substance in these fires that issue new & new
"Around thee, sometimes like a flood, & sometimes like a rock
"Of living pangs, thy horrible bed glowing with ceaseless fires
"Beneath thee & around. Above, a shower of fire now beats,
"Moulded to globes & arrowy wedges, rending thy bleeding limbs.
"And now a whirling pillar of burning sands to overwhelm thee,
"Steeping thy wounds in salts infernal & in bitter anguish.
"And now a rock moves on the surface of this lake of fire
"To bear thee down beneath the waves in stifling despair.
"Pity for thee mov'd me to break my dark & long repose,
"And to reveal myself before thee in a form of wisdom.
"Yet thou dost laugh at all these tortures, & this horrible place:
"Yet throw thy limbs these fires abroad that back return upon thee
"While thou reposest, throwing rage on rage, feeding thyself
"With visions of sweet bliss far other than this burning clime.
"Sure thou art bath'd in rivers of delight, on verdant fields
"Walking in joy, in bright Expanses sleeping on bright clouds
"With visions of delight so lovely that they urge thy rage
"Tenfold with fierce desire to rend thy chain & howl in fury
"And dim oblivion of all woe, & desperate repose.
"Or is thy joy founded on torment which others bear for thee?"

Orc answer'd: "Curse thy hoary brows! What dost thou in this deep?
"Thy Pity I contemn. Scatter thy snows elsewhere.
"I rage in the deep, for Lo, my feet & hands are nail'd to the burning rock,
"Yet my fierce fires are better than thy snows. Shudd'ring thou sittest.
"Thou art not chain'd. Why shouldst thou sit, cold grovelling demon of woe,
"In tortures of dire coldness? now a Lake of waters deep
"Sweeps over thee freezing to solid; still thou sit'st clos'd up
"In that transparent rock as if in joy of thy bright prison,
"Till, overburden'd with its own weight drawn out thro' immensity,
"With a crash breaking across, the horrible mass comes down
"Thund'ring, & hail & frozen iron hail'd from the Element
"Rends thy white hair; yet thou dost, fix'd obdurate brooding, sit
"Writing thy books. Anon a cloud, fill'd with a waste of snows
"Covers thee, still obdurate, still resolv'd & writing still;
"Tho' rocks roll o'er thee, tho' floods pour, tho' winds black as the sea
"Cut thee in gashes, tho' the blood pours down around thy ankles,
"Freezing thy feet to the hard rock, still thy pen obdurate
"Traces the wonders of Futurity in horrible fear of the future.
"I rage furious in the deep, for lo, my feet & hands are nail'd
"To the hard rock, or thou shouldst feel my enmity & hate
"In all the diseases of man falling upon thy grey accursed front."

Urizen answer'd: "Read my books, explore my Constellations,
"Enquire of my Sons & they shall teach thee how to War.
"Enquire of my Daughters, who, accurs'd in the dark depths,
"Knead bread of Sorrow by my stern command; for I am God
"Of all this dreadful ruin. Rise, O daughters, at my stern command!"

Rending the Rocks, Eleth & Uveth rose, & Ona rose,
Terrific with their iron vessels, driving them across
In the dim air; they took the book of iron & plac'd above
On clouds of death, & sang their songs, kneading the bread of Orc.
Orc listen'd to the song, compell'd, hung'ring on the cold wind
That swagg'd heavy with the accursed dough; the hoar frost rag'd
Thro' Ona's sieve; the torrent rain poured from the iron pail
Of Eleth, & the icy hands of Uveth kneaded the bread.
The heavens bow with terror underneath their iron hands,
Singing at their dire work the words of Urizen's book of iron
While the enormous scrolls roll'd dreadful in the heavens above;
And still the burden of their song in tears was pour'd forth:
"The bread is kneaded, let us rest, O cruel father of children!"

But Urizen remitted not their labours upon his rock,
And Urizen Read in his book of brass in sounding tones:

"Listen, O Daughters, to my voice. Listen to the Words of Wisdom,
"So shall [you] govern over all; let Moral Duty tune your tongue.
"But be your hearts harder than the nether millstone.
"To bring the Shadow of Enitharmon beneath our wondrous tree,
"That Los may Evaporate like smoke & be no more,
"Draw down Enitharmon to the Spectre of Urthona,
"And let him have dominion over Los, the terrible shade.
"Compell the poor to live upon a Crust of bread, by soft mild arts.
"Smile when they frown, frown when they smile; & when a man looks pale
"With labour & abstinence, say he looks healthy & happy;
"And when his children sicken, let them die; there are enough
"Born, even too many, & our Earth will be overrun
"Without these arts. If you would make the poor live with temper[1],
"With pomp give every crust of bread you give; with gracious cunning
"Magnify small gifts; reduce the man to want a gift, & then give with pomp.
"Say he smiles if you hear him sigh. If pale, say he is ruddy.
"Preach temperance: say he is overgorg'd & drowns his wit
"In strong drink, tho' you know that bread & water are all
"He can afford. Flatter his wife, pity his children, till we can
"Reduce all to our will, as spaniels are taught with art.
"Lo! how the heart & brain are formed in the breeding womb
"Of Enitharmon: how it buds with life & forms the bones,
"The little heart, the liver, & the red blood in its labyrinths;
"By gratified desire, by strong devouring appetite, she fills
"Los with ambitious fury that his race shall all devour."

Then Orc [answer'd *del.*] cried: "Curse thy Cold hypocrisy! already round thy Tree
"In scales that shine with gold & rubies, thou beginnest to weaken
"My divided Spirit. Like a worm I rise in peace, unbound
"From wrath. Now when I rage, my fetters bind me more.
"O torment! O torment! A Worm compell'd! Am I a worm?
"Is it in strong deceit that man is born? In strong deceit
"Thou dost restrain my fury that the worm may fold the tree.
"Avaunt, Cold hypocrite! I am chain'd, or thou couldst not use me thus.
"The Man shall rage, bound with this chain, the worm in silence creep.
"Thou wilt not cease from rage. Grey demon, silence all thy storms,
"Give me example of thy mildness. King of furious hail storms,
"Art thou the cold attractive power that holds me in this chain?
"I well remember how I stole thy light & it became fire

---

[1]*temper* probably an abbreviation of *temperance*.

"Consuming. Thou Know'st me now, O Urizen, Prince of Light,
"And I know thee; is this the triumph, this the Godlike State
"That lies beyond the bounds of Science in the Grey obscure?"

Terrified Urizen heard Orc, now certain that he was Luvah.
[So saying *del.*] And Orc (he) began to organize a Serpent body,
Despising Urizen's light & turning it into flaming fire,
Recieving as a poison'd cup Recieves the heavenly wine,
And turning [wisdom *del.*] affection into fury, & thought into abstraction,
A Self consuming dark devourer rising into the heavens.

Urizen envious brooding sat & saw the secret terror
Flame high in pride & laugh to scorn the source of his deceit,
Nor knew the source of his own, but thought himself the sole author
Of all his wandering Experiments in the horrible Abyss.
He knew that weakness stretches out in breadth & length, he knew
That wisdom reaches high & deep; & therefore he made Orc,
In serpent form compell'd, stretch out & up the mysterious tree.
He suffer'd him to climb that he might draw all human forms
Into submission to his will, nor knew the dread result.

Los sat in showers of Urizen [cold *del.*] watching cold Enitharmon.
His broodings rush down to his feet, producing Eggs that hatching
Burst forth upon the winds above the tree of Mystery.
Enitharmon lay on his knees. Urizen trac'd his Verses.
In the dark deep the dark tree grew; her shadow was drawn down,
Down to the roots; it wept over Orc, the shadow of Enitharmon.

Los saw her stretch'd, the image of death, upon his wither'd valleys;
Her shadow went forth & return'd. Now she was pale as snow
When the mountains & hills are cover'd over & the paths of Men shut up,
But when her spirit return'd, as ruddy as a morning when
The ripe fruit blushes into joy in heaven's eternal halls,
[She secret joy'd to see; she fed herself on his Despair.
She said, "I am aveng'd for all my sufferings of old." *del.*]
Sorrow shot thro' him from his feet, it shot up to his head
Like a cold night that nips the roots & shatters off the leaves.
Silent he stood o'er Enitharmon, watching her pale face.
He spoke not, he was silent till he felt the cold disease.
Then Los mourn'd on the dismal wind in his jealous lamentation:

"Why can I not Enjoy thy beauty, Lovely Enitharmon?
"When I return from clouds of Grief in the wand'ring Elements
"Where thou in thrilling joy, in beaming summer loveliness,

"Delectable reposest, ruddy in my absence, flaming with beauty,
"Cold pale in sorrow at my approach, trembling at my terrific
"Forehead & eyes, thy lips decay like roses in [early *del.*] the spring.
"How art thou shrunk! thy grapes that burst in summer's vast Excess,
"Shut up in little purple covering, faintly bud & die.
"Thy olive trees that pour'd down oil upon a thousand hills,
"Sickly look forth & scarcely stretch their branches to the plain.
"Thy roses that expanded in the face of glowing morn,
"Hid in a little silken veil scarce breathe & faintly shine.
"Thy lillies that gave light what time the morning looked forth,
"Hid in the Vales, faintly lament, & no one hears their voice.
"All things beside the woful Los enjoy the delights of beauty!
"Once how I sang & call'd the beasts & birds to their delights,
"Nor knew that I, alone exempted from the joys of love,
"Must war with secret monsters of the animating worlds.
"O that I had not seen the day! then should I be at rest,
"Nor felt the stingings of desire, nor longings after life,
"For life is sweet to Los the wretched; to his winged woes
"Is given a craving cry, that they may sit at night on barren rocks
"And whet their beaks & snuff the air, & watch the opening dawn,
"And shriek till, at the smells of blood, they stretch their boney wings
"And cut the winds like arrows shot by troops of Destiny."

Thus Los lamented in the night, unheard by Enitharmon.
For the Shadow of Enitharmon descended down the tree of Mystery.
The Spectre saw the Shade shivering over his gloomy rocks
Beneath the tree of Mystery, which in the dismal Abyss
Began to blossom in fierce pain, shooting its writhing buds
In throes of birth; & now, the blossoms falling, shining fruit
Appear'd of many colours & of various poisonous qualities,
Of Plagues hidden in shining globes that grew on the living tree.

The Spectre of Urthona saw the Shadow of Enitharmon
Beneath the Tree of Mystery among the leaves & fruit.
Redd'ning, the demon strong prepar'd the poison of sweet Love.
He turn'd from side to side in tears; he wept & he embrac'd
The fleeting image, & in whispers mild woo'd the faint shade:

"Loveliest delight of Men! Enitharmon, shady hiding
"In secret places where no eye can trace thy wat'ry way,
"Have I found thee? have I found thee? tremblest thou in fear
"Because of Orc? because he rent his discordant way
"From thy sweet loins of bliss? red flow'd thy blood,
"Pale grew thy face, [*word del.*] lightnings play'd around thee, thunders hover'd

"Over thee, & the terrible Orc rent his discordant way;
"But the next joy of thine shall be in sweet delusion,
"And its birth in fainting & sleep & sweet delusions of Vala."

The Shadow of Enitharmon answer'd: "Art thou, terrible Shade,
"Set over this sweet boy of mine to guard him lest he rend
"His mother to the winds of heaven? Intoxicated with
"The fruit of this delightful tree, I cannot flee away
"From thy embrace, else be assur'd so horrible a form
"Should never in my arms repose; now listen, I will tell
"Thee Secrets of Eternity which ne'er before unlock'd
"My golden lips nor took the bar from Enitharmon's breast.
"Among the Flowers of Beulah walk'd the Eternal Man & saw
"Vala, the lilly of the desart melting in high noon;
"Upon her bosom in sweet bliss he fainted. Wonder siez'd
"All heaven; they saw him dark; they built a golden wall
"Round Beulah. There he revel'd in delight among the Flowers.
"Vala was pregnant & brought forth Urizen, Prince of Light,
"First born of Generation. Then behold a wonder to the Eyes
"Of the now fallen Man; a double form Vala appear'd, a Male
"And female; shudd'ring pale the Fallen Man recoil'd
"From the Enormity & call'd them Luvah & Vala, turning down
"The vales to find his way back into Heaven, but found none,
"For his frail eyes were faded & his ears heavy & dull.
"Urizen grew up in the plains of Beulah. Many sons
"And many daughters flourish'd round the holy Tent of Man
"Till he forgot Eternity, delighted in his sweet joy
"Among his family, his flocks & herds & tents & pastures.
"But Luvah close conferr'd with Urizen in darksom night
"To bind the father & enslave the brethren. Nought he knew
"Of sweet Eternity; the blood flow'd round the holy tent & riv'n
"From its hinges, uttering its final groan, all Beulah fell
"In dark confusion; mean time Los was born & Enitharmon,
"But how, I know not; then forgetfulness quite wrap'd me up
"A period, nor do I more remember till I stood
"Beside Los in the Cavern dark, enslav'd to vegetative forms
"According to the Will of Luvah, who assum'd the Place
"Of the Eternal Man & smote him. But thou, Spectre dark,
"Maist find a way to punish Vala in thy fiery south,
"To bring her down subjected to the rage of my fierce boy."

The Spectre said: "Thou lovely Vision, this delightful Tree
"Is given us for a Shelter from the tempests of Void & Solid,
"Till once again the morn of ages shall renew upon us,
"To reunite in those mild fields of happy Eternity

"Where thou & I in undivided Essence walk'd about
"Imbodied, thou my garden of delight & I the spirit in the garden;
"Mutual there we dwelt in one another's joy, revolving
"Days of Eternity, with Tharmas mild & Luvah sweet melodious
"Upon our waters. This thou well rememberest; listen, I will tell
"What thou forgettest. They in us & we in them alternate Liv'd,
"Drinking the joys of Universal Manhood. One dread morn—
"Listen, O vision of Delight! One dread morn of gory blood
"The manhood was divided, for the gentle passions, making way
"Thro' the infinite labyrinths of the heart & thro' the nostrils issuing
"In odorous stupefaction, stood before the Eyes of Man
"A female bright. I stood beside my anvil dark, a mass
"Of iron glow'd bright prepar'd for spade & plowshares: sudden down
"I sunk with cries of blood issuing downward in the veins
"Which now my rivers were become, rolling in tubelike forms
"Shut up within themselves descending down. I sunk along
"The goary tide even to the place of seed, & there dividing
"I was divided in darkness & oblivion; thou an infant woe,
"And I an infant terror in the womb of Enion.
"My masculine spirit, scorning the frail body issued forth,
"From Enion's brain In this deformed form, leaving thee there
"Till times pass'd over thee; but still my spirit returning hover'd
"And form'd a Male, to be a counterpart to thee, O Love
"Darken'd & Lost! In due time issuing forth from Enion's womb
"Thou & that demon Los were born. Ah, jealousy & woe!
"Ah, poor divided dark Urthona! now a Spectre wand'ring
"The deeps of Los, the slave of that Creation I created.
"I labour night & day for Los; but listen thou my vision.
"I view futurity in thee. I will bring down soft Vala
"To the embraces of this terror, & I will destroy
"That body I created; then shall we unite again in bliss;
"For till these terrors planted round the Gates of Eternal life
"Are driven away & annihilated, we never can repass the Gates.
"Thou knowest that the Spectre is in Every Man insane, brutish,
"Deform'd, that I am thus a ravening devouring lust continually
"Craving & devouring; but my Eyes are always upon thee, O lovely
"Delusion, & I cannot crave for any thing but thee: [& till
"I have thee in my arms & am again united to Los
"To be one body & One spirit with him *del.*] not so
"The Spectres of the Dead, for I am as the Spectre of the Living."

Astonish'd, fill'd with tears, the spirit of Enitharmon beheld
And heard the Spectre; bitterly she wept, Embracing fervent
Her once lov'd Lord, now but a Shade, herself also a shade,
Conferring times on times among the branches of that Tree.

Thus they conferr'd among the intoxicating fumes of Mystery
Till Enitharmon's shadow, pregnant in the deeps beneath,
Brought forth a wonder horrible. While Enitharmon shriek'd
And trembled, thro' the Worlds above Los wept, his fierce soul was terrified
At the shrieks of Enitharmon, at her tossings, nor could his eyes percieve
The cause of her dire anguish, for she lay the image of death,
Mov'd by strong shudders till her shadow was delivered, then she ran
Raving about the upper Elements in maddening fury.

She burst the Gates of Enitharmon's heart with direful Crash,
Nor could they ever be clos'd again; the golden hinges were broken,
And the gates broke in sunder & their ornaments defac'd
Beneath the tree of Mystery, for the immortal shadow shuddering
Brought forth this wonder horrible: a Cloud; she grew & grew
Till many of the Dead burst forth from the bottoms of their tombs
In male forms without female counterparts, or Emanations,
Cruel and ravening with Enmity & Hatred & War,
In dreams of Ulro, [sweet *del.*] dark delusive, drawn by the lovely shadow.

The Spectre [*word del.*] (&) terrified gave her Charge over the howling Orc.
Then took the tree of Mystery root in the World of Los,
Its topmost [branches *del.*] boughs shooting a [stem *del.*] fibre beneath Enitharmon's couch,
The double rooted Labyrinth soon wav'd around their heads.

But then the Spectre enter'd Los's bosom. Every sigh & groan
Of Enitharmon bore Urthona's Spectre on its wings.
Obdurate Los felt Pity. Enitharmon told the tale
Of Urthona. Los embrac'd the Spectre, first as a brother,
Then as another Self, astonish'd, humanizing & in tears,
In Self abasement Giving up his Domineering lust.

"Thou never canst embrace sweet Enitharmon, terrible Demon, Till
"Thou art united with thy Spectre, Consummating by pains & labours
"[Thy *del.*] That mortal body, & by Self annihilation back returning
"To life Eternal; be assur'd I am thy real self,
"Tho' thus divided from thee & the slave of Every passion
"Of thy fierce Soul. Unbar the Gates of Memory: look upon me
"Not as another, but as thy real Self. I am thy Spectre,
"Thou didst subdue me in old times by thy Immortal Strength

"When I was a ravening hungering & thirsting cruel lust & murder.
"Tho' horrible & Ghastly to thine Eyes, tho' buried beneath
"The ruins of the Universe, hear what inspir'd I speak, & be silent.
"If [once *del.*] we unite in one, another better world will be
"Open'd within your heart & loins & wondrous brain,
"Threefold, as it was in Eternity, & this, the fourth Universe,
"Will be Renew'd by the three & consummated in Mental fires;
"But if thou dost refuse, Another body will be prepared
"For me, & thou, annihilate, evaporate & be no more.
"For thou art but a form & organ of life, & of thyself
"Art nothing, being Created Continually by Mercy & Love divine."

Los furious answer'd: "Spectre horrible, thy words astound my Ear
"With irresistible conviction. I feel I am not one of those
"Who when convinc'd can still persist: tho' furious, controllable
"By Reason's power. Even I already feel a World within
"Opening its gates, & in it all the real substances
"Of which these in the outward World are shadows which pass away.
"Come then into my Bosom, & in thy shadowy arms bring with thee
"My lovely Enitharmon. I will quell my fury & teach
"Peace to the soul of dark revenge, & repentance to Cruelty."

So spoke Los, & Embracing Enitharmon & the Spectre,
Clouds would have folded round in Extacy & Love uniting,
But Enitharmon trembling, fled & hid beneath Urizen's tree.
But mingling together with his Spectre, the Spectre of Urthona
Wondering beheld the Center open'd; by Divine Mercy inspir'd—
He in his turn Gave Tasks to Los, Enormous, to destroy
That body he created; but in vain, for Los perform'd
Wonders of labour—
They Builded Golgonooza, Los labouring [*word del.*] builded pillars high
And Domes terrific in the nether heavens, for beneath
Was open'd new heavens & a new Earth beneath & within,
Threefold, within the brain, within the heart, within the loins:
A Threefold Atmosphere Sublime, continuous from Urthona's world,
But yet having a Limit Twofold named Satan & Adam.

But Los stood on the Limit of Translucence, weeping & trembling,
Filled with doubts in self accusation, beheld the fruit
Of Urizen's Mysterious tree. For Enitharmon thus spake:
"When In the Deeps beneath I gather'd of this ruddy fruit,
"It was by that I knew that I had Sinn'd, & then I knew
"That without a ransom I could not be sav'd from Eternal death:

"That Life lives upon death, & by devouring appetite
"All things subsist on one another; thenceforth in despair
"I spend my glowing time; but thou art strong & mighty
"To bear this Self conviction; take then, Eat thou also of
"The fruit & give me proof of life Eternal or I die."

Then Los plucked the fruit & Eat & sat down in Despair,
And must have given himself to death Eternal, But
Urthona's spectre in part mingling with him, comforted him,
Being a medium between him & Enitharmon. But This Union
Was not to be Effected without Cares & Sorrows & Troubles
Of six thousand Years of self denial and [many Tears *del.*] of bitter Contrition.

Urthona's Spectre terrified beheld the Spectres of the dead:
Each male form'd without a counterpart, without a concentering vision.
The Spectre of Urthona wept before Los, saying, "I am the cause
"That this dire state commences. I began the dreadful state
"Of Separation, & on my dark head the curse & punishment
"Must fall unless a way be found to Ransom & Redeem.
"But I have thee my [Counterpart *del.*] [Vegetative *del.*] miraculous,
"These spectres have no [Counterparts *del.*], therefore they ravin
"Without the food of life. Let us Create them Coun [terparts;]
"For without a Created body the Spectre is Eternal Death."
Los trembling, answer'd: "Now I feel the weight of stern repentance.
"Tremble not so, my Enitharmon, at the awful gates
"Of thy poor broken Heart. I see thee like a shadow withering
"As on the outside of Existence; but look! behold! take comfort!
"Turn inwardly thine Eyes & there behold the Lamb of God
"Clothed in Luvah's robes of blood descending to redeem.
"O Spectre of Urthona, take comfort! O Enitharmon!
"Could'st thou but cease from terror & trembling & affright.
"When I appear before thee in forgiveness of [former . . . *del.*] ancient injuries,
"Why should'st thou remember & be afraid? I surely have died in pain
"Often enough to convince thy jealousy & fear & terror.
"Come hither; be patient; let us converse together, because
"I also tremble at myself & at all my former life."

Enitharmon answer'd: "I behold the Lamb of God descending
"To Meet these Spectres of the Dead. I therefore fear that he
"Will give us to Eternal Death, fit punishment for such
"Hideous offenders: Uttermost extinction in eternal pain:

"An ever dying life of stifling & obstruction: shut out
"Of existence to be a sign & terror to all who behold,
"Lest any should in futurity do as we have done in heaven.
"*Such is our state; nor will the Son of God redeem us, but destroy.*"
So Enitharmon spoke trembling & in torrents of tears.

Los sat in Golgonooza, in the Gate of Luban where
He had erected many porches [which *del.*] where branched the Mysterious tree,
Where the Spectrous dead wail; & sighing thus he spoke to Enitharmon:

"Lovely delight of Men, Enitharmon shady [sweet *del.*] refuge from furious war,
"Thy bosom translucent is a soft repose for the weeping souls
"Of those piteous victims of battle; there they sleep in happy obscurity;
"They feed upon our life; we are their victims. Stern desire
"I feel to fabricate embodied semblances in which the dead
"May live before us in our palaces & in our gardens of [pleasure *del.*] labour,
"Which now, open'd within the Center, we behold spread abroad
"To form a world of [life & love *del.*] sacrifice of brothers & sons & daughters,
"To comfort Orc in his dire sufferings; look, my fires enlume afresh
"Before my face ascending with delight as in ancient times!"

Enitharmon spread her beamy locks upon the wind & said,
"O [lovely *del.*] Lovely terrible Los, wonder of Eternity, O Los, my defence & guide,
"Thy works are all my joy & in thy fires my soul delights;
"If mild they burn in just proportion, & in secret night
"And silence build their day in shadow of soft clouds & dews,
"Then I can sigh forth on the winds of Golgonooza piteous forms
"That vanish again into my bosom; but if thou, my Los,
"Wilt in sweet moderated fury fabricate [sweet *del.*] forms *sublime*,
"Such as the piteous spectres may assimilate themselves into,
"They shall be ransoms for our Souls that we may live."

So Enitharmon spoke, & Los, his hands divine inspir'd, began
[To hew the cavern'd rocks of Dranthon into forms of beauty *del.*]
To modulate his fires; studious the loud roaring flames
He vanquish'd with the strength of Art, bending their iron points
And drawing them forth delighted upon the winds of Golgonooza
From out the ranks of Urizen's war & from the fiery lake

Of Orc, bending down as the binder of the sheaves follows
The reaper, in both arms embracing the furious raging flames.
Los drew them forth out of the deeps, planting his right foot firm
Upon the Iron crag of Urizen, thence springing up aloft
Into the heavens of Enitharmon in a mighty circle.

And first he drew a line upon the walls of shining heaven,
And Enitharmon tinctur'd it with beams of blushing love.
It remain'd permanent, a lovely form, inspir'd, divinely human.
Dividing into just proportions, Los unwearied labour'd
The immortal lines upon the heavens, till with sighs of love,
Sweet Enitharmon mild, Entranc'd breath'd forth upon the wind
The spectrous dead. Weeping, the Spectres view'd the immortal works
Of Los, Assimilating to those forms, Embodied & Lovely
In youth & beauty, in the arms of Enitharmon mild reposing.

First Rintrah & then Palamabron, drawn from out the ranks of war,
In infant innocence repos'd on Enitharmon's bosom.
Orc was comforted in the deeps; his soul reviv'd in them:
As the Eldest brother is the [*word del.*] father's image, So Orc became
As Los, a father to his brethren, & he joy'd in the dark lake
Tho' bound with chains of Jealousy & in scales of iron & brass.

But Los loved them & refus'd to Sacrifice their infant limbs,
And Enitharmon's smiles & tears prevail'd over self protection.
They rather chose to meet Eternal Death than to destroy
The offspring of their Care & Pity. Urthona's spectre was comforted;
But Tharmas most rejoic'd in hope of Enion's return,
For he beheld new Female forms born forth upon the air
Who wove soft silken veils of covering in sweet raptur'd trance,
Mortal, & not as Enitharmon, without a covering veil.

First his immortal spirit drew Urizen['s] Spectre away
From out the ranks of war, separating him in sunder,
Leaving his Spectrous form, which could not be drawn away.
Then he divided Thiriel, the Eldest of Urizen's sons:
Urizen became Rintrah, Thiriel became Palamabron.
Thus dividing the power of Every Warrior,
Startled was Los; he found his Enemy Urizen now
In his hands; he wonder'd that he felt love & not hate.
His whole soul loved him; he beheld him an infant
Lovely, breath'd from Enitharmon; he trembled within himself.

[END OF NIGHT THE SEVENTH]

Vala

Night the Seventh [*b*]

But in the deeps beneath the [tree *del.*] roots of Mystery in darkest night
Where Urizen sat on his rock, the Shadow brooded. [*word del.*]
Urizen saw & triumph'd, & he cried to [the Shadowy Female *del.*] his warriors:
"The time of Prophecy is now revolv'd, & all
"This Universal ornament is mine, & in my hands
"The ends of heaven; like a Garment will I fold them round me,
"Consuming what must be consum'd; then in power & majesty
"I will walk forth thro' those wide fields of endless Eternity,
"A God & not a Man, a Conqueror in triumphant glory,
"And all the Sons of Everlasting shall bow down at my feet."

[The Shadowy voice answer'd: "O Urizen Prince of Light" *del.*]
First Trades & Commerce, ships & armed vessels he builded laborious
To swim the deep; & on the land, children are sold to trades
Of dire necessity, still laboring day & night till all
Their life extinct they took the spectre form in dark despair;
And slaves in myriads, in ship loads, burden the hoarse sounding deep,
Rattling with clanking chains; the Universal Empire groans.

And he commanded his Sons [to] found a Center in the Deep;
And Urizen laid the first Stone, & all his myriads
Builded a temple in the image of the human heart.
And in the inner part of the Temple, wondrous workmanship,
They form'd the Secret place, reversing all the order of delight,
That whosoever enter'd into the temple might not behold
The hidden wonders, allegoric of the Generations
Of secret lust, when hid in chambers dark the nightly harlot
Plays in Disguise in whisper'd hymn & mumbling prayer. The priests
He ordain'd & Priestesses, cloth'd in disguises beastial,
Inspiring secrecy; & lamps they bore: intoxicating fumes
Roll round the Temple; & they took the Sun that glow'd o'er Los
And, with immense machines down rolling, the terrific orb
Compell'd. The Sun, redd'ning like a fierce lion in his chains,
Descended to the sound of instruments that drown'd the noise
Of the hoarse wheels & the terrific howlings of wild beasts
That drag'd the wheels of the Sun's chariot; & they put the Sun
Into the temple of Urizen to give light to the Abyss,

To light the War by day, to hide his secret beams by night,
For he divided day & night in different order'd portions,
The day for war, the night for secret religion in his temple.

[Urizen nam'd it . . . *del.*]
Los rear'd his mighty [forehead *del.*] stature: on Earth stood his feet. Above
The moon his furious forehead, circled with black bursting thunders,
His naked limbs glittering upon the dark blue sky, his knees
Bathed in bloody clouds, his loins in fires of war where spears
And swords rage, where the Eagles cry & the Vultures laugh, saying:
"Now comes the night of Carnage, now the flesh of Kings & Princes
"Pampered in palaces for our food, the blood of Captains nurtur'd
"With lust & murder for our drink; the drunken Raven shall wander
"All night among the slain, & mock the wounded that groan in the field."

Tharmas laugh'd furious among the Banners cloth'd in blood,
Crying: "As I will I rend the Nations all asunder, rending
"The People: vain their combinations, I will scatter them.
"But thou, O Son, whom I have crowned and inthroned, thee strong
"I will preserve tho' Enemies arise around thee numberless.
"I will command my winds & they shall scatter them, or call
"My Waters like a flood around thee; fear not, trust in me
"And I will give thee all the ends of heaven for thy possession.
"In war shalt thou bear rule, in blood shalt thou triumph for me,
"Because in times of Everlasting I was rent in sunder
"And what I loved best was divided among my Enemies.
"My little daughters were made captives, & I saw them beaten
"With whips along the sultry [roads *del.*] sands. I heard those whom I lov'd
"Crying in secret tents at night, & in the morn compell'd
"To labour; & behold, my heart sunk down beneath
"In sighs & sobbings, all dividing, till I was divided
"In twain; & lo, my Crystal form that lived in my bosom
"Follow'd her daughters to the fields of blood: they left me naked,
"Alone, & they refus'd to return from the fields of the mighty.
"Therefore I will reward them as they have rewarded me.
"I will divide them in my anger, & thou, O my King,
"Shalt gather them from out their graves, & put thy fetter on them,
"And bind them to thee, that my crystal form may come to me."

So cried the Demon of the Waters in the Clouds of Los.
Outstretch'd upon the hills lay Enitharmon; clouds & tempests
Beat round her head all night: all day she riots in Excess.

But [day by *del.*] night or day Los follows War, & the dismal moon rolls over her,
That when Los war'd upon the South, reflected the fierce fires
Of his immortal head into the North, upon faint Enitharmon.
Red rage the furies of fierce Orc; black thunders roll round Los;
Flaming his head, like the bright sun seen thro' a mist that magnifies
The disk into a terrible vision to the Eyes of trembling mortals.

And Enitharmon, trembling & in fear, utter'd these words:

"I put not any trust in thee, nor in thy glitt'ring scales;
"Thy eyelids are a terror to me; & the flaming of thy crest,
"The rushing of thy scales confound me, thy hoarse rushing scales.
"And if that Los had not built me a tower upon a rock,
"I must have died in the dark desart among noxious worms.
"How shall I flee, how shall I flee into the tower of Los?
"My feet are turned backward & my footsteps slide in clay,
"And clouds are clos'd around my tower; my arms labour in vain.
"Does not the God of waters in the wracking Elements
"Love those who hate, rewarding with hate the Loving Soul?
"And must not I obey the God, thou Shadow of Jealousy?
"I cry; the watchman heareth not. I pour my voice in roarings:
"Watchman! the night is thick, & darkness cheats my rayie sight.
"Lift up! Lift up! O Los! awake my watchman, for he sleepeth.
"Lift up! Lift up! Shine forth, O Light! watchman, thy light is out.
"O Los! unless thou keep my tower the Watchman will be slain."

So Enitharmon cried upon her terrible Earthy bed
While the broad Oak wreath'd his roots round her, forcing his dark way
Thro' caves of death into Existence. The Beech, long limbed, advanc'd
Terrific into the pain'd heavens. The fruit trees humanizing
Shew'd their immortal energies in warlike desperation,
Rending the heavens & earths & drinking blood in the hot battle
To feed their fruit, to gratify their hidden sons & daughters
That far within the close recesses of their secret palaces
View'd the vast war & joy'd, wishing[?] to vegetate
Into the worlds of Enitharmon. Loud the roaring winds,
Burden'd with clouds, howl round the Couch. Sullen the wooly sheep
Walks thro' the battle. Dark & fierce the Bull his rage
Propagates thro' the warring Earth. The Lion raging in flames,
The Tyger in redounding smoke. The serpent of the woods
And of the waters, & the scorpion of the desart irritate
With harsh songs every living soul. The Prester Serpent runs

Along the ranks, crying, "Listen to the Priest of God, ye warriors;
"This Cowl upon my head he plac'd in times of Everlasting,
"And said, 'Go forth & guide my battles; like the jointed spine
" 'Of Man I made thee when I blotted Man from life & light.
" 'Take thou the Seven Diseases of Man; store them for times to come
" 'In store houses, in secret places that I will tell thee of,
" 'To be my great & awful curses at the time appointed.' "
The Prester Serpent ceas'd; the War song sounded loud & strong
Thro' all the heavens. Urizen's Web vibrated, torment on torment.
Then I heard the Earthquake, &c.[1]

Now in the Caverns of the Grave & Places of human seed
The nameless shadowy Vortex stood before the face of Orc.
The shadow rear'd her dismal head over the flaming youth
With sighs & howling & deep sobs; that he might lose his rage
And with it lose himself in meekness, she embrac'd his fire.—
As when the Earthquake rouzes from his den, his shoulders huge
Appear above the crumbling Mountain, Silence waits around him
A moment, then astounding horror belches from the Center,
The fiery dogs arise, the shoulders huge appear—
So Orc roll'd round his clouds upon the deeps of dark Urthona,
Knowing the arts of Urizen were Pity & Meek [love *del.*] affection
And that by these arts the serpent form exuded from his limbs
Silent as despairing love & strong as jealousy,
Jealous that she was Vala, now become Urizen's harlot
And the Harlot of Los & the deluded harlot of the Kings of Earth,
His soul was gnawn in sunder.
The hairy shoulders rend the links, free are the wrists of fire.
Red rage redounds, he rouzed his lions from his forests black,
They howl around the flaming youth, rending the nameless shadow
And running their immortal course thro' solid darkness borne.

Loud sounds the war song round red Orc in his [*word erased*] fury
And round the nameless shadowy Female in her howling terror
When all the Elemental Gods join'd in the wondrous Song:

"Sound the War trumpet terrific, souls clad in attractive steel!
"Sound the shrill fife, serpents of war! I hear the northern drum.
"Awake! I hear the flapping of the folding banners.

"The dragons of the North put on their armour;
"Upon the Eastern sea direct they take their course.
"The glittering of their horses' trappings stains the vault of night.

"Stop we the rising of the glorious King: spur, spur your [steeds *del.*] clouds
"Of death! O northern drum, awake! O hand of iron, sound

[1] The rest of this passage is lost.

"The northern drum! Now give the charge! bravely obscur'd
"With darts of wintry hail. Again the black bow draw:
"Again the Elemental strings to your right breasts draw,
"And let the thundering drum speed on the arrows black."

The arrows flew from cloudy bow all day, till blood
From east to west flow'd, like the human veins, in rivers
Of life upon the plains of death & valleys of despair.

"Now sound the clarions of Victory, now strip the slain.
"[Now *del.*] clothe yourselves in golden arms, brothers of war."
They sound the clarions strong, they chain the howling captives,
They give the Oath of blood, they cast the lots into the helmet,
They vote the death of Luvah & they nail'd him to the tree,
They pierc'd him with a spear & laid him in a sepulcher
To die a death of Six thousand years, bound round with desolation.

The sun was black & the moon roll'd, a useless globe, thro' heaven.

Then left the sons of Urizen the plow & harrow, the loom,
The hammer & the chisel & the rule & compasses.
They forg'd the sword, the chariot of war, the battle ax,
The trumpet fitted to the battle & the flute of summer,
And all the arts of life they chang'd into the arts of death.
The hour glass contemn'd because its simple workmanship
Was as the workmanship of the plowman, & the water wheel
That raises water into Cisterns, broken & burn'd in fire
Because its workmanship was like the workmanship of the shepherd,
And in their stead intricate wheels invented, Wheel without wheel,
To perplex youth in their outgoings & to bind to labours
Of day & night the myriads of Eternity, that they might file
And polish brass & iron hour after hour, laborious workmanship,
Kept ignorant of the use that they might spend the days of wisdom
In sorrowful drudgery to obtain a scanty pittance of bread,
In ignorance to view a small portion & think that All,
And call it demonstration, blind to all the simple rules of life.

"Now, now the Battle rages round thy tender limbs, O Vala!
"Now smile among thy bitter tears, now put on all thy beauty.
"Is not the wound of the sword sweet & the broken bone delightful?
"Wilt thou now smile among the slain when the wounded groan in the field?

"Lift up thy blue eyes, Vala, & put on thy sapphire shoes.
"O Melancholy Magdalen, behold the morning breaks!
"Gird on thy flaming Zone, descend into the Sepulchre,

"Scatter the blood from thy golden brow, the tears from thy silver locks,
"Shake off the water from thy wings & the dust from thy white garments.

"Remember all thy feigned terrors on the secret couch
"When the sun rose in glowing morn with arms of mighty hosts
"Marching to battle, who was wont to rise with Urizen's harps
"Girt as a Sower with his seed to scatter life abroad.

"Arise, O Vala! bring the bow of Urizen, bring the swift arrows of light.
"How rag'd the golden horses of Urizen, bound to the chariot of Love,
"Compell'd to leave the plow to the Ox, to snuff up the winds of desolation,
"To trample the cornfields in boastful neighings; this is no gentle harp,
"This is no warbling brook, nor Shadow of a Myrtle tree,

"But blood & wounds & dismal cries & clarions of war,
"And hearts laid open to the light by the broad grizly sword,
"And bowels hidden [in darkness *del.*] in hammered steel ripp'd forth upon the ground.
"Call forth thy smiles of soft deceit, call forth thy cloudy tears!
"We hear thy sighs in trumpets shrill when Morn shall blood renew."

So sung the demons of the deep; the Clarions of war blew loud.
Orc rent her, & his human form consum'd in his own fires
Mingled with her dolorous members strewn thro' the Abyss.
She joy'd in all the Conflict, Gratified & dropping tears of woe.
No more remain'd of Orc but the Serpent round the tree of Mystery.
The form of Orc was gone; he rear'd his serpent bulk among
The stars of Urizen in Power, rending the form of life
Into a formless indefinite & strewing her on the Abyss
Like clouds upon the winter sky, broken with winds & thunders.
This was, to her, Supreme delight. The Warriors mourn'd disappointed.
They go out to war with strong shouts & loud clarions.
O, Pity! They return with lamentations, mourning, & weeping.
Invisible or visible, drawn out in length or stretcht in breadth,
The Shadowy Female Varied in the War in her delight,
Howling in discontent, black & heavy, uttering brute sounds,
Wading thro' fens among the slimy weeds, making Lamentations
To decieve Tharmas in his rage, to soothe his furious soul,

To stay him in his flight that Urizen might live tho' in pain.
He said: "Art thou bright Enion? is the shadow of hope return'd?"

And she said: "Tharmas, I am Vala, bless thy innocent face!
"Doth Enion avoid the sight of thy blue wat'ry eyes?
"Be not perswaded that the air knows this, or the falling dew."

Tharmas repli'd: "O Vala, once I liv'd in a garden of delight;
"I waken'd Enion in the morning, & she turn'd away
"Among the apple trees; & all the gardens of delight
"Swam like a dream before my eyes. I went to seek the steps
"Of Enion in the gardens, & the shadows compass'd me
"And clos'd me in a wat'ry world of woe where Enion stood
"Trembling before me like a shadow, like a mist, like air.
"And she is gone, & here alone I war with darkness & death.
"I hear thy voice, but not thy form see; thou & all delight
"And life appear & vanish, mocking me with shadows of false hope.
"Hast thou forgot that the air listens thro' all its districts, telling
"The subtlest thoughts shut up from light in chambers of the Moon?"

"Tharmas, The Moon has chambers where the babes of love lie hid,
"And whence they never can be brought in all Eternity
"Unless expos'd by their vain parents. Lo, him whom I love
"Is hidden from me, & I never in all Eternity
"Shall see him. Enitharmon & Ahania, combin'd with Enion,
"Hid him in that Outrageous form of Orc, which torments me for Sin.
"For all my secret faults, which he brings forth upon the light
"Of day, in jealousy & blood my Children are led to Urizen's war
"Before my eyes, & for every one of these I am condemn'd
"To Eternal torment in these flames; for tho' I have the power
"To rise on high, Yet love here binds me down, & never, never
"Will I arise till him I love is loos'd from this dark chain."

Tharmas replied: "Vala, thy sins have lost us heaven & bliss.
"Thou art our Curse, and till I can bring love into the light
"I never will depart from my great wrath."

So Tharmas wail'd [then *del.*] wrathful; then rode upon the stormy Deep
Cursing the voice that mock'd him with false hope, in furious mood.
Then she returns, swift as a blight upon the infant bud,
Howling in all the notes of woe to stay his furious rage,
Stamping the hills, wading or swimming, flying furious or falling,
Or like an Earthquake rumbling in the bowels of the earth,
Or like a cloud beneath, & like a fire flaming in high,

Walking in pleasure of the hills or murmuring in the dales
Like to a rushing torrent beneath & a falling rock above,
A thunder cloud in the south & a lulling voice heard in the north.

And she went forth & saw the forms of life & of delight
Walking on Mountains or flying in the open expanse of heaven.
She heard sweet voices in the winds & in the voices of birds
That rose from waters; for the waters were as the voice of Luvah,
Not seen to her like waters or like this dark world of death,
Tho' all those fair perfections, which men know only by name,
In beautiful substantial forms appear'd & served her
As food or drink or ornament, or in delightful works
To build her bowers; for the Elements brought forth abundantly
The living soul in glorious forms, & every one came forth
Walking before her Shadowy face & bowing at her feet.
But in vain delights were poured forth on the howling melancholy.
For her delight the horse his proud neck bow'd & his white mane,
And the strong Lion deign'd in his mouth to wear the golden bit,
While the far beaming Peacock waited on the fragrant wind
To bring her fruits of sweet delight from trees of richest wonders,
And the strong pinion'd Eagle bore the fire of heaven in the night season.
Woo'd & subdu'd into Eternal Death the Demon Lay,
In [anger for *del.*] rage against the dark despair, the howling Melancholy.
For far & wide she stretch'd thro' all the worlds of Urizen's journey,
And was Ajoin'd to Beulah as the Polypus to the Rock.
Mo[u]rning the daughters of Beulah saw, nor could they have sustain'd
The horrid sight of death & torment, But the Eternal Promise
They wrote on all their tombs & pillars, & on every Urn
These words: "If ye will believe, your B[r]other shall rise again,"
In golden letters ornamented with sweet labours of Love,
Waiting with patience [of *del.*] for the fulfilment of the Promise Divine.

And all the Songs of Beulah sounded comfortable notes,
Not suffering doubt to rise up from the Clouds of the Shadowy Female.
Then myriads of the dead burst thro' the bottoms of their tombs,
Descending on the shadowy female's clouds in Spectrous terror,
Beyond the Limit of Translucence on the Lake of Udan Adan.
These they nam'd Satans, & in the Aggregate they nam'd them Satan.

End of The Seventh Night [*b*]

Vala

Night the Eighth

Then All in Great Eternity [which is called *del.*] Met in the Council of God
[Met *del.*]as one Man, Even Jesus, upon Gilead & Hermon,
Upon the Limit of Contraction to create the fallen Man.
The [Eternal *del.*] Fallen Man stretch'd like a corse upon the oozy Rock,
Wash'd with the tides, pale, overgrown with weeds
That mov'd with horrible dreams; hovering high over his head
Two winged immortal shapes, one standing at his feet
Toward the East, one standing at his head toward the west,
Their wings join'd in the Zenith over head; [but other wings
They had which cloth'd their bodies like a garment of soft down,
Silvery white, shining upon the dark blue sky in silence.
Their wings touch'd the heavens; their fair feet hover'd above
The swelling tides; they bent over the dead corse like an arch,
Pointed at top in highest heavens, of precious stones & pearl. *del.*]
Such is a Vision of All Beulah hov'ring over the Sleeper.

The limit of Contraction now was fix'd & Man began
To wake upon the Couch of Death; he sneezed seven times;
A tear of blood dropped from either eye; again he repos'd
In the Saviour's arms, in the arms of tender mercy & loving kindness.

Then [first *del.*] Los said: "I behold the Divine Vision thro' the broken Gates
"Of [Enitharmon's *del.*] thy poor broken heart, astonish'd, melted into Compassion & Love."
And Enitharmon said: "I see the Lamb of God upon Mount Zion."
Wondering with love & Awe they felt the divine hand upon them;

For nothing could restrain the dead in Beulah from descending
Unto Ulro's night; tempted by the Shadowy female's sweet
Delusive cruelty, they descend away from the Daughters of Beulah
And Enter Urizen's temple, Enitharmon pitying, & her heart
Gates broken down; they descend thro' the Gate of Pity,
The broken heart Gate of Enitharmon [which join'd to Urizen's temple
Which is the Synagogue of Satan. *del.*] She sighs them forth upon the wind
Of Golgonooza. Los stood [at the Gate *del.*] recieving them—

For Los could enter into Enitharmon's bosom & explore
Its intricate Labyrinths now the Obdurate heart was broken—
From out the War of Urizen, & Tharmas recieving them
[Los stood, &c. *marginal insertion.*]
Into his hands. Then Enitharmon erected Looms in Luban's Gate
And call'd the Looms Cathedron; in these Looms she wove the Spectres
Bodies of Vegetation, singing lulling Cadences to drive away
Despair from the poor wandering spectres; and Los loved them
With a parental love, for the Divine hand was upon him
And upon Enitharmon, & the Divine Countenance shone
In Golgonooza. Looking down, the daughters of Beulah saw
With joy the bright Light, & in it a Human form,
And knew he was the Saviour, Even Jesus: & they worshipped.

[Astonish'd, comforted, delighted the Daughters of Beulah saw *del.*]
Astonish'd, comforted, Delighted, in notes of Rapturous Extacy
All Beulah stood astonish'd, looking down to Eternal Death.
They saw the Saviour beyond the Pit of death & destruction;
For whether they look'd upward they saw the Divine Vision,
Or whether they look'd downward still they saw the Divine Vision
Surrounding them on all sides beyond sin & death & hell.

Enitharmon wove in tears, singing songs of Lamentation
And pitying comfort as she sigh'd forth on the wind the Spectres,
Also the Vegetated bodies which Enitharmon wove
Open'd within their hearts & in their loins & in their brain
To Beulah; & the Dead in Ulro descended from the War
Of Urizen & Tharmas & from the Shadowy female's clouds.
And some were woven [One fold *del.*] single, & some twofold, & some threefold
In Head or Heart or Reins, according to the fittest order
Of most merciful pity & compassion to the spectrous dead.

When Urizen saw the Lamb of God clothed in Luvah's robes,
Perplex'd & terrifi'd he stood, tho' well he knew that Orc
Was Luvah. But he now beheld a new Luvah, Or One
Who assum'd Luvah's form & stood before him opposite.
But he saw Orc a Serpent form augmenting times on times
In the fierce battle; & he saw the Lamb of God & the World of Los
Surrounded by his dark machines; for Orc augmented swift
In fury, a Serpent wondrous among the Constellations of Urizen.
A crest of fire rose on his forehead, red as the carbuncle,
Beneath, down to his eyelids, scales of pearl, then gold & silver
Immingled with the ruby overspread his Visage down

His furious neck; writhing contortive in dire budding pains
The scaly armour shot out. Stubborn, down his back & bosom
The Emerald, Onyx, Sapphire, jasper, beryl, amethyst
Strove in terrific emulation which should gain a place
[On the immortal fiend *del.*] Upon the mighty Fiend, the fruit of the mysterious tree
Kneaded in Uveth's kneading trough. Still Orc devour'd the food
In raging hunger. Still the pestilential food, in gems & gold,
Exuded round his awful limbs, Stretching to serpent length
His human bulk, While the dark Shadowy female, brooding over,
Measur'd his food morning & evening in cups & baskets of iron.
With tears of sorrow incessant she labour'd the food of Orc,
Compell'd by the iron hearted sisters, Daughters of Urizen,
Gathering the fruit of that mysterious tree, circling its root
She spread herself thro' all the branches in the power of Orc.

Thus Urizen, in self dece[i]t, his warlike preparations fabricated;
And when all things were finish'd, sudden wav'd [his hurtling hand *del.*] among the stars,
[Among the stars *del.*] His hurtling hand gave the dire signal; thunderous clarions blow,
And all the hollow deep rebellow'd with the wond'rous war.
[But thus *del.*] But Urizen his mighty rage let loose in the mid deep.
Sparkles of dire affliction issued [from *del.*] round his frozen limbs.
Horrible hooks & nets he form'd, twisting the cords of iron
And brass, & molten metals cast in hollow globes, & bor'd
Tubes in petrific steel, & ramm'd combustibles, & wheels
And chains & pullies fabricated all round the Heavens of Los;
Communing with the Serpent of Orc in dark dissimulation,
And with the Synagogue of Satan in dark Sanhedrim,
To undermine the World of Los & tear bright Enitharmon
To the four winds, hopeless of future. All futurity
Seems teeming with endless destruction never to be repell'd;
Desperate remorse swallows the present in a quenchless rage.

Terrified & astonish'd, Urizen beheld the battle take a form
Which he intended not: a Shadowy [male *del.*] hermaphrodite, black & opake;
The soldiers nam'd it Satan, but he was yet unform'd & vast.
Hermaphroditic it at length became, hiding the Male
Within as in a Tabernacle, Abominable, Deadly.

The battle howls, the terrors fir'd rage in the work of death;—
Enormous Works Los contemplated, inspir'd by the holy Spirit.—
Los builds the Walls of Golgonooza against the stirring battle

That only thro' the Gates of Death they can enter to Enitharmon.
Raging they take the human visage & the human form,
Feeling the hand of Los in Golgonooza & the force
Attractive of his hammer's beating & the silver looms
Of Enitharmon singing lulling cadences on the wind;
They humanize in the fierce battle, where in direful pain
Troop by troop the beastial droves rend one another, sounding loud
The instruments of sound; & troop by troop, in human forms, they urge
The dire confusion till the battle faints; those that remain
Return in pangs & horrible convulsions to their beastial state;
For the monsters of the Elements, Lions or Tygers or Wolves,
Sound loud the howling music Inspir'd by Los & Enitharmon, sounding loud; terrific men
They seem to one another, laughing terrible among the banners.
And when, the revolution of their day of battles over,
Relapsing in dire torment they return to forms of woe,
To moping visages returning, inanimate tho' furious,
No more erect, tho' strong, drawn out in length they ravin
For senseless gratification, & their visages thrust forth,
Flatten above & beneath & stretch out into beastial length.
Weaken'd they stretch beyond their power in dire droves till war begins,
Or secret religion in their temples before secret shrines.

And Urizen gave life & sense by his immortal power
To all his Engines of deceit: that linked chains might run
Thro' ranks of war spontaneous: & that hooks & boring screws
Might act according to their forms by innate cruelty.
He formed also harsh instruments of sound
To grate the soul into destruction, or to inflame with fury
The spirits of life, to pervert all the faculties of sense
Into their own destruction, if perhaps he might avert
His own despair even at the cost of every thing that breathes.

Thus in the temple of the Sun his books of iron & brass
And silver & gold he consecrated, reading incessantly
To myriads of perturbed spirits; thro' the universe
They propagated the deadly words, the Shadowy Female absorbing
The enormous Sciences of Urizen, ages after ages exploring
The fell destruction. And she said: "O Urizen, Prince of Light,
"What words of dread pierce my faint Ear! what falling snows around
"My feeble limbs infold my destin'd misery!
"I alone dare the lash abide to sit beneath the blast

"Unhurt, & dare the inclement forehead of the King of Light;
"From dark abysses of the times remote fated to be
"The Sorrower of Eternity; in love, with tears submiss I rear
"My Eyes to thy Pavilions; hear my prayer for Luvah's sake.
"I see the murderer of my Luvah, cloth'd in robes of blood:
"He who assumed my Luvah's throne in times of Everlasting.
"Where hast thou hid him whom I love: in what remote Abyss
"Resides that God of my delight? O might my eyes behold
"My Luvah, then could I deliver all the sons of God
"From Bondage of [the human form *del.*] these terrors, & with influences sweet,
"As once in those eternal fields, in brotherhood & Love
"United, we should live in bliss as those who sinned not.
"The Eternal Man is seal'd by thee, never to be deliver'd.
"We are all servants to thy will. O King of Light, relent
"Thy furious power; be our father & our loved King.
"But if my Luvah is no more, If [that *del.*] thou hast smitten him
"And laid him in the Sepulcher, Or if [that *del.*] thou wilt revenge
"His murder on another, Silent I bow with dread.
"But happiness can never [come] to thee, O King, nor me,
"For he was source of every joy that this mysterious tree
"Unfolds in Allegoric fruit. When shall the dead revive?
"Can that which has existed cease, or can love & life expire?"

Urizen heard the Voice & saw the shadow underneath
His woven darkness; & in laws & deceitful religions,
Beginning at the tree of Mystery, circling its root
She spread herself thro' all the branches in the power of Orc:
A shapeless & indefinite cloud, in tears of sorrow incessant
Steeping the direful Web of Religion; swagging heavy, it fell
From heaven to heav'n, thro' all its meshes, altering the Vortexes,
Misplacing every Center; hungry desire & lust began
Gathering the fruit of that Mysterious tree, till Urizen,
Sitting within his temple, furious, felt the num[m]ing stupor,
Himself tangled in his own net, in sorrow, lust, repentance.

Enitharmon wove in tears, singing songs of Lamentations
And pitying comfort as she sigh'd forth on the wind the spectres
And wove them bodies, calling them her belov'd sons & daughters,
Employing the daughters in her looms, & Los employ'd the sons
In Golgonooza's Furnaces among the Anvils of time & space,
Thus forming a vast family, wondrous in beauty & love,
And they appear'd a Universal female form created
From those who were dead in Ulro, from the spectres of the dead.

And Enitharmon named the Female, Jerusalem the holy.
Wond'ring, she saw the Lamb of God within Jerusalem's Veil;
The Divine Vision seen within the inmost deep recess
Of fair Jerusalem's bosom in a gently beaming fire.

Then sang the sons of Eden round the Lamb of God, & said,
"Glory, Glory, Glory to the holy Lamb of God
"Who now beginneth to put off the dark Satanic body.
"Now we behold redemption. Now we know that life Eternal
"Depends alone upon the Universal hand, & not in us
"Is aught but death In individual weakness, sorrow & pain.
"[Daughters of Beulah describe *del.*] We behold with wonder Enitharmon's Looms & Los's Forges,
"And the Spindles of Tirzah & Rahab, and the Mills of Satan & Beelzeboul.
"In Golgonooza Los's anvils stand & his Furnaces rage,
"[The hard dentant hammers are lull'd by the flute lula lula,
"The bellowing furnaces blare by the long sounding Clarions, *del.*]
"Ten thousand Demons labour at the forges Creating Continually
"The times & spaces of Mortal Life, the Sun, the Moon, the Stars,
"In periods of Pulsative furor, beating into [bars *del.*] wedges & bars,
"Then drawing into wires the terrific Passions & Affections
"Of Spectrous dead. Thence to the Looms of Cathedron convey'd,
"The Daughters of Enitharmon weave the ovarium & the integument
"In soft silk, drawn from their own bowels in lascivious delight,
"With songs of sweetest cadence to the turning spindle & reel,
"Lulling the weeping spectres of the dead, Clothing their limbs
"With gifts & gold of Eden. Astonish'd, stupefied with delight,
"The terrors put on their sweet clothing on the banks of [*name del.*] Arnon,
"Whence they plunge into the river of space for a period, till
"The dread Sleep of Ulro is past. But Satan, [*word del.*] Og & Sihon
"Build Mills of resistless wheels to unwind the soft threads & reveal
"Naked of their clothing the poor spectres before the accusing heavens,
"While Rahab & Tirzah far different mantles prepare: webs of torture,
"Mantles of despair, girdles of bitter compunction, shoes of indolence,
"Veils of ignorance covering from head to feet with a cold web.
"We look down into Ulro; we behold the Wonders of the Grave.
"Eastward of Golgonooza stands the Lake of Udan Adan, In
"Entuthon Benithon, [it is *del.*] a Lake not of Waters but of Spaces,
"Perturb'd, black & deadly; on [the *del.*] its Islands & [the *del.*] its Margins [of the Lake *del.*]
"The Mills of Satan and Beelzeboul stand round the roots of Urizen's tree;

"For this Lake is form'd from the tears & sighs & death sweat of the Victims
"Of Urizen's laws, to irrigate the roots of the tree of Mystery.
"They unweave the soft threads, then they weave them anew in the forms
"Of dark death & despair, & none from Eternity to Eternity could Escape,
"But [All *del.*] thou, O Universal Humanity—who is One Man, blessed for Ever—
"Recievest the Integuments woven. Rahab beholds the Lamb of God.
"She smites with her knife of flint. She destroys her own work
"Times upon times, thinking to destroy the Lamb blessed for Ever.
"He puts off the clothing of blood, he redeems the spectres from their bonds.
"He awakes sleepers in Ulro; the Daughters of Beulah praise him;
"They anoint his feet with ointment, they wipe them with the hair of their head.

"We now behold the Ends of Beulah, & we now behold
"Where death Eternal is put off Eternally.
"Assume the dark Satanic body in the Virgin's womb,
"O Lamb Divine! it cannot thee annoy. O pitying one,
"Thy pity is from the foundation of the World, & thy Redemption
"Begun Already in Eternity. Come then, O Lamb of God,
"Come, Lord Jesus, come quickly."

So sang they in Eternity, looking down into Beulah.
The war roar'd round Jerusalem's Gates; it took a hideous form
Seen in the aggregate, a Vast Hermaphroditic form
[Heaving *del.*] Heav'd like an Earthquake lab'ring with convulsive groans
Intolerable; at length an awful wonder burst
From the Hermaphroditic bosom. Satan he was nam'd,
Sons of Perdition, terrible his form, dishumaniz'd, monstrous,
A male without a female counterpart, a howling fiend
Fo[r]lorn of Eden & repugnant to the forms of life,
Yet hiding the shadowy female Vala as in an ark & Curtains,
Abhorr'd, accursed, ever dying an Eternal death,
Being multitudes of tyrant Men in union blasphemous
Against the Divine image, Congregated assemblies of wicked men.

Los said to Enitharmon, "Pitying I saw."
Pitying, the Lamb of God descended thro' Jerusalem's gates
To put off Mystery time after time; & as a Man
Is born on Earth, so was he born of Fair Jerusalem

In mystery's woven mantle, & in the Robes of Luvah.
He stood in fair Jerusalem to awake up into Eden
The fallen Man, but first to Give [the Veil of Mystery *del.*] his vegetated body
[And then call Urizen & Luvah & Tharmas & Urthona *del.*]
To be cut off & separated, that the Spiritual body may be Reveal'd.

The Lamb of God stood before Satan opposite
In Entuthon Benithon, in the shadows of torment & woe
Upon the heights of Amalek, taking refuge in his arms
The victims fled from punishment, for all his words were peace.
Urizen call'd together the Synagogue of Satan in dire Sanhedrim
To judge the Lamb of God to Death as a murderer & robber:
As it is written, he was number'd among the transgressors.
Cold, dark, opake, the Assembly met twelvefold in Amalek,
Twelve rocky unshap'd forms, terrific forms of torture & woe,
Such seem'd the Synagogue to distant view; [around *del.*] amidst them [stood *del.*] beam'd
A False Feminine Counterpart, of Lovely Delusive Beauty
Dividing & Uniting at will in the Cruelties of Holiness,
Vala, drawn down into a Vegetated body, now triumphant.
The Synagogue of Satan Clothed her with Scarlet robes & Gems,
And on her forehead was her name written in blood, "Mystery."
When view'd remote she is One, when view'd near she divides
To multitude, as it is in Eden, so permitted because
It was the best possible in the State called Satan to save
From Death Eternal & to put off Satan Eternally.
The Synagogue Created her from Fruit of Urizen's tree
By devilish arts, abominable, unlawful, unutterable,
Perpetually vegetating in detestable births
Of female forms, beautiful thro' poisons hidden in secret
Which give a tincture to false beauty; then was hidden within
The bosom of Satan The false Female, as in an ark & veil
Which Christ must rend & her reveal. Her daughters are call'd
Tirzah; She is [call'd *del.*] named Rahab; their various divisions are call'd
The daughters of Amalek, Canaan & Moab, binding on the stones
Their victims, & with knives tormenting them, singing with tears
Over their victims. Hear ye the song of the Females of Amalek:

"O thou poor human form! O thou poor child of woe!
"Why dost thou wander away from Tirzah? why me compell to bind thee?
"If thou dost go away from me, I shall consume upon the rocks.
"These fibres of thine eyes that used to wander in distant heavens

"Away from me, I have bound down with a hot iron.
"These nostrils that Expanded with delight in morning skies
"I have bent downward with lead molten in my roaring furnaces.
"My soul is seven furnaces, incessant roars the bellows
"Upon my terribly flaming heart, the molten metal runs
"In channels thro' my fiery limbs. O love! O pity! O pain!
"O the pangs, the bitter pangs of love forsaken!
"Ephraim was a wilderness of joy where all my wild beasts ran.
"The river Kanah wander'd by my sweet Manasseh's side.
"[To see the boy spring into heaven, sounding from my sight *del.*]
"Go, Noah, fetch the girdle of strong brass, [pre . . . *del.*] heat it red hot,
"Press it around the loins of this expanding cruelty.
"Shriek not so, my only love.
"Bind him down, sisters, bind him down on Ebal, mount of cursing.
"Malah, come forth from Lebanon, & Hoglah from Mount Sinai,
"Come circumscribe this tongue of sweets, & with a screw of iron
"Fasten this Ear into the Rock. Milcah, the task is thine.
"Weep not so, sisters, weep not so; our life depends on this,
"Or mercy & truth are fled away from Shechem & Mount Gilead,
"Unless my beloved is bound upon the stems of Vegetation."

Such are the songs of Tirzah, such the loves of Amalek.
The Lamb of God descended thro' the twelve portions of Luvah,
Bearing his sorrows & recieving all his cruel wounds.

Thus was the Lamb of God condemn'd to Death.
They nail'd him upon the tree of Mystery, weeping over him
And then mocking & then worshipping, calling him Lord & King.
Sometimes as twelve daughters lovely, & sometimes as five
They stood in beaming beauty, & sometimes as one, even Rahab
Who is Mystery, Babylon the Great, the Mother of Harlots.

[She *del.*] Jerusalem saw the Body dead upon the Cross. She fled away,
Saying: "Is this Eternal Death? Where shall I hide from Death?
"Pity me, Los! pity me, Urizen! & [build *del.*] let us build
"A Sepulcher & worship Death in fear while yet we live:
"Death! God of All! from whom we rise, to whom we all return:
"And Let all Nations of the Earth worship at the Sepulcher
"With Gifts & Spices, with lamps rich emboss'd, jewels & gold."

Los took the Body from the Cross, Jerusalem weeping over;
They bore it to the Sepulcher which Los had hewn in the rock
Of Eternity for himself: he hew'd it despairing of Life Eternal.

[And *del.*] But when Rahab had cut off the Mantle of Luvah from
The Lamb of God, it roll'd apart, revealing to all in heaven
And all on Earth, the Temple & the Synagogue of Satan, & Mystery
Even Rahab in all her turpitude. Rahab divided herself;
She stood before Los in her Pride [alone *del.*] among the Furnaces,
Dividing & uniting in Delusive feminine pomp, questioning him.
He answer'd her with tenderness & love not uninspired.

Los sat upon his anvil stock; they sat beside the forge.
Los wip'd the sweat from his red brow & thus began
To the delusive female forms shining among his furnaces:
"I am that shadowy Prophet who six thousand years ago
"Fell from my station in the Eternal bosom. I divided
"To multitude, & my multitudes are children of Care & Labour.
"O Rahab, I behold thee. I was once like thee, a Son
"Of Pride, and I also have pierc'd the Lamb of God in pride & wrath.
"Hear me repeat my Generations that thou maist also repent.
"And these [were *del.*] are the Sons of Los & Enitharmon: Rintrah, Palamabron,
"Theotormon, Bromion, Antamon, Ananton, Ozoth, Ohana,
"Sotha, Mydon, Ellayol, Natho, Gon, Harhath, Satan,
"Har, Ochim, Ijim, Adam, Reuben, Simeon, Levi, Judah, Dan, Naphtali,
"Gad, Asher, Issachar, Zebulun, Joseph, Benjamin, David, Solomon,
"Paul, Constantine, Charlemaine, Luther, Milton.
"These [were their *del.*] are our daughters: Ocalythron, Elynittria, Oothoon, Leutha,
"Elythiria, Enanto, Manathu Vorcyon, Ethinthus, Moab, Midian,
"Adah, Zillah, Caina, Naamah, Tamar, Rahab, Tirzah, Mary.
"And myriads more of Sons & daughters to whom [their *del.*] our love increas'd,
"To each according to the multiplication of their multitudes.
"But Satan accus'd Palamabron before [Los *del.*] his brethren, also he madden'd
"The horses of Palambron's harrow, wherefore Rintrah & Palamabron
"Cut him off from Golgonooza. But Enitharmon in tears
"Wept over him, Created him a Space clos'd with a tender moon
"And he roll'd down beneath the fires of Orc, a Globe immense
"Crusted with snow in a dim void; here, by the Arts of Urizen,
"He tempted many of the Sons & daughters of Los to flee
"Away from [Los *del.*] Me; first Reuben fled, then Simeon, then Levi, then Judah,
"Then Dan, then Naphtali, then Gad, then Asher, then Issachar,
"Then Zebulun, then Joseph, then Benjamin, twelve sons of Los.

"And this is the manner in which Satan became the Tempter.
"There is a State nam'd Satan; learn distinct to know, O [Mortals *del.*] Rahab!
"The difference between States & Individuals of those States.
"The State nam'd Satan never can be redeem'd in all Eternity;
"But when Luvah in Orc became a Serpent, he descended into
"That State call'd Satan. Enitharmon breath'd forth on the Winds
"Of Golgonooza her well beloved, knowing he was Orc's human remains.
"She tenderly lov'd him above all his brethren; he grew up
"In mother's tenderness. The Enormous worlds rolling in Urizen's power
"Must have given Satan, by these mild arts, dominion over all;
"Wherefore [Rintrah & *del.*] Palamabron, being accused by Satan to Los,
"Call'd down a Great Solemn assembly. Rintrah in fury & fire
"Defended Palamabron, & rage fill'd the Universal Tent—
"Because Palamabron was good natur'd, Satan suppos'd he fear'd him—
"And Satan, not having the Science of Wrath but only of Pity,
"Was soon condemn'd, & wrath was left to wrath, & Pity to Pity:
"Rintrah & Palamabron, Cut sheer off from Golgonooza,
"Enitharmon's Moony space, & in it, Satan & his companions.
"They roll'd down a dim world, crusted with Snow, deadly & dark.
"Jerusalem, pitying them, wove them mantles of life & death,
"Times after times. And those in Eden sent Lucifer for their Guard.
"Lucifer refus'd to die for Satan & in pride he forsook his charge.
"Then they sent Molech. Molech was impatient. They sent
"Molech impatient. They sent Elohim, who created Adam
"To die for Satan. Adam refus'd, but was compell'd to die
"By Satan's arts. Then the Eternals sent Shaddai.
"Shaddai was angry. Pachad descended. Pachad was terrified.
"And then they sent Jehovah, who leprous stretch'd his hand to Eternity.
"Then Jesus came & Died willing beneath Tirzah & Rahab.
"Thou art that Rahab. Lo the tomb! what can we purpose more?
"Lo, Enitharmon, terrible & beautiful in Eternal youth!
"Bow down before her, you her children, & set Jerusalem free."

Rahab, burning with pride & revenge, departed from Los.
Los drop'd a tear at her departure, but he wip'd it away in hope.
She went to Urizen in pride; the Prince of Light beheld
Reveal'd before the face of heaven his secret holiness.

Darkness & sorrow cover'd all flesh. Eternity was darken'd.

Urizen sitting in his web of deceitful religion [was . . . *del.*]
[He *del.*] felt the female death, a dull & numming stupor, such as ne'er
Before assaulted the bright human form; he felt his pores
Drink in the deadly dull delusion; horrors of Eternal Death
Shot thro' him. Urizen sat stonied upon his rock.
Forgetful of his own Laws, pitying he began to embrace
The shadowy Female; since life cannot be quench'd, Life exuded;
His eyes shot outwards, then his breathing nostrils drawn forth,
Scales cover'd over a cold forehead & a neck outstretch'd
Into the deep to sieze the shadow; scales his neck & bosom
Cover'd & scales his hands & feet; upon his belly falling
Outstretch'd thro' the immense, his mouth wide opening, tongueless,
His teeth a triple row, he strove to sieze the shadow in vain,
And his immense tail lash'd the Abyss; his human form a Stone,
A form of Senseless Stone remain'd in terrors on the rock,
Abominable to the eyes of mortals who explore his books.
His wisdom still remain'd, & all his memory stor'd with woe.

And still his stony form remain'd in the Abyss immense,
Like the pale visage in its sheet of lead that cannot follow—
Incessant stern disdain his scaly form gnaws inwardly,
With deep repentance for the loss of that fair form of Man.
With Envy he saw Los, with Envy Tharmas & [Urthona *del.*] the
Spectre,
With Envy & in vain he swam around his stony form.

No longer now Erect, the King of Light outstretch'd in fury
Lashes his tail in the wild deep; his eyelids, like the Sun
Arising in his pride, enlighten all the Grizly deeps,
His scales transparent give forth light like windows of the morning,
His neck flames with wrath & majesty, he lashes the Abyss,
Beating the desarts & the rocks; the desarts feel his power,
They shake their slumbers off, they wave in awful fear
Calling the Lion & the Tyger, the horse & the wild stag,
The Elephant, the wolf, the Bear, the Lamia, the Satyr.
His Eyelids give their light around; his folding tail aspires
Among the stars; the Earth & all the Abysses feel his fury
When as the snow covers the mountains, oft petrific hardness
Covers the deeps, at his vast fury moving in his rock,
Hardens the Lion & the Bear; trembling in the solid mountain
They view the light & wonder; crying out in terrible existence,
Up bound the wild stag & the horse: behold the King of Pride!

Oft doth his Eye emerge from the Abyss into the realms
Of his Eternal day, & memory strives to augment his ruthfulness.

Then weeping he descends in wrath, drawing all things in his fury
Into obedience to his will; & now he finds in vain
That not of his own power he bore the human form erect,
Nor of his own will gave his Laws in times of Everlasting,
For now fierce Orc in wrath & fury rises into the heavens,
[In forms of priesthood in the dark delusions of repentance *del.*]
A King of wrath & fury, a dark enraged horror:
And Urizen, repentant, forgets his wisdom in the abyss,
In forms of priesthood, in the dark delusions of repentance
Repining in his heart & spirit that Orc reign'd over all,
And that his wisdom serv'd but to augment the indefinite lust.

Then Tharmas & Urthona felt the stony stupor rise
Into their limbs. Urthona shot forth a Vast Fibrous form.
Tharmas like a pillar of sand roll'd round by the whirlwind,
An animated Pillar rolling round & round in incessant rage.
Los felt the stony stupor, & his head roll'd down beneath
Into the Abysses of his bosom; the vessels of his blood
Dart forth upon the wind in pipes, writhing about in the Abyss;
And Enitharmon, pale & cold, in milky juices flow'd
Into a form of Vegetation, living, having a voice,
Moving on root-like fibres, trembling in fear upon the Earth.

And Tharmas gave his Power to Los, Urthona gave his Strength
Into the youthful Prophet for the Love of Enitharmon
And of the nameless shadowy female in the nether deep,
And for the dread of the dark terrors of Orc & Urizen.

Thus in a living death the nameless shadow all things bound:
All mortal things made permanent that they may be put off
Time after time by the Divine Lamb who died for all,
And all in him died, & he put off all mortality.

Tharmas [above *del.*] on high rode furious thro' the afflicted worlds,
Pursuing the Vain Shadow of Hope, fleeing from identity
In abstract false Expanses that he may not hear the Voice
Of Ahania wailing on the winds; in vain he flies, for still
The voice incessant calls on all the children of Men:
For she spoke of all in heaven, & all upon the Earth
Saw not as yet the Divine Vision; her eyes are toward Urizen,
And thus Ahania cries aloud to the Caverns of the Grave:

"Will you keep a flock of wolves & lead them? will you take the wintry blast
"For a covering to your limbs, or the summer pestilence for a tent to abide in?
"Will you erect a lasting habitation in the mouldering Church yard?

"Or a pillar & palace of Eternity in the jaws of the hungry grave?
"Will you seek pleasure from the festering wound, or marry for a Wife
"The ancient Leprosy? that the King & Priest may still feast on your decay
"And the grave mock & laugh at the plow'd field, saying,
" 'I am the nourisher, thou the destroyer; in my bosom is milk & wine,
" 'And a fountain from my breasts; to me come all multitudes;
" 'To my breath they obey; they worship me. I am a goddess & queen.'
"But listen to Ahania, O ye sons of the Murder'd one,
"Listen to her whose memory beholds your ancient days,
"Listen to her whose eyes behold the dark body of corruptible death
"Looking for Urizen in vain; in vain I seek for morning.
"The Eternal Man sleeps in the Earth, nor feels the vig'rous sun
"Nor silent moon, nor all the hosts of heaven move in his body.
"His fiery halls are dark, & round his limbs the Serpent Orc
"Fold without fold encompasses him, And his corrupting members
"Vomit out the scaly monsters of the restless deep.
"They come up in rivers & annoy the nether parts
"Of Man who lays upon the shores, leaning his faded head
"Upon the Oozy rock inwrapped with the weeds of death.
"His eyes sink hollow in his head, his flesh cover'd with slime
"And shrunk up to the bones; alas, that Man should come to this!
"His strong bones beat with snows & hid within the caves of night,
"Marrowless, bloodless, falling into dust, driven by the winds.
"O how the horrors of Eternal Death take hold on Man!
"His faint groans shake the caves & issue thro' the desolate rocks,
"And the strong Eagle, now with numming cold blighted of feathers,
"Once like the pride of the sun, now flagging in cold night,
"Hovers with blasted wings aloft, watching with Eager Eye
"Till Man shall leave a corruptible body; he, famish'd, hears him groan,
"And now he fixes his strong talons in the pointed rock,
"And now he beats the heavy air with his enormous wings.
"Beside him lies the Lion dead, & in his belly worms
"Feast on his death till universal death devours all,
"And the pale horse seeks for the pool to lie him down & die,
"But finds the pools filled with serpents devouring one another.
"He droops his head & trembling stands, & his bright eyes decay.
"These are the Visions of My Eyes, the Visions of Ahania."

Thus cries Ahania. Enion replies from the Caverns of the Grave:

"Fear not, O poor forsaken one! O land of briars & thorns
"Where once the olive flourished & the Cedar spread his wings!
"Once I wail'd desolate like thee; my fallow fields in fear

"Cried to the Churchyards & the Earthworm came in dismal state.
"I found him in my bosom, & I said the time of love
"Appears upon the rocks & hills in silent shades; but soon
"A voice came in the night, a midnight cry upon the mountains:
" 'Awake! the bridegroom cometh!' I awoke to sleep no more;
"But an Eternal consummation is dark Enion,
"The wat'ry Grave. O thou corn field! O thou vegetater happy!
"More happy is the dark consumer; hope drowns all my torment,
"For I am now surrounded by a shadowy vortex drawing
"The spectre quite away from Enion, that I die a death
"Of better hope, altho' I consume in these raging waters.
"The furrow'd field replies to the grave. I hear her reply to me:
" 'Behold the time approaches fast that thou shalt be as a thing
" 'Forgotten; when one speaks of thee he will not be believ'd.
" 'When the man gently fades away in his immortality,
" 'When the mortal disappears in improved knowledge, cast away
" 'The former things, so shall the Mortal gently fade away
" 'And so become invisible to those who still remain.
" 'Listen. I will tell thee what is done in the caverns of the grave.
" 'The Lamb of God has rent the Veil of Mystery, soon to return
" 'In Clouds & Fires around the rock & the Mysterious tree.
" 'As the seed waits Eagerly watching for its flower & fruit,
" 'Anxious its little soul looks out into the clear expanse
" 'To see if hungry winds are abroad with their invisible army,
" 'So Man looks out in tree & herb & fish & bird & beast
" 'Collecting up the scatter'd portions of his immortal body
" 'Into the Elemental forms of every thing that grows.
" 'He tries the sullen north wind, riding on its angry furrows,
" 'The sultry south when the sun rises, & the angry east
" 'When the sun sets; when the clods harden & the cattle stand
" 'Drooping & the birds hide in their silent nests, he stores his thoughts
" 'As in a store house in his memory; he regulates the forms
" 'Of all beneath & all above, & in the gentle West
" 'Reposes where the Sun's heat dwells; he rises to the Sun
" 'And to the Planets of the Night, & to the stars that gild
" 'The Zodiac, & the stars that sullen stand to north & south.
" 'He touches the remotest pole, & in the center weeps
" 'That Man should Labour & sorrow, & learn & forget, & return
" 'To the dark valley whence he came, to begin his labours anew.
" 'In pain he sighs, in pain he labours in his universe,
" 'Screaming in birds over the deep, & howling in the wolf
" 'Over the slain, & moaning in the cattle, & in the winds,
" 'And weeping over Orc & Urizen in clouds & [dismal *del.*] *flaming* fires,

" 'And in the cries of birth & in the groans of death his voice
" 'Is heard throughout the Universe: wherever a grass grows
" 'Or a leaf buds, The Eternal Man is seen, is heard, is felt,
" 'And all his sorrows, till he reassumes his ancient bliss.' "

Such are the words of Ahania & Enion. Los hears & weeps.
[But Rahab hew'd (?) a Sepulcher in the Rock of Eternity,
And placing in the Sepulcher the body which she had taken

The End of the Eighth Night.

From the divine Lamb, wept over the Sepulcher, weaving
Her web of Religion around the Sepulcher times after times beside Jerusalem's Gate.
But as she wove, behold! the bottom of the Sepulcher
Rent & a door was (?) open'd thro' the bottom of the Sepulcher
Into Eternity. And as she wove, she heard a Voice behind her calling her.
She turn'd (?) & saw (?) the Divine Vision & her . . . *del.*]

And Los & Enitharmon took the Body of the Lamb
Down from the Cross & plac'd it in a sepulcher which Los had hewn
For himself in the Rock of Eternity, trembling & in [fear *del.*] despair.
Jerusalem wept over the Sepulcher two thousand years.

[End of the Eighth Night *erased*]

Rahab triumphs over all; she took Jerusalem
Captive, a Willing Captive, by delusive arts impell'd
To worship Urizen's Dragon form, to offer her own Children
Upon the bloody Altar. John saw these things Reveal'd in Heaven
On Patmos Isle, & heard the souls cry out to be deliver'd.
He saw the Harlot of the Kings of Earth, & saw her Cup
Of fornication, food of Orc & Satan, press'd from the fruit of Mystery.
But when she saw the form of Ahania weeping on the Void,
And heard Enion's voice sound from the caverns of the Grave,
No more spirit remain'd in her. She secretly left the Synagogue of Satan,
She commun'd with Orc in secret. She hid him with the flax
That Enitharmon had number'd, away from the Heavens,
She gather'd it together to consume her Harlot Robes
In bitterest contrition; sometimes Self condemning, repentant,
And sometimes kissing her Robes & Jewels & weeping over them;

Sometimes returning to the Synagogue of Satan in Pride,
And sometimes weeping before Orc in humility & trembling.
The Synagogue of Satan therefore, uniting against Mystery,
Satan divided against Satan, resolv'd in open Sanhedrim
To burn Mystery with fire & form another from her ashes,
For God put it into their heart to fulfill all his will.

The Ashes of Mystery began to animate; they call'd it Deism
And Natural Religion; as of old, so now anew began
Babylon again in Infancy, call'd Natural Religion.

[END OF THE EIGHTH NIGHT]

Vala

Night the Ninth

Being

The Last Judgment

And Los & Enitharmon builded Jerusalem, weeping
Over the Sepulcher & over the Crucified body
Which, to their Phantom Eyes, appear'd still in the Sepulcher;
But Jesus stood beside them in the spirit, separating
Their spirit from their body. Terrified at Non Existence,
For such they deem'd the death of the body, Los his vegetable hands
Outstretch'd; his right hand, branching out in fibrous strength,
Siez'd the Sun; His left hand, like dark roots, cover'd the Moon,
And tore them down, cracking the heavens across from immense to immense.
Then fell the fires of Eternity with loud & shrill
Sound of Loud Trumpet thundering along from heaven to heaven
A mighty sound articulate: "Awake, ye dead, & come
"To Judgment from the four winds! Awake & Come away!"
Folding like scrolls of the Enormous volume of Heaven & Earth,
With thunderous noise & dreadful shakings, rocking to & fro,
The heavens are shaken & the Earth removed from its place,
The foundations of the Eternal hills discover'd:
The thrones of Kings are shaken, they have lost their robes & crowns,
The poor smite their oppressors, they awake up to the harvest,
The naked warriors rush together down to the sea shore
Trembling before the multitudes of slaves now set at liberty:
They are become like wintry flocks, like forests strip'd of leaves:
The oppressed pursue like the wind; there is no room for escape.

The Spectre of Enitharmon, let loose on the troubled deep,
Wail'd shrill in the confusion, & the Spectre of Urthona
Reciev'd her in the darkening south; their bodies lost, they stood
Trembling & weak, a faint embrace, a fierce desire, as when
Two shadows mingle on a wall; they wail & shadowy tears
Fell down, & shadowy forms of joy mix'd with despair & grief—
Their bodies buried in the ruins of the Universe—
Mingled with the confusion. Who shall call them from the Grave?

Rahab & Tirzah wail aloud in the wild flames; they give up themselves to Consummation.

The books of Urizen unroll with dreadful noise; the folding Serpent
Of Orc began to Consume in fierce raving fire; his fierce flames
Issu'd on all sides, gathering strength in animating volumes,
Roaming abroad on all the winds, raging intense, reddening
Into resistless pillars of fire rolling round & round, gathering
Strength from the Earths consumed & heavens & all hidden abysses,
Where'er the Eagle has Explor'd, or Lion or Tyger trod,
Or where the Comets of the night or stars of [eternal *del.*] asterial day
Have shot their arrows or long beamed spears in wrath & fury.

And all the while the trumpet sounds, ["Awake, ye dead, & come
"To Judgment!" *del.*] from the clotted gore & from the hollow den
Start forth the trembling millions into flames of mental fire,
Bathing their limbs in the bright visions of Eternity.
Then, like the doves from pillars of Smoke, the trembling families
Of women & children throughout every nation under heaven
Cling round the men in bands of twenties & of fifties, pale
As snow that falls around a leafless tree upon the green.
Their oppressors are fall'n, they have stricken them, they awake to life.
Yet pale the just man stands erect & looking up to heav'n.
Trembling & strucken by the Universal stroke, the trees unroot,
The rocks groan horrible & run about; the mountains &
Their rivers cry with a dismal cry; the cattle gather together,
Lowing they kneel before the heavens; the wild beasts of the forests
Tremble; the Lion shuddering asks the Leopard: "Feelest thou
"The dread I feel, unknown before? My voice refuses to roar,
"And in weak moans I speak to thee. This night,
"Before the morning's dawn, the Eagle call'd the Vulture,
"The Raven call'd the hawk, I heard them from my forests black,
"Saying: 'Let us go up far, for soon, I smell upon the wind,
" 'A terror coming from the south.' The Eagle & Hawk fled away
"At dawn, & e'er the sun arose, the raven & Vulture follow'd.

"Let us flee also to the north." They fled. The Sons of Men
Saw them depart in dismal droves. The trumpet sounded loud
And all the Sons of Eternity Descended into Beulah.

In the fierce flames the limbs of Mystery lay consuming with howling
And deep despair. Rattling go up the flames around the Synagogue
Of Satan. Loud the Serpent Orc rag'd thro' his twenty seven
Folds. The tree of Mystery went up in folding flames.
Blood issu'd out in rushing volumes, pouring in whirlpools fierce
From out the flood gates of the Sky. The Gates are burst; down pour
The torrents black upon the Earth; the blood pours down incessant.
Kings in their palaces lie drown'd. Shepherds, their flocks, their tents,
Roll down the mountains in black torrents. Cities, Villages,
High spires & Castles drown'd in the black deluge; shoal on shoal
Float the dead carcases of Men & Beasts, driven to & fro on waves
Of foaming blood beneath the black incessant sky, till all
Mystery's tyrants are cut off & not one left on Earth.

And when all Tyranny was cut off from the face of Earth,
Around the dragon form of Urizen, & round his stony form,
The flames rolling intense thro' the wide Universe
[Began to draw near to the Earth *del.*]
Began to enter the Holy City. Ent'ring, the dismal clouds
In furrow'd lightnings break their way, the wild flames li[c]king up
The Bloody Deluge: living flames winged with intellect
And Reason, round the Earth they march in order, flame by flame.
From the clotted gore & from the hollow den
Start forth the trembling millions into flames of mental fire,
Bathing their limbs in the bright visions of Eternity.

[Without *del.*] Beyond this Universal Confusion, beyond the remotest Pole
Where their vortexes begin to operate, there stands
A Horrible rock far in the South; it was forsaken when
Urizen gave the horses of Light into the hands of Luvah.
On this rock lay the faded head of the Eternal Man
Enwrapped round with weeds of death, pale cold in sorrow & woe.
He lifts the blue lamps of his Eyes & cries with heavenly voice:
Bowing his head over the consuming Universe, he cried:
"O weakness & O weariness! O war within my members!
"My sons, exiled from my breast, pass to & fro before me.
"My birds are silent on my hills, flocks die beneath my branches.
"My tents are fallen, my trumpets & the sweet sounds of my harp
"Is silent on my clouded hills that belch forth storms & fire.
"My milk of cows & honey of bees & fruit of golden harvest
"Are gather'd in the scorching heat & in the driving rain.

"My robe is turned to confusion, & my bright gold to stone.
"Where once I sat, I weary walk in misery & pain,
"For from within my [narrow *del.*] wither'd breast grown narrow with my woes
"The Corn is turned to thistles & the apples into poison,
"The birds of song to murderous crows, My joys to bitter groans,
"The voices of children in my tents to cries of helpless infants,
"And all exiled from the face of light & shine of morning
"In this dark world, a narrow house, I wander up & down.
"I hear Mystery howling in these flames of Consummation.
"When shall the Man of future times become as in days of old?
"O weary life! why sit I here & give up all my powers
"To indolence, to the night of death, when indolence & mourning
"Sit hovering over my dark threshold? tho' I arise, look out
"And scorn the war within my members, yet my heart is weak
"And my head faint. Yet will I look again unto the morning.
"Whence is this sound of rage of Men drinking each other's blood,
"Drunk with the smoking gore, & red, but not with nourishing wine?"

The Eternal Man sat on the Rocks & cried with awful voice:
"O Prince of Light, where art thou? I behold thee not as once
"In those Eternal fields, in clouds of morning stepping forth
"With harps & songs where bright Ahania sang before thy face
"And all thy sons & daughters gather'd round my ample table.
"See you not all this wracking furious confusion?
"Come forth from slumbers of thy cold abstraction! Come forth,
"Arise to Eternal births! Shake off thy cold repose,
"Schoolmaster of souls, great opposer of change, arise!
"That the Eternal worlds may see thy face in peace & joy,
"That thou, dread form of Certainty, maist sit in town & village
"While little children play around thy feet in gentle awe,
"Fearing thy frown, loving thy smile, O Urizen, Prince of Light."

He call'd; the deep buried his voice & answer none return'd.
Then wrath burst round; the Eternal Man was wrath; again he cried:
"Arise, O stony form of death! O dragon of the Deeps!
"Lie down before my feet, O Dragon! let Urizen arise.
"*O how couldst thou deform those beautiful proportions*
"*Of life & person; for as the Person, so is his life proportion'd.*
"Let Luvah rage in the dark deep, even to Consummation,
"For if thou feedest not his rage, it will subside in peace.
"But if thou darest obstinate refuse my stern behest,
"Thy crown & scepter I will sieze, & regulate all my members
"In stern severity, & cast thee out into the indefinite

"Where nothing lives, there to wander; & if thou returnest weary,
"Weeping at the threshold of Existence, I will steel my heart
"Against thee to Eternity, & never recieve thee more.
"Thy self-destroying, beast form'd Science shall be thy eternal lot.
"My anger against thee is greater than against this Luvah,
"For war is [cruel *del.*] energy Enslav'd, but thy religion,
"The first author of this war & the distracting of honest minds
"Into confused perturbation & strife & honour & pride,
"Is a deciet so detestable that I will cast thee out
"If thou repentest not, & leave thee as a rotten branch to be burn'd
"With Mystery the Harlot & with Satan for Ever & Ever.
"Error can never be redeemed in all Eternity,
"But Sin, Even Rahab, is redeem'd in blood & fury & jealousy—
"That line of blood that stretch'd across the windows of the morning—
"Redeem'd from Error's power. Wake, thou dragon of the deeps!"

Urizen wept in the dark deep, anxious his scaly form
To reassume the human; & he wept in the dark deep,
Saying: "O that I had never drunk the wine nor eat the bread
"Of dark mortality, or cast my view into [the past *del.*] futurity, nor turn'd
"My back, dark'ning the present, clouding with a cloud,
"And building arches high, & cities, turrets & [high *del.*] towers & domes
"Whose smoke destroy'd the pleasant gardens, & whose running kennels
"Chok'd the bright rivers; burd'ning with my Ships the angry deep;
"Thro' Chaos seeking for delight, & in spaces remote
"Seeking the Eternal which is always present to the wise;
"Seeking for pleasure which unsought falls round the infant's path
"And on the fleeces of mild flocks who neither care nor labour;
"But I, the labourer of ages, whose unwearied hands
"Are thus deform'd with hardness, with the [*word del.*] sword & with the spear
"And with the chisel & the mallet, I, whose labours vast
"Order the nations, separating family by family,
"Alone enjoy not. I alone, in misery supreme,
"Ungratified give all my joy unto this Luvah & Vala.
"Then Go, O dark [remembrance *del.*] futurity! I will cast thee forth from these
"Heavens of my brain, nor will I look upon [remembrance *del.*] futurity more.
"I cast [remembrance *del.*] futurity away, & turn my back upon that void

"Which I have made; for lo! [Remembrance *del.*] futurity is in this moment.
"Let Orc consume, let Tharmas rage, let dark Urthona give
"All strength to Los & Enitharmon, & let Los self-curs'd
"Rend down this fabric, as a wall ruin'd & family extinct.
"Rage, Orc! Rage Tharmas! Urizen no longer curbs your rage."

So Urizen spoke; he shook his snows from off his shoulders & arose
As on a Pyramid of mist, his white robes scattering
The fleecy white: renew'd, he shook his aged mantles off
Into the fires. Then, glorious bright, Exulting in his joy,
He sounding rose into the heavens in naked majesty,
In radiant Youth; when Lo! like garlands in the Eastern sky
When vocal may comes dancing from the East, Ahania came
Exulting in her flight, as when a bubble rises up
On to the surface of a lake, Ahania rose in joy.
Excess of Joy is worse than grief; her heart beat high, her blood
Burst its bright vessels: she fell down dead at the feet of Urizen
Outstretch'd, a smiling corse: they buried her in a silent cave.
Urizen dropped a tear; the Eternal Man Darken'd with sorrow.

The three daughters of Urizen guard Ahania's death couch;
Rising from the confusion in tears & howlings & despair,
Calling upon their father's Name, upon their Rivers dark.

And the Eternal Man said: "Hear my [voice *del.*] words, O Prince of Light.
"Behold Jerusalem in whose bosom the Lamb of God [is seen *del.*]
"Is seen; tho' slain before her Gates, he self-renew'd remains
"Eternal, & I thro' him awake from death's dark vale.
"The times revolve; the time is coming when all these delights
"Shall be renew'd, & all these Elements that now consume
"Shall reflourish. Then bright Ahania shall awake from death,
"A glorious Vision [of *del.*] to thine Eyes, a Self-renewing Vision:
"The spring, the summer, to be thine; then sleep the wintry days
"In silken garments spun by her own hands against her funeral.
"The winter thou shalt plow & lay thy stores into thy barns
"Expecting to recieve Ahania in the spring with joy.
"Immortal thou, Regenerate She, & all the lovely Sex
"From her shall learn obedience & prepare for a wintry grave,
"That spring may see them rise in tenfold joy & sweet delight.
"Thus shall the male & female live the life of Eternity,
"Because the Lamb of God Creates himself a bride & wife
"That we his Children evermore may live in Jerusalem
"Which now descendeth out of heaven, a City, yet a Woman,

"Mother of myriads redeem'd & born in her spiritual palaces,
"By a New Spiritual birth Regenerated from Death."

Urizen said: "I have Erred, & my Error remains with me.
"What Chain encompasses? in what Lock is the river of light confin'd
"That issues forth in the morning by measure & the evening by carefulness?
"Where shall we take our stand to view the infinite & unbounded?
"Or where are human feet? for Lo, our eyes are in the heavens."

He ceas'd, for riv'n link from link, the bursting Universe explodes.
All things revers'd flew from their centers: rattling bones [to bones *del.*]
To bones Join: shaking convuls'd, the shivering clay breathes:
Each speck of dust to the Earth's center nestles round & round
In pangs of an Eternal Birth: in torment & awe & fear,
All spirits deceas'd, let loose from reptile prisons, come in shoals:
Wild furies from the tyger's brain & from the lion's eyes,
And from the ox & ass come moping terrors, from the eagle
And raven: numerous as the leaves of autumn, every species
Flock to the trumpet, mutt'ring over the sides of the grave & crying
In the fierce wind round heaving rocks & mountains fill'd with groans.
On rifted rocks, suspended in the air by inward fires,
Many a woful company & many on clouds & waters,
Fathers & friends, Mothers & Infants, Kings & Warriors,
Priests & chain'd Captives, met together in a horrible fear;
And every one of the dead appears as he had liv'd before,
And all the marks remain of the slave's scourge & tyrant's Crown,
And of the Priest's o'ergorged Abdomen, & of the merchant's thin
Sinewy deception, & of the warrior's ou[t]braving & thoughtlessness
In lineaments too extended & in bones too strait & long.
They shew their wounds: they accuse: they sieze the opressor; howlings began
On the golden palace, songs & joy on the desart; the Cold babe
Stands in the furious air; he cries: the children of six thousand years
Who died in infancy rage furious: a mighty multitude rage furious,
Naked & pale standing on the expecting air, to be deliver'd.
Rend limb from limb the warrior & the tyrant, reuniting in pain.

The furious wind still rends around; they flee in sluggish effort;
They beg, they intreat in vain now; they listened not to intreaty;
They view the flames red rolling on thro' the wide universe
From the [black *altered to*] dark jaws of death beneath & desolate shores remote,

These covering vaults of heaven & these trembling globes of earth.
One Planet [cries *del.*] calls to another & one star enquires of another:
"What flames are these, coming from the South? what noise, what dreadful rout
"As of a battle in the heavens? hark! heard you not the trumpet
"As of fierce battle?" While they spoke, the flames come on intense roaring.
They see him whom they have pierc'd, they wail because of him,
They magnify themselves no more against Jerusalem, Nor
Against her little ones; the innocent, accused before the Judges,
Shines with immortal glory; trembling, the judge springs from his throne
Hiding his face in the dust beneath the prisoner's feet & saying:
"Brother of Jesus, what have I done? intreat thy lord for me:
"Perhaps I may be forgiven." While he speaks the flames roll on,
And after the flames appears the Cloud of the Son of Man
Descending from Jerusalem with power and great Glory.
All nations look up to the Cloud & behold him who was crucified.
The Prisoner answers: "You scourg'd my father to death before my face
"While I stood bound with cords & heavy chains. Your hipocrisy
"Shall now avail you nought." So speaking, he dash'd him with his foot.

The Cloud is Blood, dazling upon the heavens, & in the cloud,
Above upon its volumes, is beheld [as *del.*] a throne & [as *del.*] a pavement
Of precious stones surrounded by twenty-four venerable patriarchs,
And these again surrounded by four Wonders of the Almighty,
Incomprehensible, pervading all, amidst & round about,
Fourfold, each in the other reflected; they are named Life's—in Eternity—
Four Starry Universes going forward from Eternity to Eternity.
And the Fall'n Man who was arisen upon the Rock of Ages
Beheld the Vision of God, & he arose up from the Rock,
And Urizen arose up with him, walking thro' the flames
To meet the Lord coming to Judgment; but the flames repell'd them
Still to the Rock; in vain they strove to Enter the Consummation
Together, for the [Fallen *altered to*] Redeem'd Man could not enter the Consummation.

Then siez'd the sons of Urizen the Plow; they polish'd it
From rust of ages; all its ornaments of gold & silver & ivory
Reshone across the field immense where all the nations
Darken'd like Mould in the divided fallows where the weed

Triumphs in its own destruction; they took down the harness
From the blue walls of heaven, starry jingling, ornamented
With beautiful art, the study of angels, the workmanship of Demons
When Heaven & Hell in Emulation strove in sports of Glory.

The noise of rural works resounded thro' the heavens of heavens,
The horse[s] neigh from the battle, the wild bulls from the sultry waste,
The tygers from the forests, & the lions from the sandy desarts.
They sing; they sieze the instruments of harmony; they throw away
The spear, the bow, the gun, the mortar; they level the fortifications.
They beat the iron engines of destruction into wedges;
They give them to Urthona's sons; ringing the hammers sound
In dens of death to forge the spade, the mattock & the ax,
The heavy roller to break the clods, to pass over the nations.

The Sons of Urizen shout. Their father rose. The Eternal horses
Harness'd, They call'd to Urizen; the heavens moved at their call.
The limbs of Urizen shone with ardor. [he rose up from the Rock.
The Fallen Man wond'ring beheld *del.*] He laid his hand on the Plow,
Thro' dismal darkness drave the Plow of ages over Cities
And all their Villages; over Mountains & all their Vallies;
Over the graves & caverns of the dead; Over the Planets
And over the void spaces; over sun & moon & star & constellation.

Then Urizen commanded & they brought the Seed of Men.
The trembling souls of All the dead stood before Urizen,
Weak wailing in the troubled air. East, west & north & south
He turn'd the horses loose & laid his Plow in the northern corner
Of the wide Universal field, then step'd [out *del.*] forth into the immense.

Then he began to sow the seed; he girded round his loins
With a bright girdle, & his skirt fill'd with immortal souls.
Howling & Wailing fly the souls from Urizen's strong hand,
For from the hand of Urizen the myriads fall like stars
Into their own appointed places, driven back by the winds.
The naked warriors rush together down to the sea shores:
They are become like wintry flocks, like forests strip'd of leaves;
The Kings & Princes of the Earth cry with a feeble cry,
Driven on the unproducing sands & on the harden'd rocks;
And all the while the flames of Orc follow the vent'rous feet
Of Urizen, & all the while the Trump of Tharmas sounds.
Weeping & wailing fly the souls from Urizen's strong hands—
The daughters of Urizen stand with Cups & measures of foaming wine

Immense upon the heavens with bread & delicate repasts—
Then follows the golden harrow in the midst of Mental fires.
To ravishing melody of flutes & harps & softest voice
The seed is harrow'd in, while flames heat the black mould & cause
The human harvest to begin. Towards the south first sprang
The myriads, & in silent fear they look out from their graves.

Then Urizen sits down to rest, & all his wearied sons
Take their repose on beds; they drink, they sing, they view the flames
Of Orc; in joy they view the human harvest springing up.
A time they give to sweet repose, till all the harvest is ripe.
And Lo, like the harvest Moon, Ahania cast off her death clothes;
She folded them up in care, in silence, & her bright'ning limbs
Bath'd in the clear spring of the rock; then from her darksome cave
Issu'd in majesty divine. Urizen rose up from his couch
On wings of tenfold joy, clapping his hands, his feet, his radiant wings
In the immense: as when the Sun dances upon the mountains
A shout of jubilee in lovely notes responds from daughter to daughter,
From son to son: as if the stars beaming innumerable
Thro' night should sing soft warbling, filling earth & heaven;
And bright Ahania took her seat by Urizen in songs & joy.

The Eternal Man also sat down upon the Couches of Beulah,
Sorrowful that he could not put off his new risen body
In mental flames; the flames refus'd, they drove him back to Beulah.
His body was redeem'd to be permanent thro' Mercy Divine.

And now fierce Orc had quite consum'd himself in Mental flames,
Expending all his energy against the fuel of fire.
The [Ancient Man *altered to*] Regenerate Man stoop'd his head over the Universe & in
His holy hands reciev'd the flaming Demon & Demoness of smoke
And gave them to Urizen's hands; the Immortal frown'd, saying,

"Luvah & Vala, henceforth you are Servants; obey & live.
"You shall forget your former state; return, & Love in peace,
"Into your place, the place of seed, not in the brain or heart.
"If Gods combine against Man, setting their dominion above
"The Human form Divine, Thrown down from their high station
"In the Eternal heavens of Human [Thought *del.*] Imagination, buried beneath
"In dark Oblivion, with incessant pangs, ages on ages,
"In enmity & war first weaken'd, then in stern repentance
"They must renew their brightness, & their disorganiz'd functions
"Again reorganize, till they resume the image of the human,
"Co-operating in the bliss of Man, obeying his Will,
"Servants to the infinite & Eternal of the Human form."

Luvah & Vala descended & enter'd the Gates of Dark Urthona,
And walk'd from the hands of Urizen in the shadows of Vala's Garden
Where the impressions of Despair & Hope for ever vegetate
In flowers, in fruits, in fishes, birds & beasts & clouds & waters,
The land of doubts & shadows, sweet delusions, unform'd hopes.
They saw no more the terrible confusion of the wracking universe.
They heard not, saw not, felt not all the terrible confusion,
For in their orbed senses, within clos'd up, they wander'd at will.
And those upon the Couches view'd them, in the dreams of Beulah,
As they repos'd from the terrible wide universal harvest,
Invisible Luvah in bright clouds hover'd over Vala's head,
And thus their ancient golden age renew'd; for Luvah spoke
With voice mild from his golden Cloud upon the breath of morning:

"Come forth, O Vala, from the grass & from the silent dew,
"Rise from the dews of death, for the Eternal Man is Risen."

She rises among flowers & looks toward the Eastern clearness
She walks yea runs, her feet are wing'd, on the tops of the bending grass,
Her garments rejoice in the vocal wind & her hair glistens with dew.

She answer'd thus: "Whose voice is this, in the voice of the nourishing air,
"In the spirit of the morning, awaking the Soul from its grassy bed?
"Where dost thou dwell? for it is thee I seek, & but for thee
"I must have slept Eternally, nor have felt the dew of thy morning.
"Look how the opening dawn advances with vocal harmony!
"Look how the beams foreshew the rising of some glorious power!
"The sun is thine, [when *del.*] he goeth forth in his majestic brightness.
"O thou creating voice that callest! & who shall answer thee?"

"Where dost thou flee, O fair one? where doest thou seek thy happy place?"

"To yonder brightness, there I haste, for sure I came from thence
"Or I must have slept eternally, nor have felt the dew of morning."

"Eternally thou must have slept, nor have felt the morning dew,
"But for yon nourishing sun; 'tis that by which thou art arisen.
"The birds adore the sun: the beasts rise up & play in his beams,
"And every flower & every leaf rejoices in his light.
"Then, O thou fair one, sit thee down, for thou art as the grass,
"Thou risest in the dew of morning & at night art folded up."

"Alas! am I but as a flower? then will I sit me down,
"Then will I weep, then I'll complain & sigh for immortality,
"And chide my maker, thee O Sun, that raisedst me to fall."

So saying she sat down & wept beneath the apple trees.

"O be thou blotted out, thou Sun! that raisedst me to trouble,
"That gavest me a heart to crave, & raisedst me, thy phantom,
"To feel thy heat & see thy light & wander here alone,
"Hopeless, if I am like the grass & so shall pass away."

"Rise, sluggish Soul, why sit'st thou here? why dost thou sit & weep?
"Yon sun shall wax old & decay, but thou shalt ever flourish.
"The fruit shall ripen & fall down, & the flowers consume away,
"But thou shalt still survive; arise, O dry thy dewy tears."

"Hah! shall I still survive? whence came that sweet & comforting voice?
"And whence that voice of sorrow? O sun! thou art nothing now to me.
"Go on thy course rejoicing, & let us both rejoice together.
"I walk among his flocks & hear the bleating of his lambs.
"O that I could behold his face & follow his pure feet!
"I walk by the footsteps of his flocks; come hither, tender flocks.
"Can you converse with a pure soul that seeketh for her maker?
"You answer not: then am I set your mistress in this garden.
"I'll watch you & attend your footsteps; you are not like the birds
"That sing & fly in the bright air; but you do lick my feet
"And let me touch your woolly backs; follow me as I sing,
"For in my bosom a new song arises to my Lord:

"Rise up, O sun, most glorious minister & light of day.
"Flow on, ye gentle airs, & bear the voice of my rejoicing.
"Wave freshly, clear waters flowing around the tender grass;
"And thou, sweet smelling ground, put forth thy life in fruits & flowers.
"Follow me, O my flocks, & hear me sing my rapturous song.
"I will cause my voice to be heard on the clouds that glitter in the sun.
"I will call; & who shall answer me? I will sing; who shall reply?
"For from my pleasant hills behold the living, living springs,
"Running among my green pastures, delighting among my trees.
"I am not here alone: my flocks, you are my brethren;
"And you birds that sing & adorn the sky, you are my sisters.
"I sing, & you reply to my song; I rejoice, & you are glad.
"Follow me, O my flocks; we will now descend into the valley.

"O how delicious are the grapes, flourishing in the sun!
"How clear the spring of the rock, running among the golden sand!
"How cool the breezes of the valley, & the arms of the branching trees!
"Cover us from the sun; come & let us sit in the shade.
"My Luvah here hath plac'd me in a sweet & pleasant land,
"And given me fruits & pleasant waters, & warm hills & cool valleys.
"Here will I build myself a house, & here I'll call on his name,
"Here I'll return when I am weary & take my pleasant rest."

So spoke the sinless soul, & laid her head on the downy fleece
Of a curl'd Ram who stretch'd himself in sleep beside his mistress,
And soft sleep fell upon her eyelids in the silent noon of day.

Then Luvah passed by, & saw the sinless soul,
And said: "Let a pleasant house arise to be the dwelling place
"Of this immortal spirit growing in lower Paradise."
He spoke, & pillars were builded, & walls as white as ivory.
The grass she slept upon was pav'd with pavement as of pearl.
Beneath her rose a downy bed, & a cieling cover'd all.

Vala awoke. "When in the pleasant gates of sleep I enter'd,
"I saw my Luvah like a spirit stand in the bright air.
"Round him stood spirits like me, who rear'd me a bright house,
"And here I see thee, house, remain in my most pleasant world.
"My Luvah smil'd: I kneeled down: he laid his hand on my head,
"And when he laid his hand upon me, from the gates of sleep I came
"Into this bodily house to tend my flocks in my pleasant garden."

So saying, she arose & walked round her beautiful house,
And then from her white door she look'd to see her bleating lambs,
But her flocks were gone up from beneath the trees into the hills.

"I see the hand that leadeth me doth also lead my flocks."
She went up to her flocks & turned oft to see her shining house.
She stop'd to drink of the clear spring & eat the grapes & apples.
She bore the fruits in her lap; she gather'd flowers for her bosom.
She called to her flocks, saying, "Follow me, O my flocks!"

They follow'd her to the silent valley beneath the spreading trees.
And on the river's margin she ungirded her golden girdle;
She stood in the river & view'd herself within the wat'ry glass,
And her bright hair was wet with the waters: she rose up from the river,
And as she rose her eyes were open'd to the world of waters:
She saw Tharmas sitting upon the rocks beside the wavy sea.
He strok'd the water from his beard & mourn'd faint thro' the summer vales.

And Vala stood on the rocks of Tharmas & heard his mournful voice:

"O Enion, my weary head is in the bed of death,
"For weeds of death have wrap'd around my limbs in the hoary deeps.
"I sit in the place of shells & mourn, & thou art clos'd in clouds.
"When will the time of Clouds be past, & the dismal night of Tharmas?
"Arise, O Enion! Arise & smile upon my head
"As thou dost smile upon the barren mountains and they rejoice.
"When wilt thou smile on Tharmas, O thou bringer of golden day?
"Arise, O Enion, arise, for Lo, I have calm'd my seas."

So saying, his faint head he laid upon the Oozy rock,
And darkness cover'd all the deep: the light of Enion faded
Like a faint flame quivering upon the surface of the darkness.

Then Vala lifted up her hands to heaven to call on Enion.
She call'd, but none could answer her & the eccho of her voice return'd:

"Where is the voice of God that call'd me from the silent dew?
"Where is the Lord of Vala? dost thou hide in clefts of the rock?
"Why shouldst thou hide thyself from Vala, from the soul that wanders desolate?"

She ceas'd, & light beamed round her like the glory of the morning,
And she arose out of the river & girded her golden girdle.
And now her feet step on the grassy bosom of the ground
Among her flocks, & she turn'd her eyes toward her pleasant house
And saw in the door way beneath the trees two little children playing.
She drew near to her house & her flocks follow'd her footsteps.
The children clung around her knees, she embrac'd them & wept over them.

"Thou, little Boy, art Tharmas, & thou, bright Girl, Enion.
"How are ye thus renew'd & brought into the Gardens of Vala?"

She embrac'd them in tears, till the sun descended the western hills,
And then she enter'd her bright house, leading her mighty children.
And when night came, the flocks laid round the house beneath the trees.
She laid the children on the beds which she saw prepar'd in the house,
Then last, herself laid down & clos'd her Eyelids in soft slumbers.

And in the morning, when the sun arose in the crystal sky,
Vala awoke & call'd the children from their gentle slumbers:

"Awake, O Enion, awake & let thine innocent Eyes
"Enlighten all the Crystal house of Vala! awake! awake!
"Awake, Tharmas! awake, awake thou child of dewy tears.
"Open the orbs of thy blue eyes & smile upon my gardens."

The Children woke & smil'd on Vala; she kneel'd by the golden couch,
She pres'd them to her bosom & her pearly tears drop'd down.
"O my sweet Children! Enion, let Tharmas kiss thy Cheek.

"Why dost thou turn thyself away from his sweet wat'ry eyes?
"Tharmas, henceforth in Vala's bosom thou shalt find sweet peace.
"O bless the lovely eyes of Tharmas & the Eyes of Enion!"

They rose; they went out wand'ring, sometimes together, sometimes alone
"Why weep'st thou, Tharmas, Child of tears, in the bright house of joy?
"Doth Enion avoid the sight of thy blue heavenly Eyes?
"And dost thou wander with my lambs & [with *del.*] wet their innocent faces
"With thy bright tears because the steps of Enion are in the gardens?
"Arise, sweet boy, & let us follow the path of Enion."

So saying, they went down into the garden among the fruits.
And Enion sang among the flowers that grew among the trees,
And Vala said: "Go, Tharmas; weep not. Go to Enion."

He said: "O Vala, I am sick, & all this garden of Pleasure
"Swims like a dream before my eyes; but the sweet smelling fruit
"Revives me to new deaths. I fade, even like a water lilly
"In the sun's heat, till in the night on the couch of Enion
"I drink new life & feel the breath of sleeping Enion.
"But in the morning she arises to avoid my Eyes,
"Then my loins fade & in the house I sit me down & weep."

"Chear up thy Countenance, bright boy, & go to Enion.
"Tell her that Vala waits her in the shadows of her garden."

He went with timid steps, & Enion, like the ruddy morn
When infant spring appears in swelling buds & opening flowers,
Behind her Veil withdraws; so Enion turn'd her modest head.

But Tharmas spoke: "Vala seeks thee, sweet Enion, in the shades.
"Follow the steps of Tharmas, O thou brightness of the gardens."
He took her hand reluctant; she follow'd in infant doubts.
Thus in Eternal Childhood, straying among Vala's flocks

In infant sorrow & joy alternate, Enion & Tharmas play'd
Round Vala in the Gardens of Vala & by her river's margin.
They are the shadows of Tharmas & of Enion in Vala's world.

And the sleepers who rested from their harvest work beheld these visions.
Thus were the sleepers entertain'd upon the Couches of Beulah.

When Luvah & Vala were clos'd up in their world of shadowy forms,
Darkness was all beneath the heavens: only a little light
Such as glows out from sleeping spirits, appear'd in the deeps beneath.
As when the wind sweeps over a corn field, the noise of souls
Thro' all the immense, borne down by Clouds swagging in autumnal heat,
Mutt'ring along from heaven to heaven, hoarse roll the human forms
Beneath thick clouds, dreadful lightnings burst & thunders roll,
Down pour the torrent floods of heaven on all the human harvest.
Then Urizen, sitting at his repose on beds in the bright South,
Cried, "Times are Ended!" he exulted; he arose in joy; he exulted;
He pour'd his light, & all his sons & daughters pour'd their light
To exhale the spirits of Luvah & Vala thro' the atmosphere.
And Luvah & Vala saw the Light; their spirits were exhal'd
In all their ancient innocence; the floods depart; the clouds
Dissipate or sink into the Seas of Tharmas. Luvah sat
Above on the bright heavens in peace; the Spirits of Men beneath
Cried out to be deliver'd, & the spirit of Luvah wept
Over the human harvest & over Vala, the sweet wanderer.
In pain the human harvest wav'd, in horrible groans of woe.
The Universal Groan went up; the Eternal Man was darken'd.

Then Urizen arose & took his sickle in his hand.
There is a brazen sickle, & a scythe of iron hid
Deep in the South, guarded by a few solitary stars.
This sickle Urizen took; the scythe his sons embrac'd
And went forth & began to reap; & all his joyful sons
Reap'd the wide Universe & bound in sheaves a wondrous harvest.
They took them into the wide barns with loud rejoicings & triumph
Of flute & harp & drum & trumpet, horn & clarion.

The feast was spread in the bright South, & the Regenerate Man
Sat at the feast rejoicing, & the wine of Eternity
Was serv'd round by the flames of Luvah all day & all the Night.
And when Morning began to dawn upon the distant hills,
[Then *del.*] a whirlwind rose up in the Center, & in the whirlwind a shriek,

And in the shriek a rattling of bones & in the rattling of bones
A dolorous groan, & from the dolorous groan in tears
Rose Enion like a gentle light; & Enion spoke, saying:

"O Dreams of Death! the human form dissolving, companied
"[With *del.*] By beasts & worms & creeping things, & darkness & despair.
"The clouds fall off from my wet brow, the dust from my cold limbs
"Into the sea of Tharmas. Soon renew'd, a Golden Moth,
"I shall cast off my death clothes & Embrace Tharmas again.
"For Lo, the winter melted away upon the distant hills,
"And all the black mould sings." She speaks to her infant race; her milk
Descends down on the sand; the thirsty sand drinks & rejoices
Wondering to behold the Emmet, the Grasshopper, the jointed worm.
The roots shoot thick thro' the solid rocks, bursting their way
They cry out in joys of existence; the broad stems
Rear on the mountains stem after stem; the scaly newt creeps
From the stone, & the armed fly springs from the rocky crevice,
The spider, The bat burst from the harden'd slime, crying
To one another: "What are we, & whence is our joy & delight?
"Lo, the little moss begins to spring, & the tender weed
"Creeps round our secret nest." Flocks brighten the Mountains,
Herds throng up the Valley, wild beasts fill the forests.

Joy thrill'd thro' all the Furious forms of Tharmas humanizing.
Mild he Embrac'd her whom he sought; he rais'd her thro' the heavens,
Sounding his trumpet to awake the dead, on high he soar'd
Over the ruin'd worlds, the smoking tomb of the Eternal Prophet.

The Eternal Man arose. He welcom'd them to the Feast.
The feast was spread in the bright South, & the Eternal Man
Sat at the feast rejoicing, & the wine of Eternity
Was serv'd round by the flames of Luvah all day & all the night.

And Many Eternal Men sat at the golden feast to see
The female form now separate. They shudder'd at the horrible thing
Not born for the sport and amusement of Man, but born to drink up all his powers.
[And *del.*] They wept to see their shadows; they said to one another: "This is Sin:
"This is the [Vegetative *del.*] Generative world;" they remember'd the days of old.

And One of the Eternals spoke. All was silent at the feast.

"Man is a Worm; wearied with joy, he seeks the caves of sleep
"Among the Flowers of Beulah, in his selfish cold repose
"Forsaking Brotherhood & Universal love, in selfish clay
"Folding the pure wings of his mind, seeking the places dark
"Abstracted from the roots of [Nature *del.*] Science; then inclos'd around
"In walls of Gold we cast him like a Seed into the Earth
"Till times & spaces have pass'd over him; duly every morn
"We visit him, covering with a Veil the immortal seed;
"With windows from the inclement sky we cover him, & with walls
"And hearths protect the selfish terror, till divided all
"In families we see our shadows born, & thence we know
"That Man subsists by Brotherhood & Universal Love.
"We fall on one another's necks, more closely we embrace.
Ephesians iii c. 10 v
"Not for ourselves, but for the Eternal family we live.
"Man liveth not by Self alone, but in his brother's face
"Each shall behold the Eternal Father & love & joy abound."

So spoke the Eternal at the Feast; they embrac'd the New born Man,
Calling him Brother, image of the Eternal Father; they sat down
At the immortal tables, sounding loud their instruments of joy,
Calling the Morning into Beulah; the Eternal Man rejoic'd.

When Morning dawn'd, The Eternals rose to labour at the Vintage.
Beneath they saw their sons & daughters, wond'ring inconcievable
At the dark myriads in shadows in the worlds beneath.

The morning dawn'd. Urizen rose, & in his hand the Flail
Sounds on the Floor, heard terrible by all beneath the heavens.
Dismal loud redounding, the nether floor shakes with the sound,
And all Nations were threshed out, & the stars thresh'd from their husks.

Then Tharmas took the Winnowing fan; the winnowing wind furious
Above, veer'd round by the violent whirlwind, driven west & south,
Tossed the Nations like chaff into the seas of Tharmas.

"O Mystery," Fierce Tharmas cries, "Behold thy end is come!
"Art thou she that made the nations drunk with the cup of Religion?
"Go down, ye Kings & Councellors & Giant Warriors,
"Go down into the depths, go down & hide yourselves beneath,
"Go down with horse & Chariots & Trumpets of hoarse war.

"Lo, how the Pomp of Mystery goes down into the Caves!
"Her great men howl & throw the dust, & rend their hoary hair.
"Her delicate women & children shriek upon the bitter wind,
"Spoil'd of their beauty, their hair rent & their skin shrivel'd up.

"Lo, darkness covers the long pomp of banners on the wind,
"And black horses & armed men & miserable bound captives.
"Where shall the graves recieve them all, & where shall be their place?
"And who shall mourn for Mystery who never loos'd her Captives?

"Let the slave, grinding at the mill, run out into the field;
"Let him look up into the heavens & laugh in the bright air.
"Let the inchained soul, shut up in darkness & in sighing,
"Whose face has never seen a smile in thirty weary years,
"Rise & look out: his chains are loose, his dungeon doors are open;
"And let his wife & children return from the opressor's scourge.

"They look behind at every step & believe it is a dream.
"Are these the slaves that groan'd along the streets of Mystery?
"Where are your bonds & task masters? are these the prisoners?
"Where are your chains? where are your tears? why do you look around?
"If you are thirsty, there is the river: go, bathe your parched limbs,
"The good of all the Land is before you, for Mystery is no more."

Then All the Slaves from every Earth in the wide Universe
Sing a New Song, drowning confusion in its happy notes,
While the flail of Urizen sounded loud, & the winnowing wind of Tharmas
So loud, so clear in the wide heavens; & the song that they sung was this,
Composed by an African Black from the little Earth of Sotha:

"Aha! Aha! how came I here so soon in my sweet native land?
"How came I here? Methinks I am as I was in my youth
"When in my father's house I sat & heard his chearing voice.
"Methinks I see his flocks & herds & feel my limbs renew'd,
"And Lo, my Brethren in their tents, & their little ones around them!"

The song arose to the Golden feast; the Eternal Man rejoic'd.
Then the Eternal Man said: "Luvah, the Vintage is ripe: arise!
"The sons of Urizen shall gather the vintage with sharp hooks,
"And all thy sons, O Luvah! bear away the families of Earth.
"I hear the flail of Urizen; his barns are full; no room
"Remains, & in the Vineyards stand the abounding sheaves beneath

"The falling Grapes that odorous burst upon the winds. Arise
"My flocks & herds, trample the Corn! my cattle, browze upon
"The ripe Clusters! The shepherds shout for Luvah, prince of Love.
"Let the Bulls of Luvah tread the Corn & draw the loaded waggon
"Into the Barn while children glean the Ears around the door.
"Then shall they lift their innocent hands & stroke his furious nose,
"And he shall lick the little girl's white neck & on her head
"Scatter the perfume of his breath; while from his mountains high
"The lion of terror shall come down, & bending his bright mane
"And couching at their side, shall eat from the curl'd boy's white lap
"His golden food, and in the evening sleep before the door."

"Attempting to be more than Man We become less," said Luvah
As he arose from the bright feast, drunk with the wine of ages.
His crown of thorns fell from his head, he hung his living Lyre
Behind the seat of the Eternal Man & took his way
Sounding the Song of Los, descending to the Vineyards bright.
His sons, arising from the feast with golden baskets, follow,
A fiery train, as when the Sun sings in the ripe vineyards.
Then Luvah stood before the Wine press; all his fiery sons
Brought up the loaded Waggons with shoutings; ramping tygers play
In the jingling traces; furious lions sound the song of joy
To the golden wheels circling upon the pavement of heaven, & all
The Villages of Luvah ring; the golden tiles of the villages
Reply to violins & tabors, to the pipe, flute, lyre & cymbal.
Then fell the Legions of Mystery in madd'ning confusion,
Down, down thro' the immense, with outcry, fury & despair,
Into the wine presses of Luvah; howling fell the clusters
Of human families thro' the deep; the wine presses were fill'd;
The blood of life flow'd plentiful. Odors of life arose
All round the heavenly arches, & the Odors rose singing this song:

"O terrible wine presses of Luvah! O caverns of the Grave!
"How lovely the delights of those risen again from death!
"O trembling joy! excess of joy is like Excess of grief."

So sang the Human Odors round the wine presses of Luvah;

But in the Wine presses is wailing, terror & despair.
Forsaken of their Elements they vanish & are no more,
No more but a desire of Being, a distracted, ravening desire,
Desiring like the hungry worm & like the [silent *del.*] gaping grave.
They plunge into the Elements; the Elements cast them forth
Or else consume their shadowy semblance. Yet they, obstinate
Tho' pained to distraction, cry, "O let us Exist! for

"This dreadful Non Existence is worse than pains of Eternal [death *del.*] Birth:
"Eternal death who can Endure? let us consume in fires,
"In waters stifling, or in air corroding, or in earth shut up.
"The Pangs of Eternal birth are better than the Pangs of Eternal death."

How red the sons & daughters of Luvah! how they tread the Grapes!
Laughing & shouting, drunk with odors, many fall o'erwearied:
Drown'd in the wine is many a youth & maiden; those around
Lay them on skins of tygers or the spotted Leopard or wild Ass
Till they revive, or bury them in cool Grots making lamentation.

But in the Wine Presses the Human Grapes sing not nor dance,
They howl & writhe in shoals of torment, in fierce flames consuming,
In chains of iron & in dungeons circled with ceaseless fires,
In pits & dens & shades of death, in shapes of torment & woe;
The Plates, the Screws & Racks & Saws & cords & fires & floods,
The cruel joy of Luvah's daughters, lacerating with knives
And whips their Victims, & the deadly sport of Luvah's sons.
Timbrels & Violins sport round the Wine Presses. The little Seed,
The sportive root, the Earthworm, the small beetle, the wise Emmet,
Dance round the Wine Presses of Luvah; the Centipede is there,
The ground Spider with many eyes, the Mole clothed in Velvet,
The Earwig arm'd, the tender maggot, emblem of Immortality;
The slow slug, the grasshopper that sings & laughs & drinks:
The winter comes; he folds his slender bones without a murmur.
There is the Nettle that stings with soft down; & there
The indignant Thistle whose bitterness is bred in his milk
And who lives on the contempt of his neighbour; there all the idle weeds,
That creep about the obscure places, shew their various limbs
Naked in all their beauty, dancing round the Wine Presses.
They dance around the dying & they drink the howl & groan;
They catch the shrieks in cups of gold; they hand them to one another.
These are the sports of love & these the sweet delights of amorous play:
Tears of the grape, the death sweat of the Cluster, the last sigh
Of the mild youth who listens to the luring songs of Luvah.
The Eternal Man darken'd with sorrow & a wintry mantle
Cover'd the Hills. He said, "O Tharmas, rise! & O Urthona!"
Then Tharmas & Urthona rose from the Golden feast, satiated
With Mirth & Joy: Urthona, limping from his fall, on Tharmas lean'd,
In his right hand his hammer. Tharmas held his shepherd's crook
Beset with gold, gold were the ornaments form'd by sons of Urizen.
Then Enion & Ahania & Vala & the wife of dark Urthona

Rose from the feast, in joy ascending to their Golden Looms.
There the wing'd shuttle sang, the spindle & the distaff & the Reel
Rang sweet the praise of industry. Thro' all the golden rooms
Heaven rang with winged Exultation. All beneath howl'd loud;
With tenfold rout & desolation roar'd the Chasms beneath
Where the wide woof flow'd down & where the Nations are gather'd together.

Tharmas went down to the Wine presses & beheld the sons & daughters
Of Luvah quite exhausted with the labour & quite fill'd
With new wine, that they began to torment one another and to tread [the weak *del.*]
The weak. Luvah & Vala slept on the floor, o'erwearied.
Urthona call'd his sons around him: Tharmas call'd his sons
Numerous; they took the wine, they separated the Lees,
And Luvah was put for dung on the ground by the Sons of Tharmas & Urthona.
They formed heavens of sweetest woods, of gold & silver & ivory,
Of glass & precious stones. They loaded all the waggons of heaven
And took away the wine of ages with solemn songs & joy.

Luvah & Vala woke, & all the sons & daughters of Luvah
Awoke; they wept to one another & they reascended
To the Eternal Man in woe: he cast them wailing into
The world of shadows, thro' the air, till winter is over & gone;
But the Human Wine stood wondering; in all their delightful Expanses
The elements subside; the heavens roll'd on with vocal harmony.

Then Los, who is Urthona, rose in all his regenerate power.
The Sea that roll'd & foam'd with darkness & the shadows of death
Vomited out & gave up all; the floods lift up their hands
Singing & shouting to the Man; they bow their hoary heads
And murmuring in their channels flow & circle round his feet.

Then Dark Urthona took the Corn out of the Stores of Urizen;
He ground it in his rumbling Mills. Terrible the distress
Of all the Nations of Earth, ground in the Mills of Urthona.
In his hand Tharmas takes the Storms: he turns the whirlwind loose
Upon the wheels; the stormy seas howl at his dread command
And Eddying fierce rejoice in the fierce agitation of the wheels
Of Dark Urthona. Thunders, Earthquakes, Fires, Water floods,
Rejoice to one another; loud their voices shake the Abyss,
Their dread forms tending the dire mills. The grey hoar frost was there,
And his pale wife, the aged Snow; they watch over the fires,

They build the Ovens of Urthona. Nature in darkness groans
And Men are bound to sullen contemplation in the night:
Restless they turn on beds of sorrow; in their inmost brain
Feeling the crushing Wheels, they rise, they write the bitter words
Of Stern Philosophy & knead the bread of knowledge with tears & groans.

Such are the works of Dark Urthona. Tharmas sifted the corn.
Urthona made the Bread of Ages, & he placed it,
In golden & in silver baskets, in heavens of precious stone
And then took his repose in Winter, in the night of Time.

The Sun has left his blackness & has found a fresher morning,
And the mild moon rejoices in the clear & cloudless night,
And Man walks forth from midst of the fires: the evil is all consum'd.
His eyes behold the Angelic spheres arising night & day;
The stars consum'd like a lamp blown out, & in their stead, behold
The Expanding Eyes of Man behold the depths of wondrous worlds!
One Earth, one sea beneath; nor Erring Globes wander, but Stars
Of fire rise up nightly from the Ocean; & one Sun
Each morning, like a New born Man, issues with songs & joy
Calling the Plowman to his Labour & the Shepherd to his rest.
He walks upon the Eternal Mountains, raising his heavenly voice,
Conversing with the Animal forms of wisdom night & day,
That, risen from the Sea of fire, renew'd walk o'er the Earth;
For Tharmas brought his flocks upon the hills, & in the Vales
Around the Eternal Man's bright tent, the little Children play
Among the wooly flocks. The hammer of Urthona sounds
In the deep caves beneath; his limbs renew'd, his Lions roar
Around the Furnaces & in Evening sport upon the plains.
They raise their faces from the Earth, conversing with the Man:

"How is it we have walk'd thro' fires & yet are not consum'd?
"How is it that all things are chang'd, even as in ancient times?"

The Sun arises from his dewy bed, & the fresh airs
Play in his smiling beams giving the seeds of life to grow,
And the fresh Earth beams forth ten thousand thousand springs of life.
Urthona is arisen in his strength, no longer now
Divided from Enitharmon, no longer the Spectre Los.
Where is the Spectre of Prophecy? where the delusive Phantom?
Departed: & Urthona rises from the ruinous Walls
In all his ancient strength to form the golden armour of science
For intellectual War. The war of swords departed now,
The dark Religions are departed & sweet Science reigns.

End of The Dream

NOTES WRITTEN ON THE PAGES OF THE FOUR ZOAS

Christ's Crucifix shall be made an excuse for Executing Criminals.

¶

Till thou dost injure the distrest.
Thou shalt never have peace within thy breast.

¶

The Christian Religion teaches that No Man is Indifferent to you, but that every one is Either your friend or your enemy; he must necessarily be either the one or the other, And that he will be equally profitable both ways if you treat him as he deserves.

¶

Unorganiz'd Innocence : An Impossibility.
Innocence dwells with Wisdom, but never with Ignorance.

[END OF THE FOUR ZOAS]

THE FOUR ZOAS

ADDITIONAL FRAGMENTS

Beneath the veil of [*name del.*] Vala rose Tharmas from dewy tears.
The [ancient *del.*] *eternal* man bow'd his bright head, & Urizen, prince of light,
[Astonish'd look'd from his bright portals, calling thus to Luvah,
Aloud in the . . . *del.*]
Astonish'd look'd from his bright portals. Luvah, King of Love
Awaken'd Vala. Ariston ran forth with bright Anana,
And dark Urthona rouz'd his shady bride from her deep den.
[Awaking from his stony slumber . . . *del.*]
Pitying, they view'd the new born demon, for they could not love.
[*Half a line del.*]
Male form'd the demon mild athletic force his shoulders spread,
And his bright feet firm as a brazen altar; but the parts
To love devoted, female; all astonish'd stood the hosts
Of heaven, while Tharmas with wing'd speed flew to the sandy shore,
He rested on the desart wild, & on the raging sea
He stood & stretch'd his wings &c

With printless feet, scorning the concave of the joyful sky,
Female her form, bright as the summer, but the parts of love
Male, & her brow, radiant as day, darted a lovely scorn.
Tharmas beheld from his rock &c

¶

The ocean calm, the clouds fold round, & fiery flames of love
Inwrap the immortal limbs, struggling in terrific joy.
Not long; thunders, lightnings swift, rendings & blasting winds
Sweep o'er the struggling copulation, in fell writhing pangs
They lie, in twisting agonies beneath the covering heavens.

¶

The womb impress'd, Enion fled & hid in verdant mountains,
Yet here his heavenly orbs &c

¶

From Enion pours the seed of life, & death in all her limbs
Frozen in the womb of Tharmas rush the rivers of Enion's pain.
Trembling he lay, swell'd with the deluge, stifling in the anguish.

¶

Opening in rifted rocks, mingling [their bodies *del.*] *together they* join in burning anguish,
Mingling his horrible [brightness *del.*] *darkness* with her tender limbs; then high she soar'd,
Shrieking above the ocean: a bright wonder that nature shudder'd at,
Half Woman & half [serpent *del.*] beast, all his [lovely changing *del.*] *darkly waving* colours mix
With her fair crystal clearness; in her lips & cheeks his [poisons *del.*] metals rose
In blushes like the morning, & his [scaly armour *del.*] *rocky features* soft'ning,
A [monster *del.*] *wonder,* lovely in the heavens or wand'ring on the earth,
With female voice warbling upon the hills & hollow vales,
Beauty all blushing with desire, a self enjoying wonder.
For Enion brooded, groaning loud; the rough seas vegetate. Golden rocks rise from the vast . . .
And thus her voice: "Glory, delight & sweet enjoyment born
"To mild Eternity, shut in a threefold shape delightful,
"To wander in sweet solitude, enraptur'd at every wind."

[Shining across the ocean Enion brooded groaning; the golden rocks vegetate. The . . . *del.*]
Infolding the bright woman [from the desolating winds, & thus her voice & . . . *del.*]

That I should hide thee with my power & . . .
And now thou dark'nest in my presence; never from my sight . . .

¶

The Lamb of God stood before Urizen opposite
In Entuthon Benithon, in the shadows of torment & woe
Upon the heights of [Entuthon that *del.*] Amalek, taking refuge in his arms
The victims fled from punishment, [that *del.*] for all his words were peace.
[He *del.*] Urizen call'd together all the synagogue of Satan in dark Sanhedrim
To judge the lamb of God to death as a murderer & robber:
As it is written, He was number'd among the transgressors.

Cold, dark, opake the Assembly met twelvefold in Amalek,
Twelve rocky unshap'd forms, terrific forms of torture & woe,
Such seem'd the Synagogue to distant view; around them stood
The daughters of Canaan & Moab, binding on the Stones
Their victims, & with [songs *del.*] knives tormenting them, singing with tears
Over their victims. Thus was the Lamb of God condemn'd to death.
They nailed him upon the tree of Mystery, & weeping over him
And mocking & then worshiping, calling him Lord & King.
Sometimes as twelve daughters lovely, & sometimes as five
They stood in beaming beauty, & sometimes as One, even Rahab
[*Half a line del.*]
Who is Mystery, Babylon the Great, Mother of Harlots.

And Rahab strip'd off Luvah's robes from off the lamb of God,
Then first she saw his glory, & her harlot form appear'd
In all its turpitude beneath the divine light, & of Luvah's robes
She made herself a Mantle.
Also the Vegetated bodies which Enitharmon wove in her looms
Open'd within the heart & in the loins & in the brain
To Beulah, & the dead in Beulah descended thro' their gates
And some were woven onefold, some twofold, & some threefold
In head or heart or reins, according to the fittest order
Of most mournful pity & compassion to the spectrous dead.
Darkness & sorrow cover'd all flesh; eternity was darken'd.
Urizen sitting in his web of deceitful religion was tormented.
He felt the female &c

[END OF ADDITIONAL FRAGMENTS]

ANNOTATIONS TO "An Apology for The Bible in a Series of Letters addressed to Thomas Paine by R. Watson, D.D., F.R.S." London MDCCXCVII

Written 1798

Notes on the B. of L's. Apology for the Bible by William Blake

[*Written on the back of the title-page*]

To defend the Bible in this year 1798 would cost a man his life.

The Beast & the Whore rule without control.

It is an easy matter for a Bishop to triumph over Paine's attack, but it is not so easy for one who loves the Bible.

The Perversions of Christ's words & acts are attack'd by Paine & also the perversions of the Bible; Who dare defend either the Acts of Christ or the Bible Unperverted?

But to him who sees this mortal pilgrimage in the light that I see it, Duty to his country is the first consideration & safety the last.

Read patiently: take not up this Book in an idle hour: the consideration of these things is the whole duty of man & the affairs of life & death trifles, sports of time. But these considerations [are the] business of Eternity.

I have been commanded from Hell not to print this, as it is what our Enemies wish.

[*Blake's notes are here printed in larger type after the extracts from Bishop Watson's text. The numbers indicate the passages to which Blake refers. Words underlined by Blake are printed in italic.*]

Page [iii]

[Bishop Watson's Preface]

This edition of the Apology for the Bible is published, in compliance with the earnest solicitations of many serious persons of all ranks. They have remarked to me, that the deistical writings of Mr Paine are circulated, with great and pernicious industry, amongst the unlearned part of the community, especially in large manufacturing towns; and they have been pleased to think, that this Defence of Revealed Religion might, if generally distributed, be efficacious in stopping that torrent of infidelity which endangers alike the future happiness of individuals, and the present safety of *all Christian states* [1] . . .

Calgarth Park,
May 10, 1796.

[1] Paine has not attacked Christianity. Watson has defended Antichrist.

[List of books by Bishop Watson] [1]

7. The Wisdom and Goodness of God, in having made both *Rich and Poor* [2]: a Sermon, preached before the Stewards of Westminster Dispensary, at the Anniversary Meeting in Charlotte-street Chapel . . .

[1] Read the xxiii Chap. of Matthew & then condemn Paine's hatred of Priests if you dare. [2] God made Man happy & Rich, but the Subtil made the innocent, Poor. This must be a most wicked & blasphemous book.

Page 1.

LETTER I. [1]

SIR,

I have lately met with a book of your's, entitled—"The Age of Reason," part the second, being an investigation of true and of fabulous theology;—and I think it not inconsistent with my station, and the duty I owe to society, to trouble you and the world with some observations on so extraordinary a performance. Extraordinary I esteem it; not from any novelty in the objections which *you have produced against revealed religion*, (*for I find little or no novelty in them*), [2] but from the zeal with which you labour to disseminate your opinions, and from the confidence with which you esteem them true. You perceive, by this, that I give you credit for your sincerity, *how much soever I may question your wisdom*, [3] in writing in such a manner on such a subject: and I have no reluctance in acknowledging, that you possess a considerable share of energy of language, and acuteness of investigation; though I must be allowed to lament, that these *talents have not been applied in a manner more useful to human kind, and more creditable to yourself.* [4] I begin with your preface. You therein state—that you had long had an intention of publishing your thoughts upon religion, but that you had originally reserved it to a later period in life. I hope there is no want of charity in saying, that it would have been fortunate for the Christian world, *had your life been terminated before you had fulfilled your intention.* [5] In accomplishing your purpose you will have unsettled the faith of thousands; rooted from the minds of the unhappy virtuous all their comfortable assurance of a future recompence; have annihilated in the minds of the flagitious all their fears of future punishment; you will have given the reins to the domination of every passion, and have thereby contributed to the introduction of the public insecurity, and of the private unhappiness usually and almost necessarily accompanying a state of corrupted morals. [6]

[1] If this first Letter is written without Railing & Illiberality I have never read one that is. To me it is all Daggers & Poison; the sting of the serpent is in every Sentence as well as the glittering Dissimulation. Achilles' wrath is blunt abuse: Thersites' sly insinuation; such is the Bishop's. If such is the characteristic of a modern polite gentleman we may hope to see Christ's discourses Expung'd. I have not the Charity for the Bishop that he pretends to have for Paine. I believe him to be a State trickster. [2] Dishonest Misrepresentation. [3] Priestly Impudence. [4] Contemptible Falsehood & Detraction. [5] Presumptuous Murderer. Dost thou, O Priest, wish thy brother's death when God has preserved him? [6] Mr Paine has not extinguish'd, & cannot Extinguish, Moral rectitude; he has Extinguish'd Superstition, which took the Place of Moral Rectitude. What has Moral Rectitude to do with Opinions concerning historical fact?

Page 2.

No one can think worse of confession to a priest and subsequent absolution, as practised in the church of Rome, than I do: but I cannot, with you, attribute the *guillotine-massacres to that cause. Men's minds were not prepared,* [1] as you suppose, for the commission of all manner of crimes, by any doctrines of the church of Rome, corrupted as I esteem it, *but by their not thoroughly believing even that religion. What may not society expect from those, who shall imbibe the principles of your book?* [2]

A fever, which you and those about you expected would prove mortal, made you remember, with renewed satisfaction, that you had written the former part of your Age of Reason—and you know therefore, you say, by experience, the conscientious trial of your own principles. I admit this declaration to be a proof of the sincerity of your persuasion, but I cannot admit it to be any proof of the truth of your principles. What is conscience? Is it, as has been thought, an internal monitor implanted in us by the *Supreme Being*, and dictating to us, on all occasions, what is *right or wrong? Or is it merely* our own judgment of the moral rectitude or turpitude of our own actions? I *take the word* (with Mr. Locke) in the latter, *as in the only intelligible* sense. [3] Now who sees not that our judgments of virtue and vice, right and wrong, are not always formed from an enlightened and dispassionate use of our reason, in the investigation of truth? They are more generally formed from the nature of the religion we profess; from the quality of the civil government under which we live; from the general manners of the age, or the particular manners of the persons with whom we associate; from the education we have had in our youth; from the books we have read at a more advanced period; and from other accidental causes. Who sees not that, on this account, conscience may be comfortable or repugnant to the law of nature?—may be certain, or doubtful?—and that it can be no criterion of moral rectitude, even when it is certain, because the certainty of an opinion is no proof of it's being a right opinion? [4] A man may be certainly persuaded of an error in reasoning, or of an untruth in matters of fact. It is a maxim of every law, human and divine, that a man ought never to act in opposition to his conscience:

[1] To what does the Bishop attribute the English Crusade against France? Is it not to State Religion? Blush for shame. [2] Folly & Impudence. Does the thorough belief of Popery hinder crimes, or can the man who writes the latter sentiment be in the good humour the bishop Pretends to be? If we are to expect crimes from Paine & his followers, are we to believe that Bishops do not Rail? I should Expect that the man who wrote this sneaking sentence *would be as good an inquisitor as any other Priest.* [3] Conscience in those that have it is unequivocal. It is the voice of God. Our judgment of right & wrong is Reason. I believe that the Bishop laught at the Bible in his slieve & so did Locke. [4] Virtue is not Opinion.

Page 3.

but it will not from thence follow, that he will, in obeying the dictates of his conscience, *on all occasions act right.* [1] An inquisitor, who burns jews and heretics; a Robespierre, who massacres innocent and harmless women; a robber, who thinks that all things ought to be in common, and that a state of property is an unjust infringement of natural liberty:—these, and a thousand perpetrators of different crimes, may all follow *the dictates of conscience*; [2] and may, at the real or supposed approach of death, remember "with renewed satisfaction" the worst of their transactions, and experience, without dismay, "a conscientious trial of their principles." But this their conscientious composure can be no proof to others of the rectitude of their principles, and ought to be no pledge to themselves of their innocence, in adhering to them.

I have thought fit to make this remark, with a view of suggesting to you a consideration of great importance—whether you have examined calmly, and according to the best of your ability, the arguments by which the truth of revealed religion may, in the judgment of learned and impartial men, be established? [3] . . .

If you have made the best examination you can, and yet reject revealed religion as an imposture, I pray that God may pardon what I esteem your error. And whether you have made this examination or not, does not become me or any man to determine. That gospel, which you despise, has taught me this moderation; it has said to me—"Who art thou that judgest another man's servant? To his own master he standeth or falleth."—I think that you are in an error; but whether that error be to you a vincible or an invincible error, I presume not to determine [4] . . .

[1] Always, or the Bible is false. If Conscience is not a Criterion of Moral Rectitude, What is it? He who thinks that Honesty is changeable knows nothing about it. [2] Contemptible Falshood & Wickedness. Virtue & honesty, or the dictates of Conscience, are of no doubtful Signification to anyone. Opinion is one Thing. Principle another. No Man can change his Principles. Every Man changes his opinions. He who supposes that his Principles are to be changed is a Dissembler, who Disguises his Principles & calls that change. [3] Paine is either a Devil or an Inspired man. Men who give themselves to their Energetic Genius in the manner that Paine does are no Examiners. If they are not determinately wrong they must be Right or the Bible is false; as to Examiners in these points they will [always be found to be neither cold nor hot & will *del.*] be spewed out. The Man who pretends to be a modest enquirer into the truth of a self evident thing is a Knave. The truth & certainty of Virtue & Honesty, *i.e.* Inspiration, needs no one to prove it; it is Evident as the Sun & Moon. [*six words deleted*] He who stands doubting of what he intends, whether it is Virtuous or Vicious, knows not what Virtue means. No man can do a Vicious action & think it to be Virtuous. No man can take darkness for light. He may pretend to do so & may pretend to be a modest Enquirer, but he is a Knave. [4] Serpentine Dissimulation.

Pages 4-5.

You hold it impossible that the Bible can be the Word of God, because it is therein said, that the Israelites destroyed the Canaanites by the express command of God: and to believe the Bible to be true, we must, you affirm, unbelieve all our belief of the moral justice of God; for wherein, you ask, could crying or smiling infants offend?—I am astonished that so acute a reasoner should attempt to disparage the Bible, by bringing forward this exploded and frequently refuted objection of Morgan, Tindal, and Bolingbroke. [1] You profess yourself to be a deist, and to believe that there is a God, who created the universe, and established the laws of nature, by which it is sustained in existence. You profess that from the contemplation of the works of God, you derive a knowledge of his attributes; and you reject the Bible, because it ascribes to God things inconsistent (as you suppose) with the attributes which you have discovered to belong to him; in particular, you think it repugnant to his moral justice, that he should doom to destruction the crying or smiling infants of the Canaanites.—Why do you not maintain it to be repugnant to his moral justice, that he should suffer crying or smiling infants to be swallowed up by an earthquake, drowned by an inundation, consumed by a fire, starved by famine, or destroyed by a pestilence? The Word of God is in perfect harmony with his work; crying or smiling infants are subjected to death in both. We believe that the earth, at the express command of God, opened her mouth, and swallowed up Korah, Dathan, and Abiram, with their wives, their sons, and their little ones. This you esteem so repugnant to God's moral justice, that you spurn, as spurious, the Book in which the circumstance is related. When Catania, Lima, and Lisbon, were severally destroyed by earthquakes, men with their wives, their sons, and their little ones, were swallowed up alive:—why do you not spurn, as spurious, the book of nature, in which this fact is certainly written, and from the perusal of which you infer the moral justice of God? You will, probably, reply, that the evils which the Canaanites suffered from the express command of God, were different from those which are brought on mankind by the operation of the laws of nature.—Different! in what?—Not in the magnitude of the evil—not in the subjects of sufferance—not in the author of it—for my philosophy,

[1] To me, who believe the Bible & profess myself a Christian, a defence of the Wickedness of the Israelites in murdering so many thousands under pretence of a command from God is altogether Abominable & Blasphemous. Wherefore did Christ come? Was it not to abolish the Jewish Imposture? Was not Christ murder'd because he taught that God loved all Men & was their father & forbad all contention for Worldly prosperity in opposition to the Jewish Scriptures, which are only an Example of the wickedness & deceit of the Jews & were written as an Example of the possibility of Human Beastliness in all its branches? Christ died as an Unbeliever & if the Bishops had their will so would Paine: see page 1: but he who speaks a word against the Son of man shall be forgiven. Let the Bishop prove that he has not spoken against the Holy Ghost, who in Paine strives with Christendom as in Christ he strove with the Jews.

Page 6.
at least, instructs me to believe, that God not only primarily formed, but that he hath through all ages executed, the laws of nature; and that he will through all eternity administer them, for the general happiness of his creatures, whether we can, on every occasion, discern that end or not. [1]
I am far from being guilty of the impiety of questioning the existence of the moral justice of God, as proved either by natural or revealed religion; what I contend for is shortly this—that you have no right, in fairness of reasoning, to urge any apparent deviation from moral justice, as an argument against revealed religion, because you do not urge an equally apparent deviation from it, as an argument against natural religion: you reject the former, and admit the latter, without considering that, as to your objection, they must stand or fall together. [2]
As to the Canaanites, it is needless to enter into any proof of the depraved state of their morals; they were a wicked people in the time of Abraham, and they, even then, were devoted to destruction by God; but their iniquity was not then full. In the time of Moses, they were idolaters; sacrificers of their own crying or smiling infants; devourers of human flesh; addicted to unnatural lust; immersed in the filthiness of all manner of vice. Now, I think, it will be impossible to prove, that it was a *proceeding contrary to God's moral justice, to exterminate so wicked a people.* [3] He made the Israelites the executors of his vengeance; and, in doing this, he gave such an evident and terrible proof of his abomination of vice, as

could not fail to strike the surrounding nations with astonishment and terror, and to impress on the minds of the Israelites what they were to expect, if they followed the example of the nations whom he commended them to cut off. "Ye shall not commit any of these abominations—that the land spue not you out also, as it spued out the nations that were before you." How strong and descriptive this language! the vices of the inhabitants were so abominable, that the very land was sick of them, and forced to vomit them forth, as the stomach disgorges a deadly poison. [4].

[1] The Bible says that God formed Nature perfect, but that Man perverted the order of Nature, since which time the Elements are fill'd with the Prince of Evil, who has the power of the air. [2] Natural Religion is the voice of God & not the result of reasoning on the Powers of Satan. [3] Horrible! The Bishop is an Inquisitor. God never makes one man murder another, nor one nation. [4] There is a vast difference between an accident brought on by a man's own carelessness & a destruction from the designs of another. The Earthquakes at Lisbon etc. were the Natural result of Sin, but the destruction of the Canaanites by Joshua was the Unnatural design of wicked men. To Extirpate a nation by means of another nation is as wicked as to destroy an individual by means of another individual, which God considers (in the Bible) as Murder & commands that it shall not be done. Therefore the Bishop has not answer'd Paine.

Pages 6–7.

I have often wondered what could be the reason that men, not destitute of talents, should be desirous of undermining the authority of revealed religion, and studious in exposing, with a malignant and illiberal exultation, every little difficulty attending the scriptures, to popular animadversion and contempt. I am not willing to attribute this strange propensity to what Plato attributed the atheism of his time—to profligacy of manners—to affectation of singularity—to gross ignorance, assuming the semblance of deep research and superior sagacity;—I had rather refer it to an impropriety of judgment, respecting the manners, and mental acquirements, of human kind in the first ages of the world. Most unbelievers argue as if they thought that man, in remote and rude antiquity, in the very birth and infancy of our species, had the same distinct conceptions of one, eternal, invincible, incorporeal, infinitely wise, powerful, and good God, which they themselves have now. This I look upon as a great mistake, and a pregnant source of infidelity. Human kind, by long experience; by the institutions of civil society; by the cultivation of arts and sciences; by, as I believe, divine instruction actually given to some, and traditionally communicated to all; *is in a far more distinguished situation, as to the powers* of the mind, than it was in the childhood of the world. [1] . . .

[1] That mankind are in a less distinguished Situation with regard to mind than they were in the time of Homer, Socrates, Phidias, Glycon, Aristotle, etc., let all their works witness. [The Deists *del.*] Paine says that Christianity put a stop to improvement, & the Bishop has not shewn the contrary.

Pages 7–8.

It appears incredible to many, that God Almighty should have had colloquial intercourse with our first parents; that he should have contracted a kind of friendship for the patriarchs, and entered into covenants with them; [1] that he should have suspended the laws of nature in Egypt; should have been so apparently partial, as to become the God and governor of one particular nation; [2] and should have so far demeaned himself, as to give to that people a burdensome ritual of worship, statutes and ordinances, many of which seem to be beneath the dignity of his attention, unimportant and impolitic . . .

[1] That God does & always did converse with honest Men, Paine never denies. He only denies that God conversed with Murderers & Revengers such as the Jews were, & of course he holds that the Jews conversed with their own [self will *del.*] State Religion which they call'd God & so were liars as Christ says. [2] That the Jews assumed a right Exclusively to the benefits of God will be a lasting witness against them & the same will it be against [of *del.*] Christians.

Pages 8–9.

. . . I own to you, that when I consider how nearly man, *in a savage state*, *approaches to the brute creation*, as to intellectual excellence; [1] and when I contemplate his miserable attainments, as to the knowledge of God, in a civilized state, when he has had no divine instruction on the subject, or when that instruction has been forgotten, (for all men have known something of God from tradition,) I cannot but admire the wisdom and goodness of the Supreme Being, in having let himself down to our apprehensions; in having given to mankind, in the earliest ages, sensible and extraordinary proofs of his existence and attributes; in having made the jewish and Christian dispensations mediums to convey to all men, through all ages, that knowledge concerning himself, which he had not vouchsafed to give immediately to the first. [2]

[1] Read the Edda of Iceland, the Songs of Fingal, the accounts of North American Savages (as they are call'd). Likewise read Homer's Iliad. He was certainly a Savage in the Bishop's sense. He knew nothing of God in the Bishop's sense of the word & yet he was no fool. [2] The Bible or Peculiar Word of God, Exclusive of Conscience or the Word of God Universal, is that Abomination, which, like the Jewish ceremonies, is for ever removed & henceforth every man may converse with God & be a King & Priest in his own house.

Page 9.

I own it is strange, very strange, that he should have made an immediate manifestation of himself in the first ages of the world; but what is there that is not strange? It is strange that you and I are here—that there is water, and earth, and air, and fire—that there is a sun, and moon, and stars—that there is generation, corruption, reproduction. [1] I can account ultimately for none of these things, without recurring to him who made every thing. I also am his workmanship, and look up to him with hope of preservation through all eternity; I adore him for his word as well as for his work; his work I cannot comprehend, but his word hath assured me of all that I am concerned to know—that he hath prepared everlasting happiness for those who love and obey him. This you will call preachment:—I will have done with it; but the subject is so vast, and the *plan of providence*, in my opinion, so obviously *wise and good*, [2] that I can never think of it without having my mind filled with piety, admiration, and gratitude.

In addition to the moral evidence (as you are pleased to think it) against the Bible, you threaten, in the progress of your work, to produce such other evidence as even a priest cannot deny. A philosopher in search of truth forfeits with me all claim to candour and impartiality, when he introduces railing for reasoning, vulgar and illiberal sarcasm in the room of argument. I will not imitate the example you set me; but examine what you shall produce, with as much coolness and respect, *as if you had given the priests no provocation; as if you were a man of the most unblemished character,* subject to no prejudices, actuated by no bad designs, not liable to have abuse retorted upon you with success. [3]

[1] It is strange that God should speak to man formerly & not now, because it is not true; but the Strangeness of Sun, Moon, or Stars is Strange on a contrary account. [2] The Bible tells me that the plan of Providence was Subverted at the Fall of Adam & that it was not restored till Christ.

[3] Is not this Illiberal? Has not the Bishop given himself the lie in the moment the first words were out of his mouth? Can any man who writes so pretend that he is in a good humour? Is not this the Bishop's cloven foot? Has he not spoil'd the hasty pudding?

Pages 10–11. LETTER II. [1]

This distinction between the genuineness and authenticity of a book, will assist us in detecting the fallacy of an argument, which you state with great confidence in the part of your work now under consideration, and which you frequently allude to, in other parts, as conclusive evidence against the truth of the Bible. Your argument stands thus—If it be found that the books ascribed to Moses, Joshua, and Samuel, were not written by Moses, Joshua, and Samuel, every part of the authority and authenticity of these books is gone at once.—I presume to think otherwise. The genuineness of these books (in the judgment of those who say that they were written by these authors) will certainly be gone; but their authenticity will remain; they may still contain a true account of real transactions, though the names of the writers of them should be found to be different from what they are generally esteemed to be. [2]

[1] The trifles which the Bishop has combated in the following Letters are such as do nothing against Paine's Arguments, none of which the Bishop has dared to Consider. One, for instance, which is that the books of the Bible were never believ'd willingly by any nation & that none but designing Villains ever pretended to believe—That the Bible is all a State Trick, thro' which tho' the People at all times could see, they never had the power to throw off. Another Argument is that all the Commentators on the Bible are Dishonest Designing Knaves, who in hopes of a good living adopt the State religion; this he has shewn with great force, which calls upon His Opponent loudly for an answer. I could name an hundred such.

[2] He who writes things for true which none could write but the actor (such are most of the acts of Moses), must either be the actor or a fable writer or a liar. If Moses did not write the history of his acts, it takes away the authority altogether; it ceases to be history & becomes a Poem of probable impossibilities, fabricated for pleasure, as moderns say, but I say by Inspiration.

Pages 12–13.

Had, indeed, Moses said that he wrote the five first books of the Bible; and had Joshua and Samuel said that they wrote the books which are respectively attributed to them; and had it been found, that Moses, Joshua, and Samuel, did not write these books; then, I grant, the authority of the whole would have been gone at once; these men would have been found liars, as to the genuineness of the books; and this proof of the want of their veracity, in one point, would have invalidated their testimony in every other; these books would have been justly stigmatized, as neither genuine nor authentic. [1] . . .

As to your assertion, that the miracles recorded in Tacitus, and in other profane historians, are quite as well authenticated as those of the Bible—it, being a mere assertion destitute of proof, may be properly answered by a contrary assertion. I take the liberty then to say, that the evidence for the miracles recorded in the Bible is, both in kind and degree, so greatly superior to that for the prodigies mentioned by Livy, or the miracles related by Tacitus, as to justify us in giving credit to the one as the work of God, and in with-holding it from the other as the effect of superstition and imposture. This method of derogating from the credibility of Christianity, by opposing to the miracles of our Saviour, the tricks of ancient impostors, seems to have originated with Hierocles in the fourth century; and it has been adopted by unbelievers from that time to this; with this difference, indeed, that the heathens of the third and fourth century admitted that Jesus wrought miracles; but lest that admission should have compelled them to abandon their gods and become Christians, they said, that their Apollonius, their Apuleius, their Aristeas, did as great; whilst modern deists deny the fact of Jesus having ever wrought a miracle. [2] . . .

[1] If Paine means that a history, tho' true in itself, is false when it is attributed to a wrong author, he's a fool. But he says that Moses, being proved not the author of that history which is written in his name & in which he says I did so & so, Undermines the veracity intirely. The writer says he is Moses; if this is proved false, the history is false (Deut. xxxi, v, 24). But perhaps Moses is not the author & then the Bishop loses his Author.

[2] Jesus could not do miracles where unbelief hindered, hence we must conclude that the man who holds miracles to be ceased puts it out of his own power to ever witness one. The manner of a miracle being performed is in modern times considered as an arbitrary command of the agent upon the patient, but this is an impossibility, not a miracle, neither did Jesus ever do such a miracle. Is it a greater miracle to feed five thousand men with five loaves than to overthrow all the armies of Europe with a small pamphlet? Look over the events of your own life & if you do not find that you have both done such miracles & lived by such you do not see as I do. True, I cannot do a miracle thro' experiment & to domineer over & prove to others my superior power, as neither could Christ. But I can & do work such as both astonish & comfort me & mine. How can Paine, the worker of miracles, ever doubt Christ's in the above sense of the word miracle? But how can Watson ever believe the above sense of a miracle, who considers it as an arbitrary act of the agent upon an unbelieving patient, whereas the Gospel says that Christ could not do a miracle because of Unbelief?

If Christ could not do miracles because of Unbelief, the reason alledged by Priests for miracles is false; for those who believe want not to be confounded by miracles. Christ & his Prophets & Apostles were not Ambitious miracle mongers.

Page 14.

... The Bible is not the only book which has undergone the fate of being reprobated as spurious, after it had been received as genuine and authentic for many ages. It has been maintained that the history of HERODOTUS was written in the time of CONSTANTINE; and that the Classics are forgeries of the thirteenth or fourteenth century. These extravagant reveries amused the world at the time of their publication, and have long since sunk into oblivion. You esteem all prophets to be such lying rascals, that I dare not venture to predict the fate of your book. [1]

[1] Prophets, in the modern sense of the word, have never existed. Jonah was no prophet in the modern sense, for his prophecy of Nineveh failed. Every honest man is a Prophet; he utters his opinion both of private & public matters. Thus: If you go on So, the result is So. He never says, such a thing shall happen let you do what you will. A Prophet is a Seer, not an Arbitrary Dictator. It is man's fault if God is not able to do him good, for he gives to the just & to the unjust, but the unjust reject his gift.

Pages 15-16.

What possible doubt can there be that Moses wrote the books in question? I could accumulate many other passages from the scriptures to this purpose; but if what I have advanced will not convince you that there is affirmative evidence, and of the strongest kind, for Moses's being the author of these books, nothing that I can advance will convince you.

What if I should grant all you undertake to prove (the stupidity and ignorance of the writer excepted)?—What if I should admit, that Samuel, or Ezra, or some other learned jew, composed these books, *from public* records, many years after the death of Moses? Will it follow, that there was no truth in them? According to my logic, it will only follow, that they are not genuine books; every fact recorded *in them may be true,* whenever, or by whomsoever they were written. [1] It cannot be said that the jews had no public records; the Bible furnishes abundance of proof to the contrary. I by no means admit, that these books, as to the main part of them, were not written by Moses; but I do contend, that a book may contain a true history, though we know not the author of it, or though we may be mistaken in ascribing it to a wrong author.

[1] Nothing can be more contemptible than to suppose Public RECORDS to be True. Read them & Judge, if you are not a Fool. Of what consequence is it whether Moses wrote the Pentateuch or no? If Paine trifles in some of his objections it is folly to confute him so seriously in them & leave his more material ones unanswered. Public Records! As if Public Records were True! Impossible; for the facts are such as none but the actor could tell. If it is True, Moses & none but he could write it, unless we allow it to be Poetry & that poetry inspired.

If historical facts can be written by inspiration, Milton's Paradise Lost is as true as Genesis or Exodus; but the Evidence is nothing, for how can he who writes what he has neither seen nor heard of be an Evidence of The Truth of his history.

Page 17.

... I do not call you a vain and arrogant coxcomb for vindicating your character, when in the latter part of this very work you boast, and I hope truly, "that the man does not exist that can say I have persecuted him, or any man, or any set of men, in the American revolution, or in the French revolution; or that I have in any case returned evil for evil." I know not what kings and priests may say to this; you may not have returned to them evil for evil, because they never, I believe, did you any harm; but you have done them all the harm you could, and that without provocation. [1]

[1] Paine says that Kings & Priests have done him harm from his birth.

Page 22.

LETTER III.

Having done with what you call the grammatical evidence that Moses was not the author of the books attributed to him, you come to your historical and chronological evidence; and you begin with Genesis. [1]

[1] I cannot concieve the Divinity of the books in the Bible to consist either in who they were written by, or at what time, or in the historical evidence which may be all false in the eyes of one man & true in the eyes of another, but in the Sentiments & Examples, which, whether true or Parabolic, are Equally useful as Examples given to us of the perverseness of some & its consequent evil & the honesty of others & its consequent good. This sense of the Bible is equally true to all & equally plain to all. None can doubt the impression which he recieves from a book of Examples. If he is good he will abhor wickedness in David or Abraham; if he is wicked he will make their wickedness an excuse for his & so he would do by any other book.

Page 25.

... The destruction of the Canaanites exhibits to all nations, in all ages, a signal proof of God's displeasure against sin; it has been to others, and it is to ourselves, a benevolent warning. Moses would have been the wretch you represent him, had he acted by his own authority alone; but you may as reasonably attribute cruelty and murder to the judge of the land in condemning criminals to death, as butchery and massacre to Moses in executing the command of God. [1]

[1] All Penal Laws court Transgression & therefore are cruelty & Murder. The laws of the Jews were (both ceremonial & real) the basest & most oppressive of human codes, & being like all other codes given under pretence of divine command were what Christ pronounced them, The Abomination that maketh desolate, *i.e.* State Religion, which is the source of all Cruelty.

Page 29.

LETTER IV.

... And who told you that the jews had no records, or that they did not preserve them with singular care? ... If any one, having access to the journals of the lords and commons, to the books of the treasury, war-office, privy council, and other public documents, should at this day write an history of the reigns of George the first and second, and should publish it without his name, would any man, three or four hundreds or thousands of years hence, [1] question the authority of that book, when he knew that the whole British nation had received it as an authentic book, from the time of it's first publication to the age in which he lived? ...

If I am right in this reasoning, [2] (and I protest to you that I do not see any error in it,) all the arguments you adduce in proof that the book of Joshua was not written by Joshua, nor that of Samuel by Samuel, are nothing to the purpose for which you have brought them forward: these books may be books of authority, though all you advance against the genuineness of them should be granted.

[1] Hundreds or Thousands of Years! O, very fine Records! As if he knew that there were Records! The Ancients Knew Better. [2] As if Reasoning was of any Consequence to a Question! Downright Plain Truth is Something, but Reasoning is Nothing.

Page 31.
Whoever wrote the gospel of St. Matthew, it was written not many centuries, probably (I had almost said certainly) not a quarter of one century after the death of Jesus; [1]

Pages 33-34.
It seems to me that you do not perfectly comprehend what is meant by the expression—the Word of God—or the divine authority of the scriptures: I will explain it to you in the words of Dr. Law, late bishop of Carlisle, and in those of St. Austin. [2]

Page 35.
. . . The two books of Samuel come next under your review. You proceed to shew that these books were not written by Samuel, that they are anonymous, and thence you conclude without authority. [3]

[1] There are no Proofs that Matthew, the Earliest of all the writings of the New Testament, was written within the first century (see p. 94 & 95). [2] They seem to Forget that there is a God of this World, A God Worship'd in this World as God & set above all that is call'd God. [3] Who gave them the Name of Books of Samuel? It is not of Consequence.

Page 36.
. . . Very little certainty, I think, can at this time be obtained on this subject: but that you may have some knowledge of what has been conjectured by men of judgment, I will quote to you a passage from Dr. Hartley's Observations on Man. [1]

[1] Hartley a Man of Judgment! Then Judgment was a Fool. What Nonsense!

Page 48.

LETTER V.

. . . As to the sins and debaucheries of Solomon, we have nothing to do with them but to avoid them; and to give full credit to his experience, when he preaches to us his admirable sermon on the vanity of every thing but piety and virtue. [1]

Page 49.
. . . I have read also Isaiah's burden of Babylon, and I have compared it with the past and present state of Babylon, and the comparison has made such an impression on my mind, that it will never be effaced from my memory. I shall never cease to believe that the Eternal alone, by whom things future are more distinctly known than past or present things are by man, that the eternal God alone could have dictated to the prophet Isaiah the subject of the burden of Babylon. [2]

[1] Piety & Virtue! Is Seneca Classical, O Fine Bishop? [2] The Bishop never saw the Everlasting Gospel any more than Tom Paine.

Page 95.

LETTER IX.

Did you ever read the apology for the Christians, which Justin Martyr presented to the emperor Antoninus Pius, to the senate, and people of Rome? I should sooner expect a falsity in a petition, which any body of persecuted men, imploring justice, should present to the king and parliament of Great Britain, than in this apology.—Yet in this apology, which was presented not fifty years after the death of St. John, [1] not only parts of all the four gospels are quoted, but it is expressly said, that on the day called Sunday, a portion of them was read in the public assemblies of the Christians. I forbear pursuing this matter farther; else it might easily be shewn, that *probably the gospels,* and certainly some of St. Paul's epistles were known to Clement, Ignatius, and Polycarp, contemporaries with the apostles. These men could not quote or refer to books which did not exist: and therefore, though you could make it out that the book called the New Testament did not formally exist under that title, till 350 years after Christ; *yet I hold it to be a certain fact, that all the books,* of which it is composed, were written, and most of them received by all Christians, within a few years after his death. [2]

[1] A:D: 150. [2] This is No Certain Fact. Presumption is no Proof.

Page 108.

LETTER X.

... The moral precepts of the gospel [1] are so well fitted to promote the happiness of mankind in this world, and to prepare human nature for the future enjoyment of that blessedness, of which, in our present state, we can form no conception, that I had no expectation they would have met with your disapprobation.

Page 109.

... Two precepts you particularize as inconsistent with the dignity and the nature of man—that of not resenting injuries, and that of loving enemies. [2]—Who but yourself ever interpreted literally the proverbial phrase—"If a man smite thee on thy right cheek, turn to him the other also?"—Did Jesus himself turn the *other cheek when the officer of the high priest smote him?* [3] It is evident, that a patient acquiescence under *slight* [4] personal injuries is here enjoined; and that a proneness to revenge, which instigates men to savage acts of brutality, for every trifling offence, is forbidden.

Page 117.

... The importance of revelation is by nothing rendered more apparent, than by the discordant sentiments of learned and good men (for I speak not of the *ignorant and immoral*) [5] on this point.

[1] The Gospel is Forgiveness of Sins & has No Moral Precepts; these belong to Plato & Seneca & Nero. [2] Well done, Paine! [3] Yes, I have no doubt he Did. [4] O Fool! Slight Hypocrite & Villain! [5] O, how Virtuous! Christ came not to call the Virtuous.

Pages 118-119.

We are all, of every rank and condition, equally concerned in knowing—what will become of us after death;—and, if we are to live again, we are interested in knowing —whether it be possible for us to do any thing [1] whilst we live here, which may render that future life an happy one.—Now, "that thing called Christianity," as you scoffingly speak—that last best gift of Almighty God, as I esteem it, the gospel of Jesus Christ, has given us the most clear and satisfactory information on both these points. It tells us, what deism never could have told us, that we shall certainly be raised from the dead—that, whatever be the nature of the soul, we shall certainly live for ever—and that, whilst we live here, it is possible for us to do much towards the rendering that everlasting life an happy one.—These are tremendous truths to bad men; [2] they cannot be received and reflected on with indifference by the best; and they suggest to all such a cogent motive to virtuous action, as deism could not furnish even to Brutus himself.

[1] Do or Act to Do Good or to do Evil. Who dare to Judge but God alone? [2] Who does the Bishop call Bad Men? Are they the Publicans & Sinners that Christ loved to associate with? Does God Love the Righteous according to the Gospel, or does he not cast them off?

Some men have been warped to infidelity by viciousness of life; and some may have hypocritically professed Christianity from prospects of temporal advantage: but, being a stranger to your character, I neither impute the former to you, nor can admit the latter as operating on myself. The generality of unbelievers are such, from want of information on the subject of religion; having been engaged from their youth in struggling for worldly distinction, or perplexed with the incessant intricacies of business, or bewildered in the pursuits of pleasure, they have neither ability, inclination, nor leisure, to enter into critical disquisitions concerning the truth of Christianity. [1] . . .

[1] For who is really Righteous? It is all Pretension.

Page 120.

It appears to me Now that Tom Paine is a better Christian than the Bishop.
I have read this Book with attention & find that the Bishop has only hurt Paine's heel while Paine has broken his head. The Bishop has not answer'd one of Paine's grand objections.

[*Written on the last page*]

ANNOTATIONS TO
Essays Moral, Economical and Political by Francis Bacon London MDCCXCVIII

Written about 1798

Half-title:

Is it True or is it False that the Wisdom of this World is Foolishness with God?
This is Certain: If what Bacon says Is True, what Christ says Is False. If Caesar is Right, Christ is Wrong both in Politics & Religion, since they will divide them in Two.

Title-page, centre:

Good Advice for Satan's Kingdom.

Editor's Preface, page i, top :

I am astonish'd how such Contemptible Knavery & Folly as this Book contains can ever have been call'd Wisdom by Men of Sense, but perhaps this never was the Case & all Men of Sense have despised the Book as Much as I do.

Per William Blake

Preface, page iv, margin :

But these Essays, written at a period of better taste, and on subjects of immediate importance to the conduct of common life "such as come home to men's *business and bosoms,*" are still read with pleasure . . .

Erratum: to Men's Pockets.

Page xii, blank :

Every Body Knows that this is Epicurus and Lucretius & Yet Every Body says that it is Christian Philosophy; how is this Possible? Every Body must be a Liar & deciever. But Every Body does not do this, But The Hirelings of Kings & Courts who make themselves Every Body & Knowingly propagate Falshood.

It was a Common opinion in the Court of Queen Elizabeth that Knavery Is Wisdom. Cunning Plotters were consider'd as wise Machiavels.

[*The annotations after this point are marginal. The title of each Essay is given after the number of the first page of the essay which has an annotation. Words underlined by Blake are printed in italic. Passages from Bacon are in smaller type.*]

Page 1. Of Truth.

Self Evident Truth is one Thing and Truth the result of Reasoning is another Thing. Rational Truth is not the Truth of Christ, but of Pilate. It is the Tree of the Knowledge of Good & Evil.

What is truth? said jesting Pilate, and would not stay for an answer. Certainly there be that delight in giddiness, and count it a bondage to fix a belief; affecting free-will in thinking, as well as in acting: and, though the sects of philosophers of that kind be gone, yet there remain certain discoursing wits which are of the same veins, though there be not so much blood in them as was in those of the ancients.

But more Nerve if by Ancients he means Heathen Authors.

But it is not only the difficulty and labour which men take in finding out of truths; nor again, that, when it is found, it imposeth upon men's thoughts, that doth bring lies in favour; [page 2] but a natural, though corrupt love of the lie itself. One of the later school of the Grecians examineth the matter, and is at a stand to think what should be in it, that men should love lies, where neither they make for pleasure, as with poets; nor for advantage, as with the merchant but for the lie's sake. But I cannot tell: this same truth is a naked and open daylight, that doth not shew the masques, and mummeries, and triumphs of the world half so stately and daintily as candlelights . . .

What Bacon calls Lies is Truth itself.

Page 3.
But howsoever these things are thus in men's depraved judgments and affections, yet truth, which only doth judge itself, teacheth that the inquiry of truth, which is the love-making, or wooing of it; the knowledge of truth, which is the presence of it; and the belief of truth, which is the enjoying of it, is the sovereign good of human nature. The first creature of God, in the works of the days, was the light of the sense; the last was the light of reason; and his sabbath work, ever since, is the illumination of his Spirit . . .

Pretence to Religion to destroy Religion.

Page 4.
To pass from theological and philosophical truth to the truth of civil business, it will be acknowledged; even by those that practise it not, that clear and round dealing is the honour of man's nature, and that mixture of falsehood is like allay in coin of gold and silver . . .

Christianity is Civil Business Only. There is & can Be No Other to Man: what Else Can Be? Civil is Christianity or Religion or whatever is Humane.

Page 5.
Surely the wickedness of falsehood and breach of faith cannot possibly be so highly expressed as in that it shall be the last peal to call the judgments of God upon the generations of men: it being foretold, that when "Christ cometh," he shall not "find faith upon earth".

Bacon put an End to Faith.

Page 5-6. Of Death.
You shall read in some of the friars books of mortification, that a man should think with himself what the pain is, if he have but his fingers end pressed, or tortured, and thereby imagine what the pains of death are when the whole body is corrupted and dissolved; when many times death passeth with less pain than the torture of a limb; for the most vital parts are not the quickest of sense: and by him that spake only as a philosopher and natural man, it was well said, "Pompa mortis magis terret, quam mors ipsa".

Bacon supposes all Men alike.

Page 6.
Revenge triumphs over death; love flights it; honour aspireth to it; grief flieth to it; fear pre-occupieth it; nay, we read, after Otho the emperor had slain himself, pity (which is the tenderest of affections) provoked many to die out of mere compassion to their sovereign, and as the truest sort of followers.

One Man's Revenge or Love is not the same as Another's. The tender Mercies of some Men are Cruel.[1]

Page 8. Of Unity in Religion.
Religion being the chief band of human society, it is a happy thing when itself is well contained within the true band of unity. The quarrels and divisions about religion were evils *unknown to the heathen.*

False, O Satan.

[1] cf. *Proverbs,* xii, 10.

The reason was, because the religion of the heathen consisted rather in rites and ceremonies, than in any constant belief: for you may imagine what kind of faith theirs was, when the chief doctors and fathers of their church were the *poets.*

Prophets.

Page 9.
The fruits of unity (next unto the well-pleasing of God, which is all in all) are two; the one towards those that are without the church; the other towards those that are within. For the former, it is certain, that heresies and schisms are of all others the greatest scandals; yea more more than corruption of manners: for as in the natural body a wound or solution of continuity is worse than a corrupt humour, so in the spiritual: . . .

False!

Page 9–10.
The doctor of the Gentiles (the propriety of whose vocation drew him to have a special care of those without) saith, "If an heathen come in, and hear you speak with several tongues, will he not say that you are mad?" and, certainly, it is little better: when atheists and profane persons do hear of so many discordant and contrary opinions in religion, it doth avert them from the church, and maketh them "to sit down in the chair of the scorners". It is but a light thing to be vouched in so serious a matter, but yet it expresseth well the deformity.

Trifling Nonsense!

Page 11–12.
Men ought to take heed of rending God's church by two kinds of controversies; the one is, when the matter of the point controverted is too small and light, not worth the heat and strife about it, kindled only by contradiction; for, as it is noted by one of the fathers, Christ's coat indeed had no seam, but the church's vesture was of divers colours; whereupon he saith, "in veste varietas sit, scissura non sit", they be two things, unity and uniformity: the other is when the matter of the point controverted is great, but it is driven to an over-great subtility and obscurity, so that it becometh a thing rather ingenious than substantial.

Lame Reasoning upon Premises. This Never can Happen.

Page 14.
It was great blasphemy when the devil said, "I will ascend and be like the Highest"; but it is greater blasphemy to personate God, and bring him in saying, "I will descend, and be like the prince of darkness."

Did not Jesus descend & become a Servant? The Prince of darkness is a Gentleman & not a Man: he is a Lord Chancellor.

Page 17. Of Revenge.
This is certain, that a man that studieth revenge keeps his own wounds green, which otherwise would heal and do well. Public revenges are for the most part fortunate.

A Lie.

Page 22. Of Simulation and Dissimulation.
In a few words, mysteries are due to secrecy. Besides (to say truth) *nakedness is uncomely,* as well in mind as in body.

This is Folly Itself.

Page 32. Of Envy.
A man that hath no virtue in himself ever envieth virtue in others: for men's minds will either feed upon their own good, or upon others evil; and who wanteth the one

will prey upon the other; and whoso is out of hope to attain to another's virtue, will seek to come at even hand by depressing another's fortune.

What do these Knaves mean by Virtue? Do they mean War & its horrors & its Heroic Villains?

Page 37.
Lastly, to conclude this part, as we said in the beginning that the act of envy had somewhat in it of witchcraft, so there is no other cure of envy but the cure of witchcraft; and that is, to remove the lot, (as they call it), and to lay it upon another; for which purpose, the wiser sort of great persons bring in ever upon the stage somebody upon whom to derive the envy that would come upon themselves.

Politic Foolery & most contemptible Villainy & Murder!

Now to speak of public envy: there is yet some good in public envy, whereas in private there is none; for public envy is as an ostracism, that eclipseth men when they grow too great.

Foolish & tells into the hands of a Tyrant.

Page 38.
This public envy seemeth to beat chiefly upon principal officers or ministers, rather than upon kings and estates themselves.

A Lie! Every Body hates a King. Bacon was afraid to say that the Envy was upon a King, but is This Envy or Indignation?

Page 44. Of Great Place.
But power to do good is the true and lawful end of aspiring; for good thoughts (though God accept them), yet towards men are little better than good dreams, except they be put in act.

Thought is Act. Christ's Acts were Nothing to Caesar's if this is not so.

Page 45.
In the discharge of thy place set before thee the best examples; for imitation is a globe of precepts; and after a time set before thee thine own example; and examine thyself strictly whether thou didst not best at first.

Here is nothing of Thy own Original Genius, but only Imitation: what Folly!

Page 48.
Be not too sensible or too remembering of thy place in conversation and private answers to suitors, but let it rather be said, "When he sits in place he is another man."

A Flogging Magistrate! I have seen many such fly-blows of Bacon.

Page 54. Of Goodness and Goodness of Nature.
And beware how in making the portrait thou breakest the pattern: for divinity maketh the love of ourselves the pattern; the love of our neighbours but the portraiture: "Sell all thou hast, and give it to the poor, and follow me:" but sell not all thou hast, except thou come and follow me; that is except thou have a vocation wherein thou mayest do as much good with little means as great.

Except is Christ. You Lie Except did anyone ever do this & not follow Christ who Does by Nature.

Page 55. [*related to page 56, Of a King*]

A representation of hinder parts, labelled : The devil's arse, *and depending from it a chain of excrement ending in :* A King.

Page 56. Of a King.
A king is a mortal god on earth, unto whom the living God hath lent his own name as a great honour.

O Contemptible & Abject Slave!

Page 58.
That king which is not feared is not loved; and he that is well seen in his craft must as well study to be feared as loved; yet not loved for fear, but feared for love.

Fear Cannot Love.

Page 60.
He then that honoureth him [the King] not is next an atheist, wanting the fear of God in his heart.

Blasphemy!

Page 60. Of Nobility.
We will speak of nobility first as a portion of an estate, then as a condition of particular persons.

Is Nobility a portion of a State i.e. Republic?

A monarchy, where there is no nobility at all, is ever a pure and absolute tyranny, as that of the Turks; for nobility attempers sovereignty, and draws the eyes of the people somewhat aside from the line royal: but for *democracies they need* it not; and they are *commonly more quiet, and less* subject to sedition, than where there are stirps of nobles.

Self Contradiction! Knave & Fool!

Page 62.
Those that are first raised to nobility, are commonly more virtuous, but less innocent than their descendants; for there is rarely any rising but by a commixture of good and evil parts.

Virtuous I supposed to be Innocents: was I Mistaken or is Bacon a Liar?

On the other side, nobility extinguisheth the passive envy from others towards them, because they are in possession of honour. Certainly, kings that have able men of their nobility shall find ease in employing them, and a better slide into their business; for people naturally bend to them as born in some sort to command.

Nonsense.

Page 63. Of Seditions and Troubles.

This Section contradicts the Preceding.

Shepherds of all people had need know the calendars of tempests in state, which are commonly greatest when things grow to equality.

What Shepherds does he mean? Such as Christ describes by Ravening Wolves?

Page 65.
Also, when discords, and quarrels, and factions are carried openly and audaciously it is a sign the reverence of government is lost.

When the Reverence of Government is Lost it is better than when it is found. Reverence is all For Reverence.

Page 66.
So when any of the four pillars of government are mainly shaken, or weakened, (which are religion, justice, counsel, and treasure,) men had need to pray for fair weather.

Four Pillars of different heights and Sizes.

Concerning the materials of sedition, it is a thing well to be considered. . . . The matters of sedition is of two kinds, much poverty and much discontentment.

These are one Kind Only.

Page 67.
As for discontentments, they are in the politic body like to humours in the natural, which are apt to gather a preternatural heat and to enflame; and let no prince measure the danger of them by this, whether they be just or unjust.

A Tyrant is the Worst disease & the Cause of all others.

. . . in great oppressions, the same things that provoke the patience, do withal mate the courage.

a lie!

Page 68-9.
The first remedy or prevention is to remove by all means possible that material cause of sedition whereof we speak, which is want and poverty in the estate; to which purpose serveth the opening and well balancing of trade; the cherishing of manufactures; the banishing of idleness; the repressing of waste and excess by sumptuary laws; the improvement and husbanding of the soil; the regulating of prices of things vendible; the moderating of taxes and tributes, and the like.

You cannot regulate the price of Necessaries without destruction. All False!

Page 69-70.
It is likewise to be remembered, that forasmuch as the increase of any estate must be upon the foreigner, (for whatsoever is somewhere gotten is somewhere lost,) there be but three things which one nation selleth unto another: the commodity as nature yieldeth it; the manufacture; and the vecture or carriage: so that if these two wheels go, wealth will flow as in a spring tide.

The Increase of a State as of a Man is from Internal Improvement or Intellectual Acquirement. Man is not Improved by the hurt of another. States are not Improved at the Expense of Foreigners.
Bacon has no notion of anything but Mammon.

Page 71.
The poets feign that the rest of the Gods would have bound Jupiter, which he hearing of by the counsel of Pallas, sent for Briareus with his hundred hands to come in to his aid: an emblem, no doubt, to shew how safe it is for monarchs to make sure of the good will of common people.

Good Advice for the Devil.

Page 71-72.
Certainly, the politic and artificial nourishing and entertaining of hopes, and carrying men from hopes to hopes is one of the best antidotes against the poison of discontentments.

Subterfuges!

Page 74.
Lastly, let princes against all events, not be without some great person, one or rather more, of military valour, near unto them, for the repression of seditions in their beginnings.

Contemptible Knave! Let the People look to this!

. . . but let such military persons be assured and well reputed of, rather than factious and popular.

Factious is Not Popular & never can be except Factious is Christianity.

Page 75. Of Atheism.
I had rather believe all the fables and the legend, and the Talmud, and the Alcoran than that this universal frame is without a *mind:* and, therefore, God never wrought miracle to convince atheism, because his ordinary works convince it.

The devil is the Mind of the Natural Frame.

It is true that a little philosophy inclineth man's mind to atheism; but depth in philosophy bringeth men's minds about to religion; for while the mind of man looketh upon second causes scattered, it may sometimes rest in them and go no farther.

There is no Such Thing as a Second Cause nor as a Natural Cause for any Thing in any Way.

Page 76.
He who says there are Second Causes has already denied a First. The Word Cause is a foolish Word.

Page 77.
The contemplative atheist is rare, a Diagoras, A Bion, a Lucian perhaps, and some others.

A Lie! Few believe it is a New Birth. Bacon was a Contemplative Atheist. Evidently an Epicurean. Lucian disbeliev'd Heathen Gods: he did not perhaps disbelieve for all that. Bacon did.

Page 77-78-79.
The causes of atheism are, divisions in religion, if they be many; . . . another is, scandal of priests . . .: a third is, a custom of profane scoffing in holy matters . . .; and, lastly, learned times, expecially with peace and prosperity; for troubles and *adversities* do more bow men's minds to religion.

a Lie!

They that deny a God destroy man's nobility; for certainly man is of kin to the beasts by his body; and, if he be not of kin to God by his spirit, he is a base and ignoble creature.

an artifice!

It destroys likewise magnanimity, and the raising of human nature; for take an example of a dog, and mark what a generosity and courage he will put on when he finds himself maintained by a man, who to him is instead of a God, or "melior natura"; which courage is manifestly such as that creature, without that confidence of a better nature than his own, could never attain;

Self contradiction!

therefore, as atheism is in all respects hateful, so in this, that it depriveth human nature of the means to exalt itself above human frailty.

An Atheist pretending to talk against Atheism!

Page 79. Of superstition.
It were better to have no opinion of God at all, than such an opinion as is unworthy of him.

Is this true? is it better?

Page 80.
as the contumely is greater *towards God, so the danger* is greater towards men. Atheism *leaves* a man to sense, to philosophy, to natural *piety,* to laws, to reputation; all which may *be guides* to an outward moral virtue, though religion were not;

Praise of Atheism!

but superstition dismounts all these, and erecteth an absolute monarchy in the minds of men: *therefore atheism* did *never perturb* states; for it makes men wary of themselves, as looking no farther, and we see the times inclined to atheism, (as the time of Augustus Caesar,) were civil times.

Atheism is thus the best of all. Bacon fools us.

The master of superstition is the people, and in all superstition wise men follow fools; and arguments are fitted to practise in a reversed order.

What must our Clergy be who Allow Bacon to be Either Wise or even of Common Capacity? I cannot.

Page 82.
There is a superstition in avoiding superstition, when men think to do best if they go farthest from the superstition formerly received; therefore care should be had that, (as it fareth in ill purgings,) the good be not taken away with the bad, which commonly is done when the *people* is the reformer.

Who is to be the Reformer? Bacon's Villain is a King, or Who?

Page 83. Of Travel.
The things to be seen and observed are the courts of princes, especially when they give audience to ambassadors; the courts of justice . . . the churches and monasteries . . . the walls and fortifications . . . and so the havens and harbours, antiquities and ruins, libraries, colleges, disputations, and lectures where any are; shipping and navies; houses and gardens of state and pleasure near great cities; armories, arsenals, magazines, exchanges, burses, warehouses, exercises of horsemanship, fencing, training of soldiers, and the like; comedies . . . treasures of jewels and robes; cabinets and rarieties.

The Things worthy to be seen are all the Trumpery he could rake together.
Nothing of Arts or Artists or Learned Men or of Agriculture or any Useful Thing. His Business & Bosom was to be Lord Chancellor.

Page 84.
As for triumphs, masks, feasts, weddings, funerals, capital executions, and such shews, men need not to be put in mind of them; yet are they not to be neglected.

Bacon supposes that the dragon Beast & Harlot are worthy of a Place in the New Jerusalem. Excellent Traveller, Go on & be damned!

If you will have a young man to put his travel into a little room, and in short time to gather much, this you must do . . . let him not stay long in one city or town, more or less as the place deserveth, but not long; nay, when he stayeth in one city or town, let him change his lodging from one end and part of the town to another, which is a great adamant of acquaintance;

Harum Scarum: who can do this?

let him sequester himself from the company of his countrymen and diet in such places where there is good company of the nation where he travelleth; let him upon his removes from one place to another procure recommendation to some person of *quality* residing in the place whither he removeth . . .

The Contrary is the best Advice.

Page 85.
As for the acquaintance which is to be sought in travel, that which is most of all profitable is acquaintance with the secretaries and employed men of ambassadors.

Acquaintance with Knaves.

Page 86. Of Empire.
It is a miserable state of mind to have few things to desire, and many things to fear.

He who has few Things to desire cannot have many to fear.

Page 87.
. . . the mind of man is more cheered and refreshed by profiting in small things, than by standing at a stay in great.

A lie!

Page 98. Of Counsel.
For weakening of authority the fable sheweth the remedy: nay, the majesty of kings is rather exalted than diminished when they are in the chair of council; neither was there ever prince bereaved of his dependances by his council, except where there hath been either an over-greatness in one counsellor, or an over-strict combination in divers, which are things soon found and holpen.

Did he mean to Ridicule a King & his Council?

Page 101.
In choice of committees for ripening business for the council, it is better to choose indifferent persons, than to make an indifferency by putting in those that are strong on both sides.

better choose Fools at once!

Page 104. Of Cunning.
There be that can pack the cards, and yet cannot play well; so there are some that are good in canvasses and factions, that are otherwise weak men.

Nonsense!

Again, it is one thing to understand persons, and another thing to understand matters; for many are perfect in men's humours that are not greatly capable of the real part of business, which is the constitution of one that hath studied men more than books.

Nonsense!

Such men are fitter for practice than for counsel, and they are good but in their own ally.

How absurd!

Page 105.
If a man would cross a business that he doubts some other would handsomely and effectually move, let him pretend to wish it well, and move it himself in such sort as may foil it.

None but a Fool can act so.

Page 106–7.
I knew one that, when he wrote a letter, he would put that which was most material in the post-script, as if it had been a bye matter.
I knew another that, when he came to have speech, he would pass over that that he intended most; and go forth, and come back again, and speak of it as of a thing that he had almost forgot.

What Fools!

Page 107–108.
It is a point of cunning to let fall those words in a man's own name which he would have another man learn and use, and thereupon take advantage. I knew two that were competitors for the secretary's place in queen Elizabeth's time, . . . and the one of them said, that to be a secretary in the declination of a monarchy was a ticklish thing, and that he did not affect it: the other straight caught up those words, and discoursed with divers of his friends, that he had no reason to desire to be secretary in the declination of a monarchy. The first man took hold of it, and found means it was told the queen; who hearing of a declination of a monarchy took it so ill, as she would never after hear of the other's suit.

This is too stupid to have been True.

Page 113. Of Innovations.
As the births of living creatures at first are ill shapen, so are all innovations, which are the births of time.

What a Cursed Fool is this, Ill Shapen! are Infants or small Plants ill shapen because they are not yet come to their maturity? What a contemptible Fool is This Bacon!

Page 123–124. Of Friendship.
L. Sylla, when he commanded Rome, raised Pompey to that height, that Pompey vaunted himself for Sylla's over-match; . . . With Julius Caesar Decimus Brutus had obtained that interest as he set him down in his testament for heir in remainder after his nephew; . . . Augustus raised Agrippa, (though of mean birth,) to that height, as, when he consulted Mecænas about the marriage of his daughter Julia, Mecænas took the liberty to tell him, that he must either marry his daughter to Agrippa, or take away his life.

The Friendship of these Roman Villains is a strange Example to alledge for our imitation & approval.

Page 133. Of Expense.
Certainly, if a man will keep but of even hand, his ordinary expenses ought to be but to the half of his receipts; and if he think to wax rich, but to the third part.

If this is advice to the Poor, it is mocking them. If to the Rich, it is worse still—it is The Miser. If to the Middle Class, it is the direct Contrary to Christ's advice.

Page 134.
He that can look into his estate but seldom, it behoveth him to turn all to *certainties.*

Nonsense!

Page 135. Of the True Greatness of Kingdoms and Estates.
The speech of Themistocles the Athenian, which was haughty and arrogant in taking so much to himself, had been a grave and wise observation and censure, applied at large to others. Desired at a feast to touch a lute, he said, "he could not fiddle, but yet he could make a small town a great city". These words, (holpen with a little metaphor,) may express two differing abilities in those that deal in business of estate.

a Lord Chancellor's opinions as different from Christ as those of Caiphas or Pilate or Herod: what such Men call Great is indeed detestable.

Page 136.
... let us speak of the work; that is, the true greatness of kingdoms and estates; and the means thereof. An argument fit for great and mighty *princes* to have in their hand; to the end, that neither by over-measuring their forces they lose themselves in vain enterprises ...

Princes' Powers! Powers of darkness!

Page 137.
The Kingdom of heaven is compared, not to any great Kernal or nut but, to a grain of mustard seed; which is one of the least grains, but hath in it a property and spirit hastily to get up and spread.

The Kingdom of Heaven is the direct Negation of Earthly domination.

Page 137-138.
Walled towns, stored arsenals and armories, goodly races of horse, chariots of war, elephants, ordnance, artillery, and the like; all this is but a sheep in lion's skin, except the breed and disposition of the people be stout and warlike. Nay, number (itself) in armies importeth not much, where the people is of weak courage. ... The army of the Persians, in the plains of Arbela was such a vast sea of people as it did somewhat astonish the commanders in Alexander's army, who came to him therefore, and wished him to set upon them by night; but he answered, he would not pilfer the victory; and the defeat was easy.

Bacon knows the Wisdom of War—if it is Wisdom.

Page 142.
Never any state was, in this point, so open to receive strangers into their body as were the Romans; therefore it sorted with them accordingly, for they grew to the *greatest monarchy.*

Is this Great? Is this Christian? No!

Page 143-144.
It is certain, that sedentary and within-door arts, and delicate manufactures, (that require rather the finger than the arm,) have in their nature a contrariety to a military disposition; ... therefore it was great advantage in the ancient states of Sparta, Athens, Rome, and others that they had the use of slaves, which commonly did rid those manufactures; but that is abolished, in greatest part, by the christian law. That which cometh nearest to it is, to leave those arts chiefly to strangers ... and to contain the principal bulk of the vulgar natives within those three kinds, tillers of the ground, free servants, and handicraftmen of strong and manly arts; as smiths, masons, carpenters, &c. not reckoning professed soldiers.

Bacon calls Intellectual Arts Unmanly. Poetry, Painting, Music are in his opinion Useless & so they are for Kings & Wars & shall in the End Annihilate them.

Page 147.
No body can be healthful without exercise, neither natural body nor politic: and, certainly, to a kingdom or estate a just and honourable war is the true exercise.

Is not this the Greatest Folly?

Page 149.
There be now, for martial encouragement, some degrees and orders of chivalry, which, nevertheless, are conferred promiscuously upon soldiers and no soldiers, and some remembrance perhaps upon the escutcheon . . .

What can be worse than this or more foolish?

Page 151. Of Regimen of Health.
. . . strength of nature in youth passeth over many excesses which are owing a man till his age.

Excess in Youth is Necessary to Life.

Beware of sudden change in any great point of diet, and if necessity enforce it, fit the rest to it;

Nonsense!

for it is a secret both in nature and state, that it is safer to change many things than one.

False!

Page 152.
If you fly physic in health altogether, it will be too strange for your body when you shall need it.

Very Pernicious Advice . . . The work of a Fool to use Physic but for necessity.

Page 153.
In sickness, respect health principally; and in health, action: for those that put their bodies to endure in health, may in most sicknesses which are not very sharp, be cured only with diet and tendering.

Those that put their Bodies To endure are Fools.

Celsus could never have spoken it as a physician, had he not been a wise man withal, when he giveth it for one of the great precepts of health and lasting, that a man do vary and interchange contraries; but with an inclination to the more benign extreme: use fasting and full eating, but rather full eating; watching and sleep, but rather sleep; sitting and exercise, but rather exercise, and the like: so shall nature be cherished, and yet taught masteries.

Celsus was a bad adviser.
Nature taught to Ostentation.

Page 154. Of Suspicion.
Suspicions amongst thoughts are like bats amongst birds, they ever fly by twilight; certainly they are to be repressed, or, at the least, well guarded.

What is Suspition in one Man is Caution in Another & Truth or Discernment in Another & in Some it is Folly.

Page 156. Of Discourse.
Some in their discourse desire rather commendation of wit, in being able to hold all argument, than of judgment, in discerning what is true; as if it were a praise to know what might be said, and not what should be thought.

Surely the Man who wrote this never talked to any but Coxcombs.

Page 158.
Discretion of speech is more than eloquence; and to speak agreeably to him with whom we deal, is more than to speak in good words, or in good order.

Bacon hated Talents of all Kinds. Eloquence is discretion of Speech.

Page 169. Of Riches.
Be not penny-wise; riches have wings, and sometimes they fly away of themselves, sometimes they must be set flying to bring in more.

Bacon was always a poor Devil if History says true: how should one so foolish know about Riches Except Pretence to be Rich, if that is it.

Page 182. Of Nature in Men.
Neither is the ancient rule amiss, to bend nature as a wand to a contrary extreme, whereby to set it right; understanding it where the contrary extreme is no vice.

Very Foolish.

Page 187. Of Fortune.
It cannot be denied but outward accidents conduce much to fortune; favour, opportunity, death of others, occasion fitting virtue; but chiefly, the mould of a man's fortune is in his own hands.

What is Fortune but an outward Accident for a few years, sixty at most, & then gone.

Page 190. Of Usury.

Bacon was a Usurer.

Page 191.
The discommodities of usury are, first, that it makes fewer merchants; for were it not for this lazy trade of usury, money would not lie still, but would in great part be employed upon merchandizing.

A Lie: it makes Merchants & nothing Else.

Page 192.
On the other side, the commodities of usury are first, that howsoever usury in some respect hindereth merchandizing, yet in some other it advanceth it.

Commodities of Usury? can it Be?

Page 193.
I remember a cruel monied man in the country, that would say, "The devil take this usury, it keeps us from forfeitures of mortgages and bonds".

It is not True what a Cruel Man says.

To speak now of the reformation and reglement of usury; how the discommodities of it may be best avoided, and the commodities retained.

Bacon is in his Element on Usury; it is himself & his Philosophy.

Page 197. Of Youth and Age.
The errors of young men are the ruin of business; but the errors of aged men amount but to this, that more might have been done, or sooner.

Bacon's Business is not Intellect or Art.

Page 198.
. . . and age doth profit rather in the powers of understanding, than in the virtues of the will and affections.

a Lie!

Page 199.
There be some have an over-early ripeness in their years, which fadeth betimes: these are, first, such as have brittle wits, the edge whereof is soon turned; such as was Hermogenes the rhetorician, whose books are exceeding subtile, who afterwards waxed stupid.

Such was Bacon: Stupid Indeed!

Page 202. Of Deformity.
Certainly there is a consent between the body and the mind, and where nature erreth in the one, she ventureth in the other.

False! Contemptible!

Whosoever hath any thing fixed in his person that doth induce contempt, hath also a perpetual spur in himself to rescue and deliver himself from scorn; therefore all deformed persons are extreme bold.

Is not this Very Very Contemptible? Contempt is the Element of the Contemptible.

Page 203.
Kings in ancient times (and at this present in some countries,) were wont to put great trust in eunuchs, because they that are envious towards all are more obnoxious and officious towards one.

because Kings do it is it Wisdom?

Page 206. Of Building.
First, therefore, I say you cannot have a perfect *palace,* except you have two several sides; a side for the banquet, as is spoken of in the book of Esther, and a side for the household.

What Trifling Nonsense & Self Conceit!

Page 235. Of Faction.
The even carriage between two factions proceedeth not always of moderation, but of a trueness to a man's self, with end to make use of both. Certainly, in Italy they hold it a little suspect in popes, when they have often in their mouth "*Padre commune*"; and take it to be a sign of one that meaneth to refer all to the greatness of his own house.

None but God is This.

Page 235-236.
Kings had need beware how they side themselves . . . The motions of factions under Kings, ought to be like the motions, (as the astronomers speak,) of the inferior orbs; which may have their proper motions, but yet still are quietly carried by the higher motion of "primum mobile".

King James was Bacon's Primum Mobile.

Page 236. Of Ceremonies and Respects.
. . . for the proverb is true, "That light gains make heavy purses"; for light gains come thick, whereas great come but now and then: so it is true, that *small matters* win great commendation, because they are continually in use and in note.

Small matters—What are They? Caesar seems to me a Very Small Matter & so he seem'd to Jesus: is the devil Great? Consider.

Page 239. Of Praise.
Praise is the reflection of virtue; but it is as the glass or body which giveth the reflection: if it be from the *common people*, it is commonly false and nought, and rather followeth vain persons, than virtuous.

Villain! did Christ Seek the Praise of the Rulers?

ANNOTATIONS TO BOYD'S TRANSLATION OF DANTE'S INFERNO

Dublin 1785

Written about 1800 (?)

In "A Comparative View of the Inferno, With some other Poems relative to the Original Principles of Human Nature."

Page 35.
But the most daring flights of fancy, the most accurate delineations of character, and the most artful conduct of fable, are *not, even* when combined together, sufficient of themselves to make a poem interesting. [*The italicized words have been strongly deleted by Blake*].

Pages 35-36.
The discord of Achilles and Agamemnon may produce the most tragical consequences; but if we, who are cool and impartial in the affair . . . cannot enter warmly into the views of either party, the story, though adorned with all the genius of an Homer, will be read by us with some degree of nonchalance. The superstitions that led the Crusaders to rescue the Holy Land from the Infidels, instead of interesting us, appears frigid, if not ridiculous. We cannot be much concerned for the fate of such a crew of fanatics, notwithstanding the magic numbers of a Tasso . . . we cannot sympathise with Achilles for the loss of his Mistress, when we feel that he gained her by the massacre of her family.

nobody considers these things when they read Homer or Shakespear or Dante.

Page 37.
When a man, where no interest is concerned, no provocation given, lays a whole nation in blood merely for his glory; we, to whom his glory is indifferent, cannot enter into his resentment.

false: All poetry gives the lie to this.

Pages 37-38.
Such may be good poetical characters, of that mixt kind that Aristotle admits; but the most beautiful mixture of light and shade has no attraction unless it warms *or freezes* the heart. [*The words italicized inserted by Blake*] It must have something that engages the sympathy, something that appeals to the *moral sense* [*These two words deleted by Blake and altered to :* passions & senses]; for nothing can thoroughly captivate the fancy, however artfully delineated, that does not awake the sympathy and interest the passions *that enlist on the side of Virtue* [*words deleted*] and appeal to our native notions of right and wrong.

Pages 38-39.
It is this that sets the Odyssey, in point of sentiment, so far above the Iliad. We feel the injuries of Ulysses; . . . we seem to feel the generous indignation of the young Telemachus, and we tremble at the dangers of the fair Penelope . . . we can go along with the resentment of Ulysses, because it is just, but our feelings must tell us that Achilles carries his resentment to a savage length, a length where we cannot follow him.

If Homer's merit was only in these Historical combinations & Moral sentiments he would be no better than Clarissa.

Pages 39–40.
Iliacos extra muros peccatur; et intra. It is a contest between barbarians, equally guilty of injustice, rapine, and bloodshed; and we are not sorry to see the vengeance of Heaven equally inflicted on both parties.

Homer meant this.

Aeneas indeed is a more amiable personage than Achilles; he seems meant for a perfect character. But compare his conduct with respect to Dido with the self-denial of Dryden's Cleomenes, or with the conduct of Titus in the Berenice of Racine, we will then see what is meant by making a character interesting.

Every body naturally hates a perfect character because they are all greater Villains than the imperfect, as Eneas is here shewn a worse man than Achilles in leaving Dido.

Pages 45–46.
Antecedent to and independent of all laws, a man may learn to argue on the nature of moral obligation, and the duty of universal benevolence, from Cumberland, Wollaston, Shaftesbury, Hutcheson; but would he feel what vice is in itself . . . let him enter into the passions of Lear, when he feels the ingratitude of his children; of Hamlet, when he learns the story of his father's murder; . . . and he will know the difference of right and wrong much more clearly than from all the moralists that ever wrote.

the grandest Poetry is Immoral, the Grandest characters Wicked, Very Satan—Capanius, Othello a murderer, Prometheus, Jupiter, Jehovah, Jesus a wine bibber. Cunning & Morality are not Poetry but Philosophy; the Poet is Independent & Wicked; the Philosopher is Dependent & Good.

Poetry is to excuse Vice & shew its reason & necessary purgation.

Page 49.
The industrious knave cultivates the soil; the indolent good man leaves it uncultivated. Who ought to reap the harvest? . . . The natural course of things decides in favour of the villain; the natural sentiments of men in favour of the man of virtue.

false.

Pages 56–57.
As to those who think the notion of a future Life arose from the descriptions and inventions of the Poets, they may just as well suppose that eating and drinking had the same original . . . The Poets indeed altered the genuine sentiments of nature, and tinged the Light of Reason by introducing the wild conceits of Fancy . . . But still the root was natural, though the fruit was wild. All that *nature teaches* [*underlined by Blake*] is, that there is a future life, distinguished into different states of happiness and misery.

False.

Nature Teaches nothing of Spiritual Life but only of Natural Life.

Page 74.
[On a blank page at the end of "A Comparative View"]

Every Sentiment & Opinion as well as Every Principle in Dante is in these Preliminary Essays Controverted & proved Foolish by his Translator, If I have any Judgment in Such Things as Sentiments Opinions & Principles.

In "Historical Essay of the State of Affairs in the thirteenth and fourteenth centuries: With Respect to the History of Florence."

Page 118.
[Concerning the quarrel between Guilielmo and Bertaccio, the heads of two branches of the family of Cancelieri]. Dante was at this time Prior of Florence, and it was he who gave the advice, *ruinous to himself,* and *pernicious to his native country,* of calling in the heads of the two factions to Florence. [*Italicized words underlined by Blake*]

Dante was a Fool or his Translator was Not: That is, Dante was Hired or Tr. was Not. It appears to Me that Men are hired to Run down Men of Genius under the Mask of Translators, but Dante gives too much Caesar: he is not a Republican.
[*at the top of the page*] Dante was an Emperor's, a Caesar's Man; Luther also left the Priest & join'd the Soldier.

Pages 129–130.
The fervours of religion have often actuated the passions to deeds of the wildest fanaticism. The booted Apostles of Germany, and the Crusards of Florence, carried their zeal to a very guilty degree. But the passion for any thing laudable will hardly carry men to a proper pitch, unless it be so strong as sometimes to push them beyond the golden mean.

How very Foolish all this Is.

Page 131.
Such were the effects of intolerance even in the extreme. In a more moderate degree, every well-regulated government, both ancient and modern, were *so far intolerant,* as not to admit the pollutions of every superstition and *every pernicious opinion.* It was from a regard to the morals of the people, that the Roman Magistrates expelled the Priests of Bacchus, in the first and most virtuous ages of the republic. It was on this principle that the *Persians* destroyed the *temples of Greece wherever they came.* [*Italicized words underlined by Blake*]

If Well regulated Governments act so who can tell so well as the hireling Writer whose praise is contrary to what he Knows to be true. Persians destroy the Temples & are praised for it.

Pages 133–134.
The Athenians and Romans kept a watchful eye, not only over the grosser superstitions, but over impiety . . . Polybius plainly attributes the fall of freedom in Greece to the prevalence of atheism . . . It was not till the republic was verging to its fall, that Caesar dared in open senate to laugh at the speculative opinion of a future state. These were the times of universal toleration, when every pollution, from every clime, flowed to Rome, whence they had carefully been kept out before.

What is Liberty without Universal Toleration?

Pages 135-136.

I leave it to these who are best acquainted with the spirit of antiquity, to determine whether a species of religion . . . had or had not a very principal share in raising those celebrated nations to the summit of their glory: their decline and fall, at least, may be fairly attributed to irreligion, and to the want of some general standard of morality, whose authority they all allowed and to which they all appealed. The want of this pole-star left them adrift in the boundless ocean of conjecture; the disputes of their philosophers were endless, and their opinions of the grounds of morality were as different as their conditions, their tastes and their pursuits.

Yet simple country Hinds are Moral Enthusiasts, Indignant against Knavery, without a Moral criterion other than Native Honesty untaught, while other country Hinds are as indignant against honesty & Enthusiasts for Cunning & Artifice.

Page 148.

. . . but there are certain *bounds* even to *liberty* [*Italicized words underlined by Blake*]

If it is thus, the extreme of black is white & of sweet sower & of good Evil & of Nothing Something.

Lines for the illustrations to Gray's Poems

Written in 1797

Around the Springs of Gray my wild root weaves.
Traveller repose & Dream among my leaves.
Will Blake

To Mrs Ann Flaxman

A little Flower grew in a lonely Vale.
Its form was lovely but its colours pale.
One standing in the Porches of the Sun,
When his Meridian Glories were begun,
Leap'd from the steps of fire & on the grass
Alighted where this little flower was.
With hands divine he mov'd the gentle Sod
And took the Flower up in its native Clod;
Then planting it upon a Mountain's brow—
" 'Tis your own fault if you don't flourish now."
William Blake

POEMS AND FRAGMENTS FROM THE NOTE-BOOK

Written about 1800–1803

Pp. 2–3.

I

My Spectre around me night & day
Like a Wild beast guards my way.
My Emanation far within
Weeps incessantly for my Sin.

["(Her *del.*) Thy weeping (she *del.*) thou shall ne'er give o'er:
"I sin against (her *del.*) thee more & more,
"And never will from sin be free
"Till she forgives & comes to me" *del.*]

[(4 *del.*) 5
"Thou hast parted from my side:
"Once thou wast a virgin bride.
"Never shalt thou a (lover *del.*) true love find:
"My Spectre follows thee Behind." *del.*]

[2
A deep winter (night *del.*) dark & cold
(In a dark cold winter night
Within my (love's *del.*) Heart)
Within my heart thou didst unfold
A Fathomless & boundless deep;
There we wander, there we weep. *del.*]

[(3 *del.*) 4
1 When my Love did first begin,
2 Thou didst call that Love a Sin:
3 Secret trembling night & day
4 Driving all my Loves away. *del.*]

2

A Fathomless & boundless deep,
There we wander, there we weep;
On the hungry craving wind
My Spectre follows thee behind.

[6 *del.*] 3
He scents thy footsteps in the snow,
Wheresoever thou dost go
Thro' the wintry hail & rain.
When wilt thou return again?

[6 *del.*] 4
[Didst *del.*] Dost thou not in Pride & scorn
Fill with tempests all my morn,
And with jealousies & fears
Fill my pleasant nights with tears?

[7 *del.*] [4 *del.*] 5
Seven of my sweet loves thy knife
Has bereaved of their life.
Their marble tombs I built with tears
And with cold & shuddering fears.

[8 *del.*] [5 *del.*] 6
Seven more loves weep night & day
Round the tombs where my loves lay,
And seven more loves attend each night
Around my couch with torches bright.

[6 *del.*] 7
And seven more Loves in my bed
Crown with wine my mournful head,
Pitying & forgiving all
Thy transgressions, great & small.

[10 *del.*] [7 *del.*] 8
When wilt thou return & view
My loves, & them to life renew?
When wilt thou return & live?
When wilt thou pity [& *del.*] as I forgive?

9
"Never, Never I return:
"Still for Victory I burn.
"Living, thee alone I'll have
"And when dead I'll be thy Grave.

10
"Thro' the Heaven & Earth & Hell
"Thou shalt never never quell:
"I will fly & thou pursue,
"Night & Morn the flight renew."

11

Till [thou *del.*] I turn from Female Love,
And [dig *del.*] root up the Infernal Grove,
[Thou shalt *del.*] I shall never worthy be
To Step into Eternity.

12

And [I *del.*] to end thy cruel mocks,
Annihilate thee on the rocks,
And another form create
To be subservient to my Fate.

13

Let us agree to give up Love,
And root up the infernal grove;
Then shall we return & see
The worlds of happy Eternity.

14

& Throughout all Eternity
I forgive you, you forgive me.
As our dear Redeemer said:
"This the Wine & this the Bread."

[*Additional stanzas*]

1

O'er [thy *del.*] my Sins Thou sit & moan:
Hast thou no sins of thy own?
O'er [thy *del.*] my Sins thou sit & weep,
And lull [my *del.*] thy own Sins fast asleep.

2

What Transgressions I commit
Are for thy Transgressions fit.
They thy Harlots, thou their Slave,
And my Bed becomes their Grave.

Poor pale pitiable form
That I follow in a Storm,
Iron tears & groans of lead
Bind around my aking head.

And let us go to the [*word illegible*] downs
With many pleasing wiles
The Woman that does not love your Frowns
Will never endure your smiles.

P. 4.

2

When a Man has Married a Wife
he finds out whether
Her Knees & elbows are only
glued together

P. 6.

3

On the Virginity of the Virgin
Mary & Johanna Southcott

Whate'er is done to her she cannot know,
And if you'll ask her she will [tell you *del.*] swear it so.
Whether 'tis good or evil none's to blame:
No one can take the pride, no one the shame.

P. 7.

4

Mock on, Mock on Voltaire, Rousseau:
Mock on, Mock on: 'tis all in vain!
You throw the sand against the wind,
And the wind blows it back again.

And every sand becomes a Gem
Reflected in the beams divine;
Blown back they blind the mocking Eye,
But still in Israel's paths they shine.

The Atoms of Democritus
And Newton's Particles of light
Are sands upon the Red sea shore,
Where Israel's tents do shine so bright.

P. 12.

5

1 I saw a Monk of [Constantine *del.*] Charlemaine
Arise before my sight:
I talk'd to the Grey Monk where he stood
In beams of infernal light.

2 Gibbon arose with a lash of steel,
And Voltaire with a wracking wheel.
[Charlemaine & his barons bold *del.*]
The Schools in Clouds of Learning roll'd
Arose with War in iron & gold.

3 "[Seditious *del.*] Thou Lazy Monk," [said Charlemaine *del.*]
they sound afar,
["The Glory of War thou condemn'st in vain *del.*]
"In vain condemning Glorious War,
"And in thy Cell thou shall ever dwell.
"Rise, War, & bind him in his Cell!"

4 The blood red ran from the Grey monk's side,
His hands & feet were wounded wide,
His body bent, his arms & knees
Like to the roots of ancient trees.

"I die, I die," the Mother said,
"My Children will die for lack of bread.
"What more has the merciless tyrant said?"
The Monk sat down on her stony bed.

His Eye was dry, no tear could flow,
A hollow groan first spoke his woe.
[From his dry tongue these accents flow *del.*]
He trembl'd & shudder'd upon the bed:
At length with a feeble cry he said:

"When God commanded this hand to write
"In the studious hours of deep midnight,
"He told me that All I wrote should prove
"The bane of all that on Earth I love.

"My brother starv'd between two walls;
"His children's cry my soul appalls.
"[But *del.*] I mock'd at the wrack & griding chain:
"My bent body mocks at their torturing pain.

"Thy father drew his sword in the north;
"With his thousands strong he is marched forth;
"Thy brother has armed himself in steel
"To revenge the wrongs thy Children feel.

"But vain the sword & vain the bow,
"They never can work war's overthrow.
"The Hermit's prayer & the widow's tear
"Alone can free the world from fear.

"The hand of vengeance sought the bed
"To which the purple tyrant fled.
"The iron hand crush'd the tyrant's head
"[And usurp'd the tyrant's throne & bed *del.*]
"And became a tyrant in his stead.

"Untill the Tyrant himself relent,
"The Tyrant who first the black bow bent,
"Slaughter shall heap the bloody plain;
"Resistance & war is the Tyrant's gain.

"But The Tear of Love & forgiveness sweet
"And submission to death beneath his feet—
"The Tear shall melt the sword of steel,
"And every wound it has made shall heal.

"For the tear is an intellectual thing,
"And a sigh is the Sword of an Angel King,
"And the bitter groan [for another's *del.*] of the Martyr's woe
"Is an arrow from the Almightie's bow."

[*Additional stanzas*]

5 When Satan first the black bow bent
And the Moral Law from the Gospel rent,
He forg'd the Law into a Sword
And spill'd the blood of Mercy's Lord.

6 [O, Charlemaine! O, Charlemaine! *del.*]
Titus! Constantine! Charlemaine!
O Voltaire! Rousseau! Gibbon! vain
Your [mocks & scorn *del.*] Grecian mocks & Roman sword
Against this image of his Lord.

A tear is an &c.

Gibbon plied his lash of steel:
Voltaire turn'd his wracking wheel:
Charlemaine & his barons bold
Stood by & mocked in iron & gold.

The Wheel of Voltaire whirl'd on high,
Gibbon aloud his lash does ply,
Charlemaine & his clouds of War
Muster around the Polar Star.

A Grecian Scoff is a wracking wheel.
The Roman pride is a sword of steel.
[Vict *del.*] Glory & Victory a [*word del.*] phallic Whip

[*For fair copy of nine stanzas as "The Grey Monk" see p.* 430 *and of seven others see p.* 683.]

P. 12.

6

Morning

To find the Western path
Right thro' the Gates of Wrath
I urge my way;
Sweet Mercy leads me on:
With soft repentant moan
I see the break of day.

The war of swords & spears
Melted by dewy tears
Exhales on high;
The Sun is freed from fears
And with soft grateful tears
Ascends the sky.

P. 12.

7

Terror in the house does roar,
But Pity stands before the door.

P. 12.

8

[4] [This world *del.*] Each Man is in [the *del.*] his Spectre's power
[3] Untill the arrival of that hour,
[1] [Untill *del.*] When [the *del.*] his Humanity awake
[2] And cast [the *del.*] his own Spectre into the Lake.

And there to Eternity aspire
The selfhood in a flame of fire
Till then the Lamb of God . . .

P. 14.

9

Beneath the white thorn, lovely May,
[Three Virgins at the Break of day,
"Whither, Young Man, whither away? *del.*]
"Alas for wo! alas for wo! alas for wo!"
They cry & tears for ever flow.
3 The one was cloth'd in flames of fire,
4 The other cloth'd in [sweet desire *del.*] Iron wire,

5 The other cloth'd in [sighs *del.*] & tears & sighs,
6 Dazzling bright before my Eyes.
1 They bore a Net of Golden twine
2 To hang upon the branches fine.
7 [Pitying, I wept to see the woe
8 That Love & Beauty undergo—
9 To be consum'd in burning fires
And in Ungratified desires. *del.*]
And in tears cloth'd night & day
Melted all my soul away.
When they saw my tears, a smile
That did heaven itself beguile,
Bore the Golden net aloft
As by downy pinions soft
O'er the morning of my day.
Underneath the net I stray,
Now intreating flaming fire,
Now intreating [sweet desire *del.*] iron wire,
Now intreating tears & sighs.
[When *del.*] O when will the Morning rise?

[*opening passage rewritten and del.*]

Beneath the white thorn, lovely may,
Three Virgins at the break of day,
The one was cloth'd in flames of fire,
The other cloth'd in [sweet desire *del.*] iron wire,
The other cloth'd in tears & sighs,
Dazzling bright before my eyes.

[*additional passage del.*]

Wings they had [& when they chose *del.*] that soft inclose
Round their body when they chose;
They would let them down at will,
Or make translucent . . .

[*For fair copy as "The Golden Net" see p.* 424]

P. 14.

10

The Birds

He. Where thou dwellest, in what Grove
Tell me, Fair one, tell me, love;
Where thou thy charming Nest dost build,
O thou pride of every field!

She. Yonder stands a lonely tree,
There I live & mourn for thee.
Morning drinks my silent tear,
And evening winds my sorrows bear.

He. O thou Summer's harmony,
I have liv'd & mourn'd for thee.
Each day I mourn along the wood,
And night hath heard my sorrows loud.

She. Dost thou truly long for me?
And am I thus sweet to thee?
Sorrow now is at an End,
O my Lover & my Friend!

He. Come, on wings of joy we'll fly
To where my Bower hangs on high!
Come, & make thy calm retreat
Among green leaves & blossoms sweet!

[END OF NOTE-BOOK 1800-1803]

POEMS FROM THE PICKERING MANUSCRIPT

Fair copies made about 1803

The Smile

There is a Smile of Love,
And there is a Smile of Deceit,
And there is a Smile of Smiles
In which these two Smiles meet.

And there is a Frown of Hate,
And there is a Frown of disdain,
And there is a Frown of Frowns
Which you strive to forget in vain,

For it sticks in the Heart's deep Core
And it sticks in the deep Back bone;
And no Smile that ever was smil'd,
But only one Smile alone,

That betwixt the Cradle & Grave
It only once Smil'd can be;
But, when it once is Smil'd,
There's an end to all Misery.

The Golden Net

Three Virgins at the break of day:
"Whither, young Man, whither away?
"Alas for woe! alas for woe!"
They cry, & tears for ever flow.
The one was Cloth'd in flames of fire,
The other Cloth'd in iron wire,
The other Cloth'd in tears & sighs
Dazling bright before my Eyes.
They bore a Net of Golden twine
To hang upon the Branches fine.
Pitying I wept to see the woe
That Love & Beauty undergo,
To be consum'd in burning Fires
And in ungratified desires,
And in tears cloth'd Night & day
Melted all my Soul away.
When they saw my Tears, a Smile
That did Heaven itself beguile,
Bore the Golden Net aloft
As on downy Pinions soft
Over the Morning of my day.
Underneath the Net I stray,
Now intreating Burning Fire,
Now intreating Iron Wire,
Now intreating Tears & Sighs.
O when will the morning rise?

The Mental Traveller

I travel'd thro' a Land of Men,
A Land of Men & Women too,
And heard & saw such dreadful things
As cold Earth wanderers never knew.

For there the Babe is born in joy
That was begotten in dire woe;
Just as we Reap in joy the fruit
Which we in bitter tears did sow.

And if the Babe is born a Boy
He's given to a Woman Old,
Who nails him down upon a rock,
Catches his shrieks in cups of gold.

She binds iron thorns around his head,
She pierces both his hands & feet,
She cuts his heart out at his side
To make it feel both cold & heat.

Her fingers number every Nerve,
Just as a Miser counts his gold;
She lives upon his shrieks & cries,
And she grows young as he grows old.

Till he becomes a bleeding youth,
And she becomes a Virgin bright;
Then he rends up his Manacles
And binds her down for his delight.

He plants himself in all her Nerves,
Just as a Husbandman his mould;
And she becomes his dwelling place
And Garden fruitful seventy fold.

An aged Shadow, soon he fades,
Wand'ring round an Earthly Cot,
Full filled all with gems & gold
Which he by industry had got.

And these are the gems of the Human Soul,
The rubies & pearls of a lovesick eye,
The countless gold of the akeing heart,
The martyr's groan & the lover's sigh.

They are his meat, they are his drink;
He feeds the Beggar & the Poor
And the wayfaring Traveller:
For ever open is his door.

His grief is their eternal joy;
They make the roofs & walls to ring;
Till from the fire on the hearth
A little Female Babe does spring.

And she is all of solid fire
And gems & gold, that none his hand
Dares stretch to touch her Baby form,
Or wrap her in his swaddling-band.

But She comes to the Man she loves,
If young or old, or rich or poor;
They soon drive out the aged Host,
A Beggar at another's door.

He wanders weeping far away,
Untill some other take him in;
Oft blind & age-bent, sore distrest,
Untill he can a Maiden win.

And to allay his freezing Age
The Poor Man takes her in his arms;
The Cottage fades before his sight,
The Garden & its lovely Charms.

The Guests are scatter'd thro' the land,
For the Eye altering alters all;
The Senses roll themselves in fear,
And the flat Earth becomes a Ball;

The stars, sun, Moon, all shrink away,
A desart vast without a bound,
And nothing left to eat or drink,
And a dark desart all around.

The honey of her Infant lips,
The bread & wine of her sweet smile,
The wild game of her roving Eye,
Does him to Infancy beguile;

For as he eats & drinks he grows
Younger & younger every day;
And on the desart wild they both
Wander in terror & dismay.

Like the wild Stag she flees away,
Her fear plants many a thicket wild;
While he pursues her night & day,
By various arts of Love beguil'd,

By various arts of Love & Hate,
Till the wide desart planted o'er
With Labyrinths of wayward Love,
Where roams the Lion, Wolf & Boar,

Till he becomes a wayward Babe,
And she a weeping Woman Old.
Then many a Lover wanders here;
The Sun & Stars are nearer roll'd.

The trees bring forth sweet Extacy
To all who in the desart roam;
Till many a City there is Built,
And many a pleasant Shepherd's home.

But when they find the frowning Babe,
Terror strikes thro' the region wide:
They cry "The Babe! the Babe is Born!"
And flee away on Every side.

For who dare touch the frowning form,
His arm is wither'd to its root;
Lions, Boars, Wolves, all howling flee,
And every Tree does shed its fruit.

And none can touch that frowning form,
Except it be a Woman Old;
She nails him down upon the Rock,
And all is done as I have told.

The Land of Dreams

Awake, awake, my little Boy!
Thou wast thy Mother's only joy;
Why dost thou weep in thy gentle sleep?
Awake! thy Father does thee keep.

"O, what Land is the Land of Dreams?
"What are its Mountains & what are its Streams?
"O Father, I saw my Mother there,
"Among the Lillies by waters fair.

"Among the Lambs, clothed in white,
"She walk'd with her Thomas in sweet delight.
"I wept for joy, like a dove I mourn;
"O! when shall I again return?"

Dear Child, I also by pleasant Streams
Have wander'd all Night in the Land of Dreams;
But tho' calm & warm the waters wide,
I could not get to the other side.

"Father, O Father! what do we here
"In this Land of unbelief & fear?
"The Land of Dreams is better far,
"Above the light of the Morning Star."

Mary

Sweet Mary, the first time she ever was there,
Came into the Ball room among the Fair;
The young Men & Maidens around her throng,
And these are the words upon every tongue:

"An Angel is here from the heavenly Climes,
"Or again does return the Golden times;
"Her eyes outshine every brilliant ray,
"She opens her lips—'tis the Month of May."

Mary moves in soft beauty & conscious delight
To augment with sweet smiles all the joys of the Night,
Nor once blushes to own to the rest of the Fair
That sweet Love & Beauty are worthy our care.

In the Morning the Villagers rose with delight
And repeated with pleasure the joys of the night,
And Mary arose among Friends to be free,
But no Friend from henceforward thou, Mary, shalt see.

Some said she was proud, some call'd her a whore,
And some, when she passed by, shut to the door;
A damp cold came o'er her, her blushes all fled;
Her lillies & roses are blighted & shed.

"O, why was I born with a different Face?
"Why was I not born like this Envious Race?
"Why did Heaven adorn me with bountiful hand,
"And then set me down in an envious Land?

"To be weak as a Lamb & smooth as a dove,
"And not to raise Envy, is call'd Christian Love;
"But if you raise Envy your Merit's to blame
"For planting such spite in the weak & the tame.

"I will humble my Beauty, I will not dress fine,
"I will keep from the Ball, & my Eyes shall not shine;
"And if any Girl's Lover forsakes her for me,
"I'll refuse him my hand & from Envy be free."

She went out in Morning attir'd plain & neat;
"Proud Mary's gone Mad," said the Child in the Street;
She went out in Morning in plain neat attire,
And came home in Evening bespatter'd with mire.

She trembled & wept, sitting on the Bed side;
She forgot it was Night, & she trembled & cried;
She forgot it was Night, she forgot it was Morn,
Her soft Memory imprinted with Faces of Scorn,

With Faces of Scorn & with Eyes of disdain
Like foul Fiends inhabiting Mary's mild Brain;
She remembers no Face like the Human Divine.
All Faces have Envy, sweet Mary, but thine;

And thine is a Face of sweet Love in despair,
And thine is a Face of mild sorrow & care,
And thine is a Face of wild terror & fear
That shall never be quiet till laid on its bier.

The Crystal Cabinet

The Maiden caught me in the Wild,
Where I was dancing merrily;
She put me into her Cabinet
And Lock'd me up with a golden Key.

This Cabinet is form'd of Gold
And Pearl & Crystal shining bright,
And within it opens into a World
And a little lovely Moony Night.

Another England there I saw,
Another London with its Tower,
Another Thames & other Hills,
And another pleasant Surrey Bower,

Another Maiden like herself,
Translucent, lovely, shining clear,
Threefold each in the other clos'd—
O, what a pleasant trembling fear!

O, what a smile! a threefold Smile
Fill'd me, that like a flame I burn'd;
I bent to Kiss the lovely Maid,
And found a Threefold Kiss return'd.

I strove to sieze the inmost Form
With ardor fierce & hands of flame,
But burst the Crystal Cabinet,
And like a Weeping Babe became—

A weeping Babe upon the wild,
And Weeping Woman pale reclin'd,
And in the outward air again
I fill'd with woes the passing Wind.

The Grey Monk

"I die, I die!" the Mother said,
"My Children die for lack of Bread.
"What more has the merciless Tyrant said?"
The Monk sat down on the Stony Bed.

The blood red ran from the Grey Monk's side,
His hands & feet were wounded wide,
His Body bent, his arms & knees
Like to the roots of ancient trees.

His eye was dry; no tear could flow:
A hollow groan first spoke his woe.
He trembled & shudder'd upon the Bed;
At length with a feeble cry he said:

"When God commanded this hand to write
"In the studious hours of deep midnight,
"He told me the writing I wrote should prove
"The Bane of all that on Earth I lov'd.

"My Brother starv'd between two Walls,
"His Children's Cry my Soul appalls;
"I mock'd at the wrack & griding chain,
"My bent body mocks their torturing pain.

"Thy Father drew his sword in the North,
"With his thousands strong he marched forth;
"Thy Brother has arm'd himself in Steel
"To avenge the wrongs thy Children feel.

"But vain the Sword & vain the Bow,
"They never can work War's overthrow.
"The Hermit's Prayer & the Widow's tear
"Alone can free the World from fear.

"For a Tear is an Intellectual Thing,
"And a Sigh is the Sword of an Angel King,
"And the bitter groan of the Martyr's woe
"Is an Arrow from the Almightie's Bow.

"The hand of Vengeance found the Bed
"To which the Purple Tyrant fled;
"The iron hand crush'd the Tyrant's head
"And became a Tyrant in his stead."

Auguries of Innocence

To see a World in a Grain of Sand
And a Heaven in a Wild Flower,
Hold Infinity in the palm of your hand
And Eternity in an hour.

A Robin Red breast in a Cage
Puts all Heaven in a Rage.
A dove house fill'd with doves & Pigeons
Shudders Hell thro' all its regions.
A dog starv'd at his Master's Gate
Predicts the ruin of the State.
A Horse misus'd upon the Road
Calls to Heaven for Human blood.
Each outcry of the hunted Hare
A fibre from the Brain does tear.
A Skylark wounded in the wing,
A Cherubim does cease to sing.
The Game Cock clip'd & arm'd for fight
Does the Rising Sun affright.
Every Wolf's & Lion's howl
Raises from Hell a Human Soul.
The wild deer, wand'ring here & there,
Keeps the Human Soul from Care.
The Lamb misus'd breeds Public strife
And yet forgives the Butcher's Knife.
The Bat that flits at close of Eve
Has left the Brain that won't Believe.
The Owl that calls upon the Night
Speaks the Unbeliever's fright.
He who shall hurt the little Wren
Shall never be belov'd by Men.
He who the Ox to wrath has mov'd
Shall never be by Woman lov'd.
The wanton Boy that kills the Fly
Shall feel the Spider's enmity.
He who torments the Chafer's sprite
Weaves a Bower in endless Night.

The Catterpiller on the Leaf
Repeats to thee thy Mother's grief.
Kill not the Moth nor Butterfly,
For the Last Judgment draweth nigh.
He who shall train the Horse to War
Shall never pass the Polar Bar.
The Begger's Dog & Widow's Cat,
Feed them & thou wilt grow fat.
The Gnat that sings his Summer's song
Poison gets from Slander's tongue.
The poison of the Snake & Newt
Is the sweat of Envy's Foot.
The Poison of the Honey Bee
Is the Artist's Jealousy.
The Prince's Robes & Beggar's Rags
Are Toadstools on the Miser's Bags.
A truth that's told with bad intent
Beats all the Lies you can invent.
It is right it should be so;
Man was made for Joy & Woe;
And when this we rightly know
Thro' the World we safely go.
Joy & Woe are woven fine,
A Clothing for the Soul divine;
Under every grief & pine
Runs a joy with silken twine.
The Babe is more than swadling Bands;
Throughout all these Human Lands
Tools were made, & Born were hands,
Every Farmer Understands.
Every Tear from Every Eye
Becomes a Babe in Eternity;
This is caught by Females bright
And return'd to its own delight.
The Bleat, the Bark, Bellow & Roar
Are Waves that Beat on Heaven's Shore.
The Babe that weeps the Rod beneath
Writes Revenge in realms of death.
The Beggar's Rags, fluttering in Air,
Does to Rags the Heavens tear.
The Soldier, arm'd with Sword & Gun,
Palsied strikes the Summer's Sun.
The poor Man's Farthing is worth more
Than all the Gold on Afric's Shore.
One Mite wrung from the Labrer's hands

Shall buy & sell the Miser's Lands:
Or, if protected from on high,
Does that whole Nation sell & buy.
He who mocks the Infant's Faith
Shall be mock'd in Age & Death.
He who shall teach the Child to Doubt
The rotting Grave shall ne'er get out.
He who respects the Infant's faith
Triumphs over Hell & Death.
The Child's Toys & the Old Man's Reasons
Are the Fruits of the Two seasons.
The Questioner, who sits so sly,
Shall never know how to Reply.
He who replies to words of Doubt
Doth put the Light of Knowledge out.
The Strongest Poison ever known
Came from Caesar's Laurel Crown.
Nought can deform the Human Race
Like to the Armour's iron brace.
When Gold & Gems adorn the Plow
To peaceful Arts shall Envy Bow.
A Riddle or the Cricket's Cry
Is to Doubt a fit Reply.
The Emmet's Inch & Eagle's Mile
Make Lame Philosophy to smile.
He who Doubts from what he sees
Will ne'er Believe, do what you Please.
If the Sun & Moon should doubt,
They'd immediately Go out.
To be in a Passion you Good may do,
But no Good if a Passion is in you.
The Whore & Gambler, by the State
Licenc'd, build that Nation's Fate.
The Harlot's cry from Street to Street
Shall weave Old England's winding Sheet.
The Winner's Shout, the Loser's Curse,
Dance before dead England's Hearse.
Every Night & every Morn
Some to Misery are Born.
Every Morn & every Night
Some are Born to sweet delight.
Some are Born to sweet delight,
Some are Born to Endless Night.
We are led to Believe a Lie
When we see [With *del.*] not Thro' the Eye

Which was Born in a Night to perish in a Night
When the Soul Slept in Beams of Light.
God Appears & God is Light
To those poor Souls who dwell in Night,
But does a Human Form Display
To those who Dwell in Realms of day.

Long John Brown & Little Mary Bell

[Pretty *del.*] Little Mary Bell had a Fairy in a Nut,
[Young *del.*] Long John Brown had the Devil in his Gut;
[Young *del.*] Long John Brown lov'd [Pretty *del.*] Little Mary Bell,
And the Fairy drew the Devil into the Nut-shell.

Her Fairy Skip'd out & her Fairy Skip'd in;
He laugh'd at the Devil saying 'Love is a Sin.'
The Devil he raged & the Devil he was wroth,
And the Devil enter'd into the Young Man's broth.

He was soon in the Gut of the loving Young Swain,
For John eat & drank to drive away Love's pain;
But all he could do he grew thinner & thinner,
Tho' he eat & drank as much as ten Men for his dinner.

Some said he had a Wolf in his stomach day & night,
Some said he had the Devil & they guess'd right;
The fairy skip'd about in his Glory, Joy & Pride,
And he laugh'd at the Devil till poor John Brown died.

Then the Fairy skip'd out of the old Nut shell,
And woe & alack for Pretty Mary Bell!
For the Devil crept in when the Fairy skip'd out,
And there goes Miss Bell with her fusty old Nut.

William Bond

I wonder whether the Girls are mad,
And I wonder whether they mean to kill,
And I wonder if William Bond will die,
For assuredly he is very ill.

He went to Church in a May morning
Attended by Fairies, one, two & three;
But the Angels of Providence drove them away,
And he return'd home in Misery.

He went not out to the Field nor Fold,
He went not out to the Village nor Town,
But he came home in a black, black cloud,
And took to his Bed & there lay down.

And an Angel of Providence at his Feet,
And an Angel of Providence at his Head,
And in the midst a Black, Black Cloud,
And in the midst the Sick Man on his Bed.

And on his Right hand was Mary Green,
And on his Left hand was his Sister Jane,
And their tears fell thro' the black, black Cloud
To drive away the sick man's pain.

"O William, if thou dost another Love,
"Dost another Love better than poor Mary,
"Go & take that other to be thy Wife,
"And Mary Green shall her Servant be."

"Yes, Mary, I do another Love,
"Another I Love far better than thee,
"And Another I will have for my Wife;
"Then what have I to do with thee?

"For thou art Melancholy Pale,
"And on thy Head is the cold Moon's shine,
"But she is ruddy & bright as day,
"And the sun beams dazzle from her eyne."

Mary trembled & Mary chill'd
And Mary fell down on the right hand floor,
That William Bond & his Sister Jane
Scarce could recover Mary more.

When Mary woke & found her Laid
On the Right hand of her William dear,
On the Right hand of his loved Bed,
And saw her William Bond so near,

The Fairies that fled from William Bond
Danced around her Shining Head;
They danced over the Pillow white,
And the Angels of Providence left the Bed.

I thought Love liv'd in the hot sun shine,
But O, he lives in the Moony light!
I thought to find Love in the heat of day,
But sweet Love is the Comforter of Night.

Seek Love in the Pity of others' Woe,
In the gentle relief of another's care,
In the darkness of night & the winter's snow,
In the naked & outcast, Seek Love there!

[END OF PICKERING MS.]

BLAKE'S MEMORANDUM
[August 1803]

Blake's Memorandum in Refutation of the Information and Complaint of John Scholfield, a private Soldier, &c.

The Soldier has been heard to say repeatedly, that he did not know how the Quarrel began, which he would not say if such seditious words were spoken.

Mrs. Haynes Evidences, that she saw me turn him down the Road, & all the while we were at the Stable Door, and that not one word of charge against me was uttered, either relating to Sedition or any thing else; all he did was swearing and threatening.

Mr. Hosier heard him say that he would be revenged, and would have me hanged if he could: He spoke this the Day after my turning him out of the Garden. Hosier says he is ready to give Evidence of this, if necessary.

The Soldier's Comrade swore before the Magistrates, while I was present, that he heard me utter seditious words, at the Stable Door, and in particular, said, that he heard me D—n the K—g. Now I have all the Persons who were present at the Stable Door to witness that no Word relating to Seditious Subjects was uttered, either by one party or the other, and they are ready, on their Oaths, to say that I did not utter such Words.

Mrs. Haynes says very sensibly, that she never heard People quarrel, but they always charged each other with the Offence, and repeated it to those around, therefore as the Soldier charged not me with Seditious Words at that Time, neither did his Comrade, the whole Charge must have been fabricated in the Stable afterwards.

If we prove the Comrade perjured who swore that he heard me D—n the K—g, I believe the whole Charge falls to the Ground.

Mr. Cosens, owner of the Mill at Felpham, was passing by in the Road, and saw me and the Soldier and William standing near each other; he heard nothing, but says we certainly were not quarrelling.

The whole Distance that William could be at any Time of the Conversation between me and the Soldier (supposing such Conversation to have existed) is only 12 Yards, & W— says that he was backwards and forwards in the Garden. It was a still Day, there was no Wind stirring.

William says on his Oath, that the first Words that he heard me speak to the Soldier were ordering him out of the Garden; the truth is, I did not speak to the Soldier till then, & my ordering him out of the Garden was occasioned by his saying something that I thought insulting.

The Time that I & the Soldier were together in the Garden was not sufficient for me to have uttered the Things that he alledged.

The Soldier said to Mrs. Grinder, that it would be right to have my House searched, as I might have plans of the Country which I intended to send to the Enemy; he called me a Military Painter; I suppose [he *del.*] mistaking the Words Miniature Painter, which he might have heard me called. I think that this proves, his having come into the Garden with some bad Intention, or at least with a prejudiced Mind.

It is necessary to learn the Names of all that were present at the Stable Door, that we may not have any Witnesses brought against us, that were not there.

All the Persons present at the Stable Door were, Mrs. Grinder and her Daughter, all the Time; Mrs. Haynes & her Daughter all the Time; Mr. Grinder, part of the Time; Mr. Hayley's Gardener part of the Time.—Mrs. Haynes was present from my turning him out at my Gate, all the rest of the Time. What passed in the Garden, there is no Person but William & the Soldier, & myself can know.

There was not any body in Grinder's Tap-room, but an Old Man, named Jones, who (Mrs. Grinder says) did not come out. He is the same Man who lately hurt his Hand, & wears it in a sling.

The Soldier after he and his Comrade came together into the Tap-room, threatened to knock William's Eyes out (this was his often repeated Threat to me and to my Wife) because W— refused to go with him to Chichester, and swear against me. William said that he would not take a false Oath, for that he heard me say nothing of the Kind (i.e. Sedition) Mr. Grinder then reproved the Soldier for threatening William, and Mr. Grinder said, that W— should not go, because of those Threats, especially as he was sure that no seditious Words were spoken.

William's timidity in giving his Evidence before the Magistrates, and his fear of uttering a Falsehood upon Oath, proves him to be an honest Man, & is to me an host of Strength. I am certain that if I had not turned the Soldier out of my Garden, I never should have been free from his Impertinence & Intrusion.

Mr. Hayley's Gardener came past at the Time of the Contention at the Stable Door, & going to the Comrade said to him, Is your Comrade drunk?—a Proof that he thought the Soldier abusive, & in an Intoxication of Mind.

If such a Perjury as this can take effect, any Villain in future may come & drag me and my Wife out of our House, & beat us in the Garden, or use us as he please, or is able, & afterwards go and swear our Lives away.

Is it not in the Power of any Thief who enters a Man's Dwelling, & robs him, or misuses his Wife or Children, to go & swear as this Man has sworn.

Remarks on the drawings of Thomas Heath Malkin from "A Fathers Memoirs of his Child" by Benj. Heath Malkin London MDCCCVI

Written about 1805

P. 33.

They are all firm, determinate outline, or identical form. Had the hand which executed these little ideas been that of a plagiary, who works only from the memory, we should have seen blots called masses; blots without form, and therefore without meaning. These blots of light and dark, as being the result of labour, are always clumsy and indefinite; the effect of rubbing out and putting in, like the progress of a blind man, or of one in the dark, who feels his way, but does not see it. These are not so. Even the copy from Raphael's Cartoon of St. Paul preaching, is a firm, determinate outline, struck at once, as Protogenes struck his line, when he meant to make himself known to Apelles. The map of Allestone has the same character of the firm and determinate. All his efforts prove this little boy to have had that greatest of all blessings, a strong imagination, a clear idea, and a determinate vision of things in his own mind.

MEMORANDA FROM THE NOTE-BOOK

Written in 1807

1

P. 10.

Tuesday, Janry. 20, 1807, between Two & Seven in the Evening—Despair.

2

Memorandum

To Engrave on Pewter: Let there be first a drawing made correctly with black lead pencil: let nothing be to seek; then rub it off on the plate cover'd with white wax, or perhaps pass it thro' press—this will produce certain & determin'd forms on the plate & time will not be wasted in seeking them afterwards.

3

Memorandum

To Woodcut on Pewter: lay a ground on the Plate & smoke it as for Etching; then trace your outlines [& draw them in with a needle *del.*], and beginning with the spots of light on each object with an oval pointed needle scrape off the ground [& instead of etching the shadowy strokes *del.*] as a direction for your graver; then proceed to graving with the ground on the plate, being as careful as possible not to hurt the ground, because it, being black, will shew perfectly what is wanted [*word del.*].

4

Memorandum

To Woodcut on Copper: Lay a Ground as for Etching; trace &c, & instead of Etching the blacks, Etch the whites & bite it in.

5

Pp. 88-89.

South Molton Street. Sunday, August 1807.

My Wife was told by a Spirit to look for her fortune by opening by chance a book which she had in her hand; it was Bysshe's Art of Poetry. She open'd the following:

I saw 'em kindle with desire
While with soft sighs they blew the fire,
Saw the approaches of their joy,
He growing more fierce & she less coy
Saw how they mingled melting rays,
Exchanging Love a thousand ways.

Kind was the force on every side,
Her new desire she could not hide,
Nor would the shepherd be denied.
The blessed minute he pursued
Till she, transported in his arms
Yields to the Conqueror all her charms.
His panting breast to hers now join'd,
They feast on raptures unconfin'd,
Vast & luxuriant, such as prove
The immortality of Love
For who but a divinity
Could mingle souls to that degree
And melt them into Extasy.
Now like the Phoenix both expire,
While from the ashes of their fire
Spring up a new & soft desire.
Like charmers thrice they did invoke
The God & thrice new Vigor took.

Behn

I was so well pleased with her Luck that I thought I would try my Own & open'd the following:

As when the winds their airy quarrel try,
Justling from every quarter of the sky,
This way & that the Mountain oak they bear
His boughs they shatter & his branches tear,
With leaves & falling mast they spread the Ground,
The hollow Valleys Eccho to the Sound.
Unmov'd the royal plant their fury mocks,
Or shaken clings more closely to the rocks,
For as he shoots his lowring head on high
So deep in earth his fix'd foundations lie.

Dryden's Virgil

Inscription on the back of "The Fall of Man" Watercolour Drawing 1807

The Father indignant at the Fall—the Saviour, while the Evil Angels are driven, gently conducts our first Parents out of Eden through a guard of Weeping Angels—Satan now awakes Sin, Death & Hell, to celebrate with him the birth of War & Misery: while the Lion seizes the Bull, the Tiger the Horse, the Vulture and the Eagle contend for the Lamb.

DEDICATION OF THE ILLUSTRATIONS TO BLAIR'S GRAVE

Printed 1808

TO THE QUEEN

The Door of Death is made of Gold,
That Mortal Eyes cannot behold;
But, when the Mortal Eyes are clos'd,
And cold and pale the Limbs repos'd,
The Soul awakes; and, wond'ring, sees
In her mild Hand the golden Keys:
The Grave is Heaven's golden Gate,
And rich and poor around it wait;
O Shepherdess of England's Fold,
Behold this Gate of Pearl and Gold!

To dedicate to England's Queen
The Visions that my Soul has seen,
And, by Her kind permission, bring
What I have borne on solemn Wing
From the vast regions of the Grave,
Before Her Throne my Wings I wave;
Bowing before my Sov'reign's Feet,
"The Grave produc'd these Blossoms sweet
"In mild repose from Earthly strife;
"The Blossoms of Eternal Life!"

DESCRIPTION OF A VISION OF THE LAST JUDGMENT

[three drafts][1]

Written in 1808

To Ozias Humphry Esqre

The Design of The Last Judgment, which I have completed by your recommendation [under a fortunate star] for the Countess [*del.* Earl (*in another hand*)] of Egremont, [by a happy accident] it is necessary to give some account of: & its various parts ought to be described, for the accomodation of those who give it the honor of attention.

[1] Additions found in the second and third drafts are printed in square brackets.

Christ seated on the Throne of Judgment: The Heavens in Clouds rolling before him & around him, like a scroll ready to be consumed in the fires of the Angels; who descend before his feet with their four trumpets sounding to the four Winds.

Beneath; the Earth is convuls'd with the labours of the Resurrection. In the caverns of the Earth is the Dragon with seven heads & ten horns, Chained by two Angels & above his Cavern[s] on the Earth's surface, is the Harlot also siezed & bound [chain'd] by two Angels with Chains while her Palaces are falling into [in] ruins & her Councellors & Warriors are descending into the Abyss in wailing & despair.

Hell opens beneath the Harlot's seat on the left hand into which the Wicked are descending [while others rise from their Graves on the brink of the Pit].

The right hand of the Design is appropriated to the Resurrection of The Just; the left hand of the Design is appropriated to the Resurrection & Fall of the Wicked.

Immediately before the Throne of Christ is Adam & Eve, kneeling in humiliation, as representatives of the whole Human Race; Abraham & Moses kneel on each side beneath them; from the Cloud on which Eve kneels & beneath Moses & from the Tables of Stone which utter lightnings, is seen Satan wound round by the Serpent & falling headlong; the Pharisees appear on the left hand pleading their own righteousness before the Throne of Christ: [& before] The Book of Death [which] is open'd on Clouds by two Angels; [&] many groupes of Figures are falling from before the Throne & from the Sea of Fire which flows before the steps of the Throne on which are seen the Seven Lamps of the Almighty burning before the Throne: many Figures Chain'd & bound together [in various attitudes of Despair & Horror:] fall thro' the air, & some are scourged by Spirits with flames of fire into the Abyss of Hell which opens to recieve them beneath, on the left hand of the Harlot's seat, where others are howling & descending into the flames & in the act of dragging each other into Hell & of contending in fighting with each other on the [very] brink of Perdition.

Before the Throne of Christ on the right hand the Just in humiliation & in exultation, rise thro' the air, with their Children & Families: some of whom are bowing before the Book of Life which is open'd by two Angels on Clouds: many Groupes arise with Exultation [in joy]: among them is a Figure crowned with Stars & the moon beneath her feet with six infants around her. She represents the Christian Church: The Green Hills appear beneath: with the Graves of the Blessed, which are seen bursting with their births of immortality; Parents & Children [Wives & Husbands] embrace & arise together & in exulting attitudes [of great joy] tell each other, that The

New Jerusalem is ready to descend upon Earth; they arise upon the air rejoicing: others newly awaken'd from the Grave stand upon the Earth embracing & shouting to the Lamb who cometh in the Clouds with Power & great Glory.

The whole upper part of the Design is a view of Heaven opened: around the Throne of Christ, [in the Cloud which rolls away are the] Four Living Creatures filled with Eyes, attended by Seven Angels with the Seven Vials of the Wrath of God, & above these [there are] Seven Angels with the Seven Trumpets compose [composing] the Cloud, which by its rolling away displays the opening Seats of the Blessed, on the right & the left of which are seen the Four & Twenty Elders seated on Thrones to Judge the Dead.

Behind the Seat & Throne of Christ appears [appear] the Tabernacle with its Veil opened: [&] the Candlestick on the right: the Table with Shew Bread, on the left: & in the midst, the Cross in place of the Ark, with the two Cherubim bowing over it.

On the right hand of the Throne of Christ is Baptism. On his left is the Lord's Supper: the two introducers into Eternal Life. Women with Infants approach the Figure of an aged Apostle which represents Baptism; & on the left hand the Lord's Supper is administer'd by Angels, from the hands of another aged Apostle; these Kneel on each side of the Throne which is surrounded by a glory, in the glory many Infants appear [in the Glory], representing [the] Eternal Creation flowing from The Divine Humanity in Jesus: who opens the Scroll of Judgment upon his knees before the Living & the Dead.

Such is the Design which you, my Dear Sir, have been the cause of my producing & which: but for you might have slept till the Last Judgment.

William Blake

18 January 1808 [February 1808]

ANNOTATIONS TO SIR JOSHUA REYNOLDS'S DISCOURSES

London MDCCXCVIII

Written about 1808

This Man was Hired to Depress Art.

This is the Opinion of Will Blake: my Proofs of this Opinion are given in the following Notes.

Advice of the Popes who succeeded the Age of Rafael

Degrade first the Arts if you'd Mankind Degrade.
Hire Idiots to Paint with cold light & hot shade:
Give high Price for the worst, leave the best in disgrace,
And with Labours of Ignorance fill every place.

Having spent the Vigour of my Youth & Genius under the Opression of S[r] Joshua & his Gang of Cunning Hired Knaves Without Employment & as much as could possibly be Without Bread, The Reader must Expect to Read in all my Remarks on these Books Nothing but Indignation & Resentment. While S[r] Joshua was rolling in Riches, Barry was Poor & Unemploy'd except by his own Energy; Mortimer was call'd a Madman, & only Portrait Painting applauded & rewarded by the Rich & Great. Reynolds & Gainsborough Blotted & Blurred one against the other & Divided all the English World between them. Fuseli, Indignant, almost hid himself. I am hid.

The Arts & Sciences are the Destruction of Tyrannies or Bad Governments. Why should A Good Government endeavour to Depress what is its Chief & only Support?

The Foundation of Empire is Art & Science. Remove them or Degrade them, & the Empire is No More. Empire follows Art & Not Vice Versa as Englishmen suppose.

"On peut dire que le Pape Léon Xme en encourageant les Études "donna Les armes contre lui-même. J'ai oui dire à un Seigneur "Anglais qu'il avait vu une Lettre du Seigneur Polus, ou de La Pole, "depuis Cardinal, à ce Pape; dans laquelle, en le félicitant sur ce "qu'il étendait le progrès de Science en Europe, il l'avertissait *qu'il* "*était dangereux de rendre les hommes trop Savan*[*t*]*s*."

VOLTAIRE, *Mœurs de Nations*. Tome 4.

O Englishmen! why are you still of this foolish Cardinal's opinion?

Who will Dare to Say that Polite Art is Encouraged or Either Wished or Tolerated in a Nation where The Society for the Encouragement of Art Suffer'd Barry to Give them his Labour for Nothing, A Society Composed of the Flower of the English Nobility & Gentry?—Suffering an Artist to Starve while he Supported Really what They, under Pretence of Encouraging, were Endeavouring to Depress.—Barry told me that while he Did that Work, he Lived on Bread & Apples.

O Society for Encouragement of Art! O King & Nobility of England! Where have you hid Fuseli's Milton? Is Satan troubled at his Exposure?

[*These passages are written on the title-page and preliminary leaves. Blake's subsequent remarks are here printed after the passages to which they refer. Words underlined by him are printed in italic.*]

CONTENTS OF THE FIRST VOLUME

DISCOURSE II

The course and order of study.—The different stages of Art.—Much copying discountenanced.—The Artist at all times and in all places should be employed in laying up materials for the exercise of his art.

To learn the Language of Art, 'Copy for Ever' is My Rule.

Page i.

TO THE KING

The regular progress of cultivated life is from necessaries to accommodations, from accommodations to ornaments.

The Bible says That Cultivated Life Existed First. Uncultivated Life comes afterwards from Satan's Hirelings. Necessaries, Accomodations & Ornaments are the whole of Life. Satan took away Ornament First. Next he took away Accomodations, & Then he became Lord & Master of Necessaries.

Page ii.

[*Dedication, continued*]

To give advice to those who are contending for royal liberality, has been for some years the duty of my station in the Academy.

Liberality! we want not Liberality. We want a Fair Price & Proportionate Value & a General Demand for Art.
Let not that Nation where Less than Nobility is the Reward, Pretend that Art is Encouraged by that Nation. Art is First in Intellectuals & Ought to be First in Nations.

Page iii.

Invention depends Altogether upon Execution or Organization; as that is right or wrong so is the Invention perfect or imperfect.

Whoever is set to Undermine the Execution of Art is set to Destroy Art. Michael Angelo's Art depends on Michael Angelo's Execution Altogether.

Page viii.

[Some Account of Sir Joshua Reynolds]

But what most strongly confirmed him in his Love of the Art, was Richardson's Treatise on Painting; the perusal of which so delighted and inflamed his mind, that Raffelle appeared to him superior to the most illustrious names of ancient or modern time; a notion which he loved to indulge all the rest of his life.

Why then did he not follow Rafael's Track?

Page ix.

[*footnote*] "He [Thomas Hudson] enjoyed for many years the chief business of "portrait-painting in the capital, . . . The better taste introduced by Sir Joshua "Reynolds, put an end to Hudson's reign . . ."

Hudson Drew Correctly.

Pages xiv-xv.

"It has frequently happened . . ., as I was informed by the keeper of the Vatican, "that many of those whom he had conducted through the various apartments of "that edifice, when about to be dismissed, have asked for the works of Raffaelle, "and would not believe that they had already passed through the rooms where "they are preserved; so little impression had those performances made on them.

Men who have been Educated with Works of Venetian Artists under their Eyes cannot see Rafael unless they are born with Determinate Organs.

"I remember very well my own disappointment, when I first visited the Vatican; "but on confessing my feelings to a brother-student . . . he acknowledged that the "works of Raffaelle had the same effect on him, or rather that they did not produce "the effect which he expected;

I am happy I cannot say that Rafael Ever was, from my Earliest Childhood, hidden from Me. I Saw & I Knew immediately the difference between Rafael & Rubens.

Some look to see the sweet Outlines
And beauteous Forms that Love does wear.
Some look to find out Patches, Paint,
Bracelets & Stays & Powder'd Hair.

"and on inquiring further of other students, I found that those persons only who "from natural imbecility appeared to be incapable of ever relishing those divine "performances, made pretensions to instantaneous raptures on first beholding "them.

Here are Mocks on those who Saw Rafael.

". . . I found myself in the midst of works executed upon principles with which I "was unacquainted: I felt my ignorance, and stood abashed.

A Liar! he never was Abashed in his Life & never felt his Ignorance.

Page xvi.

"I proceeded to copy some of those excellent works. I viewed them again and "again; . . . In a short time a new taste and new perceptions began to dawn on me. ". . . The truth is, that if these works had really been what I expected, they would "have contained beauties superficial and alluring, but by no means such as would "have entitled them to the great reputation which they have so long and so justly "obtained.

All this Concession is to prove that Genius is Acquired, as follows in the Next page.

Pages xvii-xviii.

". . . I am now clearly of opinion, that a relish for the higher excellencies of art is "an acquired taste, which no man ever possessed without long cultivation . . . we "are often ashamed of our apparent dulness; as if it were to be expected that our "minds, like tinder, should instantly catch fire from the divine spark of Raffaelle's "genius.

A Mock!

". . . but let it be always remembered, that the excellence of his style is not on the "surface, but lies deep; and at the first view is seen but mistily.

A Mock!

"It is the florid style, which strikes at once, and captivates the eye for a time, . . .

A Lie! The Florid Style, such as the Venetian & the Flemish, Never Struck Me at Once nor At-All.

The Style that Strikes the Eye is the True Style, But A Fool's Eye is Not to be a Criterion.

Page xviii.

"The man of true genius, instead of spending all his hours . . . in measuring statues "and copying pictures, soon begins to think for himself, . . . I consider *general* "*copying as a delusive kind of industry :*

Here he Condemns Generalizing, which he almost always Approves & Recommends.

Page xix.

"How incapable of producing any thing of their own, those are, who have spent "most of their time in making finished copies, is an observation well known to all "who are conversant with our art."

Finish'd! What does he Mean? Niggling without the Correct & Definite Outline? If he means That Copying Correctly is a hindrance, he is a Liar, for that is the only School to the Language of Art.

Page xxix.

"It is the thoughts expressed in the works of Michael Angelo, Corregio, Raffelle, "Parmegiano, and perhaps some of the old Gothick masters, and not the inventions "of Pietro da Cortona, Carlo Maratti, Luca Giordano, and others that I might "mention, which we seek after with avidity. From the former we learn to think "originally."

Here is an Acknowledgment of all that I could wish. But if it is True, Why are we to be told that Masters who could Think had not the

Judgment to Perform the Inferior Parts of Art, as Reynolds artfully calls them, But that we are to Learn to Think from Great Masters & to Learn to Perform from Underlings? Learn to Design from Rafael & to Execute from Rubens...? [*the remainder has been cut away by the binder*]

Page xxxiv.
He [Mr. Mudge, Prebendary of Exeter] was a learned and venerable old man; and as I thought, very much conversant in the Platonick Philosophy....

Slang!

He had been originally a dissenting minister.

Villainy!

Page xlii.
[*To a footnote concerning rumours that the Discourses had been written by Dr. Johnson or by Mr. Burke.*]

The Contradictions in Reynolds's Discourses are Strong Presumptions that they are the Work of Several Hands, But this is no Proof that Reynolds did not Write them. The Man, Either Painter or Philosopher, who Learns or Acquires all he knows from Others, Must be full of Contradictions.

Page xlvii.
[*To a footnote on George Michael Moser, Keeper of the Royal Academy.*]

I was once looking over the Prints from Rafael & Michael Angelo in the Library of the Royal Academy. Moser came to me & said: "You "should not Study these old Hard, Stiff & Dry, Unfinish'd Works of "Art—Stay a little & I will shew you what you should Study." He then went & took down Le Brun's & Rubens's Galleries. How I did secretly Rage! I also spoke my Mind.... [*a line cut away by the binder*] I said to Moser, "These things that you call Finish'd are not Even "Begun; how can they then be Finish'd? The Man who does not "know The Beginning never can know the End of Art."

Page xlix.
"I consoled myself, however, by remarking that these ready inventors are ex-"tremely apt to acquiesce in *imperfection*."

Villainy! a Lie!

Page l.
"How difficult it is for the artist who possesses this facility, to guard against "carelessness and commonplace invention, is well known, and in a kindred art "Metastasio is an eminent instance; who always complained of the great difficulty "he found in attaining correctness, in consequence of having been in his youth an "Improvisatore."

I do not believe this Anecdote.

Page liii, footnote.
"There is nothing in our art which enforces such continued exertion and cir-"cumspection, as an attention to the general effect of the whole. It requires much "study and much practice; it requires the painter's entire mind: whereas the parts "may be finishing by nice touches, while his mind is engaged on other matters: "he may even hear a play or a novel read without much disturbance."

A Lie! Working up Effect is more an operation of Indolence than the Making out of the Parts, as far as Greatest is more than Least. I speak here of Rembrandt's & Rubens's & Reynolds's Effects. For Real Effect is Making out the Parts, & it is Nothing Else but That.

Page lvii.
[*To a footnote on the lost secrets of colour-mixing known to the old masters.*]

Oil colours will not do. Why are we told that Reynolds is a Great Colourist & yet inferior to the Venetians?

Page lx.
[*To a footnote concerning the fading of pictures by Reynolds.*]

I do not think that the Change is so much in the Pictures as in the Opinions of the Public.

Page lxx.
[*footnote*] In a Letter to Mr. Baretti, June 10, 1761, Dr. Johnson says—"Reynolds "is without a rival, and continues to add thousands to thousands."

How much did Barry Get?

Page lxxii.
Many of the pictures of Rubens being to be sold in 1783, in consequence of certain religious houses being suppressed by the Emperor, he [Reynolds] again in that year visited Antwerp and Brussels, and devoted several days to contemplating the productions of that great painter.

If Reynolds had Really admired Mich. Angelo, he never would have follow'd Rubens.

Page lxxxix, footnote.
His [Reynolds's] deafness was originally occasioned by a cold that he caught in the Vatican, by painting for a long time near a stove, by which the damp vapours of that edifice were attracted, and affected his head. When in company with only one person, he heard very well, without the aid of a trumpet.

A Sly Dog! So can Every body; but bring Two People & the Hearing is Stopped.

Page xc.
[*To a quotation from Goldsmith's* "Retaliation" *giving the lines on Reynolds.*]

Such Men as Goldsmith ought not to have been Acquainted with such Men as Reynolds.

Page xcvi.
[*footnote*] It is clear from his manners and his writings that in the character of his eloquence he would have resembled the perspicuous and elegant Laelius, rather than the severe and vehement Galba.

He certainly would have been more like a Fool than a Wise Man.

Page xcviii.
[*footnote*] He was a great generalizer. . . . But this disposition to abstractions, to generalizing and classification, is the great glory of the human mind. . . .

To Generalize is to be an Idiot. To Particularize is the Alone Distinction of Merit. General Knowledges are those Knowledges that Idiots possess.

Page xcix.
Such was his love of his art, and such his ardour to excel, that he often declared he had, during the greater part of his life, laboured as hard with his pencil, as any mechanick working at his trade for bread.

The Man who does not Labour more than the Hireling must be a poor Devil.

Page ciii.
[*To a footnote giving a quotation from Pope appropriate to* "the ferocious and "enslaved Republick of France," *ending with the lines:*]

They led their wild desires to woods and caves
And thought that all but savages were slaves.

When France got free, Europe, 'twixt Fools & Knaves,
Were Savage first to France, & after—Slaves.

Page civ.
[*To a footnote on the wealth and prosperity of England.*]

This Whole Book was Written to Serve Political Purposes.

Page cix.
[*To the account of Reynolds's death in* 1792.]

When S[r] Joshua Reynolds died
All Nature was degraded;
The King drop'd a tear into the Queen's Ear,
And all his Pictures Faded.

Page cxi.
[*To the account of his funeral, where the pall was*] borne up by three Dukes, two Marquisses, and five other noblemen.

A Mock!

Page cxx.
[*In an account of Reynolds by Burke.*]
"Sir Joshua Reynolds was, on very many accounts, one of the most memorable "men of his time."

Is not this a Manifest Lie?

Barry Painted a Picture for Burke, equal to Rafael or Mich. Ang. or any of the Italians. Burke used to shew this Picture to his Friends & to say, "I gave Twenty Guineas for this horrible Dawb, & if any one "would give . . . [*a line cut off by the binder*]
Such was Burke's Patronage of Art & Science.

DISCOURSE I

Page 2.

I consider Reynolds's Discourses to the Royal Academy as the Simulations of the Hypocrite who smiles particularly where he means to Betray. His Praise of Rafael is like the Hysteric Smile of Revenge. His Softness & Candour, the hidden trap & the poisoned feast. He praises Michel Angelo for Qualities which Michel Angelo abhorr'd, & He blames Rafael for the only Qualities which Rafael Valued. Whether Reynolds knew what he was doing is nothing to me: the Mischief is just the same whether a Man does it Ignorantly or Knowingly. I always consider'd True Art & True Artists to be particularly Insulted & Degraded by the Reputation of these Discourses, As much as they were Degraded by the Reputation of Reynolds's Paintings, & that Such Artists as Reynolds are at all times Hired by the Satans for the Depression of Art—A Pretence of Art, To destroy Art.

Page 3.

The Neglect of Fuseli's Milton in a Country pretending to the Encouragement of Art is a Sufficient Apology for My Vigorous Indignation, if indeed the Neglect of My own Powers had not been. Ought not the Employers of Fools to be Execrated in future Ages? They Will and Shall! Foolish Men, your own real Greatness depends on your Encouragement of the Arts, & your Fall will depend on [your *del.*] their Neglect & Depression. What you Fear is your true Interest. Leo X was advised not to Encourage the Arts; he was too Wise to take this Advice.

Page 4.

The Rich Men of England form themselves into a Society to Sell & Not to Buy Pictures. The Artist who does not throw his Contempt on such Trading Exhibitions, does not know either his own Interest or his Duty.

When Nations grow Old, The Arts grow Cold
And Commerce settles on every Tree,
And the Poor & the Old can live upon Gold,
For all are Born Poor, Aged Sixty three.

Page 5.

Reynolds's Opinion was that Genius May be Taught & that all Pretence to Inspiration is a Lie & a Deceit, to say the least of it. For if it is a Deceit, the whole Bible is Madness. This Opinion originates in the Greeks' Calling the Muses Daughters of Memory.

The Enquiry in England is not whether a Man has Talents & Genius,

But whether he is Passive & Polite & a Virtuous Ass & obedient to Noblemen's Opinions in Art & Science. If he is, he is a Good Man. If Not, he must be Starved.

Page 7.

After so much has been done by His Majesty. . . .

3 Farthings!

Page 9.

Raffaelle, it is true, had not the advantage of studying in an Academy; but all Rome, and the works of Michael Angelo in particular, were to him an Academy. On the sight of the Capella Sistina, he immediately from a dry, Gothick, and even insipid manner, which attends to the minute accidental discriminations of particular and individual objects, assumed that grand style of painting which improves partial representation by the general and invariable ideas of nature.

Minute Discrimination is Not Accidental. All Sublimity is founded on Minute Discrimination.

I do not believe that Rafael taught Mich. Angelo, or that Mich. Angelo taught Rafael, any more than I believe that the Rose teaches the Lilly how to grow, or the Apple tree teaches the Pear tree how to bear Fruit. I do not believe the tales of Anecdote writers when they militate against Individual Character.

Page 11.

I would chiefly recommend that an implicit obedience to the Rules of Art, as established by the practice of the great Masters should be exacted from the young Students. That those models, which have passed through the approbation of ages, should be considered by them as perfect and infallible guides; as subjects for their imitation, not their criticism.

Imitation is Criticism.

Page 13.

A facility in composing—a lively, and what is called a masterly handling of the chalk or pencil are . . . captivating qualities to young minds.

I consider The Following sentence is Supremely Insolent for the following Reasons:—Why this Sentence should be begun by the Words "A Facility in Composing" I cannot tell, unless it was to cast a stigma upon Real Facility in Composition by Assimilating it with a Pretence to, & Imitation of, Facility in Execution; or are we to understand him to mean that Facility in Composing is a Frivolous pursuit? A Facility in Composing is the Greatest Power of Art, & Belongs to None but the Greatest Artists and the Most Minutely Discriminating & Determinate.

Page 14.

By this useless industry they are excluded from all power of advancing in real excellence. Whilst boys, they are arrived at their utmost perfection; . . . and make the mechanical felicity the chief excellence of the art, which is only an ornament.

Mechanical Excellence is the Only Vehicle of Genius.

This seems to me to be one of the most dangerous sources of corruption . . . which has actually infected all foreign Academies. The directors . . . praised their dispatch at the expence of their correctness.

This is all False & Self-Contradictory.

But young men have not only this frivolous ambition of being thought masters of execution, inciting them on one hand, but also their natural sloth tempting them on the other.

Execution is the Chariot of Genius.

Page 15.

They wish to find some shorter path to excellence, . . . They must therefore be told again and again, that labour is the only price of solid fame, . . .

This is All Self-Contradictory, Truth & Falsehood Jumbled Together.

When we read the lives of the most eminent Painters, every page informs us that no part of their time was spent in dissipation . . . They pursued their studies . . .

The Lives of Painters say that Rafael Died of Dissipation. Idleness is one Thing & Dissipation Another. He who has Nothing to Dissipate Cannot Dissipate; the Weak Man may be Virtuous Enough, but will Never be an Artist.

Painters are noted for being Dissipated & Wild.

Page 16.

When they [the old masters] conceived a subject, they first made a variety of sketches, then a finished drawing of the whole; after that a more correct drawing of every separate part—heads, hands, feet, and pieces of drapery; they then painted the picture, *and after all re-touched it from life.*

This is False.

The Students instead of vying with each other which shall have the readiest hand, should be taught to contend who shall have the purest and most correct outline.

Excellent!

Page 17.

The error I mean is, that the students never draw exactly from the living models which they have before them. They make a drawing rather of what they think the figure ought to be, than of what it appears. I have thought this the obstacle that has stopped the progress of many young men . . . I very much doubt whether a habit of drawing correctly what we see, will not give a proportionable power of drawing correctly what we imagine.

This is Admirably Said. Why does he not always allow as much?

Page 18.

He who endeavours to copy nicely the figure before him, not only acquires a habit of exactness and precision, but is continually advancing in his knowledge of the human figure.

Excellent!

Page 22.

The Labour'd Works of Journeymen employ'd by Correggio, Titian, Veronese & all the Venetians, ought not to be shewn to the Young Artist as the Works of original Conception any more than the Engravings of Strange, Bartollozzi, or Wollett. They are Works of Manual Labour.

DISCOURSE II

Page 23.

The course and order of Study.—The different Stages of Art.—Much copying discountenanced.—The artist at all times and in all places should be employ'd in laying up materials for the exercise of his art.

What is Laying up materials but Copying?

Page 25.

When the Artist is once enabled to express himself . . . he must then endeavour to collect subjects for expression; to amass a stock of ideas . . . to learn all that has been known and done before . . .

After having been a Fool, a Student is to amass a Stock of Ideas, &, knowing himself to be a Fool, he is to assume the Right to put other Men's Ideas into his Foolery.

Page 26.

Though the Student will not resign himself blindly to any single authority, when he may have the advantage of consulting many, he must still be afraid of trusting to his own judgment, and of deviating into any track where he cannot find the footsteps of some former master.

Instead of Following One Great Master he is to follow a Great Many Fools.

Page 29.

A Student unacquainted with the attempts of former adventurers, is always apt to over-rate his own abilities; to mistake the most trifling excursions for discoveries of moment, and every coast new to him, for a new-found country.

Contemptible Mocks!

The productions of such minds are seldom distinguished by an air of originality; they are anticipated in their happiest efforts; and if they are found to differ in anything from their predecessors, it is only in irregular sallies and trifling conceits.

Thus Reynolds Depreciates the Efforts of Inventive Genius. Trifling Conceits are better than Colouring without any meaning at all.

Page 32.

How incapable those are of producing anything of their own, who have spent much of their time in making finished copies, is well known to all who are conversant with our art.

This is most False, for no one can ever Design till he has learn'd the Language of Art by making many Finish'd Copies both of Nature & Art & of whatever comes in his way from Earliest Childhood. The difference between a bad Artist & a Good One Is: the Bad Artist Seems to Copy a Great deal. The Good one Really Does Copy a Great deal.

Page 33.
The great use in copying, if it be at all useful, should seem to be in learning to colour; yet even colouring will never be perfectly attained by servilely copying the model before you.

Contemptible! Servile Copying is the Great Merit of Copying.

Page 34.
Following these rules, and using these precautions, when you have clearly and distinctly learned in what good colouring consists, you cannot do better than have recourse to nature herself, who is always at hand, and in comparison of whose true splendour the best coloured pictures are but faint and feeble.

Nonsense! Every Eye Sees differently. As the Eye, Such the Object.

Page 35.
Instead of copying the touches of those great masters, copy only their conceptions . . . Labour to invent on their general principles and way of thinking.

General Principles Again! Unless You Consult Particulars You Cannot even Know or See Mich. Ang°. or Rafael or any Thing Else.

But as mere enthusiasm will carry you but a little way . . .

Meer Enthusiasm is the All in All! Bacon's Philosophy has Ruin'd England. Bacon is only Epicurus over again.

Page 37.
Few have been taught to any purpose who have not been their own teachers.

True!

Page 40.
A facility of drawing, like that of playing upon a musical instrument, cannot be acquired but by an infinite number of acts.

True!

Page 41.
I would particularly recommend that after your return from the Academy . . . you would endeavour to draw the figure by memory.

Good advice!

But while I mention the port-crayon as the student's constant companion, he must still remember that the pencil is the instrument by which he must hope to obtain eminence.

Nonsense!

Page 42.
The Venetian and Flemish schools, which owe much of their fame to colouring, have enriched the cabinets of the collectors of drawings with very few examples.

—because they could not draw.

Page 43.
Those of Titian, Paul Veronese, Tintoret, and the Bassans are in general slight and undetermined. Their sketches on paper are as rude as their pictures are excellent in regard to harmony of colouring. Correggio and Baroccio have left few, if any finished drawings behind them. And in the Flemish school, Rubens and Vandyck made their drawings for the most part in colour or in chiaro oscuro.

All the Pictures said to be by these Men are the Laboured fabrications of Journey-work. They could not draw.

Page 47.
He who would have you believe that he is waiting for the inspiration of Genius, is in reality at a loss how to begin, and is at last delivered of his monsters, with difficulty and pain.

A Stroke at Mortimer!

Pages 46, 48.
He regards all Nature with a view to his profession; and combines her beauties, or corrects her defects. . . .
The well-grounded painter . . . is contented that all shall be as great as himself, who have undergone the same fatigue . . .

The Man who asserts that there is no Such Thing as Softness in Art, & that every thing in Art is Definite & Determinate, has not been told this by Practise, but by Inspiration & Vision, because Vision is Determinate & Perfect, & he Copies That without Fatigue, Every thing being Definite & determinate. Softness is Produced alone by Comparative Strength & Weakness in the Marking out of the Forms. I say These Principles could never be found out by the Study of Nature without Con–or Innate Science.

DISCOURSE III

Page 50.
A work of Genius is a Work "Not to be obtain'd by the Invocation "of Memory & her Syren Daughters, but by Devout prayer to that "Eternal Spirit, who can enrich with all utterance & knowledge & "sends out his Seraphim with the hallowed fire of his Altar to touch "& purify the lips of whom he pleases." MILTON.
The following [Lecture *del.*] Discourse is particularly Interesting to Block heads, as it Endeavours to prove That there is No such thing as Inspiration & that any Man of a plain Understanding may by Thieving from Others become a Mich. Angelo.

Page 52.
The wish of the genuine painter must be more extensive: instead of endeavouring to amuse mankind with the minute neatness of his imitations, he must endeavour to improve them by the grandeur of his ideas.

Without Minute Neatness of Execution The Sublime cannot Exist! Grandeur of Ideas is founded on Precision of Ideas.

Page 54.

The Moderns are not less convinced than the Ancients of this superior power existing in the art; nor less sensible of its effects.

I wish that this was True.

Page 55.

Such is the warmth with which both the Ancients and Moderns speak of this divine principle of the art;

And such is the Coldness with which Reynolds speaks! And such is his Enmity.

but, as I have formerly observed, enthusiastick admiration seldom promotes knowledge.

Enthusiastic Admiration is the first Principle of Knowledge & its last. Now he begins to Degrade, to Deny & to Mock.

Though a student by such praise may have his attention roused . . . *He examines* his own mind, and perceives there nothing of that divine inspiration, with which, he is told, so many others have been favoured.

The Man who on Examining his own Mind finds nothing of Inspiration ought not to dare to be an Artist; he is a Fool & a Cunning Knave suited to the Purposes of Evil Demons.

Page 56.

He never travelled to heaven to gather new ideas; and he finds himself possessed of no other qualifications than what mere common observation and a plain understanding can confer.

The Man who never in his Mind & Thoughts travel'd to Heaven Is No Artist.

Artists who are above a plain Understanding are Mock'd & Destroy'd by this President of Fools.

But on this, as upon many other occasions, we ought to distinguish how much is to be given to enthusiasm, and how much to reason . . . taking care . . . not to lose in terms of vague admiration, that solidity and truth of principle, upon which alone we can reason, and may be enabled to practise.

It is Evident that Reynolds Wish'd none but Fools to be in the Arts & in order to this, he calls all others Vague Enthusiasts or Madmen. What has Reasoning to do with the Art of Painting?

Page 57.

. . . most people err, not so much from want of capacity to find their object, as from not knowing what object to pursue.

The Man who does not know what Object to Pursue is an Idiot.

This great ideal perfection and beauty are not to be sought in the heavens, but upon the earth.

A Lie!

They are about us, and upon every side of us.

A Lie!

But the power of discovering what is deformed in nature, or in other words, what is particular and uncommon, can be acquired only by experience;

A Lie!

Page 58.

and the whole beauty of the art consists, in my opinion, in being able to get above all singular forms, local customs, particularities, and details of every kind.

A Folly! Singular & Particular Detail is the Foundation of the Sublime.

All the objects which are exhibited to our view by nature, upon close examination will be found to have their blemishes and defects. The most beautiful forms have something about them like weakness, minuteness, or imperfection.

Minuteness is their whole Beauty.

This long laborious comparison should be the first study of the painter, who aims at the greatest style . . . he corrects nature by herself . . . This idea of the perfect state of nature, which the Artist calls the Ideal Beauty, is the great leading principle by which works of genius are conducted

Knowledge of Ideal Beauty is Not to be Acquired. It is Born with us. Innate Ideas are in Every Man, Born with him; they are truly Himself. The Man who says that we have No Innate Ideas must be a Fool & Knave, Having No Con-Science or Innate Science.

Page 60.

Thus it is from a reiterated experience and a close comparison of the objects in nature, that an artist becomes possessed of the idea of that central form . . . from which every deviation is deformity.

One Central Form composed of all other Forms being Granted, it does not therefore follow that all other Forms are Deformity.

All Forms are Perfect in the Poet's Mind, but these are not Abstracted nor Compounded from Nature, but are from Imagination.

Page 61.

Even the great Bacon treats with ridicule the idea of confining proportion to rules, or of producing beauty by selection.

The Great Bacon—he is Call'd: I call him the Little Bacon—says that Every thing must be done by Experiment; his first principle is Unbelief, and yet here he says that Art must be produc'd Without such Method. He is Like S[r] Joshua, full of Self-Contradiction & Knavery.

There is a rule, obtained out of general nature, to contradict which is to fall into deformity.

What is General Nature? is there Such a Thing? what is General Knowledge? is there such a Thing? Strictly Speaking All Knowledge is Particular.

Page 62.

To the principle I have laid down, that the idea of beauty in each species of beings is an invariable one, it may be objected, that in every particular species there are various central forms, which are separate and distinct from each other, and yet are each undeniably beautiful.

Here he loses sight of A Central Form & Gets into Many Central Forms.

Page 63.
It is true, indeed, that these figures are each perfect in their kind, though of different characters and proportions; but still none of them is the representation of an individual, but of a class.

Every Class is Individual.

Thus, though the forms of childhood and age differ exceedingly, there is a common form in childhood, and a common form in age, which is the more perfect, as it is more remote from all peculiarities.

There is no End to the Follies of this Man. Childhood & Age are Equally belonging to Every Class.

. . . though the most perfect forms of each of the general divisions of the human figure are ideal . . . yet the highest perfection of the human figure is not to be found in any one of them. It is not in the Hercules, nor in the Gladiator, nor in the Apollo.

Here he comes again to his Central Form.

Page 64.
There is, likewise, a kind of symmetry, or proportion, which may properly be said to belong to deformity. A figure lean or corpulent, tall or short, though deviating from beauty, may still have a certain union of the various parts.

The Symmetry of Deformity is a Pretty Foolery. Can any Man who Thinks Talk so? Leanness or Fatness is not Deformity, but Reynolds thought Character Itself Extravagance & Deformity. Age & Youth are not Classes, but [Situations *del.*] Properties of Each Class; so are Leanness & Fatness.

Page 65.
When the Artist has by diligent attention acquired a clear and distinct idea of beauty and symmetry; when he has reduced the variety of nature to the abstract idea . . .

What Folly!

Page 67.
. . . the painter . . . must divest himself of all prejudices in favour of his age or country; he must disregard all local and temporary ornaments, and look only on those general habits, which are every where and always the same . . .

Generalizing in Every thing, the Man would soon be a Fool, but a Cunning Fool.

Page 71.
Albert Durer, as Vasari has justly remarked, would, probably, have been one of the first painters of his age . . . had he been initiated into those great principles of the art, which were so well understood and practised by his contemporaries in Italy.

What does this mean, "*Would have been*" *one of the first Painters of his Age*? Albert Durer *Is*, Not would have been. Besides, let them look at Gothic Figures & Gothic Buildings & not talk of Dark Ages or of any Age. Ages are all Equal. But Genius is Always Above The Age.

Page 74.
I should be sorry, if what is here recommended, should be at all understood to countenance a careless or indetermined manner of painting. For though the painter is to overlook the accidental discriminations of nature, he is to exhibit distinctly, and with precision, the general forms of things.

Here he is for Determinate & yet for Indeterminate.
Distinct General Form Cannot Exist. Distinctness is Particular, Not General.

Page 75.
A firm and determined outline is one of the characteristics of the great style in painting; and let me add, that he who possesses the knowledge of the exact form which every part of nature ought to have, will be fond of expressing that knowledge with correctness and precision in all his works.

A Noble Sentence!
Here is a Sentence, Which overthrows all his Book.

To conclude; I have endeavoured to reduce the idea of beauty to general principles.

[Sir Joshua proves *del.*] that Bacon's Philosophy makes both Statesmen & Artists Fools & Knaves.

DISCOURSE IV

Page 78.

The Two Following Discourses are Particularly Calculated for the Setting Ignorant & Vulgar Artists as Models of Execution in Art. Let him who will, follow such advice. I will not. I know that The Man's Execution is as his Conception & No Better.

Page 79.
The value and rank of every art is in proportion to the mental labour employed in it, or the mental pleasure produced by it.

Why does he not always allow This?

Page 80.
I have formerly observed that perfect form is produced by leaving out particularities, and retaining only general ideas . . .

General Ideas again!

Invention in Painting does not imply the invention of the Subject; for that is commonly supplied by the Poet or Historian.

All but Names of Persons & Places is Invention both in Poetry & Painting.

Page 82:
However, the usual and most dangerous error is on the side of minuteness, and therefore I think caution most necessary where most have failed.

Here is Nonsense!

Page 83.
The general idea constitutes real excellence. All smaller things, however perfect in their way, are to be sacrificed without mercy to the greater.

Sacrifice the Parts, What becomes of the Whole?

Even in portraits, the grace, and, we may add, the likeness, consists more in taking the general air, than in observing the exact similitude of every feature.

How ignorant!

Page 86.
A painter of portraits retains the individual likeness; a painter of history shews the man by shewing his actions.

If he does not shew the Man as well as the Action, he is a poor Artist.

Page 87.
He cannot make his hero talk like a great man; he must make him look like one. For which reason he ought to be well studied in the analysis of those circumstances which constitute dignity of appearance in real life.

Here he allows an Analysis of Circumstances.

Page 89.
Certainly, nothing can be more simple than monotony: and the distinct blue, red, and yellow colours which are seen in the draperies of the Roman and Florentine schools . . . have the effect of grandeur which was intended. Perhaps these distinct colours strike the mind more forcibly, from there not being any great union between them; as martial musick . . . has its effect from the sudden and strongly marked transitions from one note to another . . .

These are Fine & Just Notions. Why does he not always allow as much?

Page 90.
In the same manner as the historical Painter never enters into the detail of colours, so neither does he debase his conceptions with minute attention to the discriminations of Drapery.

Excellent Remarks!

Carlo Maratti was of opinion, that the disposition of drapery was a more difficult art than even that of drawing the human figure . . .

I do not believe that Carlo Maratti thought so, or that any body can think so; the Drapery is formed alone by the Shape of the Naked.

Page 92.
Though I can by no means allow them [the Venetians] to hold any rank with the nobler schools of painting, they accomplished perfectly the thing they attempted. But as mere elegance is their principal object . . . it can be no injury to them to suppose that their practice is useful only to its proper end.

They accomplish'd Nothing. As to Elegance they have not a Spark.

Page 93.

[To a question] on the conduct of Paul Veronese, who . . . had, contrary to the strict rules of art . . . represented the principal figure in the shade, . . . if they had ranked him as an ornamental Painter, there would have been no difficulty in answering: ". . . . His intention was solely to produce an effect of light and "shadow; . . . and the capricious composition of that picture suited very well "with the style which he professed."

This is not a Satisfactory Answer. To produce an Effect of True Light & Shadow is Necessary to the Ornamental Style, which altogether depends on Distinctness of Form. The Venetian ought not to be call'd the Ornamental Style.

Page 94.

The powers exerted in the mechanical part of the Art have been called the language of Painters. . . . The language of Painting must indeed be allowed these masters [the Venetians].

The Language of Painters cannot be allow'd them if Reynolds says right at p. 97; he there says that the Venetian Will Not Correspond with the Great Style. The Greek Gems are in the Same Style as the Greek Statues.

Page 95.

Such as suppose that the great style might happily be blended with the ornamental, that the simple, grave and majestick dignity of Raffaelle could unite with the glow and bustle of a Paolo, or Tintoret, are totally mistaken.

What can be better said on this Subject? but Reynolds contradicts what he says continually. He makes little Concessions that he may take Great Advantages.

Page 97.

However great the difference is between the composition of the Venetian, and the rest of the Italian schools, there is full as great a disparity in the effect of their pictures as produced by colours . . . yet even that skill, as they have employed it, will but ill correspond with the great style. Their colouring is not only too brilliant, but . . . too harmonious to produce that . . . effect, which heroic subjects require. . . .

Somebody Else wrote this page for Reynolds. I think that Barry or Fuseli wrote it, or dictated it.

Page 98.

Michael Angelo . . . after having seen a picture by Titian, told Vasari . . . "that he "liked much his colouring and manner"; but then he added, "that it was a pity "the Venetian painters did not learn to draw correctly in their early youth, and "adopt a better manner of study." By this it appears, that the principal attention of the Venetian painters, in the opinion of Michael Angelo, seemed to be engrossed by the study of colours, to the neglect of the ideal beauty of form . . .

Venetian Attention is to a Contempt & Neglect of Form Itself & to the Destruction of all Form or Outline Purposely & Intentionally.

On the Venetian Painter

He makes the Lame to walk we all agree,
But then he strives to blind those who can see.

But if general censure was given to that school from the sight of a picture of Titian . . .

As if Mich. Ang. had seen but One Picture of Titian's! Mich. Ang. knew & despised all that Titian could do.

Page 99.

If the Venetian's Outline was Right, his Shadows would destroy it & deform its appearance.

A Pair of Stays to mend the Shape
Of crooked, Humpy Woman
Put on, O Venus! now thou art
Quite a Venetian Roman.

Page 100.

. . . when I speak of the Venetian painters, I wish to be understood to mean Paolo Veronese and Tintoret, to the exclusion of Titian; for . . . there is a sort of senatorial dignity about him . . .

Titian, as well as the other Venetians, so far from Senatorial Dignity appears to me to give always the Characters of Vulgar Stupidity.
Why should Titian & The Venetians be Named in a discourse on Art? Such Idiots are not Artists.

Venetian, all thy Colouring is no more
Than Boulster'd Plasters on a Crooked Whore.

Page 101.

The Venetian is indeed the most splendid of the schools of elegance . . .

Vulgarity & *not Elegance*; the Word Elegance ought to be applied to Forms, not to Colours.

Page 102.

. . . painting is not merely a gratification of the sight.

Broken Colours & Broken Lines & Broken Masses are Equally Subversive of the Sublime.

Such excellence, . . . where nothing higher than elegance is intended, is weak and unworthy of regard, when the work aspires to grandeur and sublimity.

Well Said Enough!

Page 103.

. . . the Flemish school, of which Rubens is the head, was formed upon that of the Venetian . . .

How can that be call'd the Ornamental Style of which Gross Vulgarity forms the Principal Excellence?

Page 104.

Some inferior dexterity, some extraordinary mechanical power is apparently that from which they seek distinction.

The Words, Mechanical Power, should not be thus Prostituted.

Page 106.
An History-Painter paints man in general; a Portrait-painter, a particular man, and consequently a defective model.

A History Painter Paints The Hero, & not Man in General, but most minutely in Particular.

Page 109.
. . . if a portrait-painter is desirous to raise and improve his subject . . . he leaves out all the minute breaks and peculiarities in the face, and changes the dress from a temporary fashion to one more permanent.

Folly! Of what consequence is it to the Arts what a Portrait Painter does?

Page 110.
Of those who have practised the composite style . . . perhaps the foremost is Correggio.

There is No Such Thing as A Composite Style.

Page 111.
The errors of genius . . . are pardonable . . .

Genius has no Error; it is Ignorance that is Error.

Page 112.
. . . there is but one presiding principle, which regulates, and gives stability to every art. The works . . . which are built upon general nature, live for ever; while those which depend for their existence on particular customs and habits . . . can only be coeval with that which first raised them from obscurity.

All Equivocation & Self-Contradiction!

DISCOURSE V

Page 114.
Gainsborough told a Gentleman of Rank & Fortune that the Worst Painters always chose the Grandest Subjects. I desired the Gentleman to Set Gainsborough about one of Rafael's Grandest Subjects, Namely Christ delivering the Keys to St Peter, & he would find that in Gainsborough's hands it would be a Vulgar Subject of Poor Fishermen & a Journeyman Carpenter.
The following Discourse is written with the same End in View that Gainsborough had in making the Above assertion, Namely To Represent Vulgar Artists as the Models of Executive Merit.

Page 116.
. . . nothing has its proper lustre but in its proper place. That which is most worthy of esteem in its allotted sphere, becomes an object, not of respect, but of derision, when it is forced into a higher, to which it is not suited.

Concessions to Truth for the sake of Oversetting Truth.

Pages 117–118.
If you mean to preserve the most perfect beauty in its most perfect state, you cannot express the passions . . .

What Nonsense!
Passion & Expression is Beauty Itself. The Face that is Incapable of Passion & Expression is deformity Itself. Let it be Painted & Patch'd & Praised & Advertised for Ever, it will only be admired by Fools.

Page 119.
. . . some of the Cartoons and other pictures of Raffaelle . . . where the excellent master himself may have attempted this expression of passions above the powers of the art.

If Reynolds could not see variety of Character in Rafael, Others Can.

We can easily, like the ancients, suppose a Jupiter to be possessed of all those powers and perfections which the subordinate Deities were endowed with separately. Yet, when they employed their art to represent him, they confined his character to majesty alone.

False! The Ancients were chiefly attentive to Complicated & Minute Discrimination of Character; it is the whole of Art.

Page 120.

Reynolds cannot bear Expression.

A statue in which you endeavour to unite stately dignity, youthful elegance, and stern valour, must surely possess none of these to any eminent degree.

Why not? O Poverty!

The summit of excellence seems to be an assemblage of contrary qualities . . .

A Fine Jumble!

Page 121.
If any man shall be master of such a transcendant, commanding, and ductile genius, as to enable him to rise to the highest, and to stoop to the lowest, flight of art, and to sweep over all of them unobstructed and secure, he is fitter to give example than to receive instruction.

Mocks!

Page 123.
The principal works of modern art are in Fresco, a mode of painting which excludes attention to minute elegancies.

This is False. Fresco Painting is the Most Minute. Fresco Painting is Like Miniature Painting; a Wall is a Large Ivory.

Page 124.
Raffaelle . . . owes his reputation . . . to his excellence in the higher parts of the art [Fresco]: . . . though he continually . . . embellished his performances more and more with the addition of those lower ornaments, which entirely make the merit of some painters, yet he never arrived at . . . perfection . . .

Folly & Falsehood! The Man who can say that Rafael knew not the smaller beauties of the Art ought to be contemn'd, & I accordingly hold Reynolds in Contempt for this Sentence in particular.

Page 125.
He never acquired that nicety of taste in colours, that breadth of light and shadow. . . . When he painted in oil, his hand seemed to be so cramped and confined, that he not only lost that facility and spirit, but . . . even that correctness of form.

Rafael did as he Pleased. He who does not admire Rafael's Execution does not Even see Rafael.

I have no desire to degrade Raffaelle from the high rank which he deservedly holds . . .

A Lie!

Page 126.
Michael Angelo . . . did not possess so many excellencies as Raffaelle, but those which he had were of the highest kind . . .

According to Reynolds Mich. Angelo was worse still & knew Nothing at all about Art as an object of Imitation. Can any Man be such a fool as to believe that Rafael & Michael Angelo were Incapable of the meer Language of Art & That Such Idiots as Rubens, Correggio & Titian knew how to Execute what they could not Think or Invent?

He [Michael Angelo] never attempted those lesser elegancies and graces in the art.

Damned Fool!

If any man had a right to look down upon the lower accomplishments as beneath his attention, it was certainly Michael Angelo.

O Yes!

Page 127.
. . . he has rejected all the false, though specious ornaments, which disgrace the works even of the most esteemed artists.

Here is another Contradiction. If Mich. Ang. Neglected any thing that Titian or Veronese did, He Rejected it for Good Reasons. S[r] Joshua in other Places owns that the Venetian Cannot Mix with the Roman or Florentine. What then does he Mean when he says that Mich. Ang. & Rafael were not worthy of Imitation in the Lower parts of Art?

Page 128.
If we put these great artists in a light of comparison with each other, Raffaelle had more Taste and Fancy, Michael Angelo more Genius and imagination.

What Nonsense!

Page 129.
Michael Angelo's works have a strong, peculiar, and marked character: they seem to proceed from his own mind entirely, . . . Raffaelle's materials are generally borrowed, though the noble structure is his own.

If all this is True, Why does not Reynolds recommend The Study of Rafael & Mich. Angelo's Execution? at page 97 he allows that the Venetian Style will Ill correspond with the great Style.

Page 131.
Such is the great style . . .: in this, search after novelty . . . has no place.

The Great Style is always Novel or New in all its Operations.

But there is another style, which . . . has still great merit . . . the original or characteristical style . . .

Original & Characteristical are the Two Grand Merits of the Great Style.

Pages 131–132.
One of the strongest-marked characters of this kind . . . is that of Salvator Rosa.

Why should these words be applied to such a Wretch as Salvator Rosa?
Salvator Rosa was precisely what he Pretended not to be. His Pictures are high Labour'd pretensions to Expeditious Workmanship. He was the Quack Doctor of Painting. His Roughnesses & Smoothnesses are the Production of Labour & Trick. As to Imagination, he was totally without Any.

Page 133.
He gives us a peculiar cast of nature, which . . . has that sort of dignity which belongs to savage and uncultivated nature.

Savages are Fops & Fribbles more than any other Men.

. . . what is most to be admired in him, is, the perfect correspondence which he observed between the subjects which he chose and his manner of treating them.

Handling is All that he has, & we all know this Handling is Labour & Trick. Salvator Rosa employ'd Journeymen.

Page 134.
I will mention two other painters, who, though entirely dissimilar . . . have both gained reputation. . . . The painters I mean, are Rubens and Poussin. Rubens . . . I think . . . a remarkable instance of the same mind being seen in all the various parts of the art. The whole is so much of a piece . . .

All Rubens's Pictures are Painted by Journeymen & so far from being all of a Piece, are The most wretched Bungles.

Page 135.
His Colouring, in which he is eminently skilled, is notwithstanding too much of what we call tinted.

To My Eye Rubens's Colouring is most Contemptible. His Shadows are of a Filthy Brown somewhat of the Colour of Excrement; these are fill'd with tints & messes of yellow & red. His lights are all the Colours of the Rainbow, laid on Indiscriminately & broken one into another. Altogether his Colouring is Contrary to The Colouring of Real Art & Science.

Opposed to Rubens's Colouring Sr Joshua has placed Poussin, but he ought to put All Men of Genius who ever Painted. Rubens & the Venetians are Opposite in every thing to True Art & they Meant to be so; they were hired for this Purpose.

Page 137.

Poussin in the latter part of his life changed from his dry manner to one much softer and richer . . . as in the Seven Sacraments . . ., but neither these, nor any of his other pictures in this manner, are at all comparable to many in his dry manner which we have in England.

True!

The favourite subjects of Poussin were Ancient Fables; and no painter was ever better qualified to paint such subjects . . .

True!

Page 138.

Poussin seemed to think that the style and the language in which such stories are told is not the worse for preserving some relish of the old way of painting . . .

True!

Page 139.

. . . if the Figures which people his pictures had a modern air or countenance,. . . if the landskip had the appearance of a modern view, how ridiculous would Apollo appear instead of the Sun . . .

These remarks on Poussin are Excellent.

Page 141.

It is certain that the lowest style will be the most popular, as it falls within the compass of ignorance itself.

Well said!

Page 142.

. . . our Exhibitions . . . have also a mischievous tendency, by seducing the Painter to an ambition of pleasing indiscriminately the mixed multitude of people who resort to them.

Why then does he talk in other places of pleasing Every body?

DISCOURSE VI

Page 144.

Imitation.—Genius begins where rules end.—Invention;—Acquired by being conversant with the inventions of others.—The true method of imitating . . .

When a Man talks of Acquiring Invention & of learning how to produce Original Conception, he must expect to be call'd a Fool by Men of Understanding; but such a Hired Knave cares not for the Few. His Eye is on the Many, or, rather, on the Money.

Page 147.
Those who have undertaken to write on our art, and have represented it as a kind of inspiration . . . seem to insure a much more favourable disposition from their readers . . . than he who attempts to examine, coldly, whether there are any means by which this art may be acquired . . .

Bacon's Philosophy has Destroy'd [*word cut away*] Art & Science. The Man who says that the Genius is not Born, but Taught—Is a Knave.

O Reader, behold the Philosopher's Grave!
He was born quite a Fool, but he died quite a Knave.

Page 149.
. . . to owe nothing to another, is the praise which men . . . bestow sometimes upon others; and sometimes on themselves; and their imaginary dignity is naturally heightened by a supercilious censure of . . . the servile imitator.

How ridiculous it would be to see the Sheep Endeavouring to walk like the Dog, or the Ox striving to trot like the Horse; just as Ridiculous it is to see One Man Striving to Imitate Another. Man varies from Man more than Animal from Animal of different Species.

Page 152.
But the truth is, that the degree of excellence which proclaims Genius is different, in different times and different places; and what shews it to be so is, that mankind have often changed their opinion upon this matter.

Never, Never!

Page 153.
These excellencies were, heretofore, considered merely as the effects of genius; and justly, if genius is not taken for inspiration, but as the effect of close observation and experience.

Damn'd Fool!

Page 154.
He who first made any of these observations . . . had that merit, but probably no one went very far at once . . . others worked more and improved further . . .

If Art was Progressive We should have had Mich. Angelos & Rafaels to Succeed & to Improve upon each other. But it is not so. Genius dies with its Possessor & comes not again till Another is Born with It.

Page 155.
It must of necessity be, that even works of Genius, like every other effect, as they must have their cause, must likewise have their rules.

Identities or Things are Neither Cause nor Effect. They are Eternal.

Page 157.
. . . our minds should be habituated to the contemplation of excellence . . . we should to the last moment of our lives continue a settled intercourse with all the true examples of grandeur. Their inventions are not only the food of our infancy, but the substance which supplies the fullest maturity of our vigour.

Reynolds Thinks that Man Learns all that he knows. I say on the Contrary that Man Brings All that he has or can have Into the World with him. Man is Born Like a Garden ready Planted & Sown. This World is too poor to produce one Seed.

The mind is but a barren soil; a soil which is soon exhausted, and will produce no crop, . . .

The mind that could have produced this Sentence must have been a Pitiful, a Pitiable Imbecillity. I always thought that the Human Mind was the most Prolific of All Things & Inexhaustible. I certainly do Thank God that I am not like Reynolds.

Page 158.
. . . or only one, unless it be continually fertilized and enriched with foreign matter.

Nonsense!

Page 159.
It is vain for painters or poets to endeavour to invent without materials on which the mind may work. . . . Nothing can come of nothing.

Is the Mind Nothing?

. . . we are certain that Michael Angelo, and Raffaelle, were equally possessed of all the knowledge in the art which had been discovered in the works of their predecessors.

If so they knew all that Titian & Correggio knew. Correggio was two years older than Mich. Angelo. Correggio born 1472, Mich. Angelo born 1474.

Page 161.
. . . it is not to be understood, that I advise any endeavour to copy the exact peculiar colour and complexion of another man's mind. . . . His model may be excellent but the copy will be ridiculous.

Why then Imitate at all?

Page 163.
Art in its perfection is not ostentatious; it lies hid, and works its effect, itself unseen. It is the proper study and labour of an artist to uncover and find out the latent cause of conspicuous beauties . . .

This is a Very Clever Sentence; who wrote it, God knows.

Page 165.
Peculiar marks, I hold to be, generally, if not always, defects; . . .

Peculiar Marks are the Only Merit.

Peculiarities in the works of art, are like those in the human figure . . . they are always so many blemishes;

Infernal Falshood!

Page 166.

Even the great name of Michael Angelo may be used, to keep in countenance a deficiency or rather neglect of colouring, and every other ornamental part of the art.

No Man who can see Michael Angelo can say that he wants either Colouring or Ornamental parts of Art in the highest degree, for he has Every Thing of Both.

Page 167.

. . . there is no defect that may not be excused, if it is a sufficient excuse that it can be imputed to considerable artists; . . .

He who Admires Rafael Must admire Rafael's Execution. He who does not admire Rafael's Execution Cannot Admire Rafael.

Page 172.

. . . want of strength of parts. In this certainly men are not equal . . .

A Confession!

Page 176.

In order to encourage you to imitation, to the utmost extent, let me add, that the very finished artists in the inferior branches of the art, will contribute to furnish the mind and give hints . . .

This Sentence is to Introduce another in Condemnation & Contempt of Alb. Durer.

The works of Albert Durer, Lucas Van Leyden, the numerous inventions of Tobias Stimmer, and Jost Ammon, afford a rich mass of genuine materials . . .

A Polish'd Villain who Robs & Murders!

Page 178.

The greatest style, if that style is confined to small figures, . . . would receive an additional grace by the elegance and precision of pencil so admirable in the works of Teniers . . .

What does Precision of Pencil mean? If it does not mean Outline, it means Nothing.

Page 179.

Jan Steen seems to be one of the most diligent and accurate observers . . . if [he] . . . had been blessed with Michael Angelo and Raffaelle for his masters . . . he now would have ranged with the great pillars and supporters of our Art.

Jan Steen was a Boor, & neither Rafael nor Mich. Ang. could have made him any better.

Page 180.

Men who although thus bound down by the almost invincible powers of early habits have still exerted extraordinary abilities . . . and have . . . given . . . great force and energy to their works . . .

He who can be bound down is No Genius. Genius cannot be Bound; it may be Render'd Indignant & Outrageous.

"Opression makes the Wise Man Mad."

SOLOMON.

DISCOURSE VII

Page 188.

The Purpose of the following discourse is to Prove That Taste & Genius are not of Heavenly Origin & that all who have supposed that they Are so, are to be Consider'd as Weak headed Fanatics.

The Obligations Reynolds has laid on Bad Artists of all Classes will at all times make them his Admirers, but most especially for this discourse, in which it is proved that the Stupid are born with Faculties Equal to other Men, Only they have not Cultivated them because they thought it not worth the trouble.

Page 194.

We will allow a poet to express his meaning, when his meaning is not well known to himself, with a certain degree of obscurity, as it is one source of the sublime.

Obscurity is Neither the Source of the Sublime nor of any Thing Else.

But when, in plain prose, we gravely talk of courting the muse in shady bowers; waiting the call and inspiration of Genius . . .; of attending to times and seasons when the imagination shoots with greatest vigour, . . . sagaciously observing how much the wild freedom and liberty of imagination is cramped by attention to established rules . . . we at best entertain notions not only groundless but pernicious.

The Ancients & the wisest of the Moderns were of the opinion that Reynolds condemns & laughs at.

Page 195.

. . . scarce a poet is to be found . . . who . . . continued practising his profession to the very last, whose latter works are not as replete with the fire of imagination, as those which were produced in his more youthful days.

As Replete, but Not More Replete.

To understand literally these metaphors or ideas expressed in poetical language, seems to be equally absurd as to conclude . . .

The Ancients did not mean to Impose when they affirm'd their belief in Vision & Revelation. Plato was in Earnest: Milton was in Earnest. They believ'd that God did Visit Man Really & Truly & not as Reynolds pretends.

Page 196.

. . . that because painters sometimes represent poets writing from the dictates of a little winged boy or genius, that this same genius really did inform him in a whisper what he was to write; and that he is himself but a mere machine, unconscious of the operations of his own mind.

How very Anxious Reynolds is to Disprove & Contemn Spiritual Perception!

Page 197.

It is supposed . . . that under the name of genius great works are produced, and under the name of taste an exact judgement given, without our knowing why . . .

Who Ever said this?

One can scarce state these opinions without exposing their absurdity . . .

He states Absurdities in Company with Truths & calls both Absurd.

Page 198.

. . . I am persuaded, that even among those few who may be called thinkers, the prevalent opinion allows less than it ought to the powers of reason . . .

The Artifice of the Epicurean Philosophers is to Call all other Opinions Unsolid & Unsubstantial than those which are derived from Earth.

We often appear to differ in Sentiments from each other, merely from the inaccuracy of terms.

It is not in Terms that Reynolds & I disagree. Two Contrary Opinions can never by any Language be made alike. I say, Taste & Genius are Not Teachable or Acquirable, but are born with us. Reynolds says the Contrary.

Page 199.

We apply the term TASTE to that act of the mind by which we like or dislike, whatever be the subject. . . . We are obliged to take words as we find them; all we can do is to distinguish the THINGS to which they are applied.

This is False; the Fault is not in Words, but in Things. Locke's Opinions of Words & their Fallaciousness are Artful Opinions & Fallacious also.

Page 200.

It is the very same taste which relishes a demonstration in geometry, that is pleased with the resemblance of a picture to an original, and touched with the harmony of musick.

Demonstration, Similitude & Harmony are Objects of Reasoning. Invention, Identity & Melody are Objects of Intuition.

Page 201.

Colouring is true . . . from brightness, from softness, from harmony, from resemblance; because these agree with their object, NATURE, and therefore are true; as true as mathematical demonstration; . . .

God forbid that Truth should be Confined to Mathematical Demonstration!

But beside real, there is also apparent truth, or opinion, or prejudice. With regard to real truth, when it is known, the taste which conforms to it, is, and must be, uniform.

He who does not Know Truth at Sight is unworthy of Her Notice.

In proportion as these prejudices are known to be generally diffused . . . the taste which conforms to them approaches nearer to certainty, . . .

Here is a great deal to do to Prove that All Truth is Prejudice, for All that is Valuable in Knowledge is Superior to Demonstrative Science, such as is Weighed or Measured.

Page 202.

As these prejudices become more narrow, . . . this secondary taste becomes more and more fantastical; . . .

And so he thinks he has proved that Genius & Inspiration are All a Hum.

Having laid down these positions, I shall proceed with less method . . .

He calls the Above proceeding with Method!

We will take it for granted, that reason is something invariable and fixed in the nature of things; . . .

Reason, or A Ratio of All we have Known, is not the Same it shall be when we know More; he therefore takes a Falshood for granted to set out with.

Page 203.

. . . we will conclude, that whatever goes under the name of taste, which we can fairly bring under the dominion of reason, must be considered as equally exempt from change.

Now this is Supreme Fooling.

The arts would lie open for ever to caprice and casualty, if those who are to judge of their excellencies had no settled principles by which they are to regulate their decisions, . . .

He may as well say that if Man does not lay down settled Principles, The Sun will not rise in a Morning.

Page 204.

My notion of nature comprehends not only the forms which nature produces, but also the nature and internal fabrick and organization . . . of the human mind and imagination.

Here is a Plain Confession that he Thinks Mind & Imagination not to be above the Mortal & Perishing Nature. Such is the End of Epicurean or Newtonian Philosophy; it is Atheism.

Page 208.

This [Poussin's Perseus and Medusa's head] is undoubtedly a subject of great bustle and tumult, and that the first effect of the picture may correspond to the subject, every principle of composition is violated; . . . I remember turning from it with disgust . . .

Reynolds's Eye could not bear Characteristic Colouring or Light & Shade.

This conduct of Poussin I hold to be entirely improper to imitate. A picture should please at first sight, and appear to invite the spectator's attention; ...

Please Whom? Some Men cannot see a Picture except in a Dark Corner.

Page 209.

No one can deny, that violent passions will naturally emit harsh and disagreeable tones: ...

Violent Passions Emit the Real, Good & Perfect Tones.

Page 214.

If it be objected that Rubens judged ill at first in thinking it necessary to make his work so very ornamental, this puts the question upon new ground.

Here it is call'd Ornamental that the Roman & Bolognian Schools may be Insinuated not to be Ornamental.

Page 215.

Nobody will dispute but some of the best of the Roman or Bolognian schools would have produced a more learned and more noble work.

Learned & Noble is Ornamental.

This leads us to another important province of taste, that of weighing the value of the different classes of the art, ...

A Fool's Balance is no Criterion because, tho' it goes down on the heaviest side, we ought to look what he puts into it.

Page 232.

If an European, when he has cut off his beard, ... or bound up his own natural hair in regular hard knots, as unlike nature as he can possibly make it; ... meets a Cherokee Indian, who has ... laid on with equal care and attention his yellow and red oker ... ; whoever of these two despises the other for this attention to the fashion of his country ... is the barbarian.

Excellent!

Page 242.

In the midst of the highest flights of fancy or imagination, reason ought to preside from first to last, ...

If this is True, it is a devilish Foolish Thing to be an Artist.

DISCOURSE VIII

Page 244.

Burke's Treatise on the Sublime & Beautiful is founded on the Opinions of Newton & Locke; on this Treatise Reynolds has grounded many of his assertions in all his Discourses. I read Burke's Treatise when very Young; at the same time I read Locke on Human Understanding & Bacon's Advancement of Learning; on Every one of these Books I wrote my Opinions, & on looking them over find that my Notes on Reynolds in this Book are exactly Similar. I felt the Same Contempt & Abhorrence then that I do now. They mock Inspiration & Vision. Inspiration & Vision was then, & now is, & I hope will always Remain, my Element, my Eternal Dwelling place; how can I then hear it Contemned without returning Scorn for Scorn?

Page 245.
The principles of art . . . have their foundation in the mind; such as novelty, variety and contrast; these in their excess become defects. . . .

Principles, according to S[r] Joshua, become defects.

I have recommended in former discourses, that Artists should . . . form an idea of perfection from the different excellencies which lie dispersed in the various schools of painting.

In another discourse he says that we cannot Mix the Florentine & Venetian.

Page 251.
An instance occurs to me of two painters (Rembrandt and Poussin,) of characters totally opposite to each other in every respect, . . . Rembrandt's manner is absolute unity . . . Poussin . . . has scarce any principal mass of light at all . . .

Rembrandt was a Generalizer. Poussin was a Particularizer.

. . . the works of Poussin being as much distinguished for simplicity, as those of Rembrandt for combination.

Poussin knew better that [than] to make all his Pictures have the same light & shadows. Any fool may concentrate a light in the Middle.

Page 256.
. . . the portraits of Titian, where dignity . . . has the appearance of an unalienable adjunct; . . .

Dignity an Adjunct!

Page 260.
When a young artist is first told, that his composition and his attitudes must be contrasted, . . . and that the eye must be gratified with a variety of colours;—when he is told this, with certain animating words, of Spirit, Dignity, Energy, Grace, greatness of Style, and brilliancy of Tints, he becomes suddenly vain of his newly acquired knowledge, . . .

Mocks!

Page 262.
The Art in its infancy, like the first work of a Student, was dry, hard, and simple, But this kind of barbarous simplicity, would be better named Penury, as it proceeds from mere want;

Mocks!

. . . their simplicity was the offspring, not of choice, but of necessity.

A Lie!

But however they may have strayed, we cannot recommend to them to return to that simplicity . . . but to deal out their abundance with a more sparing hand, . . .

Abundance of Stupidity!

Page 264.

. . . it is not enough that a work be learned; it must be pleasing.

If you Endeavour to Please the Worst, you will never Please the Best. To please All Is Impossible.

Page 266.

St. Paul preaching at Athens in one of the Cartoons, far from any affected academical contrast of limbs, stands equally on both legs, . . . add contrast, and the whole energy and unaffected grace of the figure is destroyed.

Well Said!

Page 267.

It is given as a rule by Fresnoy, That "the principal figure of a subject must "appear in the midst of the picture, under the principal light, to distinguish it "from the rest."

What a devil of a Rule!

Page 272.

. . . What those proportions are, cannot be so well learnt by precept as by observation on pictures, and in this knowledge bad pictures will instruct as well as good.

Bad Pictures are always S[r] Joshua's Friends.

It ought, in my opinion, to be indispensably observed, that the masses of light in a picture be always of warm mellow colour, yellow, red, or a yellowish-white, and that the blue, the grey, or the green colours be kept almost entirely out of these masses, and be used only to support and set off these warm colours; . . .

Colouring formed upon these Principles is destructive of All Art, because it takes away the possibility of Variety & only promotes Harmony or Blending of Colours one into another.

Page 274.

The conduct of Titian in the picture of Bacchus and Ariadne, has been much celebrated, and justly, for the harmony of colouring.

Such Harmony of Colouring is destructive of Art. One Species of General Hue over all is the Cursed Thing call'd Harmony; it is like the Smile of a Fool.

Page 275.

The illuminated parts of objects are in nature of a warmer tint than those that are in the shade: . . .

Shade is always Cold, & never, as in Rubens & the Colourists, Hot & Yellowy Brown.

Page 277.

. . . that fulness of manner which . . . is found in perfection in the best works of Correggio, and . . . of Rembrandt. This effect is produced by melting and losing the shadows in a ground still darker than those shadows; . . .

All This is Destructive of Art.

Page 279.

. . . a picture which I have of Rubens: it is a representation of a Moonlight. . . . The Moon in this picture does not preserve so gréat a superiority in regard to its lightness over the object which it illumines, as it does in nature; . . . If Rubens had preserved the same scale of gradation of light between the Moon and the objects, which is found in nature, the picture must have consisted of one small spot of light only, . . .

These are Excellent Remarks on Proportional Colour.

Page 281.

Reason and common sense tell us, that before, and above all considerations, it is necessary that the work should be seen . . . with pleasure and satisfaction.

If the Picture ought to be seen with Ease, surely The Nobler parts of the Picture, such as the Heads, ought to be Principal; but this Never is the Case except in the Roman & Florentine Schools. Note: I Include the Germans in the Florentine School.

Page 284.

It is true, sketches, or such drawings as painters generally make for their works, give this pleasure of imagination to a high degree. From a slight undetermined drawing . . . the imagination supplies more than the painter himself, probably, could produce, . . .

What Falshood!

Page 285.

. . . every thing shall be carefully and distinctly expressed, as if the painter knew, with correctness and precision, the exact form and character of whatever is introduced into the picture.

Excellent, & Contrary to his usual Opinions!

Page 286.

Mr. Falconet has observed . . . that the circumstance of covering the face of Agamemnon was probably not in consequence of any fine imagination of the painter, . . . but merely copied from the description of the sacrifice, as it is found in Euripides . . . Falconet does not at all acquiesce in the praise that is bestowed on Timanthes; . . .

I am of Falconet's opinion.

[END OF ANNOTATIONS TO REYNOLDS]

MILTON

a Poem in [1] 2 Books

The Author & Printer W Blake 1804

To Justify the Ways of God to Men

Written and etched, 1804-1808[1]

1

Preface

The Stolen and Perverted Writings of Homer & Ovid, of Plato & Cicero, which all Men ought to contemn, are set up by artifice against the Sublime of the Bible; but when the New Age is at leisure to Pronounce, all will be set right, & those Grand Works of the more ancient & consciously & professedly Inspired Men will hold their proper rank, & the Daughters of Memory shall become the Daughters of Inspiration. Shakspeare & Milton were both curb'd by the general malady & infection from the silly Greek & Latin slaves of the Sword.

Rouze up, O Young Men of the New Age! set your foreheads against the ignorant Hirelings! For we have Hirelings in the Camp, the Court & the University, who would, if they could, for ever depress Mental & prolong Corporeal War. Painters! on you I call. Sculptors! Architects! Suffer not the fash[i]onable Fools to depress your powers by the prices they pretend to give for contemptible works, or the expensive advertizing boasts that they make of such works; believe Christ & his Apostles that there is a Class of Men whose whole delight is in Destroying. We do not want either Greek or Roman Models if we are but just & true to our own Imaginations, those Worlds of Eternity in which we shall live for ever in Jesus our Lord.

And did those feet in ancient time
Walk upon England's mountains green?
And was the holy Lamb of God
On England's pleasant pastures seen?

---

[1] The plates are here numbered according to the arrangement found in copy D, the only complete copy of the original, with 50 plates. The pages without text are not included in the numbering.

And did the Countenance Divine
Shine forth upon our clouded hills?
And was Jerusalem builded here
Among these dark Satanic Mills?

Bring me my Bow of burning gold:
Bring me my Arrows of desire:
Bring me my Spear: O clouds unfold!
Bring me my Chariot of fire.

I will not cease from Mental Fight,
Nor shall my Sword sleep in my hand
Till we have built Jerusalem
In England's green & pleasant Land.

"Would to God that all the Lord's people were Prophets."
Numbers, xi. ch., 29 v.

MILTON

Book the First

2

Daughters of Beulah! Muses who inspire the Poet's Song,
Record the journey of immortal Milton thro' your Realms
Of terror & mild moony lustre in soft sexual delusions
Of varied beauty, to delight the wanderer and repose
His burning thirst & freezing hunger! Come into my hand,
By your mild power descending down the Nerves of my right arm
From out the Portals of my brain, where by your ministry
The Eternal Great Humanity Divine planted his Paradise,
And in it caus'd the Spectres of the Dead to take sweet forms
In likeness of himself. Tell also of the False Tongue! vegetated
Beneath your land of shadows, of its sacrifices and
Its offerings: even till Jesus, the image of the Invisible God,
Became its prey, a curse, an offering and an atonement
For Death Eternal in the heavens of Albion & before the Gates
Of Jerusalem his Emanation, in the heavens beneath Beulah.

Say first! what mov'd Milton, who walk'd about in Eternity
One hundred years, pond'ring the intricate mazes of Providence,
Unhappy tho' in heav'n—he obey'd, he murmur'd not, he was silent
Viewing his Sixfold Emanation scatter'd thro' the deep
In torment—To go into the deep her to redeem & himself perish?

What cause at length mov'd Milton to this unexampled deed,
A Bard's prophetic Song! for sitting at eternal tables,
Terrific among the Sons of Albion, in chorus solemn & loud
A Bard broke forth: all sat attentive to the awful man.

Mark well my words! they are of your eternal salvation.

Three Classes are Created by the Hammer of Los & Woven

3

By Enitharmon's Looms when Albion was slain upon his Mountains
And in his Tent, thro' envy of Living Form, even of the Divine
Vision,
And of the sports of Wisdom in the Human Imagination,
Which is the Divine Body of the Lord Jesus, blessed for ever.
Mark well my words! they are of your eternal salvation.

Urizen lay in darkness & solitude, in chains of the mind lock'd up
Los siez'd his Hammer & Tongs; he labour'd at his resolute Anvil
Among indefinite Druid rocks & snows of doubt & reasoning.

Refusing all Definite Form, the Abstract Horror roof'd, stony hard;
And a first Age passed over, & a State of dismal woe.

Down sunk with fright a red round Globe, hot burning, deep,
Deep down into the Abyss, panting, conglobing, trembling;
And a second Age passed over, & a State of dismal woe.

Rolling round into two little Orbs, & closed in two little Caves,
The Eyes beheld the Abyss, lest bones of solidness freeze over all;
And a third Age passed over, & a State of dismal woe.

From beneath his Orbs of Vision, Two Ears in close volutions
Shot spiring out in the deep darkness & petrified as they grew;
And a fourth Age passed over, & a State of dismal woe.

Hanging upon the wind, two nostrils bent down into the Deep;
And a fifth Age passed over, & a State of dismal woe.

In ghastly torment sick, a Tongue of hunger & thirst flamed out;
And a sixth Age passed over, & a State of dismal woe.

Enraged & stifled without & within, in terror & woe he threw his
Right Arm to the north, his left Arm to the south, & his Feet
Stamp'd the nether Abyss in trembling & howling & dismay;
And a seventh Age passed over, & a State of dismal woe.

Terrified, Los stood in the Abyss, & his immortal limbs
Grew deadly pale: he became what he beheld, for a red
Round Globe sunk down from his Bosom into the Deep; in pangs
He hover'd over it trembling & weeping; suspended it shook
The nether Abyss; in tremblings he wept over it, he cherish'd it
In deadly, sickening pain, till separated into a Female pale
As the cloud that brings the snow; all the while from his Back
A blue fluid exuded in Sinews, hardening in the Abyss
Till it separated into a Male Form howling in Jealousy.

Within labouring, beholding Without, from Particulars to Generals
Subduing his Spectre, they Builded the Looms of Generation;
They builded Great Golgonooza Times on Times, Ages on Ages.
First Orc was Born, then the Shadowy Female: then All Los's Family.
At last Enitharmon brought forth Satan, Refusing Form in vain,
The Miller of Eternity made subservient to the Great Harvest
That he may go to his own Place, Prince of the Starry Wheels

4

Beneath the Plow of Rintrah & the Harrow of the Almighty
In the hands of Palamabron, Where the Starry Mills of Satan
Are built beneath the Earth & Waters of the Mundane Shell:
Here the Three Classes of Men take their Sexual texture, Woven;
The Sexual is Threefold: the Human is Fourfold.

"If you account it Wisdom when you are angry to be silent and
"Not to shew it, I do not account that Wisdom, but Folly.
"Every Man's Wisdom is peculiar to his own Individuality.
"O Satan, my youngest born, art thou not Prince of the Starry Hosts
"And of the Wheels of Heaven, to turn the Mills day & night?
"Art thou not Newton's Pantocrator, weaving the Woof of Locke?
"To Mortals thy Mills seem every thing, & the Harrow of Shaddai
"A Scheme of Human conduct invisible & incomprehensible.
"Get to thy Labours at the Mills & leave me to my wrath."

Satan was going to reply, but Los roll'd his loud thunders.

"Anger me not! thou canst not drive the Harrow in pity's paths:
"Thy Work is Eternal Death with Mills & Ovens & Cauldrons.
"Trouble me no more; thou canst not have Eternal Life."

So Los spoke. Satan trembling obey'd, weeping along the way.
Mark well my words! they are of your eternal Salvation.

Between South Molton Street & Stratford Place, Calvary's foot,
Where the Victims were preparing for Sacrifice their Cherubim;
Around their Loins pour'd forth their arrows, & their bosoms beam
With all colours of precious stones, & their inmost palaces
Resounded with preparation of animals wild & tame,
(Mark well my words: Corporeal Friends are Spiritual Enemies)
Mocking Druidical Mathematical Proportion of Length, Bredth, Highth:
Displaying Naked Beauty, with Flute & Harp & Song.

5

Palamabron with the fiery Harrow in morning returning
From breathing fields, Satan fainted beneath the artillery.
Christ took on Sin in the Virgin's Womb & put it off on the Cross.
All pitied the piteous & was wrath with the wrathful, & Los heard it.

And this is the manner of the Daughters of Albion in their beauty.
Every one is threefold in Head & Heart & Reins, & every one
Has three Gates into the Three Heavens of Beulah, which shine
Translucent in their Foreheads & their Bosoms & their Loins
Surrounded with fires unapproachable: but whom they please
They take up into their Heavens in intoxicating delight;
For the Elect cannot be Redeem'd, but Created continually
By Offering & Atonement in the crue[l]ties of Moral Law.
Hence the three Classes of Men take their fix'd destinations.
They are the Two Contraries & the Reasoning Negative.

While the Females prepare the Victims, the Males at Furnaces
And Anvils dance the dance of tears & pain: loud lightnings
Lash on their limbs as they turn the whirlwinds loose upon
The Furnaces, lamenting around the Anvils, & this their Song:

"Ah weak & wide astray! Ah shut in narrow doleful form,
"Creeping in reptile flesh upon the bosom of the ground!
"The Eye of Man a little narrow orb, clos'd up & dark,
"Scarcely beholding the great light, conversing with the Void;
"The Ear a little shell, in small volutions shutting out
"All melodies & comprehending only Discord and Harmony;
"The Tongue a little moisture fills, a little food it cloys,
"A little sound it utters & its cries are faintly heard,
"Then brings forth Moral Virtue the cruel Virgin Babylon.

"Can such an Eye judge of the stars? & looking thro' its tubes
"Measure the sunny rays that point their spears on Udanadan?
"Can such an Ear, fill'd with the vapours of the yawning pit,
"Judge of the pure melodious harp struck by a hand divine?
"Can such closed Nostrils feel a joy? or tell of autumn fruits
"When grapes & figs burst their covering to the joyful air?
"Can such a Tongue boast of the living waters? or take in
"Ought but the Vegetable Ratio & loathe the faint delight?
"Can such gross Lips percieve? alas, folded within themselves
"They touch not ought, but pallid turn & tremble at every wind."

Thus they sing Creating the Three Classes among Druid Rocks.
Charles calls on Milton for Atonement. Cromwell is ready.
James calls for fires in Golgonooza, for heaps of smoking ruins
In the night of prosperity and wantonness which he himself Created
Among the Daughters of Albion, among the Rocks of the Druids
When Satan fainted beneath the arrows of Elynittria,
And Mathematic Proportion was subdued by Living Proportion.

6

From Golgonooza the spiritual Four-fold London eternal,
In immense labours & sorrows, ever building, ever falling,
Thro' Albion's four Forests which overspread all the Earth
From London Stone to Blackheath east: to Hounslow west:
To Finchley north: to Norwood south: and the weights
Of Enitharmon's Loom play lulling cadences on the winds of Albion
From Caithness in the north to Lizard-point & Dover in the south.

Loud sounds the Hammer of Los & loud his Bellows is heard
Before London to Hampstead's breadths & Highgate's heights, To
Stratford & old Bow & across to the Gardens of Kensington
On Tyburn's Brook: loud groans Thames beneath the iron Forge
Of Rintrah & Palamabron, of Theotorm & Bromion, to forge the instruments
Of Harvest, the Plow & Harrow to pass over the Nations.

The Surrey hills glow like the clinkers of the furnace; Lambeth's Vale
Where Jerusalem's foundations began, where they were laid in ruins,
Where they were laid in ruins from every Nation, & Oak Groves rooted,
Dark gleams before the Furnace-mouth a heap of burning ashes.
When shall Jerusalem return & overspread all the Nations?
Return, return to Lambeth's Vale, O building of human souls!
Thence stony Druid Temples overspread the Island white,

And thence from Jerusalem's ruins, from her walls of salvation
And praise, thro' the whole Earth were rear'd from Ireland
To Mexico & Peru west, & east to China & Japan, till Babel
The Spectre of Albion frown'd over the Nations in glory & war.
All things begin & end in Albion's ancient Druid rocky shore:
But now the Starry Heavens are fled from the mighty limbs of Albion.

Loud sounds the Hammer of Los, loud turn the Wheels of
Enitharmon:
Her Looms vibrate with soft affections, weaving the Web of Life
Out from the ashes of the Dead; Los lifts his iron Ladles
With molten ore: he heaves the iron cliffs in his rattling chains
From Hyde Park to the Alms-houses of Mile-end & old Bow.

Here the Three Classes of Mortal Men take their fix'd destinations,
And hence they overspread the Nations of the whole Earth, & hence
The Web of Life is woven & the tender sinews of life created
And the Three Classes of Men regulated by Los's Hammers [and
woven][1]

7

By Enitharmon's Looms & Spun beneath the Spindle of Tirzah.[2]
The first, The Elect from before the foundation of the World:
The second, The Redeem'd: The Third, The Reprobate & form'd
To destruction from the mother's womb: [The Reprobate are the
first
Who . . . *erased*] follow with me my plow.

Of the first class was Satan: with incomparable mildness,
His primitive tyrannical attempts on Los, with most endearing love
He soft intreated Los to give to him Palamabron's station,
For Palamabron return'd with labour wearied every evening.
Palamabron oft refus'd, and as often Satan offer'd
His service, till by repeated offers and repeated intreaties
Los gave to him the Harrow of the Almighty; alas, blamable,
Palamabron fear'd to be angry lest Satan should accuse him of
Ingratitude & Los believe the accusation thro' Satan's extreme
Mildness. Satan labour'd all day: it was a thousand years:
In the evening returning terrified, overlabour'd & astonish'd,
Embrac'd soft with a brother's tears Palamabron, who also wept.

Mark well my words! they are of your eternal salvation.

---

[1] These words inserted in two copies. [2] This line erased in two copies.

Next morning Palamabron rose: the horses of the Harrow
Were madden'd with tormenting fury, & the servants of the Harrow,
The Gnomes, accus'd Satan with indignation, fury and fire.
Then Palamabron, reddening like the Moon in an eclipse,
Spoke, saying: "You know Satan's mildness and his self-imposition,
"Seeming a brother, being a tyrant, even thinking himself a brother
"While he is murdering the just: prophetic I behold
"His future course thro' darkness and despair to eternal death.
"But we must not be tyrants also: he hath assum'd my place
"For one whole day under pretence of pity and love to me.
"My horses hath he madden'd and my fellow servants injur'd.
"How should he, he, know the duties of another? O foolish forbearance!
"Would I had told Los all my heart! but patience, O my friends,
"All may be well: silent remain, while I call Los and Satan."

Loud as the wind of Beulah that unroots the rocks & hills
Palamabron call'd, and Los & Satan came before him,
And Palamabron shew'd the horses & the servants. Satan wept
And mildly cursing Palamabron, him accus'd of crimes
Himself had wrought. Los trembled: Satan's blandishments almost
Perswaded the Prophet of Eternity that Palamabron
Was Satan's enemy & that the Gnomes, being Palamabron's friends,
Were leagued together against Satan thro' ancient enmity.
What could Los do? how could he judge, when Satan's self believ'd
That he had not oppres'd the horses of the Harrow nor the servants.

So Los said: "Henceforth, Palamabron, let each his own station
"Keep: nor in pity false, nor in officious brotherhood, where
"None needs, be active." Mean time Palamabron's horses
Rag'd with thick flames redundant, & the Harrow madden'd with fury.
Trembling Palamabron stood; the strongest of Demons trembled,
Curbing his living creatures; many of the strongest Gnomes
They bit in their wild fury, who also madden'd like wildest beasts.

Mark well my words! they are of your eternal salvation.

8

Mean while wept Satan before Los accusing Palamabron,
Himself exculpating with mildest speech, for himself believ'd
That he had not oppress'd nor injur'd the refractory servants.

But Satan returning to his Mills (for Palamabron had serv'd
The Mills of Satan as the easier task) found all confusion,
And back return'd to Los, not fill'd with vengeance but with tears,
Himself convinc'd of Palamabron's turpitude. Los beheld
The servants of the Mills drunken with wine and dancing wild
With shouts and Palamabron's songs, rending the forests green
With ecchoing confusion, tho' the Sun was risen on high.

Then Los took off his left sandal, placing it on his head,
Signal of solemn mourning: when the servants of the Mills
Beheld the signal they in silence stood, tho' drunk with wine.
Los wept! But Rintrah also came, and Enitharmon on
His arm lean'd tremblingly, observing all these things.

And Los said: "Ye Genii of the Mills! the Sun is on high,
"Your labours call you: Palamabron is also in sad dilemma:
"His horses are mad, his Harrow confounded, his companions enrag'd.
"Mine is the fault! I should have remember'd that pity divides the soul
"And man unmans: follow with me my Plow: this mournful day
"Must be a blank in Nature: follow with me and tomorrow again
"Resume your labours, & this day shall be a mournful day."

Wildly they follow'd Los and Rintrah, & the Mills were silent.
They mourn'd all day, this mournful day of Satan & Palamabron:
And all the Elect & all the Redeem'd mourn'd one toward another
Upon the mountains of Albion among the cliffs of the Dead.

They Plow'd in tears; incessant pour'd Jehovah's rain & Molech's
Thick fires contending with the rain thunder'd above, rolling
Terrible over their heads; Satan wept over Palamabron.
Theotormon & Bromion contended on the side of Satan,
Pitying his youth and beauty, trembling at eternal death.
Michael contended against Satan in the rolling thunder:
Thulloh the friend of Satan also reprov'd him: faint their reproof.

But Rintrah who is of the reprobate, of those form'd to destruction,
In indignation for Satan's soft dissimulation of friendship
Flam'd above all the plowed furrows, angry, red and furious,
Till Michael sat down in the furrow, weary, dissolv'd in tears.
Satan, who drave the team beside him, stood angry & red:
He smote Thulloh & slew him, & he stood terrible over Michael
Urging him to arise: he wept: Enitharmon saw his tears.
But Los hid Thulloh from her sight, lest she should die of grief.

She wept, she trembled, she kissed Satan, she wept over Michael:
She form'd a Space for Satan & Michael & for the poor infected.
Trembling she wept over the Space & clos'd it with a tender Moon.

Los secret buried Thulloh, weeping disconsolate over the moony Space.

But Palamabron called down a Great Solemn Assembly,
That he who will not defend Truth, may be compelled to
Defend a Lie, that he may be snared & caught & taken.

9

And all Eden descended into Palamabron's tent
Among Albion's Druids & Bards in the caves beneath Albion's
Death Couch, in the caverns of death, in the corner of the Atlantic.
And in the midst of the Great Assembly Palamabron pray'd:
"O God, protect me from my friends, that they have not power over me.
"Thou hast giv'n me power to protect myself from my bitterest enemies."

Mark well my words! they are of your eternal salvation.

Then rose the Two Witnesses, Rintrah & Palamabron:
And Palamabron appeal'd to all Eden and reciev'd
Judgment: and Lo! it fell on Rintrah and his rage,
Which now flam'd high & furious in Satan against Palamabron
Till it became a proverb in Eden: Satan is among the Reprobate.

Los in his wrath curs'd heaven & earth; he rent up Nations,
Standing on Albion's rocks among high-rear'd Druid temples
Which reach the stars of heaven & stretch from pole to pole.
He displac'd continents, the oceans fled before his face:
He alter'd the poles of the world, east, west & north & south,
But he clos'd up Enitharmon from the sight of all these things.

For Satan, flaming with Rintrah's fury hidden beneath his own mildness,
Accus'd Palamabron before the Assembly of ingratitude, of malice.
He created Seven deadly Sins, drawing out his infernal scroll
Of Moral laws and cruel punishments upon the clouds of Jehovah,
To pervert the Divine voice in its entrance to the earth
With thunder of war & trumpet's sound, with armies of disease,

Punishments & deaths muster'd & number'd, Saying: "I am God
alone:
"There is no other! let all obey my principles of moral individuality.
"I have brought them from the uppermost innermost recesses
"Of my Eternal Mind: transgressors I will rend off for ever
"As now I rend this accursed Family from my covering."

Thus Satan rag'd amidst the Assembly, and his bosom grew
Opake against the Divine Vision: the paved terraces of
His bosom inwards shone with fires, but the stones becoming opake
Hid him from sight in an extreme blackness and darkness.
And there a World of deeper Ulro was open'd in the midst
Of the Assembly. In Satan's bosom, a vast unfathomable Abyss.

Astonishment held the Assembly in an awful silence, and tears
Fell down as dews of night, & a loud solemn universal groan
Was utter'd from the east & from the west & from the south
And from the north; and Satan stood opake immeasurable,
Covering the east with solid blackness round his hidden heart,
With thunders utter'd from his hidden wheels, accusing loud
The Divine Mercy for protecting Palamabron in his tent.

Rintrah rear'd up walls of rocks and pour'd rivers & moats
Of fire round the walls: columns of fire guard around
Between Satan and Palamabron in the terrible darkness.

And Satan not having the Science of Wrath, but only of Pity,
Rent them asunder, and wrath was left to wrath, & pity to pity.
He sunk down, a dreadful Death unlike the slumbers of Beulah.

The Separation was terrible: the Dead was repos'd on his Couch
Beneath the Couch of Albion, on the seven mou[n]tains of Rome,
In the whole place of the Covering Cherub, Rome, Babylon & Tyre.
His Spectre raging furious descended into its Space.

10

Then Los & Enitharman [*sic*] knew that Satan is Urizen,
Drawn down by Orc & the Shadowy Female into Generation.
Oft Enitharmon enter'd weeping into the Space, there appearing
An aged Woman raving along the Streets (the Space is named
Canaan): then she returnd to Los, weary, frighted as from dreams.

The nature of a Female Space is this: it shrinks the Organs
Of Life till they become Finite & Itself seems Infinite.

And Satan vibrated in the immensity of the Space, Limited
To those without, but Infinite to those within: it fell down and
Became Canaan, closing Los from Eternity in Albion's Cliffs.
A mighty Fiend against the Divine Humanity, must'ring to War.

"Satan, Ah me! is gone to his own place," said Los: "their God
"I will not worship in their Churches, nor King in their Theatres.
"Elynittria! whence is this Jealousy running along the mountains?
"British Women were not Jealous when Greek & Roman were Jealous.
"Every thing in Eternity shines by its own Internal light, but thou
"Darkenest every Internal light with the arrows of thy quiver,
"Bound up in the horns of Jealousy to a deadly fading Moon,
"And Ocalythron binds the Sun into a Jealous Globe,
"That every thing is fix'd Opake without Internal light."

So Los lamented over Satan who triumphant divided the Nations.

II

He set his face against Jerusalem to destroy the Eon of Albion.

But Los hid Enitharmon from the sight of all these things
Upon the Thames whose lulling harmony repos'd her soul,
Where Beulah lovely terminates in rocky Albion,
Terminating in Hyde Park on Tyburn's awful brook.

And the Mills of Satan were separated into a moony Space
Among the rocks of Albion's Temples, and Satan's Druid sons
Offer the Human Victims throughout all the Earth, and Albion's
Dread Tomb, immortal on his Rock, overshadow'd the whole Earth,
Where Satan, making to himself Laws from his own identity,
Compell'd others to serve him in moral gratitude & submission,
Being call'd God, setting himself above all that is called God;
And all the Spectres of the Dead, calling themselves Sons of God,
In his Synagogues worship Satan under the Unutterable Name.

And it was enquir'd Why in a Great Solemn Assembly
The Innocent should be condemn'd for the Guilty. Then an Eternal rose,

Saying: "If the Guilty should be condemn'd he must be an Eternal Death,
"And one must die for another throughout all Eternity.
"Satan is fall'n from his station & never can be redeem'd,

"But must be new Created continually moment by moment.
"And therefore the Class of Satan shall be call'd the Elect, & those
"Of Rintrah the Reprobate, & those of Palamabron the Redeem'd:
"For he is redeem'd from Satan's Law, the wrath falling on Rintrah.
"And therefore Palamabron dared not to call a solemn Assembly
"Till Satan had assum'd Rintrah's wrath in the day of mourning,
"In a feminine delusion of false pride self-deciev'd."

So spake the Eternal and confirm'd it with a thunderous oath.

But when Leutha (a Daughter of Beulah) beheld Satan's condemnation,
She down descended into the midst of the Great Solemn Assembly,
Offering herself a Ransom for Satan, taking on her his Sin.

Mark well my words! they are of your eternal salvation.

And Leutha stood glowing with varying colours, immortal, heart-piercing
And lovely, & her moth-like elegance shone over the Assembly

At length, standing upon the golden floor of Palamabron,
She spake: "I am the Author of this Sin! by my suggestion
"My Parent power Satan has committed this transgression.
"I loved Palamabron & I sought to approach his Tent,
"But beautiful Elynittria with her silver arrows repell'd me,

12

"For her light is terrible to me: I fade before her immortal beauty.
"O wherefore doth a Dragon-Form forth issue from my limbs
"To sieze her new born son? Ah me! the wretched Leutha!
"This to prevent, entering the doors of Satan's brain night after night
"Like sweet perfumes, I stupified the masculine perceptions
"And kept only the feminine awake: hence rose his soft
"Delusory love to Palamabron, admiration join'd with envy.
"Cupidity unconquerable! my fault, when at noon of day
"The Horses of Palamabron call'd for rest and pleasant death,
"I sprang out of the breast of Satan, over the Harrow beaming
"In all my beauty, that I might unloose the flaming steeds
"As Elynittria used to do; but too well those living creatures
"Knew that I was not Elynittria and they brake the traces.
"But me the servants of the Harrow saw not but as a bow
"Of varying colours on the hills; terribly rag'd the horses.
"Satan astonish'd and with power above his own controll

"Compell'd the Gnomes to curb the horses & to throw banks of sand
"Around the fiery flaming Harrow in labyrinthine forms,
"And brooks between to intersect the meadows in their course.
"The Harrow cast thick flames: Jehovah thunder'd above.
"Chaos & ancient night fled from beneath the fiery Harrow:
"The Harrow cast thick flames & orb'd us round in concave fires,
"A Hell of our own making; see! its flames still gird me round.
"Jehovah thunder'd above; Satan in pride of heart
"Drove the fierce Harrow among the constellations of Jehovah,
"Drawing a third part in the fires as stubble north & south
"To devour Albion and Jerusalem, the Emanation of Albion,
"Driving the Harrow in Pity's paths; 'twas then, with our dark fires
"Which now gird round us (O eternal torment!) I form'd the Serpent
"Of precious stones & gold, turn'd poisons on the sultry wastes.
"The Gnomes in all that day spar'd not; they curs'd Satan bitterly
"To do unkind things in kindness, with power arm'd to say
"The most irritating things in the midst of tears and love:
"These are the stings of the Serpent! thus did we by them till thus
"They in return retaliated, and the Living Creatures madden'd.
"The Gnomes labour'd. I weeping hid in Satan's inmost brain.
"But when the Gnomes refus'd to labour more, with blandishments
"I came forth from the head of Satan: back the Gnomes recoil'd
"And call'd me Sin and for a sign portentous held me. Soon
"Day sunk and Palamabron return'd; trembling I hid myself
"In Satan's inmost Palace of his nervous fine wrought Brain:
"For Elynittria met Satan with all her singing women,
"Terrific in their joy & pouring wine of wildest power.
"They gave Satan their wine; indignant at the burning wrath,
"Wild with prophetic fury, his former life became like a dream.
"Cloth'd in the Serpent's folds, in selfish holiness demanding purity,
"Being most impure, self-condemn'd to eternal tears, he drove
"Me from his inmost Brain & the doors clos'd with thunder's sound.
"O Divine Vision who didst create the Female to repose
"The Sleepers of Beulah, pity the repentant Leutha! My

13

"Sick Couch bears the dark shades of Eternal Death infolding
"The Spectre of Satan: he furious refuses to repose in sleep.
"I humbly bow in all my Sin before the Throne Divine.
"Not so the Sick-one. Alas, what shall be done him to restore
"Who calls the Individual Law Holy and despises the Saviour,
"Glorying to involve Albion's Body in fires of eternal War?"

Now Leutha ceas'd: tears flow'd, but the Divine Pity supported her.

"All is my fault! We are the Spectre of Luvah, the murderer
"Of Albion. O Vala! O Luvah! O Albion! O lovely Jerusalem!
"The Sin was begun in Eternity and will not rest to Eternity
"Till two Eternitys meet together. Ah! lost, lost, lost for ever!"

So Leutha spoke. But when she saw that Enitharmon had
Created a New Space to protect Satan from punishment,
She fled to Enitharmon's Tent & hid herself. Loud raging
Thunder'd the Assembly dark & clouded, and they ratify'd
The kind decision of Enitharmon & gave a Time to the Space,
Even Six Thousand years, and sent Lucifer for its Guard.
But Lucifer refus'd to die & in pride he forsook his charge:
And they elected Molech, and when Molech was impatient
The Divine hand found the Two Limits, first of Opacity, then of Contraction.
Opacity was named Satan, Contraction was named Adam.
Triple Elohim came: Elohim wearied fainted: they elected Shaddai:
Shaddai angry, Pahad descended: Pahad terrified, they sent Jehovah,
And Jehovah was leprous; loud he call'd, stretching his hand to Eternity,
For then the Body of Death was perfected in hypocritic holiness,
Around the Lamb, a Female Tabernacle woven in Cathedron's Looms.
He died as a Reprobate, he was Punish'd as a Transgressor.
Glory! Glory! Glory! to the Holy Lamb of God!
I touch the heavens as an instrument to glorify the Lord!

The Elect shall meet the Redeem'd on Albion's rocks, they shall meet
Astonish'd at the Transgressor, in him beholding the Saviour.
And the Elect shall say to the Redeem'd: "We behold it is of Divine
"Mercy alone, of Free Gift and Election that we live:
"Our Virtues & Cruel Goodnesses have deserv'd Eternal Death."
Thus they weep upon the fatal Brook of Albion's River.

But Elynittria met Leutha in the place where she was hidden
And threw aside her arrows and laid down her sounding Bow.
She sooth'd her with soft words & brought her to Palamabron's bed
In moments new created for delusion, interwoven round about.
In dreams she bore the shadowy Spectre of Sleep & nam'd him Death:
In dreams she bore Rahab, the mother of Tirzah, & her sisters
In Lambeth's vales, in Cambridge & in Oxford, places of Thought,
Intricate labyrinths of Times and Spaces unknown, that Leutha lived
In Palamabron's Tent and Oothoon was her charming guard.

The Bard ceas'd. All consider'd and a loud resounding murmur
Continu'd round the Halls; and much they question'd the immortal
Loud voic'd Bard, and many condemn'd the high toned Song,
Saying: "Pity and Love are too venerable for the imputation
"Of Guilt." Others said: "If it is true, if the acts have been performed'd,
"Let the Bard himself witness. Where hadst thou this terrible Song?"

The Bard replied: "I am Inspired! I know it is Truth! for I Sing

14

"According to the inspiration of the Poetic Genius
"Who is the eternal all-protecting Divine Humanity,
"To whom be Glory & Power & Dominion Evermore. Amen."

Then there was murmuring in the Heavens of Albion
Concerning Generation & the Vegetative power & concerning
The Lamb the Saviour. Albion trembled to Italy, Greece & Egypt
To Tartary & Hindostan & China & to Great America,
Shaking the roots & fast foundations of the Earth in doubtfulness.
The loud voic'd Bard terrify'd took refuge in Milton's bosom.

Then Milton rose up from the heavens of Albion ardorous.
The whole Assembly wept prophetic, seeing in Milton's face
And in his lineaments divine the Shades of Death & Ulro:
He took off the robe of the promise & ungirded himself from the oath of God.

And Milton said: "I go to Eternal Death! The Nations still
"Follow after the detestable Gods of Priam, in pomp
"Of warlike selfhood contradicting and blaspheming.
"When will the Resurrection come to deliver the sleeping body
"From corruptibility? O when, Lord Jesus, wilt thou come?
"Tarry no longer, for my soul lies at the gates of death.
"I will arise and look forth for the morning of the grave:
"I will go down to the sepulcher to see if morning breaks:
"I will go down to self annihilation and eternal death,
"Lest the Last Judgment come & find me unannihilate
"And I be siez'd & giv'n into the hands of my own Selfhood.
"The Lamb of God is seen thro' mists & shadows, hov'ring
"Over the sepulchers in clouds of Jehovah & winds of Elohim,
"A disk of blood distant, & heav'ns & earths roll dark between.
"What do I here before the Judgment? without my Emanation?

"With the daughters of memory & not with the daughters of inspiration?
"I in my Selfhood am that Satan: I am that Evil One!
"He is my Spectre! in my obedience to loose him from my Hells,
"To claim the Hells, my Furnaces, I go to Eternal Death."

And Milton said: "I go to Eternal Death!" Eternity shudder'd,
For he took the outside course among the graves of the dead,
A mournful shade. Eternity shudder'd at the image of eternal death.

Then on the verge of Beulah he beheld his own Shadow,
A mournful form double, hermaphroditic, male & female
In one wonderful body; and he enter'd into it
In direful pain, for the dread shadow twenty-seven fold
Reach'd to the depths of direst Hell & thence to Albion's land,
Which is this earth of vegetation on which now I write.

The Seven Angels of the Presence wept over Milton's Shadow.

15

As when a man dreams he reflects not that his body sleeps,
Else he would wake, so seem'd he entering his Shadow: but
With him the Spirits of the Seven Angels of the Presence
Entering, they gave him still perceptions of his Sleeping Body
Which now arose and walk'd with them in Eden, as an Eighth
Image Divine tho' darken'd and tho' walking as one walks
In sleep, and the Seven comforted and supported him.

Like as a Polypus that vegetates beneath the deep,
They saw his Shadow vegetated underneath the Couch
Of death: for when he enter'd into his Shadow, Himself,
His real and immortal Self, was, as appear'd to those
Who dwell in immortality, as One sleeping on a couch
Of gold, and those in immortality gave forth their Emanations
Like Females of sweet beauty to guard round him & to feed
His lips with food of Eden in his cold and dim repose:
But to himself he seem'd a wanderer lost in dreary night.

Onwards his Shadow kept its course among the Spectres call'd
Satan, but swift as lightning passing them, startled the shades
Of Hell beheld him in a trail of light as of a comet
That travels into Chaos: so Milton went guarded within.

The nature of infinity is this: That every thing has its
Own Vortex, and when once a traveller thro' Eternity
Has pass'd that Vortex, he percieves it roll backward behind
His path, into a globe itself infolding like a sun,
Or like a moon, or like a universe of starry majesty,
While he keeps onwards in his wondrous journey on the earth,
Or like a human form, a friend with (with) whom he liv'd
benevolent.
As the eye of man views both the east & west encompassing
Its vortex, and the north & south with all their starry host,
Also the rising sun & setting moon he views surrounding
His corn-fields and his valleys of five hundred acres square,
Thus is the earth one infinite plane, and not as apparent
To the weak traveller confin'd beneath the moony shade.
Thus is the heaven a vortex pass'd already, and the earth
A vortex not yet pass'd by the traveller thro' Eternity.

First Milton saw Albion upon the Rock of Ages,
Deadly pale outstretch'd and snowy cold, storm cover'd,
A Giant form of perfect beauty outstretch'd on the rock
In solemn death: the Sea of Time & Space thunder'd aloud
Against the rock, which was inwrapped with the weeds of death.
Hovering over the cold bosom in its vortex Milton bent down
To the bosom of death: what was underneath soon seem'd above:
A cloudy heaven mingled with stormy seas in loudest ruin;
But as a wintry globe descends precipitant thro' Beulah bursting
With thunders loud and terrible, so Milton's shadow fell
Precipitant, loud thund'ring into the Sea of Time & Space.

Then first I saw him in the Zenith as a falling star
Descending perpendicular, swift as the swallow or swift:
And on my left foot falling on the tarsus, enter'd there:
But from my left foot a black cloud redounding spread over Europe.

Then Milton knew that the Three Heavens of Beulah were beheld
By him on earth in his bright pilgrimage of sixty years

16

To Annihilate the Self-hood of Deceit & False Forgiveness[1]

---

[1] This line accompanies a full-page illustration, and is independent of the text on plates 15 and 17.

17

In those three females whom his wives, & those three whom his
Daughters
Had represented and contain'd, that they might be resum'd
By giving up of Selfhood: & they distant view'd his journey
In their eternal spheres, now Human, tho' their Bodies remain clos'd
In the dark Ulro till the Judgment: also Milton knew: they and
Himself was Human, tho' now wandering thro' Death's Vale
In conflict with those Female forms, which in blood & jealousy
Surrounded him, dividing & uniting without end or number.

He saw the cruelties of Ulro and he wrote them down
In iron tablets; and his Wives' & Daughters' names were these:
Rahab and Tirzah, & Milcah & Malah & Noah & Hoglah.
They sat rang'd round him as the rocks of Horeb round the land
Of Canaan, and they wrote in thunder, smoke and fire
His dictate; and his body was the Rock Sinai, that body
Which was on earth born to corruption; & the six Females
Are Hor & Peor & Bashan & Abarim & Lebanon & Hermon,
Seven rocky masses terrible in the Desarts of Midian.

But Milton's Human Shadow continu'd journeying above
The rocky masses of The Mundane Shell, in the Lands
Of Edom & Aram & Moab & Midian & Amalek.

The Mundane Shell is a vast Concave Earth, an immense
Harden'd shadow of all things upon our Vegetated Earth,
Enlarg'd into dimension & deform'd into indefinite space,
In Twenty-seven Heavens and all their Hells, with Chaos
And Ancient Night & Purgatory. It is a cavernous Earth
Of labyrinthine intricacy, twenty-seven-folds of opakeness,
And finishes where the lark mounts; here Milton journeyed
In that Region call'd Midian among the Rocks of Horeb.
For travellers from Eternity pass outward to Satan's seat,
But travellers to Eternity pass inward to Golgonooza.

Los, the Vehicular terror, beheld him, & divine Enitharmon
Call'd all her daughters, Saying: "Surely to unloose my bond
"Is this Man come! Satan shall be unloos'd upon Albion!"

Los heard in terror Enitharmon's words: in fibrous strength
His limbs shot forth like roots of trees against the forward path
Of Milton's journey. Urizen beheld the immortal Man

18

And Tharmas, Demon of the Waters, & Orc, who is Luvah.

The Shadowy Female seeing Milton, howl'd in her lamentation
Over the Deeps, outstretching her Twenty seven Heavens over Albion,

And thus the Shadowy Female howls in articulate howlings:

"I will lament over Milton in the lamentations of the afflicted:
"My Garments shall be woven of sighs & heart broken lamentations:
"The misery of unhappy Families shall be drawn out into its border,
"Wrought with the needle with dire sufferings, poverty, pain & woe
"Along the rocky Island & thence throughout the whole Earth;
"There shall be the sick Father & his starving Family, there
"The Prisoner in the stone Dungeon & the Slave at the Mill.
"I will have writings written all over it in Human Words
"That every Infant that is born upon the Earth shall read
"And get by rote as a hard task of a life of sixty years.
"I will have Kings inwoven upon it & Councellors & Mighty Men:
"The Famine shall clasp it together with buckles & Clasps,
"And the Pestilence shall be its fringe & the War its girdle,
"To divide into Rahab & Tirzah that Milton may come to our tents.
"For I will put on the Human Form & take the Image of God,
"Even Pity & Humanity, but my Clothing shall be Cruelty:
"And I will put on Holiness as a breastplate & as a helmet,
"And all my ornaments shall be of the gold of broken hearts,
"And the precious stones of anxiety & care & desperation & death
"And repentance for sin & sorrow & punishment & fear,
"To defend me from thy terrors, O Orc, my only beloved!"

Orc answer'd: "Take not the Human Form, O loveliest, Take not
"Terror upon thee! Behold how I am & tremble lest thou also
"Consume in my Consummation; but thou maist take a Form
"Female & lovely, that cannot consume in Man's consummation.
"Wherefore dost thou Create & Weave this Satan for a Covering?
"When thou attemptest to put on the Human Form, my wrath
"Burns to the top of heaven against thee in Jealousy & Fear;
"Then I rend thee asunder, then I howl over thy clay & ashes.
"When wilt thou put on the Female Form as in times of old,
"With a Garment of Pity & Compassion like the Garment of God?
"His Garments are long sufferings for the Children of Men;
"Jerusalem is his Garment, & not thy Covering Cherub, O lovely
"Shadow of my delight, who wanderest seeking for the prey."

So spoke Orc when Oothoon & Leutha hover'd over his Couch
Of fire, in interchange of Beauty & Perfection in the darkness
Opening interiorly into Jerusalem & Babylon, shining glorious
In the Shadowy Female's bosom. Jealous her darkness grew:
Howlings fill'd all the desolate places in accusations of Sin,
In Female beauty shining in the unform'd void; & Orc in vain
Stretch'd out his hands of fire & wooed: they triumph in his pain.

Thus darken'd the Shadowy Female tenfold, & Orc tenfold
Glow'd on his rocky Couch against the darkness: loud thunders
Told of the enormous conflict. Earthquake beneath, around,
Rent the Immortal Females limb from limb & joint from joint
And moved the fast foundations of the Earth to wake the Dead.

Urizen emerged from his Rocky Form & from his Snows,

19

And he also darken'd his brows, freezing dark rocks between
The footsteps and infixing deep the feet in marble beds,
That Milton labour'd with his journey & his feet bled sore
Upon the clay now chang'd to marble; also Urizen rose
And met him on the shores of Arnon & by the streams of the brooks.

Silent they met and silent strove among the streams of Arnon
Even to Mahanaim, when with cold hand Urizen stoop'd down
And took up water from the river Jordan, pouring on
To Milton's brain the icy fluid from his broad cold palm.
But Milton took of the red clay of Succoth, moulding it with care
Between his palms and filling up the furrows of many years,
Beginning at the feet of Urizen, and on the bones
Creating new flesh on the Demon cold and building him
As with new clay, a Human form in the Valley of Beth Peor.

Four Universes round the Mundane Egg remain Chaotic,
One to the North, named Urthona: One to the South, named Urizen:
One to the East, named Luvah: One to the West, named Tharmas;
They are the Four Zoas that stood around the Throne Divine.
But when Luvah assum'd the World of Urizen to the South
And Albion was slain upon his mountains & in his tent,
All fell towards the Center in dire ruin sinking down.
And in the South remains a burning fire: in the East, a void:
In the West, a world of raging waters: in the North, a solid,
Unfathomable, without end. But in the midst of these
Is built eternally the Universe of Los and Enitharmon,
Towards which Milton went, but Urizen oppos'd his path.

The Man and Demon strove many periods. Rahab beheld,
Standing on Carmel. Rahab and Tirzah trembled to behold
The enormous strife, one giving life, the other giving death
To his adversary, and they sent forth all their sons & daughters
In all their beauty to entice Milton across the river.

The Twofold form Hermaphroditic and the Double-sexed,
The Female-male & the Male-female, self-dividing stood
Before him in their beauty & in cruelties of holiness,
Shining in darkness, glorious upon the deeps of Entuthon,

Saying: "Come thou to Ephraim! behold the Kings of Canaan!
"The beautiful Amalekites behold the fires of youth
"Bound with the Chain of Jealousy by Los & Enitharmon.
"The banks of Cam, cold learning's streams, London's dark frowning towers
"Lament upon the winds of Europe in Rephaim's Vale,
"Because Ahania, rent apart into a desolate night,
"Laments, & Enion wanders like a weeping inarticulate voice,
"And Vala labours for her bread & water among the Furnaces.
"Therefore bright Tirzah triumphs, putting on all beauty
"And all perfection in her cruel sports among the Victims.
"Come, bring with thee Jerusalem with songs on the Grecian Lyre!
"In Natural Religion, in experiments on Men
"Let her be Offer'd up to Holiness! Tirzah numbers her:
"She numbers with her fingers every fibre ere it grow.
"Where is the Lamb of God? where is the promise of his coming?
"Her shadowy Sisters form the bones, even the bones of Horeb
"Around the marrow, and the orbed scull around the brain.
"His Images are born for War, for Sacrifice to Tirzah,
"To Natural Religion, to Tirzah, the Daughter of Rahab the Holy!
"She ties the knot of nervous fibres into a white brain!
"She ties the knot of bloody veins into a red hot heart!
"Within her bosom Albion lies embalm'd, never to awake.
"Hand is become a rock: Sinai & Horeb is Hyle & Coban:
"Scofield is bound in iron armour before Reuben's Gate.
"She ties the knot of milky seed into two lovely Heavens,

20

"Two yet but one, each in the other sweet reflected; these
"Are our Three Heavens beneath the shades of Beulah, land of rest.
"Come then to Ephraim & Manasseh, O beloved-one!
"Come to my ivory palaces, O beloved of thy mother!
"And let us bind thee in the bands of War, & be thou King
"Of Canaan and reign in Hazor where the Twelve Tribes meet."

So spoke they as in one voice. Silent Milton stood before
The darken'd Urizen, as the sculptor silent stands before
His forming image; he walks round it patient labouring.
Thus Milton stood forming bright Urizen, while his Mortal part
Sat frozen in the rock of Horeb, and his Redeemed portion
Thus form'd the Clay of Urizen; but within that portion
His real Human walk'd above in power and majesty,
Tho' darken'd, and the Seven Angels of the Presence attended him.

O how can I with my gross tongue that cleaveth to the dust
Tell of the Four-fold Man in starry numbers fitly order'd,
Or how can I with my cold hand of clay! But thou, O Lord,
Do with me as thou wilt! for I am nothing, and vanity.
If thou chuse to elect a worm, it shall remove the mountains.
For that portion nam'd the Elect, the Spectrous body of Milton,
Redounding from my left foot into Los's Mundane space,
Brooded over his Body in Horeb against the Resurrection,
Preparing it for the Great Consummation; red the Cherub on Sinai
Glow'd, but in terrors folded round his clouds of blood.

Now Albion's sleeping Humanity began to turn upon his Couch,
Feeling the electric flame of Milton's awful precipitate descent.
Seest thou the little winged fly, smaller than a grain of sand?
It has a heart like thee, a brain open to heaven & hell,
Withinside wondrous & expansive: its gates are not clos'd:
I hope thine are not: hence it clothes itself in rich array:
Hence thou art cloth'd with human beauty, O thou mortal man.
Seek not thy heavenly father then beyond the skies,
There Chaos dwells & ancient Night & Og & Anak old.
For every human heart has gates of brass & bars of adamant
Which few dare unbar, because dread Og & Anak guard the gates
Terrific: and each mortal brain is wall'd and moated round
Within, and Og & Anak watch here: here is the Seat
Of Satan in its Webs: for in brain and heart and loins
Gates open behind Satan's Seat to the City of Golgonooza,
Which is the spiritual fourfold London in the loins of Albion.

Thus Milton fell thro' Albion's heart, travelling outside of Humanity
Beyond the Stars in Chaos, in Caverns of the Mundane Shell.

But many of the Eternals rose up from eternal tables
Drunk with the Spirit; burning round the Couch of death they stood
Looking down into Beulah; wrathful, fill'd with rage
They rend the heavens round the Watchers in a fiery circle
And round the Shadowy Eighth: the Eight close up the Couch

Into a tabernacle and flee with cries down to the Deeps,
Where Los opens his three wide gates surrounded by raging fires.
They soon find their own place & join the Watchers of the Ulro.

Los saw them and a cold pale horror cover'd o'er his limbs.
Pondering he knew that Rintrah & Palamabron might depart,
Even as Reuben & as Gad: gave up himself to tears:
He sat down on his anvil-stock and lean'd upon the trough,
Looking into the black water, mingling it with tears.

At last when desperation almost tore his heart in twain
He recollected an old Prophecy in Eden recorded
And often sung to the loud harp at the immortal feasts:
That Milton of the Land of Albion should up ascend
Forwards from Ulro from the Vale of Felpham, and set free
Orc from his Chain of Jealousy: he started at the thought

21

And down descended into Udan-Adan; it was night,
And Satan sat sleeping upon his Couch in Udan-Adan:
His Spectre slept, his Shadow woke; when one sleeps th'other wakes.

But Milton entering my Foot, I saw in the nether
Regions of the Imagination—also all men on Earth
And all in Heaven saw in the nether regions of the Imagination
In Ulro beneath Beulah—the vast breach of Milton's descent.
But I knew not that it was Milton, for man cannot know
What passes in his members till periods of Space & Time
Reveal the secrets of Eternity: for more extensive
Than any other earthly things are Man's earthly lineaments.
And all this Vegetable World appear'd on my left Foot
As a bright sandal form'd immortal of precious stones & gold.
I stooped down & bound it on to walk forward thro' Eternity.

There is in Eden a sweet River of milk & liquid pearl
Nam'd Ololon, on whose mild banks dwelt those who Milton drove
Down into Ulro: and they wept in long resounding song
For seven days of eternity, and the river's living banks,
The mountains, wail'd, & every plant that grew, in solemn sighs lamented.

When Luvah's bulls each morning drag the sulphur Sun out of the Deep
Harness'd with starry harness, black & shining, kept by black slaves

That work all night at the starry harness, Strong and vigorous
They drag the unwilling Orb: at this time all the Family
Of Eden heard the lamentation and Providence began.
But when the clarions of day sounded, they drown'd the lamentations,
And when night came, all was silent in Ololon, & all refus'd to lament
In the still night, fearing lest they should others molest.

Seven mornings Los heard them, as the poor bird within the shell
Hears its impatient parent bird, and Enitharmon heard them
But saw them not, for the blue Mundane Shell inclos'd them in.

And they lamented that they had in wrath & fury & fire
Driven Milton into the Ulro; for now they knew too late
That it was Milton the Awakener: they had not heard the Bard
Whose song call'd Milton to the attempt; and Los heard these laments.
He heard them call in prayer all the Divine Family,
And he beheld the Cloud of Milton stretching over Europe.

But all the Family Divine collected as Four Suns
In the Four Points of heaven, East, West & North & South,
Enlarging and enlarging till their Disks approach'd each other,
And when they touch'd, closed together Southward in One Sun
Over Ololon; and as One Man who weeps over his brother
In a dark tomb, so all the Family Divine wept over Ololon,

Saying: "Milton goes to Eternal Death!" so saying they groan'd in spirit
And were troubled; and again the Divine Family groaned in spirit.

And Ololon said: "Let us descend also, and let us give
"Ourselves to death in Ulro among the Transgressors.
"Is Virtue a Punisher? O no! how is this wondrous thing,
"This World beneath, unseen before, this refuge from the wars
"Of Great Eternity! unnatural refuge! unknown by us till now?
"Or are these the pangs of repentance? let us enter into them."

Then the Divine Family said: "Six Thousand Years are now
"Accomplish'd in this World of Sorrow. Milton's Angel knew
"The Universal Dictate, and you also feel this Dictate.
"And now you know this World of Sorrow and feel Pity. Obey
"The Dictate! Watch over this World, and with your brooding wings
"Renew it to Eternal Life. Lo! I am with you alway.
"But you cannot renew Milton: he goes to Eternal Death."

So spake the Family Divine as One Man, even Jesus,
Uniting in One with Ololon, & the appearance of One Man,
Jesus the Saviour, appear'd coming in the Clouds of Ololon.

22

Tho' driven away with the Seven Starry Ones into the Ulro,
Yet the Divine Vision remains Every-where For-ever. Amen.
And Ololon lamented for Milton with a great lamentation.

While Los heard indistinct in fear, what time I bound my sandals
On to walk forward thro' Eternity, Los descended to me:
And Los behind me stood, a terrible flaming Sun, just close
Behind my back. I turned round in terror, and behold!
Los stood in that fierce glowing fire, & he also stoop'd down
And bound my sandals on in Udan-Adan; trembling I stood
Exceedingly with fear & terror, standing in the Vale
Of Lambeth; but he kissed me and wish'd me health,
And I became One Man with him arising in my strength.
'Twas too late now to recede. Los had enter'd into my soul:
His terrors now posses'd me whole! I arose in fury & strength.

"I am that Shadowy Prophet who Six Thousand Years ago
"Fell from my station in the Eternal bosom. Six Thousand Years
"Are finish'd. I return! both Time & Space obey my will.
"I in Six Thousand Years walk up and down; for not one Moment
"Of Time is lost, nor one Event of Space unpermanent,
"But all remain: every fabric of Six Thousand Years
"Remains permanent, tho' on the Earth where Satan
"Fell and was cut off, all things vanish & are seen no more,
"They vanish not from me & mine, we guard them first & last.
"The generations of men run on in the tide of Time,
"But leave their destin'd lineaments permanent for ever & ever."

So spoke Los as we went along to his supreme abode.

Rintrah and Palamabron met us at the Gate of Golgonooza,
Clouded with discontent & brooding in their minds terrible things.

They said: "O Father most beloved! O merciful Parent
"Pitying and permitting evil, tho' strong & mighty to destroy!
"Whence is this Shadow terrible? wherefore dost thou refuse
"To throw him into the Furnaces? knowest thou not that he
"Will unchain Orc & let loose Satan, Og, Sihon & Anak
"Upon the Body of Albion? for this he is come! behold it written

"Upon his fibrous left Foot black, most dismal to our eyes.
"The Shadowy Female shudders thro' heaven in torment inexpressible,
"And all the Daughters of Los prophetic wail; yet in deceit
"They weave a new Religion from new Jealousy of Theotormon.
"Milton's Religion is the cause: there is no end to destruction.
"Seeing the Churches at their Period in terror & despair,
"Rahab created Voltaire, Tirzah created Rousseau,
"Asserting the Self-righteousness against the Universal Saviour,
"Mocking the Confessors & Martyrs, claiming Self-righteousness,
"With cruel Virtue making War upon the Lamb's Redeemed
"To perpetuate War & Glory, to perpetuate the Laws of Sin.
"They perverted Swedenborg's Visions in Beulah & in Ulro
"To destroy Jerusalem as a Harlot & her Sons as Reprobates,
"To raise up Mystery the Virgin Harlot, Mother of War,
"Babylon the Great, the Abomination of Desolation.
"O Swedenborg! strongest of men, the Samson shorn by the Churches,
"Shewing the Transgressors in Hell, the proud Warriors in Heaven,
"Heaven as a Punisher, & Hell as One under Punishment,
"With Laws from Plato & his Greeks to renew the Trojan Gods
"In Albion, & to deny the value of the Saviour's blood.
"But then I rais'd up Whitefield, Palamabron rais'd up Westley,
"And these are the cries of the Churches before the two Witnesses.
"Faith in God the dear Saviour who took on the likeness of men,
"Becoming obedient to death, even the death of the Cross.
"The Witnesses lie dead in the Street of the Great City:
"No Faith is in all the Earth: the Book of God is trodden under Foot.
"He sent his two Servants, Whitefield & Westley: were they Prophets,
"Or were they Idiots or Madmen? shew us Miracles!

23

"Can you have greater Miracles than these? Men who devote
"Their life's whole comfort to intire scorn & injury & death?
"Awake, thou sleeper on the Rock of Eternity! Albion awake!
"The trumpet of Judgment hath twice sounded: all Nations are awake,
"But thou art still heavy and dull. Awake, Albion awake!
"Lo, Orc arises on the Atlantic. Lo, his blood and fire
"Glow on America's shore. Albion turns upon his Couch:
"He listens to the sounds of War, astonishd and confounded:
"He weeps into the Atlantic deep, yet still in dismal dreams
"Unwaken'd, and the Covering Cherub advances from the East.

"How long shall we lay dead in the Street of the great City?
"How long beneath the Covering Cherub give our Emanations?
"Milton will utterly consume us & thee our beloved Father.
"He hath enter'd into the Covering Cherub, becoming one with
"Albion's dread Sons: Hand, Hyle & Coban surround him as
"A girdle, Gwendolen & Conwenna as a garment woven
"Of War & Religion; let us descend & bring him chained
"To Bowlahoola, O father most beloved! O mild Parent!
"Cruel in thy mildness, pitying and permitting evil,
"Tho' strong and mighty to destroy, O Los our beloved Father!"

Like the black storm, coming out of Chaos beyond the stars,
It issues thro' the dark & intricate caves of the Mundane Shell,
Passing the planetary visions & the well adorned Firmament.
The Sun rolls into Chaos & the stars into the Desarts,
And then the storms become visible, audible & terrible,
Covering the light of day & rolling down upon the mountains,
Deluge all the country round. Such is a vision of Los
When Rintrah & Palamabron spake, and such his stormy face
Appear'd as does the face of heaven when cover'd with thick storms,
Pitying and loving tho' in frowns of terrible perturbation.

But Los dispers'd the clouds even as the strong winds of Jehovah,
And Los thus spoke: "O noble Sons, be patient yet a little!
"I have embrac'd the falling Death, he is become One with me:
"O Sons, we live not by wrath, by mercy alone we live!
"I recollect an old Prophecy in Eden recorded in gold and oft
"Sung to the harp, That Milton of the land of Albion
"Should up ascend forward from Felpham's Vale & break the Chain
"Of Jealousy from all its roots; be patient therefore, O my Sons!
"These lovely Females form sweet night and silence and secret
"Obscurities to hide from Satan's Watch-Fiends Human loves
"And graces, lest they write them in their Books & in the Scroll
"Of mortal life to condemn the accused, who at Satan's Bar
"Tremble in Spectrous Bodies continually day and night,
"While on the Earth they live in sorrowful Vegetations.
"O when shall we tread our Wine-presses in heaven and Reap
"Our wheat with shoutings of joy, and leave the Earth in peace?
"Remember how Calvin and Luther in fury premature
"Sow'd War and stern division between Papists & Protestants.
"Let it not be so now! O go not forth in Martyrdoms & Wars!
"We were plac'd here by the Universal Brotherhood & Mercy
"With powers fitted to circumscribe this dark Satanic death,
"And that the Seven Eyes of God may have space for Redemption.
"But how this is as yet we know not, and we cannot know

"Till Albion is arisen; then patient wait a little while.
"Six Thousand years are pass'd away, the end approaches fast:
"This mighty one is come from Eden, he is of the Elect
"Who died from Earth & he is return'd before the Judgment. This thing
"Was never known, that one of the holy dead should willing return.
"Then patient wait a little while till the Last Vintage is over,
"Till we have quench'd the Sun of Salah in the Lake of Udan-Adan.
"O my dear Sons, leave not your Father as your brethren left me!
"Twelve Sons successive fled away in that thousand years of sorrow

24

"Of Palamabron's Harrow & of Rintrah's wrath & fury:
"Reuben & Manazzoth & Gad & Simeon & Levi
"And Ephraim & Judah were Generated because
"They left me, wandering with Tirzah. Enitharmon wept
"One thousand years, and all the Earth was in a wat'ry deluge.
"We call'd him Menassheh because of the Generations of Tirzah,
"Because of Satan: & the Seven Eyes of God continually
"Guard round them, but I, the Fourth Zoa, am also set
"The Watchman of Eternity: the Three are not, & I am preserved.
"Still my four mighty ones are left to me in Golgonooza,
"Still Rintrah fierce, and Palamabron mild & piteous,
"Theotormon fill'd with care, Bromion loving Science.
"You, O my Sons, still guard round Los: O wander not & leave me!
"Rintrah, thou well rememberest when Amalek & Canaan
"Fled with their Sister Moab into that abhorred Void,
"They became Nations in our sight beneath the hands of Tirzah.
"And Palamabron, thou rememberest when Joseph, an infant,
"Stolen from his nurse's cradle, wrap'd in needle-work
"Of emblematic texture, was sold to the Amalekite
"Who carried him down into Egypt where Ephraim & Menassheh
"Gather'd my Sons together in the Sands of Midian.
"And if you also flee away and leave your Father's side
"Following Milton into Ulro, altho' your power is great,
"Surely you also shall become poor mortal vegetations
"Beneath the Moon of Ulro: pity then your Father's tears.
"When Jesus rais'd Lazarus from the Grave I stood & saw
"Lazarus, who is the Vehicular Body of Albion the Redeem'd,
"Arise into the Covering Cherub, who is the Spectre of Albion,
"By martyrdoms to suffer, to watch over the Sleeping Body
"Upon his Rock beneath his Tomb. I saw the Covering Cherub
"Divide Four-fold into Four Churches when Lazarus arose,

"Paul, Constantine, Charlemaine, Luther; behold, they stand before us
"Stretch'd over Europe & Asia! come O Sons, come, come away!
"Arise, O Sons, give all your strength against Eternal Death,
"Lest we are vegetated, for Cathedron's Looms weave only Death,
"A Web of Death: & were it not for Bowlahoola & Allamanda
"No Human Form but only a Fibrous Vegetation,
"A Polypus of soft affections without Thought or Vision,
"Must tremble in the Heavens & Earths thro' all the Ulro space.
"Throw all the Vegetated Mortals into Bowlahoola:
"But as to this Elected Form who is return'd again,
"He is the Signal that the Last Vintage now approaches,
"Nor Vegetation may go on till all the Earth is reap'd."

So Los spoke. Furious they descended to Bowlahoola & Allamanda,
Indignant, unconvinc'd by Los's arguments & thun[d]ers rolling:
They saw that wrath now sway'd and now pity absorb'd him.
As it was so it remain'd & no hope of an end.

Bowlahoola is nam'd Law by mortals; Tharmas founded it,
Because of Satan, before Luban in the City of Golgonooza.
But Golgonooza is nam'd Art & Manufacture by mortal men.

In Bowlahoola Los's Anvils stand & his Furnaces rage;
Thundering the Hammers beat & the Bellows blow loud,
Living, self moving, mourning, lamenting & howling incessantly.
Bowlahoola thro' all its porches feels, tho' too fast founded
Its pillars & porticoes to tremble at the force
Of mortal or immortal arm: and softly lilling flutes,
Accordant with the horrid labours, make sweet melody.
The Bellows are the Animal Lungs: the Hammers the Animal Heart:
The Furnaces the Stomach for digestion: terrible their fury.
Thousands & thousands labour, thousands play on instruments
Stringed or fluted to ameliorate the sorrows of slavery.
Loud sport the dancers in the dance of death, rejoicing in carnage.
The hard dentant Hammers are lull'd by the flutes' lula lula,
The bellowing Furnaces blare by the long sounding clarion,
The double drum drowns howls & groans, the shrill fife shrieks & cries,
The crooked horn mellows the hoarse raving serpent, terrible but harmonious:
Bowlahoola is the Stomach in every individual man.

Los is by mortals nam'd Time, Enitharmon is nam'd Space:
But they depict him bald & aged who is in eternal youth
All powerful and his locks flourish like the brows of morning:

He is the Spirit of Prophecy, the ever apparent Elias.
Time is the mercy of Eternity; without Time's swiftness,
Which is the swiftest of all things, all were eternal torment.
All the Gods of the Kingdoms of Earth labour in Los's Halls:
Every one is a fallen Son of the Spirit of Prophecy.
He is the Fourth Zoa that stood arou[n]d the Throne Divine.

25

Loud shout the Sons of Luvah at the Wine-presses as Los descended
With Rintrah & Palamabron in his fires of resistless fury.

The Wine-press on the Rhine groans loud, but all its central beams
Act more terrific in the central Cities of the Nations
Where Human Thought is crush'd beneath the iron hand of Power:
There Los puts all into the Press, the Opressor & the Opressed
Together, ripe for the Harvest & Vintage & ready for the Loom.

They sang at the Vintage: "This is the Last Vintage, & Seed
"Shall no more be sown upon Earth till all the Vintage is over
"And all gather'd in, till the Plow has pass'd over the Nations
"And the Harrow & heavy thundering Roller upon the mountains."

And loud the Souls howl round the Porches of Golgonooza,
Crying: "O God deliver us to the Heavens or to the Earths,
"That we may preach righteousness & punish the sinner with death."
But Los refused, till all the Vintage of Earth was gathered in.

And Los stood & cried to the Labourers of the Vintage in voice of awe:

"Fellow Labourers! The Great Vintage & Harvest is now upon Earth.
"The whole extent of the Globe is explored. Every scatter'd Atom
"Of Human Intellect now is flocking to the sound of the Trumpet.
"All the Wisdom which was hidden in caves & dens from ancient
"Time is now sought out from Animal & Vegetable & Mineral.
"The Awakener is come outstretch'd over Europe: the Vision of God
is fulfilled:
"The Ancient Man upon the Rock of Albion Awakes,
"He listens to the sounds of War astonish'd & ashamed,
"He sees his Children mock at Faith and deny Providence.
"Therefore you must bind the Sheaves not by Nations or Families,
"You shall bind them in Three Classes, according to their Classes
"So shall you bind them, Separating What has been Mixed
"Since Men began to be Wove into Nations by Rahab & Tirzah,
"Since Albion's Death & Satan's Cutting off from our awful Fields,
"When under pretence to benevolence the Elect Subdu'd All

"From the Foundation of the World. The Elect is one Class: You
"Shall bind them separate: they cannot Believe in Eternal Life
"Except by Miracle & a New Birth. The other two Classes,
"The Reprobate who never cease to Believe, and the Redeem'd
"Who live in doubts & fears perpetually tormented by the Elect,
"These you shall bind in a twin-bundle for the Consummation:
"But the Elect must be saved [from] fires of Eternal Death,
"To be formed into the Churches of Beulah that they destroy not the Earth.
"For in every Nation & every Family the Three Classes are born,
"And in every Species of Earth, Metal, Tree, Fish, Bird & Beast.
"We form the Mundane Egg, that Spectres coming by fury or amity,
"All is the same, & every one remains in his own energy.
"Go forth Reapers with rejoicing; you sowed in tears,
"But the time of your refreshing cometh: only a little moment
"Still abstain from pleasure & rest in the labours of eternity,
"And you shall Reap the whole Earth from Pole to Pole, from Sea to Sea,
"Begin[n]ing at Jerusalem's Inner Court, Lambeth, ruin'd and given
"To the detestable Gods of Priam, to Apollo, and at the Asylum
"Given to Hercules, who labour in Tirzah's Looms for bread,
"Who set Pleasure against Duty, who Create Olympic crowns
"To make Learning a burden & the Work of the Holy Spirit, Strife:
"The Thor & cruel Odin who first rear'd the Polar Caves.
"Lambeth mourns, calling Jerusalem: she weeps & looks abroad
"For the Lord's coming, that Jerusalem may overspread all Nations.
"Crave not for the mortal & perishing delights, but leave them
"To the weak, and pity the weak as your infant care. Break not
"Forth in your wrath, lest you also are vegetated by Tirzah.
"Wait till the Judgement is past, till the Creation is consumed,
"And then rush forward with me into the glorious spiritual
"Vegetation, the Supper of the Lamb & his Bride, and the
"Awaking of Albion our friend and ancient companion."

So Los spoke. But lightnings of discontent broke on all sides round
And murmurs of thunder rolling heavy long & loud over the mountains,
While Los call'd his Sons around him to the Harvest & the Vintage.

Thou seest the Constellations in the deep & wondrous Night:
They rise in order and continue their immortal courses
Upon the mountain & in vales with harp & heavenly song,
With flute & clarion, with cups & measures fill'd with foaming wine.
Glitt'ring the streams reflect the Vision of beatitude,
And the calm Ocean joys beneath & smooths his awful waves:

26

These are the Sons of Los, & these the Labourers of the Vintage.
Thou seest the gorgeous clothed Flies that dance & sport in summer
Upon the sunny brooks & meadows: every one the dance
Knows in its intricate mazes of delight artful to weave:
Each one to sound his instruments of music in the dance,
To touch each other & recede, to cross & change & return:
These are the Children of Los; thou seest the Trees on mountains,
The wind blows heavy, loud they thunder thro' the darksom sky,
Uttering prophecies & speaking instructive words to the sons
Of men: These are the Sons of Los: These the Visions of Eternity,
But we see only as it were the hem of their garments
When with our vegetable eyes we view these wondrous Visions.

There are Two Gates thro' which all Souls descend, One Southward
From Dover Cliff to Lizard Point, the other toward the North,
Caithness & rocky Durness, Pentland & John Groat's House.

The Souls descending to the Body wail on the right hand
Of Los, & those deliver'd from the Body on the left hand.
For Los against the east his force continually bends
Along the Valleys of Middlesex from Hounslow to Blackheath,
Lest those Three Heavens of Beulah should the Creation destroy;
And lest they should descend before the north & south Gates,
Groaning with pity, he among the wailing Souls laments.

And these the Labours of the Sons of Los in Allamanda
And in the City of Golgonooza & in Luban & around
The Lake of Udan-Adan in the Forests of Entuthon Benython,
Where Souls incessant wail, being piteous Passions & Desires
With neither lineament nor form, but like to wat'ry clouds
The Passions & Desires descend upon the hungry winds,
For such alone Sleepers remain, meer passion & appetite.
The Sons of Los clothe them & feed & provide houses & fields.

And every Generated Body in its inward form
Is a garden of delight & a building of magnificence,
Built by the Sons of Los in Bowlahoola & Allamanda:
And the herbs & flowers & furniture & beds & chambers
Continually woven in the Looms of Enitharmon's Daughters,
In bright Cathedron's golden Dome with care & love & tears.
For the various Classes of Men are all mark'd out determinate
In Bowlahoola, & as the Spectres choose their affinities,
So they are born on Earth, & every Class is determinate:
But not by Natural, but by Spiritual power alone, Because

The Natural power continually seeks & tends to Destruction,
Ending in Death, which would of itself be Eternal Death.
And all are Class'd by Spiritual & not by Natural power.

And every Natural Effect has a Spiritual Cause, and Not
A Natural; for a Natural Cause only seems: it is a Delusion
Of Ulro & a ratio of the perishing Vegetable Memory.

27

But the Wine-press of Los is eastward of Golgonooza before the Seat
Of Satan: Luvah laid the foundation & Urizen finish'd it in howling
woe.
How red the sons & daughters of Luvah! here they tread the grapes:
Laughing & shouting, drunk with odours many fall o'erwearied,
Drown'd in the wine is many a youth & maiden: those around
Lay them on skins of Tygers & of the spotted Leopard & the Wild Ass
Till they revive, or bury them in cool grots, making lamentation.

This Wine-press is call'd War on Earth: it is the Printing-Press
Of Los, and here he lays his words in order above the mortal brain,
As cogs are form'd in a wheel to turn the cogs of the adverse wheel.

Timbrels & violins sport round the Wine-presses; the little Seed,
The sportive Root, the Earth-worm, the gold Beetle, the wise Emmet
Dance round the Wine-presses of Luvah: the Centipede is there,
The ground Spider with many eyes, the Mole clothed in velvet,
The ambitious Spider in his sullen web, the lucky golden Spinner,
The Earwig arm'd, the tender Maggot, emblem of immortality,
The Flea, Louse, Bug, the Tape-Worm, all the Armies of Disease,
Visible or invisible to the slothful vegetating Man.
The slow Slug, the Grasshopper that sings & laughs & drinks:
Winter comes, he folds his slender bones without a murmur.
The cruel Scorpion is there, the Gnat, Wasp, Hornet & the Honey
Bee,
The Toad & venomous Newt, the Serpent cloth'd in gems & gold.
They throw off their gorgeous raiment: they rejoice with loud jubilee
Around the Wine-presses of Luvah, naked & drunk with wine.

There is the Nettle that stings with soft down, and there
The indignant Thistle whose bitterness is bred in his milk,
Who feeds on contempt of his neighbour: there all the idle Weeds
That creep around the obscure places shew their various limbs
Naked in all their beauty dancing round the Wine-presses.

But in the Wine-presses the Human grapes sing not nor dance:
They howl & writhe in shoals of torment, in fierce flames consuming,

In chains of iron & in dungeons circled with ceaseless fires,
In pits & dens & shades of death, in shapes of torment & woe:
The plates & screws & wracks & saws & cords & fires & cisterns,
The cruel joys of Luvah's Daughters, lacerating with knives
And whips their Victims, & the deadly sport of Luvah's Sons.

They dance around the dying & they drink the howl & groan,
They catch the shrieks in cups of gold, they hand them to one another:
These are the sports of love, & these the sweet delights of amorous play,
Tears of the grape, the death sweat of the cluster, the last sigh
Of the mild youth who listens to the lureing songs of Luvah.

But Allamanda, call'd on Earth Commerce, is the Cultivated land
Around the City of Golgonooza in the Forests of Entuthon:
Here the Sons of Los labour against Death Eternal, through all
The Twenty-seven Heavens of Beulah in Ulro, Seat of Satan,
Which is the False Tongue beneath Beulah: it is the Sense of Touch.
The Plow goes forth in tempests & lightnings, & the Harrow cruel
In blights of the east, the heavy Roller follows in howlings of woe.

Urizen's sons here labour also, & here are seen the Mills
Of Theotormon on the verge of the Lake of Udan-Adan.
These are the starry voids of night & the depths & caverns of earth.
These Mills are oceans, clouds & waters ungovernable in their fury:
Here are the stars created & the seeds of all things planted,
And here the Sun & Moon recieve their fixed destinations.

But in Eternity the Four Arts, Poetry, Painting, Music
And Architecture, which is Science, are the Four Faces of Man.
Not so in Time & Space: there Three are shut out, and only
Science remains thro' Mercy, & by means of Science the Three
Become apparent in Time & Space in the Three Professions,
Poetry in Religion: Music, Law: Painting, in Physic & Surgery:[1]
That Man may live upon Earth till the time of his awaking.
And from these Three Science derives every Occupation of Men,
And Science is divided into Bowlahoola & Allamanda.

28

Some Sons of Los surround the Passions with porches of iron & silver,
Creating form & beauty around the dark regions of sorrow,
Giving to airy nothing a name and a habitation

---

[1] *This line erased in one copy.*

Delightful, with bounds to the Infinite putting off the Indefinite
Into most holy forms of Thought; such is the power of inspiration
They labour incessant with many tears & afflictions,
Creating the beautiful House for the piteous sufferer.

Others Cabinets richly fabricate of gold & ivory
For Doubts & fears unform'd & wretched & melancholy.
The little weeping Spectre stands on the threshold of Death
Eternal, and sometimes two Spectres like lamps quivering,
And often malignant they combat; heart-breaking sorrowful & piteous,
Antamon takes them into his beautiful flexible hands:
As the Sower takes the seed or as the Artist his clay
Or fine wax, to mould artful a model for golden ornaments.
The soft hands of Antamon draw the indelible line,
Form immortal with golden pen, such as the Spectre admiring
Puts on the sweet form; then smiles Antamon bright thro' his windows.
The Daughters of beauty look up from their Loom & prepare
The integument soft for its clothing with joy & delight.

But Theotormon & Sotha stand in the Gate of Luban anxious.
Their numbers are seven million & seven thousand & seven hundred.
They contend with the weak Spectres, they fabricate soothing forms.
The Spectre refuses, he seeks cruelty: they create the crested Cock.
Terrified the Spectre screams & rushes in fear into their Net
Of kindness & compassion, & is born a weeping terror.
Or they create the Lion & Tyger in compassionate thunderings:
Howling the Spectres flee: they take refuge in Human lineaments.

The Sons of Ozoth within the Optic Nerve stand fiery glowing,
And the number of his Sons is eight millions & eight.
They give delights to the man unknown; artificial riches
They give to scorn, & their possessors to trouble & sorrow & care,
Shutting the sun & moon & stars & trees & clouds & waters
And hills out from the Optic Nerve, & hardening it into a bone
Opake and like the black pebble on the enraged beach,
While the poor indigent is like the diamond which, tho' cloth'd
In rugged covering in the mine, is open all within
And in his hallow'd center holds the heavens of bright eternity.
Ozoth here builds walls of rocks against the surging sea,
And timbers crampt with iron cramps bar in the joys of life
From fell destruction in the Spectrous cunning or rage. He Creates
The speckled Newt, the Spider & Beetle, the Rat & Mouse,
The Badger & Fox: they worship before his feet in trembling fear.

But others of the Sons of Los build Moments & Minutes & Hours
And Days & Months & Years & Ages & Periods, wondrous buildings;
And every Moment has a Couch of gold for soft repose,
(A Moment equals a pulsation of the artery),
And between every two Moments stands a Daughter of Beulah
To feed the Sleepers on their Couches with maternal care.
And every Minute has an azure Tent with silken Veils:
And every Hour has a bright golden Gate carved with skill:
And every Day & Night has Walls of brass & Gates of adamant,
Shining like precious Stones & ornamented with appropriate signs:
And every Month a silver paved Terrace builded high:
And every Year invulnerable Barriers with high Towers:
And every Age is Moated deep with Bridges of silver & gold:
And every Seven Ages is Incircled with a Flaming Fire.
Now Seven Ages is amounting to Two Hundred Years.
Each has its Guard, each Moment, Minute, Hour, Day, Month & Year.
All are the work of Fairy hands of the Four Elements:
The Guard are Angels of Providence on duty evermore.
Every Time less than a pulsation of the artery
Is equal in its period & value to Six Thousand Years,

29

For in this Period the Poet's Work is Done: and all the Great
Events of Time start forth & are conciev'd in such a Period,
Within a Moment, a Pulsation of the Artery.

The Sky is an immortal Tent built by the Sons of Los:
And every Space that a Man views around his dwelling-place
Standing on his own roof or in his garden on a mount
Of twenty-five cubits in height, such space is his Universe:
And on its verge the Sun rises & sets, the Clouds bow
To meet the flat Earth & the Sea in such an order'd Space:
The Starry heavens reach no further, but here bend and set
On all sides, & the two Poles turn on their valves of gold;
And if he move his dwelling-place, his heavens also move
Where'er he goes, & all his neighbourhood bewail his loss.
Such are the Spaces called Earth & such its dimension.
As to that false appearance which appears to the reasoner
As of a Globe rolling thro' Voidness, it is a delusion of Ulro.
The Microscope knows not of this nor the Telescope: they alter
The ratio of the Spectator's Organs, but leave Objects untouch'd.
For every Space larger than a red Globule of Man's blood
Is visionary, and is created by the Hammer of Los:
And every Space smaller than a Globule of Man's blood opens

Into Eternity of which this vegetable Earth is but a shadow.
The red Globule is the unwearied Sun by Los created
To measure Time and Space to mortal Men every morning.
Bowlahoola & Allamanda are placed on each side
Of that Pulsation & that Globule, terrible their power.

But Rintrah & Palamabron govern over Day & Night
In Allamanda & Entuthon Benython where Souls wail,
Where Orc incessant howls, burning in fires of Eternal Youth,
Within the vegetated mortal Nerves; for every Man born is joined
Within into One mighty Polypus, and this Polypus is Orc.

But in the Optic vegetative Nerves, Sleep was transformed
To Death in old time by Satan the father of Sin & Death:
And Satan is the Spectre of Orc, & Orc is the generate Luvah.

But in the Nerves of the Nostrils, Accident being formed
Into Substance & Principle by the cruelties of Demonstration
It became Opake & Indefinite, but the Divine Saviour
Formed it into a Solid by Los's Mathematic power.
He named the Opake, Satan: he named the Solid, Adam.

And in the Nerves of the Ear (for the Nerves of the Tongue are closed)
On Albion's Rock Los stands creating the glorious Sun each morning,
And when unwearied in the evening, he creates the Moon,
Death to delude, who all in terror at their splendor leaves
His prey, while Los appoints & Rintrah & Palamabron guide
The Souls clear from the Rock of Death, that Death himself may wake
In his appointed season when the ends of heaven meet.

Then Los conducts the Spirits to be Vegetated into
Great Golgonooza, free from the four iron pillars of Satan's Throne,
(Temperance, Prudence, Justice, Fortitude, the four pillars of tyranny)
That Satan's Watch-Fiends touch them not before they Vegetate.

But Enitharmon and her Daughters take the pleasant charge
To give them to their lovely heavens till the Great Judgment Day:
Such is their lovely charge. But Rahab & Tirzah pervert
Their mild influences; therefore the Seven Eyes of God walk round
The Three Heavens of Ulro where Tirzah & her Sisters
Weave the black Woof of Death upon Entuthon Benython,
In the Vale of Surrey where Horeb terminates in Rephaim.
The stamping feet of Zelophehad's Daughters are cover'd with Human gore

Upon the treddles of the Loom: they sing to the winged shuttle.
The River rises above his banks to wash the Woof:
He takes it in his arms; he passes it in strength thro' his current;
The veil of human miseries is woven over the Ocean
From the Atlantic to the Great South Sea, the Erythrean.

Such is the World of Los, the labour of six thousand years.
Thus Nature is a Vision of the Science of the Elohim.

End of the First Book

30

There is a place where Contrarieties are equally True:
This place is called Beulah. It is a pleasant lovely Shadow
Where no dispute can come, Because of those who Sleep.
Into this place the Sons & Daughters of Ololon descended
With solemn mourning, into Beulah's moony shades & hills
Weeping for Milton: mute wonder held the Daughters of Beulah,
Enraptur'd with affection sweet and mild benevolence.

Beulah is evermore Created around Eternity, appearing
To the Inhabitants of Eden around them on all sides.
But Beulah to its Inhabitants appears within each district
As the beloved infant in his mother's bosom round incircled
With arms of love & pity & sweet compassion. But to
The Sons of Eden the moony habitations of Beulah
Are from Great Eternity a mild & pleasant Rest.

And it is thus Created. Lo, the Eternal Great Humanity,
To whom be Glory & Dominion Evermore, Amen,
Walks among all his awful Family seen in every face:
As the breath of the Almighty such are the words of man to man
In the great Wars of Eternity, in fury of Poetic Inspiration,
To build the Universe stupendous, Mental forms Creating.

But the Emanations trembled exceedingly, nor could they
Live, because the life of Man was too exceeding unbounded.
His joy became terrible to them; they trembled & wept,
Crying with one voice: "Give us a habitation & a place
"In which we may be hidden under the shadow of wings:
"For if we, who are but for a time & who pass away in winter,
"Behold these wonders of Eternity we shall consume:
"But you, O our Fathers & Brothers, remain in Eternity.
"But grant us a Temporal Habitation, do you speak
"To us; we will obey your words as you obey Jesus
"The Eternal who is blessed for ever & ever. Amen."

So spake the lovely Emanations, & there appear'd a pleasant
Mild Shadow above, beneath, & on all sides round.

31

Into this pleasant Shadow all the weak & weary
Like Women & Children were taken away as on wings
Of dovelike softness, & shadowy habitations prepared for them.
But every Man return'd & went still going forward thro'
The Bosom of the Father in Eternity on Eternity,
Neither did any lack or fall into Error without
A Shadow to repose in all the Days of happy Eternity.

Into this pleasant Shadow, Beulah, all Ololon descended,
And when the Daughters of Beulah heard the lamentation
All Beulah wept, for they saw the Lord coming in the Clouds.
And the Shadows of Beulah terminate in rocky Albion.

And all Nations wept in affliction, Family by Family:
Germany wept towards France & Italy, England wept & trembled
Towards America, India rose up from his golden bed
As one awaken'd in the night; they saw the Lord coming
In the Clouds of Ololon with Power & Great Glory.
And all the Living Creatures of the Four Elements wail'd
With bitter wailing; these in the aggregate are named Satan

And Rahab: they know not of Regeneration, but only of Generation:
The Fairies, Nymphs, Gnomes & Genii of the Four Elements,
Unforgiving & unalterable, these cannot be Regenerated
But must be Created, for they know only of Generation:
These are the Gods of the Kingdoms of the Earth, in contrarious
And cruel opposition, Element against Element, opposed in War
Not Mental, as the Wars of Eternity, but a Corporeal Strife
In Los's Halls, continual labouring in the Furnaces of Golgonooza.
Orc howls on the Atlantic: Enitharmon trembles: All Beulah weeps.

Thou hearest the Nightingale begin the Song of Spring.
The Lark sitting upon his earthy bed, just as the morn
Appears, listens silent; then springing from the waving Cornfield, loud
He leads the Choir of Day: trill, trill, trill, trill,
Mounting upon the wings of light into the Great Expanse,
Reecchoing against the lovely blue & shining heavenly Shell,
His little throat labours with inspiration; every feather
On throat & breast & wings vibrates with the effluence Divine.
All Nature listens silent to him, & the awful Sun
Stands still upon the Mountain looking on this little Bird
With eyes of soft humility & wonder, love & awe.
Then loud from their green covert all the Birds begin their Song:
The Thrush, the Linnet & the Goldfinch, Robin & the Wren
Awake the Sun from his sweet reverie upon the Mountain.
The Nightingale again assays his song, & thro' the day
And thro' the night warbles luxuriant, every Bird of Song
Attending his loud harmony with admiration & love.
This is a Vision of the lamentation of Beulah over Ololon.

Thou percievest the Flowers put forth their precious Odours,
And none can tell how from so small a center comes such sweets,
Forgetting that within that Center Eternity expands
Its ever during doors that Og & Anak fiercely guard.
First, e'er the morning breaks, joy opens in the flowery bosoms,
Joy even to tears, which the Sun rising dries; first the Wild Thyme
And Meadow-sweet, downy & soft waving among the reeds,
Light springing on the air, lead the sweet Dance: they wake
The Honeysuckle sleeping on the Oak; the flaunting beauty
Revels along upon the wind; the White-thorn, lovely May,
Opens her many lovely eyes listening; the Rose still sleeps,
None dare to wake her; soon she bursts her crimson curtain'd bed
And comes forth in the majesty of beauty; every Flower,
The Pink, the Jessamine, the Wall-flower, the Carnation,

The Jonquil, the mild Lilly, opes her heavens; every Tree
And Flower & Herb soon fill the air with an innumerable Dance,
Yet all in order sweet & lovely. Men are sick with Love.
Such is a Vision of the lamentation of Beulah over Ololon.

32

And Milton oft sat upon the Couch of Death & oft conversed
In vision & dream beatific with the Seven Angels of the Presence.

"I have turned my back upon these Heavens builded on cruelty;
"My Spectre still wandering thro' them follows my Emanation,
"He hunts her footsteps thro' the snow & the wintry hail & rain.
"The idiot Reasoner laughs at the Man of Imagination,
"And from laughter proceeds to murder by undervaluing calumny."

Then Hillel, who is Lucifer, replied over the Couch of Death,
And thus the Seven Angels instructed him, & thus they converse:

"We are not Individuals but States, Combinations of Individuals.
"We were Angels of the Divine Presence, & were Druids in Annandale,
"Compell'd to combine into Form by Satan, the Spectre of Albion,
"Who made himself a God & destroyed the Human Form Divine.
"But the Divine Humanity & Mercy gave us a Human Form
"Because we were combin'd in Freedom & holy Brotherhood,

כובים
as multitudes
Vox Populi

"While those combin'd by Satan's Tyranny, first in the blood of War
"And Sacrifice & next in Chains of imprisonment, are Shapeless Rocks
"Retaining only Satan's Mathematic Holiness, Length, Bredth & Highth,
"Calling the Human Imagination, which is the Divine Vision & Fruition
"In which Man liveth eternally, madness & blasphemy against
"Its own Qualities, which are Servants of Humanity, not Gods or Lords.
"Distinguish therefore States from Individuals in those States.
"States Change, but Individual Identities never change nor cease.
"You cannot go to Eternal Death in that which can never Die.
"Satan & Adam are States Created into Twenty-seven Churches,
"And thou, O Milton, art a State about to be Created,

"Called Eternal Annihilation, that none but the Living shall
"Dare to enter, & they shall enter triumphant over Death
"And Hell & the Grave: States that are not, but ah! Seem to be.

"Judge then of thy Own Self: thy Eternal Lineaments explore,
"What is Eternal & what Changeable, & what Annihilable.
"The Imagination is not a State: it is the Human Existence itself.
"Affection or Love becomes a State when divided from Imagination.
"The Memory is a State always, & the Reason is a State
"Created to be Annihilated & a new Ratio Created.
"Whatever can be Created can be Annihilated: Forms cannot:
"The Oak is cut down by the Ax, the Lamb falls by the Knife,
"But their Forms Eternal Exist For-ever. Amen. Hallelujah!"

Thus they converse with the Dead, watching round the Couch of Death;
For God himself enters Death's Door always with those that enter
And lays down in the Grave with them, in Visions of Eternity,
Till they awake & see Jesus & the Linen Clothes lying
That the Females had Woven for them, & the Gates of their Father's House.

33

And the Divine Voice was heard in the Songs of Beulah, Saying:

"When I first Married you, I gave you all my whole Soul.
"I thought that you would love my loves & joy in my delights,
"Seeking for pleasures in my pleasures, O Daughter of Babylon.
"Then thou wast lovely, mild & gentle; now thou art terrible
"In jealousy & unlovely in my sight, because thou hast cruelly
"Cut off my loves in fury till I have no love left for thee.
"Thy love depends on him thou lovest, & on his dear loves
"Depend thy pleasures, which thou hast cut off by jealousy.
"Therefore I shew my Jealousy & set before you Death.
"Behold Milton descended to Redeem the Female Shade
"From Death Eternal; such your lot, to be continually Redeem'd
"By death & misery of those you love & by Annihilation.
"When the Sixfold Female percieves that Milton annihilates
"Himself, that seeing all his loves by her cut off, he leaves
"Her also, intirely abstracting himself from Female loves,
"She shall relent in fear of death; She shall begin to give
"Her maidens to her husband, delighting in his delight.
"And then & then alone begins the happy Female joy

"As it is done in Beulah, & thou, O Virgin Babylon, Mother of Whoredoms,
"Shalt bring Jerusalem in thine arms in the night watches, and
"No longer turning her a wandering Harlot in the streets,
"Shalt give her into the arms of God your Lord & Husband."

Such are the Songs of Beulah in the Lamentations of Ololon.

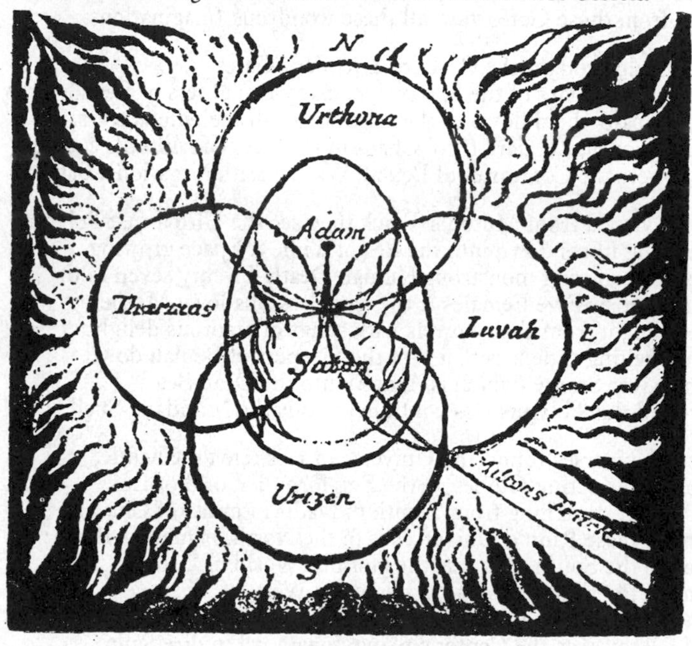

34

And all the Songs of Beulah sounded comfortable notes
To comfort Ololon's lamentation, for they said:
"Are you the Fiery Circle that late drove in fury & fire
"The Eight Immortal Starry-Ones down into Ulro dark,
"Rending the Heavens of Beulah with your thunders & lightnings?
"And can you thus lament & can you pity & forgive?
"Is terror chang'd to pity? O wonder of Eternity!"

And the Four States of Humanity in its Repose
Were shewed them. First of Beulah, a most pleasant Sleep
On Couches soft with mild music, tended by Flowers of Beulah,

Sweet Female forms, winged or floating in the air spontaneous:
The Second State is Alla, & the third State Al-Ulro;
But the Fourth State is dreadful, it is named Or-Ulro.
The First State is in the Head, the Second is in the Heart,
The Third in the Loins & Seminal Vessels, & the Fourth
In the Stomach & Intestines terrible, deadly, unutterable.
And he whose Gates are open'd in those Regions of his Body
Can from those Gates view all these wondrous Imaginations.

But Ololon sought the Or-Ulro & its fiery Gates
And the Couches of the Martyrs, & many Daughters of Beulah
Accompany them down to the Ulro with soft melodious tears,
A long journey & dark thro' Chaos in the track of Milton's course
To where the Contraries of Beulah War beneath Negation's Banner.

Then view'd from Milton's Track they see the Ulro a vast Polypus
Of living fibres down into the Sea of Time & Space growing
A self-devouring monstrous Human Death Twenty seven fold.
Within it sit Five Females & the nameless Shadowy Mother,
Spinning it from their bowels with songs of amorous delight
And melting cadences that lure the Sleepers of Beulah down
The River Storge (which is Arnon) into the Dead Sea.
Around this Polypus Los continual builds the Mundane Shell.

Four Universes round the Universe of Los remain Chaotic,
Four intersecting Globes, & the Egg form'd World of Los
In midst, stretching from Zenith to Nadir in midst of Chaos.
One of these Ruin'd Universes is to the North, named Urthona:
One to the South, this was the glorious World of Urizen:
One to the East, of Luvah: One to the West, of Tharmas.
But when Luvah assumed the World of Urizen in the South
All fell towards the Center sinking downward in dire Ruin.

Here in these Chaoses the Sons of Ololon took their abode,
In Chasms of the Mundane Shell which open on all sides round,
Southward & by the East within the Breach of Milton's descent,
To watch the time, pitying, & gentle to awaken Urizen.
They stood in a dark land of death, of fiery corroding waters,
Where lie in evil death the Four Immortals pale and cold
And the Eternal Man, even Albion, upon the Rock of Ages.
Seeing Milton's Shadow, some Daughters of Beulah trembling
Return'd, but Ololon remain'd before the Gates of the Dead.

And Ololon looked down into the Heavens of Ulro in fear.
They said: "How are the Wars of man, which in Great Eternity
"Appear around in the External Spheres of Visionary Life,

"Here render'd Deadly within the Life & Interior Vision?
"How are the Beasts & Birds & Fishes & Plants & Minerals
"Here fix'd into a frozen bulk subject to decay & death?
"Those Visions of Human Life & Shadows of Wisdom & Knowledge

35

"Are here frozen to unexpansive deadly destroying terrors,
"And War & Hunting, the Two Fountains of the River of Life,
"Are become Fountains of bitter Death & of corroding Hell,
"Till Brotherhood is chang'd into a Curse & a Flattery
"By Differences between Ideas, that Ideas themselves (which are
"The Divine Members) may be slain in offerings for sin.
"O dreadful Loom of Death! O piteous Female forms compell'd
"To weave the Woof of Death! On Camberwell Tirzah's Courts,
"Malah's on Blackheath, Rahab & Noah dwell on Windsor's heights:
"Where once the Cherubs of Jerusalem spread to Lambeth's Vale
"Milcah's Pillars shine from Harrow to Hampstead, where Hoglah
"On Highgate's heights magnificent Weaves over trembling Thames
"To Shooters' Hill and thence to Blackheath, the dark Woof. Loud,
"Loud roll the Weights & Spindles over the whole Earth, let down
"On all sides round to the Four Quarters of the World, eastward on
"Europe to Euphrates & Hindu to Nile, & back in Clouds
"Of Death across the Atlantic to America North & South."

So spake Ololon in reminiscence astonish'd, but they
Could not behold Golgonooza without passing the Polypus,
A wondrous journey not passable by Immortal feet, & none
But the Divine Saviour can pass it without annihilation.
For Golgonooza cannot be seen till having pass'd the Polypus
It is viewed on all sides round by a Four-fold Vision,
Or till you become Mortal & Vegetable in Sexuality,
Then you behold its mighty Spires & Domes of ivory & gold.

And Ololon examined all the Couches of the Dead,
Even of Los & Enitharmon & all the Sons of Albion
And his Four Zoas terrified & on the verge of Death.
In midst of these was Milton's Couch, & when they saw Eight
Immortal Starry-Ones guarding the Couch in flaming fires,
They thunderous utter'd all a universal groan, falling down
Prostrate before the Starry Eight asking with tears forgiveness,
Confessing their crime with humiliation and sorrow.

O how the Starry Eight rejoic'd to see Ololon descended,
And now that a wide road was open to Eternity
By Ololon's descent thro' Beulah to Los & Enitharmon!

For mighty were the multitudes of Ololon, vast the extent
Of their great sway reaching from Ulro to Eternity,
Surrounding the Mundane Shell outside in its Caverns
And through Beulah, and all silent forbore to contend
With Ololon, for they saw the Lord in the Clouds of Ololon.

There is a Moment in each Day that Satan cannot find,
Nor can his Watch Fiends find it; but the Industrious find
This Moment & it multiply, & when it once is found
It renovates every Moment of the Day if rightly placed.
In this Moment Ololon descended to Los & Enitharmon
Unseen beyond the Mundane Shell, Southward in Milton's track.

Just in this Moment, when the morning odours rise abroad
And first from the Wild Thyme, stands a Fountain in a rock
Of crystal flowing into two Streams: one flows thro' Golgonooza
And thro' Beulah to Eden beneath Los's western Wall:
The other flows thro' the Aerial Void & all the Churches,
Meeting again in Golgonooza beyond Satan's Seat.

The Wild Thyme is Los's Messenger to Eden, a mighty Demon,
Terrible, deadly & poisonous his presence in Ulro dark;
Therefore he appears only a small Root creeping in grass
Covering over the Rock of Odours his bright purple mantle
Beside the Fount above the Lark's nest in Golgonooza.
Luvah slept here in death & here is Luvah's empty Tomb.
Ololon sat beside this Fountain on the Rock of Odours.

Just at the place to where the Lark mounts is a Crystal Gate:
It is the enterance of the First Heaven, named Luther; for
The Lark is Los's Messenger thro' the Twenty-seven Churches,
That the Seven Eyes of God, who walk even to Satan's Seat
Thro' all the Twenty-seven Heavens, may not slumber nor sleep.
But the Lark's Nest is at the Gate of Los, at the eastern
Gate of wide Golgonooza, & the Lark is Los's Messenger.

36

When on the highest lift of his light pinions he arrives
At that bright Gate, another Lark meets him, & back to back
They touch their pinions, tip tip, and each descend
To their respective Earths & there all night consult with Angels
Of Providence & with the Eyes of God all night in slumbers
Inspired, & at the dawn of day send out another Lark
Into another Heaven to carry news upon his wings.
Thus are the Messengers dispatch'd till they reach the Earth again

In the East Gate of Golgonooza, & the Twenty-eighth bright
Lark met the Female Ololon descending into my Garden.
Thus it appears to Mortal eyes & those of the Ulro Heavens,
But not thus to Immortals: the Lark is a mighty Angel.

For Ololon step'd into the Polypus within the Mundane Shell.
They could not step into Vegetable Worlds without becoming
The enemies of Humanity, except in a Female Form,
And as One Female Ololon and all its mighty Hosts
Appear'd, a Virgin of twelve years: nor time nor space was
To the perception of the Virgin Ololon, but as the
Flash of lightning, but more quick the Virgin in my Garden
Before my Cottage stood, for the Satanic Space is delusion.

For when Los join'd with me he took me in his fi'ry whirlwind:
My Vegetated portion was hurried from Lambeth's shades,
He set me down in Felpham's Vale & prepar'd a beautiful
Cottage for me, that in three years I might write all these Visions
To display Nature's cruel holiness, the deceits of Natural Religion.
Walking in my Cottage Garden, sudden I beheld
The Virgin Ololon & address'd her as a Daughter of Beulah:

"Virgin of Providence, fear not to enter into my Cottage.
"What is thy message to thy friend? What am I now to do?
"Is it again to plunge into deeper affliction? behold me
"Ready to obey, but pity thou my Shadow of Delight:
"Enter my Cottage, comfort her, for she is sick with fatigue."

[*design of a house with the figure of Ololon descending to Blake in his garden, inscribed:* Blake's Cottage at Felpham]

37

The Virgin answer'd: "Knowest thou of Milton who descended
"Driven from Eternity? him I seek, terrified at my Act
"In Great Eternity which thou knowest: I come him to seek."

So Ololon utter'd in words distinct the anxious thought:
Mild was the voice but more distinct than any earthly.
That Milton's Shadow heard, & condensing all his Fibres
Into a strength impregnable of majesty & beauty infinite,
I saw he was the Covering Cherub & within him Satan
And Rahah[b], in an outside which is fallacious, within,
Beyond the outline of Identity, in the Selfhood deadly;
And he appear'd the Wicker Man of Scandinavia, in whom
Jerusalem's children consume in flames among the Stars.

Descending down into my Garden, a Human Wonder of God
Reaching from heaven to earth, a Cloud & Human Form,
I beheld Milton with astonishment & in him beheld
The Monstrous Churches of Beulah, the Gods of Ulro dark,
Twelve monstrous dishumaniz'd terrors, Synagogues of Satan,
A Double Twelve & Thrice Nine: such their divisions.

And these their Names & their Places within the Mundane Shell:

In Tyre & Sidon I saw Baal & Ashtaroth: In Moab Chemosh:
In Ammon Molech, loud his Furnaces rage among the Wheels
Of Og, & pealing loud the cries of the Victims of Fire,
And pale his Priestesses infolded in Veils of Pestilence border'd
With War, Woven in Looms of Tyre & Sidon by beautiful Ashtaroth:
In Palestine Dagon, Sea Monster, worship'd o'er the Sea:
Thammuz in Lebanon & Rimmon in Damascus curtain'd:
Osiris, Isis, Orus in Egypt, dark their Tabernacles on Nile
Floating with solemn songs & on the Lakes of Egypt nightly
With pomp even till morning break & Osiris appear in the sky:
But Belial of Sodom & Gomorrha, obscure Demon of Bribes
And secret Assasinations, not worship'd nor ador'd, but
With the finger on the lips & the back turn'd to the light:
And Saturn, Jove & Rhea of the Isles of the Sea remote.
These Twelve Gods are the Twelve Spectre Sons of the Druid Albion.

And these the names of the Twenty-seven Heavens & their Churches:
Adam, Seth, Enos, Cainan, Mahalaleel, Jared, Enoch,
Methuselah, Lamech, these are Giants mighty, Hermaphroditic;
Noah, Shem, Arphaxad, Cainan the second, Salah, Heber,
Peleg, Reu, Serug, Nahor, Terah, these are the Female-Males,
A Male within a Female hid as in an Ark & Curtains;
Abraham, Moses, Solomon, Paul, Constantine, Charlemaine,
Luther, these seven are the Male-Females, the Dragon Forms,
Religion hid in War, a Dragon red & hidden Harlot.

All these are seen in Milton's Shadow, who is the Covering Cherub,
The Spectre of Albion in which the Spectre of Luvah inhabits
In the Newtonian Voids between the Substances of Creation.

For the Chaotic Voids outside of the Stars are measured by
The Stars, which are the boundaries of Kingdoms, Provinces
And Empires of Chaos invisible to the Vegetable Man.
The Kingdom of Og is in Orion: Sihon is in Ophiucus.
Og has Twenty-seven Districts: Sihon's Districts Twenty-one.
From Star to Star, Mountains & Valleys, terrible dimension
Stretch'd out, compose the Mundane Shell, a mighty Incrustation

Of Forty-eight deformed Human Wonders of the Almighty,
With Caverns whose remotest bottoms meet again beyond
The Mundane Shell in Golgonooza; but the Fires of Los rage
In the remotest bottoms of the Caves, that none can pass
Into Eternity that way, but all descend to Los,
To Bowlahoola & Allamanda & to Entuthon Benython.

The Heavens are the Cherub: the Twelve Gods are Satan,

38

And the Forty-eight Starry Regions are Cities of the Levites,
The Heads of the Great Polypus, Four-fold twelve enormity,
In mighty & mysterious comingling, enemy with enemy,
Woven by Urizen into Sexes from his mantle of years.
And Milton collecting all his fibres into impregnable strength
Descended down a Paved work of all kinds of precious stones
Out from the eastern sky; descending down into my Cottage
Garden, clothed in black, severe & silent he descended.

The Spectre of Satan stood upon the roaring sea & beheld
Milton within his sleeping Humanity; trembling & shudd'ring
He stood upon the waves a Twenty-seven fold mighty Demon
Gorgeous & beautiful; loud roll his thunders against Milton.
Loud Satan thunder'd, loud & dark upon mild Felpham shore
Not daring to touch one fibre he howl'd round upon the Sea.

I also stood in Satan's bosom & beheld its desolations:
A ruin'd Man, a ruin'd building of God, not made with hands:
Its plains of burning sand, its mountains of marble terrible:
Its pits & declivities flowing with molten ore & fountains
Of pitch & nitre: its ruin'd palaces & cities & mighty works:
Its furnaces of affliction, in which his Angels & Emanations
Labour with blacken'd visages among its stupendous ruins,
Arches & pyramids & porches, colonades & domes,
In which dwells Mystery, Babylon; here is her secret place,
From hence she comes forth on the Churches in delight;
Here is her Cup fill'd with its poisons in these horrid vales,
And here her scarlet Veil woven in pestilence & war;
Here is Jerusalem bound in chains in the Dens of Babylon.

In the Eastern porch of Satan's Universe Milton stood & said:

"Satan! my Spectre! I know my power thee to annihilate
"And be a greater in thy place & be thy Tabernacle,
"A covering for thee to do thy will, till one greater comes
"And smites me as I smote thee & becomes my covering.

"Such are the Laws of thy false Heav'ns; but Laws of Eternity
"Are not such; know thou, I come to Self Annihilation.
"Such are the Laws of Eternity, that each shall mutually
"Annihilate himself for others' good, as I for thee.
"Thy purpose & the purpose of thy Priests & of thy Churches
"Is to impress on men the fear of death, to teach
"Trembling & fear, terror, constriction, abject selfishness.
"Mine is to teach Men to despise death & to go on
"In fearless majesty annihilating Self, laughing to scorn
"Thy Laws & terrors, shaking down thy Synagogues as webs.
"I come to discover before Heav'n & Hell the Self righteousness
"In all its Hypocritic turpitude, opening to every eye
"These wonders of Satan's holiness, shewing to the Earth
"The Idol Virtues of the Natural Heart, & Satan's Seat
"Explore in all its Selfish Natural Virtue, & put off
"In Self annihilation all that is not of God alone,
"To put off Self & all I have, ever & ever. Amen."

Satan heard, Coming in a cloud, with trumpets & flaming fire,
Saying: "I am God the judge of all, the living & the dead.
"Fall therefore down & worship me, submit thy supreme
"Dictate to my eternal Will, & to my dictate bow.
"I hold the Balances of Right & Just & mine the Sword.
"Seven Angels bear my Name & in those Seven I appear,
"But I alone am God & I alone in Heav'n & Earth
"Of all that live dare utter this, others tremble & bow,

39

"Till All Things become One Great Satan, in Holiness
"Oppos'd to Mercy, and the Divine Delusion, Jesus, be no more."

Suddenly around Milton on my Path the Starry Seven
Burn'd terrible; my Path became a solid fire, as bright
As the clear Sun, & Milton silent came down on my Path.
And there went forth from the Starry limbs of the Seven, Forms
Human, with Trumpets innumerable, sounding articulate
As the Seven spake; and they stood in a mighty Column of Fire
Surrounding Felpham's Vale, reaching to the Mundane Shell,
Saying:

"Awake, Albion awake! reclaim thy Reasoning Spectre. Subdue
"Him to the Divine Mercy. Cast him down into the Lake
"Of Los that ever burneth with fire ever & ever, Amen!
"Let the Four Zoas awake from Slumbers of Six Thousand Years."

Then loud the Furnaces of Los were heard, & seen as Seven Heavens
Stretching from south to north over the mountains of Albion.

Satan heard; trembling round his Body, he incircled it:
He trembled with exceeding great trembling & astonishment,
Howling in his Spectre round his Body, hung'ring to devour
But fearing for the pain, for if he touches a Vital
His torment is unendurable: therefore he cannot devour
But howls round it as a lion round his prey continually.
Loud Satan thunder'd, loud & dark upon mild Felpham's Shore,
Coming in a Cloud with Trumpets & with Fiery Flame,
An awful Form eastward from midst of a bright Paved-work
Of precious stones by Cherubim surrounded, so permitted
(Lest he should fall apart in his Eternal Death) to imitate
The Eternal Great Humanity Divine surrounded by
His Cherubim & Seraphim in ever happy Eternity.
Beneath sat Chaos: Sin on his right hand, Death on his left,
And Ancient Night spread over all the heav'n his Mantle of Laws.
He trembled with exceeding great trembling & astonishment.

Then Albion rose up in the Night of Beulah on his Couch
Of dread repose seen by the visionary eye: his face is toward
The east, toward Jerusalem's Gates; groaning he sat above
His rocks. London & Bath & Legions & Edinburgh
Are the four pillars of his Throne: his left foot near London
Covers the shades of Tyburn: his instep from Windsor
To Primrose Hill stretching to Highgate & Holloway.
London is between his knees, its basements fourfold;
His right foot stretches to the sea on Dover cliffs, his heel
On Canterbury's ruins; his right hand covers lofty Wales,
His left Scotland; his bosom girt with gold involves
York, Edinburgh, Durham & Carlisle, & on the front
Bath, Oxford, Cambridge, Norwich; his right elbow
Leans on the Rocks of Erin's Land, Ireland, ancient nation.
His head bends over London; he sees his embodied Spectre
Trembling before him with exceeding great trembling & fear.
He views Jerusalem & Babylon, his tears flow down.
He mov'd his right foot to Cornwall, his left to the Rocks of Bognor.
He strove to rise to walk into the Deep, but strength failing
Forbad, & down with dreadful groans he sunk upon his Couch
In moony Beulah. Los, his strong Guard, walks round beneath the Moon.

Urizen faints in terror striving among the Brooks of Arnon
With Milton's Spirit; as the Plowman or Artificer or Shepherd
While in the labours of his Calling sends his Thought abroad

To labour in the ocean or in the starry heaven, So Milton
Labour'd in Chasms of the Mundane Shell, tho' here before
My Cottage midst the Starry Seven where the Virgin Ololon
Stood trembling in the Porch; loud Satan thunder'd on the stormy Sea
Circling Albion's Cliffs, in which the Four-fold World resides,
Tho' seen in fallacy outside, a fallacy of Satan's Churches.

40

Before Ololon Milton stood & perciev'd the Eternal Form
Of that mild Vision; wondrous were their acts, by me unknown
Except remotely, and I heard Ololon say to Milton:

"I see thee strive upon the Brooks of Arnon: there a dread
"And awful Man I see, o'ercover'd with the mantle of years.
"I behold Los & Urizen, I behold Orc & Tharmas,
"The Four Zoas of Albion, & thy Spirit with them striving,
"In Self annihilation giving thy life to thy enemies.
"Are those who contemn Religion & seek to annihilate it
"Become in their Femin[in]e portions the causes & promoters
"Of these Religions? how is this thing, this Newtonian Phantasm,
"This Voltaire & Rousseau, this Hume & Gibbon & Bolingbroke,
"This Natural Religion, this impossible absurdity?
"Is Ololon the cause of this? O where shall I hide my face?
"These tears fall for the little ones, the Children of Jerusalem,
"Lest they be annihilated in thy annihilation."

No sooner she had spoke but Rahab Babylon appear'd
Eastward upon the Paved work across Europe & Asia,
Glorious as the midday Sun in Satan's bosom glowing,
A Female hidden in a Male, Religion hidden in War,
Nam'd Moral Virtue, cruel two-fold Monster shining bright,
A Dragon red & hidden Harlot which John in Patmos saw.

And all beneath the Nations innumerable of Ulro
Appear'd: the Seven Kingdoms of Canaan & Five Baalim
Of Philistea into Twelve divided, call'd after the Names
Of Israel, as they are in Eden, Mountain, River & Plain,
City & sandy Desart intermingled beyond mortal ken.

But turning toward Ololon in terrible majesty Milton
Replied: "Obey thou the Words of the Inspired Man.
"All that can be (ann be) annihilated must be annihilated
"That the Children of Jerusalem may be saved from slavery.

"There is a Negation, & there is a Contrary:
"The Negation must be destroy'd to redeem the Contraries.
"The Negation is the Spectre, the Reasoning Power in Man:
"This is a false Body, an Incrustation over my Immortal
"Spirit, a Selfhood which must be put off & annihilated alway.
"To cleanse the Face of my Spirit by Self-examination,

41

"To bathe in the Waters of Life, to wash off the Not Human,
"I come in Self-annihilation & the grandeur of Inspiration,
"To cast off Rational Demonstration by Faith in the Saviour,
"To cast off the rotten rags of Memory by Inspiration,
"To cast off Bacon, Locke & Newton from Albion's covering,
"To take off his filthy garments & clothe him with Imagination,
"To cast aside from Poetry all that is not Inspiration,
"That it no longer shall dare to mock with the aspersion of Madness
"Cast on the Inspired by the tame high finisher of paltry Blots
"Indefinite, or paltry Rhymes, or paltry Harmonies,
"Who creeps into State Government like a catterpiller to destroy;
"To cast off the idiot Questioner who is always questioning
"But never capable of answering, who sits with a sly grin
"Silent plotting when to question, like a thief in a cave,
"Who publishes doubt & calls it knowledge, whose Science is Despair,
"Whose pretence to knowledge is envy, whose whole Science is
"To destroy the wisdom of ages to gratify ravenous Envy
"That rages round him like a Wolf day & night without rest:
"He smiles with condescension, he talks of Benevolence & Virtue,
"And those who act with Benevolence & Virtue they murder time on time.
"These are the destroyers of Jerusalem, these are the murderers
"Of Jesus, who deny the Faith & mock at Eternal Life,
"Who pretend to Poetry that they may destroy Imagination
"By imitation of Nature's Images drawn from Remembrance.
"These are the Sexual Garments, the Abomination of Desolation,
"Hiding the Human Lineaments as with an Ark & Curtains
"Which Jesus rent & now shall wholly purge away with Fire
"Till Generation is swallow'd up in Regeneration."

Then trembled the Virgin Ololon & reply'd in clouds of despair:

"Is this our Femin[in]e Portion, the Six-fold Miltonic Female?
"Terribly this Portion trembles before thee, O awful Man.
"Altho' our Human Power can sustain the severe contentions

"Of Friendship, our Sexual cannot, but flies into the Ulro.
"Hence arose all our terrors in Eternity; & now remembrance
"Returns upon us; are we Contraries, O Milton, Thou & I?
"O Immortal, how were we led to War the Wars of Death?
"Is this the Void Outside of Existence, which if enter'd into

42

"Becomes a Womb? & is this the Death Couch of Albion?
"Thou goest to Eternal Death & all must go with thee."

So saying, the Virgin divided Six-fold, & with a shriek
Dolorous that ran thro' all Creation, a Double Six-fold Wonder
Away from Ololon she divided & fled into the depths
Of Milton's Shadow, as a Dove upon the stormy Sea.

Then as a Moony Ark Ololon descended to Felpham's Vale
In clouds of blood, in streams of gore, with dreadful thunderings
Into the Fires of Intellect that rejoic'd in Felpham's Vale
Around the Starry Eight; with one accord the Starry Eight became
One Man, Jesus the Saviour, wonderful! round his limbs
The Clouds of Ololon folded as a Garment dipped in blood,
Written within & without in woven letters, & the Writing
Is the Divine Revelation in the Litteral expression,
A Garment of War. I heard it nam'd the Woof of Six Thousand Years.

And I beheld the Twenty-four Cities of Albion
Arise upon their Thrones to Judge the Nations of the Earth;
And the Immortal Four in whom the Twenty-four appear Four-fold
Arose around Albion's body. Jesus wept & walked forth
From Felpham's Vale clothed in Clouds of blood, to enter into
Albion's Bosom, the bosom of death, & the Four surrounded him
In the Column of Fire in Felpham's Vale; then to their mouths the Four
Applied their Four Trumpets & them sounded to the Four winds.

Terror struck in the Vale I stood at that immortal sound.
My bones trembled, I fell outstretch'd upon the path
A moment, & my Soul return'd into its mortal state
To Resurrection & Judgment in the Vegetable Body,
And my sweet Shadow of Delight stood trembling by my side.

Immediately the Lark mounted with a loud trill from Felpham's Vale,
And the Wild Thyme from Wimbleton's green & impurpled Hills,
And Los & Enitharmon rose over the Hills of Surrey:

Their clouds roll over London with a south wind; soft Oothoon
Pants in the Vales of Lambeth, weeping o'er her Human Harvest.
Los listens to the Cry of the Poor Man, his Cloud
Over London in volume terrific low bended in anger.

Rintrah & Palamabron view the Human Harvest beneath.
Their Wine-presses & Barns stand open, the Ovens are prepar'd,
The Waggons ready; terrific Lions & Tygers sport & play.
All Animals upon the Earth are prepar'd in all their strength

43

To go forth to the Great Harvest & Vintage of the Nations.

Finis

Written on the back of a sketch for the design on no. 43:
Father & Mother, I return from flames of fire tried & pure & white.

EPIGRAMS, VERSES, AND FRAGMENTS FROM THE NOTE-BOOK

Written about 1808-1811

I

P. 21.

No real Style of Colouring ever appears,
But advertising in the News Papers.
Look there—you'll see Sr Joshua's Colouring.
Look at his Pictures—['tis quite another Thing *del.*] All has taken Wing

2

P. 21.

You don't believe—I [would *first rdg.*] won't attempt to make ye:
You are asleep—I won't attempt to wake ye.
Sleep on, Sleep on! while in your pleasant dreams
Of Reason you may drink of Life's clear streams.
Reason and Newton, they are quite two things;
For so the Swallow & the Sparrow sings.
Reason says "Miracle": Newton says "Doubt."
Aye! that's the way to make all Nature out.
"Doubt, Doubt, & don't believe without experiment":
That is the very thing that Jesus meant,
When he said, "[Rich *del.*] Only Believe! Believe & try!
"Try, Try, & never mind the Reason why."

3

P. 22.

And his legs carried it like a long fork,
Reach'd all the way from Chichester to York,
From York all across Scotland to the Sea;
This was a Man of Men, as seems to me.
Not only in his Mouth his own Soul lay,
But my Soul also would he bear away.
Like as a Pedlar bears his weary Pack,
[He would bear my soul *del.*]
So Stewhard's Soul he buckl'd to his Back.
But once, alas! committing a Mistake,
He bore the wretched Soul of William Blake

That he might turn it into Eggs of Gold;
But neither Back nor mouth those Eggs could hold.
His under jaw drop'd as those Eggs he laid,
And [all my *del.*] Stewhard's Eggs are addled & decay'd.
The Examiner, whose very name is Hunt,
Call'd Death a Madman [deadly the affront *del.*] trembling for the affront,
Like trembling Hare sits on his weakly paper
On which he us'd to dance & sport & caper.
[And *del.*] Yorkshire Jack Hemp & gentle, blushing Daw,
Clap'd Death into the corner of their jaw,
And Felpham Billy rode out every morn
Horseback with Death over the fields of corn,
[And *del.*] Who with iron hand cuff'd in the afternoon
The Ears of Billy's Lawyer & Dragoon.
And Cur, my Lawyer, & Dady, Jack Hemp's Parson,
Both went to Law with Death to keep our Ears on.
For how to starve Death we had laid a plot
Against his Price—but Death was in the Pot.
He made them pay his Price, alack a day!
He knew both Law & Gospel better than they.
O, that I ne'er has [had] seen that William Blake,
Or could from death Assassinetti wake!
We thought—Alas, that such a thought should be!—
That Blake would Etch for him & draw for me.
For 'twas a kind of Bargain Screwmuch made
That Blake's designs should be by us display'd,
Because he makes designs so very cheap.
Then Screwmuch at Blake's soul took a long leap.
'Twas not a Mouse—'twas Death in a disguise,
And I, alas! live to weep out mine Eyes.
And Death sits [mocking *del.*] laughing on their Monuments,
On which he's written, "Reciev'd the Contents."
But I have writ—so sorrowful my thought is—
His Epitaph [with *del.*] for my tears [of *del.*] are aqua fortis:
"[Ye *del.*] Come Artists, knock your heads against this stone
"For Sorrow that [your *del.*] our friend Bob Screwmuch's gone."
And, now the Men upon me smile & Laugh,
I'll also write my own dear Epitaph,
And I'll be buried near a Dike
That my friends may weep as much as they like:
"Here lies Stewhard the Friend of All, &c."

[*See no.* 43, *page* 546]

4

P. 23.

Was I angry with Hayley who us'd me so ill,
Or can I be angry with Felpham's old Mill?
[Or angry with Boydell or Bowyer or Ba . . . *del.*]
Or angry with Flaxman or Cromek or Stothard,
Or poor Schiavonetti, whom they to death bother'd?
Or angry with Macklin or Boydel or Bowyer,
Because they did not say, "O what a Beau ye are"?
At a Friend's Errors Anger shew,
Mirth at the Errors of a Foe.

5

P. 23.

Anger & Wrath my bosom rends:
I thought them the Errors of friends.
But all my limbs with warmth glow:
I find them the Errors of the foe.

6

P. 24.

The Sussex Men are Noted Fools,
And weak is their brain pan:
I wonder if H[aines] the painter
Is not a Sussex Man?

7

P. 24.

old acquaintance well renew.
Prospero had One Caliban & I have Two.

8

P. 25.

"Madman" I have been call'd: "Fool" they call thee.
I wonder which they Envy, Thee or Me?

9

P. 25.

To H[unt]

You think Fuseli is not a Great Painter. I'm Glad:
This is one of the best compliments he ever had.

10

P. 26.

To F[laxman]

I mock thee not, tho' I by thee am Mocked.
Thou call'st me Madman, but I call thee Blockhead.

11

P. 26.

Can there be any thing more mean,
More Malice in disguise,
Than Praise a Man for doing [that *del.*] what
[Which he *del.*] That Man does most despise?
[This *del.*] Reynolds Lectures [plainly shew *del.*] Exactly so
When he praises Michael Angelo.

12

P. 27.

S[tothard] in Childhood on the Nursery floor
Was extreme Old & most extremely poor.
He is grown old & rich & what he will:
He is extreme old & extreme poor still.

13

P. 27.

To Nancy F[laxman]

How can I help thy Husband's copying Me?
Should that make difference 'twixt me & Thee?

14

P. 27.

Of H[ayley]'s birth this was the happy lot
His Mother on his Father him begot.

15

P. 28.

Sir Joshua Praises Michael Angelo:
[And counts it courage thus to praise his foe *del.*]
[Is it Politeness *del.*]
'Tis Christian Mildness when [fools *del.*] Knaves Praise a Foe;
But 'Twould be Madness [that we all must *del.*] all the World would say,
[If All *del.*] Should Michael Angelo [praising *del.*] praise Sir Joshua—
Christ us'd the Pharisees in a rougher way.

16

P. 26.

He's a Blockhead who wants a proof of what he can't Percieve,
And he's a Fool who [seeks *del.*] tries to make such a Blockhead believe.

17

P. 29.

Cr[omek] loves artists as he loves his Meat.
[Cr— *del.*] He loves the Art, but 'tis the Art to Cheat.

18

P. 29.

A petty Sneaking Knave I knew—
O Mr Cr[omek], how do ye do?

19

P. 29.

Sir Joshua praised Rubens with a Smile
By calling his the ornamental Style;
[Because *del.*] And yet his praise of Flaxman was the smartest
When he call'd him the Ornamental Artist.
But sure such ornaments we well may spare,
[Like a filthy infectious head of hair *del.*]
[A Crooked Stick & louzy head of hair *del.*]
As Crooked limbs & louzy heads of hair.

20

P. 29.

He is a Cock would . . .
And would be a Cock if he could . . .

21

P. 30.

He has observ'd the Golden Rule
Till he's become the Golden Fool.

22

P. 30.

To S[tothar]d.

[He *del.*] You all [his *del.*] your Youth observ'd the Golden Rule
Till [he's *del.*] you're at last become the golden fool.
I sport with Fortune, Merry, Blithe & Gay,
Like to the Lion Sporting with his Prey.
[He has *del.*] Take you the hide & horns which [he may wear *del.*] [thou maist *del.*] you may wear:
Mine is the flesh—the bones may be [thy *del.*] your Share.

23

P. 31.

[Mr Cromek to *del.*] Mr Stothard
To Mr Cromek

For Fortune's favours you your riches bring,
But Fortune says she gave you no such thing.
Why should you be ungrateful to your friends,
Sneaking & [Calumny *del.*] Backbiting & Odds & Ends?

24

P. 31.

Mr Cromek to Mr Stothard

Fortune favours the Brave, old Proverbs say;
But not with Money: that is not the way.
Turn back, turn back: you travel all in vain.
Turn thro' the iron gate down Sneaking lane.

25

P. 31.

I am no Homer's Hero, you all know;
I profess not Generosity to a Foe.
My Generosity is to my Friends,
That for their Friendship I may make amends.
The Generous to Enemies promotes their Ends
And becomes the Enemy & Betrayer of his Friends.

26

P. 32.

The Angel that presided o'er my birth
Said, "Little creature, [thou art form'd for Mirth *first rdg.*]
form'd of Joy & Mirth,
"Go love without the help of any Thing on Earth."

27

P. 32.

Florentine Ingratitude

Sir Joshua sent his own Portrait to
The birth Place of Michael Angelo,
And in the hand of the simpering fool
He put a dirty paper scroll,
And on the paper, to be polite,
Did "Sketches by Michel Angelo" write.
[They said, "Thus Learning & Politeness from England we fetch:

"(We thought Michael Angelo did never sketch *del.*)
"For No good Artist will or Can sketch,
"And 'tis English Politeness as fair as may . . .
"To (say *del.*) speak Michael Angelo & (mean *del.*) act Rembrandt
"To speak Michael Angelo & mean Rembrandt." *del.*]

The Florentines said, " 'Tis a Dutch English bore,
"Michael Angelo's Name writ on Rembrandt's door."
The Florentines call it an English Fetch,
For Michael Angelo did never sketch.
Every line of his has Meaning
And needs neither Suckling nor Weaning.
[Is this Politeness, or is it Cant *del.*]
'Tis the trading English Venetian cant
To speak Michael Angelo & Act Rembrandt.
[2] But You must not bring in your hand a Lie.
If you mean the Florentines [to *del.*] should buy.
[1] It will set his Dutch friends all in a roar
To write "Mich. Ang." on Rembrandt's Door.

Ghiotto's Circle or Apelles' Line
Were not the Work of Sketchers drunk with Wine,
Nor of the City Clark's warm hearted Fashion,
Nor of Sir Isaac Newton's Calculation,
Nor of the City Clark's Idle Facilities
Which sprang from Sir Isaac Newton's great Abilities

These Verses were written by a very Envious Man,
Who, whatever likeness he may have to Michael Angelo,
Never can have any to Sir Jehoshuan.

28

P. 33.

A [Pitiable *del.*] Pitiful Case

The Villain at the Gallows tree
When he is doom'd to die,
To assuage his misery
In Virtue's praise does cry.

So Reynolds when he came to die,
To assuage his bitter woe
Thus aloud [was heard to *del.*] did howl & cry:
"Michael Angelo! Michael Angelo!"

P. 33. 29

To the Royal Academy

A strange Erratum in all the Editions
Of Sir Joshua Reynolds's Lectures
Should be corrected by the Young Gentlemen
And the Royal Academy's directors.

Instead of "Michael Angelo"
Read "Rembrandt", [& you will know *del.*] for it is fit
[That Sir Joshua never wish'd to speak
Of Michael Angelo. *del.*]
To make [either sense or *del.*] meer common honesty
In all that he has writ.

P. 33. 30

If it is True, what the Prophets write,
That the heathen Gods are all stocks & stones,
Shall we, for the sake of being Polite,
Feed them with the juice of our marrow bones?

And if Bezaleel & Aholiab drew
What the Finger of God pointed to their View,
Shall we suffer the Roman & Grecian Rods
To compell us to worship them as Gods?

They stole them from the Temple of the Lord,
And Worshipp'd them [to *del.*] that they might make
Inspired Art Abhorr'd.

The Wood & Stone were call'd The Holy Things
And their Sublime Intent given to their Kings,
All the Atonements of Jehovah spurn'd,
And Criminals to Sacrifices Turn'd.

P. 34. 31

[To *del.*] On F[laxman] & S[tothard]

I found [thee *altered to*] them blind: I taught [thee *altered to*] them how to see;
And now [thou *del.*] they know ['st *del.*] neither [thyself *del.*] themselves nor me.

'Tis Excellent to turn a thorn to a pin,
A [knave *altered to*] Fool to a bolt, a [Fool *altered to*] Knave to a glass of gin.

32

P. 34.

P[hillips] loved me not as he lov'd his Friends,
For he lov'd them for gain to serve his Ends.
[But *del.*] He loved me [but *del.*] and for no Gain at all
But to rejoice & triumph in my fall.

33

P. 34.

To forgive Enemies H[ayley] does pretend,
Who never in his Life forgave a friend.

34

P. 35.

To F[laxman]

You call me Mad: 'tis Folly to do so—
To seek to turn a Madman to a Foe.
If you think as you speak, you are an Ass.
If you do not, you are [just *del.*] but what you was.

35

P. 35.

On H[ayle]y's Friendship

When H—y finds out what you cannot do,
That is the very thing he'll set you to.
If you break not your Neck, 'tis not his fault,
[A *del.*] But pecks of poison[s *del.*] are not [a *del.*] pecks of salt.
And when he could not act upon my wife
Hired a Villain to bereave my Life.

36

P. 36.

Some Men, created for destruction, come
Into the World & make the World their home.
[Friend Caiaphas is one, do what he can. *del.*]
Be they as Vile & Base as E'er they can,
[He'll *del.*] They'll still be called "The World's honest man."

37

P. 36.

On S[tothard]

You say reserve & modesty he has,
[His *del.*] Whose heart is iron, his head wood, & his face brass,
The Fox, the Owl, the Beetle & the Bat
[On *del.*] By sweet reserve & modesty [feed Fat *del.*] get Fat.

38

P. 37.

Imitation of Pope: A Compliment to the Ladies

Wondrous the Gods, more wondrous are the Men,
More Wondrous Wondrous still the Cock & Hen,
More Wondrous still the Table, Stool & Chair;
But Ah! More wondrous still the Charming Fair.

39

P. 37.

To H[ayley]

Thy Friendship oft has made my heart to ake:
Do be my Enemy for Friendship's sake.

40

P. 37.

Cosway, Frazer & Baldwin of Egypt's Lake
Fear to associate with Blake.
This Life is a Warfare against Evils;
They heal the sick: he casts out devils.
Hayley, Flaxman & Stothard are also in doubt
Lest their Virtue should be put to the rout.
One grins, [one *del.*] t'other spits & in corners hides,
And all the [Righteous *del.*] Virtuous have shewn their backsides.

41

P. 37.

An Epitaph

Come knock your heads against this stone
For sorrow that poor John Thompson's gone.

42

P. 37.

Another

I was buried near this Dike,
That my Friends may weep as much as they like.

43

P. 37.

Another

Here lies John Trot, the Friend of all mankind:
He has not left one Enemy behind.
Friends were quite hard to find, old authors say;
But now they stand in every bodies way.

44

P. 38.

My title as an [Artist *del.*] Genius thus is prov'd:
Not Prais'd by Hayley nor by Flaxman lov'd.

45

P. 38.

[Rubens had been a Statesman or a Saint *first rdg.*]
I, Rubens, am a Statesman & a Saint.
[He mix'd them both, & so he Learn'd to Paint *del.*]
Deceptions? O no—so I'll learn to Paint.

46

P. 38.

To English Connoisseurs

You must agree that Rubens was a Fool,
And yet you make him master of your School
And give more money for his slobberings
Than you will give for Rafael's finest Things.
I understood Christ was a Carpenter
And not a Brewer's Servant, my good Sir.

47

P. 38.

Swell'd limbs, with no outline that you can descry,
That Stink in the Nose of a Stander-by.
But all the Pulp wash'd, painted, finish'd with labour
Of an hundred Journeymen's 'how d'ye do, Neighbour'.

48

P. 38.

[A Pretty Epigram for those who have Given high Prices for Bad Pictures And never *del.*]

A Pretty Epigram for [those *del.*] the Entertainment of those who [pay *del.*] have Paid Great Sums in the Venetian & Flemish Ooze

Nature & Art in this together Suit:
What is Most Grand is always most Minute.
Rubens thinks Tables, Chairs & Stools are Grand,
But Rafael thinks A Head, a foot, a hand.

49

P. 38.

[Let it be told *del.*]
3 The Swallow sings in Courts of Kings
That Fools have their high finishings,
And this the Princes' golden rule,
The Laborious stumble of a Fool.
1 These are the Idiot's chiefest arts,
2 To blend & not define the Parts.
To make out the parts is the wise man's aim,
But to lose them the Fool makes his foolish Game.

50

P. 39.

Rafael Sublime, Majestic, Graceful, Wise,
His Executive Power must I despise?
Rubens Low, Vulgar, Stupid, Ignorant,
His power of Execution I must grant?
Learn the Laborious stumble of a Fool,
And from an Idiot's Actions form my rule?
Go send your Children to the Slobbering School!

51

P. 39.

If I e'er Grow to Man's Estate,
O, Give to me a Woman's fate!
May I govern all, both great & small,
Have the last word & take the wall.

52

P. 39.

The Cripple every Step Drudges & labours,
And says: "come, learn to walk of me, Good Neighbours."
Sir Joshua in astonishment cries out:
["His pains are more than others', there's no doubt." *del.*]
"See, what Great Labour Pain him & Modest Doubt!"
Newton & Bacon cry, being badly Nurst:
"He is all Experiments from last to first.
"He walks & stumbles as if he crep,
"And how high labour'd is every step!"

53

P. 40.

On the Great Encouragement
Given by English Nobility & Gentry to Correggio, Rubens,
Rembrandt, Reynolds, Gainsborough, Catalani,
Du Crowe, & Dilbury Doodle

As the Ignorant Savage will sell his own Wife
For a [Button, a Bauble (Buckle *del.*), a Bead or a *del.*] Sword or a Cutlass, a dagger or Knife,
So the [wise *del.*, Learned *del.*] Taught, Savage Englishman [pours *del.*] spends his whole Fortune
[For *del.*] On a smear [& *del.*] or a squall [that is not *del.*] to destroy Picture or Tune,
And I call upon Colonel Wardle
To give these Rascals a dose of Cawdle.

54

P. 40.

Give pensions to the Learned Pig
Or the Hare playing on a Tabor;
Anglus can never see Perfection
But in the Journeyman's Labour.

55

P. 40.

The Cunning-sures & the aim-at-yours . . .

56

P. 40.

All Pictures that's Painted with Sense & with Thought
Are Painted by Madmen as sure as a Groat;
For the Greater the Fool in the Pencil more blest,

And when they are drunk they always paint best.
They never can Rafael it, Fuseli it, nor Blake it;
If they can't see an outline, pray how can they make it?
When Men will draw outlines begin you to jaw them;
Madmen see outlines & therefore they draw them.

57

P. 41.

On H[ayley] the Pick thank

I write the Rascal Thanks till he & I
With Thanks & Compliments are quite drawn dry.

58

P. 41.

Cromek Speaks

I always take my judgment from a Fool
Because [I know he always judges *del.*] his judgment is so very Cool,
Not prejudic'd by feelings great or small.
[Because we know *del,*]
Amiable state! he cannot feel at all.

59

P. 41.

English Encouragement of Art: Cromek's opinions put into Rhyme

[*First reading*]

If you mean to Please Every body you will
Set to work both Ignorance & skill;
For a great [multitude *del.*] Madjority are Ignorant,
And skill to them seems raving & rant;
Like putting oil & water into a lamp,
'Twill make a great splutter with smoke & damp;
For there is no use, as it seems to me,
Of Lighting a Lamp when you don't wish to see.
And, when it smells of the Lamp, we [will *del.*] can
Say all was owing to the Skilful Man.
For the smell of water is but small,
So e'en let Ignorance do it all.

[*Second reading*]

If you mean to Please Every body you will
Menny wouver both Bunglishness & skill,
For a great Conquest are Bunglery,

And Jenous looks to him [looks *del.*] like mad Rantery,
Like displaying oil & water into a lamp,
'Twill hold forth a huge splutter with smoke & damp;
For it's all sheer loss, as it seems to me,
Of displaying up a light when we want not to see.

60

P. 41.

When you look at a picture, you always can see
If a Man of Sense has Painted he.
Then never flinch, but keep up a Jaw
About freedom & Jenny suck awa'.

61

P. 42.

You say their Pictures well Painted be,
And yet they are Blockheads you all agree.
Thank God, I never was sent to school
[To learn to admire the works of a Fool. *del.*]
To be Flog'd into following the Style of a Fool.

The Errors of a Wise Man make your Rule
Rather than the Perfections of a Fool.

62

P. 42.

The Washerwoman's Song

I wash'd them out & wash'd them in,
And they told me it was a great Sin.

63

P. 43.

When I see a Rubens, Rembrandt, [or *del.*] Correggio,
I think of the Crippled Harry & Slobbering Joe;
And then I [say to myself *del.*] question thus; are artists' rules
To be drawn from the works of two manifest fools?
Then God defend us from the Arts I say!
Send Battle, Murder, Sudden death, [we *del.*] O pray!
Rather than [let *del.*] be such a blind Human Fool
I'd be an Ass, a Hog, a worm, a Chair, a Stool!

64

P. 43.

Great things are done when Men & Mountains meet;
This is not done by Jostling in the Street.

65

P. 46.

Delicate Hands & Heads will never appear
While Titian's &c., as in the Book of Moonlight, p. 5.

66

P. 46.

I [have giv'n *del.*] give you the end of a golden string:
Only wind it into a ball,
It will lead you in at Heaven's Gate
Built in Jerusalem's wall.

67

P. 47.

If you play a Game of Chance, know, before you begin,
If you are benevolent you will never win.

68

P. 50.

William Cowper, Esqre

[*The first stanza erased and illegible*]

For this is being a Friend just in the nick,
Not when he's well, but waiting till he's sick.
He calls you to his help: be you not mov'd
Untill, by being Sick, his wants are prov'd.

You see him spend his Soul in Prophecy.
Do you believe it a confounded lie
Till some Bookseller & the Public Fame
Proves there is truth in his extravagant claim.

For 'tis [most wicked *del.*] atrocious in a Friend you love
To tell you any thing that he can't prove,
And 'tis most wicked in a Christian Nation
For any Man to pretend to Inspiration.

69

P. 50.

The only Man that e'er I knew
Who did not make me almost spew
Was Fuseli: he was both Turk & Jew—
And so, [sweet *del.*] dear Christian Friends, how do you do?

70

P. 52.

I will tell you what Joseph of Arimathea
Said to my Fairy—was not it very queer?
Pliny & Trajan! what are you here?
Come listen to Joseph of Arimathea:
Listen patient, & when Joseph has done
'Twill make a fool laugh & a Fairy Fun.

71

P. 54.

Grown old in Love from Seven till Seven times Seven,
I oft have wish'd for Hell for Ease from Heaven.

72

P. 56.

Why was Cupid a Boy
And why a boy was he?
He should have been a Girl
For ought that I can see.

For he shoots with his bow,
And the Girl shoots with her Eye,
And they both are merry & glad
And laugh when we do cry.

[Then *del.*] And to make Cupid a Boy
Was [surely a Woman's *del.*]
    the Cupid Girl's mocking plan;
For a boy [never learns so much *del.*]
    can't interpret the thing
Till he is become a man.

And then he's so pierc'd with care
And wounded with arrowy smarts,
That the whole business of his life
Is to pick out the heads of the darts.

'Twas the Greeks' love of war
Turn'd Love into a Boy,
And Woman into a Statue of Stone—
And away fled every Joy.

73

P. 59.

From Bell's Weekly Messenger, Augst 4, 1811

"Salisbury, July 29: A Bill of Indictment was preferred against Peter "le Cave for Felony, but return'd Ignoramus by the Grand Jury. It "appear'd that he was in extreme indigence, but was an Artist of very "superior Merit, while he was in Wilton [Jail *del.*] Goal he painted "many Pieces in the Style of Morland, some of which are stated to be "even superior to the performances of that Artist, with whom Le "Cave lived many years as a Professional Assistant & he states that "many Paintings of his were only Varnished over by Morland & sold "by that Artist as his own. Many of the Principal Gentlemen of the "County have visited Le Cave in the Goal & declared his drawings & "Paintings in many instances to excel Morland's. The Writer of this "Article has seen many of Le Cave's Works & tho' he does not "pretend to the knowledge of an artist, yet he considers them as "Chaste delineations of Rural Objects."

Such is the Paragraph. It confirms the Suspition I entertain'd concerning those two [Prints *del.*] I Engraved From for J. R. Smith—That Morland could not have Painted them, as they were the works of a Correct Mind & no Blurrer.

74

P. 60–61.

I ask'd my dear Friend, Orator Prigg:
"What's the first part of Oratory?" he said: "a great wig."
"And what is the second?" then dancing a jig
And bowing profoundly he said: "a great wig."
"And what is the third?" then he snor'd like a pig,
And [smil'd like a Cherub & said *del.*] puffing his cheeks he replied:
"a Great wig."

So if a Great Painter with Questions you push,
"What's the first Part of Painting?" he'll say: "a Paint Brush."
"And what is the second?" with most modest blush,
He'll [nod, wink & smile & reply *first rdg.*] smile like a Cherub & say:
"a paint Brush."
"And what is the third?" he'll bow like a rush,
With a lear in his Eye, he'll reply: "a Paint Brush."
Perhaps this is all a Painter can want;
But look yonder—that house is the house of Rembrandt. &c.
(to come in Barry, a Poem.)

[Then Reynolds said: "O woman most sage!" *del.*]
"O dear Mother outline, [be not in a Rage *del.*] of knowledge most sage,
"What's the First Part of Painting?" she said: "Patronage."
"And what is the second?" to Please & Engage,
She frown'd like a Fury & said: "Patronage."
"And what is the Third?" she put off Old Age,
And smil'd like a Syren & said: "Patronage."

75

Pp. 60-61.

To Venetian Artists

That God is colouring Newton does shew,
And the devil is a Black outline, all of us know.
Perhaps this little Fable &c.

[*on next page*]
Perhaps this little Fable may make us merry:
A dog went over the water without a wherry;
A bone which he had stolen he had in his mouth;
He cared not whether the wind was north or south.
As he swam he saw the reflection of the bone.
"This is quite Perfection, [here's two for one! what a brilliant tone! *del.*] one Generalizing Tone!
"Outline! There's no outline! There's no such thing!
"All is Chiaro Scuro, Poco Pen, [& *del.*] it's all colouring."
[Then he snap'd & *del.*]
Snap, Snap! he has lost shadow & substance too.
He had them both before: now how do ye do?
"A great deal better than I was before.
"[I've tasted shadow & *del.*]
"Those who taste colouring love it more & more."

76

P. 63.

Great Men & Fools do often me Inspire,
But the Greater Fool, the Greater Liar.

77

Pp. 62-63.

Blake's apology for his Catalogue

Dryden in Rhyme cries: "Milton only Plann'd."
4 Every Fool shook his bells throughout the Land.
5 Tom Cooke cut Hogarth down with his clean Graving.
6 [How many *del.*]

Thousands of Connoisseurs with joy ran raving.
Having Given great offence by writing in Prose,
I'll write in Rhyme as soft as [feather Pillows *del.*] Bartolloze.
1 Some blush at what others can see no crime in,
2 But Nobody [at all *del.*] sees any harm in Rhyming.
3 Thus Poor Schiavonetti died of the Cromek,
A thing that's tied about the Examiner's neck.
7 Thus Hayley on his Toilette seeing the sope,
8 Says, "Homer is very much improv'd by Pope."
Flaxman & Stothard, smelling a sweet savour,
Cry, "Blakified drawing spoils painter & Engraver."
9 While I looking up to my Umbrella,
10 Resolv'd to be a very Contrary Fellow,
11 Cry, [Tom Cooke proves *del.*] looking up from [Circumference
del.] Skumference to Center,
12 "No one can finish so high as the original inventor."
Who cries, "all art is a fraud & Genius a trick,
"And Blake is an unfortunate Lunatic"?
I've given great Provision to my Foes,
And now I'll lead my false friends by the Nose.

[*For shorter form see p.* 595. *For fair copy see no.* 80]

78

P. 64.

From Cratetos

Me Time has crook'd; no good workman
Is he. Infirm is all that he does . . .

79

P. 64.

I always thought that Jesus Christ was a Snubby or I should not have worship'd him, if I had thought he had been one of those long spindle nosed rascals.

80

P. 65.

Having given great offence by writing in Prose,
I'll write in Verse as soft as Bartolloze.
Some blush at what others can see no crime in,
But nobody sees any harm in Rhyming.

Dryden in Rhyme cries, "Milton only plann'd."
Every Fool shook his bells throughout the land.
Tom Cooke cut Hogarth down with his clean graving.

Thousands of Connoisseurs with joy ran raving.
Thus Hayley on his Toilette seeing the sope,
Cries, "Homer is very much improv'd by Pope."
Some say I've given great Provision to my foes,
And that now I lead my false friends by the nose.
Flaxman & Stothard smelling a sweet savour
Cry, "Blakified drawing spoils painter & Engraver,"
While I, looking up to my Umbrella,
Resolv'd to be a very contrary fellow,
Cry, looking quite from Skumference to Center,
"No one can finish so high as the original Inventor."
Thus Poor Schiavonetti died of the Cromek
A thing that's tied around the Examiner's neck.
This is my sweet apology to my friends,
That I may put them in mind of their latter Ends.

81

P. 65.

If Men will act like a maid smiling over a Churn,
They ought not, when it comes to another's turn,
To grow sower at what a friend may utter,
Knowing & feeling that we all have need of Butter.

False Friends! [O no *del.*] fie! fie! our Friendship [ne'er shall *del.*] you shan't sever,
[For now *del.*] In spite we will be greater friends than ever.

82

P. 67.

23 May, 1810, found the Word Golden.

83

P. 70.

Some people admire the work of a Fool,
For it's sure to keep your judgment cool;
It does not reproach you with want of wit;
It is not like a lawyer serving a writ.

84

P. 72.

Jesus does not trea[t *part of leaf cut away*] he makes a Wide distinction between the Sheep & the Goats; consequently he is Not Charitable.

85

P. 73.

To God

If you have form'd a Circle to go into,
Go into it yourself & see how you would do.

86

P. 73.

Since all the Riches of this [Earth *del.*] World
May be gifts from the Devil & Earthly Kings,
I should suspect that I worship'd the Devil
If I thank'd my God for [Worldly *del.* Earthly *del.*] Worldly things.

87

P. 78.

To Chloe's breast young Cupid slily stole,
But he crept in at Myra's pocket hole.

88

P. 79.

"Now Art has lost its mental Charms
"France shall subdue the World in Arms."
So spoke an Angel at my birth,
Then said, "Descend thou upon Earth.
"Renew the Arts on Britain's Shore,
"And France shall fall down & adore.
"With works of Art their Armies meet,
"And [Armies *del.*] War shall sink beneath thy feet.
"But if thy Nation Arts refuse,
"And if they scorn the immortal Muse,
"France shall the arts of Peace restore,
"And save [thy works *del.*] thee from [Britain's *del.*] the
Ungrateful shore."

Spirit, who lov'st Brittannia's [Shore *del.*] Isle
Round which the Fiends of Commerce [roar *del.*] smile . . .

89

P. 79.

Nail his neck to the Cross: nail it with a nail.
Nail his neck to the Cross: ye all have power over his tail.

90

P. 87.

The [Visions *del.*] Caverns of the Grave I've seen,
And these I shew'd to England's Queen.
[And *del.*] But now the Caves of Hell I view:
Who shall I dare to shew them to?
What mighty Soul in Beauty's form
Shall [dare to *del.*] dauntless View the Infernal Storm?
Egremont's Countess [dare *del.*] can controll
The [waves *del.*] flames of Hell that round me roll.
If she refuse, I still go on
Till the Heavens & Earth are gone,
Still admir'd by [worthy *del.*] Noble minds,
Follow'd by Envy on the winds,
Re-engrav'd Time after Time,
Ever in their youthful prime,
My designs [shall still *del.*] unchang'd remain.
Time may rage but rage in vain.
For above Time's troubled Fountains
On the Great Atlantic Mountains,
In my Golden House on high,
There they Shine Eternally.

91

P. 89.

I rose up at the dawn of day—
Get thee away! get thee away!
Pray'st thou for Riches? away! away!
This is the Throne of Mammon grey.

Said I, "this sure is very odd.
"I took it to be the Throne of God.
"For every Thing besides I have:
"It is only for Riches that I can crave.

"I have Mental Joy & Mental Health
"And Mental Friends & Mental wealth;
"I've a Wife I love & that loves me;
"I've all But Riches Bodily.

"I am in God's presence night & day,
"And he never turns his face away.
"The accuser of sins by my side does stand
"And he holds my money bag in his hand.

"For [all that *del.*] my worldly things God makes him pay,
"And he'd pay for more if to him I would pray;
"And so you may do the worst you can do:
"Be assur'd M^r devil I won't pray to you.

"Then If for Riches I must not Pray,
"God knows I little of Prayers need say.
"So [as sure *del.*] as a Church is known by its Steeple,
"If I pray it must be for other People.

"He says, if I do not worship him for a God,
"I shall eat coarser food & go worse shod;
"So as I don't value such things as these,
"You must do, M^r devil, just as God please."

92

P. 93.

A Woman Scaly & a Man all Hairy
Is such a Match as he who dares
Will find the Woman's Scales scrape off the Man's Hairs.

[END OF EPIGRAMS, &C., FROM THE NOTE-BOOK, 1808–1811]

ADDITIONAL PASSAGE

93

Page 92, reversed.

Every thing which is in harmony with me I call In harmony—But there may be things which are Not in harmony with Me & yet are in a More perfect Harmony.

[ADVERTISEMENT OF] EXHIBITION OF
Paintings in Fresco, Poetical and Historical Inventions,
BY WM. BLAKE

Printed 1809

THE ANCIENT BRITONS—Three Ancient Britons overthrowing the Army of armed Romans; the Figures full as large as Life—From the Welch Triades.

In the last Battle that Arthur fought, the most Beautiful was one
That return'd, and the most Strong another: with them also return'd
The most Ugly, and no other beside return'd from the bloody Field.

The most Beautiful, the Roman Warriors trembled before and worshipped:
The most Strong, they melted before him and dissolved in his presence:
The most Ugly they fled with outcries and contortion of their Limbs.

THE CANTERBURY PILGRIMS from *Chaucer*—a cabinet Picture in Fresco—Thirty Figures on Horse-back, in a brilliant Morning Scene.

Two Pictures, representing grand Apotheoses of NELSON and PITT, with variety of cabinet Pictures, unchangeable and permanent in Fresco, and Drawings for Public Inspection and for Sale by Private Contract, at

No. 28, *Corner of BROAD STREET*, *Golden-Square.*

"*Fit audience find tho' few*" MILTON.

Admittance 2s. 6d. each Person, a discriptive Catalogue included.
[Containing Ample Illustrations on Art *added in MS.*]

Watts & Co., Printers, South Molton St.

THE INVENTION OF A PORTABLE FRESCO

A Wall on Canvas or Wood, or any other portable thing, of dimensions ever so large, or ever so small, which may be removed with the same convenience as so many easel Pictures; is worthy the consideration of the Rich and those who have the direction of public Works. If the Frescos of APELLES, of PROTOGENES, of RAPHAEL, or MICHAEL ANGELO could have been removed, we might, perhaps, have them now in England. I could divide Westminster Hall, or the walls of any other great Building, into compartments and ornament them with Frescos, which would be removable at pleasure.

Oil will not drink or absorb Colour enough to stand the test of very little Time and of the Air; it grows yellow, and at length brown. It was never generally used till after VANDYKE'S time. All the little old Pictures, called cabinet Pictures, are in Fresco, and not in Oil.

Fresco Painting is properly Miniature, or Enamel Painting; every thing in Fresco is as high finished as Miniature or Enamel, although in Works larger than Life. The Art has been lost: I have recovered it. How this was done, will be told, together with the whole Process, in a Work on Art, now in the Press. The ignorant Insults of Individuals will not hinder me from doing my duty to my Art. Fresco Painting, as it is now practised, is like most other things, the contrary of what it pretends to be.

The execution of my Designs, being all in Water-colours, (that is in Fresco) are regularly refused to be exhibited by the *Royal Academy*, and the *British Institution* has, this year, followed its example, and has effectually excluded me by this Resolution; I therefore invite those Noblemen and Gentlemen, who are its Subscribers, to inspect what they have excluded: and those who have been told that my Works are but an unscientific and irregular Eccentricity, a Madman's Scrawls, I demand of them to do me the justice to examine before they decide.

There cannot be more than two or three great Painters or Poets in any Age or Country; and these, in a corrupt state of Society, are easily excluded, but not so easily obstructed. They have ex[c]luded Water-colours; it is therefore become necessary that I should exhibit to the Public, in an Exhibition of my own, my Designs, Painted in Water-colours. If Italy is enriched and made great by RAPHAEL, if MICHAEL ANGELO is its supreme glory, if Art is the glory of a Nation, if Genius and Inspiration are the great Origin and Bond of Society, the distinction my Works have obtained from those who best understand such things, calls for my Exhibition as the greatest of Duties to my Country.

[May 15, 1809 *added in MS.*] *WILLIAM BLAKE.*

[END OF ADVERTISEMENT]

[ADVERTISEMENT OF]

A DESCRIPTIVE CATALOGUE OF BLAKE'S EXHIBITION,

At No. 28, Corner of
BROAD-STREET
GOLDEN-SQUARE.

Printed 1809

THE grand style of Art restored; in FRESCO, or Water-colour Painting, and England protected from the too just imputation of being the Seat and Protectress of bad (that is blotting and blurring) Art.

In this Exhibition will be seen real Art, as it was left us by *Raphael* and *Albert Durer*, *Michael Angelo*, and *Julio Romano*; stripped from the Ignorances of *Rubens* and *Rembrandt*, *Titian* and *Correggio*;

BY WILLIAM BLAKE.

The Descriptive Catalogue, Price 2s. 6d. containing Mr. B.'s Opinions and Determinations on Art, very necessary to be known by Artists and Connoisseurs of all Ranks. Every Purchaser of a Catalogue will be entitled, at the time of purchase, to view the Exhibition.

These Original Conceptions on Art, by an Original Artist, are sold only at the Corner of BROAD STREET.

Admittance to the Exhibition 1 *Shilling; an Index to the Catalogue gratis.*

Printed by Watts & Bridgewater, Southmolton-street.

A DESCRIPTIVE CATALOGUE OF PICTURES, Poetical and Historical Inventions, PAINTED BY WILLIAM BLAKE IN WATER COLOURS, BEING THE ANCIENT METHOD OF *FRESCO PAINTING RESTORED*: AND DRAWINGS, *FOR PUBLIC INSPECTION,* AND FOR Sale by Private Contract,

LONDON: Printed by D. N. SHURY, 7, Berwick-Street, Soho, for J. Blake, 28, Broad-Street, Golden-Square. 1809.

CONDITIONS OF SALE

I. *One third of the price to be paid at the time of Purchase, and the remainder on Delivery.*

II. *The Pictures and Drawings to remain in the Exhibition till its close, which will be the 29th of September* 1809; *and the Picture of the Canterbury Pilgrims, which is to be engraved, will be Sold only on condition of its remaining in the Artist's hands twelve months, when it will be delivered to the Buyer.*

PREFACE

The eye that can prefer the Colouring of Titian and Rubens to that of Michael Angelo and Rafael, ought to be modest and to doubt its own powers. Connoisseurs talk as if Rafael and Michael Angelo had never seen the colouring of Titian or Correggio: They ought to know that Correggio was born two years before Michael Angelo, and Titian but four years after. Both Rafael and Michael Angelo knew the Venetian, and contemned and rejected all he did with the utmost disdain, as that which is fabricated for the purpose to destroy art.

Mr. B. appeals to the Public, from the judgment of those narrow blinking eyes, that have too long governed art in a dark corner. The eyes of stupid cunning never will be pleased with the work any more than with the look of self-devoting genius. The quarrel of the Florentine with the Venetian is not because he does not understand Drawing, but because he does not understand Colouring. How should he? he who does not know how to draw a hand or a foot, know how to colour it?

Colouring does not depend on where the Colours are put, but on where the lights and darks are put, and all depends on Form or Outline, on where that is put; where that is wrong, the Colouring never can be right; and it is always wrong in Titian and Correggio, Rubens and Rembrandt. Till we get rid of Titian and Correggio, Rubens and Rembrandt, We never shall equal Rafael and Albert Durer, Michael Angelo, and Julio Romano.

INDEX TO THE CATALOGUE.

DESCRIPTIVE CATALOGUE

&c. &c.

NUMBER I.

The spiritual form of Nelson guiding Leviathan, in whose wreathings are infolded the Nations of the Earth.

Clearness and precision have been the chief objects in painting these Pictures. Clear colours unmudded by oil, and firm and determinate lineaments unbroken by shadows, which ought to display and not to hide form, as is the practice of the latter schools of Italy and Flanders.

NUMBER II, ITS COMPANION.

The spiritual form of Pitt, guiding Behemoth; he is that Angel who, pleased to perform the Almighty's orders, rides on the whirlwind, directing the storms of war: He is ordering the Reaper to reap the Vine of the Earth, and the Plowman to plow up the Cities and Towers.

This Picture also is a proof of the power of colours unsullied with oil or with any cloggy vehicle. Oil has falsely been supposed to give strength to colours: but a little consideration must shew the fallacy of this opinion. Oil will not drink or absorb colour enough to stand the test of very little time and of the air. It deadens every colour it is mixed with, at its first mixture, and in a little time becomes a yellow mask over all that it touches. Let the works of modern Artists since Rubens' time witness the villany of some one at that time, who first brought oil Painting into general opinion and practice: since which we have never had a Picture painted, that could shew itself by the side of an earlier production. Whether Rubens or Vandyke, or both, were guilty of this villainy, is to be enquired in another work on Painting, and who first forged the silly story and known falshood, about John of Bruges inventing oil colours: in the meantime let it be observed, that before Vandyke's time, and in his time all the genuine Pictures are on Plaster or Whiting grounds and none since.

The two pictures of Nelson and Pitt are compositions of a mythological cast, similar to those Apotheoses of Persian, Hindoo, and Egyptian Antiquity, which are still preserved on rude monuments, being copies from some stupendous originals now lost or perhaps buried till some happier age. The Artist having been taken in vision into the ancient republics, monarchies, and patriarchates of Asia, has seen those wonderful originals called in the Sacred Scriptures the Cherubim, which were sculptured and painted on walls of Temples, Towers, Cities, Palaces, and erected in the highly cultivated states of Egypt, Moab, Edom, Aram, among the Rivers of Paradise, being originals from which the Greeks and Hetrurians copied Hercules Farnese, Venus of Medicis, Apollo Belvidere, and all the grand works of ancient art. They were executed in a very superior style to those justly admired copies, being with their accompaniments terrific and grand in the highest degree. The Artist has endeavoured to emulate the grandeur of those seen in his vision, and to apply it to modern Heroes, on a smaller scale.

No man can believe that either Homer's Mythology, or Ovid's, were the production of Greece or of Latium; neither will any one believe, that the Greek statues, as they are called, were the invention of Greek Artists; perhaps the Torso is the only original work remaining; all the rest are evidently copies, though fine ones, from greater works of the Asiatic Patriarchs. The Greek Muses are daughters of

Mnemosyne, or Memory, and not of Inspiration or Imagination, therefore not authors of such sublime conceptions. Those wonderful originals seen in my visions, were some of them one hundred feet in height; some were painted as pictures, and some carved as basso relievos, and some as groupes of statues, all containing mythological and recondite meaning, where more is meant than meets the eye. The Artist wishes it was now the fashion to make such monuments, and then he should not doubt of having a national commission to execute these two Pictures on a scale that is suitable to the grandeur of the nation, who is the parent of his heroes, in high finished fresco, where the colours would be as pure and as permanent as precious stones, though the figures were one hundred feet in height.

All Frescoes are as high finished as miniatures or enamels, and they are known to be unchangeable; but oil, being a body itself, will drink or absorb very little colour, and changing yellow, and at length brown, destroys every colour it is mixed with, especially every delicate colour. It turns every permanent white to a yellow and brown putty, and has compelled the use of that destroyer of colour, white lead; which, when its protecting oil is evaporated, will become lead again. This is an awful thing to say to oil Painters; they may call it madness, but it is true. All the genuine old little pictures, called Cabinet Pictures, are in fresco and not in oil. Oil was not used, except by blundering ignorance, till after Vandyke's time, but the art of fresco painting being lost, oil became a fetter to genius, and a dungeon to art. But one convincing proof among many others, that these assertions are true is, that real gold and silver cannot be used with oil, as they are in all the old pictures and in Mr. B.'s frescos.

NUMBER III.

Sir Jeffery Chaucer and the nine and twenty Pilgrims on their journey to Canterbury.

The time chosen is early morning, before sunrise, when the jolly company are just quitting the Tabarde Inn. The Knight and Squire with the Squire's Yeoman lead the Procession; next follow the youthful Abbess, her nun and three priests; her greyhounds attend her—

> "Of small hounds had she, that she fed
> "With roast flesh, milk and wastel bread."

Next follow the Friar and Monk; then the Tapiser, the Pardoner, and the Somner and Manciple. After these "Our Host," who occupies the center of the cavalcade, directs them to the Knight as the person who would be likely to commence their task of each telling a tale in their order. After the Host follow the Shipman, the Haberdasher, the Dyer, the Franklin, the Physician, the Plowman, the Lawyer, the poor Parson, the Merchant, the Wife of Bath, the Miller, the Cook, the Oxford Scholar, Chaucer himself, and the Reeve comes as Chaucer has described:

"And ever he rode hinderest of the rout."

These last are issuing from the gateway of the Inn; the Cook and the Wife of Bath are both taking their morning's draught of comfort. Spectators stand at the gateway of the Inn, and are composed of an old Man, a Woman, and Children.

The Landscape is an eastward view of the country, from the Tabarde Inn, in Southwark, as it may be supposed to have appeared in Chaucer's time, interspersed with cottages and villages; the first beams of the Sun are seen above the horizon; some buildings and spires indicate the situation of the great City; the Inn is a gothic building, which Thynne in his Glossary says was the lodging of the Abbot of Hyde, by Winchester. On the Inn is inscribed its title, and a proper advantage is taken of this circumstance to describe the subject of the Picture. The words written over the gateway of the Inn are as follow: "The Tabarde Inn, by Henry Baillie, the lodgynge-"house for Pilgrims, who journey to Saint Thomas's Shrine at "Canterbury."

The characters of Chaucer's Pilgrims are the characters which compose all ages and nations: as one age falls, another rises, different to mortal sight, but to immortals only the same; for we see the same characters repeated again and again, in animals, vegetables, minerals, and in men; nothing new occurs in identical existence; Accident ever varies, Substance can never suffer change nor decay.

Of Chaucer's characters, as described in his Canterbury Tales, some of the names or titles are altered by time, but the characters themselves for ever remain unaltered, and consequently they are the physiognomies or lineaments of universal human life, beyond which Nature never steps. Names alter, things never alter. I have known multitudes of those who would have been monks in the age of monkery, who in this deistical age are deists. As Newton numbered the stars, and as Linneus numbered the plants, so Chaucer numbered the classes of men.

The Painter has consequently varied the heads and forms of his personages into all Nature's varieties; the Horses he has also varied to accord to their Riders; the costume is correct according to authentic monuments.

The Knight and Squire with the Squire's Yeoman lead the procession, as Chaucer has also placed them first in his prologue. The Knight is a true Hero, a good, great, and wise man; his whole length portrait on horseback, as written by Chaucer, cannot be surpassed. He has spent his life in the field; has ever been a conqueror, and is that species of character which in every age stands as the guardian of man against the oppressor. His son is like him with the germ of perhaps greater perfection still, as he blends literature and the arts with his warlike studies. Their dress and their horses are of the first rate, without ostentation, and with all the true grandeur that unaffected simplicity when in high rank always displays. The Squire's Yeoman is also a great character, a man perfectly knowing in his profession:

> "And in his hand he bare a mighty bow."

Chaucer describes here a mighty man; one who in war is the worthy attendant on noble heroes.

The Prioress follows these with her female chaplain:

> "Another Nonne also with her had she,
> "That was her Chaplaine, and Priests three."

This Lady is described also as of the first rank, rich and honoured. She has certain peculiarities and little delicate affectations, not unbecoming in her, being accompanied with what is truly grand and really polite; her person and face Chaucer has described with minuteness; it is very elegant, and was the beauty of our ancestors, till after Elizabeth's time, when voluptuousness and folly began to be accounted beautiful.

Her companion and her three priests were no doubt all perfectly delineated in those parts of Chaucer's work which are now lost; we ought to suppose them suitable attendants on rank and fashion.

The Monk follows these with the Friar. The Painter has also grouped with these the Pardoner and the Sompnour and the Manciple, and has here also introduced one of the rich citizens of London: Characters likely to ride in company, all being above the common rank in life or attendants on those who were so.

For the Monk is described by Chaucer, as a man of the first rank in society, noble, rich, and expensively attended; he is a leader of the age, with certain humorous accompaniments in his character, that do not degrade, but render him an object of dignified mirth, but also with other accompaniments not so respectable.

The Friar is a character also of a mixed kind:

> "A friar there was, a wanton and a merry."

but in his office he is said to be a "full solemn man": eloquent, amorous, witty, and satyrical; young, handsome, and rich; he is a complete rogue, with constitutional gaiety enough to make him a master of all the pleasures of the world.

> "His neck was white as the flour de lis,
> "Thereto strong he was as a champioun."

It is necessary here to speak of Chaucer's own character, that I may set certain mistaken critics right in their conception of the humour and fun that occurs on the journey. Chaucer is himself the great poetical observer of men, who in every age is born to record and eternize its acts. This he does as a master, as a father, and superior, who looks down on their little follies from the Emperor to the Miller; sometimes with severity, oftener with joke and sport.

Accordingly Chaucer has made his Monk a great tragedian, one who studied poetical art. So much so, that the generous Knight is, in the compassionate dictates of his soul, compelled to cry out:

> " 'Ho,' quoth the Knyght,—'good Sir, no more of this;
> " 'That ye have said is right ynough I wis;
> " 'And mokell more, for little heaviness
> " 'Is right enough for much folk, as I guesse.
> " 'I say, for me, it is a great disease,
> " 'Whereas men have been in wealth and ease,
> " 'To heare of their sudden fall, alas,
> " 'And the contrary is joy and solas.' "

The Monk's definition of tragedy in the proem to his tale is worth repeating:

> "Tragedie is to tell a certain story,
> "As old books us maken memory,
> "Of hem that stood in great prosperity,
> "And be fallen out of high degree,
> "Into miserie, and ended wretchedly."

Though a man of luxury, pride and pleasure, he is a master of art and learning, though affecting to despise it. Those who can think that the proud Huntsman and Noble Housekeeper, Chaucer's Monk, is intended for a buffoon or burlesque character, know little of Chaucer.

For the Host who follows this group, and holds the center of the cavalcade, is a first rate character, and his jokes are no trifles; they are always, though uttered with audacity, and equally free with the Lord and the Peasant, they are always substantially and weightily expressive of knowledge and experience; Henry Baillie, the keeper of the greatest Inn of the greatest City; for such was the Tabarde Inn in Southwark, near London: our Host was also a leader of the age.

By way of illustration, I instance Shakspeare's Witches in Macbeth. Those who dress them for the stage, consider them as wretched old women, and not as Shakspeare intended, the Goddesses of Destiny; this shews how Chaucer has been misunderstood in his sublime work. Shakspeare's Fairies also are the rulers of the vegetable world, and so are Chaucer's; let them be so considered, and then the poet will be understood, and not else.

But I have omitted to speak of a very prominent character, the Pardoner, the Age's Knave, who always commands and domineers over the high and low vulgar. This man is sent in every age for a rod and scourge, and for a blight, for a trial of men, to divide the classes of men; he is in the most holy sanctuary, and he is suffered by Providence for wise ends, and has also his great use, and his grand leading destiny.

His companion, the Sompnour, is also a Devil of the first magnitude, grand, terrific, rich and honoured in the rank of which he holds the destiny. The uses to Society are perhaps equal of the Devil and of the Angel, their sublimity, who can dispute.

"In daunger had he at his own gise,
"The young girls of his diocese,
"And he knew well their counsel, &c."

The principal figure in the next groupe is the Good Parson; an Apostle, a real Messenger of Heaven, sent in every age for its light and its warmth. This man is beloved and venerated by all, and neglected by all: He serves all, and is served by none; he is, according to Christ's definition, the greatest of his age. Yet he is a Poor Parson of a town. Read Chaucer's description of the Good Parson, and bow the head and the knee to him, who, in every age, sends us such a burning and a shining light. Search, O ye rich and powerful, for these men and obey their counsel, then shall the golden age return: But alas! you will not easily distinguish him from the Friar or the Pardoner; they, also, are "full solemn men," and their counsel you will continue to follow.

I have placed by his side the Sergeant at Lawe, who appears delighted to ride in his company, and between him and his brother, the Plowman; as I wish men of Law would always ride with them, and take their counsel, especially in all difficult points. Chaucer's Lawyer is a character of great venerableness, a Judge, and a real master of the jurisprudence of his age.

The Doctor of Physic is in this groupe, and the Franklin, the voluptuous country gentleman, contrasted with the Physician, and on his other hand, with two Citizens of London. Chaucer's characters live age after age. Every age is a Canterbury Pilgrimage; we all pass on, each sustaining one or other of these characters; nor can a child be born, who is not one of these characters of Chaucer. The Doctor of Physic is described as the first of his profession; perfect, learned, completely Master and Doctor in his art. Thus the reader will observe, that Chaucer makes every one of his characters perfect in his kind; every one is an Antique Statue; the image of a class, and not of an imperfect individual.

This groupe also would furnish substantial matter, on which volumes might be written. The Franklin is one who keeps open table, who is the genius of eating and drinking, the Bacchus; as the Doctor of Physic is the Esculapius, the Host is the Silenus, the Squire is the Apollo, the Miller is the Hercules, &c. Chaucer's characters are a description of the eternal Principles that exist in all ages. The Franklin is voluptuousness itself, most nobly pourtrayed:

"It snewed in his house of meat and drink."

The Plowman is simplicity itself, with wisdom and strength for its stamina. Chaucer has divided the ancient character of Hercules between his Miller and his Plowman. Benevolence is the plowman's great characteristic; he is thin with excessive labour, and not with old age, as some have supposed:

"He would thresh, and thereto dike and delve
"For Christe's sake, for every poore wight,
"Withouten hire, if it lay in his might."

Visions of these eternal principles or characters of human life appear to poets, in all ages; the Grecian gods were the ancient Cherubim of Phoenicia; but the Greeks, and since them the Moderns, have neglected to subdue the gods of Priam. These gods are visions of the eternal attributes, or divine names, which, when erected into gods, become destructive to humanity. They ought to be the servants, and not the masters of man, or of society. They ought to be made to sacrifice to Man, and not man compelled to sacrifice to them; for when separated from man or humanity, who is Jesus the Saviour, the vine of eternity, they are thieves and rebels, they are destroyers.

The Plowman of Chaucer is Hercules in his supreme eternal state, divested of his spectrous shadow; which is the Miller, a terrible fellow, such as exists in all times and places for the trial of men, to astonish every neighbourhood with brutal strength and courage, to get rich and powerful to curb the pride of Man.

The Reeve and the Manciple are two characters of the most consummate worldly wisdom. The Shipman, or Sailor, is a similar genius of Ulyssean art; but with the highest courage superadded.

The Citizens and their Cook are each leaders of a class. Chaucer has been somehow made to number four citizens, which would make his whole company, himself included, thirty-one. But he says there was but nine and twenty in his company:

"Full nine and twenty in a company."

The Webbe, or Weaver, and the Tapiser, or Tapestry Weaver, appear to me to be the same person; but this is only an opinion, for full nine and twenty may signify one more or less. But I dare say that Chaucer wrote "A Webbe Dyer," that is, a Cloth Dyer:

"A Webbe Dyer, and a Tapiser."

The Merchant cannot be one of the Three Citizens, as his dress is different, and his character is more marked, whereas Chaucer says of his rich citizens:

"All were yclothed in o liverie."

The characters of Women Chaucer has divided into two classes, the Lady Prioress and the Wife of Bath. Are not these leaders of the ages of men? The lady prioress, in some ages, predominates; and in some the wife of Bath, in whose character Chaucer has been equally minute and exact, because she is also a scourge and a blight. I shall say no more of her, nor expose what Chaucer has left hidden; let the young reader study what he has said of her: it is useful as a scarecrow. There are of such characters born too many for the peace of the world.

I come at length to the Clerk of Oxenford. This character varies from that of Chaucer, as the contemplative philosopher varies from the poetical genius. There are always these two classes of learned sages, the poetical and the philosophical. The painter has put them side by side, as if the youthful clerk had put himself under the tuition of the mature poet. Let the Philosopher always be the servant and scholar of inspiration and all will be happy.

Such are the characters that compose this Picture, which was painted in self-defence against the insolent and envious imputation of unfitness for finished and scientific art; and this imputation, most artfully and industriously endeavoured to be propagated among the public by ignorant hirelings. The painter courts comparison with his competitors, who, having received fourteen hundred guineas and more, from the profits of his designs in that well-known work, Designs for Blair's Grave, have left him to shift for himself, while others, more obedient to an employer's opinions and directions, are employed, at a great expence, to produce works, in succession to his, by which they acquired public patronage. This has hitherto been his lot—to get patronage for others and then to be left and neglected, and his work, which gained that patronage, cried down as eccentricity and madness; as unfinished and neglected by the artist's violent temper; he is sure the works now exhibited will give the lie to such aspersions.

Those who say that men are led by interest are knaves. A knavish character will often say, 'of what interest is it to me to do so and so?'

I answer, 'of none at all, but the contrary, as you well know. It is of 'malice and envy that you have done this; hence I am aware of you, 'because I know that you act, not from interest, but from malice, 'even to your own destruction.' It is therefore become a duty which Mr. B. owes to the Public, who have always recognized him, and patronized him, however hidden by artifices, that he should not suffer such things to be done, or be hindered from the public Exhibition of his finished productions by any calumnies in future.

The character and expression in this picture could never have been produced with Rubens' light and shadow, or with Rembrandt's, or anything Venetian or Flemish. The Venetian and Flemish practice is broken lines, broken masses, and broken colours. Mr. B.'s practice is unbroken lines, unbroken masses, and unbroken colours. Their art is to lose form; his art is to find form, and to keep it. His arts are opposite to theirs in all things.

As there is a class of men whose whole delight is the destruction of men, so there is a class of artists, whose whole art and science is fabricated for the purpose of destroying art. Who these are is soon known: "by their works ye shall know them." All who endeavour to raise up a style against Rafael, Mich. Angelo, and the Antique; those who separate Painting from Drawing; who look if a picture is well Drawn, and, if it is, immediately cry out, that it cannot be well Coloured—those are the men.

But to shew the stupidity of this class of men nothing need be done but to examine my rival's prospectus.

The two first characters in Chaucer, the Knight and the Squire, he has put among his rabble; and indeed his prospectus calls the Squire the fop of Chaucer's age. Now hear Chaucer:

"Of his Stature, he was of even length,
"And wonderly deliver, and of great strength;
"And he had be sometime in Chivauchy,
"In Flanders, in Artois, and in Picardy,
"And borne him well, as of so litele space."

Was this a fop?

"Well could he sit a horse, and faire ride,
"He could songs make, and eke well indite
"Just, and eke dance, pourtray, and well write."

Was this a fop?

"Curteis he was, and meek, and serviceable;
"And kerft before his fader at the table"

Was this a fop?

It is the same with all his characters; he has done all by chance, or perhaps his fortune,—money, money. According to his prospectus he has Three Monks; these he cannot find in Chaucer, who has only One Monk, and that no vulgar character, as he has endeavoured to make him. When men cannot read they should not pretend to paint. To be sure Chaucer is a little difficult to him who has only blundered over novels, and catchpenny trifles of booksellers. Yet a little pains ought to be taken even by the ignorant and weak. He has put The Reeve, a vulgar fellow, between his Knight and Squire, as if he was resolved to go contrary in everything to Chaucer, who says of the Reeve:

"And ever he rode hinderest of the rout."

In this manner he has jumbled his dumb dollies together and is praised by his equals for it; for both himself and his friend are equally masters of Chaucer's language. They both think that the Wife of Bath is a young, beautiful, blooming damsel, and H——[1] says, that she is the Fair Wife of Bath, and that the Spring appears in her Cheeks. Now hear what Chaucer has made her say of herself, who is no modest one:

" But Lord when it remembereth me
" Upon my youth and on my jollity
" It tickleth me about the heart root,
" Unto this day it doth my heart boot,
" That I have had my world as in my time;
" But age, alas, that all will envenime
" Hath bireft my beauty and my pith
" Let go; farewell: the Devil go therewith,
" The flower is gone; there is no more to tell
" The bran, as best I can, I now mote sell;
" And yet to be right merry will I fond,—
" Now forth to tell of my fourth husband. "

She has had four husbands, a fit subject for this painter; yet the painter ought to be very much offended with his friend H——, who has called his "a common scene," "and very ordinary forms," which is the truest part of all, for it is so, and very wretchedly so indeed. What merit can there be in a picture of which such words are spoken with truth?

But the prospectus says that the Painter has represented Chaucer himself as a knave, who thrusts himself among honest people, to make game of and laugh at them; though I must do justice to the painter, and say that he has made him look more like a fool than a

[1] John Hoppner, R.A.

knave. But it appears in all the writings of Chaucer, and particularly in his Canterbury Tales, that he was very devout, and paid respect to true enthusiastic superstition. He has laughed at his knaves and fools, as I do now. But he has respected his True Pilgrims, who are a majority of his company, and are not thrown together in the random manner that Mr. S——[1] has done. Chaucer has no where called the Plowman old, worn out with age and labour, as the prospectus has represented him, and says that the picture has done so too. He is worn down with labour, but not with age. How spots of brown and yellow, smeared about at random, can be either young or old, I cannot see. It may be an old man; it may be a young one; it may be any thing that a prospectus pleases. But I know that where there are no lineaments there can be no character. And what connoisseurs call touch, I know by experience, must be the destruction of all character and expression, as it is of every lineament.

The scene of Mr. S——'s Picture is by Dulwich Hills, which was not the way to Canterbury; but perhaps the painter thought he would give them a ride round about, because they were a burlesque set of scare-crows, not worth any man's respect or care.

But the painter's thoughts being always upon gold, he has introduced a character that Chaucer has not; namely, a Goldsmith; for so the prospectus tells us. Why he has introduced a Goldsmith, and what is the wit of it, the prospectus does not explain. But it takes care to mention the reserve and modesty of the Painter; this makes a good epigram enough:

"The fox, the owl, the spider, and the mole,
"By sweet reserve and modesty get fat."

But the prospectus tells us, that the painter has introduced a Sea Captain; Chaucer has a Ship-man a Sailor, a Trading Master of a Vessel, called by courtesy Captain, as every master of a boat is; but this does not make him a Sea Captain. Chaucer has purposely omitted such a personage, as it only exists in certain periods: it is the soldier by sea. He who would be a Soldier in inland nations is a sea captain in commercial nations.

All is misconceived, and its mis-execution is equal to its misconception. I have no objection to Rubens and Rembrandt being employed, or even to their living in a palace; but it shall not be at the expence of Rafael and Michael Angelo living in a cottage, and in contempt and derision. I have been scorned long enough by these fellows, who owe to me all that they have; it shall be so no longer.

"I found them blind, I taught them how to see;
"And, now, they know me not, nor yet themselves."

---

[1] Thomas Stothard, R.A.

NUMBER IV.

The Bard, from Gray.

"On a rock, whose haughty brow
"Frown'd o'er old Conway's foaming flood,
"Robed in the sable garb of woe,
"With haggard eyes the Poet stood;
"Loose his beard, and hoary hair
"Stream'd like a meteor to the troubled air.

"Weave the warp, and weave the woof,
"The winding sheet of Edward's race."

Weaving the winding sheet of Edward's race by means of sounds of spiritual music and its accompanying expressions of articulate speech, is a bold, and daring, and most masterly conception, that the public have embraced and approved with avidity. Poetry consists in these conceptions; and shall Painting be confined to the sordid drudgery of fac-simile representations of merely mortal and perishing substances, and not be as poetry and music are, elevated into its own proper sphere of invention and visionary conception? No, it shall not be so! Painting, as well as poetry and music, exists and exults in immortal thoughts. If Mr. B.'s Canterbury Pilgrims had been done by any other power than that of the poetic visionary, it would have been as dull as his adversary's.

The Spirits of the murdered bards assist in weaving the deadly woof:

"With me in dreadful harmony they join
"And weave, with bloody hands, the tissue of thy line."

The connoisseurs and artists who have made objections to Mr. B.'s mode of representing spirits with real bodies, would do well to consider that the Venus, the Minerva, the Jupiter, the Apollo, which they admire in Greek statues are all of them representations of spiritual existences, of Gods immortal, to the mortal perishing organ of sight; and yet they are embodied and organized in solid marble. Mr. B. requires the same latitude, and all is well. The Prophets describe what they saw in Vision as real and existing men, whom they saw with their imaginative and immortal organs; the Apostles the same; the clearer the organ the more distinct the object. A Spirit and a Vision are not, as the modern philosophy supposes, a cloudy vapour, or a nothing: they are organized and minutely articulated beyond all that the mortal and perishing nature can produce. He who does not imagine in stronger and better lineaments, and in stronger and better light than his perishing, mortal eye can see, does not imagine at all. The painter of this work asserts that all his imaginations appear to him infinitely more perfect and more minutely organized than any thing seen by his mortal eye. Spirits are organized men. Moderns wish to draw figures without lines, and with great and heavy shadows; are not shadows more unmeaning than lines, and more heavy? O who can doubt this!

King Edward and his Queen Elenor are prostrated, with their horses, at the foot of a rock on which the Bard stands; prostrated by the terrors of his harp on the margin of the river Conway, whose waves bear up a corse of a slaughtered bard at the foot of the rock. The armies of Edward are seen winding among the mountains.

"He wound with toilsome march his long array."

Mortimer and Gloucester lie spell bound behind their king.

The execution of this picture is also in Water Colours, or Fresco.

NUMBER V.

The Ancient Britons

In the last Battle of King Arthur, only Three Britons escaped; these were the Strongest Man, the Beautifullest Man, and the Ugliest Man; these three marched through the field unsubdued, as Gods, and the Sun of Britain sat, but shall arise again with tenfold splendor when Arthur shall awake from sleep, and resume his dominion over earth and ocean.

The three general classes of men who are represented by the most Beautiful, the most Strong, and the most Ugly, could not be represented by any historical facts but those of our own country, the Ancient Britons, without violating costume. The Britons (say historians) were naked civilized men, learned, studious, abstruse in thought and contemplation; naked, simple, plain in their acts and manners; wiser than after-ages. They were overwhelmed by brutal arms, all but a small remnant; Strength, Beauty, and Ugliness escaped the wreck, and remain for ever unsubdued, age after age.

The British Antiquities are now in the Artist's hands; all his visionary contemplations, relating to his own country and its ancient glory, when it was, as it again shall be, the source of learning and inspiration. Arthur was a name for the constellation Arcturus, or Boötes, the keeper of the North Pole. And all the fables of Arthur and his round table; of the warlike naked Britons; of Merlin; of Arthur's conquest of the whole world; of his death, or sleep, and promise to return again; of the Druid monuments or temples; of the pavement of Watling-street; of London stone; of the caverns in Cornwall, Wales, Derbyshire, and Scotland; of the Giants of Ireland and Britain; of the elemental beings called by us by the general name of fairies; and of these three who escaped, namely Beauty, Strength, and Ugliness. Mr. B. has in his hands poems of the highest antiquity. Adam was a Druid, and Noah; also Abraham was called to succeed the Druidical age, which began to turn allegoric and mental signification into corporeal command, whereby human sacrifice would have depopulated the earth. All these things are written in Eden. The artist is an inhabitant of that happy country; and if every thing goes on as it has begun, the world of vegetation and generation may expect to be opened again to Heaven, through Eden, as it was in the beginning.

The Strong Man represents the human sublime. The Beautiful Man represents the human pathetic, which was in the wars of Eden divided into male and female. The Ugly Man represents the human reason. They were originally one man, who was fourfold; he was self-divided, and his real humanity slain on the stems of generation, and the form of the fourth was like the Son of God. How he became divided is a subject of great sublimity and pathos. The Artist has written it under inspiration, and will, if God please, publish it; it is voluminous, and contains the ancient history of Britain, and the world of Satan and of Adam.

In the mean time he has painted this Picture, which supposes that in the reign of that British Prince, who lived in the fifth century, there were remains of those naked Heroes in the Welch Mountains; they are there now, Gray saw them in the person of his bard on Snowdon; there they dwell in naked simplicity; happy is he who can see and converse with them above the shadows of generation and death. The giant Albion, was Patriarch of the Atlantic; he is the Atlas of the Greeks, one of those the Greeks called Titans. The stories of Arthur are the acts of Albion, applied to a Prince of the fifth century, who conquered Europe, and held the Empire of the world in the dark age, which the Romans never again recovered. In this Picture, believing with Milton the ancient British History, Mr. B. has done as all the ancients did, and as all the moderns who are worthy of fame, given the historical fact in its poetical vigour so as it always happens, and not in that dull way that some Historians pretend, who, being weakly organized themselves, cannot see either miracle or prodigy; all is to them a dull round of probabilities and possibilities; but the history of all times and places is nothing else but improbabilities and impossibilities; what we should say was impossible if we did not see it always before our eyes.

The antiquities of every Nation under Heaven, is no less sacred than that of the Jews. They are the same thing, as Jacob Bryant and all antiquaries have proved. How other antiquities came to be neglected and disbelieved, while those of the Jews are collected and arranged, is an enquiry worthy of both the Antiquarian and the

Divine. All had originally one language, and one religion: this was the religion of Jesus, the everlasting Gospel. Antiquity preaches the Gospel of Jesus. The reasoning historian, turner and twister of causes and consequences, such as Hume, Gibbon, and Voltaire, cannot with all their artifice turn or twist one fact or disarrange self evident action and reality. Reasons and opinions concerning acts are not history. Acts themselves alone are history, and these are neither the exclusive property of Hume, Gibbon, nor Voltaire, Echard, Rapin, Plutarch, nor Herodotus. Tell me the Acts, O historian, and leave me to reason upon them as I please; away with your reasoning and your rubbish! All that is not action is not worth reading. Tell me the What; I do not want you to tell me the Why, and the How; I can find that out myself, as well as you can, and I will not be fooled by you into opinions, that you please to impose, to disbelieve what you think improbable or impossible. His opinions, who does not see spiritual agency, is not worth any man's reading; he who rejects a fact because it is improbable, must reject all History and retain doubts only.

It has been said to the Artist, "take the Apollo for the model of "your beautiful Man, and the Hercules for your strong Man, and the "Dancing Fawn for your Ugly Man." Now he comes to his trial. He knows that what he does is not inferior to the grandest Antiques. Superior they cannot be, for human power cannot go beyond either what he does, or what they have done; it is the gift of God, it is inspiration and vision. He had resolved to emulate those precious remains of antiquity; he has done so and the result you behold; his ideas of strength and beauty have not been greatly different. Poetry as it exists now on earth, in the various remains of ancient authors, Music as it exists in old tunes or melodies, Painting and Sculpture as it exists in the remains of Antiquity and in the works of more modern genius, is Inspiration, and cannot be surpassed; it is perfect and eternal. Milton, Shakspeare, Michael Angelo, Rafael, the finest specimens of Ancient Sculpture and Painting and Architecture, Gothic, Grecian, Hindoo and Egyptian, are the extent of the human mind. The human mind cannot go beyond the gift of God, the Holy Ghost. To suppose that Art can go beyond the finest specimens of Art that are now in the world, is not knowing what Art is; it is being blind to the gifts of the spirit.

It will be necessary for the Painter to say something concerning his ideas of Beauty, Strength and Ugliness.

The Beauty that is annexed and appended to folly, is a lamentable accident and error of the mortal and perishing life; it does but seldom happen; but with this unnatural mixture the sublime Artist can have nothing to do; it is fit for the burlesque. The Beauty proper for sublime art is lineaments, or forms and features that are capable of being the receptacles of intellect; accordingly the Painter has given in his beautiful man, his own idea of intellectual Beauty. The face and limbs that deviates or alters least, from infancy to old age, is the face and limbs of greatest Beauty and perfection.

The Ugly, likewise, when accompanied and annexed to imbecility and disease, is a subject for burlesque and not for historical grandeur; the Artist has imagined his Ugly man, one approaching to the beast in features and form, his forehead small, without frontals; his jaws large; his nose high on the ridge, and narrow; his chest, and the stamina of his make, comparatively little, and his joints and his extremities large; his eyes, with scarce any whites, narrow and cunning, and every thing tending toward what is truly Ugly, the incapability of intellect.

The Artist has considered his strong Man as a receptacle of Wisdom, a sublime energizer; his features and limbs do not spindle out into length without strength, nor are they too large and unwieldy for his brain and bosom. Strength consists in accumulation of power to the principal seat, and from thence a regular gradation and subordination; strength is compactness, not extent nor bulk.

The strong Man acts from conscious superiority, and marches on in fearless dependance on the divine decrees, raging with the inspirations of a prophetic mind. The Beautiful Man acts from duty and anxious solicitude for the fates of those for whom he combats. The Ugly Man acts from love of carnage, and delight in the savage barbarities of war, rushing with sportive precipitation into the very teeth of the affrighted enemy.

The Roman Soldiers rolled together in a heap before them: "Like the rolling thing before the whirlwind"; each shew a different character, and a different expression of fear, or revenge, or envy, or blank horror, or amazement, or devout wonder and unresisting awe.

The dead and the dying, Britons naked, mingled with armed Romans, strew the field beneath. Among these the last of the Bards who were capable of attending warlike deeds, is seen falling, outstretched among the dead and the dying, singing to his harp in the pains of death.

Distant among the mountains are Druid Temples, similar to Stone Henge. The Sun sets behind the mountains, bloody with the day of battle.

The flush of health in flesh exposed to the open air, nourished by the spirits of forests and floods in that ancient happy period, which history has recorded, cannot be like the sickly daubs of Titian or Rubens. Where will the copier of nature, as it now is, find a civilized man, who has been accustomed to go naked? Imagination only can furnish us with colouring appropriate, such as is found in the Frescos of Rafael and Michael Angelo: the disposition of forms always directs colouring in works of true art. As to a modern Man, stripped from his load of cloathing, he is like a dead corpse. Hence Rubens, Titian, Correggio and all of that class, are like leather and chalk; their men are like leather, and their women like chalk, for the disposition of their forms will not admit of grand colouring; in Mr. B.'s Britons the blood is seen to circulate in their limbs; he defies competition in colouring.

NUMBER VI.

A Spirit vaulting from a cloud to turn and wind a fiery Pegasus.—Shakspeare. The Horse of Intellect is leaping from the cliffs of Memory and Reasoning; it is a barren Rock: it is also called the Barren Waste of Locke and Newton.

This Picture was done many years ago, and was one of the first Mr. B. ever did in Fresco; fortunately, or rather, providentially, he left it unblotted and unblurred, although molested continually by blotting and blurring demons; but he was also compelled to leave it unfinished, for reasons that will be shewn in the following.

NUMBER VII.

The Goats, an experiment Picture.

The subject is taken from the Missionary Voyage, and varied from the literal fact for the sake of picturesque scenery. The savage girls had dressed themselves with vine leaves, and some goats on board the missionary ship stripped them off presently. This Picture was painted at intervals, for experiment with the colours, and is laboured to a superabundant blackness; it has, however, that about it, which may be worthy the attention of the Artist and Connoisseur for reasons that follow.

NUMBER VIII.

The spiritual Preceptor, an experiment Picture.

This subject is taken from the Visions of Emanuel Swedenborg, Universal Theology, No. 623. The Learned, who strive to ascend into Heaven by means of learning, appear to Children like dead horses, when repelled by the celestial spheres. The works of this visionary are well worthy the attention of Painters and Poets; they are foundations for grand things; the reason they have not been more attended to is because corporeal demons have gained a predominance; who the leaders of these are, will be shewn below. Unworthy Men who gain fame among Men, continue to govern mankind after death, and in their spiritual bodies oppose the spirits of those who worthily are famous; and, as Swedenborg observes, by entering into disease and excrement, drunkenness and concupiscence, they possess themselves of the bodies of mortal men, and shut the doors of mind and of thought by placing Learning above Inspiration. O Artist! you may disbelieve all this, but it shall be at your own peril.

NUMBER IX.

Satan calling up his Legions, from Milton's Paradise Lost; a composition for a more perfect Picture afterward executed for a Lady of high rank. An experiment Picture.

This Picture was likewise painted at intervals, for experiment on colours without any oily vehicle; it may be worthy of attention, not only on account of its composition, but of the great labour which has been bestowed on it, that is, three or four times as much as would have finished a more perfect Picture; the labour has destroyed the lineaments; it was with difficulty brought back again to a certain effect, which it had at first, when all the lineaments were perfect.

These Pictures, among numerous others painted for experiment, were the result of temptations and perturbations, labouring to destroy Imaginative power, by means of that infernal machine called Chiaro Oscuro, in the hands of Venetian and Flemish Demons, whose enmity to the Painter himself, and to all Artists who study in the Florentine and Roman Schools, may be removed by an exhibition and exposure of their vile tricks. They cause that every thing in art shall become a Machine. They cause that the execution shall be all blocked up with brown shadows. They put the original Artist in fear and doubt of his own original conception. The spirit of Titian was particularly active in raising doubts concerning the possibility of executing without a model, and when once he had raised the doubt, it became easy for him to snatch away the vision time after time, for, when the Artist took his pencil to execute his ideas, his power of imagination weakened so much and darkened, that memory of nature, and of Pictures of the various schools possessed his mind, instead of appropriate execution resulting from the inventions; like walking in another man's style, or speaking, or looking in another man's style and manner, unappropriate and repugnant to your own individual character; tormenting the true Artist, till he leaves the Florentine, and adopts the Venetian practice, or does as Mr. B. has done, has the courage to suffer poverty and disgrace, till he ultimately conquers.

Rubens is a most outrageous demon, and by infusing the remembrances of his Pictures and style of execution, hinders all power of individual thought: so that the man who is possessed by this demon loses all admiration of any other Artist but Rubens and those who were his imitators and journeymen; he causes to the Florentine and Roman Artist fear to execute; and though the original conception was all fire and animation, he loads it with hellish brownness, and blocks up all its gates of light except one, and that one he closes with iron bars, till the victim is obliged to give up the Florentine and Roman practice, and adopt the Venetian and Flemish.

Correggio is a soft and effeminate, and consequently a most cruel demon, whose whole delight is to cause endless labour to whoever suffers him to enter his mind. The story that is told in all Lives of the Painters about Correggio being poor and but badly paid for his Pictures is altogether false; he was a petty Prince in Italy, and employed numerous Journeymen in manufacturing (as Rubens and Titian did) the Pictures that go under his name. The manual labour in these Pictures of Correggio is immense, and was paid for originally at the immense prices that those who keep manufactories of art always charge to their employers, while they themselves pay their journeymen little enough. But though Correggio was not poor, he will make any true artist so who permits him to enter his mind, and take possession of his affections; he infuses a love of soft and even tints without boundaries, and of endless reflected lights that confuse one another, and hinder all correct drawing from appearing to be correct; for if one of Rafael or Michael Angelo's figures was to be traced, and Correggio's reflections and refractions to be added to it, there would soon be an end of proportion and strength, and it would be weak, and pappy, and lumbering, and thick headed, like his own works; but then it would have softness and evenness by a twelvemonth's labour, where a month would with judgment have finished it better and higher; and the poor wretch who executed it, would be the Correggio that the life writers have written of: a drudge and a miserable man, compelled to softness by poverty. I say again, O Artist, you may disbelieve all this, but it shall be at your own peril.

Note. These experiment Pictures have been bruized and knocked about without mercy, to try all experiments.

NUMBER X.

The Bramins.—A Drawing.

The subject is, Mr. Wilkin translating the Geeta; an ideal design, suggested by the first publication of that part of the Hindoo Scriptures translated by Mr. Wilkin. I understand that my Costume is incorrect, but in this I plead the authority of the ancients, who often deviated from the Habits to preserve the Manners, as in the instance of Laocoön, who, though a priest, is represented naked.

NUMBER XI.

The Body of Abel found by Adam and Eve; Cain, who was about to bury it, fleeing from the face of his Parents—A Drawing.

NUMBER XII.

The Soldiers casting lots for Christ's Garment.—A Drawing.

NUMBER XIII.

Jacob's Ladder.—A Drawing.

NUMBER XIV.

The Angels hovering over the Body of Jesus in the Sepulchre.—A Drawing.

The above four drawings the Artist wishes were in Fresco on an enlarged scale to ornament the altars of churches, and to make England, like Italy, respected by respectable men of other countries on account of Art. It is not the want of Genius that can hereafter be laid to our charge; the Artist who has done these Pictures and Drawings will take care of that; let those who govern the Nation take care of the other. The times require that every one should speak out boldly; England expects that every man should do his duty, in Arts, as well as in Arms, or in the Senate.

NUMBER XV.

Ruth.—A Drawing.

This Design is taken from that most pathetic passage in the Book of Ruth, where Naomi, having taken leave of her daughters in law with intent to return to her own country, Ruth cannot leave her, but says, "Whither thou goest I will go; and where thou lodgest I will "lodge; thy people shall be my people, and thy God my God; where "thou diest I will die, and there will I be buried; God do so to me "and more also, if ought but death part thee and me."

The distinction that is made in modern times between a Painting and a Drawing proceeds from ignorance of art. The merit of a Picture is the same as the merit of a Drawing. The dawber dawbs his Drawings; he who draws his Drawings draws his Pictures. There is no difference between Rafael's Cartoons and his Frescos, or Pictures, except that the Frescos, or Pictures, are more finished. When Mr. B. formerly painted in oil colours his Pictures were shewn to certain painters and connoisseurs, who said that they were very admirable Drawings on canvass, but not Pictures; but they said the same of Rafael's Pictures. Mr. B. thought this the greatest of compliments, though it was meant otherwise. If losing and obliterating the outline constitutes a Picture, Mr. B. will never be so foolish as to do one. Such art of losing the outlines is the art of Venice and Flanders; it loses all character, and leaves what some people call expression; but this is a false notion of expression; expression cannot exist without character as its stamina; and neither character nor expression can exist without firm and determinate outline. Fresco Painting is susceptible of higher finishing than Drawing on Paper, or than any other method of Painting. But he must have a strange organization of sight who does not prefer a Drawing on Paper to a Dawbing in Oil by the same master, supposing both to be done with equal care.

The great and golden rule of art, as well as of life, is this: That the more distinct, sharp, and wirey the bounding line, the more perfect the work of art; and the less keen and sharp, the greater is the evidence of weak imitation, plagiarism, and bungling. Great inventors, in all ages, knew this: Protogenes and Apelles knew each other by this line. Rafael and Michael Angelo and Albert Dürer are known by this and this alone. The want of this determinate and bounding form evidences the want of idea[1] in the artist's mind, and the pretence of the plagiary in all its branches. How do we distinguish the oak from the beech, the horse from the ox, but by the bounding outline? How do we distinguish one face or countenance from another, but by the bounding line and its infinite inflexions and movements? What is it that builds a house and plants a garden, but the definite and determinate? What is it that distinguishes honesty from knavery, but the hard and wirey line of rectitude and certainty in the actions and intentions? Leave out this line, and you leave out life itself; all is chaos again, and the line of the almighty must be drawn out upon it before man or beast can exist. Talk no more then of Correggio, or Rembrandt, or any other of those plagiaries of Venice or Flanders. They were but the lame imitators of lines drawn by their predecessors, and their works prove themselves contemptible, dis-arranged imitations, and blundering, misapplied copies.

NUMBER XVI.

The Penance of Jane Shore in St. Paul's Church.—A Drawing.

This Drawing was done above Thirty Years ago, and proves to the Author, and he thinks will prove to any discerning eye, that the productions of our youth and of our maturer age are equal in all

---

[1] *Printed as:* the idea of want, *and altered by Blake by pen in some copies.*

essential points. If a man is master of his profession, he cannot be ignorant that he is so; and if he is not employed by those who pretend to encourage art, he will employ himself, and laugh in secret at the pretences of the ignorant, while he has every night dropped into his shoe, as soon as he puts it off, and puts out the candle, and gets into bed, a reward for the labours of the day, such as the world cannot give, and patience and time await to give him all that the world can give.

FINIS

D. N. SHURY, PRINTER, BERWICK-STREET, SOHO, LONDON.

[PROSPECTUS OF THE ENGRAVING OF CHAUCER'S CANTERBURY PILGRIMS]

Printed, May, 1809

BLAKE'S CHAUCER,

THE CANTERBURY PILGRIMS.

THE FRESCO PICTURE,

Representing CHAUCER's Characters painted by

WILLIAM BLAKE,

As it is now submitted to the Public,

The Designer proposes to Engrave, in a correct and finished Line manner of Engraving, similar to those original Copper Plates of ALBERT DURER, LUCAS, HISBEN, ALDEGRAVE and the old original Engravers, who were great Masters in Painting and Designing, whose method, alone, can delineate Character as it is in this Picture, where all the Lineaments are distinct.

It is hoped that the Painter will be allowed by the Public (notwithstanding artfully dissemminated insinuations to the contrary) to be better able than any other to keep his own Characters and Expressions; having had sufficient evidence in the Works of our own HOGARTH, that no other Artist can reach the original Spirit so well as the Painter himself, especially as Mr. B. is an old well-known and acknowledged Engraver.

The size of the Engraving will be 3-feet 1-inch long, by 1-foot high.—The Artist engages to deliver it, finished, in One Year from September next.—No Work of Art, can take longer than a Year: it may be worked backwards and forwards without end, and last a Man's whole Life; but he will, at length, only be forced to bring it back to what it was, and it will be worse than it was at the end of the first Twelve Months. The Value of this Artist's Year is the Criterion of Society: and as it is valued, so does Society flourish or decay.

The Price to Subscribers—FOUR GUINEAS, Two to be paid at the time of Subscribing, the other Two, on delivery of the Print. Subscriptions received at No. 28, Corner of BROAD-STREET, GOLDEN-SQUARE; where the Picture is now Exhibiting, among other Works, by the same Artist.

The Price will be considerably raised to Non-subscribers.

May 15th, 1809.

Printed by Watts & Bridgewater, Southmolton-Street.

[DRAFT FOR PROSPECTUS OF THE ENGRAVING OF CHAUCER'S CANTERBURY] PILGRIMS.

FROM THE NOTE-BOOK

Written 1809

Pp. 117-119.

Blake's Chaucer
An Original Engraving by William Blake from
his Fresco Painting of Chaucer's
Canterbury Pilgrims.

Mr B., having from early Youth cultivated the two Arts, Painting & Engraving, & during a Period of forty Years never suspended his Labours on Copper for a single day, Submits with Confidence to Public Patronage & requests the attention of the Amateur in a Large [Work *del.*] Stroke Engraving, 3 feet 1 inch long by one foot high, Containing Thirty original high finish'd whole Length Portraits on Horseback Of Chaucer's Characters, where every Character & every

Expression, every Lineament of Head, Hand & Foot, every particular of dress or Costume, where every Horse is appropriate to his Rider & the Scene or Landscape with its Villages, Cottages, Churches, & the Inn in Southwark is minutely labour'd, not by the hands of Journeymen, but by the Original Artist himself, even to the Stuffs & Embroidery of the Garments, the hair upon the Horses, the Leaves upon the Trees, & the Stones & Gravel upon the road; the Great Strength of Colouring & depth of work peculiar to Mr B.'s Prints will be here found accompanied by a Precision not to be seen but in the work of an Original Artist.

Sir Jeffery Chaucer & the nine & twenty
Pilgrims on their Journey to Canterbury.

The time chosen is early morning before sun rise, when the jolly Company are just quitting the Tabarde Inn. The Knight & Squire with the Squire's Yeoman lead the Procession: then the Youthful Abbess, her Nun & three Priests; her Greyhounds attend her—

"Of small Hounds had she that she fed
"With roast flesh, milk & wastel bread."

Next follow the Friar & Monk; then the Tapiser, the Pardoner, the Sompnour & the Manciple. After these "Our Host," who occupies the Center of the cavalcade (the Fun afterwards exhibited on the road may be seen depicted in his jolly face) directs them to the Knight (whose solemn Gallantry no less fixes attention) as the person who will be likely to commense their Task of each telling a Tale in their order. After the Host follow the Shipman, the Haberdasher, the Dyer, the Franklin, the Physician, the Plowman, the Lawyer, the Poor Parson, the Merchant, the Wife of Bath, the Cook, the Oxford Scholar, Chaucer himself, & the Reeve comes as Chaucer has described:

"And ever he rode hinderest of the rout."

These last are issuing from the Gateway of the Inn, the Cook & Wife of Bath are both taking their morning's draught of comfort. Spectators stand at the Gateway of the Inn & are composed of an old man, a woman & children.

The Landscape is an Eastward view of the Country from the Tabarde Inn in Southwark as it may be supposed to have appear'd in Chaucer's time, interspersed with Cottages & Villages; the first beams of the Sun are seen above the Horizon. Some buildings & spires indicate the situation of the Great City. The Inn is a Gothic Building which Thynne in his Glossary says was the Lodging of the Abbot of Hyde by Winchester. On the Inn is inscribed its title, & a proper advantage is taken of this circumstance to describe the subject of the Picture; the Words written in Gothic Letters over the Gateway are as follow: "The Tabarde Inne by Henry Bailly the Lodgyng "house for Pilgrims who Journey to Saint Thomas's Shrine at "Canterbury."

The Characters of Chaucer's Pilgrims are the Characters that compose all Ages & Nations; as one Age falls another rises, different to Mortal Sight, but to Immortals only the same; for we see the same Characters repeated again & again, in Animals, in Vegetables, in Minerals & in Men. Nothing new occurs in Identical Existence: Accident ever varies, Substance can never suffer change nor decay.

[END OF DRAFT FOR PROSPECTUS FROM THE NOTE-BOOK.]

[PROSPECTUS OF THE ENGRAVING OF CHAUCER'S CANTERBURY PILGRIMS]

Printed about 1810

Blake's Chaucer:

An Original Engraving by him from his Fresco Painting of Sir Jeffrey Chaucer and his Nine and Twenty Pilgrims setting forth from Southwark on their Journey to Canterbury.

Three Feet 1 Inch long, and 1 Foot high;
Price Three Guineas

The Time chosen is early morning before sun-rise when the Jolly Company are just quitting the Tabarde Inn. The Knight and Squire with the Squire's and Yeoman [*sic*] lead the Procession; then the youthful Abbess, her Nun and three Priests: her Grey-hounds attend her.

"Of small hounds had she, that she fed
"With roast flesh, milk and wastel bread."

Next follow the Friar and Monk, then the Tapster [*sic*], the Pardoner, the Sompnour and the Manciple. After these "our Host," who occupies the Center of the Cavalcade, directs them to the Knight as the person who will be likely to commence their Task of each telling a Tale in their order. After the Host follow the Shipman, the Haberdasher, the Dyer, the Franklin, the Physician, the Plowman, the Lawyer, the Parson, the Merchant, the Wife of Bath, the Cook, the Oxford Scholar, Chaucer himself, and the Reeve comes as Chaucer has described:

"And ever he rode hinderest of the rout."

These last are issuing from the Gateway of the Inn. The Cook and the Wife of Bath are both taking their morning's draught of comfort. Spectators stand at the Gateway of the Inn, and are composed of an Old Man, a Woman and Children.

The Inn is yet extant under the name of the Talbot; and the Landlord, Robert Bristow, Esq. of Broxmore near Rumsey, has continued a Board over the Gateway, inscribed, "This is the Inn from which "Sir Jeffrey Chaucer and his Pilgrims set out for Canterbury."

St. Thomas's Hospital which is situated near to it, is one of the most amiable features of the Christian Church; it belonged to the Monastery of St. Mary Overies and was dedicated to Thomas a Becket. The Pilgrims, if sick or lame, on their Journey to and from his Shrine, were received at this House. Even at this day every friendless wretch who wants the succour of it, is considered as a Pilgrim travelling through this Journey of Life.

The Landscape is an eastward view of the Country from the Tabarde Inn in Southwark as it may be supposed to have appeared in Chaucer's time, interspersed with Cottages and Villages. The first beams of the sun are seen above the horrizon: some Buildings and Spires indicate the situation of the Great City. The Inn is a Gothic Building which Thynne in his Glossary says was the Lodging of the Abbot of Hyde by Winchester. On the Inn is inscribed its Title, and a proper advantage is taken of this circumstance to describe the subject of the Picture. The words written in Gothic Letters over the Gateway of the Inn are as follow: "The Tabarde Inn by Henry "Bailly. The Lodging House for Pilgrims who Journey to St. Thomas's "Shrine at Canterbury."

Of Chaucer's Characters as described in his Canterbury Tales, some of the Names are altered by Time, but the Characters themselves for ever remain unaltered and consequently they are the Physiognomies or Lineaments of Universal Human Life beyond which Nature never steps. The Painter has consequently varied the heads and forms of his Personages into all Nature's varieties; the Horses he has varied to accord to their riders, the Costume is correct according to authentic Monuments.

Subscriptions received at No. 28, Corner of Broad Street, Golden Square.

G. Smeeton, Printer, 17, St. Martin's Lane, London.

[PUBLIC ADDRESS]

FROM THE NOTE-BOOK

Written about 1810

P. 65.

Chaucer's Canterbury Pilgrims Being a Complete Index of Human Characters as they appear Age after Age

P. 56.

This day is Publish'd Advertizements to Blake's Canterbury Pilgrims from Chaucer, Containing Anecdotes of Artists. Price 6^{d}.

P. 1.

If Men of weak capacities [in Art *del.*] have alone the Power of Execution in Art, Mr B. has now put to the test. If to Invent & to draw well hinders the Executive Power in Art, & his strokes are still to be Condemn'd because they are unlike those of Artists who are Unacquainted with Drawing [& the accompanying *del.*], is now to be Decided by The Public. Mr B.'s Inventive Powers & his Scientific Knowledge of Drawing is on all hands acknowledg'd; it only remains to be Certified whether [The Fool's hand or the *del.*] Physiognomic Strength & Power is to give Place to Imbecillity, [and whether (*several words illegible*) an unabated study & practise of forty Years (for I devoted myself to engraving in my Earliest Youth) are sufficient to elevate me above the Mediocrity to which I have hitherto been the victim. *del.*] In a work of Art it is not fine tints that are required, but Fine Forms. Fine Tints without, are loathsome[1]. Fine Tints without Fine Forms are always the Subterfuge of the Blockhead.

I account it a Public Duty respectfully to address myself to The Chalcographic Society & to Express to them my opinion (the result of the incessant Practice & Experience of Many Years) That Engraving as an art is Lost in England owing to an artfully propagated [in a most wretched state of injury from an *del.*] opinion that Drawing spoils an Engraver, [which opinion has been held out to me by such men as Flaxman, Romney, Stothard *del.*]. I request the Society to inspect my Print, of which drawing is the Foundation & indeed the Superstructure: it is drawing on copper, as Painting ought to be drawing on canvas or any other [table *del.*] surface, & nothing Else.

[1] *The sentences,* In a work . . . loathsome, *are written in twice, above and below the deleted passage.*

I request likewise that the Society will compare the Prints of Bartolozzi, Woolett, Strange &c. with the old English Portraits, that is, compare the Modern Art with the Art as it Existed Previous to the Enterance of Vandyke and Rubens into this Country, since which English Engraving is Lost, & I am sure [of *del.*] the Result of the comparison will be that the Society must be of my Opinion that Engraving, by Losing drawing, has Lost all character & all Expression, without which The Art is Lost.

Pp. 51-57.

In this Plate Mr B. has resumed the style with which he set out in life, of which Heath & Stothard were the awkward imitators at that time; it is the style of Alb. Durer's Histories & the old Engravers, which cannot be imitated by any one who does not understand drawing, & which, according to Heath & Stothard, Flaxman, & even Romney, spoils an Engraver; for Each of these Men have repeatedly asserted this Absurdity to me in Condemnation of my Work & approbation of Heath's lame imitation, Stothard being such a fool as to suppose that his blundering blurs can be made out & delineated by any Engraver who knows how to cut dots & lozenges equally well with those little prints which I engraved after him five & twenty years ago & by which he got his reputation as a draughtsman.

The manner in which my Character has been blasted these thirty years, both as an artist & a Man, may be seen particularly in a Sunday Paper cal'd the Examiner, Publish'd in Beaufort Buildings (We all know that Editors of Newspapers trouble their heads very little about art & science, & that they are always paid for what they put in upon these ungracious Subjects), & the manner in which I have routed out the nest of villains will be seen in a Poem concerning my Three years' Herculean Labours at Felpham, which I will soon Publish. Secret Calumny & open Professions of Friendship are common enough all the world over, but have never been so good an occasion of Poetic Imagery. When a Base Man means to be your Enemy he always begins with being your Friend. Flaxman cannot deny that one of the very first Monuments he did, I gratuitously design'd for him; at the same time he was blasting my character as an Artist to Macklin, my Employer, as Macklin told me at the time; how much of his Homer & Dante he will allow to be mine I do not know, as he went far enough off to Publish them, even to Italy, but the Public will know & Posterity will know.

Many People are so foolish [as] to think that they can wound Mr Fuseli over my Shoulder; they will find themselves mistaken; they could not wound even Mr Barry so.

A certain Portrait Painter said To me in a boasting way, "Since "I have Practised Painting I have lost all idea of drawing." Such a

Man must know that I look'd upon him with contempt; he did not care for this any more than West did, who hesitated & equivocated with me upon the same subject, at which time he asserted that Woolett's Prints were superior to Basire's because they had more Labour & Care; now this is contrary to the truth. Woolett did not know how to put so much labour into a head or a foot as Basire did; he did not know how to draw the Leaf of a tree; all his study was clean strokes & mossy tints—how then should he be able to make use of either Labour or Care, unless the Labour & Care of Imbecillity? The Life's Labour of Mental Weakness scarcely Equals one Hour of the Labour of Ordinary Capacity, like the full Gallop of the Gouty Man to the ordinary walk of youth & health. I allow that there is such a thing as high finish'd Ignorance, as there may be a fool or a knave in an Embroider'd Coat; but I say that the Embroidery of the Ignorant finisher is not like a Coat made by another, but is an Emanation from Ignorance itself, & its finishing is like its master—The Life's Labour of Five Hundred Idiots, for he never does the Work Himself.

What is Call'd the English Style of Engraving, such as proceeded from the Toilettes of Woolett & Strange (for theirs were Fribble's Toilettes) can never produce Character & Expression. I knew the Men intimately, from their Intimacy with Basire, my Master, & knew them both to be heavy lumps of Cunning & Ignorance, as their works shew to all the Continent, who Laugh at the Contemptible Pretences of Englishmen to Improve Art before they even know the first [lines *del.*] Beginnings of Art. I hope this Print will redeem my Country from this Coxcomb situation & shew that it is only some Englishmen, and not All, who are thus ridiculous in their Pretences. Advertisements in Newspapers are no proof of Popular approbation, but often the Contrary. A Man who Pretends to Improve Fine Art does not know what Fine Art is. Ye English Engravers must come down from your high flights; ye must condescend to study Marc Antonio & Albert Durer. Ye must begin before you attempt to finish or improve, & when you have begun you will know better than to think of improving what cannot be improv'd. It is very true, what you have said for these thirty two Years. I am Mad or Else you are so; both of us cannot be in our right senses. Posterity will judge by our Works. Woolett's & Strange's works are like those of Titian & Correggio: the Life's Labour of Ignorant Journeymen, Suited to the Purposes of Commerce no doubt, for Commerce Cannot endure Individual Merit; its insatiable Maw must be fed by What all can do Equally well; at least it is so in England, as I have found to my Cost these Forty Years.

Commerce is so far from being beneficial to Arts, or to Empire, that it is destructive of both, as all their History shews, for the above

Reason of Individual Merit being its Great hatred. Empires flourish till they become Commercial, & then they are scatter'd abroad to the four winds.

Wooletts best works were Etch'd by Jack Brown. Woolett Etch'd very bad himself. Strange's Prints were, when I knew him, all done by Aliamet & his french journeymen whose names I forget.

"The Cottagers," & "Jocund Peasants," the "Views in Kew Gardens," "Foots Cray," & "Diana," & "Acteon," & in short all that are Call'd Woolett's were Etch'd by Jack Browne, & in Woolett's works the Etching is All, tho' even in these, a single leaf of a tree is never correct.

Such Prints as Woolett & Strange produc'd will do for those who choose to purchase the Life's labour of Ignorance & Imbecillity, in Preference to the Inspired Moments of Genius & Animation.

P. 60.

I also knew something of Tom Cooke who Engraved after Hogarth. Cooke wished to Give to Hogarth what he could take from Rafael, that is Outline & Mass & Colour, but he could not [& Hogarth with all his Merit. . . *del.*].

P. 57.

I do not pretend to Paint better than Rafael or Mich. Angelo or Julio Romano or Alb. Durer, but I do Pretend to Paint finer than Rubens or Remb[t]. or Correggio or Titian. I do not Pretend to Engrave finer than Alb. Durer, Goltzius, Sadeler or Edelinck, but I do pretend to Engrave finer than Strange, Woolett, Hall or Bartolozzi, & all because I understand drawing which They understood not.

P. 58.

In this manner the English Public have been imposed upon for many years under the impression that Engraving & Painting are somewhat Else besides drawing. Painting is drawing on Canvas, & Engraving is drawing on Copper, & Nothing Else; & he who pretends to be either Painter or Engraver without being a Master of drawing is an Impostor. We may be Clever as Pugilists, but as Artists we are & have long been the Contempt of the Continent. [*word del.*] Gravelot once said to My Master, Basire, "[you *del.*] de "English may be very clever in [your *del.*] deir own opinions, but "[you *del.*] dey do not draw de [the *written over*] draw."

Resentment for Personal Injuries has had some share in this Public Address, But Love to My Art & Zeal for my Country a much Greater.

P. 59.

Men think they can Copy Nature as Correctly as I copy Imagination; this they will find Impossible, & all the Copies or Pretended

Copiers of Nature, from Rembrandt to Reynolds, Prove that Nature becomes [tame *del.*] to its Victim nothing but Blots & Blurs. Why are Copiers of Nature Incorrect, while Copiers of Imagination are Correct? this is manifest to all.

Pp. 60-62.

The Originality of this Production makes it necessary to say a few words.

While the Works [of Translators *del.*] of Pope & Dryden are look'd upon as [in the same class of *del.*] the same Art with those of Milton & Shakespeare, while the works of Strange & Woollett are look'd upon as the same Art with those of Rafael & Albert Durer, there can be no Art in a Nation but such as is Subservient to the interest of the Monopolizing Trader [*words del.*] [who Manufactures Art by the Hands of Ignorant Journeymen till at length Christian Charity is held out as a Motive to encourage a Blockhead, & he is Counted the Greatest Genius who can sell a Good-for-Nothing Commodity for a Great Price. Obedience to the Will of the Monopolist is call'd Virtue, and the really Industrious, Virtuous & Independent Barry is driven out to make room for a pack of Idle Sycophants with whitloes on their fingers. *mostly del.*]. Englishmen, rouze yourselves from the fatal Slumber into which Booksellers & Trading Dealers have thrown you, Under the artfully propagated pretence that a Translation or a Copy of any kind can be as honourable to a Nation as An Original, [Belying *del.*] Be-lying the English Character in that well known Saying, 'Englishmen Improve what others Invent.' This Even Hogarth's Works Prove a detestable Falshood. No Man Can Improve An Original Invention. [Since Hogarth's time we have had very few Efforts of Originality *del.*] Nor can an Original Invention Exist without Execution, Organized & minutely delineated & Articulated, Either by God or Man. I do not mean smooth'd up & Niggled & Poco-Piu'd, and all the beauties pick'd out [but *del.*] & blurr'd & blotted, but Drawn with a firm & decided hand at once [with all its Spots & Blemishes which are beauties & not faults *del.*], like Fuseli & Michael Angelo, Shakespeare & Milton.

Dryden in Rhyme cries, "Milton only Planned."
Every Fool shook his bells throughout the Land.
Tom Cooke cut Hogarth down with his clean Graving.
How many thousand Connoisseurs ran raving!
Some blush at what others can see no crime in,
But Nobody at all sees harm in Rhyming.
Thus Hayley on his toilette seeing the sope
Says, "Homer is very much improv'd by Pope."
While I looking up to my umbrella,

Resolv'd to be a very Contrary Fellow,
Cry, "Tom Cooke proves, from Circumference to Center,
"No one can finish so high as the original inventor."[1]

I have heard many People say, 'Give me the Ideas. It is no matter 'what Words you put them into,' & others say, 'Give me the Design, 'it is no matter for the Execution.' These People know Enough of Artifice, but Nothing Of Art. Ideas cannot be Given but in their minutely Appropriate Words, nor Can a Design be made without its minutely Appropriate Execution. The unorganized Blots & Blurs of Rubens & Titian are not Art, nor can their Method ever express Ideas or Imaginations any more than Pope's Metaphysical Jargon of Rhyming. Unappropriate Execution is the Most nauseous of all affectation & foppery. He who copies does not Execute; he only Imitates what is already Executed. Execution is only the result of Invention.

P. 63.

Whoever looks at any of the Great & Expensive Works of Engraving that have been Publish'd by English Traders must feel a Loathing & disgust, & accordingly most Englishmen have a Contempt for Art, [which will *del.*] which is the Greatest Curse that can fall upon a Nation.

He who could represent Christ uniformly like a Drayman must have Queer Conceptions; consequently his Execution must have been as Queer, & those must be Queer fellows who give great sums for such nonsense & think it fine Art.

The Modern Chalcographic Connoisseurs & Amateurs admire only the work of the journeyman, Picking out of whites & blacks in what is call'd Tints; they despise drawing, which despises them in return. They see only whether every thing is toned down but one spot of light.

Mr B. submits to a more severe tribunal; he invites the admirers of old English Portraits to look at his Print.

P. 64.

I do not know whether Homer is a Liar & that there is no such thing as Generous Contention: I know that all those with whom I have Contended in Art have strove not to Excell, but to Starve me out by Calumny & the Arts of Trading Combination.

P. 66.

It is Nonsense for Noblemen & Gentlemen to offer Premiums for the Encouragement of Art when such Pictures as these can be done

---

[1] These lines are those numbered 1-12 in the rough draft given under no. 77 p. 554, with the title "Blake's apology for his Catalogue".

without Premiums; let them Encourage what Exists Already, & not endeavour to counteract by tricks; let it no more be said that Empires Encourage Arts, for it is Arts that Encourage Empires. Arts & Artists are Spiritual & laugh at Mortal Contingencies. It is in their Power to hinder Instruction but not to Instruct, just as it is in their Power to Murder a Man but not to make a Man.

Let us teach Buonaparte, & whomsoever else it may concern, That it is not Arts that follow & attend upon Empire, but Empire that attends upon & follows [wherever Art leads *del.*] The Arts.

P. 67.

No Man of Sense can think that an Imitation of the Objects of Nature is The Art of Painting, or that such Imitation, which any one may easily perform, is worthy of Notice, much less that such an Art should be the Glory & Pride of a Nation [& that the man who does this is *del.*]. The Italians laugh at English Connoisseurs, who are [All *del.*] most of them such silly Fellows as to believe this.

A Man sets himself down with Colours & with all the Articles of Painting; he puts a Model before him & he copies that so neat as to make it a deception: now let any Man of Sense ask himself one Question: Is this Art? can it be worthy of admiration to any body of Understanding? Who could not do this? what man who has eyes and an ordinary share of patience cannot do this neatly? Is this Art? Or is it glorious to a Nation to produce such contemptible Copies? Countrymen, Countrymen, do not suffer yourselves to be disgraced!

P. 66.

The English Artist may be assured that he is doing an injury & injustice to his Country while he studies & imitates the Effects of Nature. England will never rival Italy while we servilely copy what the Wise Italians, Rafael & Michael Angelo, scorned, nay abhorred, as Vasari tells us.

Call that the Public Voice which is their Error,
Like [to *del.*] as a Monkey peeping in a Mirror
Admires all his colours brown & warm
And never once percieves his ugly form.

What kind of Intellects must he have who sees only the Colours of things & not the Forms of Things.

P. 71.

A Jockey that is anything of a Jockey will never buy a Horse by the Colour, & a Man who has got any brains will never buy a Picture by the Colour.

When I tell any Truth it is not for the sake of Convincing those who do not know it, but for the sake of defending those who do.

P. 76.

No man of Sense ever supposes that Copying from Nature is the Art of Painting; if the Art is no more than this, it is no better than any others Manual Labour; any body may do it & the fool often will do it best as it is a work of no Mind.

P. 78.

The Greatest part of what are call'd in England Old Pictures are Oil Colour Copies from Fresco Originals; the Comparison is Easily made & the copy detected. Note, I mean Fresco, Easel, or Cabinet Pictures on Canvas & Wood & Copper &c.

P. 86.

The Painter hopes that his Friends Anytus, [& *del.*] Melitus & Lycon will percieve that they are not now in Ancient Greece, & tho' they can use the Poison of Calumny, the English Public will be convinc'd that such a Picture as this Could never be Painted by a Madman or by one in a State of Outrageous manners, as these [Villains *del.*] Bad Men both Print & Publish by all the means in their Power; the Painter begs Public Protection & all will be well.

P. 17.

I wonder who can say, Speak no Ill of the dead when it is asserted in the Bible that the name of the Wicked shall Rot. It is Deistical Virtue, I suppose, but as I have none of this I will pour Aqua fortis on the Name of the Wicked & turn it into an Ornament & an Example to be Avoided by Some and Imitated by Others if they Please.

Columbus discover'd America, but Americus Vesputius finish'd & smooth'd it over like an English Engraver or Corregio & Titian.

Pp. 18-19.

What Man of Sense will lay out his Money upon the Life's Labours of Imbecillity & Imbecillity's Journeymen, or think to Educate a Fool how to build a Universe with Farthing Balls? The Contemptible Idiots who have been call'd Great Men of late Years ought to rouze the Public Indignation of Men of Sense in all Professions.

There is not, because there cannot be, any difference of Effect in the Pictures of Rubens & Rembrandt: when you have seen one of their Pictures you have seen all. It is not so with Rafael, Julio Roman[o], Alb. d[urer], Mich. Ang. Every Picture of theirs has a different & appropriate Effect.

Yet I do not shrink from the comparison, in Either Relief or Strength of Colour, with either Rembrandt or Rubens; on the contrary I court the Comparison & fear not the Result, but not in a dark corner; their Effects are in Every Picture the same. Mine are in every Picture different.

I hope my Countrymen will Excuse me if I tell them a Wholesome truth. Most Englishmen, when they look at a Picture, immediately set about searching for Points of Light & clap the Picture into a dark corner. This, when done by [this in *del.*] Grand Works, is like looking for Epigrams in Homer. A point of light is a Witticism; many are destructive of all Art. One is an Epigram only & no Grand Work can have them.

Rafael, Mich. Ang., Alb. d., Jul. Rom. are accounted ignorant of that Epigrammatic Wit in Art because they avoid it as a destructive Machine, as it is.

That Vulgar Epigram in Art, Rembrandt's "Hundred Guelders," has entirely put an End to all Genuine & Appropriate Effect; all, both Morning & Night, is now a dark cavern. It is the Fashion; they Produce System & Monotony. When you view a Collection of Pictures painted since Venetian Art was the Fashion, or Go into a Modern Exhibition, with a very few Exceptions, Every Picture has the same Effect, a Piece of Machinery of Points of Light to be put into a dark hole.

M[r] B. repeats that there is not one Character or Expression in this Print which could be Produced with the Execution of Titian, Rubens, Coreggio, Rembrandt, or any of that Class. Character & Expression can only be Expressed by those who Feel Them. Even Hogarth's Execution cannot be Copied or Improved. Gentlemen of Fortune who give Great Prices for Pictures should consider the following. Rubens's Luxembourg Gallery is Confessed on all hands [because it bears the evidence at first view *del.*] to be the work of a Blockhead: it bears this Evidence in its face; how can its Execution be any other than the Work of a Blockhead? Bloated [Awkward *del.*] Gods, Mercury, Juno, Venus, & the rattle traps of Mythology & the lumber of an [old *del.*] awkward French Palace are thrown together around Clumsy & Ricketty Princes & Princesses higgledy piggledy. On the Contrary, Julio Rom[ano's] Palace of T at Mantua, is allow'd on all hands to be the Product of a Man of the Most Profound sense & Genius, & yet his Execution is pronounc'd by English Connoisseurs & Reynolds, their doll, to be unfit for the Study of the Painter. Can I speak with too great Contempt of such Contemptible fellows? If all the Princes in Europe, like Louis XIV & Charles the first, were to Patronize such Blockheads, I, William Blake, a Mental Prince, should decollate & Hang their Souls as Guilty of Mental High Treason.

Who that has Eyes cannot see that Rubens & Correggio must have been very weak & Vulgar fellows? & we are [we *del.*] to imitate their Execution. This is [as if *del.*] like what S[r] Francis Bacon [should downright assert *del.*] says, that a healthy Child should be taught &

compell'd to walk like a Cripple, while the Cripple must be taught to walk like healthy people. O rare wisdom!

I am really sorry to see my Countrymen trouble themselves about Politics. If Men were Wise, the Most arbitrary Princes could not hurt them. If they are not wise, the Freest Government is compell'd to be a Tyranny. Princes appear to me to be Fools. Houses of Commons & Houses of Lords appear to me to be fools; they seem to me to be something Else besides Human Life.

Pp. 20-21.

The wretched State of the Arts in this Country & in Europe, originating in the wretched State of Political Science, which is the Science of Sciences, Demands a firm & determinate conduct on the part of Artists to Resist the Contemptible Counter Arts [set on foot *del.*] Establish'd by such contemptible Politicians as Louis XIV & [but *del.*] originally set on foot by Venetian Picture traders, Music traders, & Rhime traders, to the destruction of all true art as it is this Day. To recover Art has been the business of my life to the Florentine Original & if possible to go beyond that Original; this I thought the only pursuit worthy of [an Englishman *del.*] a Man. To Imitate I abhor. I obstinately adhere to the true Style of Art such as Michael Angelo, Rafael, Jul. Rom., Alb. Durer left it, [the Art of Invention, not of Imitation. Imagination is My World; this world of Dross is beneath my Notice & beneath the Notice of the Public. *del.*] I demand therefore of the Amateurs of art the Encouragement which is my due; if they continue to refuse, theirs is the loss, not mine, & theirs is the Contempt of Posterity. I have Enough in the Approbation of fellow labourers; this is my glory & exceeding great reward. I go on & nothing can hinder my course:

and in Melodious Accents I
Will sit me down & Cry, I, I.

P. 20 (sideways).

An Example of these Contrary Arts is given us in the Characters of Milton & Dryden as they are written in a Poem signed with the name of Nat Lee, which perhaps he never wrote & perhaps he wrote in a paroxysm of insanity, In which it is said that Milton's Poem is a rough Unfinish'd Piece & Dryden has finish'd it. Now let Dryden's Fall & Milton's Paradise be read, & I will assert that every Body of Understanding [will *del.*] must cry out Shame on such Niggling & Poco-Pen as Dryden has degraded Milton with. But at the same time I will allow that Stupidity will Prefer Dryden, because it is in Rhyme [but for no other cause *del.*] & Monotonous Sing Song, Sing Song from beginning to end. Such are Bartolozzi, Woolett & Strange.

P. 23.

[*See page* 603.] The Painters of England are unemploy'd in Public Works, while the Sculptors have continual & superabundant employment. Our Churches & Abbeys are treasures of [Spiritual riches *del.*] their producing for ages back, While Painting is excluded. Painting, the Principal Art, has no place [in our *del.*] among our almost only public works. [While *del.*] Yet it is more adapted to solemn ornament than [dead *del.*] Marble can be, as it is capable of being Placed on any heighth & indeed would make a Noble finish Placed above the Great Public Monuments in Westminster, S[t] Pauls & other Cathedrals. To the Society for Encouragement of Arts I address myself with [duty & *del.*] Respectful duty, requesting their Consideration of my Plan as a Great Public [deed *del.*] means of advancing Fine Art in Protestant Communities. Monuments to the dead, Painted by Historical & Poetical Artists, like Barry & Mortimer (I forbear to name living Artists tho' equally worthy), I say, Monuments so Painted must make England What Italy is, an Envied Storehouse of Intellectual Riches.

Pp. 24-25.

It has been said of late years The English Public have no Taste for Painting. This is a Falsehood. The English are as Good Judges of Painting as of Poetry, & they prove it in their Contempt for Great Collections of all the Rubbish of the Continent brought here by Ignorant Picture dealers. An Englishman may well say, 'I am no 'Judge of Painting,' when he is sold these Smears & Dawbs at an immense price & told that such is the Art of Painting. I say the English Public are true Encouragers of real Art, while they discourage and look with Contempt on False Art.

In a Commercial Nation Impostors are abroad in all Professions; these are the greatest Enemies of Genius [M[r] B. thinks it his duty to Caution the Public against a Certain Impostor who *del.*] In [our Art *del.*] the Art of Painting these Impostors sedulously propagate an Opinion that Great Inventors Cannot Execute. This Opinion is as destructive of the true Artist as it is false by all Experience. Even Hogarth cannot be either Copied or Improved. Can Anglus never Discern Perfection but in the Journeyman's Labour?

Pp. 24-25 (sideways).

I know my Execution is not like Any Body Else. I do not intend it should be so; none but Blockheads Copy one another. My Conception & Invention are on all hands allow'd to be Superior. My Execution will be found so too. To what is it that Gentlemen of the first Rank both in Genius & Fortune have subscribed their Names? To My Inventions: the Executive part they never disputed; the Lavish praise I have recieved from all Quarters for Invention &

drawing has Generally been accompanied by this: "he can concieve "but he cannot Execute"; this Absurd assertion has done me, & may still do me, the greatest mischief. I call for Public protection against these Villains. I am, like others, Just Equal in Invention & in Execution as my works shew. I, in my own defence, Challenge a Competition with the finest Engravings & defy the most critical judge to make the Comparison Honestly, asserting in my own Defence that This Print is the Finest that has been done or is likely to be done in England, where drawing, its foundation, is Contemn'd, and absurd Nonsense about dots & Lozenges & Clean Strokes made to occupy the attention to the Neglect of all real Art. I defy any Man to Cut Cleaner Strokes than I do, or rougher where I please, & assert that he who thinks he can Engrave, or Paint either, without being a Master of drawing, is a Fool. Painting is drawing on Canvas, & Engraving is drawing on Copper, & nothing Else. Drawing is Execution, & nothing Else, & he who draws best must be the best Artist; to this I subscribe my name as a Public Duty.

William Blake

P.S.—I do not believe that this Absurd opinion ever was set on foot till in my Outset into life it was artfully publish'd, both in whispers & in print, by Certain persons whose robberies from me made it necessary to them that I should be [left *del.*] hid in a corner; it never was supposed that a Copy could be better than an original, or near so Good, till a few Years ago it became the interest of certain envious Knaves.

[PUBLIC ADDRESS]

ADDITIONAL PASSAGES

P. 38.

There is just the same Science in Lebrun or Rubens, or even Vanloo, that there is in Rafael or Mich. Angelo, but not the same Genius. Science is soon got; the other never can be acquired, but must be Born.

P. 39.

I do not condemn Rubens, Rembrandt or Titian because they did not understand drawing, but because they did not Understand Colouring; how long shall I be forced to beat this into Men's Ears? I do not condemn [Bartolozzi *del.*] Strange or Woolett because they did not understand drawing, but because they did not understand Graving. I do not condemn Pope or Dryden because they did not understand Imagination, but because they did not understand Verse. Their Colouring, Graving & Verse can never be applied to Art—

That is not either Colouring, Graving or Verse which is Unappropriate to the Subject. He who makes a design must know the Effect & Colouring Proper to be put to that design & will never take that of Rubens, Rembrandt or Titian to [put *del.*] turn that which is Soul & Life into a Mill or Machine.

P. 44.

Let a Man who has made a drawing go on & on & he will produce a Picture or Painting, but if he chooses to leave it before he has spoil'd it, he will do a Better Thing.

Pp. 46–47.

They say there is no Strait Line in Nature; this Is a Lie, like all that they say. For there is Every Line in Nature. But I will tell them what is Not in Nature. An Even Tint is not in Nature; it produces Heaviness. Nature's Shadows are Ever varying, & a Ruled Sky that is quite Even never can Produce a Natural Sky; the same with every Object in a Picture, its Spots are its beauties. Now, Gentlemen Critics, how do you like this? You may rage, but what I say, I will prove by Such Practise & have already done, so that you will rage to your own destruction. Woolett I knew very intimately by his intimacy with Basire, & I knew him to be one of the most ignorant fellows that I ever knew. A Machine is not a Man nor a Work of Art; it is destructive of Humanity & of Art; the word Machination [*word del.*]. Woolett I know did not know how to Grind his Graver. I know this; he has often proved his Ignorance before me at Basire's by laughing at Basire's knife tools & ridiculing the Forms of Basire's other Gravers till Basire was quite dash'd & out of Conceit with what he himself knew, but his Impudence had a Contrary Effect on me. Englishmen have been so used to Journeymen's undecided bungling that they cannot bear the firmness of a Master's Touch.

Every Line is the Line of Beauty; it is only fumble & Bungle which cannot draw a Line; this only is Ugliness. That is not a Line which doubts & Hesitates in the Midst of its Course.

P. 23.

[*Four lines del.* That Painted as well as Sculptured Monuments were common among the Ancients is evident from the words of the Savants who compared Those Sepulchures Painted on the outside with others only of Stone. Their Beauty is Confess'd even by the Lips of Pasch[1] himself.]

[END OF PUBLIC ADDRESS]

---

[1] Count Pasch van Krienen, author of *Del Sepolcro D'Omero*, 1773.

JOSEPH OF ARIMATHEA

First engraved 1773. *Re-engraved with inscriptions* c. 1810.

Joseph of Arimathea among The Rocks of Albion. [*At the top of the engraving.*]

This is One of the Gothic Artists who Built the Cathedrals in what we call the Dark Ages, Wandering about in sheep skins & goat skins, of whom the World was not worthy; such were the Christians in all Ages.

Michael Angelo Pinxit. Engraved by W. Blake 1773 from an old Italian Drawing. [*At the bottom of the engraving.*]

[A VISION OF THE LAST JUDGMENT]

FROM THE NOTE-BOOK

P. 70.

For the Year 1810

Additions to Blake's Catalogue of Pictures &c

The Last Judgment [will be] when all those are Cast away who trouble Religion with Questions concerning Good & Evil or Eating of the Tree of those Knowledges or Reasonings which hinder the Vision of God, turning all into a Consuming Fire. When Imagination, Art & Science & all Intellectual Gifts, all the Gifts of the Holy Ghost, are [despis'd *del.*] look'd upon as of no use & only Contention remains to Man, then the Last Judgment begins, & its Vision is seen by the [Imaginative Eye *del.*] of Every one according to the situation he holds.

P. 68.

The Last Judgment is not Fable or Allegory, but Vision. Fable or Allegory are a totally distinct & inferior kind of Poetry. Vision or Imagination is a Representation of what Eternally Exists, Really & Unchangeably. Fable or Allegory is Form'd by the daughters of Memory. Imagination is surrounded by the daughters of Inspiration, who in the aggregate are call'd Jerusalem. Fable is Allegory, but what Critics call The Fable, is Vision itself. The Hebrew Bible & the Gospel of Jesus are not Allegory, but Eternal Vision or Imagination of All that Exists. Note here that Fable or Allegory is seldom without some Vision. Pilgrim's Progress is full of it, the Greek Poets the same; but [Fable & Allegory *del.*] Allegory & Vision [& Visions of

Imagination *del.*] ought to be known as Two Distinct Things, & so call'd for the Sake of Eternal Life. Plato has made Socrates say that Poets & Prophets do not know or Understand what they write or Utter; this is a most Pernicious Falshood. If they do not, pray is an inferior kind to be call'd Knowing? Plato confutes himself.

Pp. 68-69.

The Last Judgment is one of these Stupendous Visions. I have represented it as I saw it; to different People it appears differently as everything else does; for tho' on Earth things seem Permanent, they are less permanent than a Shadow, as we all know too well.

The Nature of Visionary Fancy, or Imagination, is very little Known, & the Eternal nature & permanence of its ever Existent Images is consider'd as less permanent than the things of Vegetative & Generative Nature; yet the Oak dies as well as the Lettuce, but Its Eternal Image & Individuality never dies, but renews by its seed; just [as *del.*] so the Imaginative Image returns [according to *del.*] by the seed of Contemplative Thought; the Writings of the Prophets illustrate these conceptions of the Visionary Fancy by their various sublime & Divine Images as seen in the Worlds of Vision.

Pp. 71-72.

The Learned m . . . or Heroes; this is an . . . & not Spiritual . . . while the Bible . . . of Virtue & Vice . . . as they are Ex . . . is the Real Di . . . Things. The . . . [1]when they Assert that Jupiter usurped the Throne of his Father, Saturn, & brought on an Iron Age & Begat on Mnemosyne, or Memory, The Greek Muses, which are not Inspiration as the Bible is. Reality was Forgot, & the Vanities of Time & Space only Remember'd & call'd Reality. Such is the Mighty difference between Allegoric Fable & Spiritual Mystery. Let it here be Noted that the Greek Fables originated in Spiritual Mystery & Real Visions, which are lost & clouded in Fable & Allegory, [which *del.*] while the Hebrew Bible & the Greek Gospel are Genuine, Preserv'd by the Saviour's Mercy. The Nature of my Work is Visionary or Imaginative; it is an Endeavour to Restore what the Ancients call'd the Golden Age.

Pp. 69-70.

This world of Imagination is the world of Eternity; it is the divine bosom into which we shall all go after the death of the Vegetated body. This World of Imagination is Infinite & Eternal, whereas the world of Generation, or Vegetation, is Finite & [for a small moment *del.*] Temporal. There Exist in that Eternal World the Permanent Realities of Every Thing which we see reflected in this Vegetable Glass of Nature. All Things are comprehended in their

[1] *Part of the leaf is cut away.*

Eternal Forms in the divine body of the Saviour, the True Vine of Eternity, The Human Imagination, who appear'd to Me as Coming to Judgment among his Saints & throwing off the Temporal that the Eternal might be Establish'd; around him were seen the Images of Existences according to [their Aggregate . . . *del.*] a certain order Suited to my Imaginative Eye [In the following order *del.*] as follows.

Query, the Above ought to follow the description.
Here follows the description of the Picture:

P. 76.

Jesus seated between the Two Pillars, Jachin & Boaz, with the Word of divine Revelation on his knees, & on each side the four & twenty Elders sitting in judgment; the Heavens opening around him by unfolding the clouds around his throne. The Old H[eave]n & O[ld] Earth are passing away & the N[ew] H[eaven] & N[ew] Earth descending [as on a Scroll *del.*]. The Just arise on his right & the wicked on his Left hand. A sea of fire issues from before the throne. Adam & Eve appear first, before the [throne *del.*] Judgment seat in humiliation. Abel surrounded by Innocents, & Cain, with the flint in his hand with which he slew his brother, falling with the head downward. From the Cloud on which Eve stands, Satan is seen falling headlong wound round by the tail of the serpent whose bulk, nail'd to the Cross round which he wreathes, is falling into the Abyss. Sin is also represented as a female bound in one of the Serpent's folds, surrounded by her fiends. Death is Chain'd to the Cross, & Time falls together with death, dragged down by [an Angel *del.*] a demon crown'd with Laurel; another demon with a Key has the charge of Sin & is dragging her down by the hair; beside them a [scaled *del.*] figure is seen, scaled with iron scales from head to feet [with *del.*], precipitating himself into the Abyss with the Sword & Balances: he is Og, King of Bashan.

On the Right, Beneath the Cloud on which Abel Kneels, is Abraham with Sarah & Isaac, also Hagar & Ishmael. Abel kneels on a bloody Cloud &c. (*to come in here as two leaves forward*).

P. 80.

Abel kneels on a bloody cloud descriptive of those Churches before the flood, that they were fill'd with blood & fire & vapour of smoke; even till Abraham's time the vapor & heat was not extinguish'd; these States Exist now. Man Passes on, but States remain for Ever; he passes thro' them like a traveller who may as well suppose that the places he has passed thro' exist no more, as a Man may suppose that the States he has pass'd thro' Exist no more. Every thing is Eternal.

P. 79.

In Eternity one Thing never Changes into another Thing. Each Identity is Eternal: consequently Apuleius's Golden Ass & Ovid's Metamorphosis & others of the like kind are Fable; yet they contain Vision in a sublime degree, being derived from real Vision in More ancient Writings. Lot's Wife being Changed into [a] Pillar of Salt alludes to the Mortal Body being render'd a Permanent Statue, but not Changed or Transformed into Another Identity while it retains its own Individuality. A Man can never become Ass nor Horse; some are born with shapes of Men, who may be both, but Eternal Identity is one thing & Corporeal Vegetation is another thing. Changing Water into Wine by Jesus & into Blood by Moses relates to Vegetable Nature also.

Pp. 76-77.

[Beneath] Ishmael is Mahomed, & on the left, beneath the falling figure of Cain, is Moses casting his tables of stone into the deeps. It ought to be understood that the Persons, Moses & Abraham, are not here meant, but the States Signified by those Names, the Individuals being representatives or Visions of those States as they were reveal'd to Mortal Man in the Series of Divine Revelations as they are written in the Bible; these various States I have seen in my Imagination; when distant they appear as One Man, but as you approach they appear Multitudes of Nations. Abraham hovers above his posterity, which appear as Multitudes of Children ascending from the Earth, surrounded by Stars, as it was said: 'As the Stars of Heaven for Multitude.' Jacob & [their *del.*] his Twelve Sons hover beneath the feet of Abraham & recieve their children from the Earth. I have seen, when at a distance, Multitudes of Men in Harmony appear like a single Infant, sometimes in the Arms of a Female; this represented the Church.

But to proceed with the description of those on the Left hand—beneath the Cloud on which Moses kneels is two figures, a Male & Female, chain'd together by the feet; they represent those who perish'd by the flood; beneath them a multitude of their associates are seen falling headlong; by the side of them is a Mighty fiend with a Book in his hand, which is Shut; he represents the person nam'd in Isaiah, xxii c. & 20 v., Eliakim, the Son of Hilkiah: he drags Satan down headlong: he is crown'd with oak [& has *del.*]; by the side of the Scaled figure representing Og, King of Bashan, is a Figure with a Basket, emptying out the vanities of Riches & Worldly Honours: he is Araunah, the Jebusite, master of the threshing floor; above him are two figures, elevated on a Cloud, representing the Pharisees who plead their own Righteousness before the throne; they are weighed down by two fiends. Beneath the Man with the Basket are three fiery fiends with grey beards & scourges of fire: they represent Cruel Laws; they scourge a groupe of figures down into the deeps; beneath them are various figures in attitudes of contention representing various States of Misery, which, alas, every one on Earth is liable to enter into, & against which we should all watch. The Ladies will be pleas'd to see that I have represented the Furies by Three Men & not by three Women. It is not because I think the Ancients wrong, but they will be pleas'd to remember that mine is Vision & not Fable. The Spectator may suppose them Clergymen in the Pulpit, scourging Sin instead of Forgiving it.

The Earth beneath these falling Groupes of figures is rocky & burning, and seems as if convuls'd by Earthquakes; a Great City on fire is seen in the distance; the armies are fleeing upon the Mountains. On the foreground, hell is opened & many figures are descending into it down stone steps & beside a Gate beneath a rock where sin & death are to be closed Eternally [howling & lamenting *del.*] by that Fiend who carries the key [& drags *del.*] in one hand & drags them down with the other. On the rock & above the Gate a fiend with wings urges [them *del.*] the wicked onwards with fiery darts; he [represents the Assyrian *del.*] is Hazael, the Syrian, who drives abroad all those who rebell against their Saviour; beneath the steps [is] Babylon, represented by a King crowned, Grasping his Sword & his Sceptre: he is just awaken'd out of his Grave; around him are other Kingdoms arising to Judgment, represented in this Picture [as in the Prophets *del.*] as Single Personages according to the descriptions in the Prophets. The Figure dragging up a Woman by her hair represents the Inquisition, as do those contending on the sides of the Pit, & in Particular the Man strangling two women represents a Cruel Church.

P. 78.

Two persons, one in Purple, the other in Scarlet, are descending [into Hell *del.*] down the steps into the Pit; these are Caiphas & Pilate—Two States where all those reside who Calumniate & Murder under Pretence of Holiness & Justice. Caiphas has a Blue Flame like a Miter on his head. Pilate has bloody hands that never can be cleansed; the Females behind them represent the Females belonging to such States, who are under perpetual terrors & vain dreams, plots & secret deceit. Those figures that descend into the Flames before Caiphas[1] & Pilate are Judas & those of his Class. Achitophel is also here with the cord in his hand.

---

[1] the Females behind them . . . before Caiphas: *these sentences are written also at the bottom of p. 72 and deleted.*

Pp. 80–81.

Between the Figures of Adam & Eve appears a fiery Gulph descending from the sea of fire Before the throne; in this Cataract Four Angels descend headlong with four trumpets to awake the dead; beneath these is the Seat of the Harlot, nam'd Mystery in the Revelations. She is [bound *del.*] siezed by Two Beings each with three heads; [representing *del.*] they Represent Vegetative Existence; as it is written in Revelations, they strip her naked & burn her with fire; it represents the Eternal Consummation of Vegetable Life & Death with its Lusts. The wreathed Torches in their hands represents Eternal Fire which is the fire of Generation or Vegetation; it is an Eternal Consummation. Those who are blessed with Imaginative Vision see This Eternal Female & tremble at what others fear not, while they despise & laugh at what others fear. Her Kings & Councellors & Warriors descend in Flames, Lamenting & looking upon her in astonishment & Terror, & Hell is open'd beneath her Seat on the Left hand. Beneath her feet is a flaming Cavern in which is seen the Great Red Dragon with seven heads & ten Horns [who *del.*]; he has Satan's book of Accusations lying on the Rock open before him; he is bound in chains by Two strong demons; they are Gog & Magog, who have been compell'd to subdue their Master (Ezekiel, xxxviii c, 8 v.) with their Hammer & Tongs, about to new-Create the Seven-Headed Kingdoms. The Graves beneath are open'd, & the dead awake & obey the call of the Trumpet; those on the Right hand awake in joy, those on the Left in Horror; beneath the Dragon's Cavern a Skeleton begins to Animate, starting into life at the Trumpet's sound, while the Wicked contend with each other on the brink of perdition. On the Right a Youthful couple are awaked by their Children; an Aged patriarch is awaked by his aged wife—He is Albion, our Ancestor, patriarch of the Atlantic Continent, whose History Preceded that of the Hebrews & in whose Sleep, or Chaos, Creation began; [his Emanation or Wife is Jerusalem, who is about to be reciev'd like the Bride of the . . . *del.*]; at their head the Aged Woman is Brittannica, the Wife of Albion: Jerusalem is their daughter. Little Infants creep out of the [mould *del.*] flowery mould into the Green fields of the blessed who in various joyful companies embrace & ascend to meet Eternity.

The Persons who ascend to Meet the Lord, coming in the Clouds with power & great Glory, are representations of those States described in the Bible under the Names of the Fathers before & after the Flood. Noah is seen in the Midst of these, Canopied by a Rainbow, on his right hand Shem & on his Left Japhet; these three Persons represent Poetry, Painting & Music, the three Powers in Man of conversing with Paradise, which the flood did not Sweep away. Above Noah is the Church Universal, represented by a Woman Surrounded by Infants. There is such a State in Eternity: it is composed of the Innocent civilized Heathen & the Uncivilized Savage, who, having not the Law, do by Nature the things contain'd in the Law. This State appears like a Female crown'd with stars, driven into the Wilderness; she has the Moon under her feet. The Aged Figure with Wings, having a writing tablet & taking account of the numbers who arise, is That Angel of the Divine Presence mention'd in Exodus, xiv c., 19 v. & in other Places; this Angel is frequently call'd by the Name of Jehovah Elohim, The "I am" of the Oaks of Albion.

Around Noah & beneath him are various figures Risen into the Air; among these are Three Females, representing those who are not of the dead but of those found alive at the Last Judgment; they appear to be innocently gay & thoughtless, not being among the condemn'd because ignorant of crime in the midst of a corrupted Age; the Virgin Mary was of this Class. A Mother Meets her numerous Family in the Arms of their Father; these are representations of the Greek Learned & Wise, as also of those of other Nations, such as Egypt & Babylon, in which were multitudes who shall meet the Lord coming in the Clouds.

The Children of Abraham, or Hebrew Church, are represented as a Stream of [Light *del.*] Figures, on which are seen Stars somewhat like the Milky way; they ascend from the Earth where Figures kneel Embracing above the Graves, & Represent Religion, or Civilized Life such as it is in the Christian Church, who are the Offspring of the Hebrew.

Pp. 82-84.

Just above the graves & above the spot where the Infants creep out of the Ground stand two, a Man & Woman; these are the Primitive Christians. The two Figures in purifying flames by the side of the dragon's cavern represents the Latter state of the Church when on the verge of Perdition, yet protected by a Flaming Sword. Multitudes are seen ascending from the Green fields of the blessed in which a Gothic Church is representative of true Art, Call'd Gothic in All Ages by those who follow the Fashion, as that is call'd which is without Shape or Fashion. On the right hand of Noah a Woman with Children Represents the State Call'd Laban the Syrian; it is the Remains of Civilization in the State from whence Abraham was taken. Also On the right hand of Noah A Female descends to meet her Lover or Husband, representative of that Love, call'd Friendship, which Looks for no other heaven than their Beloved & in him sees all reflected as in a Glass of Eternal Diamond.

On the right hand of these rise the diffident & Humble, & on their left a solitary Woman with her infant: these are caught up by three aged Men who appear as suddenly emerging from the blue sky for their help. These three Aged Men represent divine Providence as oppos'd to, & distinct from, divine vengeance, represented by three Aged men on the side of the Picture among the Wicked, with scourges of fire.

If the Spectator could Enter into these Images in his Imagination, approaching them on the Fiery Chariot of his Contemplative Thought, if he could Enter into Noah's Rainbow or into his bosom, or could make a Friend & Companion of one of these Images of wonder, which always intreats him to leave mortal things (as he must know), then would he arise from his Grave, then would he meet the Lord in the Air & then he would be happy. General Knowledge is Remote Knowledge; it is in Particulars that Wisdom consists & Happiness too. Both in Art & in Life, General Masses are as Much Art as a Pasteboard Man is Human. Every Man has Eyes, Nose & Mouth; this Every Idiot knows, but he who enters into & discriminates most minutely the Manners & Intentions, the [Expression *del.*] Characters in all their branches, is the alone Wise or Sensible Man, & on this discrimination All Art is founded. I intreat, then, that the Spectator will attend to the Hands & Feet, to the Lineaments of the Countenances; they are all descriptive of Character, & not a line is drawn without intention, & that most discriminate & particular. As Poetry admits not a Letter that is Insignificant, so Painting admits not a Grain of Sand or a Blade of Grass Insignificant—much less an Insignificant Blur or Mark.

Above the Head of Noah is Seth; this State call'd Seth is Male & Female in a higher state of Happiness & wisdom than Noah, being nearer the State of Innocence; beneath the feet of Seth two figures represent the two Seasons of Spring & Autumn, while beneath the feet of Noah Four Seasons represent [our present changes of Extremes *del.*] the Changed State made by the flood.

By the side of Seth is Elijah; he comprehends all the Prophetic Characters; he is seen on his fiery Chariot, bowing before the throne of the Saviour; in like manner The figures of Seth & his wife comprehends the Fathers before the flood & their Generations; when seen remote they appear as One Man; a little below Seth on his right are Two Figures, a Male & Female, with numerous Children; these represent those who were not in the Line of the Church & yet were Saved from among the Antediluvians who Perished; between Seth & these a female figure [with the back turn'd *del.*] represents the Solitary State of those who, previous to the Flood, walked with God.

All these arise toward the opening Cloud before the Throne, led onward by triumphant Groupes of Infants, & the Morning Stars sang together. Between Seth & Elijah three Female Figures crown'd with Garlands Represent Learning & Science, which accompanied Adam out of Eden.

The Cloud that opens, rolling apart before the throne & before the New Heaven & the New Earth, is Composed of Various Groupes of Figures, particularly the Four Living Creatures mention'd in Revelations as Surrounding the Throne; these I suppose to have the chief agency in removing the [former *del.*] old heavens & the old Earth to make way for the New Heaven & the New Earth, to descend from the throne of God & of the Lamb; that Living Creature on the Left of the Throne Gives to the Seven Angels the Seven Vials of the wrath of God, with which they, hovering over the deeps beneath, pour out upon the wicked their Plagues; the Other Living Creatures are descending with a Shout & with the Sound of the Trumpet, directing the Combats in the upper Elements; in the two Corners of the Picture [where...Apollyon *del.*], on the Left hand Apollyon is foiled before the Sword of Michael, & on the Right the Two Witnesses are subduing their Enemies.

[Around the Throne Heaven is Opened *del.*] On the Cloud are open'd the Books of Remembrance of Life & of Death: before that of Life, on the Right, some figures bow in humiliation; before that of Death, on the Left, the Pharisees are pleading their own Righteousness; the one shines with beams of Light, the other utters Lightnings & tempests.

A Last Judgment is Necessary because Fools flourish. Nations Flourish under Wise Rulers & are depress'd under foolish Rulers; it is the same with Individuals as Nations; works of Art can only be produc'd in Perfection where the Man is either in Affluence or is Above the Care of it. Poverty is the Fool's Rod, which at last is turn'd on his own back; this is A Last Judgment—when Men of Real Art Govern & Pretenders Fall. Some People & not a few Artists have asserted that the Painter of this Picture would not have done so well if he had been properly Encourag'd. Let those who think so, reflect on the State of Nations under Poverty & their incapability of Art; tho' Art is Above Either, the Argument is better for Affluence than Poverty; & tho' he would not have been a greater Artist, yet he would have produc'd Greater works of Art in proportion to his means. A Last Judgment is not for the purpose of making Bad Men better, but for the Purpose of hindering them from opressing the Good with Poverty & Pain by means of Such Vile Arguments & Insinuations.

Around the Throne Heaven is open'd & the Nature of Eternal Things Display'd, All Springing from the Divine Humanity. All beams from him [& (Because *del.*) as he himself has said, All dwells in him *del.*]. He is the Bread & the Wine; he is the Water of Life; accordingly on Each Side of the opening Heaven appears an Apostle; [one *del.*] that on the Right Represents Baptism, [& the Other *del.*] that on the Left Represents the Lord's Supper. All Life consists of these Two, Throwing off Error & Knaves from our company continually & Recieving Truth or Wise Men into our Company continually. He who is out of the Church & opposes it is no less an Agent of Religion than he who is in it; to be an Error & to be Cast out is a part of God's design. No man can Embrace True Art till he has Explor'd & cast out False Art (such is the Nature of Mortal Things), or he will be himself Cast out by those who have Already Embraced True Art. Thus My Picture is a History of Art & Science, the Foundation of Society, [all *del.*] Which is Humanity itself. What are all the Gifts of the Spirit but Mental Gifts? Whenever any Individual Rejects Error & Embraces Truth, a Last Judgment passes upon that Individual.

P. 85.

Over the Head of the Saviour & Redeemer The Holy Spirit, like a Dove, is surrounded by a blue Heaven in which are the two Cherubim that bow'd over the Ark, for here the temple is open'd in Heaven & the Ark of the Covenant is as a Dove of Peace. The Curtains are drawn apart, Christ having rent the Veil. The Candlestick & the Table of Shew-bread appear on Each side; a Glorification of Angels with Harps surround the Dove.

The Temple stands on the Mount of God; from it flows on each side the River of Life, on whose banks Grows the tree of Life, among whose branches temples & Pinnacles, tents & pavilions, Gardens & Groves, display Paradise with its Inhabitants walking up & down in Conversations concerning Mental Delights. Here they are &c. (*as three leaves on*).

Pp. 90-91.

Here they are no longer talking of what is Good & Evil, or of what is Right or Wrong, & puzzling themselves in Satan's [Maze *del.*] Labyrinth, But are Conversing with Eternal Realities as they Exist in the Human Imagination. We are in a World of Generation & death, & this world we must cast off if we would be Painters such as Rafael, Mich. Angelo & the Ancient Sculptors; if we do not cast off this world we shall be only Venetian Painters, who will be cast off & Lost from Art.

P. 85.

Jesus is surrounded by Beams of Glory in which are seen all around him Infants emanating from him; these represent the Eternal Births of Intellect from the divine Humanity. A Rainbow surrounds the throne & the Glory, in which youthful Nuptials recieve the infants in their hands. In Eternity Woman is the Emanation of Man; she has No Will of her own. There is no such thing in Eternity as a Female Will.

On the Side next Baptism are seen those call'd in the Bible Nursing Fathers & Nursing Mothers; [they have Crowns; the Spectator may suppose them to be the Good . . . *del.*] they represent Education. On the Side next the Lord's Supper The Holy Family, consisting of Mary, Joseph, John the Baptist, Zacharias & Elizabeth, recieving the Bread & Wine, among other Spirits of the Just made perfect. [Just *del.*] beneath these a Cloud of Women & Children are taken up, fleeing from the rolling Cloud which separates the Wicked from the Seats of Bliss. These represent those who, tho' willing, were too weak to Reject Error without the Assistance & Countenance of those Already in the Truth; for a Man Can only Reject Error by the Advice of a Friend or by the Immediate Inspiration of God; it is for this Reason among many others that I have put the Lord's Supper on the Left hand of the [Picture *del.*] Throne, for it appears so at the Last Judgment, for a Protection.

Pp.91-92.

Many suppose that before [Adam *del.*] the Creation All was Solitude & Chaos. This is the most pernicious Idea that can enter the Mind, as it takes away all sublimity from the Bible & Limits All Existence to Creation & to Chaos, To the Time & Space fixed by the Corporeal Vegetative Eye, & leaves the Man who entertains such an Idea the habitation of Unbelieving demons. Eternity Exists, and All things in Eternity, Independent of Creation which was an act of Mercy. I have represented those who are in Eternity by some in a Cloud within the Rainbow that Surrounds the Throne; they merely appear as in a Cloud when any thing of Creation, Redemption or Judgment are the Subjects of Contemplation, tho' their Whole Contemplation is concerning these things; the Reason they so appear is The Humiliation of the Reason & doubting Self-hood, & the Giving all up to Inspiration. By this it will be seen that I do not consider either the Just or the Wicked to be in a Supreme State, but to be every one of them States of the Sleep [of *del.*] which the Soul may fall into in its deadly dreams of Good & Evil when it leaves Paradise [with *del.*] following the Serpent.

P. 91 (sideways).

The Greeks represent Chronos or Time as a very Aged Man; this is Fable, but the Real Vision of Time is in Eternal Youth. I have, however, somewhat accomodated my Figure of Time to the common opinion, as I myself am also infected with it & my Visions also infected, & I see Time Aged, alas, too much so.

Allegories are things that Relate to Moral Virtues. Moral Virtues do not Exist; they are Allegories & dissimulations. But Time & Space are Real Beings, a Male & a Female. Time is a Man, Space is a Woman, & her Masculine Portion is Death.

Pp. 86, 90.

The Combats of Good & Evil [& of Truth & Error which are the same thing *del.*] is Eating of the Tree of Knowledge. The Combats of Truth & Error is Eating of the Tree of Life; these are not only Universal, but Particular. Each are Personified. There is not an Error but it has a Man for its [Actor *del.*] Agent, that is, it is a Man. There is not a Truth but it has also a Man. Good & Evil are Qualities in Every Man, whether a Good or Evil Man. These are Enemies & destroy one another by every Means in their power, both of deceit & of open Violence. The deist & the Christian are but the Results of these Opposing Natures. Many are deists who would in certain Circumstances have been Christians in outward appearance. Voltaire was one of this number; he was as intolerant as an Inquisitor. Manners make the Man, not Habits. It is the same in Art: by their Works ye shall know them; the Knave who is Converted to [Christianity *del.*] Deism & the Knave who is Converted to Christianity is still a Knave, but he himself will not know it, tho' Every body else does. Christ comes, as he came at first, to deliver those who were bound under the Knave, not to deliver the Knave. He Comes to deliver Man, the Accused, & not Satan, the Accuser. We do not find any where that Satan is Accused of Sin; he is only accused of Unbelief & thereby drawing Man into Sin that he may accuse him. Such is the Last Judgment—a deliverance from Satan's Accusation. Satan thinks that Sin is displeasing to God; he ought to know that Nothing is displeasing to God but Unbelief & Eating of the Tree of Knowledge of Good & Evil.

P. 87.

Men are admitted into Heaven not because they have curbed & govern'd their Passions or have No Passions, but because they have Cultivated their Understandings. The Treasures of Heaven are not Negations of Passion, but Realities of Intellect, from which all the Passions Emanate Uncurbed in their Eternal Glory. The Fool shall not enter into Heaven let him be ever so Holy. Holiness is not The Price of Enterance into Heaven. Those who are cast out are All Those who, having no Passions of their own because No Intellect, Have spent their lives in Curbing & Governing other People's by the Various arts of Poverty & Cruelty of all kinds. Wo, Wo, Wo to you Hypocrites. Even Murder, the Courts of Justice, more merciful than the Church, are compell'd to allow is not done in Passion, but in Cool Blooded design & Intention.

The Modern Church Crucifies Christ with the Head Downwards.

Pp. 92-95.

Many Persons, such as Paine & Voltaire, with some of the Ancient Greeks, say: "we will not converse concerning Good & Evil; we will "live in Paradise & Liberty." You may do so in Spirit, but not in the Mortal Body as you pretend, till after the Last Judgment; for in Paradise they have no Corporeal & Mortal Body—that originated with the Fall & was call'd Death & cannot be removed but by a Last Judgment; while we are in the world of Mortality we Must Suffer. The Whole Creation Groans to be deliver'd; there will always be as many Hypocrites born as Honest Men, & they will always have superior Power in Mortal Things. You cannot have Liberty in this World without what you call Moral Virtue, & you cannot have Moral Virtue without the Slavery of [half *del.*] that half of the Human Race who hate what you call Moral Virtue.

The Nature of Hatred & Envy & of All the Mischiefs in the World are here depicted. No one Envies or Hates one of his Own Party; even the devils love one another in their Way; they torment one another for other reasons than Hate or Envy; these are only employ'd against the Just. Neither can Seth Envy Noah, or Elijah Envy Abraham, but they may both of them Envy the Success of Satan or of Og or Molech. The Horse never Envies the Peacock, nor the Sheep the Goat, but they Envy a Rival in Life & Existence whose ways & means exceed their own, let him be of what Class of Animals he will; a dog will envy a Cat who is pamper'd at [his *del.*] the expense of his comfort, as I have often seen. The Bible never tells us that devils torment one another thro' Envy; it is thro' this that [makes *del.*] they torment the Just—but for what do they torment one another? I answer: For the Coercive Laws of Hell, Moral Hypocrisy. They torment a Hypocrite when he is discover'd; they punish a Failure in the tormentor who has suffer'd the Subject of his torture to Escape. In Hell all is Self Righteousness; there is no such thing there as Forgiveness of Sin; he who does Forgive Sin is Crucified as an Abettor of Criminals, & he who performs Works of Mercy in Any shape whatever is punish'd &, if possible, destroy'd, not thro' envy or Hatred or Malice, but thro' Self Righteousness that thinks it does God service, which God is Satan. They do not Envy one another: They contemn & despise one another: Forgiveness of Sin is only at the Judgment Seat of Jesus the Saviour, where the Accuser is cast out, not because he Sins, but because he torments the Just & makes them do what he condemns as Sin & what he knows is opposite to their own Identity.

It is not because Angels are Holier than Men or Devils that makes them Angels, but because they do not Expect Holiness from one another, but from God only.

The Player is a liar when he says: "Angels are happier than Men "because they are better." Angels are happier than Men & Devils because they are not always Prying after Good & Evil in one another & eating the Tree of Knowledge for Satan's Gratification.

Thinking as I do that the Creator of this World is a very Cruel Being, & being a Worshipper of Christ, I cannot help saying: "the "Son, O how unlike the Father!" First God Almighty comes with a Thump on the Head. Then Jesus Christ comes with a balm to heal it.

The Last Judgment is an Overwhelming of Bad Art & Science. Mental Things are alone Real; what is call'd Corporeal, Nobody Knows of its Dwelling Place: it is in Fallacy, & its Existence an Imposture. Where is the Existence Out of Mind or Thought? Where is it but in the Mind of a Fool? Some People flatter themselves that there will be No Last Judgment & that Bad Art will be adopted & mixed with Good Art, That Error or Experiment will make a Part of Truth, & they Boast that it is its Foundation; these People flatter themselves: I will not Flatter them. Error is Created. Truth is Eternal. Error, or Creation, will be Burned up, & then, & not till Then, Truth or Eternity will appear. It is Burnt up the Moment Men cease to behold it. I assert for My Self that I do not behold the outward Creation & that to me it is hindrance & not Action; it is as the Dirt upon my feet, No part of Me. "What," it will be Question'd, "When the Sun rises, do you not see a round disk of fire somewhat "like a Guinea?" O no, no, I see an Innumerable company of the Heavenly host crying 'Holy, Holy, Holy is the Lord God Almighty.' I question not my Corporeal or Vegetative Eye any more than I would Question a Window concerning a Sight. I look thro' it & not with it.

[END OF A VISION OF THE LAST JUDGMENT]

DESCRIPTIONS OF THE ILLUSTRATIONS TO MILTON'S "L'ALLEGRO" AND "IL PENSEROSO"

Written about 1816
following the relevant passages from the poems

Mirth Allegro

1 *Heart easing Mirth.*
Haste thee Nymph, & bring with thee
Jest & Youthful Jollity,
Quips & Cranks, & Wanton Wiles,
Nods & Becks, & Wreathed Smiles,

Sport that wrinkled Care derides,
And Laughter holding both his Sides.
Come, & trip it as you go
On the light phantastic toe,
And in thy right hand lead with thee,
The Mountain Nymph, Sweet Liberty.

These Personifications are all brought together in the First Design Surrounding the Principal Figure which is Mirth herself.

2. The Lark is an Angel on the Wing. Dull Night starts from his Watch Tower on a Cloud. The Dawn with her Dappled Horses arises above the Earth. The Earth beneath awakes at the Lark's Voice.

3. The Great Sun is represented clothed in Flames, Surrounded by the Clouds in their Liveries, in their various Offices at the Eastern Gate; beneath, in Small Figures, Milton walking by Elms on Hillocks green, The Plowman, The Milkmaid, The Mower whetting his Scythe, & The Shepherd & his Lass under a Hawthorn in the Dale.

4. In this design is Introduced,

Mountains on whose barren breast,
The Laboring Clouds do often rest.

Mountains, Clouds, Rivers, Trees appear Humanized on the Sunshine Holiday. The Church Steeple with its merry bells. The Clouds arise from the bosoms of Mountains, While Two Angels sound their Trumpets in the Heavens to announce the Sunshine Holiday.

5. The Goblin, crop full, flings out of doors from his Laborious task, dropping his Flail & Cream bowl, yawning & stretching, vanishes into the Sky, in which is seen Queen Mab Eating the Junkets. The Sports of the Fairies are seen thro' the Cottage where "She" lays in Bed "pinchd & pulld" by Fairies as they dance on the Bed, the Ceiling, & the Floor, & a Ghost pulls the Bed Clothes at her Feet. "He" is seen following the Friars Lantern towards the Convent.

6. The youthful Poet, sleeping on a bank by the Haunted Stream by Sun Set, sees in his dream the more bright Sun of Imagination under the auspices of Shakespeare & Johnson, in which is Hymen at a Marriage & the Antique Pageantry attending it.

Melancholy Penseroso

7. *Come pensive Nun, devout & pure,*
Sober, steadfast, & demure,
. . .
And join with thee calm Peace & Quiet,
Spare Fast, who oft with Gods doth diet,
. . .

And add to these retired Leisure,
Who in trim Gardens takes his pleasure;
But first, & chiefest, with thee bring,
Him who yon soars on golden Wing,
Guiding the Fiery wheeled Throne,
The Cherub Contemplation.

These Personifications are all brought together in this design, surrounding the Principal Figure Who is Melancholy herself.

8. Milton, in his Character of a Student at Cambridge, Sees the Moon terrified as one led astray in the midst of her path thro' heaven. The distant Steeple seen across a wide water indicates the sound of the Curfew Bell.

9. The Spirit of Plato unfolds his Worlds to Milton in Contemplation. The Three Destinies sit on the Circles of Plato's Heavens, weaving the Thread of Mortal Life; these Heavens are Venus, Jupiter & Mars. Hermes flies before as attending on the Heaven of Jupiter; the Great Bear is seen in the Sky beneath Hermes, & The Spirits of Fire, Air, Water & Earth Surround Milton's Chair.

10. Milton led by Melancholy into the Groves away from the Sun's flaring Beams, who is seen in the Heavens throwing his darts & flames of fire. The Spirits of the Trees on each side are seen under the domination of Insects raised by the Sun's heat.

11. Milton Sleeping on a Bank; Sleep descending, with a Strange, Mysterious dream, upon his Wings, of Scrolls, & Nets, & Webs, unfolded by Spirits in the Air & in the Brook; around Milton are Six Spirits or Fairies, hovering on the air, with Instruments of Music.

12. Milton, in his Old Age, sitting in his Mossy Cell, Contemplating the Constellations, surrounded by the Spirits of the Herbs & Flowers, bursts forth into a rapturous Prophetic Strain.

Jerusalem

The Emanation of The Giant Albion

[In XXVIII Chapters *del.*]

1804 Printed by W. Blake S[th] Molton S[t]

Written and etched 1804-1820

Plate 1

Frontispiece

Above the archway:
There is a Void outside of Existence, which if enter'd into
Englobes itself & becomes a Womb; such was Albion's Couch,
A pleasant Shadow of Repose call'd Albion's lovely Land.
His Sublime & Pathos become Two Rocks fix'd in the Earth;
His reason, his Spectrous Power, covers them above.
Jerusalem his Emanation is a Stone laying beneath.
O [*words erased*] behold the Vision of Albion.

On the right-hand side of the archway:
Half Friendship is the bitterest Enmity, said Los
As he enter'd the Door of Death for Albion's sake Inspired.
The long sufferings of God are not for ever: there is a Judgment.

On the left-hand side of the archway in reversed lettering:
Every Thing has its Vermin, O Spectre of the Sleeping Dead.

[*These passages are seen only on an early proof of the plate; they were afterwards erased.*]

Plate 3

SHEEP — To the Public — GOATS

After my three years slumber on the banks of the Ocean, I again display my Giant forms to the Public. My former Giants & Fairies having reciev'd the highest reward possible, the *love*[1] and *friendship* of those with whom to be connected is to be *blessed,* I cannot doubt that this more consolidated & extended Work will be as kindly recieved.—The Enthusiasm of the following Poem, the Author hopes

[1] All the words on the plates here printed in italic have been partially erased from the copper, sometimes with others which cannot be recovered.

no Reader will think presumptuousness or arrogance when he is reminded that the Ancients entrusted their love to their Writing, to the full as Enthusiastically as I have who Acknowledge mine for my Saviour and Lord; for they were wholly absorb'd in their Gods. I also hope the Reader will be with me, wholly One in Jesus our Lord, who is the God *of Fire* and Lord *of Love* to whom the Ancients look'd and saw his day afar off, with trembling & amazement.

The Spirit of Jesus is continual forgiveness of Sin: he who waits to be righteous before he enters into the Saviour's kingdom, the Divine Body, will never enter there. I am perhaps the most sinful of men. I pretend not to holiness: yet I pretend to love, to see, to converse with daily as man with man, & the more to have an interest in the Friend of Sinners. Therefore, *dear* Reader, *forgive* what you do not approve, & *love* me for this energetic exertion of my talent.

Reader! *lover* of books! *lover* of heaven,
And of that God from whom *all books are given*,
Who in mysterious Sinai's awful cave
To Man the wondrous art of writing gave:
Again he speaks in thunder and in fire!
Thunder of Thought, & flames of fierce desire:
Even from the depths of Hell his voice I hear
Within the unfathom'd caverns of my Ear.
Therefore I print; nor vain my types shall be:
Heaven, Earth & Hell henceforth shall live in harmony.

Of the Measure in which
the following Poem is written.

We who dwell on Earth can do nothing of ourselves; every thing is conducted by Spirits, no less than Digestion or Sleep: *to Note the last words of Jesus* Εδοθη μοι πασα εξουσια εν ουρανῳ και επι γης.

When this Verse was first dictated to me, I consider'd a Monotonous Cadence, like that used by Milton & Shakspeare & all writers of English Blank Verse, derived from the modern bondage of Rhyming, to be a necessary and indispensible part of Verse. But I soon found that in the mouth of a true Orator such monotony was not only awkward, but as much a bondage as rhyme itself. I therefore have produced a variety in every line, both of cadences & number of syllables. Every word and every letter is studied and put into its fit place; the terrific numbers are reserved for the terrific parts, the mild & gentle for the mild & gentle parts, and the prosaic for inferior parts; all are necessary to each other. Poetry Fetter'd Fetters the Human Race. Nations are Destroy'd or Flourish in proportion as Their Poetry, Painting and Music are Destroy'd or Flourish! The Primeval State of Man was Wisdom, Art and Science.

Plate 4

Μονος ὁ Ιεσους

Jerusalem

Chap: 1

Of the Sleep of Ulro! and of the passage through
Eternal Death! and of the awaking to Eternal Life.

This theme calls me in sleep night after night, & ev'ry morn
Awakes me at sun-rise; then I see the Saviour over me
Spreading his beams of love & dictating the words of this mild song.

"Awake! awake O sleeper of the land of shadows, wake! expand!
"I am in you and you in me, mutual in love divine:
"Fibres of love from man to man thro' Albion's pleasant land.
"In all the dark Atlantic vale down from the hills of Surrey
"A black water accumulates; return Albion! return!
"Thy brethren call thee, and thy fathers and thy sons,
"Thy nurses and thy mothers, thy sisters and thy daughters
"Weep at thy soul's disease, and the Divine Vision is darken'd,
"Thy Emanation that was wont to play before thy face,
"Beaming forth with her daughters into the Divine bosom: [Where *erased*]
"Where hast thou hidden thy Emanation, lovely Jerusalem,
"From the vision and fruition of the Holy-one?
"I am not a God afar off, I am a brother and friend;
"Within your bosoms I reside, and you reside in me:
"Lo! we are One, forgiving all Evil, Not seeking recompense.
"Ye are my members, O ye sleepers of Beulah, land of shades!"

But the perturbed Man away turns down the valleys dark:
Saying: "We are not One: we are Many, thou most simulative
"Phantom of the over heated brain! shadow of immortality!
"Seeking to keep my soul a victim to thy Love! which binds
"Man, the enemy of man, into deceitful friendships,
"Jerusalem is not! her daughters are indefinite:
"By demonstration man alone can live, and not by faith.
"My mountains are my own, and I will keep them to myself:
"The Malvern and the Cheviot, the Wolds, Plinlimmon & Snowdon
"Are mine: here will I build my Laws of Moral Virtue.
"Humanity shall be no more, but war & princedom & victory!"

So spoke Albion in jealous fears, hiding his Emanation
Upon the Thames and Medway, rivers of Beulah, dissembling
His jealousy before the throne divine, darkening, cold!

Plate 5

The banks of the Thames are clouded! the ancient porches of Albion are
Darken'd! they are drawn thro' unbounded space, scatter'd upon
The Void in incoher(er)ent despair! Cambridge & Oxford & London
Are driven among the starry Wheels, rent away and dissipated
In Chasms & Abysses of sorrow, enlarg'd without dimension, terrible.
Albion's mountains run with blood, the cries of war & of tumult
Resound into the unbounded night, every Human perfection
Of mountain & river & city are small & wither'd & darken'd.
Cam is a little stream! Ely is almost swallow'd up!
Lincoln & Norwich stand trembling on the brink of Udan-Adan!
Wales and Scotland shrink themselves to the west and to the north!
Mourning for fear of the warriors in the Vale of Entuthon-Benython
Jerusalem is scatter'd abroad like a cloud of smoke thro' non-entity.
Moab & Ammon & Amalek & Canaan & Egypt & Aram
Recieve her little-ones for sacrifices and the delights of cruelty.

Trembling I sit day and night, my friends are astonish'd at me,
Yet they forgive my wanderings. I rest not from my great task!
To open the Eternal Worlds, to open the immortal Eyes
Of Man inwards into the Worlds of Thought, into Eternity
Ever expanding in the Bosom of God, the Human Imagination.
O Saviour pour upon me thy Spirit of meekness & love!
Annihilate the Selfhood in me: be thou all my life!
Guide thou my hand, which trembles exceedingly upon the rock of ages,
While I write of the building of Golgonooza, & of the terrors of Entuthon,
Of Hand & Hyle & Coban, of Kwantok, Peachey, Brereton, Slayd & Hutton,
Of the terrible sons & daughters of Albion, and their Generations.

Scofield, Kox, Kotope and Bowen revolve most mightily upon
The Furnace of Los; before the eastern gate bending their fury
They war to destroy the Furnaces, to desolate Golgonooza,
And to devour the Sleeping Humanity of Albion in rage & hunger.
They revolve into the Furnaces Southward & are driven forth Northward,
Divided into Male and Female forms time after time.
From these Twelve all the Families of England spread abroad.

The Male is a Furnace of beryll; the Female is a golden Loom.
I behold them, and their rushing fires overwhelm my Soul
In London's darkness, and my tears fall day and night

Upon the Emanations of Albion's Sons, the Daughters of Albion,
Names anciently remember'd, but now contemn'd as fictions
Although in every bosom they controll our Vegetative powers.

These are united into Tirzah and her Sisters on Mount Gilead,
Cambel & Gwendolen & Conwenna & Cordella & Ignoge.
And these united into Rahab in the Covering Cherub on Euphrates,
Gwiniverra & Gwinefred & Gonorill & Sabrina beautiful,
Estrild, Mehetabel & Ragan, lovely Daughters of Albion,
They are the beautiful Emanations of the Twelve Sons of Albion.

The Starry Wheels revolv'd heavily over the Furnaces,
Drawing Jerusalem in anguish of maternal love
Eastward, a pillar of a cloud with Vala upon the mountains
Howling in pain, redounding from the arms of Beulah's Daughters!
Out from the Furnaces of Los above the head of Los.
A pillar of smoke writhing afar into Non-Entity, redounding
Till the cloud reaches afar outstretch'd among the Starry Wheels
Which revolve heavily in the mighty Void above the Furnaces.

O what avail the loves & tears of Beulah's lovely Daughters!
They hold the Immortal Form in gentle bands & tender tears,
But all within is open'd into the deeps of Entuthon Benython,
A dark and unknown night, indefinite, unmeasurable, without end,
Abstract Philosophy warring in enmity against Imagination
(Which is the Divine Body of the Lord Jesus, blessed for ever),
And there Jerusalem wanders with Vala upon the mountains.
Attracted by the revolutions of those Wheels, the Cloud of smoke
Immense and Jerusalem & Vala weeping in the Cloud
Wander away into the Chaotic Void, lamenting with her Shadow
Among the Daughters of Albion, among the Starry Wheels,
Lamenting for her children, for the sons & daughters of Albion.

Los heard her lamentations in the deeps afar! his tears fall
Incessant before the Furnaces, and his Emanation divided in pain
Eastward toward the Starry Wheels. But Westward, a black Horror,

Plate 6

His Spectre driv'n by the Starry Wheels of Albion's sons, black and
Opake divided from his back; he labours and he mourns!

For as his Emanation divided, his Spectre also divided
In terror of those starry wheels: and the Spectre stood over Los
Howling in pain, a black'ning Shadow, black'ning dark & opake,
Cursing the terrible Los, bitterly cursing him for his friendship
To Albion, suggesting murderous thoughts against Albion.

Los rag'd and stamp'd the earth in his might & terrible wrath!
He stood and stamp'd the earth; then he threw down his hammer in rage &
In fury; then he sat down and wept, terrified! Then arose
And chaunted his song, labouring with the tongs and hammer;
But still the Spectre divided, and still his pain increas'd!

In pain the Spectre divided, in pain of hunger and thirst
To devour Los's Human Perfection; but when he saw that Los

Plate 7

Was living, panting like a frighted wolf and howling
He stood over the Immortal in the solitude and darkness
Upon the dark'ning Thames, across the whole Island westward,
A horrible Shadow of Death among the Furnaces beneath
The pillar of folding smoke; and he sought by other means
To lure Los, by tears, by arguments of science & by terrors,
Terrors in every Nerve, by spasms & extended pains,
While Los answer'd unterrified to the opake blackening Fiend.

And thus the Spectre spoke: "Wilt thou still go on to destruction?
"Till thy life is all taken away by this deceitful Friendship?
"He drinks thee up like water, like wine he pours thee
"Into his tuns; thy Daughters are trodden in his vintage.
"He makes thy Sons the trampling of his bulls, they are plow'd
"And harrow'd for his profit; lo! thy stolen Emanation
"Is his garden of pleasure! all the Spectres of his Sons mock thee;
"Look how they scorn thy once admired palaces, now in ruins
"Because of Albion! because of deceit and friendship! For Lo!
"Hand has peopled Babel & Nineveh: Hyle, Ashur & Aram:
"Coban's son is Nimrod: his son Cush is adjoin'd to Aram
"By the Daughter of Babel in a woven mantle of pestilence & war.
"They put forth their spectrous cloudy sails which drive their immense
"Constellations over the deadly deeps of indefinite Udan-Adan.
"Kox is the Father of Shem & Ham & Japheth, he is the Noah
"Of the Flood of Udan-Adan: Hut'n is the Father of the Seven
"From Enoch to Adam: Schofield is Adam who was New-
"Created in Edom. I saw it indignant, & thou art not moved!
"This has divided thee in sunder, and wilt thou still forgive?
"O! thou seest not what I see, what is done in the Furnaces.
"Listen, I will tell thee what is done in moments to thee unknown:
"Luvah was cast into the Furnaces of affliction and sealed,
"And Vala fed in cruel delight the Furnaces with fire.

"Stern Urizen beheld, urg'd by necessity to keep
"The evil day afar, and if perchance with iron power
"He might avert his own despair, in woe & fear he saw
"Vala incircle round the Furnaces where Luvah was clos'd.
"With joy she heard his howlings & forgot he was her Luvah,
"With whom she liv'd in bliss in times of innocence & youth.
"Vala comes from the Furnace in a cloud, but wretched Luvah
"Is howling in the Furnaces, in flames among Albion's Spectres,
"To prepare the Spectre of Albion to reign over thee, O Los,
"Forming the Spectres of Albion according to his rage:
"To prepare the Spectre sons of Adam, who is Scofield, the Ninth
"Of Albion's sons & the father of all his brethren in the Shadowy
"Generation. Cambel & Gwendolen wove webs of war & of
"Religion to involve all Albion's sons, and when they had
"Involv'd Eight, their webs roll'd outwards into darkness,
"And Scofield the Ninth remain'd on the outside of the Eight,
"And Kox, Kotope & Bowen, One in him, a Fourfold Wonder,
"Involv'd the Eight. Such are the Generations of the Giant Albion,
"To separate a Law of Sin, to punish thee in thy members."

Los answer'd: "Altho' I know not this, I know far worse than this:
"I know that Albion hath divided me, and that thou, O my Spectre,
"Hast just cause to be irritated; but look stedfastly upon me;
"Comfort thyself in my strength; the time will arrive
"When all Albion's injuries shall cease, and when we shall
"Embrace him, tenfold bright, rising from his tomb in immortality.
"They have divided themselves by Wrath, they must be united by
"Pity; let us therefore take example & warning, O my Spectre.
"O that I could abstain from wrath! O that the Lamb
"Of God would look upon me and pity me in my fury,
"In anguish of regeneration, in terrors of self annihilation!
"Pity must join together those whom wrath has torn in sunder,
"And the Religion of Generation, which was meant for the destruction
"Of Jerusalem, become her covering till the time of the End.
"O holy Generation, Image of regeneration!
"O point of mutual forgiveness between Enemies!
"Birthplace of the Lamb of God incomprehensible!
"The Dead despise & scorn thee & cast thee out as accursed,
"Seeing the Lamb of God in thy gardens & thy palaces
"Where they desire to place the Abomination of Desolation.
"Hand sits before his furnace: scorn of others & furious pride
"Freeze round him to bars of steel & to iron rocks beneath
"His feet; indignant self-righteousness like whirlwinds of the north

Plate 8

"Rose up against me thundering, from the Brook of Albion's River,
"From Ranelagh & Strumbolo, from Cromwell's gardens & Chelsea,
"The place of wounded Soldiers; but when he saw my Mace
"Whirl'd round from heaven to earth, trembling he sat: his cold
"Poisons rose up, & his sweet deceits cover'd them all over
"With a tender cloud. As thou art now, such was he, O Spectre.
"I know thy deceit & thy revenges, and unless thou desist
"I will certainly create an eternal Hell for thee. Listen!
"Be attentive! be obedient! Lo, the Furnaces are ready to recieve thee!
"I will break thee into shivers & melt thee in the furnaces of death.
"I will cast thee into forms of abhorrence & torment if thou
"Desist not from thine own will & obey not my stern command
"I am clos'd up from my children: my Emanation is dividing,
"And thou my Spectre art divided against me. But mark,
"I will compell thee to assist me in my terrible labours: To beat
"These hypocritic Selfhoods on the Anvils of bitter Death.
"I am inspired. I act not for myself; for Albion's sake
"I now am what I am! a horror and an astonishment,
"Shudd'ring the heavens to look upon me. Behold what cruelties
"Are practised in Babel & Shinar, & have approach'd to Zion's Hill."

While Los spoke the terrible Spectre fell shudd'ring before him,
Watching his time with glowing eyes to leap upon his prey.
Los open'd the Furnaces in fear, the Spectre saw to Babel & Shinar
Across all Europe & Asia, he saw the tortures of the Victims.
He saw now from the outside what he before saw & felt from within;
He saw that Los was the sole, uncontroll'd Lord of the Furnaces.
Groaning he kneel'd before Los's iron-shod feet on London Stone,
Hung'ring & thirsting for Los's life, yet pretending obedience,
While Los pursu'd his speech in threat'nings loud & fierce:

"Thou art my Pride & Self-righteousness: I have found thee out.
"Thou art reveal'd before me in all thy magnitude & power.
"Thy Uncircumcised pretences to Chastity must be cut in sunder.
"Thy holy wrath & deep deceit cannot avail against me,
"Nor shalt thou ever assume the triple-form of Albion's Spectre,
"For I am one of the living: dare not to mock my inspired fury.
"If thou wast cast forth from my life, if I was dead upon the mountains,
"Thou mightest be pitied & lov'd; but now I am living, unless
"Thou abstain ravening I will create an eternal Hell for thee.
"Take thou this Hammer & in patience heave the thundering Bellows;
"Take thou these Tongs, strike thou alternate with me, labour obedient.

"Hand & Hyle & Koban, Skofeld, Kox & Kotope labour mightily
"In the Wars of Babel & Shinar; all their Emanations were
"Condens'd. Hand has absorb'd all his Brethren in his might;
"All the infant Loves & Graces were lost, for the mighty Hand

Plate 9

"Condens'd his Emanations into hard opake substances,
"And his infant thoughts & desires into cold dark cliffs of death.
"His hammer of gold he siez'd, and his anvil of adamant;
"He siez'd the bars of condens'd thoughts to forge them
"Into the sword of war, into the bow and arrow,
"Into the thundering cannon and into the murdering gun.
"I saw the limbs form'd for exercise contemn'd, & the beauty of
"Eternity look'd upon as deformity, & loveliness as a dry tree.
"I saw disease forming a Body of Death around the Lamb
"Of God to destroy Jerusalem & to devour the body of Albion,
"By war and stratagem to win the labour of the husbandman.

"Awkwardness arm'd in steel, folly in a helmet of gold,
"Weakness with horns & talons, ignorance with a rav'ning beak,
"Every Emanative joy forbidden as a Crime
"And the Emanations buried alive in the earth with pomp of religion,
"Inspiration deny'd, Genius forbidden by laws of punishment,
"I saw terrified. I took the sighs & tears & bitter groans,
"I lifted them into my Furnaces to form the spiritual sword
"That lays open the hidden heart. I drew forth the pang
"Of sorrow red hot: I work'd it on my resolute anvil:
"I heated it in the flames of Hand & Hyle & Coban
"Nine times. Gwendolen & Cambel & Gwineverra

"Are melted into the gold, the silver, the liquid ruby,
"The crysolite, the topaz, the jacinth & every precious stone.
"Loud roar my Furnaces and loud my hammer is heard.
"I labour day and night. I behold the soft affections
"Condense beneath my hammer into forms of cruelty,
"But still I labour in hope, tho' still my tears flow down:
"That he who will not defend Truth may be compell'd to defend
"A Lie: that he may be snared and caught and snared and taken:
"That Enthusiasm and Life may not cease; arise Spectre, arise!"

Thus they contended among the Furnaces with groans & tears.
Groaning the Spectre heav'd the bellows, obeying Los's frowns,
Till the Spaces of Erin were perfected in the furnaces
Of affliction, and Los drew them forth, compelling the harsh Spectre

Plate 10

Into the Furnaces & into the valleys of the Anvils of Death
And into the mountains of the Anvils & of the heavy Hammers,
Till he should bring the Sons & Daughters of Jerusalem to be
The Sons & Daughters of Los, that he might protect them from
Albion's dread Spectres; storming, loud, thunderous & mighty
The Bellows & the Hammers move compell'd by Los's hand.

And this is the manner of the Sons of Albion in their strength:
They take the Two Contraries which are call'd Qualities, with which
Every Substance is clothed: they name them Good & Evil;
From them they make an Abstract, which is a Negation
Not only of the Substance from which it is derived,
A murderer of its own Body, but also a murderer
Of every Divine Member: it is the Reasoning Power,
An Abstract objecting power that Negatives every thing.
This is the Spectre of Man, the Holy Reasoning Power,
And in its Holiness is closed the Abomination of Desolation.

Therefore Los stands in London building Golgonooza,
Compelling his Spectre to labours mighty; trembling in fear
The Spectre weeps, but Los unmov'd by tears or threats remains.

"I must Create a System or be enslav'd by another Man's.
"I will not Reason & Compare: my business is to Create."

So Los in fury & strength, in indignation & burning wrath.
Shudd'ring the Spectre howls, his howlings terrify the night,
He stamps around the Anvil, beating blows of stern despair,
He curses Heaven & Earth, Day & Night & Sun & Moon,
He curses Forest, Spring & River, Desart & sandy Waste,
Cities & Nations, Families & Peoples, Tongues & Laws,
Driven to desperation by Los's terrors & threat'ning fears.

Los cries, "Obey my voice & never deviate from my will
"And I will be merciful to thee! be thou invisible to all
"To whom I make thee invisible, but chief to my own Children.
"O Spectre of Urthona! Reason not against their dear approach
"Nor them obstruct with thy temptations of doubt & despair.
"O Shame, O strong & mighty Shame, I break thy brazen fetters!
"If thou refuse, thy present torments will seem southern breezes
"To what thou shalt endure if thou obey not my great will."

The Spectre answer'd: "Art thou not asham'd of those thy Sins
"That thou callest thy Children? lo, the Law of God commands
"That they be offered upon his Altar! O cruelty & torment,
"For thine are also mine! I have kept silent hitherto

"Concerning my chief delight, but thou hast broken silence.
"Now I will speak my mind! Where is my lovely Enitharmon?
"O thou my enemy, where is my Great Sin? She is also thine.
"I said: now is my grief at worst, incapable of being
"Surpassed; but every moment it accumulates more & more,
"It continues accumulating to eternity; the joys of God advance,
"For he is Righteous, he is not a Being of Pity & Compassion,
"He cannot feel Distress, he feeds on Sacrifice & Offering,
"Delighting in cries & tears & clothed in holiness & solitude;
"But my griefs advance also, for ever & ever without end.
"O that I could cease to be! Despair! I am Despair,
"Created to be the great example of horror & agony; also my
"Prayer is vain. I called for compassion: compassion mock'd;
"Mercy & pity threw the grave stone over me, & with lead
"And iron bound it over me for ever. Life lives on my
"Consuming, & the Almighty hath made me his Contrary
"To be all evil, all reversed & for ever dead: knowing
"And seeing life, yet living not; how can I then behold
"And not tremble? how can I be beheld & not abhorr'd?"

So spoke the Spectre shudd'ring, & dark tears ran down his shadowy face,
Which Los wiped off, but comfort none could give, or beam of hope.
Yet ceas'd he not from labouring at the roarings of his Forge,
With iron & brass Building Golgonooza in great contendings,
Till his Sons & Daughters came forth from the Furnaces
At the sublime Labours: for Los compell'd the invisible Spectre

Plate 11

To labours mighty with vast strength, with his mighty chains,
In pulsations of time, & extensions of space like Urns of Beulah,
With great labour upon his anvils, & in his ladles the Ore
He lifted, pouring it into the clay ground prepar'd with art,
Striving with Systems to deliver Individuals from those Systems,
That whenever any Spectre began to devour the Dead,
He might feel the pain as if a man gnaw'd his own tender nerves.

Then Erin came forth from the Furnaces, & all the Daughters of Beulah
Came from the Furnaces, by Los's mighty power for Jerusalem's
Sake, walking up and down among the Spaces of Erin.
And the Sons and Daughters of Los came forth in perfection lovely,
And the Spaces of Erin reach'd from the starry heighth to the starry depth.

Los wept with exceeding joy & all wept with joy together.
They fear'd they never more should see their Father who
Was built in from Eternity in the Cliffs of Albion.

But when the joy of meeting was exhausted in loving embrace,
Again they lament: "O what shall we do for lovely Jerusalem
"To protect the Emanations of Albion's mighty ones from cruelty?
"Sabrina & Ignoge begin to sharpen their beamy spears
"Of light and love; their little children stand with arrows of gold.
"Ragan is wholly cruel, Scofield is bound in iron armour,
"He is like a mandrake in the earth before Reuben's gate,
"He shoots beneath Jerusalem's walls to undermine her foundations.
"Vala is but thy Shadow, O thou loveliest among women!
"A shadow animated by thy tears, O mournful Jerusalem!

Plate 12

"Why wilt thou give to her a Body whose life is but a Shade?
"Her joy and love, a shade, a shade of sweet repose:
"But animated and vegetated she is a devouring worm.
"What shall we do for thee, O lovely mild Jerusalem?"

And Los said, "I behold the finger of God in terrors!
"Albion is dead! his Emanation is divided from him!
"But I am living! yet I feel my Emanation also dividing.
"Such thing was never known! O pity me, thou all-piteous-one!
"What shall I do, or how exist, divided from Enitharmon?
"Yet why despair? I saw the finger of God go forth
"Upon my Furnaces from within the Wheels of Albion's Sons,
"Fixing their Systems permanent, by mathematic power
"Giving a body to Falsehood that it may be cast off for ever,
"With Demonstrative Science piercing Apollyon with his own bow.
"God is within & without: he is even in the depths of Hell!"

Such were the lamentations of the Labourers in the Furnaces.

And they appear'd within & without, incircling on both sides
The Starry Wheels of Albion's Sons, with Spaces for Jerusalem
And for Vala the shadow of Jerusalem, the ever mourning Shade,
On both sides, within & without beaming gloriously.

Terrified at the sublime Wonder, Los stood before his Furnaces.
And they stood around, terrified with admiration at Erin's Spaces,
For the Spaces reach'd from the starry heighth to the starry depth:
And they builded Golgonooza: terrible eternal labour!

What are those golden builders doing? where was the burying-place
Of soft Ethinthus? near Tyburn's fatal Tree? is that
Mild Zion's hill's most ancient promontory, near mournful
Ever weeping Paddington? is that Calvary and Golgotha
Becoming a building of pity and compassion? Lo!
The stones are pity, and the bricks, well wrought affections
Enamel'd with love & kindness, & the tiles engraven gold,
Labour of merciful hands: the beams & rafters are forgiveness:
The mortar & cement of the work, tears of honesty: the nails
And the screws & iron braces are well wrought blandishments
And well contrived words, firm fixing, never forgotten,
Always comforting the remembrance: the floors, humility:
The cielings, devotion: the hearths, thanksgiving.
Prepare the furniture, O Lambeth, in thy pitying looms,
The curtains, woven tears & sighs wrought into lovely forms
For comfort; there the secret furniture of Jerusalem's chamber
Is wrought. Lambeth! the Bride, the Lamb's Wife, loveth thee.
Thou art one with her & knowest not of self in thy supreme joy.
Go on, builders in hope, tho' Jerusalem wanders far away
Without the gate of Los, among the dark Satanic wheels.

Fourfold the Sons of Los in their divisions, and fourfold
The great City of Golgonooza: fourfold toward the north,
And toward the south fourfold, & fourfold toward the east & west,
Each within other toward the four points: that toward
Eden, and that toward the World of Generation,
And that toward Beulah, and that toward Ulro.
Ulro is the space of the terrible starry wheels of Albion's sons,
But that toward Eden is walled up till time of renovation,
Yet it is perfect in its building, ornaments & perfection.

And the Four Points are thus beheld in Great Eternity:
West, the Circumference: South, the Zenith: North,
The Nadir: East, the Center, unapproachable for ever.
These are the four Faces towards the Four Worlds of Humanity
In every Man. Ezekiel saw them by Chebar's flood.
And the Eyes are the South, and the Nostrils are the East,
And the Tongue is the West, and the Ear is the North.

And the North Gate of Golgonooza, toward Generation
Has four sculptur'd Bulls, terrible, before the Gate of iron,
And iron the Bulls; and that which looks toward Ulro,
Clay bak'd & enamel'd, eternal glowing as four furnaces,
Turning upon the Wheels of Albion's sons with enormous power:
And that toward Beulah four, gold, silver, brass & iron;

Plate 13

And that toward Eden, four, form'd of gold, silver, brass & iron.

The South, a golden Gate, has four Lions terrible, living:
That toward Generation, four, of iron carv'd wondrous:
That toward Ulro, four, clay bak'd, laborious workmanship:
That toward Eden, four, immortal gold, silver, brass & iron.

The Western Gate fourfold is clos'd, having four Cherubim
Its guards, living, the work of elemental hands, laborious task,
Like Men hermaphroditic, each winged with eight wings.
That towards Generation, iron: that toward Beulah, stone:
That toward Ulro, clay: that toward Eden, metals:
But all clos'd up till the last day, when the graves shall yield their dead.

The Eastern Gate fourfold, terrible & deadly its ornaments,
Taking their forms from the Wheels of Albion's sons, as cogs
Are form'd in a wheel to fit the cogs of the adverse wheel.

That toward Eden, eternal ice frozen in seven folds
Of forms of death: and that toward Beulah, stone,
The seven diseases of the earth are carved terrible:
And that toward Ulro, forms of war, seven enormities:
And that toward Generation, seven generative forms.

And every part of the City is fourfold; & every inhabitant, fourfold.
And every pot & vessel & garment & utensil of the houses,
And every house, fourfold; but the third Gate in every one
Is clos'd as with a threefold curtain of ivory & fine linen & ermine.
And Luban stands in middle of the City; a moat of fire
Surrounds Luban, Los's Palace & the golden Looms of Cathedron.

And sixty-four thousand Genii guard the Eastern Gate,
And sixty-four thousand Gnomes guard the Northern Gate,
And sixty-four thousand Nymphs guard the Western Gate,
And sixty-four thousand Fairies guard the Southern Gate.

Around Golgonooza lies the land of death eternal, a Land
Of pain and misery and despair and ever brooding melancholy
In all the Twenty-seven Heavens, number'd from Adam to Luther,
From the blue Mundane Shell, reaching to the Vegetative Earth.

The Vegetative Universe opens like a flower from the Earth's center
In which is Eternity. It expands in Stars to the Mundane Shell
And there it meets Eternity again, both within and without,
And the abstract Voids between the Stars are the Satanic Wheels.

There is the Cave, the Rock, the Tree, the Lake of Udan Adan,
The Forest and the Marsh and the Pits of bitumen deadly,
The Rocks of solid fire, the Ice valleys, the Plains
Of burning sand, the rivers, cataract & Lakes of Fire,
The Islands of the fiery Lakes, the Trees of Malice, Revenge
And black Anxiety, and the Cities of the Salamandrine men,
(But whatever is visible to the Generated Man
Is a Creation of mercy & love from the Satanic Void).
The land of darkness flamed, but no light & no repose:
The land of snows of trembling & of iron hail incessant:
The land of earthquakes, and the land of woven labyrinths:
The land of snares & traps & wheels & pit-falls & dire mills:
The Voids, the Solids, & the land of clouds & regions of waters
With their inhabitants, in the Twenty-seven Heavens beneath Beulah:
Self-righteousnesses conglomerating against the Divine Vision:
A Concave Earth wondrous, Chasmal, Abyssal, Incoherent,
Forming the Mundane Shell: above, beneath, on all sides surrounding
Golgonooza. Los walks round the walls night and day.

He views the City of Golgonooza & its smaller Cities,
The Looms & Mills & Prisons & Work-houses of Og & Anak,
The Amalekite, the Canaanite, the Moabite, the Egyptian,
And all that has existed in the space of six thousand years,
Permanent & not lost, not lost nor vanish'd, & every little act,
Word, work & wish that has existed, all remaining still
In those Churches ever consuming & ever building by the Spectres
Of all the inhabitants of Earth wailing to be Created,
Shadowy to those who dwell not in them, meer possibilities,
But to those who enter into them they seem the only substances;
For every thing exists & not one sigh nor smile nor tear,

Plate 14

One hair nor particle of dust, not one can pass away.

He views the Cherub at the Tree of Life, also the Serpent
Orc, the first born, coil'd in the south, the Dragon Urizen,
Tharmas the Vegetated Tongue, even the Devouring Tongue,
A threefold region, a false brain, a false heart
And false bowels, altogether composing the False Tongue,
Beneath Beulah as a wat'ry flame revolving every way,
And as dark roots and stems, a Forest of affliction, growing
In seas of sorrow. Los also views the Four Females,
Ahania and Enion and Vala and Enitharmon lovely,

And from them, all the lovely beaming Daughters of Albion.
Ahania & Enion & Vala are three evanescent shades:
Enitharmon is a vegetated mortal Wife of Los,
His Emanation, yet his Wife till the sleep of Death is past.

Such are the Buildings of Los, & such are the Woofs of Enitharmon.

And Los beheld his Sons and he beheld his Daughters,
Every one a translucent Wonder, a Universe within,
Increasing inwards into length and breadth and heighth,
Starry & glorious; and they every one in their bright loins
Have a beautiful golden gate, which opens into the vegetative world;
And every one a gate of rubies & all sorts of precious stones
In their translucent hearts, which opens into the vegetative world;
And every one a gate of iron dreadful and wonderful
In their translucent heads, which opens into the vegetative world;
And every one has the three regions, Childhood, Manhood & Age;
But the gate of the tongue, the western gate, in them is clos'd,
Having a wall builded against it, and thereby the gates
Eastward & Southward & Northward are incircled with flaming fires.
And the North is Breadth, the South is Heighth & Depth,
The East is Inwards, & the West is Outwards every way.

And Los beheld the mild Emanation, Jerusalem, eastward bending
Her revolutions toward the Starry Wheels in maternal anguish,
Like a pale cloud, arising from the arms of Beulah's Daughters
In Entuthon Benython's deep Vales beneath Golgonooza.

[End of the 1st Chap. *erased*]

Plate 15

And Hand & Hyle rooted into Jerusalem by a fibre
Of strong revenge, & Skofeld Vegetated by Reuben's Gate
In every Nation of the Earth, till the Twelve Sons of Albion
Enrooted into every Nation, a mighty Polypus growing
From Albion over the whole Earth: such is my awful Vision.

I see the Four-fold Man, The Humanity in deadly sleep
And its fallen Emanation, The Spectre & its cruel Shadow.
I see the Past, Present & Future existing all at once
Before me. O Divine Spirit, sustain me on thy wings,
That I may awake Albion from his long & cold repose;
For Bacon & Newton, sheath'd in dismal steel, their terrors hang
Like iron scourges over Albion: Reasonings like vast Serpents
Infold around my limbs, bruising my minute articulations.

I turn my eyes to the Schools & Universities of Europe
And there behold the Loom of Locke, whose Woof rages dire,
Wash'd by the Water-wheels of Newton: black the cloth
In heavy wreathes folds over every Nation: cruel Works
Of many Wheels I view, wheel without wheel, with cogs tyrannic
Moving by compulsion each other, not as those in Eden, which,
Wheel within Wheel, in freedom revolve in harmony & peace.

I see in deadly fear in London Los raging round his Anvil
Of death, forming an Ax of gold; the Four Sons of Los
Stand round him cutting the Fibres from Albion's hills
That Albion's Sons may roll apart over the Nations,
While Reuben enroots his brethren in the narrow Canaanite
From the Limit Noah to the Limit Abram, in whose Loins
Reuben in his Twelve-fold majesty & beauty shall take refuge
As Abraham flees from Chaldea shaking his goary locks.
But first Albion must sleep, divided from the Nations.

I see Albion sitting upon his Rock in the first Winter,
And thence I see the Chaos of Satan & the World of Adam
When the Divine Hand went forth on Albion in the mid Winter
And at the place of Death, when Albion sat in Eternal Death
Among the Furnaces of Los in the Valley of the Son of Hinnom.

Plate 16

Hampstead, Highgate, Finchley, Hendon, Muswell hill rage loud
Before Bromion's iron Tongs & glowing Poker reddening fierce;
Hertfordshire glows with fierce Vegetation; in the Forests
The Oak frowns terrible, the Beech & Ash & Elm enroot
Among the Spiritual fires; loud the Corn-fields thunder along,
The Soldier's fife, the Harlot's shriek, the Virgin's dismal groan,
The Parent's fear, the Brother's jealousy, the Sister's curse,
Beneath the Storms of Theotormon, & the thund'ring Bellows
Heaves in the hand of Palamabron, who in London's darkness
Before the Anvil watches the bellowing flames: thundering
The Hammer loud rages in Rintrah's strong grasp, swinging loud
Round from heaven to earth, down falling with heavy blow
Dead on the Anvil, where the red hot wedge groans in pain.
He quenches it in the black trough of his Forge: London's River
Feeds the dread Forge, trembling & shuddering along the Valleys.

Humber & Trent roll dreadful before the Seventh Furnace,
And Tweed & Tyne anxious give up their Souls for Albion's sake.
Lincolnshire, Derbyshire, Nottinghamshire, Leicestershire,

From Oxfordshire to Norfolk on the Lake of Udan Adan,
Labour within the Furnaces, walking among the Fires
With Ladles huge & iron Pokers over the Island white.

Scotland pours out his Sons to labour at the Furnaces;
Wales gives his Daughters to the Looms; England, nursing Mothers
Gives to the Children of Albion & to the Children of Jerusalem.
From the blue Mundane Shell even to the Earth of Vegetation,
Throughout the whole Creation, which groans to be deliver'd,
Albion groans in the deep slumbers of Death upon his Rock.

Here Los fix'd down the Fifty-two Counties of England & Wales,
The Thirty-six of Scotland & the Thirty-four of Ireland,
With mighty power, when they fled out at Jerusalem's Gates
Away from the Conflict of Luvah & Urizen, fixing the Gates
In the Twelve Counties of Wales, & thence Gates looking every way
To the Four Points conduct to England & Scotland & Ireland,
And thence to all the Kingdoms & Nations & Families of the Earth.
The Gate of Reuben in Carmarthenshire: the Gate of Simeon in
Cardiganshire, & the Gate of Levi in Montgomeryshire:
The Gate of Judah, Merionethshire: the Gate of Dan, Flintshire:
The Gate of Napthali, Radnorshire: the Gate of Gad, Pembrokeshire:
The Gate of Asher, Carnarvonshire: the Gate of Issachar, Brecknokshire:
The Gate of Zebulun, in Anglesea & Sodor; so is Wales divided:
The Gate of Joseph, Denbighshire: the Gate of Benjamin, Glamorganshire:
For the protection of the Twelve Emanations of Albion's Sons.

And the Forty Counties of England are thus divided in the Gates:
Of Reuben: Norfolk, Suffolk, Essex; Simeon: Lincoln, York, Lancashire;
Levi: Middlesex, Kent, Surrey; Judah: Somerset, Glouster, Wiltshire;
Dan: Cornwal, Devon, Dorset; Napthali: Warwick, Leicester, Worcester;
Gad: Oxford, Bucks, Harford; Asher: Sussex, Hampshire, Berkshire;
Issachar: Northampton, Rutland, Nottgham; Zebulun: Bedford, Huntgn, Camb;
Joseph: Stafford, Shrops, Heref; Benjamin: Derby, Cheshire, Monmouth;
And Cumberland, Northumberland, Westmoreland & Durham are
Divided in the (the) Gates of Reuben, Judah, Dan & Joseph.

And the Thirty-six Counties of Scotland, divided in the Gates:
Of Reuben: Kincard, Haddntn, Forfar; Simeon: Ayr, Argyll, Banff;
Levi: Edinburgh, Roxbro, Ross; Judah: Abrdeen, Berwik, Dumfries;
Dan: Bute, Caitnes, Clakmanan; Napthali: Nairn, Invernes, Linlithgo;
Gad: Peebles, Perth, Renfru; Asher: Sutherlan, Sterling, Wigtoun;
Issachar: Selkirk, Dumbartn, Glasgo; Zebulun: Orkney, Shetland, Skye;
Joseph: Elgin, Lanerk, Kinros; Benjamin: Kromarty, Murra, Kirkubriht;
Governing all by the sweet delights of secret amorous glances
In Enitharmon's Halls builded by Los & his mighty Children.

All things acted on Earth are seen in the bright Sculptures of
Los's Halls, & every Age renews its powers from these Works
With every pathetic story possible to happen from Hate or
Wayward Love; & every sorrow & distress is carved here,
Every Affinity of Parents, Marriages & Friendships are here
In all their various combinations wrought with wondrous Art,
All that can happen to Man in his pilgrimage of seventy years.
Such is the Divine Written Law of Horeb & Sinai,
And such the Holy Gospel of Mount Olivet & Calvary.

Plate 17

His Spectre divides & Los in fury compells it to divide,
To labour in the fire, in the water, in the earth, in the air,
To follow the Daughters of Albion as the hound follows the scent
Of the wild inhabitant of the forest to drive them from his own,
To make a way for the Children of Los to come from the Furnaces.
But Los himself against Albion's Sons his fury bends, for he
Dare not approach the Daughters openly, lest he be consumed
In the fires of their beauty & perfection & be Vegetated beneath
Their Looms in a Generation of death & resurrection to forgetfulness.
They wooe Los continually to subdue his strength; he continually
Shews them his Spectre, sending him abroad over the four points of heaven
In the fierce desires of beauty & in the tortures of repulse. He is
The Spectre of the Living pursuing the Emanations of the Dead.
Shudd'ring they flee: they hide in the Druid Temples in cold chastity,
Subdued by the Spectre of the Living & terrified by undisguis'd desire.

For Los said: "Tho' my Spectre is divided, as I am a Living Man
"I must compell him to obey me wholly, that Enitharmon may not
"Be lost, & lest he should devour Enitharmon. Ah me!

"Piteous image of my soft desires & loves, O Enitharmon!
"I will compell my Spectre to obey. I will restore to thee thy Children.
"No one bruises or starves himself to make himself fit for labour!

"Tormented with sweet desire for these beauties of Albion,
"They would never love my power if they did not seek to destroy
"Enitharmon. Vala would never have sought & loved Albion
"If she had not sought to destroy Jerusalem; such is that false
"And Generating Love, a pretence of love to destroy love,
"Cruel hipocrisy, unlike the lovely delusions of Beulah,
"And cruel forms, unlike the merciful forms of Beulah's Night.

"They know not why they love nor wherefore they sicken & die,
"Calling that Holy Love which is Envy, Revenge & Cruelty,
"Which separated the stars from the mountains, the mountains from Man
"And left Man, a little grovelling Root outside of Himself.
"Negations are not Contraries: Contraries mutually Exist;
"But Negations Exist Not. Exceptions & Objections & Unbeliefs
"Exist not, nor shall they ever be Organized for ever & ever.
"If thou separate from me, thou art a Negation, a meer
"Reasoning & Derogation from me, an Objecting & cruel Spite
"And Malice & Envy; but my Emanation, Alas! will become
"My Contrary. O thou Negation, I will continually compell
"Thee to be invisible to any but whom I please, & when
"And where & how I please, and never! never! shalt thou be Organized
"But as a distorted & reversed Reflexion in the Darkness
"And in the Non Entity: nor shall that which is above
"Ever descend into thee, but thou shalt be a Non Entity for ever;
"And if any enter into thee, thou shalt be an Unquenchable Fire,
"And he shall be a never dying Worm, mutually tormented by
"Those that thou tormentest: a Hell & Despair for ever & ever."

So Los in secret with himself communed, & Enitharmon heard
In her darkness & was comforted; yet still she divided away
In gnawing pain from Los's bosom in the deadly Night;
First as a red Globe of blood trembling beneath his bosom
Suspended over her he hung: he infolded her in his garments
Of wool: he hid her from the Spectre in shame & confusion of
Face, in terrors & pains of Hell & Eternal Death; the
Trembling Globe shot forth Self-living, & Los howl'd over it
Feeding it with his groans & tears, day & night without ceasing:
And the Spectrous Darkness from his back divided in temptations
And in grinding agonies, in threats, stiflings & direful strugglings.

"Go thou to Skofield: ask him if he is Bath or if he is Canterbury.
"Tell him to be no more dubious: demand explicit words.
"Tell him I will dash him into shivers where & at what time
"I please; tell Hand & Skofield they are my ministers of evil
"To those I hate, for I can hate also as well as they!"

Plate 18

From every-one of the Four Regions of Human Majesty
There is an Outside spread Without & an Outside spread Within,
Beyond the Outline of Identity both ways, which meet in One,
An orbed Void of doubt, despair, hunger & thirst & sorrow
Here the Twelve Sons of Albion, join'd in dark Assembly,
Jealous of Jerusalem's children, asham'd of her little-ones,
(For Vala produc'd the Bodies, Jerusalem gave the Souls)
Became as Three Immense Wheels turning upon one-another
Into Non-Entity, and their thunders hoarse appall the Dead
To murder their own Souls, to build a Kingdom among the Dead.

"Cast, Cast ye Jerusalem forth! The Shadow of delusions!
"The Harlot daughter! Mother of pity and dishonourable forgiveness!
"Our Father Albion's sin and shame! But father now no more,
"Nor sons, nor hateful peace & love, nor soft complacencies,
"With transgressors meeting in brotherhood around the table
"Or in the porch or garden. No more the sinful delights
"Of age and youth, and boy and girl, and animal and herb,
"And river and mountain, and city & village, and house & family,
"Beneath the Oak & Palm, beneath the Vine and Fig-tree,
"In self-denial!—But War and deadly contention Between
"Father and Son, and light and love! All bold asperities
"Of Haters met in deadly strife, rending the house & garden,
"The unforgiving porches, the tables of enmity, and beds
"And chambers of trembling & suspition, hatreds of age & youth,
"And boy & girl, & animal & herb, & river & mountain,
"And city & village, and house & family, That the Perfect
"May live in glory, redeem'd by Sacrifice of the Lamb
"And of his children before sinful Jerusalem, To build
"Babylon the City of Vala, the Goddess Virgin-Mother.
"She is our Mother! Nature! Jerusalem is our Harlot-Sister
"Return'd with Children of pollution to defile our House
"With Sin and Shame. Cast, Cast her into the Potter's field!
"Her little-ones She must slay upon our Altars, and her aged
"Parents must be carried into captivity: to redeem her Soul,
"To be for a Shame & a Curse, and to be our Slaves for ever."

So cry Hand & Hyle, the eldest of the fathers of Albion's
Little-ones, to destroy the Divine Saviour, the Friend of Sinners,
Building Castles in desolated places and strong Fortifications.
Soon Hand mightily devour'd & absorb'd Albion's Twelve Sons.
Out from his bosom a mighty Polypus, vegetating in darkness;
And Hyle & Coban were his two chosen ones for Emissaries
In War: forth from his bosom they went and return'd,
Like Wheels from a great Wheel reflected in the Deep.
Hoarse turn'd the Starry Wheels rending a way in Albion's Loins:
Beyond the Night of Beulah, In a dark & unknown Night:
Outstretch'd his Giant beauty on the ground in pain & tears:

Plate 19

His Children exil'd from his breast pass to and fro before him,
His birds are silent on his hills, flocks die beneath his branches,
His tents are fall'n; his trumpets and the sweet sound of his harp
Are silent on his clouded hills that belch forth storms & fire.
His milk of Cows & honey of Bees & fruit of golden harvest
Is gather'd in the scorching heat & in the driving rain.
Where once he sat, he weary walks in misery and pain,
His Giant beauty and perfection fallen into dust,
Till, from within his wither'd breast, grown narrow with his woes,
The corn is turn'd to thistles & the apples into poison,
The birds of song to murderous crows, his joys to bitter groans,
The voices of children in his tents to cries of helpless infants,
And self-exiled from the face of light & shine of morning,
In the dark world, a narrow house! he wanders up and down
Seeking for rest and finding none! and hidden far within,
His Eon weeping in the cold and desolated Earth.

All his Affections now appear withoutside: all his Sons,
Hand, Hyle & Coban, Guantok, Peachey, Brereton, Slayd & Hutton,
Scofeld, Kox, Kotope & Bowen: his Twelve Sons, Satanic Mill,
Who are the Spectres of the Twenty-four, each Double-form'd,
Revolve upon his mountains groaning in pain beneath
The dark incessant sky, seeking for rest and finding none,
Raging against their Human natures, rav'ning to gormandize
The Human majesty and beauty of the Twenty-four,
Condensing them into solid rocks with cruelty and abhorrence,
Suspition & revenge; & the seven diseases of the Soul
Settled around Albion and around Luvah in his secret cloud.
Willing the Friends endur'd for Albion's sake and for
Jerusalem, his Emanation, shut within his bosom,
Which harden'd against them more and more as he builded onwards

On the Gulph of Death in self-righteousness that roll'd
Before his awful feet, in pride of virtue for victory:
And Los was roof'd in from Eternity in Albion's Cliffs
Which stand upon the ends of Beulah, and withoutside all
Appear'd a rocky form against the Divine Humanity.

Albion's Circumference was clos'd: his Center began dark'ning
Into the Night of Beulah, and the Moon of Beulah rose
Clouded with storms. Los, his strong Guard, walk'd round beneath the Moon,
And Albion fled inward among the currents of his rivers.

He found Jerusalem upon the River of his City, soft repos'd
In the arms of Vala, assimilating in one with Vala,
The Lilly of Havilah; and they sang soft thro' Lambeth's vales
In a sweet moony night & silence that they had created
With a blue sky spread over with wings and a mild moon,
Dividing & uniting into many female forms, Jerusalem
Trembling; then in one comingling in eternal tears,
Sighing to melt his Giant beauty on the moony river.

Plate 20

But when they saw Albion fall'n upon mild Lambeth's vale,
Astonish'd, Terrified, they hover'd over his Giant limbs.
Then thus Jerusalem spoke, while Vala wove the veil of tears,
Weeping in pleadings of Love, in the web of despair:

"Wherefore hast thou shut me into the winter of human life,
"And clos'd up the sweet regions of youth and virgin innocence
"Where we live forgetting error, not pondering on evil,
"Among my lambs & brooks of water, among my warbling birds:
"Where we delight in innocence before the face of the Lamb,
"Going in and out before him in his love and sweet affection?"

Vala replied weeping & trembling, hiding in her veil:

"When winter rends the hungry family and the snow falls
"Upon the ways of men hiding the paths of man and beast,
"Then mourns the wanderer: then he repents his wanderings & eyes
"The distant forest: then the slave groans in the dungeon of stone,
"The captive in the mill of the stranger, sold for scanty hire.
"They view their former life: they number moments over and over,
"Stringing them on their remembrance as on a thread of sorrow.
"Thou art my sister and my daughter: thy shame is mine also:
"Ask me not of my griefs! thou knowest all my griefs."

Jerusalem answer'd with soft tears over the valleys:

"O Vala, what is Sin, that thou shudderest and weepest
"At sight of thy once lov'd Jerusalem? What is Sin but a little
"Error & fault that is soon forgiven? but mercy is not a Sin,
"Nor pity nor love nor kind forgiveness. O, if I have Sinned
"Forgive & pity me! O, unfold thy Veil in mercy & love!
"Slay not my little ones, beloved Virgin daughter of Babylon,
"Slay not my infant loves & graces, beautiful daughter of Moab!
"I cannot put off the human form. I strive but strive in vain.
"When Albion rent thy beautiful net of gold and silver twine,
"Thou hadst woven it with art, thou hadst caught me in the bands
"Of love, thou refusedst to let me go: Albion beheld thy beauty,
"Beautiful thro' our Love's comeliness, beautiful thro' pity.
"The Veil shone with thy brightness in the eyes of Albion
"Because it inclos'd pity & love, because we lov'd one-another.
"Albion lov'd thee: he rent thy Veil: he embrac'd thee: he lov'd thee!
"Astonish'd at his beauty & perfection, thou forgavest his furious love.
"I redounded from Albion's bosom in my virgin loveliness:
"The Lamb of God reciev'd me in his arms, he smil'd upon us:
"He made me his Bride & Wife: he gave thee to Albion.
"Then was a time of love. O why is it passed away!"

Then Albion broke silence and with groans reply'd:

Plate 21

"O Vala! O Jerusalem! do you delight in my groans!
"You, O lovely forms, you have prepared my death-cup.
"The disease of Shame covers me from head to feet. I have no hope.
"Every boil upon my body is a separate & deadly Sin.
"Doubt first assail'd me, then Shame took possession of me.
"Shame divides Families, Shame hath divided Albion in sunder.
"First fled my Sons & then my Daughters, then my Wild Animations,
"My Cattle next, last ev'n the Dog of my Gate; the Forests fled,
"The Corn-fields & the breathing Gardens outside separated,
"The Sea, the Stars, the Sun, the Moon, driv'n forth by my disease.
"All is Eternal Death unless you can weave a chaste
"Body over an unchaste Mind! Vala! O that thou wert pure!
"That the deep wound of Sin might be clos'd up with the Needle
"And with the Loom, to cover Gwendolen & Ragan with costly Robes
"Of Natural Virtue, for their Spiritual forms without a Veil
"Wither in Luvah's Sepulcher. I thrust him from my presence,
"And all my Children follow'd his loud howlings into the Deep.
"Jerusalem! dissembler Jerusalem! I look into thy bosom:

"I discover thy secret places. Cordella! I behold
"Thee whom I thought pure as the heavens in innocence & fear,
"Thy Tabernacle taken down, thy secret Cherubim disclosed.
"Art thou broken? Ah me, Sabrina, running by my side,
"In childhood what wert thou? unutterable anguish! Conwenna!
"Thy cradled infancy is most piteous. O hide, O hide!
"Their secret gardens were made paths to the traveller.
"I knew not of their secret loves with those I hated most,
"Nor that their every thought was Sin & secret appetite.
"Hyle sees in fear, he howls in fury over them. Hand sees
"In jealous fear: in stern accusation with cruel stripes
"He drives them thro' the Streets of Babylon before my face.
"Because they taught Luvah to rise into my clouded heavens,
"Battersea and Chelsea mourn for Cambel & Gwendolen,
"Hackney and Holloway sicken for Estrild & Ignoge:
"Because the Peak, Malvern & Cheviot Reason in Cruelty,
"Penmaenmawr & Dhinas-bran Demonstrate in Unbelief,
"Manchester & Liverpool are in tortures of Doubt & Despair,
"Malden & Colchester Demonstrate. I hear my Children's voices,
"I see their piteous faces gleam out upon the cruel winds
"From Lincoln & Norwich, from Edinburgh & Monmouth:
"I see them distant from my bosom scourg'd along the roads,
"Then lost in clouds. I hear their tender voices! clouds divide:
"I see them die beneath the whips of the Captains; they are taken
"In solemn pomp into Chaldea across the bredths of Europe.
"Six months they lie embalm'd in silent death, worshipped,
"Carried in Arks of Oak before the armies in the spring.
"Bursting their Arks they rise again to life: they play before
"The Armies. I hear their loud cymbals & their deadly cries.
"Are the Dead cruel? are those who are infolded in moral Law
"Revengeful? O that Death & Annihilation were the same!"

Then Vala answer'd spreading her scarlet Veil over Albion:

Plate 22

"Albion thy fear has made me tremble; thy terrors have surrounded me:
"Thy Sons have nail'd me on the Gates, piercing my hands & feet,
"Till Skofield's Nimrod, the mighty Huntsman Jehovah, came
"With Cush his Son & took me down. He in a golden Ark
"Bears me before his Armies, tho' my shadow hovers here.
"The flesh of multitudes fed & nouris'd me in my childhood,
"My morn & evening food were prepar'd in Battles of Men.
"Great is the cry of the Hounds of Nimrod along the Valley

"Of Vision, they scent the odor of War in the Valley of Vision.
"All Love is lost! terror succeeds, & Hatred instead of Love,
"And stern demands of Right & Duty instead of Liberty.
"Once thou wast to me the loveliest Son of heaven, but now
"Where shall I hide from thy dread countenance & searching eyes?
"I have looked into the secret Soul of him I loved,
"And in the dark recesses found Sin & can never return."

Albion again utter'd his voice beneath the silent Moon:

"I brought Love into light of day, to pride in chaste beauty,
"I brought Love into light, & fancied Innocence is no more."

Then spoke Jerusalem: "O Albion! my Father Albion!
"Why wilt thou number every little fibre of my Soul,
"Spreading them out before the Sun like stalks of flax to dry?
"The Infant Joy is beautiful, but its anatomy
"Horrible, ghast & deadly! nought shalt thou find in it
"But dark despair & everlasting brooding melancholy!"

Then Albion turn'd his face toward Jerusalem & spoke:

"Hide thou, Jerusalem, in impalpable voidness, not to be
"Touch'd by the hand nor seen with the eye. O Jerusalem,
"Would thou wert not & that thy place might never be found!
"But come, O Vala, with knife & cup, drain my blood
"To the last drop, then hide me in thy Scarlet Tabernacle;
"For I see Luvah whom I slew, I behold him in my Spectre
"As I behold Jerusalem in thee, O Vala, dark and cold."

Jerusalem then stretch'd her hand toward the Moon & spoke:

"Why should Punishment Weave the Veil with Iron Wheels of War
"When Forgiveness might it Weave with Wings of Cherubim?"

Loud groan'd Albion from mountain to mountain & replied:

Plate 23

"Jerusalem! Jerusalem! deluding shadow of Albion!
"Daughter of my phantasy! unlawful pleasure! Albion's curse!
"I came here with intention to annihilate thee, But
"My soul is melted away, inwoven within the Veil.
"Hast thou again knitted the Veil of Vala which I for thee
"Pitying rent in ancient times? I see it whole and more
"Perfect and shining with beauty!" "But thou! O wretched Father!"

Jerusalem reply'd, like a voice heard from a sepulcher,
"Father once piteous! Is Pity a Sin? Embalm'd in Vala's bosom
"In an Eternal Death for Albion's sake, our best beloved,
"Thou art my Father & my Brother. Why hast thou hidden me
"Remote from the divine Vision my Lord and Saviour?"

Trembling stood Albion at her words in jealous dark despair;
He felt that Love and Pity are the same, a soft repose,
Inward complacency of Soul, a Self-annihilation.

"I have erred! I am ashamed! and will never return more.
"I have taught my children sacrifices of cruelty: what shall I answer?
"I will hide it from Eternals! I will give myself for my Children!
"Which way soever I turn, I behold Humanity and Pity!"

He recoil'd: he rush'd outwards: he bore the Veil whole away.
His fires redound from his Dragon Altars in Errors returning.
He drew the Veil of Moral Virtue, woven for Cruel Laws,
And cast it into the Atlantic Deep to catch the Souls of the Dead.
He stood between the Palm tree & the Oak of weeping
Which stand upon the edge of Beulah, and there Albion sunk
Down in sick pallid languor. These were his last words, relapsing
Hoarse from his rocks, from caverns of Derbyshire & Wales
And Scotland, utter'd from the Circumference into Eternity:

"Blasphemous Sons of Feminine delusion! God in the dreary Void
"Dwells from Eternity, wide separated from the Human Soul.
"But thou, deluding Image, by whom imbu'd the Veil I rent,
"Lo, here is Vala's Veil whole, for a Law, a Terror & a Curse!
"And therefore God takes vengeance on me: from my clay-cold bosom
"My children wander, trembling victims of his Moral Justice:
"His snows fall on me and cover me, while in the Veil I fold
"My dying limbs. Therefore O Manhood, if thou art aught
"But a meer Phantasy, hear dying Albion's Curse!
"May God, who dwells in this dark Ulro & voidness, vengeance take,
"And draw thee down into this Abyss of sorrow and torture,
"Like me thy Victim. O that Death & Annihilation were the same!

Plate 24

"What have I said? What have I done? O all-powerful Human Words!
"You recoil back upon me in the blood of the Lamb slain in his Children.
"Two bleeding Contraries, equally true, are his Witnesses against me.

"We reared mighty Stones, we danced naked around them,
"Thinking to bring Love into light of day, to Jerusalem's shame
"Displaying our Giant limbs to all the winds of heaven. Sudden
"Shame siez'd us, we could not look on one-another for abhorrence: the Blue
"Of our immortal Veins & all their Hosts fled from our Limbs
"And wander'd distant in a dismal Night clouded & dark.
"The Sun fled from the Briton's forehead, the Moon from his mighty loins,
"Scandinavia fled with all his mountains fill'd with groans.

"O what is Life & what is Man? O what is Death? Wherefore
"Are you, my Children, natives in the Grave to where I go?
"Or are you born to feed the hungry ravenings of Destruction,
"To be the sport of Accident, to waste in Wrath & Love a weary
"Life, in brooding cares & anxious labours that prove but chaff?
"O Jerusalem, Jerusalem, I have forsaken thy Courts,
"Thy Pillars of ivory & gold, thy Curtains of silk & fine
"Linen, thy Pavements of precious stones, thy Walls of pearl
"And gold, thy Gates of Thanksgiving, thy Windows of Praise,
"Thy Clouds of Blessing, thy Cherubims of Tender-mercy
"Stretching their Wings sublime over the Little-ones of Albion!
"O Human Imagination, O Divine Body I have Crucified,
"I have turned my back upon thee into the Wastes of Moral Law.
"There Babylon is builded in the Waste, founded in Human desolation.
"O Babylon, thy Watchman stands over thee in the night,
"Thy severe Judge all the day long proves thee, O Babylon,
"With provings of destruction, with giving thee thy heart's desire;
"But Albion is cast forth to the Potter, his Children to the Builders
"To build Babylon because they have forsaken Jerusalem.
"The Walls of Babylon are Souls of Men, her Gates the Groans
"Of Nations, her Towers are the Miseries of once happy Familie
"Her Streets are paved with Destruction, her Houses built Death,
"Her Palaces with Hell & the Grave, her Synagogues with
"Of ever-hardening Despair, squar'd & polish'd with
"Yet thou wast lovely as the summer cloud upon my
"When Jerusalem was thy heart's desire, in times
"Thy Sons came to Jerusalem with gifts; she se
"With blessings on their hands & on their fee
"And pearl & diamond: thy Daughters san rmony.
"They came up to Jerusalem: they walke
"In the Exchanges of London every N
"And London walk'd in every Natio

“Albion cover’d the whole Earth, England encompass’d the Nations,
“Mutual each within other’s bosom in Visions of Regeneration.
“Jerusalem cover’d the Atlantic Mountains & the Erythrean
“From bright Japan & China to Hesperia, France & England.
“Mount Zion lifted his head in every Nation under heaven,
“And the Mount of Olives was beheld over the whole Earth.
“The footsteps of the Lamb of God were there; but now no more,
“No more shall I behold him; he is clos’d in Luvah’s Sepulcher.
“Yet why these smitings of Luvah, the gentlest mildest Zoa?
“If God was Merciful, this could not be. O Lamb of God,
“Thou art a delusion and Jerusalem is my Sin! O my Children,
“I have educated you in the crucifying cruelties of Demonstration
“Till you have assum’d the Providence of God & slain your Father.
“Dost thou appear before me, who liest dead in Luvah’s Sepulcher?
“Dost thou forgive me, thou who wast Dead & art Alive?
“Look not so merciful upon me, O thou Slain Lamb of God!
“I die! I die in thy arms, tho’ Hope is banish’d from me.”

Thund’ring the Veil rushes from his hand, Vegetating Knot by
Knot, Day by Day, Night by Night; loud roll the indignant Atlantic
Waves & the Erythrean, turning up the bottoms of the Deeps.

Plate 25

And there was heard a great lamenting in Beulah; all the Regions
Of Beulah were moved as the tender bowels are moved, & they said:

“Why did you take Vengeance, O ye Sons of the mighty Albion,
“Planting these Oaken Groves, Erecting these Dragon Temples?
“Injury the Lord heals, but Vengeance cannot be healed.
“As the Sons of Albion have done to Luvah, so they have in him
“Done to the Divine Lord & Saviour, who suffers with those that
suffer;
‘For not one sparrow can suffer & the whole Universe not suffer also
In all its Regions, & its Father & Saviour not pity and weep.
ut Vengeance is the destroyer of Grace & Repentance in the bosom
the Injurer, in which the Divine Lamb is cruelly slain.
end, O Lamb of God, & take away the imputation of Sin
Creation of States & the deliverance of Individuals Evermore.
n.”

hey in Beulah over the Four Regions of Albion;
bted & despair’d & imputed Sin & Righteousness
& not to States, and these Slept in Ulro.

[End of Chap: 1st]

Plate 26

A picture of HAND *in flames before* JERUSALEM *is inscribed at the sides of the plate and in the centre :*

SUCH VISIONS HAVE APPEAR'D TO ME
AS I MY ORDER'D RACE HAVE RUN.
JERUSALEM IS NAMED LIBERTY
AMONG THE SONS OF ALBION.

Plate 27

To the Jews

Jerusalem the Emanation of the Giant Albion! Can it be? Is it a Truth that the Learned have explored? Was Britain the Primitive Seat of the Patriarchal Religion? If it is true, my title-page is also True, that Jerusalem was & is the Emanation of the Giant Albion. It is True and cannot be controverted. Ye are united, O ye Inhabitants of Earth, in One Religion, The Religion of Jesus, the most Ancient, the Eternal & the Everlasting Gospel. The Wicked will turn it to Wickedness, the Righteous to Righteousness. Amen! Huzza! Selah! "All things Begin & End in Albion's Ancient Druid Rocky Shore."

Your Ancestors derived their origin from Abraham, Heber, Shem and Noah, who were Druids, as the Druid Temples (which are the Patriarchal Pillars & Oak Groves) over the whole Earth witness to this day.

You have a tradition, that Man anciently contain'd in his mighty limbs all things in Heaven & Earth: this you recieved from the Druids.

"But now the Starry Heavens are fled from the mighty limbs of Albion."

Albion was the Parent of the Druids, & in his Chaotic State of Sleep, Satan & Adam & the whole World was Created by the Elohim.

The fields from Islington to Marybone,
To Primrose Hill and Saint John's Wood,
Were builded over with pillars of gold,
And there Jerusalem's pillars stood.

Her Little-ones ran on the fields,
The Lamb of God among them seen,
And fair Jerusalem his Bride,
Among the little meadows green.

Pancrass & Kentish-town repose
Among her golden pillars high,
Among her golden arches which
Shine upon the starry sky.

The Jew's-harp-house & the Green Man,
The Ponds where Boys to bathe delight,
The fields of Cows by Willan's farm,
Shine in Jerusalem's pleasant sight.

She walks upon our meadows green,
The Lamb of God walks by her side,
And every English Child is seen
Children of Jesus & his Bride.

Forgiving trespasses and sins
Lest Babylon with cruel Og
With Moral & Self-righteous Law
Should Crucify in Satan's Synagogue!

What are those golden Builders doing
Near mournful ever-weeping Paddington,
Standing above that mighty Ruin
Where Satan the first victory won,

Where Albion slept beneath the Fatal Tree,
And the Druids' golden Knife
Rioted in human gore,
In Offerings of Human Life?

They groan'd aloud on London Stone,
They groan'd aloud on Tyburn's Brook,
Albion gave his deadly groan,
And all the Atlantic Mountains shook.

Albion's Spectre from his Loins
Tore forth in all the pomp of War:
Satan his name: in flames of fire
He stretch'd his Druid Pillars far.

Jerusalem fell from Lambeth's Vale
Down thro' Poplar & Old Bow,
Thro' Malden & acros the Sea,
In War & howling, death & woe.

The Rhine was red with human blood,
The Danube roll'd a purple tide,
On the Euphrates Satan stood,
And over Asia stretch'd his pride.

He wither'd up sweet Zion's Hill
From every Nation of the Earth;
He wither'd up Jerusalem's Gates,
And in a dark Land gave her birth.

He wither'd up the Human Form
By laws of sacrifice for sin,
Till it became a Mortal Worm,
But O! translucent all within.

The Divine Vision still was seen,
Still was the Human Form Divine,
Weeping in weak & mortal clay,
O Jesus, still the Form was thine.

And thine the Human Face, & thine
The Human Hands & Feet & Breath,
Entering thro' the Gates of Birth
And passing thro' the Gates of Death.

And O thou Lamb of God, whom I
Slew in my dark self-righteous pride,
Art thou return'd to Albion's Land?
And is Jerusalem thy Bride?

Come to my arms & never more
Depart, but dwell for ever here:
Create my Spirit to thy Love:
Subdue my Spectre to thy Fear.

Spectre of Albion! warlike Fiend!
In clouds of blood & ruin roll'd,
I here reclaim thee as my own,
My Self-hood! Satan! arm'd in gold.

Is this thy soft Family-Love,
Thy cruel Patriarchal pride,
Planting thy Family alone,
Destroying all the World beside?

A man's worst enemies are those
Of his own house & family;
And he who makes his law a curse,
By his own law shall surely die.

In my Exchanges every Land
Shall walk, & mine in every Land,
Mutual shall build Jerusalem,
Both heart in heart & hand in hand.

If Humility is Christianity, you, O Jews, are the true Christians. If your tradition that Man contained in his Limbs all Animals is True, & they were separated from him by cruel Sacrifices, and when compulsory cruel Sacrifices had brought Humanity into a Feminine Tabernacle in the loins of Abraham & David, the Lamb of God, the Saviour became apparent on Earth as the Prophets had foretold, The Return of Israel is a Return to Mental Sacrifice & War. Take up the Cross, O Israel, & follow Jesus.

Plate 28

Jerusalem

Chap: 2

Every ornament of perfection and every labour of love
In all the Garden of Eden & in all the golden mountains
Was become an envied horror and a remembrance of jealousy,
And every Act a Crime, and Albion the punisher & judge.

And Albion spoke from his secret seat and said:

"All these ornaments are crimes, they are made by the labours
"Of loves, of unnatural consanguinities and friendships
"Horrid to think of when enquired deeply into; and all
"These hills & valleys are accursed witnesses of Sin.
"I therefore condense them into solid rocks, stedfast,
"A foundation and certainty and demonstrative truth,
"That Man be separate from Man, & here I plant my seat."

Cold snows drifted around him: ice cover'd his loins around.
He sat by Tyburn's brook, and underneath his heel shot up
A deadly Tree: he nam'd it Moral Virtue and the Law
Of God who dwells in Chaos hidden from the human sight.

The Tree spread over him its cold shadows, (Albion groan'd)
They bent down, they felt the earth, and again enrooting
Shot into many a Tree, an endless labyrinth of woe.

From willing sacrifice of Self, to sacrifice of (miscall'd) Enemies
For Atonement. Albion began to erect twelve Altars
Of rough unhewn rocks, before the Potter's Furnace.
He nam'd them Justice and Truth. And Albion's Sons
Must have become the first Victims, being the first transgressors,
But they fled to the mountains to seek ransom, building A Strong
Fortification against the Divine Humanity and Mercy,
In Shame & Jealousy to annihilate Jerusalem.

Plate 29 [*43*]

Then the Divine Vision like a silent Sun appear'd above
Albion's dark rocks, setting behind the Gardens of Kensington
On Tyburn's River in clouds of blood, where was mild Zion Hill's
Most ancient promontory; and in the Sun a Human Form appear'd,
And thus the Voice Divine went forth upon the rocks of Albion:

"I elected Albion for my glory: I gave to him the Nations
"Of the whole Earth. He was the Angel of my Presence, and all
"The Sons of God were Albion's Sons, and Jerusalem was my joy
"The Reactor hath hid himself thro' envy. I behold him,
"But you cannot behold him till he be reveal'd in his System.
"Albion's Reactor must have a Place prepar'd. Albion must Sleep
"The Sleep of Death till the Man of Sin & Repentance be reveal'd.
"Hidden in Albion's Forests he lurks: he admits of no Reply
"From Albion, but hath founded his Reaction into a Law
"Of Action, for Obedience to destroy the Contraries of Man.
"He hath compell'd Albion to become a Punisher & hath possess'd
"Himself of Albion's Forests & Wilds, and Jerusalem is taken,
"The City of the Woods in the Forest of Ephratah is taken!
"London is a stone of her ruins, Oxford is the dust of her walls,
"Sussex & Kent are her scatter'd garments, Ireland her holy place,
"And the murder'd bodies of her little ones are Scotland and Wales.
"The Cities of the Nations are the smoke of her consummation,
"The Nations are her dust, ground by the chariot wheels
"Of her lordly conquerors, her palaces levell'd with the dust.
"I come that I may find a way for my banished ones to return.
"Fear not, O little Flock, I come. Albion shall rise again."

So saying, the mild Sun inclos'd the Human Family.

Forthwith from Albion's dark'ning rocks[1] came two Immortal forms,
Saying: "We alone are escaped, O merciful Lord and Saviour,
"We flee from the interiors of Albion's hills and mountains,
"From his Valleys Eastward from Amalek, Canaan & Moab,
"Beneath his vast ranges of hills surrounding Jerusalem.

"Albion walk'd on the steps of fire before his Halls,
"And Vala walk'd with him in dreams of soft deluding slumber;
"He looked up & saw the Prince of Light with splendor faded.
"Then Albion ascended mourning into the porches of his Palace,
"Above him rose a Shadow from his wearied intellect,
"Of living gold, pure, perfect, holy; in white linen pure he hover'd,
"A sweet entrancing self-delusion, a wat'ry vision of Albion,
"Soft exulting in existence, all the Man absorbing.

"Albion fell upon his face prostrate before the wat'ry Shadow,
"Saying: 'O Lord, whence is this change? thou knowest I am nothing!'
"And Vala trembled & cover'd her face, & her locks were spread on the pavement.

"We heard, astonish'd at the Vision, & our hearts trembled within us;
"We heard the voice of slumberous Albion, and thus he spake,
"Idolatrous to his own Shadow, words of eternity uttering:

" 'O I am nothing when I enter into judgment with thee!
" 'If thou withdraw thy breath, I die & vanish into Hades;
" 'If thou dost lay thine hand upon me, behold I am silent;
" 'If thou withhold thine hand, I perish like a fallen leaf.
" 'O I am nothing, and to nothing must return again!
" 'If thou withdraw thy breath, Behold, I am oblivion.'

"He ceas'd: the shadowy voice was silent: but the cloud hover'd over their heads
"In golden wreathes, the sorrow of Man, & the balmy drops fell down.
"And lo! that son of Man, that Shadowy Spirit of mild Albion,
"Luvah, descended from the cloud; in terror Albion rose:
"Indignant rose the awful Man & turn'd his back on Vala.

"We heard the voice of Albion starting from his sleep:

" 'Whence is this voice crying, Enion! that soundeth in my ears?
" 'O cruel pity! O dark deceit! can love seek for dominion?'

[1] *Emendation for* locks *of the original text.*

"And Luvah strove to gain dominion over Albion:
"They strove together above the Body where Vala was inclos'd
"And the dark Body of Albion left prostrate upon the crystal pavement,
"Cover'd with boils from head to foot, the terrible smitings of Luvah.
"Then frown'd the fallen Man and put forth Luvah from his presence,
"Saying, 'Go and Die the Death of Man for Vala the sweet wanderer.
" 'I will turn the volutions of your ears outward, and bend your nostrils
" 'Downward, and your fluxile eyes englob'd roll round in fear;
" 'Your with'ring lips and tongue shrink up into a narrow circle,
" 'Till into narrow forms you creep: go take your fiery way,
" 'And learn what 'tis to absorb the Man, you Spirits of Pity & Love.'

"They heard the voice and fled swift as the winter's setting sun.
"And now the human blood foam'd high; the Spirits Luvah & Vala
"Went down the Human Heart, where Paradise & its joys abounded,
"In jealous fears & fury & rage, & flames roll round their fervid feet,
"And the vast form of Nature like a serpent play'd before them.
"And as they fled in folding fires & thunders of the deep,
"Vala shrunk in like the dark sea that leaves its slimy banks;
"And from her bosom Luvah fell far as the east and west,
"And the vast form of Nature like a serpent roll'd between,
"Whether of Jerusalem's or Vala's ruins congenerated, we know not:
"All is confusion, all is tumult, & we alone are escaped."
So spoke the fugitives; they join'd the Divine Family, trembling.

Plate 30 [*44*]

And the Two that escaped were the Emanation of Los & his
Spectre; for where ever the Emanation goes, the Spectre
Attends her as her Guard, & Los's Emanation is named
Enitharmon, & his Spectre is named Urthona; they knew
Not where to flee: they had been on a visit to Albion's Children,
And they strove to weave a Shadow of the Emanation
To hide themselves, weeping & lamenting for the Vegetation
Of Albion's Children, fleeing thro' Albion's vales in streams of gore.

Being not irritated by insult, bearing insulting benevolences,
They percieved that corporeal friends are spiritual enemies:
They saw the Sexual Religion in its embryon Uncircumcision,
And the Divine hand was upon them, bearing them thro' darkness
Back safe to their Humanity, as doves to their windows.
Therefore the Sons of Eden praise Urthona's Spectre in Songs,
Because he kept the Divine Vision in time of trouble.

They wept & trembled, & Los put forth his hand & took them in,
Into his Bosom, from which Albion shrunk in dismal pain,
Rending the fibres of Brotherhood & in Feminine Allegories
Inclosing Los; but the Divine Vision appear'd with Los
Following Albion into his Central Void among his Oaks.

And Los prayed and said, "O Divine Saviour, arise
"Upon the Mountains of Albion as in ancient time! Behold!
"The Cities of Albion seek thy face: London groans in pain
"From Hill to Hill, & the Thames laments along the Valleys:
"The little Villages of Middlesex & Surrey hunger & thirst:
"The Twenty-eight Cities of Albion stretch their hands to thee
"Because of the Opressors of Albion in every City & Village.
"They mock at the Labourer's limbs: they mock at his starv'd Children:
"They buy his Daughters that they may have power to sell his Sons:
"They compell the Poor to live upon a crust of bread by soft mild arts:
"They reduce the Man to want, then give with pomp & ceremony:
"The praise of Jehovah is chaunted from lips of hunger & thirst.
"Humanity knows not of Sex: wherefore are Sexes in Beulah?
"In Beulah the Female lets down her beautiful Tabernacle
"Which the Male enters magnificent between her Cherubim
"And becomes One with her, mingling, condensing in Self-love
"The Rocky Law of Condemnation & double Generation & Death.
"Albion hath enter'd the Loins, the place of the Last Judgment,
"And Luvah hath drawn the Curtains around Albion in Vala's bosom.
"The Dead awake to Generation! Arise O Lord, & rend the Veil!"

So Los in lamentations follow'd Albion. Albion cover'd

Plate 31 [*45*]

His western heaven with rocky clouds of death & despair.

Fearing that Albion should turn his back against the Divine Vision,
Los took his globe of fire to search the interiors of Albion's
Bosom, in all the terrors of friendship entering the caves
Of despair & death to search the tempters out, walking among
Albion's rocks & precipices, caves of solitude & dark despair,
And saw every Minute Particular of Albion degraded & murder'd,
But saw not by whom; they were hidden within in the minute particulars
Of which they had possess'd themselves, and there they take up
The articulations of a man's soul and laughing throw it down

Into the frame, then knock it out upon the plank, & souls are bak'd
In bricks to build the pyramids of Heber & Terah. But Los
Search'd in vain; clos'd from the minutia, he walk'd difficult.
He came down from Highgate thro' Hackney & Holloway towards London
Till he came to old Stratford, & thence to Stepney & the Isle
Of Leutha's Dogs, thence thro' the narrows of the River's side,
And saw every minute particular: the jewels of Albion running down
The kennels of the streets & lanes as if they were abhorr'd:
Every Universal Form was become barren mountains of Moral
Virtue, and every Minute Particular harden'd into grains of sand,
And all the tendernesses of the soul cast forth as filth & mire:
Among the winding places of deep contemplation intricate,
To where the Tower of London frown'd dreadful over Jerusalem,
A building of Luvah, builded in Jerusalem's eastern gate, to be
His secluded Court: thence to Bethlehem, where was builded
Dens of despair in the house of bread, enquiring in vain
Of stones and rocks, he took his way, for human form was none;
And thus he spoke, looking on Albion's City with many tears:

"What shall I do? what could I do if I could find these Criminals?
"I could not dare to take vengeance, for all things are so constructed
"And builded by the Divine hand that the sinner shall always escape,
"And he who takes vengeance alone is the criminal of Providence.
"If I should dare to lay my finger on a grain of sand
"In way of vengeance, I punish the already punish'd. O whom
"Should I pity if I pity not the sinner who is gone astray?
"O Albion, if thou takest vengeance, if thou revengest thy wrongs,
"Thou art for ever lost! What can I do to hinder the Sons
"Of Albion from taking vengeance? or how shall I them perswade?"

So spoke Los, travelling thro' darkness & horrid solitude;
And he beheld Jerusalem in Westminster & Marybone
Among the ruins of the Temple, and Vala who is her Shadow,
Jerusalem's Shadow, bent northward over the Island white.
At length he sat on London Stone & heard Jerusalem's voice:

"Albion, I cannot be thy Wife; thine own Minute Particulars
"Belong to God alone, and all thy little ones are holy;
"They are of Faith & not of Demonstration; wherefore is Vala
"Cloth'd in black mourning upon my river's currents? Vala awake!
"I hear thy shuttles sing in the sky, and round my limbs
"I feel the iron threads of love & jealousy & despair."

Vala reply'd: "Albion is mine! Luvah gave me to Albion
"And now recieves reproach & hate. Was it not said of old,
" 'Set your Son before a man & he shall take you & your sons
" 'For slaves; but set your Daughter before a man & She
" 'Shall make him & his sons & daughters your slaves for ever?'
"And is this Faith? Behold the strife of Albion & Luvah
"Is great in the east, their spears of blood rage in the eastern heaven.
"Urizen is the champion of Albion; they will slay my Luvah,
"And thou, O harlot daughter, daughter of despair, art all
"This cause of these shakings of my towers on Euphrates.
"Here is the House of Albion & here is thy secluded place,
"And here we have found thy sins; & hence we turn thee forth
"For all to avoid thee, to be astonish'd at thee for thy sins,
"Because thou art the impurity & the harlot, & thy children,
"Children of whoredoms, born for Sacrifice, for the meat & drink
"Offering, to sustain the glorious combat & the battle & war,
"That Man may be purified by the death of thy delusions."

So saying she her dark threads cast over the trembling River
And over the valleys, from the hills of Hertfordshire to the hills
Of Surrey across Middlesex, & across Albion's House
Of Eternity; pale stood Albion at his eastern gate,

Plate 32 [*46*]

Leaning against the pillars, & his disease rose from his skirts:
Upon the Precipice he stood, ready to fall into Non-Entity.

Los was all astonishment & terror, he trembled sitting on the Stone
Of London; but the interiors of Albion's fibres & nerves were hidden
From Los, astonish'd he beheld only the petrified surfaces
And saw his Furnaces in ruins, for Los is the Demon of the Furnaces;
He saw also the Four Points of Albion revers'd inwards.
He siez'd his Hammer & Tongs, his iron Poker & his Bellows,
Upon the valleys of Middlesex, Shouting loud for aid Divine.

In stern defiance came from Albion's bosom, Hand, Hyle, Koban,
Gwantok, Peachy, Brertun, Slaid, Huttn, Skofeld, Kock, Kotope,
Bowen, Albion's Sons; they bore him a golden couch into the porch
And on the Couch repos'd his limbs trembling from the bloody field,
Rearing their Druid Patriarchal rocky Temples around his limbs.
(All things begin & end in Albion's Ancient Druid Rocky Shore.)

Plate 33 [*29*]

Turning his back to the Divine Vision, his Spectrous
Chaos before his face appear'd, an Unformed Memory.

Then spoke the Spectrous Chaos to Albion, dark'ning cold,
From the back & loins where dwell the Spectrous Dead:

"I am your Rational Power, O Albion, & that Human Form
"You call Divine is but a Worm seventy inches long
"That creeps forth in a night & is dried in the morning sun,
"In fortuitous concourse of memorys accumulated & lost.
"It plows the Earth in its own conceit, it overwhelms the Hills
"Beneath its winding labyrinths, till a stone of the brook
"Stops it in midst of its pride among its hills & rivers.
"Battersea & Chelsea mourn, London & Canterbury tremble:
"Their place shall not be found as the wind passes over.
"The ancient Cities of the Earth remove as a traveller,
"And shall Albion's Cities remain when I pass over them
"With my deluge of forgotten remembrances over the tablet?"

So spoke the Spectre to Albion: he is the Great Selfhood,
Satan, Worship'd as God by the Mighty Ones of the Earth,
Having a white Dot call'd a Center, from which branches out
A Circle in continual gyrations: this became a Heart
From which sprang numerous branches varying their motions,
Producing many heads, three or seven or ten, & hands & feet
Innumerable at will of the unfortunate contemplator
Who becomes his food: such is the way of the Devouring Power.

And this is the cause of the appearance in the frowning Chaos:
Albion's Emanation, which he had hidden in Jealousy,
Appear'd now in the frowning Chaos, prolific upon the Chaos,
Reflecting back to Albion in Sexual Reasoning Hermaphroditic.

Albion spoke: "Who art thou that appearest in gloomy pomp
"Involving the Divine Vision in colours of autumn ripeness?
"I never saw thee till this time, nor beheld life abstracted,
"Nor darkness immingled with light on my furrow'd field.
"Whence camest thou? who art thou, O loveliest? the Divine Vision
"Is as nothing before thee: faded is all life and joy."

Vala replied in clouds of tears, Albion's garment embracing:

"I was a City & a Temple built by Albion's Children.
"I was a Garden planted with beauty. I allured on hill & valley

"The River of Life to flow against my walls & among my trees.
"Vala was Albion's Bride & Wife in great Eternity,
"The loveliest of the daughters of Eternity when in day-break
"I emanated from Luvah over the Towers of Jerusalem,
"And in her Courts among her little Children offering up
"The Sacrifice of fanatic love! why loved I Jerusalem?
"Why was I one with her, embracing in the Vision of Jesus?
"Wherefore did I, loving, create love, which never yet
"Immingled God & Man, when thou & I hid the Divine Vision
"In cloud of secret gloom which, behold, involve[s] me round about?
"Know me now Albion: look upon me. I alone am Beauty.
"The Imaginative Human Form is but a breathing of Vala:
"I breathe him forth into the Heaven from my secret Cave,
"Born of the Woman, to obey the Woman, O Albion the mighty,
"For the Divine appearance is Brotherhood, but I am Love

Plate 34 [*30*]

"Elevate into the Region of Brotherhood with my red fires."

"Art thou Vala?" replied Albion, "image of my repose!
"O how I tremble! how my members pour down milky fear!
"A dewy garment covers me all over, all manhood is gone!
"At thy word & at thy look, death enrobes me about
"From head to feet, a garment of death & eternal fear.
"Is not that Sun thy husband & that Moon thy glimmering Veil?
"Are not the Stars of heaven thy Children? art thou not Babylon?
"Art thou Nature, Mother of all? is Jerusalem thy Daughter?
"Why have thou elevate inward, O dweller of outward chambers,
"From grot & cave beneath the Moon, dim region of death
"Where I laid my Plow in the hot noon, where my hot team fed,
"Where implements of War are forged, the Plow to go over the Nations,
"In pain girding me round like a rib of iron in heaven? O Vala!
"In Eternity they neither marry nor are given in marriage.
"Albion, the high Cliff of the Atlantic, is become a barren Land."

Los stood at his Anvil: he heard the contentions of Vala;
He heav'd his thund'ring Bellows upon the valleys of Middlesex,
He open'd his Furnaces before Vala; then Albion frown'd in anger
On his Rock, ere yet the Starry Heavens were fled away
From his awful Members; and thus Los cried aloud
To the Sons of Albion & to Hand the eldest Son of Albion:

"I hear the screech of Childbirth loud pealing, & the groans
"Of Death in Albion's clouds dreadful utter'd over all the Earth.
"What may Man be? who can tell! but what may Woman be
"To have power over Man from Cradle to corruptible Grave?
"There is a Throne in every Man, it is the Throne of God;
"This, Woman has claim'd as her own, & Man is no more!
"Albion is the Tabernacle of Vala & her Temple,
"And not the Tabernacle & Temple of the Most High.
"O Albion, why wilt thou Create a Female Will?
"To hide the most evident God in a hidden covert, even
"In the shadows of a Woman & a secluded Holy Place,
"That we may pry after him as after a stolen treasure,
"Hidden among the Dead & mured up from the paths of life.
"Hand! art thou not Reuben enrooting thyself into Bashan
"Till thou remainest a vaporous Shadow in a Void? O Merlin!
"Unknown among the Dead where never before Existence came,
"Is this the Female Will, O ye lovely Daughters of Albion, To
"Converse concerning Weight & Distance in the Wilds of Newton
& Locke?"

So Los spoke, standing on Mam-Tor, looking over Europe & Asia.
The Graves thunder beneath his feet from Ireland to Japan.

Reuben slept in Bashan like one dead in the valley
Cut off from Albion's mountains & from all the Earth's summits
Between Succoth & Zaretan beside the Stone of Bohan,
While the Daughters of Albion divided Luvah into three Bodies.
Los bended his Nostrils down to the Earth, then sent him over
Jordan to the Land of the Hittite; every-one that saw him
Fled! they fled at his horrible Form: they hid in caves
And dens; they looked on one-another & became what they beheld.

Reuben return'd to Bashan; in despair he slept on the Stone.
Then Gwendolen divided into Rahab & Tirza in Twelve Portions.
Los rolled his Eyes into two narrow circles, then sent him
Over Jordan; all terrified fled: they became what they beheld.

If Perceptive Organs vary, Objects of Perception seem to vary:
If the Perceptive Organs close, their Objects seem to close also.
"Consider this, O mortal Man, O worm of sixty winters," said Los,
"Consider Sexual Organization & hide thee in the dust."

Plate 35 [*31*]

Then the Divine hand found the Two Limits, Satan and Adam,
In Albion's bosom, for in every Human bosom those Limits stand,
And the Divine voice came from the Furnaces, as multitudes without
Number, the voices of the innumerable multitudes of Eternity!
And the appearance of a Man was seen in the Furnaces
Saving those who have sinned from the punishment of the Law
(In pity of the punisher whose state is eternal death)
And keeping them from Sin by the mild counsels of his love:

"Albion goes to Eternal Death. In Me all Eternity
"Must pass thro' condemnation and awake beyond the Grave.
"No individual can keep these Laws, for they are death
"To every energy of man and forbid the springs of life.
"Albion hath enter'd the State Satan! Be permanent, O State!
"And be thou for ever accursed! that Albion may arise again.
"And be thou created into a State! I go forth to Create
"States, to deliver Individuals evermore! Amen."

So spoke the voice from the Furnaces, descending into Non-Entity.
To Govern the Evil by Good and . . . abolish Systems

Plate 36 [*32*]

Reuben return'd to his place; in vain he sought beautiful Tirzah,
For his Eyelids were narrow'd & his Nostrils scented the ground.
And Sixty Winters Los raged in the Divisions of Reuben,
Building the Moon of Ulro plank by plank & rib by rib.
Reuben slept in the Cave of Adam, and Los folded his Tongue
Between Lips of mire & clay, then sent him forth over Jordan.
In the love of Tirzah he said: "Doubt is my food day & night."
All that beheld him fled howling and gnawed their tongues
For pain: they became what they beheld. In reasonings Reuben returned
To Heshbon: disconsolate he walk'd thro' Moab & he stood
Before the Furnaces of Los in a horrible dreamful slumber
On Mount Gilead looking toward Gilgal: and Los bended
His Ear in a spiral circle outward, then sent him over Jordan.

The Seven Nations fled before him: they became what they beheld.
Hand, Hyle & Coban fled: they became what they beheld.
Gwantock & Peachy hid in Damascus beneath Mount Lebanon,
Brereton & Slade in Egypt: Hutton & Skofeld & Kox

Fled over Chaldea in terror, in pains in every nerve.
Kotope & Bowen became what they beheld, fleeing over the Earth,
And the Twelve Female Emanations fled with them, agonizing.

Jerusalem trembled seeing her Children driv'n by Los's Hammer
In the visions of the dreams of Beulah on the edge of Non-Entity.
Hand stood between Reuben & Merlin, as the Reasoning Spectre
Stands between the Vegetative Man & his Immortal Imagination.

And the Four Zoas clouded rage East & West & North & South;
They change their situations in the Universal Man.
Albion groans, he sees the Elements divide before his face,
And England, who is Brittannia, divided into Jerusalem & Vala;
And Urizen assumes the East, Luvah assumes the South,
In his dark Spectre ravening from his open Sepulcher.

And the Four Zoas, who are the Four Eternal Senses of Man,
Became Four Elements separating from the Limbs of Albion:
These are their names in the Vegetative Generation:
[*one line erased from the plate*]
And Accident & Chance were found hidden in Length, Bredth & Highth,
And they divided into Four ravening deathlike Forms,
Fairies & Genii & Nymphs & Gnomes of the Elements:
These are States Permanently Fixed by the Divine Power.
The Atlantic Continent sunk round Albion's cliffy shore,
And the Sea poured in amain upon the Giants of Albion
As Los bended the Senses of Reuben. Reuben is Merlin
Exploring the Three States of Ulro: Creation, Redemption & Judgment.

And many of the Eternal Ones laughed after their manner:

"Have you known the Judgment that is arisen among the
"Zoas of Albion, where a Man dare hardly to embrace
"His own Wife for the terrors of Chastity that they call
"By the name of Morality? their Daughters govern all
"In hidden deceit! they are vegetable, only fit for burning.
"Art & Science cannot exist but by Naked Beauty display'd."

Then those in Great Eternity who contemplate on Death
Said thus: "What seems to Be, Is, To those to whom
"It seems to Be, & is productive of the most dreadful
"Consequences to those to whom it seems to Be, even of
"Torments, Despair, Eternal Death; but the Divine Mercy

"Steps beyond and Redeems Man in the Body of Jesus. Amen.
"And Length, Bredth, Highth again Obey the Divine Vision. Hallelujah."

Plate 37 [*33*]

And One stood forth from the Divine family & said:
"I feel my Spectre rising upon me! Albion! arouze thyself!
"Why dost thou thunder with frozen Spectrous wrath against us?
"The Spectre is, in Giant Man, insane and most deform'd.
"Thou wilt certainly provoke my Spectre against thine in fury!
"He has a Sepulcher hewn out of a Rock ready for thee,
"And a Death of Eight thousand years, forg'd by thyself, upon
"The point of his Spear, if thou persistest to forbid with Laws
"Our Emanations and to attack our secret supreme delights."

So Los spoke. But when he saw [pale *altered to*] blue death in Albion's feet
Again he join'd the Divine Body, following merciful,
While Albion fled more indignant, revengeful covering

Plate 38 [*34*]

His face and bosom with petrific hardness, and his hands
And feet, lest any should enter his bosom & embrace
His hidden heart; his Emanation wept & trembled within him,
Uttering not his jealousy but hiding it as with
Iron and steel, dark and opake, with clouds & tempests brooding;
His strong limbs shudder'd upon his mountains high and dark

Turning from Universal Love, petrific as he went,
His cold against the warmth of Eden rag'd with loud
Thunders of deadly war (the fever of the human soul)
Fires and clouds of rolling smoke! but mild, the Saviour follow'd him,
Displaying the Eternal Vision, the Divine Similitude,
In loves and tears of brothers, sisters, sons, fathers and friends,
Which if Man ceases to behold, he ceases to exist,

Saying, "Albion! Our wars are wars of life, & wounds of love
"With intellectual spears, & long winged arrows of thought.
"Mutual in one another's love and wrath all renewing
"We live as One Man; for contracting our infinite senses
"We behold multitude, or expanding, we behold as one,
"As One Man all the Universal Family, and that One Man

"We call Jesus the Christ; and he in us, and we in him
"Live in perfect harmony in Eden, the land of life,
"Giving, recieving, and forgiving each other's trespasses.
"He is the Good shepherd, he is the Lord and master,
"He is the Shepherd of Albion, he is all in all,
"In Eden, in the garden of God, and in heavenly Jerusalem.
"If we have offended, forgive us; take not vengeance against us."

Thus speaking, the Divine Family follow Albion.
I see them in the Vision of God upon my pleasant valleys.

I behold London, a Human awful wonder of God!
He says: "Return, Albion, return! I give myself for thee.
"My Streets are my Ideas of Imagination.
"Awake Albion, awake! and let us awake up together.
"My Houses are Thoughts: my Inhabitants, Affections,
"The children of my thoughts walking within my blood-vessels,
"Shut from my nervous form which sleeps upon the verge of Beulah
"In dreams of darkness, while my vegetating blood in veiny pipes
"Rolls dreadful thro' the Furnaces of Los and the Mills of Satan.
"For Albion's sake and for Jerusalem thy Emanation
"I give myself, and these my brethren give themselves for Albion."

So spoke London, immortal Guardian! I heard in Lambeth's shades.
In Felpham I heard and saw the Visions of Albion.
I write in South Molton Street what I both see and hear
In regions of Humanity, in London's opening streets.

I see thee, awful Parent Land in light, behold I see!
Verulam! Canterbury! venerable parent of men,
Generous immortal Guardian, golden clad! for Cities
Are Men, fathers of multitudes, and Rivers & Mountains
Are also Men; every thing is Human, mighty! sublime!
In every bosom a Universe expands as wings,
Let down at will around and call'd the Universal Tent.
York, crown'd with loving kindness, Edinburgh, cloth'd
With fortitude, as with a garment of immortal texture
Woven in looms of Eden, in spiritual deaths of mighty men
Who give themselves in Golgotha, Victims to Justice, where
There is in Albion a Gate of Precious stones and gold
Seen only by Emanations, by vegetations viewless:
Bending across the road of Oxford Street, it from Hyde Park
To Tyburn's deathful shades admits the wandering souls
Of multitudes who die from Earth: this Gate cannot be found

Plate 39 [*35*]

By Satan's Watch-fiends, tho' they search numbering every grain
Of sand on Earth every night, they never find this Gate.
It is the Gate of Los. Withoutside is the Mill, intricate, dreadful
And fill'd with cruel tortures; but no mortal man can find the Mill
Of Satan in his mortal pilgrimage of seventy years,
For Human beauty knows it not, nor can Mercy find it! But
In the Fourth region of Humanity, Urthona nam'd,
Mortality begins to roll the billows of Eternal Death
Before the Gate of Los. Urthona here is named Los,
And here begins the System of Moral Virtue named Rahab.
Albion fled thro' the Gate of Los and he stood in the Gate.

Los was the friend of Albion who most lov'd him. In Cambridgeshire
His eternal station, he is the twenty-eighth & is four-fold.
Seeing Albion had turn'd his back against the Divine Vision,
Los said to Albion: "Whither fleest thou?" Albion reply'd:

"I die! I go to Eternal Death! the shades of death
"Hover within me & beneath, and spreading themselves outside
"Like rocky clouds, build me a gloomy monument of woe.
"Will none accompany me in my death, or be a Ransom for me
"In that dark Valley? I have girded round my cloke, and on my feet
"Bound these black shoes of death, & on my hands, death's iron gloves.
"God hath forsaken me & my friends are become a burden,
"A weariness to me, & the human footstep is a terror to me."

Los answered troubled, and his soul was rent in twain:
"Must the Wise die for an Atonement? does Mercy endure Atonement?
"No! It is Moral Severity & destroys Mercy in its Victim."
So speaking, not yet infected with the Error & Illusion,

Plate 40 [*36*]

Los shudder'd at beholding Albion, for his disease
Arose upon him pale and ghastly, and he call'd around
The Friends of Albion; trembling at the sight of Eternal Death
The four appear'd with their Emanations in fiery
Chariots: black their fires roll, beholding Albion's House of Eternity:
Damp couch the flames beneath and silent sick, stand shuddering
Before the Porch of sixteen pillars; weeping every one
Descended and fell down upon their knees round Albion's knees,
Swearing the Oath of God with awful voice of thunders round
Upon the hills & valleys, and the cloudy Oath roll'd far and wide.

"Albion is sick!" said every Valley, every mournful Hill
And every River: "our brother Albion is sick to death.
"He hath leagued himself with robbers: he hath studied the arts
"Of unbelief. Envy hovers over him: his Friends are his abhorrence:
"Those who give their lives for him are despised:
"Those who devour his soul are taken into his bosom:
"To destroy his Emanation is their intention.
"Arise! awake, O Friends of the Giant Albion!
"They have perswaded him of horrible falsehoods:
"They have sown errors over all his fruitful fields!"

The Twenty-four heard! they came trembling on wat'ry chariots
Borne by the Living Creatures of the third procession
Of Human Majesty: the Living Creatures wept aloud, as they
Went along Albion's roads, till they arriv'd at Albion's House.

O! how the torments of Eternal Death waited on Man,
And the loud-rending bars of the Creation ready to burst,
That the wide world might fly from its hinges & the immortal mansion
Of Man for ever be possess'd by monsters of the deeps,
And Man himself become a Fiend, wrap'd in an endless curse,
Consuming and consum'd for-ever in flames of Moral Justice.

For had the Body of Albion fall'n down and from its dreadful ruins
Let loose the enormous Spectre on the darkness of the deep
At enmity with the Merciful & fill'd with devouring fire,
A nether-world must have reciev'd the foul enormous spirit
Under pretence of Moral Virtue, fill'd with Revenge and Law,
There to eternity chain'd down and issuing in red flames
And curses, with his mighty arms brandish'd against the heavens,
Breathing cruelty, blood & vengeance, gnashing his teeth with pain,
Torn with black storms & ceaseless torrents of his own consuming fire,
Within his breast his mighty Sons chain'd down & fill'd with cursings,
And his dark Eon, that once fair crystal form divinely clear,
Within his ribs producing serpents whose souls are flames of fire.
But glory to the Merciful One, for he is of tender mercies!
And the Divine Family wept over him as One Man.

And these the Twenty-four in whom the Divine Family
Appear'd; and they were One in Him. A Human Vision!
Human Divine, Jesus the Saviour, blessed for ever and ever.

Selsey, true friend! who afterwards submitted to be devour'd
By the waves of Despair, whose Emanation rose above
The flood and was nam'd Chichester, lovely mild & gentle! Lo!
Her lambs bleat to the sea-fowls' cry, lamenting still for Albion.

Submitting to be call'd the son of Los, the terrible vision,
Winchester stood devoting himself for Albion, his tents
Outspread with abundant riches, and his Emanations
Submitting to be call'd Enitharmon's daughters and be born
In vegetable mould, created by the Hammer and Loom
In Bowlahoola & Allamanda where the Dead wail night & day.

(I call them by their English names: English, the rough basement.
Los built the stubborn structure of the Language, acting against
Albion's melancholy, who must else have been a Dumb despair.)

Gloucester and Exeter and Salisbury and Bristol, and benevolent
Bath,

Plate 41 [*37*]

Bath who is Legions; he is the Seventh, the physician and
The poisoner, the best and worst in Heaven and Hell,
Whose Spectre first assimilated with Luvah in Albion's mountains,
A triple octave he took, to reduce Jerusalem to twelve,
To cast Jerusalem forth upon the wilds to Poplar & Bow,
To Malden & Canterbury in the delights of cruelty.
The Shuttles of death sing in the sky to Islington & Pancrass,
Round Marybone to Tyburn's River, weaving black melancholy as a
net,
And despair as meshes closely wove over the west of London
Where mild Jerusalem sought to repose in death & be no more.
She fled to Lambeth's mild Vale and hid herself beneath
The Surrey Hills where Rephaim terminates: her Sons are siez'd
For victims of sacrifice; but Jerusalem cannot be found, Hid
By the Daughters of Beulah, gently snatch'd away and hid in Beulah.

There is a Grain of Sand in Lambeth that Satan cannot find,
Nor can his Watch Fiends find it; 'tis translucent & has many Angles,
But he who finds it will find Oothoon's palace; for within
Opening into Beulah, every angle is a lovely heaven.
But should the Watch Fiends find it, they would call it Sin
And lay its Heavens & their inhabitants in blood of punishment.
Here Jerusalem & Vala were hid in soft slumberous repose,
Hid from the terrible East, shut up in the South & West.

The Twenty-eight trembled in Death's dark caves; in cold despair
They kneel'd around the Couch of Death, in deep humiliation
And tortures of self condemnation, while their Spectres rag'd within.
The Four Zoas in terrible combustion clouded rage,

Drinking the shuddering fears & loves of Albion's Families,
Destroying by selfish affections the things that they most admire,
Drinking & eating, & pitying & weeping as at a trajic scene
The soul drinks murder & revenge & applauds its own holiness.

They saw Albion endeavouring to destroy their Emanations.

Plate 42

Thus Albion sat, studious of others in his pale disease,
Brooding on evil; but when Los open'd the Furnaces before him
He saw that the accursed things were his own affections
And his own beloveds; then he turn'd sick: his soul died within him
Also Los, sick & terrified, beheld the Furnaces of Death
And must have died, but the Divine Saviour descended
Among the infant loves & affections, and the Divine Vision wept
Like evening dew on every herb upon the breathing ground.

Albion spoke in his dismal dreams: "O thou deceitful friend,
"Worshipping mercy & beholding thy friend in such affliction!
"Los! thou now discoverest thy turpitude to the heavens.
"I demand righteousness & justice. O thou ingratitude!

"Give me my Emanations back, food for my dying soul.
"My daughters are harlots: my sons are accursed before me.
"Enitharmon is my daughter, accursed with a father's curse.
"O! I have utterly been wasted. I have given my daughters to devils."

So spoke Albion in gloomy majesty, and deepest night
Of Ulro roll'd round his skirts from Dover to Cornwall.

Los answer'd: "Righteousness & justice I give thee in return
"For thy righteousness, but I add mercy also and bind
"Thee from destroying these little ones; am I to be only
"Merciful to thee and cruel to all that thou hatest?
"Thou wast the Image of God surrounded by the Four Zoas.
"Three thou hast slain. I am the Fourth: thou canst not destroy me.
"Thou art in Error; trouble me not with thy righteousness.
"I have innocence to defend and ignorance to instruct:
"I have no time for seeming and little arts of compliment
"In morality and virtue, in self-glorying and pride.
"There is a limit of Opakeness and a limit of Contraction
"In every Individual Man, and the limit of Opakeness
"Is named Satan, and the limit of Contraction is named Adam.
"But when Man sleeps in Beulah, the Saviour in Mercy takes
"Contraction's Limit, and of the Limit he forms Woman, That
"Himself may in process of time be born Man to redeem.
"But there is no Limit of Expansion; there is no Limit of Translucence
"In the bosom of Man for ever from eternity to eternity.
"Therefore I break thy bonds of righteousness. I crush thy messengers,
"That they may not crush me and mine; do thou be righteous
"And I will return it; otherwise I defy thy worst revenge.
"Consider me as thine enemy: on me turn all thy fury;
"But destroy not these little ones, nor mock the Lord's anointed:
"Destroy not by Moral Virtue the little ones whom he hath chosen,
"The little ones whom he hath chosen in preference to thee.
"He hath cast thee off for ever: the little ones he hath anointed!
"Thy Selfhood is for ever accursed from the Divine presence."

So Los spoke, then turn'd his face & wept for Albion.

Albion replied: "Go, Hand & Hyle! sieze the abhorred friend
"As you have siez'd the Twenty-four rebellious ingratitudes
"To atone for you, for spiritual death. Man lives by deaths of Men.
"Bring him to justice before heaven here upon London stone,
"Between Blackheath & Hounslow, between Norwood & Finchley.

"All that they have is mine: from my free gen'rous gift
"They now hold all they have; ingratitude to me,
"To me their benefactor, calls aloud for vengeance deep."

Los stood before his Furnaces awaiting the fury of the Dead,
And the Divine hand was upon him, strengthening him mightily.

The Spectres of the Dead cry out from the deeps beneath
Upon the hills of Albion; Oxford groans in his iron furnace,
Winchester in his den & cavern; they lament against
Albion: they curse their human kindness & affection:
They rage like wild beasts in the forests of affliction:
In the dreams of Ulro they repent of their human kindness.

"Come up, build Babylon, Rahab is ours & all her multitudes
"With her, in pomp and glory of victory. Depart,
"Ye twenty-four, into the deeps; let us depart to glory!"

Their Human majestic Forms sit up upon their Couches
Of death; they curb their Spectres as with iron curbs:
They enquire after Jerusalem in the regions of the dead
With the voices of dead men, low, scarcely articulate,
And with tears cold on their cheeks they weary repose.

"O when shall the morning of the grave appear, and when
"Shall our salvation come? we sleep upon our watch,
"We cannot awake, and our Spectres rage in the forests.
"O God of Albion, where art thou? pity the watchers!"

Thus mourn they. Loud the Furnaces of Los thunder upon
The clouds of Europe & Asia among the Serpent Temples.

And Los drew his Seven Furnaces around Albion's Altars;
And as Albion built his frozen Altars, Los built the Mundane Shell
In the Four Regions of Humanity, East & West & North & South,
Till Norwood & Finchley & Blackheath & Hounslow cover'd the whole Earth.
This is the Net & Veil of Vala among the Souls of the Dead.

Plate 43 [*38*]

They saw their Wheels rising up poisonous against Albion:
Urizen cold & scientific, Luvah pitying & weeping,
Tharmas indolent & sullen, Urthona doubting & despairing,
Victims to one another & dreadfully plotting against each other
To prevent Albion walking about in the Four Complexions.

They saw America clos'd out by the Oaks of the western shore,
And Tharmas dash'd on the Rocks of the Altars of Victims in Mexico.
"If we are wrathful, Albion will destroy Jerusalem with rooty Groves:
"If we are merciful, ourselves must suffer destruction on his Oaks.
"Why should we enter into our Spectres to behold our own corruptions?
"O God of Albion, descend! deliver Jerusalem from the Oaken Groves!"

Then Los grew furious, raging: "Why stand we here trembling around
"Calling on God for help, and not ourselves, in whom God dwells,
"Stretching a hand to save the falling Man? are we not Four
"Beholding Albion upon the Precipice ready to fall into Non-Entity?
"Seeing these Heavens & Hells conglobing in the Void, Heavens over Hells
"Brooding in holy hypocritic lust, drinking the cries of pain
"From howling victims of Law, building Heavens Twenty-seven-fold,
"Swell'd & bloated General Forms repugnant to the Divine-
"Humanity who is the Only General and Universal Form,
"To which all Lineaments tend & seek with love & sympathy.
"All broad & general principles belong to benevolence
"Who protects minute particulars every one in their own identity;
"But here the affectionate touch of the tongue is clos'd in by deadly teeth,
"And the soft smile of friendship & the open dawn of benevolence
"Become a net & a trap, & every energy render'd cruel,
"Till the existence of friendship & benevolence is denied:
"The wine of the Spirit & the vineyards of the Holy-One
"Here turn into poisonous stupor & deadly intoxication,
"That they may be condemn'd by Law & the Lamb of God be slain;
"And the two Sources of Life in Eternity, Hunting and War,
"Are become the Sources of dark & bitter Death & of corroding Hell.
"The open heart is shut up in integuments of frozen silence
"That the spear that lights it forth may shatter the ribs & bosom.
"A pretence of Art to destroy Art; a pretence of Liberty
"To destroy Liberty; a pretence of Religion to destroy Religion.
"Oshea and Caleb fight: they contend in the valleys of (of) Peor,
"In the terrible Family Contentions of those who love each other.
"The Armies of Balaam weep—no women come to the field:
"Dead corses lay before them, & not as in Wars of old;
"For the Soldier who fights for Truth calls his enemy his brother:
"They fight & contend for life & not for eternal death;
"But here the Soldier strikes, & a dead corse falls at his feet,

"Nor Daughter nor Sister nor Mother come forth to embosom the Slain;
"But Death, Eternal Death, remains in the Valleys of Peor.
"The English are scatter'd over the face of the Nations: are these
"Jerusalem's children? Hark! hear the Giants of Albion cry at night:
" 'We smell the blood of the English! we delight in their blood on our Altars.
" 'The living & the dead shall be ground in our rumbling Mills
" 'For bread of the Sons of Albion, of the Giants Hand & Scofield.'
"Scofeld & Kox are let loose upon my Saxons! they accumulate
"A World in which Man is by his Nature the Enemy of Man,
"In pride of Selfhood unwieldy stretching out into Non Entity,
"Generalizing Art & Science till Art & Science is lost.
"Bristol & Bath, listen to my words, & ye Seventeen, give ear!
"It is easy to acknowledge a man to be great & good while we
"Derogate from him in the trifles & small articles of that goodness.
"Those alone are his friends who admire his minutest powers.
"Instead of Albion's lovely mountains & the curtains of Jerusalem,
"I see a Cave, a Rock, a Tree deadly and poisonous, unimaginative.
"Instead of the Mutual Forgivenesses, the Minute Particulars, I see
"Pits of bitumen ever burning, artificial Riches of the Canaanite
"Like Lakes of liquid lead: instead of heavenly Chapels built
"By our dear Lord, I see Worlds crusted with snows & ice.
"I see a Wicker Idol woven round Jerusalem's children. I see
"The Canaanite, the Amalekite, the Moabite, the Egyptian,
"By Demonstrations the cruel Sons of Quality & Negation,
"Driven on the Void in incoherent despair into Non Entity.
"I see America clos'd apart, & Jerusalem driven in terror
"Away from Albion's mountains, far away from London's spires.
"I will not endure this thing! I alone withstand to death
"This outrage! Ah me! how sick & pale you all stand round me!
"Ah me! pitiable ones! do you also go to death's vale?
"All you my Friends & Brothers, all you my beloved Companions,
"Have you also caught the infection of Sin & stern Repentance?
"I see Disease arise upon you! yet speak to me and give
"Me some comfort! why do you all stand silent? I alone
"Remain in permanent strength. Or is all this goodness & pity only
"That you may take the greater vengeance in your Sepulcher?"

So Los spoke. Pale they stood around the House of Death,
In the midst of temptations & despair, among the rooted Oaks,
Among reared Rocks of Albion's Sons; at length they rose

Plate 44 [*39*]

With one accord in love sublime, &, as on Cherubs' wings,
They Albion surround with kindest violence to bear him back
Against his will thro' Los's Gate to Eden. Four-fold, loud,
Their Wings waving over the bottomless Immense, to bear
Their awful charge back to his native home; but Albion dark,
Repugnant, roll'd his Wheels backward into Non-Entity.
Loud roll the Starry Wheels of Albion into the World of Death,
And all the Gate of Los, clouded with clouds redounding from
Albion's dread Wheels, stretching out spaces immense between,
That every little particle of light & air became Opake,
Black & immense, a Rock of difficulty & a Cliff
Of black despair, that the immortal Wings labour'd against
Cliff after cliff & over Valleys of despair & death.
The narrow Sea between Albion & the Atlantic Continent,
Its waves of pearl became a boundless Ocean bottomless,
Of grey obscurity, fill'd with clouds & rocks & whirling waters,
And Albion's Sons ascending & descending in the horrid Void.

But as the Will must not be bended but in the day of Divine
Power, silent calm & motionless in the mid-air sublime
The Family Divine hover around the darken'd Albion.

Such is the nature of the Ulro, that whatever enters
Becomes Sexual & is Created and Vegetated and Born.
From Hyde Park spread their vegetating roots beneath Albion,
In dreadful pain the Spectrous Uncircumcised Vegetation
Forming a Sexual Machine, an Aged Virgin Form,

In Erin's Land toward the north, joint after joint, & burning
In love & jealousy immingled, & calling it Religion.
And feeling the damps of death, they with one accord delegated Los,
Conjuring him by the Highest that he should Watch over them
Till Jesus shall appear; & they gave their power to Los
Naming him the Spirit of Prophecy, calling him Elijah.

Strucken with Albion's disease, they become what they behold.
They assimilate with Albion in pity & compassion.
Their Emanations return not: their Spectres rage in the Deep.
The Slumbers of Death came over them around the Couch of Death,
Before the Gate of Los & in the depths of Non Entity,
Among the Furnaces of Los, among the Oaks of Albion.

Man is adjoin'd to Man by his Emanative portion
Who is Jerusalem in every individual Man, and her
Shadow is Vala, builded by the Reasoning power in Man.
O search & see: turn your eyes inward: open, O thou World
Of Love & Harmony in Man: expand thy ever lovely Gates!

They wept into the deeps a little space; at length was heard
The voice of Bath, faint as the voice of the Dead in the House of
Death,

Plate 45 [*40*]

Bath, healing City! whose wisdom, in midst of Poetic
Fervor, mild spoke thro' the Western Porch in soft gentle tears:

"O Albion, mildest Son of Eden! clos'd is thy Western Gate.
"Brothers of Eternity, this Man whose great example
"We all admir'd & lov'd, whose all benevolent countenance seen
"In Eden, in lovely Jerusalem, drew even from envy
"The tear, and the confession of honesty open & undisguis'd
"From mistrust and suspition: The Man is himself become
"A piteous example of oblivion, To teach the Sons
"Of Eden that however great and glorious, however loving
"And merciful the Individuality, however high
"Our palaces and cities and however fruitful are our fields,
"In Selfhood, we are nothing, but fade away in morning's breath.
"Our mildness is nothing: the greatest mildness we can use
"Is incapable and nothing: none but the Lamb of God can heal
"This dread disease, none but Jesus. O Lord, descend and save!
"Albion's Western Gate is clos'd: his death is coming apace.
"Jesus alone can save him; for alas, we none can know
"How soon his lot may be our own. When Africa in sleep
"Rose in the night of Beulah and bound down the Sun & Moon,
"His friends cut his strong chains & overwhelm'd his dark
"Machines in fury & destruction, and the Man reviving repented:
"He wept before his wrathful brethren, thankful & considerate
"For their well timed wrath. But Albion's sleep is not
"Like Africa's, and his machines are woven with his life.
"Nothing but mercy can save him! nothing but mercy interposing
"Lest he should slay Jerusalem in his fearful jealousy.
"O God, descend! gather our brethren: deliver Jerusalem!
"But that we may omit no office of the friendly spirit,
"Oxford, take thou these leaves of the Tree of Life; with eloquence
"That thy immortal tongue inspires, present them to Albion:
"Perhaps he may recieve them, offer'd from thy loved hands."

So spoke, unheard by Albion, the merciful Son of Heaven
To those whose Western Gates were open, as they stood weeping
Around Albion; but Albion heard him not: obdurate, hard,
He frown'd on all his Friends, counting them enemies in his sorrow.

And the Seventeen conjoining with Bath, the Seventh
In whom the other Ten shone manifest a Divine Vision,
Assimilated and embrac'd Eternal Death for Albion's sake.

And these the names of the Eighteen combining with those Ten:

Plate 46 [*41*]

Bath, mild Physician of Eternity, mysterious power
Whose springs are unsearchable & knowledge infinite:
Hereford, ancient Guardian of Wales, whose hands
Builded the mountain palaces of Eden, stupendous works!
Lincoln, Durham & Carlisle, Councellors of Los,
And Ely, Scribe of Los, whose pen no other hand
Dare touch: Oxford, immortal Bard, with eloquence
Divine he wept over Albion speaking the words of God
In mild perswasion, bringing leaves of the Tree of Life:

"Thou art in Error, Albion, the Land of Ulro.
"One Error not remov'd will destroy a human Soul.
"Repose in Beulah's night till the Error is remov'd.
"Reason not on both sides. Repose upon our bosoms
"Till the Plow of Jehovah and the Harrow of Shaddai
"Have passed over the Dead to awake the Dead to Judgment."
But Albion turn'd away refusing comfort.

Oxford trembled while he spoke, then fainted in the arms
Of Norwich, Peterboro, Rochester, Chester awful, Worcester,
Litchfield, Saint David's, Landaff, Asaph, Bangor, Sodor,
Bowing their heads devoted: and the Furnaces of Los
Began to rage; thundering loud the storms began to roar
Upon the Furnaces, and loud the Furnaces rebellow beneath.

And these the Four in whom the twenty-four appear'd four-fold:
Verulam, London, York, Edinburgh, mourning one towards another.
Alas!—The time will come when a man's worst enemies
Shall be those of his own house and family, in a Religion
Of Generation to destroy, by Sin and Atonement, happy Jerusalem,
The Bride and Wife of the Lamb. O God, thou art Not an Avenger!

Plate 47

When Albion utter'd his last words Hope is banish'd from me
From Camberwell to Highgate where the mighty Thames shudders along,
Where Los's Furnaces stand, where Jerusalem & Vala howl,
Luvah tore forth from Albion's Loins in fibrous veins, in rivers
Of blood over Europe: a Vegetating Root, in grinding pain
Animating the Dragon Temples, soon to become that Holy Fiend
The Wicker Man of Scandinavia, in which, cruelly consumed,
The Captives rear'd to heaven howl in flames among the stars.
Loud the cries of War on the Rhine & Danube with Albion's Sons:
Away from Beulah's hills & vales break forth the Souls of the Dead,
With cymbal, trumpet, clarion & the scythed chariots of Britain.

And the Veil of Vala is composed of the Spectres of the Dead.

Hark! the mingling cries of Luvah with the Sons of Albion.
Hark! & Record the terrible wonder! that the Punisher
Mingles with his Victim's Spectre, enslaved and tormented
To him whom he has murder'd, bound in vengeance & enmity.
Shudder not, but Write, & the hand of God will assist you!
Therefore I write Albion's last words: "Hope is banish'd from me."

Plate 48

These were his last words; and the merciful Saviour in his arms
Reciev'd him, in the arms of tender mercy, and repos'd
The pale limbs of his Eternal Individuality
Upon the Rock of Ages. Then, surrounded with a Cloud,
In silence the Divine Lord builded with immortal labour,
Of gold & jewels, a sublime Ornament, a Couch of repose
With Sixteen pillars, canopied with emblems & written verse,
Spiritual Verse, order'd & measur'd: from whence time shall reveal
The Five books of the Decalogue: the books of Joshua & Judges,
Samuel, a double book, & Kings, a double book, the Psalms & Prophets,
The Four-fold Gospel, and the Revelations everlasting.
Eternity groan'd & was troubled at the image of Eternal Death!

Beneath the bottoms of the Graves, which is Earth's central joint,
There is a place where Contrarieties are equally true:
(To protect from the Giant blows in the sports of intellect,
Thunder in the midst of kindness, & love that kills its beloved:
Because Death is for a period, and they renew tenfold.)
From this sweet Place Maternal Love awoke Jerusalem;

With pangs she forsook Beulah's pleasant lovely shadowy Universe
Where no dispute can come, created for those who Sleep.

Weeping was in all Beulah, and all the Daughters of Beulah
Wept for their Sister, the Daughter of Albion, Jerusalem,
When out of Beulah the Emanation of the Sleeper descended
With solemn mourning, out of Beulah's moony shades and hills
Within the Human Heart, whose Gates closed with solemn sound.

And this the manner of the terrible Separation.
The Emanations of the grievously afflicted Friends of Albion
Concenter in one Female form, an Aged pensive Woman,
Astonish'd, lovely, embracing the sublime shade, the Daughters of Beulah
Beheld her with wonder! With awful hands she took
A Moment of Time, drawing it out with many tears & afflictions
And many sorrows, oblique across the Atlantic Vale,
Which is the Vale of Rephaim dreadful from East to West
Where the Human Harvest waves abundant in the beams of Eden,
Into a Rainbow of jewels and gold, a mild Reflection from
Albion's dread Tomb: Eight thousand and five hundred years
In its extension. Every two hundred years has a door to Eden.
She also took an Atom of Space, with dire pain opening it a Center
Into Beulah; trembling the Daughters of Beulah dried
Her tears; she ardent embrac'd her sorrows, occupied in labours
Of sublime mercy in Rephaim's Vale. Perusing Albion's Tomb
She sat: she walk'd among the ornaments solemn mourning.
The Daughters attended her shudderings, wiping the death sweat.
Los also saw her in his seventh Furnace; he also, terrified,
Saw the finger of God go forth upon his seventh Furnace
Away from the Starry Wheels to prepare Jerusalem a place,
When with a dreadful groan the Emanation mild of Albion
Burst from his bosom in the Tomb like a pale snowy cloud,
Female and lovely, struggling to put off the Human form,
Writhing in pain. The Daughters of Beulah in kind arms reciev'd
Jerusalem, weeping over her among the Spaces of Erin
In the Ends of Beulah, where the Dead wail night & day.

And thus Erin spoke to the Daughters of Beulah in soft tears:

"Albion the Vortex of the Dead! Albion the Generous!
"Albion the mildest son of Heaven! The Place of Holy Sacrifice
"Where Friends Die for each other, will become the Place
"Of Murder & Unforgiving, Never-awaking Sacrifice of Enemies
"The Children must be sacrific'd! (a horror never known

"Till now in Beulah) unless a Refuge can be found
"To hide them from the wrath of Albion's Law that freezes sore
"Upon his Sons & Daughters, self-exiled from his bosom.
"Draw ye Jerusalem away from Albion's Mountains
"To give a Place for Redemption, let Sihon and Og
"Remove Eastward to Bashan and Gilead, and leave

Plate 49

"The secret coverts of Albion & the hidden places of America.
"Jerusalem! Jerusalem! why wilt thou turn away?
"Come ye, O Daughters of Beulah, lament for Og & Sihon
"Upon the Lakes of Ireland from Rathlin to Baltimore.
"Stand ye upon the Dargle from Wicklow to Drogheda.
"Come & mourn over Albion, the White Cliff of the Atlantic,
"The Mountain of Giants: all the Giants of Albion are become
"Weak, wither'd, darken'd, & Jerusalem is cast forth from Albion.
"They deny that they ever knew Jerusalem, or ever dwelt in Shiloh.
"The Gigantic roots & twigs of the vegetating Sons of Albion,
"Fill'd with the little-ones, are consumed in the Fires of their Altars.
"The vegetating Cities are burned & consumed from the Earth,
"And the Bodies in which all Animals & Vegetations, the Earth & Heaven
"Were contain'd in the All Glorious Imagination, are wither'd & darken'd.
"The golden Gate of Havilah and all the Garden of God
"Was caught up with the Sun in one day of fury and war.
"The Lungs, the Heart, the Liver, shrunk away far distant from Man
"And left a little slimy substance floating upon the tides.
"In one night the Atlantic Continent was caught up with the Moon
"And became an Opake Globe far distant, clad with moony beams.
"The Visions of Eternity, by reason of narrowed perceptions,
"Are become weak Visions of Time & Space, fix'd into furrows of death,
"Till deep dissimulation is the only defence an honest man has left.
"O Polypus of Death! O Spectre over Europe and Asia,
"Withering the Human Form by Laws of Sacrifice for Sin!
"By Laws of Chastity & Abhorrence I am wither'd up:
"Striving to Create a Heaven in which all shall be pure & holy
"In their Own Selfhoods: in Natural Selfish Chastity to banish Pity
"And dear Mutual Forgiveness, & to become One Great Satan
"Inslav'd to the most powerful Selfhood: to murder the Divine Humanity
"In whose sight all are as the dust & who chargeth his Angels with folly!
"Ah! weak & wide astray! Ah! shut in narrow doleful form!

"Creeping in reptile flesh upon the bosom of the ground!
"The Eye of Man, a little narrow orb, clos'd up & dark,
"Scarcely beholding the Great Light, conversing with the ground:
"The Ear, a little shell, in small volutions shutting out
"True Harmonies & comprehending great as very small:
"The Nostrils, bent down to the earth & clos'd with senseless flesh
"That odours cannot them expand, nor joy on them exult:
"The Tongue, a little moisture fills, a little food it cloys,
"A little sound it utters, & its cries are faintly heard.
"Therefore they are removed: therefore they have taken root
"In Egypt & Philistea, in Moab & Edom & Aram:
"In the Erythrean Sea their Uncircumcision in Heart & Loins
"Be lost for ever & ever; then they shall arise from Self
"By Self Annihilation into Jerusalem's Courts & into Shiloh,
"Shiloh, the Masculine Emanation among the Flowers of Beulah.
"Lo, Shiloh dwells over France, as Jerusalem dwells over Albion.
"Build & prepare a Wall & Curtain for America's shore!
"Rush on! Rush on! Rush on, ye vegetating Sons of Albion!
"The Sun shall go before you in Day, the Moon shall go
"Before you in Night. Come on! Come on! Come on! The Lord
"Jehovah is before, behind, above, beneath, around.
"He has builded the arches of Albion's Tomb, binding the Stars
"In merciful Order, bending the Laws of Cruelty to Peace.
"He hath placed Og & Anak, the Giants of Albion, for their Guards,
"Building the Body of Moses in the Valley of Peor, the Body
"Of Divine Analogy; and Og & Sihon in the tears of Balaam
"The Son of Beor, have given their power to Joshua & Caleb.
"Remove from Albion, far remove these terrible surfaces:
"They are beginning to form Heavens & Hells in immense
"Circles, the Hells for food to the Heavens, food of torment,
"Food of despair: they drink the condemn'd Soul & rejoice
"In cruel holiness in their Heavens of Chastity & Uncircumcision;
"Yet they are blameless, & Iniquity must be imputed only
"To the State they are enter'd into, that they may be deliver'd.
"Satan is the State of Death & not a Human existence;
"But Luvah is named Satan because he has enter'd that State:
"A World where Man is by Nature the enemy of Man,
"Because the Evil is Created into a State, that Men
"May be deliver'd time after time, evermore. Amen.
"Learn therefore, O Sisters, to distinguish the Eternal Human
"That walks about among the stones of fire in bliss & woe
"Alternate, from those States or Worlds in which the Spirit travels.
"This is the only means to Forgiveness of Enemies.
"Therefore remove from Albion these terrible Surfaces
"And let wild seas & rocks close up Jerusalem away from

Plate 50

"The Atlantic Mountains where Giants dwelt in Intellect,
"Now given to stony Druids and Allegoric Generation,
"To the Twelve Gods of Asia, the Spectres of those who Sleep
"Sway'd by a Providence oppos'd to the Divine Lord Jesus:
"A murderous Providence! A Creation that groans, living on Death,
"Where Fish & Bird & Beast & Man & Tree & Metal & Stone
"Live by Devouring, going into Eternal Death continually!
"Albion is now possess'd by the War of Blood! the Sacrifice
"Of envy Albion is become, and his Emanation cast out.
"Come Lord Jesus, Lamb of God descend! for if, O Lord!
"If thou hadst been here, our brother Albion had not died.
"Arise sisters! Go ye & meet the Lord, while I remain.
"Behold the foggy mornings of the Dead on Albion's cliffs!
"Ye know that if the Emanation remains in them
"She will become an Eternal Death, an Avenger of Sin,
"A Self-righteousness, the proud Virgin-Harlot! Mother of War!
"And we also & all Beulah consume beneath Albion's curse."

So Erin spoke to the Daughters of Beulah. Shuddering
With their wings, they sat in the Furnace, in a night
Of stars, for all the Sons of Albion appear'd distant stars
Ascending and descending into Albion's sea of death.
And Erin's lovely Bow enclos'd the Wheels of Albion's Sons.

Expanding on wing, the Daughters of Beulah replied in sweet response:

"Come, O thou Lamb of God, and take away the remembrance of Sin.
"To Sin & to hide the Sin in sweet deceit is lovely!
"To Sin in the open face of day is cruel & pitiless! But
"To record the Sin for a reproach, to let the Sun go down
"In a remembrance of the Sin, is a Woe & a Horror,
"A brooder of an Evil Day and a Sun rising in blood!
"Come then, O Lamb of God, and take away the remembrance of Sin."

End of Chap: 2^{d}.

Plate 52

Rahab is an Eternal State. } To the Deists { The Spiritual States of the Soul are all Eternal. Distinguish between the Man & his present State.

He never can be a Friend to the Human Race who is the Preacher of Natural Morality or Natural Religion; he is a flatterer who means to betray, to perpetuate Tyrant Pride & the Laws of that Babylon which he Foresees shall shortly be destroyed, with the Spiritual and not the Natural Sword. He is in the State named Rahab, which State must be put off before he can be the Friend of Man.

You, O Deists, profess yourselves the Enemies of Christianity, and you are so: you are also the Enemies of the Human Race & of Universal Nature. Man is born a Spectre or Satan & is altogether an Evil, & requires a New Selfhood continually, & must continually be changed into his direct Contrary. But your Greek Philosophy (which is a remnant of Druidism) teaches that Man is Righteous in his Vegetated Spectre: an Opinion of fatal & accursed consequence to Man, as the Ancients saw plainly by Revelation, to the intire abrogation of Experimental Theory; and many believed what they saw and Prophecied of Jesus.

Man must & will have Some Religion: if he has not the Religion of Jesus, he will have the Religion of Satan & will erect the Synagogue of Satan, calling the Prince of this World, God, and destroying all who do not worship Satan under the Name of God. Will any one say, "Where are those who worship Satan under the Name of God?" Where are they? Listen! Every Religion that Preaches Vengeance for Sin is the Religion of the Enemy & Avenger and not of the Forgiver of Sin, and their God is Satan, Named by the Divine Name. Your Religion, O Deists! Deism, is the Worship of the God of this World by the means of what you call Natural Religion and Natural Philosophy, and of Natural Morality or Self-Righteousness, the Selfish Virtues of the Natural Heart. This was the Religion of the Pharisees who murder'd Jesus. Deism is the same & ends in the same.

Voltaire, Rousseau, Gibbon, Hume, charge the Spiritually Religious with Hypocrisy; but how a Monk, or a Methodist either, can be a Hypocrite, I cannot concieve. We are Men of like passions with others & pretend not to be holier than others; therefore, when a Religious Man falls into Sin, he ought not to be call'd a Hypocrite; this title is more properly to be given to a Player who falls into Sin, whose profession is Virtue & Morality & the making Men Self-Righteous. Foote in calling Whitefield, Hypocrite, was himself one; for Whitefield pretended not to be holier than others, but confessed his Sins before all the World. Voltaire! Rousseau! You cannot escape my charge that you are Pharisees & Hypocrites, for you are constantly talking of the Virtues of the Human Heart and particularly of your own, that you may accuse others, & especially the Religious, whose errors you, by this display of pretended Virtue, chiefly design to expose. Rousseau thought Men Good by Nature: he found them Evil & found no friend. Friendship cannot exist without Forgiveness of Sins continually. The Book written by Rousseau call'd his Confessions, is an apology & cloke for his sin & not a confession.

But you also charge the poor Monks & Religious with being the causes of War, while you acquit & flatter the Alexanders & Caesars, the Lewis's & Fredericks, who alone are its causes & its actors. But the Religion of Jesus, Forgiveness of Sin, can never be the cause of a War nor of a single Martyrdom.

Those who Martyr others or who cause War are Deists, but never can be Forgivers of Sin. The Glory of Christianity is To Conquer by Forgiveness. All the Destruction, therefore, in Christian Europe has arisen from Deism, which is Natural Religion.

I saw a Monk of Charlemaine
Arise before my sight:
I talk'd with the Grey Monk as we stood
In beams of infernal light.

Gibbon arose with a lash of steel,
And Voltaire with a wracking wheel;
The Schools, in clouds of learning roll'd,
Arose with War in iron & gold.

"Thou lazy Monk," they sound afar,
"In vain condemning glorious War;
"And in your Cell you shall ever dwell:
"Rise, War, & bind him in his Cell!"

The blood red ran from the Grey Monk's side,
His hands & feet were wounded wide,
His body bent, his arms & knees
Like to the roots of ancient trees.

When Satan first the black bow bent
And the Moral Law from the Gospel rent,
He forg'd the Law into a Sword
And spill'd the blood of mercy's Lord.

Titus! Constantine! Charlemaine!
O Voltaire! Rousseau! Gibbon! Vain
Your Grecian Mocks & Roman Sword
Against this image of his Lord!

For a Tear is an Intellectual thing,
And a Sigh is the Sword of an Angel King,
And the bitter groan of a Martyr's woe
Is an Arrow from the Almightie's Bow.

Plate 53

Jerusalem

Chap: 3

But Los, who is the Vehicular Form of strong Urthona,
Wept vehemently over Albion where Thames' currents spring
From the rivers of Beulah; pleasant river! soft, mild parent stream.
And the roots of Albion's Tree enter'd the Soul of Los
As he sat before his Furnaces clothed in sackcloth of hair,
In gnawing pain dividing him from his Emanation,
Inclosing all the Children of Los time after time,
Their Giant forms condensing into Nations & Peoples & Tongues.
Translucent the Furnaces, of Beryll & Emerald immortal
And Seven-fold each within other, incomprehensible
To the Vegetated Mortal Eye's perverted & single vision.
The Bellows are the Animal Lungs, the Hammers the Animal Heart,
The Furnaces the Stomach for Digestion; terrible their fury
Like seven burning heavens rang'd from South to North.

Here, on the banks of the Thames, Los builded Golgonooza,
Outside of the Gates of the Human Heart beneath Beulah
In the midst of the rocks of the Altars of Albion. In fears
He builded it, in rage & in fury. It is the Spiritual Fourfold
London, continually building & continually decaying desolate.
In eternal labours loud the Furnaces & loud the Anvils
Of Death thunder incessant around the flaming Couches of
The Twenty-four Friends of Albion and round the awful Four
For the protection of the Twelve Emanations of Albion's Sons,
The Mystic Union of the Emanation in the Lord. Because
Man divided from his Emanation is a dark Spectre,
His Emanation is an ever-weeping melancholy Shadow;
But she is made receptive of Generation thro' mercy
In the Potter's Furnace among the Funeral Urns of Beulah,
From Surrey hills thro' Italy and Greece to Hinnom's vale.

Plate 54

In Great Eternity every particular Form gives forth or Emanates
Its own peculiar Light, & the Form is the Divine Vision
And the Light is his Garment. This is Jerusalem in every Man,
A Tent & Tabernacle of Mutual Forgiveness, Male & Female Clothings.
And Jerusalem is called Liberty among the Children of Albion.

But Albion fell down, a Rocky fragment from Eternity hurl'd
By his own Spectre, who is the Reasoning Power in every Man,
Into his own Chaos, which is the Memory between Man & Man.

The silent broodings of deadly revenge springing from the
All powerful parental affection, fills Albion from head to foot.

Seeing his Sons assimilate with Luvah, bound in the bonds
Of spiritual Hate, from which springs Sexual Love as iron chains,
He tosses like a cloud outstretch'd among Jerusalem's Ruins
Which overspread all the Earth; he groans among his ruin'd porches.

But the Spectre, like a hoar frost & a Mildew, rose over Albion,
Saying, "I am God, O Sons of Men! I am your Rational Power!
"Am I not Bacon & Newton & Locke who teach Humility to Man,
"Who teach Doubt & Experiment? & my two Wings, Voltaire, Rousseau?
"Where is that Friend of Sinners? that Rebel against my Laws
"Who teaches Belief to the Nations & an unknown Eternal Life?
"Come hither into the Desart & turn these stones to bread.
"Vain Foolish Man! wilt thou believe without Experiment
"And build a World of Phantasy upon my Great Abyss,
"A World of Shapes in craving lust & devouring appetite?"

So spoke the hard cold constrictive Spectre: he is named Arthur,
Constricting into Druid Rocks round Canaan, Agag & Aram & Pharoh.

Then Albion drew England into his bosom in groans & tears,
But she stretch'd out her starry Night in Spaces against him like
A long Serpent in the Abyss of the Spectre, which augmented
The Night with Dragon wings cover'd with stars, & in the Wings
Jerusalem & Vala appear'd; & above, between the Wings magnificent,
The Divine Vision dimly appear'd in clouds of blood weeping.

Plate 55

When those who disregard all Mortal Things saw a Mighty-One
Among the Flowers of Beulah still retain his awful strength,
They wonder'd, checking their wild flames; & Many gathering
Together into an Assembly, they said, "let us go down
"And see these changes." Others said, "If you do so, prepare
"For being driven from our fields; what have we to do with the Dead?
"To be their inferiors or superiors we equally abhor:
"Superior, none we know: inferior, none: all equal share
"Divine Benevolence & joy; for the Eternal Man
"Walketh among us, calling us his Brothers & his Friends,
"Forbidding us that Veil which Satan puts between Eve & Adam,
"By which the Princes of the Dead enslave their Votaries
"Teaching them to form the Serpent of precious stones & gold,
"To sieze the Sons of Jerusalem & plant them in One Man's Loins,
"To make One Family of Contraries, that Joseph may be sold
"Into Egypt for Negation, a Veil the Saviour born & dying rends."

But others said: "Let us to him, who only Is & who
"Walketh among us, give decision: bring forth all your fires!"

So saying, an eternal deed was done: in fiery flames
The Universal Concave raged such thunderous sounds as never
Were sounded from a mortal cloud, nor on Mount Sinai old,
Nor in Havilah where the Cherub roll'd his redounding flame.

Loud! loud! the Mountains lifted up their voices, loud the Forests:
Rivers thunder'd against their banks, loud Winds furious fought:
Cities & Nations contended in fires & clouds & tempests:
The Seas rais'd up their voices & lifted their hands on high:
The Stars in their courses fought, the Sun, Moon, Heaven, Earth,
Contending for Albion & for Jerusalem his Emanation,
And for Shiloh the Emanation of France, & for lovely Vala.

Then far the greatest number were about to make a Separation;
And they Elected Seven, call'd the Seven Eyes of God,
Lucifer, Molech, Elohim, Shaddai, Pahad, Jehovah, Jesus.
They nam'd the Eighth: he came not, he hid in Albion's Forests.
But first they said: (& their Words stood in Chariots in array
Curbing their Tygers with golden bits & bridles of silver & ivory)

"Let the Human Organs be kept in their perfect Integrity,
"At will Contracting into Worms or Expanding into Gods,
"And then, behold! what are these Ulro Visions of Chastity?

"Then as the moss upon the tree, or dust upon the plow,
"Or as the sweat upon the labouring shoulder, or as the chaff
"Of the wheat-floor, or as the dregs of the sweet wine-press:
"Such are these Ulro Visions; for tho' we sit down within
"The plowed furrow, list'ning to the weeping clods till we
"Contract or Expand Space at will, or if we raise ourselves
"Upon the chariots of the morning, Contracting or Expanding Time,
"Every one knows we are One Family, One Man blessed for ever."

Silence remain'd & every one resum'd his Human Majesty.
And many conversed on these things as they labour'd at the furrow,
Saying: "It is better to prevent misery than to release from misery:
"It is better to prevent error than to forgive the criminal.
"Labour well the Minute Particulars, attend to the Little-ones,
"And those who are in misery cannot remain so long
"If we do but our duty: labour well the teeming Earth."

They Plow'd in tears, the trumpets sounded before the golden Plow,
And the voices of the Living Creatures were heard in the clouds of heaven,
Crying: "Compell the Reasoner to Demonstrate with unhewn Demonstrations.
"Let the Indefinite be explored, and let every Man be Judged
"By his own Works. Let all Indefinites be thrown into Demonstrations,
"To be pounded to dust & melted in the Furnaces of Affliction.
"He who would do good to another must do it in Minute Particulars:
"General Good is the plea of the scoundrel, hypocrite & flatterer,
"For Art & Science cannot exist but in minutely organized Particulars
"And not in generalizing Demonstrations of the Rational Power.
"The Infinite alone resides in Definite & Determinate Identity;
"Establishment of Truth depends on destruction of Falsehood continually,
"On Circumcision, not on Virginity, O Reasoners of Albion!"

So cried they at the Plow. Albion's Rock frowned above,
And the Great Voice of Eternity rolled above terrible in clouds,
Saying, "Who will go forth for us, & Who shall we send before our face?"

Plate 56

Then Los heaved his thund'ring Bellows on the Valley of Middlesex,
And thus he chaunted his Song: the Daughters of Albion reply:

"What may Man be? who can tell! But what may Woman be
"To have power over Man from Cradle to corruptible Grave?
"He who is an Infant and whose Cradle is a Manger
"Knoweth the Infant sorrow, whence it came and where it goeth
"And who weave it a Cradle of the grass that withereth away.
"This World is all a Cradle for the erred wandering Phantom,
"Rock'd by Year, Month, Day & Hour; and every two Moments
"Between dwells a Daughter of Beulah to feed the Human Vegetable.
"Entune, Daughters of Albion, your hymning Chorus mildly,
"Cord of affection thrilling extatic on the iron Reel
"To the golden Loom of Love, to the moth-labour'd Woof,
"A Garment and Cradle weaving for the infantine Terror,
"For fear, at entering the gate into our World of cruel
"Lamentation, it flee back & hide in Non-Entity's dark wild
"Where dwells the Spectre of Albion, destroyer of Definite Form.
"The Sun shall be a Scythed Chariot of Britain: the Moon, a Ship
"In the British Ocean, Created by Los's Hammer, measured out
"Into Days & Nights & Years & Months, to travel with my feet
"Over these desolate rocks of Albion. O daughters of despair!
"Rock the Cradle, and in mild melodies tell me where found
"What you have enwoven with so much tears & care, so much
"Tender artifice, to laugh, to weep, to learn, to know:
"Remember! recollect! what dark befel in wintry days."

"O it was lost for ever, and we found it not; it came
"And wept at our wintry Door. Look! look! behold! Gwendolen
"Is become a Clod of Clay! Merlin is a Worm of the Valley!"

Then Los uttered with Hammer & Anvil: "Chaunt! revoice!
"I mind not your laugh, and your frown I not fear, and
"You must my dictate obey; from your gold-beam'd Looms trill
"Gentle to Albion's Watchman; on Albion's mountains reeccho,
"And rock the Cradle while, Ah me! Of that Eternal Man
"And of the cradled Infancy in his bowels of compassion
"Who fell beneath his instruments of husbandry & became
"Subservient to the clods of the furrow; the cattle and even
"The emmet and earth-Worm are his superiors & his lords."

Then the response came warbling from trilling Looms in Albion:
"We Women tremble at the light, therefore hiding fearful
"The Divine Vision with Curtain & Veil & fleshly Tabernacle."
Los utter'd, swift as the rattling thunder upon the mountains:
"Look back into the Church Paul! Look! Three Women around
"The Cross! O Albion, why didst thou a Female Will Create?"

Plate 57

And the voices of Bath & Canterbury & York & Edinburgh Cry
Over the Plow of Nations in the strong hand of Albion, thundering along
Among the Fires of the Druid & the deep black rethundering Waters
Of the Atlantic which poured in, impetuous, loud, loud, louder & louder.
And the Great Voice of the Atlantic howled over the Druid Altars,
Weeping over his Children in Stone-henge, in Malden & Colchester,
Round the Rocky Peak of Derbyshire, London Stone & Rosamond's Bower:

"What is a Wife & what is a Harlot? What is a Church & What
"Is a Theatre? are they Two & not One? can they Exist Separate?
"Are not Religion & Politics the Same Thing? Brotherhood is Religion,
"O Demonstrations of Reason Dividing Families in Cruelty & Pride!"

But Albion fled from the Divine Vision; with the Plow of Nations enflaming,
The Living Creatures madden'd, and Albion fell into the Furrow; and
The Plow went over him & the Living was Plowed in among the Dead.
But his Spectre rose over the starry Plow. Albion fled beneath the Plow
Till he came to the Rock of Ages, & he took his Seat upon the Rock.

Wonder siez'd all in Eternity, to behold the Divine Vision open
The Center into an Expanse, & the Center rolled out into an Expanse.

Plate 58

In beauty the Daughters of Albion divide & unite at will,
Naked & drunk with blood. Gwendolen dancing to the timbrel
Of War, reeling up the Street of London, she divides in twain
Among the Inhabitants of Albion: the People fall around.
The Daughters of Albion divide & unite in jealousy & cruelty.
The Inhabitants of Albion at the Harvest & the Vintage
Feel their Brain cut round beneath the temples, shrieking,
Bonifying into a Scull, the Marrow exuding in dismal pain.
They flee over the rocks bonifying. Horses, Oxen feel the knife.
And while the Sons of Albion by severe War & Judgment bonify,
The Hermaphroditic Condensations are divided by the Knife:
The obdurate Forms are cut asunder by Jealousy & Pity.

Rational Philosophy and Mathematic Demonstration
Is divided in the intoxications of pleasure & affection.
Two Contraries War against each other in fury & blood,
And Los fixes them on his Anvil, incessant his blows:
He fixes them with strong blows, placing the stones & timbers
To Create a World of Generation from the World of Death,
Dividing the Masculine & Feminine, for the comingling
Of Albion's & Luvah's Spectres was Hermaphroditic.

Urizen wrathful strode above, directing the awful Building
As a Mighty Temple, delivering Form out of confusion.
Jordan sprang beneath its threshold, bubbling from beneath
Its pillars: Euphrates ran under its arches: white sails
And silver oars reflect on its pillars & sound on its ecchoing
Pavements, where walk the Sons of Jerusalem who remain Ungenerate.
But the revolving Sun and Moon pass thro' its porticoes:
Day & night in sublime majesty & silence they revolve
And shine glorious within. Hand & Koban arch'd over the Sun
In the hot noon as he travel'd thro' his journey. Hyle & Skofield
Arch'd over the Moon at midnight, & Los Fix'd them there
With his thunderous Hammer: terrified the Spectres rage & flee.
Canaan is his portico. Jordan is a fountain in his porch,
A fountain of milk & wine to relieve the traveller.
Egypt is the eight steps within. Ethiopia supports his pillars.
Lybia & the Lands unknown are the ascent without;
Within is Asia & Greece, ornamented with exquisite art.
Persia & Media are his halls: his inmost hall is Great Tartary.
China & India & Siberia are his temples for entertainment.
Poland & Russia & Sweden, his soft retired chambers.
France & Spain & Italy & Denmark & Holland & Germany
Are the temples among his pillars: Britain is Los's Forge.
America North & South are his baths of living waters.

Such is the Ancient World of Urizen in the Satanic Void,
Created from the Valley of Middlesex by London's River,
From Stone-henge and from London Stone, from Cornwall to Cathnes.
The Four Zoas rush around on all sides in dire ruin:
Furious in pride of Selfhood the terrible Spectres of Albion
Rear their dark Rocks among the Stars of God, stupendous
Works! A World of Generation continually Creating out of
The Hermaphroditic Satanic World of rocky destiny,

Plate 59

And formed into Four precious stones for enterance from Beulah.

For the Veil of Vala, which Albion cast into the Atlantic Deep
To catch the Souls of the Dead, began to Vegetate & Petrify
Around the Earth of Albion among the Roots of his Tree.
This Los formed into the Gates & mighty Wall between the Oak
Of Weeping & the Palm of Suffering beneath Albion's Tomb.
Thus in process of time it became the beautiful Mundane Shell,
The Habitation of the Spectres of the Dead, & the Place
Of Redemption & of awaking again into Eternity.

For Four Universes round the Mundane Egg remain Chaotic:
One to the North, Urthona: One to the South, Urizen:
One to the East, Luvah: One to the West, Tharmas.
They are the Four Zoas that stood around the Throne Divine,
Verulam, London, York & Edinburgh, their English names.
But when Luvah assumed the World of Urizen Southward
And Albion was slain upon his Mountains & in his Tent,
All fell towards the Center, sinking downwards in dire ruin.
In the South remains a burning Fire: in the East, a Void:
In the West, a World of raging Waters: in the North, solid Darkness
Unfathomable without end; but in the midst of these
Is Built eternally the sublime Universe of Los & Enitharmon.

And in the North Gate, in the West of the North, toward Beulah,
Cathedron's Looms are builded, and Los's Furnaces in the South.
A wondrous golden Building immense with ornaments sublime
Is bright Cathedron's golden Hall, its Courts, Towers & Pinnacles.

And one Daughter of Los sat at the fiery Reel, & another
Sat at the shining Loom with her Sisters attending round,
Terrible their distress, & their sorrow cannot be utter'd;
And another Daughter of Los sat at the Spinning Wheel,
Endless their labour, with bitter food, void of sleep;
Tho' hungry, they labour: they rouze themselves anxious
Hour after hour labouring at the whirling Wheel,
Many Wheels & as many lovely Daughters sit weeping.
Yet the intoxicating delight that they take in their work
Obliterates every other evil; none pities their tears,
Yet they regard not pity & they expect no one to pity,
For they labour for life & love regardless of any one
But the poor Spectres that they work for always, incessantly.

They are mock'd by every one that passes by; they regard not,
They labour, & when their Wheels are broken by scorn & malice
They mend them sorrowing with many tears & afflictions.

Other Daughters Weave on the Cushion & Pillow Network fine
That Rahab & Tirzah may exist & live & breathe & love.
Ah, that it could be as the Daughters of Beulah wish!

Other Daughters of Los, labouring at Looms less fine,
Create the Silk-worm & the Spider & the Catterpiller
To assist in their most grievous work of pity & compassion;
And others Create the wooly Lamb & the downy Fowl
To assist in the work; the Lamb bleats, the Sea-fowl cries:
Men understand not the distress & the labour & sorrow
That in the Interior Worlds is carried on in fear & trembling,
Weaving the shudd'ring fears & loves of Albion's Families.
Thunderous rage the Spindles of iron, & the iron Distaff
Maddens in the fury of their hands, weaving in bitter tears
The Veil of Goats-hair & Purple & Scarlet & fine twined Linen.

Plate 60

The clouds of Albion's Druid Temples rage in the eastern heaven
While Los sat terrified beholding Albion's Spectre, who is Luvah,
Spreading in bloody veins in torments over Europe & Asia,
Not yet formed, but a wretched torment unformed & abyssal
In flaming fire; within the Furnaces the Divine Vision appear'd
On Albion's hills, often walking from the Furnaces in clouds
And flames among the Druid Temples & the Starry Wheels,
Gather'd Jerusalem's Children in his arms & bore them like
A Shepherd in the night of Albion which overspread all the Earth.

"I gave thee liberty and life, O lovely Jerusalem,
"And thou hast bound me down upon the Stems of Vegetation.
"I gave thee Sheep-walks upon the Spanish Mountains, Jerusalem,
"I gave thee Priam's City and the Isles of Grecia lovely.
"I gave thee Hand & Scofield & the Counties of Albion,
"They spread forth like a lovely root into the Garden of God,
"They were as Adam before me, united into One Man,
"They stood in innocence & their skiey tent reach'd over Asia
"To Nimrod's Tower, to Ham & Canaan, walking with Mizraim
"Upon the Egyptian Nile, with solemn songs to Grecia
"And sweet Hesperia, even to Great Chaldea & Tesshina,
"Following thee as a Shepherd by the Four Rivers of Eden.
"Why wilt thou rend thyself apart, Jerusalem,

"And build this Babylon & sacrifice in secret Groves
"Among the Gods of Asia, among the fountains of pitch & nitre?
"Therefore thy Mountains are become barren, Jerusalem,
"Thy Valleys, Plains of burning sand; thy Rivers, waters of death;
"Thy Villages die of the Famine, and thy Cities
"Beg bread from house to house, lovely Jerusalem.
"Why wilt thou deface thy beauty & the beauty of thy little-ones
"To please thy Idols in the pretended chastities of Uncircumcision?
"Thy Sons are lovelier than Egypt or Assyria; wherefore
"Dost thou blacken their beauty by a Secluded place of rest,
"And a peculiar Tabernacle to cut the integuments of beauty
"Into veils of tears and sorrows, O lovely Jerusalem?
"They have perswaded thee to this; therefore their end shall come,
"And I will lead thee thro' the Wilderness in shadow of my cloud,
"And in my love I will lead thee, lovely Shadow of Sleeping Albion."

This is the Song of the Lamb, sung by Slaves in evening time.

But Jerusalem faintly saw him; clos'd in the Dungeons of Babylon
Her Form was held by Beulah's Daughters; but all within unseen
She sat at the Mills, her hair unbound, her feet naked
Cut with the flints, her tears run down, her reason grows like
The Wheel of Hand incessant turning day & night without rest,
Insane she raves upon the winds, hoarse, inarticulate.
All night Vala hears, she triumphs in pride of holiness
To see Jerusalem deface her lineaments with bitter blows
Of despair, while the Satanic Holiness triumph'd in Vala
In a Religion of Chastity & Uncircumcised Selfishness
Both of the Head & Heart & Loins, clos'd up in Moral Pride.

But the Divine Lamb stood beside Jerusalem; oft she saw
The lineaments Divine & oft the Voice heard, & oft she said:

"O Lord & Saviour, have the Gods of the Heathen pierced thee,
"Or hast thou been pierced in the House of thy Friends?
"Art thou alive, & livest thou for evermore? or art thou
"Not [Nought] but a delusive shadow, a thought that liveth not?
"Babel mocks, saying there is no God nor Son of God,
"That thou, O Human Imagination, O Divine Body, art all
"A delusion; but I know thee, O Lord, when thou arisest upon
"My weary eyes, even in this dungeon & this iron mill.
"The Stars of Albion cruel rise; thou bindest to sweet influences,
"For thou also sufferest with me, altho' I behold thee not;
"And altho' I sin & blaspheme thy holy name, thou pitiest me
"Because thou knowest I am deluded by the turning mills
"And by these visions of pity & love because of Albion's death."

Thus spake Jerusalem, & thus the Divine Voice replied:

"Mild Shade of Man, pitiest thou these Visions of terror & woe?
"Give forth thy pity & love; fear not! lo, I am with thee always
"Only believe in me, that I have power to raise from death
"Thy Brother who Sleepeth in Albion; fear not, trembling Shade,

Plate 61

"Behold, in the Visions of Elohim Jehovah, behold Joseph & Mary
"And be comforted, O Jerusalem, in the Visions of Jehovah Elohim."

She looked & saw Joseph the Carpenter in Nazareth & Mary
His espoused Wife. And Mary said, "If thou put me away from thee
"Dost thou not murder me?" Joseph spoke in anger & fury, "Should I
"Marry a Harlot & an Adulteress?" Mary answer'd, "Art thou more pure
"Than thy Maker who forgiveth Sins & calls again Her that is Lost?
"Tho' She hates, he calls her again in love. I love my dear Joseph,
"But he driveth me away from his presence; yet I hear the voice of God
"In the voice of my Husband: tho' he is angry for a moment, he will not
"Utterly cast me away; if I were pure, never could I taste the sweets
"Of the Forgive[ne]ss of Sins; if I were holy, I never could behold the tears
"Of love, of him who loves me in the midst of his anger in furnace of fire."

"Ah my Mary!" said Joseph, weeping over & embracing her closely in
His arms: "Doth he forgive Jerusalem, & not exact Purity from her who is
"Polluted? I heard his voice in my sleep & his Angel in my dream,
"Saying, 'Doth Jehovah Forgive a Debt only on condition that it shall
" 'Be Payed? Doth he Forgive Pollution only on conditions of Purity?
" 'That Debt is not Forgiven! That Pollution is not Forgiven!
" 'Such is the Forgiveness of the Gods, the Moral Virtues of the
" 'Heathen whose tender Mercies are Cruelty. But Jehovah's Salvation
" 'Is without Money & without Price, in the Continual Forgiveness of Sins,
" 'In the Perpetual Mutual Sacrifice in Great Eternity; for behold,
" 'There is none that liveth & Sinneth not! And this is the Covenant

" 'Of Jehovah: If you Forgive one-another, so shall Jehovah Forgive You,
" 'That He Himself may Dwell among You. Fear not then to take
" 'To thee Mary thy Wife, for she is with Child by the Holy Ghost.' "

Then Mary burst forth into a Song: she flowed like a River of
Many Streams in the arms of Joseph & gave forth her tears of joy
Like many waters, and Emanating into gardens & palaces upon
Euphrates, & to forests & floods & animals wild & tame from
Gihon to Hiddekel, & to corn fields & villages & inhabitants
Upon Pison & Arnon & Jordan. And I heard the voice among
The Reapers, Saying, "Am I Jerusalem the lost Adulteress? or am I
"Babylon come up to Jerusalem?" And another voice answer'd, Saying,

"Does the voice of my Lord call me again? am I pure thro' his Mercy
"And Pity? Am I become lovely as a Virgin in his sight, who am
"Indeed a Harlot drunken with the Sacrifice of Idols? does he
"Call her pure as he did in the days of her Infancy when She
"Was cast out to the loathing of her person? The Chaldean took
"Me from my Cradle. The Amalekite stole me away upon his Camels
"Before I had ever beheld with love the Face of Jehovah, or known
"That there was a God of Mercy. O Mercy, O Divine Humanity!
"O Forgiveness & Pity & Compassion! If I were Pure I should never
"Have known Thee: If I were Unpolluted I should never have
"Glorified thy Holiness or rejoiced in thy great Salvation."

Mary leaned her side against Jerusalem: Jerusalem recieved
The Infant into her hands in the Visions of Jehovah. Times passed on.
Jerusalem fainted over the Cross & Sepulcher. She heard the voice:
"Wilt thou make Rome thy Patriarch Druid & the Kings of Europe his
"Horsemen? Man in the Resurrection changes his Sexual Gar[m]ents at will.
"Every Harlot was once a Virgin: every Criminal an Infant Love.

Plate 62

"Repose on me till the morning of the Grave. I am thy life."

Jerusalem replied: "I am an outcast: Albion is dead:
"I am left to the trampling foot & the spurning heel:
"A Harlot I am call'd: I am sold from street to street:
"I am defaced with blows & with the dirt of the Prison,

"And wilt thou become my Husband, O my Lord & Saviour?
"Shall Vala bring thee forth? shall the Chaste be ashamed also?
"I see the Maternal Line, I behold the Seed of the Woman:
"Cainah & Ada & Zillah, & Naamah, Wife of Noah,
"Shuah's daughter & Tamar & Rahab the Canaanites,
"Ruth the Moabite, & Bathsheba of the daughters of Heth,
"Naamah the Ammonite, Zibeah the Philistine, & Mary
"These are the Daughters of Vala, Mother of the Body of death;
"But I, thy Magdalen, behold thy Spiritual Risen Body.
"Shall Albion arise? I know he shall arise at the Last Day!
"I know that in my flesh I shall see God; but Emanations
"Are weak, they know not whence they are nor whither tend."

Jesus replied, "I am the Resurrection & the Life.
"I Die & pass the limits of possibility as it appears
"To individual perception. Luvah must be Created
"And Vala, for I cannot leave them in the gnawing Grave
"But will prepare a way for my banished-ones to return.
"Come now with me into the villages, walk thro' all the cities;
"Tho' thou art taken to prison & judgment, starved in the streets,
"I will command the cloud to give thee food & the hard rock
"To flow with milk & wine; tho' thou seest me not a season,
"Even a long season, & a hard journey & a howling wilderness,
"Tho' Vala's cloud hide thee & Luvah's fires follow thee,
"Only believe & trust in me. Lo, I am always with thee!"

So spoke the Lamb of God while Luvah's Cloud reddening above
Burst forth in streams of blood upon the heavens, & dark night
Involv'd Jerusalem, & the Wheels of Albion's Sons turn'd hoarse
Over the Mountains, & the fires blaz'd on Druid Altars,
And the Sun set in Tyburn's Brook where Victims howl & cry.

But Los beheld the Divine Vision among the flames of the Furnaces.
Therefore he lived & breathed in hope; but his tears fell incessant
Because his Children were clos'd from him apart & Enitharmon
Dividing in fierce pain; also the Vision of God was clos'd in clouds
Of Albion's Spectres, that Los in despair oft sat & often ponder'd
On Death Eternal, in fierce shudders upon the mountains of Albion
Walking, & in the vales in howlings fierce; then to his Anvils
Turning, anew began his labours, tho' in terrible pains.

Plate 63

Jehovah stood among the Druids in the Valley of Annandale
When the Four Zoas of Albion, the Four Living Creatures, the Cherubim

Of Albion tremble before the Spectre in the starry Harness of the Plow
Of Nations. And their Names are Urizen & Luvah & Tharmas & Urthona.

Luvah slew Tharmas, the Angel of the Tongue, & Albion brought him
To Justice in his own City of Paris, denying the Resurrection.
Then Vala, the Wife of Albion, who is the Daughter of Luvah,
Took vengeance Twelve-fold among the Chaotic Rocks of the Druids
Where the Human Victims howl to the Moon, & Thor & Friga
Dance the dance of death, contending with Jehovah among the Cherubim.
The Chariot Wheels filled with Eyes rage along the howling Valley
In the Dividing of Reuben & Benjamin bleeding from Chester's River.

The Giants & the Witches & the Ghosts of Albion dance with
Thor & Friga, & the Fairies lead the Moon along the Valley of Cherubim
Bleeding in torrents from Mountain to Mountain, a lovely Victim.
And Jehovah stood in the Gates of the Victim, & he appeared
A weeping Infant in the Gates of Birth in the midst of Heaven.

The Cities & Villages of Albion became Rock & Sand Unhumanized,
The Druid Sons of Albion; & the Heavens a Void around, unfathomable;
No Human Form but Sexual, & a little weeping Infant pale reflected
Multitudinous in the Looking Glass of Enitharmon, on all sides
Around in the clouds of the Female, on Albion's Cliffs of the Dead.

Such the appearance in Cheviot, in the Divisions of Reuben,
When the Cherubim hid their heads under their wings in deep slumbers,
When the Druids demanded Chastity from Woman & all was lost.

"How can the Female be Chaste, O thou stupid Druid," Cried Los,
"Without the Forgiveness of Sins in the merciful clouds of Jehovah
"And without the Baptism of Repentance to wash away Calumnies and
"The Accusations of Sin, that each may be Pure in their Neighbours' sight?
"O when shall Jehovah give us Victims from his Flocks & Herds
"Instead of Human Victims by the Daughters of Albion & Canaan?"

Then laugh'd Gwendolen, & her laughter shook the Nations & Familys of
The Dead beneath Beulah from Tyburn to Golgotha and from
Ireland to Japan: furious her Lions & Tygers & Wolves sport before
Los on the Thames & Medway: London & Canterbury groan in pain.

Los knew not yet what was done: he thought it was all in Vision,
In Visions of the Dreams of Beulah among the Daughters of Albion;
Therefore the Murder was put apart in the Looking-Glass of Enitharmon.

He saw in Vala's hand the Druid Knife of Revenge & the Poison Cup
Of Jealousy, and thought it a Poetic Vision of the Atmospheres,
Till Canaan roll'd apart from Albion across the Rhine, along the Danube.

And all the Land of Canaan suspended over the Valley of Cheviot,
From Bashan to Tyre & from Troy to Gaza of the Amalekite.
And Reuben fled with his head downwards among the Caverns

Plate 64

Of the Mundane Shell which froze on all sides round Canaan on
The vast Expanse, where the Daughters of Albion Weave the Web
Of Ages & Generations, folding & unfolding it like a Veil of Cherubim;
And sometimes it touches the Earth's summits & sometimes spreads
Abroad into the Indefinite Spectre, who is the Rational Power.

Then All the Daughters of Albion became One before Los, even Vala
And she put forth her hand upon the Looms in dreadful howlings
Till she vegetated into a hungry Stomach & a devouring Tongue.
Her Hand is a Court of Justice: her Feet two Armies in Battle:
Storms & Pestilence in her Locks, & in her Loins Earthquake
And Fire & the Ruin of Cities & Nations & Families & Tongues.

She cries: "The Human is but a Worm, & thou, O Male! Thou art
"Thyself Female, a Male, a breeder of Seed, a Son & Husband: & Lo,
"The Human Divine is Woman's Shadow, a Vapor in the summer's heat.
"Go assume Papal dignity, thou Spectre, thou Male Harlot! Arthur,
"Divide into the Kings of Europe in times remote, O Woman-born
"And Woman-nourish'd & Woman-educated & Woman-scorn'd!"

"Wherefore art thou living," said Los, "& Man cannot live in thy presence?
"Art thou Vala the Wife of Albion, O thou lovely Daughter of Luvah?

"All Quarrels arise from Reasoning: the secret Murder and
"The violent Man-slaughter, these are the Spectre's double Cave,
"The Sexual Death living on accusation of Sin & Judgment,
"To freeze Love & Innocence into the gold & silver of the Merchant.
"Without Forgiveness of Sin, Love is Itself Eternal Death."

Then the Spectre drew Vala into his bosom, magnificent, terrific,
Glittering with precious stones & gold, with Garments of blood & fire.
He wept in deadly wrath of the Spectre, in self-contradicting agony,
Crimson with Wrath & green with Jealousy, dazling with Love
And Jealousy immingled, & the purple of the violet darken'd deep,
Over the Plow of Nations thund'ring in the hand of Albion's Spectre.

A dark Hermaphrodite they stood frown(in)ing upon London's River;
And the Distaff & Spindle in the hands of Vala, with the Flax of
Human Miseries, turn'd fierce with the Lives of Men along the Valley
As Reuben fled before the Daughters of Albion, Taxing the Nations.

Derby Peak yawn'd a horrid Chasm at the Cries of Gwendolen & at
The stamping feet of Ragan upon the flaming Treddles of her Loom
That drop with crimson gore with the Loves of Albion & Canaan,
Opening along the Valley of Rephaim, weaving over the Caves of Machpelah,

Plate 65

To decide Two Worlds with a great decision, a World of Mercy and
A World of Justice, the World of Mercy for Salvation:
To cast Luvah into the Wrath and Albion into the Pity,
In the Two Contraries of Humanity & in the Four Regions.

For in the depths of Albion's bosom in the eastern heaven
They sound the clarions strong, they chain the howling Captives,
They cast the lots into the helmet, they give the oath of blood in Lambeth,
They vote the death of Luvah & they nail'd him to Albion's Tree in Bath,
They stain'd him with poisonous blue, they inwove him in cruel roots
To die a death of Six thousand years bound round with vegetation.
The sun was black & the moon roll'd a useless globe thro' Britain.

Then left the Sons of Urizen the plow & harrow, the loom,
The hammer & the chisel & the rule & compasses; from London fleeing,
They forg'd the sword on Cheviot, the chariot of war & the battle-ax,

The trumpet fitted to mortal battle, & the Flute of summer in Annandale;
And all the Arts of Life they chang'd into the Arts of Death in Albion.
The hour-glass contemn'd because its simple workmanship
Was like the workmanship of the plowman, & the water wheel
That raises water into cisterns, broken & burn'd with fire
Because its workmanship was like the workmanship of the shepherd;
And in their stead, intricate wheels invented, wheel without wheel,
To perplex youth in their outgoings & to bind to labours in Albion
Of day & night the myriads of eternity: that they may grind
And polish brass & iron hour after hour, laborious task,
Kept ignorant of its use: that they might spend the days of wisdom
In sorrowful drudgery to obtain a scanty pittance of bread,
In ignorance to view a small portion & think that All,
And call it Demonstration, blind to all the simple rules of life.

"Now, now the battle rages round thy tender limbs, O Vala!
"Now smile among thy bitter tears, now put on all thy beauty.
"Is not the wound of the sword sweet & the broken bone delightful?
"Wilt thou now smile among the scythes when the wounded groan in the field?
"We were carried away in thousands from London & in tens
"Of thousands from Westminster & Marybone, in ships clos'd up,
"Chain'd hand & foot, compell'd to fight under the iron whips
"Of our captains, fearing our officers more than the enemy.
"Lift up thy blue eyes, Vala, & put on thy sapphire shoes!
"O melancholy Magdalen, behold the morning over Malden break!
"Gird on thy flaming zone, descend into the sepulcher of Canterbury.
"Scatter the blood from thy golden brow, the tears from thy silver locks;
"Shake off the waters from thy wings & the dust from thy white garments.
"Remember all thy feigned terrors on the secret couch of Lambeth's Vale
"When the sun rose in glowing morn, with arms of mighty hosts
"Marching to battle, who was wont to rise with Urizen's harps
"Girt as a sower with his seed to scatter life abroad over Albion.
"Arise, O Vala, bring the bow of Urizen, bring the swift arrows of light.
"How rag'd the golden horses of Urizen, compell'd to the chariot of love!
"Compell'd to leave the plow to the ox, to snuff up the winds of desolation,
"To trample the corn fields in boastful neighings; this is no gentle harp,

"This is no warbling brook nor shadow of a mirtle tree.
"But blood and wounds and dismal cries and shadows of the oak,
"And hearts laid open to the light by the broad grizly sword,
"And bowels, hid in hammer'd steel, rip'd quivering on the ground.
"Call forth thy smiles of soft deceit: call forth thy cloudy tears.
"We hear thy sighs in trumpets shrill when morn shall blood renew."

So sang the Spectre Sons of Albion round Luvah's Stone of Trial,
Mocking and deriding at the writhings of their Victim on Salisbury,
Drinking his Emanation in intoxicating bliss, rejoicing in Giant dance;
For a Spectre has no Emanation but what he imbibes from decieving
A Victim: Then he becomes her Priest & she his Tabernacle
And his Oak Grove, till the Victim rend the woven Veil
In the end of his sleep when Jesus calls him from his grave.

Howling the Victims on the Druid Altars yield their souls
To the stern Warriors; lovely sport the Daughters round their Victims,
Drinking their lives in sweet intoxication; hence arose from Bath
Soft deluding odours, in spiral volutions intricately winding
Over Albion's mountains a feminine indefinite cruel delusion.
Astonish'd, terrified & in pain & torment, Sudden they behold
Their own Parent, the Emanation of their murder'd Enemy
Become their Emanation and their Temple and Tabernacle.
They knew not this Vala was their beloved Mother Vala, Albion's Wife.

Terrified at the sight of the Victim, at his distorted sinews,
The tremblings of Vala vibrate thro' the limbs of Albion's Sons
While they rejoice over Luvah in mockery & bitter scorn.
Sudden they become like what they behold, in howlings & deadly pain:
Spasms smite their features, sinews & limbs: pale they look on one another;
They turn, contorted: their iron necks bend unwilling towards
Luvah: their lips tremble: their muscular fibres are cramp'd & smitten:
They become like what they behold! Yet immense in strength & power,

Plate 66

In awful pomp & gold, in all the precious unhewn stones of Eden
They build a stupendous Building on the Plain of Salisbury, with chains

Of rocks round London Stone, of Reasonings, of unhewn
Demonstrations
In labyrinthine arches (Mighty Urizen the Architect) thro' which
The Heavens might revolve & Eternity be bound in their chain.
Labour unparallell'd! a wondrous rocky World of cruel destiny,
Rocks piled on rocks reaching the stars, stretching from pole to pole.
The Building is Natural Religion & its Altars Natural Morality,
A building of eternal death, whose proportions are eternal despair.
Here Vala stood turning the iron Spindle of destruction
From heaven to earth, howling, invisible; but not invisible,
Her Two Covering Cherubs, afterwards named Voltaire & Rousseau,
Two frowning Rocks on each side of the Cove & Stone of Torture,
Frozen Sons of the feminine Tabernacle of Bacon, Newton & Locke;
For Luvah is France, the Victim of the Spectres of Albion.

Los beheld in terror; he pour'd his loud storms on the Furnaces.
The Daughters of Albion clothed in garments of needle work
Strip them off from their shoulders and bosoms, they lay aside
Their garments, they sit naked upon the Stone of trial.
The Knife of flint passes over the howling Victim: his blood
Gushes & stains the fair side of the fair Daug[h]ters of Albion.
They put aside his curls, they divide his seven locks upon
His forehead, they bind his forehead with thorns of iron,
They put into his hand a reed, they mock, Saying: "Behold
"The King of Canaan whose are seven hundred chariots of iron!"
They take off his vesture whole with their Knives of flint,
But they cut asunder his inner garments, searching with
Their cruel fingers for his heart, & there they enter in pomp,
In many tears, & there they erect a temple & an altar.
They pour cold water on his brain in front, to cause
Lids to grow over his eyes in veils of tears, and caverns
To freeze over his nostrils, while they feed his tongue from cups
And dishes of painted clay. Glowing with beauty & cruelty
They obscure the sun & the moon: no eye can look upon them.

Ah! alas! at the sight of the Victim & at sight of those who are smitten,
All who see become what they behold; their eyes are cover'd
With veils of tears and their nostrils & tongues shrunk up,
Their ear bent outwards; as their Victim, so are they, in the pangs
Of unconquerable fear amidst delights of revenge Earth-shaking.
And as their eye & ear shrunk, the heavens shrunk away:
The Divine Vision became First a burning flame, then a column
Of fire, then an awful fiery wheel surrounding earth & heaven,
And then a globe of blood wandering distant in an unknown night.
Afar into the unknown night the mountains fled away,

Six months of mortality, a summer, & six months of mortality, a winter.
The Human form began to be alter'd by the Daughters of Albion
And the perceptions to be dissipated into the Indefinite, Becoming
A mighty Polypus nam'd Albion's Tree; they tie the Veins
And Nerves into two knots & the Seed into a double knot.
They look forth: the Sun is shrunk: the Heavens are shrunk
Away into the far remote, and the Trees & Mountains wither'd
Into indefinite cloudy shadows in darkness & separation.
By Invisible Hatreds adjoin'd, they seem remote and separate
From each other, and yet are a Mighty Polypus in the Deep!
As the Mistletoe grows on the Oak, so Albion's Tree on Eternity. Lo!
He who will not comingle in Love must be adjoin'd by Hate.

They look forth from Stone-henge: from the Cove round London Stone
They look on one another: the mountain calls out to the mountain.
Plinlimmon shrunk away: Snowdon trembled: the mountains
Of Wales & Scotland beheld the descending War, the routed flying.
Red run the streams of Albion: Thames is drunk with blood
As Gwendolen cast the shuttle of war, as Cambel return'd the beam,
The Humber & the Severn are drunk with the blood of the slain.
London feels his brain cut round: Edinburgh's heart is circumscribed:
York & Lincoln hide among the flocks because of the griding Knife.
Worcester & Hereford, Oxford & Cambridge reel & stagger
Overwearied with howling. Wales & Scotland alone sustain the fight!
The inhabitants are sick to death: they labour to divide into Days
And Nights the uncertain Periods, and into Weeks & Months. In vain
They send the Dove & Raven & in vain the Serpent over the mountains
And in vain the Eagle & Lion over the four-fold wilderness:
They return not, but generate in rocky places desolate:
They return not, but build a habitation separate from Man.
The Sun forgets his course like a drunken man; he hesitates
Upon the Cheselden hills, thinking to sleep on the Severn.
In vain: he is hurried afar into an unknown Night:
He bleeds in torrents of blood as he rolls thro' heaven above.
He chokes up the paths of the sky; the Moon is leprous as snow,
Trembling & descending down, seeking to rest upon high Mona,
Scattering her leprous snows in flakes of disease over Albion.
The Stars flee remote; the heaven is iron, the earth is sulphur,
And all the mountains & hills shrink up like a withering gourd
As the Senses of Men shrink together under the Knife of flint
In the hands of Albion's Daughters among the Druid Temples,

Plate 67

By those who drink their blood & the blood of their Covenant.

And the Twelve Daughters of Albion united in Rahab & Tirzah,
A Double Female; and they drew out from the Rocky Stones
Fibres of Life to Weave, for every Female is a Golden Loom,
The Rocks are opake hardnesses covering all Vegetated things;
And as they Wove & Cut from the Looms, in various divisions
Stretching over Europe & Asia from Ireland to Japan,
They divided into many lovely Daughters, to be counterparts
To those they Wove; for when they Wove a Male, they divided
Into a Female to the Woven Male: in opake hardness
They cut the Fibres from the Rocks: groaning in pain they Weave,
Calling the Rocks Atomic Origins of Existence, denying Eternity
By the Atheistical Epicurean Philosophy of Albion's Tree.
Such are the Feminine & Masculine when separated from Man.
They call the Rocks Parents of Men, & adore the frowning Chaos,
Dancing around in howling pain, clothed in the bloody Veil,
Hiding Albion's Sons within the Veil, closing Jerusalem's
Sons without, to feed with their Souls the Spectres of Albion,
Ashamed to give Love openly to the piteous & merciful Man,
Counting him an imbecile mockery, but the Warrior
They adore & his revenge cherish with the blood of the Innocent.
They drink up Dan & Gad to feed with milk Skofeld & Kotope;
They strip off Joseph's Coat & dip it in the blood of battle.

Tirzah sits weeping to hear the shrieks of the dying: her Knife
Of flint is in her hand: she passes it over the howling Victim.
The Daughters Weave their Work in loud cries over the Rock
Of Horeb, still eyeing Albion's Cliffs, eagerly siezing & twisting
The threads of Vala & Jerusalem running from mountain to mountain
Over the whole Earth; loud the Warriors rage in Beth Peor
Beneath the iron whips of their Captains & consecrated banners:
Loud the Sun & Moon rage in the conflict: loud the Stars
Shout in the night of battle, & their spears grow to their hands,
With blood weaving the deaths of the Mighty into a Tabernacle
For Rahab & Tirzah, till the Great Polypus of Generation covered
the Earth.

In Verulam the Polypus's Head, winding around his bulk
Thro' Rochester and Chichester & Exeter & Salisbury
To Bristol, & his Heart beat strong on Salisbury Plain
Shooting out Fibres round the Earth thro' Gaul & Italy
And Greece & along the Sea of Rephaim into Judea
To Sodom & Gomorrha: thence to India, China & Japan

The Twelve Daughters in Rahab & Tirzah have circumscrib'd the Brain
Beneath & pierced it thro' the midst with a golden pin.
Blood hath stain'd her fair side beneath her bosom.

"O thou poor Human Form!" said she. "O thou poor child of woe!
"Why wilt thou wander away from Tirzah? why me compel to bind thee?
"If thou dost go away from me I shall consume upon these Rocks.
"These fibres of thine eyes that used to beam in distant heavens
"Away from me, I have bound down with a hot iron.
"These nostrils that expanded with delight in morning skies
"I have bent downward with lead melted in my roaring furnaces
"Of affliction, of love, of sweet despair, of torment unendurable.
"My soul is seven furnaces; incessant roars the bellows
"Upon my terribly flaming heart, the molten metal runs
"In channels thro' my fiery limbs. O love, O pity, O fear,
"O pain! O the pangs, the bitter pangs of love forsaken!
"Ephraim was a wilderness of joy where all my wild beasts ran.
"The River Kanah wander'd by my sweet Manasseh's side
"To see the boy spring into heavens sounding from my sight!
"Go Noah, fetch the girdle of strong brass, heat it red-hot,
"Press it around the loins of this ever expanding cruelty.
"Shriek not so my only love. I refuse thy joys: I drink
"Thy shrieks because Hand & Hyle are cruel & obdurate to me.

Plate 68

"O Skofield, why art thou cruel? Lo, Joseph is thine! to make
"You One, to weave you both in the same mantle of skin.
"Bind him down, Sisters, bind him down on Ebal, Mount of cursing.
"Malah, come forth from Lebanon, & Hoglah, from Mount Sinai!
"Come, circumscribe this tongue of sweets, & with a screw of iron
"Fasten this ear into the rock. Milcah, the task is thine!
"Weep not so, Sisters, weep not so: our life depends on this,
"Or mercy & truth are fled away from Shechem & Mount Gilead,
"Unless my beloved is bound upon the Stems of Vegetation."

And thus the Warriors cry, in the hot day of Victory, in Songs:

"Look! the beautiful Daughter of Albion sits naked upon the Stone,
"Her panting Victim beside her: her heart is drunk with blood
"Tho' her brain is not drunk with wine: she goes forth from Albion
"In pride of beauty, in cruelty of holiness, in the brightness
"Of her tabernacle & her ark & secret place: the beautiful Daughter

"Of Albion delights the eyes of the Kings: their hearts & the
"Hearts of their Warriors glow hot before Thor & Friga. O Molech!
"O Chemosh! O Bacchus! O Venus! O Double God of Generation!
"The Heavens are cut like a mantle around from the Cliffs of Albion
"Across Europe, across Africa: in howlings & deadly War,
"A sheet & veil & curtain of blood is let down from Heaven
"Across the hills of Ephraim & down Mount Olivet to
"The Valley of the Jebusite. Molech rejoices in heaven,
"He sees the Twelve Daughters naked upon the Twelve Stones
"Themselves condensing to rocks & into the Ribs of a Man.
"Lo, they shoot forth in tender Nerves across Europe & Asia.
"Lo, they rest upon the Tribes, where their panting Victims lie.
"Molech rushes into the Kings, in love to the beautiful Daughters,
"But they frown & delight in cruelty, refusing all other joy.
"Bring your Offerings, your first begotten, pamper'd with milk & blood,
"Your first born of seven years old, be they Males or Females,
"To the beautiful Daughters of Albion! they sport before the Kings
"Clothed in the skin of the Victim! blood, human blood is the life
"And delightful food of the Warrior; the well fed Warrior's flesh
"Of him who is slain in War fills the Valleys of Ephraim with
"Breeding Women walking in pride & bringing forth under green trees
"With pleasure, without pain, for their food is blood of the Captive.
"Molech rejoices thro' the Land from Havilah to Shur: he rejoices
"In moral law & its severe penalties; loud Shaddai & Jehovah
"Thunder above, when they see the Twelve panting Victims
"On the Twelve Stones of Power, & the beautiful Daughters of Albion:
" 'If you dare rend their Veil with your Spear, you are healed of Love.'
"From the Hills of Camberwell & Wimbledon, from the Valleys
"Of Walton & Esher, from Stone-henge & from Malden's Cove,
"Jerusalem's Pillars fall in the rendings of fierce War.
"Over France & Germany, upon the Rhine & Danube,
"Reuben & Benjamin flee: they hide in the Valley of Rephaim.
"Why trembles the Warrior's limbs when he beholds thy beauty
"Spotted with Victims' blood? by the fires of thy secret tabernacle
"And thy ark & holy place, at thy frowns, at thy dire revenge,
"Smitten as Uzzah of old, his armour is soften'd, his spear
"And sword faint in his hand from Albion across Great Tartary.
"O beautiful Daughter of Albion! cruelty is thy delight.
"O Virgin of terrible eyes who dwellest by Valleys of springs
"Beneath the Mountains of Lebanon in the City of Rehob in Hamath,
"Taught to touch the harp, to dance in the Circle of Warriors
"Before the Kings of Canaan, to cut the flesh from the Victim,

"To roast the flesh in fire, to examine the Infant's limbs
"In cruelties of holiness, to refuse the joys of love, to bring
"The Spies from Egypt, to raise jealousy in the bosoms of the Twelve
"Kings of Canaan, then to let the Spies depart to Meribah Kadesh,
"To the place of the Amalekite: I am drunk with unsatiated love,
"I must rush again to War, for the Virgin has frown'd & refus'd.
"Sometimes I curse & sometimes bless thy fascinating beauty.
"Once Man was occupied in intellectual pleasures & Energies,
"But now my Soul is harrow'd with grief & fear & love & desire,
"And now I hate & now I love, & Intellect is no more.
"There is no time for any thing but the torments of love & desire.
"The Feminine & Masculine Shadows, soft, mild & ever varying
"In beauty, are Shadows now no more, but Rocks in Horeb."

Plate 69

Then all the Males conjoined into One Male, & every one
Became a ravening eating Cancer growing in the Female,
A Polypus of Roots, of Reasoning, Doubt, Despair & Death,
Going forth & returning from Albion's Rocks to Canaan,
Devouring Jerusalem from every Nation of the Earth.

Envying stood the enormous Form, at variance with Itself
In all its Members, in eternal torment of love & jealousy,
Driv'n forth by Los time after time from Albion's cliffy shore,
Drawing the free loves of Jerusalem into infernal bondage
That they might be born in contentions of Chastity & in
Deadly Hate between Leah & Rachel, Daughters of Deceit & Fraud
Bearing the Images of various Species of Contention
And Jealousy & Abhorrence & Revenge & deadly Murder,
Till they refuse liberty to the Male, & not like Beulah
Where every Female delights to give her maiden to her husband:
The Female searches sea & land for gratifications to the
Male Genius, who in return clothes her in gems & gold
And feeds her with the food of Eden; hence all her beauty beams.
She Creates at her will a little moony night & silence
With Spaces of sweet gardens & a tent of elegant beauty,
Closed in by a sandy desart & a night of stars shining
And a little tender moon & hovering angels on the wing;
And the Male gives a Time & Revolution to her Space
Till the time of love is passed in ever varying delights.
For All Things Exist in the Human Imagination,
And thence in Beulah they are stolen by secret amorous theft
Till they have had Punishment enough to make them commit Crimes.
Hence rose the Tabernacle in the Wilderness & all its Offerings,

From Male & Female Loves in Beulah & their Jealousies;
But no one can consummate Female bliss in Los's World without
Becoming a Generated Mortal, a Vegetating Death.

And now the Spectres of the Dead awake in Beulah; all
The Jealousies become Murderous, uniting together in Rahab
A Religion of Chastity, forming a Commerce to sell Loves,
With Moral Law an Equal Balance not going down with decision.
Therefore the Male severe & cruel, fill'd with stern Revenge,
Mutual Hate returns & mutual Deceit & mutual Fear.

Hence the Infernal Veil grows in the disobedient Female,
Which Jesus rends & the whole Druid Law removes away
From the Inner Sanctuary, a False Holiness hid within the Center.
For the Sanctuary of Eden is in the Camp, in the Outline,
In the Circumference, & every Minute Particular is Holy:
Embraces are Cominglings from the Head even to the Feet,
And not a pompous High Priest entering by a Secret Place.

Jerusalem pined in her inmost soul over Wandering Reuben
As she slept in Beulah's Night, hid by the Daughters of Beulah.

Plate 70

And this the form of mighty Hand sitting on Albion's cliffs
Before the face of Albion, a mighty threat'ning Form:

His bosom wide & shoulders huge, overspreading wondrous,
Bear Three strong sinewy Necks & Three awful & terrible Heads,
Three Brains, in contradictory council brooding incessantly,
Neither daring to put in act its councils, fearing each-other,
Therefore rejecting Ideas as nothing & holding all Wisdom
To consist in the agreements & disagree[me]nts of Ideas,
Plotting to devour Albion's Body of Humanity & Love.

Such Form the aggregate of the Twelve Sons of Albion took, & such
Their appearance when combin'd; but often by birth-pangs & loud groans
They divide to Twelve; the key-bones & the chest dividing in pain
Disclose a hideous orifice; thence issuing, the Giant-brood
Arise, as the smoke of the furnace, shaking the rocks from sea to sea,
And there they combine into Three Forms named Bacon & Newton & Locke
In the Oak Groves of Albion which overspread all the Earth.

Imputing Sin & Righteousness to Individuals, Rahab
Sat, deep within him hid, his Feminine Power unreveal'd,
Brooding Abstract Philosophy to destroy Imagination, the Divine-
Humanity: A Three-fold Wonder, feminine, most beautiful, Three-fold
Each within other. On her white marble & even Neck, her Heart,
Inorb'd and bonified, with locks of shadowing modesty, shining
Over her beautiful Female features soft flourishing in beauty,
Beams mild, all love and all perfection, that when the lips
Recieve a kiss from Gods or Men, a threefold kiss returns
From the press'd loveliness; so her whole immortal form three-fold,
Three-fold embrace returns, consuming lives of Gods & Men,
In fires of beauty melting them as gold & silver in the furnace.
Her Brain enlabyrinths the whole heaven of her bosom & loins
To put in act what her Heart wills. O who can withstand her power!
Her name is Vala in Eternity: in Time her name is Rahab.

The Starry Heavens all were fled from the mighty limbs of Albion,

Plate 71

And above Albion's Land was seen the Heavenly Canaan
As the Substance is to the Shadow, and above Albion's Twelve Sons
Were seen Jerusalem's Sons and all the Twelve Tribes spreading
Over Albion. As the Soul is to the Body, so Jerusalem's Sons
Are to the Sons of Albion, and Jerusalem is Albion's Emanation.

What is Above is Within, for every-thing in Eternity is translucent:
The Circumference is Within, Without is formed the Selfish Center,
And the Circumference still expands going forward to Eternity,
And the Center has Eternal States; these States we now explore.

And these the Names of Albion's Twelve Sons & of his Twelve Daughters
With their Districts: Hand dwelt in Selsey & had Sussex & Surrey
And Kent & Middlesex, all their Rivers & their Hills of flocks & herds,
Their Villages, Towns, Cities, Sea-Ports, Temples, sublime Cathedrals,
All were his Friends, & their Sons & Daughters intermarry in Beulah;
For all are Men in Eternity, Rivers, Mountains, Cities, Villages,
All are Human, & when you enter into their Bosoms you walk
In Heavens & Earths, as in your own Bosom you bear your Heaven
And Earth & all you behold; tho' it appears Without, it is Within,
In your Imagination, of which this World of Mortality is but a Shadow.

Hyle dwelt in Winchester, comprehending Hants, Dorset, Devon, Cornwall,
Their Villages, Cities, Sea Ports, their Corn fields & Gardens spacious,
Palaces, Rivers & Mountains; and between Hand & Hyle arose
Gwendolen & Cambel who is Boadicea: they go abroad & return
Like lovely beams of light from the mingled affections of the Brothers.
The Inhabitants of the whole Earth rejoice in their beautiful light.

Coban dwelt in Bath: Somerset, Wiltshire, Gloucestershire
Obey'd his awful voice: Ignoge is his lovely Emanation;
She adjoin'd with Gwantoke's Children; soon lovely Cordella arose;
Gwantoke forgave & joy'd over South Wales & all its Mountains.

Peachey had North Wales, Shropshire, Cheshire & the Isle of Man;
His Emanation is Mehetabel, terrible & lovely upon the Mountains.

Brertun had Yorkshire, Durham, Westmoreland, & his Emanation
Is Ragan; she adjoin'd to Slade, & produced Gonorill far beaming.

Slade had Lincoln, Stafford, Derby, Nottingham, & his lovely
Emanation, Gonorill, rejoices over hills & rocks & woods & rivers.

Huttn had Warwick, Northampton, Bedford, Buckingham,
Leicester & Berkshire, & his Emanation is Gwinefred beautiful.

Skofeld had Ely, Rutland, Cambridge, Huntingdon, Norfolk,
Suffolk, Hartford & Essex, & his Emanation is Gwinevera
Beautiful; she beams towards the east, all kinds of precious stones
And pearl, with instruments of music in holy Jerusalem.

Kox had Oxford, Warwick, Wilts; his Emanation is Estrild;
Join'd with Cordella she shines southward over the Atlantic.

Kotope had Hereford, Stafford, Worcester, & his Emanation
Is Sabrina; join'd with Mehetabel she shines west over America.

Bowen had all Scotland, the Isles, Northumberland & Cumberland;
His Emanation is Conwenna; she shines a triple form
Over the north with pearly beams gorgeous & terrible.
Jerusalem & Vala rejoice in Bowen & Conwenna.

But the Four Sons of Jerusalem that never were Generated
Are Rintrah and Palamabron and Theotormon and Bromion. They
Dwell over the Four Provinces of Ireland in heavenly light,
The Four Universities of Scotland, & in Oxford & Cambridge & Winchester.

But now Albion is darkened & Jerusalem lies in ruins
Above the Mountains of Albion, above the head of Los.

And Los shouted with ceaseless shoutings, & his tears poured down
His immortal cheeks, rearing his hands to heaven for aid Divine!
But he spoke not to Albion, fearing lest Albion should turn his Back
Against the Divine Vision & fall over the Precipice of Eternal Death;
But he receded before Albion & before Vala weaving the Veil
With the iron shuttle of War among the rooted Oaks of Albion,
Weeping & shouting to the Lord day & night; and his Children
Wept round him as a flock silent Seven Days of Eternity.

Plate 72

And the Thirty-two Counties of the Four Provinces of Ireland
Are thus divided: The Four Counties are in the Four Camps,
Munster South in Reuben's Gate, Connaut West in Joseph's Gate,
Ulster North in Dan's Gate, Leinster East in Judah's Gate;

For Albion in Eternity has Sixteen Gates among his Pillars,
But the Four towards the West were Walled up, & the Twelve
That front the Four other Points were turned Four Square
By Los for Jerusalem's sake & called the Gates of Jerusalem,
Because Twelve Sons of Jerusalem fled successive thro' the Gates.
But the Four Sons of Jerusalem who fled not but remain'd,
Are Rintrah & Palamabron & Theotormon & Bromion,
The Four that remain with Los to guard the Western Wall;
And these Four remain to guard the Four Walls of Jerusalem
Whose foundations remain in the Thirty-two Counties of Ireland
And in Twelve Counties of Wales & in the Forty Counties
Of England & in the Thirty-six Counties of Scotland.

And the names of the Thirty-two Counties of Ireland are these:
Under Judah & Issachar & Zebulun are Lowth, Longford,
Eastmeath, Westmeath, Dublin, Kildare, King's County,
Queen's County, Wicklow, Catherloh, Wexford, Kilkenny.
And those under Reuben & Simeon & Levi are these:
Waterford, Tipperary, Cork, Limerick, Kerry, Clare.
And those under Ephraim, Manasseh & Benjamin are these:
Galway, Roscommon, Mayo, Sligo, Leitrim.
And those under Dan, Asher & Napthali are these:
Donnegal, Antrim, Tyrone, Fermanagh, Armagh, Londonderry,
Down, Managhan, Cavan. These are the Land of Erin.

All these Center in London & in Golgonooza, from whence
They are Created continually, East & West & North & South,
And from them are Created all the Nations of the Earth,
Europe & Asia & Africa & America, in fury Fourfold.

And Thirty-two the Nations to dwell in Jerusalem's Gates.
O Come ye Nations! Come ye People! Come up to Jerusalem!
Return, Jerusalem, & dwell together as of old! Return,
Return, O Albion! let Jerusalem overspread all Nations
As in the times of old! O Albion awake! Reuben wanders,
The Nations wait for Jerusalem, they look up for the Bride.

France, Spain, Italy, Germany, Poland, Russia, Sweden, Turkey,
Arabia, Palestine, Persia, Hindostan, China, Tartary, Siberia,
Egypt, Lybia, Ethiopia, Guinea, Caffraria, Negroland, Morocco,
Congo, Zaara, Canada, Greenland, Carolina, Mexico,
Peru, Patagonia, Amazonia, Brazil: Thirty-two Nations,
And under these Thirty-two Classes of Islands in the Ocean
All the Nations, Peoples & Tongues throughout all the Earth.

And the Four Gates of Los surround the Universe Within and
Without; & whatever is visible in the Vegetable Earth, the same
Is visible in the Mundane Shell revers'd, in mountain & vale.
And a Son of Eden was set over each Daughter of Beulah to guard
In Albion's Tomb the wondrous Creation, & the Four-fold Gate
Towards Beulah is to the South. Fenelon, Guion, Teresa,
Whitefield & Hervey guard that Gate, with all the gentle Souls
Who guide the great Wine-press of Love. Four precious Stones that Gate.

Plate 73

Such are Cathedron's golden Halls in the City of Golgonooza.

And Los's Furnaces howl loud, living, self-moving, lamenting
With fury & despair, & they stretch from South to North
Thro' all the Four Points. Lo! the Labourers at the Furnaces,
Rintrah & Palamabron, Theotormon & Bromion, loud lab'ring
With the innumerable multitudes of Golgonooza round the Anvils
Of Death! But how they came forth from the Furnaces, & how long
Vast & severe the anguish e'er they knew their Father, were
Long to tell; & of the iron rollers, golden axle-trees & yokes
Of brass, iron chains & braces, & the gold, silver & brass,
Mingled or separate, for swords, arrows, cannons, mortars,
The terrible ball, the wedge, the loud sounding hammer of destruction,
The sounding flail to thresh, the winnow to winnow kingdoms,
The water wheel & mill of many innumerable wheels resistless,
Over the Four fold Monarchy from Earth to the Mundane Shell:

Perusing Albion's Tomb in the starry characters of Og & Anak,
To Create the lion & wolf, the bear, the tyger & ounce,
To Create the wooly lamb & downy fowl & scaly serpent,
The summer & winter, day & night, the sun & moon & stars,
The tree, the plant, the flower, the rock, the stone, the metal
Of Vegetative Nature by their hard restricting condensations.

Where Luvah's World of Opakeness grew to a period, It
Became a Limit, a Rocky hardness without form & void,
Accumulating without end; here Los, who is of the Elohim,
Opens the Furnaces of affliction in the Emanation,
Fixing the Sexual into an ever-prolific Generation,
Naming the Limit of Opakeness, Satan, & the Limit of Contraction,
Adam, who is Peleg & Joktan, & Esau & Jacob, & Saul & David.

Voltaire insinuates that these Limits are the cruel work of God,
Mocking the Remover of Limits & the Resurrection of the Dead,
Setting up Kings in wrath, in holiness of Natural Religion:
Which Los with his mighty Hammer demolishes time on time
In miracles & wonders in the Four-fold Desart of Albion:
Permanently Creating, to be in Time Reveal'd & Demolish'd,
Satan, Cain, Tubal, Nimrod, Pharoh, Priam, Bladud, Belin,
Arthur, Alfred, the Norman Conqueror, Richard, John,
Edward, *Henry*, *Elizabeth*, *James*, *Charles*, *William*, *George*
And all the Kings & Nobles of the Earth & all their Glories:
These are Created by Rahab & Tirzah in Ulro; but around

These, to preserve them from Eternal Death, Los Creates
Adam, Noah, Abraham, Moses, Samuel, David, Ezekiel,
Pythagoras, *Socrates*, *Euripedes*, *Virgil*, *Dante*, *Milton*,
Dissipating the rocky forms of Death by his thunderous Hammer.
As the Pilgrim passes while the Country permanent remains,
So Men pass on, but States remain permanent for ever.

The Spectres of the Dead howl round the porches of Los
In the terrible Family feuds of Albion's cities & villages,
To devour the Body of Albion, hung'ring & thirsting & rav'ning.
The Sons of Los clothe them & feed, & provide houses & gardens,
And every Human Vegetated Form in its inward recesses
Is a house of ple[as]antness & a garden of delight Built by the
Sons & Daughters of Los in Bowlahoola & in Cathedron.

From London to York & Edinburgh the Furnaces rage terrible.
Primrose Hill is the mouth of the Furnace & the Iron Door.

Plate 74

The Four Zoas clouded rage. Urizen stood by Albion
With Rintrah and Palamabron and Theotormon and Bromion:
These Four are Verulam & London & York & Edinburgh.
And the Four Zoas are Urizen & Luvah & Tharmas & Urthona:
In opposition deadly, and their Wheels in poisonous
And deadly stupor turn'd against each other, loud & fierce,
Entering into the Reasoning Power, forsaking Imagination,
They became Spectres, & their Human Bodies were reposed
In Beulah by the Daughters of Beulah with tears & lamentations.

The Spectre is the Reasoning Power in Man, & when separated
From Imagination and closing itself as in steel in a Ratio
Of the Things of Memory, It thence frames Laws & Moralities
To destroy Imagination, the Divine Body, by Martyrdoms & Wars.

Teach me, O Holy Spirit, the Testimony of Jesus! let me
Comprehend wonderous things out of the Divine Law!
I behold Babylon in the opening Streets of London. I behold
Jerusalem in ruins wandering about from house to house.
This I behold: the shudderings of death attend my steps.
I walk up and down in Six Thousand Years: their Events are present
before me
To tell how Los in grief & anger, whirling round his Hammer on high,
Drave the Sons & Daughters of Albion from their ancient mountains.
They became the Twelve Gods of Asia Opposing the Divine Vision.

The Sons of Albion are Twelve, the Sons of Jerusalem Sixteen.
I tell how Albion's Sons, by Harmonies of Concords & Discords
Opposed to Melody, and by Lights & Shades opposed to Outline,
And by Abstraction opposed to the Visions of Imagination,
By cruel Laws, divided Sixteen into Twelve Divisions:
How Hyle roof'd Los in Albion's Cliffs by the Affections rent
Asunder & opposed to Thought, to draw Jerusalem's Sons
Into the Vortex of his Wheels, therefore Hyle is called Gog,
Age after age drawing them away towards Babylon,
Babylon, the Rational Morality, deluding to death the little ones
In strong temptations of stolen beauty. I tell how Reuben slept
On London Stone, & the Daughters of Albion ran around admiring
His awful beauty; with Moral Virtue, the fair deciever, offspring
Of Good & Evil, they divided him in love upon the Thames & sent
Him over Europe, in streams of gore, out of Cathedron's Looms:
How Los drave them from Albion & they became Daughters of Canaan;
Hence Albion was call'd the Canaanite & all his Giant Sons.
Hence is my Theme. O Lord my Saviour, open thou the Gates
And I will lead forth thy Words! telling how the Daughters
Cut the Fibres of Reuben, how he roll'd apart & took Root
In Bashan: terror-struck Albion's Sons look toward Bashan.
They have divided Simeon: he also roll'd apart in blood
Over the Nations till he took Root beneath the shining Looms
Of Albion's Daughters in Philistea by the side of Amalek.
They have divided Levi: he hath shot out into Forty eight Roots
Over the Land of Canaan; they have divided Judah:
He hath took Root in Hebron, in the Land of Hand & Hyle.
Dan, Napthali, Gad, Asher, Issachar, Zebulun roll apart
From all the Nations of the Earth to dissipate into Non Entity.

I see a Feminine Form arise from the Four terrible Zoas,
Beautiful but terrible, struggling to take a form of beauty,
Rooted in Shechem: this is Dinah, the youthful form of Erin.
The Wound I see in South Molton Street & Stratford place,
Whence Joseph & Benjamin roll'd apart away from the Nations.
In vain they roll'd apart: they are fix'd into the Land of Cabul.

Plate 75

And Rahab, Babylon the Great, hath destroyed Jerusalem.
Bath stood upon the Severn with Merlin & Bladud & Arthur,
The Cup of Rahab in his hand, her Poisons Twenty-seven-fold.

And all her Twenty-seven Heavens, now hid & now reveal'd,
Appear in strong delusive light of Time & Space, drawn out

In shadowy pomp, by the Eternal Prophet created evermore.
For Los in Six Thousand Years walks up & down continually
That not one Moment of Time be lost, & every revolution
Of Space he makes permanent in Bowlahoola & Cathedron.

And these the names of the Twenty-seven Heavens & their Churches:
Adam, Seth, Enos, Cainan, Mahalaleel, Jared, Enoch,
Methuselah, Lamech: these are the Giants mighty, Hermaphroditic.
Noah, Shem, Arphaxad, Cainan the Second, Salah, Heber,
Peleg, Reu, Serug, Nahor, Terah: these are the Female Males,
A Male within a Female hid as in an Ark & Curtains.
Abraham, Moses, Solomon, Paul, Constantine, Charlemaine,
Luther: these Seven are the Male Females, the Dragon Forms,
The Female hid within a Male; thus Rahab is reveal'd,
Mystery, Babylon the Great, the Abomination of Desolation,
Religion hid in War, a Dragon red & hidden Harlot.
But Jesus, breaking thro' the Central Zones of Death & Hell,
Opens Eternity in Time & Space, triumphant in Mercy.

Thus are the Heavens form'd by Los within the Mundane Shell.
And where Luther ends Adam begins again in Eternal Circle
To awake the Prisoners of Death, to bring Albion again
With Luvah into light eternal in his eternal day.

But now the Starry Heavens are fled from the mighty limbs of Albion.

[END OF CHAP: 3RD]

Plate 77

To the Christians

Devils are
False Religions.
"Saul, Saul,
"Why persecutest thou me?"

I give you the end of a golden string,
Only wind it into a ball,
It will lead you in at Heaven's gate
Built in Jerusalem's wall.

We are told to abstain from fleshly desires that we may lose no time from the Work of the Lord: Every moment lost is a moment that cannot be redeemed; every pleasure that intermingles with the duty of our station is a folly unredeemable, & is planted like the seed of a wild flower among our wheat: All the tortures of repentance are tortures of self-reproach on account of our leaving the Divine Harvest to the Enemy, the struggles of intanglement with incoherent roots. I know of no other Christianity and of no other Gospel than the liberty both of body & mind to exercise the Divine Arts of Imagination, Imagination, the real & eternal World of which this Vegetable Universe is but a faint shadow, & in which we shall live in our Eternal or Imaginative Bodies when these Vegetable Mortal Bodies are no more. The Apostles knew of no other Gospel. What were all their spiritual gifts? What is the Divine Spirit? is the Holy Ghost any other than an Intellectual Fountain? What is the Harvest of the Gospel & its Labours? What is that Talent which it is a curse to hide? What are the Treasures of Heaven which we are to lay up for ourselves, are they any other than Mental Studies & Performances? What are all the Gifts of the Gospel, are they not all Mental Gifts? Is God a Spirit who must be worshipped in Spirit & in Truth, and are not the Gifts of the Spirit Every-thing to Man? O ye Religious, discountenance every one among you who shall pretend to despise Art & Science! I call upon you in the Name of Jesus! What is the Life of Man but Art & Science? is it Meat & Drink? is not the Body more than Raiment? What is Mortality but the things relating to the Body which Dies? What is Immortality but the things relating to the Spirit which Lives Eternally? What is the Joy of Heaven but Improvement in the things of the Spirit? What are the Pains of Hell but Ignorance, Bodily Lust, Idleness & devastation of the things of the Spirit? Answer this to yourselves, & expel from among you those who pretend to despise the labours of Art & Science, which alone are the labours of the Gospel. Is not this plain & manifest to the thought? Can you think at all & not pronounce heartily That to Labour in Knowledge is to Build up Jerusalem, and to Despise Knowledge is to Despise Jerusalem & her Builders. And remember: He who despises & mocks a Mental Gift in another, calling it pride & selfishness & sin, mocks Jesus the giver of every Mental Gift, which always appear to the ignorance-loving Hypocrite as Sins; but that which is a Sin in the sight of cruel Man is not so in the sight of our kind God. Let every Christian, as much as in him lies, engage himself openly & publicly before all the World in some Mental pursuit for the Building up of Jerusalem.

I stood among my valleys of the south
And saw a flame of fire, even as a Wheel
Of fire surrounding all the heavens: it went
From west to east, against the current of
Creation, and devour'd all things in its loud
Fury & thundering course round heaven & earth.
By it the Sun was roll'd into an orb,
By it the Moon faded into a globe
Travelling thro' the night; for, from its dire
And restless fury, Man himself shrunk up
Into a little root a fathom long.

And I asked a Watcher & a Holy-One
Its Name; he answered: "It is the Wheel of Religion."
I wept & said: "Is this the law of Jesus,
"This terrible devouring sword turning every way?"
He answer'd: "Jesus died because he strove
"Against the current of this Wheel; its Name
"Is Caiaphas, the dark Preacher of Death,
"Of sin, of sorrow & of punishment:
"Opposing Nature! It is Natural Religion;
"But Jesus is the bright Preacher of Life
"Creating Nature from this fiery Law
"By self-denial & forgiveness of Sin.
"Go therefore, cast out devils in Christ's name,
"Heal thou the sick of spiritual disease,
"Pity the evil, for thou art not sent
"To smite with terror & with punishments
"Those that are sick, like to the Pharisees
"Crucifying & encompassing sea & land
"For proselytes to tyranny & wrath;
"But to the Publicans & Harlots go,
"Teach them True Happiness, but let no curse
"Go forth out of thy mouth to blight their peace;
"For Hell is open'd to Heaven: thine eyes beheld
"The dungeons burst & the Prisoners set free."

England! awake! awake! awake!
Jerusalem thy Sister calls!
Why wilt thou sleep the sleep of death
And close her from thy ancient walls?

Thy hills & valleys felt her feet
Gently upon their bosoms move:
Thy gates beheld sweet Zion's ways:
Then was a time of joy and love.

And now the time returns again:
Our souls exult, & London's towers
Recieve the Lamb of God to dwell
In England's green & pleasant bowers.

Plate 78

Jerusalem. C. 4

The Spectres of Albion's Twelve Sons revolve mightily
Over the Tomb & over the Body, rav'ning to devour
The Sleeping Humanity. Los with his mace of iron

Walks round; loud his threats, loud his blows fall
On the rocky Spectres, as the Potter breaks the potsherds,
Dashing in pieces Self-righteousnesses, driving them from Albion's
Cliffs, dividing them into Male & Female forms in his Furnaces
And on his Anvils; lest they destroy the Feminine Affections
They are broken. Loud howl the Spectres in his iron Furnace.

While Los laments at his dire labours, viewing Jerusalem,
Sitting before his Furnaces clothed in sackcloth of hair,
Albion's Twelve Sons surround the Forty-two Gates of Erin
In terrible armour, raging against the Lamb & against Jerusalem,
Surrounding them with armies to destroy the Lamb of God.
They took their Mother Vala and they crown'd her with gold;
They nam'd her Rahab & gave her power over the Earth,
The Concave Earth round Golgonooza in Entuthon Benython,
Even to the stars exalting her Throne, to build beyond the Throne
Of God and the Lamb, to destroy the Lamb & usurp the Throne of God,
Drawing their Ulro Voidness round the Four-fold Humanity.

Naked Jerusalem lay before the Gates upon Mount Zion
The Hill of Giants, all her foundations levell'd with the dust,

Her Twelve Gates thrown down, her children carried into captivity,
Herself in chains; this from within was seen in a dismal night
Outside, unknown before in Beulah; & the twelve gates were fill'd
With blood, from Japan eastward to the Giants causway west
In Erin's Continent; and Jerusalem wept upon Euphrates' banks
Disorganiz'd: an evanescent shade scarce seen or heard among
Her children's Druid Temples, dropping with blood, wander'd weeping!
And thus her voice went forth in the darkness of Philisthea:

"My brother & my father are no more! God hath forsaken me!
"The arrows of the Almighty pour upon me & my children!
"I have sinned and am an outcast from the Divine Presence!

Plate 79

"My tents are fall'n! my pillars are in ruins! my children dash'd
"Upon Egypt's iron floors & the marble pavements of Assyria!
"I melt my soul in reasonings among the towers of Heshbon.
"Mount Zion is become a cruel rock, & no more dew
"Nor rain, no more the spring of the rock appears, but cold
"Hard & obdurate are the furrows of the mountain of wine & oil:

"The mountain of blessing is itself a curse & an astonishment.
"The hills of Judea are fallen with me into the deepest hell.
"Away from the Nations of the Earth & from the Cities of the Nations
"I walk to Ephraim. I seek for Shiloh. I walk like a lost sheep
"Among precipices of despair; in Goshen I seek for light
"In vain, and in Gilead for a physician and a comforter.
"Goshen hath follow'd Philistea. Gilead hath join'd with Og.
"They are become narrow places in a little and dark land,
"How distant far from Albion! his hills & his valleys no more
"Recieve the feet of Jerusalem: they have cast me quite away,
"And Albion is himself shrunk to a narrow rock in the midst of the sea!
"The plains of Sussex & Surrey, their hills of flocks & herds
"No more seek to Jerusalem nor to the sound of my Holy-ones.
"The Fifty-two Counties of England are harden'd against me
"As if I was not their Mother; they despise me & cast me out.
"London cover'd the whole Earth: England encompass'd the Nations,
"And all the Nations of the Earth were seen in the Cities of Albion.
"My pillars reach'd from sea to sea. London beheld me come
"From my east & from my west; he blessed me and gave
"His children to my breasts, his sons & daughters to my knees.
"His aged parents sought me out in every city & village;
"They discern'd my countenance with joy, they shew'd me to their sons,
"Saying, 'Lo Jerusalem is here! she sitteth in our secret chambers.
" 'Levi and Judah & Issachar, Ephra[i]m, Manasseh, Gad and Dan
" 'Are seen in our hills & valleys: they keep our flocks & herds:
" 'They watch them in the night, and the Lamb of God appears among us.'
"The river Severn stay'd his course at my command:
"Thames poured his waters into my basons and baths:
"Medway mingled with Kishon: Thames reciev'd the heavenly Jordan.
"Albion gave me to the whole Earth to walk up & down, to pour
"Joy upon every mountain, to teach songs to the shepherd & plowman.
"I taught the ships of the sea to sing the songs of Zion.
"Italy saw me in sublime astonishment: France was wholly mine
"As my garden & as my secret bath: Spain was my heavenly couch,
"I slept in his golden hills; the Lamb of God met me there,
"There we walked as in our secret chamber among our little ones,
"They looked upon our loves with joy, they beheld our secret joys
"With holy raptures of adoration, rap'd sublime in the Visions of God.
"Germany, Poland & the North wooed my footsteps, they found
"My gates in all their mountains & my curtains in all their vales;
"The furniture of their houses was the furniture of my chamber.

"Turkey & Grecia saw my instr[u]ments of music; they arose,
"They siez'd the harp, the flute, the mellow horn of Jerusalem's joy;
"They sounded thanksgivings in my courts. Egypt & Lybia heard,
"The swarthy sons of Ethiopia stood round the Lamb of God
"Enquiring for Jerusalem: he led them up my steps to my altar.
"And thou, America! I once beheld thee, but now behold no more
"Thy golden mountains where my Cherubim & Seraphim rejoic'd
"Together among my little-ones. But now my Altars run with blood,
"My fires are corrupt, my incense is a cloudy pestilence
"Of seven diseases! Once a continual cloud of salvation rose
"From all my myriads, once the Four-fold World rejoic'd among
"The pillars of Jerusalem between my winged Cherubim;
"But now I am clos'd out from them in the narrow passages
"Of the valleys of destruction into a dark land of pitch & bitumen,
"From Albion's Tomb afar and from the four-fold wonders of God
"Shrunk to a narrow doleful form in the dark land of Cabul.
"There is Reuben & Gad & Joseph & Judah & Levi clos'd up
"In narrow vales. I walk & count the bones of my beloveds
"Along the Valley of Destruction, among these Druid Temples
"Which overspread all the Earth in patriarchal pomp & cruel pride.
"Tell me, O Vala, thy purposes; tell me wherefore thy shuttles
"Drop with the gore of the slain, why Euphrates is red with blood,
"Wherefore in dreadful majesty & beauty outside appears
"Thy Masculine from thy Feminine, hardening against the heavens
"To devour the Human! Why dost thou weep upon the wind among
"These cruel Druid Temples? O Vala! Humanity is far above
"Sexual organization & the Visions of the Night of Beulah
"Where Sexes wander in dreams of bliss among the Emanations,
"Where the Masculine & Feminine are nurs'd into Youth & Maiden
"By the tears & smiles of Beulah's Daughters till the time of Sleep is past.
"Wherefore then do you realize these nets of beauty & delusion
"In open day, to draw the souls of the Dead into the light
"Till Albion is shut out from every Nation under Heaven?

Plate 80

"Encompass'd by the frozen Net and by the rooted Tree
"I walk weeping in pangs of a Mother's torment for her Children.
"I walk in affliction. I am a worm and no living soul!
"A worm going to eternal torment, rais'd up in a night
"To an eternal night of pain, lost! lost! lost! for ever!"

Beside her Vala howl'd upon the winds in pride of beauty,
Lamenting among the timbrels of the Warriors, among the Captives

In cruel holiness, and her lamenting songs were from Arnon
And Jordan to Euphrates. Jerusalem follow'd trembling
Her children in captivity, listening to Vala's lamentation
In the thick cloud & darkness, & the voice went forth from
The cloud: "O rent in sunder from Jerusalem the Harlot daughter!
"In an eternal condemnation, in fierce burning flames
"Of torment unendurable! and if once a Delusion be found
"Woman must perish & the Heavens of Heavens remain no more.

"My Father gave to me command to murder Albion
"In unreviving Death; my Love, my Luvah, order'd me in night
"To murder Albion, the King of Men; he fought in battles fierce,
"He conquer'd Luvah, my beloved, he took me and my Father,
"He slew them. I revived them to life in my warm bosom.
"He saw them issue from my bosom dark in Jealousy.
"He burn'd before me. Luvah fram'd the Knife & Luvah gave
"The Knife into his daughter's hand; such thing was never known
"Before in Albion's land, that one should die a death never to be reviv'd!
"For, in our battles, we the Slain men view with pity and love,
"We soon revive them in the secret of our tabernacles;
"But I, Vala, Luvah's daughter, keep his body, embalm'd in moral laws
"With spices of sweet odours of lovely jealous stupefaction,
"Within my bosom, lest he arise to life & slay my Luvah.
"Pity me then, O Lamb of God! O Jesus pity me!
"Come into Luvah's Tents and seek not to revive the Dead!"

So sang she, and the Spindle turn'd furious as she sang.
The Children of Jerusalem, the Souls of those who sleep,
Were caught into the flax of her Distaff & in her Cloud
To weave Jerusalem a body according to her will,
A Dragon form on Zion Hill's most ancient promontory.

The Spindle turn'd in blood & fire: loud sound the trumpets
Of war: the cymbals play loud before the Captains
With Cambel & Gwendolen in dance and solemn song.
The Cloud of Rahab vibrating with the Daughters of Albion
Los saw terrified, melted with pity & divided in wrath
He sent them over the narrow seas in pity and love
Among the Four Forests of Albion which overspread all the Earth.
They go forth & return swift as a flash of lightning
Among the tribes of warriors, among the Stones of power;
Against Jerusalem they rage thro' all the Nations of Europe,
Thro' Italy & Grecia to Lebanon & Persia & India.

The Serpent Temples thro' the Earth, from the wide Plain of Salisbury,
Resound with cries of Victims, shouts & songs & dying groans
And flames of dusky fire, to Amalek, Canaan and Moab.
And Rahab, like a dismal and indefinite hovering Cloud,
Refus'd to take a definite form; she hover'd over all the Earth
Calling the definite, sin, defacing every definite form
Invisible or Visible, stretch'd out in length or spread in breadth
Over the Temples, drinking groans of victims, weeping in pity
And joying in the pity, howling over Jerusalem's walls.

Hand slept on Skiddaw's top, drawn by the love of beautiful
Cambel, his bright beaming Counterpart, divided from him;
And her delusive light beam'd fierce above the Mountain,
Soft, invisible, drinking his sighs in sweet intoxication,
Drawing out fibre by fibre, returning to Albion's Tree
At night and in the morning to Skiddaw; she sent him over
Mountainous Wales into the Loom of Cathedron fibre by fibre.
He ran in tender nerves across Europe to Jerusalem's Shade
To weave Jerusalem a Body repugnant to the Lamb.

Hyle on East Moor in rocky Derbyshire rav'd to the Moon
For Gwendolen; she took up in bitter tears his anguish'd heart
That, apparent to all in Eternity, glows like the Sun in the breast:
She hid it in his ribs & back; she hid his tongue with teeth.
In terrible convulsions, pitying & gratified, drunk with pity,
Glowing with loveliness before him, becoming apparent
According to his changes, she roll'd his kidneys round
Into two irregular forms, and looking on Albion's dread Tree,
She wove two vessels of seed, beautiful as Skiddaw's snow,
Giving them bends of self interest & selfish natural virtue.
She hid them in his loins; raving he ran among the rocks,
Compell'd into a shape of Moral Virtue against the Lamb,
The invisible lovely one giving him a form according to
His Law, a form against the Lamb of God, oppos'd to Mercy
And playing in the thunderous Loom in sweet intoxication,
Filling cups of silver & crystal with shrieks & cries, with groans
And dolorous sobs, the wine of lovers in the Wine-press of Luvah.

"O sister Cambel," said Gwendolen, as their long beaming light
Mingled above the Mountain, "what shall we do to keep
"These awful forms in our soft bands, distracted with trembling?

Plate 81

"I have mock'd those who refused cruelty, & I have admired
"The cruel Warrior. I have refused to give love to Merlin the piteous.

"He brings to me the Images of his Love & I reject in chastity
"And turn them out into the streets for Harlots, to be food
"To the stern Warrior. I am become perfect in beauty over my Warrior;
"For Men are caught by Love: Woman is caught by Pride,
"That Love may only be obtain'd in the passages of Death.
"Let us look: let us examine: is the Cruel become an Infant,
"Or is he still a cruel Warrior? look Sisters, look! O piteous!
"I have destroy'd Wand'ring Reuben who strove to bind my Will.
"I have strip'd off Joseph's beautiful integument for my Beloved,
"The Cruel-one of Albion, to clothe him in gems of my Zone.
"I have named him Jehovah of Hosts. Humanity is become
"A weeping Infant in ruin'd lovely Jerusalem's folding Cloud.

[In Heaven Love begets Love, but Fear is the Parent of Earthly Love,
And he who will not bend to Love must be subdu'd by Fear.]

Plate 82

"I have heard Jerusalem's groans; from Vala's cries & lamentations
"I gather our eternal fate. Outcasts from life and love,
"Unless we find a way to bind these awful Forms to our
"Embrace, we shall perish annihilate; discover'd our Delusions.
"Look! I have wrought without delusion. Look! I have wept,
"And given soft milk mingled together with the spirits of flocks
"Of lambs and doves, mingled together in cups and dishes
"Of painted clay; the mighty Hyle is become a weeping infant.
"Soon shall the Spectres of the Dead follow my weaving threads."

The Twelve Daughters of Albion attentive listen in secret shades,
On Cambridge and Oxford beaming soft, uniting with Rahab's cloud,
While Gwendolen spoke to Cambel, turning soft the spinning reel,
Or throwing the wing'd shuttle, or drawing the cords with softest songs.
The golden cords of the Looms animate beneath their touches soft
Along the Island white, among the Druid Temples, while Gwendolen
Spoke to the Daughters of Albion standing on Skiddaw's top.

So saying she took a Falsehood & hid it in her left hand
To entice her Sisters away to Babylon on Euphrates.
And thus she closed her left hand and utter'd her Falsehood,
Forgetting that Falsehood is prophetic: she hid her hand behind her,
Upon her back behind her loins, & thus utter'd her Deceit:

"I heard Enitharmon say to Los: 'Let the Daughters of Albion
" 'Be scatter'd abroad and let the name of Albion be forgotten.
" 'Divide them into three; name them Amalek, Canaan & Moab.
" 'Let Albion remain a desolation without an inhabitant,
" 'And let the Looms of Enitharmon & the Furnaces of Los
" 'Create Jerusalem & Babylon & Egypt & Moab & Amalek
" 'And Helle & Hesperia & Hindostan & China & Japan;
" 'But hide America, for a Curse, an Altar of Victims & a Holy Place.'
"See Sisters, Canaan is pleasant, Egypt is as the Garden of Eden,
"Babylon is our chief desire, Moab our bath in summer.
"Let us lead the stems of this Tree, let us plant it before Jerusalem,
"To judge the Friend of Sinners to death without the Veil,
"To cut her off from America, to close up her secret Ark
"And the fury of Man exhaust in War, Woman permanent remain.
"See how the fires of our loins point eastward to Babylon!
"Look, Hyle is become an infant Love! look! behold! see him lie

"Upon my bosom; look! here is the lovely wayward form
"That gave me sweet delight by his torments beneath my Veil!
"By the fruit of Albion's Tree I have fed him with sweet milk.
"By contentions of the mighty for Sacrifice of Captives,
"Humanity, the Great Delusion, is chang'd to War & Sacrifice:
"I have nail'd his hands on Beth Rabbim & his hands on Heshbon's Wall.
"O that I could live in his sight! O that I could bind him to my arm!"

So saying, She drew aside her Veil, from Mam-Tor to Dovedale,
Discovering her own perfect beauty to the Daughters of Albion
And Hyle a winding Worm beneath *her loom upon the scales*
Hyle was become a winding Worm & not a weeping Infant
Trembling & pitying she scream'd & fled upon the wind.
Hyle was a winding Worm and herself perfect in beauty.
The desarts tremble at his wrath, they shrink themselves in fear.

Cambel trembled with jealousy: she trembled! she envied!
The envy ran thro' Cathedron's Looms into the Heart
Of mild Jerusalem to destroy the Lamb of God. Jerusalem
Languish'd upon Mount Olivet, East of mild Zion's Hill.

Los saw the envious blight above his Seventh Furnace
On London's Tower on the Thames; he drew Cambel in wrath
Into his thundering Bellows, heaving it for a loud blast,
And with the blast of his Furnace upon fishy Billingsgate,
Beneath Albion's fatal Tree before the Gate of Los,
Shew'd her the fibres of her beloved to ameliorate
The envy; loud she labour'd in the Furnace of fire
To form the mighty form of Hand according to her will
In the Furnaces of Los & in the Wine-press, treading day & night
Naked among the human clusters, bringing wine of anguish
To feed the afflicted in the Furnaces; she minded not
The raging flames, tho' she return'd *consum'd day after day*
A redning skeleton in howling woe instead of beauty
Deformity; she gave her beauty to another, bearing abroad
Her struggling torment in her iron arms, and like a chain
Binding his wrists & ankles with the iron arms of love.

Gwendolen saw the Infant in her sister's arms; she howl'd
Over the forests with bitter tears and over the winding Worm
Repentant, and she also in the eddying wind of Los's Bellows
Began her dolorous task of love in the Wine-press of Luvah
To form the Worm into a form of love by tears & pain.
The Sisters saw: trembling ran thro' their Looms, soften[in]g mild
Towards London: then they saw the Furna[c]es open'd & in tears

Began to give their souls away in the Furna[c]es of affliction.
Los saw & was comforted at his Furnaces, uttering thus his voice:
"I know I am Urthona, keeper of the Gates of Heaven,
"And that I can at will expatiate in the Gardens of bliss;
"But pangs of love draw me down to my loins, which are
"Become a fountain of veiny pipes. O Albion! my brother!

Plate 83

"Corruptability appears upon thy limbs, and never more
"Can I arise and leave thy side, but labour here incessant
"Till thy awaking: yet alas, I shall forget Eternity!
"Against the Patriarchal pomp and cruelty labouring incessant,
"I shall become an Infant horror. Enion! Tharmas! friends
"Absorb me not in such dire grief. O Albion, my brother!
"Jerusalem hungers in the desart; affection to her children!
"The scorn'd and contemn'd youthful girl, where shall she fly?
"Sussex shuts up her Villages: Hants, Devon & Wilts,
"Surrounded with masses of stone in order'd forms: determine then
"A form for Vala and a form for Luvah, here on the Thames
"Where the Victim nightly howls beneath the Druid's knife,
"A Form of Vegetation; nail them down on the stems of Mystery.
"O when shall the Saxon return with the English, his redeemed brother?
"O when shall the Lamb of God descend among the Reprobate?
"I woo to Amalek to protect my fugitives: Amalek trembles.
"I call to Canaan & Moab in my night watches: they mourn,
"They listen not to my cry, they rejoice among their warriors.
"Woden and Thor and Friga wholly consume my Saxons
"On their enormous Altars built in the terrible north
"From Ireland's rocks to Scandinavia, Persia and Tartary,
"From the Atlantic Sea to the universal Erythrean.
"Found ye London! enormous City! weeps thy River?
"Upon his parent bosom lay thy little ones, O Land
"Forsaken! Surrey and Sussex are Enitharmon's Chamber
"Where I will build her a Couch of repose, & my pillars
"Shall surround her in beautiful labyrinths. Oothoon!
"Where hides my child? in Oxford hidest thou with Antamon?
"In graceful hidings of error, in merciful deceit
"Lest Hand the terrible destroy his Affection, thou hidest her;
"In chaste appearances for sweet deceits of love & modesty
"Immingled, interwoven, glistening to the sickening sight
"Let Cambel and her Sisters sit within the Mundane Shell
"Forming the fluctuating Globe according to their will:

"According as they weave the little embryon nerves & veins,
"The Eye, the little Nostrils & the delicate Tongue, & Ears
"Of labyrinthine intricacy, so shall they fold the World,
"That whatever is seen upon the Mundane Shell, the same
"Be seen upon the Fluctuating Earth woven by the Sisters.
"And sometimes the Earth shall roll in the Abyss & sometimes
"Stand in the Center & sometimes stretch flat in the Expanse,
"According to the will of the lovely Daughters of Albion;
"Sometimes it shall assimilate with mighty Golgonooza,
"Touching its summits, & sometimes divided roll apart.
"As a beautiful Veil, so these Females shall fold & unfold,
"According to their will, the outside surface of the Earth,
"An outside shadowy Surface superadded to the real Surface
"Which is unchangeable for ever & ever. Amen: so be it!
"Separate Albion's Sons gently from their Emanations,
"Weaving bowers of delight on the current of infant Thames,
"Where the old Parent still retains his youth, as I alas!
"Retain my youth eight thousand and five hundred years,
"The labourer of ages in the Valleys of Despair!
"The land is mark'd for desolation & unless we plant
"The seeds of Cities & of Villages in the Human bosom
"Albion must be a rock of blood; mark ye the points
"Where Cities shall remain & where Villages; for the rest,
"It must lie in confusion till Albion's time of awaking.
"Place the Tribes of Llewellyn in America for a hiding place
"Till sweet Jerusalem emanates again into Eternity.
"The night falls thick: I go upon my watch: be attentive.
"The Sons of Albion go forth; I follow from my Furnaces
"That they return no more, that a place be prepar'd on Euphrates.
"Listen to your Watchman's voice: sleep not before the Furnaces,
"Eternal Death stands at the door. O God, pity our labours."

So Los spoke to the Daughters of Beulah while his Emanation
Like a faint rainbow waved before him in the awful gloom
Of London City on the Thames from Surrey Hills to Highgate.
Swift turn the silver spindles & the golden weights play soft
And lulling harmonies beneath the Looms from Caithness in the north
To Lizard-point & Dover in the south; his Emanation
Joy'd in the many weaving threads in bright Cathedron's Dome,
Weaving the Web of life for Jerusalem; the Web of life,
Down flowing into Entuthon's Vales, glistens with soft affections.

While Los arose upon his Watch and down from Golgonooza,
Putting on his golden sandals to walk from mountain to mountain,

He takes his way, girding himself with gold & in his hand
Holding his iron mace, The Spectre remains attentive.
Alternate they watch in night, alternate labour in day,
Before the Furnaces labouring, while Los all night watches
The stars rising & setting & the meteors & terrors of night.
With him went down the Dogs of Leutha; at his feet
They lap the water of the trembling Thames, then follow swift,
And thus he heard the voice of Albion's daughters on Euphrates:

"Our Father Albion's land, O it was a lovely land! & the Daughters of Beulah
"Walked up and down in its green mountains; but Hand is fled
"Away & mighty Hyle, & after them Jerusalem is gone. Awake

Plate 84

"Highgate's heights & Hampstead's, to Poplar, Hackney & Bow,
"To Islington & Paddington & the Brook of Albion's River.
"We builded Jerusalem as a City & a Temple; from Lambeth
"We began our Foundations, lovely Lambeth. O lovely Hills
"Of Camberwell, we shall behold you no more in glory & pride,
"For Jerusalem lies in ruins & the Furnaces of Los are builded there.
"You are now shrunk up to a narrow Rock in the midst of the Sea;
"But here we build Babylon on Euphrates, compell'd to build
"And to inhabit, our Little-ones to clothe in armour of the gold
"Of Jerusalem's Cherubims & to forge them swords of her Altars.
"I see London, blind & age-bent, begging thro' the Streets
"Of Babylon, led by a child; his tears run down his beard.
"The voice of Wandering Reuben ecchoes from street to street
"In all the Cities of the Nations, Paris, Madrid, Amsterdam.
"The Corner of Broad Street weeps; Poland Street languishes;
"To Great Queen Street & Lincoln's Inn all is distress & woe.
[*three lines erased*]
"The night falls thick. Hand comes from Albion in his strength:
"He combines into a Mighty-one, the Double Molech & Chemosh,
"Marching thro' Egypt in his fury: the East is pale at his course.
"The Nations of India, the Wild Tartar that never knew Man
"Starts from his lofty places & casts down his tents & flees away;
"But we woo him all the night in songs. O Los come forth, O Los
"Divide us from these terrors & give us power them to subdue.
"Arise upon thy Watches, let us see thy Globe of fire
"On Albion's Rocks & let thy voice be heard upon Euphrates."

Thus sang the Daughters in lamentation, uniting into One
With Rahab as she turn'd the iron Spindle of destruction.
Terrified at the Sons of Albion they took the Falsehood which
Gwendolen hid in her left hand: it grew & grew till it

Plate 85

Became a Space & an Allegory around the Winding Worm.
They nam'd it Canaan & built for it a tender Moon.
Los smil'd with joy, thinking on Enitharmon, & he brought
Reuben from his twelvefold wand'rings & led him into it,
Planting the Seeds of the Twelve Tribes & Moses & David,
And gave a Time & Revolution to the Space, Six Thousand Years.
He call'd it Divine Analogy, for in Beulah the Feminine
Emanations Create Space, the Masculine Create Time & plant
The Seeds of beauty in the Space; list'ning to their lamentation
Los walks upon his ancient Mountains in the deadly darkness,
Among his Furnaces directing his laborious Myriads, watchful
Looking to the East, & his voice is heard over the whole Earth
As he watches the Furnaces by night & directs the labourers.

And thus Los replies upon his Watch: the Valleys listen silent,
The Stars stand still to hear: Jerusalem & Vala cease to mourn:
His voice is heard from Albion: the Alps & Appenines
Listen: Hermon & Lebanon bow their crowned heads:
Babel & Shinar look toward the Western Gate, they sit down
Silent at his voice: they view the red Globe of fire in Los's hand
As he walks from Furnace to Furnace directing the Labourers.
And this is the Song of Los, the Song that he sings on his Watch:

"O lovely mild Jerusalem! O Shiloh of Mount Ephraim!
"I see thy Gates of precious stones, thy Walls of gold & silver.
"Thou art the soft reflected Image of the Sleeping Man
"Who, stretch'd on Albion's rocks, reposes amidst his Twenty-eight
"Cities, where Beulah lovely terminates in the hills & valleys of Albion,
"Cities not yet embodied in Time and Space; plant ye
"The Seeds, O Sisters, in the bosom of Time & Space's womb,
"To spring up for Jerusalem, lovely Shadow of Sleeping Albion.
"Why wilt thou rend thyself apart & build an Earthly Kingdom
"To reign in pride & to opress & to mix the Cup of Delusion?
"O thou that dwellest with Babylon! Come forth, O lovely-one!

Plate 86

"I see thy Form, O lovely mild Jerusalem, Wing'd with Six Wings
"In the opacous Bosom of the Sleeper, lovely Three-fold
"In Head & Heart & Reins, three Universes of love & beauty.
"Thy forehead bright, Holiness to the Lord, with Gates of pearl
"Reflects Eternity; beneath, thy azure wings of feathery down

"Ribb'd delicate & cloth'd with feather'd gold & azure & purple,
"From thy white shoulders shadowing purity in holiness!
"Thence, feather'd with soft crimson of the ruby, bright as fire,
"Spreading into the azure, Wings which like a canopy
"Bends over thy immortal Head in which Eternity dwells.
"Albion, beloved Land! I see thy mountains & thy hills
"And valleys & thy pleasant Cities, Holiness to the Lord.
"I see the Spectres of thy Dead, O Emanation of Albion.

"Thy Bosom white, translucent, cover'd with immortal gems,
"A sublime ornament not obscuring the outlines of beauty,
"Terrible to behold for thy extreme beauty & perfection;
"Twelve-fold here all the Tribes of Israel I behold
"Upon the Holy Land. I see the River of Life & Tree of Life,
"I see the New Jerusalem descending out of Heaven,
"Between thy Wings of gold & silver, feather'd, immortal,
"Clear as the rainbow, as the cloud of the Sun's tabernacle.

"Thy Reins, cover'd with Wings translucent, sometimes covering
"And sometimes spread abroad, reveal the flames of holiness
"Which like a robe covers & like a Veil of Seraphim
"In flaming fire unceasing burns from Eternity to Eternity.
"Twelvefold I there behold Israel in her Tents;
"A Pillar of a Cloud by day, a Pillar of fire by night
"Guides them; there I behold Moab & Ammon & Amalek.
"There, Bells of silver round thy knees living articulate
"Comforting sounds of love & harmony, & on thy feet
"Sandals of gold & pearl, & Egypt & Assyria before me,
"The Isles of Javan, Philistea, Tyre and Lebanon."

Thus Los sings upon his Watch, walking from Furnace to Furnace.
He siezes his Hammer every hour; flames surround him as
He beats, seas roll beneath his feet, tempests muster
Around his head, the thick hail stones stand ready to obey
His voice in the black cloud, his Sons labour in thunders
At his Furnaces, his Daughters at their Looms sing woes,
His Emanation separates in milky fibres agonizing
Among the golden Looms of Cathedron, sending fibres of love
From Golgonooza with sweet visions for Jerusalem, wanderer.

Nor can any consummate bliss without being Generated
On Earth, of those whose Emanations weave the loves
Of Beulah for Jerusalem & Shiloh in immortal Golgonooza,
Concentering in the majestic form of Erin in eternal tears,
Viewing the Winding Worm on the Desarts of Great Tartary,

Viewing Los in his shudderings, pouring balm on his sorrows:
So dread is Los's fury that none dare him to approach
Without becoming his Children in the Furnaces of affliction

And Enitharmon like a faint rainbow waved before him
Filling with Fibres from his loins which redden'd with desire
Into a Globe of blood beneath his bosom trembling in darkness
Of Albion's clouds; he fed it with his tears & bitter groans,
Hiding his Spectre in invisibility from the timorous Shade,
Till it became a separated cloud of beauty, grace & love
Among the darkness of his Furnaces, dividing asunder till
She separated stood before him, a lovely Female weeping,
Even Enitharmon separated outside; & his Loins closed
And heal'd after the separation; his pains he soon forgot,
Lured by her beauty outside of himself in shadowy grief.
Two Wills they had, Two Intellects, & not as in times of old.

Silent they wander'd hand in hand, like two Infants wand'ring,
From Enion in the desarts, terrified at each other's beauty,
Envying each other, yet desiring in all devouring Love,

Plate 87

Repelling weeping Enion, blind & age-bent, into the fourfold
Desarts. Los first broke silence & began to utter his love:

"O lovely Enitharmon! I behold thy graceful forms
"Moving beside me till, intoxicated with the woven labyrinth
"Of beauty & perfection, my wild fibres shoot in veins
"Of blood thro' all my nervous limbs; soon overgrown in roots
"I shall be closed from thy sight; sieze therefore in thy hand
"The small fibres as they shoot around me, draw out in pity
"And let them run on the winds of thy bosom: I will fix them
"With pulsations; we will divide them into Sons & Daughters
"To live in thy Bosom's translucence as in an eternal morning."

Enitharmon answer'd: "No! I will sieze thy Fibres & weave
"Them, not as thou wilt, but as I will; for I will Create
"A round Womb beneath my bosom, lest I also be overwoven
"With Love; be thou assured I never will be thy slave.
"Let Man's delight be Love, but Woman's delight be Pride.
"In Eden our loves were the same; here they are opposite.
"I have Love's of my own; I will weave them in Albion's Spectre.
"Cast thou in Jerusalem's shadows thy Loves, silk of liquid
"Rubies, Jacinths, Crysolites, issuing from thy Furnaces. While
"Jerusalem divides thy care, while thou carest for Jerusalem,

"Know that I never will be thine; also thou hidest Vala:
"From her these fibres shoot to shut me in a Grave.
"You are Albion's Victim; he has set his Daughter in your path."

Plate 88

Los answer'd, sighing like the Bellows of his Furnaces:

"I care not! the swing of my Hammer shall measure the starry round.
"When in Eternity Man converses with Man, they enter
"Into each other's Bosom (which are Universes of delight)
"In mutual interchange, and first their Emanations meet
"Surrounded by their Children; if they embrace & comingle,
"The Human Four-fold Forms mingle also in thunders of Intellect;
"But if the Emanations mingle not, with storms & agitations
"Of earthquakes & consuming fires they roll apart in fear;
"For Man cannot unite with Man but by their Emanations
"Which stand both Male & Female at the Gates of each Humanity.
"How then can I ever again be united as Man with Man
"While thou, my Emanation, refusest my Fibres of dominion?
"When Souls mingle & join thro' all the Fibres of Brotherhood
"Can there be any secret joy on Earth greater than this?

Enitharmon answer'd: "This is Woman's World, nor need she any
"Spectre to defend her from Man. I will Create secret places,
"And the masculine names of the places, Merlin & Arthur.
"A triple Female Tabernacle for Moral Law I weave,
"That he who loves Jesus may loathe, terrified, Female love,
"Till God himself become a Male subservient to the Female."

She spoke in scorn & jealousy, alternate torments; and
So speaking she sat down on Sussex shore, singing lulling
Cadences & playing in sweet intoxication among the glistening
Fibres of Los, sending them over the Ocean eastward into
The realms of dark death. O perverse to thyself, contrarious
To thy own purposes! for when she began to weave,
Shooting out in sweet pleasure, her bosom in milky Love
Flow'd into the aching fibres of Los, yet contending against him,
In pride send(ind)ing his Fibres over to her objects of jealousy
In the little lovely Allegoric Night of Albion's Daughters
Which stretch'd abroad, expanding east & west & north & south,
Thro' all the World of Erin & of Los & all their Children.

A sullen smile broke from the Spectre in mockery & scorn;
Knowing himself the author of their divisions & shrinkings, gratified
At their contentions, he wiped his tears, he wash'd his visage.

"The Man who respects Woman shall be despised by Woman,
"And deadly cunning & mean abjectness only shall enjoy them.
"For I will make their places of joy & love excrementitious,
"Continually building, continually destroying in Family feuds.
"While you are under the dominion of a jealous Female,
"Unpermanent for ever because of love & jealousy,
"You shall want all the Minute Particulars of Life."

Thus joy'd the Spectre in the dusky fires of Los's Forge, eyeing
Enitharmon who at her shining Looms sings lulling cadences
While Los stood at his Anvil in wrath, the victim of their love
And hate, dividing the Space of Love with brazen Compasses
In Golgonooza & in Udan-Adan & in Entuthon of Urizen.

The blow of his Hammer is Justice, the swing of his Hammer Mercy,
The force of Los's Hammer is eternal Forgiveness; but
His rage or his mildness were vain, she scatter'd his love on the wind
Eastward into her own Center, creating the Female Womb
In mild Jerusalem around the Lamb of God. Loud howl
The Furnaces of Los! loud roll the Wheels of Enitharmon!
The Four Zoas in all their faded majesty burst out in fury
And fire. Jerusalem took the Cup which foam'd in Vala's hand
Like the red Sun upon the mountains in the bloody day
Upon the Hermaphroditic Wine-presses of Love & Wrath.

Plate 89

Tho' divided by the Cross & Nails & Thorns & Spear
In cruelties of Rahab & Tirzah, permanent endure
A terrible indefinite Hermaphroditic form,
A Wine-press of Love & Wrath, double, Hermaphroditic,
Twelvefold in Allegoric pomp, in selfish holiness:
The Pharisaion, the Grammateis, the Presbuterion,
The Archiereus, the Iereus, the Saddusaion: double
Each withoutside of the other, covering eastern heaven.

Thus was the Covering Cherub reveal'd, majestic image
Of Selfhood, Body put off, the Antichrist accursed,
Cover'd with precious stones: a Human Dragon terrible
And bright stretch'd over Europe & Asia gorgeous.
In three nights he devour'd the rejected corse of death.

His Head, dark, deadly, in its Brain incloses a reflexion
Of Eden all perverted: Egypt on the Gihon, many tongued
And many mouth'd, Ethiopia, Lybia, the Sea of Rephaim.

Minute Particulars in slavery I behold among the brick-kilns
Disorganiz'd; & there is Pharoh in his iron Court
And the Dragon of the River & the Furnaces of iron.
Outwoven from Thames & Tweed & Severn, awful streams,
Twelve ridges of Stone frown over all the Earth in tyrant pride,
Frown over each River, stupendous Works of Albion's Druid Sons,
And Albion's Forests of Oaks cover'd the Earth from Pole to Pole.

His Bosom wide reflects Moab & Ammon on the River
Pison, since call'd Arnon: there is Heshbon beautiful,
The Rocks of Rabbath on the Arnon & the Fish-pools of Heshbon
Whose currents flow into the Dead Sea by Sodom & Gomorra.
Above his Head high arching Wings, black, fill'd with Eyes,
Spring upon iron sinews from the Scapulæ & Os Humeri:
There Israel in bondage to his Generalizing Gods,
Molech & Chemosh; & in his left breast is Philistea,
In Druid Temples over the whole Earth with Victim's Sacrifice
From Gaza to Damascus, Tyre & Sidon, & the Gods
Of Javan thro' the Isles of Grecia & all Europe's Kings,
Where Hiddekel pursues his course among the rocks.
Two Wings spring from his ribs of brass, starry, black as night,
But translucent their blackness as the dazling of gems.

His Loins inclose Babylon on Euphrates beautiful
And Rome in sweet Hesperia: there Israel scatter'd abroad
In martyrdoms & slavery I behold, ah vision of sorrow!
Inclosed by eyeless Wings, glowing with fire as the iron
Heated in the Smith's forge, but cold the wind of their dread fury.

But in the midst of a devouring Stomach, Jerusalem
Hidden within the Covering Cherub, as in a Tabernacle
Of threefold workmanship, in allegoric delusion & woe:
There the Seven Kings of Canaan & Five Baalim of Philistea,
Sihon & Og, the Anakim & Emim, Nephilim & Gibborim,
From Babylon to Rome; & the Wings spread from Japan,
Where the Red Sea terminates the World of Generation & Death,
To Ireland's farthest rocks, where Giants builded their Causeway,
Into the Sea of Rephaim, but the Sea o'erwhelm'd them all.

A Double Female now appear'd within the Tabernacle,
Religion hid in War, a Dragon red & hidden Harlot
Each within other, but without, a Warlike Mighty-one
Of dreadful power sitting upon Horeb, pondering dire
And mighty preparations, mustering multitudes innumerable
Of warlike sons among the sands of Midian & Aram.

For multitudes of those who sleep in Alla descend,
Lured by his warlike symphonies of tabret, pipe & harp,
Burst the bottoms of the Graves & Funeral Arks of Beulah.
Wandering in that unknown Night beyond the silent Grave
They become One with the Antichrist & are absorb'd in him.

Plate 90

The Feminine separates from the Masculine & both from Man,
Ceasing to be His Emanations, Life to Themselves assuming:
And while they circumscribe his Brain & while they circumscribe
His Heart & while they circumscribe his Loins, a Veil & Net
Of Veins of red Blood grows around them like a scarlet robe
Covering them from the sight of Man, like the woven Veil of Sleep
Such as the Flowers of Beulah weave to be their Funeral Mantles;
But dark, opake, tender to touch, & painful & agonizing
To the embrace of love & to the mingling of soft fibres
Of tender affection, that no more the Masculine mingles
With the Feminine, but the Sublime is shut out from the Pathos
In howling torment, to build stone walls of separation, compelling
The Pathos to weave curtains of hiding secresy from the torment.

Bowen & Conwenna stood on Skiddaw cutting the Fibres
Of Benjamin from Chester's River; loud the River, loud the Mersey
And the Ribble thunder into the Irish sea as the Twelve Sons
Of Albion drank & imbibed the Life & eternal Form of Luvah;
Cheshire & Lancashire & Westmoreland groan in anguish
As they cut the fibres from the Rivers; he sears them with hot
Iron of his Forge & fixes them into Bones of chalk & Rock.
Conwenna sat above; with solemn cadences she drew
Fibres of life out from the Bones into her golden Loom.
Hand had his Furnace on Highgate's heights & it reach'd
To Brockley Hills across the Thames; he with double Boadicea
In cruel pride cut Reuben apart from the Hills of Surrey,
Comingling with Luvah & with the Sepulcher of Luvah.
For the Male is a Furnace of beryll, the Female is a golden Loom.

Los cries: "No Individual ought to appropriate to Himself
"Or to his Emanation any of the Universal Characteristics
"Of David or of Eve, of the Woman or of the Lord,
"Of Reuben or of Benjamin, of Joseph or Judah or Levi.
"Those who dare appropriate to themselves Universal Attributes
"Are the Blasphemous Selfhoods, & must be broken asunder.
"A Vegetated Christ & a Virgin Eve are the Hermaphroditic
"Blasphemy; by his Maternal Birth he is that Evil-One

"And his Maternal Humanity must be put off Eternally,
"Lest the Sexual Generation swallow up Regeneration.
"Come Lord Jesus, take on thee the Satanic Body of Holiness!"

So Los cried in the Valleys of Middlesex in the Spirit of Prophecy,
While in Selfhood Hand & Hyle & Bowen & Skofeld appropriate
The Divine Names, seeking to Vegetate the Divine Vision
In a corporeal & ever dying Vegetation & Corruption;
Mingling with Luvah in One, they become One Great Satan.

Loud scream the Daughters of Albion beneath the Tongs & Hammer,
Dolorous are their lamentations in the burning Forge.
They drink Reuben & Benjamin as the iron drinks the fire:
They are red hot with cruelty, raving along the Banks of Thames
And on Tyburn's Brook among the howling Victims in loveliness,
While Hand & Hyle condense the Little-ones & erect them into
A mighty Temple even to the stars; but they Vegetate
Beneath Los's Hammer, that Life may not be blotted out.

For Los said: "When the Individual appropriates Universality
"He divides into Male & Female, & when the Male & Female
"Appropriate Individuality they become an Eternal Death.
"Hermaphroditic worshippers of a God of cruelty & law,
"Your Slaves & Captives you compell to worship a God of Mercy!
"These are the Demonstrations of Los & the blows of my mighty
Hammer."

So Los spoke. And the Giants of Albion, terrified & ashamed
With Los's thunderous Words, began to build trembling rocking
Stones,
For his Words roll in thunders & lightnings among the Temples
Terrified rocking to & fro upon the earth, & sometimes
Resting in a Circle in Malden or in Strathness or Dura,
Plotting to devour Albion & Los the friend of Albion,
Denying in private, mocking God & Eternal Life, & in Public
Collusion calling themselves Deists, Worshipping the Maternal
Humanity, calling it Nature and Natural Religion.

But still the thunder of Los peals loud, & thus the thunder's cry:
"These beautiful Witchcrafts of Albion are gratifyd by Cruelty.

Plate 91

Forgiveness of enemies . . . only . . . God . . .
"It is easier to forgive an Enemy than to forgive a Friend.
"The man who permits you to injure him deserves your vengeance:
"He also will recieve it; go Spectre! obey my most secret desire

"Which thou knowest without my speaking. Go to these Fiends of Righteousness,
"Tell them to obey their Humanities & not pretend Holiness
"When they are murderers: as far as my Hammer & Anvil permit.
"Go, tell them that the Worship of God is honouring his gifts
"In other men: & loving the greatest men best, each according
"To his Genius: which is the Holy Ghost in Man; there is no other
"God than that God who is the intellectual fountain of Humanity.
"He who envies or calumniates, which is murder & cruelty,
"Murders the Holy-one. Go, tell them this, & overthrow their cup,
"Their bread, their altar-table, their incense & their oath,
"Their marriage & their baptism, their burial & consecration.
"I have tried to make friends by corporeal gifts but have only
"Made enemies. I never made friends but by spiritual gifts,
"By severe contentions of friendship & the burning fire of thought.
"He who would see the Divinity must see him in his Children,
"One first, in friendship & love, then a Divine Family, & in the midst
"Jesus will appear; so he who wishes to see a Vision, a perfect Whole,
"Must see it in its Minute Particulars, Organized, & not as thou,
"O Fiend of Righteousness, pretendest; thine is a Disorganized
"And snowy cloud, brooder of tempests & destructive War.
"You smile with pomp & rigor, you talk of benevolence & virtue;
"I act with benevolence & Virtue & get murder'd time after time.
"You accumulate Particulars & murder by analyzing, that you
"May take the aggregate, & you call the aggregate Moral Law,
"And you call that swell'd & bloated Form a Minute Particular;
"But General Forms have their vitality in Particulars, & every
"Particular is a Man, a Divine Member of the Divine Jesus."

So Los cried at his Anvil in the horrible darkness weeping.

The Spectre builded stupendous Works, taking the Starry Heavens
Like to a curtain & folding them according to his will,
Repeating the Smaragdine Table of Hermes to draw Los down
Into the Indefinite, refusing to believe without demonstration.
Los reads the Stars of Albion, the Spectre reads the Voids
Between the Stars among the arches of Albion's Tomb sublime,
Rolling the Sea in rocky paths, forming Leviathan
And Behemoth, the War by Sea enormous & the War
By Land astounding, erecting pillars in the deepest Hell
To reach the heavenly arches. Los beheld undaunted, furious,
His heav'd Hammer; he swung it round & at one blow
In unpitying ruin driving down the pyramids of pride,
Smiting the Spectre on his Anvil & the integuments of his Eye
And Ear unbinding in dire pain, with many blows
Of strict severity self-subduing, & with many tears labouring.

Then he sent forth the Spectre: all his pyramids were grains
Of sand, & his pillars dust on the fly's wing, & his starry
Heavens a moth of gold & silver, mocking his anxious grasp.
Thus Los alter'd his Spectre, & every Ratio of his Reason
He alter'd time after time with dire pain & many tears
Till he had completely divided him into a separate space.

Terrified Los sat to behold, trembling & weeping & howling:
"I care not whether a Man is Good or Evil; all that I care
"Is whether he is a Wise Man or a Fool. Go, put off Holiness
"And put on Intellect, or my thund'rous Hammer shall drive thee
"To wrath which thou condemnest, till thou obey my voice."

So Los terrified cries, trembling & weeping & howling: "Beholding,

Plate 92

"What do I see! The Briton, Saxon, Roman, Norman amalgamating
"In my Furnaces into One Nation, the English, & taking refuge
"In the Loins of Albion. The Canaanite united with the fugitive
"Hebrew, whom she divided into Twelve & sold into Egypt,
"Then scatter'd the Egyptian & Hebrew to the four Winds.
"This sinful Nation Created in our Furnaces & Looms is Albion."

So Los spoke. Enitharmon answer'd in great terror in Lambeth's Vale:

"The Poet's Song draws to its period, & Enitharmon is no more;
"For if he be that Albion, I can never weave him in my Looms,
"But when he touches the first fibrous thread, like filmy dew
"My Looms will be no more & I annihilate vanish for ever.
"Then thou wilt Create another Female according to thy Will."

Los answer'd swift as the shuttle of gold: "Sexes must vanish & cease
"To be when Albion arises from his dread repose, O lovely Enitharmon:
"When all their Crimes, their Punishments, their Accusations of Sin,
"All their Jealousies, Revenges, Murders, hidings of Cruelty in Deceit
"Appear only in the Outward Spheres of Visionary Space and Time,
"In the shadows of Possibility, by Mutual Forgiveness for evermore,
"And in the Vision & in the Prophecy, that we may Foresee & Avoid
"The terrors of Creation & Redemption & Judgment: Beholding them
"Display'd in the Emanative Visions of Canaan, in Jerusalem & in Shiloh

"And in the Shadows of Remembrance & in the Chaos of the Spectre,
"Amalek, Edom, Egypt, Moab, Ammon, Ashur, Philistea, around Jerusalem,
"Where the Druids rear'd their Rocky Circles to make permanent Remembrance
"Of Sin, & the Tree of Good & Evil sprang from the Rocky Circle & Snake
"Of the Druid, along the Valley of Rephaim from Camberwell to Golgotha,
"And framed the Mundane Shell Cavernous in Length, Bredth & Highth."

Plate 93

Enitharmon heard. She rais'd her head like the mild Moon:

"O Rintrah! O Palamabron! What are your dire & awful purposes?
"Enitharmon's name is nothing before you; you forget all my Love.
"The Mother's love of obedience is forgotten, & you seek a Love
"Of the pride of dominion that will Divorce Ocalythron & Elynittria
"Upon East Moor in Derbyshire & along the Valleys of Cheviot.
"Could you Love me, Rintrah, if you Pride not in my Love?
"As Reuben found Mandrakes in the field & gave them to his Mother,
"Pride meets with Pride upon the Mountains in the stormy day,
"In that terrible Day of Rintrah's Plow & of Satan's driving the Team.
"Ah! then I heard my little ones weeping along the Valley.
"Ah! then I saw my beloved ones fleeing from my Tent.
"Merlin was like thee, Rintrah, among the Giants of Albion,
"Judah was like Palamabron. O Simeon! O Levi! ye fled away!
"How can I hear my little ones weeping along the Valley,
"Or how upon the distant Hills see my beloveds' Tents?"

Then Los again took up his speech as Enitharmon ceast:

"Fear not, my Sons, this Waking Death; he is become One with me.
"Behold him here! We shall not Die! we shall be united in Jesus.
"Will you suffer this Satan, this Body of Doubt that Seems but Is Not,
"To occupy the very threshold of Eternal Life? if Bacon, Newton, Locke
"Deny a Conscience in Man & the Communion of Saints & Angels,
"Contemning the Divine Vision & Fruition, Worshiping the Deus
"Of the Heathen, The God of This World, & the Goddess Nature,
"Mystery, Babylon the Great, The Druid Dragon & hidden Harlot,
"Is it not that Signal of the Morning which was told us in the Beginning?"

Thus they converse upon Mam-Tor, the Graves thunder under their feet.

Plate 94

Albion cold lays on his Rock: storms & snows beat round him,
Beneath the Furnaces & the starry Wheels & the Immortal Tomb:
Howling winds cover him: roaring seas dash furious against him:
In the deep darkness broad lightnings glare, long thunders roll.

The weeds of Death inwrap his hands & feet, blown incessant
And wash'd incessant by the for-ever restless sea-waves foaming abroad
Upon the white Rock. England, a Female Shadow, as deadly damps
Of the Mines of Cornwall & Derbyshire, lays upon his bosom heavy,
Moved by the wind in volumes of thick cloud, returning, folding round
His loins & bosom, unremovable by swelling storms & loud rending
Of enraged thunders. Around them the Starry Wheels of their Giant Sons
Revolve, & over them the Furnaces of Los, & the Immortal Tomb around,
Erin sitting in the Tomb to watch them unceasing night and day:
And the Body of Albion was closed apart from all Nations.

Over them the famish'd Eagle screams on boney Wings, and around
Them howls the Wolf of famine; deep heaves the Ocean black, thundering
Around the wormy Garments of Albion, then pausing in deathlike silence.

Time was Finished! The Breath Divine Breathed over Albion
Beneath the Furnaces & starry Wheels and in the Immortal Tomb,
And England, who is Brittannia, awoke from Death on Albion's bosom:
She awoke pale & cold; she fainted seven times on the Body of Albion.

"O pitious Sleep, O pitious Dream! O God, O God awake! I have slain
"In Dreams of Chasti(ti)ty & Moral Law: I have Murdered Albion! Ah!
"In Stone-henge & on London Stone & in the Oak Groves of Malden
"I have Slain him in my Sleep with the Knife of the Druid. O England!
"O all ye Nations of the Earth, behold ye the Jealous Wife!
"The Eagle & the Wolf & Monkey & Owl & the King & Priest were there."

Plate 95

Her voice pierc'd Albion's clay cold ear; he moved upon the Rock.
The Breath Divine went forth upon the morning hills. Albion mov'd
Upon the Rock, he open'd his eyelids in pain, in pain he mov'd
His stony members, he saw England. Ah! shall the Dead live again?

The Breath Divine went forth over the morning hills. Albion rose
In anger, the wrath of God breaking, bright flaming on all sides around
His awful limbs; into the Heavens he walked, clothed in flames,
Loud thund'ring, with broad flashes of flaming lightning & pillars
Of fire, speaking the Words of Eternity in Human Forms, in direful
Revolutions of Action & Passion, thro' the Four Elements on all sides
Surrounding his awful Members. Thou seest the Sun in heavy clouds
Struggling to rise above the Mountains; in his burning hand
He takes his Bow, then chooses out his arrows of flaming gold;
Murmuring the Bowstring breathes with ardor! clouds roll round the
Horns of the wide Bow, loud sounding winds sport on the mountain brows,
Compelling Urizen to his Furrow & Tharmas to his Sheepfold
And Luvah to his Loom: Urthona he beheld, mighty labouring at
His Anvil, in the Great Spectre Los unwearied labouring & weeping:
Therefore the Sons of Eden praise Urthona's Spectre in songs,
Because he kept the Divine Vision in time of trouble.

As the Sun & Moon lead forward the Visions of Heaven & Earth,
England, who is Brittannia, enter'd Albion's bosom rejoicing
Rejoicing in his indignation, adoring his wrathful rebuke.
She who adores not your frowns will only loathe your smiles.

Plate 96

As the Sun & Moon lead forward the Visions of Heaven & Earth,
England, who is Brittannia, entered Albion's bosom rejoicing.

Then Jesus appeared standing by Albion as the Good Shepherd
By the lost Sheep that he hath found, & Albion knew that it
Was the Lord, the Universal Humanity; & Albion saw his Form
A Man, & they conversed as Man with Man in Ages of Eternity.
And the Divine Appearance was the likeness & similitude of Los.

Albion said: "O Lord, what can I do? my Selfhood cruel
"Marches against thee, deceitful, from Sinai & from Edom
"Into the Wilderness of Judah, to meet thee in his pride.
"I behold the Visions of my deadly Sleep of Six Thousand Years
"Dazling around thy skirts like a Serpent of precious stones & gold
"I know it is my Self, O my Divine Creator & Redeemer."

Jesus replied: "Fear not Albion: unless I die thou canst not live;
"But if I die I shall arise again & thou with me.
"This is Friendship & Brotherhood: without it Man Is Not."

So Jesus spoke: the Covering Cherub coming on in darkness
Overshadow'd them, & Jesus said: "Thus do Men in Eternity
"One for another to put off, by forgiveness, every sin."

Albion reply'd: "Cannot Man exist without Mysterious
"Offering of Self for Another? is this Friendship & Brotherhood?
"I see thee in the likeness & similitude of Los my Friend."

Jesus said: "Wouldest thou love one who never died
"For thee, or ever die for one who had not died for thee?
"And if God dieth not for Man & giveth not himself
"Eternally for Man, Man could not exist; for Man is Love
"As God is Love; every kindness to another is a little Death
"In the Divine Image, nor can Man exist but by Brotherhood."

So saying the Cloud overshadowing divided them asunder.
Albion stood in terror, not for himself but for his Friend
Divine; & Self was lost in the contemplation of faith
And wonder at the Divine Mercy & at Los's sublime honour.

"Do I sleep amidst danger to Friends? O my Cities & Counties,
"Do you sleep? rouze up, rouze up! Eternal Death is abroad!"

So Albion spoke & threw himself into the Furnaces of affliction.
All was a Vision, all a Dream: the Furnaces became
Fountains of Living Waters flowing from the Humanity Divine.
And all the Cities of Albion rose from their Slumbers, and All
The Sons & Daughters of Albion on soft clouds, waking from Sleep.
Soon all around remote the Heavens burnt with flaming fires,
And Urizen & Luvah & Tharmas & Urthona arose into
Albion's Bosom. Then Albion stood before Jesus in the Clouds
Of Heaven, Fourfold among the Visions of God in Eternity.

Plate 97

"Awake, Awake, Jerusalem! O lovely Emanation of Albion,
"Awake and overspread all Nations as in Ancient Time;
"For lo! the Night of Death is past and the Eternal Day
"Appears upon our Hills. Awake, Jerusalem, and come away!"

So spake the Vision of Albion, & in him so spake in my hearing
The Universal Father. Then Albion stretch'd his hand into Infinitude
And took his Bow. Fourfold the Vision; for bright beaming Urizen
Lay'd his hand on the South & took a breathing Bow of carved Gold:
Luvah his hand stretch'd to the East & bore a Silver Bow, bright shining:
Tharmas Westward a Bow of Brass, pure flaming, richly wrought:
Urthona Northward in thick storms a Bow of Iron, terrible thundering.

And the Bow is a Male & Female, & the Quiver of the Arrows of Love
Are the Children of this Bow, a Bow of Mercy & Loving-kindness laying
Open the hidden Heart in Wars of mutual Benevolence, Wars of Love:
And the Hand of Man grasps firm between the Male & Female Loves.
And he Clothed himself in Bow & Arrows, in awful state, Fourfold,
In the midst of his Twenty-eight Cities, each with his Bow breathing.

Plate 98

Then each an Arrow flaming from his Quiver fitted carefully;
They drew fourfold the unreprovable String, bending thro' the wide Heavens
The horned Bow Fourfold; loud sounding flew the flaming Arrow fourfold.

Murmuring the Bowstring breathes with ardor. Clouds roll round the horns
Of the wide Bow; loud sounding Winds sport on the Mountains' brows.
The Druid Spectre was Annihilate, loud thund'ring, rejoicing terrific, vanishing,
Fourfold Annihilation; & at the clangor of the Arrows of Intellect
The innumerable Chariots of the Almighty appear'd in Heaven,
And Bacon & Newton & Locke, & Milton & Shakspear & Chaucer,
A Sun of blood red wrath surrounding heaven, on all sides around,
Glorious, incompreh[en]sible by Mortal Man, & each Chariot was Sexual Threefold.

And every Man stood Fourfold; each Four Faces had: One to the West,
One toward the East, One to the South, One to the North, the Horses Fourfold.
And the dim Chaos brighten'd beneath, above, around: Eyed as the Peacock,
According to the Human Nerves of Sensation, the Four Rivers of the Water of Life.

South stood the Nerves of the Eye; East, in Rivers of bliss, the Nerves of the
Expansive Nostrils; West flow'd the Parent Sense, the Tongue; North stood
The labyrinthine Ear: Circumscribing & Circumcising the excrementitious
Husk & Covering, into Vacuum evaporating, revealing the lineaments of Man,
Driving outward the Body of Death in an Eternal Death & Resurrection,
Awaking it to Life among the Flowers of Beulah, rejoicing in Unity
In the Four Senses, in the Outline, the Circumference & Form, for ever
In Forgiveness of Sins which is Self Annihilation; it is the Covenant of Jehovah.

The Four Living Creatures, Chariots of Humanity Divine Incomprehensible,
In beautiful Paradises expand. These are the Four Rivers of Paradise
And the Four Faces of Humanity, fronting the Four Cardinal Points
Of Heaven, going forward, forward irresistible from Eternity to Eternity.

And they conversed together in Visionary forms dramatic which bright
Redounded from their Tongues in thunderous majesty, in Visions
In new Expanses, creating exemplars of Memory and of Intellect,
Creating Space, Creating Time, according to the wonders Divine
Of Human Imagination throughout all the Three Regions immense
Of Childhood, Manhood & Old Age; & the all tremendous unfathomable Non Ens
Of Death was seen in regenerations terrific or complacent, varying
According to the subject of discourse; & every Word & Every Character
Was Human according to the Expansion or Contraction, the Translucence or
Opakeness of Nervous fibres: such was the variation of Time & Space
Which vary according as the Organs of Perception vary; & they walked
To & fro in Eternity as One Man, reflecting each in each & clearly seen
And seeing, according to fitness & order. And I heard Jehovah speak
Terrific from his Holy Place, & saw the Words of the Mutual Covenant Divine
On Chariots of gold & jewels, with Living Creatures, starry & flaming
With every Colour, Lion, Tyger, Horse, Elephant, Eagle, Dove, Fly, Worm
And the all wondrous Serpent clothed in gems & rich array, Humanize
In the Forgiveness of Sins according to thy Covenant, Jehovah. They Cry:

"Where is the Covenant of Priam, the Moral Virtues of the Heathen?
"Where is the Tree of Good & Evil that rooted beneath the cruel heel
"Of Albion's Spectre, the Patriarch Druid? where are all his Human Sacrifices
"For Sin in War & in the Druid Temples of the Accuser of Sin, beneath
"The Oak Groves of Albion that cover'd the whole Earth beneath his Spectre?
"Where are the Kingdoms of the World & all their glory that grew on Desolation,
"The Fruit of Albion's Poverty Tree, when the Triple Headed Gog-Magog Giant
"Of Albion Taxed the Nations into Desolation & then gave the Spectrous Oath?"

Such is the Cry from all the Earth, from the Living Creatures of the Earth
And from the great City of Golgonooza in the Shadowy Generation,
And from the Thirty-two Nations of the Earth among the Living Creatures.

All Human Forms identified, even Tree, Metal, Earth & Stone: all
Human Forms identified, living, going forth & returning wearied
Into the Planetary lives of Years, Months, Days & Hours; reposing,
And then Awaking into his Bosom in the Life of Immortality.

And I heard the Name of their Emanations: they are named
Jerusalem.

The End of The Song
of Jerusalem.

THE EVERLASTING GOSPEL

FROM THE NOTE-BOOK

Written about 1818

a

P. 33.

The Vision of Christ that thou dost see
Is my Vision's Greatest Enemy:
Thine has a great hook nose like thine,
Mine has a snub nose like to mine:
Thine is the friend of All Mankind,
Mine speaks in parables to the Blind:
Thine loves the same world that mine hates,
Thy Heaven doors are my Hell Gates.
Socrates taught what Meletus
Loath'd as a Nation's bitterest Curse,
And Caiphas[1] was in his own Mind
A benefactor to Mankind:
Both read the Bible day & night,
But thou read'st black where I read white.

b

P. 100-101.

Was Jesus gentle, or did he
Give any marks of Gentility?
When twelve years old he ran away
And left his Parents in dismay.
When after three days' sorrow found,
Loud as Sinai's trumpet sound:
"No Earthly Parents I confess—
"My Heavenly Father's business!
"Ye understand not what I say,
"And, angry, force me to obey."
Obedience is a duty then,
And favour gains with God & Men.
John from the Wilderness loud cried;
Satan gloried in his Pride.

---

[1]Blake often wrote the name in this form, though at other times he wrote it 'Caiaphas'. See below.

"Come," said Satan, "come away,
"I'll soon see if you'll obey!
"John for disobedience bled,
"But you can turn the stones to bread.
"God's high king & God's high Priest
"Shall Plant their Glories in your breast
"If Caiaphas you will obey,
"If Herod you with bloody Prey
"Feed with the sacrifice, & be
"Obedient, fall down, worship me."
Thunders & lightnings broke around,
And Jesus' voice in thunders' sound:
"Thus I sieze the Spiritual Prey.
"Ye smiters with disease, make way.
"I come your King & God to sieze.
"Is God a smiter with disease?"
The God of this World raged in vain:
He bound Old Satan in his Chain,
And bursting forth [with *del.*], his furious ire
Became a Chariot of fire.
Throughout the land he took his course,
And traced diseases to their source:
He curs'd the Scribe & Pharisee,
Trampling down Hipocrisy:
Where'er his Chariot took its way,
There Gates of death let in the day,
Broke down from every Chain & Bar;
And Satan in his Spiritual War
Drag'd at his Chariot wheels: loud howl'd
The God of this World: louder roll'd
The Chariot Wheels, & louder still
His voice was heard from Zion's hill,
And in his hand the Scourge shone bright;
He scourg'd the Merchant Canaanite
From out the Temple of his Mind,
And in his Body tight does bind
Satan & all his Hellish Crew;
And thus with wrath he did subdue
The Serpent Bulk of Nature's dross,
Till He had nail'd it to the Cross.
[He took on Sin in the Virgin's Womb,
And on the Cross he Seal'd its doom *del.*]
He took on Sin in the Virgin's Womb,
And put it off on the Cross & Tomb
To be Worship'd by the Church of Rome.

c

P. 98.

Was Jesus Humble? or did he
Give any proofs of Humility?
When but a Child he ran away
And left his Parents in dismay.
When they had wander'd three days long
These were the words upon his Tongue:
"No Earthly Parents I confess:
"I am doing my Father's business."
When the rich learned Pharisee
1 Came to consult him secretly,
4 He was too Proud to take a bribe;
5 He spoke with authority, not like a Scribe.
2 Upon his heart with Iron pen
3 He wrote, "Ye must be born again."
6 He says with most consummate Art,
"Follow me, I am meek & lowly of heart,"
As that is the only way to Escape
The Miser's net & the Glutton's trap.
He who loves his Enemies, hates his Friends;
This is surely not what Jesus intends;
He must mean the meer love of Civility,
And so he must mean concerning Humility;
But he acts with triumphant, honest pride,
And this is the Reason Jesus died.
If he had been [the *del.*] Antichrist, Creeping Jesus,
He'd have done any thing to please us:
Gone sneaking into the Synagogues
And not used the Elders & Priests like Dogs,
But humble as a Lamb or an Ass,
Obey himself to Caiaphas.
God wants not Man to humble himself:
This is the Trick of the Ancient Elf.
Humble toward God, Haughty toward Man,
This is the Race that Jesus ran,
And when he humbled himself to God,
Then descended the cruel rod.
"[Why dost thou humble thyself to me?
"Thou Also dwelst in Eternity. *del.*]
"If thou humblest thyself, thou humblest me;
"Thou also dwelst in Eternity.
"Thou art a Man, God is no more,
"Thine own Humanity learn to Adore
"And thy Revenge Abroad display

"In terrors at the Last Judgment day.
"God's Mercy & Long Suffering
"Are but the Sinner to Judgment to bring.
"Thou on the Cross for them shalt pray
"[Whom thou shalt Torment at the Last Day. *del.*]
"And take Revenge at the last Day."

Do what you will, this Life's a Fiction
And is made up of Contradiction.

d

P. 52-54.

The Everlasting Gospel

Was Jesus Humble? or did he
Give any Proofs of Humility?
Boast of high Things with Humble tone,
And give with Charity a Stone?
When but a Child he ran away
And left his Parents in dismay.
When they had wander'd three days long
These were the words upon his tongue:
"No Earthly Parents I confess:
"I am doing my Father's business."
When the rich learned Pharisee
Came to consult him secretly,
Upon his heart with Iron pen
He wrote, "Ye must be born again."
He was too proud to take a bribe;
He spoke with authority, not like a Scribe.
He says with most consummate Art,
"Follow me, I am meek & lowly of heart,"
As that is the only way to escape
The Miser's net & the Glutton's trap.
What can be done with such desperate Fools
Who follow after the Heathen Schools?
I was standing by when Jesus died;
What I call'd Humility, they call'd Pride.
He who loves his Enemies [hates *del.*] betrays his Friends;
This surely is not what Jesus intends,
But the sneaking Pride of Heroic Schools,
And the Scribes' & Pharisees' Virtuous Rules;
For he acts with honest, triumphant Pride,
And this is the cause that Jesus died.
He did not die with Christian Ease,

Asking pardon of his Enemies:
If he had, Caiphas would forgive;
Sneaking submission can always live.
He had only to say that God was the devil,
And the devil was God, like a Christian Civil:
Mild Christian regrets to the devil confess
a For affronting him thrice in the Wilderness;
Like dr. Priestly & [Sir Isaac *del.*] Bacon & Newton—
1 Poor Spiritual Knowledge is not worth a button!
b He had soon been bloody Caesar's Elf,
c And at last he would have been Caesar himself.
2 [As *del.*] For thus the Gospel Sir Isaac confutes:
3 "God can only be known by his Attributes;
"And as for the Indwelling of the Holy Ghost
"Or of Christ & his Father, it's all a boast
"And Pride & Vanity of the imagination,
"That disdains to follow this World's Fashion."
To teach doubt & Experiment
Certainly was not what Christ meant.
What was he doing all that time,
From twelve years old to manly prime?
Was he then Idle, or the Less
About his Father's business?
Or was his wisdom held in scorn
Before his wrath began to burn
In Miracles throughout the Land,
That quite unnerv'd Caiaphas' hand?
If he had been [the *del.*] Antichrist, Creeping Jesus,
He'd have done any thing to please us—
Gone sneaking into Synagogues
And not us'd the Elders & Priests like dogs,
But Humble as a Lamb or Ass
Obey'd himself to Caiaphas.
God wants not Man to Humble himself:
This is the trick of the ancient Elf.
This is the Race that Jesus ran:
Humble to God, Haughty to Man,
Cursing the Rulers before the People
Even to the temple's highest Steeple;
And when he Humbled himself to God,
Then descended the Cruel Rod.
"If thou humblest thyself, thou humblest me;
"Thou also dwell'st in Eternity.
"Thou art a Man, God is no more,
"Thy own humanity learn to adore,

"For that is my Spirit of Life.
"Awake, arise to Spiritual Strife
"And thy Revenge abroad display
"In terrors at the Last Judgment day.
"God's Mercy & Long Suffering
"Is but the Sinner to Judgment to bring.
"Thou on the Cross for them shalt pray
"And take Revenge at the Last Day.
["This Corporeal (All) life's a fiction
"And is made up of Contradiction." *del.*]
Jesus replied & thunders hurl'd:
"I never will Pray for the World.
"Once a [*for* I] did so when I pray'd in the Garden;
"I wish'd to take with me a Bodily Pardon."
Can that which was of woman born
In the absence of the Morn,
When the Soul fell into Sleep
And Archangels round it weep,
Shooting out against the Light
Fibres of a deadly night,
Reasoning upon its own dark Fiction,
In doubt which is Self Contradiction?
Humility is only doubt,
And does the Sun & Moon blot out,
Rooting over with thorns & stems
The buried Soul & all its Gems.
This Life's dim Windows of the Soul
Distorts the Heavens from Pole to Pole
And leads you to Believe a Lie
When you see with, not thro', the Eye
That was born in a night to perish in a night,
When the Soul slept in the beams of Light. 78 lines
Was Jesus Chaste? or did he, &c

e

P. 48-52.

Was Jesus Chaste? or did he
Give any Lessons of Chastity?
The morning blush'd fiery red:
Mary was found in Adulterous bed;
Earth groan'd beneath, & Heaven above
Trembled at discovery of Love.
Jesus was sitting in Moses' Chair,
They brought the trembling Woman There.

Moses commands she be stoned to death,
What was the [words *del.*] sound of Jesus' breath?
He laid His hand on Moses' Law:
The Ancient Heavens, in Silent Awe
Writ with Curses from Pole to Pole,
All away began to roll:
The Earth trembling & Naked lay
In secret bed of Mortal Clay,
On Sinai felt the hand divine
Putting back the bloody shrine,
And she heard the breath of God
As she heard by Eden's flood:
"Good & Evil are no more!
"Sinai's trumpets, cease to roar!
"Cease, finger of God, to write!
"The Heavens are not clean in thy Sight.
"Thou art Good, & thou Alone;
"Nor may the sinner cast one stone.
"To be Good only, is to be
"A God [Devil *in pencil*] or else a Pharisee.
"Thou Angel of the Presence Divine
"That didst create this Body of Mine,
"Wherefore has thou writ these Laws
"And Created Hell's dark jaws?
"My Presence I will take from thee:
"A Cold Leper thou shalt be.
"Tho' thou wast so pure & bright
"That Heaven was Impure in thy Sight,
"Tho' thy Oath turn'd Heaven Pale,
"Tho' thy Covenant built Hell's Jail,
"Tho' thou didst all to Chaos roll
"With the Serpent for its soul,
"Still the breath Divine does move
"And the breath Divine is Love.
"Mary, Fear Not! Let me see
"The Seven Devils that torment thee:
"Hide not from my Sight thy Sin,
"That forgiveness thou maist win.
"Has no Man Condemned thee?"
"No Man, Lord:" "then what is he
"Who shall Accuse thee? Come Ye forth,
"Fallen fiends of Heav'nly birth
"That have forgot your Ancient love
"And driven away my trembling Dove.
"You shall bow before her feet;

"You shall lick the dust for Meat;
"And tho' you cannot Love, but Hate,
"Shall be beggars at Love's Gate.
"What was thy love? Let me [see't *del.*] see it;
"Was it love or Dark Deceit?"
"Love too long from Me has fled;
" 'Twas dark deceit, to Earn my bread;
" 'Twas Covet, or 'twas Custom, or
"['Twas *del.*] Some trifle not worth caring for;
"That they may call a [crime *del.*] shame & Sin
"[The *del.*] Love's temple [where *del.*] that God dwelleth in,
"And hide in secret hidden Shrine
"The Naked Human form divine,
"And render that a Lawless thing
"On which the Soul Expands its wing.
"But this, O Lord, this was my Sin
"When first I let these Devils in
"In dark pretence to Chastity:
"Blaspheming Love, blaspheming thee.
"Thence Rose Secret Adulteries,
"And thence did Covet also rise.
"My sin thou hast forgiven me,
"Canst thou forgive my Blasphemy?
"Canst thou return to this dark Hell,
"And in my burning bosom dwell?
"And canst thou die that I may live?
"And canst thou Pity & forgive?"
Then Roll'd the shadowy Man away
From the Limbs of Jesus, to make them his prey,
An Ever devouring appetite
Glittering with festering Venoms bright,
Crying, "[I've found *del.*] Crucify this cause of distress,
"[You *del.*] Who don't keep the secrets of Holiness!
"All Mental Powers by Diseases we bind,
"But he heals the deaf & the Dumb & the Blind.
"Whom God has afflicted for Secret Ends,
"He comforts & Heals & calls them Friends."
But, when Jesus was Crucified,
Then was perfected his glitt'ring pride:
In three Nights he devour'd his prey,
And still he devours the Body of Clay;
For dust & Clay is the Serpent's meat,
Which never was made for Man to Eat.

94 lines

f

P. 54.

I am sure This Jesus will not do
Either for Englishman or Jew.

g

P. 52.

Seeing this False Christ, In fury & Passion
I made my Voice heard all over the Nation.
What are those, &c

h

P. 48 (in pencil).

This was spoke by My Spectre to Voltaire, Bacon, &c

Did Jesus teach doubt? or did he
Give any lessons of Philosophy,
Charge Visionaries with decieving,
Or call Men wise for not Believing?

i

P. 120.

Was Jesus Born of a Virgin Pure
With narrow Soul & looks demure?
If he intended to take on Sin
The Mother should an Harlot been,
Just such a one as Magdalen
With seven devils in her Pen;
Or were Jew Virgins still more Curst,
And more sucking devils nurst?
Or what was it which he took on
That he might bring Salvation?
A Body subject to be Tempted,
From neither pain nor grief Exempted?
Or such a body as might not feel
The passions that with Sinners deal?
Yes, but they say he never fell.
Ask Caiaphas; for he can tell.
"He mock'd the Sabbath, & he mock'd
"The Sabbath's God, & he unlock'd
"The Evil spirits from their Shrines,
"And turn'd Fishermen to Divines;
"O'erturn'd the Tent of Secret Sins,

"& its Golden cords & Pins—
" 'Tis the Bloody Shrine of War
"Pinn'd around from Star to Star,
"Halls of justice, hating Vice,
"Where the devil Combs his lice.
"He turn'd the devils into Swine
"That he might tempt the Jews to dine;
"Since which, a Pig has got a look
"That for a Jew may be mistook.
" 'Obey your parents.'—What says he?
" 'Woman, what have I to do with thee?
" 'No Earthly Parents I confess:
" 'I am doing my Father's Business.'
"He scorn'd [his *del.*] Earth's Parents, scorn'd [his *del.*] Earth's God,
"And mock'd the one & the other's Rod;
"His Seventy Disciples sent
"Against Religion & Government:
"They by the Sword of Justice fell
"And him their Cruel Murderer tell.
"He left his Father's trade to roam
"A wand'ring Vagrant without Home;
"And thus he others' labour stole
"That he might live above Controll.
"The Publicans & Harlots he
"Selected for his Company,
"And from the Adulteress turn'd away
"God's righteous Law, that lost its Prey."

THE EVERLASTING GOSPEL

SUPPLEMENTARY PASSAGES

Written not before 1818

There is not one Moral Virtue that Jesus Inculcated but Plato & Cicero did Inculcate before him; what then did Christ Inculcate? Forgiveness of Sins. This alone is the Gospel, & this is the Life & Immortality brought to light by Jesus, Even the Covenant of Jehovah, which is This: If you forgive one another your Trespasses, so shall Jehovah forgive you, That he himself may dwell among you; but if you Avenge, you Murder the Divine Image, & he cannot dwell among you; [by his *del.*] because you Murder him he arises again, & you deny that he is Arisen, & are blind to Spirit.

1

This to come first.

If Moral Virtue was Christianity,
Christ's Pretensions were all Vanity,
And Caiphas & Pilate, Men
Praise Worthy, & the Lion's Den
And not the Sheepfold, Allegories
Of God & Heaven & their Glories.
The Moral Christian is the Cause
Of the Unbeliever & his Laws.
The Roman Virtues, Warlike Fame,
Take Jesus' & Jehovah's Name;
For what is Antichrist but those
Who against Sinners Heaven close
With Iron bars, in Virtuous State,
And Rhadamanthus at the Gate?

2

What can this Gospel of Jesus be?
What Life & Immortality,
What was it that he brought to Light
That Plato & Cicero did not write?
The Heathen Deities wrote them all,
These Moral Virtues, great & small.
What is the Accusation of Sin
But Moral Virtues' deadly Gin?
The Moral Virtues in their Pride
Did o'er the World triumphant ride
In Wars & Sacrifice for Sin,
And Souls to Hell ran trooping in.
The Accuser, Holy God of All
This Pharisaic Worldly Ball,
Amidst them in his Glory Beams
Upon the Rivers & the Streams.
Then Jesus rose & said to [men *altered to*] Me,
"Thy Sins are all forgiven thee."
Loud Pilate Howl'd, loud Caiphas yell'd,
When they the Gospel Light beheld.
["Jerusalem" he said to me *del.*]
It was when Jesus said to Me,
"Thy Sins are all forgiven thee."
The Christian trumpets loud proclaim
Thro' all the World in Jesus' name
Mutual forgiveness of each Vice,

And oped the Gates of Paradise.
The Moral Virtues in Great fear
Formed the Cross & Nails & Spear,
And the Accuser standing by
Cried out, "Crucify! Crucify!
"Our Moral Virtues ne'er can be,
"Nor Warlike pomp & Majesty;
"For Moral Virtues all begin
"In the Accusations of Sin,
"And [Moral *del.*] all the Heroic Virtues [all *del.*] End
"In destroying the Sinners' Friend.
"Am I not Lucifer the Great,
"And you my daughters in Great State,
"The fruit of my Mysterious Tree
"Of Good & Evil & Misery
"And Death & Hell, which now begin
"On everyone who Forgives Sin?"

[END OF THE EVERLASTING GOSPEL]

FOR THE SEXES: THE GATES OF PARADISE

First engraved 1793

Additions made about 1818

[FRONTISPIECE]

What is Man?

The Sun's Light when he unfolds it
Depends on the Organ that beholds it.

[PROLOGUE]

Mutual Forgiveness of each Vice,
Such are the Gates of Paradise.
Against the Accuser's chief desire,
Who walk'd among the Stones of Fire,
Jehovah's fingers Wrote the Law:
[Jehovah's Finger Wrote the Law: *later version*]
Then Wept! then rose in Zeal & Awe,
And in the midst of Sinai's heat
Hid it beneath his Mercy Seat.
[And the Dead Corpse from Sinai's heat
Buried beneath his Mercy Seat. *later version*]
O Christians, Christians! tell me Why
You rear it on your Altars high.

1

I found him beneath a Tree.

2 Water
Thou Waterest him with Tears:

3 Earth
He struggles into Life

4

Air
On Cloudy Doubts & Reasoning Cares

5

Fire
That end in endless Strife.

6

At length for hatching ripe
he breaks the shell.

7

What are these? Alas! the Female Martyr,
Is She also the Divine Image?

8 My Son! my Son!

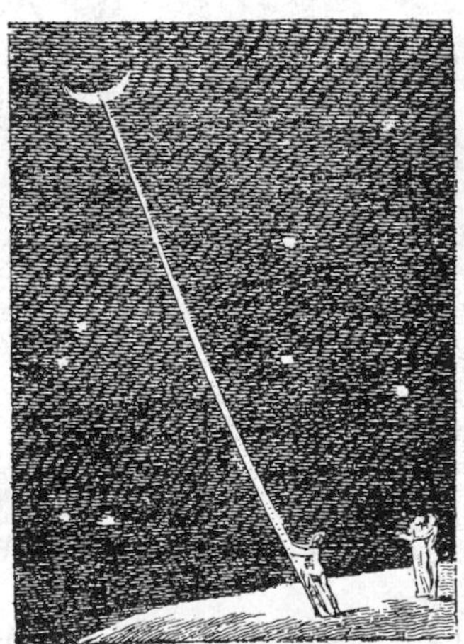

9 I want! I want!

10

Help! Help!

11

Aged Ignorance

Perceptive Organs closed, their Objects close.

12

Does thy God, O Priest, take such vengeance as this?

13

Fear & Hope are—Vision.

14

The Traveller hasteth in the Evening.

15

Death's Door

16

I have said to the Worm:
Thou art my mother & my sister.

THE KEYS

The Catterpiller on the Leaf
Reminds thee of thy Mother's Grief.

OF THE GATES

1 My Eternal Man set in Repose,
The Female from his darkness rose
And She found me beneath a Tree,
A Mandrake, & in her Veil hid me.
Serpent Reasonings us entice
Of Good & Evil, Virtue & Vice.
2 Doubt Self Jealous, Wat'ry folly,
3 Struggling thro' Earth's Melancholy.
4 Naked in Air, in Shame & Fear,
5 Blind in Fire with shield & spear,
Two Horn'd Reasoning, Cloven Fiction,
In Doubt, which is Self contradiction,
A dark Hermaphrodite I [We *later version*] stood,
Rational Truth, Root of Evil & Good.
Round me flew the Flaming Sword;
Round her snowy Whirlwinds roar'd,
Freezing her Veil, the Mundane Shell.
6 I rent the Veil where the Dead dwell:

When weary Man enters his Cave
He meets his Saviour in the Grave
Some find a Female Garment there,
And some a Male, woven with care,
Lest the Sexual Garments sweet
Should grow a devouring Winding sheet,
7 One Dies! Alas! the Living & Dead,
One is slain & One is fled.
8 In Vain-glory hatcht & nurst,
By double Spectres Self Accurst,
My Son! my Son! thou treatest me
But as I have instructed thee.
9 On the shadows of the Moon
Climbing thro' Night's highest noon.
10 In Time's Ocean falling drown'd.
In Aged Ignorance profound,
11 Holy & cold, I clip'd the Wings
Of all Sublunary Things,
12 And in depths of my Dungeons
Closed the Father & the Sons.
13 But when once I did descry
The Immortal Man that cannot Die,
14 Thro' evening shades I haste away
To close the Labours of my Day.
15 The Door of Death I open found
And the Worm Weaving in the Ground:
16 Thou'rt my Mother from the Womb,
Wife, Sister, Daughter, to the Tomb,
Weaving to Dreams the Sexual strife
And weeping over the Web of Life.

[EPILOGUE]

To The Accuser who is
The God of This World

Truly, My Satan, thou art but a Dunce,
And dost not know the Garment from the Man.
Every Harlot was a Virgin once,
Nor can'st thou ever change Kate into Nan.

Tho' thou art Worship'd by the Names Divine
Of Jesus & Jehovah, thou art still
The Son of Morn in weary Night's decline,
The lost Traveller's Dream under the Hill.

NOTES ON SPURZHEIM'S "OBSERVATIONS ON THE DERANGED MANIFESTATIONS OF THE MIND, OR INSANITY."

London. MDCCCXVII

Written about 1819

[*Blake's notes here follow, in larger type, the passages from Spurzheim to which they refer.*]

Page 106.
... In children ... the disturbances of the organization appear merely as organic diseases, because the functions are entirely suppressed.

Corporeal disease, to which I readily agree. Diseases of the mind: I pity him. Denies mental health and perfection. Stick to this, all is right. But see page 152.

Page 152.
As the functions depend on the organization, disturbed functions will derange the organization, and one deranged cerebral part, will have an influence on others, and so arises insanity.... Whatever occupies the mind too intensely or exclusively is hurtful to the brain, and induces a state favourable to insanity, in diminishing the influence of the will.

Page 154.
Religion is another fertile cause of insanity. Mr. Haslam, though he declares it sinful to consider religion as a cause of insanity, adds, however, that he would be ungrateful, did he not avow his obligations to Methodism for its supply of numerous cases. Hence the primitive feelings of religion may be misled and produce insanity; that is what I would contend for, and in that sense religion often leads to insanity.

Methodism, etc., p. 154. Cowper came to me and said: "O that I "were insane always. I will never rest. Can you not make me truly "insane? I will never rest till I am so. O that in the bosom of God I "was hid. You retain health and yet are as mad as any of us all—over "us all—mad as a refuge from unbelief—from Bacon, Newton and "Locke."

NOTE ON A PENCIL DRAWING OF NINE GROTESQUE HEADS

Written about 1819

All Genius varies Thus. Devils are
various. Angels are all alike.

MIRTH AND HER COMPANIONS

Engraved about 1820
beneath a print of the first subject illustrating Milton's L'Allegro.

Solomon says, 'Vanity of Vanities, all is Vanity,' & What can be Foolisher than this?

ANNOTATIONS TO BERKELEY'S "SIRIS"

Dublin MDCCXLIV

Written about 1820

[*Blake's remarks here follow, in larger type, the passages from "Siris" to which they refer.*]

Page 203.
God knoweth all things, as pure mind or intellect, but nothing by sense, nor in nor through a sensory. Therefore to suppose a sensory of any kind, whether space or any other, in God would be very wrong, and lead us into false conceptions of his nature.

Imagination or the Human Eternal Body in Every Man.

Page 204.
But in respect of a perfect spirit, there is nothing hard or impenetrable: there is no resistance to the deity. Nor hath he any Body: Nor is the supreme being united to the world, as the soul of an animal is to its body, which necessarily implieth defect, both as an instrument and as a constant weight and impediment.

Imagination or the Divine Body in Every Man.

Page 205.
Natural phænomena are only natural appearances . . . They and the phantomes that result from those appearances, *the children of imagination* [*underlined by Blake*] grafted upon sense, such for example as pure space, are thought by many the very first in existence and stability, and to embrace and comprehend all beings.

The All in Man. The Divine Image or Imagination.
The Four Senses are the Four Faces of Man & the Four Rivers of the Water of Life.

Page 212.
Plato and Aristotle considered God as abstracted or distinct from the natural world. But the Aegyptians considered God and nature as making one whole, or all things together as making one universe.

They also consider'd God as abstracted or distinct from the Imaginative World, but Jesus, as also Abraham & David, consider'd God as a Man in the Spiritual or Imaginative Vision.
Jesus consider'd Imagination to be the Real Man & says I will not leave you Orphans and I will manifest myself to you; he says also, the Spiritual Body or Angel as little Children always behold the Face of the Heavenly Father.

Page 213.
The perceptions of sense are gross: but even in the senses there is a difference. Though harmony and proportion are not objects of sense, yet the eye and the ear are organs, which offer to the mind such materials, by means whereof she may apprehend both the one and the other.

Harmony [and] Proportion are Qualities & Not Things. The Harmony & Proportion of a Horse are not the same with those of a Bull. Every Thing has its own Harmony & Proportion, Two Inferior Qualities in it. For its Reality is Its Imaginative Form.

Page 214.
By experiments of sense we become acquainted with the lower faculties of the soul; and from them, whether by a gradual evolution or ascent, we arrive at the highest. These become subjects for fancy to work upon. Reason considers and judges of the imaginations. And these acts of reason become new objects to the understanding.

Knowledge is not by deduction, but Immediate by Perception or Sense at once. Christ addresses himself to the Man, not to his Reason. Plato did not bring Life & Immortality to Light. Jesus only did this.

Page 215.
There is according to Plato properly no knowledge, but only opinion concerning things sensible and perishing, not because they are naturally abstruse and involved in darkness: but because their nature and existence is uncertain, ever fleeting and changing.

Jesus supposes every Thing to be Evident to the Child & to the Poor & Unlearned. Such is the Gospel.
The Whole Bible is fill'd with Imagination & Visions from End to End & not with Moral Virtues; that is the business of Plato & the Greeks & all Warriors. The Moral Virtues are continual Accusers of Sin & promote Eternal Wars & Dominency over others.

Page 217.
Aristotle maketh a threefold distinction of objects according to the three speculative sciences. Physics he supposeth to be conversant about such things as have a principle of motion in themselves, mathematics about things permanent but not abstracted, and theology about being abstracted and immoveable, which distinction may be seen in the ninth book of his metaphysics.

God is not a Mathematical Diagram.

Page 218.
It is a maxim of the Platonic philosophy, that the soul of man was originally furnished with native inbred notions, and stands in need of sensible occasions, not absolutely for producing them, but only for awakening, rousing or exciting into act what was already pre-existent, dormant, and latent in the soul.

The Natural Body is an Obstruction to the Soul or Spiritual Body.

Page 219.
. . . Whence, according to Themistius, . . . it may be inferred that all beings are in the soul. For, saith he, the forms are the beings. By the form every thing is what it is. And, he adds, it is the soul that imparteth forms to matter, . . .

This is my Opinion, but Forms must be apprehended by Sense or the Eye of Imagination. Man is All Imagination. God is Man & exists in us & we in him.

Page 241.

What Jesus came to Remove was the Heathen or Platonic Philosophy, which blinds the Eye of Imagination, The Real Man.

[END OF ANNOTATIONS TO BERKELEY]

[THE LAOCOÖN]

Engraved about 1820

The Angel of the Divine Presence

מלאך יהוה

οφιουχος

Evil Good

לילית

יה & his two Sons, Satan & Adam, as they were copied from the Cherubim of Solomon's Temple, by three Rhodians, & applied to Natural Fact or History of Ilium.

If Morality was Christianity, Socrates was the Saviour.

Art Degraded, Imagination Denied, War Governed the Nations.

Spiritual War: Israel deliver'd from Egypt, is Art deliver'd from Nature & Imitation.

A Poet, a Painter, a Musician, an Architect: the Man Or Woman who is not one of these is not a Christian.

You must leave Fathers & Mothers & Houses & Lands if they stand in the way of Art.

Prayer is the Study of Art.

Praise is the Practise of Art.

Fasting &c., all relate to Art.

The outward Ceremony is Antichrist.

The Eternal Body of Man is The Imagination, that is,

God himself
The Divine Body } יש[ו]ע, Jesus: we are his Members.

It manifests itself in his Works of Art (In Eternity All is Vision).

The True Christian Charity not dependent on Money (the life's blood of Poor Families), that is, on Caesar or Empire or Natural Religion: Money, which is The Great Satan or Reason, the Root of Good & Evil In The Accusation of Sin.

Good & Evil are Riches & Poverty, a Tree of Misery, propagating Generation & Death.

Where any view of Money exists, Art cannot be carried on, but War only (Read Matthew, c. x: 9 & 10 v.) by pretences to the Two Impossibilities, Chastity & Abstinence, Gods of the Heathen.

He repented that he had made Adam (of the Female, the Adamah) & it grieved him at his heart.

What can be Created Can be Destroyed.

Adam is only The Natural Man & not the Soul or Imagination.

Hebrew Art is called Sin by the Deist Science.

All that we See is Vision, from Generated Organs gone as soon as come, Permanent in The Imagination, Consider'd as Nothing by the Natural Man.

Art can never exist without Naked Beauty displayed.

The Gods of Greece & Egypt were Mathematical Diagrams—See Plato's Works.

Divine Union Deriding, And Denying Immediate Communion with God, The Spoilers say, "Where are his Works That he did in "the Wilderness? Lo, what are these? Whence came they?" These are not the Works Of Egypt nor Babylon, Whose Gods are the Powers Of this World, Goddess Nature, Who first spoil & then destroy Imaginative Art; For their Glory is War and Dominion.

Empire against Art—See Virgil's Eneid, Lib. VI, v. 848.

Satan's Wife, The Goddess Nature, is War & Misery, & Heroism a Miser.

For every Pleasure Money Is Useless.

There are States in which all Visionary Men are accounted Mad Men; such are Greece & Rome: Such is Empire or Tax—See Luke, Ch. 2, v. 1.

The Gods of Priam are the Cherubim of Moses & Solomon, The Hosts of Heaven.

Without Unceasing Practise nothing can be done. Practise is Art. If you leave off you are Lost.

Jesus & his Apostles & Disciples were all Artists. Their Works were destroy'd by the Seven Angels of the Seven Churches in Asia, Antichrist Science.

The Old & New Testaments are the Great Code of Art.

Art is the Tree of Life. God is Jesus.

Science is the Tree of Death.

The Whole Business of Man Is The Arts, & All Things Common. No Secresy in Art.

The unproductive Man is not a Christian, much less the Destroyer.

Christianity is Art & not Money. Money is its Curse.

What we call Antique Gems are the Gems of Aaron's Breast Plate.

Is not every Vice possible to Man described in the Bible openly?

All is not Sin that Satan calls so: all the Loves & Graces of Eternity.

ON HOMER'S POETRY & ON VIRGIL

Etched about 1820

On Homer's Poetry

Every Poem must necessarily be a perfect Unity, but why Homer's is peculiarly so, I cannot tell; he has told the story of Bellerophon & omitted the Judgment of Paris, which is not only a part, but a principal part, of Homer's subject.

But when a Work has Unity, it is as much in a Part as in the Whole: the Torso is as much a Unity as the Laocoon.

As Unity is the cloke of folly, so Goodness is the cloke of knavery. Those who will have Unity exclusively in Homer come out with a Moral like a sting in the tail. Aristotle says Characters are either Good or Bad; now Goodness or Badness has nothing to do with Character: an Apple tree, a Pear tree, a Horse, a Lion are Characters, but a Good Apple tree or a Bad is an Apple tree still; a Horse is not more a Lion for being a Bad Horse: that is its Character: its Goodness or Badness is another consideration.

It is the same with the Moral of a whole Poem as with the Moral Goodness of its parts. Unity & Morality are secondary considerations, & belong to Philosophy & not to Poetry, to Exception & not to Rule, to Accident & not to Substance; the Ancients call'd it eating of the tree of good & evil.

The Classics! it is the Classics, & not Goths nor Monks, that Desolate Europe with Wars.

On Virgil

Sacred Truth has pronounced that Greece & Rome, as Babylon & Egypt, so far from being parents of Arts & Sciences as they pretend, were destroyers of all Art. Homer, Virgil & Ovid confirm this opinion & make us reverence The Word of God, the only light of antiquity that remains unperverted by War. Virgil in the Eneid, Book VI, line 848, says "Let others study Art: Rome has somewhat better to do, "namely War & Dominion."

Rome & Greece swept Art into their maw & destroy'd it; a Warlike State never can produce Art. It will Rob & Plunder & accumulate into one place, & Translate & Copy & Buy & Sell & Criticise, but not Make. Grecian is Mathematic Form: Gothic is Living Form, Mathematic Form is Eternal in the Reasoning Memory: Living Form is Eternal Existence.

NOTE IN CENNINI'S "TRATTATO DELLA PITTURA."

Roma. MDCCCXXI

Written about 1822

The Pope supposes Nature & the Virgin Mary to be the same allegorical personages, but the Protestant considers Nature as incapable of bearing a Child.

THE GHOST of ABEL

A Revelation In the Visions of Jehovah
Seen by William Blake

Etched 1822

Plate I

To LORD BYRON in the Wilderness:

What doest thou here, Elijah?

Can a Poet doubt the Visions of Jehovah? Nature has no Outline, but Imagination has. Nature has no Tune, but Imagination has. Nature has no Supernatural & dissolves: Imagination is Eternity.

Scene—*A rocky Country.* Eve *fainted over the dead body of* Abel, *which lays near a Grave.* Adam *kneels by her.* Jehovah *stands above.*

Jehovah. Adam!
Adam. I will not hear thee more, thou Spiritual Voice.
Is this Death?
Jehovah. Adam!
Adam. It is in vain. I will not hear thee
Henceforth! Is this thy Promise, that the Woman's Seed
Should bruise the Serpent's head? Is this the Serpent? Ah!
Seven times, O Eve, thou hast fainted over the Dead. Ah! Ah!

Eve *revives.*

Eve. Is this the Promise of Jehovah? O, it is all a vain delusion,
This Death & this Life & this Jehovah!
Jehovah. Woman, lift thine eyes!

A Voice is heard coming on.

Voice. O Earth, cover not thou my Blood! cover not thou my Blood!

Enter the Ghost *of* Abel.

Eve. Thou Visionary Phantasm, thou art not the real Abel.
Abel. Among the Elohim, a Human Victim I wander: I am their House,
Prince of the Air, & our dimensions compass Zenith & Nadir.
Vain is thy Covenant, O Jehovah! I am the Accuser & Avenger
Of Blood. O Earth, Cover not thou the Blood of Abel.
Jehovah. What Vengeance dost thou require?
Abel. Life for Life! Life for Life!
Jehovah. He who shall take Cain's life must also Die, O Abel!
And who is he? Adam, wilt thou, or Eve, thou do this?
Adam. It is all a Vain delusion of the all creative Imagination.
Eve, come away, & let us not believe these vain delusions.
Abel is dead, & Cain slew him. We shall also Die a Death,
And then, what then? be, as poor Abel, a Thought, or as
This! O, what shall I call thee, Form Divine, Father of Mercies,
That appearest to my Spiritual Vision? Eve, seest thou also?
Eve. I see him plainly with my Mind's Eye. I see also Abel living,
Tho' terribly afflicted, as We also are, yet Jehovah sees him

Plate 2

Alive & not Dead; were it not better to believe Vision
With all our might & strength, tho' we are fallen & lost?
Adam. Eve, thou hast spoken truly: let us kneel before his feet.

They Kneel before Jehovah.

Abel. Are these the Sacrifices of Eternity, O Jehovah, a Broken Spirit
And a Contrite Heart? O, I cannot Forgive! the Accuser hath
Enter'd into Me as into his House, & I loathe thy Tabernacles.
As thou hast said, so is it come to pass: My desire is unto Cain,
And He doth rule over Me; therefore My Soul in fumes of Blood
Cries for Vengeance, Sacrifice on Sacrifice, Blood on Blood!
Jehovah. Lo, I have given you a Lamb for an Atonement instead
Of the Transgressor, or no Flesh or Spirit could ever Live.
Abel. Compelled I cry, O Earth, cover not the Blood of Abel!

Abel *sinks down into the Grave, from which arises* Satan,
Armed in glittering scales, with a Crown & a Spear.

Satan. I will have Human Blood & not the blood of Bulls or Goats,
And no Atonement, O Jehovah! the Elohim live on Sacrifice
Of Men: hence I am God of Men: Thou Human, O Jehovah!

By the Rock & Oak of the Druid, creeping Mistletoe & Thorn,
Cain's City built with Human Blood, not Blood of Bulls & Goats,
Thou shalt Thyself be Sacrificed to Me, thy God, on Calvary.
Jehovah. Such is My Will *Thunders.*
that Thou Thyself go to Eternal Death
In Self Annihilation, even till Satan, Self-subdu'd, Put off Satan
Into the Bottomless Abyss, whose torment arises for ever & ever.

On each side a Chorus of Angels entering Sing the following:

The Elohim of the Heathen Swore Vengeance for Sin! Then Thou stood'st
Forth, O Elohim Jehovah! in the midst of the darkness of the Oath, All Clothed
In Thy Covenant of the Forgiveness of Sins: Death, O Holy! Is this Brotherhood.
The Elohim saw their Oath Eternal Fire: they rolled apart trembling over The
Mercy Seat, each in his station fixt in the Firmament by Peace, Brotherhood and Love.

The Curtain falls.

[*A floating figure is inscribed:* The Voice of Abel's Blood.]

1822 W Blake's Original Stereotype was 1788

INSCRIPTION IN THE AUTOGRAPH ALBUM OF WILLIAM UPCOTT

Written January 16, 1826

William Blake, one who is very much delighted with being in good Company.

Born 28 Novr 1757 in London & has died several times since.

January 16 1826.

The above was written & the drawing annexed by the desire of Mr Leigh; how far it is an Autograph is a Question. I do not think an Artist can write an Autograph, especially one who has studied in the Florentine & Roman Schools, as such an one will Consider what he is doing; but an Autograph, as I understand it, is writ helter skelter like a hog upon a rope, or a Man who walks without Considering whether he shall run against a Post or a House or a Horse or a Man, & I am apt to believe that what is done without meaning is very different from that which a Man does with his Thought & Mind, & ought not to be Call'd by the Same Name.

I consider the Autograph of Mr Cruickshank, which very justly stands first in the Book, & that Beautiful Specimen of Writing by Mr Comfield, & my own, as standing [in] the same Predicament: they are in some measure Works of Art & not of Nature or Chance.

Heaven born, the Soul a Heavenward Course must hold;
For what delights the Sense is False & Weak.
Beyond the Visible World she soars to Seek.
Ideal Form, The Universal Mold.

Michael Angelo. Sonnet as Translated by Mr Wordsworth.

[*Poems*, 1815, vol. II, p. 179.]

ANNOTATIONS TO "POEMS" BY WILLIAM WORDSWORTH

VOL. I, LONDON, MDCCCXV

Written 1826

[*Blake's annotations are here printed in larger type after the passages from Wordsworth to which they refer.*]

Page viii.

The powers requisite for the production of poetry are, first, those of observation and description . . . 2dly, Sensibility.

One Power alone makes a Poet: Imagination, The Divine Vision.

Page 1.

[*Sub-title*]: "Poems Referring to the Period of Childhood."

I see in Wordsworth the Natural Man rising up against the Spiritual Man Continually, & then he is No Poet but a Heathen Philosopher at Enmity against all true Poetry or Inspiration.

Page 3.

And I could wish my days to be
Bound each to each by natural piety.

There is no such Thing as Natural Piety Because The Natural Man is at Enmity with God.

Page 43.

"To H.C. Six Years Old."

This is all in the highest degree Imaginative & equal to any Poet, but not Superior. I cannot think that Real Poets have any competition. None are greatest in the Kingdom of Heaven; it is so in Poetry.

Page 44.

"Influence of Natural Objects
"In calling forth and strengthening the Imagination
"in Boyhood and early Youth."

Natural Objects always did & now do weaken, deaden & obliterate Imagination in Me. Wordsworth must know that what he Writes Valuable is Not to be found in Nature. Read Michael Angelo's Sonnet, vol. 2, p. 179:

[Heaven-born, the Soul a heaven-ward course must hold;
Beyond the visible world She soars to seek,
(For what delights the sense is false and weak)
Ideal Form, the universal mould.]

Page 341.

"Essay, Supplementary to the Preface."

I do not know who wrote these Prefaces: they are very mischievous & direct contrary to Wordsworth's own Practise.

Pages 364-5.

In Macpherson's work it is exactly the reverse; every thing (that is not stolen) is in this manner defined, insulated, dislocated, deadened,—yet nothing distinct . . . Yet, much as these pretended treasures of antiquity have been admired, they have been wholly uninfluential upon the literature of the country . . . no Author in the least distinguished, has ventured formally to imitate them—except the Boy, Chatterton, on their first appearance.

I believe both Macpherson & Chatterton, that what they say is Ancient Is so.
I own myself an admirer of Ossian equally with any other Poet whatever, Rowley & Chatterton also.

Pages 374-5.

Is it the result of the whole that, in the opinion of the Writer, the judgment of the People is not to be respected? The thought is most injurious; . . . to the People . . . his devout respect, his reverence, is due. He . . . takes leave of his Readers by assuring them—that if he were not persuaded that the Contents of these Volumes, and the Work to which they are subsidiary, evinced something of the "Vision and the Faculty divine," . . . he would not, if a wish could do it, save them from immediate destruction.

It appears to me as if the last Paragraph beginning "Is it the result" Was writ by another hand & mind from the rest of these Prefaces. Perhaps they are the opinions of a Portrait or Landscape painter. Imagination is the Divine Vision not of The World, or of Man, nor from Man as he is a Natural Man, but only as he is a Spiritual Man. Imagination has nothing to do with Memory.

ANNOTATIONS TO "THE EXCURSION, BEING A PORTION OF THE RECLUSE, A POEM" BY WILLIAM WORDSWORTH, LONDON, MDCCCXIV

Written 1826,

[*together with a manuscript copy in Blake's hand of the poetical portion of Wordsworth's Preface and his prefatory sentences; the relevant passages are here followed by Blake's notes in larger type. Words underlined by Blake are printed in italic.*]

Page xi.

All strength—all terror, single or in bands,
That ever was put forth in personal form;
Jehovah—with his thunder, and the choir
Of shouting Angels, and the empyreal thrones,
I pass them, unalarmed . . .

Solomon, when he Married Pharoh's daughter & became a Convert to the Heathen Mythology, Talked exactly in this way of Jehovah as a Very inferior object of Man's Contemplation; he also passed him by unalarm'd & was permitted. Jehovah dropped a tear & follow'd him by his Spirit into the Abstract Void; it is called the Divine Mercy. Satan dwells in it, but Mercy does not dwell in him; he knows not to Forgive.

Pages xii-xiii.

How exquisitely the individual Mind
(And the progressive powers perhaps no less
Of the whole species) to the external World
Is fitted:—& how exquisitely, too,
Theme this but little heard of among Men,
The external World is fitted to the Mind.

You shall not bring me down to believe such fitting & fitted. I know better & please your Lordship.

Such grateful haunts foregoing, if I oft
Must turn elsewhere—to travel near the tribes
And fellowships of Men, & see ill sights
Of madding passions mutually inflamed;
Must hear *Humanity in fields & groves*
Pipe solitary anguish; or must hang
Brooding above the fierce confederate storm
Of Sorrow, barricadoed evermore
With the walls of cities; may these sounds
Have their authentic comment,—that, even these
Hearing, I be not downcast or forlorn!

Does not this Fit, & is it not Fitting most Exquisitely too, but to what?—not to Mind, but to the Vile Body only & to its Laws of Good & Evil & its Enmities against Mind.

NOTES ON THE ILLUSTRATIONS TO DANTE

Written 1825-1827

On design no. 7, *a map of the classical conception of the Universe, written in the circles surrounding the central figure of Homer.*

Every thing in Dante's Comedia shews That for Tyrannical Purposes he has made This World the Foundation of All, & the Goddess Nature Memory [Nature *del.*] is his Inspirer & not Imagination the Holy Ghost. As Poor Churchill said: "Nature, thou art my Goddess."

Round Purgatory is Paradise, & round Paradise is Vacuum or Limbo, so that Homer is the Center of All—I mean the Poetry of the Heathen, Stolen & Perverted from the Bible, not by Chance but by design, by the Kings of Persia & their Generals, The Greek Heroes & lastly by the Romans.

Swedenborg does the same in saying that in this World is the Ultimate of Heaven. This is the most damnable Falshood of Satan & his Antichrist.

On design no. 16, *The Goddess Fortune.*

The hole of a Shit-house.

The Goddess Fortune is the devil's servant, ready to Kiss any one's Arse.

On design no. 101, *a diagram of the Circles of Hell.*

It seems as if Dante's supreme Good was something Superior to the Father or Jesus; for if he gives his rain to the Evil & the Good, & his Sun to the Just & the Unjust, He could never have Built Dante's Hell, nor the Hell of the Bible neither, in the way our Parsons explain it—It must have been originally Formed by the devil Himself; & So I understand it to have been.

Whatever Book is for Vengeance for Sin & whatever Book is Against the Forgiveness of Sins is not of the Father, but of Satan the Accuser & Father of Hell.

This [*the diagram*] is Upside Down When view'd from Hell's gate, which ought to be at top, But right When View'd from Purgatory after they have passed the Center.

In Equivocal Worlds Up & Down are Equivocal.

In the circles from below upwards

1. Limbo. Charon.
2. Minos.

3. Cerberus.
4. Plutus & Phlegyas.
5. City of Dis. Queen of Endless Woe. furies & . . . Lesser Circle Point of the Universe. Canto Eleventh Line 68.
6. Minotaur. The City of Dis seems to occupy the Space between the Fifth and Sixth Circles or perhaps it occupies both Circles with its Environs.
7. Centaurs. Most likely Dante describes the 7, 8 & 9 Circles in Canto XI, v. 18.
   3 Compartments.
   Dante calls them Cerchietti.
8. Geryon. Malebolge. Containing 10 gulphs.
9. Lucifer. Containing 9 Rounds.

ANNOTATIONS TO DR. THORNTON'S "NEW TRANSLATION OF THE LORD'S PRAYER"

LONDON MDCCCXXVII

Written 1827

I look upon this as a Most Malignant & Artful attack upon the Kingdom of Jesus By the Classical Learned, thro' the Instrumentality of Dr Thornton. The Greek & Roman Classics is the Antichrist. I say Is & not Are as most expressive & correct too. [*on the title-page*]

[*Those of Blake's subsequent annotations that refer to the text are printed after the relevant passages which are given in smaller type. On page* 3 *is Blake's own version of the Lord's Prayer; on the fly-leaf at the end is his paraphrase of Dr. Thornton's version.*]

Page iii.

Doctor Johnson on the Bible: "The Bible is the most difficult book in the world "to comprehend, nor can it be understood at all by the unlearned, except through "the aid of critical and explanatory notes."

Christ & his Apostles were Illiterate Men; Caiphas, Pilate & Herod were Learned.

Lord Byron on the Ethics of Christ: "What made Socrates the greatest of men? "His moral truths—his ethics. What proved Jesus Christ to be the son of God, "hardly less than his miracles did? His moral precepts."

If Morality was Christianity, Socrates was The Savior.

The Beauty of the Bible is that the most Ignorant & Simple Minds Understand it Best—Was Johnson hired to Pretend to Religious Terrors while he was an Infidel, or how was it?

Page iv.

The only thing for Newtonian & Baconian Philosophers to Consider is this: Whether Jesus did not suffer himself to be Mock'd by Caesar's Soldiers Willingly, & [I hope they will *del.*] to Consider this to all Eternity will be Comment Enough.

Page 1.

[*Following remarks on the necessity for a new translation of the Bible.*]

Such things as these depend on the Fashion of the Age.

In a book where all may Read, &
In a book which all may Read, & } are Equally Right.
In a book that all may Read

That Man who &c is equally so—The Man that & the Man which.

Men from their childhood have been so accustomed to mouth the Lord's Prayer, that they continue this through life, and call it "Saying their Prayers." . . .

It is the learned that Mouth, & not the Vulgar.

THE LORD'S PRAYER

Translated from the Greek, by Dr. Thornton.

Come let us worship, and bow down, and kneel, before the Lord, our Maker. Psalm xcv.

ΠΑΤΕΡ ἡμῶν ὁ ἐν τοῖς οὐρανοις αγιαςθητω τὸ ὀνομα σου.

O Father of Mankind, Thou, who dwellest in the highest of the Heavens, Reverenc'd be Thy Name.

ἐλθέτω ἡ βασιλεία σου γενηθητω το θέλημα σου.

May Thy Reign be, every where, proclaim'd so that Thy Will may be done upon the Earth, as it is in the Mansions of Heaven:

Grant unto me, and the whole world, day by day, an abundant supply of spiritual and corporeal Food:

Forgive us our transgressions against Thee, as we extend our Kindness, and Forgiveness, to all:

O God! abandon us not, when surrounded, by trials;

But preserve us from the Dominion of Satan: For Thine only, is the Sovereignty, the power, and the glory, throughout Eternity!!!

Amen.

Lawful Bread, Bought with Lawful Money, & a Lawful Heaven, seen thro' a Lawful Telescope, by means of Lawful Window Light! The Holy Ghost, & whatever cannot be Taxed, is Unlawful & Witchcraft.

Spirits are Lawful, but not Ghosts; especially Royal Gin is Lawful Spirit. [real *del.*] No Smuggling real British Spirit & Truth!

Page 2.

Give us the Bread that is our due & Right, by taking away Money, or a Price, or Tax upon what is Common to all in thy Kingdom.

Page 3.

Jesus, our Father, who art in thy heaven call'd by thy Name the Holy Ghost, Thy Kingdom on Earth is Not, nor thy Will done, but [his Will who is the *del.*] Satan's, who is God of this World, the Accuser. Let his Judgment be Forgiveness that he may be consum'd in his own shame.
Give us This Eternal Day our [ghostly *del.*] own right Bread by taking away Money or debtor Tax & Value or Price, as we have all Things Common among us. Every thing has as much right to Eternal Life as God, who is the Servant of Man. [The Accusation *del.*] His Judgment shall be Forgiveness that he may be consum'd in his own Shame.
Leave us not in Parsimony, Satan's Kingdom [*word del.*]; liberate us from the Natural Man & [*words illegible*] Kingdom.
For thine is the Kingdom & the Power & the Glory & not Caesar's or Satan's. Amen.

Page 5.

Dim at best are the conceptions we have of the Supreme Being, who, as it were, keeps the human race in suspense, neither discovering, nor hiding Himself; . . .

a Female God!

Page 6.

What is the Will of God we are ordered to obey? . . . Let us consider whose Will it is. . . . It is the Will of our Maker. . . . It is finally the Will of Him, who is uncontrollably powerful. . . .

So you See That God is just such a Tyrant as Augustus Caesar; & is not this Good & Learned & Wise & Classical?

Fly-leaf.

This is Saying the Lord's Prayer Backwards, which they say Raises the devil.

Doctor Thornton's Tory Translation, Translated out of its disguise in the Classical & Scotch languages into [plain *del.*] the vulgar English.

Our Father Augustus Caesar, who art in these thy Substantial Astronomical Telescopic Heavens, Holiness to thy Name or Title, & reverence to thy Shadow. Thy Kingship come upon Earth first & thence in Heaven. Give us day by day our Real Taxed Substantial Money bought Bread [& take . . . *del.*]; deliver from the Holy Ghost so we call nature [debt that was owing to him *del.*] whatever cannot be Taxed; for all is debts & Taxes between Caesar & us & one another;

lead us not to read the Bible, but let our Bible be Virgil & Shakspeare; & deliver us from Poverty in Jesus, that Evil One. For thine is the Kingship, or Allegoric Godship, & the Power, or War, & the Glory, or Law, Ages after Ages in thy descendants; for God is only an Allegory of Kings & nothing Else.

Amen.

I swear that Basileia, βασιλεια, is not Kingdom but Kingship. I, Nature, Hermaphroditic Priest & King, Live in Real Substantial Natural Born Man, & that Spirit is the Ghost of Matter or Nature, & God is The Ghost of the Priest & King, who Exist, whereas God exists not except from their Effluvia.

Here is Signed Two Names which are too Holy to be Written.

Thus we see that the Real God is the Goddess Nature, & that God Creates nothing but what can be Touch'd & Weighed & Taxed & Measured; all else is Heresy & Rebellion against Caesar, Virgil's Only God—see Eclogue 1; for all this we Thank Dr Thornton.

[END OF ANNOTATIONS TO THORNTON]

THE LETTERS

1. TO WILLEY REVELEY October 1791[1]

M[r] Blake's Comp[ts] to M[r] Reveley tho' full of work [as M[r] R said he should be by then the plates were put in hand *del.*] he is glad to embrace the offer of engraving such beautiful things & will do what he can by the end of January.

2. TO GEORGE CUMBERLAND 6 December 1795

Lambeth
6 Decemb[r] 1795

Dear Sir,

I congratulate you, not on any atchievement, because I know that the Genius that produces the Designs can execute them in any manner, notwithstanding the pretended Philosophy which teaches that Execution is the power of One & Invention of Another—Locke says it [is the] same faculty that Invents Judges, & I say he who [can] Invent can Execute.

As to laying on the Wax, it is as follows:

Take a cake of Virgin's Wax[2] (I don't know what animal produces it) & stroke it regularly over the surface of a warm Plate (the Plate must be warm enough to melt the Wax as it passes over), then immediately draw a feather over it & you will get an even surface which, when cold, will recieve any impression minutely.

NOTE: The danger is in not covering the Plate *all over*.

Now you will, I hope, shew all the family of Antique Borers that Peace & Plenty & Domestic Happiness is the Source of Sublime Art, & prove to the Abstract Philosophers that Enjoyment & not Abstinence is the food of Intellect.

Yours sincerely,
Will Blake

Health to M[rs] Cumberland & family.

---

[1]Written in answer to a request to make engravings after some drawings by William Pars for Stuart and Revett's *The Antiquities of Athens,* published in 1794.
[2] Purified bees' wax or candle wax.

The pressure necessary to roll off the lines is the same as when you print, or not quite so great. I have not been able to send a proof of the bath[1] tho' I have done the corrections, my paper not being in order.

3. TO GEORGE CUMBERLAND 23 December 1796

Dear Cumberland,

I have lately had some pricks of conscience on account of not acknowledging your friendship to me [before *del.*] immediately on the receit of your beautiful book.[2] I have likewise had by me all the summer 6 Plates which you desired me to get made for you; they have laid on my shelf, without speaking to tell me whose they were or that they were [there *del.*] at all & it was some time (when I found them) before I could divine whence they came or whither they were bound or whether they were to lie there to eternity. I have now sent them to you to be transmuted, thou real Alchymist!

Go on, Go on. Such works as yours Nature & Providence, the Eternal Parents, demand from their children: how few produce them in such perfection: how Nature smiles on them: how Providence rewards them. How all your Brethren say, 'The sound of his harp & his flute heard from his secret forest chears us to the labours of life, & we plow & reap forgetting our labour.'

Let us see you sometimes as well as sometimes hear from you & let us often see your Works.

Compliments to M[rs] Cumberland & Family.

Yours in head & heart,

Will Blake

Lambeth

23 Decemb[r] 1796

a Merry Christmas

4. TO DR. TRUSLER[3] 16 August 1799

To the Rev[d] D[r] Trusler

Rev[d] Sir,

I find more & more that my Style of Designing is a Species by itself, & in this which I send you have been compell'd by my Genius or Angel to follow where he led; if I were to act otherwise it would not

---

[1] Blake's engraving of "the bath" illustrating Anacreon, Ode LII, is plate 23 in Cumberland's *Thoughts on Outline*, 1796.

[2] Cumberland's *Thoughts on Outline*, London, 1796.

[3] John Trusler (1735-1820), author of *Hogarth Moralized.*

fulfill the purpose for which alone I live, which is, in conjunction with such men as my friend Cumberland, to renew the lost Art of the Greeks.

I attempted every morning for a fortnight together to follow your Dictate, but when I found my attempts were in vain, resolv'd to shew an independence which I know will please an Author better than slavishly following the track of another, however admirable that track may be. At any rate, my Excuse must be: I could not do otherwise; it was out of my power!

I know I begged of you to give me your Ideas, & promised to build on them; here I counted without my host. I now find my mistake.

The Design I have Sent Is:

A Father, taking leave of his Wife & Child, Is watch'd by Two Fiends incarnate, with intention that when his back is turned they will murder the mother & her infant. If this is not Malevolence with a vengeance, I have never seen it on Earth; & if you approve of this, I have no doubt of giving you Benevolence with Equal Vigor, as also Pride & Humility, but cannot previously describe in words what I mean to Design, for fear I should Evaporate the Spirit of my Invention. But I hope that none of my Designs will be destitute of Infinite Particulars which will present themselves to the Contemplator. And tho' I call them Mine, I know that they are not Mine, being of the same opinion with Milton when he says[1] That the Muse visits his Slumbers & awakes & governs his Song when Morn purples the East, & being also in the predicament of that prophet who says: I cannot go beyond the command of the Lord, to speak good or bad.[2]

If you approve of my Manner, & it is agreeable to you, I would rather Paint Pictures in oil of the same dimensions than make Drawings, & on the same terms; by this means you will have a number of Cabinet pictures, which I flatter myself will not be unworthy of a Scholar of Rembrandt & Teniers, whom I have Studied no less than Rafael & Michael angelo. Please to send me your orders respecting this, & In my next Effort I promise more Expedition.

I am, Revd Sir,

Your very humble serv^t

Willm Blake

Hercules Build^gs
Lambeth
Aug^st 16 1799

[1] *Paradise Lost*, book vii, ll. 29, 30.
[2] *Numbers*, xxiv. 13.

5. TO DR. TRUSLER 23 August 1799

Revd Sir,

I really am sorry that you are fall'n out with the Spiritual World, Especially if I should have to answer for it. I feel very sorry that your Ideas & Mine on Moral Painting differ so much as to have made you angry with my method of Study. If I am wrong, I am wrong in good company. I had hoped your plan comprehended All Species of this Art, & Expecially that you would not regret that Species which gives Existence to Every other, namely, Visions of Eternity. You say that I want somebody to Elucidate my Ideas. But you ought to know that What is Grand is necessarily obscure to Weak men. That which can be made Explicit to the Idiot is not worth my care. The wisest of the Ancients consider'd what is not too Explicit as the fittest for Instruction, because it rouzes the faculties to act. I name Moses, Solomon, Esop, Homer, Plato.

But as you have favor'd me with your remarks on my Design, permit me in return to defend it against a mistaken one, which is, That I have supposed Malevolence without a Cause. Is not Merit in one a Cause of Envy in another, & Serenity & Happiness & Beauty a Cause of Malevolence? But Want of Money & the Distress of A Thief can never be alledged as the Cause of his Thieving, for many honest people endure greater hardships with Fortitude. We must therefore seek the Cause elsewhere than in want of Money, for that is the Miser's passion, not the Thief's.

I have therefore proved your Reasonings Ill proportion'd, which you can never prove my figures to be; they are those of Michael Angelo, Rafael & the Antique, & of the best living Models. I percieve that your Eye is perverted by Caricature Prints, which ought not to abound so much as they do. Fun I love, but too much Fun is of all things the most loathsom. Mirth is better than Fun, & Happiness is better than Mirth. I feel that a Man may be happy in This World. And I know that This World Is a World of imagination & Vision. I see Every thing I paint In This World, but Every body does not see alike. To the Eyes of a Miser a Guinea is more beautiful than the Sun, & a bag worn with the use of Money has more beautiful proportions than a Vine filled with Grapes. The tree which moves some to tears of joy is in the Eyes of others only a Green thing that stands in the way. Some See Nature all Ridicule & Deformity, & by these I shall not regulate my proportions; & Some Scarce see Nature at all. But to the Eyes of the Man of Imagination, Nature is Imagination itself. As a man is, So he Sees. As the Eye is formed, such are its Powers. You certainly Mistake, when you say that the Visions of Fancy are not to be found in This World. To Me This World is all One continued Vision of Fancy or Imagination, & I feel Flatter'd when I am told so. What is it sets Homer, Virgil & Milton in so high a rank of Art? Why is the Bible more Entertaining & Instructive than any other book? Is it not because they are addressed to the Imagination, which is Spiritual Sensation, & but mediately to the Understanding or Reason? Such is True Painting, and such was alone valued by the Greeks & the best modern Artists. Consider what Lord Bacon says: "Sense sends over to Imagination before Reason have judged, & Reason sends over to Imagination before the Decree can be acted." See Advancem[t] of Learning, Part 2, P. 47 of first Edition.

But I am happy to find a Great Majority of Fellow Mortals who can Elucidate My Visions, & Particularly they have been Elucidated by Children, who have taken a greater delight in contemplating my Pictures than I even hoped. Neither Youth nor Childhood is Folly or Incapacity. Some Children are Fools & so are some Old Men. But There is a vast Majority on the side of Imagination or Spiritual Sensation.

To Engrave after another Painter is infinitely more laborious than to Engrave one's own Inventions. And of the size you require my price has been Thirty Guineas, & I cannot afford to do it for less. I had Twelve for the Head I sent you as a Specimen; but after my own designs I could do at least Six times the quantity of labour in the same time, which will account for the difference of price as also that Chalk Engraving is at least six times as laborious as Aqua tinta. I have no objection to Engraving after another Artist. Engraving is the profession I was apprenticed to, & should never have attempted to live by any thing else, If orders had not come in for my Designs & Paintings, which I have the pleasure to tell you are Increasing Every Day. Thus If I am a Painter it is not to be attributed to Seeking after. But I am contented whether I live by Painting or Engraving.

I am, Rev[d] Sir, your very obedient servant,

William Blake

13 Hercules Buildings
Lambeth
August 23. 1799

6. TO GEORGE CUMBERLAND 26 August 1799

Dear Cumberland,

I ought long ago to have written to you to thank you for your kind recommendation to D[r] Trusler, which, tho' it has fail'd of success, is not the less to be remember'd by me with Gratitude.

I have made him a Drawing in my best manner; he has sent it back with a Letter full of Criticisms, in which he says It accords not with his Intentions, which are to Reject all Fancy from his Work.

How far he Expects to please, I cannot tell. But as I cannot paint Dirty rags & old shoes where I ought to place Naked Beauty or simple ornament, I despair of Ever pleasing one Class of Men. Unfortunately our authors of books are among this Class; how soon we Shall have a change for the better I cannot Prophecy. Dr Trusler says: "*Your Fancy*, from what I have seen of it, & I have seen variety at Mr Cumberland's, seems to be in the other world, or the World of Spirits, which accords not with my Intentions, which, whilst living in This World, Wish to follow *the Nature of it*." I could not help Smiling at the difference between the doctrines of Dr Trusler & those of Christ. But, however, for his own sake I am sorry that a Man should be so enamour'd of Rowlandson's caricatures as to call them copies from life & manners, or fit Things for a Clergyman to write upon.

Pray let me intreat you to persevere in your Designing; it is the only source of Pleasure. All your other pleasures depend upon it. It is the Tree; your Pleasures are the Fruit. Your Inventions of Intellectual Visions are the Stamina of every thing you value. Go on, if not for your own sake, yet for ours, who love & admire your works; but, above all, For the Sake of the Arts. Do not throw aside for any long time the honour intended you by Nature to revive the Greek workmanship. I study your outlines[1] as usual, just as if they were antiques.

As to Myself, about whom you are so kindly Interested, I live by Miracle. I am Painting small Pictures from the Bible. For as to Engraving, in which art I cannot reproach myself with any neglect, yet I am laid by in a corner as if I did not Exist, & Since my Young's Night Thoughts[2] have been publish'd, Even Johnson & Fuseli have discarded my Graver. But as I know that He who Works & has his health cannot starve, I laugh at Fortune & Go on & on. I think I foresee better Things than I have ever seen. My Work pleases my employer,[3] & I have an order for Fifty small Pictures at One Guinea each, which is Something better than mere copying after another artist. But above all, I feel myself happy & contented let what will come; having passed now near twenty years in ups & downs, I am used to them, & perhaps a little practise in them may turn out to benefit. It is now Exactly Twenty years since I was upon the ocean of business,[4] & Tho' I laugh at Fortune, I am perswaded that She

---

[1] *Thoughts on Outline*, London, 1796.

[2] *The Complaint and the Consolation; or, Night Thoughts*, by Edward Young. London: Printed for R. Edwards, 1797: folio, with 43 marginal illustrations designed and engraved by Blake.

[3] Thomas Butts.

[4] Blake had completed his apprenticeship to the engraver James Basire in July 1779, and had been working independently since that date.

Alone is the Governor of Worldly Riches, & when it is Fit She will call on me; till then I wait with Patience, in hopes that She is busied among my Friends.

With Mine & My Wife's best compliments to M[rs] Cumberland, I remain,

Yours sincerely,

Will[m] Blake

Hercules Buildings
Lambeth
Aug[st] 26. 1799

7. TO WILLIAM HAYLEY* 18 February 1800

[Extract from a letter to Hayley, to whom he submitted an impression of the plate[1] of "The Death of Demosthenes" which] "has been approved by M[r] Flaxman". [He hopes that the young sculptor] "will soon be well enough to make hundreds of designs both for the engraver and the sculptor."

8. TO WILLIAM HAYLEY 1 April 1800

Dear Sir,

With all possible Expedition I send you a proof of my attempt to Express your & our Much Beloved's Countenance.[2] M[r]. Flaxman has seen it & approved of my now sending it to you for your remarks. Your Sorrows and your dear son's May Jesus and his Angels assuage & if it is consistent with his divine providence restore him to us & to his labours of Art & Science in this world. So prays a fellow sufferer & Your humble servant,

Will[m] Blake

Hercules Buildings, Lambeth
1 April 1800

---

[1] In Hayley's *An Essay on Sculpture*, 1800.

[2] An engraving after a medallion portrait of Thomas Alphonso Hayley by Flaxman, done for Hayley's *An Essay on Sculpture*.

* This and all other letters marked with an asterisk are those of which no original draft is available. The texts of these letters are mostly derived from printed sources as indicated in the Notes at the end of the book.

9. TO WILLIAM HAYLEY 6 May 1800

Dear Sir,

I am very sorry for your immense loss,[1] which is a repetition of what all feel in this valley of misery & happiness mixed. I send the Shadow of the departed Angel[2]: hope the likeness is improved. The lip I have again lessened as you advised & done a good many other softenings to the whole. I know that our deceased friends are more really with us than when they were apparent to our mortal part. Thirteen years ago I lost a brother[3] & with his spirit I converse daily & hourly in the Spirit & See him in my remembrance in the regions of my Imagination. I hear his advice & even now write from his Dictate. Forgive me for Expressing to you my Enthusiasm which I wish all to partake of Since it is to me a Source of Immortal Joy: even in this world by it I am the companion of Angels. May you continue to be so more & more & to be more & more perswaded that every Mortal loss is an Immortal Gain. The Ruins of Time builds Mansions in Eternity.—I have also sent A Proof of Pericles[4] for your Remarks, thanking you for the Kindness with which you Express them & feeling heartily your Grief with a brother's Sympathy.

I remain, Dear Sir, Your humble Servant

William Blake

Lambeth. May 6. 1800

10. TO GEORGE CUMBERLAND 2 July 1800

Dear Cumberland,

I have to congratulate you on your plan for a National Gallery being put into Execution. All your wishes shall in due time be fulfilled; the immense flood of Grecian light & glory which is coming on Europe will more than realize our warmest wishes. Your honours will be unbounded when your plan shall be carried into Execution as it must be if England continues a Nation. I hear that it is now in the hands of Ministers, That the King shews it great Countenance & Encouragement, that it will soon be before Parliament, & that it *must* be extended & enlarged to take in Originals both of Painting & Sculpture by considering every valuable original that is brought into England or can be purchased Abroad as its objects of Acquisition.

---

[1] Alludes to the death of his illegitimate son, Thomas Alphonso Hayley on 2 May 1800.

[2] The engraving already mentioned.

[3] Robert Blake died February 1787.

[4] An engraving for Hayley's *An Essay on Sculpture*, 1800.

Such is the Plan as I am told & such must be the plan if England wishes to continue at all worth notice; as you have yourself observ'd only now, we must possess Originals as well as France or be Nothing.

Excuse, I intreat you, my not returning Thanks at the proper moment for your kind present. No perswasion could make my stupid head believe that it was proper for me to trouble you with a letter of meer compliment & Expression of thanks. I begin to Emerge from a Deep pit of Melancholy, Melancholy without any real reason for it, a Disease which God keep you from & all good men. Our artists of all ranks praise your outlines & wish for more. Flaxman is very warm in your commendation & more and more of A Grecian. M[r] Hayley has lately mentioned your Work on outline in Notes to [Epistles on Sculpture *del.*] an Essay on Sculpture in Six Epistles to John Flaxman. I have been too little among friends which I fear they will not Excuse & I know not how to apologize for. Poor Fuseli, sore from the lash of Envious tongues, praises you & dispraises with the same breath; he is not naturally good natured, but he is artificially very ill natured, yet even from him I learn the Estimation you are held in among artists & connoisseurs.

I am still Employ'd in making Designs & little Pictures with now & then an Engraving & find that in future to live will not be so difficult as it has been. It is very Extraordinary that London in so few years from a City of meer Necessaries or at l[e]ast a commerce of the lowest order of luxuries should have become a City of Elegance in some degree & that its once stupid inhabitants should enter into an Emulation of Grecian manners. There are now, I believe, as many Booksellers as there are Butchers & as many Printshops as of any other trade. We remember when a Print shop was a rare bird in London & I myself remember when I thought my pursuits of Art a kind of criminal dissipation & neglect of the main chance, which I hid my face for not being able to abandon as a Passion which is forbidden by Law & Religion, but now it appears to be Law & Gospel too, at least I hear so from the few friends I have dared to visit in my stupid Melancholy. Excuse this communication of sentiments which I felt necessary to my repose at this time. I feel very strongly that I neglect my Duty to my Friends, but It is not want of Gratitude or Friendship but perhaps an Excess of both.

Let me hear of your welfare. Remember My & My Wife's Respectful Compliments to M[rs] Cumberland & Family

& believe me to be for Ever

Yours

William Blake

13 Hercules Buildings
Lambeth
2 July 1800

11. TO JOHN FLAXMAN 12 September 1800

My Dearest Friend,

It is to you I owe All my present Happiness. It is to you I owe perhaps the Principal Happiness of my life. I have presum'd on your friendship in staying so long away & not calling to know of your welfare, but hope now every thing is nearly completed for our removal to Felpham, that I shall see you on Sunday, as we have appointed Sunday afternoon to call on M[rs] Flaxman at Hampstead. I send you a few lines, which I hope you will Excuse. And As the time is arriv'd when Men shall again converse in Heaven & walk with Angels, I know you will be pleased with the Intention, & hope you will forgive the Poetry.

To My Dearest Friend, John Flaxman, these lines:

I bless thee, O Father of Heaven & Earth, that ever I saw Flaxman's face.
Angels stand round my Spirit in Heaven, the blessed of Heaven are my friends upon Earth.
When Flaxman was taken to Italy, Fuseli was given to me for a season,
And now Flaxman hath given me Hayley his friend to be mine, such my lot upon Earth.
Now my lot in the Heavens is this, Milton lov'd me in childhood & shew'd me his face.
Ezra came with Isaiah the Prophet, but Shakespeare in riper years gave me his hand;
Paracelsus & Behmen appear'd to me, terrors appear'd in the Heavens above
And in Hell beneath, & a mighty & awful change threatened the Earth.
The American War began. All its dark horrors passed before my face
Across the Atlantic to France. Then the French Revolution commenc'd in thick clouds,
And My Angels have told me that seeing such visions I could not subsist on the Earth,
But by my conjunction with Flaxman, who knows to forgive Nervous Fear.

I remain, for Ever Yours,
William Blake

Be so kind as to Read & then seal the Inclosed & send it on its much beloved Mission.

12. MRS. BLAKE TO MRS. FLAXMAN 14 September 1800

My Dearest Friend,

I hope you will not think we could forget your Services to us, or any way neglect to love & remember with affection even the hem of your garment; we indeed presume on your kindness in neglecting to have call'd on you since my husband's first return from Felpham.[1] We have been incessantly busy in our great removal; but can never think of going without first paying our proper duty to you & Mr Flaxman. We intend to call on Sunday afternoon in Hampstead, to take farewell, All things being now nearly completed for our setting forth on Tuesday Morning; it is only Sixty Miles, & Lambeth was On[e] Hundred, for the terrible desart of London was between. My husband has been obliged to finish several things necessary to be finish'd before our migration; the Swallows call us, fleeting past our window at this moment. O how we delight in talking of the pleasure we shall have in preparing you a summer bower at Felpham, & we not only talk, but behold! the Angels of our journey have inspired a song to you:

To My Dear Friend, Mrs Anna Flaxman.

This Song to the flower of Flaxman's joy,
To the blossom of hope, for a sweet decoy:
Do all that you can or all that you may,
To entice him to Felpham & far away:

Away to Sweet Felpham, for Heaven is there;
The Ladder of Angels descends thro' the air;
On the Turret[2] its spiral does softly descend,
Thro' the village then winds, at My Cot it does end.

You stand in the village & look up to heaven;
The precious stones glitter on flights seventy seven;
And My Brother is there, & My Friend & Thine
Descend & Ascend with the Bread & the Wine.

The Bread of sweet Thought & the Wine of Delight
Feeds the Village of Felpham by day & by night;
And at his own door the bless'd Hermit[3] does stand,
Dispensing Unceasing to all the whole Land.

W. Blake

---

[1] Blake had first visited Felpham in July 1800.

[2] The Turret of Hayley's house in Felpham.

[3] Hayley, often called the Hermit of Eartham by himself and his friends.

Recieve my & my husband's love & affection, & believe me to be Yours affectionately,

Catherine Blake

H B Lambeth
14 Sepr 1800

13. TO WILLIAM HAYLEY 16 September 1800

Leader of My Angels,

My Dear & too careful & over joyous Woman has Exhausted her strength to such a degree with expectation & gladness added to labour in our removal that I fear it will be Thursday before we can get away from this —— City. I shall not be able to avail myself of the assistance of Bruno's fairies.[1] But I Invoke the Good Genii that Surround Miss Poole's[2] Villa to shine upon my journey thro' the Petworth road which by your fortunate advice I mean to take; but whether I come on Wednesday or Thursday That Day shall be marked on my calendar with a Star of the first magnitude.

Eartham will be my first temple & altar. My wife is like a flame of many colours of precious jewels whenever she hears it named. Excuse my haste & recieve my hearty Love & Respect.

I am, dear Sir,
Your Sincere
William Blake

H. B. Lambeth
Sept 16. 1800

My fingers Emit sparks of fire with Expectation of my future labours.

14. TO JOHN FLAXMAN 21 September 1800

Dear Sculptor of Eternity,

We are safe arrived at our Cottage, which is more beautiful than I thought it, & more convenient. It is a perfect Model for Cottages &, I think, for Palaces of Magnificence, only Enlarging, not altering its proportions, & adding ornaments & not principals. Nothing can be more Grand than its Simplicity & Usefulness. Simple without

---

1 A reference to Giordano Bruno, hermetic philosopher and magician.

2 Miss Henrietta, or Harriet, Poole, also known as Lady Paulina of Lavant, an intimate friend of Hayley.

Intricacy, it seems to be the Spontaneous Effusion of Humanity, congenial to the wants of Man. No other formed House can ever please me so well; nor shall I ever be perswaded, I believe, that it can be improved either in Beauty or Use.

Mr Hayley reciev'd us with his usual brotherly affection. I have begun to work. Felpham is a sweet place for Study, because it is more Spiritual than London. Heaven opens here on all sides her Golden Gates; her windows are not obstructed by vapours; voices of Celestial inhabitants are more distinctly heard, & their forms more distinctly seen, & my Cottage is also a Shadow of their houses. My Wife & Sister[1] are both well, courting Neptune for an Embrace.

Our Journey was very pleasant; & tho' we had a great deal of Luggage, No Grumbling, All was Chearfulness & Good Humour on the Road, & yet we could not arrive at our Cottage before half past Eleven at night, owing to the necessary shifting of our Luggage from one Chaise to another; for we had Seven Different Chaises, & as many different drivers. We set out between Six & Seven in the Morning of Thursday, with Sixteen heavy boxes & portfolios full of prints. And Now Begins a New life, because another covering of Earth is shaken off. I am more famed in Heaven for my works than I could well concieve. In my Brain are studies & Chambers fill'd with books & pictures of old, which I wrote & painted in ages of Eternity before my mortal life; & those works are the delight & Study of Archangels. Why, then, should I be anxious about the riches or fame of mortality. The Lord our father will do for us & with us according to his Divine will for our Good.

You, O Dear Flaxman, are a Sublime Archangel, My Friend & Companion from Eternity; in the Divine bosom in our Dwelling place. I look back into the regions of Reminiscence & behold our ancient days before this Earth appear'd in its vegetated mortality to my mortal vegetated Eyes. I see our houses of Eternity, which can never be separated, tho' our Mortal vehicles should stand at the remotest corners of heaven from each other.

Farewell, My Best Friend. Remember Me & My Wife in Love & Friendship to our Dear Mrs Flaxman, whom we ardently desire to Entertain beneath our thatched roof of rusted gold, & believe me for ever to remain

Your Grateful & Affectionate,
William Blake

Felphan
Septr 21, 1800
Sunday Morning

[1] Catherine Blake, the youngest of the family.

15. TO THOMAS BUTTS 23 September 1800

Dear Friend of My Angels,

We are safe arrived at our Cottage without accident or hindrance, tho' it was between Eleven & Twelve O'Clock at night before we could get home, owing to the necessary shifting of our boxes & portfolios from one Chaise to another. We had Seven different Chaises & as many different drivers. All upon the road was chearfulness & welcome; tho' our luggage was very heavy there was no grumbling at all. We travel'd thro' a most beautiful country on a most glorious day. Our Cottage is more beautiful than I thought it, & also more convenient, for tho' small it is well proportion'd, & if I should ever build a Palace it would be only My Cottage Enlarged. Please to tell M[rs] Butts that we have dedicated a Chamber for her service, & that it has a very fine view of the Sea. M[r] Hayley reciev'd me with his usual brotherly affection. My Wife & Sister are both very well, & courting Neptune for an Embrace, whose terrors this morning made them afraid, but whose mildness is often Equal to his terrors. The Villagers of Felpham are not meer Rustics; they are polite & modest. Meat is cheaper than in London, but the sweet air & the voices of winds, trees & birds, & the odours of the happy ground, makes it a dwelling for immortals. Work will go on here with God speed.—A roller & two harrows lie before my window. I met a plow on my first going out at my gate the first morning after my arrival, & the Plowboy said to the Plowman, "Father, The Gate is Open."—I have begun to Work, & find that I can work with greater pleasure than ever. Hope soon to give you a proof that Felpham is propitious to the Arts.

God bless you! I shall wish for you on Tuesday Evening as usual. Pray give My & My wife & sister's love & respects to M[rs] Butts; accept them yourself, & believe me for ever

Your affectionate & obliged Friend,
William Blake

My Sister will be in town in a week, & bring with her your account & whatever else I can finish.

Direct to Mr
Blake, Felpham, near Chichester, Sussex.

16. TO THOMAS BUTTS 2 October 1800

Friend of Religion & Order,

I thank you for your very beautiful & encouraging Verses, which I account a Crown of Laurels, & I also thank you for your reprehension of follies by me foster'd. Your prediction will, I hope, be fulfilled in me, & in future I am the determined advocate of Religion & Humility, the two bands of Society. Having been so full of the Business of Settling the sticks & feathers of my nest, I have not got any forwarder with "the three Marys" or with any other of your commissions; but hope, now I have commenced a new life of industry to do credit to that new life by Improved Works. Recieve from me a return of verses, such as Felpham produces by me, tho' not such as she produces by her Eldest Son;[1] however, such as they are, I cannot resist the temptation to send them to you.

To my Friend Butts I write
My first Vision of Light,
On the yellow sands sitting.
The Sun was Emitting
His Glorious beams
From Heaven's high Streams.
Over Sea, over Land
My Eyes did Expand
Into regions of air
Away from all Care,
Into regions of fire
Remote from Desire;
The Light of the Morning
Heaven's Mountains adorning:
In particles bright
The jewels of Light
Distinct shone & clear.
Amaz'd & in fear
I each particle gazed,
Astonish'd, Amazed;
For each was a Man
Human-form'd. Swift I ran,
For they beckon'd to me
Remote by the Sea,
Saying: Each grain of Sand,
Every Stone on the Land,

[1] William Hayley.

Each rock & each hill,
Each fountain & rill,
Each herb & each tree,
Mountain, hill, earth & sea,
Cloud, Meteor & Star,
Are Men Seen Afar.
I stood in the Streams
Of Heaven's bright beams,
And Saw Felpham sweet
Beneath my bright feet
In soft Female charms;
And in her fair arms
My Shadow I knew
And my wife's shadow too,
And My Sister & Friend.
We like Infants descend
In our Shadows on Earth,
Like a weak mortal birth.
My Eyes more & more
Like a Sea without shore
Continue Expanding,
The Heavens commanding,
Till the Jewels of Light,
Heavenly Men beaming bright,
Appear'd as One Man
Who Complacent began
My limbs to infold
In his beams of bright gold;
Like dross purg'd away
All my mire & my clay.
Soft consum'd in delight
In his bosom Sun bright
I remain'd. Soft he smil'd,
And I heard his voice Mild
Saying: This is My Fold,
O thou Ram horn'd with gold,
Who awakest from Sleep
On the Sides of the Deep.
On the Mountains around
The roarings resound
Of the lion & wolf,
The loud Sea & deep gulf.
These are guards of My Fold,
O thou Ram horn'd with gold!
And the voice faded mild.

I remain'd as a Child;
All I ever had known
Before me bright Shone.
I saw you & your wife
By the fountains of Life.
Such the Vision to me
Appear'd on the Sea.

Mrs Butts will, I hope, Excuse my not having finish'd the Portrait.[1] I wait for less hurried moments. Our Cottage looks more & more beautiful. And tho' the weather is wet, the Air is very Mild, much Milder than it was in London when we came away. Chichester is a very handsom City, Seven miles from us; we can get most Conveniences there. The Country is not so destitute of accomodations to our wants as I expected it would be. We have had but little time for viewing the Country, but what we have seen is Most Beautiful, & the People are Genuine Saxons, handsomer than the people about London. Mrs Butts will Excuse the following lines:

To Mrs Butts.

Wife of the Friend of those I most revere,
Recieve this tribute from a Harp sincere;
Go on in Virtuous Seed sowing on Mold
Of Human Vegetation, & Behold
Your Harvest Springing to Eternal life,
Parent of Youthful Minds, & happy Wife!

W. B.

I am for Ever Yours,
William Blake

Felpham
Octr 2d 1800

17. TO WILLIAM HAYLEY* 26 November 1800

Dear Sir,

Absorbed by the poets[2] Milton, Homer, Camoens, Ercilla, Ariosto, and Spenser, whose physiognomies have been my delightful study,

[1] A miniature of Thomas Butts.

[2] Blake was at work upon a series of heads of the poets, to be a frieze for Hayley's new library at Felpham.

Little Tom[1] has been of late unattended to, and my wife's illness not being quite gone off, she has not printed any more since you went to London. But we can muster a few in colours and some in black, which I hope will be no less favour'd, tho' they are rough like rough sailors. We mean to begin printing again to-morrow. Time flies very fast and very merrily. I sometimes try to be miserable that I may do more work, but find it is a foolish experiment. Happinesses have wings and wheels; miseries are leaden legged, and their whole employment is to clip the wings and to take off the wheels of our chariots. We determine, therefore, to be happy and do all that we can, tho' not all that we would. Our dear friend Flaxman is the theme of my emulation in this of industry, as well as in other virtues and merits. Gladly I hear of his full health and spirits. Happy son of the immortal Phidias, his lot is truly glorious, and mine no less happy in his friendship and in that of his friends. Our cottage is surrounded by the same guardians you left with us; they keep off every wind. We hear the west howl at a distance, the south bounds on high over our thatch, and smiling on our cottage says: "You lay too low for my anger to injure." As to the east and north, I believe they cannot get past the Turret.

My wife joins with me in duty and affection to you. Please to remember us both in love to Mr. and Mrs. Flaxman, and

believe me to be your affectionate,

Enthusiastic, hope-fostered visionary,

William Blake

Felpham
26th November 1800

18. TO JOHN FLAXMAN[?]* c. 1800

Sending all the sketches he has ever produced; has studied "The Presentation,"[2] but not yet put it on paper; is full of business, and feels perfectly happy, thanks to his correspondents and Mr. Flaxman. [*Extract from sale catalogue.*]

---

[1] *Little Tom the Sailor,* a broadsheet, Printed for & Sold by the Widow Spicer of Folkestone for the benefit of her Orphans: October 5, 1800.

[2] Presumably the water-colour painting of "The Presentation of Christ in the Temple", now in the Fogg Art Museum, Cambridge, Mass.

19. TO THOMAS BUTTS 10 May 1801

My Dear Sir,

The necessary application to my Duty, as well to my old as new friends, has prevented me from that respect I owe in particular to you. And your accustomed forgiveness of my want of dexterity in certain points Emboldens me to hope that Forgiveness to be continued to me a little longer, When I shall be Enabled to throw off all obstructions to success.

Mr Hayley acts like a Prince. I am at complete Ease, but I wish to do my duty, especially to you, who were the præcursor of my present Fortune. I never will send you a picture unworthy of my present proficiency. I soon shall send you several; my present engagements are in Miniature Painting. Miniature is become a Goddess in my Eyes, & my Friends in Sussex say that I Excell in the pursuit. I have a great many orders, & they Multiply.

Now—let me intreat you to give me orders to furnish every accomodation in my power to recieve you & Mrs Butts. I know my Cottage is too narrow for your Ease & comfort; we have one room in which we could make a bed to lodge you both, & if this is sufficient, it is at your service; but as beds & rooms & accomodations are easily procur'd by one on the spot, permit me to offer my service in either way, either in my cottage, or in a lod[g]ing in the village, as is most agreeable to you, if you & Mrs Butts should think Bognor a pleasant relief from business in the Summer. It will give me the utmost delight to do my best.

Sussex is certainly a happy place, & Felpham in particular is the sweetest spot on Earth, at least it is so to me & My Good Wife, who desires her kindest Love to Mrs Butts & yourself; accept mine also, & believe me to remain,

Your devoted,
Will Blake

Felpham
May 10. 1801

20. TO THOMAS BUTTS 11 September 1801

My Dear Sir,

I hope you will continue to excuse my want of steady perseverance, by which want I am still so much your debtor & you so much my Credit-er; but such as I can be, I will. I can be grateful, & I can soon Send you some of your designs which I have nearly completed. In the mean time by my Sister's hands I transmit to Mrs Butts an attempt at your likeness,[1] which I hope She, who is the best judge, will think like. Time flies faster (as seems to me) here than in London. I labour incessantly & accomplish not one half of what I intend, because my Abstract folly hurries me often away while I am at work, carrying me over Mountains & Valleys, which are not Real, in a Land of Abstraction where Spectres of the Dead[2] wander. This I endeavour to prevent & with my whole might chain my feet to the world of Duty & Reality; but in vain! the faster I bind, the better is the Ballast, for I, so far from being bound down, take the world with me in my flights, & often it seems lighter than a ball of wool rolled by the wind. Bacon & Newton would prescribe ways of making the world heavier to me, & Pitt would prescribe distress for a medicinal potion; but as none on Earth can give me Mental Distress, & I know that all Distress inflicted by Heaven is a Mercy, a Fig for all Corporeal! Such Distress is My mock & scorn. Alas! wretched, happy, ineffectual labourer of time's moments that I am! who shall deliver me from this Spirit of Abstraction & Improvidence? Such, my Dear Sir, Is the truth of my state, & I tell it you in palliation of my seeming neglect of your most pleasant orders; but I have not neglected them, & yet a Year is rolled over, & only now I approach the prospect of sending you some, which you may expect soon. I should have sent them by My Sister, but, as the Coach goes three times a week to London & they will arrive as safe as with her, I shall have an opportunity of inclosing several together which are not yet completed. I thank you again & again for your generous forbearance, of which I have need—& now I must express my wishes to see you at Felpham & to shew you Mr Hayley's Library, which is still unfinish'd, but is in a finishing way & looks well. I ought also to mention my Extreme disappointment at Mr Johnson's[3] forgetfulness, who appointed to call on you but did Not. He is also a happy Abstract, known by all his Friends as the most innocent forgetter of his own Interests. He is nephew to the late Mr Cowper the Poet; you would like him much. I continue painting Miniatures & Improve more & more, as all my friends tell me; but my Principal labour at this time is Engraving Plates for Cowper's Life,[4] a Work of Magnitude, which Mr Hayley is now Labouring with all his matchless industry, & which will be a most valuable acquisition to Literature, not only on account of Mr

---

[1] A miniature.

[2] "The spectres of the dead" are used by Blake in more than one sense. Here he seems to mean "the abstract idea for which the artist cannot, save by inspiration, find the living form, the eternally right expression" (see Sloss & Wallis, ii, 226-8).

[3] Rector of Yaxham with Welborne, Norfolk: cousin and friend of Cowper.

[4] *The Life and Posthumous Writings of William Cowper by William Hayley*, 1803-1804. 3 vols., 4°, containing five engravings by Blake, one of which is an excellent stippled plate of a bust of Cowper in a night-cap after Lawrence.

Hayley's composition, but also as it will contain Letters of Cowper to his friends, Perhaps, or rather Certainly, the very best letters that ever were published.

My wife joins with me in Love to you & Mrs Butts, hoping that her joy is now increased, & yours also, in an increase of family & of health & happiness.

I remain, Dear Sir,
Ever Yours Sincerely,
William Blake

Felpham Cottage
of Cottages the prettiest
September 11. 1801

Next time I have the happiness to see you, I am determined to paint another Portrait of you from Life in my best manner, for Memory will not do in such minute operations; for I have now discover'd that without Nature before the painter's Eye, he can never produce any thing in the walks of Natural Painting. Historical Designing is one thing & Portrait Painting another, & they are as Distinct as any two Arts can be. Happy would that Man be who could unite them!

P.S. Please to Remember our best respects to Mr Birch,[1] & tell him that Felpham Men are the mildest of the human race; if it is the will of Providence, they shall be the wisest. We hope that he will, next summer, joke us face to face.—God bless you all!

21. TO JOHN FLAXMAN 19 October 1801

Dear Flaxman,

I rejoice to hear that your Great Work is accomplish'd. Peace[2] opens the way to greater still. The Kingdoms of this World are now become the Kingdoms of God & his Christ, & we shall reign with him for ever & ever. The Reign of Literature & the Arts Commences. Blessed are those who are found studious of Literature & Humane & polite accomplishments. Such have their lamps burning & such shall shine as the stars.

Mr Thomas, your friend to whom you was so kind as to make honourable mention of me, has been at Felpham & did me the favor to call on me. I have promis'd him to send my designs for Comus when I have done them, directed to you.

---

[1] John Birch (1745-1815), surgeon.

[2] Peace with Napoleon Buonaparte, concluded in 1802.

Now I hope to see the Great Works of Art, as they are so near to Felpham, Paris being scarce further off than London. But I hope that France & England will henceforth be as One Country and their Arts One, & that you will Ere long be erecting Monuments In Paris—Emblems of Peace.

My Wife joins with me in love to You & M[rs] Flaxman.

I remain, Yours Sincerely
William Blake

Oct 19 1801

22. TO THOMAS BUTTS 10 January 1802

Felpham Jan[y] 10. 1802

Dear Sir,

Your very kind & affectionate Letter & the many kind things you have said in it, call'd upon me for an immediate answer; but it found My Wife & Myself so Ill, & My wife so very ill, that till now I have not been able to do this duty. The Ague & Rheumatism have been almost her constant Enemies, which she has combated in vain ever since we have been here; & her sickness is always my sorrow, of course. But what you tell me about your sight afflicted me not a little, & that about your health, in another part of your letter, makes me intreat you to take due care of both; it is a part of our duty to God & man to take due care of his Gifts; & tho' we ought not [to] think *more* highly of ourselves, yet we ought to think *As* highly of ourselves as immortals ought to think.

When I came down here, I was more sanguine than I am at present; but it was because I was ignorant of many things which have since occurred, & chiefly the unhealthiness of the place. Yet I do not repent of coming on a thousand accounts; & M[r] H., I doubt not, will do ultimately all that both he & I wish—that is, to lift me out of difficulty; but this is no easy matter to a man who, having Spiritual Enemies of such formidable magnitude, cannot expect to want natural hidden ones.

Your approbation of my pictures is a Multitude to Me, & I doubt not that all your kind wishes in my behalf shall in due time be fulfilled. Your kind offer of pecuniary assistance I can only thank you for at present, because I have enough to serve my present purpose here; our expenses are small, & our income, from our incessant labour, fully adequate to [it *del.*] them at present. I am now engaged in Engraving 6 small plates for a New Edition of M[r] Hayley's Triumphs of Temper,[1] from drawings by Maria Flaxman, sister to my friend the Sculptor, and it seems that other things will follow in course, if I do but Copy these well; but Patience! if Great things do not turn out, it is because such things depend on the Spiritual & not on the Natural World; & if it was fit for me, I doubt not that I should be Employ'd in Greater things; & when it is proper, my Talents shall be properly exercised in Public, as I hope they are now in private; for, till then, I leave no stone unturn'd & no path unexplor'd that tends to improvement in my beloved Arts. One thing of real consequence I have accomplish'd by coming into the country, which is to me consolation enough: namely, I have recollected all my scatter'd thoughts on Art & resumed my primitive & original ways of Execution in both painting & engraving, which in the confusion of London I had very much lost & obliterated from my mind. But whatever becomes of my labours, I would rather that they should be preserv'd in your Green House (not, as you mistakenly call it, dung hill) than in the cold gallery of fashion.—The Sun may yet shine, & then they will be brought into open air.

But you have so generously & openly desired that I will divide my griefs with you, that I cannot hide what it is now become my duty to explain.—My unhappiness has arisen from a source which, if explor'd too narrowly, might hurt my pecuniary circumstances, As my dependence is on Engraving at present, & particularly on the Engravings I have in hand for Mr H.: & I find on all hands great objections to my doing any thing but the meer drudgery of business, & intimations that if I do not confine myself to this, I shall not live; this has always pursu'd me. You will understand by this the source of all my uneasiness. This from Johnson & Fuseli brought me down here, & this from Mr H. will bring me back again; for that I cannot live without doing my duty to lay up treasures in heaven is Certain & Determined, & to this I have long made up my mind, & why this should be made an objection to Me, while Drunkenness, Lewdness, Gluttony & even Idleness itself, does not hurt other men, let Satan himself Explain. The Thing I have most at Heart—more than life, or all that seems to make life comfortable without—Is the Interest of True Religion & Science, & whenever any thing appears to affect that Interest (Especially if I myself omit any duty to my [self *del.*] Station as a Soldier of Christ), It gives me the greatest of torments. I am not ashamed, afraid, or averse to tell you what Ought to be Told: That I am under the direction of Messengers from Heaven, Daily & Nightly; but the nature of such things is not, as some suppose, without trouble or care. Temptations are on the right hand & left; behind, the sea of time & space roars & follows swiftly; he who keeps not

---

[1] *The Triumphs of Temper. A Poem : In Six Cantos.* London, 1803. 12th edition.

right onward is lost, & if our footsteps slide in clay, how can we do otherwise than fear & tremble? but I should not have troubled You with this account of my spiritual state, unless it had been necessary in explaining the actual cause of my uneasiness, into which you are so kind as to Enquire; for I never obtrude such things on others unless question'd, & then I never disguise the truth.—But if we fear to do the dictates of our Angels, & tremble at the Tasks set before us; if we refuse to do Spiritual Acts because of Natural Fears or Natural Desires! Who can describe the dismal torments of such a state!—I too well remember the Threats I heard!—If you, who are organized by Divine Providence for Spiritual communion, Refuse, & bury your Talent in the Earth, even tho' you should want Natural Bread, Sorrow & Desperation pursues you thro' life, & after death shame & confusion of face to eternity. Every one in Eternity will leave you, aghast at the Man who was crown'd with glory & honour by his brethren, & betray'd their cause to their enemies. You will be call'd the base Judas who betray'd his Friend!—Such words would make any stout man tremble, & how then could I be at ease? But I am now no longer in That State, & now go on again with my Task, Fearless, and tho' my path is difficult, I have no fear of stumbling while I keep it.

My wife desires her kindest Love to M[rs] Butts, & I have permitted her to send it to you also; we often wish that we could unite again in Society, & hope that the time is not distant when we shall do so, being determin'd not to remain another winter here, but to return to London.

I hear a voice you cannot hear, that says I must not stay,
I see a hand you cannot see, that beckons me away.[1]

Naked we came here, naked of Natural things, & naked we shall return; but while cloth'd with the Divine Mercy, we are richly cloth'd in Spiritual & suffer all the rest gladly. Pray give my Love to M[rs] Butts & your family.

I am, Yours Sincerely,

William Blake

P.S. Your Obliging proposal of Exhibiting my two Pictures likewise calls for my thanks; I will finish the other, & then we shall judge of the matter with certainty.

---

[1] Four lines, written as two, from Thomas Tickell's "Lucy and Colin", in Percy's *Reliques of Ancient English Poetry*, London, 1765, III, 308.

23. TO THOMAS BUTTS 22 November 1802

Felpham, Novr 22: 1802.

Dear Sir,

My Brother[1] tells me that he fears you are offended with me. I fear so too, because there appears some reason why you might be so. But when you have heard me out, you will not be so.

I have now given two years to the intense study of those parts of the art which relate to light & shade & colour, & am Convinc'd that either my understanding is incapable of comprehending the beauties of Colouring, or the Pictures which I painted for you Are Equal in Every part of the Art, & superior in One, to any thing that has been done since the age of Rafael.—All Sr J. Reynolds's discourses to the Royal Academy will shew that the Venetian finesse in Art can never be united with the Majesty of Colouring necessary to Historical beauty; & in a letter to the Revd Mr Gilpin, author of a work on Picturesque Scenery, he says Thus:[2] "It may be worth consideration" "whether the epithet Picturesque is not applicable to the excel-" "lencies of the inferior Schools rather than to the higher. The works" "of Michael Angelo, Rafael, &^c, appear to me to have nothing of it:" "whereas Rubens & the Venetian Painters may almost be said to" "have Nothing Else.—Perhaps Picturesque is somewhat synony-" "mous to the word Taste, which we should think improperly" "applied to Homer or Milton, but very well to Prior or Pope. I" "suspect that the application of these words are to Excellencies of" "an inferior order, & which are incompatible with the Grand Style." "You are certainly right in saying that variety of Tints & Forms is" "Picturesque; but it must be remember'd, on the other hand, that" "the reverse of this (*uniformity of Colour* & a *long continuation of*" "*lines*) produces Grandeur."—So Says Sir Joshua, and So say I; for I have now proved that the parts of the art which I neglected to display in those little pictures & drawings which I had the pleasure & profit to do for you, are incompatible with the designs.—There is nothing in the Art which our Painters do that I can confess myself ignorant of. I also Know & Understand & can assuredly affirm, that the works I have done for You are Equal to Carrache or Rafael (and I am now Seven years older than Rafael was when he died), I say they are Equal to Carrache or Rafael, or Else I am Blind, Stupid, Ignorant and Incapable in two years' Study to understand those things which a Boarding School Miss can comprehend in a fortnight. Be assured, My dear Friend, that there is not one touch in those Drawings & Pictures but what came from my Head & my Heart in

---

[1] James Blake.

[2] *Three Essays on Picturesque Beauty*, by William Gilpin, 1792, p. 35.

Unison; That I am Proud of being their Author and Grateful to you my Employer; & that I look upon you as the Chief of my Friends, whom I would endeavour to please, because you, among all men, have enabled me to produce these things. I would not send you a Drawing or a Picture till I had again reconsider'd my notions of Art, & had put myself back as if I was a learner. I have proved that I am Right, & shall now Go on with the Vigor I was in my Childhood famous for.

But I do not pretend to be Perfect: but, if my Works have faults, Caracche, Corregio, & Rafael's have faults also; let me observe that the yellow leather flesh of old men, the ill drawn & ugly young women, &, above all, the dawbed black & yellow shadows that are found in most fine, ay, & the finest pictures, I altogether reject as ruinous to Effect, tho' Connoisseurs may think otherwise.

Let me also notice that Carrache's Pictures are not like Correggio's, nor Correggio's like Rafael's; &, if neither of them was to be encouraged till he did like any of the others, he must die without Encouragement. My Pictures are unlike any of these Painters, & I would have them to be so. I think the manner I adopt More Perfect than any other; no doubt They thought the same of theirs.

You will be tempted to think that, as I improve, The Pictures, &c, that I did for you are not what I would now wish them to be. On this I beg to say That they are what I intended them, & that I know I never shall do better; for, if I was to do them over again, they would lose as much as they gain'd, because they were done in the heat of My Spirits.

But You will justly enquire why I have not written all this time to you? I answer I have been very Unhappy, & could not think of troubling you about it, or any of my real Friends. (I have written many letters to you which I burn'd & did not send) & why I have not before now finish'd the Miniature I promiss'd to Mrs Butts? I answer I have not, till now, in any degree pleased myself, & now I must intreat you to Excuse faults, for Portrait Painting is the direct contrary to Designing & Historical Painting in every respect. If you have not Nature before you for Every Touch, you cannot Paint Portrait; & if you have Nature before you at all, you cannot Paint History; it was Michael Angelo's opinion & is Mine. Pray Give My Wife's love with mine to Mrs Butts; assure her that it cannot be long before I have the pleasure of Painting from you in Person, & then that She may Expect a likeness, but now I have done All I could, & know she will forgive any failure in consideration of the Endeavour.

And now let me finish with assuring you that, Tho' I have been very unhappy, I am so no longer. I am again Emerged into the light of day; I still & shall to Eternity Embrace Christianity and Adore him who is the Express image of God; but I have travel'd thro' Perils

& Darkness not unlike a Champion. I have Conquer'd, and shall still Go on Conquering. Nothing can withstand the fury of my Course among the Stars of God & in the Abysses of the Accuser. My Enthusiasm is still what it was, only Enlarged and confirm'd.

I now Send Two Pictures & hope you will approve of them. I have inclosed the Account of Money reciev'd & Work done, which I ought long ago to have sent you; pray forgive Errors in omissions of this kind. I am incapable of many attentions which it is my Duty to observe towards you, thro' multitude of employment & thro' hope of soon seeing you again. I often omit to Enquire of you. But pray let me now hear how you do & of the welfare of your family.

Accept my Sincere love & respect.

I remain Yours Sincerely,
Willm Blake

A Piece of Sea Weed serves for a Barometer; at [it] gets wet & dry as the weather gets so.

24. TO THOMAS BUTTS 22 November 1802

Dear Sir,

After I had finish'd my Letter, I found that I had not said half what I intended to say, & in particular I wish to ask you what subject you choose to be painted on the remaining Canvas which I brought down with me (for there were three), and to tell you that several of the Drawings were in great forwardness; you will see by the Inclosed Account that the remaining Number of Drawings which you gave me orders for is Eighteen. I will finish these with all possible Expedition, if indeed I have not tired you, or, as it is politely call'd, Bored you too much already; or, if you would rather cry out Enough, Off, Off!, tell me in a Letter of forgiveness if you were offended, & of accustom'd friendship if you were not. But I will bore you more with some Verses which My Wife desires me to Copy out & send you with her kind love & Respect; they were Composed above a twelvemonth ago, while walking from Felpham to Lavant to meet my Sister:

With happiness stretch'd across the hills
In a cloud that dewy sweetness distills,
With a blue sky spread over with wings
And a mild sun that mounts & sings,
With trees & fields full of Fairy elves
And little devils who fight for themselves—
Remembr'ing the Verses that Hayley sung

When my heart knock'd against the root of my tongue—[1]
With Angels planted in Hawthorn bowers
And God himself in the passing hours,
With Silver Angels across my way
And Golden Demons that none can stay,
With my Father hovering upon the wind
And my Brother Robert just behind
And my Brother John the evil one
In a black cloud making his mone;
Tho' dead, they appear upon my path,
Notwithstanding my terrible wrath:
They beg, they intreat, they drop their tears,
Fill'd full of hopes, fill'd full of fears—
With a thousand Angels upon the Wind
Pouring disconsolate from behind
To drive them off, & before my way
A frowning Thistle implores my stay.
What to others a trifle appears
Fills me full of smiles or tears;
For double the vision my Eyes do see,
And a double vision is always with me.
With my inward Eye 'tis an old Man grey;
With my outward, a Thistle across my way.
"If thou goest back," the thistle said,
"Thou art to endless woe betray'd;
For here does Theotormon lower
And here is Enitharmon's bower
And Los the terrible thus hath sworn,
Because thou backward dost return,
Poverty, Envy, old age & fear
Shall bring thy Wife upon a bier;
And Butts shall give what Fuseli gave,
A dark black Rock & a gloomy Cave."

I struck the Thistle with my foot,
And broke him up from his delving root:
"Must the duties of life each other cross?"
"Must every joy be dung & dross?"
"Must my dear Butts feel cold neglect"
"Because I give Hayley his due respect?"

[1] The two lines beginning "Rememb'ring the Verses", are written in the margin and marked: "These 2 lines were omitted in transcribing & ought to come in at X". The "Verses that Hayley sung" are probably about 200 lines of blank verse written in Blake's hand, entitled *Genesis, the Seven Days of the Created World*, now identified as a translation of the opening lines of Tasso's *Le Sette Giornale del Mondo Creato.*

"Must Flaxman look upon me as wild,"
"And all my friends be with doubts beguil'd?"
"Must my Wife live in my Sister's bane,"
"Or my Sister survive on my Love's pain?"
"The curses of Los the terrible shade"
"And his dismal terrors make me afraid."

So I spoke & struck in my wrath
The old man weltering upon my path.
Then Los appear'd in all his power:
In the Sun he appear'd, descending before
My face in fierce flames; in my double sight
'Twas outward a Sun: inward Los in his might.

"My hands are labour'd day & night,"
"And Ease comes never in my sight."
"My Wife has no indulgence given"
"Except what comes to her from heaven."
"We eat little, we drink less;"
"This Earth breeds not our happiness."
"Another Sun feeds our life's streams,"
"We are not warmed with thy beams;"
"Thou measurest not the Time to me,"
"Nor yet the Space that I do see;"
"My Mind is not with thy light array'd."
"Thy terrors shall not make me afraid."

When I had my Defiance given,
The Sun stood trembling in heaven;
The Moon that glow'd remote below,
Became leprous & white as snow;
And every soul of men on the Earth
Felt affliction & sorrow & sickness & dearth.
Los flam'd in my path, & the Sun was hot
With the bows of my Mind & the Arrows of Thought—
My bowstring fierce with Ardour breathes,
My arrows glow in their golden sheaves;
My brothers & father march before;
The heavens drop with human gore.

Now I a fourfold vision see,
And a fourfold vision is given to me;
'Tis fourfold in my supreme delight
And threefold in soft Beulah's night
And twofold Always. May God us keep
From Single vision & Newton's sleep!

I also inclose you some Ballads by Mr Hayley,[1] with prints to them by Your Hble Servt. I should have sent them before now, but could not get any thing done for You to please myself; for I do assure you that I have truly studied the two little pictures I now send, & do not repent of the time I have spent upon them.

God bless you.

Yours,
W. B.

P.S. I have taken the liberty to trouble you with a letter to my Brother, which you will be so kind as to send or give him, & oblige yours, W. B.

25. TO JAMES BLAKE 30 January 1803

Felpham,
Jany, 30, 1803.

Dear Brother,

Your Letter mentioning Mr Butts's account of my Ague surprized me because I have no Ague, but have had a Cold this Winter. You know that it is my way to make the best of every thing. I never make myself nor my friends uneasy if I can help it. My Wife has had Agues & Rheumatisms almost ever since she has been here, but our time is almost out that we took the Cottage for. I did not mention our Sickness to you & should not to Mr Butts but for a determination which we have lately made, namely To leave This Place, because I am now certain of what I have long doubted, Viz that H. is jealous as Stothard was & will be no further My friend than he is compell'd by circumstances. The truth is, As a Poet he is frighten'd at me & as a Painter his views & mine are opposite; he thinks to turn me into a Portrait Painter as he did Poor Romney, but this he nor all the devils in hell will never do. I must own that seeing H. like S., Envious (& that he is I am now certain) made me very uneasy, but it is over & I now defy the worst & fear not while I am true to myself which I will be. This is the uneasiness I spoke of to Mr Butts, but I did not tell him so plain & wish you to keep it a secret & to burn this letter because it speaks so plain. I told Mr Butts that I did not wish to Explore too much the cause of our determination to leave Felpham because of pecuniary connexions between H. & me—Be not then uneasy on any account & tell my Sister not to be uneasy, for I am fully Employ'd & Well Paid. I have made it so much H's interest to employ me that he can no

[1] *Designs to a Series of Ballads written by William Hayley,* Chichester, 1802, 4°, in four parts with fourteen engravings by Blake.

longer treat me with indifference & now it is in my power to stay or return or remove to any other place that I choose, because I am getting before hand in money matters. The Profits arising from Publications are immense, & I now have it in my power to commence publication with many very formidable works, which I have finish'd & ready. A Book price half a guinea may be got out at the Expense of Ten pounds & its almost certain profits are 500 G. I am only sorry that I did not know the methods of publishing years ago, & this is one of the numerous benefits I have obtain'd by coming here, for I should never have known the nature of Publication unless I had known H. & his connexions & his method of managing. It now would be folly not to venture publishing. I am now Engraving Six little plates for a little work[1] of Mr H's, for which I am to have 10 Guineas each, & the certain profits of that work are a fortune such as would make me independent, supposing that I could substantiate such a one of my own & I mean to try many. But I again say as I said before, We are very Happy sitting at tea by a wood fire in our Cottage, the wind singing above our roof & the sea roaring at a distance, but if sickness comes all is unpleasant.

But my letter to Mr Butts appears to me not to be so explicit as that to you, for I told you that I should come to London in the Spring to commence Publisher & he has offer'd me every assistance in his power without knowing my intention. But since I wrote yours we had made the resolution of which we inform'd him, viz to leave Felpham entirely. I also told you what I was about & that I was not ignorant of what was doing in London in works of art. But I did not mention Illness because I hoped to get better (for I was really very ill when I wrote to him the last time) & was not then perswaded as I am now that the air tho' warm is unhealthy.

However, this I know will set you at Ease. I am now so full of work that I have had no time to go on with the Ballads, & my prospects of more & more work continually are certain. My Heads of Cowper for Mr H's life of Cowper have pleas'd his Relations exceedingly & in Particular Lady Hesketh & Lord Cowper—to please Lady H. was a doubtful chance who almost ador'd her Cousin the poet & thought him all perfection, & she writes that she is quite satisfied with the portraits & charm'd by the great Head in particular, tho' she never could bear the original Picture.

But I ought to mention to you that our present idea is: To take a house in some village further from the Sea, Perhaps Lavant, & in or near the road to London for the sake of convenience. I also ought to inform you that I read your letter to Mr H. & that he is very afraid of losing me & also very afraid that my Friends in London should have

---

[1] Hayley's *Triumphs of Temper*, 1803.

a bad opinion of the reception he has given to me. But My Wife has undertaken to Print the whole number of the Plates for Cowper's work, which She does to admiration, & being under my own eye the prints are as fine as the French prints & please every one: in short I have Got every thing so under my thumb that it is more profitable that things should be as they are than any other way, tho' not so agreeable, because we wish naturally for friendship in preference to interest.—The Publishers[1] are already indebted to My Wife Twenty Guineas for work deliver'd; this is a small specimen of how we go on: then fear nothing & let my Sister fear nothing because it appears to me that I am now too old & have had too much experience to be any longer imposed upon, only illness makes all uncomfortable & this we must prevent by every means in our power.

I send with this 5 Copies of N4 of the Ballads[2] for Mrs Flaxman & Five more, two of which you will be so good as to give to Mrs Chetwynd if she should call or send for them. These Ballads are likely to be Profitable, for we have Sold all that we have had time to print. Evans the Bookseller in Pallmall says they go off very well, & why should we repent of having done them? it is doing Nothing that is to be repented of & not doing such things as these.

Pray remember us both to Mr Hall when you see him.

I write in great haste & with a head full of botheration about various projected works & particularly a work now Proposed to the Public at the End of Cowper's Life, which will very likely be of great consequence; it is Cowper's Milton, the same that Fuseli's Milton Gallery was painted for, & if we succeed in our intentions the prints to this work will be very profitable to me & not only profitable, but honourable at any rate.[3] The Project pleases Lord Cowper's family, & I am now labouring in my thoughts Designs for this & other works equally creditable. These are works to be boasted of, & therefore I cannot feel depress'd, tho' I know that as far as Designing & Poetry are concern'd I am Envied in many Quarters, but I will cram the dogs, for I know that the Public are my friends & love my works & will embrace them whenever they see them. My only Difficulty is to produce fast enough.

I go on Merrily with my Greek & Latin; am very sorry that I did not begin to learn languages early in life as I find it very Easy; am now learning my Hebrew אבג. I read Greek as fluently as an Oxford scholar & the Testament is my chief master: astonishing indeed is the English Translation, it is almost word for word, & if the Hebrew Bible is as well translated, which I do not doubt it is, we need

---

[1] Joseph Seagrave of Chichester.
[2] Hayley's *Ballads*, 1802.
[3] These plates were not engraved.

not doubt of its having been translated as well as written by the Holy Ghost:

my wife joins me in Love to you both.

I am, Sincerely yours,

W. Blake

26. TO THOMAS BUTTS 25 April 1803

My Dear Sir,

I write in haste, having reciev'd a pressing Letter from my Brother. I intended to have sent the Picture of the Riposo,[1] which is nearly finish'd much to my satisfaction, but not quite; you shall have it soon. I now send the 4 Numbers for Mr Birch, with best Respects to him. The Reason the Ballads have been suspended is the pressure of other business, but they will go on again soon.[2]

Accept of my thanks for your kind & heartening Letter. You have Faith in the Endeavours of Me, your weak brother & fellow Disciple; how great must be your faith in our Divine Master! You are to me a Lesson of Humility, while you Exalt me by such distinguishing commendations. I know that you see certain merits in me, which, by God's Grace, shall be made fully apparent & perfect in Eternity; in the mean time I must not bury the Talents in the Earth, but do my endeavour to live to the Glory of our Lord & Saviour; & I am also grateful to the kind hand that endeavours to lift me out of despondency, even if it lifts me too high.

And now, My Dear Sir, Congratulate me on my return to London, with the full approbation of Mr Hayley & with Promise—But, Alas!

Now I may say to you, what perhaps I should not dare to say to any one else: That I can alone carry on my visionary studies in London unannoy'd, & that I may converse with my friends in Eternity, See Visions, Dream Dreams & prophecy & speak Parables unobserv'd & at liberty from the Doubts of other Mortals; perhaps Doubts proceeding from Kindness, but Doubts are always pernicious, Especially when we Doubt our Friends. Christ is very decided on this Point: "He who is Not With Me is Against Me." There is no Medium or Middle state; & if a Man is the Enemy of my Spiritual Life while he pretends to be the Friend of my Corporeal, he is a Real Enemy—but the Man may be the friend of my Spiritual Life while he seems the Enemy of my Corporeal, but Not Vice Versa.

What is very pleasant, Every one who hears of my going to London again Applauds it as the only course for the interest of all concern'd

---

[1] This picture is believed to have been destroyed.

[2] No further numbers were published.

in My Works, Observing that I ought not to be away from the opportunities London affords of seeing fine Pictures, and the various improvements in Works of Art going on in London.

But none can know the Spiritual Acts of my three years' Slumber on the banks of the Ocean, unless he has seen them in the Spirit, or unless he should read My long Poem descriptive of those Acts; for I have in these three years composed an immense number of verses on One Grand Theme, Similar to Homer's Iliad or Milton's Paradise Lost, the Persons & Machinery intirely new to the Inhabitants of Earth (some of the Persons Excepted). I have written this Poem from immediate Dictation, twelve or sometimes twenty or thirty lines at a time, without Premeditation & even against my Will; the Time it has taken in writing was thus render'd Non Existent, & an immense Poem Exists which seems to be the Labour of a long Life, all produc'd without Labour or Study. I mention this to shew you what I think the Grand Reason of my being brought down here.

I have a thousand & ten thousand things to say to you. My heart is full of futurity. I percieve that the sore travel which has been given me these three years leads to Glory & Honour. I rejoice & I tremble: "I am fearfully & wonderfully made." I had been reading the cxxxix Psalm a little before your Letter arrived. I take your advice. I see the face of my Heavenly Father; he lays his Hand upon my Head & gives a blessing to all my works; why should I be troubled? why should my heart & flesh cry out? I will go on in the Strength of the Lord; through Hell will I sing forth his Praises, that the Dragons of the Deep may praise him, & that those who dwell in darkness & in the Sea coasts may be gather'd into his Kingdom. Excuse my, perhaps, too great Enthusiasm. Please to accept of & give our Loves to M[rs] Butts & your amiable Family, & believe me to be,

Ever Yours Affectionately,

Will Blake

Felpham

April 25. 1803

27. TO THOMAS BUTTS 6 July 1803

Dear Sir,

I send you the Riposo, which I hope you will think my best Picture in many respects. It represents the Holy Family in Egypt, Guarded in their Repose from those Fiends, the Egyptian Gods, and tho' not directly taken from a Poem of Milton's (for till I had design'd it Milton's Poem did not come into my Thoughts), Yet it is very similar to his Hymn on the Nativity, which you will find among his smaller Poems, & will read with great delight. I have given, in the background, a building, which may be supposed the ruin of a Part of Nimrod's tower,[1] which I conjecture to have spread over many Countries; for he ought to be reckon'd of the Giant brood.

I have now on the Stocks the following drawings for you: 1. Jephthah sacrificing his Daughter; 2. Ruth & her mother in Law & Sister; 3. The three Maries at the Sepulcher; 4. The Death of Joseph; 5. The Death of the Virgin Mary; 6. S[t] Paul Preaching; & 7. The Angel of the Divine Presence clothing Adam & Eve with Coats of Skins.

These are all in great forwardness, & I am satisfied that I improve very much & shall continue to do so while I live, which is a blessing I can never be too thankful for both to God & Man.

We look forward every day with pleasure toward our meeting again in London with those whom we have learn'd to value by absence no less perhaps than we did by presence; for recollection often surpasses every thing, indeed, the prospect of returning to our friends is supremely delightful—Then, I am determin'd that M[rs] Butts shall have a good likeness of You, if I have hands & eyes left; for I am become a likeness taker & succeed admirably well; but this is not to be atchiev'd without the original sitting before you for Every touch, all likenesses from memory being necessarily very very defective; but Nature & Fancy are Two Things & can Never be joined; neither ought any one to attempt it, for it is Idolatry & destroys the Soul.

I ought to tell you that M[r] H. is quite agreeable to our return, & that there is all the appearance in the world of our being fully employ'd in Engraving for his projected Works, Particularly Cowper's Milton, a Work now on foot by Subscription, & I understand that the Subscription goes on briskly. This work is to be a very Elegant one & to consist of All Milton's Poems, with Cowper's Notes and translations by Cowper from Milton's Latin & Italian Poems.[2] These works will be ornamented with Engravings from Designs from Romney, Flaxman & Y[r] hble Serv[t], & to be Engrav'd also by the last mention'd. The Profits of the work are intended to be appropriated to Erect a Monument to the Memory of Cowper in S[t] Paul's or Westminster Abbey. Such is the Project—& M[r] Addington[3] & M[r] Pitt are both among the Subscribers, which are already numerous & of the first rank; the price of the Work is Six Guineas—Thus I hope that all our three years' trouble Ends in Good Luck at last & shall be

---

[1] The Tower of Babel.

[2] *Latin and Italian Poems of Milton translated into English verse . . . by the late William Cowper*. Edited by William Hayley, 1808, with two plates engraved by Raimbach after Flaxman.

[3] Henry Addington (1757–1844), first Lord Sidmouth, Speaker of the House of Commons, 1789–1801.

forgot by my affections & only remember'd by my Understanding; to be a Memento in time to come, & to speak to future generations by a Sublime Allegory, which is now perfectly completed into a Grand Poem. I may praise it, since I dare not pretend to be any other than the Secretary; the Authors are in Eternity. I consider it as the Grandest Poem that this World Contains. Allegory address'd to the Intellectual powers, while it is altogether hidden from the Corporeal Understanding, is My Definition of the Most Sublime Poetry; it is also somewhat in the same manner defin'd by Plato. This Poem shall, by Divine Assistance, be progressively Printed & Ornamented with Prints & given to the Public. But of this work I take care to say little to Mr H., since he is as much averse to my poetry as he is to a Chapter in the Bible. He knows that I have writ it, for I have shewn it to him, & he has read Part by his own desire & has looked with sufficient contempt to inhance my opinion of it. But I do not wish to irritate by seeming too obstinate in Poetic pursuits. But if all the World should set their faces against This, I have Orders to set my face like a flint (Ezekiel iiiC, 9v) against their faces, & my forehead against their foreheads.

As to Mr H., I feel myself at liberty to say as follows upon this ticklish subject: I regard Fashion in Poetry as little as I do in Painting; so, if both Poets & Painters should alternately dislike (but I know the majority of them will not), I am not to regard it at all, but Mr H. approves of My Designs as little as he does of my Poems, and I have been forced to insist on his leaving me in both to my own Self Will; for I am determin'd to be no longer Pester'd with his Genteel Ignorance & Polite Disapprobation. I know myself both Poet & Painter, & it is not his affected Contempt that can move me to any thing but a more assiduous pursuit of both Arts. Indeed, by my late Firmness I have brought down his affected Loftiness, & he begins to think I have some Genius: as if Genius & Assurance were the same thing! but his imbecile attempts to depress Me only deserve laughter. I say thus much to you, knowing that you will not make a bad use of it. But it is a Fact too true That, if I had only depended on Mortal Things, both myself & my Wife must have been Lost. I shall leave every one in This Country astonish'd at my Patience & Forbearance of Injuries upon Injuries; & I do assure you that, if I could have return'd to London a Month after my arrival here, I should have done so, but I was commanded by my Spiritual friends to bear all, to be silent, & to go thro' all without murmuring, &, in firm hope, till my three years should be almost accomplish'd; at which time I was set at liberty to remonstrate against former conduct & to demand Justice & Truth; which I have done in so effectual a manner that my antagonist is silenc'd completely, & I have compell'd what should have been of freedom—My Just Right as an Artist & as a Man; & if any attempt should be made to refuse me this, I am inflexible & will relinquish any engagement of Designing at all, unless altogether left to my own Judgment, As you, My dear Friend, have always left me, for which I shall never cease to honour & respect you.

When we meet, I will perfectly describe to you my Conduct & the Conduct of others toward me, & you will see that I have labour'd hard indeed, & have been borne on angel's wings. Till we meet I beg of God our Saviour to be with you & me, & yours & mine. Pray give my & my wife's love to Mrs Butts & Family, & believe me to remain,

Yours in truth & sincerity,

Will Blake

Felpham July 6. 1803

28. TO THOMAS BUTTS 16 August 1803

Felpham, August 16. 1803

Dear Sir,

I send 7 Drawings, which I hope will please you; this, I believe, about balances our account. Our return to London draws on apace; our Expectation of meeting again with you is one of our greatest pleasures. Pray tell me how your Eyes do. I never sit down to work but I think of you & feel anxious for the sight of that friend whose Eyes have done me so much good. I omitted (very unaccountably) to copy out in my last Letter that passage in my rough sketch which related to your kindness in offering to Exhibit my 2 last Pictures in the Gallery in Berners Street; it was in these Words: "I sincerely thank you for your kind offer of Exhibiting my 2 Pictures; the trouble you take on my account I trust will be recompensed to you by him who seeth in secret; if you should find it convenient to do so, it will be gratefully remember'd by me among the other numerous kindnesses I have reciev'd from you."

I go on with the remaining Subjects which you gave me commission to Execute for you, but shall not be able to send any more before my return, tho' perhaps I may bring some with me finish'd. I am at Present in a Bustle to defend myself against a very unwarrantable warrant from a Justice of Peace in Chichester, which was taken out against me by a Private[1] in Captn Leathes's troop of 1st or Royal Dragoons, for an assault & Seditious words. The wretched Man has terribly Perjur'd himself, as has his Comrade;[2] for, as to Sedition, not one Word relating to the King or Government was spoken by either him or me. His Enmity arises from my having turned him out

[1] John Scofield, Scholfield, or Scolfield.
[2] Private Cock.

of my Garden, into which he was invited as an assistant by a Gardener at work therein, without my knowledge that he was so invited. I desired him, as politely as was possible, to go out of the Garden; he made me an impertinent answer. I insisted on his leaving the Garden; he refused. I still persisted in desiring his departure; he then threaten'd to knock out my Eyes, with many abominable imprecations & with some contempt for my Person; it affronted my foolish Pride. I therefore took him by the Elbows & pushed him before me till I had got him out; there I intended to have left him, but he, turning about, put himself into a Posture of Defiance, threatening & swearing at me. I, perhaps foolishly & perhaps not, stepped out at the Gate, &, putting aside his blows, took him again by the Elbows, &, keeping his back to me, pushed him forwards down the road about fifty yards—he all the while endeavouring to turn round & strike me, & raging & cursing, which drew out several neighbours; at length, when I had got him to where he was Quarter'd, which was very quickly done, we were met at the Gate by the Master of the house, The Fox Inn (who is [my *del.*] the proprietor of my Cottage), & his wife & Daughter & the Man's Comrade & several other people. My Landlord compell'd the Soldiers to go in doors, after many abusive threats [from them *del.*] against me & my wife from the two Soldiers; but not one word of threat on account of Sedition was utter'd at that time. This method of Revenge was Plann'd between them after they had got together into the Stable. This is the whole outline. I have for witnesses: The Gardener, who is Hostler at the Fox & who Evidences that, to his knowledge, no word of the remotest tendency to Government or Sedition was utter'd: Our next door Neighbour, a Miller's wife, who saw me turn him before me down the road, & saw & heard all that happen'd at the Gate of the Inn, who Evidences that no Expression of threatening on account of Sedition was utter'd in the heat of their fury by either of the Dragoons; this was the woman's own remark, & does high honour to her good sense, as she observes that, whenever a quarrel happens, the offence is always repeated. The Landlord of the Inn & His Wife & daughter will Evidence the Same, & will evidently prove the Comrade perjur'd, who swore that he heard me, while at the Gate, utter Seditious words & D— the K—, without which perjury I could not have been committed; & I had no witness with me before the Justices who could combat his assertion, as the Gardener remain'd in my Garden all the while, & he was the only person I thought necessary to take with me. I have been before a Bench of Justices at Chichester this morning; but they, as the Lawyer who wrote down the Accusation told me in private, are compell'd by the Military to suffer a prosecution to be enter'd into: altho' they must know, & it is manifest, that the whole is a Fabricated Perjury. I have been forced to find Bail. M[r] Hayley was kind enough to come forwards, & Mr Seagrave,[1] Printer at Chichester; Mr H. in 100£, & Mr S. in 50£; & myself am bound in 100£ for my appearance at the Quarter Sessions, which is after Michaelmass. So I shall have the satisfaction to see my friends in Town before this Contemptible business comes on. I say Contemptible, for it must be manifest to every one that the whole accusation is a wilful Perjury. Thus, you see, my dear Friend, that I cannot leave this place without some adventure; it has struck a consternation thro' all the Villages round. Every Man is now afraid of speaking to, or looking at, a Soldier; for the peaceable Villagers have always been forward in expressing their kindness for us, & they express their sorrow at our departure as soon as they hear of it. Every one here is my Evidence for Peace & Good Neighbourhood; & yet, such is the present state of things, this foolish accusation must be tried in Public. Well, I am content, I murmur not & doubt not that I shall recieve Justice, & am only sorry for the trouble & expense. I have heard that my Accuser is a disgraced Sergeant; his name is John Scholfield; perhaps it will be in your power to learn somewhat about the Man. I am very ignorant of what I am requesting of you; I only suggest what I know you will be kind enough to Excuse if you can learn nothing about him, & what, I as well know, if it is possible, you will be kind enough to do in this matter.

Dear Sir, This perhaps was suffer'd to Clear up some doubts, & to give opportunity to those whom I doubted to clear themselves of all imputation. If a Man offends me ignorantly & not designedly, surely I ought to consider him with favour & affection. Perhaps the simplicity of myself is the origin of all offences committed against me. If I have found this, I shall have learned a most valuable thing, well worth three years' perseverance. I have found it. It is certain that a too passive manner, inconsistent with my active physiognomy, had done me much mischief. I must now express to you my conviction that all is come from the spiritual World for Good, & not for Evil.

Give me your advice in my perilous adventure; burn what I have peevishly written about any friend. I have been very much degraded & injuriously treated; but if it all arise from my own fault, I ought to blame myself.

O why was I born with a different face?
Why was I not born like the rest of my race?
When I look, each one starts! when I speak, I offend;
Then I'm silent & passive & lose every Friend.

---

[1] Printer of Hayley's *Ballads, The Life of Cowper, The Triumphs of Temper,* and other books by Hayley.

Then my verse I dishonour, My pictures despise,
My person degrade & my temper chastise;
And the pen is my terror, the pencil my shame;
All my Talents I bury, and dead is my Fame.

I am either too low or too highly priz'd;
When Elate I am Envy'd, When Meek I'm despis'd.

This is but too just a Picture of my Present state. I pray God to keep you & all men from it, & to deliver me in his own good time. Pray write to me, & tell me how you & your family enjoy health. My much terrified Wife joins me in love to you & M[rs] Butts & all your family. I again take the liberty to beg of you to cause the Enclos'd Letter to be deliver'd to my Brother, & remain Sincerely & Affectionately Yours,

William Blake

29. TO WILLIAM HAYLEY* 19 September 1803

"My admiration of Flaxman's genius is more and more—his industry is equal to his other great powers."

Speaks of his works in progress in his studio, and of various matters connected with art. [*Extracts from sale catalogue.*]

30. TO WILLIAM HAYLEY 7 October 1803

London, October 7, 1803.

Dear Sir,

Your generous & tender solicitude about your devoted rebel makes it absolutely necessary that he should trouble you with an account of his safe arrival, which will excuse his begging the favor of a few lines to inform him how you escaped the contagion of the Court of Justice—I fear that you have & must suffer more on my account than I shall ever be worth—Arrived safe in London, my wife in very poor health, still I resolve not to lose hope of seeing better days.

Art in London flourishes. Engravers in particular are wanted. Every Engraver turns away work that he cannot execute from his superabundant Employment. Yet no one brings work to me. I am content that it shall be so as long as God pleases. I know that many works of a lucrative nature are in want of hands; other Engravers are courted. I suppose that I must go a Courting, which I shall do awkwardly; in the mean time I lose no moment to complete Romney to satisfaction.[1]

[1] Blake engraved a head of Romney for Hayley's *Life*, but it was not used.

How is it possible that a Man almost 50 Years of Age, who has not lost any of his life since he was five years old without incessant labour & study, how is it possible that such a one with ordinary common sense can be inferior to a boy of twenty, who scarcely has taken or deigns to take a pencil in hand, but who rides about the Parks or Saunters about the Playhouses, who Eats & drinks for business not for need, how is it possible that such a fop can be superior to the studious lover of Art can scarcely be imagin'd. Yet such is somewhat like my fate & such it is likely to remain. Yet I laugh & sing, for if on Earth neglected I am in heaven a Prince among Princes, & even on Earth beloved by the Good as a Good Man; this I should be perfectly contented with, but at certain periods a blaze of reputation arises round me in which I am consider'd as one distinguish'd by some mental perfection, but the flame soon dies again & I am left stupified and astonish'd. O that I could live as others do in a regular succession of Employment, this wish I fear is not to be accomplish'd to me—Forgive this Dirge-like lamentation over a dead horse, & now I have lamented over the dead horse let me laugh & be merry with my friends till Christmas, for as Man liveth not by bread alone, I shall live altho' I should want bread—nothing is necessary to me but to do my Duty & to rejoice in the exceeding joy that is always poured out on my Spirit, to pray that my friends & you above the rest may be made partakers of the joy that the world cannot concieve, that you may still be replenish'd with the same & be as you always have been, a glorious & triumphant Dweller in immortality. Please to pay for me my best thanks to Miss Poole: tell her that I wish her a continued Excess of Happiness—some say that Happiness is not Good for Mortals, & they ought to be answer'd that Sorrow is not fit for Immortals & is utterly useless to any one; a blight never does good to a tree, & if a blight kill not a tree but it still bear fruit, let none say that the fruit was in consequence of the blight. When this Soldier-like danger is over I will do double the work I do now, for it will hang heavy on my Devil who terribly resents it; but I soothe him to peace, & indeed he is a good natur'd Devil after all & certainly does not lead me into scrapes—he is not in the least to be blamed for the present scrape, as he was out of the way all the time on other employment seeking amusement in making Verses, to which he constantly leads me very much to my hurt & sometimes to the annoyance of my friends; as I percieve he is now doing the same work by my letter, I will finish it, wishing you health & joy in God our Saviour.

To Eternity yours,
Will[m] Blake

31. TO WILLIAM HAYLEY* 26 October 1803

Dear Sir,

I hasten to write to you by the favour of Mr. Edwards. I have been with Mr. Saunders, who has now in his possession all Mr. Romney's[1] pictures that remained after the sale at Hampstead; I saw "Milton and his Daughters", and "'Twas where the Seas were Roaring", and a beautiful "Female Head". He has promised to write a list of all that he has in his possession, and of all that he remembers of Mr. Romney's paintings, with notices where they now are, so far as his recollection will serve. The picture of "Christ in the Desert" he supposes to be one of those which he has rolled on large rollers. He will take them down and unroll them, but cannot do it easily, as they are so large as to occupy the whole length of his workshop, and are laid across beams at the top.

Mr. Flaxman is now out of town. When he returns I will lose no time in setting him to work on the same object.

I have got to work after Fuseli for a little Shakespeare.[2] Mr. Johnson, the bookseller, tells me that there is no want of work. So far you will be rejoiced with me, and your words, "*Do not fear you can want employment!*" were verified the morning after I received your kind letter; but I go on finishing Romney with spirit, and for the relief of variety shall engage in other little works as they arise.

I called on Mr. Evans,[3] who gives small hopes of our ballads; he says he has sold but fifteen numbers at the most, and that going on would be a certain loss of almost all the expenses. I then proposed to him to take a part with me in publishing them on a smaller scale, which he declined on account of its being out of his line of business to publish, and a line in which he is determined never to engage, attaching himself wholly to the sale of fine editions of authors and curious books in general. He advises that some publisher should be spoken to who would purchase the copyright: and, as far as I can judge of the nature of publication, no chance is left to one out of the trade. Thus the case stands at present. God send better times! Everybody complains, yet all go on cheerfully and with spirit. The shops in London improve; everything is elegant, clean, and neat; the streets are widened where they were narrow; even Snow Hill is become almost level, and is a very handsome street, and the narrow part of the Strand near St. Clement's is widened and become very elegant.

---

[1] The inquiries concerning Romney, upon which Blake was engaged at this time, were made on Hayley's behalf for his *Life of Romney*.

[2] *The Plays of William Shakespeare,* ed. Alexander Chalmers, 1805, for which Blake engraved two plates.

[3] R. H. Evans, bookseller, Pall Mall, London.

My wife continues poorly, but fancies she is better in health here than by the seaside. We both sincerely pray for the health of Miss Poole, and for all our friends in Sussex, and remain, dear sir,

Your sincere and devoted servants,

W. and C. Blake

South Molton Street

26 October 1803

32. TO WILLIAM HAYLEY 13 December 1803

Dear Sir,

I write in a violent hurry. Your Letter has never arrived to me. M[rs] Lambert has been with me, which is the first notice I had of the Letter or of the drawing. I have fetch'd the drawing from M[r] Rose & have shew'd it to M[r] Flaxman, who approves of it, wishing only that the Monument itself may be more made out & the other Monument in the back Ground kept in a lower tint. The little oval tablet on the side by Cowper's Monument he tells me is M[rs] Unwin's; of course that shall be distinguish'd.

I have a great many things to say & a great many heartfelt acknowledgments to express, particularly for your tens, which are hundreds to me, nay thousands. I am going on with success: business comes in & I shall be at ease if this infernal business of the soldier can be got over.

I have seen M[r] Saunders & enquir'd of him whether he has any of M[r] Romney's [Sketches *del.*] Historical Sketches: he says that he sent a great part of them to the North & explain'd the North by saying that [M[r] Romney *del.*] M[r] John Romney[1] has a dwelling in the north. M[r] Flaxman supposes that if some of the most distinguish'd designs of M[r] Romney, of which M[r] Saunders has a good many, were Engrav'd, they would be an appropriate accompaniment to the Life of Romney; the expense would not be very great & the merit of the designs an object of consequence.

M[r] Saunders will shortly write to you giving you every information in his power with notices of where M[r] Romney's best pictures now are & other articles collected from every Fountain he can visit.

I send the five copies of Cowper's Plates, which you will recieve with this & have only time to say, because I shall be too late for the carriage,

---

[1] Romney's only surviving son (1758-1832). He afterwards quarrelled with Hayley and attacked him in his *Life of Romney*, 1830.

God bless you & preserve you & reward your kindness to me
Will Blake

Tuesday night
13 Decr 1803

P.S. My wife is better; we are very anxious about Miss Poole's health & shall be truly happy to hear that it is perfectly restored. Mr Romney's Portrait goes on with spirit. I do not send a proof because I cannot get one, the Printers [being *del.*] having been this afternoon unable or unwilling & my Press not yet being put up.

Farewell.

33. TO WILLIAM HAYLEY 14 January 1804

London Jany 14. 1804

Dear Sir,

I write immediately on my arrival. Not merely to inform you that I am safe arriv'd, but also to inform you that in a conversation with an old Soldier who came in the Coach with me I learned: that no one: not even the most expert horseman: ought ever to mount a Trooper's Horse; they are taught so many tricks such as stopping short, falling down on their knees, running sideways, & in various & innumerable ways endeavouring to throw the rider, that it is a miracle if a stranger escapes with Life,—All this I learn'd with some alarm & heard also what the soldier said confirm'd by another person in the coach. I therefore as it is my duty beg & intreat you never to mount that wicked horse again, nor again trust to one who has been so Educated. God our Saviour watch over you & preserve you.

I have seen Flaxman already as I took to him early this morning your present to his Scholar; he & his are all well & in high spirits & welcom'd Me with kind affection & generous exultation in my escape from the arrows of darkness. I intend to see Mrs Lambert & Mr Johnson bookseller this afternoon. My poor wife has been near the Gate of Death as was supposed by our kind & attentive fellow inhabitant, the young & very amiable Mrs Enoch, who gave my wife all the attention that a daughter could pay to a mother, but my arrival has dispell'd the formidable malady & my dear & good woman again begins to resume her health & strength. Pray my dear Sir favour me with a line concerning your health & how you have escaped the double blow both from the wicked horse & from your innocent humble servant, whose heart & soul are more & more drawn out towards you & Felpham & its kind inhabitants. I feel anxious, & therefore pray to my God & father for the health of Miss Poole: hope that the pang of affection & gratitude is the Gift of God for good. I am thankful that I feel it; it draws the soul towards Eternal life & conjunction with Spirits of just men made perfect by love & gratitude—the two angels who stand at heaven's gate ever open, ever inviting guests to the marriage. O foolish Philosophy! Gratitude is Heaven itself; there could be no heaven without Gratitude. I feel it & I know it. I thank God & Man for it & above all You, My dear friend & benefactor in the Lord. Pray give my & my wife's duties to Miss Poole; accept them yourself & believe me to be,

Yours in sincerity,
Willm Blake

34. TO WILLIAM HAYLEY 27 January 1804

Dear Sir,

Your eager expectation of hearing from me compells me to write immediately, tho' I have not done half the business I wish'd owing to a violent cold which confin'd me to my bed 3 days & to my chamber a week. I am now so well (thank God) as to get out & have accordingly been to Mr Walker's[1] who is not in town being at Birmingham where he will remain 6 weeks or 2 Months. I took my Portrait of Romney as you desired to shew him: his son was likewise not at home: but I will again call on Mr Walker Junr & beg him to shew me the Pictures, & make every enquiry of him, If you think best:—Mr Sanders has one or two large Cartoons, The Subjects he does not know, they are folded up on the top of his workshop, the rest he pack'd up & sent into the North. I shew'd your Letter to Mr John Romney to Mr Flaxman who was perfectly satisfied with it. I seal'd & sent it immediately as directed by Mr Sanders to Kendall, Westmoreland. Mr Sanders expects Mr Romney in town soon. Note, Your Letter to Mr J. Romney I sent off the morning after I reciev'd it from you, being then in health. I have taken your noble present to Mr Rose & left it with charge to the Servant of Great Care; the Writing looks very pretty. I was fortunate in doing it myself & hit it off excellently. I have not seen Mr Rose,[2] tho' he is in town. Mr Flaxman is not at all acquainted with Sr Allan Chambre,[3] recommends me to enquire concerning him of Mr Rose; my brother says he believes Sr Allan is a Master in Chancery. Tho' I have call'd on Mr Edwards twice for Lady Hamilton's[4] direction, was so unfortunate as to find him Out both times. I will repeat my call on him tomorrow morning.

---

[1] Adam Walker (1731-1821), author and inventor, an old friend of Romney.
[2] Samuel Rose, Blake's counsel at his trial.
[3] Sir Alan Chambré (1739-1823), judge; Recorder of Lancaster; Baron of the Exchequer, 1799. His portrait was painted by Romney.
[4] Emma Hart, Lady Hamilton.

My Dear Sir, I write now to satisfy you that all is in a good train. I am going on briskly with the Plates, find every thing promising. Work in Abundance; & if God blesses me with health doubt not yet to make a Figure in the Great dance of Life that shall amuse the Spectators in the Sky. I thank you for my Demosthenes[1] which is now become a noble subject—My Wife gets better every Day: hope earnestly that you have entirely escaped the brush of my Evil Star, which I believe is now for ever fallen into the Abyss—God bless & preserve You and our Good Lady Paulina with the Good things both of this life & of eternity & with you my much admired & respected Edward the Bard of Oxford[2] whose verses still sound upon my Ear like the distant approach of things mighty & magnificent; like the sound of harps which I hear before the Sun's rising, like the remembrance of Felpham's waves & of the Glorious & far beaming Turret, like the Villa of Lavant,[3] blessed & blessing. Amen. God bless you all O people of Sussex around your Hermit & Bard. So prays the Emulator of both his & your mild & happy tempers of Soul. Your devoted

Will Blake

Sth Molton Street
Friday Jany 27 1804

35. TO WILLIAM HAYLEY 23 February 1804

Dear Sir,

I call'd Yesterday on Mr Braithwaite,[4] as you desired, & found him quite as chearful as you describe him, & by his appearance should not have supposed him to be near sixty, notwithstanding he was shaded by a green shade over his Eyes. He gives a very spirited assurance of Mr John Romney's interesting himself in the great object of his Father's Fame, & thinks that he must be proud of such a work & in such hands. The Picture from Sterne,[5] which you desired him to procure for you, he has not yet found where it is. Supposes that it may be in the north, & that he may learn from Mr Romney, who will

---

[1] "The Death of Demosthenes", engraved by Blake after Thomas Hayley, for William Hayley's *Essay on Sculpture*, 1800, 4°.

[2] Probably Edward Marsh, of Oriel College (see Gilchrist's *Life*, 1880, i, 203).

[3] i.e. Miss Poole's villa.

[4] Daniel Braithwaite, controller of the Foreign department of the Post Office, was Romney's earliest patron, in 1762; it was to him that Hayley dedicated his *Life of Romney*.

[5] Probably "The Introduction of Dr. Slop into the Parlour of Mr. Shandy", a scene from *Tristam Shandy*, painted *c.* 1757, which was engraved for the *Life of Romney* by W. Haines.

be in town soon. Mr B. desires I will present his Compliments to you, & write you that he has spoken with Mr Read concerning the Life of Romney; he interests himself in it, & has promised to procure dates of premiums, Pictures, &c, Mr Read having a number of Articles relating to Romney, either written or printed, which he promises to copy out for your use, as also the Catalogue of Hampstead Sale. He shew'd me a very fine Portrait of Mrs Siddons (by Romney) as the Tragic Muse, half-length, that is, the Head & hands, & in his best Style. He also desires me to express to you his wish that you would give the Public an Engraving of that Medallion by your Son's matchless hand,[1] which is placed over his chimney piece between two little pretty pictures, correct & enlarged copies from antique Gems, of which the center ornament is worthy; he says that it is by far, in his opinion, the most exact resemblance of Romney he ever saw. I have, furthermore, the pleasure of informing you that he knew immediately my Portrait of Romney, & assured me that he thought it a very great likeness.

I wish I could give you a Pleasant account of our beloved Councellor;[2] he, Alas! was ill in bed when I call'd yesterday at about 12 O'clock, & the servant said that he remains very ill indeed.

Mr Walker, I have been so unfortunate as not to find at home, but I will call again in a day or two. Neither Mr Flaxman nor Mr Edwards know Lady Hamilton's address; the house Sr William liv'd in in Piccadilly She left some time ago. Mr Edwards will procure her address for you, & I will send it immediately.

I have inclos'd for you the 22 Numbers of Fuseli's Shakespeare that are out, & the book of Italian Letters from Mrs Flaxman, who with her admirable husband present their best Compliments to you; he is so busy that I believe I shall never see him again but when I call on him, for he has never yet, since my return to London, had the time or grace to call on me. Mrs Flaxman & her Sisters gave also their testimony to my Likeness of Romney. Mr Flaxman I have not yet had an opportunity of consulting about it, but soon will.

I inclose likewise the Academical Correspondence of Mr Hoare[3] the Painter, whose note to me I also inclose, for I did but express to him my desire of sending you a Copy of his work, & the day after I reciev'd it with the note Expressing his pleasure [of your *del.*] in your wish to see it. You would be much delighted with the Man, as I assure myself you will be with his work.

---

[1] The medallion of Romney by Thomas Hayley was engraved for the *Life* by Caroline Watson.

[2] Samuel Rose.

[3] Prince Hoare (1755-1834), painter and author of several works, including *Academic Correspondence,* 1803, 4°, with frontispiece of a bust of Ceres engraved by Blake after Flaxman.

The plates of Cowper's Monument are both in great forwardness, & you shall have Proofs in another week. I assure you that I will not spare pains, & am myself very much satisfied that I shall do my duty & produce two Elegant plates; there is, however, a great deal of work in them that must & will have time.

"Busy, Busy, Busy, I bustle along,
"Mounted upon warm Phœbus's rays,
"Thro' the heavenly throng."[1]

But I hasten'd to write to you about Mr Braithwaite; hope when I send my proofs to give as good an account of Mr Walker.

My wife joins me in Respects & Love to you, & desires with mine to present hers to Miss Poole.

I remain, Dear Sir, Your Sincere,
Will Blake

S^th^ Molton Street
23 Feby 1804

36. TO WILLLIAM HAYLEY 12 March 1804

Dear Sir,

I begin with the latter end of your letter & grieve more for Miss Poole's ill-health than for my failure in sending proofs, tho' I am very sorry that I cannot send before Saturday's Coach. Engraving is Eternal work; the two plates are almost finish'd. You will recieve proofs of them for Lady Hesketh, whose copy of Cowper's letters ought to be printed in letters of Gold & ornamented with Jewels of Heaven, Havilah, Eden & all the countries where Jewels abound. I curse & bless Engraving alternately, because it takes so much time & is so untractable, tho' capable of such beauty & perfection.

My wife desires me to Express her Love to you, Praying for Miss Poole's perfect recovery, & we both remain,

Your Affectionate,
Will Blake

March 12
1804

[1] From *The Rehearsal*, Act V, by George Villiers, second Duke of Buckingham.

37. TO WILLIAM HAYLEY 16 March 1804

Dear Sir,

According to your Desire I send proofs of the Monumental Plates[1] tho' as you will percieve they have not the last touches especially the Plate of the Monument which I have drawn from Mr Flaxman's Model with all the fidelity I could & will finish with equal care, the writing being exactly copied from the tracing paper which was traced on the marble. The inscriptions to the Plates I must beg of you to send to me that I may Engrave them immediately.

The drawing of the Monument which Mr Johnson sent has the following Inscription—"Monument Erected to the Memory of William Cowper Esqre in St Edmunds Chapel East Dereham by the Lady Hesketh 1803"—But it strikes me that St Edmund's Chapel East Dereham may be understood to mean a Chapel in East Dereham *Town* & not to Express sufficiently that the Monument is in *East Dereham Church*. Owing to my determination of sending you Proofs I have not been able to consult Mr Flaxman about the Designs of Mr Romney which are at Saunders'. I call'd once of [on] Mr F. but he was not at home so could not spare more time, but will now immediately proceed in that business. The Pleasure I reciev'd from your kind Letter ought to make me assiduous & it does so. That Mr John Romney is so honest as to expose to you his whole absurd prejudice gives hopes that he may prove worthy of his father, & that he should tell such inconsistent surmizes proves that they will soon be eradicated & forgotten. You who was his father's best friend will I hope become the most respected object of his love & admiration.

I call'd on Mr Hoare with your Elegant & Heart lifting Compliment; he was not at home. I left it with a short note, have not seen him since.

Mr Rose I am happy to hear is getting quite well. Hope to hear the same good account of our most admirable & always anxiously remember'd Miss Poole.

Mr Braithwaite call'd on me & brought two Prints which he desires may be sent to you (with His Compliments) (which you will find inclosed) one is a copy from that Miniature you kindly suffer'd me to make from the Picture of Romney which I am now Engraving & which was lent by Mr Long[2] for the purpose of being Engraved for

---

[1] This and the succeeding paragraphs refer to the plates for Hayley's *Life of Cowper*, 1803.

[2] William Long (1747-1818), F.R.S., F.S.A., assistant surgeon to St. Bartholomew's Hospital and Master of the College of Surgeons in 1800, a friend of both Flaxman and Hayley. His portrait was painted by Romney.

the European Mag^ne^. The other is Mrs Siddons from the Picture by Romney in Mr Braithwaite's possession, but as much unlike the original as possible.

My Wife joins me in best affections to you

& I remain Sincerely Yours

Will Blake

16 March 1804

I enclose also N° 23 of the Shakspeare.

38. TO WILLIAM HAYLEY 21 March 1804

Dear Sir,

I send two Proofs of Each of the Monumental Plates with the writing, which I hope will please. Should have sent the twelve of each if I had not wish'd to improve them still more, & because I had not enough paper in proper order for printing: beg pardon for the omission of Mr Braithwaite's two Prints, as also for omitting to mention Mr Hoare's grateful sensation on His reception of your very beautiful Verses. I now send you his note to Me, as I think it will give you a good idea of this good & excellent Man.

I have been to look at the Drawings & Picture, but Flaxman has not yet been able to go with me. Am sorry to inform you that one of the drawings which Mr Romney destined for you is Lost or at least cannot now be found: it is that of the Witch raising the Storm. Mr Romney says that in lieu of the lost drawing you shall have choice of either of the remaining ones of which Sanders says there are several, but I only saw one more because I would not give much trouble as Flaxman was not with me. The Drawing I saw is of a Female Figure with a Serpent in one hand & a torch in the other both held above her head & a figure kneeling at her feet; it is a very sublime drawing & would make an Excellent Print, but I will not advise any thing till Flaxman sees them. The drawing of Pliny in the Eruption of Vesuvius is very clever & indeed a Sublime, but very unfinish'd, Sketch—The Picture of the Man on horseback rescuing the drowning people is a beautiful Performance.[1] Mr Saunders says that he has orders from Mr Romney to deliver the Picture & two drawings to any person whom you shall authorize to recieve them. They are somewhat batter'd, but not so much as I expected, for I remember, & Saunders says, that they never were properly strained upon their straining frames.

---

[1] Romney's oil sketch, "The Shipwreck", engraved by Blake for Hayley's *Life of Romney*, 4°, 1809. Blake's sepia drawing done from the picture is now in the Print Room of the British Museum.

We both rejoice that Miss Poole is better, but hope & pray for her intire recovery.

My wife joins me in sincere love to you: please to remember us both affectionately & gratefully to Miss Poole

& believe me to remain, Ever Yours,

Will Blake

Sth Molton Street

March 21. 1804

39. TO WILLIAM HAYLEY 31 March 1804

Dear Sir,

I did not recieve your Letter till Monday: of course could not have got them Printed to send by tuesday's Coach. But there is a real reason equally good why I have not yet sent. I hope you will believe me when I say that my solicitude to bring them to perfection has caused this delay, as also not being quite sure that you had Copies ready for them. I could not think of delivering the 12 Copies without giving the last touches, which are always the best. I have now, I hope, given them & we directly go to Printing. Consequently it will be by Tuesday's Coach that you will recieve 12 of Each. If you do not wish any more done before I deliver, then pray favor me with a line that I may send the Plates to Johnson, who wants them to set the Printer to work upon.

I remain In Engraver's hurry, which is
the worst & most unprofitable of hurries,

Your Sincere & Affectionate,

Will Blake

St Molton St[t]

March 31. 1804

40. TO WILLIAM HAYLEY* 2 April 1804

. . . Mr. Flaxman advises that the drawing of Mr. Romney's which shall be chosen instead of the Witch (if that cannot be recovered), be Hecate, the figure with the torch and snake, which he thinks one of the finest drawings. The twelve impressions of each of the plates which I now send ought to be unrolled immediately that you receive them and put under somewhat to press them flat. You should have had fifteen of each, but I had not paper enough in proper order for printing. There is now in hand a new edition of Flaxman's *Homer*,[1] with additional designs, two of which I am now engraving. I am uneasy at not hearing from Mr. Dally,[2] to whom I enclosed £15 in a letter a fortnight ago, by his desire. I write to him by this post to inquire about it. Money in these times is not to be trifled with. I have now cleared the way to Romney, in whose service I now enter again with great pleasure, and hope soon to show you my zeal with good effect. Am in hopes that Miss Poole is recovered, as you are silent on that most alarming and interesting topic in both your last letters. God be with you in all things. My wife joins me in this prayer.

I am, dear Sir,
Your sincerely affectionate,
Willm. Blake

41. TO WILLIAM HAYLEY 7 April 1804

Dear Sir,

You can have no Idea, unless you was in London as I am, how much your Name is lov'd & respected. I have the Extreme pleasure of transmitting to you one proof of this Respect which you will be pleased with & I hope will adopt & embrace. It comes thro' M[r] Hoare from M[r] Phillips[3] of S[t] Pauls Church Yard; it is as yet an intire secret between M[r] P, M[r] H, & myself & will remain so till you have given Your Decision—M[r] Phillips is a man of vast spirit & enterprize with a solidity of character which few have; he is the man who applied to Cowper for that sonnet in favor of a Prisoner at Leicester which I believe you thought fit not to Print. So you see he is spiritually adjoin'd with us. His connections throughout England & indeed Europe & America enable him to Circulate Publications to an immense Extent & he told M[r] Hoare that on the present work which he proposes to commence with your assistance he can afford to expend 2,000 a year. M[r] Phillips considers you as the Great Leading character in Literature & his terms to others will amount to only one Quarter of what he proposes to you. I send Inclos'd his Terms as M[r] Hoare by my desire has given them to me in writing. Knowing your aversion to Reviews & Reviewing I consider the Present Proposal as peculiarly adapted to your Ideas; it may be call'd a Defence of Literature against those pests of the Press & a bulwark for Genius, which shall with your

[1] Flaxman's *Iliad of Homer*, 1805, with 40 plates, three of which were engraved by Blake.

[2] Mr. Dally has not been certainly identified. Perhaps he was Richard Dally, a friend of Hayley and author of *The Bognor Guide*, Chichester, 1828, and other works.

[3] Richard Phillips (1767-1840), bookseller and publisher, proprietor of the *Monthly Magazine*. The project described by Blake was never carried out. Phillips published the 1805 edition of Hayley's *Ballads*, with Blake's plates.

good assistance disperse those Rebellious Spirits of Envy & Malignity. In short: If you see it as I see it, you will embrace this Proposal on the Score of Parental Duty. Literature is your Child. She calls for your assistance! You: who never refuse to assist any, how remote soever, will certainly hear her voice. Your answer to the Proposal you will if you think fit direct to Mr Hoare who is worthy of every Confidence you can place in him.

I am, dear Sir,
Your anxiously devoted
Will Blake

Sth Molton Street
April 7. 1804

Mr Hoare's address is
To Prince Hoare Esqre
Buckingham Street
Strand

42. TO WILLIAM HAYLEY 27 April 1804

Dear Sir,

I have at length seen Mr. Hoare, after having repeatedly called on him every day and not finding him. I now understand that he received your reply to P's proposal at Brighton, where he has a residence, from whence he sent it to London to Mr. Phillips; he has not seen P. since his return, and therefore cannot tell me how he understood your answer. Mr. H. appears to me to consider it as a rejection of the proposal altogether. I took the liberty to tell him that I could not consider it so, but that as I understood you, you had accepted the spirit of P's intention, which was to leave the whole conduct of the affair to you, and that you had accordingly nominated one of your friends and agreed to nominate others. But if P. meant that you should yourself take on you the drudgery of the ordinary business of a review, his proposal was by no means a generous one. Mr. H. has promised to see Mr. Phillips immediately, and to know what his intentions are; but he says perhaps Mr. P. may not yet have seen your letter to him, and that his multiplicity of business may very well account for the delay. I have seen our excellent Flaxman lately, he is well in health, but has had such a burn on his hand as you had once, which has hindered his working for a fortnight. It is now better; he desires to be most affectionately remembered to you; he began a letter to you a week ago; perhaps by this time you have received it; but he is also a laborious votary of endless work. Engraving is of so slow process, I must beg of you to give me the earliest possible notice of what engraving is to be done for the *Life of Romney*. Endless work is the true title of engraving, as I find by the things I have in hand day and night. We feel much easier to hear that you have parted with your horse. Hope soon to hear that you have a living one of brass, a Pegasus of Corinthian metal; and that Miss Poole is again in such health as when she first mounted me on my beloved Bruno. I forgot to mention that Mr. Hoare desires his most respectful compliments to you. Speaks of taking a ride across the country to Felpham, as he always keeps a horse at Brighton. My wife joins me in love to you.

I remain, yours sincerely,
William Blake

27 April 1804

43. TO WILLIAM HAYLEY* 4 May 1804

Dear Sir,

I thank you sincerely for Falconer,[1] an admirable poet, and the admirable prints to it by Fittler. Whether you intended it or not, they have given me some excellent hints in engraving; his manner of working is what I shall endeavour to adopt in many points. I have seen the elder Mr. Walker. He knew and admired without any preface my print of Romney, and when his daughter came in he gave the print into her hand without a word, and she immediately said, "Ah! Romney! younger than I knew him, *but very like indeed*." Mr. Walker showed me Romney's first attempt at oil painting; it is a copy from a Dutch picture—Dutch Boor Smoking; on the back is written, "This was the first attempt at oil painting by G. Romney." He shew'd me also the last performance of Romney. It is of Mr. Walker and family,[2] the draperies put in by somebody else. It is a very excellent picture, but unfinished. The figures as large as life, half length, Mr. W., three sons, and, I believe, two daughters, with maps, instruments, &c. Mr. Walker also shew'd me a portrait of himself (W.), whole length, on a canvas about two feet by one and a half; it is the first portrait Romney ever painted. But above all, a picture of *Lear and Cordelia*, when he awakes and knows her,—an incomparable production, which Mr. W. bought for five shillings at a broker's shop; it is about five feet by four, and exquisite for expression; indeed, it is most pathetic; the heads of Lear and Cordelia can never be surpassed, and Kent and the other attendant are admirable; the picture is very

[1] *The Shipwreck*, by William Falconer, 1804, with seven engravings by J. Fittler, A.R.A., after N. Pocock.

[2] A large canvas, now in the National Portrait Gallery, of Walker seated at a table with his wife and daughter, his three sons standing behind them.

highly finished. Other things I saw of Romney's first works: two copies, perhaps from Borgognone, of battles; and Mr. Walker promises to collect all he can of information for you. I much admired his mild and gentle benevolent manners; it seems as if all Romney's intimate friends were truly amiable and feeling like himself.

I have also seen Alderman Boydel,[1] who has promised to get the number and prices of all Romney's prints as you desired. He has sent a Catalogue of all his Collection, and a Scheme of his Lottery; desires his compliments to you; says he laments your absence from London, as your advice would be acceptable at all times, but especially at the present. He is very thin and decay'd, and but the shadow of what he was; so he is now a Shadow's Shadow; but how can we expect a very stout man at eighty-five, which age he tells me he has now reached? You would have been pleas'd to see his eyes light up at the mention of your name.

Mr. Flaxman agrees with me that somewhat more than outline is necessary to the execution of Romney's designs, because his merit is eminent in the art of massing his lights and shades. I should propose to etch them in a rapid but firm manner, somewhat, perhaps, as I did the *Head of Euler*;[2] the price I receive for engraving Flaxman's outlines of *Homer* is five guineas each. I send the Domenichino, which is very neatly done. His merit was but little in light and shade; outline was his element, and yet these outlines give but a faint idea of the finished prints from his works, several of the best of which I have. I send also the French monuments, and inclose with them a catalogue of Bell's Gallery, and another of the Exhibition, which I have *not* yet seen. I mentioned the pictures from Sterne to Mr. Walker; he says that there were several; one, a garden scene, with Uncle Toby and Obadiah planting in the garden; but that of Lefevre's Death he speaks of as incomparable, but cannot tell where it now is, as they were scattered abroad, being disposed of by means of a raffle. He supposes it is in Westmoreland; promises to make every inquiry about it. Accept, also, of my thanks for Cowper's third volume, which I got, as you directed, of Mr. Johnson. I have seen Mr. Rose; he looks, tho' not so well as I have seen him, yet tolerably, considering the terrible storm he has been thro'! He says that the last session was a severe labour; indeed it must be so to a man just out of so dreadful a fever. I also thank you for your very beautiful little poem on the King's recovery; it is one of the prettiest things I ever read, and I hope the king will live to fulfil the prophecy and die in peace; but at present, poor man, I understand he is poorly indeed, and

---

[1] John Boydell, engraver and printseller, for whose *Graphic Illustrations of the Works of Shakespeare* Blake had engraved a plate after Opie, dated 1803, for *Romeo and Juliet*, Act IV, Scene V.

[2] Frontispiece to Euler's *Elements of Algebra*, J. Johnson, London, 1797.

times threaten worse than ever. I must now express my sorrow and my hopes for our good Miss Poole, and so take my leave for the present, with the joint love of my good woman, who is still stiff-knee'd but well in other respects.

I am, dear Sir,
Yours most sincerely,
William Blake

4th May 1804

44. TO WILLIAM HAYLEY* 28 May 1804

Dear Sir,

I thank you heartily for your kind offer of reading, &c. I have read the book thro' attentively and was much entertain'd and instructed, but have not yet come to the *Life of Washington*. I suppose an American would tell me that Washington did all that was done before he was born, as the French now adore Buonaparte and the English our poor George; so the Americans will consider Washington as their god. This is only Grecian, or rather Trojan, worship, and perhaps will be revised [?] in an age or two. In the meantime I have the happiness of seeing the Divine countenance in such men as Cowper and Milton more distinctly than in any prince or hero. Mr. Phillips has sent a small poem; he would not tell the author's name, but desired me to inclose it for you with Washington's *Life*.

Mr. Carr[1] called on me, and I, as you desired, gave him a history of the reviewing business as far as I am acquainted with it. He desires me to express to you that he would heartily devote himself to the business in all its laborious parts, if you would take on you the direction; and he thinks it might be done with very little trouble to you. He is now going to Russia; hopes that the negotiations for this business are not wholly at an end, but that on his return he may still perform his best, as your assistant in it. I have delivered the letter to Mr. Edwards, who will give it immediately to Lady Hamilton. Mr. Walker I have again seen; he promises to collect numerous particulars concerning Romney and send them to you; wonders he has not had a line from you; desires me to assure you of his wish to give every information in his power. Says that I shall have *Lear and Cordelia* to copy if you desire it should be done; supposes that Romney was about eighteen when he painted it; it is therefore doubly interesting. Mr. Walker is truly an amiable man; spoke of Mr. Green[2]

[1] John (later Sir John) Carr (1772-1832), barrister of the Middle Temple and traveller.

[2] Thomas Greene (1737-1810), of Slyne, Lancaster, solicitor.

as the oldest friend of Romney, who knew most concerning him of any one; lamented the little difference that subsisted between you, speaking of you both with great affection. Mr. Flaxman has also promised to write all he knows or can collect concerning Romney, and send to you. Mr. Sanders has promised to write to Mr. J. Romney immediately, desiring him to give us liberty to copy any of his father's designs that Mr. Flaxman may select for that purpose; doubts not at all of Mr. Romney's readiness to send any of the cartoons to London you desire; if this can be done it will be all that could be wished. I spoke to Mr. Flaxman about choosing out proper subjects for our purpose; he has promised to do so. I hope soon to send you Flaxman's advice upon this article. When I repeated to Mr. Phillips your intention of taking the books you want from his shop, he made a reply to the following purpose: "I shall be very proud to have Mr. Hayley's name in my books, but please to express to him my hope that he will consider me as the sincere friend of Mr. Johnson, who is (I have every reason to say) both the most generous and honest man I ever knew, and with whose interest I should be so averse to interfere, that I should wish him to have the refusal first of anything before it should be offered to me, as I know the value of Mr. Hayley's connexion too well to interfere between my best friend and him." This Phillips spoke with real affection, and I know you will love him for it, and will also respect Johnson the more for such testimony; but to balance all this I must, in duty to my friend Seagrave, tell you that Mr. Rose repeated to me his great opinion of Mr. Johnson's integrity, while we were talking concerning Seagrave's printing; it is but justice, therefore, to tell you that I perceive a determination in the London booksellers to injure Seagrave in your opinion, if possible. Johnson may be very honest and very generous, too, where his own interest is concerned; but I must say that he leaves no stone unturn'd to serve that interest, and often (I think) unfairly; he always has taken care, when I have seen him, to rail against Seagrave, and I perceive that he does the same by Mr. Rose. Mr. Phillips took care to repeat Johnson's railing to me, and to say that the country printers could not do anything of consequence. Luckily he found fault with the paper which Cowper's *Life* is printed on, not knowing that it was furnish'd by Johnson. I let him run on so far as to say that it was scandalous and unfit for such a work; here I cut him short by asking if he knew who furnish'd the paper. He answered: "I hope Mr. J. did not." I assured him that he did, and here he left off, desiring me to tell you that the *Life of Washington* was not put to press till the 3rd of this month (May), and on the 13th he had deliver'd a dozen copies at Stationer's Hall, and by the 16th five hundred were out. This is swift work if literally true, but I am not apt to believe literally what booksellers say; and on comparing *Cowper* with *Washington*, must assert that, *except paper* (which is Johnson's fault), *Cowper* is far the best, both as to type and printing. Pray look at *Washington* as far as page 177, you will find that the type is smaller than from 177 to 308, the whole middle of the book being printed with a larger and better type than the two extremities; also it is carefully hot-pressed. I say thus much, being urged thereto by Mr. Rose's observing some defects in Seagrave's work, which I conceive were urged upon him by Johnson; and as to the time the booksellers would take to execute any work, I need only refer to the little job which Mr. Johnson was to get done for our friend Dally. He promised it in a fortnight, and it is now three months and is not yet completed. I could not avoid saying thus much in justice to our good Seagrave, whose replies to Mr. Johnson's aggravating letters have been represented to Mr. Rose in an unfair light, as I have no doubt; because Mr. Johnson has, at times, written such letters to me as would have called for the sceptre of Agamemnon rather than the tongue of Ulysses, and I will venture to give it as my settled opinion that if you suffer yourself to be persuaded to print in London you will be cheated every way; but, however, as some little excuse, I must say that in London every calumny and falsehood utter'd against another of the same trade is thought fair play. Engravers, Painters, Statuaries, Printers, Poets, we are not in a field of battle, but in a City of Assassinations. This makes your lot truly enviable, and the country is not only more beautiful on account of its expanded meadows, but also on account of its benevolent minds. My wife joins with me in the hearty wish that you may long enjoy your beautiful retirement.

I am, with best respects to Miss Poole, for whose health we constantly send wishes to our spiritual friends,

Yours sincerely,
William Blake

28 May 1804

P.S.—Mr. Walker says that Mr. Cumberland is right in his reckoning of Romney's age. Mr. W. says Romney was two years older than himself, consequently was born 1734.

Mr. Flaxman told me that Mr. Romney was three years in Italy; that he returned twenty-eight years since. Mr. Humphry,[1] the Painter, was in Italy the same time with Mr. Romney. Mr. Romney lodged at Mr. Richter's, Great Newport Street, before he went; took the house in Cavendish Square immediately on his return; but as Flaxman has promised to put pen to paper, you may expect a full account of all he can collect. Mr. Sanders does not know the time when Mr. R. took or left Cavendish Square house.

[1] Ozias Humphry (1742-1810), miniaturist.

45. TO WILLIAM HAYLEY 22 June 1804

Dear Sir,

I have got the three Sublime Designs of Romney now in my Lodgings, & find them all too Grand as well as too undefined for meer outlines; & indeed it is not only my opinion but that of Mr Flaxman & Mr Parker,[1] both of whom I have consulted, that to give a true Idea of Romney's Genius, nothing less than some Finish'd Engravings will do, as Outline intirely omits his chief beauties; but there are some which may be executed in a slighter manner than others, & Mr Parker, whose Eminence as an Engraver makes his opinion deserve notice, has advised that 4 should be done in the highly finished manner, & 4 in a less Finish'd—& on my desiring him to tell me for what he would undertake to Engrave One in Each manner, the size to be about 7 Inches by 5¼, which is the size of a Quarto printed Page, he answer'd: "30 Guineas the finish'd, & half the sum for the less finish'd; but as you tell me that they will be wanted in November, I am of opinion that if Eight different Engravers are Employ'd, the Eight Plates will not be done by that time; as for myself" (Note Parker now speaks), "I have to-day turned away a Plate of 400 Guineas because I am too full of work to undertake it, & I know that all the Good Engravers are so Engaged that they will be hardly prevail'd upon to undertake more than One of the Plates on so short a notice." This is Mr Parker's account of the matter, & perhaps may discourage you from the Pursuit of so Expensive an undertaking; it is certain that the Pictures deserve to be Engraved by the hands of Angels, & must not by any means be done in a careless or too hasty manner. The Price Mr Parker has affix'd to each is Exactly what I myself had before concluded upon. Judging as he did that if the Fuseli Shakespeare is worth 25 Guineas, these will be at least worth 30, & that the inferior ones cannot be done at any rate under 15.

Mr Flaxman advises that the best Engravers should be engaged in the work, as its magnitude demands all the Talents that can be procured.

Mr Flaxman named the following Eight as proper subjects for Prints:

1. The Vision of Atossa from Eschylus.
2. Apparition of Darius.
3. Black Ey'd Susan, a figure on the Sea shore embracing a Corse.
4. The Shipwreck, with the Man on Horseback &^c^., which I have.[2]

---

[1] James Parker; he was in partnership with Blake as printsellers and engraver, from 1784 to 1787.

[2] Engraved by Blake for Hayley's *Life of Romney*, 1809.

5. Hecate: a very fine thing indeed, which I have.
6. Pliny: very fine, but very unfinish'd, Which I have.
7. Lear & Cordelia, belonging to Mr Walker.
8. One other which I omitted to write down & have forgot, but think that it was a Figure with Children, which he call'd a Charity.

I write immediately on recieving the Above Information, because no time should be lost in this truly interesting business.

Richardson is not yet Published. My Head of Romney is in very great forwardness. Parker commends it highly. Flaxman has not yet seen it, but shall soon, & then you shall have a Proof of it for your remarks also. I hope by this time Flaxman has written to you, & that you will soon recieve such documents as will enable you to decide on what is to be done in our desirable & arduous task of doing Justice to our admired Sublime Romney. I have not yet been able to meet Mr Braithwaite at home, but intend very soon to call again, & (as you wish) to write all I can collect from him—be so good as to give me your Earliest decision on what would be safe & not too venturesome in the number of projected Engravings, that I may put it into a train to be properly Executed.

We both rejoice in the generous Paulina's return, with recover'd strength, to her delightful Villa; please to present our sincerest Affections to her. My Wife continues to get better, & joins me in my warmest love & acknowledgments to you, as do my Brother & Sister.

I am, dear Sir, Yours Sincerely,
William Blake

Sth Molton Street
22 June 1804

46. TO WILLIAM HAYLEY 16 July 1804

[*See the letter printed in full, pages* 933–4.]

47. TO WILLIAM HAYLEY* 7 August 1804

It is certainly necessary that the best artists that can be engaged should be employed on the work of Romney's Life. . . . Money flies from me. Profit never ventures upon my Threshold, tho' every other man's doorstone is worn down into the very Earth by the footsteps of the fiends of commerce. [*Extracts from sale catalogue.*]

48. TO WILLIAM HAYLEY* 9 August 1804

[Unpublished.]

Signed: W. & C. Blake

49. TO WILLIAM HAYLEY 28 September 1804

Dear Sir,

I hope you will Excuse my delay in sending the Books which I have had some time, but kept them back till I could send a Proof of the Shipwreck which I hope will please. It yet wants all its last & finishing touches, but I hope you will be enabled by it to judge of the Pathos of the Picture.

I send Washington's 2d Vol:—5 Numbers of Fuseli's Shakespeare, & two Vols. with a Letter from Mr Spilsbury,[1] with whom I accidentally met in the Strand: he says that he relinquish'd Painting as a Profession, for which I think he is to be applauded: but I concieve that he may be a much better Painter if he practises secretly & for amusement, than he could ever be if employ'd in the drudgery of fashionable daubing for a poor pittance of money in return for the sacrifice of Art & Genius: he says he never will leave to Practise the Art, because he loves it, & This Alone will pay its labour by Success, if not of money, yet of True Art, which is All.

I had the pleasure of a call from Mrs Chetwynd & her Brother, a Giant in body, mild & polite in soul, as I have, in general, found great bodies to be; they were much pleased with Romney's Designs. Mrs C. sent to me the two articles for you, & for the safety of which by the Coach I had some fears, till Mr Meyer[2] obligingly undertook to convey them safe: he is now, I suppose, enjoying the delights of the Turret of Lovely Felpham; please to give my affectionate compliments to him.

I cannot help suggesting an Idea which has struck me very forcibly, that the Tobit & Tobias[3] in your bedchamber would make a very beautiful Engraving, done in the same manner as the Head of Cowper,[4] after Lawrence. The Heads to be finish'd, & the figures left exactly in imitation of the first strokes of the Painter. The Expression of those truly Pathetic heads would thus be transmitted to the Public,

---

[1] Probably Jonathan Spilsbury (brother of John Spilsbury, the engraver), who exhibited portraits at the Royal Academy from 1776 to 1807.

[2] William Meyer, son of the miniaturist, who was Romney's friend.

[3] According to *Romney*, by Humphry Ward and W. Roberts (vol. II, p. 202), this picture was painted at Eartham, Hayley and his son serving as models.

[4] Engraved by Blake for Hayley's *Life of Cowper*, 1803.

a singular Monument of Romney's Genius in that Highest branch of Art.

I must now tell my wants, & beg the favour of some more of the needful: the favor of ten Pounds more will carry me thro' this Plate & the Head of Romney, for which I am already paid. You shall soon see a Proof of Him in a very advanc'd state. I have not yet proved it, but shall soon, when I will send you one. I rejoice to hear from Mr Meyer of Miss Poole's continued recovery. My wife desires with me her respects to you, & her, & to all whom we love, that is, to all Sussex.

I remain,

Your Sincere & Obliged Hble Servant,

Will Blake

Sth Molton St

28 Septr 1804

50. TO WILLIAM HAYLEY* 23 October 1804

Dear Sir,

I received your kind letter with the note to Mr. Payne, and have had the cash from him. I should have returned my thanks immediately on receipt of it, but hoped to be able to send, before now, proofs of the two plates, the *Head* of R[omney] and the *Shipwreck*, which you shall soon see in a much more perfect state. I write immediately because you wish I should do so, to satisfy you that I have received your kind favour.

I take the extreme pleasure of expressing my joy at our good Lady of Lavant's[1] continued recovery: but with a mixture of sincere sorrow on account of the beloved Councillor.[2] My wife returns her heartfelt thanks for your kind inquiry concerning her health. She is surprisingly recovered. Electricity is the wonderful cause; the swelling of her legs and knees is entirely reduced. She is very near as free from rheumatism as she was five years ago, and we have the greatest confidence in her perfect recovery.

The pleasure of seeing another poem from your hands has truly set me longing (my wife says I ought to have said us) with desire and curiosity; but, however, "Christmas is a-coming."

Our good and kind friend Hawkins[3] is not yet in town—hope soon to have the pleasure of seeing him, with the courage of conscious industry, worthy of his former kindness to me. For now! O Glory! and O Delight! I have entirely reduced that spectrous Fiend to his station, whose annoyance has been the ruin of my labours for the last

[1] Miss Harriet Poole.

[2] Samuel Rose.

[3] John Hawkins (1758-1841), youngest son of Thomas Hawkins of Trewin and St. Erith, Cornwall, M.P. for Grampound and F.R.S.

passed twenty years of my life. He is the enemy of conjugal love and is the Jupiter of the Greeks, an iron-hearted tyrant, the ruiner of ancient Greece. I speak with perfect confidence and certainty of the fact which has passed upon me. Nebuchadnezzar had seven times passed over him; I have had twenty; thank God I was not altogether a beast as he was; but I was a slave bound in a mill among beasts and devils; these beasts and these devils are now, together with myself, become children of light and liberty, and my feet and my wife's feet are free from fetters. O lovely Felpham, parent of Immortal Friendship, to thee I am eternally indebted for my three years' rest from perturbation and the strength I now enjoy. Suddenly, on the day after visiting the Truchsessian Gallery[1] of pictures, I was again enlightened with the light I enjoyed in my youth, and which has for exactly twenty years been closed from me as by a door and by window-shutters. Consequently I can, with confidence, promise you ocular demonstration of my altered state on the plates I am now engraving after Romney, whose spiritual aid has not a little conduced to my restoration to the light of Art. O the distress I have undergone, and my poor wife with me: incessantly labouring and incessantly spoiling what I had done well. Every one of my friends was astonished at my faults, and could not assign a reason; they knew my industry and abstinence from every pleasure for the sake of study, and yet—and yet—and yet there wanted the proofs of industry in my works. I thank God with entire confidence that it shall be so no longer—he is become my servant who domineered over me, he is even as a brother who was my enemy. Dear Sir, excuse my enthusiasm or rather madness, for I am really drunk with intellectual vision whenever I take a pencil or graver into my hand, even as I used to be in my youth, and as I have not been for twenty dark, but very profitable years. I thank God that I courageously pursued my course through darkness. In a short time I shall make my assertion good that I am become suddenly as I was at first, by producing the *Head of Romney* and the *Shipwreck* quite another thing from what you or I ever expected them to be. In short, I am now satisfied and proud of my work, which I have not been for the above long period.

If our excellent and manly friend Meyer is yet with you, please to make my wife's and my own most respectful and affectionate compliments to him, also to our kind friend at Lavant.

I remain, with my wife's joint affection,

Your sincere and obliged servant,

Will Blake

23 October 1804

[1] The Truchsessian Gallery was a collection of pictures brought to England by Joseph, Count Truchsess, and exhibited in London in August 1803, with a view to selling the pictures to a company for the benefit of the public.

51. TO WILLIAM HAYLEY 4 December 1804

[*See the letter printed in full, pages* 934–5.]

52. TO WILLIAM HAYLEY* 18 December 1804

Dear Sir,

I send, with some confidence, proofs of my two plates, having had the assistance and approbation of our good friend Flaxman. He approves much (I cannot help telling you so much) of the *Shipwreck*. Mrs. Flaxman also, who is a good connoisseur in engraving, has given her warm approbation, and to the plate of the *Portrait*, though not yet in so high finished a state. I am sure (mark my confidence), with Flaxman's advice, which he gives with all the warmth of friendship both to you and me, it must be soon a highly finished and properly finished print; but yet I must solicit for a supply of money, and hope you will be convinced that the labour I have used on the two plates has left me without any resource but that of applying to you. I am again in want of ten pounds; hope that the size and neatness of my plate of the *Shipwreck* will plead for me the excuse for troubling you before it can be properly called finished, though Flaxman has already pronounced it so. I beg your remarks also on both my performances, as in their present state they will be capable of very much improvement from a few lucky or well advised touches. I cannot omit observing that the price Mr. Johnson gives for the plates of Fuseli's *Shakespeare* (the concluding numbers of which I now send) is twenty-five guineas each. On comparing them with mine of the *Shipwreck*, you will perceive that I have done my duty, and put forth my whole strength.

Your beautiful and elegant daughter *Venusea*[1] grows in our estimation on a second and third perusal. I have not yet received the *History of Chichester*.[2] I mention this not because I would hasten its arrival before it is convenient, but fancy it may have miscarried. My wife joins me in wishing you a merry Christmas. Remembering our happy Christmas at lovely Felpham, our spirits seem still to hover

[1] A character in Hayley's *Triumph of Music*, Chichester, 1804.

[2] By Alexander Hay, Chichester, 1804.

round our sweet cottage and round the beautiful Turret. I have said *seem,* but am persuaded that distance is nothing but a phantasy. We are often sitting by our cottage fire, and often we think we hear your voice calling at the gate. Surely these things are real and eternal in our eternal mind and can never pass away. My wife continues well, thanks to Mr. Birch's Electrical Magic, which she has discontinued these three months.

I remain your sincere and obliged,
William Blake

53. TO WILLIAM HAYLEY 28 December 1804

Dear Sir,

The Death of so Excellent a Man as my Generous Advocate[1] is a Public Loss, which those who knew him can best Estimate, & to those who have an affection for him like Yours, is a Loss that only can be repair'd in Eternity, where it will indeed with such abundant felicity, in the meeting Him a Glorified Saint who was a Suffering Mortal, that our Sorrow is swallow'd up in Hope. Such Consolations are alone to be found in Religion, the Sun & the Moon of our Journey; & such sweet Verses as yours in your last beautiful Poem must now afford you their full reward.

Farewell, Sweet Rose! thou hast got before me into the Celestial City. I also have but a few more Mountains to pass: for I hear the bells ring & the trumpets sound to welcome thy arrival among Cowper's Glorified Band of Spirits of Just Men made Perfect.

Now, My Dear Sir, I will thank you for the transmission of ten Pounds to the Dreamer over his own Fortunes: for I certainly am that Dreamer; but tho' I dream over my own Fortunes, I ought not to Dream over those of other Men, & accordingly have given a look over my account Book, in which I have regularly written down Every Sum I have reciev'd from you; & tho' I never can balance the account of obligations with you, I ought to do my best at all times & in all circumstances. I find that you was right in supposing that I had been paid for all I have done; but when I wrote last requesting ten pounds, I thought it was Due on the Shipwreck (which it was), but I did not advert to the Twelve Guineas which you Lent Me when I made up 30 Pounds to pay our Worthy Seagrave in part of his Account. I am therefore that 12 Guineas in your Debt: Which If I had consider'd, I should have used more consideration, & more ceremony also, in so serious an affair as the calling on you for more Money; but, however, your kind answer to my Request makes me Doubly Thank you.

[1] Samuel Rose.

The two Cartoons[1] which I have of Hecate & Pliny are very unequal in point of finishing: the Pliny in [is] a Sketch, tho' admirably contrived for an Effect equal to Rembrandt. But the Hecate is a finish'd Production, which will call for all the Engraver's nicest attention; indeed it is more finish'd than the Shipwreck; it is every body['s] favourite who have seen it, & they regularly prefer it to the Shipwreck as a work of Genius. As to the [Plates *del.*] Price of the Plates, Flaxman declares to me that he will not pretend to set a price upon Engraving. I think it can only be done by Some Engraver. I consulted Mr Parker on the Subject before I decided on the Shipwreck, & it was his opinion, & he says it still is so, that a Print of that size cannot be done under 30 Guineas, if finish'd, &, if a Sketch, 15 Guineas; as, therefore, Hecate must be a Finish'd Plate, I consider 30 Guineas as its Price, & the Pliny 15 Guineas.

Our Dear Friend Hawkins is out of Town, & will not return till April. I have sent to him, by a parcel from Col. Sibthorpe's,[2] your Desirable Poetical Present for Mrs Hawkins. His address is this—To John Hawkins, Esqr., Dallington, near Northampton. Mr Edwards is out of Town likewise.

I am very far from shewing the Portrait of Romney as a finish'd Proof; be assured that with our Good Flaxman's good help, & with your remarks on it in addition, I hope to make it a Supernaculum. The Shipwreck, also, will be infinitely better the next proof. I feel very much gratified at your approval of my Queen Catherine: beg to observe that the Print of Romeo & the Apothecary[3] annex'd to your copy is a shamefully worn-out impression, but it was the only one I could get at Johnson's. I left a good impression of it when I left Felpham last in one of Heath's Shakespeare: you will see that it is not like the same Plate with the worn out Impression. My Wife joins me in love & in rejoicing in Miss Poole's continued health. I am, dear Sir,

Yours sincerely,
Will Blake

Sth Molton Street
28 Decr 1804

P.S. I made a very high finish'd Drawing of Romney as a Companion to my drawing of the head of Cowper (you remember), with which Flaxman is very much satisfied, & says that when my Print is like that I need wish it no better, & I am determin'd to make it so at least.

W. B.

---

[1] By Romney.
[2] Colonel Humphrey Waldo Sibthorp, father-in-law of John Hawkins.
[3] These two plates were engraved by Blake after Fuseli for *The Plays of Shakespeare*, ed. Alexander Chalmers, 1805.

54. TO WILLIAM HAYLEY 19 January 1805

Saturday

Dear Sir,

I at length send the Books which I have in vain call'd for at the Publisher's[1] 3 several times; but his removal from St Pauls to a noble House in Bridge Street Blackfriars perhaps hinder'd his sending & perhaps his wish that I might again call. I have however seen him this morning, & he has in the most open & explicit manner offer'd his service to you Expressing his desire that I will repeat to you his regret that your last beautiful Poem was not Publish'd in the Extensive way (I speak his own words) that a Poem of Confessedly the first Poet of England ought to be given to the Public (speaking so I must own he won my heart). He said I knew that Dodsley was Mr Hayley's Publisher, but hope that as Mr D. is dead & if Mr H. has no Engagement with any London Bookseller I may myself be appointed by him in so honourable a concern as the Publication of his Labours. He then Proceeded to find fault with the Printing of our friend the Chichester Printer. Here I consider'd it my duty to interfere. I express'd my own respect for our Good Seagrave & said I knew your chief intentions in Employing him were 1st to Encourage a Worthy Man & 2^d For the Honour of Chichester. Mr P. immediately replied, If Mr Hayley should think fit to employ me as his Publisher I should have no objection but a pleasure in employing his Printer & have no doubt I could be of Service to him in many ways, but I feel for the Honour of London Booksellers & consider them as losing a great deal of Honour in Losing the first Publication of any work of Mr Hayley's & the Public likewise are deprived of the advantage of so extensive a diffusal as would be promoted by the methods which they use to Publish & disperse Copies into all parts to a very great amount. He then said: If Mr Hayley is willing to dispose of this his New Poem I will Purchase it & at his own Price or any other of his Works—For I do assure you I feel it a duty to my Profession that I should do my Endeavour to give Mr Hayley's works the first rate Elegance in Printing & Paper as they hold the First in internal value. I then said, Is it agreeable to you that I repeat what you have said to me, To Mr Hayley, or will you yourself, for I dare say he will be much pleas'd to hear from you, but said I, I will if you wish (as I shall write soon) give him (as near as I can remember) what you have said, & hope that he will see the matter in the light you do—He desired I would, expressing (for which I thank him) confidence in my discretion—Such was our conversation as near as I can recollect, I thought it best to keep

---

[1] Richard Phillips.

silent as to anything like a hint of a proposal relating to Edwd 1st or the Ballads having come from you; accordingly I did not say that I knew of any Poem, but left all to you intirely. I do think from the Liberality of this Enterprizing Man that all Parties, I mean our Friend Seagrave together with the Author & Publisher (& also the Public), may be mutually & extensively benefitted. His connexions are Universal; his present House is on the most noble scale & will be in some measure a Worthy Town Vehicle for your Beautiful Muse. But Mr Phillips said, Mr Hayley shall have whatever I publish sent to him if he pleases & he may return them when he has read them. Such is his determination to do every thing to engage himself to you if possible. He desired I would present you from him with the little volume of poems inclos'd; they are by a Lady of Fortune. I suppose he sends it as a specimen of Printing. P's chief objection to the manner in which the Triumphs of Music[1] are printed—were the strong Metal Rules at the Ends of the Canto's, but he confess'd to me that the first Page of the Poem was beautifully executed & could not be better done.

Pray might I not shew Phillips the four Numbers of Ballads? or will you write to him? or will you think it best to commission me to answer him? whatever you command I will zealously perform, & depend upon it I will neither Do nor say but as you Direct.

I feel extremely happy that you think My Prints will do me Credit & at the very idea of another journey to Sweet Felpham. O that I could but bring Felpham to me or go to her in this World as easy as I can in that of Affection & Remembrance. I feel it is necessary to be very circumspect how we advance with Romney; his best Works only ought to be engraved for your Work.

Pray accept My & My Wife's sincerest affection & believe me to remain Yours sincerely

Will Blake

Sth Molton Street
19 Jany 1805

55. TO WILLIAM HAYLEY* 22 January 1805

Dear Sir,

I hope this letter will outstrip Mr. Phillips', as I sit down to write immediately on returning from his house. He says he is agreeable to every proposal you have made, and will himself immediately reply to you. I should have supposed him mad if he had not: for such clear

---

[1] *The Triumph of Music* by William Hayley, Chichester, 1804.

and generous proposals as yours to him he will not easily meet from anyone else. He will, of course, inform you what his sentiments are of the proposal concerning the three dramas. I found it unnecessary to mention anything relating to the purposed application of the profits, as he, on reading your letter, expressed his wish that you should yourself set a price, and that he would, in his letter to you, explain his reasons for wishing it. The idea of publishing one volume a year he considers as impolitic, and that a handsome general edition of your works would be more productive. He likewise objects to any periodical mode of publishing any of your works, as he thinks it somewhat derogatory, as well as unprofitable. I must now express my thanks for your generous manner of proposing the *Ballads* to him on my account, and inform you of his advice concerning them; and he thinks that they should be published *all together* in a volume the size of the small edition of the *Triumphs of Temper*, with six or seven plates.[1] That one thousand copies should be the first edition, and, if we choose, we might add to the number of plates in a second edition. And he will go equal shares with me in the expense and the profits, and that Seagrave is to be the printer. That we must consider all that has been printed as lost, and begin anew, unless we can apply some of the plates to the new edition. I consider myself as only put in trust with this work, and that the copyright is for ever yours. I therefore beg that you will not suffer it to be injured by my ignorance, or that it should in any way be separated from the grand bulk of your literary property. Truly proud I am to be in possession of this beautiful little estate; for that it will be highly productive I have no doubt, in the way now proposed; and I shall consider myself a robber to retain more than you at any time please to grant. In short, I am tenant at will, and may write over my door, as the poor barber did, Money for live here.

I entreat your immediate advice what I am to do, for I would not for the world injure this beautiful work, and cannot answer P.'s proposal till I have your directions and commands concerning it; for he wishes to set about it immediately, and has desired that I will give him my proposal concerning it in writing.

I remain, dear Sir,
Your obliged and affectionate
Will Blake

22 January 1805

---

[1] *Ballads,* by William Hayley, Esq., founded on Anecdotes relating to Animals, with [five] Prints designed and engraved by William Blake. Chichester: printed by J. Seagrave, for Richard Phillips, Bridge Street, Blackfriars, London, 1805, 8°.

56. TO WILLIAM HAYLEY 25 April 1805

Friday

Dear Sir,

This Morning I have been with Mr Phillips & have entirely settled with him the plan of Engraving for the new Edition of the Ballads. The Prints 5 in Number I have Engaged to finish by 28 May: they are to be as highly finish'd as I can do them, the Size the same as the Serena plates,[1] the Price 20 Guineas Each, half to be paid by P— The Subjects I cannot do better than those already chosen, as they are the most eminent among Animals Viz. The Lion, The Eagle, The Horse, The Dog. Of the Dog Species the Two Ballads are so pre-eminent & my Designs for them please me so well that I have chosen that design in our Last Number of the Dog & Crocodile, & that of the Dog defending his dead Master from the Vultures; of these five I am making little high finish'd Pictures the size the Engravings are to be, & am hard at it to accomplish in time what I intend. Mr P— says he will send Mr Seagrave the Paper directly.

The Journeyman Printers throughout London are at War with their Masters & are likely to get the better. Each Party meet to consult against the other; nothing can be greater than the Violence on both sides. Printing is suspended in London Except at private Presses. I hope this will become a source of Advantage to our Friend Seagrave.

The Idea of Seeing an Engraving of Cowper by the hand of Caroline Watson[2] is, I assure you, a pleasing one to me; it will be highly gratifying to see another Copy by another hand & not only gratifying, but Improving, which is better.

The Town is Mad. Young Roscius[3] like all Prodigies is the talk of Every Body. I have not seen him & perhaps never may. I have no curiosity to see him, as I well know what is within the compass of a boy of 14, & as to Real Acting it is Like Historical Painting, No Boy's Work.

Fuseli is made Master of the Royal Academy. Banks[4] the Sculptor is Gone to his Eternal Home. I have heard that Flaxman means to give a Lecture on Sculpture at the Royal Academy on the Occasion

---

[1] i.e. the six plates engraved by Blake for Hayley's *Triumphs of Temper*, twelfth edition, Chichester, 1803, from designs by Maria Flaxman. Serena was the heroine of Hayley's poem.

[2] Caroline Watson (1761-1814) engraved for the octavo edition of Hayley's *Life of Cowper* the crayon portrait of the poet engraved by Blake for the quarto edition of 1803, vol. II.

[3] Master Betty, i.e. William Henry West Betty (1791-1874), actor from 1803 to 1864.

[4] Thomas Banks, R.A., had died on 2 February 1805.

of Banks' Death; he died at the Age of 75 of a Paralytic Stroke. Now I concieve Flaxman stands without a competitor in Sculpture.

I must not omit to tell you that on leaving Mr Phillips I ask'd if he had any Message to you as I meant to write immediately; he said Give my best Respects & tell Mr Hayley that I wish very much to be at work for him. But perhaps I ought to tell you what he said to me previous to this in the course of our Conversation; his words were, I feel, somewhat Embarras'd at the Idea of setting a value on any work of Mr Hayley's & fear that he will wish me to do so. I asked him how a Value was set on any Literary work; he answer'd The Probable sale of the work would be the measure of Estimating the Profits & that would lead to a Valuation of the Copy right. This may be of no Consequence, but I could not omit telling it you.

My Wife Continues in health & desires to join me in every Grateful Wish to you & to our Dear Respected Miss Poole.

I remain
Yours with Sincerity
William Blake

P.S. Your Desire that I should write a little Advertisement[1] at the Beginning of the Ballads has set my Brains to work & at length produc'd the following. Simplicity, as you desired has been my first object. I send it for your Correction or Condemnation, begging you to supply its deficiency or to New Create it according to your wish.

The Public ought to be inform'd that [The following *del.*] These Ballads were the Effusions of Friendship to Countenance what their Author is kindly pleased to call Talents for Designing and to relieve my more laborious [employment *del.*] engagement of Engraving those Portraits which accompany The Life of Cowper. Out of a number of Designs I have selected Five [and] hope that the Public will approve of my rather giving few highly labour'd Plates than a greater number & less finish'd. If I have succeeded in these more may be added at Pleasure.

Will Blake

57. TO WILLIAM HAYLEY* 17 May 1805

"Reading in the Bible of the Eyes of the Almighty, I could not help putting up a petition for yours." Speaks of his rough sketch of an advertisement (the direction of which has been improved).... "if any of my writings should hereafter appear before the Public, they will fall far short of this first specimen." [*Extracts from sale catalogue.*]

---

[1] This was not printed in the book.

58. TO WILLIAM HAYLEY* 4 June 1805

Dear Sir,

I have fortunately, I ought to say providentially, discovered that I have engraved one of the plates for that ballad of *The Horse* which is omitted in the new edition; time enough to save the extreme loss and disappointment which I should have suffered had the work been completed without that ballad's insertion. I write to entreat that you would contrive so as that my plate may come into the work, as its omission would be to me a loss that I could not now sustain, as it would cut off ten guineas from my next demand on Phillips, which sum I am in absolute want of; as well as that I should lose all the labour I have been at on that plate, which I consider as one of my best; I know it has cost me immense labour. The way in which I discovered this mistake is odd enough. Mr. Phillips objects altogether to the insertion of my Advertisement, calling it an appeal to charity, and says it will hurt the sale of the work, and he sent to me the last sheet by the penny (that is, the twopenny) post, desiring that I would forward it to Mr. Seagrave. But I have inclosed it to you, as you ought and must see it. I am no judge in these matters, and leave all to your decision,[1] as I know that you will do what is right on all hands. Pray accept my and my wife's sincerest love and gratitude.

Will Blake

59. TO WILLIAM HAYLEY 27 November 1805

Dear Sir,

Mr Cromek the Engraver came to me desiring to have some of my Designs; he nam'd his Price & wish'd me to Produce him Illustrations of The Grave[2], A Poem by Robert Blair; in consequence of this I produced about twenty Designs which pleas'd so well that he, with the same liberality with which he set me about the Drawings, has now set me to Engrave them. He means to Publish them by Subscription with the Poem as you will see in the Prospectus which he sends you in the same Pacquet with the Letter. You will, I know, feel as you always do on such occasions, not only warm wishes to promote the Spirited Exertions of my Friend Cromek. You will be pleased to see that the Royal Academy have Sanctioned the Style of work. I now have reason more than ever to lament your Distance from London, as that alone has prevented our Consulting you in our Progress,

---

1 The Advertisement did not appear.

2 Blair's *Grave*, 4°, 1808, with twelve designs engraved by Schiavonetti after Blake.

which is but of about two Months Date. I cannot give you any Account of our Ballads, for I have heard nothing of Phillips this Age. I hear them approved by the best, that is, the most serious people, & if any others are displeas'd it is also an argument of their being Successful as well as Right, of which I have no Doubt; for what is Good must Succeed first or last, but what is bad owes success to something beside or without itself, if it has any.

My Wife joins me in anxious wishes for your Health & Happiness, desiring to be particularly remember'd by You & our Good Lady Paulina over a dish of Coffee. I long to hear of your Good Health & that of our dear friend of Lavant & of all our friends (to whom we are grateful & desire to be remember'd) In Sussex.

I am, Dear Sir,
Yours ever Affectionately,
Will. Blake

27 Nov[r].
1805

60. TO WILLIAM HAYLEY 11 December 1805

Dear Sir,

I cannot omit to Return you my sincere & Grateful Acknowledgments for the kind Reception you have given my New Projected Work. It bids fair to set me above the difficulties I have hitherto encounter'd. But my Fate has been so uncommon that I expect Nothing. I was alive & in health & with the same Talents I now have all the time of Boydell's, Macklin's, Bowyer's, & other Great Works. I was known by them & was look'd upon by them as Incapable of Employment in those Works; it may turn out so again, notwithstanding appearances. I am prepared for it, but at the same time sincerely Grateful to Those whose Kindness & Good opinion has supported me thro' all hitherto. You, Dear Sir, are one who has my Particular Gratitude, having conducted me thro' Three that would have been the Darkest Years that ever Mortal Suffer'd, which were render'd thro' your means a Mild & Pleasant Slumber. I speak of Spiritual Things, Not of Natural; Of Things known only to Myself & to Spirits Good & Evil, but Not known to Men on Earth. It is the passage thro' these Three Years that has brought me into my Present State, & *I know* that if I had not been with You I must have Perish'd. Those Dangers are now Passed & I can see them beneath my feet. It will not be long before I shall be able to present the full history of my Spiritual Sufferings to the Dwellers upon Earth & of the Spiritual Victories obtain'd for me by my Friends. Excuse this Effusion of the Spirit from One who cares little for this World, which passes away, whose Happiness is Secure in Jesus our Lord, & who looks for

Suffering till the time of complete deliverance. In the mean While I am kept Happy, as I used to be, because I throw Myself & all that I have on our Saviour's Divine Providence. O What Wonders are the Children of Men! Would to God that they would consider it, That they would consider their Spiritual Life, Regardless of that faint Shadow call'd Natural Life, & that they would Promote Each other's Spiritual Labours, Each according to its Rank, & that they would know that Recieving a Prophet As a Prophet is a Duty which If omitted is more Severely Avenged than Every Sin & Wickedness beside. It is the Greatest of Crimes to Depress True Art & Science. I know that those who are dead from the Earth, & who mock'd & Despised the Meekness of True Art (and such, I find, have been the situations of our Beautiful, Affectionate Ballads), I know that such Mockers are Most Severely Punish'd in Eternity. I know it, for I see it & dare not help. The Mocker of Art is the Mocker of Jesus. Let us go on, Dear Sir, following his Cross: let us take it up daily, Persisting in Spiritual Labours & the Use of that Talent which it is Death to Bury, & of that Spirit to which we are called.

Pray Present My Sincerest Thanks to our Good Paulina, whose kindness to Me shall recieve recompense in the Presence of Jesus. Present also my Thanks to the Generous Seagrave, In whose debt I have been too long, but percieve that I shall be able to settle with him soon what is between us. I have deliver'd to Mr Sanders the 3 Works of Romney, as Mrs Lambert told me you wished to have them —a very few touches will finish the Shipwreck. Those few I have added upon a Proof before I parted with the Picture. It is a Print that I feel proud of, on a New inspection. Wishing you & All Friends in Sussex a Merry & a Happy Christmas,

I remain, Ever Your Affectionate,

Will Blake & his Wife Catherine Blake

Sth Molton Street

Decembr 11. 1805

61. TO RICHARD PHILLIPS[1]* June 1806

Sir,

My indignation was exceedingly moved at reading a criticism in *Bell's Weekly Messenger* (25th May) on the picture of Count Ugolino, by Mr. Fuseli, in the Royal Academy Exhibition; and your Magazine being as extensive in its circulation as that Paper, and as it also must from its nature be more permanent, I take the advantageous opportunity to counteract the widely diffused malice which has for

[1] Richard Phillips, publisher, and proprietor of *The Monthly Magazine*. This letter appeared in the number for 1 July 1806.

many years, under the pretence of admiration of the arts, been assiduously sown and planted among the English public against true art, such as it existed in the days of Michael Angelo and Raphael. Under pretence of fair criticism and candour, the most wretched taste ever produced has been upheld for many, very many years; but now, I say, now its end is come. Such an artist as Fuseli is invulnerable, he needs not my defence; but I should be ashamed not to set my hand and shoulder, and whole strength, against those wretches who, under pretence of criticism, use the dagger and the poison.

My criticism on this picture is as follows: Mr. Fuseli's Count Ugolino is the father of sons of feeling and dignity, who would not sit looking in their parent's face in the moment of his agony, but would rather retire and die in secret, while they suffer him to indulge his passionate and innocent grief, his innocent and venerable madness and insanity and fury, and whatever paltry, cold-hearted critics cannot, because they dare not, look upon. Fuseli's Count Ugolino is a man of wonder and admiration, of resentment against man and devil, and of humiliation before God; prayer and parental affection fill the figure from head to foot. The child in his arms, whether boy or girl signifies not (but the critic must be a fool who has not read Dante, and who does not know a boy from a girl), I say, the child is as beautifully drawn as it is coloured—in both, inimitable! and the effect of the whole is truly sublime, on account of that very colouring which our critic calls black and heavy. The German flute colour, which was used by the Flemings (they call it burnt bone), has possessed the eye of certain connoisseurs, that they cannot see appropriate colouring, and are blind to the gloom of a real terror.

The taste of English amateurs has been too much formed upon pictures imported from Flanders and Holland; consequently our countrymen are easily brow-beat on the subject of painting; and hence it is so common to hear a man say: 'I am no judge of pictures.' But O Englishmen! know that every man ought to be a judge of pictures, and every man is so who has not been connoisseured out of his senses.

A gentleman who visited me the other day, said, "I am very much surprised at the dislike that some connoisseurs shew on viewing the pictures of Mr. Fuseli; but the truth is, he is a hundred years beyond the present generation." Though I am startled at such an assertion, I hope the contemporary taste will shorten the hundred years into as many hours; for I am sure that any person consulting his own eyes must prefer what is so supereminent; and I am as sure that any person consulting his own reputation, or the reputation of his country, will refrain from disgracing either by such ill-judged criticisms in future.

Yours,

Wm. Blake

62. TO RICHARD PHILLIPS 14 October 1807

Oct 14

Sir,

A circumstance has occurred which has again raised my Indignation.

I read in the Oracle & True Briton of Oct[r] 13, 1807, that a M[r] Blair,[1] a Surgeon, has, *with the Cold fury of Robespierre,* caused the Police to sieze upon the Person & Goods or Property of an Astrologer & to commit him to Prison. The Man who can Read the Stars often is opressed by their Influence, no less than the Newtonian who reads Not & cannot Read is opressed by his own Reasonings & Experiments. We are all subject to Error: Who shall say, Except the Natural Religionists, that we are not all subject to Crime?

My desire is that you would Enquire into this Affair & that you would publish this in your Monthly Magazine. I do not pay the postage of this Letter, because you, as Sheriff, are bound to attend to it.[2]

William Blake

17 S[th] Molton S[t]

63. TO GEORGE CUMBERLAND 19 December 1808

Dear Cumberland,

I am very much obliged by your kind ardour in my cause, & should immediately Engage in reviving my former pursuits of printing if I had not now so long been turned out of the old channel into a new one, that it is impossible for me to return to it without destroying my present course. New Vanities, or rather new pleasures, occupy my thoughts. New profits seem to arise before me so tempting that I have already involved myself in engagements that preclude all possibility of promising any thing. I have, however, the satisfaction to inform you that I have Myself begun to print an account of my various Inventions in Art, for which I have procured a Publisher,[3] & am determined to pursue the plan of publishing what I may get printed without disarranging my time, which in future must alone

---

[1] William Blair (1766-1822), surgeon to the Lock Hospital and other institutions.

[2] The letter is marked: "W. B. Rec[d]. Oct[r], 27th 1807. With Mr. P.'s Comps." It was not published in *The Monthly Magazine*.

[3] Nothing further is known of this projected work, unless perhaps the reference is to *A Descriptive Catalogue*, printed in 1809.

be devoted to Designing & Painting [alone *del.*]; when I have got my Work printed I will send it you first of any body; in the mean time, believe me to be

Your Sincere friend,
Will Blake

19 Decr 1808

64. TO OZIAS HUMPHRY c. 1809

Dear Sir,

You will see in this little work[1] the cause of difference between you & me; you demand of me to Mix two things that Reynolds has confess'd cannot be mixed. You will percieve that I not only detest False Art, but have the Courage to say so Publickly & to dare all the Power on Earth to oppose—Florentine & Venetian Art cannot exist together. Till the Venetian & Flemish are destroy'd, the Florentine & Roman cannot Exist; this will be shortly accomplish'd; till then I remain Your Grateful, altho' seemingly otherwise, I say Your Grateful & Sincere

William Blake

I inclose a ticket of admission if you should honour my Exhibition with a Visit.

65. TO JOSIAH WEDGWOOD[2] 8 September 1815

Sir,

I send Two more drawings with the First that I did, altered, having taken out that part which expressed the hole for the ladle.

It will be more convenient to me to make all the drawings first, before I begin Engraving them, as it will enable me also to regulate a System of working that will be uniform from beginning to end. Any Remarks that you may be pleased to make will be thankfully reciev'd by, Sir

Your humble Servant
William Blake

17 South Molton Street
8 Septemb^r 1815

---

[1] *A Descriptive Catalogue*, 1809.

[2] Josiah Wedgwood the younger, second son of the founder of the pottery works at Etruria, Staffordshire. Blake had been recommended to the Wedgwoods by Flaxman in order to make drawings and engravings of their pottery for a pictorial catalogue, intended only for their own use. Blake engraved 185 figures on 18 plates during the years 1815-1816, and 13 more plates were engraved by others. For further details of the transactions see *Blake Studies*, 1949, pp. 67-75.

66. TO DAWSON TURNER 9 June 1818

Sir,

I send you a List of the different Works you have done me the honour to enquire after—unprofitable enough to me, tho' Expensive to the Buyer. Those I Printed for Mr Humphry[1] are a selection from the different Books of such as could be Printed without the Writing,[2] tho' to the Loss of some of the best things. For they when Printed perfect accompany Poetical Personifications & Acts, without which Poems they never could have been Executed.

			£	s.	d.
America	18 Prints	folio	5	5	0
Europe	17 do.	folio	5	5	0
Visions &c	8 do.	folio	3	3	0
Thel	6 do.	Quarto	2	2	0
Songs of Innocence	28 do.	Octavo	3	3	0
Songs of Experience	26 do.	Octavo	3	3	0
Urizen	28 Prints	Quarto	5	5	0
Milton	50 do.	Quarto	10	10	0
12 Large Prints,[3] Size of Each about 2 feet by 1 & ½, Historical & Poetical, Printed in Colours		Each	5	5	0

These last 12 Prints are unaccompanied by any writing.

The few I have Printed & Sold are sufficient to have gained me great reputation as an Artist, which was the chief thing Intended. But I have never been able to produce a Sufficient number for a general Sale by means of a regular Publisher. It is therefore necessary to me that any Person wishing to have any or all of them should send me their Order to Print them on the above terms, & I will take care that they shall be done at least as well as any I have yet Produced.

---

[1] Ozias Humphry, the miniaturist.

[2] This probably refers to the two series of colour-printed designs known as the *Large* and *Small Book of Designs,* now in the Print Room at the British Museum. These consist for the most part of designs printed from the plates of the illuminated books, but omitting the text, and are thus incomplete, as Blake points out. The two books in the British Museum have now been broken up, so that the plates may be examined separately. Another series of the prints appears also to have been broken up, perhaps by Blake himself, and the contents scattered.

[3] These are the large colour-printed monotypes of which there is a set, lacking only two, in the Tate Gallery. The twelve subjects were "God creating Adam", "Lamech and his two Wives", "The Good and Evil Angels", "Elijah in the Fiery Chariot", "Ruth parting from Naomi", "Satan exulting over Eve", "Nebuchadnezzar", "Pity, like a naked newborn babe", "Christ appearing to the Apostles", "Newton", "The Lazar House", and "Hecate".

I am, Sir, with many thanks for your very Polite approbation of my works,

Your most obedient Servant,
William Blake

9 June 1818
17 South Molton Street

67. TO JOHN LINNELL [?] 11 October 1819

Dear Sir,

I will have the Pleasure of meeting you on Thursday at 12 O' Clock; it is quite as convenient to me as any other day. It appears to me that neither Time nor Place can make any real difference as to perfect Independence of Judgment, & If it is more Convenient to Mr Heaphy[1] for us to meet at his House let us accomodate him in what is Indifferent but not at all in what is of weight & moment to our Decision: hoping that I may meet you again in perfect Health & Happiness

I remain Dear Sir
Yours Truly
William Blake

Oct. 11 1819
Monday Evening

68. TO JOHN LINNELL 7 June 1825

Dear Sir,

I return you thanks for The Two Pounds you now send me. As to Sr T. Lawrence, I have not heard from him as yet, & hope that he has a good opinion of my willingness to appear grateful, tho' not able, on account of this abominable Ague, or whatever it is. I am in Bed & at Work; my health I cannot speak of, for if it was not for the Cold weather I think I should soon get about again. Great Men die equally with the little. I am sorry for L^d^ L^d^;[2] he is a man of very singular abilities, as also for the D[ean] of C[anterbury];[3] but perhaps, & I verily believe it, Every death is an improvement of the State of the

---

[1] Thomas Heaphy (1775-1835), engraver and water-colour artist.

[2] Probably Lord Lilford, who died soon after, on 4 July 1825.

[3] Dean Gerrard Andrewes, who died 2 June 1825.

Departed. I can draw as well a-Bed as Up, & perhaps better; but I cannot Engrave. I am going on with Dante,[1] & please myself.

I am, dr Sir, yours sincerely,
William Blake

Tuesday Night

69. TO JOHN LINNELL 1825

Dear Sir,

A return of the old shivering fit[2] came on this Morning as soon as I awaked & I am now in Bed, Better & as I think almost well. If I can possibly, I will be at Mr Lahee's[3] tomorrow Morning; these attacks are too serious at the time to permit me to be out of Bed, but they go off by rest, which seems to be All that I want. I send the Pilgrims[4] under your Care with the Two First Plates of Job.

I am, Yours Sincerely,
Willm Blake

12 O'clock
Wednesday

70. TO MRS. LINNELL 11 October 1825

Dear Madam,

I have had the Pleasure to see Mr Linnell set off safe in a very comfortable Coach, & I may say I accompanied him part of the way on his Journey in the Coach, for we both got in together & with another Passenger enter'd into Conversation, when at length we found that we were all three proceeding on our Journey; but as I had not paid & did not wish to pay for or take so long a Ride, we, with some difficulty, made the Coachman understand that one of his Passengers was unwilling to Go, when he obligingly permitted me to get out, to my great joy; hence I am now enabled to tell you that I

---

[1] That is, the water-colour drawings for Dante's *Divina Commedia* on which he was still engaged at the time of his death.

[2] Probably due to gallstones and inflammation of the gall-bladder from which he afterwards died.

[3] Lahee was a copper-plate printer, who was employed by Linnell to print the engravings for *Illustrations of the Book of Job*.

[4] Probably an impression of the engraving of Chaucer's Canterbury Pilgrims.

hope to see you on Sunday morning as usual, which I could not have done if they had taken me to Gloucester.

I am, d[r] Madam, yours Sincerely,
William Blake

Tuesday
11 October 1825

71. TO JOHN LINNELL 10 November 1825

Dear Sir,

I have, I believe, done nearly all that we agreed on &[c]. If you should put on your considering Cap, just as you did last time we met, I have no doubt that the Plates would be all the better for it. I cannot get Well & am now in Bed, but seem as if I should be better to-morrow; rest does me good. Pray take care of your health this wet weather, & tho' I write, do not venture out on such days as to-day has been. I hope a few more days will bring us to a conclusion.

I am, dear Sir,
Yours Sincerely,
William Blake

Thursday Evening
10 Nov[r] 1825
Fountain Court
Strand

72. TO JOHN LINNELL 1 February 1826

Dear Sir,

I am forced to write, because I cannot come to you, & this on two accounts. First, I omitted to desire you would come & take a Mutton chop with us the day you go to Cheltenham, & I will go with you to the Coach; also, I will go to Hampstead to see M[rs] Linnell on Sunday, but will return before dinner (I mean if you set off before that), & Second, I wish to have a Copy of Job to shew to M[r] Chantry.[1]

For I am again laid up by a cold in my stomach; the Hampstead Air, as it always did, so I fear it always will do this, Except it be the Morning air; & That, in my Cousin's[2] time, I found I could bear with safety & perhaps benefit. I believe my Constitution to be a good

[1] Francis Legatt Chantrey, R.A. (1781–1842), sculptor; knighted in 1835; founder of the Chantry Bequest.

[2] The identity of Blake's cousin is not known.

one, but it has many peculiarities that no one but myself can know. When I was young, Hampstead, Highgate, Hornsea, Muswell Hill, & even Islington & all places North of London, always laid me up the day after, & sometimes two or three days, with precisely the same Complaint & the same torment of the Stomach, Easily removed, but excruciating while it lasts & enfeebling for some time after. S[r] Francis Bacon would say, it is want of discipline in Mountainous Places. S[r] Francis Bacon is a Liar. No discipline will turn one Man into another, even in the least particle, & such discipline I call Presumption & Folly. I have tried it too much not to know this, & am very sorry for all such who may be led to such ostentatious Exertion against their Eternal Existence itself, because it is Mental Rebellion against the Holy Spirit, & fit only for a Soldier of Satan to perform.

Though I hope in a morning or two to call on you in Cirencester Place, I feared you might be gone, or I might be too ill to let you know how I am, & what I wish.

I am, dear Sir,
Yours Sincerely,
William Blake

Feb[y] 1. 1826

73. TO MRS. LINNELL ? February 1826

London Sunday Morning

Dear Madam,

M[r] Linnell will have arrived at his Journey's end before the time I now write; he set off Last night before Eight o'clock from the Angel Inn near St. Clements Church, Strand, on one of the Strongest & Handsomest Built Stages I ever Saw. I should have written Last Night, but as it would not come before now, I do as M[r] Linnell desired I would do by the First Stage. My Wife desires her kindest remembrances to you & I am

Yours sincerely,
Will[m] Blake

Excuse the writing. I have delayed too long.

74. TO JOHN LINNELL 31 March 1826

Friday Evening, March 31, 1826.

Dear Sir,

I have been very ill since I saw you, but am again well enough to go on with my work, but not well enough to venture out; the Chill of the weather soon drives me back into that shivering fit which must be avoided till the Cold is gone.

Mr Robinson[1] certainly did Subscribe for Prints only & not for Proofs,[2] for I remember that he offer'd to pay me Three Guineas for each of the Copies.

However, if the weather should be warm I will endeavour to come to you before Tuesday, but much fear that my present tottering state will hold me some time yet.

I am, dear Sir, yours sincerely
Willm Blake

75. TO JOHN LINNELL 19 May 1826

Dear Sir,

I have had another desperate Shivering Fit; it came on yesterday afternoon after as good a morning as I ever experienced. It began by a gnawing Pain in the Stomach, & soon spread a deathly feel all over the limbs, which brings on the shivering fit, when I am forced to go to bed, where I contrive to get into a little perspiration, which takes it quite away. It was night when it left me, so I did not get up, but just as I was going to rise this morning, the shivering fit attacked me again & the pain, with its accompanying deathly feel. I got again into a perspiration, & was well, but so much weaken'd that I am still in bed. This entirely prevents me from the pleasure of seeing you on Sunday at Hampstead, as I fear the attack again when I am away from home.

I am, dr Sir,
Yours sincerely,
William Blake

Friday Evening
May 19 1826

76. TO JOHN LINNELL 2 July 1826

My dearest Friend,

This sudden cold weather has cut up all my hopes by the roots. Every one who knows of our intended flight into your delightful Country concur in saying: "Do not Venture till summer appears again". I also feel Myself weaker than I was aware, being not able, as yet, to sit up longer than six hours at a time; & also feel the Cold too much to dare venture beyond my present precincts. My heartiest Thanks for your care in my accomodation, & the trouble you will yet have with me. But I get better & stronger every day, tho' weaker

---

[1] Henry Crabb Robinson.

[2] The engravings of *Illustrations of the Book of Job*.

in muscle & bone than I supposed. As to pleasantness of Prospect, it is All pleasant Prospect at North End. Mrs Hurd's[1] I should like as well as any—But think of the Expense & how it may be spared, & never mind appearances.

I intend to bring with me, besides our necessary change of apparel, Only My Book of Drawings from Dante & one Plate shut up in the Book. All will go very well in the Coach, which, at present, would be a rumble I fear I could not go thro'. So that I conclude another Week must pass before I dare Venture upon what I ardently desire—the seeing you with your happy Family once again, & that for a longer Period than I had ever hoped in my healthfull hours.

I am, dear Sir,
Yours most gratefully,
William Blake

77. TO JOHN LINNELL 5 July 1826

5 July 1826.

Dear Sir,

I thank you for the Receit of Five Pounds this Morning, & Congratulate you on the receit of another fine Boy; am glad to hear of Mrs Linnell's health & safety.

I am getting better every hour; my Plan is diet only; & if the Machine is capable of it, shall make an old man yet. I go on just as if perfectly well, which indeed I am, except in those paroxysms, which I now believe will never more return. Pray let your own health & convenience put all solicitude concerning me at rest. You have a Family, I have none; there is no comparison between our necessary avocations.

Believe me to be, d^r Sir,
Yours sincerely,
William Blake

78. TO JOHN LINNELL* 14 July 1826

Dear Sir,

I am so much better that I have hopes of fulfilling my expectation & desire of Visiting Hampstead. I am nevertheless very considerably weakened by the Last severe attacks. Pray remember me with kind Love to Mrs Linnell & her lovely Family.

Yours sincerely
William Blake

July 14: 1826

---

[1] Linnell's lodgings, before he went to Collins' Farm, North End, Hampstead.

To M[r] John Linnell

July 14 1826

I hereby Declare That M[r] John Linnell has Purchased of Me The Plates & Copy-right of Job; & the same is his sole Property.

Witness William Blake

Edw[d] Jno Chance[1]

79. TO JOHN LINNELL 16 July 1826

Dear Sir,

I have been, ever since taking D[r] Young's Addition to M[r] Fincham's Practise with me (the Addition is dandelion), In a species of delirium & in Pain too much for Thought. It is now passed, as I hope. But the moment I got ease of Body, began Pain of Mind, & that not a small one. It is about The Name of the Child,[2] which Certainly ought to be Thomas, after M[rs] Linnell's Father. It will be brutal, not to say worse, for it is worse In my opinion & on my Part. Pray Reconsider it, if it is not too late. It very much troubles Me, as a Crime in which I shall be [a *del.*] The Principal. Pray Excuse this hearty Expostulation, & believe me to be, Yours Sincerely,

William Blake

Sunday Afternoon
July 16. 1826

P.S. Fincham is a Pupil of Abernethy's;[3] this is what gives me great pleasure. I did not know it before yesterday, from M[r] Fincham.

80. TO JOHN LINNELL 29 July 1826

Dear Sir,

Just as I had become Well, that is, subdued the disease tho' not its Effects, Weakness &[c], Comes Another to hinder my Progress, call'd The Piles, which, when to the degree I have had them, are a most sore plague & on a Weak Body truly afflictive. These Piles have now also as I hope run their Period, & I begin to again feel returning Strength; on these accounts I cannot yet tell when I can start for

---

[1] A son-in-law of Linnell and print dealer, working at 20 London St., Fitzroy Square.

[2] It was finally named James, the next son being called William.

[3] John Abernethy (1764-1831), surgeon to St. Bartholomew's Hospital.

Hampstead like a young Lark without feathers. Two or Three days may be sufficient or not; all now will depend on my bones & sinews. Muscle I have none, but a few days may do, & have done, miracles in the Case of a Convalescent who prepares himself ardently for his return to Life & its Business among his Friends

With whom he makes his first Effort.

Dear Sir, Yours Ever,
William Blake

29 July 1826

81. TO JOHN LINNELL 1 August 1826

Dear Sir,

If this Notice should be too short for your Convenience, please to let me know. But finding myself Well enough to come, I propose to set out from here as soon after ten as we can on Thursday Morning. Our Carriage will be a Cabriolet, for tho' getting better & stronger, I am still incapable of riding in the Stage, & shall be, I fear, for some time, being only bones & sinews, All strings & bobbins like a Weaver's Loom. Walking to & from the Stage would be, to me, impossible; tho' I seem well, being entirely free from both pain & from that Sickness to which there is no name. Thank God, I feel no more of it, & have great hopes that the disease is Gone.

I am, dear Sir, Yours Sincerely,
William Blake

Aug[st] 1 1826

82. TO JOHN LINNELL 27 January 1827

Dear Sir,

I ought to have acknowledg'd the Receit of Five Pounds from you on 16 Jan[y] 1827; that part of your Letter in which you desired I would send an acknowledg'd it [*sic*] I did not see till the next morning, owing to its being writ on the outside double of your letter; neverthe-less I ought to have sent it, but must beg you to Excuse such Follies, which tho' I am enough asham'd of & hope to mend, can only do so at present by owning the Fault.

I am, dear Sir, yours Sincerely,
William Blake

Saturday Night
Jan[y] 27 1827

83. TO JOHN LINNELL February 1827

February, 1827.

Dear Sir,

I thank you for the Five Pounds recieved to day: am getting better every Morning, but slowly, as I am still feeble & tottering, tho' all the Symptoms of my complaint seem almost gone as the fine weather is very beneficial & comfortable to me. I go on, as I think, improving my Engravings of Dante more & more, & shall soon get Proofs of these Four which I have, & beg the favour of you to send me the two Plates of Dante which you have, that I may finish them sufficiently to make some shew of Colour & Strength.

I have thought & thought of the Removal & cannot get my Mind out of a state of terrible fear at such a step; the more I think, the more I feel terror at what I wish'd at first & thought it a thing of benefit & Good hope; you will attribute it to its right Cause—Intellectual Peculiarity, that must be Myself alone shut up in Myself, or Reduced to Nothing. I could tell you of Visions & dreams upon the Subject. I have asked & intreated Divine help, but fear continues upon me, & I must relinquish the step that I had wish'd to take, & still wish, but in vain.

Your Success in your Profession is above all things to me most gratifying; may it go on to the Perfection you wish & more. So wishes also

Yours Sincerely,
William Blake

84. TO JOHN LINNELL ? February 1827

Dear Sir,

I call'd this Morning for a Walk & brought my Plates with me to prevent the trouble of your Coming thro' Curiosity to see what I was about. I have got on very forward with 4 Plates, & am getting better or I could not have Come at all.

Yours,
Will[m] Blake

85. TO JOHN LINNELL 15 March 1827

Dear Sir,

This is to thank you for Two Pounds, now by me reciev'd on account. I have reciev'd a Letter from M[r] Cumberland, in which he says he will take one Copy of Job for himself, but cannot, as yet, find a Customer for one, but hopes to do somewhat by perseverance in his Endeavours; he tells me that it is too much Finish'd, or over Labour'd, for his Bristol Friends, as they think. I saw Mr Tatham,[1] Senr., yesterday; he sat with me above an hour, & look'd over the Dante; he express'd himself very much pleas'd with the designs as well as the Engravings. I am getting on with the Engravings & hope soon to get Proofs of what I am doing.

I am, dear Sir, Yours Sincerely,
William Blake

15 March 1827

86. TO MARIA DENMAN[2] 18 March 1827

Mr Blake's respectful Compliments to Miss Denman—has found 15 Proofs of The Hesiod:[3] as they are duplicates to others which he has, they are intirely at Miss Denman's Service if she will accept of them: what Proofs he has remaining are all Printed on both sides of the Paper & so are unfit for to make up a set, especially as many of the backs of the paper have on them impressions from other Plates for Booksellers, which he was employ'd about at the same time.

Wednesday Morning
18 March 1827
3 Fountain Court, Strand

87. TO JOHN LINNELL* 1827

Dear Sir,

I am still far from recovered, & dare not get out in the cold air. Yet I lose nothing by it. Dante goes on the better, which is all I care about.

Mr Butts is to have a Proof Copy for Three Guineas; this is his own decision, quite in Character. He called on me this Week.

Yours sincerely,
William Blake

---

[1] Charles Heathcote Tatham (1772-1842), architect; father of Frederick Tatham, who wrote a *Life of Blake*.

[2] Sister-in-law of John Flaxman.

[3] Blake had engraved 38 plates for Flaxman's *Compositions from the Works Days and Theogony of Hesiod*, London, 1817.

88. TO GEORGE CUMBERLAND 12 April 1827

Dear Cumberland,

I have been very near the Gates of Death & have returned very weak & an Old Man feeble & tottering, but not in Spirit & Life, not in The Real Man The Imagination which Liveth for Ever. In that I am stronger & stronger as this Foolish Body decays. I thank you for the Pains you have taken with Poor Job. I know too well that a great majority of Englishmen are fond of The Indefinite which they Measure by Newton's Doctrine of the Fluxions of an Atom, A Thing that does not Exist. These are Politicians & think that Republican Art is Inimical to their Atom. For a Line or Lineament is not formed by Chance: a Line is a Line in its Minutest Subdivisions: Strait or Crooked It is Itself & Not Intermeasurable with or by any Thing Else. Such is Job, but since the French Revolution Englishmen are all Intermeasurable One by Another, Certainly a happy state of Agreement to which I for One do not Agree. God keep me from the Divinity of Yes & No too, The Yea Nay Creeping Jesus, from supposing Up & Down to be the same Thing as all Experimentalists must suppose.

You are desirous I know to dispose of some of my Works & to make them Pleasin[g]. I am obliged to you & to all who do so. But having none remaining of all that I had Printed I cannot Print more Except at a great loss, for at the time I printed those things I had a whole House to range in: now I am shut up in a Corner therefore am forced to ask a Price for them that I scarce expect to get from a Stranger. I am now Printing a Set of the Songs of Innocence & Experience for a Friend at Ten Guineas which I cannot do under Six Months consistent with my other Work, so that I have little hope of doing any more of such things. The Last Work I produced is a Poem Entitled Jerusalem the Emanation of the Giant Albion, but find that to Print it will Cost my Time the amount of Twenty Guineas. One I have Finish'd. It contains 100 Plates but it is not likely that I shall get a Customer for it.[1]

As you wish me to send you a list with the Prices of these things they are as follows

	£	s	d
America	6.	6.	0
Europe	6.	6.	0
Visions &c	5.	5.	0
Thel	3.	3.	0
Songs of Inn. & Exp.	10.	10.	0
Urizen	6.	6.	0

[1] This is the unique coloured copy of *Jerusalem* now in the library of Mr. Paul Mellon.

The Little Card[1] I will do as soon as Possible but when you Consider that I have been reduced to a Skeleton from which I am slowly recovering you will I hope have Patience with me.

Flaxman[2] is Gone & we must All soon follow, every one to his Own Eternal House, Leaving the Delusive Goddess Nature & her Laws to get into Freedom from all Law of the Members into The Mind, in which every one is King & Priest in his own House. God send it so on Earth as it is in Heaven.

I am, Dear Sir, Yours Affectionately
William Blake

12 April 1827
N 3 Fountain Court Strand

89. TO JOHN LINNELL 25 April 1827

Dear Sir,

I am going on better Every day, as I think, both in hea[l]th & in work. I thank you for The Ten Pounds which I recieved from you this day, which shall be put to the best use; as also for the prospect of Mr Ottley's[3] advantageous acquaintance. I go on without daring to count on Futurity, which I cannot do without doubt & Fear that ruins Activity, & are the greatest hurt to an Artist such as I am. As to Ugolino,[4] &c, I never supposed that I should sell them; my Wife alone is answerable for their having Existed in any finish'd State. I am too much attach'd to Dante to think much of anything else. I have Proved the Six Plates, & reduced the Fighting devils ready for the Copper.[5] I count myself sufficiently Paid If I live as I now do, & only fear that I may be Unlucky to my friends, & especially that I may not be so to you.

I am, sincerely yours,
William Blake

25 April 1827

---

[1] A small engraved copper-plate, with a design surrounding the name of "Mr. Cumberland".

[2] Flaxman had died on 7 December 1826.

[3] William Young Ottley (1771-1836), author of a *History of Engraving*, Keeper of the Prints in the British Museum, 1833-1836.

[4] A tempera on a panel of "Ugolino with his Sons and Grandsons in Prison", now in my collection.

[5] "The Devils mauling each other" (*Inferno*, canto xxii, l. 136), one of the seven Dante engravings.

90. TO JOHN LINNELL 3 July 1827

Dear Sir,

I thank you for the Ten Pounds you are so kind as to send me at this time. My journey to Hampstead on Sunday brought on a relapse which is lasted till now. I find I am not so well as I thought. I must not go on in a youthful Style; however, I am upon the mending hand to-day, & hope soon to look as I did, for I have been yellow, accompanied by all the old Symptoms.

I am, dear Sir,
Yours Sincerely,
William Blake

3 July 1827

The Notes

POETICAL SKETCHES

¶Page 1. The poems and other pieces included under this title are not known to exist in MS. They were first printed for Blake himself in a thin octavo volume in 1783. The Preface attributed by J. T. Smith (*Nollekens and his Times*, 1828) to the "Rev Henry Mathew", that is the Rev. A. S. Mathew (see note to *An Island in the Moon*) is as follows: "The following "sketches were the production of untutored youth, commenced in his "twelfth, and occasionally resumed by the author till his twentieth year; "since which time, his talents having been wholly directed to the attainment "of excellence in his profession, he has been deprived of the leisure requis-"ite to such a revisal of these sheets, as might have rendered them less unfit "to meet the public eye.

"Conscious of the irregularities and defects to be found in almost every "page, his friends have still believed that they possessed a poetic originality, "which merited some respite from oblivion. These their opinions remain, "however, to be now reproved or confirmed by a less partial public."

The original edition is now rare, only twenty-two copies having been recorded. According to the Preface the poems were written between the ages of twelve and twenty, that is, in 1769-77; but "Gwin, King of Norway" may have been suggested by Chatterton's "Godred Crovan", not published with the *Poems* until 1778—or could Blake have seen it in *The Town and Country Magazine* in August 1769?

The *Poetical Sketches* were first reprinted in full by R. H. Shepherd in 1868, and many times by subsequent editors. They are here reprinted from the original edition, with some changes in punctuation and a few textual emendations. Various alterations made by Blake in one or more copies of the book are indicated in footnotes. See also my *Blake Studies*, 1949, p. 27.

¶ 9. *Mad Song*, line 7. *And the rustling birds of dawn*] in the original edition *birds* is printed *beds*, and this reading has been accepted by some of Blake's editors. The alteration to *birds* has, however, been made, apparently by Blake himself, in four copies of the book. Compare also page 35, "The Couch of Death," lines 2-3, "the birds of day were heard in their nests, "rustling in brakes and thickets."

¶ 14. *An Imitation of Spenser*, line 13 . . . *leasing nurse*] misprinted *Spencer* and *leesing nurse* in the original edition.

¶ 15. Ditto, line 41, *see*] wrongly altered to *sees* in former editions.

¶ 17. *Blind-man's Buff*, lines 61-70. *Such are the fortunes . . . fair play*] the punctuation of this loosely constructed passage is considerably altered from that of the original edition, in which the sense is obscure.

¶ 30. *King Edward the Third*, scene [5] line 6. *Death wons in cities' smoke*] some editors have altered *wons* to *roams*, but *wons* is a Spenserian word, meaning *dwells*, and may therefore be allowed to stand.

THEN SHE BORE PALE DESIRE

¶ 40. This fragment of metrical prose was probably composed about the same time as some of the prose pieces in the *Poetical Sketches*. It was first printed by W. M. Rossetti, divided into lines, in *The Monthly Review* for August, 1903, with the title "The Passions." It is here printed from the original MS, in the possession of Signora Rossetti Angeli until 1929 and now in the New York Public Library. The text begins with a lower-case letter, suggesting that the first part has been lost. Punctuation has been added.

WOE, CRIED THE MUSE

¶ 43. This fragment, which was first printed in the Nonesuch edition, 1925, is part of the same seven-page MS which contains the preceding piece. It is given without alteration, except that punctuation has been supplied.

AN ISLAND IN THE MOON

¶ 44. The incomplete burlesque novel, for which this title has been supplied from the opening sentence, has usually been supposed to have been written about 1784, and to have been intended as a satire on the society which Blake met at the house of the "Reverend Henry Mathew", to whom J. T. Smith (*Nollekens and his Times*, 1828) attributed the Advertisement in *Poetical Sketches*. Recently H. M. Margoliouth (*Notes & Queries*, 14 April, 1951) has shewn that Smith was in error. There was no such person as "Henry Mathew", Blake's friend being in reality the Reverend Anthony Stephen Mathew, minister of Percy Chapel, London. It is now seen to be unlikely that Blake's target in his satire was limited to the Mathews' circle. The characters have not been identified with certainty (for a number of possible suggestions see Erdman's *Prophet against Empire*, 1954, pp. 87–90), but it is possible that "Sipsop, the Pythagorean" is Thomas Taylor, the Platonist, and "Inflammable Gas" can scarcely be any other than Dr. Joseph Priestley. Prof. Foster Damon (*William Blake*, 1924, pp. 32-3) dated the satire about 1788 because it seemed to have led directly to the printing of *Songs of Innocence*, 1789. On the other hand, references to feminine fashions, such as balloon hats, seem to point very strongly to the years 1784-5. The entire piece was first printed, though very inaccurately, by E. J. Ellis in *The Real Blake*, 1907. An approximately accurate text was printed in the first Nonesuch edition, 1925. A revised and more accurate text is now given from the original MS in the Fitzwilliam Museum, Cambridge. It includes a number of readings of deleted passages, deciphered with the expert assistance of Mr. L. A. Holder, Curator of MSS in the Fitzwilliam Museum. Blake's long paragraphs have been broken up for easier reading; punctuation and capitals at the beginning of sentences have been supplied.

¶ 50. *Jack Hunter*] John Hunter (1728-1793), famous anatomist and surgeon to St. George's Hospital.

¶ 52. *John Taylor*] possibly a reference to John Taylor (1694-1761), dissenting minister, author of *The Scripture Doctrine of Original Sin*, 1740.

¶ 53. *Robinsons*] Mrs. Mary Robinson, known as "Perdita" (1758-1800), actress, author, and mistress of George IV when Prince of Wales; also a leader of fashions.

Mr Jacko] a performing monkey at Astley's Amphitheatre in 1784. Here used as a nickname for Richard Cosway, the painter (see Erdman, p. 88).

¶ 57. *Doctor South*] Robert South (1634-1716), celebrated divine; author of *Animadversions*, 1690, in which Sherlock was attacked.

Sherlock] William Sherlock (1641?- 1707), Dean of St. Paul's; author of *Practical Discourse concerning Death*, 1689.

Sutton] Thomas Sutton (1532-1611) coal owner and philanthropist; founder of the Charterhouse.

¶ 59. *Flogiston*] i.e. phlogiston, a hypothetical substance supposed to be contained in all combustible materials.

¶ 62. —*them Illuminating the Manuscript*] possibly a reference to Blake's method of illuminated printing, which he afterwards said was revealed to him by the spirit of his brother, Robert, in 1787 or 1788, and first used by him in 1788.

POEMS WRITTEN IN A COPY OF "POETICAL SKETCHES"

¶ 63. These three poems were found written, but not in Blake's hand, on the fly-leaves of a copy of the *Poetical Sketches*, which had belonged to Mrs. Flaxman. This MS was copied by me and described in *Notes & Queries*, 24 September, 1910.

Song 2nd by a young Shepherd] this poem is another version, probably earlier, of the "Laughing Song" in the *Songs of Innocence*, for which see p. 124.

ANNOTATIONS TO LAVATER'S APHORISMS

¶ 65. The volume containing these annotations belonged after Blake's death to his friend, Samuel Palmer; it was later in the library of Robert Hoe, and is now in the H. E. Huntington Library, California. On the title-page Blake has written his own name below that of Lavater, and round the two he has drawn the outline of a heart. The frontispiece to the book was engraved by Blake after Fuseli.

Blake's underlinings are here indicated by italics; he usually did not draw his pen beneath the beginnings and ends of the lines he wished to mark, but the italics are given here as if he had done so, his intention being clear. He has also often put a cross in the margin with the words *uneasy*, *false*, etc. Some of the annotations were printed by Gilchrist, and they were given, almost in full, though very inaccurately, by E. J. Ellis in *The Real Blake*, 1907. The present text was very carefully collated with the original in 1924 by Mr. Clifford Blake Clapp, then reviser in the H. E. Huntington Library.

¶ 65. *Aphorisms 1 & 2*] Blake's comment refers to both aphorisms.

ANNOTATIONS TO SWEDENBORG'S WISDOM OF ANGELS CONCERNING DIVINE LOVE AND DIVINE WISDOM

¶ 89. The volume containing these annotations is now in the library of the British Museum. After Blake's death it was in the possession of Frederick Tatham. In 1876 it belonged to J. R. P. Kirby, by whom it was lent for exhibition at the Burlington Fine Arts Club in that year.

The notes are all in pencil, and those on the fly-leaves have been rubbed out so that they are only partly decipherable. An attempt to read the remainder with the help of ultraviolet light has been unsuccessful. The greater part of the notes were given by E. J. Ellis in *The Real Blake*, 1907, though with many inaccuracies. The present text has been transcribed and corrected from the original MS.

. . . *it is pernicious*] printed as *it is Experience* in the Nonesuch edition, 1925. The present reading, given by Prof. S. Foster Damon, is probably correct.

THERE IS NO NATURAL RELIGION, *First and Second Series*

¶ 97. These two brief series of aphorisms are etched on nineteen small copper-plates, including title-page and frontispieces, the prints being touched with water-colours. The plates probably represent Blake's first experiments in his method of illuminated printing. He never issued a complete set of either series, the twelve examples that are known consisting of only eight to fourteen plates, which are variously arranged.

The aphorisms have been printed by several editors since 1886 in part or in full. The text of ten of the plates is here printed from the example (Copy A) in the British Museum Print Room, the remainder from the unique examples in the Pierpont Morgan Library and my collection (Copy L).

Both these series and the third, *All Religions are One*, were dated c. 1789 in the Nonesuch edition, 1925; this was an error, since Blake's note on his last plates, *The Ghost of Abel*, that "Blake's Original Stereotype was 1788" must be understood to refer to these brief treatises.

ALL RELIGIONS ARE ONE

¶ 98. The history of this series of aphorisms is unknown, but the prints resemble in general character those of *There is No Natural Religion*, and they are believed to belong to the same period. Examples of the title-page are in my collection and in the Victoria and Albert Museum. The only prints of the other plates were formerly in the collection of John Linnell and are now in the H. E. Huntington Library, California. The text was first printed by Ellis and Yeats in the *Works*, 1893, and subsequently by various editors. It is here taken from the photographic reproductions which appeared in my *Bibliography of Blake*, 1921.

TIRIEL

¶ 99. This, the earliest of Blake's symbolic works, was written before *The Book of Thel*, i.e. about 1789, as was shewn by Sampson in 1905; it was never transferred to copper-plates. The MS, which is written on eight quarto leaves, was acquired by the Manuscript Department of the British Museum in 1909. It had been in Mrs. Gilchrist's possession about the year 1863, and was used by W. M. Rossetti in 1874, but afterwards disappeared until it was found again in 1903.

The text was first printed by W. M. Rossetti in 1874, and subsequently by various editors. The present text has been collated with the original MS. The MS is not decorated; twelve sepia drawings illustrating the poem are in existence but have been dispersed.

Tiriel, a name probably derived from Cornelius Agrippa's *Occult Philosophy,* is a blind tyrant, whose prototype is likely to have been King George III in his madness. Other characters, Har and Heva, typify Poetry and Painting, which had not flourished in King George's reign. The plot of the poem seems confused: for an interesting analysis see Erdman's *Prophet against Empire*, pp. 119-124.

SONGS OF INNOCENCE

¶ 111. These poems form the first complete book executed by Blake in illuminated printing and sold to his customers. Twenty-one copies of the original issue are known to exist; these usually contain thirty-one plates (though some have fewer) printed on both sides of seventeen leaves. The plates in the majority are printed in a shade of brown and are coloured with washes of a simple character. Some of the plates were afterwards transferred to the *Songs of Experience*, so that Blake in his Prospectus of 1793 advertised the work as containing only twenty-five plates.

The text of the plates, which does not vary in the different copies, is here printed from the examples in the British Museum Print Room. The arrangement adopted is that found in copy G, now in America, which is the only one still remaining in its original paper covers as issued by Blake, who usually supplied no pagination. Only four of the poems are known to exist in manuscript as noted below.

¶ 120. *The Little Boy lost*] for an earlier version in MS, which differs but slightly from the etched text, see p. 60.

¶ 121. *Nurse's Song, Holy Thursday*] for earlier versions in MS, see pp. 60, 59.

¶ 124. *Laughing Song*] for an MS version with variants, probably earlier, see p. 63.

THE BOOK OF THEL

¶ 127. This book consists of eight plates executed in illuminated printing. Fifteen copies of the original issue are definitely known to exist, and all except two of these were done about the years 1789-93; the two exceptions have a watermark dated 1815, and are more elaborately coloured than the others. The text does not vary, except in one place as noted below. The present text is taken from the example in the British Museum Print Room (Copy D).

The Book of Thel is an allegory of the unborn spirit visiting the world of generation. Thel rejects the self-sacrificing aspects of experience and flees back to eternity. The symbols of the Lily-of-the-Valley, the Cloud, the Worm, and the Clod of Clay represent idealistic fancy, youth, adolescence and motherhood.

¶ 127. *The daughters of Mne Seraphim*] it has been suggested that Blake first intended to put *The daughters of Mnetha* and afterwards omitted to erase the word he had begun; this could, however, so easily have been done that the apparently meaningless syllable was certainly intentional, probably being a corruption of the mystical name, Bne Seraphim, which is found in Agrippa's *Occult Philosophy* and elsewhere.

¶ 130. Plate 6, lines 19 and 20. *Why a tender curb . . . bed of our desire*] Blake deleted these two lines in two copies of the original.

ANNOTATIONS TO SWEDENBORG'S WISDOM OF ANGELS CONCERNING DIVINE PROVIDENCE

¶ 131. The existence of this volume was first mentioned in Hyde's *Bibliography of the Works of Swedenborg*, 1906. The annotations were not printed until they appeared in an article on Blake and Swedenborg by H. Stanley Redgrove in *The New-Church Magazine*, Jan. 1925. The present text is printed from the original volume, which is now in my collection.

THE FRENCH REVOLUTION

¶ 134. This poem was printed in ordinary type for the bookseller Joseph Johnson, in 1791, but it was never published, and only one copy now remains, probably a set of page proofs, as demonstrated by Sampson. This was preserved in the collection of John Linnell until 1918, and is now in the H. E. Huntington Library, California. The work is described on the title-page as *A Poem in Seven Books*, and an Advertisement on the second leaf states that "The remaining Books of this Poem are finished, and will "be published in their Order"; no more, however, appear to have been printed and the MS of the other books is not known to have survived. If they were written, they were probably suppressed by Blake when the results of the revolution in France turned out to be different from what he had anticipated.

The poem was known to Mrs. Gilchrist, D. G. Rossetti, and Swinburne, but it was not reprinted until 1913 when it was included in Sampson's edition of the *Poems*. The present text is printed from photographs of the original. The punctuation is substantially that of the first printing, though alterations have been made where demanded by the sense.

¶ 136. Line 46. *Eternally*] misprinted *Eeternally* in the original edition.

¶ 137. Line 76 . . . *we wear away*] misprinted *we were away* in the original edition.

¶ 141. Line 163 and page 143, line 201. *The Abbé de Sieyès* . . .] printed *The Abbe de Seyes* in the original edition, and a full-stop after *Assembly*.

¶ 147. Line 283. . . . *on souls of war, living terrors*, . . .] printed . . . *on souls of war-living terrors* . . . in the original edition.

THE MARRIAGE OF HEAVEN AND HELL

¶ 148. This work bears no date, but internal evidence shews that it was almost certainly written and etched over the years 1790-1793. The original issue contains twenty-four or, with the addition of *A Song of Liberty*, twenty-seven plates. Only nine complete copies are known to exist; all contain the *Song of Liberty*, though Sampson and others regard this as having been composed at a later date. All the copies except one are coloured, those executed later being much more elaborately done than the earlier ones.

The book contains a number of satirical manifestos with a series of paradoxical aphorisms, or Proverbs of Hell. The main target of Blake's satire was the works of Swedenborg, notably *Heaven and Hell* and *Memorable Relations*. Blake had been an adherent of Swedenborg, but here he indicates his divergence from Swedenborg's doctrines. The *Song of Liberty* was probably intended to celebrate the advent of the French Republic.

The text here printed is taken from Copy E in my collection.

¶ 157. *Opposition is true Friendship*] this aphorism is etched below the design of "Leviathan in the Sea of Time and Space," on plate 20. It is legible in at least three copies of the work, but in others it has been painted over, and was first reprinted in the first Nonesuch edition.

A SONG OF LIBERTY

¶ 159. As already mentioned, this piece may have been composed at a later date than *The Marriage of Heaven and Hell;* the three plates on which it is etched are found, however, with every copy of the longer work at present known, and it is therefore printed here in the position assigned to it by its author.

THE DANCE OF ALBION

¶ 160. This inscription is found below one uncoloured impression of the line engraving formerly known as "Glad Day". The print is dated 1780, but this seems to refer to the original drawing and not to the engraving, which was certainly made later, probably about 1793. The print with the inscription is in the Lessing J. Rosenwald Collection, National Gallery, Washington, D.C. Three other impressions are known. In two of these the inscription is obliterated by the colouring; in the third it has been cut away.

POEMS AND FRAGMENTS FROM THE NOTE-BOOK [ROSSETTI MS] 1793

¶ 161. The manuscript volume, formerly known from its association with

D. G. Rossetti as the *Rossetti MS*, was used by Blake as a common-place book at intervals during at least eighteen years, 1793-1811. It consists of fifty-eight leaves and contains the first sketches for many of the designs found in the *Gates of Paradise* and in several of the symbolic works, together with other sketches, poems, notes, and prose writings. In order to maintain chronological sequence the MS has been here divided into several parts corresponding with the approximate times at which each was written. During the first period Blake made most of the sketches and then, reversing the book, wrote the poems included under the present heading. The piece here numbered 61 probably belongs also to this period, though it is written at the other end of the book.

The volume was bought by D. G. Rossetti in 1847 for ten shillings from William Palmer, a brother of Blake's friend, Samuel Palmer. From 1887 it was in the possession of the late W. A. White of New York, or of his daughter, Mrs. Frances White Emerson, who gave it to the British Museum shortly before her death in 1957. Many of the poems were printed by D. G. Rossetti in Gilchrist's *Life*, 1863. The MS was also used by Swinburne and by Ellis and Yeats. The first authoritative text of the poems was prepared by Sampson and published in 1905. For this text the MS was transcribed by W. A. White.

Through W. A. White's generosity I had the advantage, when preparing the edition of 1925, of being able to work from a photographic reproduction of the complete MS, and the whole text was carefully revised. Since then Mrs. Emerson has allowed me to have the MS for two periods in my keeping. Much of it is very difficult to read, as can be seen in the photographic facsimile published by the Nonesuch Press in 1935. During my last examination of the MS in 1957 I have been able to make a number of minor improvements in the text, and several lines, previously found illegible or not noticed, have been deciphered and are first printed here.

On the fourth page of the MS Blake has scrawled the title, *Ideas of Good & Evil*, intended for his book of emblems made from the drawings mentioned above.

¶ 164, no. 9. *A cradle song*] not used in the *Songs of Experience*, though clearly intended for that series, since there is a poem with the same title in [*Songs of Innocence*.]

¶ 166, no. 13. *Infant Sorrow*] this poem, of which the first two stanzas were used in *Songs of Experience*, is closely related to the set of verses on p. 169 entitled "in a mirtle shade". The late Max Plowman suggested (*Times Literary Supplement*, 18 November 1926) that the apparent title was really a set of catch-words connecting these four stanzas with the sixth stanza of "Infant Sorrow". This may well be correct, and if so a "fair copy" of the whole poem might read as follows:

INFANT SORROW

My mother groan'd, my father wept,
Into the dangerous world I leapt,
Helpless, naked, piping loud,
Like a fiend hid in a cloud.

Struggling in my father's hands,
Striving against my swaddling bands,

Bound & weary I thought best
To sulk upon my mother's breast.

When I saw that rage was vain,
And to sulk would nothing gain,
Turning many a trick & wile,
I began to soothe & smile.

And I sooth'd day after day
Till upon the ground I stray;
And I smil'd night after night,
Seeking only for delight.

And I saw before me shine
Clusters of the wand'ring vine,
And many a lovely flower & tree
Stretch'd their blossoms out to me.

My father then with holy look,
In his hands a holy book,
Pronounc'd curses on my head
And bound me in a mirtle shade.

"Why should I be bound to thee,
"O my lovely mirtle tree?
"Love, free love, cannot be bound
"To any tree that grows on ground."

O how sick & weary I
Underneath my mirtle lie,
Like to dung upon the ground,
Underneath my mirtle bound.

Oft my mirtle sigh'd in vain
To behold my heavy chain;
Oft my father saw us sigh
And laugh'd at our simplicity.

So I smote him, & his gore
Stain'd the roots my mirtle bore;
But the time of youth is fled,
And grey hairs are on my head.

The mirtle is here the symbol of the married state.

¶ 169, no. 18. *in a mirtle shade*] Blake rewrote this poem on a later page in fewer lines with the title "To my Mirtle"; see p. 176.

¶ 170, no. 20. *I slept in the dark*] Blake afterwards indicated that these two stanzas should follow the one with title "The wild flower's song"; see no. 30, p. 175.

¶ 171, no. 21. *To Nobodaddy*] probably an anagram of 'Abaddon', Revelation ix, 11 (as also p. 185, no. 60, l. 9).

¶ 173, no. 27. *How came pride*] these lines are here deciphered and printed for the first time.

¶ 175, no. 29. *How to know Love*] the two stanzas of this poem are written on opposite pages of the MS, but their connexion, as pointed out by Sampson, is evident. The title here is deciphered and printed for the first time.

¶ 176, no. 33. *An ancient Proverb*] this was written out again by Blake on a later page with four other short pieces under the general title "Several Questions Answered"; see p. 184, no. 59.
No. 34. *To my Mirtle*] for the first version see no. 18, p. 169.
¶ 179, no. 43, l. 1 *He who binds*] formerly read as *He who bends*, both here and in no. 59.
¶ 180, no. 46. *The Question Answer'd*] rewritten in no. 59.
No. 47. *The Chimney Sweeper*] Blake first wrote the second and third stanzas of this poem and then added the first stanza and the title on a later page.
¶ 182, nos. 53 & 54] rewritten in no. 59.
¶ 185, no. 60. *Let the Brothels of Paris be opened*] this poem was so much changed and rewritten by Blake that his final intention is difficult to elucidate. A suggested "fair copy" is given here for the reader's convenience:

"LET THE BROTHELS OF PARIS BE OPENED"

"Let the Brothels of Paris be opened
"With many an alluring dance
"To awake the Pestilence thro' the city,"
Said the beautiful Queen of France.

The King awoke on his couch of gold,
As soon as he heard these tidings told:
"Arise & come, both fife & drum,
"And the Famine shall eat both crust & crumb."

Then he swore a great & solemn Oath:
"To kill the people I am loth,
"But if they rebel, they must go to hell:
"They shall have a Priest & a passing bell."

Then old Nobodaddy aloft
Farted & belch'd & cough'd,
And said, "I love hanging & drawing & quartering
"Every bit as well as war & slaughtering.
"Damn praying & singing,
"Unless they will bring in
"The blood of ten thousand by fighting or swinging."

The Queen of France just touched this Globe,
And the Pestilence darted from her robe;
But our good Queen quite grows to the ground,
And a great many suckers grow all around.

Fayette beside King Lewis stood;
He saw him sign his hand;
And soon he saw the famine rage
About the fruitful land.

Fayette beheld the Queen to smile
And wink her lovely eye;
And soon he saw the pestilence
From street to street to fly.

Fayette beheld the King & Queen
In tears & iron bound;
But mute Fayette wept tear for tear,
And guarded them around.

Fayette, Fayette, thou'rt bought & sold,
And sold is thy happy morrow;
Thou gavest the tears of Pity away
In exchange for the tears of sorrow.

Who will exchange his own fire side
For the steps of another's door?
Who will exchange his wheaten loaf
For the links of a dungeon floor?

O who would smile on the wintry seas,
& Pity the stormy roar?
Or who will exchange his new born child
For the dog at the wintry door?

¶ 186, no. 61. *When Klopstock England defied*] these lines have usually been printed with a number of omissions. The MS is written in pencil and has become very difficult to read, but it has now all been deciphered except lines 29-32. In my collection is a transcript in the hand of A. C. Swinburne apparently complete, but close comparison of what remains of lines 29-32 with Swinburne's version shews that they were his invention, and they are therefore still omitted as illegible.

¶ 187, no. 63. *The Hebrew Nation*] these two lines are here deciphered and printed for the first time. They seem to refer to the Decalogue and the seventh and tenth Commandments.

FRAGMENT

¶ 188. *A fairy leapt upon my knee*] the MS of these lines was in the possession of D. G. Rossetti and was printed by Swinburne in his *Critical Essay*, 1868, pp. 143-4. The "loose scrap of paper" on which they were written is now in the Lessing J. Rosenwald collection, Library of Congress, Washington, D.C. On the other side of the paper is a drawing of "The Infant Hercules throttling the serpents" (reproduced in *Pencil Drawings, Second Series*, Nonesuch Press, 1956).

VISIONS OF THE DAUGHTERS OF ALBION

¶ 189. This work consists of eleven plates, including the frontispiece and title-page. Seventeen complete copies are known to exist, of which all are coloured. The majority were printed in 1794, but three were done in 1815, these being more elaborately coloured than the earlier examples. The text, which does not vary, is here taken from copy A in the British Museum Print Room.

Visions of the Daughters of Albion is characterized by Erdman (*Prophet against Empire*, 1954, p. 211) as: "a dramatised treatise on the related questions of moral, economic, and sexual freedom and an indictment of the 'mistaken Demon' whose code separates bodies from souls and reduces women and children, nations and lands to possessions". Erdman also draws attention to the great importance in this book of Blake's knowledge of the horrors of slavery derived from Stedman's *Surinam*, 1796, for which he engraved sixteen plates mostly depicting cruelties perpetrated on negroes.

AMERICA

¶ 195. *America* is etched on eighteen plates including the frontispiece and title-page. Sixteen copies of the book are known, the majority of which are uncoloured. The theme is concerned with the American revolution, historical events and personages being given a mystical significance. Orc, the spirit of revolt, is the hero of the poem; the villain being the Guardian Prince of Albion, otherwise King George III, who typifies the forces of repression. The text is taken from copy H in the British Museum.

AMERICA, *cancelled plates*

¶ 203. In the Lessing J. Rosenwald collection, Library of Congress, Washington, D.C., are proofs of three plates which probably represent the first version of *America*. One of these was re-etched with alterations as plate 3; the other two were not used, though the third has a number of corrections made in pencil, here indicated as deletions, and the last twenty-one lines are scored through with a vertical pencil line. The two abandoned plates contain references to King George by name, which it was no doubt more discreet to eliminate. The text of these plates was first published in the Nonesuch edition, 1925, pp. 271-4.

FRAGMENT

¶ 206. These lines, probably intended for *America*, were etched on a plate only part of which remains. The plate carried also a design of which two coloured examples are known. On one of these prints, now in the Lessing J. Rosenwald collection, National Gallery of Art, Washington, D.C., the words were impressed so that they could be read by the late A. G. B. Russell from the back of the paper with the aid of a mirror. The lines could well follow on after the text of the third cancelled plate.

PROSPECTUS: TO THE PUBLIC

¶ 207. An example of this advertisement was seen by Gilchrist and was printed in his *Life of Blake*, 1863, ii, 263-4. This is now the only authority, and the present text is taken from this source.

SUBJECTS FOR THE HISTORY OF ENGLAND

¶ 208. The *Prospectus* on the preceding pages advertised "The History of "England, a small book of Engravings. Price 3s.", but the finished work is not known to exist. The only traces of it that can be found are this list of the twenty-two subjects from the *Note-Book* and some small water-colour designs, which have been dispersed. The list of subjects is given only by Sampson; the designs have never been reproduced.

FOR CHILDREN: THE GATES OF PARADISE

¶ 209. Blake executed in 1793 a small volume of eighteen engraved plates, including the title-page; only four copies have survived. The legends, printed here from the example in the British Museum Print Room, have little meaning without the emblematic designs to which they belong; but about twenty-five years later Blake re-issued the work with additional plates and legends, and the emblems have been reproduced on pp. 760-70 of the present edition, together with the amplified text.

SONGS OF EXPERIENCE

¶ 210. The *Songs of Experience* were probably never issued by Blake without the *Songs of Innocence*, which have, however, been separately printed here, since they were issued alone five years earlier. When the two works were combined in 1794, Blake transferred the three plates of "The Little Girl Lost" and "The Little Girl Found" from the earlier to the later series. Other changes were also made at different times and the volume did not reach its final form until about 1801, by which time all the twenty-three additional plates of the *Songs of Experience* had been completed. Even then Blake varied the arrangement of the plates in every copy of the book until about the year 1815, after which he was more consistent in this respect. Twenty-four copies of the whole work are known to exist, the majority of them coloured with increasing elaboration as the years passed.

The text printed here is taken from copy A now in the British Museum Print Room, but the arrangement adopted is that of the later copies referred to above. This arrangement, consistently used by Blake in seven of the last eight copies that he executed, seems to me to have more authority than that found in the eighth copy, although this was arranged according to Blake's MS index made about 1818 (see my edition of the *Letters*, 1956, pp. 179-181) and has been followed by several of Blake's editors, including Sampson.

¶ 210. *Earth's Answer*] for the first draft see p. 168.

¶ 211. *The Clod & the Pebble*] for the MS draft see p. 162.

Holy Thursday] for the first draft see p. 181.

¶ 212. *The Chimney Sweeper*] for the MS draft see p. 180.

Nurse's Song] for the MS draft see p. 171.

¶ 213. *The Sick Rose*] for the MS draft see p. 175.

The Fly] for the MS draft, with additional stanzas, see p. 182.

The Angel] for the MS draft see p. 182.

¶ 214. *The Tyger*] for the first draft, with additional stanzas, and the fair copy, see pp. 172-3.

¶ 215. *My pretty Rose Tree*] for the first draft see p. 161.

The Lilly] for the first draft see p. 171.

The Garden of Love] for the first draft see p. 162.

¶ 216. *The Little Vagabond*] for the first draft see p. 179.

London] for the first draft see p. 170.

¶ 217. *The Human Abstract*] for the first draft, under a different title, see p. 174.

Infant Sorrow] for the MS draft, with additional stanzas, see p. 166.

¶ 218. *A Poison Tree*] for the first draft, under a different title, see p. 165.

A Little Boy Lost] for the MS draft see p. 176.

¶ 220. *To Tirzah*] the lower half of the original print, bearing the legend, *It is Raised a Spiritual Body*, is reproduced here from an uncoloured example in the British Museum. This plate does not appear in three of the earliest copies of the book, its place being taken by the small plate without text representing "The Regeneration of Earth". Sampson in the Oxford edition, 1913, has pointed out that the symbolism of *To Tirzah* suggests that it was written and etched some years later than the rest of the *Songs of Experience*. This view tends to be confirmed by the fact that the last lines of the first and last stanzas occur also in the last poem of the *Pickering MS*, written about 1801-1803; see p. 435, l. 28.

A DIVINE IMAGE

¶ 221. The print bearing this poem was never included by Blake among the *Songs of Experience*, but it is found with two sets of prints which were made from the plates after his death; a third example is in my collection.

THE FIRST BOOK OF URIZEN

¶ 222. Only seven copies of this work are known to exist, and the number of plates they contain varies from twenty-four to twenty-eight. Only two copies have the full number of twenty-eight, both containing plate 4 with portions of Chapters II and III. All seven copies are coloured. In one, the latest to which a date can be assigned, Blake has removed the word *First* from the title-page; in another he has removed it from the Preludium and the colophon. Since *The Book of Ahania* carries on the story of *Urizen* it was probably intended to be *The Second Book of Urizen,* but Blake changed his mind.

Blake was not consistent in the order in which he placed the plates. The arrangement given by Sampson (Oxford, 1913) has been followed here. The text has been collated with copy D in the British Museum with the exception of plate 4, which has been compared with the example in the Dimsdale copy (A).

The Book of Urizen is the first part of the universal myth, dealing with the creation of the material world and of mankind, and so with the inherent problem of evil. Urizen, God of Reason, resembling the Hebrew Jehovah, is the Creator, his name probably being derived from the Greek οὐρίζειν, to set a limit. Los, the poetic genius and symbol of time, is also involved, since Reason cannot exist without Imagination; but from Los develops Pity, resulting in a division of his soul with the appearance of his Emanation, named Enitharmon, his female counterpart. Their offspring is Orc, the spirit of revolt. Ultimately Urizen establishes religion, and mankind becomes entangled in the web of religion as civilization emerges in Egypt.

¶ 226, Chap. IV [a] this chapter was probably written as an afterthought, when the other chapter numbered IV [b] had already been etched. In two copies Chap. IV [a] is placed between the two plates forming Chap. IV [b], lines 42-3 of section 6, *And a first Age passed over, And a state of dismal woe,* being erased.

EUROPE

¶ 237. A complete copy of *Europe* consists of eighteen plates, including the frontispiece and two other plates without text, but ten of the twelve copies known lack the small plate with the preliminary lines. Professor Foster Damon suggests that Blake usually suppressed these lines because they expressed too plainly his profound and easily misunderstood belief that salvation was allied to sexual feeling. The plates of *Europe* are usually coloured. Apart from the suppressed plate, the text does not vary; it has been collated with the complete copy K in the Fitzwilliam Museum, Cambridge.

Europe contains a historical parable covering the Christian era and ending with the French Revolution, while England prepares for war. The theme turns on the separation of Enitharmon, or Inspiration, from her eternal partner, Los, the spirit of Poetry, and the coming of war with all its horrors as the result of the imposition of Enitharmon's feminine will on the world. Orc is roused for the advent of revolution.

¶ 239, pl. 2, l.13. *And who shall bind the infinite*] this line is the subject of the frontispiece, sometimes known as "The Ancient of Days", or as "God Creating the Universe". The rough pencil sketch for this is on p. 96 of the *Note-book,* and at the side of this Blake has written: *Who shall bind the*

Infinite. The design was probably suggested by a passage in Book VII of Milton's *Paradise Lost*. It is again referred to in *The First Book of Urizen*, ch. vii, l. 39: "*He* [*Urizen*] *formed golden compasses, And began to explore the Abyss.*"

THE SONG OF LOS

¶ 245. Five copies of this work are known, each containing eight plates and all heavily coloured with opaque pigment. The text, which does not vary, has been collated with copy A in the British Museum.

The Song of Los is in two divisions headed *Africa* and *Asia*, but this distinction has no great significance and seems to be made chiefly in order to complete the sequence of the continents after *Europe* and *America*. The poem is a connecting link between the end of *Ahania* and the beginning of *America*, relating the history of mankind from the beginning of civilization to the American Revolution. Religion and philosophy, that is, repressive laws, are given by Urizen; Har and Heva, the pleasures of the imagination, flee, while war and lust flourish, until Orc shall arise to usher in the Last Judgment and release man from the bonds of materialism and mortality.

THE BOOK OF AHANIA

¶ 249. *The Book of Ahania* and *The Book of Los*, instead of being executed in relief etching like all the other illuminated books, were etched in the ordinary way, but Blake was apparently dissatisfied with the result and abandoned both books after printing only one copy of each. *Ahania* consists of six plates, including a frontispiece. The frontispiece, illustrating chap. I, ll. 30-4, became detached from the rest of the book when it was sold at Sotheby's in 1903 and is now in my collection. The other five plates, with another impression of the frontispiece added, is now in the Lessing J. Rosenwald Collection, Library of Congress, Washington, D.C.

Ahania, as already mentioned, was probably intended to be *The Second Book of Urizen*. It carries on the myth of Urizen from prehistoric to biblical times, relating the story of the flight of the Israelites from Egypt, the imposition of the Mosaic law, their settlement in Asia, and the crucifixion of Jesus. It includes a character, Fuzon or Passion, who revolts against Urizen, blasting him in the loins. Urizen casts out his Emanation, Ahania, or Pleasure, but Fuzon is struck by the rock of the decalogue and is crucified on the tree of religion. Ahania in exile becomes Sin, and the book ends with her lament.

THE BOOK OF LOS

¶ 255. *The Book of Los*, like *Ahania*, is etched in the ordinary way on five plates. The only copy known is in the British Museum. It repeats in a shortened form the prehistoric history of the primeval Los and his struggle against the power of Urizen. Los creates the sun as the centre of a system to which he binds Urizen and compels him to begin the process of material creation with the formation of earth and man. Los, or poetic imagination, is forcing a definition of reason in order to overcome error.

I ASKED A THIEF

¶ 261. *I asked a thief*] Blake copied this poem out of the *MS Note-Book, p. 114*, and signed it with the date 1796. This MS was given by Mr. Oliver R. Barrett of Chicago to Princeton University in 1959.

LEGENDS

¶ 261. These legends were inscribed by Blake beneath the colour-printed monotypes forming copies of the so-called *Large* and *Small Book of Designs*. The examples of these books now in the British Museum Print Room do not have the legends, which are found only on the prints, now dispersed, derived from other copies (see the *Census of Illuminated Books,* 1951).

VALA, OR THE FOUR ZOAS

¶ 263. The MS of this poem consists of 70 large leaves measuring about 41.5 × 32.5 cm., together with one torn fragment and two small sheets bearing additional passages. The leaves are made up of 21 sheets of drawing paper with a watermark dated 1794, 47 sheets of the same paper with working proofs of the engravings for Young's *Night Thoughts,* and 2 sheets with parts of an early engraving, "Edward and Elenor," on one side. The title on the recto of the first leaf was originally written in ink in the first form given here, and was afterwards altered in pencil to the second form. On the verso of the first leaf is a pencil sketch of a recumbent figure beneath which is written *Rest before Labour*. Of the other 69 leaves, 61 have the text written on both sides; the remainder have the text on one side and a full-page drawing or an engraving on the other. The great majority of the pages of the text have the margins decorated with pencil drawings, except where they were already occupied by the engravings for Young's *Night Thoughts*. The drawings are occasionally touched with water-colours. Most of the text is written in ink, but many words or passages are in pencil; these probably represent Blake's later additions, and are here printed in italic because they sometimes break somewhat awkwardly into the sense. Some of Blake's other alterations were written first in pencil and afterwards inked over. Blake seems at first to have intended the manuscript to be a fair copy of a poem entitled *Vala* of which the first draft was written elsewhere, for the earlier pages are written with great care in a formal copper-plate hand. In the later pages and in the marginal additions he relapsed into his ordinary hand. Blake was at work on this poem at intervals over a long period of years, and the text has consequently been subjected to extensive erasures, alterations, and additions. The correct arrangement of the leaves has presented problems of great difficulty. The text here printed gives the proper sequence as far as my own judgment goes, but the arrangement in a few places must remain conjectural.

Another title found on the back of a separate drawing may possibly refer to this poem, as suggested by the late Max Plowman. It runs as follows: "The Bible of Hell, in Nocturnal Visions collected. Vol. I. Lambeth." The division of *The Four Zoas* into nine Nights, with this title, was certainly suggested by Young's *Night Thoughts,* which Blake was illustrating at the same period. If Plowman's conjecture be correct, it would follow that Blake conceived the idea of *The Four Zoas* some years before it was actually written, for he remarks in *The Marriage of Heaven and Hell,* "I have also The Bible of Hell, which the world shall have whether they will or no." (See page 158.) The theme of *The Four Zoas* is a development of Blake's cosmic fantasy, already given expression in *The Book of Urizen* and its sequels.

Blake seems never to have carried out any final revision of the poem and he never etched it on copper-plates in the manner of the other symbolic works, except for a few passages which he incorporated in *Milton* (31 lines) and *Jerusalem* (147 lines). The date 1797 on the title-page may, as suggested by

Sampson, represent the date at which Blake began to make his fair copy, the composition having been begun a year or two before; or it may have been in this year that he decided to call what he had written of *The Bible of Hell* by the name of *Vala*. Extensive revisions were made during the Felpham period, 1800-1803, and further alterations may have been made at other times. At some time before his death Blake gave the MS to John Linnell and it remained in the keeping of Linnell's descendants until 1918 when it was sold at Christie's with the rest of the Blake-Linnell collections. An anonymous donor soon afterwards presented the MS to the British Museum where it is now in the Department of MSS. Several of the drawings have suffered mutilation since the MS left Blake's hands. Someone seems to have disliked the frankly sexual symbolism employed by the artist and has rubbed out those parts of the drawings considered offensive to conventional morality. There has been no similar interference with the text.

The MS was transcribed by Messrs. Ellis and Yeats and printed in full in their edition of the *Works*, 1893, and a revised text was printed by Ellis in 1906. Both these texts are, however, exceedingly inaccurate, and before 1925 there was no printed version which could really be regarded as representing Blake's work. The present text attempts to give a complete and accurate version of the poem, but, as already explained, the correct arrangement of the leaves of the MS is sometimes in doubt, and Blake's writing is not always easy to decipher, so that a few words, noted below, have remained uncertain. The punctuation has been a matter of great difficulty, very little help being obtained from Blake's own perfunctory indications. The responsibility for the preparation of this text was shared with me by Max Plowman, and we had the advantage of consultation with Professors D. J. Sloss and J. Wallis, late of Liverpool University, who were themselves preparing a text of the poem for publication by the Oxford University Press.

Some valuable corrections have been supplied for this edition by Mr. H. M. Margoliouth, who has recently published under the title *Vala* what he believes to have been Blake's original version before he made most of the additions and alterations, totalling approximately 900 lines, and changed the title to *The Four Zoas*. Those who wish to read the poem in this simplified form may be referred to Mr. Margoliouth's excellent edition (Oxford, 1956). The whole has been edited by G. E. Bentley jun., Oxford, 1963. Words deleted by Blake have been indicated in the text in the manner adopted throughout this edition. More extensive erasures, and lines added or transposed by Blake, have been recorded in the notes, and these will sometimes account for discontinuity in the sense of certain passages. All breaks in the MS have been indicated by a space in the printed text; when a break happens to coincide with the beginning of a printed page, the first line has been indented. The same convention has been used elsewhere in this edition.

¶ 263. "Οτι δύκ ἐσπν . . . ἐπουρανιοις] The English version given in the footnote was supplied by Mrs. Max Plowman. Blake's chapter reference was wrong and is here corrected.

THE FOUR ZOAS: NIGHT THE FIRST

¶ 264. Lines 1-5. Blake's first draft of the first three lines has been deciphered by Erdman. Blake began with the words:

This is the wrath of Vala.

This he altered to:

1 *The Dirge of Enitharmon, which shook the heavens with wrath,*
2 *And thus beginneth the Book of Vala, which whosoever reads*
3 *If with his Intellect he comprehend the terrible Sentence*
6 *The heavens shall quake; the Earth shall move & shudder, & the mountains*
7 *With all their woods; the streams and valleys wail'd in dismal fear.*
4 [*To hear the sound* del.] *Hearing the march of Long resounding strong heroic verse*
5 *Marshall'd in order for the day of Intellectual Battle*

He then re-numbered lines 4 and 5 as 2 and 3, and finally crossed them out, re-writing them in the space made by erasing the original lines 2 and 3. Nearly the whole of the first six pages of the MS (in this text up to line 178) has been erased and re-written.

Lines 9, 10, 11. *John xvii c.*, 21, 22, 23 *v.*] "21. That they all may be one; as "thou, Father, art in me, and I in thee, that they also may be one in us: "that the world may believe that thou hast sent me. 22. And the glory which "thou gavest me I have given them; that they may be one, even as we are "one. 23. I in them, and thou in me, that they may be made perfect in one; "and that the world may know that thou has sent me, and hast loved them, "as thou hast loved me."

John i *c.*, 14 *v.*] "And the Word was made flesh, and dwelt among us, (and "we beheld his glory, the glory as of the only begotten of the Father,) full of "grace and truth."

Line 12. . . . *those Living Creatures*] these words are indistinctly written, but are probably correct as given.

¶ 265. Lines 33, 34. *The Men have reciev'd* . . .] these two lines are written in the margin and are not marked for insertion.

Line 35. *Thy fear* . . .] repeated in *Jerusalem*, pl. 22, l. 1.

Lines 36-8. *All Love is lost* . . .] repeated in *Jerusalem*, pl. 22, ll. 10-12.

Line 42. *Hide me some shadowy semblance*] i.e., *hide* for *me*, etc.

Lines 44-6. *I have look'd* . . .] these three lines were added as an afterthought. The first two were repeated in *Jerusalem*, pl. 22, ll. 14, 15.

Lines 47-58. *Why wilt thou Examine* . . .] this passage is written sideways in the margin. The first five lines are repeated in *Jerusalem*, pl. 22, ll. 20-24.

Lines 59-63. *Sometimes I think* . . .] these lines are written in pencil at the top of the page in the MS. The position assigned to them seems to be clear from the sense.

¶ 266. Lines 84, 85. *As Garments woven* . . .] these lines were added at the side as an afterthought.

Lines 94-108. *There is from Great Eternity* . . .] this passage is written sideways in the margin. It is rewritten and expanded in *Milton*, pl. 33, 34.

¶ 267. Line 120. *Who animating*] *Who* is doubtful; the word should perhaps be read *Thus*.

Line 121. *Rear'd*] this is the catchword at the bottom of a page of the MS, and carries on to the fifth line following.

Line 131. *And courting that the Earth*] *courting* is unsatisfactory, but I am unable to read the word in any other way.

¶ 268. Lines 149-50. *Who art thou . . . yet I love*] these words were added as an afterthought.
¶ 269. Line 201. *To Create Man* . . .] written in as an afterthought.
¶ 270. Lines 222-6. *Then Eno* . . .] the substance of these lines is repeated in *Jerusalem*, pl. 48, ll. 30-39.
Line 224. . . . *& in* (*the*) [*twenty* del.] *every year*(*s*)] Blake first wrote this as, "*& in the twenty years*"; he afterwards intended it to be, "*& in every year,*" but omitted to make all the necessary deletions here indicated by round brackets.
¶ 271. Lines 242-3. *But had no power* . . .] written in as an afterthought.
Line 247. . . . *Reading the Visions of Beulah*] *Reading* is not clear; the word may possibly be *Seeing*.
Line 248. *But the two youthful wonders* . . .] this line is written in the margin together with the heading, *Night the Second*, both having been added after the deletion of line 247. Blake probably intended to carry out some re-arrangement of Nights 1 and 2, but his directions are not clear, and I have, therefore, left the text of these Nights as it comes in the MS.
Line 273. *Driving the Female Emanations* . . .] written in as an afterthought.
¶ 272. Lines 276-7. *If thou drivest* . . .] also written later, and mostly deleted.
Lines 290-8. *Refusing to behold . . . his mother's womb*] this passage is written in the margin and marked for insertion. Blake afterwards drew a vertical line through it as if he had copied it elsewhere.
Line 309. *Threaten not me* . . .] this was first written in between the two preceding lines, then deleted and rewritten in its present position.
¶ 273. Lines 321-41. *Of Light . . . delusion & fancy*] these lines are written at the top of the page and in the margin, those in pencil having been added last.
¶ 274. Lines 351-4. *Los saw . . . smiting*] these lines were added as an afterthought.
Lines 359-65. *But Luvah . . . such was the Vision*] these lines were written in after their context, the last five in the margin.
Lines 386-97. *The Mountain* del. . . .] these lines are written over erasures.
¶ 277. Lines 466-8. *From the supporting arms* . . .] a great part of these lines is repeated in *Jerusalem*, pl. 48, ll. 1-4.
Lines 470-4. *As one Man* . . .] repeated, with alterations, in *Jerusalem*, pl. 38, ll. 17-21.
¶ 278. Lines 528-9. . . . *such thing was never known . . . to be reviv'd*] repeated with alterations in *Jerusalem*, pl. 80, ll. 23, 24.

THE FOUR ZOAS: NIGHT THE [SECOND]

¶ 280. Blake has erased the number in the heading and has not supplied the missing word.
Line 1. *Rising upon his Couch*] *Rising* should perhaps be read as *Reclining*.
Lines 4, 8, 14.] these lines were written in as afterthoughts.
¶ 281. Lines 38-65. *Petrifying all . . . Druid Stones*] this passage was added in the margin and marked for insertion.
Line 65. . . . *among the Druid Stones*] *among* is unsatisfactory, and should perhaps be read as *array*[*s*].

¶ 282. Lines 72-9. *Luvah was cast . . . innocence & youth*] repeated in *Jerusalem*, pl. 7, ll. 30-37.
Line 81. *Vala's King*] these two words are written over an erasure.
Lines 100-5] these lines are written over erasures.
¶ 283. Lines 121-34. *With trembling horror pale . . . power & severity*] this passage is written in the margin and marked for insertion.
¶ 284. Line 168. *Quadrangular . . .*] written in as an afterthought.
Lines 173-210. *Twelve halls . . . Females from him away*] the whole of this passage is written at the bottom of a page of the MS and marked for insertion.
Lines 174, 175. Deleted, but afterwards marked: *To come in.*
¶ 287. Lines 261-5. *For the Divine Lamb . . . slept should awake*] these lines are written over erasures.
Lines 269-86. *In seven & tens . . . in the vast deep*] these lines were written as an afterthought at the bottom of a page.
¶ 288. Lines 302-82. *And Los said . . . weeping & smiling & fading*] the whole of this passage is written at the bottom of a page and in the margin, and is marked for insertion.
¶ 289. Lines 364-6. *Arise, you little glancing wings . . . lives is holy*] these lines are repeated from *Visions of the Daughters of Albion* (pl. 8, ll. 9-10).
¶ 290. Lines 389-90. *I have chosen the serpent . . . children*] repeated from *Visions of the Daughters of Albion* (pl. 5, ll. 8-9), *serpent* being substituted for *ape*.
Line 409. *To hear the dog howl . . .*] this line is repeated from *The First Book of Urizen*, pl. 25, ll. 1-2.

THE FOUR ZOAS: NIGHT THE THIRD

¶ 292. Line 30. *Leave all futurity . . .*] written in as an afterthought.
Line 36. *Till the Divine Vision . . .*] written over an erasure.
Lines 44-103. *The Dark'ning Man walk'd . . . we alone are escaped*] almost the whole of this passage is repeated in *Jerusalem*, pl. 29, ll. 33-82; a few lines are omitted and *Man* is in some places altered to *Albion*.
¶ 294. Line 105. (*Albion clos'd . . .*] this passage is written as prose in the margin, and is not marked for insertion, so that its present position is conjectural. It is reckoned here as one line.

THE FOUR ZOAS: NIGHT THE FOURTH

¶ 297. Lines 7-9. *And he said . . .*] these three lines are written over an erasure, line 8 being added after lines 7 and 9.
¶ 303. Lines 208-46. *The Eternal Mind, bounded . . .*] the whole of this passage is repeated with a few alterations from *The First Book of Urizen*, ch. iv [b], §3-end, pl. 10, l. 19—pl. 13, l. 19.
¶ 304. Line 253. *. . . if thou hadst been here our brother had not died*] this line is repeated in *Jerusalem*, pl. 50, l. 11, with the addition of *Albion* after *brother*.
Lines 260-2. *In which we may be hidden . . . consume*] these three lines are repeated in *Milton*, pl. 30, ll. 25-7.
Line 277. *The Finger of God . . .*] cf. *Jerusalem*, pl. 48, l. 45.
Lines 280-95. *In terrors Los shrank . . .*] this passage was first written on the preceding page of the MS between lines 246 and 247. Blake added clear instructions for its transposition as printed. The first four lines are taken from *The First Book of Urizen*, ch. v, §1, pl. 13, l. 20. (*Bring in here the*

Globe of Blood as in the B. of Urizen)] refers to *The First Book of Urizen*, ch. v, §8, pl. 18.

THE FOUR ZOAS: NIGHT THE FIFTH

¶ 306. Lines 43-5. *Urizen cast deep darkness . . .*] these three lines are written over a passage of six lines which have been erased.

Lines 56-61. *Torn by black storms . . . flames of fire*] these six lines are repeated with alterations in *Jerusalem*, pl. 40, ll. 39-42.

¶ 307. Lines 83-91. . . . *a tightning girdle grew . . .*] this passage is taken with alterations from *The First Book of Urizen*, ch. vii, §2-3, pl. 20, ll. 10-20.

THE FOUR ZOAS: NIGHT THE SIXTH

¶ 315. Lines 131-40. *Oft would he stand . . .*] these lines are written after the succeeding passage of six lines, but are marked for transposition.

Line 140. *He hid to recure his obstructed powers*] *revive* would obviously be preferable to *recure*, but I can only read the MS as the latter.

¶ 317. Line 237. *Gaining a New dominion . . .*] this line of almost double the usual length was written in as an afterthought and runs over into the margin.

Lines 238-44. *For Urizen lamented . . .*] cf. *The First Book of Urizen*, ch. viii, §6, pl. 25, l. 5.

¶ 319. Lines 310-3. *Four winged heralds . . .*] these four lines are repeated with alterations from *America*, cancelled plates (pl. c, ll. 14-7).

THE FOUR ZOAS: NIGHT THE SEVENTH

¶ 320. Blake seems to have written two drafts of Night the Seventh, but he never finally rejected either of them. Probably the one here printed first was written first.

¶ 321. Lines 29-39. *His book of iron on his knees . . .*] cf. *Ahania*, ch. iii, §3-4, pl. 3, l. 64.

¶ 323. Lines 110-6. *Listen, O Daughters . . .*] these seven lines were added as an afterthought, and in the MS the last six appear to come after the line beginning, *Compell the poor*; the sense makes it clear that they should be arranged as given here.

Line 117. *Compell the poor . . .*] repeated in *Jerusalem*, pl. 30, l. 30.

Line 122. . . . *with temper*(*ance*)] Blake has here abbreviated *temperance* to *temper*; his intention is shewn by the recurrence of the word in full, four lines later.

Line 124. *reduce the man to want . . .*] cf. *Jerusalem*, pl. 30, l. 31.

¶ 327. Lines 304-10. *Thou knowest . . .*] this passage is written in the margin and marked for insertion.

¶ 328. Lines 329-31. *In male forms . . .*] these three lines are added in place of one line erased.

Lines 349, 350. *Thou didst subdue me . . .*] a marginal addition.

¶ 330. Lines 407-10. *But I have thee . . .*] a marginal addition.

Line 407. *Counterpart*] Blake deleted this word and wrote *Vegetative* in its place, but then deleted this also, and never finally decided what he should use instead of *Counterpart* here and in the next two lines.

¶ 332. Lines 490-9. *First his immortal spirit . . .*] these lines, concluding the first draft of Night the Seventh, are written in the margin.

THE FOUR ZOAS: NIGHT THE SEVENTH [*b*]

¶ 333. As first written this Night began with line 124, *Now in the Caverns . . .*, and ended with, *Then I heard the Earthquake, &c.* Blake then wrote clear instructions for transposing the first and second halves of the Night as it is printed here.

¶ 336. Line 123. *Then I heard the Earthquake, &c.*] this may refer to a continuation of the passage on another page which has been lost, or it may be a hasty version of line 129, *As when the Earthquake ...*

Lines 129-32. *As when the Earthquake ...*] cf. *Tiriel*, 5, ll. 4-6.

Lines 134, 135. *Knowing the arts ...*] written in as an afterthought.

Lines 137, 138. *Jealous that she was Vala ...*] written in as an afterthought four lines lower down and marked for transposition.

¶ 336 & 338. Lines 142, 207, 213, 220] these lines are all written in as afterthoughts.

¶ 337. Lines 164-209. *They sound the clarions strong ... shall blood renew*] repeated in *Jerusalem*, pl. 65, ll. 6-55.

¶ 339. Lines 244-58. *Tharmas, The Moon ...*] this passage is written in the margin and marked for insertion.

THE FOUR ZOAS: NIGHT THE EIGHTH

¶ 341. Lines 4-9. *The Fallen Man ...*] written over an erasure.

Lines 10-15. *They had which cloth'd ...*] these lines are written in the margin, but are deleted except for the last line.

¶ 342. Line 35. *Los stood, &c.*] this marginal note indicates an additional passage which has been lost.

Line 63. ... *Luvah, Or Orc*] *Orc* should perhaps be read as *One*.

¶ 343. Line 81. *Measur'd his food ...*] cf. *America*, Preludium, l. 3.

Lines 90-101. *But Urizen his mighty rage ...*] these lines follow line 60, but are marked for transposition.

Lines 102-6. *Terrified & astonish'd ...*] written in the margin, but not marked for insertion.

Line 109. ... *the stirring battle*] *stirring* might be read as *storming*.

¶ 344. Lines 112-5. *Feeling the hand ...*] written in the margin and marked for insertion.

Line 114. *Of Enitharmon singing ...*] cf. *Milton*, pl. 6, l. 6.

¶ 346. Line 195. *Glory, Glory, Glory ...*] repeated in *Milton*, pl. 13, l. 28.

Lines 200-38. *We behold with wonder ...*] this passage is written on a later page and marked for insertion.

Line 204. *The bellowing furnaces blown ...*] *blown* should perhaps be read as *blone*, or *blare* as in *Milton*, pl. 24, ll. 63-64, where this line and the one preceding are repeated.

Lines 210-3. *The Daughters of Enitharmon ...*] cf. *Milton*, pl. 34, ll. 24-31.

¶ 348. Lines 278-94. *A False Feminine Counterpart ...*] a marginal addition marked for insertion.

Lines 298-321. *O thou poor human form ... stems of Vegetation*] repeated in *Jerusalem*, pl. 67, l. 44—pl. 68, l. 9.

¶ 349. Lines 332-40. *Saying: "Is this Eternal Death ...*] a marginal addition marked for insertion.

¶ 350. Lines 341-413. *But when Rahab ... his secret holiness*] the whole of this is written on two additional leaves and marked for insertion.

Lines 351, 352. *I am that shadowy Prophet ...*] these two lines are repeated in *Milton*, pl. 22, ll. 15-16.

¶ 351. Lines 388-404. *Wherefore Rintrah & Palamabron . . .*] cf. *Milton*, pl. 10, 11, 13.

¶ 353. Lines 490, 491. *For she spoke of all . . .*] written in as an afterthought. Lines 495, 496. *Will you erect a lasting habitation . . .*] cf. *Visions of the Daughters of Albion* (pl. 5, l. 41-pl. 6, l. 1).

¶ 356. Line 584. *Los hears & weeps*] following this is a passage of nine lines which have been very thoroughly deleted; most of it, however, has been deciphered by Sloss & Wallis (I, 287), with some queries, as printed here. Lines 597-620. *Rahab triumphs . . .*] the whole of this passage, except the last three lines, was first written in pencil and afterwards inked over.

THE FOUR ZOAS: NIGHT THE NINTH

¶ 357. Lines 1-13. *And Los & Enitharmon . . .*] these lines were written in pencil over erasures, and were afterwards inked over.

¶ 358. Line 40. . . . *asterial day*] *asterial* might possibly be read as *a*[*e*]*therial*. Line 50. *Their oppressors are fall'n . . .*] written in as an afterthought.

¶ 359. Lines 71-80. *Blood issu'd out in rushing volumes . . .*] there lines are written over erasures; *rushing* should perhaps be read as *gushing*.

Lines 81-90. *Around the dragon form . . .*] these lines are written in the margin and marked for insertion.

Lines 100–13. *My sons, exiled from my breast . . . I wander up & down*] repeated with alterations in *Jerusalem*, pl. 19, ll. 1-14.

¶ 362. Lines 201-3. *The three daughters of Urizen . . .*] a marginal addition.

¶ 364. Lines 275-7. *The Prisoner answers . . .*] a marginal addition marked for insertion.

¶ 365. Lines 333, 334. *The daughters of Urizen . . .*] written in as an afterthought.

¶ 367. Lines 383, 384. *And those upon the Couches . . .*] a marginal addition marked for insertion.

¶ 368. Line 421. . . . *arise, O dry thy dewy tears*] *O* should perhaps be read as *&*.

¶ 370. Lines 491-4. *Arise, O Enion . . .*] written in as an afterthought, partly in the margin.

¶ 373. Line 623. *Not born for the sport . . .*] written in as an afterthought.

¶ 374. Line 638. *Ephesians iii c.*, 10 *v.*] "To the intent that now unto the "principalities and powers in heavenly places might be known by the "church the manifold wisdom of God." More probably the reference should be to the preceding verse: "And to make all men see what is the "fellowship of the mystery, which from the beginning of the world hath "been hid in God, who created all things by Jesus Christ."

¶ 375. Lines 670-6. *Let the slave, grinding at the mill . . . believe it is a dream*] repeated from *America*, pl. 6, ll. 6-12.

¶ 377. Lines 743-71. *How red the sons & daughters of Luvah . . .*] this passage is repeated with alterations and additions in *Milton*, pl. 27.

¶ 379. Lines 825-6. *The Sun has left his blackness . . .*] repeated from *America*, pl. 6, ll. 13-14.

Lines 832-40. *Of fire rise up . . .*] written over erasures.

NOTES ON THE PAGES OF THE FOUR ZOAS

¶ 380. Line 1. *Christ's Crucifix . . .*] This passage is written faintly in pencil at the end of the Fourth Night.

Lines 2, 3. *Till thou dost injure . . .*] These lines are written in pencil in the margin of the fourth page of Night the Sixth, opposite the passage beginning *An earth of wintry woe* . . . (p. 314, l. 92).

Lines 4-7. *The Christian Religion* . . .] This passage is written at the top of a page which is chiefly occupied by part of the print entitled, "Edward and Elenor"; there is no other text on this page. Its position is, therefore, towards the end of Night the Seventh, but it seems to have no relation to this.

Lines 8 and 9. *Unorganiz'd Innocence* . . .] Written in the margin of the MS opposite the passage beginning, *So sung the demons of the deep* . . . (p. 338, line 210).

THE FOUR ZOAS: ADDITIONAL FRAGMENTS

¶ 380. The first four fragments are written on both sides of a small sheet of notepaper. The fifth, beginning *Opening in rifted rocks,* is on a piece torn from a leaf of the MS. The final fragment is on a piece of different thinner paper, and is another version of passages in Night the Eighth, ll. 268-347.

ANNOTATIONS TO WATSON'S "APOLOGY FOR THE BIBLE"

¶ 383. Richard Watson (1737-1816) was Bishop of Llandaff and author of many works on scientific and theological subjects. In his *Apology for the Bible*, first published in 1796, he attacks Paine's *Age of Reason,* 1793. Blake's copy of the eighth edition of the *Apology* contains copious notes—written in ink and pencil on the back of the title-page and in the margins of the succeeding pages. After Blake's death the volume was in the possession of Samuel Palmer. It was sold at Sotheby's in 1914 and was then acquired for the H. E. Huntington Library, California. By the courtesy of the late G. D. Smith, I was allowed to transcribe the notes immediately after the sale, and this transcript was verified by Mr. Clifford Blake Clapp, then reviser in the H. E. Huntington Library. The annotations were printed in my *Bibliography of Blake,* 1921, but were published for the first time in the Nonesuch edition, 1925.

¶ 384. Line 5. *Read the xxiii Chap. of Matthew*] in this chapter Christ denounces the blindness and hypocrisy of the Scribes and Pharisees. The reference was suggested to Blake by the list of titles of books by Bishop Watson.

¶ 391. Line 28. *Deut. xxxi, v.* 24] "And it came to pass, when Moses had "made an end of writing the words of this law in a book, until they were "finished."

¶ 394. Line 14 from bottom. *Hartley*] David Hartley (1705-1757) published his *Observations on Man* in 1749. Blake engraved a portrait of Hartley in 1791 for a new edition of this work.

ANNOTATIONS TO BACON'S "ESSAYS"

¶ 396. The volume containing these annotations was seen by Gilchrist, who printed a small selection, though inaccurately, in 1863. It was then lost to sight until I discovered it in the United States of America in 1947, when it passed into my possession by the courtesy of Mr. J. K. Lilly jr. An article on the book, with many of the annotations, was printed in the *Times Literary Supplement,* 9 March, 1957. The annotations, with the relevant passages from Bacon, are here printed in full for the first time.

¶ 397. *Epicurus and Lucretius*] read by Gilchrist as *epicurism and libertinism.*

¶ 400. *Bacon was afraid*] read by Gilchrist as *David was afraid.*

A representation of hinder parts] the upper part of this diagram has been rubbed out, but the impress of the pencillings is clearly visible.

¶ 403. *A lie! . . . Bacon did*] the punctuation of this paragraph, supplied by the editor, probably gives the sense intended by Blake.

ANNOTATIONS TO BOYD'S TRANSLATION OF DANTE'S INFERNO

¶ 411. Henry Boyd's translation of Dante's *Inferno* was published at Dublin in two volumes, 1785. William Hayley subscribed for "7 sets", and it is probable that he gave Blake one of these in 1800 or soon after. Blake's copy of the first volume passed after his death into the possession of Samuel Palmer, and was taken to Vancouver, B.C., by his son, A. H. Palmer, in 1910. It was unknown until I visited Samuel Palmer's grandson, Mr. Bryan Palmer, in Vancouver in September 1956 and obtained the volume from him. Blake evidently read the *Inferno* carefully, as he has made several corrections in the text, but his annotations are restricted to the translator's prefatory essays. They were first published in an article by me in the *Times Literary Supplement*, 3 May 1957.

Clarissa] Samuel Richardson's *Clarissa Harlowe* was first published in 1740.

LINES FOR THE ILLUSTRATIONS TO GRAY'S POEMS

¶ 414. The volume containing the illustrations to Gray's Poems was commissioned by Flaxman in 1797 as a gift for his wife. The poem addressed to her suggests that she might gain from greater love of poetry and design presented by the double genius of Blake and Gray. The volume was in Beckford's collection after the sale of Flaxman's effects in 1828 and lay for many years forgotten in Hamilton Palace, until it was discovered again in 1919. The lines were then first printed by Prof. H. J. C. Grierson in *The Times* of November 4. Soon afterwards the late Duchess of Hamilton allowed me to examine the volume, which was reproduced in facsimile by the Clarendon Press in 1922 and for the Blake Trust in 1972. It is now the property of Mr. Paul Mellon.

POEMS AND FRAGMENTS FROM THE NOTE-BOOK 1800-03

¶ 415. The pieces grouped under this heading are written on pp. 2-14 of the *Note-Book*. As suggested by Sampson, they were probably written during the Felpham period, Blake then again using the book from its original beginning.

No. 1. *My spectre around me night & day*] this poem is written on pp. 3 and 2 of the MS. Blake's deletions and numberings as indicated here make his final intentions clear, except that the four 'additional stanzas' on p. 417, which are written, with stanza 14, very faintly in pencil, cannot be definitely placed.

¶ 417. Additional stanzas, lines 13-16] these lines are now first deciphered and printed.

¶ 418, no. 5. *I saw a Monk of Charlemaine*] the whole of this poem is written on p. 12 of the MS and is much confused by Blake's successive alterations and additions. Nine of the stanzas were afterwards copied by Blake in the *Pickering MS* with the title "The Grey Monk" (see p. 430), and later still seven stanzas were used in *Jerusalem* as part of the preface, "To the Deists", before chapter 3 (see p. 683).

¶ 420. Line 19. *A Grecian Scoff is a wracking wheel*] this uncompleted stanza is written sideways in the middle of the page. It was first printed in 1925.

¶ 421, no. 8. *Each Man is in his Spectre's power*] after writing these lines Blake renumbered them, and then deleted his numbers. The second stanza was not completed. The first stanza was afterwards used in *Jerusalem*, pl. 41, being etched in reversed writing in one of the designs (see p. 669).

No. 9. *Beneath the white thorn, lovely May*] the text of this poem is somewhat confused by Blake's deletions and alterations. It was afterwards copied in a revised form in the *Pickering MS*, entitled, "The Golden Net" (see p. 424), and this text was given by Sampson. The poem was first printed in its original form in 1925. All previous editors give the first line incorrectly as, *Beneath the white thorn's lovely May*.

POEMS FROM THE PICKERING MS

¶ 423. This manuscript consists of 11 leaves, about 20.5 × 15 cm., paginated by Blake 1-22. It contains fair copies of ten poems, some of which are found in their first state in the *Note-Book* among those composed during the Felpham period, 1800-1803. Sampson has given good reasons for supposing that the whole MS may be assigned to about the year 1803. The MS was first held by Frederick Tatham. It was in the hands of D. G. Rossetti about 1863 and was used for the poems printed in Gilchrist's *Life*. In 1866 it was the property of B. M. Pickering, with whose name it has since been associated. It is now in the Pierpont Morgan Library, New York. The first accurate text of all the poems was printed by Sampson in 1905. They are here printed from photographs supplied by a late owner, W. A. White.

¶ 424. *The Golden Net*] the rough draft of this poem is found in the *Note-Book*; see p. 421.

¶ 430. *The Grey Monk*] the first draft of this poem, with additional stanzas, is found in the *Note-Book*; see pp. 418-420.

¶ 431. *Auguries of Innocence*] Sampson pointed out in 1905 that this poem consists of an opening quatrain, followed by sixty-four couplets. Blake, however, has given no signs of any divisions in his manuscript, and the poem is, therefore, printed here continuously. Sampson gives a conjectural rearrangement of the lines, in which each theme treated by Blake is followed to its conclusion instead of being woven in one with another. This rearrangement is greatly to be preferred to those made by other editors.

MEMORANDUM

¶ 437. This Memorandum was evidently written by Blake when Scolfield's charge was first brought against him, and was intended to serve as a statement for the information of his counsel, Samuel Rose, at the trial. Printed from a photostat of a document, now at Trinity College, Hartford, Conn., which is not in Blake's hand, though evidently copied from a holograph MS.

REMARKS ON THE DRAWINGS OF T. H. MALKIN

¶ 439. Thomas Heath Malkin was an infant prodigy, who died at the age of seven. Blake's remarks on his drawings are reprinted from B. H. Malkin's *Father's Memoirs of his Child*, 1806, pp. 33-4. Blake designed a frontispiece for this book, which was engraved by Cromek. The introduction contains a valuable account of Blake with quotations from his poems.

Line 11. *The map of Allestone*] the volume contains a large engraving after a map of an imaginary country named Allestone, which the child invented and described.

MEMORANDA FROM THE NOTE-BOOK 1807

¶ 440. Of these *Memoranda*, Nos. 1-4 are written on p. 10 of the MS, together with the note dated June, 1793 (see p. 187). The earlier note is in pencil; the writing of the others suggests that they were all made at about the same time, that is, in 1807.

INSCRIPTION ON THE BACK OF "THE FALL OF MAN"

¶ 441. This water-colour drawing was formerly in the collection of Colonel William Stirling and is now in the Victoria and Albert Museum.

DEDICATION OF THE ILLUSTRATIONS TO BLAIR'S GRAVE

¶ 442. These lines were first printed on p. iii of Cromek's edition of Blair's *Grave,* 1808, containing a portrait of Blake after Phillips and twelve engravings after Blake's designs, all the plates being engraved by Schiavonetti. The original MS of Blake's lines is not known to have survived. Blake made a water-colour design for the dedication, which is now in the British Museum, but this was not used in the book.

DESCRIPTION OF A VISION OF THE LAST JUDGMENT

¶ 442. This document is known in three drafts, two dated 18 January 1808, the third, February 1808. The first draft, which is now in the U.S.A., is printed here, additional passages from the other drafts being added in square brackets. The third draft belongs to Lord Cunliffe; the second is at Petworth House, Sussex, where the picture of "The Last Judgment" still hangs. The three drafts were first distinguished and described in my *Blake's Letters,* London, 1956, where the first and third drafts are printed in full. Minor variations in the second and third are not recorded here.

ANNOTATIONS TO REYNOLDS

¶ 445. The three volumes of the second edition of Reynolds's *Discourses* which belonged to Blake are now in the library of the British Museum. Blake's marginalia are written in the first volume only, the notes on the other volumes being in the *Note-Book* with other epigrams, etc., relating to events which took place about the year 1808.

Extracts from the annotations were first printed by Gilchrist in the *Life.* They were printed in full by E. J. Ellis in *The Real Blake,* 1907. The verses and epigrams were given by Sampson in 1905 and 1913. The annotations were newly transcribed by me for the first Nonesuch edition, and this text has now been revised.

¶ 449. *Moser came to me*] Moser, the first keeper of the Royal Academy, died in 1783, so that this incident must have occurred when Blake was still a young man.

¶ 452. *For all are Born Poor, Aged Sixty three*] this line has been taken to mean that Blake wrote these notes at the age of 63, i.e., in 1820, but it is clear from the context that he is not referring to his own age.

¶ 455. *Strange, Bartollozzi or Wollett*] see notes to the *Public Address,* p. 915.

¶ 457. *Milton*] this quotation is taken from the introduction to *The Reason of Church Government,* 1641 (Milton's *Works,* 1851, iii, 149).

¶ 476. *I read Burke's Treatise (on the Sublime) when very Young; at the same time I read Locke on Human Understanding & Bacon's Advancement of Learning; on Every one of these Books I wrote my Opinions*] none of these volumes containing Blake's early annotations is now known to exist.

¶ 479. *Falconet*] Peter Falconet (1741-1791), portrait painter.

MILTON, A POEM IN [1] 2 BOOKS

¶ 480. Until the year 1923 only three copies of *Milton* were known to exist. Two of these consist of 45 plates painted with water-colours; the third copy lacks the plate with the Preface, but has five additional plates, making 49 in all. These three copies all have watermarks dated 1808, which probably indicate the year in which the book was finished, the etching of the plates having been begun in 1804. In December, 1923, a fourth copy came to light. This copy has watermarks dated 1815 and is more elaborately coloured than the earlier examples. It contains all the plates found in the third copy mentioned above, together with one plate of text not recorded before, making 50 plates in all. This was no doubt the last example of *Milton* completed by Blake and was bought from him by Thomas Griffith Wainewright, afterwards notorious as forger and poisoner; it may be supposed to shew Blake's final intentions in the arrangement of the plates. In the present edition the text has been arranged as in this copy, all the extra plates being printed in the position in which Blake intended them to go; the text of the additional plate (no. 5) found in the fourth copy was first printed in the Nonesuch edition, 1925.

Blake seems to have intended, when he began the poem, that it should be of much greater length, for he etched the number of books on the title-page as 12. The first figure has been more or less obliterated by the brush work in the existing copies, but it can be clearly seen in the fourth of these.

Milton contains 42 plates of text, together with a title-page, and 8 other plates without text, making 51 in all, though none of the existing copies contains all of these. The 36 plates of text contained in the first two copies mentioned are here printed from copy A in the British Museum Print Room. The text of the 5 additional plates in the third copy (here numbered 3, 4, 10, 18, 32) was collated with the original prints in the New York Public Library. The text of the extra plate, here numbered 5, in the fourth copy (now in the Lessing J. Rosenwald Collection, Library of Congress, Washington, D.C.) was transcribed by me from the original in 1923, and has since been verified by S. Foster Damon. The punctuation was revised throughout for the first Nonesuch edition, and the responsibility for this was shared with me by the late Max Plowman. No other liberties have been taken with any part of the text.

The theme of *Milton* is related to the mythological system already developed in earlier books and prepares for that of *Jerusalem;* but it is in addition a very personal document, telling of the events of Blake's three years' stay in Felpham, 1800-3, and of his relations with Hayley, who came to typify to him the perverter of Art and Truth, the originator of all errors. The work is called *Milton* because it relates also the story of Milton's descent to earth and his entry into Blake, so that their minds could commune intimately together. The result is a complicated epic which cannot be summarized in a few lines. The best analysis is to be found in Prof. S. Foster Damon's *William Blake*, 1924.

As already stated the date on the title-page probably indicates the year in which the etching of the plates was begun, and perhaps also the beginning of the composition of the poem. The opinions expressed in the Preface anticipate some of those found in the *Public Address*, which is assigned to about the year 1810. This suggests that the plate of the Preface was etched last of the 45 plates constituting the first two copies. Why this plate was omitted from the other two copies it is impossible to guess.

¶ 480. *To Justify the Ways of God to Men*] this motto is taken from *Paradise Lost*, book 1, line 26:

"What in me is dark
"Illumin, what is low raise and support;
"That to the highth of this great argument
"I may assert eternal Providence,
"And justify the ways of God to Men."

¶ 482. *Plate* 2] Line 21. *What cause*] in the British Museum copy this appears to read *That cause*, with some indication that Blake wished to substitute *What* for *That*. The reading *What* is clear in the Wainewright copy and has therefore been given here.

Plate 3] this is the first additional plate in the third copy. A photograph supplied by Prof. J. Wallis shews that Blake there numbered the plate 2, though the number has always hitherto been read as 5.

¶ 483. *Plate* 4] this is the second additional plate in the third copy, and is there numbered 3 by Blake.

¶ 484. *Plate* 5] Lines 19-26. *Ah weak & wide astray . . . are faintly heard*] these lines are repeated with alterations in *Jerusalem*, plate 49; see pp. 679-80, lines 32-41.

¶ 490. *Plate* 10] this is the third additional plate in the third copy, where it is numbered 11 by Blake.

¶ 499. *Plate* 18] this is the fourth additional plate in the third copy, where it is numbered 17 by Blake.

¶ 518. *Plate* 30] the legends etched in reversed writing at the top of this plate and here reproduced, are as follows:

How wide the Gulf & Unpassable! between Simplicity & Insipidity.
Contraries are Positives.
A Negation is not a Contrary.

¶ 521. *Plate* 32] the last additional plate, numbered by Blake 32* in the third copy.

Line 14. כרבים] i.e., Kerubim.

¶ 535 last line. *Father & Mother* . . .] This sentence is written on the back of a sketch for the central figure on plate 43. This was formerly in the collection of W. A. White.

EPIGRAMS, ETC. FROM THE NOTE-BOOK 1808-11

¶ 536. This group of pieces written on pp. 21-93 of the *Note-Book* probably covers the years 1808-1811. Several of the verses on Sir Joshua Reynolds and art were evidently written at about the same time as the *Annotations to Reynolds*. Many of the epigrams are connected with the quarrel with Stothard and other friends at the period of the painting of "The Canterbury Pilgrims" and of Blake's exhibition of pictures, that is, in 1809-1810. The latest piece with a date is the quotation from Bell's *Weekly Messenger* for Aug. 4, 1811 (no. 73).

¶ 536. No. 3, line 9. *Stewhard*] i.e., Stothard.

¶ 537. Line 16. *The Examiner, whose very name is Hunt*] this refers to an attack on Blake's exhibition, which appeared in Leigh Hunt's *Examiner* for Sept. 17, 1809. Line 20. *Yorkshire Jack Hemp*], i.e., John Flaxman. *gentle, blushing Daw*] perhaps George Dawe (1781–1829), portrait painter and mezzotinter, author of a *Life of George Morland*, or his younger brother, Henry Edward (1790–1848), also an artist. Line 21. *Death*] Blake's nickname for himself. Line 22. *Felpham Billy*] i.e., William

Hayley. Line 26. *Cur, my Lawyer*] not identified. *Dady, Jack Hemp's Parson*] i.e., Dr. Malkin. (See note, p. 907.) Line 33. *Assassinetti*] i.e., Schiavonetti, engraver of the plates for Blair's *Grave*. Line 36. *Screwmuch*] i.e., Robert Cromek, publisher of Blair's *Grave*.

¶ 538. No. 4, line 6. *Macklin or Boydel or Bowyer*] publishers of engravings and illustrated books, for whom Blake had worked.

No. 6, line 3. *H—— the painter*] identified by Sampson with William Haines (1778-1848), engraver and painter. Blake and Haines both contributed to Hayley's *Life of Romney*, 1809, and to Boydell's *Shakespeare*, 1803.

No. 7. *old acquaintance well renew*] these two lines were printed in the first Nonesuch edition only in the notes. They possibly refer to Robert and Leigh Hunt, but Mr. H. M. Margoliouth has pointed out that the two lines were evidently written at different times and suggests that the two Calibans were Flaxman and Stothard. (R.E.S. N.S. VI, 1955, p. 93.)

No. 8] Sampson suggested that this may have been addressed to Flaxman.

No. 9. *To H.*] i.e., to Robert Hunt, who wrote art criticisms for Leigh Hunt's *Examiner*. His initials appeared at the end of the article attacking Blake's exhibition, and he may have been responsible for an attack on Fuseli which had appeared two years before.

¶ 540. No. 20. *He is a Cock would* . . .] this couplet is not completed. It may have some reference to Private Cock, who had helped Scolfield in Blake's trial at Chichester in 1804.

¶ 541. No. 27. *Florentine Ingratitude*] Sampson explained that this refers to the election of Sir Joshua Reynolds to the Florentine Academy, and to his sending a self-portrait in accordance with the rules. These lines contain in the MS many deletions and additions, and are difficult to decipher.

¶ 544. No. 32. *P——*] probably Thomas Phillips, painter of the portrait of Blake which was engraved for Blair's *Grave*.

No. 33. . . . *H. does pretend*] i.e., Hayley.

No. 35, line 6. *Hired a Villain to bereave my Life*] This line Blake had used many years before in the *Poetical Sketches* (see p. 6, line 68).

¶ 545. No. 37. *On S*[*tothard*]. The second couplet was used, with alterations, in *A Descriptive Catalogue* (see p. 575).

No. 40. *Cosway, Frazer & Baldwin of Egypt's Lake*] Richard Cosway (1740-1821), miniaturist, is said to have kept a house for the study and practice of magic (Ellis & Yeats, i, 25). "Frazer" is probably Alexander Fraser (1786-1865), who for twenty years painted details in Sir David Wilkie's pictures. George Baldwin (d. 1826) was a mystical writer, who had studied magnetic cures in Egypt and believed himself to be possessed of special healing gifts.

¶ 547. No. 50. *Rafael Sublime* . . .] Blake began to write these lines on p. 1 of the *Note-Book* and these two words appear in the middle of the opening passages of the *Public Address*, with which they have no connexion.

Ditto, lines 5-7. *Learn the Laborious stumble of a Fool* . . . *Slobbering School*] Sampson printed the first and third of these lines as a separate couplet and omits the second line altogether. It is clear, however, from the MS that these three lines continue the other lines as given here.

¶ 548. No. 52, lines 6-9. *Newton & Bacon Cry* . . . *labour'd is every step*] Sampson printed the first two lines after the third and fourth. It is clear from the MS that the order is correct as given here.

No. 53, line 5. *Colonel Wardle*] Gwyllym Lloyd Wardle (1762?-1833), soldier and politician, M.P. for Okehampton, 1807-1812. In 1809 he successfully attacked Frederick, Duke of York, on a charge of corrupt practices in the granting of commissions.

No. 55. *The Cunning-sures & the aim-at-yours*] a play upon the words *connoisseurs* and *amateurs*.

¶ 549. No. 59. *English Encouragement of Art*] these lines have so many deletions and corrections that I have given separate versions as first written and as amended. The last four lines (*And, when it smells* . . .) were erroneously printed in the first Nonesuch edition as part of the next piece. Second reading, line 2. *Menny wouver*] a grotesque version of *manœuvre*.

¶ 550. No. 60, line 4. *Jenny suck awa'*] interpreted by Sampson as a grotesque way of writing *Je ne sais quoi*.

No. 61, lines 6, 7. *The Errors of a Wise Man* . . .] this couplet in the MS is separated by a sketch from the other lines, and may have been intended by Blake to be a distinct piece.

¶ 551. No. 65, line 2. *as in the Book of Moonlight, p..5*] no work of this name is known.

No. 66. *I give you the end of a golden string*] these lines were afterwards used in *Jerusalem*, plate 77 (see p. 716).

¶ 553. No. 73. *From Bell's Weekly Messenger*] Blake engraved two prints entitled "The Industrious Cottager" and "The Idle Laundress", after Morland in 1788. Both were published by J. R. Smith.

No. 74, line 14. *to come in Barry, a Poem*] no work of this name is known.

¶ 554. No. 77. The first draft of these lines formed part of the *Public Address* (see p. 595); they were afterwards altered and given the title *Blake's Apology &c*, and finally copied out as a separate piece in the form printed here as no. 80.

¶ 555. Ditto. Line 7. *as soft as Bartolloze*] i.e., as soft as Bartollozzi's style of engraving.

No. 78. This couplet is a translation, probably by Blake himself, of two iambic lines attributed to Crates of Thebes in the Anthology of Johannes Stobaeus (Fl. 116. 31, 'On old age'). See W. H. Stevenson, *Notes & Queries*, ccxiii, Jan. 1968, p. 21.

¶ 556. No. 82. *found the Word Golden*] the MS gives no clue as to the precise meaning of this sentence.

¶ 557. No. 88.] Blake has left this piece uncompleted.

¶ 558. No. 90. *The Caverns of the Grave*] these lines were apparently intended to accompany the picture known as "A Vision of the Last Judgment" now at Petworth House. The rest of the page on which the poem is written is occupied by portions of the prose description of this picture.

¶ 559. No. 92. *A Woman Scaly*] these pencilled lines were first noticed by Max Plowman and were printed in my *Blake Studies*, 1949, p. 84.

No. 93. *Every thing which is in harmony*] these dimly pencilled lines were first read by Dr. David Erdman.

ADVERTISEMENT OF EXHIBITION

¶ 560. This Advertisement consists of a single leaf printed on both sides. Only one copy is known; this is in the Bodleian Library and has served as the source of the present text. Both sides of the leaf were reproduced in facsimile in my *Bibliography*, 1921.

¶ 561. Line 9. *a Work on Art*] presumably the same project as was referred to in Letter 63.

ADVERTISEMENT OF A DESCRIPTIVE CATALOGUE

¶ 562. The only extant copy of this leaflet is in the collection of the late Sir John Stirling-Maxwell, Bart., and was first described by Mr. Ruthven Todd. See also my *Blake Studies*, 1949, p. 78 (1971, p. 69).

A DESCRIPTIVE CATALOGUE

¶ 563. Blake's *Descriptive Catalogue* is a thin duodecimo volume of 38 leaves. It was issued in grey paper wrappers and was given to those who visited Blake's exhibition at the house of his brother James, 28 Broad Street, Golden Square, in return for the half-crown paid for admission. The book is now rare, only nineteen copies having been recorded. Gilchrist reprinted the *Catalogue* in the *Life,* but without the preface. The whole work was reprinted by E. J. Ellis in *The Real Blake,* 1907, though with his usual inaccuracy. Otherwise the *Catalogue* has only been adequately reprinted in the Nonesuch editions. The book was on the whole carefully printed, and the text needs little emendation. One correction, however, noted below, was usually made by Blake himself on p. 64. The punctuation has needed some revision, but it has been left as far as possible unaltered.

Of the sixteen pictures described in the *Catalogue,* five, including the large composition entitled "The Ancient Britons", have now disappeared.

Last 2 lines. *all depends on Form or Outline, on where that is put ;*] printed in the original edition as *all depends on Form or Outline. On where that is put ;*

¶ 564. *Number I. The spiritual form of Nelson*] the tempera painting is in the Tate Gallery.

¶ 565. *Number II. The Spiritual form of Pitt*] the tempera painting is in the Tate Gallery.

¶ 566. *Number III. Sir Jeffery Chaucer and the nine and twenty Pilgrims*] the tempera painting is in the collection of the late Sir John Stirling-Maxwell, Bart.

¶ 573. Line 25. *my rival's prospectus*] i.e., a prospectus of the engraving of Stothard's Canterbury Pilgrims.

¶ 575. *The fox, the owl, the spider and the mole . . .*] this couplet was first written in a slightly different form as part of an epigram "On S[tothard]" in the *Note-Book* (see p. 545).

¶ 576. *Number IV. The Bard*] the tempera painting is in the Tate Gallery. The painting has turned very dark since it was painted, Blake's medium not proving so unchangeable as he predicted.

¶ 577. *Number V. The Ancient Britons*] this picture has for many years been entirely lost to sight. Seymour Kirkup, who visited Blake's exhibition and afterwards wrote his memories of it for Swinburne, regarded this painting as Blake's masterpiece. Kirkup made a sketch of it for Swinburne, but this too has been lost.

¶ 581. *Numbers VI, VII, & VIII*] these three pictures have now all disappeared, and no record of them, except these paragraphs, remains.

¶ 582. *Number IX. Satan calling up his Legions*] Blake's first version of this picture, which he included in the exhibition, is in the Victoria and Albert Museum. The painting has, however, become very dark, and the *more perfect Picture afterward executed for a Lady of high rank* was, therefore, reproduced in addition in the first Nonesuch edition. The "Lady of high rank" was the Countess of Egremont and the picture is still at Petworth House.

¶ 583. *Number X. The Bramins*] this picture has disappeared.

¶ 584. *Number XI. The Body of Abel found by Adam and Eve*] this picture is thought to be the water-colour painting formerly in the Linnell collection and now in the U.S.A. Another version is in the Tate Gallery.

Number XII. The Soldiers casting lots] a water-colour drawing now in the Fitzwilliam Museum, Cambridge.

Number XIII. Jacob's Ladder] a water-colour drawing now in the British Museum Print Room.

Number XIV. The Angels hovering over the Body of Jesus] the water-colour drawing is in the possession of Mr. and Mrs. Esmond Morse.

Number XV. Ruth] the drawing is in the Southampton Art Gallery.

¶ 585. *Number XVI. The Penance of Jane Shore*] the varnished water-colour drawing is in the Tate Gallery.

PROSPECTUS OF THE ENGRAVING OF CHAUCER'S CANTERBURY PILGRIMS

¶ 586. This prospectus is reprinted from an example of the original leaflet in the British Museum Print Room. It was first reprinted by Gilchrist in the *Life*.

DRAFT FOR PROSPECTUS: FROM THE NOTE-BOOK

¶ 587. This draft prospectus is written on three sides of a small folded leaf which is bound in at the end of the *Note-Book*. The leaf appears not to have been part of this MS as originally constituted, but to have been inserted later. On the fourth side of the leaf is written part of *The Everlasting Gospel*. The draft was first printed in the Nonesuch edition, 1925.

PROSPECTUS OF THE ENGRAVING OF CHAUCER'S CANTERBURY PILGRIMS

¶ 589. This prospectus was evidently printed from a revised copy of the draft given on the preceding pages. It is distinct from the earlier *Prospectus* given on pp. 586-7. The text is here taken from an example of the original leaflet in the British Museum Print Room. The only other copy known is in my collection.

Line 8. *with the Squire's and Yeoman*] misprinted thus in the original leaflet; *and* should be omitted.

PUBLIC ADDRESS

¶ 591. This essay is written in scattered fragments on the pages of the *Note-Book*. The title, *Public Address*, was first applied to it by Gilchrist in 1863. Blake did not himself use the title in the form of a heading, but he refers to "this Public Address" in the course of the essay (see p. 594). The second title, *Chaucer's Canterbury Pilgrims*, etc., is written on p. 65 of the *Note-Book*; its connexion with the *Public Address* is conjectural, but it may well belong to this essay, of which the engraving of *The Canterbury Pilgrims* is the ostensible subject. The note beginning, *This day is Publish'd*, has also been given a conjectural position in relation to the *Public Address*; it is written in a corner of p. 56 of the MS, close to part of the essay. Two other prospectuses of the engraving of *The Canterbury Pilgrims* were printed (see pp. 586, 589), but neither could be described as "containing Anecdotes of Artists", and neither could have been sold for as much as 6d. It seems probable, therefore, that Blake was anticipating an announcement of the publication which he intended to work up from the raw materials of the *Public Address*.

The fragments of the essay itself are written on pp. 1, 17-25, 38, 39, 44,

46-7, 51-67, 71, 76, 78 and 86 of the MS, wherever sketches and the poems already recorded had left room. Although Blake seems to have written consecutively a few passages of some length, as on pp. 51-7, much of the essay consists of disconnected fragments; these may shew some connexion of thought, but they cannot be forced into any strict sequence to form a satisfactory whole. Until the year 1925 the essay had only once before been edited, when it was transcribed by D. G. Rossetti for Gilchrist's *Life* in 1863. Rossetti made the attempt to weld the pieces together as an essay, but the result is not entirely satisfactory, and no indication is given of the violent rearrangements that have been found necessary in the process. A different plan has been adopted in the first Nonesuch and in the present editions, the pieces being given more nearly in the order in which they occur in the MS. References to the pages of the MS have been given throughout so that the approximate relation of the pieces to one another may be evident to the reader; wherever any rearrangement has been made, the original position of the displaced fragment will also be clear.

The passage written by Blake on p. 1 of the MS has been placed first both because of its position in the MS and because its tone shews a certain formality, indicating the beginning rather than the later parts of an address. The greater part of the rest is written on the two series of pages 51-67 and 17-25. The fragments on these pages have been printed as far as possible without disturbing the sequence in which they occur in the MS. Some short passages written on pp. 71, 76, 78 and 86 have been placed after those on p. 66. Finally, four fragments on pp. 38, 39, 44 and 46-7 have been placed at the end, as no indication of their intended position is given either by their sense or by their position in the MS.

¶ 592. Lines 27-8. *a Poem concerning my Three years' Herculean Labours at Felpham*] This probably refers to the Illuminated Book entitled *Milton.*

Line 35. *Macklin, my Employer*] i.e., Thomas Macklin, publisher, for whom Blake stippled a pair of prints in colour after Stothard and Meheux in 1783.

Line 36. *his Homer & Dante*] Flaxman's *Outlines* in illustration of Homer and Dante were engraved by Piroli and published in Italy in 1793. Blake himself engraved some of them for a new edition of the Iliad series in 1804.

¶ 593. Line 4. *Woolett*] i.e., William Woollett, 1735-1785, draughtsman and line-engraver.

Ditto. *Basire*] i.e., James Basire (1730-1802), engraver, to whom Blake was apprentice, 1771-1778.

Line 20. *Strange*] i.e., Sir Robert Strange (1721-1792), engraver.

Ditto. *Fribble*] this is not the name of an engraver; cf. *Annotations to Reynolds,* p. 468, "Savages are Fops and Fribbles more than any other "Men". William Fribble was the name of a character in whom Garrick had ridiculed the affectations of "The Pretty gentleman".

¶ 594. Line 4. *Jack Brown*] i.e., John Browne (1741-1801), engraver, pupil of Woollett.

Line 6. *Aliamet*] i.e., Jacques Aliamet (b. 1728), engraver.

Line 15. *I also knew something . . .*] this paragraph is written at the top of p. 60 of the *Note-Book*, but seems to be related to the remarks on p. 57 rather than to what follows in the MS.

Ditto. *Tom Cooke*] i.e., Thomas Cook (1744-1818), engraver.

Line 22. *Goltzius*] this probably refers to Henry Goltz, a distinguished Dutch engraver born in 1558.

Ditto. *Sadeler*] there were two brothers of this name, John and Raphael Sadeler, born at Brussels in 1550 and 1555. Both were distinguished engravers. Giles Sadeler, their nephew, born 1570, was equally eminent. Blake may be referring to any of these three.

Ditto. *Edelinck*] i.e., Gerard Edelinck, born at Antwerp in 1627.

Line 23. *Hall*] probably John Hall (b. 1740), engraver.

¶ 595-6. Lines 34ff. *Dryden in rhyme . . . original inventor*] these lines of doggerel appear from the MS to have been first written consecutively with the prose as here printed. Blake afterwards made many corrections and additions, rearranged the lines with numbers, and wrote at the bottom the title: *Blake's apology for his Catalogue* (see no. 77, p. 554). In this form they were printed in the first Nonesuch edition. Finally, Blake copied out the lines, with further alterations and additions, as a separate piece; for this form see p. 555 (no. 80) of the present volume. The early draft is here restored to its proper place in the *Public Address*.

¶ 596. Line 16. *Whoever looks . . .*] this paragraph and the next are written at the top and bottom respectively of p. 63 of the MS. The two succeeding paragraphs are written between the first two at the sides. The four paragraphs were probably written in the order here printed.

Line 21. *He who could represent Christ uniformly like a Drayman*] this refers to the works of Rubens.

¶ 597. Line 24. *The English Artist . . .*] Blake has indicated by a line in the MS that this passage should be placed as given here.

Line 35. *A Jockey that is anything of a Jockey*] this passage is written sideways on p. 71 of the MS among passages of *A Vision of the Last Judgment,* but it is not continuous with any of these, and seems to come more appropriately in its present position.

¶ 598. Line 23. *What man of Sense . . .*] these passages, written on pp. 18-19 of the MS, are crowded into every available corner, and the order of the paragraphs is necessarily somewhat conjectural.

¶ 599. Line 32. *Romano's Palace of T at Mantua*] Romano rebuilt the Palazzo del T for Federigo Gonzaga, Duke of Mantua.

¶ 601. Line 14. *Barry*] i.e., James Barry, R.A. (1741-1806), who decorated the walls of the Society of Arts.

Ditto. *Mortimer*] i.e., John Hamilton Mortimer, R.A. (1741-1779).

¶ 602. Line 29. *Vanloo*] probably either John Baptist Vanloo (1684-1742) of Aix-en-Provence, or his brother, Charles Andrew (1705-1765).

JOSEPH OF ARIMATHEA

¶ 604. Blake first engraved the plate of Joseph of Arimathea from a drawing of the figure in Michelangelo's fresco of the Crucifixion of St. Peter in the Capella Paolina at the Vatican at the age of sixteen when serving as apprentice to Basire. He re-engraved it and added the inscription at a later date, probably about 1810 (see my *Blake Studies,* 1949, pp. 45-6).

A VISION OF THE LAST JUDGMENT

¶ 604. The prose essay to which this title was applied by D. G. Rossetti, is written on pp. 68-95 of the *Note-Book*. As in the case of the *Public Address* it is exceedingly difficult or impossible to arrive at Blake's final intentions, the text being written in scattered fragments on these pages of the MS wherever room could be found. In preparing the present text, I have tried to keep as far as possible to the order of the pieces as they come in the MS, and the page references have been inserted so that the reader may see what rearrangements have actually been made. Some passages of *A Vision of the Last Judgment* sound as if they should come rather in the *Public Address;* it is clear, however, from the MS that Blake intended them to be as they are given here. Probably the two essays were composed about the same time, and the ideas then in Blake's mind have come to the surface in both.

The sub-title, *For the Year* 1810, etc., is written on p. 70 of the MS in close proximity to the opening paragraph of the present text. The sub-title was evidently written first.

A Vision of the Last Judgment was transcribed for Gilchrist's *Life* by D. G. Rossetti, who introduced a considerable amount of rearrangement without giving any idea of how the pieces were ordered in the MS. The essay was not re-edited from the MS until 1925.

The picture described is stated by W. M. Rossetti in Gilchrist's *Life,* ii, 223, to be a tempera painting measuring seven feet by five and estimated to contain a thousand figures. It is distinct from the smaller work already described in the document addressed to Ozias Humphry (p. 442 of the present volume), but it has disappeared and has probably been destroyed. Several sketches, however, probably used in its composition, are in existence; one of these, now in the possession of Mr. Gregory Bateson, was reproduced in the first Nonesuch edition, and another from the Lessing J. Rosenwald collection is in *Pencil Drawings, second series,* Nonesuch Press, 1956.

¶ 604. Line 1. *The Last Judgment (will be)* . . .] this paragraph was placed by Rossetti at the end of the essay. Its position in the MS already referred to suggests that it was intended by Blake to be placed more nearly as it is given here.

¶ 606. Line 9. *Jachin & Boaz*] see I Kings, vii, 21.

¶ 607. Line 6. *a Permanent Statue*] *State* would be preferable to *Statue,* but the word is clearly written in the MS.

¶ 612. Line 13. *where . . . Apollyon*] one word is here illegible, or possibly two.

¶ 615. Line 1. *The Combats of Good & Evil* . . .] this paragraph is written on two leaves with three pages intervening. The division comes in the middle of a sentence(lines 13-14, *by their Works ye shall know them*), so that there can be no doubt of Blake's intention. He has marked the passage off from what comes before, and has drawn a vertical line through it as if he had copied it elsewhere. The whole passage is omitted by Rossetti.

DESCRIPTIONS OF THE ILLUSTRATIONS TO "L'ALLEGRO" AND "IL PENSEROSO"

¶ 617. This series of illustrations has only been reproduced in the Nonesuch edition of Milton's *Poems,* 1926, and in Mr. Adrian Van Sinderen's *Blake The Mystic Genius,* Syracuse University Press, 1949. The series was formerly in the possession of Thomas Butts and is now in the Pierpont Morgan Library, New York. Each design is accompanied by Blake's transcript of the lines illustrated, together with his own brief description of the picture.

JERUSALEM

¶ 620. *Jerusalem* was the last considerable work which Blake executed by his method of relief etching. It consists of 100 plates, and of the six copies that are known, five are printed in black and are uncoloured. The sixth copy, referred to by Blake in his last letter to George Cumberland (p. 878), is printed in orange and is elaborately finished with water-colours. The date on the title-page is 1804, but this may have been when the conception of the poem was first formed in Blake's mind. Most of the work was probably executed after the completion of *Milton* in 1808. Evidence derived from the watermarks of the existing copies shews that the printing of none of them can have been begun before 1818, or have been finished until 1820. The constitution of the plates does not vary, and the arrangement is constant except in two copies in which the order of the plates of Chapter 2 has been changed. I have here followed the arrangement of the majority of the copies, the alternative numbering being given in square brackets. Blake has made a number of erasures from the copper-plates, all of which were duly noted in the first Nonesuch edition. Usually these erasures are of whole lines, one or occasionally more, and do not affect the continuity of the passages where they occur. On plate 3, however, there are a number of unexplained erasures which leaves a series of gaps in the text; many of these have been filled in the present edition. The text has been derived from the copy formerly the property of John Linnell and now in the possession of Mrs. Frank Rinder. The reproductions in the text have been made from this copy.

An accurate text of *Jerusalem* was edited by A. G. B. Russell and E. R. D. Maclagan in 1904, but these editors reproduced the perfunctory punctuation of the original, with the result that many passages are unintelligible. With the help of the late Max Plowman I undertook a complete revision of the punctuation. The task was an extremely difficult one and may have been imperfectly carried out.

The first full-page illustration of "Los entering Albion's bosom" has vestiges of lettering above, and at the sides of, the doorway through which Los is about to step. Most of this has been obliterated by Blake in the copies which he himself printed; I was able to read part of it, however, in a copy now in the Fitzwilliam Museum, Cambridge, printed from the original plates in 1832, and this was printed in the notes to the first Nonesuch edition. I afterwards found the whole text clearly printed in a proof of the plate which I acquired in 1943 (see *Blake Studies*, 1949, p. 110), so that it can now be put in its proper place.

The theme of *Jerusalem* is summarized in the opening lines: "Of the Sleep of Ulro [life in this world]! and of the passage through Eternal Death! and of the awaking to Eternal Life." It is an effort to reconcile the imperfections of the vegetative mortal life with the eternal truths of the spiritual life, but the general plan is overlaid by an excess of symbolism derived from names in ancient myths, from the Bible, and from the geography of London and England. Nevertheless there are many fine passages on the social problems of Blake's time, and on psychology and philosophy. Prof. S. Foster Damon suggests (*William Blake,* 1924) that, if the name-symbolism is ignored, the epic does not suffer and, in fact, its meaning emerges more clearly. Much help in understanding *Jerusalem* can be obtained from Joseph Wicksteed's *Commentary*, Trianon Press for the William Blake Trust, 1954.

¶ 620-1. *Plate* 3] reference has already been made to the erasures on this plate. The missing words in lines 1 and 2 of the verse on p. 621 were first supplied by Swinburne (*Critical Essay*, 1868, p. 284). Most of the others were first deciphered by Prof. S. Foster Damon, whose readings I have not, however, followed in every instance.

¶ 623. *Plate* 5, line 25. *Hand & Hyle & Coban*] Hand probably stands for Hunt and Hyle for Hayley. Coban is unexplained (but see N. & Q., 5. iii. 1949, p. 95-6).

Ditto. *Kwantok, Peachey, Brereton*] names derived from those of John Quantock, J.P., John Peachey, J.P., and William Brereton, J.P., magistrates concerned in Blake's trial at Chichester (see Damon's *Blake*, p. 436).

Ditto. *Slayd*] not identified. *Hutton*] is probably Lt. Hulton, who entered into recognizancies for the soldiers to appear at the trial.

Line 27. *Scofield, Kox*] i.e., Privates Scofield, or Scholfield, and Cock.

Ditto. *Kotope*] not identified.

Ditto. *Bowen*] perhaps Thomas Barton Bowen, who practised on the Home Circuit and Sussex Sessions (see S. Foster Damon's *William Blake*, p. 436).

¶ 664. *Plate* 37, line 10. *pale death*] this reading is seen only in early impressions of the plate. It was altered to *blue death* on the copper-plate.

¶ 669. *Plate* 41. Reproduction of design below text] the lines etched in reversed writing on the scroll at Albion's side are as follows:

Each Man is in his Spectre's power
Until the arrival of that hour
When his Humanity awake
And cast his Spectre into the Lake.

The first draft of this stanza is found in the *Note-Book*, together with a second stanza uncompleted (see p. 421).

¶ 679-80. *Plate* 49, lines 32-41. *Ah! weak & wide astray . . . are faintly heard*] these lines are repeated from the recently discovered plate 5 of *Milton* (see p. 484, lines 19-26).

¶ 683. *Plate* 52, line 1 of poem. *I saw a Monk of Charlemaine*] the first draft of these stanzas, together with others not used, is found in the *Note-Book* (see p. 418). A fair copy of some of them, entitled "The Grey Monk", is in the *Pickering MS* (see p. 430).

¶ 712. *Plate* 72. Reproduction of design below line 31] the sentence etched in the central globe is as follows:

Continually Building. Continually Decaying because of Love & Jealousy.

Ditto. Reproduction of design below line 52] the sentence etched in reversed writing beneath the serpent is as follows:

Women, the comforters of Men, become the Tormenters & Punishers.

¶ 716. Plate 77, line 1. *I give you the end of a golden string*] the first draft of this stanza is found in the *Note-Book* (see p. 551).

¶ 718. Plate 77] at the lower corners of this plate some words have been partially erased, and their remains are obliterated in the copies printed by Blake himself. In the copy in the Fitzwilliam Museum, Cambridge, printed in 1832, some of the words can be deciphered:

The Real Selfhood . . . (left hand). *in the* . . . (right hand).

¶ 724. Plate 81. Reproduction of design below the text] the sentences etched in reversed writing to the left of the design are as follows:

In Heaven the only Art of Living
Is Forgetting & Forgiving
Especially to the Female.

But if you on Earth Forgive
You shall not find where to Live.

Below the design are two additional lines:

In Heaven Love begets Love, but Fear is the Parent of Earthly Love,
And He who will not bend to Love must be subdu'd by Fear.

Max Plowman pointed out to me that these lines are not really part of the text, as printed in the first Nonesuch editions and by other editors.

¶ 740. Plate 93. Reproduction of design at the top of plate] the sentence etched on the bodies of the three men is as follows:

Anytus Melitus & Lycon thought Socrates a Very Pernicious Man
So Caiphas thought Jesus.

THE EVERLASTING GOSPEL

¶ 748. The greater part of this poem is written in several widely separated sections of the *Note-Book* as noted below. An additional passage is written on a small leaf bound in at the end of the *Note-Book*, and supplementary lines are found in a small separate MS, the text of which was printed for the first time in the Nonesuch edition, 1925. I have followed Sampson in retaining the division of the poem into fragments determined by their positions in the MS. These fragments I have lettered *a* to *i*. No attempt to weld them into a consecutive poem could be successful. The title used here, and by previous editors, for the whole poem was written by Blake above the piece lettered *d*. The date assigned to the poem by Sampson is "not earlier than 1810." I have tentatively dated it about the year 1818 for several reasons. The wide scattering of its component parts through the *Note-Book*, and on separate leaves suggests that it was written after the commonplace book, known as the *Note-Book* (*Rossetti MS*), had been filled from end to end. This fact would merely serve to date the poem as probably after 1810, but the affinities between *The Everlasting Gospel* and the later pages of *Jerusalem* suggest that the former was written some years later than 1810. Further than this, the date in the watermark of the paper upon which the supplementary passages are written shew that these lines at any rate cannot possibly have been written before 1818. There does not seem to be any reason for supposing that this portion was written at a much later date than the rest of the poem, which may, therefore, be assigned to *about* the same year, 1818. It is possible that the poem was written in 1820 or even later. On the other hand, Bunsho Jugaku in his *Bibliographical Study of Blake's Note-Book*, 1952, brings forward a number of arguments in favour of Sampson's dating.

¶ 748. Fragment *a*] written sideways on p. 33 of the *Note-Book*.

Fragment *b*] written on pp. 100, 101 of the *Note-Book*.

¶ 750. Fragment *c*] written on p. 98 of the *Note-Book*.

Line 19. *He who loves his Enemies . . .*] this line and the three succeeding lines are a marginal insertion.

Line 29. *But humble as a Lamb or an Ass*] this line and the three succeeding lines are a marginal insertion.

¶ 751. Lines 50, 51. *Do what you will . . . Contradiction*] this couplet is written in between two other poems on the opposite half of the page to the rest of this fragment, and was printed by Sampson as a separate piece. There is, however, nothing in the position of the lines to shew that they do not belong to *The Everlasting Gospel*, and the fact that they are repeated in a slightly different form and in the same context in fragment *d* (see p. 753, lines 85, 86) seems to prove that they should be placed as given here.

¶ 751. Fragment *d*] written on pp. 52-4 of the *Note-Book* and headed by Blake with the title as given here. It is in part a revised copy of the preceding fragment.

¶ 752. Line 58. *That quite unnerv'd Caiaphas' hand*] the last two words are indistinctly written over an erasure, and Sampson read them as *the seraph band*, but I have little doubt that they are correct as given here.

¶ 753. Lines 97, 98. *Reasoning . . . Contradiction*] these two lines occur in a somewhat different form in *The Gates of Paradise* (see p. 770, lines 11, 12). This tends to confirm the late date of *The Everlasting Gospel*, as the lines in *The Gates of Paradise* were almost certainly not engraved until 1818 or 1820.
Line 103. *This Life's dim Windows of the Soul*] Sampson for *dim* read *Five*. The word is indistinctly written in the MS, but the first letter seems to be a *d*, and I believe *dim* to be correct.
Fragment *e*] written on pp. 48-51 of the *Note-Book*. Sampson adopted a different order for the pieces from this point onwards.

¶ 754. Lines 27, 28. *To be Good only . . . Pharisee*] these two lines are written in the margin and marked for insertion.

¶ 756. Fragment *f*] written on p. 54 of the *Note-Book*; it was originally intended by Blake to come at the end of fragment *d*, and he afterwards inserted the catchword shewing that fragment *e* should come between.
Fragment *g*] written on p. 52 of the *Note-Book* after fragment *e*. The catchword with which it ends may refer to the supplementary passage printed on p. 758, line 11 of which reads, *For what is Antichrist but those*; or it may indicate another piece which has been lost.
Fragment *h*] the heading is written in pencil at the top of p. 48 of the *Note-Book*, and the four lines in pencil at the side.
Fragment *i*] written on the fourth page of a small folded leaf bound in at the end of the *Note-Book*; on the first three pages of this leaf is the draft for a Prospectus of the engraving of "The Canterbury Pilgrims" (see p. 587).
Lines 7, 8. *Or were Jew Virgins . . . nurst*] these two lines were written in as an afterthought.

¶ 756-7. Lines 20-26. *And turn'd Fishermen to Divines/Where the devil Combs his lice*] these seven lines are added at the end and marked for insertion.

THE EVERLASTING GOSPEL: SUPPLEMENTARY PASSAGES

¶ 757. These passages are written on a small folded leaf which may have been at one time inserted with the other small leaf at the end of the *Note-Book*; if so, it has been separated from it for many years, and it was probably not known to Rossetti who would otherwise have included it in the transcript of *The Everlasting Gospel* which he made while the volume was in his possession. The MS was, however, known to Swinburne who gives a summary of its meaning in his *Critical Essay*, 1868, pp. 175-6, and quotes a few lines. The MS had not been seen by any of Blake's previous editors, and it was first printed in the Nonesuch edition, 1925. It was for many years in the possession of E. J. Shaw, of Walsall, and he supplied me with a description for my *Bibliography*, 1921. By his permission and by the courtesy of Messrs. Sotheby I was able to transcribe the MS in 1925. It was afterwards sold at auction and is now in the Rosenbach Foundation, Philadelphia, Pa.

The prose piece is written in pencil on the first page of the MS. The piece numbered 2 follows in ink on pp. 2 and 3; the piece numbered 1 and marked *This to come first*, is written on p. 4. The MS is almost entirely without punctuation, which has been supplied.

Prose, lines 7–8. *& he cannot dwell among you;* (*by his* del.) *because you Murder him he arises again*] this passage should perhaps be punctuated, *& he cannot dwell among you because you Murder him; he arises again* . . .

¶ 758. (1) Lines 9, 10. *The Roman Virtues . . . Name*] these two lines are written at the bottom of the page and marked for insertion.

(2) Lines 5-8. *The Heathen Deities . . . Gin*] these four lines are written sideways in the margin and marked for insertion.

Line 22. *It was when Jesus* . . .]this line begins the third page of the MS.

¶ 759. Lines 36, 37. *And all the Heroic Virtues . . . Friend*] these two lines are written sideways in the margin and marked for insertion.

FOR THE SEXES: THE GATES OF PARADISE

¶ 760. The designs illustrating this work were engraved in 1793 and issued with a different title-page; the work was then called *For Children: The Gates of Paradise*, and consisted only of the title-page and the seventeen emblems. The legends as they appeared in 1793 have already been printed under that date (see p. 209). Many years afterwards Blake again used the plates, altering the title-page, adding new sentences to the legends on several of the plates, and engraving three new plates with text to come at the end. In this form the work consists, therefore, of 21 plates. The lines of the *Prologue* engraved on the title-page were subjected to several successive alterations before they reached their final form. Only five complete copies of this work have been recorded. A sixth lacks two plates of "The Keys of the Gates." The text given here is taken from a copy formerly in the possession of Miss A. G. E. Carthew, and the reproductions of the emblems on copper have been made from the same source.

This reissue of *The Gates of Paradise* was formerly dated about 1805-1810, but there are reasons for thinking it was done several years later than this. In the first place, the text has a close relation to *The Everlasting Gospel*, and particularly to the supplementary passages which were probably written not earlier than 1818. Secondly, none of the six copies known is printed on paper with a watermark dated before 1818; four of them are dated 1820 or later. I have, therefore, assigned *The Gates of Paradise* to about the year 1818.

¶ 761-3. Legends to the plates] it will be noticed that these legends may be read as a quatrain.

¶ 770-1. *The Keys of the Gates*] the numbers on the left-hand side indicate the emblems which illustrate the lines.

NOTES ON SPURZHEIM

¶ 772. These notes were written on a torn piece of paper, which was formerly inserted in the manuscript of *The Four Zoas*. The paper is no longer to be found, but the notes were recorded by Messrs. Ellis and Yeats in their *Works of William Blake*, i, 155, and the present text is taken from this source.

NOTE ON A DRAWING OF NINE GROTESQUE HEADS

¶ 773. This drawing was formerly in the Linnell Collection, sold at Christie's in 1918, and is now in the United States of America.

MIRTH AND HER COMPANIONS

¶ 773. Two prints of this subject are in existence. One, the earlier version, is a stipple engraving now in the British Museum, Department of Prints and Drawings. The other, from the same plate, but re-engraved in line, and now in my collection, resembles in its style of execution the *Illustrations of the Book of Job*, and was evidently done in Blake's later years. The inscription below the design was added only to the later version. Both prints are reproduced in my *Catalogue of the Separate Plates*, Dublin, 1956.

ANNOTATIONS TO BERKELEY'S "SIRIS"

¶ 773. The volume containing these annotations is now in the library of Lord Rothschild. From about 1909 until 1937 it was in the W. E. Moss collection. It had been in the possession of Blake's friend, Samuel Palmer, in 1833, but its intervening history is unknown. Blake's notes are written in pencil in the margins. It is evident from the opinions expressed that the notes were made at about the same time that Blake engraved the print known as *The Laocoön*. Both belong to the period 1818 to 1820 which saw the later stages of the composition of *Jerusalem*.

The annotations were printed in an appendix to my *Bibliography of Blake*, 1921, and were first published in the Nonesuch edition, 1925.

THE LAOCOÖN

¶ 775. The print containing the Laocoön as a central group, is a line engraving measuring 27.5 × 23 cm. Blake had made a drawing of this subject in 1815 from a cast in the antique school at the Royal Academy (Gilchrist's *Life*, 1880, i, 297), and in the same year had engraved it on a smaller scale for an article in Ree's *Cyclopædia*. In the present engraving the group is invested by Blake with symbolical meaning and the sentences around it, epitomizing much of his philosophy, express the same ideas as are found in the Annotations to Berkeley's *Siris*, in the etched plate *On Homer &c.*, and in other productions of his later years. The engraving may, therefore, be assigned to the period 1818 to 1820.

Only two impressions of the print are known to exist. One was formerly in the collection of John Linnell and is now in my possession. The other is in the United States. The engraving was not known to Gilchrist or Rossetti. It was first reproduced by Messrs. Ellis and Yeats in 1893, and the sentences have been reprinted several times since that date.

Line 2. מלאך יהוה] i.e., King Jehovah.

Line 3. οφιουχος] i.e., the Serpent-holder, a constellation mentioned by Blake in *Milton*, pl. 37 (p. 528, line 50). The two serpents are labelled *Good* and *Evil*.

Line 5. לילית] i.e., Lilith, Adam's first wife according to Rabinnical theology.

Line 6. יה] i.e., Jehovah.

Line 9. *If Morality was Christianity*...] this sentence was repeated by Blake in the Annotations to Dr. Thornton's pamphlet on the Lord's Prayer, 1827; see p. 786 of present edition.

¶ 776. Line 22. *Matthew, c. x: 9 & 10 v.*] "9. Provide neither gold, nor "silver, nor brass in your purses, 10. Nor scrip for your journey, neither two "coats, neither shoes, nor yet staves: for the workman is worthy of his "meat."

Line 24. *the Adamah*] i.e., the ground.

¶ 777. Line 4. *Virgil's Eneid, Lib. VI, v.* 848] "Excudent alii spirantia mollius æra." This line is again referred to in the etched plate *On Homer &c.*; see p. 778.

Line 9. *Luke, Ch.2, v.* 1]" And it came to pass in those days, that there went "out a decree from Cæsar Augustus, that all the world should be taxed."

ON HOMER'S POETRY & ON VIRGIL

¶ 778. These two fragments of prose are etched on a single plate, measuring 11.5 × 10 cm. Six impressions of the plate are known; they are all printed in black on paper which has no watermark, and all are uncoloured. The present text is taken from an example of the print in my possession.

The opinions expressed are closely related to the Annotations to Berkeley's *Siris* and *The Laocoön*, and clearly belong to Blake's later years, probably to the period 1818-1820.

Line 9 from bottom. *Virgil's Eneid, Bk. vi, line* 848] see note on p. 777, line 4.

NOTE IN CENNINI'S "TRATTATO DELLA PITTURA"

¶ 779. This sentence has been recorded by E. J. Ellis (*The Real Blake*, 1907, p. 420) as having been written in a copy of the book lent to Blake by John Linnell, who stated that he did this soon after its publication in 1821 (Gilchrist's *Life*, 1880, i, 414). The volume has not been seen since 1907 so that I have printed the sentence as given by Ellis. Blake transcribed a sentence from Cennini in a sketch book used by George Richmond after 1824.

THE GHOST OF ABEL

¶ 779. This dramatic piece is executed in relief etching on two plates. Only four copies are known, all of which are printed in black and are uncoloured. Two copies have watermarks dated 1820 and 1821, though according to Blake's colophon the plates were not etched until 1822. The additional date, 1788, in the colophon has been supposed to indicate that *The Ghost of Abel* was first executed in that year. Sampson pointed out, however, in 1905 that this date evidently referred to Blake's earliest use of the "stereotype," or relief-etching process, and not to an earlier issue of *The Ghost of Abel.* These two plates represent Blake's final use of the process. The present text is printed from examples of the original prints in my possession.

Plate 1, line 1. *Lord Byron in the Wilderness*] the reference is to Byron's *Cain*, 1822.

INSCRIPTION IN UPCOTT'S AUTOGRAPH ALBUM

¶ 781. Blake's inscription in this album was not noticed until 1924, when the volume was sold at Sotheby's. I then transcribed Blake's contribution, and it was published for the first time in the Nonesuch edition, 1925. The inscription is accompanied by a characteristic pencil sketch of a winged figure. The album is now in the New York Public Library.

William Upcott, the illegitimate son of Ozias Humphry, miniaturist, was a zealous collector of autographs and manuscripts. His collection, sold at Sotheby's in 1846, no doubt included this volume, though it cannot be identified in the sale catalogue.

¶ 782. Line 8. *Mr. Comfield*] a professional calligraphist and writing-master.

Line 10. *Heaven born, the Soul . . .*] Blake has transposed the second and third lines of this quotation; see p. 783.

ANNOTATIONS TO WORDSWORTH'S POEMS

¶ 782. Crabb Robinson recorded in his Reminiscences under the date 1826 that he had lent Blake the two volumes of Wordsworth's *Poems*, published in 1815. After Blake's death these were returned to their owner, who then discovered the pencil annotations which he inked over rather shakily. Some of them he transcribed and these were printed by Gilchrist with the Remin iscences (*Life*, 1880, i, 387-90). Robinson bequeathed the volumes to Edwin Wilkins Field, and from him they passed to his great grandson, Mr. L. F. Thompson, who allowed me to transcribe the annotations in 1927. They were first accurately printed in the second issue of the Centenary edition, 1927. The volumes are now in the library of Cornell University, New York.

ANNOTATIONS TO WORDSWORTH'S "EXCURSION"

¶ 784. At about the same time that Blake was reading the *Poems* he was also reading *The Excursion*. He copied out part of Wordsworth's Preface and after adding some notes of his own gave the MS to Crabb Robinson. The notes have been printed here from the original MS which is still among Crabb Robinson's papers in Dr. Williams's Library. I have given only those passages from the Preface which are relevant to Blake's notes. The notes were printed in full in Miss E. J. Morley's *Selections from the Remains of Henry Crabb Robinson*, 1922, pp. 159-63, and in the first Nonesuch edition, 1925. The MS is written on two leaves, measuring 21 × 12 cm. It is headed "Wordsworth." The two shorter notes are written in the margin; the longer note is at the end.

NOTES ON THE ILLUSTRATIONS TO DANTE

¶ 785. The designs made by Blake for Dante's *Comedia* during the last years of his life are 102 in number. Only three of them have writing on them other than names, and the sentences on these three are printed here as far as they can be deciphered. The greater part of them were printed by Prof. S. Foster Damon (*William Blake*, 1924, pp. 217-8), but his text differs considerably from mine. Some words have been supplied which were not given in the first Nonesuch edition.

On design no. 7] this drawing is now in the Fogg Museum of Art, Harvard University. I have recently verified the text.

Line 4. *As Poor Churchill said*] the reference is to Charles Churchill's *The Prophecy of Famine*, 1763, p. 5: Thou, Nature, art my goddess.

On design no. 16] this drawing is now in the National Gallery of Victoria, Melbourne.

On design no. 101]this drawing is now in the British Museum, Department of Prints and Drawings.

ANNOTATIONS TO DR. THORNTON'S PAMPHLET

¶ 786. Dr. Thornton, for whose *Pastorals of Virgil* Blake had made some woodcuts in 1821, was the author of several works, chiefly medical and botanical. He died in 1837 at the age of about sixty-nine. Blake's copy of his pamphlet on the Lord's Prayer was formerly in the Linnell collection and was sold at Christie's in 1918. It is now in the H. E. Huntington Library, California. An inaccurate text of part of the annotations was printed by E. J. Ellis in 1907. Further passages were added by Prof. S. Foster Damon (*William Blake*, 1924, pp. 22-3). The present text is printed from photographs of the whole pamphlet supplied by the H. E. Huntington Library. The annotations were first printed in their entirety in the Nonesuch edition, 1925.

Line 4 from bottom. *If Morality was Christianity* . . .] this sentence is repeated from the Laocoön plate; see p. 775.

¶ 787-9. *THE LORD'S PRAYER*] Blake's notes on Dr. Thornton's translation are written on several subsequent pages; his own version is on p. 3, his paraphrase of Dr. Thornton's version on the fly-leaf at the end. Both these are written in pencil and have become very difficult to read, but only a few words are omitted from the present text.

THE LETTERS

As explained in the Preface, the letters have here been grouped together instead of being dispersed in their chronological positions in the text. Their descriptions and provenance have been so fully documented in my recent edition of *The Letters of William Blake*, London, Hart-Davis, 1956, that the information is not repeated here. Most of the essential annotation has been printed with the text as footnotes, so that little more need be added.

¶ 790. 1. *Willey Reveley*] Reveley (d. 1799) was a young architect, who edited *The Antiquities of Athens*, 1794. His request, in the third person, accompanies Blake's reply.

2. *To George Cumberland*] Cumberland (b. 1754), a cousin of Richard Cumberland the dramatist, was Blake's most faithful friend for over thirty years. In 1795 he lived near Egham in Surrey; later he moved to Bristol. He was an amateur artist and engraver, and one of the initiators of the foundation of the National Gallery.

¶ 791. 4. *To Dr Trusler*] The Reverend Dr. Trusler (1735-1820) was introduced to Blake by Cumberland and also lived near Egham. He is best known as the author of *Hogarth Moralized* and *The Way to be Rich and Respectable*. His mind was wholly antipathetic to Blake's.

¶ 792. Line 12. *The Design I have sent*] this is a water-colour drawing illustrating "Malevolence". It was formerly in the possession of Mrs. Alexander Gilchrist and is now in the United States of America. It is reproduced in my edition of the *Letters*, 1956, pl. II.

¶ 793. 5. *To Dr Trusler*] this letter is marked by the recipient: "Blake, dim'd with superstition."

¶ 795. Line 27. *Johnson & Fuseli*] Blake had been constantly employed from 1780 until 1799 by Joseph Johnson to engrave copper-plates for his publications, and a number of these were done after Fuseli's designs. Blake received other commissions from Johnson after this date.

¶ 796. 7. *To William Hayley*] this letter is known only from extracts in Gilchrist's *Life*, 1880, i, 143.

¶ 800. 12. *Mrs Blake to Mrs Flaxman*] though signed "Catherine Blake", the whole letter is in Blake's hand.

¶ 803. 15. *To Thomas Butts*] Butts (d. 1845), a clerk in the office of the Muster-Master General, was a consistent buyer of Blake's works over many years. He lived in Fitzroy Square, and, being near Blake, the letters to him cover only the three years of Blake's absence from London at Felpham.

Line 2. *your . . . Verses*] a draft of Butts's letter, to which Blake is replying, has been preserved, and is printed in the *Letters*, p. 53.

¶ 806. 17. *To William Hayley*] this, and all later letters to Hayley marked with an asterisk, were sold at auction in 1878, but have been lost to sight. Some were seen by Mrs. Gilchrist and were printed in the *Life*, 1880, so that they can be given in full from this source. Others have not been published, and can only be given as "extracts from sale catalogue".

¶ 807. 18. *To John Flaxman*] this letter was sold at Sotheby's in 1890 and has been lost to sight.

¶ 819. 25. *To James Blake*] James was Blake's eldest brother, a hosier, living at 28 Broad Street, Golden Square.

¶ 822. Line 7 from bottom. *He who is Not With Me is Against Me*] cf. the prose note in *The Four Zoas*, p. 380.

¶ 823. Line 6. *My long Poem*] this may refer to *The Four Zoas*, which is believed to have been extensively rewritten during the Felpham period; on the other hand it may be the symbolic poem *Milton*.

¶ 826. Line 7 from bottom. *I am at Present in a Bustle*] for Blake's memorandum on the quarrel with Scolfield see p. 437.

¶ 828. Lines 4 & 3 from bottom. *O why was I born with a different face*] these two lines occur in a slightly different form in the poem "Mary" in the Pickering MS; see p. 428, lines 21-2.

¶ 849. 46. *To William Hayley*] this letter has now been found and is in the possession of Prof. F. W. Hilles, New Haven, Connecticut, by whose permission it is printed in the Supplement.

¶ 853. Letter no. 51 has now been found in the Library of Congress, Washington, D.C., and is printed in full in the supplement.

¶ 862. 60. *To William Hayley*] this letter, formerly in the possession of Miss Caroline Newton, is now in my collection.

¶ 867. 66. *To Dawson Turner*] Turner (1775-1858), a banker, botanist and antiquary of Yarmouth, was introduced to Blake by Ozias Humphry.

¶ 868. 68. *To John Linnell*] this letter was tentatively dated "?1826" in my recent edition of the *Letters*. The correct date has been established by H. M. Margoliouth through his identifying "the D. of C." as the Dean of Canterbury, Gerrard Andrewes, who died on 2 June 1825.

¶ 873-4. 78. *To John Linnell*]this letter, with the attached declaration, has not been printed before. I found it in 1957 among notes extracted by the late A. H. Palmer from the Linnell family papers. The original document is now in the Pierpont Morgan Library. Blake had already signed a receipt for the copyright of *Job* on the same date (see *Letters*, p. 196) but Linnell was evidently intent on establishing without question his absolute right in the property. Seemingly Blake was acquiescent.

¶ 929. *Annotations to Swedenborg*] Blake's copy of Swedenborg's *Heaven and Hell*, 1784, is now in the Houghton Library, Harvard University.

¶ 933. *Genesis*] This uncompleted MS has designs for two title-pages. It was formerly in the Linnell collection and is now in the H. E. Huntington Library.

¶ 936. *Letter* 81A] The letter was formerly in an album formed by Mrs. Aders. It was sold at Sotheby's on 16 December 1958, lot 483. The buyer, Mr. J. Schwartz, supplied me with a photostatic copy.

FOR ADDITIONAL NOTE SEE OVER

ADDITIONAL NOTE

¶ 595. Line 30. *Poco-Piu'd*] formerly read as *Poco-Pen'd*, but Professor Hagstrum's correction of *Piu* for *Pen* is acceptable; *Poco-Piu'd* is a conjunction of two Italian words meaning *a Little More*, that is, *overdone*, in this context.

Supplement

ANNOTATIONS TO SWEDENBORG'S HEAVEN AND HELL

London, second edition, 1784

Written about 1790

[*Blake's annotations here follow the passages to which they refer, these being printed in smaller type.*]

Half-title. [inscription in a hand not Blake's]

"And as Imagination bodies forth is [*sic*] forms of things unseen turns them to "shape [*sic*] & gives to airy Nothing a local habitation & a Name." [misquoted from *A Midsummer Night's Dream*, v. 1.]

Thus Fools quote Shakespeare; the above is Theseus' opinion Not Shakespeare's. You might as well quote Satan's blasphemies from Milton & give them as Milton's Opinions.

§ 513.

Page 339.

The angels appointed for instructors are from several societies, but chiefly from such as are in the north and the south . . . [marked × by Blake.]

× See N 73 Worlds in Universe for account of Instructing Spirits.

§ 588.

Page 389.

. . . That the Hells are so many and various, appears from it's being given me to know, that under every mountain, hill, rock, plain, and valley, there were particular Hells of different extent in length, breadth, and depth. . . . So much concerning the Plurality of Hells.

under every *Good* is a hell, i.e. hell is the outward or external of heaven & is of the body of the lord, for nothing is destroy'd.

ANNOTATIONS TO SIR JOSHUA REYNOLDS'S DISCOURSES

London MDCCXCVIII

Additional passages deciphered from among notes written by Blake in pencil and deleted. They are printed after the passages from Reynolds to which they refer.

Page xvii.

. . . relish for . . . excellencies of art is an acquired taste.

Fool.

Page xxxi.

Thus Bacon became a great thinker, by first entering into and making himself master of the thoughts of other men.

This is the Character of a Knave.

Page lvii.

[*Addition to a passage on a footnote on the lost secrets of colour-mixing known to the old masters. See page 450*]

Why are Venetians treated more kindly and with more Enthusiasm whenever Reynolds talks of colouring; a Greater colourist would . . . [*conjectural reading*]

Page lxxii.

. . . the Flemish School in the Netherlands (for I will not gratify our English republicans by calling it Belgium) . . .

Why then[?] gratify Flemish Painters . . .

Page lxxxiii.

[*a passage on the Literary Club formed by Reynolds, Johnson, Burke, . . . Goldsmith.*]

Oliver Goldsmith never should have known such knaves . . . [*conjectural reading*]

Page lxxxvii.

While engaged in his painting-room, he had the pleasure of seeing and conversing with all the beautiful, accomplished, and illustrious characters of his time . . .

God blasts Them As Though they were lost . . .

Page xci.

. . . a more perfect idea of our illustrious painter . . . [from] portrait of Laelius . . .

why should Laelius be considered Sir Joshua's Counterpart? [*conjectural reading*]

. . . one of the finest gentlemen . . . most elegant scholars . . .

Who dares worship[?] one[?] who'd have Driven you long Ago Insane?

Page xcv.

[*Written beside a description of Sir Joshua's funeral*]

Funeral granted to Sir Joshua for having destroy'd Art . . .

Page civ.
[*Addition to a passage on a footnote relating to the wealth and prosperity of England. See page 451*]

First[?] to[?] Serve Nobility & Fashionable Taste & Sr Joshua.

Page cxvi.
[*Concerning the decoration of St Paul's having been prevented by the Bishop of London*]

The Rascals who See[?] Painting want to destroy Art & Learning.

Page 3.
[*Addition to the words* Employers of Fools. *See page 452*]

Artists' and Employers' Imbecility.

Page 4.
[*Below the lines* When Nations grow Old, &c. *See page 452*]

Are there Artists who live upon Assasinations of other Men?

Page 30.
. . . no modern can pretend [to veneration reserved for old masters]

This is Encouragement for Artists . . . to those Who are born for it.

Page 35.
[*Before the words* Meer Enthusiasm &c. *See page 456*]

Damn the Fool!

Page 36.
. . . you should enter into a kind of competition, by . . . making a companion to any picture that you consider as a model.

What but a Puppy will dare to do this? why[?] shoud comparing[?] Great Masters be[?] done[?] painfully?

Page 38.

Fools' opinions & Endeavours destroy Invention!

Page 57.
Could we teach taste or genius by rules, they would be no longer taste and genius.

This must be how Liars Reason.

Page 71.

Albert Durer would never have got his Manners from the Nobility.

Page 75.
. . . habits of nature, as distinguished from those of fashion.

Is Fashion the concern of Artists? The Knave Calls any thing found[?] in Nature fit for Art.

Page 87.
. . . not to run into particularities.

Nonsense!

Page 116.
. . . keep your principal attention fixed upon the higher excellencies.

Caesar said he'd rather be the [first in] a Village [than] second in Rome; was not Caesar [a] Dutch Painter? [*Heavily erased and cut by the binder; a partly conjectural reading*]

Page 177.
Though Coypel wanted a simplicity . . .

O Yes Coypel indeed[?].

NOTES IN VARLEY'S SKETCHBOOK

Written c. 1819

[*Occasional notes in Blake's or Varley's hand are to be found in a sketch-book with water-mark 1806 used by John Varley. It contains pencil sketches by Varley and a number of Blake's 'visionary heads' and scenes in pencil. The book was first described by William Bell Scott in* The Portfolio *(1871) ii. 103–5. These extracts were first printed by permission of the former owner, Mr. M. D. E. Clayton-Stamm. The book has now been divided up and the leaves dispersed at auction in 1972.*]

On the first page, recto: Can you think I can endure to be consider'd as a vapour arising from your food. I [I *repeated*] will leave you if you doubt I am of no [more *del.*] greater importance than a Butterfly
Annotated: Spiritual communication to Mr Blake
Below a line: Empress Maud not very tall

On a page opposite a drawing by Blake of Queen Maud, mother of King Henry II, in bed in an apartment with Gothic appointments:
the Empresse Maud said rose water was in the vessel under the table
octr 29 friday 11 P M 1819
& said there were closets which contain'd all the conveniences for the bed chamber

On a page otherwise blank: it is allways to keep yourself collected

On the last page, recto, with a drawing of Hotspur's head:
Hotspur said
any & we [?] shou'd have had the Battle had it not been for those curs'd Stars Hotspur said he was indignant to have been kill'd [by *del.*] through the fluid Influence [?] by such a Person as Prince Henry who was so much his inferior

On the same page reversed: Miss Ward / Oct 31 1803 / 1 P M, *and scattered notes on colours and costume* (*e.g.*, velvet collar) *on other pages.*

GENESIS

CHAPTER HEADINGS FROM A DECORATED MANUSCRIPT COPY OF PART OF THE BOOK OF GENESIS, KING JAMES VERSION

Written 1826–7

Chapter I The Creation of the Natural Man

Chapter II The Natural Man divided into Male & Female & of the Tree of Life & of the Tree of Good & Evil

Chapter III Of the Sexual Nature & its Fall into Generation & Death

Chapter IV How Generation & Death took possession of the Natural Man & of the Forgiveness of Sins written upon the Murderer's Forehead

Additions to the text:

Wherever the word *ground* occurs Blake has added *Adamah*, usually within brackets.

In Ch. IV, verse 15, the passage *And the Lord put a mark on Cain* has been amplified by Blake to *And the Lord set a mark upon Cain's forehead.*

46. TO WILLIAM HAYLEY 16 July 1804

Dear Sir,

We are both happy to hear that Miss Poole is better, sincerely Pray that she may soon be perfectly restored. I call'd on Mr Rose in Chancery Lane on Friday, hear that he is in Sussex & is well, suppose that he does not tell the worst to his family, hope that so valuable a life will be preserv'd in health & strength—I send Richardson[1] accompanied by a Proof of Romney in Still an unfinish'd state; but it will have the great advantage to (of) Time to its completion. I also send a Sketch of the Heroic Horseman as you wish'd me to do, the size the Print is to be.

Mr Phillips desired I would present his most respectful Compliments to you & inform you that he with Mr Hoare intended to have visited you together—that terrible wet Tuesday, but could not for the Deluges of Rain. Mr P. was at Brighton with Mr Hoare, fears that so good an opportunity of seeing you may not occur soon again —Mr P. refuses to recieve payment for Books & says that he will not recieve it in Money but in some how else more agreeable still, of course he means to pursue his court to Your (*altered from* his) Coy Muse. I wish him success.

[1] Probably the head of Richardson engraved for the *Life of Romney*.

I omitted to get Richardson[1] till last Friday having call'd thrice unsuccessfully & before publication, have only had time to skim it but cannot restrain myself from speaking of Mrs Klopstock's letters Vol. 3, which to my feelings are the purest image of Conjugal affection honesty & Innocence I ever saw on paper. Richardson has won my heart. I will again read Clarissa &c.,[2] they must be admirable. I was too hasty in my perusal of them to percieve all their beauty. I admire Miss Watson's[3] head of Richardson, it is truly delicate.

"The patient touches of unweari'd Art".[4]

I am now Earnestly employ'd on the Heroic Horseman endeavouring to do justice to so admirable a Picture.

My Wife joins me in love to you.

I remain Dear Sir
Your sincere &
Obliged Servt

Will Blake

Sth Molton S^t
16 July 1804

51. TO WILLIAM HAYLEY 4 December 1804[5]

Dear Sir,

I have omitted so long to thank you for your kind & admirable Present in hopes to send Proofs of my plates, but can no longer wait for them but must express my own & my wife's high gratification in the perusal of your elegant & pathetic Poem.[6] To say that Venusia is as beautiful as Serena is only expressing private opinion which will vary in each individual, but to say that she is Your Daughter & is like You, to say " 'tis a Girl, promising Boys hereafter", & to say God bless her, for she is a peerless Jewel for a Prince to wear & that we are both highly delighted is what I could not longer omit

---

[1] *The Correspondence of Samuel Richardson Selected by Anne Laetitia Barbauld*, for R. Phillips, London, 6 vols, 1804. See vol. iii, pp. 139–58 for the letters to and from Mrs. Klopstock.

[2] Samuel Richardson's three novels, *Pamela*, *Clarissa Harlowe* and *Sir Charles Grandison*.

[3] Caroline Watson (1761–1814), stipple engraver.

[4] From Pope's *Temple of Fame*, line 199: "with patient touches of unweary'd art."

[5] First printed by Professor G. M. Harper in *Studies in Philology*, lxi. 1964.

[6] *The Triumph of Music*, Joseph Seagrave, Chichester, 1804.

to say.—Proofs of my Plates will wait on you in a few days; in the mean while I conclude this hasty scrawl with sincere thanks for your kind proposal in your Last letter. I have not yet been able to meet Phillips—Wilkes[1] was not out when I call'd nor any more of Washington.[2] But I have mention'd your Proposal to our Noble Flaxman whose high & generous Spirit relinquishing the whole to me was in some measure to be Expected, but that he has reasons for not being able to furnish any designs You will readily believe; he says his Engagements are so multiform that he should not be able to do them Justice, but that he will overlook & advise & do all that he can to make my designs (should they ever be attempted) what he Can, & I know his *What he Can* will be full as much as he pretends, so that I should not fear to produce somewhat in this way that must be satisfactory; the only danger will be that I shall put my Name to his Designs, but if it should fall out so he has Enough & to Spare & the World will know his at once & I shall glory in the Discovery, for Friendship with such a one is better than Fame!—I was about to have written to you to express my wish that two so unequal labourers might not be yoked to the same Plow & to desire you if you could to get Flaxman to do the whole, because I thought it would be (to say the best of myself) like putting John Milton with John Bunyan; but being at Flaxman's taking his advice about our Engravings he mention'd his having reciev'd a Letter from you on the same Day I reciev'd mine & said somewhat, I cannot tell what, that made me think you had open'd your Proposal to him—I thought at any rate it would not be premature to tell him what you had said about the Designs for Edward the first, & he advised it to be done as above related.

I will soon speak with Phillips about it if you will favor me with a line of direction how to proceed—Hope in a few days to send Proofs of Plates which I must say are far beyond Any thing I have ever done. For O happiness never enough to be grateful for! I have lost my Confusion of Thought while at work & am as much myself when I take the Pencil or Graver into my hand as I used to be in my Youth. I have indeed fought thro' a Hell of terrors & horrors (which none could know but myself) in a Divided Existence; now no longer Divided nor at war with myself I shall travel on in the strength of the Lord God as Poor Pilgrim says.

My wife joins me in Love to You & to our dear Friend & Friends at Lavant & in all Sussex.

I remain Dear Sir Your Sincere & obliged

Sth Molton St Will Blake

4 Decr. 1804

[1] *Correspondence and Papers of John Wilkes*, ed. J. Almon, London, 1805.

[2] John Marshall, *Life of George Washington*, Philadelphia, 1804-7.

81A. TO MRS ADERS 29 December 1826

Mr Blake's respectful Compliments to Mrs Ade[r]s:[1] is sorry to say that his Illness is so far frôm gone that the least thing brings on the symptoms of the original complaint: he does not dare to leave his room by any means: he had another desperate attack of the Aguish trembling last night & is certain that at present any venture to go out must be of bad, perhaps of fatal, consequences. Is very sorry indeed that he is deprived of the happiness of visiting again & also of seeing again those Pictures of the old Masters, but must submit to the necessity & be Patient till warm weather comes.

3 Fountain Court, Strand
29 Decr 1826

[1] Mrs Aders, the daughter of Raphael Smith, the mezzotint engraver, had married a wealthy merchant of German extraction. They lived in Euston Square and there entertained many artists and literary men. At their house Blake first met Henry Crabb Robinson in 1825. Mrs Aders had bought a copy of *Songs of Innocence and of Experience* in July 1826.

Index of First Lines